Academic American Encyclopedia

Areté Publishing Company, Inc.

Princeton, New Jersey

Library of Congress Cataloging in Publication Data
Main entry under title:

Academic American encyclopedia.

Includes bibliographies and index.
1. Encyclopedias and dictionaries.
AE5.A23   C31   79-27430
ISBN 0-933880-00-6
ISBN 0-933880-11-1 (vol 11)
ISBN 0-933880-22-7 (lib. bdg.)
ISBN 0-933880-33-2 (vol 11)
ISBN 0-933880-44-8 (leather)

FEB   '83

2 PHOENICIAN			ETRUSCAN **I**
⅂ EARLY HEBREW			EARLY LATIN **I**
⅂ EARLY ARAMAIC			CLASSICAL LATIN **I**
⟨ EARLY GREEK			RUSSIAN-CYRILLIC **И**
I CLASSICAL GREEK		MODERN LATIN	GERMAN-GOTHIC **ℑ**

I

I/i is the ninth letter of the English alphabet. Both the form of the letter and its position in the alphabet are derived from the Latin, which derived it from the Greek by way of the Etruscan. The Greeks, who took the form and position of the letter, along with the rest of the alphabet, from a Semitic writing system, call the letter *iota*. The Semitic name of the sign is *yodh*, and it does not represent a vowel but the consonant *y*. The Greeks used this sign to represent both the vowel *i* and the consonant *y*; this usage was taken into Etruscan and then into Latin and was continued into the Middle Ages. At that time the two sounds were finally differentiated by the use of the letters *I/i* and *J/j*, the latter being derived from the former by the addition of a curved stroke at the bottom. In modern English pronunciation, *I/i* has two basic sounds: a short *i* as in *bit* and *lip*, and a long *i* as in *bite* and *high*. Occasionally it has the sound of long *e* as in *magazine*.

I. J. GELB AND R. M. WHITING

I Ching

The *I Ching*, or *Book of Changes*, is one of the central texts of CONFUCIANISM. It consists of 64 hexagrams, each of which is made up of six divided or undivided lines, possibly created at the end of the 2d millennium BC; a cryptic, partly unintelligible text, written at the beginning of the 1st millennium BC; and a treatise on the text, the *Ten Wings*, written at the end of the 1st millennium BC. Although the book has long been used by fortune tellers, its main influence has traditionally been philosophical, particularly during the Han and Sung dynasties, when it was used to create theories of the universe based on numerology. Although rejected by the empiricist scholars of the Ch'ing dynasty, the numerological aspects of the *I Ching* have recently been reemphasized by Westerners interested in Eastern mysticism.

LENNART FRANTZELL

Bibliography: Wilhelm, Hellmut, *The Book of Changes in the Western Tradition* (1976) and *Changes*, trans. by Cary F. Baynes (1960).

See also: CHINESE LITERATURE.

iamb: see VERSIFICATION.

Iamblichus [y-am'-bli-kuhs]

Iamblichus, d. *c.*330, called "the divine" by Neoplatonists, was considered the authority for NEOPLATONISM for more than two centuries. His interpretation gave PLOTINUS's and PORPHYRY's systems of emanations (see EMANATIONISM) a mystic and religious rather than an aesthetic or logical interpretation. He differed from Plotinus in espousing a level of "ideal numbers" between The One and Mind. He added many levels of Being, arranged triadically, with two extremes and a connecting mean, each level containing gods or demons who mediated between higher and lower orders. He differed from Porphyry in his belief that proper religious observance (theurgy) was a virtue higher than that of the intellect and could persuade the benevolent gods and repel the evil demons. Iamblichus's extant writings include *Life of Pythagoras*; a treatise, *On the Egyptian Mysteries*; and an essay, *The Community of*

the Mathematical Sciences. His commentaries on Plato and Aristotle have not survived.

ROBERT S. BRUMBAUGH

Bibliography: Whittaker, Thomas, *The Neo-Platonists*, 2d ed. (1928; repr. 1961).

Iaşi [yahsh]

Iaşi (Jassy), a city in northeastern Romania 13 km (8 mi) west of the USSR border, is the capital of the district of Iaşi. It is located on the Bahlui River near its confluence with the Prut and has a population of 264,947 (1977). Metal and leather products, chemicals, drugs, textiles, furniture, foodstuffs, and candles are manufactured there. Landmarks include the Church of the Three Hierarchs (1639), Golia Cathedral (begun in 1564), and Al. I. Cuza University (1860). Iaşi, first settled in the 7th century, became a fort and customs station on trade routes during the 14th century and suffered attacks from the Tatars (1513), Turks (1538), and Russians (1686). It was the capital of Moldavia from 1565 to 1862. The 1792 Treaty of Jassy was signed here, ending the second Russo-Turkish War.

Ibadan [ee-bah'-dahn]

Ibadan is the capital of Oyo state, Nigeria. It is that country's second largest city and is located about 130 km (80 mi) northeast of Lagos, near the border of the forest and savanna zones. Ibadan's population is 1,800,000 (1976 est.). The city receives about 1,150 mm (45 in) of rainfall annually and has an average annual temperature of 26° C (80° F).

The population is primarily YORUBA. About one-third of the work force engages in agriculture on farmland located outside of the city. Cacao, cotton, corn, and palm kernels, the major crops, are processed and marketed in the city. Other industries are traditional handicrafts (weaving and dying) and furniture and soap manufacturing.

The central part of Ibadan is dominated by a commercial center with several markets and traditional mud-and-brick houses; about 70% of the population lives in this area. Modern housing is found on the periphery of the city. The University of Ibadan (1948) and the International Institute of Tropical Agriculture are located there.

The date of Ibadan's founding is unknown, but its recorded history dates from 1829. The British took control of the city in 1893. It grew as a commercial center after the arrival of the railroad in 1901.

RONALD D. GARST

Iberian Peninsula

The Iberian Peninsula, occupied by Spain and Portugal, is situated in southwestern Europe. It has an area of 580,860 km² (224,270 mi²). Separated from the rest of Europe to the north by the Pyrenees Mountains, it is bounded by the Atlantic Ocean on the north and west and the Mediterranean Sea on the south and east. The southern tip of the peninsula is separated from Africa by the Strait of Gibraltar. The name Iberia, given by the Greeks, referred to an ancient people who originally lived along the EBRO (Iberus) River.

•Five major rivers, of which the TAGUS is the largest, drain the peninsula. Two-thirds of the peninsula is composed of a great central plateau more than 600 m (2,000 ft) in elevation, known as the Meseta. This plateau, sparsely populated, has limited rainfall, poor soil, and a relatively severe climate, with cold winters and hot summers. Agriculture is most successful in the river valleys and along both coastal plains, where the winters are mild.

Ibert, Jacques   [ee-bair']

The French composer Jacques Ibert, b. Aug. 15, 1890, d. Feb. 5, 1962, best known for his orchestral suite *Escales* (Ports of Call), was a pupil of Gabriel Fauré and Andre Gédalge at the Paris Conservatory. Ibert served in the French Navy during World War I. Awarded the Prix de Rome in 1919 for a cantata, he later returned to Rome as director (1937–55) of the French Academy there. For two years (1955–57) he was managing director of the combined Paris Opéra and Opéra Comique. His most successful work, *Escales,* first performed in 1924, reflected his naval experiences. Also popular are the piano piece "The Little White Donkey" and the orchestral *Divertissement* (1930). His other compositions include operas, symphonic poems, chamber music, and songs.   HOMER ULRICH

Iberville, Pierre Le Moyne, Sieur d'   [dee-bair-veel', pee-air' luh-mwanh', sur]

The French-Canadian explorer Pierre Le Moyne, sieur d'Iberville, b. July 1661, d. July 9, 1706, is often called the Great Canadian or the Canadian Cid in honor of his numerous heroic exploits. Like his younger brother, the sieur de BIENVILLE, he was intimately associated with French exploration and colonization in the Gulf of Mexico. Early in his career he won distinction by his military prowess against the English in Canada. Between 1686 and 1697 he led five attacks on English trading posts on Hudson Bay; he also took part in a raid (1690) on Schenectady, N.Y., destroyed (1696) Fort William Henry at Pemaquid, Maine, and briefly expelled (1696) the English from St. John, Newfoundland.

In 1698, Iberville was chosen to lead an expedition to found a French colony at the mouth of the Mississippi River. He reached the Gulf of Mexico in 1699 and sought to establish a bastion at Pensacola. The Spaniards, however, had arrived at Pensacola and fortified it just before Iberville's ships sailed into the harbor. He was thus forced down the coast to Massacre (present-day Dauphin) Island in Biloxi Bay. Iberville left the administration of the new Louisiana colony to Bienville, while he brought in supplies and reinforcements. In 1706 he led an expedition that captured the West Indian island of Nevis from the English, but later in the year he succumbed to yellow fever in Havana. He was greatly mourned by the French settlers.   JACK D. L. HOLMES

Bibliography: Crouse, Nellis M., *Lemoyne d'Iberville: Soldier of New France* (1954); Gayarré, Charles E. A., *History of Louisiana,* vol. 1, 3d ed. (1885; repr. 1972).

ibex   [y'-beks]

The ibex, *Capra ibex,* is a wild goat, family Bovidae, found in mountainous areas in Europe, Asia, and North Africa. Adult males are characterized by beards and by long horns, often 75 cm (2.5 ft) and sometimes 1.2 m (4 ft) in length, that typically curve backward over the head and that have pronounced semicircular ridges spaced along their front edges. Females lack beards and have small horns, about 20 cm (8 in) long, that are straight or just slightly curved. Six subspecies, or races, of ibexes are recognized; two of these, the eastern and western Caucasian ibexes, or turs, are sometimes considered a single separate species, *C. caucasica.* A related species, *C. pyrenaica,* is known as the Spanish ibex. The Alpine ibex, *Capra i. ibex,* of the European Alps, lives above treeline at altitudes up to 3,500 m (11,500 ft), where it feeds on shrubbery and grasses. It is brownish gray, stands about 1 m (40 in) high at the shoulders, and commonly weighs up to 90 kg (200 lb). The Nubian ibex, *C. i. nubiana,* of the Middle East and the

walia, or Abyssinian ibex, *C. i. walie,* of Ethiopia are both threatened with extinction, as is the Spanish ibex.   EDWIN E. ROSENBLUM

Ibibio   [ee-bee'-bee-oh]

The Ibibio are a group of six related peoples living in southeastern Nigeria. Their total population is estimated at 1,500,000 (1973).

Most Ibibio are subsistence farmers, but two subgroups are fishermen. Market trading and handicrafts are well developed. The Ibibio language is in the Benue-Niger subfamily of the Niger-Congo languages (see AFRICAN LANGUAGES).

Traditionally, the Ibibio had no centralized government. The village is the most important political entity, and public order is maintained by powerful secret societies run by the men. Descent is traced through the male line, and polygyny is the ideal form of marriage, although monogamy is more common. Girls were traditionally fattened before marriage, sometimes for more than a year.

Traditional Ibibio religion included a great god of the sky, assisted by several spirits and souls of the dead awaiting reincarnation; ancestor worship; and witchcraft. Today many Ibibio are Christians. Ibibio artwork includes elaborately carved masks, notably those representing ancestors which are worn by the *Ekpo* ("the dead") society, and jointed figures used as marionettes.   PHOEBE MILLER

Bibliography: Talbot, D. A., *Woman's Mysteries of a Primitive People: Ibibios of Southern Nigeria* (1968).

ibis   [y'-bis]

The scarlet ibis, Eudocimus rubra, *of tropical South America is approximately 60 cm (24 in) long. It makes its nest in huge coastal colonies.*

Ibis is the common name for various wading birds having long curved bills and belonging to the family Threskiornithidae, which also includes the spoonbill. Ibises are found in most of the warmer areas of the world and are familiar among the hieroglyphics on ancient Egyptian monuments. The sacred ibis, *Threskiornis aethiopica,* of Africa was worshiped in ancient Egypt for its legendary powers. Two American species formerly confined to the extreme south have extended their ranges northward in recent years: the glossy ibis, *Plegadis falcinellus,* approximately 60 cm (24 in) in length and dark bronze blue, now reaches Maine in annual flights; and the white ibis, *Eudocimus albus,* larger and white with black wingtips, now nests in Virginia. The bird *Mycteria americana*, formerly called the wood ibis, is a stork.

Ibiza [ee-bee'-thah]

Ibiza, one of the BALEARIC ISLANDS, is situated in the western Mediterranean Sea, about 130 km (80 mi) east of the Spanish coast. Ibiza covers 572 km² (221 mi²), and its population is 45,075 (1970). The city of Ibiza is the largest settlement on the island. Composed of limestone outcrop, the island's rugged hills rise to 475 m (1,558 ft) at Atalayasa. The climate is mild, with an average annual temperature of 17° C (63° F) and annual precipitation of 1,140 mm (45 in). Many springs and the Santa Eulalia River irrigate terraced fields of almonds, figs, olives, and potatoes. Tourism, however, is the basis of the economy. In ancient times the island was settled in turn by the Phoenicians, Carthaginians, and Romans.

Ibizan hound

The Ibizan hound, or *Podenco ibicenco*, is believed to have originated on the island of Ibiza, one of the Balearic Islands off the eastern coast of Spain. Although similar to a greyhound in appearance, the breed hunts largely by scent rather than by sight. The dog is tall and lean, with a long head and tail, small eyes, and large, erect ears turned to the front. Three coat types exist—short, wire, and long—but the shorthaired variety is the one usually seen in the United States. Coat colors may be solid red, tawny (called lion), or white, or either of the darker colors mixed with white. Males stand from 60 to 74 cm (23.5 to 29 in) high at the shoulders and weigh about 22.5 kg (50 lb). Ibizan hounds were first brought to the United States in 1954 and were accepted into the American Kennel Club's miscellaneous class in 1968.

Bibliography: Braund, Kathryn, *The Uncommon Dog Breeds* (1975).

Ibn al-Muqaffa [ib'-uhn ahl-moo-kah'-fah]

Ibn al-Muqaffa was born of Persian parents about 720, but in adult life converted to Islam and perfected his Arabic so that his translations into that language from Pahlavi (Middle Persian) became models of elegant Arabic prose. His best-known work is *Kalila and Dimna*, a book of animal fables derived from the Sanskrit *Fables of Bidpai* and the *Panchatantra* through the Pahlavi. Other works by Ibn al-Muqaffa include his *Great Book of Manners* on the ethics of rulers and courtiers. He was burned at the stake for political reasons about 756.   ISSA J. BOULLATA

Bibliography: Nicholson, R. A., *A Literary History of the Arabs*, rev. ed. (1969).

Ibn Battuta [ib'-uhn bah-too'-tah]

Ibn Battuta, b. Feb. 25, 1304, d. 1368/69 or 1377, an indefatigable Arab traveler, composed the most comprehensive account of the Muslim world in the later Middle Ages. Between 1325 and 1354 he journeyed through North Africa, the Middle East, East Africa, Central Asia, India, Southeast Asia, and possibly China. On separate trips he also visited southern Spain and crossed the Sahara to the Muslim lands of West Africa.

Ibn Battuta dictated an account of his travels after his return to Morocco; the work was completed on Dec. 9, 1357. He appears initially to have followed the tradition of describing a pilgrimage to the holy places of Arabia. The extended nature of his journeys blurred this objective, however, and his account expanded into a depiction of the known world beyond Europe. The work is valuable as a major source for economic and social history, particularly for the descriptions of India, Anatolia, and the lands around the Niger River.
                                                    MICHAEL W. DOLS

Bibliography: Ibn Battuta, *The Travels of Ibn Battuta*, trans. by H. A. R. Gibb, 3 vols. (1958–71).

Ibn Ezra, Abraham ben Meir [ib'-uhn ez'-ruh, ay'-bruh-ham ben mayr]

Abraham ben Meir Ibn Ezra, c.1089–1164, was a Spanish Jewish scholar. His Bible commentaries combined traditional

Jewish interpretation with a critical method of exegesis and emphasis on grammar; his philosophical work followed the Neoplatonic tendency (see NEOPLATONISM) in medieval thought. Ibn Ezra translated an astronomical work from the Arabic into Hebrew, creating a Hebrew prose style for scientific purposes. Liturgic poetry fascinated him; many of his hymns were included in the prayer book of the synagogue. Ibn Ezra traveled widely throughout his life and won many admirers. He was probably the model for Robert Browning's poem "Rabbi Ben Ezra."   NAHUM N. GLATZER

Bibliography: Friedländer, Michael, *Essays on the Writings of Abraham Ibn Ezra* (1877; repr. 1963–64).

ibn Gabirol, Solomon ben Judah [ib'-uhn gah-bee'-rohl, sahl'-uh-muhn ben joo'-duh]

Solomon ben Judah ibn Gabirol, c.1021–c.1058, was a Jewish poet and philosopher who lived in Muslim Spain. His enormous poetic output (over 400 extant poems) were both secular and religious. By far the best known of his religious poetry is *Keter Malkhut* (*The Kingly Crown*), a long philosophical poem that Sephardic Jews still include in their prayer book for the Day of Atonement. The ideas presented are akin to those of Gabirol's chief philosophic work, *Mekor Hayyim*, parts of which have been translated under the title *The Fountain of Life*, a metaphysical discussion that combines NEOPLATONISM with traditional Jewish philosophy. His ethical treatise *The Improvement of the Moral Qualities* reflects a similar synthesis and is regarded as the first attempt to separate ethics from a purely religious framework.   JOSEPH L. BLAU

Bibliography: Davidson, Israel, ed., *The Selected Religious Poems of Solomon ibn Gabirol* (1923); Guttmann, Julius, *The Philosophies of Judaism: The History of Jewish Philosophy from Biblical Times to Franz Rosenzweig*, trans. by David W. Silverman (1964); Ibn Gabirol, Solomon ben Judah, *Solomon ibn Gabirol's Choice of Pearls*, trans. by Abraham Cohen (1925).

Ibn Khaldun [ib'-uhn kahl-doon']

Ibn Khaldun, b. May 27, 1332, d. Mar. 16, 1406, was a famous Muslim historian, sociologist, and philosopher. Born into a distinguished Arab family in Tunis, he received a thorough education. For almost 30 years thereafter, his life alternated between active involvement in the turbulent politics of North Africa and Spain and scholarly retirement. In 1382 he went to Egypt, where he became a judge and a prominent teacher of Islamic law.

Ibn Khaldun is best known for the *Muqaddimah*, an introduction to his *Kitab al-'Ibar* (Universal History). *Kitab al-'Ibar* is a valuable source for the history of North Africa, but the *Muqaddimah* is a brilliant exposition of the methodological and cultural knowledge necessary to produce a scientific history. Ibn Khaldun was interested primarily in the reasons for the rise and fall of human civilization; he contended that the basic causes of historical evolution are to be sought in the economic and social structure of society.   MICHAEL W. DOLS

Bibliography: Ibn Khaldun, *The Muquaddimah*, trans. by Franz Rosenthal, 3 vols. (1967); Mahdi, Muhsin, *Ibn Khaldun's Philosophy of History* (1957); Schmidt, Nathaniel, *Ibn Khaldun: Historian, Sociologist, Philosopher* (1930).

Ibn Saud, King of Saudi Arabia [ib'-uhn sah-ood']

Abd al-Aziz ibn Abd al-Rahman, or Ibn Saud, unified much of the Arabian peninsula to create the Kingdom of Saudi Arabia, which he ruled from 1932 until his death on Nov. 9, 1953. Born probably in 1880 at Riyadh, he was a member of the Saudi dynasty. During his youth the Saudis were eclipsed by the Ottoman-supported house of Rashid, and he spent 1891 to 1902 in exile.

In 1902, Ibn Saud spectacularly initiated the Saudi revival by retaking Riyadh, the Saudi capital, in a surprise assault. Thereafter, his authority slowly expanded to include most of Arabia. Between 1902 and 1912 he conquered central Arabia; in 1913 he expelled the Turks from eastern Arabia; between

1916 and 1922 he eliminated Rashidi power and annexed northern Arabia; between 1924 and 1926 he drove the Hashimites (see HUSAYN IBN ALI) from Mecca and western Arabia; and between 1930 and 1934 he consolidated his new borders by repulsing Yemeni incursions. His conquests were organized into the Kingdom of Saudi Arabia in 1932.

Ibn Saud's success was due to his ability as a warrior–statesman. He carefully cultivated traditional Saudi ties with the fundamentalist Muslim sect of WAHHABISM, which provided a powerful ideological appeal. Through his Ikhwan (brotherhood) movement, he organized the settlement of many nomadic tribes in agriculturally based military colonies and thus provided bases from which to spearhead Saudi expansion. At the same time he displayed great diplomatic skill, especially in his dealings with Britain, which provided both weapons and money. Although culturally conservative, Ibn Saud inadvertently initiated the revolutionary modernization of his realm in 1933 when he allowed an American oil company (later Aramco) to begin developing Saudi Arabia's vast petroleum wealth. Ibn Saud was succeeded by his son SAUD.

ROBERT G. LANDEN

Bibliography: Howarth, David, *The Desert King: Ibn Saud and His Arabia* (1964) and *The Desert King: The Life of Ibn Saud* (1968); Philby, H. S. J., *Arabian Jubilee* (1953).

Ibo   [ee'-boh]

The Ibo (Igbo) are a major ethnic group of southeastern Nigeria. Their language is in the Kwa subfamily of Niger-Congo languages (see AFRICAN LANGUAGES), and they are estimated to number 7 million (1973). Most Ibo are subsistence farmers who grow root crops and produce palm oil for export. Local and long-distance market trade is well developed. Descent is mainly patrilineal, and marriage is polygynous, formalized by the payment of bride-price. Tribal associations are common and include title societies, groups based on age, and men's secret societies. Traditional religion centers on ancestral spirits and nature worship. Oracles are powerful and highly respected. Art forms include spectacular, painted wood carvings of human heads, masks, and figures, and doors and stools carved in geometric patterns.

Traditionally the Ibo lived in hundreds of autonomous village groups ruled by councils of elders. They practiced headhunting and owned slaves in precolonial times. Because of the high population density of their home region, large numbers of Ibo migrated to other parts of Nigeria. Under British colonial and missionary influence, many became Christians. In 1963 the Ibo played a major part in establishing Nigerian independence. Political conflict in 1966 between the Ibo and the Muslim HAUSA and FULANI of northern Nigeria led to the formation of the Ibo-supported secessionist state of BIAFRA. Thousands of Ibo were killed during the bloody civil war that followed (1967–70).

PHOEBE MILLER

Bibliography: Basden, George, *Among the Ibos of Nigeria* (1921; repr. 1966); Green, M. M., *Ibo Village Affairs*, 2d ed. (1964); Isichei, Elizabeth, *A History of the Igbo People* (1976); Uchendu, Victor C., *The Igbo of Southeastern Nigeria* (1965).

Ibsen, Henrik   [ib'-suhn, hen'-rik]

Henrik Johan Ibsen was a Norwegian poet and dramatist, one of the masters of world literature, whose works form the foundation of modern drama. He was born in Skien, Norway, on Mar. 20, 1828, and died in Christiania (now Oslo) on May 23, 1906. Ibsen's lasting international reputation may be attributed on the one hand to the 2 long dramatic poems *Brand* (1866; Eng. trans., 1911) and PEER GYNT (1867; Eng. trans., 1907) of his middle years and, on the other, to a cycle of 11 primarily realistic plays with contemporary settings that he produced between 1877 and 1896. Of these, A DOLL'S HOUSE (1879; Eng. trans., 1906), GHOSTS (1881; Eng. trans., 1906), and HEDDA GABLER (1890; Eng. trans., 1907) are probably the most widely read, discussed, and performed.

Ibsen's childhood and youth were scarred by his father's bankruptcy in 1836 and the consequent change from affluence to relative poverty; his maturity was profoundly influ-

Henrik Ibsen, 19th-century Norwegian playwright, profoundly influenced the development of modern drama through his realistic themes and emphasis on the individual's search for meaning. Such masterpieces as A Doll's House *(1879) and* The Wild Duck *(1884), widely debated during Ibsen's lifetime, dramatize the tension between action and conviction in a frequently restrictive society.*

enced by the oppressive and troubled aftermath of the year of revolutions, 1848. Fending for himself from age 15, he became a druggist's apprentice in Grimstad with the intention of pursuing medicinal studies, but failure in Greek and arithmetic on the entrance examination to the University of Christiania in 1850 closed that avenue to him. He then turned to journalism and made fledgling efforts in poetry and playwriting. The latter brought him to the attention of the celebrated Ole BULL, who in 1851 offered Ibsen an appointment as codirector and dramatic author at the newly established Norwegian Theater (later the National Stage) in Bergen.

Artistically, Ibsen's tenure in Bergen (1851–57) and his subsequent appointment as artistic manager of the Christiania Norwegian Theater (1857–62) spanned 11 years more notable for failures and frustrations than any real success. These posts afforded him, nevertheless, invaluable training and experience in dramaturgy and stagecraft. In 1852, on a sabbatical in Copenhagen and Dresden, Ibsen first experienced Shakespeare in performance, and encountered the tradition of presenting Holberg's comedies, still strongly maintained on the Danish stage. He also studied the dramatic theory of Hermann Hettner, a professor of aesthetics at Jena University, whose programmatic essay *Das moderne Drama* (Modern Drama, 1852) was currently much discussed. Hettner reinforced Ibsen's awareness of the psychological truth to which serious drama should aspire, proceeding from the conflict and development of human character. Hettner also drew his attention to Friedrich Hebbel's bourgeois tragedy, *Maria Magdalena* (1843; Eng. trans., 1914), which he came to admire greatly.

In 1856, Ibsen met Suzannah Thoresen, whom he married two years later. Their son and only child, Sigurd, was born in 1859. In the main, theirs was a good marriage. They were genuinely fond and supportive of each other and were able to communicate and work effectively together. Beginning in 1864, the Ibsens lived abroad, primarily in Rome, Dresden, and Munich, on grants from the Norwegian parliament, which were awarded annually after the tremendous breakthrough that *Brand* heralded, and on the growing royalties from the playwright's creative output. His meeting with the Danish critic George Brandes in 1871 and his reading of the first part of Brandes's *Main Currents in Nineteenth-Century Literature* (1872; Eng. trans., 1901–06) not only reinforced Ibsen's belief in the necessity of a spiritual, as opposed to a political, revolution but was also the main reason why he limited his poetic vision to the sphere of contemporary life in his last 11 dramas. In 1891, as *grand seigneur* of Scandinavian letters, Ibsen returned to live in Christiania. In 1900 he suffered the first of a series of strokes that ended his literary career; he was bedridden the last 5 years of his life.

Ibsen's work as a creative writer spanned 50 years (1849–99) and yielded 25 completed plays and a sheaf of verse of fairly consistent high quality. While his total production is remarkable for its extraordinary thematic unity—dealing chiefly with the individual human being and one's self-realization in spirit and in truth—it may be divided into two phases: an initial romantic period (1849–75), during which dramatic and nondramatic verse was his principal means of expression, and a subsequent realistic one (1875–99), when he devoted himself exclusively to the more difficult art of writing the straightforward, plain language spoken in real life; he thereby laid the foundations of modern prose drama.

Present-day scholarship, while recognizing the seminal influence of *Peer Gynt*, generally considers *The Wild Duck* (1884; Eng. trans., 1907) to be Ibsen's masterpiece. The former, a dramatic poem whose central theme is the search for self amid moral chaos, stands as an artistic expression of mankind's existential dilemma. *The Wild Duck*, with its curious blend of pity and contempt for human suffering, advocates the necessity of the "vital lie" for survival in a highly imperfect world. The collective saga of the Werle and Ekdal families is both comic and tragic—the modern notion of dramatic genre becomes increasingly ambiguous—and the complex patterns of reciprocity in the network of interrelationships reinforce the modern concept of the ensemble, as opposed to the star system, in theatrical production. As in all of his mature plays, Ibsen's aim in *The Wild Duck* is to raise social, moral, and spiritual questions for his audiences.

RAYMOND JARVI

Bibliography: Bull, Francis, *Ibsen: The Man and the Dramatist* (1973); Clurman, Harold, *Ibsen* (1977); Downs, Brian W., *A Study of Six Plays by Ibsen* (1950; repr. 1972); Egan, Michael, ed., *Ibsen: The Critical Heritage* (1972); Fjelde, Rolf, ed., *Ibsen: A Collection of Critical Essays* (1965); Ibsen, Henrik, *Letters and Speeches*, ed. by Evert Sprinchorn (1964); Jaeger, Henrik, *Henrik Ibsen: A Critical Biography* (1901; repr. 1973); Koht, Halvdan, *The Life of Ibsen*, trans. by Einar Haugen and A. E. Santaniello (1970); Lyons, Charles R., *Henrik Ibsen: The Divided Consciousness* (1972); McFarlane, James, ed., *Henrik Ibsen: A Critical Anthology* (1970); Northam, John, *Ibsen: A Critical Study* (1973); Shaw, George Bernard, *The Quintessence of Ibsenism* (1904; repr. 1959).

Ibuse Masuji   [ee-boo'-say mah-soo'-jee]

The Japanese novelist Ibuse Masuji, b. Feb. 15, 1898, is noted for his warmly drawn characters and wry humor. His best-known novel, *Black Rain* (1966; Eng. trans., 1969), concerns the atomic bombing of Hiroshima and is a compelling yet remarkably unsentimental report. Ibuse's works are characterized by optimism, leisurely detachment, spare style, and sensitivity to rural and folk traditions.   EDWARD B. FOWLER

Ibycus   [ib'-i-kuhs]

A Greek lyric poet of the 6th century BC, Ibycus was noted for his erotic love poems and vivid mythological choral songs. Born in Rhegium, Italy, he later moved to Samos, where he composed narrative verse in the style of Stesichorus. According to legend, Ibycus, while being murdered by robbers, called on a flock of cranes to avenge his death. Thereafter, the phrase "the cranes of Ibycus" became synonymous with the triumph of divine justice.

Bibliography: Bowra, C. M., *Greek Lyric Poetry from Alcman to Simonides* (1936; repr. 1961).

Icarus: see DAEDALUS (mythology).

Icaza, Jorge   [ee-kah'-sah, hor'-hay]

Jorge Icaza, b. July 10, 1906, d. May 1978, was an Ecuadorean writer who was equally at home in many literary genres. The author of seven plays, six novels, and four books of short stories, primarily dealing with the ills of Ecuadorean society, Icaza won international recognition for his novel *Huasipungo* (1934; trans. as *The Villagers*, 1964). In this he used an innovative, impersonal technique and dazzling linguistic versatility to convey the brutal destruction of an Indian village by ruthless landlords and foreign investors.   KEITH ELLIS

ICBM: see BALLISTIC MISSILE.

ice, oceanic: see PACK ICE.

ice, river and lake

Ice forms in lakes and rivers whenever the surface water supercools to 0° C (32° F) or a fraction of a degree lower. The first appearance of ice in a lake usually takes the form of spicules or platelike crystals. These grow into a network of dendrites that ultimately freeze together to form a continuous ice cover, called skim ice. Skim ice may form and dissipate several times before a stable ice cover is established. This ice cover continues to thicken downward as a result of transfer of heat from the ice to the air. Such ice is generally composed of prismatic or columnar-shaped crystals oriented vertically within the ice sheet. Additional thickening may occur at the top surface when water-soaked snow freezes to form snow ice.

Freezing of lake water removes most dissolved solids; the impurities retained are usually concentrated in the crystal boundaries. These impurities during spring induce preferential melting of crystal boundaries. Such melting produces candling, or disintegration of the ice cover crystal by crystal, a major factor in its ultimate decay. Candling is usually preceded by melting of ice from the top of the ice sheet and from along the shore.

Continuous ice covers may also form on rivers that have flow velocities less than about 0.5 m/sec (1.6 ft/sec). Ice formations in more turbulent, supercooled water, however, tend to be dominated by a copious crystallization of small particles of ice called frazil. If these particles remain suspended in the water, they may never coalesce sufficiently to form a frazil ice cover, except at obstructions in the river where bridging or damming can occur—frequently the prelude to flooding. Another major problem encountered with frazil is the clogging of intakes of hydroelectric plants. Accumulations of river-ice fragments can also damage structures by exerting pressure against them.

Anchor ice may form on river bottoms. Soil and stones at the bottom may radiate enough heat on clear, cold nights to lower bottom temperature below 0° C. The volume of anchor ice can grow very quickly; solar radiation in the morning can loosen the ice and bring it quickly to the surface in large chunks.

ANTHONY J. GOW

Bibliography: Pounder, Elton R., *The Physics of Ice* (1965).

Ice Age lakes: see LAKE, GLACIAL.

ice ages

An ice age is any part of several periods or epochs of time when glaciers, especially in the form of great ice sheets (see GLACIER AND GLACIATION), covered more of the Earth's surface than they do today. The term "ice age" has been used in two senses. First, it may refer to whole glacial epochs (the Pleistocene, for example), 2.5 million to 60 million years long, when the climate in the middle latitudes fluctuated wildly from warm to cold and glaciation ranged from today's small polar ice caps to massive, semiglobal ice sheets. Alternatively, it may describe a single glacial stage (such as the Wisconsin or Illinoisan) within these epochs, lasting for approximately 19,000 to 100,000 years each, when glaciers covered perhaps 20 to 50% of the then-existing continents (see PALEOCLIMATOLOGY).

Evidence of extensive repeated glaciation has been found for at least five stretches of geologic time: the middle of the Huronian Era in Precambrian time, beginning about 1,700 million to 2,300 million years ago; the end of the Proterozoic Era, in Precambrian time, starting about 670 million years ago; the middle of the Paleozoic Era, between the Ordovician and Silurian Periods, about 420 million years ago; the late Carboniferous and early Permian Periods, late in the Paleozoic Era, beginning 290 million years ago; and the Pleistocene Epoch of the Quaternary Period (Cenozoic Era), beginning at least 2.5 million years ago.

Each ice age lasted at least three million years; most of the earlier ones lasted more than 10 million years. Some of the great ice sheets, such as the Ordovician-Silurian and the Permo-Carboniferous sheets, appear to have migrated back and forth repeatedly across a large paleocontinent over a period of 100 million years. The combined length of glacial stages of the five aforementioned ice ages was probably between 50 and 200 million years, or only 1 to 4% of the Earth's long history (4.6 billion years). Ice ages are thus unusual and very short episodes in the Earth's climatic history.

EVIDENCE

The existence of the five ice ages is verified by clear evidence coming from widely scattered parts of the Earth's surface. The knowledge that such evidence dates from the same part of one geologic period depends upon critical fossils of short duration above and below the glacial layers or upon intrusions of igneous rocks datable in years by isotopes. Beyond 10 million years ago, these dates may vary by a million years; between 290 million and 650 million years ago, by as much as 10 million years. From evidence of the last ice age, which lasted more than 2.5 million years, it can be inferred that the comings and goings of the great ice sheets were simultaneous on several continents.

The proof of glaciation over continent-sized areas lies first in the widespread deposition of a unique kind of sediment or dirt called till (see TILL AND TILLITE) that can be observed under all glaciers today. The till and related deposits additionally contain a wide variety of rock types (stones and boulders called glacial ERRATICS) such as would be derived from widely disparate areas. Third, the till and erratics lie on one of the unique erosional surfaces of glaciation, such as grooved, striated, or polished bedrock pavement. Many other features associated with glaciers today are taken as indications of ancient ice ages: "streamlined" elongated ridges on the underlying rock (see ROCHE MOUTONNÉE); crescent-shaped nesting fractures in that rock; striated or faceted stones in the till; interspersed GRAVEL layers or lenses containing many rock types or all well-rounded pebbles; fine clay and silt laminae with dropstones from icebergs deposited in glacier-dammed lakes (see VARVED DEPOSIT); and uniformly sorted massive silt (not layered) deposited by glacial winds (see LOESS).

The older the rock record of an ice age, the less it is preserved, because rocks are altered by metamorphism over long periods of time. The Quaternary deposits of the last 2.5 million years are still easy-to-dig dirt, loose and slumping except in the case of certain ice-pressed and water-dried subglacial tills. But till deposits 420 million to 290 million years old have been contracted by wetting and drying, compressed by overlying layers, and cemented by chemicals carried in groundwater. Till, gravel, and varves from these earlier ice ages are found today in the form of tillite, CONGLOMERATE, and laminated SHALE, respectively. Buried and at times tilted, layers of these glacial rocks can be found at the surface today at scattered locations in mountain and valley regions. Beds of glacial materials 1,800 million to 650 million years old have been altered further to METAMORPHIC ROCKS (PHYLLITE, QUARTZITE, and SLATE) by the heat and pressure of mountain building. These materials are even harder to identify as glacial till, except for the fact that they often rest on a smooth, striated surface—the clearest glacial evidence of all.

Ancient Ice Ages. Evidence for the oldest known glaciation occurs in basal middle-Huronian rocks, 2,300 to 1,700 million years old, of the Precambrian early Proterozoic Era. The best tillites from this ice age are in the Gowganda Series in Canada; they rest on striated pavement and have been dated as being 2,288 million (± 87 million) years old. Three altered tillites indicate three continental ice advances. This formation, which contains varied subangular erratics up to 5 m (16 ft) long and interbedded varved slates, extends across a 130,000-km² (52,000-mi²) area (only 20,000 km²/8,000 mi² is exposed) under west central Ontario near Sudbury. Other widespread formations of the same age (Kalevian) lie under Finland and South Africa. A similar formation has been found in upper Michigan, in the Fern Creek Formation, but it may date from an even earlier, Lower-Huronian interval. These deposits were laid down when all these land masses were at the North Pole.

Another drastic ice age occurred 680 million years ago, and

may or may not have triggered an enormous diversity of marine invertebrates whose fossil remains are found in the rocks of this time. On the west side of the Wasatch Mountains in Utah there is a 100-m-thick (330-ft) layer of sooty-gray phyllite rocks that were once tillites; they contain various erratic boulders up to 6 m (20 ft) long and lie on laminated or varved slates. Glacial sediments have been mapped in detail over an area of 250,000 km² (100,000 mi²) in the Adelaide geosyncline running roughly southeast to northwest through central Australia. The best tillites are preserved in eastern Greenland, Scotland, and Scandinavia and date from the late Proterozoic Era. Other tillites have been found in Belorussia and China. All have giant erractics or varied lithology, but the Bigganjargga in northern Norway has basal pavement to clinch the glacial origin.

The most recently authenticated major glaciation is the one that took place at the Ordovician-Silurian boundary, about 420 million years ago. A layer of sedimentary marine tillites and beautifully grooved pavement is found all around the Sahara. Under it is a striated pavement of Ordovician sandstone containing TRILOBITE fossils, and over it are dropstones in silt containing the remains of Silurian GRAPTOLITES. Central Africa was the Earth's south pole then, and evidence of glaciation from this period extends well up through Spain and west into eastern Brazil.

The outstanding worldwide sediment record of the Pennsylvanian (Upper Carboniferous) Period shows cycles of rise and fall in sea level. It is not clear whether or not these cycles were glacially induced, but no better explanation has been put forth. Also, the evidence for glaciation simultaneously or just into the Permian Period (about 280 million years ago) is good. A series of marine or coal-swamp (shore) beds covered by several tillites containing coals or silts and dropstones, and being overlain by varved slates, lie under areas totaling thousands of square kilometers in five widely separated continents: the Buckeye and Pagoda Formations in Antarctica, the Dwyka Series in South Africa, the Itarare Group in Brazil, the Talchir Beds in India, and certain localities in Australia. Only in Australia does there appear to have been extensive moun-

Glaciation, such as that which occurs during an ice age, leads to changes in sea level. As temperatures become lower, a land mass (A) is covered by glaciers (B), which contain much of the water originally in the ocean; thus the sea level decreases. The weight of the ice causes depression of the land that amounts to about one-third of the ice thickness. When warm conditions return and the ice melts (C), the water flows back to the ocean; an additional rise in sea level is due to the slow recovery of the depressed land.

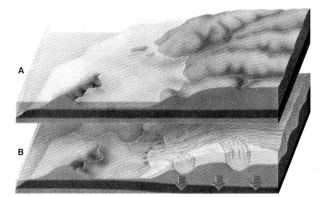

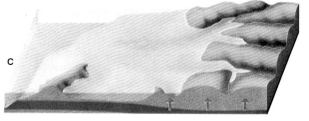

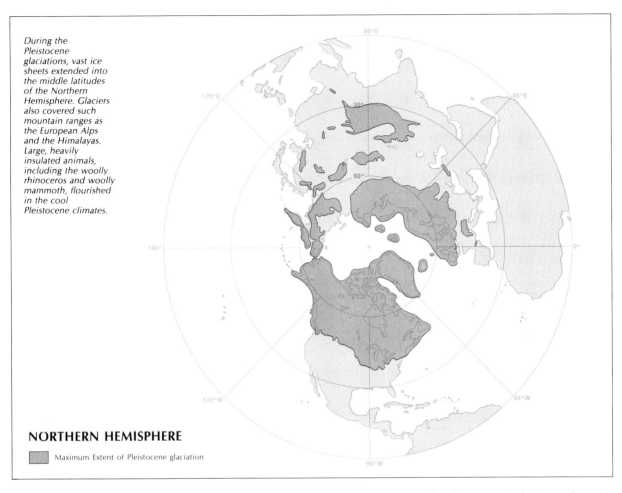

During the Pleistocene glaciations, vast ice sheets extended into the middle latitudes of the Northern Hemisphere. Glaciers also covered such mountain ranges as the European Alps and the Himalayas. Large, heavily insulated animals, including the woolly rhinoceros and woolly mammoth, flourished in the cool Pleistocene climates.

NORTHERN HEMISPHERE

Maximum Extent of Pleistocene glaciation

tain glaciation. Each area shows clear evidence of tillite resting on a fine striated and polished older rock surface. Although this evidence comes from far-flung parts of the globe, in Permo-Carboniferous time what are now today's continents then formed the paleocontinent GONDWANALAND, which was then centered about the South Pole. One gigantic ice sheet may have covered 50% of Gondwanaland.

The Permo-Carboniferous rocks are the first to clearly show the effects of an ice age upon higher forms of life. Most notable were changes in plant life all over the world. Pennsylvanian trees, including the Calamites, nearly disappeared, and two new tree genuses, *Glossopteris* and *Gangamopteris,* proliferated far and wide in the Permian Period. Faunal changes were not so extensive, because no mammals existed then. Development and change in the dog-sized amphibians and reptiles were rapid in the following Triassic Period, but their migration relates mostly to the expansions and contractions of the seas.

Quaternary Ice Age. In the Pleistocene Epoch, beginning 2.5 million years ago, ice sheets developed on highlands in North America and Europe and spread over the northern half of North America and a quarter of Eurasia, dominating the Northern Hemisphere. As sea level fell and the ice covered more land area, glaciers spread over what is now the shallow seafloor of Hudson Bay and the Barents Sea. This glacial spread comprised 52% of the Pleistocene ice-covered area. The older Antarctic and Greenland ice sheets grew somewhat larger as well. Mantles of ice developed in the group of mountain ranges stretching from southern Alaska to Colorado and California, in the European Alps, in the Ural and Caucasus Mountains, and in the Himalayas. Mountain glaciers in the Southern Hemisphere (in the South American Andes, the New Zealand Alps, and western Tasmania) extended down onto the plains. Altogether the mountain glaciers made up 16 percent of the total ice area.

The continental glaciers became very thick. Today more than half of the Antarctic ice sheet is more than 2,500 m (8,200 ft) thick; in central Greenland the ice is 2,000 m (6,600 ft) thick in most places. These have been measured by two drill holes, by sesimic (wave) sounding, by radio-echo sounding, and by precise gravity measurements. Thickness has also been calculated by using a formula involving primarily the temperature of the basal ice and the slippage at the bottom. Similar calculations applied to the much larger Pleistocene ice sheets indicate that these were over 3,000 m (10,000 ft) thick in North America and 2,500 m (8,200 ft) thick in Europe. These thicknesses are independently confirmed by the isotopic ratios of oxygen (O^{18}/O^{16}), which differ between rainfall and snowfall ice; the oxygen isotopes of microfossil sediments that fell to the seafloor during the colder stages of Quaternary time indicate that the thickness of the ice averaged 2,500 m (8,200 ft) much of the time.

The ice-age seas were lower than today's by 100 to 140 m (330 to 460 ft). Many wave-cut terraces and sea-cliffs are found that far below today's sea level. Elevated coral reefs and shore terraces, however, indicate that sea level was also 5 to 50 m (16 to 160 ft) higher than it is now during some interglacial intervals. By comparison, if all the Greenland and Antarctic ice melted today, sea level would rise nearly 65 m (215 ft). Ice-age sea levels are generally lower than those in the nonglacial 99 percent of geologic time. They certainly fluctuate wildly over the few tens of thousands of years during which the ice sheets grew and melted away. During the last ice age sea level rose or fell over 1 to 2 m (3 to 7 ft) per century. During the same period the ice crept over the land at 50 to 150 m (160 to 490 ft) per year.

These Quaternary events occurred because of changes in climate. Cirques produced by local mountain glaciers that could have existed only during glacial stages are found 1,200 to 1,700 m (4,000 to 5,600 ft) lower than today's mountain glaciers; this indicates that the temperature in mid-latitude mountain ranges during these stages was 7 C degrees (13 F degrees) cooler than it is today. Careful study of temperature and salinity requirements of hundreds of species of living ocean-surface plankton (DIATOMS, FORAMINIFERA, and RADIOLARIA) can be applied by regression curves to the undisturbed cores of ice-age ooze on the deep ocean floor. These measurements show that the surface ocean fauna and flora moved repeatedly 600 to 1,100 km (360 to 660 mi) north and then back south. Most ocean surface waters at the height of the glacial stages were at least 2 to 5 C degrees (4 to 9 F degrees) cooler and slightly less saline than today. The oxygen-isotope ratios of snow falling during the last ice age indicate that on the still-remaining ice sheets (Antarctica and Greenland ice at 1,300 and 1,150 m/4,300 and 3,800 ft depth), ice-age temperatures were as much as 6 to 8 C degrees (11 to 14 F degrees) colder, and the atmosphere was ten or more times dustier than it is today.

The Quaternary ice age had great effects—far more than previous ice ages had—upon life forms, because more-advanced life forms and more numerous species of fauna and flora were involved. The stresses of rapidly changing temperature, precipitation, and winds must have been great.

Heavily insulated animal species—such as the woolly rhinoceros, the woolly mammoth, and the musk ox—developed, while slowly evolving Cenozoic species, such as the Pliocene horse and several fish, disappeared early in this ice age. A few new species of birds, amphibians, and field mice (microtines) died out. For some reason, giant mammals developed; for example, the ancestral BISON, the imperial MAMMOTH, and a giant bear and dog. The list of extinct Pleistocene mammals is long. The large ones—the mastodon, the great beavers, the saber-tooth cats, the ground sloth, and the glyptodon—disappeared everywhere. Llamas, camels, tapirs, horses, yaks, and other species became extinct only in North America. Lower animal forms, such as mollusks and beetles, did not change much by adaptation, but they did migrate. River valleys became natural migratory highways; while some animal forms were frozen into extinction, others were able to escape the ice by migrating toward the equator.

Plant life changed little during the 2.5 million years of the Quaternary ice age. Plant pollen and spores, being quite hardy, are preserved in bogs between glacial layers and provide complete records of the interglacial spasms and approaching glacial stages. Tree genuses in those times were similar to today's; although they failed to reproduce in some colder areas, they appeared and flourished anew in warmer areas as the ice slowly moved in. In North America, spruce grew best 1,200 to 1,600 km (745 to 990 mi) further south than usual—in North Carolina, Virginia, and Ohio—suggesting temperatures 7 to 10 C degrees (13 to 18 F degrees) cooler at that time. Trees lying in the path of the ice were crushed and swept up into the till. South of the ice, in temperate latitudes, a mixture of warm-climate species on hillsides facing south and cool-climate species on those facing north coexisted. The group of warmth-loving species returned in each succeeding warm interglacial time; in Europe these species were more diverse than in America, but all the trees of that time were similar to those of today.

Today we live in a warm interlude during or just after the Quaternary ice age. All of the early development of humans came during this last ice age, and civilization has come into existence in its aftermath.

CAUSES OF GLACIATION

The only adequate source of water for such massive amounts of ice is the oceans. The creation of massive ice sheets on land thus necessarily depends on wind and weather patterns. To preserve snow from year to year, the summer climate must be cooler. There are so many ways these events could happen, and happen repeatedly, that the cause is locked into complicated OCEAN-ATMOSPHERE INTERACTIONS. It is extremely

GLACIATIONS AND INTERGLACIATIONS OF THE PLEISTOCENE EPOCH*

Approximate Ending (years ago)	North American Stages	Northern European Stages	Central European (Alpine) stages
10,000	Late Wisconsin	Weichselian	Würm
Interstadials	Mid Wisconsin	Eemian	R-W
45,000	Early Wisconsin	Saalian	Riss
Interglacial	Sangomonian	Holsteinian	M-R
125,000	Illinoian	Elsterian	Mindel
Interglacial	Yarmouth	Cromerian	G-M
690,000	Kansan	Menapian	Günz
Interglacial	Aftonian	Waalian	D-G
1,600,000	Nebraskan	Eburonian	Danube
Interglacial		Tiglian	B-D
2,000,000		Brüggenian	Biber

* In North America the glacial stages are named for the states in which good exposures of till deposits have been encountered; the interglacials, after localities (Sangamon County, Ill.; Yarmouth, Iowa; Afton Junction, Iowa) where interglacial deposits have been found. In Northern Europe the glacial and interglacial stages are named after various towns and rivers in this region. The Central European (Alpine) stages are named after Alpine streams (arranged alphabetically from earliest to latest) that are tributaries of the Danube River; the interglacials are specified by the initials of the glacial stages that precede and follow them.

difficult to know what is cause and what is effect.

For example, the stratosphere was ten times dustier during glacial times than today. Dust not only absorbs some radiation in the upper atmosphere but also reflects some of the Sun's heat back out, thus cooling the Earth's surface. At first this was thought to be volcanic dust, but volcanism has not been correlated with any of the glacial stages. Dust may have been raised because much bare ocean shelf was exposed around receding seas.

Evidence in dunes and loess blankets shows that in glacial times the wind was intensified, and the belts of westerlies were pushed toward the equator. Intensified heat exchange would also produce more clouds and precipitation; the increased cloudiness would be 80% effective in reflecting solar radiation back out into space; therefore the Earth's surface would become 1 to 2 C degrees (2 to 4 F degrees) cooler.

A varying amount of carbon dioxide in the lower atmosphere may also have had some effect. Carbon dioxide lets in short-wave sunlight, but it also prevents long-wave heat radiation from passing out of the atmosphere, thus raising the atmospheric temperature between glaciations. In glacial stages, however, surface seawater would have been 2 to 6 C degrees (4 to 11 F degrees) cooler; this cooler water could absorb more carbon dioxide from the air and thus cool the latter by 1 to 2 C degrees (2 to 4 F degrees).

When sea level was lower, many surface ocean currents no longer delivered heat to the far north (or south, in earlier ice ages); this would have dropped high-latitude temperature by 2 to 4 C degrees (4 to 7 F degrees). Once it had begun to form, the snow-ice surface itself would have then cooled the air masses contacting it by more than 5 C degrees (9 F degrees); this would have caused the further extension of sea ice that is recorded in the sandy sediments on the ocean floor. Sea ice, like clouds, is 80% effective in reflecting the radiant energy from the Sun, thus adding to the cooling effect. This also prevents free access of moisture into the air, the principal effect behind the Ewing-Donn theory of glaciation. The ice sheets, then, cut off from their source of moisture, begin to shrink, sea level correspondingly rises, and warm ocean currents begin to melt the sea ice. All these mechanisms are self-reinforcing, and each may contribute to the waxing and waning of any ice age.

Continental glaciation requires either high mountain altitudes (over 4,000 m/13,000 ft) or polar land (high ground located above 60° latitude). CONTINENTAL DRIFT and shifting polar positions play a part here. Paleomagnetic analysis of ice-age sediments is now showing that today's continents were at one time united and near one pole or the other. Also, high mountains have arisen wherever continental plates have slid into each other, as India's current collision with Asia is raising the Himalayas. Unlike the self-reinforcing mechanisms, continental drift and mountain building occur so slowly that they could contribute only to whole ice ages, not to the drastic cycling of climate characteristic of the several glacial stages.

Some trigger mechanism, most likely from outside the Earth or its atmosphere, affecting the climate seems to be necessary. Solar energy intensities have not yet been found to vary sufficiently to have single-handedly produced an ice age, but solar activity as expressed in sunspots and radio blackouts on an 11-year cycle has been shown to relate to short-term fluctuations in the Earth's climate. Longer cycles are currently being sought by statistical means.

An unproven idea is that the solar system may pass through interstellar clouds of disseminated matter; such clouds could block out some of the Sun's energy. This effect would be small, however, and no space clouds big enough or dense enough to cause glacial stages have been identified along the Earth's trail. Other trigger mechanisms suggested include the astronomical relation of the Earth to the Sun as the shape of its orbit changes (more elliptical every 92,000 years); the 1¼° variation in tilt of the Earth's axis (more tilted every 40,000 years); and the coincidence of the Earth's furthest distance from the Sun with summer tilt toward the Sun (every 21,000 years). Machine modeling of these effects makes them look very promising as possible trigger effects (see MILANKOVICH THEORY).

RICHARD P. GOLDTHWAIT

Bibliography: Charlesworth, J. K., *The Quaternary Era, with Special Reference to Its Glaciation,* 2 vols. (1957); Coleman, Arthur, *Ice Ages, Recent and Ancient* (1969); Cornwell, Ian, *The Ice Ages* (1970); Embleton, Clifford, and King, C. A. M., *Glacial and Periglacial Geomorphology,* 2 vols., 2d ed. (1975); Flint, Richard F., *Glacial and Quaternary Geology* (1971); Frenzel, Burkhard, *Climatic Fluctuations of the Ice Age,* trans. by A. E. Nairn (1973); Imbrie, John and Katherine, *The Ice Ages: Solving the Mystery* (1979); Kurten, Bjorn, *The Ice Age* (1972); Matthews, William H., *The Story of Glaciers and the Ice Age* (1974); Schultz, Gwen, *Ice Age Lost* (1974); Zeuner, F. E., *The Pleistocene Period* (1959).

ice cream

Ice cream is popular frozen food made from varying mixtures of cream and milk, sweeteners, flavorings, and air. The air is beaten into the milk mixture as it freezes, making the final product light and spoonable. Other ice cream ingredients range from the eggs used in rich French ice creams to the stabilizers and emulsifiers that are added to many commercial ice creams. Stabilizers prevent large ice crystals from forming; emulsifiers are added to smooth and fill and to render ice cream more whippable.

The differences between ice creams are a product of the quality, richness, and freshness of the ingredients. An economy ice cream may use more dried milk products and a lower percentage of milk fats; it will often contain large amounts of stabilizers and emulsifiers and will have a higher volume of air. A high-quality ice cream is denser and less airy; it will use fresh whole products, contain 16 to 20% milk fat, and use additives sparingly, if at all. Natural ice creams avoid artificial flavorings and additives, although they do use natural products to emulsify and stabilize.

In its standards for various frozen milk desserts, the U.S. Food and Drug Administration requires that most ice cream contain at least 20% milk solids by weight. Ice milk must contain a minimum of 11% milk solids; sherbet, a minimum of 2%. Maximum amounts of stabilizers and emulsifiers are also regulated. Ice cream is, however, one of the few manufactured foods where a listing of the ingredients is not required on the package label.

The confection may have been introduced to Europe in 1295, when Marco Polo returned to Italy from the Far East with a recipe for a frozen dessert that included milk; it probably resembled sherbet. Italy is credited with popularizing the dish. In 1851 ice cream making became a full-fledged industry when Baltimore milk dealer Jacob Fussell found himself oversupplied with cream and began producing ice cream in quantity. Today over 800 million gallons of ice cream are sold in the United States annually; the total reaches over 1 billion gallons when ice milk, sherbet, and water ices are included.

PAUL DICKSON

Bibliography: Arbuckle, Wendell S., *Ice Cream,* 3d ed. (1977); Dickson, Paul, *The Great American Ice Cream Book* (1972).

ice fog: see FOG.

ice hockey

Ice hockey is a sport played by two teams of six players on a rectangular surface of ice called a rink. The players, who wear ice skates, attempt to knock a circular piece of hard rubber, the puck, into one of two goals, situated at opposite ends of the rink. Players use a stick with a flat blade at one end to drive the puck forward at speeds that sometimes exceed 160 km/h (100 mph). Ice hockey has traditionally been a cold-weather sport, and Canada and the Soviet Union are the two nations with the greatest number of active players. Hockey is played by professionals and amateurs and is a popular spectator sport.

HISTORY

Records of early hockey games date back to mid-19th-century Canada. The first formal hockey game was played in Kingston, Ontario, in 1855, with teams drawn from the Royal Canadian Rifles, an Imperial Army troop. McGill University students played the game in the 1870s. The first set of hockey rules was codified by W. F. Robertson, a McGill student, who adapted the rules of field hockey for play on ice. Robertson's rules called for nine players on a side and the use of a square puck. The first amateur league was formed in 1885. In 1893 the governor general of Canada, Lord Stanley of Preston, offered a trophy (the Stanley Cup) to be awarded to the best Canadian hockey team. Today the cup is awarded annually to a professional team—the champion of the National Hockey League (NHL). In the same year (1893), hockey was first played in the United States at Yale and The Johns Hopkins universities. In 1917 several Canadian hockey teams banded together and organized the NHL. Hockey became an Olympic Games event in 1920, and in 1924 the newly founded Boston Bruins became the first professional hockey team among the previously amateur teams of the NHL. In the 1978–79 hockey season the NHL consisted of 17 professional teams in cities in the United States and Canada. The NHL was rivaled by the 6 teams of the World Hockey Association (WHA), founded in the 1972–73 season. In 1979 an agreement was reached between the two leagues to bring about the absorption of the WHA by the NHL. Beginning in the 1979-80 season the NHL had 21 teams, including 4 from the disbanded WHA.

An offensive player pivots to protect the puck from a defender (kneeling), then looks to pass off to a teammate during a game between the New York Rangers and the New York Islanders, two rival teams in the Patrick Division of the National Hockey League.

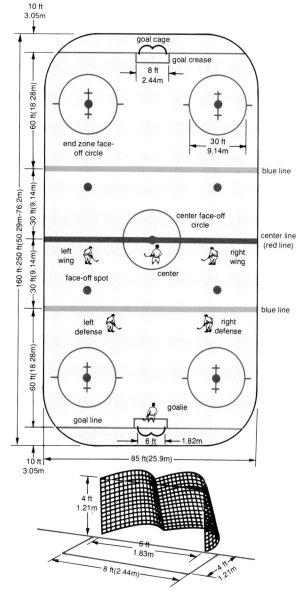

A standard hockey rink and goal appear with dimensions, markings, and players' positions. Between the blue lines lies the neutral zone, which is divided in half by a red center line. Defense players are situated in their defending zone. Forwards are positioned behind the red line. Face-off circles and spots are places where the game is started or restarted after a referee's call.

EQUIPMENT AND THE RINK

Hockey rinks vary in size, although standard International Ice Hockey Federation dimensions call for a rink 200 ft (61 m) long and 85 ft (26 m) wide, with corners rounded into the arc of a circle with a 28-ft (8.5-m) radius. The rink is enclosed by 4-ft-high (1.2-m) retaining boards and is divided into three zones—two end zones and a neutral zone. The zones are demarcated on the ice by blue lines that extend up the sides of the boards. Two red goal lines, 2 in (5 cm) wide, run the width of the rink. There is a space of 10 ft (3 m) between the goal lines and the barrier boards at each end of the ice. There are two goal cages that have openings 4 ft (1.2 m) high and 6 ft (1.8 m) wide, with the posts resting on, and 3 ft (.91 m) to either side of, the midpoint of the goal lines. The backs of the goals have a netting that stops pucks shot into the goal and makes judging a score easier. Two 12-in-wide (30-cm)

blue lines are 60 ft (18 m) toward the center of the rink from each goal line. The blue lines also extend the width of the ice. A red line, seen only in professional ice hockey, also 12 in (30 cm) wide, bisects the length of the rink between the blue lines. The blue lines designate attacking and defending zones, depending on which team controls the puck.

In the center of the rink is a red spot 12 in (30 cm) in diameter, circumscribed by a line 2 in (5 cm) wide with a 10-ft (3-m) radius. There are four other spots and circles of the same size, two in each end zone. They are located halfway between each goal post and the boards and 15 ft (4.6 m) out from the goal lines. In professional hockey four red spots of the same size are in the neutral zone midway between the boards and the center of the rink and 5 ft (1.5 m) from each blue line. The center spot is where play starts at the beginning of each period or after a goal is scored. The other spots are where play is resumed after any stop in play. Around the mouth of the goal is an area called the crease that is delineated by 2-in-wide (5-cm) red lines. The puck is a disk-shaped piece of black vulcanized rubber 3 in (7.6 cm) in diameter and 1 in (2.5 cm) thick; it weighs 5.5–6 oz (154–168 g).

Sticks are made of wood or a wood-and-fiberglass construction. The handles may be no more than 55 in (1.4 m) long, 1.25 in (3.2 cm) wide, and 0.75 in (1.9 cm) thick. The blades may be no more than 12.5 in (32 cm) long and 3 in (7.6 cm) wide. Goaltender's sticks may be wider and heavier. Ice hockey skates have a short blade that is slightly curved, which permits quick turns and stops. Goaltenders' skates have longer, flat blades for stability.

Players wear protective shoulder, hip, and elbow pads, knee and shin guards, and heavy leather gloves; some also wear helmets. Goaltenders wear massive leg and chest pads and a glove similar to a baseball mitt with which to catch flying pucks. Most goaltenders also wear a plastic face mask.

PLAY OF THE GAME

Each team consists of a goaltender, two defenders, and three

STANLEY CUP CHAMPIONS*

Year	Team	Year	Team
1917	Seattle Metropolitans	1949	Toronto Maple Leafs
1918	Toronto Arenas†	1950	Detroit Red Wings
1920	Ottawa Senators	1951	Toronto Maple Leafs
1921	Ottawa Senators	1952	Detroit Red Wings
1922	Toronto St. Patricks	1953	Montreal Canadiens
1923	Ottawa Senators	1954	Detroit Red Wings
1924	Montreal Canadiens	1955	Detroit Red Wings
1925	Victoria Cougars	1956	Montreal Canadiens
1926	Montreal Maroons	1957	Montreal Canadiens
1927	Ottawa Senators	1958	Montreal Canadiens
1928	New York Rangers	1959	Montreal Canadiens
1929	Boston Bruins	1960	Montreal Canadiens
1930	Montreal Canadiens	1961	Chicago Black Hawks
1931	Montreal Canadiens	1962	Toronto Maple Leafs
1932	Toronto Maple Leafs	1963	Toronto Maple Leafs
1933	New York Rangers	1964	Toronto Maple Leafs
1934	Chicago Black Hawks	1965	Montreal Canadiens
1935	Montreal Maroons	1966	Montreal Canadiens
1936	Detroit Red Wings	1967	Toronto Maple Leafs
1937	Detroit Red Wings	1968	Montreal Canadiens
1938	Chicago Black Hawks	1969	Montreal Canadiens
1939	Boston Bruins	1970	Boston Bruins
1940	New York Rangers	1971	Montreal Canadiens
1941	Boston Bruins	1972	Boston Bruins
1942	Toronto Maple Leafs	1973	Montreal Canadiens
1943	Detroit Red Wings	1974	Philadelphia Flyers
1944	Montreal Canadiens	1975	Philadelphia Flyers
1945	Toronto Maple Leafs	1976	Montreal Canadiens
1946	Montreal Canadiens	1977	Montreal Canadiens
1947	Toronto Maple Leafs	1978	Montreal Canadiens
1948	Toronto Maple Leafs	1979	Montreal Canadiens

* The Stanley Cup (instituted 1893) was originally presented to the amateur ice hockey champion of Canada; as of 1917 it was awarded to the professional National Hockey League champion.
† The 1919 series was discontinued after 5 games because of an influenza epidemic.

Ice hockey players require considerable protection because the game is both violent and fast paced. Forwards and defensive players (A) wear streamlined equipment to reduce wind resistance. This includes a helmet with a face mask (1), chest protector and shoulder pads (2), elbow pads (3), gloves (4), hip and thigh pads (5), knee pads and shin guards (6), and skates (7). The stick (8) is smaller than that used by the goalkeeper (15). Because a goalkeeper uses any part of his body to block the puck (9), his equipment (B) must provide even more protection. He also wears a special face mask (10); a mittlike glove (11), used to catch the puck; a fiberboard guard (12) to deflect the puck; bulky legpads (13); and reinforced skates (14).

forwards (a center and two wings). In the professional leagues play is supervised by three major officials; in amateur games two officials are used.

Play of the three 20-minute periods starts at the center spot with a face-off—the official drops the puck and the two centers try to control it.

Actual play in hockey is frequently interrupted by one of two infractions: icing and offside. A player is offside if he or she precedes the puck into the attacking zone. This rule prevents players from hovering by the goal when the puck is not in the attacking zone. A face-off is then held at one of the red spots in the neutral zone nearest to where the infraction was committed.

Icing is called when the puck crosses the center and goal lines without being touched by the opposition. An icing penalty warrants a face-off in the defensive zone of the penalized team at the red spot nearest to the location of the infraction.

Other infractions include tripping, holding, and hooking or spearing with the stick. For such fouls the offending player must leave the game for 2 minutes. More serious infractions, such as fighting, draw 5- or 10-minute penalties. The penalized team must play short-handed, while the other team, at full strength, enjoys a "power-play" situation. The penalized player may return if his or her team surrenders a goal during the time he or she spends in the "penalty box."

The team that scores more goals by the end of the third period is the winner. In the NHL ties are permitted except during playoffs, when the team to score first in an overtime period wins. In amateur play the first score in a 10-minute overtime period decides the outcome of the game. The match is declared a draw, however, if no goal is scored in the extra period. JAMES M. GREIFF

Bibliography: Chadwick, Bill, *Illustrated Ice Hockey Rules* (1976); Eskenazi, Gerald, *A Thinking Man's Guide to Pro Hockey*, rev. ed. (1976); Esposito, Phil, and Dew, Dick, *Winning Hockey: For Beginners* (1976); Fischler, Stan, and Baliotti, Dan, *This Is Hockey* (1975); Fischler, Stan and Shirley, *Fischler's Hockey Encyclopedia* (1975); Hollander, Zander, and Bock, Hal, *The Complete Encyclopedia of Ice Hockey*, rev. ed. (1974); Isaacs, Neil D., *Checking Back: The Story of NHL Hockey* (1977); Mikita, Stan, and Wass, George, *Inside Hockey* (1971).

ice plant

The common name for the genus *Mesembryanthemum*, ice plant usually refers to *M. crystallinum*, a succulent herb native to South Africa and naturalized in such places as California and southwest Asia. Found in dry sandy areas, it has whitish to pink or red flowers. Because the leaves are covered with small, glistening swellings, they appear icy.   DIANNE FAHSELT

ice skating

Ice skating is a sport in which people slide over a smooth ice surface on steel-bladed skates. About 28 million people skate in the United States, and millions more skate in other parts of the world wherever the winters are cold enough. Although most people ice skate for recreation and exercise, skating for form and speed is a highly competitive international amateur sport. Ice-skating skills are also an important part of the game of ICE HOCKEY. Ice-skating shows, such as the Ice Follies and the Ice Capades, have entertained millions of spectators. These shows also provide a means for skaters to commercially exploit their talents. The increasing number of indoor rinks has made year-round ice skating possible.

HISTORY OF ICE SKATING

Humans probably skated on ice before the birth of Christ in the Scandinavian countries. The first skates are believed to have been sharp splinters of animal bone fitted to the bottoms of boots to ease travel over ice. There are drawings and references in literature to ice skating that date from the Middle Ages. The modern word *skate* is derived from the Dutch word *schaats*, meaning "leg bone" or "shank bone." Skating as a sport developed on the lakes of Scotland and the canals of the Netherlands. In the 13th and 14th centuries wood was eventually substituted for bone skate blades, and in 1572 the first iron skates were manufactured. The iron blades reduced the friction of forward motion, and their resistance to lateral slipping enabled the skater to push himself or herself ahead. Instructional books were published, and the first skate club was founded in Edinburgh, Scotland, in 1742. The metal-bladed skates were soon brought to North America by Scottish immigrants.

(Left) *Figure skating champion Dorothy Hamill won a gold medal in the 1976 Olympic competition for her flawless performance of both compulsory figures and free-skating routines.*

(Right) *Olympic champion Irina Rodnina and her husband-partner Alexandr Zaitsev of the Soviet Union won gold medals at both the 1976 and 1980 Olympic Winter games for their performance in the paired figure-skating competition. Rodnina also won a gold medal at the 1972 Olympic games, skating with a different partner.*

Ice skating did not develop as an organized competitive sport until the introduction of steel skate blades permanently attached to leather boots. The earlier iron blades dulled quickly, and street shoes, to which they were tied with straps, lacked ankle support. Using the steel skates, a U.S. ballet dancer named Jackson Haines created a free-flowing skating technique that incorporated waltzlike movements. Ice speed skating, which had developed in the Netherlands in the 17th century, was given a boost by the innovations in skate construction. Figure skating became an Olympic event in 1908. Speed skating for men was part of the 1924 Olympic Games, but it was not until 1960 that women's speed skating was placed on the Olympic agenda.

SKATE DESIGN

The figure-skate blade differs from the ice-hockey or speed-skate blade because it is slightly concave, or "hollow ground." The hollow, which runs the length of the blade, creates two edges, which come in contact with the ice. The forward part of the blade, the toe-rake, is sawtoothed and is used for jumps and spins on the toes. The figure-skate boots, which are traditionally black for men and white for women, are made of sturdy leather and have stiffening supports at the heel and under the arch. They are tightly laced up over the ankle to help prevent the foot from rolling from one side or the other. Speed skates have a considerably longer blade and a single, thin edge. The toe of the blade is smooth and turned

up. The boot is made of lighter leather than the figure-skate boot and is lower, coming just to the top of the ankles.

COMPETITIVE ICE SKATING

Figure Skating. Figure skating is primarily a sport for amateurs. Contests are held for singles and for pairs. In the singles class a skater's talents are appraised in the compulsory-figures and free-skating categories. The compulsory-figures event requires each skater to perform 3 or 6 repetitions of 3 figures drawn from a possible 41 patterns. All figures are based on a figure-8 pattern or variations thereof. Skaters start from a stationary position and execute the figure, with attention given to the precision of the retracing of the figure, balance, control, and gracefulness. Judges award contestants up to a maximum of 6 points for each figure executed. The free-skating events involve jumps, spins, spirals, and skating coordinated with music. For singles, regular free-skating and a compulsory free-skating performance account for 60 percent of a skater's score, whereas pairs are judged only on their free-skating performance. The pairs event, in addition to free skating, may also include ice dancing. In pairs skating, the same jumps, spins, and twirls as in the singles events are used, along with lifts and partner-assisted jumps. Ice dancing differs from pairs skating: lifts are prohibited and specific movements are required.

Ice figure skating was popularized by Sonja HENIE, who won numerous amateur competitions before turning professional

(Left) *Speed skaters bend low to cut wind resistance while competing in an international meet. Although eclipsed in popularity by figure skating, speed skating is a much older sport and remains popular in northern Europe.*

(Right) *Eric Heiden, an American athlete, dominated the speed-skating competition in the 1980 Winter Olympic games, skating to victory in all five races of the sport (500 m; 1,000 m; 1,500 m; 5,000 m; 10,000 m).*

in 1936. Peggy FLEMING, Dorothy HAMILL, and Dick BUTTON also toured with ice revues after illustrious amateur careers. The typical ice show is similar to a circus on ice skates and features costumes, trick skating, and gags to entertain the audience rather than to display true figure-skating expertise.

Speed Skating. The long, narrow blades of the modern speed skate permit skaters to maintain speeds of about 48 km/h (30 mph). Formal competitions are usually held outdoors on large rinks. Men who participate in major international meets enter one of four events: 500 meters (1,650 ft), 1,500 meters (4,950 ft), 5,000 meters (16,500 ft), or 10,000 meters (33,000 ft). Women compete over courses of from 500 meters to 3,000 meters (9,900 ft). American, Scandinavian, and Japanese men speed skaters usually do well in the shorter races, whereas in the longer events Soviet and Dutch skaters usually excel. Women's speed skating is dominated by Americans and Soviets. JAMES M. GREIFF

Bibliography: Arnold, Richard, *Better Ice Skating* (1976); Deleeuw, Dianne, and Lehrman, Steve, *Figure Skating* (1978); Jonland, Einar, and Fitzgerald, Jim, *Inside Ice Skating* (1978); Ogilvie, Robert S., *Basic Ice Skating Skills* (1968); Scott, Barbara, and Kirby, Michael, *Skating for Beginners* (1953); Wild, John, *Power Skating* (1971).

iceberg

An iceberg is a large piece of ice that has broken off, or calved, from the terminus of a GLACIER into a body of water. Nearly all icebergs are found in the ocean, but all are composed of freshwater ice rather than frozen sea water. They are usually white, blue, or green, although some are black due to rock material incorporated in them.

The glaciers of Antarctica and Greenland are the sources of most icebergs. The largest icebergs are found in Antarctica; the U.S. Coast Guard icebreaker *Glacier* measured one that was 333 km (208 mi) long and 96 km (60 mi) wide. They may extend downward 300 m (1,000 ft) and reach a height of more than 60 m (200 ft). Icebergs float low; on the average, $\frac{6}{7}$ of the volume of an Arctic iceberg and $\frac{4}{5}$ of icebergs of Antarctic origin is submerged. The degree of submergence depends on the density, the rock content, and the shape of the iceberg.

Wind and ocean currents may move icebergs thousands of kilometers from their source; in 1907 and 1926 icebergs were reported as far south as Bermuda. As time passes, icebergs de-

Melting icebergs reveal typical features of coastal erosion: recent wave-cut notches (1), old notches cut when the iceberg was heavier and lower (2), water-runoff erosion (3), parent-glacier rock fragments (4), a water-eroded sea stack (5), and a wave-cut platform (6).

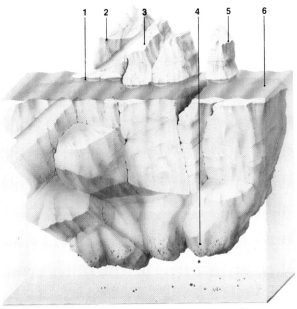

crease in size, both because contact with the ocean and air melts the ice and because storm waves break off pieces. Greenland icebergs are mostly craggy and usually melt away completely by the time they are 2 years old; Antarctic icebergs are mainly tabular because of calving from ice shelves and may survive 10 or more years.

On Apr. 14, 1912, the *Titanic,* the largest ship in the world, ran into a small iceberg on her maiden voyage across the Atlantic and sank, resulting in the death of 1,503 people. During World War II the Allies considered anchoring a flattopped Antarctic iceberg in the Atlantic to serve as a landing field for planes involved in the submarine war. Several nations have set up research stations on floating icebergs (see, for example, FLETCHER'S ICE ISLAND). The oil-rich nations of the Middle East are now giving serious thought to the possibility of towing icebergs from the Antarctic and using them as sources of water. ROBERT L. NICHOLS

Bibliography: Hult, John L., and Ostrander, N. C., *Antarctic Icebergs as a Global Fresh Water Resource* (1973); Schultz, Gwen, *Icebergs and Their Voyages* (1975).

See also: INTERNATIONAL ICE PATROL.

iceboating

The pilot of a small iceboat leans to one side to stabilize the craft's runners against the ice during a race over a frozen lake. Because these sail-powered craft are capable of achieving speeds of up to 229 km/h (143 mph), iceboating is regarded as the fastest of all winter sports.

Iceboating is the sport of sailing a boat that rides on metal runners over a smooth ice surface. A modern iceboat typically has a narrow hull constructed of a rigid, light material, a forward steering runner, an outrigged runner on both sides, and a mast that supports one or two sails. The sport is limited to regions where winters are cold enough to freeze lakes and rivers. Large bodies of water and low winter temperatures have made iceboating popular in the northern United States, Canada, Scandinavia, the Baltic Sea area, and the Netherlands. Iceboats are frequently used for racing, and organized clubs stage regattas. Larger craft have crews of two, whereas smaller boats are skippered by one person. The Ice Yacht Challenge Pennant of America, first run in 1881, is the premier race and is open to boats of all sizes from any country.

The earliest record of an iceboat is a 1768 drawing of a Dutch sloop built with runners affixed to a cross plank under the hull. The Lapps and Finns, as well as the Dutch, probably had developed iceboats by the 18th century. By 1800 there were similar vessels on the Hudson River and on the waters near Red Bank, N.J. The sport flourished among the wealthy in the late 19th century. Iceboats can travel about 4 times the speed of the wind, and in 1938 a stern-steering iceboat attained a speed of 229 km/h (143 mph) on Lake Winnebago, Wis. The adoption of synthetic sail fabric, stainless-steel rigging, and fiberglass hull materials mark improvements over the boats of the last century. In the United States iceboats are classified on the basis of either adherence to the specifications of "one design" or sail area. The largest class is for boats with more than 250 ft² (22.5 m²) of sail area. The one-design Skeeters carry 75 ft² (6.75 m²), and the most popular boat, the DN, carries 60 ft² (5.4 m²) of sail area.

Bibliography: Andresen, Jack, *Sailing on Ice* (1974); Smith, Calhoun, *Ice Boating* (1962).

icebreaker

An icebreaker is a vessel used for clearing a passage through ice-bound waters. The earliest such vessels were used on Lake Baikal and the Baltic Sea.

One of the first and most successful icebreakers was the *Ermak*, which was built for the Russian government and was launched on the River Tyne in England in 1898. The vessel had a steel hull and an enormously strengthened bow that had a very gradual slope upward from below so that the ship could glide up onto the ice and use its weight to break the ice from above, rather than by crashing forward into it. The *Ermak* had a displacement of over 8,700 tons. It was 97 m (320 ft) long with a beam of 22 m (71 ft) and depth of 13 m (43 ft). It had a speed of 15 knots, and its three aft screw propellers were protected from floating ice by the special stern construction. There was also one forward screw propeller.

The first nuclear-powered surface ship was the *Lenin*, a Russian icebreaker. Today the USSR has a fleet of three 75,000-horsepower, nuclear-powered icebreakers. The first, named the *Arktika*, commissioned in 1977, was the first surface vessel to navigate a passage to the North Pole. It traveled from Murmansk across the Barents Sea and the Arctic Ocean to the North Pole.

Current nuclear icebreakers are expected to bring a new era to Arctic shipping, which is of particular importance to the USSR and Canada. In 1978 the Canadian Coast Guard indicated interest in obtaining a nuclear-powered icebreaker. It mentioned that a considerable saving in fuel costs would be possible and that the lengthened time intervals between refuelings (15–20 months compared with about 1 month for conventional types) would enable the vessel to operate much more effectively.

ALAN E. BRANCH

icefish

Icefishes are transparent or pale fishes of three families inhabiting southern polar seas and eastern Asia. The name *icefish* is sometimes applied to the GLASSFISH, family Centropomidae, and conversely, icefishes are sometimes called glassfishes. The Asiatic icefishes, family Salangidae, are 14 species of small freshwater or freshwater-spawning (anadromous) fishes found in Japan, China, Korea, and Vietnam. They grow to about 10 cm (4 in) in length and have elongated, transparent, scaleless or nearly scaleless bodies and flattened heads. They are neotenic, reaching sexual maturity while still retaining certain larval characteristics. The crocodile icefishes, family Chaenichthyidae or Channichthyidae, are 16 to 18 species of marine fishes with large mouths, flattened snouts, and big eyes. They inhabit the oceanic waters of Antarctica and Patagonia, South America. The largest species, *Chaenocephalus aceratus,* grows to 60 cm (2 ft) long and about 1 kg (2.5 lb) in weight. The cod icefishes, or Antarctic cods, family Nototheniidae, consist of about 59 species of marine fishes inhabiting the coastal waters of Antarctica and southern South America. They are similar in appearance to the crocodile icefishes but have extendable snouts.

The blood of certain species of marine icefishes is of biological interest because its temperature may fall below the usual freezing point of fish blood (−1° C/30° F) without freezing and because it lacks red blood cells and oxygen-carrying hemoglobin and consequently has a very low oxygen capacity. Research has indicated that marine icefishes have antifreeze in their blood in the form of glycoproteins—complex compounds containing sugars and amino acids—which presumably interfere with the formation or growth of ice crystals.

Icefish blood lacking the red pigment of hemoglobin is transparent and colorless or tinted a pale yellow. Because of this colorless blood, marine icefishes are sometimes called "bloodless." The oxygen-carrying capacity of blood fluid, or plasma, without hemoglobin is low, and marine icefishes lacking hemoglobin must manage with a markedly reduced supply of oxygen. Studies have shown that the icefishes are able to survive this reduction by using several ecological features as well as certain physiological modifications that reduce energy expenditure and therefore oxygen consumption. Icefishes live in oxygen-rich water, which provides them with a plentiful initial supply. They are believed to be able to increase their oxygen intake by absorption through the skin. Antarctic waters are also cold, which tends to slow physiological processes and thus lower oxygen demand. Icefishes feed only sporadically and are inactive much of the time. Their hearts are enlarged and, although slow-beating, are able to pump three to four times the volume of blood of comparable red-blooded fishes. Their blood capillaries are believed to be also enlarged in order to reduce the energy-consuming resistance to blood flow. The continuous act of breathing, or passing water over the gills, requires little energy because it is done slowly through an enlarged, low-resistance breathing apparatus, which includes enlarged gill flaps (opercular pump) and relatively wide-spaced gill folds (lamellae).

EDWIN E. ROSENBLUM

Iceland

The Republic of Iceland is the second-largest island in Europe, after Great Britain. Located in the North Atlantic Ocean immediately south of the Arctic Circle, Iceland lies about 965 km (600 mi) west of Norway, 800 km (500 mi) northwest of Scotland, and 260 km (160 mi) southeast of Greenland. REYK-

ICELAND

Official Name: Republic of Iceland
Capital and Largest City: Reykjavik (1977 pop., 83,887)
Area: 102,952 km² (39,758 mi²)
Elevation: *Highest*—Hvannadalshnúkur, 2,119 m (6,952 ft); *lowest*—sea level, along the coast
Population: 224,000 (1979 est.). *Distribution*—87% urban, 13% rural; *density,* 2 persons per km² (6 per mi²); *annual rate of increase* (1970–76), 1.3%
Principal Language: Icelandic
Principal Religion: Evangelical Lutheran
Principal Products: *Agriculture* –beef and dairy cattle, sheep; hay, potatoes, turnips. *Manufacturing and industry*—fish processing; aluminum smelting; diatomite and cement production. *Mining*—diatomite; shell sand
Railroads: None
Roads: 144 km/89 mi (1977 paved)
Currency: 1 Icelandic króna = 100 aurar

at least two active volcanoes that cause flooding by the melt flow when they erupt. Iceland has benefited greatly from more than 800 thermal springs found in more than 250 locations, most of which remain to be tapped. The hot water provides home heating for Reykjavik and steam heat for a large, flourishing greenhouse produce industry. Iceland's many rivers are unnavigable.

Although the interior of Iceland is quite cold, the perimeter experiences an even, mild temperature, averaging −1° C (31° F) in January and 11° C (52° F) in July. Rainfall, however, varies widely: 1,270–2,030 mm (50–80 in) annually on the south coast; 380–500 mm (15–20 in) on the north; and more than 3,810 mm (150 in) in the mountainous central areas.

PEOPLE

Iceland's population is predominantly of Norwegian stock, and the rest are of Celtic origin. A high degree of homogeneity characterizes the inhabitants of an island unaffected by large inmigration. Their Icelandic language is distinct, having evolved from Old Norse. More than 95% of the population are Evangelical Lutherans.

Demography. More than one-half of Iceland's predominantly urban population lives in the Reykjavik metropolitan area along Faxa Bay. Most of the nation's urban centers are on the coast. Akureyri (1977 est. pop., 12,643), the country's second-largest city, is on the north coast at the head of Eyja Fjord. The only other cities with a population exceeding 10,000 are Hafnarfjördur and Kópavogur, parts of Reykjavik's metropolitan area.

Migration from Iceland has reflected the economic conditions. A significant exodus took place at the beginning of the 20th century, when more than 15% of the population left the island, primarily for the United States and Canada. The size of the population has increased steadily since that time.

Education and Health. Almost all educational services are provided by the government free of charge. School attendance is compulsory for all individuals between the ages of 7 and 15. The University of Iceland, founded in 1911, is state controlled. Illiteracy is virtually nonexistent.

Public health facilities, furnished by the government, are available to all at low cost. Efforts to eradicate contagious diseases have been successful; heart disease and cancer are the most frequent causes of death. The physician-patient ratio is comparable to that in the United States. The infant mortality rate is approximately 12.5 per 1,000 live births, and life expectancy is 75 years.

The Arts. Iceland's cultural heritage has been preserved in writings and art. The most significant literary contribution of the Icelanders is the SAGA, a historical tale of adventure.

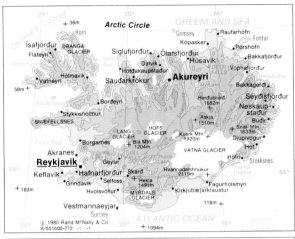

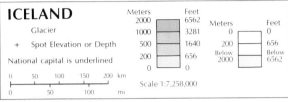

ICELAND

	Meters	Feet			
	2000	6562		Meters	Feet
Glacier	1000	3281		0	0
+ Spot Elevation or Depth	500	1640		200	656
	200	656		Below 2000	Below 6562
National capital is underlined	0	0			

0 50 100 150 200 km
0 50 100 mi
Scale 1:7,258,000

JAVIK, its capital, is on the southwest coast. Iceland, which had been under the control of Denmark since the late 14th century, did not become fully independent until 1944.

LAND

Iceland lies precariously atop the Mid-Atlantic Ridge in an area of active volcanism. SEAFLOOR SPREADING at the ridge could cause the breakup of the island in the future. Iceland has been formed by more than 150 volcanoes, 30 of which have been active since settlement during the 9th century. Most recently (1963), the offshore island of Surtsey was created by a volcanic eruption. Only one-fourth of the country can support continuous vegetation of any type; trees, mainly birches, survive on less than 1% of the land.

The rest of Iceland is barren. Glaciers cover much of the interior. Vatnajökull, in the southeastern part of Iceland, is the largest glacier, covering approximately 8,400 km² (3,240 mi²). Waterfalls, CIRQUES, and FJORDS are found throughout the island. Icefields, comprising about 11,800 km² (4,555 mi²), cover

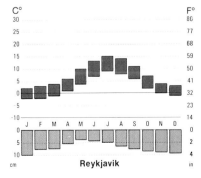

(Left) *Reykjavik, the capital, chief port, and largest city of Iceland, is situated at the southwestern end of the island. It is the world's most northerly capital.*

(Below) *Bars indicate the monthly ranges of temperature* (red) *and precipitation* (blue) *of Reykjavik, Iceland. Although Iceland is located only slightly south of the Arctic Circle, the warm waters of the North Atlantic Drift temper its climate.*

Many regions of Iceland are covered by thick layers of lava. The island, which is geologically quite young, is one of the most volcanically active areas in the world. Iceland's 200 volcanoes, many of which still erupt, represent almost every volcanic type known on Earth.

Wood carvings and woolen cloth designs are also characteristic art forms. A collection of native crafts is housed in the National Museum of Iceland (1863) in Reykjavik. The capital is also the home of the National Theatre and the country's only symphony orchestra. (See ICELANDIC LITERATURE.)

ECONOMIC ACTIVITY

Iceland's economy provides a high standard of living. Less than 1% of the population is unemployed. Agriculture employs about 15% of the work force, many of whom work in produce greenhouses. The main outdoor crop is hay, fodder for the few cattle and sheep. Potatoes and turnips are also grown.

Manufacturing and mining employ about 25% of the work force. Major industries, concentrated in Reykjavik, are fishing and fish processing (mainly cod, capelin, and herring), along with metal products, clothing, furniture, books, fertilizer, and cement. Few mineral resources exist other than diatomite, which is used in filtration systems. Imported aluminum ore is processed for reexport as finished goods. The enormous amount of electricity required to produce aluminum is found in Iceland's abundant supply of hydroelectric power and hot springs.

A general trend toward nationalization of industry, especially fishing, has been taking place. Private agricultural and industrial enterprises are also subsidized. No railroad system exists, but a dense road network provides access to all inhabited areas of the island. Nearly every village in the country can be reached by bus. Air transportation is important, both locally and internationally, through airports at Reykjavik and Keflavík. Six daily newspapers serve the country, in addition to a number of weeklies. Radio and television broadcasting facilities are state owned.

Icelandic Airlines, or Loftleidir, contributes substantially to the economy of the country. The nation's largest single employer, the airline uses Keflavík airport, which is maintained by the United States. The U.S. naval base there is the country's second-largest employer. Persons flying from the United States to Europe on Icelandic often stop over at Keflavík. Tourists, primarily Americans and West Germans, are attracted to Iceland for skiing and mountaineering.

Iceland has a favorable balance of payments. Fishing accounts for 75% of all export earnings, and aluminum makes up 17%. Machinery and transport equipment constitute 30% of all imports, followed by manufactured goods and fuels, with 20% and 12% respectively. Its principal trading partners are the United States, USSR, United Kingdom, and West Germany. Iceland is a member of the EUROPEAN FREE TRADE ASSOCIATION.

Iceland has suffered from inflation, which has averaged 40% annually over the past 5 years. Wage raises are adjusted quarterly to match cost-of-living increases. The króna has been repeatedly devalued, depreciating to slightly more than one-half its 1973 value by 1977.

GOVERNMENT

Iceland is a constitutional republic governed by a 60-member, 2-chamber general assembly (*Althing*). The president is popularly elected every 4 years by universal suffrage for all persons over 20 years of age. Real executive power is vested in the prime minister and the cabinet, currently a three-party coalition, who are subject to a potential vote of no confidence by the *Althing*. Local government consists of 23 counties and 14 independent towns. Counties are subdivided into 215 parishes or communes.

HISTORY

Discovered by Irish explorers about 800, Iceland was settled by Norwegian seafarers during the late 9th century. In 930 they created a representative governing assembly (*Althing*), the oldest parliamentary body in the world. Norwegians gained control in 1263, incorporating Iceland into the Norwegian-Danish state in 1381.

The steamship, invented in the 18th century, overcame strong currents and made access to Iceland's rocky, irregular coasts safer in the 1800s; this, along with the laying of the transoceanic cable in 1906, lessened Iceland's isolation.

In 1874, Iceland was granted a constitution and limited home rule; the subsequent Act of Union of 1918 granted full self-government under the Danish crown, with the right of either country to dissolve the union after 25 years. When Denmark fell to the Germans in 1940, Iceland was occupied by British troops to prevent a German takeover. The British were replaced in 1941 by U.S. forces that remained throughout the war. The Icelandic government proclaimed full independence on June 17, 1944, 25 years after implementation of the Act of Union.

Iceland became a charter member of the NORTH ATLANTIC TREATY ORGANIZATION (NATO) in 1949, and in 1951 reluctantly signed a treaty granting the United States the right to develop and maintain an airbase at Keflavík in return for U.S. defense of the country. Iceland has no military force of its own. The "cod wars" between Britain and Iceland in the 1960s and '70s were triggered by Iceland's extension of its offshore fishing limits to 320 km (200 mi). Tensions began to ease, however, in the late 1970s.   PAUL C. HELMREICH

Bibliography: Auden, W. H., and MacNeice, Louis, *Letters from Iceland* (1969); Griffiths, J. C., *Modern Iceland* (1969); Grondal, Benedikt, *Iceland: From Neutrality to NATO Membership* (1971); Guthmundsson, Barthi, *The Origin of the Icelanders*, trans. by Lee Hollander (1967); Magnusson, Sigurdur, *Northern Sphinx: Iceland and the Icelanders from the Settlement to the Present* (1977); Nuechterlein, Donald E., *Iceland: Reluctant Ally* (1975); Scherman, Katharine, *Daughter of Fire: A Portrait of Iceland* (1976).

Iceland spar: see CALCITE.

Icelandic language: see GERMANIC LANGUAGES.

Icelandic literature   [ys-lan'-dik]

Iceland was settled—mostly by emigrants from the area now known as Norway—in the 9th and 10th centuries, but almost two centuries passed before its earliest literature was written down. This medieval literature may be subdivided into three categories: (a) Eddic poetry, that is, mythological and heroic poems; (b) skaldic poetry, mostly occasional and praise poems composed by court poets; and (c) SAGA literature, or prose works ranging from fairly solid histories to pure fiction. Among the former type of saga literature—in which works were based on both oral tradition and written sources—are Ari Thorgilsson's *Íslendingabók* (a history of Iceland), SNORRI

STURLUSON's HEIMSKRINGLA (about Norwegian kings), and the anonymous *Knytlinga Saga* (about Danish kings). A prime example of the fictional type of saga literature is *Hrafnkel's Saga,* a short *bildungsroman.* In between, with some features of both, fall the so-called family sagas, such as *Egil's Saga* and *Njál's Saga.*

The epic tradition climaxed in the 13th century. Pre-Reformation literature also includes Eysteinn Ásgrímsson's religious poem *Lilja* (14th century), a number of popular ballads, and the *rímur,* which were cycles of epic poetry.

After the Reformation (1550), Iceland experienced three centuries of poverty, which also affected its literature, although the 17th century left behind the treasure of Hallgrímur Pétursson's *Passion Hymns.* Romanticism was brought to Iceland by Bjarni Thorarensen shortly after 1800 and blossomed in the poetry of Jónas Hallgrímsson and Grímur Thomsen, while the novelist Jón THORODDSEN foreshadowed the trend toward realism.

Among writers flourishing around 1900, Stephan G. Stephansson and Einar Benediktsson, both poets, may be mentioned. Shortly after the turn of the century some Icelanders began to write in Danish. Preeminent among these was the novelist Gunnar GUNNARSSON.

After World War I, Icelandic literature experienced a renaissance, especially in the lyric poetry of Stefán frá Hvítadal, Davíð Stefánsson, and Tómas Guðmundsson. Among the prose writers of this era, the most prominent were Thórbergur Thórðarson and Halldór LAXNESS. The latter won the Nobel Prize for literature in 1955. After World War II another generation of lyric poets took over, introducing modernistic features into the heavily traditional Icelandic context. Among the leaders of this avant-garde were Steinn Steinarr and Jón úr Vör. Among the best writers active in Iceland today are the poets Hannes Pétursson and Snorri Hjartarson and the novelists Ólafur Jóhann Sigurðsson (who is also a poet), Thor Vilhjálmsson, and Indriði G. Thorsteinsson.   AAGE JØRGENSEN

Bibliography: Beck, Richard, *A History of Icelandic Poets, 1800-1940* (1950); Einarsson, Stefán, *A History of Icelandic Literature* (1957); Hallberg, Peter, *The Icelandic Saga* (1962); Hallmundsson, Hallberg, ed., *An Anthology of Scandinavian Literature* (1966).

See also: EDDA; SKALDIC LITERATURE.

Ichikawa   (family)   [ee-chee'-kah-wah]

The Ichikawa family is the most famous of the several dozen hereditary acting families in KABUKI, a form of Japanese drama combining dance, music, and mime and supported by elaborate costuming and theatrical setting. Kabuki has flourished since the 17th century. The art of Kabuki acting is passed from the father to the natural or adopted son when he is considered capable of the inheritance.

The Ichikawa family has several branches, the most famous of which is that headed by **Ichikawa Danjuro** in Tokyo. **Danjuro I** (1660-1704) created an acting style called *aragoto,* or "bravura style," which accommodated itself well to superhuman heroic roles. It became immensely popular with the performance of *Narukami the Thunder God* in 1684. **Ichikawa Ebizo X** is expected, in time, to inherit the position of his late father **Danjuro XI,** who died in 1963, and to become **Ichikawa Danjuro XII.** Other branches of the Ichikawa family are headed by **Ichikawa Sadanji, Ichikawa Ennosuke,** and **Ichikawa Chusha.**   JAMES R. BRANDON

Bibliography: Kincaid, Zöe, *Kabuki* (1925; repr. 1965); Scott, A. C., *The Kabuki Theatre of Japan* (1955).

ichneumon fly   [ik-nue'-muhn]

Ichneumon flies are parasitic wasps in the family Ichneumonidae and are found worldwide. They resemble wasps, but are slim, with long legs and often a long terminal ovipositor used to bore a hole into their hosts. Eggs are laid on or in other insects, and the parasitic larvae kill their host. Many ichneumon flies are specific to one species of host and are therefore valuable for biological control of certain pest insects. Adult ichneumon flies are commonly found on vegetation.

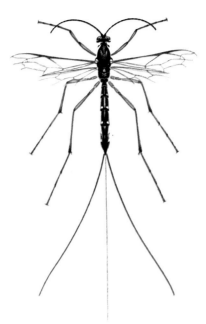

The ichneumon fly, Rhyssa persuasoria, is a slender, long-legged wasp that parasitizes the horntail, Urocerus, by piercing its larva and laying an egg inside.

ichthyology.   [ik-thee-ahl'-uh-jee]

A branch of zoology (the science of animals), ichthyology deals specifically with FISHES. Areas of study include the structure, classification, behavior, development, and distribution of fishes. In addition, ichthyology is concerned with relationships between fish and the environment, the importance of fish to humans (such as fisheries), and conservation.

Bibliography: Lagler, Karl F., et al., *Ichthyology,* 2d ed. (1977).

Ichthyornis   [ik-thee-ohr'-nuhs]

Ichthyornis (Greek: *ichthys,* "fish"; *ornis,* "bird"), an early, very primitive, and apparently toothed bird, is known from several dozen fragmentary fossil specimens found in Late Cretaceous chalk (about 100 million years old) in Kansas and Nebraska. This material includes associated jaws with teeth, as well as keeled breastbones and fused elements of the wing skeleton—the oldest evidence of powered flight in birds. *Ichthyornis* is believed to have been a shore bird, ternlike in its habits.   JOHN H. OSTROM

Bibliography: Colbert, E. H., *Evolution of the Vertebrates* (1969); Romer, A. S., *Vertebrate Paleontology* (1966).

Ichthyosaurus   [ik-thee-uh-sohr'-uhs]

Ichthyosaurus (Greek: *ichthys,* "fish"; *saurus,* "lizard") was one of a group of highly aquatic reptiles that inhabited the Mesozoic oceans from mid-Triassic time (about 210 million years ago) until late in the Cretaceous Period (65 million years ago). Specimens have been found in Lower Jurassic rocks

Ichthyosaurus, *the order of fish-lizards, flourished about 150 million years ago. It evolved from land reptiles in much the same way that present-day seals and whales evolved from land mammals.*

(less than 190 million years old) from many parts of the world. The name *fish lizard* is most appropriate, considering the fishlike form—sharp snout, large eyes, and streamlined head—of those reptiles. The fin rising from the creature's back was high and sharklike; the tail was vertical, two-lobed and fishlike; and the limbs were modified into large flippers.

JOHN H. OSTROM

Bibliography: Colbert, E. H., *Evolution of the Vertebrates* (1969); Romer, A. S., *Vertebrate Paleontology* (1966).

Ickes, Harold   [ik'-eez]

Harold LeClaire Ickes, b. Blair County, Pa., Mar. 15, 1874, d. Feb. 3, 1952, served as U.S. secretary of the interior in the administrations of Franklin D. Roosevelt and Harry S. Truman. Ickes earned his way through the University of Chicago, taking his B.A. in 1897 and returning for a law degree (1907) after several years as a Chicago newspaper reporter.

A political activist, Ickes crusaded against corruption in Chicago and for reformers at the local and state levels. A Bull Moose party supporter of Theodore Roosevelt's presidential quest in 1912, he remained a Progressive, campaigning for Robert M. La Follette in 1924, Alfred E. Smith in 1928, and Franklin Roosevelt in 1932. Ickes opposed exploitation of the nation's limited natural resources by private interests and supported federal development of electric power in the public domain.

When Franklin Roosevelt became president in 1933, he determined that a Progressive Republican should head the interior department and selected Ickes. A forceful, colorful administrator, "Honest Harold" converted that notoriously corrupt department, earlier the center of the Teapot Dome scandal, into a custodian of the nation's resources. Ickes also headed the PUBLIC WORKS ADMINISTRATION, spending nearly $6 billion on the building of public facilities—ranging from hydroelectric dams to civic and educational facilities—and on rural electrification and military modernization projects. Ickes wrote several books, including *The New Democracy* (1934) and *The Secret Diary of Harold L. Ickes* (3 vols., published posthumously 1953–54; repr. 1974).

ELLIOT A. ROSEN

Bibliography: Schlesinger, Arthur M., Jr., *The Age of Roosevelt*, 3 vols. (1957–60).

icon   [y'-kahn]

The icon (Greek *eikōn*, meaning "image") plays an essential part in the religious life of the Eastern ORTHODOX CHURCH. Most commonly a portrait of Christ, the Virgin, or one of the saints, an icon may also represent an episode from the Bible or from a saint's life. Icons usually were painted on wooden

In Eastern Orthodox religious art, icons represent a sacred image used for veneration, as in this 16th-century Russian icon of Christ. Icon painting has its roots in the Byzantine artistic tradition. It became popular in Eastern Orthodox churches after the 5th century. These sacred representations, which emphasize the mystical and symbolic elements of the subject, are usually oil paintings on wood; mosaic, ivory, and metal, however, have also been used to create icons. (Rublov Museum, Moscow.)

panels, although several miniature mosaic icons from Constantinople have survived. The preeminent place for the exhibition of icons is on the ICONOSTASIS of an Orthodox church, but portable icons can also be carried in processions, set in roadside shrines, or even kept in the home, as was especially common in Russia. Whatever their location, however, icons are not primarily aesthetic but are, rather, sacred images; as the focus of prayer and devotion, the icon is as essential to the Orthodox church as is the relic to the Roman Catholic church in the West.

The icon as a special type of sacred image developed in Byzantine art (see BYZANTINE ART AND ARCHITECTURE) in the 6th century, and many stories from that period tell of miracle-working icons and of others "not made by human hands" but regarded as produced by or descended from heaven. Such stories reflected and encouraged the veneration of the icon by many Christians and led, not surprisingly, to a puritanical reaction by those who saw this practice as little removed from pagan idol worship. ICONOCLASM, the prohibition and deliberate destruction of religious images, became official Byzantine policy in AD 726. In reaction to this policy, many Byzantine theologians, among whom Saint JOHN DAMASCENE (d. 754) was most important, developed an elaborate theory and defense of holy images and their place in worship; this theory led to the restoration of the icons in 843 and remains the Orthodox view to this day. Drawing on the doctrine of the incarnation of Christ and on Neoplatonic philosophical ideas, John argued that the holy icon through divine grace partook of the spiritual essence of the figure it depicted, and, as the product of the emanation of its holiness, constituted the essential point of direct contact between the human and divine realms.

Icons of an established type, because of their sacred function and relationship to a heavenly prototype, changed relatively little through the centuries, although new types occasionally appeared. Thus the beautiful icon known as *Our Lady of Vladimir* (c.1130; Tretyakov Gallery, Moscow), depicting the Virgin and Child embracing, painted in Constantinople in the early 12th century, reflects with its tender lyricism a new trend toward emotional and humanistic values in Byzantine art of that period. After this icon was taken to Russia, it established a type, *Umileniye* ("merciful" or "compassionate"), reproduced there for 7 centuries.

LAWRENCE NEES

Bibliography: Galavaris, George, *Icons from the Elvehjem Art Center* (1973); Hamilton, George H., *The Art and Architecture of Russia*, 2d ed. (1976); Stuart, John, *Ikons* (1975); Weitzmann, Kurt, *The Icon* (1978) and *The Monastery of Saint Catherine at Mount Sinai: The Icons* (1976); Weitzmann, Kurt, et al., *Icons from South Eastern Europe and Sinai* (1968).

See also: RUSSIAN ART AND ARCHITECTURE.

Iconium: see KONYA.

iconoclasm   [y-kahn'-oh-klazm]

Iconoclasm, a Greek term that means "image-breaking," refers to the religious doctrine that forbids the veneration of images (icons) of Christ and the saints in Christian churches. Iconoclasm provoked major controversies in the BYZANTINE EMPIRE for over a century (726–843). In 726, Emperor LEO III ordered the image of Christ at the Chalke palace in Constantinople to be destroyed. In the following years, other measures were taken to suppress the veneration of images. Reaction came from Orthodox monks, inspired by the writings of Saint JOHN DAMASCENE, and from the Roman popes, who protested against the imperial policies. Leo's son and successor, Constantine V (r. 741–75), convoked (754) a council of bishops, which confirmed the iconoclastic doctrines and practices. The veneration of images was restored in the empire during the rule of Empress IRENE, at the Second Council of Nicaea (787; see NICAEA, COUNCILS OF), but a revival of iconoclasm took place under Leo V (r. 813–20), Michael II (r. 820–29), and Theophilus (r. 829–42). The latter's widow, Empress Theodora, however, presided over the restoration of icon veneration in 843, an event still celebrated by the ORTHODOX CHURCH as the

Triumph of Orthodoxy. During the second iconoclastic period, the main spokesmen for the veneration of images were the patriarch NICEPHORUS and Saint Theodore of Studios.

The iconoclastic movement was motivated by a variety of factors that possibly included Muslim influences, as well as the concern of some that the cult of icons was a form of idolatry. The essential argument of the Orthodox defenders of the images was that, since God became man in Jesus Christ, he also assumed all human characteristics including visibility. The icon of Christ is therefore a confession of faith in Christ's divinity and humanity. The Council of Nicaea also specified that images should be venerated but not worshiped, since worship (*latria*) belongs to God alone and the worship of icons would mean idolatry. The ideas promoted by the defenders of images served as doctrinal bases for the later development of Eastern Christian art, particularly in the Byzantine Empire and in Russia.

Iconoclasm was also a feature of the Protestant REFORMATION of the 16th century; some Protestant groups still oppose the use of religious images. JOHN MEYENDORFF

Bibliography: Martin, E. J., *A History of the Iconoclastic Controversy* (1930; repr. 1977); Meyendorff, J., *Christ in Eastern Christian Thought* (1975).

See also: BYZANTINE ART AND ARCHITECTURE.

iconography [y-kuhn-ahg'-ruh-fee]

Iconography (from the Greek, *eikōn*, "image" and *graphia*, "writing") is the study of the subject matter, or content, of works of art, as opposed to their style. The content of a painting or a sculpture can convey the artist's meaning in several ways. In general, works depicting only real persons, places, and objects—that is, portraits, landscapes, still lifes, and the like—may be said to have only one level of meaning, the surface or primary level. A secondary level of meaning is added when a work contains an imagined person or a fictional or mythological scene, or when the artist attempts to render some abstract concept in concrete terms. Because these secondary levels of meaning cannot be explained in words in a painting or a sculpture, the artist must use a type of sign language—a visual shorthand, drawing on conventions and formulas that the audience will recognize. In traditional Christian art, a broken wheel placed beside the figure of a woman tells the viewer that the figure represents Saint Catherine, whereas a woman holding a bridle and reins personifies the virtue of temperance. The function of iconography is to recognize and explain images of this kind and to search literature for the origins of personages and scenes. The term *iconology* is sometimes used for the study of the way in which a work of art is related to the cultural background of its era.

In this article the word *image* denotes any portrayal of an object or action that contains a secondary meaning. The word *attribute* signifies an object, such as Saint Catherine's wheel, that is associated with a human figure simply to give that figure a recognizable identity. A *symbol*, however, is an object or figure that by itself represents something else, often an abstract idea. In many 15th- and 16th-century paintings, for example, a skull is used to represent the idea of mortality—a so-called memento mori. Finally, the artist may link together individual symbols so as to convey some thematic idea or axiom; this combining of symbols into an overall pattern is known as an *allegory*. A great fondness for allegory was shown by Italian Renaissance artists, who often constructed elaborate chains of symbols. To arrive at the allegorical or overall meaning of the painting the observer must discern the symbols' interrelationships, as well as their individual meanings.

ORIGINS AND HISTORICAL DEVELOPMENT

Ancient Greece. The earliest recorded images were those associated with the rites of ancient religions, especially those in which the deity had human form (see GREEK ART). To propitiate or petition the gods, worshipers offered sacrifices to statues in temples; the statue was thought to contain the actual presence of the deity, and the temple was considered to be its "house." This ANTHROPOMORPHISM of divinities was devel-

oped significantly by the great poet Homer (*c.*8th century BC), who organized the ancient Greek gods into a kind of family or pantheon and gave each one an individual personality and specific physical characteristics. Following Homer's lead, the classical Greek artists endowed each god with recognizable attributes: Zeus was sometimes accompanied by an eagle, the bird sacred to him; Poseidon, who ruled the sea, carried a trident; Artemis, the huntress, had a bow and quiver; and so on.

Ancient Rome. The Romans, much more than the Greeks, used art to magnify the glory of their own accomplishments (see ROMAN ART). Arches, columns, altars, and public buildings were decorated with sculpture commemorating the triumphs of Roman generals, and patrician families basked in the reflected glory of the images of the ancient gods and heroes from whom they claimed descent. Statues of the later emperors, who regarded themselves as gods, often depicted the rulers with the appropriate divine attributes. Along with symbols and attributes, allegory was well understood by the Romans. An altar, called the Ara Pacis, built (9 BC) in honor of Emperor Augustus and dedicated to peace, shows in one panel a contented and fruitful Mother Earth holding two infants in her lap and seated amid various symbols of the abundance and prosperity that Augustus's peaceful reign had brought.

Early Christian Iconography. The plethora of symbols and attributes used by the Romans contrasted sharply to the few, simple images used by the early Christians, who had to be circumspect in the face of religious persecution (see EARLY CHRISTIAN ART). On sacramental cups, seals, and lamps the Holy Spirit was symbolized by a dove, and Christ by a fish (perhaps because at the time fish was one of the elements of the sacred meal) or by a shepherd carrying a sheep on his shoulders (from Luke 15:3-7). The Savior was also represented by a monogram formed by combining the Greek letters *chi* and *rho* (XP), the first two letters of the Greek word for Christ.

Byzantine Iconography. When Christianity became (4th century) the official religion of the Roman Empire, its imagery began to reflect borrowings from the emperor's court at Constantinople (see BYZANTINE ART AND ARCHITECTURE). Christ was

The symbolic representation of Christ as the Good Shepherd of the biblical parable is a common iconographic type in Early Christian art. This 3d-century marble statue portrays a youthful, beardless Christ, developed from the Hellenic ideal of the beautiful and good Apollonian god. Many examples of the zoomorphic symbolism of Christ as the Lamb of God (Agnus Dei) itself are found in Christian iconography as well. (Lateran Museum, Rome.)

Some common Christian iconographic symbols are shown above. (1) The risen Christ is portrayed surrounded by the four evangelists: Saint Matthew as the man-angel, Saint John as the eagle, Saint Mark as the lion, and Saint Luke as the bull. (2) The passion of the crucified Christ is symbolized by the crown of thorns encircling his monogram XP (chi/rho). (3) Christ as the Lamb of God (Agnus Dei) is shown holding an unfurled banner bearing his inscriptions. (4) The dove, symbolizing the Holy Spirit, carries a lily, a symbol of purity.

no longer depicted as a youthful shepherd, but as an enthroned emperor and judge with a dignified beard. The Virgin Mary, whose cult developed rapidly after about 400, appeared crowned and robed like the empress, and saints dressed like courtiers approached the throne of God with veiled hands, as was the custom in the courts of Eastern monarchs.

The repertoire of symbolic subjects included scenes from the New Testament reflecting the annual cycle of the principal festivals of the Church. Subjects from the Old Testament, which earlier had served as examples of God's power to save—the Hebrews in the fiery furnace, Noah and the flood— now reflected the belief that, as part of God's plan, certain episodes in the Old Testament prefigured events in the New Testament. Jonah, who formerly symbolized the idea of salvation, now became the type—the original model—of Christ, whose death and resurrection was seemingly foreshadowed by Jonah's miraculous encounter with the great fish. Throughout the Middle Ages the Scriptures were ransacked for correspondences of this kind, which exemplify the iconographic principle of typology.

Medieval European Iconography. From about 1000 to 1300 the French monastery of Cluny (see MONASTIC ART AND ARCHITECTURE), which was founded in 910 and played a key role in the development of Romanesque and Gothic art, greatly influenced the course of Western European iconography (see ROMANESQUE ART AND ARCHITECTURE and GOTHIC ART AND ARCHITECTURE). Medieval sculpture and wall painting reflected the Cluniac monks' view that because all human activities and all creatures under heaven were part of the divine plan, they were all fit subjects for representation. Alongside more traditional subject matter now appeared such secular motifs as the 12 Labors of the Months, depicting the yearly cycle of husbandry; the birds and animals of the BESTIARY, an allegorical interpretation of natural history that was very popular in the Middle Ages; and strange humanoid monsters believed to inhabit the outer regions of the Earth.

Renaissance Iconography. The Renaissance period, which began in Italy in the 15th century, ushered in a radical shift in iconography (see RENAISSANCE ART AND ARCHITECTURE). As artists rediscovered the forms and images of classical antiquity, the gods and goddesses of Greek and Roman mythology once more dominated Western European iconography. Ovid's *Metamorphoses* (AD 8) provided Italian artists with scenes of the amours of the gods, and French humanist artists used the pagan divinities to personify moral qualities in allegorical compositions.

Underlying this reappearance of ancient imagery was an attempt to reconcile the classical philosophy of the ancient pagan world with Christian teaching. A popular subject was the combat between Virtue and Vice in all their manifestations: Reason against Passion, for example, in which a civilized Apollo, shown with a bow or lyre, and a chaste Diana, the huntress, would be pitted against Venus, the goddess of love, and her offspring Cupid. For detailed information about the appearance of the ancient gods, and personifications in general, Renaissance artists often had to rely on contemporary handbooks and dictionaries of classical iconography, which were no less influential for being generally inaccurate. The most widely used of these source books was Cesare Ripa's (fl. 1600) *Iconologia*, the 1603 edition of which described, with illustrations, the dress, attributes, and moral symbolism of a wide range of allegorical figures.

Impact of the Reformation. Paradoxically, the Protestant reformers of the 16th century, who rejected religious imagery as blasphemous, indirectly gave religious subject matter renewed strength in Roman Catholic countries, where art became a propaganda device used to uphold specifically Roman Catholic doctrines. Roman Catholic artists depicted the Virgin Mary treading on a serpent that symbolized the Protestant heresy, as well as such specifically Roman Catholic scenes as the celebration of the Seven Sacraments and the veneration of holy relics. Artists in Protestant regions such as the northern provinces of the Netherlands, however, turned to PORTRAITURE and LANDSCAPE PAINTING or specialized in some particular class of domestic subject (GENRE PAINTING). STILL-LIFE PAINTINGS occasionally became vehicles for allegory and at times even con-

Classical myths were rediscovered by Renaissance artists and used in the development of iconographic types. In Sandro Botticelli's Mars and Venus (1485–90) the allegory of the god of war abandoning his weapons for love is fully realized. (National Gallery, London.)

tained a veiled expression of Christian beliefs. Many such allegorical compositions used tokens of luxury or pleasure, such as jewels, coins, books, and musical instruments, as symbols of the transitory character of life, whose inevitable conclusion would be symbolized by a memento mori. The underlying message of the emptiness or vanity of life on earth lent the name *vanitas paintings* to this type of work.

Modern Trends. Beginning roughly in the last part of the 17th century the European pictorial arts were dominated by two discrete approaches to iconography. While noniconographic subject matter such as landscape, portraiture, and still life became increasingly important, widespread historicizing movements sparked the conscious revival of past artistic forms and images—NEOCLASSICISM and ROMANTICISM in art being the principal movements. Both trends reflected the lack in early modern art of a broad-based and intrinsic cultural ethos, such as Christianity in medieval art, that could provide artists with a fund of images and symbols of contemporary value.

In the 19th century the gulf between the historicizing and the noniconographic movements widened enormously. His-

toricism became the keynote of so-called academic art (see ACADEMIES OF ART), officially sanctioned by the political and academic establishment. Simultaneously, the trend toward nonsymbolic art led to the development of realism (see REALISM, art) and impressionism (see IMPRESSIONISM, art). From the romantic landscapes of John Constable and J. M. W. Turner, in which humans and their works assume increasingly insignificant roles, to the series paintings of Claude Monet, in which the painter's sole object is to depict one object or group of objects under various atmospheric and lighting conditions, avant-garde artists gradually banished every trace of literary or moral meaning from their works, concentrating instead on their impressions of the exterior world.

The eventual triumph of the impressionist viewpoint over that of the academic schools resulted inevitably in the exaltation of the role of the individual artist and the rejection of any culture-based iconographic language shared by artist and audience. Almost all of the great movements that shaped 20th-century art—CUBISM, EXPRESSIONISM, SURREALISM, ABSTRACT ART, and ABSTRACT EXPRESSIONISM—reflect extremely personal aesthetic visions that defy the kind of literary decoding necessary to interpret fully iconographic works. With the significant exceptions of Dadaism (see DADA) and POP ART (examined in the following sections), modern artistic movements by definition lie outside the realm of iconography.

JAMES HALL

DEVELOPMENT OF ICONOGRAPHIC STUDIES

Origins. With the exception of the Renaissance and baroque manuals of classical iconography, little effort was made to study systematically the forms and meanings of Western iconography until the 18th century, when classical mythology and symbolism became a necessary feature of every well-bred person's education, rather than the exclusive province of artists and scholars. This process had been stimulated by the researches of archaeologists and antiquarians, especially of Greek and Roman ruins. Johann Friedrich Christ (1700-56), the first art historian to occupy (1735-56) an academic chair, gave his lectures at Leipzig University under the heading of the archaeology of literature. Although important, these early

(Above) *During the Reformation a distinctive genre emerged in the painting of still-life compositions on the theme of* vanitas *("vanity"). This 17th-century still life by Pieter Claesz assimilated the iconographic elements of the skull and the extinguished candle, which symbolized the transitory nature of life. The type is also known as a* memento mori.

(Right) *The neoclassical movement in European art revived historical subjects as iconographic symbols. In the painting* The Battle of the Romans and the Sabines *(1799) Jacques Louis David uses the legend of the Sabine women intervening and stopping the battle to express his sentiments concerning the French Revolution. (Louvre, Paris.)*

researches remained narrowly focused on the historical derivation of symbols and themes, and no coherent theory of iconography was developed at this time.

Iconology. The next great advance in iconography as an analytical tool came in the early 1900s, when a number of art historians became interested in defining the meaning of a work of art in terms of its social heritage and purpose. Describing their research procedures by the term *iconology*, these scholars sought to reduce the entire meaning of a work of art to a textual definition. Most prominent among this new breed of art historians was the German Aby Warburg (1866–1929), who was the first to use the term *iconology*. At the 10th International Congress on the history of art, held in Rome in 1912, Warburg introduced an innovative methodology to art history by presenting a study of Italian 15th-century art in which the figures in various paintings were identified according to precise literary sources. This purely iconographic method of identification broke clearly with the stylistic method of art-historical analysis. Rather than interpreting a work within a strictly aesthetic context, Warburg and subsequent iconologists, such as Erwin PANOFSKY, pursued this method of interpreting a work of art by means of original historical texts, in contradistinction to those who analyzed art as a matter of connoisseurship, or an analysis of style.

The iconologist's interdisciplinary approach to the study of art led to a tremendous expansion in the 20th century of what was considered to be part of the study of iconography, as well as of what was considered to be art. Panofsky's publication of an essay on film titled "Style and Medium in the Motion Pictures" (1947) introduced the study of cinema as a serious art form. The art of primitive peoples, children, and the mentally impaired also received critical attention for the first time, and the use of these sources by artists such as Pablo PICASSO and Paul KLEE furthered their acceptance as objects of iconographic study.

One of the more significant developments in the mid-20th century was the publication of numerous iconographic studies of what is termed *popular culture*—which entered the vocabulary of "high" art with the early-20th-century collages of the Dadaists. Movies, comic books, advertisements, and pinup magazines all have been analyzed iconographically. This field of study was accelerated by the success of pop art, which took well-known popular icons, such as soup-can labels, and presented them in a serious aesthetic context. Rather than creating icons, artists now capitalized on the availability and popularity of existing icons. The modern iconographic approach to the study of art has reinforced this trend toward appropriating the images and symbols of popular culture for aesthetic purposes. Necessarily, this type of art has been analyzed primarily as a sociological phenomenon and only secondarily as an aesthetic event.

VALENTIN TATRANSKY

Bibliography: Beckwith, John, *Early Christian and Byzantine Art* (1970); Cirlot, J. E., *A Dictionary of Symbols*, trans. by Jack Sage, 2d ed. (1972); Demus, Otto, *Byzantine Mosaic Decoration* (1948; repr. 1976); Grabar, Andre, *Christian Iconography: A Study of Its Origins* (1968); Hall, James, *Dictionary of Subjects and Symbols in Art* (1974); Hecksher, W. S., *The Genesis of Iconology* (1967); Lasko, Peter, *Ars Sacra: 800–1200* (1973); Mâle, Émile, *Religious Art in France: 13th Century* (1913); Moore, Albert C., *The Iconography of Religions* (1977); Panofsky, Erwin, *Early Netherlandish Painting* (1953) and *Studies in Iconology* (1939; repr. 1962); Ripa, Cesare, *Baroque and Rococo Pictorial Imagery: Iconologia*, trans. by Edward A. Maser (1971); Seznec, Jean, *The Survival of the Pagan Gods*, trans. by Barbara Sessions (1953; repr. 1972); Schiller, Gertrud, *Iconography of Christian Art*, 2 vols. (1971, 1972); Wagner, Geoffrey, *Parade of Pleasure: A Study of Popular Iconography in the U.S.A.* (1955); Whittick, Arnold, *Symbols, Signs and Their Meaning* (1960).

iconostasis   [y-kuhn-ahs'-tuh-sis]

The iconostasis is the icon screen that in Eastern Orthodox churches separates the sanctuary—the area around the altar that only the clergy may enter—from the rest of the church. The clergy pass through its three doors in the elaborate symbolic processions that are an essential feature of the Eastern liturgy. In the Byzantine church the iconostasis—originally, in

the 6th century, only a low parapet, to which images were added by the 9th century—remained relatively low until the 16th century. In Russia, however, by the 14th century the iconostasis had already appeared in its final form—a solid high barrier completely blocking the congregation's view of the sanctuary and its sacred mysteries. Covered with rows of large icons arranged according to a strict formula, the Russian iconostasis embodies the basic doctrine of the incarnation of Christ as foreshadowed in the Old Testament, fulfilled in the New Testament, and reenacted in the daily sacramental liturgy so as to grant ultimate salvation to the faithful.

LAWRENCE NEES

Bibliography: Galavaris, George, *Icons from the Elvehjem Art Center* (1973); Grabar, Andre, *The Art of the Byzantine Empire* (1967); Hamilton, George H., *The Art and Architecture of Russia*, 2d ed. (1976); Mathews, Thomas F., *The Early Churches of Constantinople* (1971); Stuart, John, *Ikons* (1975).

See also: BYZANTINE ART AND ARCHITECTURE; RUSSIAN ART AND ARCHITECTURE.

ICSH: see GONADOTROPHIN; HORMONES; PITUITARY GLAND.

Ictinus   [ik-ty'-nus]

The Greek architect Ictinus, fl. 5th century BC, along with his fellow architect CALLICRATES, designed and built the PARTHENON (447–431 BC) on the ACROPOLIS of Athens. Entrusted with this project by the Athenian statesman Pericles and his artistic supervisor, the sculptor PHIDIAS, Ictinus used fine Pentelic marble throughout the Doric temple, incorporating all the refinements developed by Greek architects over the two preceding centuries. Ictinus, in collaboration with an otherwise unknown Carpion, described the construction of the Parthenon in a lost work that, fortunately, was known to the Roman architect and theorist VITRUVIUS, who described it in his treatise, *On Architecture* (1st century BC). Pausanias, in his *Description of Greece* (2d century AD), named Ictinus as the architect of the Temple of Apollo Epicurius at Bassae in Arcadia, dated by Pausanias about 420 BC. The temple is highly original, incorporating engaged interior columns and the first known use in architecture of the Corinthian order (see ARCHITECTURE). Ictinus also worked (c.440 BC) in Eleusis on the Telesterion or Hall of the Mysteries, a huge hall for religious rites with a central light source in the roof. The Telesterion, however, was begun and finished by other architects.

JOHN STEPHENS CRAWFORD

Bibliography: Dinsmoor, William, *The Architecture of Ancient Greece*, 3d ed. (1975); Tomlinson, R. A., *Greek Sanctuaries* (1976).

id: see PSYCHOANALYSIS.

Idaho   [y'-duh-hoh]

Idaho, a Pacific Northwest state, links the Great Plains and the Northwest coast. It is bounded on the north by British Columbia, on the east by Wyoming and Montana, and on the south by Utah and Nevada. Its western border with Oregon and Washington follows, in part, the course of the SNAKE RIVER. The ROCKY MOUNTAINS dominate the entire landscape except for the Snake River plain, which cuts across the southern part of the state. Idaho's wealth of natural resources, along with its scenic attractions, forms the base of its expanding economy.

LAND AND RESOURCES

The broad, arid Snake River valley arcs across the southern part of Idaho. The plain developed when a series of high ridges to the north and south of the river began to sink and their intervening valleys became filled with lava and wind-blown soils. The valley of the Snake provides an access route from the Great Plains to the Pacific Northwest. Farther north, rugged mountains of the Bitterroot, Lost River, Pioneer, and Sawtooth ranges, separated by deep canyons and interrupted by occasional prairies, make up nearly all the rest of the state. Other than that portion of the GREAT BASIN rim in the south-

IDAHO

Capital and Largest City: Boise (1979 est. pop., 111,000)
Population: 887,500 (1979 est.). *Distribution*—54% urban, 46% rural; *density,* 4 persons per km² (16 per mi²); *increase* (1970–79) 24%; *population rank,* 42d
Area: 216,412 km² (83,557 mi²), including 2,279 km² (880 mi²) of inland water; *area rank,* 13th
Elevation: *Highest*—Borah Peak, 3,859 m (12,662 ft); *lowest*—along Snake River at Lewiston, 216 m (710 ft)
Principal Products: *Manufacturing and industry*—chemicals; food and food products; lumber and wood products; construction equipment. *Agriculture*—cattle; barley, hay, potatoes, sugar beets, wheat; milk. *Mining*—silver, lead, phosphate, zinc, copper, sand, gravel
Government: *State Legislature*—35 senators, 70 representatives. *Representation in Congress*—2 U.S. senators, 2 U.S. representatives
Statehood: July 3, 1890; the 43d state
Number of Counties: 44
State Nickname: The Gem State
State Bird: Mountain bluebird
State Flower: Syringa
State Tree: White pine
State Motto: Esto Perpetua ("It is forever")

east, all of Idaho is part of the COLUMBIA RIVER basin. Almost 64% of Idaho is owned by the U.S. government. Mountains or deserts used for forestry and grazing make up almost all these public lands.

Soils. Idaho's variation in soils is a result of elevation and climatic diversity. Most of the windblown, volcanic soils in arid parts of the Snake plain are alkaline, including about 11,100 km² (4,300 mi²) of irrigated farmland. Soils receiving 279 to 356 mm (11 to 14 in) of annual precipitation are chemically neutral. Where precipitation increases to 457 mm (18 in), darker, slightly acid soils predominate. Exceptionally valuable dark, acidic windblown soils of the Palouse country near Moscow receive 432 to 635 mm (17 to 25 in) of precipitation, as do similar soils at higher elevations in southern Idaho. Mountain and forest soils, usually thin, can support only timber, although some drained mountain-basin soils yield crops.

Rivers and Lakes. Except for the Bear River in southeastern Idaho and the Kootenai, Pend d'Oreille, and Spokane systems to the north, the Snake River drains virtually the entire state. The Big Wood, Blackfoot, Boise, Clearwater, Payette, and Sal-

mon rivers flow into the Snake, along with many smaller rivers. More than 1,609 km (1,000 mi) long, this major river discharges more water than the Colorado and Sacramento rivers combined.

Idaho has four large lakes: Pend d'Oreille, Coeur d'Alene, Priest, and Bear. Thousands of small lakes and reservoirs contribute to the state's expanse of inland water. Idaho contains four of the nation's wild rivers, the Clearwater, Rapid, Salmon, and Snake.

Climate. Elevation and latitude influence the climate in Idaho. The Lewiston area, in the north, has the warmest climate, while higher cities in the southeast are much cooler. Of ten climatic regions in the state, northern canyons above Lewiston average 11° C (52° F) annually, and southwestern valleys in the Boise region average 1 degree cooler. The southeastern highlands are substantially colder (6° C/42° F).

Low humidity makes hot desert summers more tolerable; at higher elevations, particularly, daily variation in summer temperatures often approaches 22 C degrees (72 F degrees). Precipitation ranges from 152 mm (6 in) or less in desert areas to 2,504 mm (99 in) in the mountains.

Vegetation and Animal Life. Coniferous forests cover nearly 40% of the state, while pasture and range lands constitute almost one-half of the remainder. Much of Idaho's grazing land is semiarid, and more than half of the 13% used for farming requires irrigation.

Large indigenous animals include deer (white tail in the extreme north, mule deer farther south), elk, moose, mountain goats, big horn sheep, antelope, cougars, and bears. A few grizzlies inhabit remote areas. A large variety of smaller animals typical of the mountain and desert west abound throughout the state. Wilderness-preservation efforts help to maintain the wildlife population.

Resources. In addition to abundant water for irrigation and power, Idaho's commercial minerals include extensive silver, lead, zinc, and phosphate deposits. Forest products, primarily in the north, and valuable farmland contribute to the economy. Outdoor recreation areas are found throughout the state. Along the Oregon border, Hells Canyon, the deepest gorge in the nation, is a major attraction, along with Sawtooth National Recreation Area and Bear Lake.

PEOPLE

Idaho's population has grown 24% since 1970—an increase of more than twice the national rate. More than two-thirds of the state is uninhabited. Traditionally a rural state, Idaho became more than one-half urban between 1960 and 1970. Other than about 7,000 Indians, approximately the same number present at the time of initial exploration of the area, Idaho has few notable population elements. Southwestern Idaho

Boise, situated in the Boise River valley of southeastern Idaho, is the state's capital and largest city. It was founded in 1863 as a military outpost to protect the highly productive mining enterprises established in the area during the gold rush of 1862.

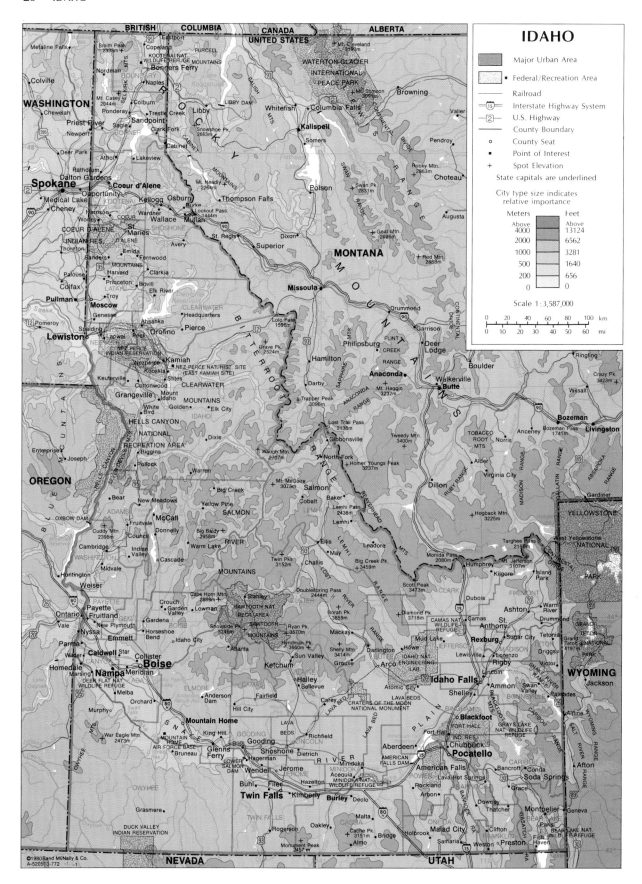

IDAHO

	Major Urban Area
	Federal/Recreation Area
	Railroad
	Interstate Highway System
	U.S. Highway
	County Boundary
o	County Seat
■	Point of Interest
+	Spot Elevation

State capitals are underlined

City type size indicates
relative importance

Meters	Feet
Above 4000	Above 13124
2000	6562
1000	3281
500	1640
200	656
0	0

Scale 1 : 3,587,000

©1980 Rand McNally & Co.
A-520513-772

(Left) *The Snake River, the largest tributary of the Columbia River, flows from east to west across southern Idaho. Used today for irrigation and the generation of hydroelectric power, the river was first charted by the Lewis and Clark Expedition in 1805.*

(Below) *Coeur d'Alene Lake, in Idaho's northern panhandle near the Washington border, lies within a historic silver- and lead-mining district. Bordering the lake on the north is Coeur d'Alene National Forest, and on the south, the Coeur d'Alene Indian Reservation.*

has the nation's major concentration of Basques, and some Japanese (reinforced by a 10,000-person relocation center from the Pacific coast during 1942–45) also live in the state. A few Chinese families remain, descendants of the Orientals who arrived after the gold rush, when most Idaho miners were Chinese. Black miners also came to Idaho with the gold rush, but the state's black population has never exceeded 1%. Among religious groups, the Mormons, about 25% of the state's population, are the largest, followed by Roman Catholics and Methodists. For more than a century, Idaho has ranked second only to Utah in concentration of Mormon population.

Idaho has no large cities; most of the urban population live in small towns. BOISE, with an estimated metropolitan area population of 154,600 in 1979, is the only place with more than 50,000 persons; LEWISTON in the north has a population exceeding 40,000, while Twin Falls and Nampa have more than 20,000. The state's relatively rapid growth since 1970 has taken place primarily in cities and in rural communities with scenic or recreational benefits.

Education. Elementary, secondary, vocational, and higher education in Idaho have been under the jurisdiction of a single state board of education since 1912. Following a professional study in 1946, the legislature consolidated the state's 1,110 school districts into few more than 100. Legislation enacted in 1965 provides for a sales tax to supplement property-tax revenues used in funding school budgets. The University of Idaho was chartered in 1889 as the major state institution of higher education. Idaho State University at POCATELLO (1901) and Boise State University (1932) are also 4-year state institutions.

Major libraries include that of the University of Idaho with more than 900,000 volumes; libraries of the other state universities; Idaho State Library; and Boise Public Library. Regional libraries serve the public libraries located throughout the state.

Cultural Institutions. Idaho has the State Historical Museum in Boise, the Idaho Museum of Natural History in Pocatello, a major museum educational program at the University of Idaho in Moscow, and about 30 county historical museums distributed throughout the state. Several symphony orchestras, including the professional Boise Philharmonic, perform in the larger communities. The Ballet Folk of Moscow and Antique Festival Theatre, headquartered in Buhl, can be seen in performances throughout the state. The SUN VALLEY Center for

the Arts and Humanities offers an extensive cultural program.

Historic Sites. Three of Idaho's eight registered National Historic Landmarks are related to the LEWIS AND CLARK EXPEDITION. Others include Fort Hall near Pocatello, City of Rocks along the California Trail, and two important buildings—the Jesuit Coeur d'Alene Mission near Cataldo and the U.S. Assay office in Boise. Nez Percé National Historical Park has sites in northern Idaho.

Communications. The *Idaho Statesman*, one of 14 dailies and the state's oldest newspaper, has been published since 1864. Almost 60 weekly papers serve the state's communities. Sixty-two radio stations, the oldest of which dates from 1922, and 11 television stations (three of them public) are located in Idaho. In addition, television stations located in Spokane, Wash., and Salt Lake City, Utah, broadcast into Idaho.

ECONOMIC ACTIVITY

Although originally dependent upon mining, Idaho developed farming and forestry as well. After 1940 industrial diversification broadened the state's economy, and tourism gained importance.

Agriculture. With total sales exceeding $1.1 billion in 1977, Idaho's farms dominated the state's economic production. Potatoes, wheat, hay, and barley are the major commodities. Values yielded by 23 different crops amount to more than

Except for a period of intensive mining in the late 19th century, the greatest share of Idaho's revenue has been derived from agriculture. (Left) Sheep graze along the Salmon River, which courses across central Idaho; in 1977 more than 490,000 head of sheep worth approximately $23 million were raised in Idaho. (Right) The Great Basin region south of Pocatello contains some of the state's most fertile farmland. The area is noted for the growing of potatoes, wheat, and sugar beets, and Idaho leads all states in the production of potatoes.

$1 million each. Many of them are irrigated and harvested by migrant workers.

Forestry and Fishing. Commercial lumber production, primarily of Douglas fir, white fir, white pine, yellow pine, and red cedar, reached 1.6 billion board feet in 1970. In 1970, Idaho ranked fifth in the nation in lumbering, with additional forestry production in paper products. Lumber value in 1978 exceeded $254 million. Idaho's 82,447 km² (31,834 mi²) of national forest land in 16 areas exceed all other states except Alaska.

In 1947 commercial rainbow trout fish farming began near Hagerman in southern Idaho, utilizing water from Thousand Springs. Soon, national markets for rainbow trout justified a $30 million-per-year industry.

Mining. Silver, with 18,356,049 troy oz extracted in 1978, lead, zinc, and phosphate accounted for most of the $280 million value of mineral recovery in 1978. Dramatic increases in gold and silver prices have led to the resumption of mining in abandoned districts as well as increasing production in the Coeur d'Alene area.

Manufacturing. Most of the state's industrial development has taken place since 1940, and Idaho's manufactured products had increased in value to $3.448 billion by 1976. Of this, 45% represents value added by manufacturing. A small population and the absence of iron and steel restricts this economic sector to agribusinesses, and wood products, mobile home, electronics, and construction-equipment manufacturing. Large land reclamation, reforestation, and highway projects within the state have been undertaken by Idaho's construction and lumber firms.

Transportation and Trade. A central mountain barrier has made railroad construction between north and south Idaho infeasible, and only one highway, surfaced in 1938, connects the two sections of the state. As a result, Spokane serves as commercial center for the northern counties, Salt Lake City for the southeast, and Boise for the southwest.

Tourism. Although Idaho's mountainous topography creates serious economic problems, recreation and tourism benefit from this natural heritage. Federal financial assistance has enabled Idaho to develop areas for tourism, such as Lava Hot Springs State Resort near Pocatello. Special attractions include the nation's pioneer ski resort at Sun Valley, developed by the Union Pacific Railroad in 1936. Nez Percé National Historical Park in the north, CRATERS OF THE MOON NATIONAL MONUMENT,

and YELLOWSTONE NATIONAL PARK on the Wyoming border attract visitors. Tourism accounted for $358 million in revenue in 1975.

GOVERNMENT

Idaho's constitution was adopted in 1889, one year before statehood. It provides for a governor and seven other state officials elected to 4-year terms. A constitutional amendment enacted in 1972 called for the reorganization of the executive branch into no more than 20 departments. Education, health and welfare, and transportation are the major departments. More than 100 state agencies are assigned to these departments. A 35-member senate and 70-member house of representatives form the legislature. The state supreme court, with five justices, heads the judicial branch. Two levels of trial courts (district and magistrate) serve all counties in the state. Legislators are elected to 2-year terms, judges and magistrates to 4-year terms, and supreme court justices to 6-year terms. All court justices are nonpartisan.

Local government consists of 44 counties and approximately 200 cities and villages. Nationally, two senators and two representatives serve Idaho in the U.S. Congress.

Idaho has gained a reputation for independent voting on a national level. An almost equal number of Democratic and Republican candidates for the presidency have received the state's electoral votes since Idaho entered the Union. Statewide elections for governor have favored Republicans nearly twice as often as Democrats.

HISTORY

Idaho has been inhabited for more than 14,000 years. A continental ice sheet extended into northern Idaho at the time of first habitation. As the ice receded, floods swept through northern valleys. The largest of these torrents—equal to ten times all the rivers of the world combined—occurred about 12,000 years ago when ancient Lake Missoula (see LAKE, GLACIAL) overflowed and washed out a 610-m-high (2,000-ft) ice dam. That catastrophe was followed by a hot, dry epoch, then another cold period. The early inhabitants hunted mammoths and other large animals now extinct. These early people migrated throughout the region.

By the 18th century, Idaho was the home of six Indian tribes: KUTENAI, Pend d'Oreille (or FLATHEAD), Coeur d'Alene, and NEZ PERCÉ in the north; and Northern SHOSHONI and Northern PAIUTE (known as Bannock) to the south.

Exploration and Fur Trade. After the Lewis and Clark Expedi-

Much of Idaho's topography is dominated by mountain ranges and rugged terrain formed through volcanic activity. (Left) The Sawtooth Mountains tower above Little Redfish Lake, a glacial body of water located in central Idaho's Sawtooth National Recreation Area. (Right) The landscape of the Craters of the Moon, Idaho's only national monument, was shaped during many centuries by lava flows. Perhaps the most impressive feature of the monument is the towering black cinder cones, some of which rise to heights of about 180 m (600 ft).

tion discovered the Salmon and Clearwater country in 1805–06, fur trappers explored the rest of Idaho in search of beaver. Idaho's Snake River area became a disputed borderland in which British and French trappers, based in Montreal and the lower Columbia River valley, competed with U.S. adventurers from Saint Louis. By 1840 trapping had almost ended, and the HUDSON'S BAY COMPANY gained control of the region. The United States acquired the southern part of the Oregon country, including all of present-day Idaho, in 1846. Hudson's Bay Company, with posts at Fort Hall and Fort Boise, continued to serve the settlers traveling to the west over the OREGON TRAIL and California Trail. Permanent white settlement began in 1860, when Mormons moved northward from Utah and miners arrived from the Pacific coast.

Mining. A series of Idaho gold rushes lured many, especially after an important mineral discovery at Pierce in 1860. Idaho was then part of Washington Territory, which extended east from Puget Sound to the continental divide. By 1862, a majority of the territory's population lived in Idaho. On Mar. 4, 1863, President Abraham Lincoln approved an act of Congress establishing the Idaho Territory. Present-day Montana and nearly all of Wyoming were included in this new mining commonwealth. Despite the departure of thousands of miners, Idaho had more than 32,000 residents in the census of 1863. Population figures declined after that time. Some of Idaho's early gold camps were quickly mined out, but others continued to produce for many years. Important lead-silver discoveries near Hailey in 1880 and in the Coeur d'Alene mines to the north in 1884 brought permanence to Idaho's mining industry. The latter became the major lead-silver region of the United States, with production exceeding a value of $2.8 billion in less than a century.

Statehood. After territories were formed in Montana (1864) and Wyoming (1868), Idaho's boundaries enclosed two areas divided by mountains. For a quarter-century, North Idaho tried without success to form a new territory with eastern Washington, or, as a last resort, rejoin Washington. The U.S. Congress voted in 1886–87 to annex North Idaho to Washington Territory, but President Grover Cleveland was persuaded not to approve that change.

Although Idaho Territory had been overwhelmingly Confederate Democratic after 1864, a coalition of Republicans and anti-Mormons gained power in 1882. By 1888, Idaho had become safely Republican. In attempting to establish control over the U.S. Congress, the Republicans voted for admission of the territory. Idaho was made a state on July 3, 1890.

Political and Economic Unrest. A silver-price collapse (1888–92), followed by a national economic panic, severely hurt Idaho. The Populist candidate James B. Weaver received the state's votes in the presidential election of 1892, as did William Jennings Bryan in 1896. Idaho thus expressed its discontent with the federal government's economic policies. Labor battles in the Coeur d'Alene mine area attracted national attention in 1892 and 1899. Sheep ranchers and cattlemen, vying for the limited range land available, clashed during that same period. By 1900, Idaho began to avail itself of national legislative programs, enacted in 1894 and 1902, directed at large-scale reclamation projects.

The state developed rapidly in the early 1900s, spurred by the commercial lumber industry. National farm and forest products markets, along with large-scale mining, developed in all parts of the state, but in 1920, a severe agriculture price

Sun Valley is located in southern Idaho's Sawtooth Mountains at an elevation of about 1,830 m (6,000 ft), which ensures plentiful snowfall for winter sports enthusiasts. Developed in 1936 as a ski resort, the region today offers year-round recreational activities.

collapse, followed by the Depression of the 1930s, intensified the state's problems; federal expenditures helped Idaho's economic recovery. Important military bases (a large naval training station on Lake Pend d'Oreille; air bases at Boise, Pocatello, and Mountain Home; and a naval gun plant at Pocatello) contributed to the state's economy after 1942. Idaho's largest federal installation, a National Reactor Testing Station located west of IDAHO FALLS, superseded Idaho's naval-gun testing area in 1949, developing nuclear power there 2 years later.

Contemporary Idaho. Issues related to maintenance of a high-quality environment and to wilderness preservation in vast mountain areas of the state have remained prominent since 1970. With extensive wilderness, and with constantly increasing pressures of economic and population growth, Idaho serves as an example for the study of contemporary environmental problems. MERLE WELLS

Bibliography: Beal, Merrill D., and Wells, Merle, *A History of Idaho,* 3 vols. (1959); Beatty, Robert O., *Idaho* (1974); Federal Writers' Project, *Idaho* (1936; repr. 1975); Jensen, Dwight, *Discovering Idaho: A History* (1977); Peterson, F. Ross, *Idaho: A Bicentennial History* (1976); Sparling, Wayne, *Southern Idaho Ghost Towns* (1974); Wells, Merle W., *Idaho: Student's Guide to Localized History* (1965).

Idaho, state universities and colleges of

Idaho's schools of higher learning are coeducational and all grant the bachelor's degree and all but one offer higher degrees. The **University of Idaho** (1889; enrollment: 7,680; library: 900,000 volumes) at Moscow, a land-grant school, has a 324-ha (800-acre) experimental farm and colleges of agriculture, forestry and range sciences, mines, law, arts and sciences, engineering, and wildlife, all of which grant bachelor's, master's, and doctor's degrees. Other schools are **Idaho State University** (1901; enrollment: 9,760; library: 1,000,000 volumes) at Pocatello and **Boise State College** (1932; enrollment: 10,420; library: 230,000 volumes) at Boise, both offering undergraduate and graduate degrees. **Lewis-Clark State College** (1894; enrollment: 1,780; library: 96,000 volumes) at Lewiston grants only undergraduate degrees.

Idaho Falls

Idaho Falls, a city with a population of 37,900 (1979 est.), is located on the Snake River in southeastern Idaho and is the seat of Bonneville County. Its economy depends on the processing of potatoes, sugar beets, and grain, all grown in the extensively irrigated region, augmented by diversified industry and a nearby U.S. government nuclear reactor. Settled as Eagle Rock in 1863, the city was renamed in 1890.

ideal gas

An ideal gas is any gas whose behavior exactly follows the relationship $PV = nRT$ (see GAS LAWS). Most real gases obey this equation of state at moderate pressures and can be treated as though they were ideal. At high pressures, low temperatures, or both, real gases show significant deviations from the ideal gas equation because of the increased attractive forces between molecules.

At standard conditions (1 atmosphere pressure and 273K), one MOLE of an ideal gas is exactly contained in a volume of 22.4 liters. These values permit the calculation of R, the ideal gas constant, which is 0.08205. GERALD C. ROPER

idealism

Idealism, the philosophical view that the mind or spirit constitutes the fundamental reality, has taken several distinct but related forms. Objective idealism accepts commonsense REALISM (the view that material objects exist) but rejects NATURALISM (according to which the mind and spiritual values have emerged from material things), whereas subjective idealism denies that material objects exist independently of human perception and thus stands opposed to both realism and naturalism.

PLATO is often considered the first idealist philosopher, chiefly because of his metaphysical doctrine of Forms. Plato considered the universal Idea or Form—for example, redness or goodness—more real than a particular instance of the form—a red object, a good action. According to Plato, the world of changing experience is unreal, and the Idea or Form—which does not change and which can be known only by reason—constitutes true reality.

The 18th-century epistemologist George BERKELEY was one of the major exponents of idealism. He held that the object of knowledge is an idea and that ideas can exist only in the mind; therefore, objects can exist only as objects of consciousness. Berkeley's dictum *esse est percipi* ("to be is to be perceived") has clear metaphysical implications. Indeed he called his theory immaterialism and intended it as a refutation of traditional MATERIALISM.

Immanuel KANT held that it is impossible to gain knowledge of the world by either reason or sense experience alone. Whereas in ordinary idealism the individual subject's awareness is the basic element of reality, in Kant's transcendental idealism the subject in general—not a particular subject, but the universal structure of all subjects—is the basic element of reality. This universal subject, the transcendental self, is the precondition of any knowledge of an objective world.

Kant's successor Johann Gottlieb FICHTE postulated a creative Ego as the ultimate source of reality, which generates all change and all knowledge. Fichte's theory was elaborated in G. W. F. HEGEL's absolute idealism. For Hegel reality is absolute Spirit or Reason, which manifests its development toward total self-consciousness in every aspect of experience from nature to human history. The English Hegelian F. H. BRADLEY argued that ordinary experience is fragmentary and contradictory and therefore appearance; reality, the Absolute, is a unified totality, which can be known only through a unique and absolute, perhaps mystical, experience. J. T. MOORE

Bibliography: Cunningham, G. Watts, *The Idealistic Argument in Recent British and American Philosophy* (1933); Ewing, A. C., ed., *The Idealist Tradition: From Berkeley to Blanshard* (1957) and *Idealism, a Critical Survey,* 3d ed. (1974); Smith, N. K., *Prolegomena to an Idealist Theory of Knowledge* (1924).

See also: EPISTEMOLOGY; ETHICS; METAPHYSICS.

identity crisis: see ADOLESCENCE; ERIKSON, ERIK; MIDDLE AGE.

ideology   [y-dee-ahl'-uh-jee]

An ideology is a system of beliefs that aspires to explain and to change the world. The concept of ideology originated in France during the late 18th century, when some thinkers and writers attacked the divine right of the French king to rule and questioned orthodox religious traditions associated with the Roman Catholic church. The philosopher DESTUTT DE TRACY coined the term *ideology* to denote a science of ideas that would be based, not on the discredited principles of faith and authority linked to the church and the monarchical state, but on knowledge gained from the human senses.

Today social scientists conceive of ideology as a systematic set of principles that link perceptions of the world to explicit moral values. An ideology not only interprets the meaning of events, but also posits the need for change in the existing situation. This definition reflects three aspects of ideology: (1) its content, (2) its functions, and (3) its style of reasoning.

What Ideology Is About. The content of political ideology is concerned with fundamental philosophical principles and the bases of political power. Ideologies such as CONSERVATISM, LIBERALISM, democratic SOCIALISM, COMMUNISM, FASCISM, and ANARCHISM all concern the nature of the self, the interaction between the self and the collectivity, the relation of the person to the physical environment, the nature of society, and the view of history. A political ideology also contains a program for political action. In this regard, the bases of political power and the interpretation of freedom and equality become especially important. Who rules now? Who ought to rule? How should the political leaders be selected? What will be the justification for the rulers' exercise of power? What public policies will they pursue; that is, how will the priority and interpretations given to freedom and equality influence their preferences for certain public policies? From this standpoint, ideology can be regarded as a set of beliefs that both justify and criticize political decisions.

What Ideology Does. In its philosophical aspects an ideology seeks to explain the key problems facing a society and to interpret key events: it provides meaning for life and history. In its policy-related aspects, ideology shapes the purposes and priorities of political action. Once leaders determine to resolve specific social problems, political ideology influences the selection of the most desirable and feasible policies. An ideology thus operates as a perceptual screen that accepts some alternatives but filters out others. Furthermore, by providing reasons for actions, ideology helps those persons holding power to gain acceptance for their policies. Leaders who do not exercise governmental power use ideology to challenge established authority, criticize existing policies, and offer proposals for change. Finally, ideologies can mobilize human efforts behind a cause, such as social equality or freedom from foreign domination and internal exploitation. By so doing, they serve to bring members of a group a shared sense of identity and solidarity.

Ideological Thought. An ideological style of reasoning involves abstract, deductive thought patterns. Ideology is thus a general, abstract, systematic set of principles, rather than a set of specific, concrete, and random beliefs. Persons who think in terms of ideology perceive concrete events in the light of abstract ideas, such as equality for the downtrodden or freedom for the enterprising. Stylistically, they also engage in deductive thinking; they deduce specific conclusions from a set of general theoretical principles. Generally, people with less formal education, those who do not play an active role in political life, and those who do not seek changes in the status quo, are unlikely to engage in an ideological style of reasoning. However, more formally educated persons, political activists, and people preferring fundamental changes in the existing situation—whether it be the radical creation of a new social order or the restoration of a previously operating order—will voice their ideas in an ideological style.

The Historical Place of Ideology. Historically, political ideology has been associated with movements for social change. An ideology encourages people to abandon their reliance on habit and routine as guides to behavior and to act instead according to a vision of a changed order. Generally, the more abstract, deductive, and comprehensive the beliefs, the more likely that an ideology will assert the need for fundamental changes. In Russia, China, Vietnam, and Cuba, Marxist-Leninist revolutionaries viewed ideology as a comprehensive, systematic program for political action to reconstruct the society.

Some writers have argued in recent years that ideology has come to an "end," in the sense that it no longer provides a guide to political action. Ideology plays its greatest role during times of drastic social change. The most intense ideological struggles have occurred when societies were experiencing institutional disintegration, challenges to established authority, war, economic collapse, and rapid industrialization. Thus, in Western Europe ideological polarization reached a peak between 1870 and 1940, when European societies faced rapid economic growth, challenges to monarchical rule, war, disillusionment with orthodox religion and conventional morality, and economic depression. In the 1960s the thaw in the cold war, increased prosperity, the growing separation between the Roman Catholic church and the state, and socialist and communist participation in governments all served to decrease the historical ideological cleavages. Marxist-Leninist political parties have paid more attention to ideology than have most European and American parties. In recent years, however, ideology has diminished in importance as a guide to communist political action. Today in the Soviet Union the pragmatic considerations of building a powerful state and an industrialized economy take precedence over Marxist-Leninist ideology. In China, after the death of Mao Tse-tung in 1976, efforts to create a new Chinese citizen and an egalitarian society became subordinated to the tasks of increasing economic productivity and technological efficiency. On the other

hand, in Latin America, Africa, and Asia, where instability characterizes the struggle for political power, ideologies are becoming more important. Various nationalist and socialist ideologies are put forward to explain political problems and suggest new solutions.   CHARLES F. ANDRAIN

Bibliography: Apter, David E., ed., *Ideology and Discontent* (1964); Bell, Daniel, *The End of Ideology*, rev. ed. (1967); Benewick, Robert, et al., *Knowledge and Belief in Politics: The Problem of Ideology* (1973); Hoffer, Eric, *The True Believer* (1951); Lane, Robert E., *Political Ideology* (1962); Putnam, Robert D., *The Beliefs of Politicians: Ideology, Conflict, and Democracy in Britain and Italy* (1973); Seliger, Martin, *Ideology and Politics* (1976); Waxman, Chaim I., ed., *The End of Ideology Debate* (1968).

Idfu: see EDFU.

Idiot, The

Fyodor DOSTOYEVSKY's novel *The Idiot* (1869; Eng. trans., 1913) portrays a morally blameless man, Prince Mishkin, whose innocent and simple nature and epileptic seizures cause him to be taken for a cretin. His Christ-like qualities, far from influencing those about him, are shown to be utterly incongruous in a sinful world. Nastasya Filipovna, who has been cruelly treated by a former lover, is attracted both to Mishkin and to the evil Rogozhin, and is unable to commit herself to either. When she is killed by Rogozhin, Mishkin's pacifism allows him to be an unwitting accomplice in the murder.

EDWARD WASIOLEK

Bibliography: Wasiolek, Edward, *Dostoevsky: The Major Fiction* (1964); Wellek, René, ed., *Dostoevsky: A Collection of Critical Essays* (1962).

idocrase [y'-duh-krays]

Idocrase, or vesuvianite, is a calcium aluminosilicate mineral (Ca_{10} Al_4 $(Mg, Fe)_2$ Si_9 O_{24} $(OH)_4$) commonly found in altered limestones. It forms prismatic crystals (tetragonal system) and columnar, granular, or massive aggregates that are usually brown or green. Hardness is $6\frac{1}{2}$, luster is vitreous to resinous, and specific gravity is 3.3–3.5. Transparent crystals sometimes are cut as gemstones, and californite, a compact, green, jade-like variety found in California, is an ornamental stone.

idol [y'-dul]

Images or statues modeled after gods or goddesses that are used in worship are called idols. In ancient cultures the practice of giving tangible expression to the realm of the spiritual was widespread, and personifications of symbols of life and fertility were common. The images, usually constructed of wood, stone, and metals, were decorated, presented with food, and prayed to by their devotees. Idols remain common in many religions of the world, including Buddhism and Hinduism as well as primitive religions.

The Judeo-Christian heritage prohibits the making and worship of images (Exod. 20:4-6; 34:17). In Judaism only the one true God, who cannot be contained in forms fashioned by humans, is worthy of worship. The New Testament depicts idolatry as any inordinate desire that places any object, person, institution, or ideology as the recipient of man's ultimate concern or affection. Idols represent all false forms of religion, which oppose the true and living God (I Cor. 8:4; I Thess. 1:9; I John 5:21). Like Judaism and Christianity, Islam prohibits the use of idols.   DOUGLAS EZELL

Bibliography: Barfield, Owen, *Saving the Appearances: A Study in Idolatry* (1957); Bevan, Edwyn, *Holy Images: An Inquiry into Idolatry and Image-Worship in Ancient Paganism and in Christianity* (1940; repr. 1978).

Idomeneus [ee-dah-may-noos']

In Greek legend Idomeneus, the son of DEUCALION and grandson of MINOS, was king of Crete. He was one of the major Greek leaders in the TROJAN WAR. According to Homer's *Odyssey*, he and his 80 ships returned uneventfully to Crete after the fall of Troy. In a later version of the legend, however, he was caught in a storm on the return voyage and vowed that if he reached home safely he would sacrifice to Poseidon the first creature he encountered. This proved to be his son. When Idomeneus fulfilled the vow, a plague fell on Crete and his subjects banished him. Mozart's opera *Idomeneo* was based on the legend.

Idris, King of Libya   [id-rees']

Idris, b. Mar. 13, 1890, was the first king (1951–69) of Libya. A grandson of al-Sanusi, he became leader of the Sanusi Muslim sect in 1917 and in 1920 was recognized as emir of Cyrenaica by the Italians, who had invaded Libya in 1911. The Italian Fascists forced him into exile in 1922, but Cyrenaica was restored (1943) to him in World War II. In 1951, Idris became king of the unified Libya. Idris and the monarchy were overthrown by a military junta led by Muammar al-Qaddafi in 1967.

Bibliography: Khadduri, Majid, *Modern Libya: A Study in Political Development* (1963).

Idrisi, al-   [id-ree'-see, ahl]

Abu Abd Allah Muhammad al Idrisi, or al-Idrisi, 1100–c.1165, was an outstanding medieval Arab geographer. He traveled widely in North Africa, Anatolia, and southwestern Europe before settling in Sicily in 1145; there he joined the court of the Norman king Roger II. Using his own observations and Greek and Arab sources, al-Idrisi wrote an outstanding geographical work that was a description of the known world, and he constructed a model of the Earth. He sent skilled men to do research and accurate drawings, and most errors in his work occurred when he relied on unchecked sources. His cartography recognized that the world is a sphere.

Bibliography: Ahmad, S. Maqbul, *Al-Sharif al-Idrisi: India and the Neighboring Territories* (1960).

idyll   [y'-dul]

The term *idyll* originally denoted a pastoral poem, generally a short one, describing the innocent rustic life of shepherds. The major classical writers of pastoral idylls were the Greeks Theocritus (3d century BC), Moschus and Bion (both 2d century BC), and the Roman Virgil (70–19 BC). Such English poets as Edmund Spenser and John Milton were influenced by the classical idylls. Later the term gradually lost its pastoral connotation and came to mean any composition, prose or verse, that had a country setting or merely a simple, appealing, or charming mood. Thus, Alfred Tennyson's *Idylls of the King* (1859–85) contains no descriptions of rustic life, although the mood and tone are those of an idyll.

Idylls of the King   [y'-dulz]

Idylls of the King, published between 1859 and 1885, are 12 poems in blank verse by Alfred Lord Tennyson that recount the adventures of King Arthur and his knights of the Round Table. Although generations of school children have become acquainted with Arthur and Arthurian legend through this popular Victorian version, Tennyson actually stripped the original medieval tales of their fey qualities and humor by elevating the language used and by focusing on the Christian elements of the story, such as the quest for the Holy Grail and Guinevere's penance for her adultery with Sir Lancelot. His chief source was Sir Thomas Malory's *Morte Darthur* (1469–70). The *Idylls* were written as public poetry, written by the reigning poet laureate and dedicated to Prince Albert, with an epilogue to Queen Victoria.   JANE COLVILLE BETTS

Bibliography: Fox, Arthur W., *Tennyson's "Idylls of the King"* (1909; repr. 1970); Pallen, Conde B., *The Meaning of the "Idylls of the King"* (1904; repr. 1965).

Ieper: see YPRES.

Ieyasu, Shogun of Japan   [ee-ay'-yah-soo, shoh'-guhn]

Ieyasu, or Tokugawa Ieyasu, 1542–1616, founded the TOKUGAWA shogunate that ruled Japan until 1868. The eldest son of Matsudaira Hirotada, lord (daimyo) of Okazaki castle in Mikawa province, he spent his youth during a period of great civil unrest as a hostage of the house of Imagawa. When freed in 1560 he formed a military alliance with the powerful NOBUNAGA. After Nobunaga's death (1582) Ieyasu competed for leadership with Nobunaga's general, HIDEYOSHI, and then allied with him during the last stages of the military unification of Japan. Ieyasu was a leading general in the defeat of the Hojo of Odowara in 1590 and received as his reward the former Hojo territories in the Kanto. He built a tightly organized administration there, centered on his castle city of Edo (later Tokyo).

When Hideyoshi died in 1598, Ieyasu was appointed a regent to his son and successor, Toyotomi Hideyori. Defeating his rivals in the Battle of Sekigahara in 1600, Ieyasu emerged as the new military leader of Japan. In 1603 he assumed the title of SHOGUN.

In 1605, Ieyasu passed the office of shogun to his son Hidetada, establishing a precedent for Tokugawa succession. He then retired to his family castle of Sumpu and prepared to eliminate Hideyori as a threat to continued Tokugawa rule. He attacked Hideyori's castle at Osaka in 1615 and eliminated Hideyoshi's successor.

Ieyasu initially sought to develop foreign trade and tolerated the Christian missionaries. He soon began establishing trade monopolies, however. This policy was continued by his Tokugawa successors and eventually led Japan into almost total isolation. Ieyasu's mausoleum at Nikko became an important shrine.   WILLIAM B. HAUSER

Bibliography: Sadler, A., *The Maker of Modern Japan* (1937; repr. 1970).

Ife   [ee'-fay]

The town of Ife (1971 est. pop., 157,200) in southwestern Nigeria was the seat of a powerful YORUBA kingdom from the 11th to the 17th century. It remains the sacred city of the Yoruba people where, according to tradition, the god Oduduwa created the Earth and established himself as *oni* (king). All later *oni* are traditionally believed to be descended from the mythological ruler of Ife, which is an important Yoruba cult center. Ife is also known for the many magnificent art objects in copper alloy, terra-cotta, and stone that have been excavated there. The most famous of these are naturalistic portrait heads of ancient kings, cast in metal by the lost-wax process, that date from the 12th to the 14th century. Scholars have suggested that these heads were probably attached to wooden effigies of the dead leaders and used in second burial ceremonies. Examples of these and other artifacts of ancient Ife are displayed in the Museum of Ife Antiquities, Ife, and in the Museum of Mankind (part of the British Museum, London).   DOUGLAS FRASER

Bibliography: Shaw, Thurstan, *Nigeria* (1978); Willett, Frank, *Ife in the History of West African Sculpture* (1967).

Ifni   [eef'-nee]

Ifni is a region located in southwestern Morocco along the Atlantic Ocean; it was formerly a possession of Spain. Its area, mostly desert, measures 1,500 km² (580 mi²). The region has a population of 45,784 (1971), most of whom are BERBERS. The main town is Sidi Ifni (1971 pop., 13,650). Fishing is the main occupation along the coast, and some goats and sheep are raised inland. The Spanish settled along the Ifni coast in 1476 and held it until 1524; they reclaimed it in 1860, although effective Spanish occupation began only in 1934. In 1969, after a decade of sporadic fighting with Morocco, Spain ceded its rights over Ifni.

Ignatius Loyola, Saint   [ig-nay'-shuhs loy-oh'-luh]

Saint Ignatius Loyola, b. 1491, d. July 31, 1556, was the founder of the Society of Jesus, or JESUITS. He was born into a noble

Saint Ignatius Loyola founded the Society of Jesus (Jesuits), a Roman Catholic order devoted to missionary work and education that was highly influential during the 16th-century Counter-Reformation. Ignatius is shown receiving Pope Paul III's blessing on the formal inauguration of the order in 1540. (Gesù Church, Rome.)

Basque family at the Loyola family castle near San Sebastian in northern Spain. He was educated at the royal court of Castile. While in the service of the viceroy of Navarre, Ignatius received a leg wound in a battle with the French in 1521. Although not very religious, he was forced through boredom to read a life of Christ while convalescing. Reflection on this reading brought about a profound change in his religious attitude.

Once recovered, Ignatius decided to set out on a pilgrimage to Jerusalem. First, however, he stopped at the famed Benedictine abbey of Montserrat in Catalonia, where he dedicated himself to God. He then spent nearly a year in a spiritual retreat at nearby Manresa. Here he had the mystical experience that would be later developed into his method of spirituality known as the *Spiritual Exercises*. He also discovered the orientation of his life's work. He traveled on as a poor man and beggar to Rome, to Venice, and finally to Jerusalem.

After his return to Spain, Ignatius studied Latin at Barcelona (1524–26) and continued his schooling with the study of philosophy at Alcalá (1526–27) and at Salamanca (1527). In 1528 he began his theological training at Paris. There he gathered his first associates, six in all (including Saint FRANCIS XAVIER), who together took vows of poverty and chastity at Montmartre in 1534. They were ordained in 1537.

The group wished to work in the Holy Land, but Europe's wars with Ottoman Turkey prevented them. As an alternative, they decided to offer their services to the pope. They were received (1538) by Pope PAUL III, and Ignatius drew up the rule of life for a new religious order, which was approved by Paul in 1540. Ignatius became the first general of the Society of Jesus.

By the time of Ignatius's death in 1556, the society had spread widely and had over a thousand members. Ignatius and his order had become a major factor in the COUNTER-REFORMATION. Besides his *Spiritual Exercises*, Ignatius also dictated an autobiography, wrote the *Constitutions* of the Society of Jesus, and left several thousand letters. His great theme was the service of God and God's greater glory. Ignatius was canonized in 1622 and is the patron of spiritual retreats. Feast day: July 31.   CYPRIAN DAVIS, O.S.B.

Bibliography: Brodrick, James P., St. Ignatius Loyola: The Pilgrim Years, 1491-1538 (1956); Dudon, Paul, St. Ignatius of Loyola, trans. by William J. Young (1949); Ignatius of Loyola, Autobiography of St. Ignatius of Loyola, trans. by Joseph F. O'Callaghan and ed. by John C. Olin (1974); St. Ignatius of Loyola: A Pictorial Biography, trans. by John Murray (1956); Purcell, Mary, The First Jesuit (1957).

Ignatius of Antioch, Saint

The third bishop of Antioch, Ignatius, d. *c.*107, was brought to Rome under Trajan and thrown to wild beasts. On the way to Rome he wrote to the Christians at Ephesus, Magnesia, Tralles, Rome, Philadelphia, and Smyrna and to Polycarp, bishop of Smyrna. These seven letters give an enlightening glimpse not only of the beliefs and internal conditions of early Christian communities, but also of the character of their author.

Ignatius wrote about the virgin birth and divinity of Christ, but stressed especially Christ's human nature. The first writer to call the church "catholic," Ignatius described it as a society of love, presided over in love by a bishop with his presbyters and deacons, and assembled "in grace, in one faith and one Jesus Christ" (Eph. 20).

Called *Theophoros* ("God-bearer"), Ignatius considered martyrdom a great honor and asked the Roman Christians not to save him. "Let me be given to the wild beasts," he wrote, "for through them I can attain unto God" (Rom. 4). Feast day: Oct. 17 (Western); Dec. 17 (Antioch); Dec. 20 (other Eastern).

Bibliography: Corwin, Virginia, Saint Ignatius and Christianity in Antioch (1960); Kleist, J. A., ed., The Epistles of St. Clement of Rome and St. Ignatius of Antioch (1946); Richardson, Cyril, The Christianity of Ignatius of Antioch (1935).

igneous rock   [ig′-nee-uhs]

Igneous rocks constitute one of the three main groups in standard rock classification, along with SEDIMENTARY ROCKS and METAMORPHIC ROCKS (see PETROGRAPHY). Igneous rocks form from the cooling and crystallization of molten or partially molten material called MAGMA.

According to some theories, the entire outer part of the Earth may have once been molten, and extensive igneous activity and volcanism (see VOLCANO) followed during early stages of the planet's development (see EARTH, GEOLOGICAL HISTORY OF). Differences in the crystallization rates and the times of formation for minerals of different compositions would have led to differentiation of rock types. Lighter elements, such as silicon, aluminum, sodium, and potassium, would have concentrated in the upper parts of the crust while heavier elements, such as iron, magnesium, and others, would have tended to sink. Such long-term igneous differentiation processes may have been one major factor contributing to the formation of the Earth's chemically and mineralogically layered structure.

The wide variety of presumably igneous rocks has long puzzled petrologists. Many workers once thought that most igneous rocks, including even granite and rhyolite, originated from chemical evolution of a single—probably basaltic—parent magma. Now the variety can apparently be better explained by the partial melting of many different source materials. Contamination of these melts by assimilation of surrounding, nonhomogeneous materials would have extended the variety. The great variety of igneous rocks may also be linked to differentiation processes occurring during sedimentary action at the Earth's surface, followed by subsequent burial and partial melting.

TYPES

Key variables in subdividing igneous rocks include mode of occurrence; grain size and texture; and mineralogy and chemistry. Rocks thought to be igneous may be subdivided into volcanic, subvolcanic (hypabyssal), plutonic, and pyroclastic types. Direct evidence of igneous origin is available only for volcanic and pyroclastic rocks, which form directly from the cooling of a viscous fluid (LAVA) or other materials that flow or erupt from volcanic vents and fissures. Geologists have inferred an igneous origin for other old rocks that have textures, chemical compositions, and mineral components identical to those of present-day volcanic rocks.

Volcanic. Volcanic rocks tend to be fine-grained (less than 1 mm/0.04 in), and their matrix usually contains glass as well as tiny crystals. Wholly glassy varieties are called OBSIDIAN. In porphyritic varieties (see PORPHYRY), larger crystals are embedded in a fine-grained groundmass. This texture probably results from extrusion of lava containing crystals already grown and developed under conditions of slow cooling below the Earth's surface; subsequent rapid cooling leads to crystallization of the finer-grained matrix.

The most common volcanic rocks are BASALT, ANDESITE, and RHYOLITE. Basalt, thought to form during partial melting of rocks in the Earth's mantle, is the most abundant volcanic rock. Andesite may form from partial melting of crustal rocks deep in fold belts. Rhyolite, composed largely of alkali FELD-

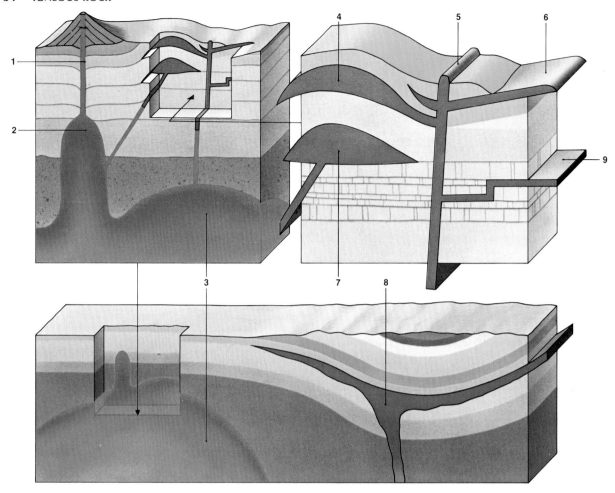

Igneous rocks are formed from solidification of magma, or molten matter from the Earth's interior. The rocks may cool as extrusive masses on the surface of the Earth or as intrusive bodies below the surface. Intrusive igneous rocks assume many different characteristic shapes. A neck (1) is solidified magma in a circular vertical feed channel of an extinct volcano. A stock (2) is a mass with a circular or elliptical shape. A batholith (3) is a huge mass, generally of granitic composition, that lies deep within the crust. Laccoliths (4, 7) are domelike masses in which the pressure of the intrusive magma has arched up the overlying sediment. A dike (5) is an inclined sheetlike body much longer than it is wide that generally occupies rock fractures and cuts across previously existing rock layers. A sill (6) is a thin band that conforms to the structural planes of the sedimentary beds around it. A lopolith (8) is a saucer-shaped mass—sometimes extremely large—that is concave upward. A transgressive sill (9) is a thin band of igneous rock that occurs in more than one horizontal plane.

SPAR and free silica (see SILICA MINERALS) such as QUARTZ, forms lava flows and tuffs. Other, less common, low-silica volcanic rocks contain neither feldspar nor quartz, but are rich in FELDSPATHOIDS such as leucite or NEPHELINE. Carbonatite, an unusual carbonate rock showing igneous characteristics, was discounted as actually being igneous until sodium carbonate lavas were observed erupting from African volcanoes.

Volcanic rocks occur in many parts of the world. A great chain of volcanoes known as the RING OF FIRE encircles the Pacific Ocean. The Mid-Atlantic Ridge is a great suboceanic chain of volcanoes, as are the East-Pacific and Indian Ocean Ridges (see MID-OCEANIC RIDGE). The EAST AFRICAN RIFT SYSTEM is largely filled with volcanic material, as is the extension of this trough northward through the Rhine Valley and the Oslo Fjord. Volcanoes rim the northern edge of the Mediterranean and cover central France. Great sheetlike flows of lava cover the Columbia River Plateau in the northwestern part of the United States and the DECCAN PLATEAU in India. Such active volcanic regions appear mostly along the borders of continental plates (see PLATE TECTONICS), with the more basaltic materials rising to the surface at divergent plate boundaries, and the more andesitic and rhyolitic materials appearing along convergent plate boundaries.

Subvolcanic. Subvolcanic rocks are fine-grained rocks occurring in dikes or sills and connected directly with volcanic

rocks. The discordant character of dikes and other types of forceful intrusions supports the theory that they were formed from a fluid. Some such rocks are medium-grained (1 to 5 mm/0.04 to 0.2 in), but their patterns of grain intergrowth and their compositions strongly resemble those of surface volcanics. Many subvolcanic rocks are porphyritic.

Plutonic. Plutonic rocks are coarse-grained (greater than 5 mm/0.2 in) or medium-grained and commonly occur in large ovoid, circular, or tabular masses. Most common among them are rocks of the GRANITE, GRANODIORITE, and GABBRO clans. The margins of the mineral grains in these rocks are tightly interlocking. Some plutonic rocks may be porphyritic. Most plutonic rocks, with the exception of some types thought to form by accumulation in layered complexes, have chemical and mineralogical equivalents among the volcanic and subvolcanic rocks.

Erosion has made it possible to trace direct gradations from some plutonic bodies to subvolcanic and volcanic structures; such bodies must be igneous. When intrusive plutonic rock seems to have cut across or broken through adjacent rocks, it is usually thought to be igneous. When rocks surrounding a mass of plutonic rocks show evidence of having been "baked" (contact metamorphism), they are considered to be of igneous origin. Many plutonic bodies appear to have formed deep within the Earth's crust and to have cooled and crystallized at depth, in environments near their melting point. Their surface exposure apparently results from uplift and erosion. Such bodies show ambiguous relationships to the rocks (usually metamorphic) surrounding them; they grade into them imperceptibly and seem to be interlayered with them, their edges being parallel to them, and showing no appearance of having either shoved aside or intruded into the surrounding rocks. Some of these plutonic bodies may be igneous, having formed by partial melting of rock masses at depth, followed by recrystallization without displacement or movement. Others may have formed by metamorphism or transformation of preexisting rocks, without any melting. The deeper the locus of formation of plutonic bodies the more ambiguous is their origin. In deep zones of the Earth's crust, igneous and metamorphic processes converge. These processes may produce similar-looking rocks, indistinguishable by present criteria. The processes themselves may indeed merge to form conditions unknown at the surface. Experimental work involving high pressures and temperatures has thrown new light on these processes and on how rock materials may behave in deep zones of the Earth's crust.

Some plutonic rocks, the so-called layered igneous rocks, also show features common in sedimentary rocks. They are inferred to be igneous because of their mineral composition and texture, as seen in the intergrowth of grains. Prominent layering in these large bodies is thought to occur because of the faster settling of larger or denser, early-formed crystals and the slower settling—or even floating—of smaller or less dense crystals. The process is similar to the settling of grains of sand in water, except that it happens at temperatures exceeding 1,000° C and at locations deep within the Earth.

Plutonic igneous rocks may also be subdivided in terms of their relationship to structural events. Some bodies were emplaced before significant folding or mountain-building events, others during folding and mountain building. The origin of bodies that formed near or at the culmination of major structural episodes is perplexing. Plutonic rocks that were emplaced after the conclusion of structural events and clearly cutting across the main fold structures are probably igneous.

Granitic rocks, including QUARTZ MONZONITE and GRANODIORITE, are the most abundant plutonic rocks. They may form from the partial melting of deeply buried sedimentary rocks during periods of mountain building. Rocks such as syenite are rich in potassium feldspar and contain no quartz.

Plutonic rocks of probable igneous origin form the cores of many of the world's great mountain ranges: the Rockies, Appalachians, Sierra Nevada, Alps, and Himalayas. In addition, the PRECAMBRIAN shields—which form the central portions of all of the continents and underlie the world's sedimentary basins—contain plutonic rocks, most of which may have been formed by the melting or partial melting of other crustal rocks, followed by subsequent slow cooling and crystallization or by more active flow, injection, and intrusion.

Pyroclastic Rocks. Igneous and sedimentary processes converge in the formation of pyroclastic rocks. Tuffs, breccias, ashflows, and other fragmental rocks have many of the same characteristics as sedimentary rocks. Ash, volcanic bombs, and other clearly igneous fragmental material are ejected from volcanoes as red-hot, molten debris. When such material falls to the ground, however, it forms deposits similar in structure to air-laid sedimentary rocks, such as wind deposits in deserts. When volcanic debris falls into water, it settles to the bottom and forms layers even more similar to sedimentary materials. Mineral composition may be the only feature by which pyroclastic rocks can be distinguished from more ordinary sedimentary rocks.

Some pyroclastic eruptions have caused great catastrophes, such as the eruptions of VESUVIUS, which buried POMPEII and HERCULANEUM, and of Mount PELÉE, which killed 35,000 people in 1902 and 1932. The great sheets of rhyolitic ash that cover wide areas in Nevada and other western states must be of similar origin.

Basic vs. Acidic. Igneous rocks are often divided into basic and acidic types. These terms relate to percentage of silica (SiO_2) rather than to hydrogen-ion content (pH). Some pe-

decreasing temperature

The Bowen reaction series, devised by Norman L. Bowen, an American physical chemist, describes the chemical mechanism through which the great variety of igneous rocks form. The series shows the general sequence of mineral formation that occurs in a cooling basaltic magma composed primarily of silicates. When molten basalt cools, various minerals begin to crystallize out of the melt in a specific order, depending on the temperature. The reaction series consists of two separate silicate branches that crystallize concurrently and converge to a third branch, which crystallizes last. Branch A is a discontinuous series in which a change occurs from one iron-magnesium-rich mineral to another in distinct steps. As the melt cools, the first mineral to crystallize is olivine (1). As the temperature continues to fall, the olivine reacts with the melt to form pyroxene (2), which in turn crystallizes and reacts to form amphibole (3), and then biotite (4). Branch B is a continuous series consisting of plagioclase feldspar in which during cooling a smooth gradation, rather than separate steps, occurs from calcium-rich anorthite (5) through mixed sodium-calcium labradorite (6) to sodium-rich albite (7). When biotite and albite have formed, the third series begins with crystallization of potassium feldspar, or orthoclase (8), then muscovite (9), and finally quartz (10).

Devil's Tower in Wyoming is believed to be the remains of hard igneous rock resulting from solidification of magma that filled the neck, or conduit, of an extinct volcano. The softer rocks of the original volcano eroded away, exposing the resistant neck.

trologists prefer the terms mafic and felsic. Ultrabasic (ultramafic) rocks, containing less than 45 percent SiO_2, include plutonic rocks such as DUNITE and PERIDOTITE, which often contain OLIVINE and PYROXENE and are free of quartz and feldspars. Some contain feldspathoids. Basic rocks contain 45 to 62 percent SiO_2 and include gabbroic (plutonic) rocks and basaltic (volcanic) rocks. Plagioclase feldspar, olivine, and pyroxene are the key minerals in these rocks, and quartz is usually absent. Intermediate rocks (52 to 66 percent SiO_2) include DIORITE (plutonic) and andesite (volcanic). These rocks contain hornblende (see AMPHIBOLE), pyroxene, and plagioclase feldspar. Quartz, potassium feldspar, and biotite (see MICA) may occur. Acidic (felsic) rocks, containing more than 66 percent SiO_2, include the granites (plutonic) and rhyolites (volcanic). Quartz and potassium feldspar are important mineral components, along with muscovite (see MICA), biotite, and hornblende.

ECONOMIC DEPOSITS

Rocks that are known or inferred to be of igneous origin are the sources of many economically important materials. Volcanic rocks are sources of sulfur and mercury. Volcanic ash-flow deposits are sources of much of the world's copper supply—specifically the porphyry copper deposits in Chile, Nevada, and Utah. The chromium-rich mineral CHROMITE is common in layered igneous complexes such as the Stillwater Complex of Montana. Low-silica complexes of probable igneous origin are sources of much asbestos, as at Thetford Mines, Quebec. Precious-metal deposits of gold, silver, and platinum are related to late stages in the formation of igneous granitic rocks. The Great Dike of Rhodesia and the Bushveld Complex of Southern Africa contain rich deposits of copper, gold, and other valuable minerals. Lead-zinc ore bodies result from late-stage concentration of these metals in cooling igneous complexes.

Many high-grade iron-ore deposits (MAGNETITE) are probably igneous, as are great nickel deposits, such as those at Sudbury, Ontario. Titanium ores occur in plagioclase-rich gabbro called anorthosite. Many anorthosites are thought to be igneous, although the absence of volcanic equivalents leads to a possibility of metamorphic origin also. Anorthosite is a low-

grade source of aluminum; no economically feasible way, however, has been found to process it. Many volcanic rocks are used in various types of construction, especially as a crushed material for road building. Plutonic rocks, lavas, and tuffs are used in house construction and as decorative stone. Volcanic ash and flows (when weathered) furnish fertile soils. The cooling of igneous rocks at depth also provides sources of GEOTHERMAL ENERGY.   WILLIAM D. ROMEY

Bibliography: Barth, T. F. W., *Theoretical Petrology*, 2d ed. (1962); Bayly, Brian, *Introduction to Petrology* (1968); Carmichael, Ian, et al., *Igneous Petrology* (1974); Hatch, Frederick H., et al., *Petrology of Igneous Rocks*, 13th ed. (1972); Hyndman, Donald, *Petrology of Igneous and Metamorphic Rocks* (1972); Macdonald, Gordon A., *Volcanoes* (1972); Romey, William D., *Field Guide to Plutonic and Metamorphic Rocks* (1971); Turner, Francis J., and Verhoogen, John, *Igneous and Metamorphic Petrology* (1960).

ignition system   [ig-nish'-uhn]

An INTERNAL-COMBUSTION ENGINE needs an ignition system for igniting the combustible mixture inside each cylinder at the proper moment. In the DIESEL ENGINE, the air inside the cylinder is compressed enough to raise the temperature above the ignition point, so that the fuel is ignited as soon as it is injected into the cylinder. This is called compression ignition. The gasoline engine, however, requires a more complex system, called spark ignition, which uses an electric spark to ignite the mixture. The two basic automotive ignition systems are the conventional breaker-point system and the newer, electronic ignition.

BREAKER-POINT IGNITION SYSTEM

The breaker-point system (see figure) consists of the source of energy (the battery), the ignition coil, distributor, ignition switch, spark plugs, and wiring. The entire electrical system includes the ignition system as a subsystem, but contains, in addition, the GENERATOR (or a related device called an alternator), the VOLTAGE REGULATOR, the starter, and electrical lights, accessories, and gauges (see AUTOMOTIVE INSTRUMENTATION).

Ignition Distributor and Coil. The ignition distributor (see figure) has two jobs. First, it opens and closes the circuit between the battery and the ignition coil. When the circuit is closed (completed), current flows in the primary circuit of the ignition coil and creates a magnetic field. When the circuit is opened (broken), the rapid decrease in the magnetic field induces (because of electromagnetic induction) a high-voltage surge of current in the secondary circuit of the ignition coil. This high-voltage surge is routed back to the distributor so the distributor can do its second job—sending the high-voltage surge to the spark plug in the engine cylinder that is nearing completion of its compression stroke and is therefore ready to fire.

The breaker-point system works in the following way. The distributor has a stationary contact point mounted on a base, a movable contact point on a spring-loaded lever, and a shaft, which is driven from the engine camshaft. As the shaft rotates, it turns a cam situated on top of the shaft. The cam has the same number of lobes as there are cylinders in the engine. As a lobe moves under the insulated rubbing block on the contact lever, it pushes the lever away so the contact points separate. Then, as the lobe moves out from under the rubbing block, the points come together again. This action serves to alternately interrupt and then complete the circuit to the ignition coil. With every interruption, the coil produces a high-voltage surge. A capacitor is connected across the contact points to prevent arcing at the points.

The high-voltage surges are distributed to the spark plugs by a rotor mounted on top of the cam and a series of metal inserts in the distributor cap, which is made of an insulating material. The rotor has a spring and a rotor blade. The spring is in contact with the center terminal on the cap, which is connected to the high-voltage terminal of the coil. Thus the high-voltage surges flow through the cap terminal to the rotor blade. As the rotor turns, the blade passes the outer terminals of the cap. When a high-voltage surge flows to the rotor blade, the blade is in a position where it is in contact with

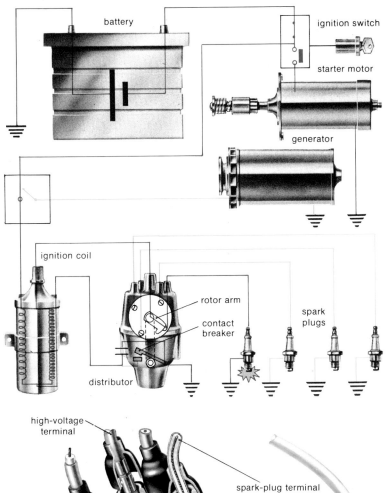

battery

ignition switch

starter motor

generator

ignition coil

rotor arm

contact breaker

spark plugs

distributor

The automotive ignition system (left) *must deliver 10,000 volts up to 300 times per second in order to keep the engine running. The electrical system, which includes the ignition system, must supply a strong current to the starter motor to start the engine. When the ignition switch is turned, current flows from the battery to the starter motor and to the ignition coil. The coil produces a high-voltage pulse (10,000 volts) that is directed to the rotor arm of the distributor, and then to the spark plugs one by one. The generator is switched into the circuit to recharge the battery when the car is in normal operation.*

The distributor (bottom left) *distributes the high-voltage pulse of the ignition coil to the spark plugs. The rotating camshaft turns the distributor shaft and opens the contact-breaker points once every revolution. This induces a high-voltage pulse in the coil that is fed to the high-voltage terminal of the distributor and then to the rotor arm. Timing is such that the pulse occurs every time the rotor arm is in contact with a spark-plug terminal, producing a spark at each plug.*

The spark plug (below) *ignites the fuel in the cylinder to drive the piston. An electric pulse (blue line) from the distributor passes to the points of the plug (inner and outer electrodes) and produces an electrical spark in the spark gap, firing the fuel. The points are made of highly corrosion-resistant metal, such as platinum, and the gap must be carefully maintained at a fixed distance. The body is insulated with ceramic to prevent an electrical discharge to the engine.*

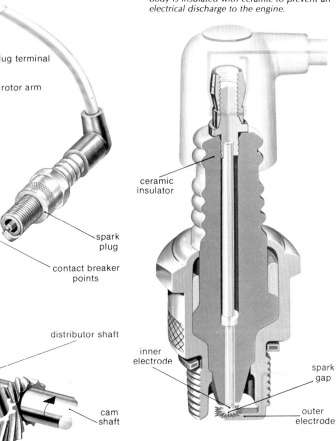

high-voltage terminal

spark-plug terminal

rotor arm

spark plug

contact breaker points

distributor shaft

cam shaft

ceramic insulator

inner electrode

spark gap

outer electrode

the outer terminal of the cap, which is connected to the spark plug that is ready to fire; the high-voltage surge, therefore, is directed to that spark plug.

Advance Mechanisms. Ignition systems include advance mechanisms that get the sparks to the spark plugs earlier in the compression strokes when the engine speed increases. This adjustment is necessary because at higher speeds the pistons are moving faster in the cylinders. If there were no advance mechanism and the spark continued to appear just before the piston reached top dead center (TDC)—the end of the compression stroke, just before the beginning of the power stroke—then at higher engine speeds the piston would be too far past TDC and already moving down on the power stroke when the spark appeared, wasting the power available from the power stroke. If, however, the spark is advanced so that it occurs earlier, then the ignited gases will be expanding at the optimal point in the cycle, and maximum power will be attained during the power stroke. Advance mechanisms vary. Mechanical, or centrifugal, advance makes use of weights and springs. As engine speed increases, centrifugal force causes the weights to move out; this motion is then used to advance the spark an appropriate amount. Vacuum advance uses the vacuum that exists in the intake manifold of the engine to accomplish the spark advance. Most modern distributors combine mechanical and vacuum advance to produce the total advance required for best operation under all conditions.

ELECTRONIC IGNITION

The electronic ignition system performs the same basic functions as the conventional systems but with one major difference: the battery-to-coil circuit is closed and opened electronically in the former rather than mechanically as in the breaker-point system. The cam is replaced with a rotor that has metal tips on it. As the rotor turns, the tips pass by a pickup-coil assembly. Each time a tip aligns with the assembly, a magnetic pulse is generated in the coil. The coil then produces a small current that is fed to an ignition-pulse amplifier. The amplified signal is used to open the battery-to-coil circuit, producing the usual high-voltage surge, which can then be fed back to the distributor cap, where it is used just as in a conventional system. Electronic ignition is now used on most new automobiles. It is more accurate over a wide range of operating conditions and requires less maintenance because it has no parts subject to mechanical wear.

Some of the newer electronic ignition systems do not use mechanical advance mechanisms. Instead, they use electronic devices to advance the spark as required. Sensors are used to detect engine variables, such as coolant temperature, piston position in the cylinder, throttle position, intake-manifold vacuum, and engine speed. The signals from these sensors are integrated in an electronic control unit, which then advances or retards the spark as required for best operation.

WILLIAM H. CROUSE

Bibliography: Blanchard, Harold F., and Ritchen, Ralph, *Motor Auto Engines and Electrical Systems,* 7th ed. (1977); Brant, Carroll, *Transistor Ignition Systems* (1976); Crouse, William H., *Automotive Electronic and Electrical Equipment,* 9th ed. (1980); Tepper, Marvin, *Electronic Ignition Systems* (1977).

Igorot   [ee-guh-roht']

Igorot (Tagalog for "mountaineer") is a general name applied to various groups of Filipinos living mainly in the mountainous interior of northern Luzon, the Philippines. Groups referred to by this term include the Bontok, Kalinga, Ibaloi (Nabaloi), Ifugao, Tinggian, and Isneg (Apayao). Ethnically they are Filipinos and speak languages affiliated with the Malayo-Polynesian linguistic family. The Igorot live in villages of raised, thatched houses and grow rice, sweet potatoes, vegetables, and fruits. The marvelous terraced rice fields of the Ifugao are world famous for their immense size and skillful engineering.

Among Igorot groups genealogical descent is traced through both parents. Although no longer practiced, warfare, including occasional HEAD-HUNTING, was frequent in earlier times among many of these groups. Most Igorot retain their traditional animistic religious beliefs, but today an increasing number are Christian. Many attend local public schools, work in mining and other industries in their region, and have adopted Christian Filipino values and customs.   DONN V. HART

Bibliography: Keesing, Felix M., *The Ethnohistory of Northern Luzon* (1962); Scott, William Henry, *The Discovery of the Igorots: Spanish Contacts with the Pagans of Northern Luzon* (1974).

Iguaçu Falls   [eeg-wuh-soo']

Iguaçu Falls, located on the Iguaçu River between Argentina and Brazil, is made up of 275 cataracts, separated by islands, that fall 60 to 80 m (200 to 280 ft) over the edge of a 4-km-wide (2.5-mi) escarpment. More than half the cataracts fall into a narrow chasm called Devil's Throat. Argentina and Brazil have both established national parks on their respective sides of the falls.

iguana   [ig-wahn'-ah]

The common iguana, I. iguana, a large lizard found from central Mexico to southern South America, basks by day on a tree branch, usually over water. When danger threatens, it submerges in the water.

The term *iguana* usually refers to the large species of typical New World lizards in the family Iguanidae. They are also classified in the infraorder Iguania, with the agamids and chameleons. Large-bodied, with robust limbs and tails, most species of iguanas live in the American tropics. Although basically a New World family of some 700 species, iguanids are also found on Madagascar and Fiji. The family as a whole is fairly well diversified in appearance and habits; it includes horned lizards, fence lizards, chuckwallas, anoles, and basilisks. The large lizards popularly called iguanas usually have compressed bodies and tails and a dorsal crest of soft spines that is more prominent in males than in females.

The common iguana, *Iguana iguana,* is widely used as food throughout its range from southern Mexico to central South America and also in the Lesser Antilles. It is an arboreal tropical forest animal, attaining more than 1.5 m (5 ft) in total length, often found in the vicinity of rivers and streams. Young iguanas have been popular as pets because of their bright green skin color, which dulls with age. Large ground iguanas, *Cyclura,* inhabit islands of the Caribbean and attain total lengths of up to 1.2 m (4 ft). Large iguanas are also found on the Galapagos Islands. The land iguanas, *Conolophus,* feed on terrestrial plants, including cactus, whereas the marine iguanas, *Amblyrhynchus cristatus,* feed on marine algae. These marine iguanas, up to 1.5 m (5 ft) in length, are the only lizards that regularly make use of the nearby marine environment—they usually swim close to shore and can dive to depths more than 35 feet to eat plants, particularly seaweed growing on the bottom. They can remain submerged for up to 30 minutes.

The common iguana eats both plants and animals, including leaves and fruit, insects, birds, and small mammals. Ground iguanas are predators of birds and small mammals but eat vegetation as well.

The spiny-tailed iguanas, or black iguanas, *Ctenosaura*, are found from Central America into northern Mexico. Less arboreal than the common iguana, they inhabit brush and scrub areas primarily, and their bodies and tails are cylindrical rather than compressed.

A relatively small iguanid, *Dipsosaurus dorsalis*, known as the desert iguana, inhabits deserts with creosote bush in the southwestern United States. It is vegetarian and grows to little more than 30 cm (1 ft) in length. Often active during the hottest part of the day when smaller lizards are under shelter, the desert iguana runs rapidly and ascends creosote bushes to eat leaves and flowers.

Iguanas lay their eggs in burrows that they excavate themselves; most nest individually, but marine iguanas nest communally, several females laying eggs in a single burrow.

STEVEN C. ANDERSON

Bibliography: Bellairs, Angus, *The Life of Reptiles,* 2 vols. (1970); Goin, Coleman J., et al., *Introduction to Herpetology,* 3d ed. (1978); Mertens, Robert, *The World of Amphibians and Reptiles* (1960); Porter, Kenneth, *Herpetology* (1972); Roberts, Mervin and Martha, *All About Iguanas* (1976); Schmidt, Karl P., and Inger, Robert F., *Living Reptiles of the World* (1957).

Iguanodon   [ig-wan'-uh-dahn]

Iguanodon was a bipedal herbivorous ornithischian DINOSAUR whose fossils appear in Late Jurassic and Early Cretaceous rocks. With massive bodies weighing more than 6 metric tons (13,200 lb), iguanodons stood up to 4.9 m (16 ft) high and were up to 9.5 m (31 ft) long. The jaws, lined with broad, leaf-shaped teeth, ended in the front with a toothless, horny beak. Arm-like forelimbs had five-fingered hands with a large sharp bony spike in place of a thumb. Four-toed feet (three functional toes and a large, spikelike thumb) produced bird-like tracks that are preserved in certain strata. Iguanodon specimens have been found principally in Europe, with fragmentary remains recently reported from the United States, in Utah, and from Mongolia. Among the first dinosaurs to be discovered (in England in 1822), *Iguanodon* became one of the best known through the discovery in 1878 of some 33 skeletons in a Belgian coal mine. The name (Greek for

The Iguanodon, *a dinosaur with spikes on its forelimbs, flourished about 100 million years ago and may have been a herbivorous twig eater.*

"iguana tooth") alludes to a vague resemblance of the teeth to those of the existing but unrelated iguana lizard.

WANN LANGSTON

Bibliography: Desmond, Adrian J., *The Hot-Blooded Dinosaurs* (1976); Swinton, W. E., *The Dinosaurs* (1970).

IGY: see INTERNATIONAL GEOPHYSICAL YEAR.

Ihara Saikaku   [ee'-hah-rah sy'-kah-koo]

Ihara Saikaku, b. Osaka, 1642, d. Aug. 10, 1693, was a Japanese novelist and Japan's greatest fiction writer of the Edo, or early modern, period (1603–1868). Beginning his literary career as a poet, he turned to writing fiction in the last decade of his life. His reputation rests on his prose work. Saikaku broke new ground in creating fiction that, while not entirely realistic, was set squarely in the milieu in which he lived. He wrote at a time when merchants in the large Japanese cities were gradually gaining acceptance as a social class. In his writings he captured the zest for living and the bawdy humor of that emerging class. Saikaku's characters ran off with their lovers and schemed to make quick commercial profit. Among his works are *The Life of an Amorous Man* (1682; Eng. trans., 1964), *The Japanese Family Storehouse* (1688; Eng. trans., 1959), and *Worldly Mental Calculations* (1692; Eng. trans., 1976).

EDWARD B. FOWLER

Bibliography: Hibbett, Howard, *The Floating World in Japanese Fiction* (1959; repr. 1970).

IJsselmeer   [y'-sul-mayr]

The IJsselmeer is a large freshwater lake in the north Netherlands that was once part of the Zuiderzee, a landlocked inlet of the North Sea. The lake was created when a 31-km-long (19-mi) dam, completed in 1932, was built from North Holland province to Friesland province. The IJsselmeer is 8 m (25 ft) above sea level and covers 3,440 km² (1,328 mi²). A road runs along the top of the dam, locks permit boat traffic, and sluices regulate the water flow. The dam was built as part of a drainage project in order to create new land, called polders. The first polder, the Wieringermeer, was finished in 1930. It was followed by the Northeast Polder (1945), East Flevoland (1957), South Flevoland (1968), and the largest, Markerwaard, which was begun in 1956. The creation of new land for agriculture, industry, and recreation continues. Much freshwater fishing is done on the IJsselmeer. Amsterdam is located on the shore of the lake.

Ik   [ik]

The Ik (Teuso) are an African people of northern Uganda and the bordering areas of Sudan and Kenya. Once a nomadic hunter-gatherer people living in equilibrium with their environment, they now occupy barren mountaintop villages in a rocky area with only scattered patches of arable soil and an uncertain water supply. Shortly before World War II the traditional hunting ground of the Ik, the Kidepo Valley in northern Uganda, was made a national park, and hunting was forbidden. The Ik were encouraged to move to nearby mountains where their attempts to farm resulted in starvation or near starvation.

Some Ik tribespeople have stayed alive by poaching in the national park or appropriating stray cattle belonging to neighboring herding peoples. Their traditional way of life has broken down almost completely. Leadership within the local group has disappeared as people have withdrawn from one another. Marriage and the family have disintegrated. Parental support generally ends at age 3, when children must learn to fend for themselves. Young children give one another some support, but adulthood begins at age 12 or 13. In 1970 the Ik population numbered about 2,000. Their prospects for survival are bleak.

PHOEBE MILLER

Bibliography: Calhoun, John B., "Plight of the Ik and Kaiadilt Is Seen as a Chilling Possible End for Man," *Smithsonian,* 3 (1972); Turnbull, Colin M., *The Mountain People* (1972).

Ikeda Hayato   [ee-kay'-dah hah-yah'-toh]

The Japanese statesman Ikeda Hayato, b. Dec. 3, 1899, d. Aug. 13, 1965, played a key role in Japan's economic recovery after World War II. An official in the ministry of finance from 1927, he was elected to the Japanese House of Representatives in 1949 and served as minister of finance (1949-52, 1956–57) and of international trade and industry (1959-60). In 1960 he assumed leadership of the Liberal-Democratic party and became prime minister. Ikeda greatly improved Japan's foreign trade position and eased internal political tensions. He resigned because of ill health in 1964.

Ikeno Taiga: see TAIGA.

Ikhanaton: see AKHENATEN.

Île-de-France   [eel-duh-frahns']

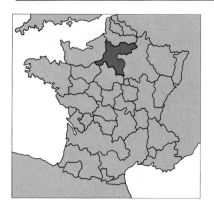

The map indicates the location of Île-de-France, a historical region of pre-Revolutionary France in the north-central portion of the country. The region was divided in 1790 among the administrative departments of Seine, Seine-et-Marne, Seine-et-Oise, Oise, and Aisne.

· The Île-de-France is a historic region and former province of north central France. PARIS and its suburbs dominate the region. A fertile depression lying at the center of the Paris Basin, the Île-de-France is drained by the SEINE RIVER and its main tributaries, the MARNE and the Oise rivers. The region's subregions—Valois, Beauce, Brie, and Soissonais—are flat, limestone plains covered with loess. Forests, such as those of FONTAINEBLEAU and Compiègne, occupy sandy areas between the plains. Industry is concentrated in the Paris area; truck farms serve the city; and wheat, barley, corn, sugar beets, and dairy cattle are raised in the region.

With its capital at Paris, this duchy (then called Francia) was the nucleus around which Hugh Capet, founder of the Capetian dynasty in 987, began the consolidation of the French state. From 1483 to 1790, when it was divided into departments, Île-de-France was a province of France.

TIMOTHY J. RICKARD

ileitis: see ENTERITIS.

ileus   [il'-ee-uhs]

Ileus, or bowel obstruction, is a condition of the small or large intestine in which the passage of intestinal contents is stopped or impaired. The bowel wall becomes swollen (edemic) and congested and the intestine distended; there is an increasing risk of peritonitis and death. Complete mechanical obstruction of the small intestine causes upper abdominal pain, vomiting, constipation, dehydration with dry tongue and skin, and a drop in blood pressure. In later stages confusion and coma can result. The most common cause is mechanical blockage, which may result from surgery, inflammatory disease, or congenital factors; impacted feces or gallstones; or tumors. Paralytic ileus is the failure of normal peristalsis. Causes include interrupted blood flow due to embolism and thrombosis of arteries, toxic effects of peritonitis, and the effects of certain metabolic states on the nerves of the bowel wall.

Iliad   [il'-ee-uhd]

The *Iliad*, an epic poem of roughly 16,000 lines in dactylic hexameter, is thought to be the earliest surviving example of Greek literature (see GREEK LITERATURE, ANCIENT). Although opinions as to its composition vary, the *Iliad* is usually ascribed to the poet HOMER, who may have dictated the poem after composing it orally. Set in the 10th and last year of the TROJAN WAR, the *Iliad* deals specifically with the Greek hero ACHILLES, who leaves the battlefield in anger after the commander in chief, AGAMEMNON, confiscates his prize of war, the maid Briseis. Without Achilles' prowess, the fortunes of the Greeks decline. Achilles returns to combat only after his friend Patroclus is slain by HECTOR, the Trojan prince. The final battle between Achilles and Hector, in which the Greek triumphs, presages the destruction of Troy. Achilles' vengeance ultimately yields to compassion when, in the most moving episode of the poem, Achilles returns Hector's body to his aged father PRIAM. Portraying the deeds and death of men in battle, the poet of the *Iliad* conveys the idea of heroic energy burning brightly in the midst of the dark futility of human existence. For richness and vitality of language the *Iliad* remains unrivaled. It has inspired a range of distinguished translators, from George Chapman in the 17th century and Alexander Pope in the 18th to Richmond Lattimore (1951) and Robert Fitzgerald (1975) in the 20th. The work has also become, by its extensive treatment of the earlier Mycenaean age, an invaluable source for historical and archaeological researchers.

CHARLES ROWAN BEYE

Bibliography: Atchity, J. K., *Homer's Iliad* (1978); Beye, Charles R., *The Iliad, the Odyssey and the Epic Tradition* (1966); Vivante, Paolo, *The Homeric Imagination* (1970); Whitman, Cedric H., *Homer and the Heroic Tradition* (1958).

Illich, Ivan   [il'-ich, ee-vahn']

Ivan Illich, b. Sept. 4, 1926, is an Austrian-born American author, educator, and social critic. Ordained a priest in 1951, he became vice-rector of the Catholic University of Puerto Rico five years later, but he was forced to leave Puerto Rico after publicly disapproving of an intervention by the bishop of Ponce in the election of 1960. He then helped to found (1961) in Cuernavaca, Mexico, the Centro Intercultural de Documentación (CIDOC), an institute to teach the Spanish language and Latin American culture. Illich left the priesthood in 1969 when his criticism of traditional missionary activity became extremely controversial. His social targets have included ethnocentrism, paternalism, bureaucracy, and the status quo. With his book *Deschooling Society* (1971), he extended his radical critique to conventional schooling and compulsory education. He subsequently produced several other works of social criticism, including *Medical Nemesis* (1975), in which he attacked the established system of medical care as the greatest of all hazards to health.

Bibliography: Gray, F., *Divine Disobedience: Profiles in Catholic Radicalism* (1970); Pease, Edward, *Encountering Ivan Illich* (1974).

Illinois   [il-uh-noy']

Illinois is a leading agricultural, manufacturing, and urban state of the north central region of the United States. It is bordered by Wisconsin on the north, Lake Michigan on the northeast, Indiana on the east and southeast, and Kentucky on the south. The Ohio River follows its southern border, and the Mississippi in the west and southwest of the state lies along its borders with Iowa and Missouri. Inhabited thousands of years ago by Indians, Illinois was explored by the French Jesuit missionary Jacques MARQUETTE and frontiersman Louis JOLLIET, who reached the area on June 20, 1673. The French changed the Indian name for the area, *Illiniwek*, meaning "the men," to Illinois. Illinois became a state on Dec. 3, 1818. Although the 24th largest state in size, its population is ranked fifth largest of all states. The state's 1990 population may reach 11.7 million if current trends continue. SPRINGFIELD became the capital in 1837. Since 1850, Illinois has been a major state in all sectors of the economy. Now it faces

ILLINOIS

Capital: Springfield (85,700, 1979 est.)
Largest City: Chicago (2,940,000, 1979 est.)
Population: 11,321,800 (1979 est.). *Distribution*—83% urban, 17% rural; *density*, 77 persons per km² (201 per mi²); *increase* (1970–79) 1.8%; *population rank*, 5th
Area: 146,075 km² (56,400 mi²), including 1,689 km² (652 mi²) of inland water; *area rank*, 24th
Elevation: *Highest*—Charles Mound, 376 m/1,235 ft; *lowest*—85 m (279 ft), along the Mississippi River in Alexander County
Principal Products: *Manufacturing and Industry*—chemicals, machinery, food products, transportation equipment, metal products, printing and publishing, electrical products. *Agriculture*—corn, soybeans, wheat and hay, beef cattle and hogs, dairy products, eggs, greenhouse and nursery products. *Mining*—coal, fluorspar, petroleum, sand and gravel, stone
Government: *State Legislature*—59 senators, 117 representatives. *Representation in Congress*—2 U.S. senators, 24 U.S. representatives
Number of Counties: 102
Statehood: Dec. 3, 1818; the 21st state
State Nickname: Prairie State
State Bird: Cardinal
State Flower: Violet
State Tree: White oak
State Motto: State Sovereignty–National Union

the problems of increasing urbanization and interregional economic competition.

LAND AND RESOURCES

Illinois is composed of about 60% prairie, 30% hills with prairie, and 10% hills. The prairies cover central, northeastern, eastern and south-central Illinois; hills with prairie are found in northwestern, western, and southern Illinois; hills characterize the DRIFTLESS AREA of the extreme northwest and the Shawnee Hills in the south.

Geologically most of Illinois consists of ancient Precambrian granite overlain by sedimentary rocks of the Pennsylvanian and Mississippian periods (280–340 million years ago). These formations underlie 80% of the state in a bowl-shaped structure extending from the Shawnee Hills in the south to the Illinois River in the north. The northern fifth of the state contains bedrock from the Silurian, Ordovician, and Cambrian geologic periods (more than 390 million years ago). After the

deposition of bedrock, four glaciers covered 90% of Illinois from 1.2 million to 13,000 years ago. Their effects are seen in glacial deposits, wind-blown soil (löess) and morainal ridges.

Soils. All Illinois soils are cultivable and fall into three soil groups: mollisols—a deep, highly organic, black prairie soil found in the northern two-thirds of the state; alfisols—a shallower, less organic, brown, forest-based soil dominant in the southern third of the state; and alluvium—a mixed, deep, water-deposited soil found in nearly all river valleys.

Drainage. Each day an average 23 billion gallons of water enter the state's drainage system. More than 500 streams and rivers and 950 lakes and reservoirs circulate and store the water. The Illinois River is the largest river within the state, draining about 64,750 km² (25,000 mi²). Other large river basins are those of the Kankakee, Sangamon, and Fox. All of the major streams drain into either the Ohio or Mississippi rivers. The Chicago River once flowed eastward into Lake Michigan, but it is now artificially controlled by a series of locks to flow west toward the Des Plaines River. Underground aquifers, found in limestone and sandstone deposits, supply water to many northern cities. Surface water provides the rest of the state's water needs.

Climate. The climate of Illinois has distinct north-south fluctuations over the 1,263-km (785-mi) length of the state. Its extent, lack of significant elevation, continental location, and dominant westerly frontal pattern influence the climate. Precipitation ranges from 1,130 mm (45 in) in southern Illinois to 880 mm (35 in) in northern Illinois. Most precipitation falls during late spring and early summer. Temperatures also vary from north to south. Winter average temperatures are −4° C (25° F) in the north and 2° C (36° F) in the south. Summer averages are 24° C (75° F) in the north and 26° C (79° F) in the south. Atmospheric storms move across the state from west to east, with convective thunderstorms during spring and summer seasons. Cold- and warm-air frontal systems cause most atmospheric storms in the fall and winter.

Vegetation. The original vegetation cover was tall prairie grasses, averaging 1.5 to 2 m (5 to 6 ft) in height. Mixed deciduous forests (oak, hickory, maple, beech, sweet gum, elm, ash, cedar, pine, tamarack, fir) covered the southern third of the state and most river valleys. Virtually all this natural vegetation has been cleared for agriculture. Wildlife includes large numbers of white-tailed deer, rabbit, squirrel, red fox, quail, and pheasant, along with several waterfowl species that fly through seasonally.

Resources. Extracted minerals include petroleum, natural gas, clay, silica, fluorspar, lead, zinc, and limestone. Illinois is the

Shawnee National Forest, covering 1,037 km² (400 mi²), has unusual rock formations, such as Camel Rock (top), and varied wildlife. Located in southwestern Illinois, the park is bordered by the Ohio River on the east and the Mississippi River on the west.

ILLINOIS

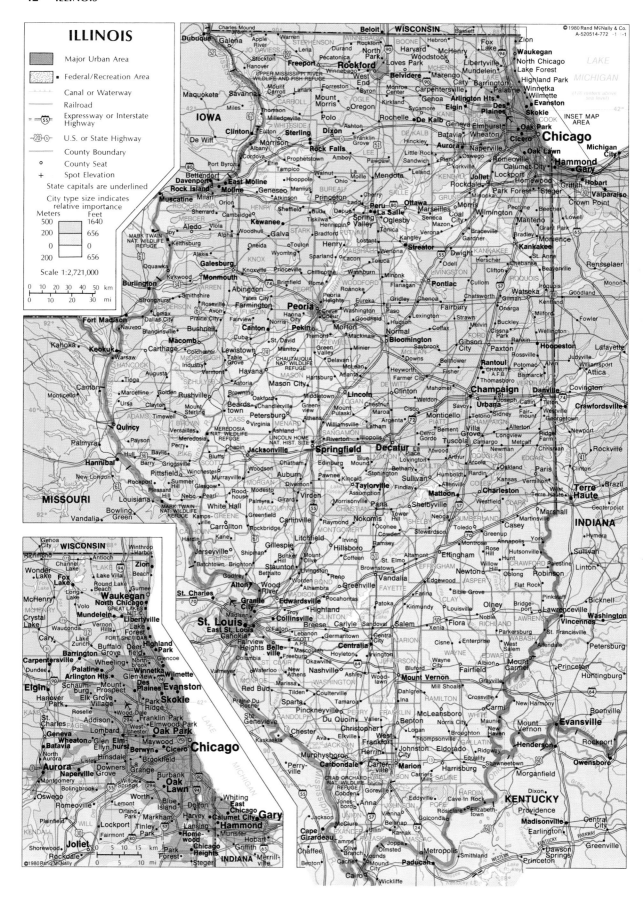

Major Urban Area

Federal/Recreation Area

Canal or Waterway

Railroad

Expressway or Interstate Highway

U.S. or State Highway

County Boundary

○ County Seat

+ Spot Elevation

State capitals are underlined

City type size indicates relative importance

Meters	Feet
500	1640
200	656
0	0
200	656

Scale 1:2,721,000

0 10 20 30 40 50 km
0 10 20 30 mi

© 1980 Rand McNally & Co.
A-520514-772 -1 -1

(Above) *Abraham Lincoln delivered (1858) his famous "House Divided" speech at the old state capitol in Springfield, Ill. Built in 1837, when Springfield became the state capital, the Greek Revival structure housed the Illinois legislature until 1887.*

(Left) *Chicago, Illinois's largest industrial city, was settled during the 1830s and rapidly became a leading port. Located at the juncture of the Mississippi and Saint Lawrence-Great Lakes systems, the city is a trade center for both agricultural commodities and industrial goods.*

fourth-largest producer of bituminous coal in the United States. The coalfield, underlying 70% of the state, has yielded 4.5 billion tons since 1882. Recent annual production was 60 million tons, with an estimated reserve of 65.7 billion tons. Since the mid-1970s, new mines have opened and more are planned. Surface water is used for agriculture, industry, city water supplies, and electrical and nuclear power plants.

PEOPLE

Although some areas in the state have fewer than one person per square mile, nine metropolitan areas account for 80% of the population: CHICAGO, ROCKFORD, PEORIA, Springfield, Rock Island-Moline, Metro-East Cluster (the Illinois portion of the SAINT LOUIS, Mo., metropolitan area), DECATUR, CHAMPAIGN-URBANA, and BLOOMINGTON-Normal. Since 1950 these cities have experienced most of the state's population increase. Growth rates are highest in the 170 suburban cities in the Chicago area, where some communities have expanded by approximately 10,000 people in ten years.

Illinois has close ties with its neighboring states. East Saint Louis, on the east bank of the Mississippi in the southwestern part of the state, is part of the Saint Louis, Mo., metropolitan area. Four bridges connect the two states at these cities. East Chicago, Hammond, and Gary, Ind., are part of the Chicago consolidated statistical area.

In 1900 less than 25% of the entire population of Illinois, but more than 75% of the population of Chicago, was foreign born. In 1970 approximately 25% of the state's population was foreign born. The largest groups were those of Polish, Irish, Italian, and German extraction. Approximately 90% of the foreign born live in the Chicago metropolitan area, which is also home for 90% of the state's blacks and the overwhelming majority of its Hispanic population.

Approximately one-third of the population is Roman Catholic. They, along with a large number of Jews, live primarily in the Chicago area. Baptist, Lutheran, Methodist, and Presbyterian congregations account for most of the state's Protestants. A significant number of Amish live here.

Education. State and local tax revenues began supporting Illinois schools in 1825. Attendance is required of all children between the ages of 7 and 16. In 1977, 2.2 million students were taught by 129,230 teachers, at a cost of $1,848 per student per year. Each school district is run locally under state provisions. State funds cover 54% of all costs, local funds 46%.

The University of Illinois, founded at Champaign-Urbana in 1867, has an enrollment of 35,000. For information on the higher education system, see ILLINOIS, STATE UNIVERSITIES OF.

Culture. The Chicago Symphony is the state's largest professional orchestra. Other cultural institutions include the Lyric Opera of Chicago, the Art Institute, the Museum of Science and Industry, the Field Museum of Natural History, the Museum of Contemporary Art, the Newberry Library, and the Du Sable Museum of African-American History, all in Chicago; the Lakeview Center for the Arts and Sciences in Peoria; and the State Museum in Springfield. The Mississippi River Arts Festival in Edwardsville and the Festival of Contemporary Arts in Urbana are annual attractions. Illinois was also a laboratory for architects Louis SULLIVAN and Frank Lloyd WRIGHT; some of their designs still stand. The Illinois Arts Council was established to assist the performing and visual arts.

Historical Sites. The heritage of Abraham LINCOLN in Illinois is preserved at Lincoln's Monument and Tomb and the Lincoln Home National Historic Site in Springfield. New Salem State Park and the Vandalia State House Memorial commemorate the beginnings of territorial settlement. CAHOKIA MOUNDS and Dickson Mounds are important relics of the state's Indian past. Other historic sites include the Stephen A. DOUGLAS Monument near Winchester, Kaskaskia Island in the Mississippi River, and the Ulysses S. Grant home in Galena.

Communications. Illinois serves as the communications center for much of the interior of the United States. In 1976, 310 AM and FM radio stations and 34 television stations served Illinois. The first Illinois newspaper, published in 1814, was the *Illinois Herald* of the territorial capital of Kaskaskia. Daily newspapers now number 920. Chicago has become an important center for book and magazine production as well.

ECONOMY

The industrial growth of the state was spurred by readily available natural resources, excellent transportation, and skilled laborers. The earliest large industries were directed toward the agricultural sector of the state's economy—meatpacking and farm-implements manufacturing.

Agriculture. In 1977, Illinois farmers produced crops valued at $6.1 billion from 691,880 km² (267,070 mi²) of farmland. The average per-acre farm output was valued at $48,000, a figure three times that of 1950. The main crops produced include corn, soybeans, wheat, barley, rye, orchard crops, and vegetables. Illinois produces 18% of the corn in the United States and 20% of the soybeans. Cattle and hog raising are also significant. The state's forested land, more than 40% of its area 200 years ago, has been cut back to little more than 10%. Annual saw timber output is now less than 1% of the U.S. total.

Fishing. The state's lakes, reservoirs, and rivers yield 20 million pounds of fish annually. Catches include carp, catfish, largemouth bass, and other species. One-half of the total amount is caught by sport-fishing enthusiasts.

Manufacturing. In 1900, Illinois was the third leading manufacturing state, but by 1976 its 17,668 industries ranked fourth in the nation in value added by manufacturing, an increase

A limestone quarry in southern Illinois produces substantial amounts of both loose stone and cut blocks, contributing to the state's high output of this important building material. Illinois's rich mineral wealth also includes large reserves of bituminous coal and oil.

Illinois's farmlands, which cover approximately 75% of the state's land area, produce crops ranging from corn and soybeans in central regions to fruit and cotton in the south. Rich soils and productive methods have given Illinois the nation's fourth highest agricultural income.

from $570 million in 1900 to $26 billion in 1976. The leading industries include chemicals, farm implements, electronics, scientific and transportation equipment, and printing. About 1.3 million persons are employed in manufacturing. The industrial center of Illinois is Chicago and its 220 suburbs, with smaller concentrations in Rockford, the Quad Cities (Rock Island, Moline, East Moline, and Davenport, Iowa), Peoria, and the Illinois portion of the Saint Louis, Mo., metropolitan area. The Midwest Stock Exchange and Chicago Mercantile Exchange are located in Chicago, as is the world's largest commodity market, the Chicago Board of Trade.

Tourism. An estimated contribution of $2 billion is made annually to the gross state product by tourists attracted to the city of Chicago and to such events as the Illinois State Fair held in Springfield. Outdoor recreational facilities are plentiful, and many are accessible throughout the year. Shawnee National Forest, covering over 5,900 km² (2,275 mi²), is composed of two separate areas in southern Illinois. Major sports stadiums located in Chicago include Soldier Field, Chicago Stadium, Wrigley Field, and Comiskey Park.

Transportation and Trade. Illinois is a major U.S. transportation hub, with ten interstate highways, the second largest railroad network, the busiest airport in the world, and three major inland waterways—the Ohio, Illinois, and Mississippi rivers. The Illinois Waterway provides an access route to the Mississippi River for Great Lakes ships via the Chicago River, Chicago Sanitary and Ship Canal, and Des Plaines and Illinois rivers. Chicago's O'Hare International Airport serves over 100,000 passengers daily. The Chicago Port Authority handled 46 million tons of commerce in 1974, using both the Navy Pier Port and Lake Calumet Port. Leading exports include food products, chemicals, paper, heavy machinery, electrical equipment, transportation equipment, scientific instruments, coal, and petroleum. Imports are dominated by iron ore and paper.

Energy. The industries of the state consume almost one-half of all electrical energy produced in Illinois. The state's 35 steam-generating plants and 7 nuclear plants have a total capacity of 28,500 megawatts—fifth in the United States.

The Illinois Environmental Protection Agency supervises landfills; controls air, soil, stream, and lake pollution; monitors noise levels; checks wastewater treatment plants; and wages court battles against polluters. One innovative project for the disposal of waste has been in operation since 1974. Sludge from the Chicago area is carried by barge on the Illi-

nois Waterway to Fulton County, where it is pumped underground to a depth of 11 miles. After sufficient time has passed for natural chemical reactions to take place, the material is pumped from the ground, pulverized, dried, and sold for fertilizer.

GOVERNMENT AND POLITICS

Illinois was one of the five states created from the NORTHWEST TERRITORY. Six different forms of government operated in Illinois before its first constitution took effect in 1818. That first document was followed by constitutions in 1848, 1870, and 1970. Its 1970 constitution included protection from discrimination for women, protection for a healthy environment, and the right of suffrage for more citizens by relaxing residency requirements. The senate and house of representatives, constituting the state's general assembly, are selected from 59 districts, each represented by one senator and three at-large representatives. The executive branch includes a team-elected governor and lieutenant governor, assisted by an attorney general, secretary of state, comptroller, and treasurer. The supreme court consists of seven judges—three from the first judicial district and one each from the four remaining districts. The appellate court judges serve each of the state judicial districts, hearing appeals from state circuit courts whose judges are elected from each of the 102 counties.

Local government consists of township, county, and city governments, each electing several officers. Cities with a population of more than 25,000 and counties with an elected chief executive have home-rule power, including the power to tax.

Illinois has been referred to as a "swing state" in national politics. On the statewide level it remained solidly Republican from the Civil War period until nearly the turn of the 20th century. Since that time, the governorship has been held by. an almost equal number of Democrats and Republicans.

HISTORY

Thousands of years before the French reached Illinois, Paleo-Indians, a nomadic people, and their descendants, archaic Indians, had explored Illinois. The culture of these hunters, dated before 5000 BC, can be studied at the Modock Rock Shelter in Randolph County. Woodland Indians were their descendants. By AD 900, Middle Mississippi Indians, who succeeded the Woodland Indians, built large earthen mounds and developed complex urban areas. These cities disappeared possibly because of overpopulation, disease, and exhaustion of resources. The descendants of the Mississippians were the

Illiniwek tribes of the 17th, 18th, and 19th centuries. After years of losing land and wars to other Indian groups and European colonists, the Illiniweks were moved to a Kansas reservation.

The French controlled areas along the Mississippi River valley in the American Bottoms between Cahokia and Kaskaskia. Their occupation, from about 1675 to 1763, left few lasting marks, as did the ineffective British rule. European control was ended by the U.S. militia of Gen. George Rogers CLARK in 1778. The area then was made a part of Virginia.

The Northwest Ordinance of 1787 charted this region and organized counties, and in 1809 the Territory of Illinois was created. During the early years of settlement by fur trappers, southern Illinois was the focus of migration to the area, especially along the Mississippi River valley and the Wabash and Ohio rivers. Granting of statehood in 1818 was controversial. The population numbered less than the required 60,000. Moreover, in order to include the Chicago port area, territorial representatives induced the U.S. Congress to draw the Illinois border 51 miles to the north of the original boundary as delimited by the Northwest Ordinance. Vandalia, along the Kaskaskia River, was chosen capital of the new state by its legislature, a position it held for 20 years. After strong pressure from Abraham Lincoln, the capital was moved to Springfield by an 1837 legislative vote.

Early statehood problems engulfed Illinois. In the 1830s the state was near bankruptcy because of government financing of canals and railroad construction. The BLACK HAWK WAR in 1832 was fought by the Indians and newly arrived settlers over possession of Illinois land. Disease was rampant and death common. Adherents to Mormonism, who had migrated from Missouri in 1839, were charged with many illegalities and finally driven from the state after their leader, Joseph SMITH, had been murdered in 1844.

The Civil War caused mixed loyalties among Illinoisans, many of whom were first- or second-generation Southerners. However, many took pride in the fact that the Union was led by a native son, Lincoln, and the state provided 250,000 soldiers to the Union army. It also was the weapons manufacturer, supplier of iron products, and major grain and meat supplier for the North.

By 1880, Illinois had become the fourth largest state in population. It was a leader in grain production and manufacturing. The huge migration of Europeans to Illinois provided labor to mine coal, run steel mills, and enhance the economy and culture of the state. By 1920, Illinois was counted among the foremost states in nearly every significant growth variable—coal mining, industry, farming, urbanization, transportation, and wholesaling. Its leadership was achieved despite having suffered through the economic slumps of the 1880s, 1890s, and early 1900s; through the labor disputes in coal mining and railroading; through the Chicago fire of 1871; and through the problems caused by organized crime. World War I and World War II boosted the economy of Illinois, which soon had five ordnance depots and numerous military training camps.

The post-World War II era was a time of industrial modification to the postwar production of consumer goods. Even though meatpacking companies began to move away from Chicago and East Saint Louis, in part because of obsolete physical plants, Illinois farms were being mechanized and upgraded for increased output. The use of hybrid seed, chemical fertilizer, herbicides, and insecticides resulted in larger crop yields. Post-World War II Illinois experienced rapid population growth. The rising number of school-age children brought about public school reform, rural school consolidations, and huge suburban educational plants. Migration streams of blacks from the South, Hispanics from Mexico and Puerto Rico, and whites from Appalachia reshaped neighborhoods in Chicago, its suburbs, and other large Illinois cities.

The future of Illinois appears to be one of continued reduction in the number of small farm owners and consolidation into huge corporate farm operations. The out-migration of whites and in-migration of blacks and Hispanics to Chicago will result in the state's largest city being dominated in number, vote, and control by poorer minorities while surrounded by more affluent white-dominated suburbs. The extensive railroad system is being trimmed because of financial losses, necessitating a growing dependence on interstate trucking systems. Illinois has grown phenomenally since the days of Lincoln, and its continued growth will insure its position as the "heartland" state of the nation.   A. DOYNE HORSLEY

Bibliography: Ahlswede, L. E., *Township Government Today* (1968); Allen, John, *Legends and Lore of Southern Illinois* (1963); Alvord, C. W., and Carter, C. E., *The Illinois Country, 1673-1818* (1965); Angle, Paul, and McCree, Mary, eds., *The Prairie State: Impressions of Illinois* (1968); Burton, W. L., *The Trembling Land: Illinois in the Age of Exploration* (1966); Carpenter, Allan, *Illinois: Land of Lincoln* (1968); Clayton, John, ed., *Illinois Fact Book and Historical Almanac, 1673-1968* (1970); Federal Writers' Project, *Illinois* (1939; repr. 1971); Havighurst, Walter, *The Heartland* (1962); Jensen, Richard J., *Illinois: A History* (1978); Kenney, David, *Basic Illinois Government*, rev. ed. (1974); Pease, Theodore C., *The Story of Illinois*, 3d ed. (1965); Walton, Clyde C., ed., *An Illinois Reader* (1970); Wheeler, Adade, with Wortman, Marlene S., *The Roads They Made: Women in Illinois History* (1977).

Illinois   (Indian tribe)

The Illinois were a large and powerful confederation of Algonquian-speaking Indian groups who dominated most of present-day Illinois, southeastern Wisconsin, and adjacent parts of Iowa and Missouri until the 1680s. The societies making up this confederacy included the Cahokia, the Kaskaskia, the Michigamea, the Moingwena, the Peoria, and the Tamaroa. Each was organized as a centralized chiefdom, and, to supplement their horticultural economy, they exploited the extensive herds of buffalo and elk once found on the Illinois prairie lands. Their name for themselves was *Ilini*, meaning simply "the people."

Illinois villages numbered about 60, and their total population probably exceeded 10,000 before 1660. They were responsible for the decimation of the WINNEBAGO tribe sometime after 1634, but in the decades afterward the Illinois were constantly under attack from the Five Nations IROQUOIS, the Santee SIOUX, the FOX, the POTAWATOMI, and other tribes. Diseases and epidemics of European origin contributed to the eventual depopulation of the Illinois. In addition, a Kaskaskia assassinated (1769) the great Ottawa leader PONTIAC, precipitating a bloody war which only a few Illinois survived. By 1885 they numbered only 150. Their descendants now live in Oklahoma.   JAMES CLIFTON

Bibliography: Kinietz, W. Vernon, *The Indians of the Western Great Lakes, 1615-1760* (1965).

Illinois, state universities of

The state universities of Illinois are coeducational and all grant both undergraduate and graduate degrees. The **University of Illinois** (1857) is a land-grant institution. Its main campus at Urbana-Champaign (enrollment: 33,950; library: 5,500,000 volumes) has colleges of law, engineering, architecture, and veterinary medicine. Chicago Circle (1965; enrollment: 20,665; library 630,000 volumes), a commuter campus, houses the medical center (1881), with colleges of nursing, pharmacy, medicine, and dentistry.

Southern Illinois University (1869) has its main branch at Carbondale (1869; enrollment: 22,540; library: 1,700,000 volumes), where there is a law school, and a branch at Edwardsville (1949; enrollment: 11,170; library: 650,000 volumes). **Illinois State University** (1857; enrollment: 19,040; library: 985,000 volumes) is at Normal. Other universities are: **Chicago State** (1869; enrollment: 7,025; library: 250,000 volumes) at Chicago, with a school of nursing; **Eastern Illinois** (1895; enrollment: 9,385; library: 425,000 volumes) at Charleston; **Governors State** (1971; enrollment: 3,815; library: 162,000 volumes) at Park Forest South; **Northeastern Illinois** (1961; enrollment: 10,150; library: 285,000 volumes) at Chicago, a commuter school; **Northern Illinois** (1899; enrollment: 21,270; library: 831,000 volumes) at DeKalb, with a campus at Oregon, Ill.; and **Western Illinois** (1899; enrollment: 13,880; library: 500,000 volumes) at Macomb.

Illinois River

The Illinois River, which is formed 72 km (45 mi) southwest of Chicago by the confluence of the Kankakee and Des Plaines rivers, flows west and then south for 440 km (273 mi) to join the Mississippi River at Grafton, Ill. The Illinois is an important part of the Illinois Waterway, a water route from the Great Lakes to the Mississippi River.

illite: see CLAY MINERALS.

illiteracy: see LITERACY AND ILLITERACY.

illuminated manuscripts

Illumination is the art of decorating handwritten books with painted pictures, ornamented letters, or geometric designs in colors and in gold and silver. The primary purpose of illumination is not to clarify a text but to beautify it and call attention to the skill that has been lavished on its creation. The heyday of manuscript illumination in the Western world was the period between about 400 and about 1450, after which the invention of the printing press and movable type led to the rapid demise of manuscript production. This article is concerned with the history of European manuscript illumination; for information on illumination in other cultures, see INDIAN ART AND ARCHITECTURE; ISLAMIC ART AND ARCHITECTURE; MOGUL ART AND ARCHITECTURE; and PERSIAN ART AND ARCHITECTURE.
Ancient and Classical Periods. Egyptian papyrus rolls are the

earliest illustrated works to have survived. The oldest example, the Ramesseum Papyrus (c.1980 BC; British Museum, London) contains figures drawn in black ink, as do copies of the BOOK OF THE DEAD that have been found in tombs. Only slight traces remain of the illustrated rolls produced between the decline of Egyptian civilization (c.1000 BC) and the 5th century AD, but it appears that by the 2d century AD the papyrus roll began to give way to the vellum codex, or leaved book. The invention of the book revolutionized manuscript illumination by permitting decorative use of layers of richly colored pigment that would have been destroyed by the continual rolling and unrolling of papyrus. Illuminators of the late classical period (4th and 5th centuries AD) produced codices of the works of the Roman poet Vergil that contain naturalistic, brightly colored figures and landscapes. In the same period early Christian illuminators adopted the prevailing styles of Greco-Roman art to ornament religious texts.
Early Western Illumination. Classical artistic forms survived in BYZANTINE ART AND ARCHITECTURE, which also assimilated some aspects of ancient Near Eastern and Oriental traditions. Forming an artistic bridge between East and West, and between classical and Christian Europe, Byzantine art exerted a profound influence on Western illuminators of the 5th through the 10th century. Also important to the development of Western illumination was CELTIC ART, in which geometric ornamental elements coexisted with the classical and Eastern motifs of Byzantium.

In the 7th and 8th centuries the monasteries of Ireland and Northern England produced fine illuminated manuscripts in

(Left) The elaborate cruciform page from the Lindisfarne Gospels, one of the finest examples of Anglo-Celtic manuscript illumination, unites Christian symbols with decorative motifs derived from Anglo-Saxon and Celtic metalwork. The blending of curvilinear and zoomorphic designs and the rich coloring testify to the advanced artistry that developed in Britain nearly 100 years before the Carolingian renaissance. (c.697–98; British Museum, London.)

(Below) The figure of Saint Matthew from the Book of Durrow reflects the highly stylized, ornamental treatment of human figures found in Anglo-Celtic art. In this early work decorative elements are confined to carefully defined regions, and ornamental motifs remain distinct. (c.680; Trinity College, Dublin.)

Christ Enthroned, one of six full-page illuminations from Charlemagne's Godescalc Gospels (781–83), reflects the artist's familiarity with Lombard and Byzantine figure traditions in its full-face, seated portrait of Christ. An early Carolingian work, the painting evidences the strong linear emphasis and ornamental design of Anglo-Celtic art. Later illuminations of the period drew more on classical forms. (Bibliothèque Nationale, Paris.)

styles that were derived mainly from Celtic metalwork and sculpture, although Mediterranean and Near Eastern motifs were also used. Anglo-Celtic illumination was purely decorative; unlike Byzantine artists, the northern monks were unconcerned with historical illustration of the text. This emphasis on purely decorative illumination led to the execution of complicated systems of interlacing ribbons, tangled knots, and spiral patterns. Also characteristic of the Anglo-Celtic tradition are elongated or twisted zoomorphic forms and stiff, hieratic human figures. Among the most important examples of early 7th-century Anglo-Celtic production are the BOOK OF KELLS, the Lindisfarne Gospels (British Museum, London) and the Book of Durrow (Trinity College, Dublin).

Anglo-Celtic manuscripts brought across the English Channel by monks played a major role in the development of Carolingian illumination (see CAROLINGIAN ART AND ARCHITECTURE) in the 8th and 9th centuries. Under Charlemagne, illumination prospered as a means of instruction. The sacramentaries, bibles, and psalters produced in Carolingian scriptoria, monastery rooms in which manuscripts were copied, combined narrative scenes from the Old Testament with richly decorated initials and sometimes included full-page illuminations with representations of the emperor. Most Carolingian illuminators drew heavily on Anglo-Celtic manuscripts and late classical art. The sketchy, impressionistic style of Hellenistic times appears clearly in the work of the palatine school of Aachen, which includes such genuinely Byzantine works as the Utrecht Psalter (University Library, Utrecht, Holland). Perhaps the most precious Carolingian manuscript is the 8th-century Godescalc Gospels (Bibliothèque Nationale, Paris); produced for the imperial court, it was written in gold and silver on purple vellum and reflects Italian influence. Other important Carolingian schools existed at Tours, Corbie, and Metz, and by the second half of the 9th century an Italian variant of the Carolingian style appeared in some scriptoria, including that at Bobbio. In Catalonia a new school produced codices, such as the Roda Bible (7th century; Bibliothèque Nationale), that combined Carolingian with Visigothic and Arabic elements.

As the Ottonian world inherited Carolingian culture, centers of illumination production shifted eastward and a revival of early Christian designs accompanied a stronger emphasis on representation of the human figure. Reichenau, the most important Ottonian school, flourished in the late 10th and the early 11th century. Using Carolingian models, Reichenau illuminators worked in a bold, firm style supplemented by a Byzantine-inspired feeling for monumental effects to produce manuscripts characterized by powerful expressiveness. Other

noted Ottonian schools were those of Regensburg, Salzburg, Mainz, and Fulda.

Simultaneously, a new school of illumination evolved at Winchester, England. In the Winchester school the Carolingian narrative style was assimilated to the continuing Anglo-Celtic tradition. The characteristics of the Winchester style include outlined, tinted figures, fluttering drapery, a generous use of gold, and wide acanthus-leaf borders—all of which are exemplified by the Benedictional of Saint Æthelwold (c.975–80; British Museum).

Romanesque Period. During the Romanesque period (c.900–c.1200) distinctive styles of illumination evolved within the overall framework of medieval Christian Europe. In art as in politics the most important unifying agent of this age was the increasing influence of the Roman Catholic church, which reached the height of its power and influence in the 12th century. As in the Carolingian era, art was preeminently didactic; religious truth took precedence over aesthetic value. Stylistically, illustrations and text were integrated more fully, and historiated initials, the favorite form of decorating the text, were often ornamented with interlacing ribbons and human and animal figures. Artists were most concerned with monumental effects, with organizing compositions into geometrical patterns, and with giving figures more massive proportions and clearly defined outlines.

Romanesque illumination also flourished in England. In addition to Winchester, important centers of illumination thrived at Canterbury, Durham, Westminster, Saint Alban's, Bury Saint Edmund's, and Hereford. Books became more luxuriously adorned than ever before as new decorative motifs—fighting men, winged dragons and other fanciful creatures—were introduced. Local Anglo-Celtic traditions survived in the use of interlacing patterns, but such outstanding works as the Winchester Bible (12th century; Winchester Cathedral library)

The angular figure of Saint John from the Grimbald Gospels (c.1025) manifests the rich blue and green coloring, the sumptuous border design, and the delicate figure style characteristic of the finest Winchester style of illumination. (British Museum, London.)

The Limbourg brothers' Zodiac man, an iconographic type associating parts of the body with astrological signs, concludes the famous calendar illuminations of their masterpiece, the Très Riches Heures du duc de Berry. *(1415–16; Musée Condé, Chantilly, France.)*

also contain elegant representations of the human figure. English miniatures are distinguished by fine composition, clinging draperies, and rich coloring—especially deep blue or green.

In France the southern schools—particularly those of Burgundy, where the religious reform movements began—produced notable manuscripts. Illuminations by the Cistercian monks are known for their remarkable initial letters, which are colored in flat reds and greens and ornamented with animal or human figures. The abbey of Cluny, at the peak of its influence in the 11th century, created gorgeous manuscripts containing gold and silver initials on purple backgrounds and showing strong Byzantine and Ottonian influence; a particularly fine example is the Cluny Lectionary. Significant northern and Flemish schools—such as Liège, Stavelot, Saint Omer, and Arras—shared a close affinity with English art, and Paris, Reims, Strasbourg, and Metz also produced fine work.

Italian illumination, which incorporated Carolingian, Ottonian, and Anglo-Celtic motifs in a predominantly Byzantine style, forged an important stylistic link between East and West. From the beginning of the 11th through the 13th century, southern Italy produced manuscripts written in the native Beneventan script, such as the Exultet Rolls of the monastery of Monte Cassino (containing joyous Easter hymns) that owed the natural organic quality of their figures to the presence of Byzantine artists. Byzantine trends also appeared in the Sicilian manuscripts illuminated during the Norman rule (c.900–c.1150), while from the late 11th through the early 13th century Rome and the Papal States turned out "Atlantic" bibles, so called for their great size and weight.

In Spain, Muslim and Christian culture merged in a style called Mozarabic, in which Coptic, Syriac, and Germanic influences, rather than Byzantine, predominated.

Gothic Period. In the 13th and 14th centuries codices became small, handy volumes, and the church's virtual monopoly on book production gave way before the rise of secular scriptoria. Liturgical texts as well as psalters, breviaries, and the new BOOK OF HOURS were produced for private devotion. New types of books, such as chronicles, romances, and medical treatises, demanded new types of representation. Initials assumed a greater importance, and illustrations became more detailed and realistic, with backgrounds drawn in careful perspective. As painters mastered a softer and more delicate style, margins acquired leafy borders that later sported flowers, fruit, and grotesques or genre scenes (see GENRE PAINTING).

Gothic illumination was dominated by French artists. In Paris a new school of painters centered at the university produced such glittering works as the Saint Louis Psalter, full of architectural detail and profusely gilded. The names of some French Gothic illuminators are known—Jean PUCELLE, for example, and later, André BEAUNEVEU and Jacquemart de HESDIN. French illumination flourished particularly in the first half of the 15th century, for example, in works by the LIMBOURG BROTHERS and Jean FOUQUET. The Limbourg brothers painted the splendid *Très Riches Heures*, a masterpiece of observation and illusionism. With Fouquet, whose works reveal an understanding of Italian forms along with Flemish influence, the Renaissance arrived in French illumination. Other important French illuminators were Jean Bourdichon (1457–1521), Simon Marmion (fl. c.1455), and the Master of Mary of Burgundy (fl. c.1470–1519).

English Gothic illuminators are famous for their delicacy of drawing, refinement of taste, use of margins full of whimsical creatures, and the softer and more rounded contours of their human figures. In this period the abbey of Saint Alban's was the primary English center of illumination. Matthew Paris, a monk at Saint Alban's and from 1217 head of the scriptorium there, left important historical writings, some of which he illustrated. Also worthy of note was the East Anglian school, centered at Norwich, that flourished in the first half of the 14th century. East Anglian manuscripts—notably the Gorleston Psalter (early 14th century; British Museum)—are replete with luxurious foliate borders, rich color schemes, profuse gilding, and ornate initials.

The finest works by Italian Gothic illuminators were illustrations similar to small panel paintings with which secular books such as legal commentaries were richly adorned. In the late 14th century the naturalistic border (with shells, foliage, and other organic forms) was introduced in northern Italy, where the Gothic style lasted longer than anywhere else in that country. Manuscript illumination continued throughout the Italian Renaissance, with schools at Florence, Siena, Ferrara, and Milan. Finally, in Italy as in the rest of Europe, printing made illumination obsolete, and wood-block prints quickly replaced miniatures.   CLAUDIA MARCHITIELLO

Bibliography: Avril, François, ed., *Manuscript Illumination at the Court of France: The Fourteenth Century* (1978); Bland, David, *A History of Book Illustration*, 2d ed. (1969); Diringer, David, *The Illuminated Book*, rev. ed. (1967); Kuehnel, Ernst, *The Minor Arts of Islam* (trans. 1970); Mitchell, Sabrina, *Medieval Manuscript Painting* (1965); Robb, D. M., *The Art of the Illuminated Manuscript* (1970); Weitzmann, K., *Studies in Classical and Byzantine Manuscript Illumination*, ed. by H. Kessler (1971); Williams, J., *Early Spanish Manuscript Illumination* (1977).

illusions

Illusions are systematic, characteristic errors in perception. They are discrepancies between the appearance of some measurable aspect of the world (such as the size, distance, location, or shape of a visible object) and the corresponding physical measures—whether of the object itself or of the light reaching the eye from the object. Illusions are different from hallucinations, in which the object is lacking or only remotely related to what is perceived. Illusions are pervasive, of practical importance in environmental design and the visual arts, and of central theoretical importance to the study of normal PERCEPTION.

Examples of what are known as the "geometrical illusions" are shown in figures 1 through 8. The lines labeled *i* and *ii* are equal in size in figures 1 through 4; parallel and straight in figures 5 through 7; and perfectly aligned in figure 8, despite

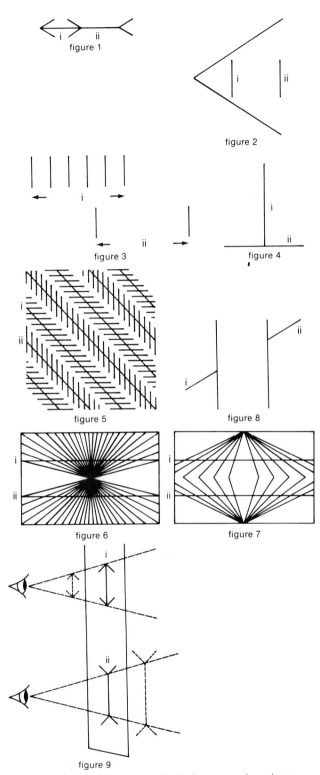

figure 1

figure 2

figure 3

figure 4

figure 5

figure 6

figure 7

figure 8

figure 9

Illusions also abound in COLOR PERCEPTION, notably in the phenomenon of simultaneous contrast, in which the appearance of a particular patch is greatly altered by changes in its surroundings. The color contrast phenomena have practical importance in painting, printing, and textile enterprises, which frequently juxtapose different colors.

Illusions are also possible in the perception of movement, notably in the case of apparent movement, known as the phi phenomenon. In the phi phenomenon, successive stationary views of an object, even though they are located in a different place in each view, are perceived as smooth, continuous motion. This phenomenon is the basis of the motion picture and television industries.

The importance of illusions to psychology depends on which theory of illusions—and of perception—is considered. No one theory explains all illusions. Indeed, each of the stronger illusions probably results from several converging factors. To the degree that the illusions can be explained in terms of purely "local" effects, they have little general importance. In one recurrent theory, for example, the geometrical illusions are explained in terms of a filling-in of acute angles (which would shorten the free line length of *i* in figure 1). Illusions have more often been explained in terms of confusion and contrast. The confusion explanation of figure 1, for example, holds that the viewer compares the areas included between the diagonals and not the line lengths.

The most general theory is that illusions result from the same processes that normally produce correct perceptions and therefore reveal how those processes work. For example, because the eye most frequently encounters diagonals like those of figure 1 as a result of linear perspective, *i* would normally be nearer than *ii* (see figure 9). To subtend equal angles at the eye as the lines do, *i* must be smaller than *ii*. In its strongest form, this theory holds that the illusions result from unconscious, inference-like processes based on the erroneous application of learned depth cues.

Three lines of research have been followed to investigate this theory. The first line of research assumes that if illusions result from perceptual learning, the strength of an illusion might increase with age and the attendant opportunity for such learning. Tests have shown that some illusions first decrease and then increase with age; others only increase; and some only decrease.

According to the second theory, if some environments provide the depth cues necessary for illusions more than do others—for example, urban environments have more parallel straight lines and rectangular corners to provide linear perspective than do savannahs and round huts—cultural differences in susceptibility to illusions might be found. Research has shown that some native cultures are less subject to illusions than others.

The third line of research maintains that if illusions are mistaken applications of perceptual experience, specific experience with a particular illusion might reduce such mistakes. Such illusion decrements do occur. For instance, repeated views of figure 1 lessen the effect on the viewer. The decrease, however, is not easy to interpret because it occurs even when the viewer receives no information that *i* and *ii* are equal, and the illusion returns in force when the left and right halves are interchanged.   JULIAN HOCHBERG

Bibliography: Coren, S. C., and Girgus, J. S., *Seeing is Deceiving: The Psychology of Visual Illusions* (1978); Gregory, R. L., *The Eye and Brain* (1966); Gregory, R. L., and Gombrich, E. H., eds., *Illusion in Nature and Art* (1974); Hochberg, Julian, *Perception*, 2d ed. (1978); Kaufman, Lloyd, *Sight and Mind* (1974); Luckiesh, Matthew, *Visual Illusions* (1922; repr. 1965).

illusionism

Illusionism comprises those painterly techniques whereby forms painted on flat planes are made to appear three-dimensional and to exist in deep space. The history of illusionism dates back to the 4th century BC in Greece; the grapes in ZEUXIS's paintings were said to seem so real that birds would peck at them. Carried to this extreme, illusionism is also known as trompe l'oeil (fool the eye). The Renaissance

appearances to the contrary. Such phenomena have long been known to architects, who know the importance of identifying the situations that produce such illusions so they can take them into account in their designs. Figure 8, for instance, is sometimes called the plumber's illusion, for obvious reasons. Knowing that an illusion is in fact an illusion, however, does not dispel it. Even after measuring lines *i* and *ii* in figure 1, the viewer will still perceive *i* as smaller.

development of one-point perspective greatly advanced illusionist technique. During the baroque period, illusionism reached its apex in the enormous ceiling paintings of various Roman churches and palaces. The vogue spread north in the succeeding rococo period and achieved fullest flower in Austria and Bavaria. The 19th-century American still-life painter William HARNETT was a master of illusionism, an abstract version of which is seen in contemporary OP ART. The term *illusionism* also refers to the creation of spatial illusions in architecture and stage design.

Bibliography: Gregory, R. L., and Gombrich, E. H., *Illusion in Nature and Art* (1974); Mastai, Marie-Louise, *Illusion in Art: A History of Pictorial Illusionism* (1975).

See also: BAROQUE ART AND ARCHITECTURE; GREEK ART; ROCOCO STYLE.

Illustrated London News, The

An English magazine, *The Illustrated London News* was founded as a monthly publication in 1842 and became a weekly in 1971. It is intended for general readers and contains articles on politics, science, literature, the arts, archaeology, and travel. The extra Christmas issue, with its special full-color seasonal features, has become a popular souvenir. The magazine has a circulation of approximately 85,000.

ROLAND E. WOLSELEY

illustration: see BOOK ILLUSTRATION.

Illyria [ih-lir'-ee-uh]

The ancient name Illyria referred to the western coastal region of the Balkan Peninsula, territory that is now included in Albania and Yugoslavia. It is widely accepted that the present-day Albanians are probably the descendants of the ancient Illyrians, an Indo-European people who originally settled there about the 10th century BC.

During the 6th century BC the Greeks established a number of colonies on the seaboard of southern Illyria. In the 3d century BC, Illyria asserted itself as an independent political power and expanded its borders southward and eastward. In 168–167 BC, however, Illyria's coastal areas were conquered by the Romans, who established the colony of Illyricum there. In succeeding decades Rome extended its control over the entire region. Some of Rome's most notable emperors, such as Aurelian, Diocletian, and Constantine I, were originally from Illyria.

After an Illyrian revolt in AD 6-9, Illyria was divided into two Roman imperial provinces, PANNONIA and DALMATIA. As a result of the administrative reorganization during the 4th century, Illyria fell to the East Roman, or Byzantine, Empire. The area was invaded by Goths, Huns, and Slavs in the following centuries, and use of the name Illyria was dropped. It was revived by Napoleon I when he included the so-called Illyrian Provinces in his empire in 1809. From 1816 to 1849 the kingdom of Illyria was an administrative subdivision of the Austrian Empire.

S. VICTOR PAPACOSMA

Bibliography: Stipčević, Aleksandar, *The Illyrians: History and Culture*, trans. by Stojana Culić Burton (1977).

See also: BALKANS.

Ilmen, Lake [il'-muhn]

Lake Ilmen, a shallow lake in the USSR, lies about 160 km (100 mi) south of Leningrad. Important for fishing and for its boat-building industry, it is ice-covered in winter and easily navigable only in late spring and summer, when melting snows and rains swell it to about 2,072 km² (800 mi²). It drains into the Volkhov River.

ilmenite [il'-muhn-yt]

The iron and titanium oxide mineral ilmenite (FeTiO$_3$) is present in small amounts in many igneous rocks and placer sands and is the principal TITANIUM ore. It forms iron black, thick tabular or acute rhombohedral crystals (hexagonal system), as well as thin plates, compact masses, and embedded grains. Hardness is 5½, luster metallic to dull, and specific gravity 4.72.

Iloilo [ee-loh-ee'-loh]

Iloilo is a city on Panay Island in the Philippines. Situated at the mouth of the Jaro River, Iloilo's harbor is protected by Guimaras Island. The population is 227,374 (1975). The economy is based on agricultural trade, and the main exports are rice, copra, hemp, and textiles. The city is the seat of the University of San Agustin (1904) and the Central Philippine University (1905).

Iloilo, the second oldest Spanish settlement in the Philippines, was established in 1571. It grew rapidly in the mid-19th century as a major sugar export center. As harbors on the nearby island of Negros were improved, the commercial status of the city declined.

image, optical

LENSES and MIRRORS are crafted to form an image of an object by modifying the path of light rays. Images can be real or virtual, enlarged or reduced in size, and erect or inverted.

A real image is one formed by rays of light actually passing through the image point, converging to a focus there. Such an image can be projected on a screen placed at the image location. A virtual image is formed from diverging rays of light that seem to come from a point within or behind the mirror or lens. Since the rays of light are diverging, they cannot be focused at any point; thus a virtual image cannot be projected on a screen. The image formed by an ordinary

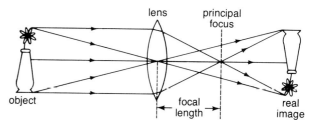

If an object is placed two focal lengths in front of a convex lens, a real and upside-down image of the same size as the object will be formed two focal lengths behind the lens.

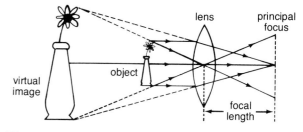

When an object is located less than one focal length from a convex lens, the image will be virtual—on the same side as the object—and will appear erect and larger than the object.

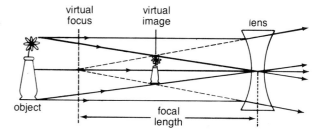

The light rays from an article placed at any distance in front of a concave lens will diverge from the opposite side of the lens to form a virtual image that is right side up and smaller in size.

plane mirror is virtual; that formed by a concave mirror (as in a reflecting telescope) is real.

A magnifying glass (convex lens) can form either a real or a virtual image, depending on the location of the object. If the object lies between the FOCAL POINT and the lens, the image will be virtual, erect, and magnified; if it is beyond the focal point, the image will be real, inverted, and either magnified or reduced, according to the following relation:

$$\frac{\text{size of image}}{\text{size of object}} = \frac{\text{image distance from lens}}{\text{object distance from lens}}$$

The ratio of the image size to the object size is the magnification of the lens.
STEPHEN FLEISHMAN

Bibliography: Born, Max, and Wolf, Emil, *Principles of Optics* (1975); Weber, Robert L., et al., *College Physics* (1974).

image and imagery

Derived from the Latin *imago* ("picture," "semblance," or "likeness"), an image is a representation of what is perceived—the registration on the mind of an object or scene. In literary criticism the term is used both for the representations produced in the mind by verbal descriptions and for the descriptions or characterizations themselves, since the mental pictures, or images, may be thought of either as separate from words or as integral features of the verbal characterizations.

In principle, imagery refers to all language that gives a vivid or concrete picture; in practice, however, studies of imagery usually concentrate on pictorial phrases used to express some abstract notion. The concept of imagery thus resembles that of figurative language (see FIGURES OF SPEECH), particularly METAPHOR and SIMILE. An important distinction, however, is that the image is not the figurative expression but what it literally denotes. For instance, in Andrew Marvell's lines, "But at my back I always hear / Time's wingèd chariot hurrying near," the phrase "wingèd chariot" is a metaphor that conveys the image of a swift vehicle. The image is the mental picture evoked by these words, and it makes vivid and concrete an idea of the swiftness of time.

Images can be classified according to the sense to which they appeal—visual, auditory, gustatory, tactile, or olfactory—and by the sphere of influence from which they are drawn, such as religious, agricultural, scientific, or domestic. The study of imagery in a particular work attempts to show how patterns of images express its theme; the study of imagery in the corpus of an author's writings leads to a description of the author's imaginative world. Such studies of imagery have become an important part of 20th century literary criticism.
JONATHAN CULLER

Bibliography: Day Lewis, Cecil, *The Poetic Image* (1947); Furbank, Philip Nicholas, *Reflections on the Word "Image"* (1970); Kermode, Frank, *The Romantic Image* (1957).

image processing

Image processing involves the manipulation of pictorial material. The usual purpose is to make the picture clearer and therefore more useful. Some image processing is carried out in various electronic devices, such as PHOTOMULTIPLIERS, television camera tubes, and image intensifiers. The digital computer, however, is the most useful and flexible device for this operation, and the remainder of this article will emphasize its applications. There are four basic types of image processing—compression, enhancement, restoration, and recognition—and each is discussed in turn.

By the 1960s digital computers had become so powerful that it was tantalizing to consider storing and manipulating an image within the computer. Initial work was carried out in university laboratories. As the numerical power of the computer increased and as more individuals became familiar with the potential of sophisticated nonlinear processes, numerous government laboratories began investigating the application of image processing to their own areas of interest. Today image-processing techniques are used in infrared, multispec-

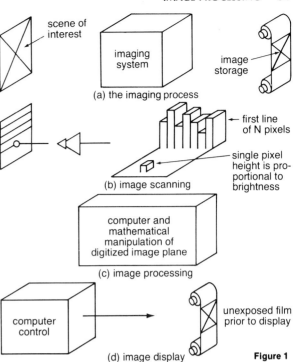

scene of interest

imaging system

image storage

(a) the imaging process

first line of N pixels

single pixel height is proportional to brightness

(b) image scanning

computer and mathematical manipulation of digitized image plane

(c) image processing

computer control

unexposed film prior to display

(d) image display

Figure 1

tral, radar, sonar, tomographic, visible, and X-ray imaging systems.

For the computer to manipulate the image it must first be "digitized," that is, recorded in terms of numbers representing the levels of brightness or energy values at each spot on the picture. The scene or picture is broken down into a number of picture elements, which are then "sampled" and converted into numerical values. A typical image is broken down into a 500×500 grid, giving 250,000 picture elements, or samples, and allowing 256 levels of brightness to be distinguished. Equipment is now available that can digitize such an image in as little as 1/30 second. Some image sensors actually record images of a size greater than 2000×3000 picture elements. These picture elements or spots on the image, also referred to as pixels or pels, are subsequently manipulated by the computer for the objectives of the user. When the computer completes its processing, the results are then retrieved from the computer and displayed in pictorial form. Figure 1 represents this process.

IMAGE COMPRESSION

Image compression is carried out in order to reduce the information (number of bits) that must be stored to preserve the image within the computer memory. Such compression techniques also reduce the number of bits needed to transmit an image over digital communication lines. This means that transmission will be speeded up for a given communication system or that the same speed can be maintained on a simpler system. Such image compression operates by removing certain inherent redundancies in pictures. Such redundancies manifest themselves as correlations between adjacent samples of image brightness. In addition, if the scene to be compressed is in color, there is an additional correlation between the color planes as well as between the pixels within a color plane. Figure 2 illustrates the technological capabilities for compressing such digital imagery using modern-day ALGO-RITHMS. The original image is displayed with a total of 24 bits per pixel (8 bits per pixel per color plane). The remaining compressed imagery is displayed with 1 bit per pixel, 1/2 bit per pixel, and 1/4 bit per pixel, corresponding to compression ratios of 24:1, 48:1, and 96:1. Degradation becomes evident at the higher compression ratios. Such compression techniques are used in imagery from spacecraft and satellites, where communication is very expensive due to power consumption; in digital television on remote expendable sensors, where

Original

1 bit

½ bit

¼ bit

Figure 2. Color Image Compression

communication must be inexpensive; and in transmission of imagery over telephone lines, where such communication takes considerable time due to the limited bandwidth of these lines.

IMAGE ENHANCEMENT

Techniques of image enhancement, or intensification, attempt to improve or make more evident some aspect of an image that is not initially apparent. Increasing contrast, sharpening edges, removing noise, and removing blurring are typical examples of enhancement procedures. The flexibility of the general-purpose digital computer makes it well suited to carry out image enhancement. The simplest types of enhancement involve the redistribution of values of picture brightness to make more evident the contrasts in extremely dark values or

Original Milkdrop

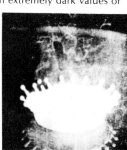

Enhanced Milkdrop

Figure 3. Dark Gray Scale Enhancement

Original Bridge

Enhanced Bridge

Figure 4. Overall Gray Scale Enhancement

extremely bright values. Figure 3 illustrates this technique. The dark background in the image is enhanced in order to bring out the subtle structure in this dark region. By this technique, however, the bright regions tend to be saturated. Figure 4 illustrates another gray-scale technique in which the bright and dark regions are simultaneously enhanced.

More sophisticated enhancement procedures can be used to sharpen edges, usually to help delineate boundaries of objects for various measurement or identification procedures. Figure 5 presents the before-and-after pictures for an edge-emphasized image of a ground scene. Note how the definition of the tower is improved in the enhanced version.

Many modern-day enhancement algorithms have become

Original

Edge Enhanced

Figure 5. Edge Enhancement

Original Latent Fingerprint

Enhanced Fingerprint

Figure 6. Adaptive Enhancement

quite sophisticated and are adaptive in nature, adjusting automatically to fit the image data. An example of this technique is presented in Figure 6, in which a latent fingerprint is considerably improved by an adaptive thresholding process. This procedure searches for subtle detail or variations around a local average brightness and emphasizes that detail.

Another enhancement procedure that has evoked some interest uses color to delineate boundaries or other information contained in an originally monochromatic (black and white) scene. Such techniques are referred to as "pseudocoloring," and one such example is illustrated in Figure 7. Here the contours of the aircraft as well as the background are made clearer through the use of color, and edge definition as well as shape can be more readily obtained.

Original

Enhanced

Figure 7. Pseudocolor Enhancement

Original

Restored

Original

Restored

Figure 8. Image Restoration

IMAGE RESTORATION

Image restoration involves the attempt to correct degradations in a scene that might be experienced during the photographic or imaging process. Examples include correcting for badly focused images, motion-blurred images, geometrical distortions—for example, distortions of NASA satellite images—radiometric correction for sensor nonlinearities, atmospheric degradations, and noise removal. The basis of image restoration is highly mathematical and statistical—much more so than the techniques for image enhancement. In restoration a definite attempt is made to model the degradation process mathematically and statistically and then to invert that process to reconstruct the original scene from the degraded image by using the model. A danger of such procedures is that attempts to undo too much of the degradation may add to the image certain aspects that were not originally present. The fields of NUMERICAL ANALYSIS and digital signal processing, however, provide useful quantitative measures to control the inherent "ill-conditioning" nature of restoration, and a variety of restoration filters have been developed for these procedures. Good examples of restoration available today include de-focus compensation and motion blur correction. Figure 8

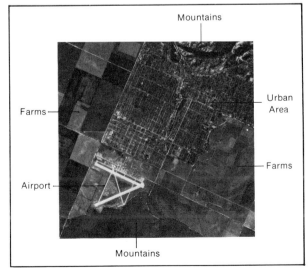

Figure 9. Image Recognition

presents some results of restoration methods applied to imagery that was badly blurred because the camera shook during exposure. In this example the blur was arbitrary but consistently the same over the entire field of view.

IMAGE RECOGNITION

Image recognition refers to the attempt to have a machine automatically recognize certain objects or structures of interest to the user (see PATTERN RECOGNITION). Examples include character recognition, airport detection, and ship classification. Coupled with image recognition is scene analysis, in which a machine attempts to describe an image in terms of homogeneous segments or regions, which themselves might be objects to recognize. As an illustration, Figure 9 provides a typical aerial image in which farmland, an airport, urban areas, and mountains are recognized. The techniques used in object and scene recognition include matched filters that look for specific shapes, texture detectors, and edge and boundary detectors. The techniques can be extended, and decisions concerning quite complex scenes can be developed. Related terms include image analysis and pictorial pattern classification.   HARRY C. ANDREWS

Bibliography: Andrews, Harry C., et al., *Computer Techniques in Image Processing* (1970) and *Digital Image Restoration* (1977); Duda, Richard O., and Hart, Peter E., *Pattern Classification and Scene Analysis* (1973); Pratt, William K., *Digital Image Processing* (1978); Rosenfeld, Azriel, *Picture Processing by Computer* (1969).

See also: NIGHT SIGHTS.

imaginary number: see COMPLEX NUMBER.

imagism   [im'-uhj-izm]

A literary movement that flourished between 1912 and 1918, imagism represents a landmark in American and British literature—a successful attempt to revitalize the language of poetry and to assign it a distinctive role. Ezra POUND said he first used the word to publicize the works of Hilda DOOLITTLE (H.D.), and he brought the movement to the attention of American readers in *Poetry* magazine. Here F. S. Flint published these rules: "Direct treatment of the 'thing,' whether subjective or objective; to use absolutely no word that did not contribute to the presentation; as regarding rhythm: to compose in sequence of the musical phrase, not in the sequence of a metronome."

These rules were not only a guide to the right image; they were also a frontal attack on the prolix, emotional, and overly metrical verse of the time. Pound drew from contemporary psychology to define the image as "that which presents an intellectual and emotional complex in an instant of time." When Amy LOWELL, who edited three anthologies (1915–17) entitled *Some Imagist Poets*, entered the movement, Pound left, calling what remained "Amygism."

Disagreement still exists about the sources of the movement. Certainly, Pound and T. E. HULME played influential roles. Whether French symbolism, impressionism, haiku, or the writings of critics such as Théophile Gautier and Ford Maddox Ford were ancestors or godparents of the movement may never be decided. Its influence on modern poetry is, however, unquestionable. Early imagist poets such as Pound, H.D., John Gould FLETCHER, Hulme, and Richard ALDINGTON were the predecessors of major poets like T. S. Eliot, Wallace Stevens, and William Carlos Williams.   JAMES HART

Bibliography: Coffman, Stanley K., *Imagism: A Chapter for the History of Modern Poetry* (1951); De Chasca, Edmund S., *John Gould Fletcher and Imagism* (1978); Gould, Jean, *Amy: The World of Amy Lowell and the Imagist Movement* (1975); Harmer, J. B., *Victory in Limbo: Imagism* (1975); Hughes, Glenn, *Imagism and the Imagist* (1931); Jones, Alun T., *The Life and Opinions of T. E. Hulme* (1960); Kenner, Hugh, *The Pound Era* (1971); Pratt, William C., ed., *The Imagist Poem* (1963); Roberts, Michael, *T. E. Hulme* (1938; repr. 1971).

imam   [im-ahm']

Imam is used in the Koran to mean leader, guide, model, or sign. These basic connotations are preserved in the four distinctive usages of later ISLAM. (1) The SUNNITES use imam as a title for the caliphs, the successors of Muhammad as leaders of the Muslim community (see CALIPHATE). One of the caliph's functions was to lead the community in Friday prayers. (2) A local group of Muslims may appoint an imam to lead them in the Friday prayers. Any Muslim of undisputed piety and sound knowledge of the Islamic faith and ritual can serve in this capacity. (3) For SHIITES, only a person from the clan of the Prophet can be the imam, for some of them only a descendant from ALI, the son-in-law of Muhammad. (4) Imam is also an honorary title given to a few of the most outstanding Muslim scholars of all centuries, such as al-Ghazali.

WILLEM A. BIJLEFELD

Imhotep [im-hoh'-tep]

Imhotep, an ancient Egyptian priest and vizier, served as architect and court official to King Zoser of the 3d dynasty (c.2686–2613 BC). His titles indicate that he was not of royal birth, but he was later deified—one of few nonroyals to achieve that distinction. As the chief sculptor and chief carpenter of Zoser, Imhotep is connected with Zoser's famous step pyramid complex at Saqqara (see PYRAMIDS). This complex, which includes the step pyramid itself, a burial chamber, a mortuary temple, and the court of the Heb Sed (festival of renewal), was, according to the late Egyptian writer Manetho, the first Egyptian building in stone. Manetho credits Imhotep with this invention.

Imhotep later came to be regarded as a sage, author of wisdom literature, and patron of scribes, and under the 26th dynasty (664–525 BC) he was deified. Many statuettes from the Late Dynastic Period show him seated with a scroll on his lap. He was identified by the Greeks with ASCLEPIUS, the god of healing; thousands flocked to his temples in search of cures. Imhotep's tomb was probably at Saqqara.

JOHN STEPHENS CRAWFORD

Bibliography: Edwards, Ionwerth, *The Pyramids of Egypt* (1977); Fakhry, Ahmed, *The Pyramids*, 2d ed. (1974); Hurry, Jamieson B., *Imhotep, the Vizier and Physician of King Zoser and Afterwards the Egyptian God of Medicine.* 2d ed. (1928; repr. 1976).

Immaculate Conception [im-mak'-yuh-luht]

The Immaculate Conception is a Roman Catholic doctrine asserting that MARY, the mother of Jesus, was preserved from the effects of ORIGINAL SIN from the first moment of her conception. The doctrine was defined as a dogma binding on Catholics by Pope Pius IX in the papal bull *Ineffabilis Deus* (1854). The doctrine as defined was debated by theologians during the Middle Ages and was rejected by Saint Thomas Aquinas. It is based on the biblical idea of Mary's holiness (Luke 1:28), early church teachings on Mary as the "new Eve," and the belief that Mary is the mother of God (Theotokos, or "God-bearer"), articulated at the Council of Ephesus (431; see EPHESUS, COUNCIL OF). The feast of the Immaculate Conception is observed on Dec. 8.

immanence, divine [im'-uh-nens]

In philosophy and theology, divine immanence refers to the omnipresence of GOD in the universe. The theory in its extreme form is PANTHEISM, in which God and the world are virtually identical. Proponents of MONOTHEISM, however, have tempered the concept of immanence by positing the parallel doctrine of divine TRANSCENDENCE. Thus, in Judaism and Christianity, God is considered omnipresent and active in human affairs as creator, sustainer, judge, and redeemer, but is also considered elevated above and distinguished from the universe.

immigration

Immigration is the act of settling as a permanent resident in a country not one's own. Since ancient times, people have left their native countries in search of adventure, to escape despotism, to avoid military service, or to improve themselves economically. Immigrants colonized the Western Hemisphere, Australia, New Zealand, Israel, Formosa, Southeast Asia, Siberia, and parts of Africa.

(Above) *In this 1851 woodcut, a kneeling Irish emigrant is blessed by a priest as he and others prepare to leave their homeland. During the 19th century, more than 1,500,000 people were forced to leave Ireland because of the potato famine. Many settled in the United States.*

(Left) *An Italian immigrant family arrives (c.1905) at Ellis Island in New York Harbor. In the early 1900s, more than 70 percent of all those immigrating to the United States came from southern and eastern Europe.*

Since World War II, some important migrations have occurred. In Europe, 12 million Germans from Poland, the Baltic states, and East Germany moved into West Germany. More than 1 million people emigrated to Israel from Europe, North Africa, Britain, and the United States between 1945 and 1965. France received immigrants from Poland, Italy, and Algeria. Large numbers of scientists and other highly trained people emigrated from developing countries such as India to Britain, and from Britain to the United States—a phenomenon that was called the "brain drain."

Most countries restrict immigration in various ways. The United States and some other countries exclude criminals, violators of narcotic laws, political subversives, prostitutes, polygamists, those likely to become public charges, the ill or afflicted, illiterates, and stowaways. In addition, some countries, including the United States, Britain, Australia, South Africa, Brazil, and the Philippine Republic, have quota restrictions that limit by country or hemisphere of origin the number of those eligible for entry. Australia excluded immigrants from Asia and Africa altogether until 1965, when it began to accept Asian and African immigrants with needed job skills. The arrival in Great Britain of several thousand British-passport-holding Asians from Kenya in 1968 led Great Britain to place U.K. citizens not born, adopted, or naturalized in Britain under strict immigration controls. In contrast, potential immigrants to Canada are graded on a point system based on

The maps depict (top) the volume of immigration into the United States by area of origin and by period (1810–60, 1860–1910, 1910–77) and (bottom) the distribution of immigrant population with the current ethnic composition of the major metropolitan areas.

that disease during his or her lifetime. A broader definition of immunity includes all of the physiological mechanisms that give an organism the ability to recognize foreign substances and neutralize or degrade them, with or without injury to the organism's own tissue. IMMUNOLOGY is the branch of medicine concerned with the body's response to foreign substances.

HISTORY

Since the 15th century the Chinese have practiced the custom of inhaling dried powders of smallpox crusts to gain protection from smallpox. The prevention of disease by inoculation of human smallpox material is hazardous, however. The first step in establishing a safer procedure was taken by Edward JENNER, who observed that people who caught cowpox, as most milkmaids inevitably did, rarely contracted smallpox. In 1796, Jenner induced a mild dose of cowpox in a young boy. A few weeks later he extracted pus from another person's smallpox sores and tried to infect the boy with smallpox. He was unsuccessful, however; the immunity provoked by the cowpox viruses apparently was also effective against smallpox organisms.

Further development of protection from disease by immunization was accomplished by Louis PASTEUR, who discovered in 1879 that cultures of chicken cholera bacillus that had been neglected lost much of their ability to cause the disease in chickens. Furthermore, fresh cultures failed to infect chickens previously inoculated with old cultures. The pathogenic organisms had become weakened or attenuated. The introduction of dead or weakened bacteria into the body to develop resistance to disease is called vaccination (from the Latin, vacca, "cow"), which is a form of passive immunity. Active immunity is immunity that results from a disease that occurs naturally. Today vaccination is used to develop the body's resistance to bacteria and viruses that cause such diseases as cholera, diphtheria, measles, mumps, whooping cough, rabies, smallpox, tetanus, typhoid, yellow fever, and poliomyelitis.

The work of Jenner and Pasteur marked the beginning of the field of immunology. Until 1900, the principal investigators in this field were French or German. Two different views emerged from their studies as to how the immune response functions. Paul EHRLICH (1854–1915) proposed the humoral theory of immunity, which emphasized the role of chemical substances (ANTIBODIES) produced by cells and released into the bloodstream as the major agents of immunity. Elie METCHNIKOFF developed the cellular theory of immunity, according to which phagocytes, the body's scavenger cells, are the major detectors of foreign material, as well as the primary defense system against infectious organisms. Today it is known that both theories are correct: both types of defense mechanism are involved in the immune system of an organism.

FUNCTIONS OF THE IMMUNE SYSTEM

In the early history of immunology, the term immunity referred primarily to the resistance of an individual to reinfection with bacteria, viruses, or parasites. Immune responses, however, are not always beneficial, nor are they associated only with resistance to infection. Because of the immune response, the entrance of foreign substances into the body sometimes has severe effects, and may even lead to death. Furthermore, the immune system has other important functions.

The role of the immune system in protecting the body against invasion by foreign organisms is the best understood. Under normal circumstances the immune system responds to foreign organisms by stimulating the production of antibodies and cells, which destroy the organisms or neutralize their toxic products. When the immune system involved in this function becomes too active, however, the result may be undesirable features, such as hypersensitivity or allergic reactions. On the other hand, when the immune response is not working properly (immunodeficient) the individual may become more susceptible to repeated infection (immunodeficiency disorders).

Another major function of the immune system is the removal of damaged or dying cells. This function may be misdi-

rected, however, resulting in an immune response against the body's own cells or tissues, producing a condition known as an autoimmune disease.

The function of the immune system most recently discovered is the system's ability to recognize and eliminate the abnormal (mutant) cells that frequently arise within the body. These mutant, or cancer, cells may occur spontaneously, or they may be induced by certain viruses (oncogenic viruses) or chemicals (mutagens). An immune system that is functioning properly can usually recognize and dispose of such cancer cells by means of a process called immune surveillance. The malfunction of this process may result in the incidence of certain types of cancer.

CELLS AND TISSUES IN THE IMMUNE RESPONSE

The ability to recognize foreignness, specificity, and memory are the key characteristics of immune defense mechanisms. The immune system of the human body must be able to recognize bacteria, viruses, and parasites in order to locate and destroy them. Specificity means that immunity to one foreign substance or organism does not necessarily provide resistance to another foreign substance, even if the two are highly similar. Memory is the ability of an organism to develop a long-lasting immunity after the initial attack by an infectious disease. For example, a person who has survived an attack of smallpox usually does not contract the disease again. The three characteristics mentioned above are invested in a single type of cell—the lymphocyte—which is one of several types of white blood cells.

Lymphocytes are carried by the circulatory and the lymphatic systems to the site of infection. Scattered along the lymphatic vessels are small swellings known as lymph nodes, which contain large numbers of lymphocytes. These nodes become hard when packed with lymphocytes that have been stimulated by the infectious organisms to divide and produce specific antibodies against specific organisms.

A major milestone in modern immunology came when two distinct types of lymphocyte were discovered: the T lymphocytes, or T cells, and the B lymphocytes, or B cells. Immunity provided by antibody molecules in the circulatory system (this type of immunity is called humoral immunity) is provided by the B cells, whereas a quite different kind of immunity (called cell-mediated immunity) is provided by T cells.

ANTIGENS

An antigen is a substance that, when introduced into an orga nism, induces an immune response consisting of the production of a circulating antibody. This type of immunity is known as humoral immunity. Protein molecules are potent antigens. Within a few days after injection, an antigen elicits large amounts of the antibody capable of interacting with it. Upon examination of the interaction of an antigen with its specific antibody, it has been found that the antibody does not recognize the entire protein molecule, but only small areas on its surface; these areas are known as antigenic deter minants. Protein molecules have several antigenic determinants, each of which can be recognized by an antibody. Because they have antigenic determinants, many carbohydrate: are also antigenic; for example, carbohydrates located on th surface of red blood cells make up the blood group antigen

ANTIBODIES

The molecules responsible for recognizing antigenic determ nants on foreign molecules or on cell surfaces are called an bodies. Antibodies are members of a related group of gamr globulin molecules known as immunoglobulins (Ig).

Each immunoglobulin molecule is made up of four distir protein chains joined together in two pairs. One pair is sm and is called a light (L) chain; the other pair is much larger and is known as a heavy (H) chain. These protein chains a unique, in that one segment at the end of each chain has sentially the same amino-acid sequence that is found in ar entire range of antibodies having different specificities. Th segment is called the constant (C) region. The arrangemen i amino acids at the other end is different for every antibod molecule of a given specificity; therefore, this region is ca J the variable (V) region. The ability of antibody molecules

first antigen

 second antigen

first antibody

second antibody

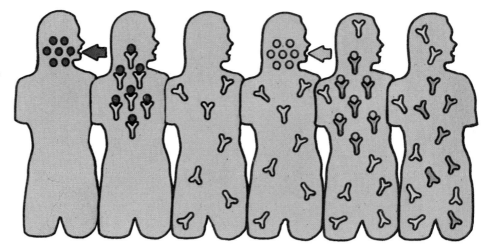

The immune system protects the body from invasion by foreign substances by attacking and destroying a particular invader and developing long-term immunity to it. When an antigen enters the bloodstream it stimulates certain B lymphocytes to differentiate (specialize) into plasma cells and divide, producing both plasma cells and memory cells. The plasma cells secrete large amounts of a specific antibody, which circulate in the blood and destroy the antigen. After the first encounter the antibodies eventually disappear, but the memory cells remain in circulation. These cells are sensitized to that particular antigen and will immediately produce new antibodies in the event of subsequent attacks, resulting in specific long-term immunity. If a second antigen is introduced, however, the process must be repeated. New plasma cells, antibodies, and memory cells are produced, and specific immunity to the second antigen is eventually acquired.

interact with many different antigens is associated with the variable regions that constitute the combining site. Five classes of immunoglobulins exist, based on structural differences in the constant regions of the heavy chains of human immunoglobulins. These differences in the heavy chains are identified by the Greek letters gamma (γ), mu (μ), alpha (α), delta (δ), and epsilon(ε), and the immunoglobulins that contain them are called IgG, IgM, IgA, IgD, and IgE, respectively. Each class has different biological and structural properties and is distributed throughout the body.

IgG, the most abundant immunoglobulin, occurs primarily in serum, as well as throughout the internal body fluids. Produced in response to bacteria, viruses, and fungi that have gained access to the body, IgG is a major line of defense against such organisms. It is the only immunoglobulin that can cross the placenta and thus is important in the defense of newborns against bacterial and viral infections.

IgM, the largest immunoglobulin, is a powerful activator of complement, protein molecules that, when activated in proper sequence, produce holes in the surface of a foreign cell, resulting in lysis, or death, of the cell. IgM, therefore, is highly efficient in destroying bacteria that have gained access to the blood.

IgA acts as a barrier against pathogenic organisms that enter via the respiratory tract and the gut. Antibody-forming B cells located in these areas produce single molecules of IgA, which are then bound together in pairs as they are secreted into the mucus lining the respiratory and digestive tracts, thus preventing bacteria and viruses from entering the tracts.

IgE triggers allergic and asthmatic reactions. Mast cells, usually situated around blood vessels, line the respiratory and digestive tracts and contain histamine and related molecules, which are released when particles such as pollen bind to the IgE molecule. These molecules, when released, cause asthma and allergic reactions.

IgD, an immunoglobulin recently discovered in serum, is the least well understood. No definite biological activity has yet been assigned to it.

ANTIBODIES IN DEFENSE

The simplest and most prevalent means by which the immune system defends the body against bacteria and viruses is by the combination of a specific antibody with the antigenic determinants located on the surface of invading organisms. An aggregate of cells, called an agglutination, is formed by antibodies bound by one of their two combining sites to one cell,

and to another cell by their other site. These aggregates are then engulfed and digested by the body's wandering scavenger cells, or large phagocytes (macrophages). In other cases, the body's antibodies bind to toxins given off by microorganisms and form large, insoluble aggregates (precipitates), which are also removed by macrophages. Precipitin and agglutination reactions are used as diagnostic tools for identifying and quantifying the antibodies of infectious organisms in blood samples and other body fluids.

Cell-mediated immunity is involved in the body's rejection of transplanted tissues; in attacking certain bacteria, viruses, and fungi; in some skin reactions resulting from contact with simple chemicals (contact dermatitis); and in immunity to cancer cells. This type of immunity occurs when the lymphocytes of a body sensitized to a particular antigen react with the antigen deposited at a particular site. Because of this interaction, the lymphocyte releases molecules, called lymphokines, that have various biological effects on other cells. Transfer factor is able to cause normal lymphocytes to release lymphokines or otherwise become activated and thus to destroy other cells. By using knowledge of the transfer ability thus gained, scientists have been able to treat individuals whose bodies cannot develop antibodies for certain bacteria, viruses, or fungi because of a hereditary defect in the cell-mediated immunity of the cells. Transfer factor is prepared from the lymphocytes of a person with good immunity to a particular disease agent and is then injected into the body of someone who is deficient in the agent. Transfer factor stimulates the lymphocytes to develop normal immunity; the body is then able to defend itself against an organism to which it was once susceptible.

Cell-mediated immunity is also involved in contact dermatitis, a reaction against small molecules such as urushiol, which is found in the sticky sap of poison ivy, poison sumac, and poison oak. Contact between urushiol and the skin causes a rash to develop within a few days.

AUTOIMMUNITY

Some of the most serious human diseases are those caused by the immune system attacking the body's own cells and tissues as though they were invaders. The pathological damage is inflicted by specific antiself antibodies or cell-mediated immunity.

RHEUMATIC FEVER, which involves damage to both joints and heart valves, is such an autoimmune disease. It begins with a streptococcal infection of the throat. Rheumatic fever is the result of an immune response to streptococcal organisms. For some reason not yet known, the patient's B and T cells mistake the patient's heart muscle and joints for the invading streptococci and attack them instead. An antigenic similarity seems to exist among the heart muscle, the joint tissues, and the streptococcal organism. MULTIPLE SCLEROSIS may also be an autoimmune disease caused by antibodies attacking the tissues of the brain.

TRANSPLANTATION IMMUNITY

When strips of skin are taken from a patient (called a donor) and grafted onto the skin of a recipient, the graft initially appears to "take"; within a few days, however, the graft becomes red, then blackens, and finally drops off or is rejected. In contrast, when skin is grafted to another part of the same patient's body, or from one identical twin to another, the graft is accepted; that is, it heals perfectly. The rejection of a graft is an immune reaction. Whether a transplant "takes" depends on preventing the organ from being rejected because of the recipient's immune response to the graft. Transplants are usually maintained by using a procedure called immunosuppression, in which the patient is given drugs designed to prevent the immune response that normally leads to rejection of the graft. The combination of drugs currently preferred includes azathioprine (Imuran) and prednisone (a corticosteroid), which act to prevent cells from growing and dividing (processes that are essential to cells involved in the immune response).

In recent years the success rate for kidney transplants has been improved substantially by matching the tissue antigens (known as the HLA system) of the donor with those of the recipient. Because of the thousands of combinations of HLA antigens on a person's cells, however, this procedure is expected to become more effective only when a large pool of potential donors is available and after the development of banks for the long-term storage of tissue.

CANCER AND IMMUNITY

Because organ transplants are closely related to CANCER, researchers are attempting to encourage the body's immune defense system to accept the cells of transplants and to reject those of cancer. By the use of immunosuppressive procedures, surgeons have, in many cases, been able to prevent the rejection of transplanted organs while learning important clues to the relationship between cancer and immunity.

The importance of the immune system in combating and controlling cancer was strongly suggested when a surgeon performing a transplant unknowingly transplanted a kidney that contained an undetected cancer. After the transplant, the patient was treated with immunosuppressive drugs. Within days, the kidney began to enlarge and look as though it were undergoing rejection. The functioning of the kidney remained normal, however, something that usually does not happen during rejection of an organ. When the patient developed chest tumors, he was taken back to the operating room, where it was discovered that the transplanted kidney was cancerous. The tumors in the lung apparently were cancers that had spread, or metastasized, from the kidney. All drug treatment was stopped, and the patient's immunity quickly returned to normal. As this occurred, the tumors in the lung and kidneys began to shrink, or regress. It appeared that, as the immune system returned to normal functioning, it was able to control the cancer growth. As the immune system did so, however, it began to destroy the grafted kidney as well, and the kidney finally had to be removed. Further evidence of the body's surveillance against the growth of cancerous cells came when it was observed that patients with kidney transplants were ten times more likely to develop cancer than were those who had not had transplants. This, too, was attributed to the immunosuppression that patients had been subjected to so that transplanted organs would be accepted.

If a connection exists between the failure of the immune system and the incidence of cancer, or its growth and spread, then any substance that stimulates the immune system is likely to help destroy or at least retard the spread of the cancer. One such substance is BCG (for "Bacillus Calmette-Guérin"), a live bacterium related to the bacillus that causes tu-

berculosis. Using a procedure called immunotherapy, BCG has been used to increase the immune response of patients suffering from various cancers. The advantage of such treatment is that it destroys every cancer cell, something no other method devised so far can do. Unlike chemotherapy and radiation therapy, immunotherapy does not destroy normal body cells. When the tumor mass is fairly large at the time of diagnosis, however, the cancerous mass must often be removed by surgery, by chemotherapy, or by radiotherapy before immunotherapy can be used effectively.   PETER ABRAMOFF

Bibliography: Abramoff, Peter, and La Via, Mariano F., *The Biology of the Immune Response* (1970); Burnet, F. M., *Immunology, Aging and Cancer* (1976) and, as ed., *Immunology: Readings from Scientific American* (1976); Glasser, Ronald J., *The Body Is the Hero* (1976); Lewin, Roger, *In Defense of the Body* (1974); Nossal, G. J., *Antibodies and Immunity*, rev. ed. (1978); Parish, H. J., *A History of Immunization* (1965); Wilson, David, *Body and Antibody* (1972).

immunity   (law)

Immunity is an exemption from a duty or legal punishment because of some special characteristic or status enjoyed by the person concerned. Many types of immunity exist under both criminal and civil law. In criminal law, a person may be granted immunity from prosecution in return for testifying for the state. Diplomatic immunity, in international law, is enjoyed by ambassadors and certain lower-level officials, as well as by members of international organizations. This immunity allows them to be free from most local laws. Legislators, judges, and witnesses are granted official immunity (usually from libel suits) with respect to statements made in the course of their duties. Governmental bodies enjoy sovereign immunity from civil lawsuits unless they consent to be sued.

immunization: see IMMUNITY (biology).

immunodeficiency disease   [im mue noh dee-fish'-en-see]

Immunodeficiency diseases are characterized by a failure of one or more parts of the immune system. Individuals with an immunodeficiency disease have very little resistance to infections and may succumb to them early in life. Most immunodeficiency diseases are acquired, or secondary. Some immunodeficiency diseases in humans can result from genetic cellular defects (see GENETIC DISEASES) and are termed *primary*.

Two major IMMUNITY systems exist in humans, and either one may be affected in immunodeficiency disease. Humoral immunity is due to ANTIBODIES that are produced by a type of lymphocyte, called B lymphocytes, in response to ANTIGENS. The antibodies, which circulate in the BLOOD and other body fluids, destroy invading bacteria, viruses, or fungi by combining with antigenic substances on their surface to form an antigen-antibody complex. Cell-mediated immunity, or delayed hypersensitivity, is due to the activities of another kind of lymphocyte, called T lymphocytes, in response to foreign antigens. The T lymphocytes do not produce antibodies but produce several mediators that are involved in immunologic processes. One of the mediators affects the B lymphocytes, stimulating them to produce antibodies. Several other mediators stimulate phagocytic cells, called macrophages, which destroy invading microorganisms by engulfing and digesting them. The B lymphocytes and T lymphocytes are so designated because of their origin in the BONE marrow and thymus gland, respectively, although both forms are derived from a common precursor cell.

An example of primary immunodeficiency disease involving B lymphocytes is X-linked infantile agammaglobulinemia, a disease in which the production of B lymphocytes is deficient or lacking because of a defect on the X chromosome. This is reflected by the deficiency or absence in the blood of gammaglobulin, the class of protein to which antibodies belong. Children with the disease are usually normal at birth, but within a few months they begin to show unusual susceptibility to pneumonia and other bacterial infection. They also have a higher than normal incidence of leukemia.

The absence or deficiency of T lymphocytes is seen in a disease called DiGeorge's syndrome, which occurs in individuals born without or with only partial thymus and parathyroid glands. The cause of DiGeorge's syndrome is unknown, and a genetic basis for the disease has not been proved. Since T lymphocytes are absent or greatly deficient, cell-mediated immunity is impaired, causing increased susceptibility to infection and death within 2 years, unless the thymus is partially present or implanted.

Several immunodeficiency diseases involve failure of both B and T lymphocytes to develop properly, thus causing severe deficiency of both humoral and cell-mediated immunity. These diseases are collectively called severe combined immunodeficiency diseases. Children with such diseases are extremely susceptible to infection and may die early in life if untreated. Immunization with live-virus vaccines can be dangerous in such children, since a lethal infection may occur even though the virus has been attenuated (weakened).

Secondary immunodeficiency diseases result from a number of organic causes. They can arise from the kidney's losing gammaglobulins (nephrotic syndrome); from radiation and cytotoxic drugs that cause bone marrow and lymphoid tissue suppression; from malnutrition and aging; from malignancies that impair phagocytosis; and from burns, diabetes, and congenital heart defects.

Some immunodeficiency diseases have been successfully treated recently by means of tissue transplantation. Transplantation of fetal thymus tissue to an individual born without a thymus can establish normal production of T lymphocytes and associated cell-mediated immunity. Bone-marrow transplantation can establish normal production of B lymphocytes and associated humoral immunity.   PETER L. PETRAKIS

Bibliography: Bergsma, Daniel, et al., *Immunodeficiency in Man and Animals* (1975; repr. 1977).

immunology   [im-mue-nahl'-uh-jee]

Immunology is the branch of medical science dealing with the body's specific responses to foreign substances. The function of the immune system is to recognize foreign, and therefore potentially harmful, microorganisms and their products and to assist their removal from the body. Immunology involves the study of the specialized cells of the immune system such as the lymphocytes, as well as ANTIBODIES, ANTIGENS, and the organs in which they are found, which include the lymph nodes, spleen, thymus, and bone marrow. Immunology also includes vaccination—the use of weakened forms of pathogenic microbes or their products to produce IMMUNITY against infectious disease. Immunological responses are generally protective and therefore beneficial to the individual; however, there are occasions when the immune response can itself be harmful, such as in the conditions called allergies (hypersensitivities) and in autoimmune diseases, where the immune system actually attacks the cells of the body as if they were foreign invaders.   MICHAEL J. TAUSSIG

Bibliography: Burnet, F. Macfarlane, *Self and Not-Self: Cellular Immunology* (1969); Roitt, Ivan M., *Essential Immunology* (1971).

See also: BLOOD; IMMUNITY; IMMUNODEFICIENCY DISEASE.

IMP

The IMP, or Interplanetary Monitoring Platform, was a series of 10 scientific satellites (part of the EXPLORER series) launched by NASA between 1963 and 1973 to probe the magnetosphere and interplanetary space during the 11-year cycle of the Sun's activity. Two of the satellites were fitted with solid propellant retro-motors to brake them into lunar orbit. The IMP satellite had a standard shape that could accommodate a variety of experiments. Each of the first seven models had an octagonal body 71 cm (28 in) wide and 30.5 cm (12 in) high. Four panels covered with solar cells and silver-cadmium batteries gave 38 W of power. Average weight was 65 kg (143 lb). Each of the final three satellites was a 16-sided polyhedron, 1.4 m (4.5 ft) in width, 1.6 m (5 ft) high, and weighing 370 kg (818 lb). Solar cells on the exterior gave 110 W of power.

Scientific instrumentation for the IMP varied with the mission, but in general was composed of magnetometers, Geiger counters, ion and electron probes, cosmic-ray detectors, plasma probes, micrometeoroid detectors, electric-field detectors, and engineering experiments in the field of radio telemetry and improved solar cells.

The IMP series was the first to measure accurately the interplanetary magnetic field, the Earth's magnetospheric boundary, and the shockwave occurring when the solar wind interacts with the Earth's magnetic field. In particular, measurements made from these satellites permitted the first detailed mapping of the "tail" of the Earth's field on the side away from the Sun.   MITCHELL SHARPE

impact crater: see METEORITE CRATERS.

impala   [im-pal'-uh]

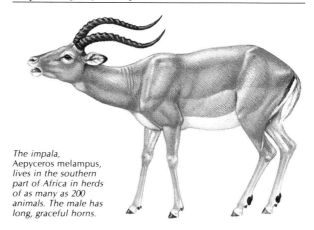

The impala, Aepyceros melampus, lives in the southern part of Africa in herds of as many as 200 animals. The male has long, graceful horns.

The impala, *Aepyceros melampus*, in the antelope and ox family, Bovidae, is a fast-running antelope of grasslands and open woodlands in central and southern Africa. It lives near water. A slight, graceful animal, the adult impala is about 1.5 m (5 ft) long, stands up to 1 m (3.3 ft) tall at the shoulder, and weighs up to 74.25 kg (165 lb). The coat is fawn or reddish brown above and whitish below. A black streak marks each side of the rump. The male has large, lyre-shaped horns. A powerful jumper, the impala can make leaps 9 m (30 ft) long and 3 m (10 ft) high. Impalas live in herds and feed on shrubs and grasses.   EVERETT SENTMAN

impasto   [im-pahs'-toh]

The term *impasto* refers to the thickness of the pigment of oil and acrylic paints applied to a surface, particularly when it is thick enough to retain the mark of the painter's brush or palette knife. Rembrandt and Peter Paul Rubens used impasto for highlights, whereas Frans Hals laid the paint in more fully in slashing strokes. A heavy, swirling, overall impasto typifies the work of Vincent van Gogh. More recently, Jackson Pollock worked layers of dripped and splattered paint, sometimes with sand added for texture, into his canvases. The term does not apply to such thin-surfaced PAINTING TECHNIQUES as TEMPERA, WATERCOLOR, and glaze.

impeachment   [im-peech'-ment]

Impeachment is the first step in the process specified in the Constitution of the United States for removing the president, vice-president, or other government official from office upon conviction of "treason, bribery, or other high crimes and misdemeanors." The House of Representatives has "the sole power of impeachment," that is, the power of bringing charges. The Senate has "the sole power to try all impeachments." A two-thirds vote is required in the Senate for conviction. When the president is to be tried, the chief justice of the United States presides. Conviction in an impeachment

President Andrew Johnson (right), the only U.S. president to be impeached, receives the summons to appear at his Senate trial in this contemporary engraving. The trial, which began in March 1868 and concluded in May, resulted in his acquittal by a single vote.

proceeding results only in removal from office and disqualification to hold "any office of honor, trust, or profit under the United States." A person convicted in an impeachment, however, is subject to further "indictment, trial, judgment, and punishment according to Law."

Impeachment originated in England, where the House of Commons would present articles of impeachment to the House of Lords, which then tried the case. A well-known instance was the impeachment and trial (1786–95) of Warren HASTINGS, first governor general of India.

The framers of the U.S. Constitution, although committed to a separation of powers and independence of the three branches of government from each other, believed that a means must be provided by which officers thought to be guilty of significant misconduct could be tried and removed. They did not want the procedure to be overly simple to invoke, nor the penalty too easily imposed—hence, the requirement of the two-thirds vote for conviction in the Senate, and the stipulation that impeachment be for "treason, bribery, and other high crimes and misdemeanors." To George Mason's suggestion that "maladministration" be a ground for impeachment, both James Madison and Gouverneur Morris objected that so vague a term would surely produce the result that tenure in office would be at the pleasure of the Senate.

Since the adoption of the Constitution, only one president, Andrew JOHNSON (1868), has been brought to trial in the Senate on charges voted by the House. The Senate failed by one vote to convict Johnson. In 1974 the House Judiciary Committee voted three charges of impeachment against President Richard M. NIXON (see WATERGATE), but he resigned from office before the charges could be voted upon by the House.

Impeachment proceedings have been brought with some frequency against federal judges. In 1804, Supreme Court justice Samuel CHASE was impeached on purely political grounds, but his acquittal (1805) effectively halted the use of impeachment to remove judges for political reasons. It has often been said that the cumbersome and time-consuming process of impeachment is unsuited to the removal of a merely venal judge. Nevertheless, because the Constitution specifies that judges hold office during good behavior, impeachment remains the only means by which a federal judge may be removed.

Certain questions concerning the impeachment process have persisted: whether it is judicial or political in nature; how to define high crimes and misdemeanors; and whether a conviction can be appealed to the Supreme Court. Although no conclusive answer can be given, it is safe to say that the judicial process of impeachment will always be infused with political motives; that the definition of high crimes and mis-

demeanors will never become entirely precise; and that once the Senate has voted to convict by a two-thirds majority, the Supreme Court is unlikely to take jurisdiction.

VALERIE A. EARLE

Bibliography: Berger, Raoul, *Impeachment: The Constitutional Problems* (1973); Black, Charles L., Jr., *Impeachment: A Handbook* (1974); Brant, Irving, *Impeachment: Trials and Errors* (1972); Schnapper, Morris B., ed., *Presidential Impeachment: A Documentary Overview* (1974); Smith, Gene, *High Crimes and Misdemeanors: The Impeachment and Trial of Andrew Johnson* (1976); White, Theodore H., *Breach of Faith: The Fall of Richard Nixon* (1975).

impedance   [im-peed'-ens]

Impedance is the apparent resistance in alternating current (AC) circuits that corresponds to true (ohmic) resistance in direct current (DC) circuits. Symbolized by the letter Z, impedance is measured in ohms and is related to the voltage E and the current I by the relation $Z = E/I$. This is, in effect, a generalized version of OHM'S LAW. Impedance is the inherent RESISTANCE of the circuit as well as inductive and capacitative REACTANCE. Because the value of reactance depends on the frequency of the applied voltage, so does the impedance.

Many electronic components, such as loudspeakers, radio transmitters, and generators, are rated according to their impedances. This enables the user to match impedances easily, that is, to add components with the same impedance. Maximum power is transferred when the input impedance of one device is identical to the output impedance of the other. For example, a home television installation is composed of the receiver, antenna, and lead-in cable. Optimum reception is obtained when the antenna and cable are selected to match the impedance of the receiver. When this cannot be done, an impedance-matching transformer may be inserted between components.

A. G. ENGELHARDT

See also: ALTERNATING CURRENT; CIRCUIT, ELECTRIC.

Imperial Valley

The Imperial Valley, located mostly in southeastern California, is an irrigated portion of the COLORADO DESERT lying below sea level. Its lowest point is 71 m/232 ft below sea level. It extends south from the SALTON SEA for about 80 km (50 mi) and is about 65–100 km (40–60 mi) wide. The valley was once part of the Gulf of California, but deposits from the COLORADO RIVER gradually cut the depression off from the gulf. The soil is fertile, and the growing season is long, but because of the arid climate, agriculture was impossible until the All-American Canal (130 km/80 mi), which brings water from the Colorado River, was completed in 1940. The Imperial Valley is now a profitable farming region where cotton, alfalfa, citrus fruits, and sugar beets are grown, and livestock is raised.

imperialism

Imperialism is the policy or practice of extending national power over other states or areas of the world, often by annexing territory. Imperialism has existed in every age. The Chou and Ch'in dynasties in ancient China (c.1027–206 BC) and the Maurya in India (c.321–c.185 BC) provide early examples of empire building. Attempts by Athens to establish political and military hegemony over the Greek city-states led to its ultimate defeat in the Peloponnesian War (431–404 BC). Alexander the Great of Macedonia created an empire reaching beyond Persia in the east that signaled the end of the Greek city-state as the basic political unit of the ancient world. In the Roman Empire, policies implicit in Alexander's rule were developed further. Although Rome remained the imperial center, rights of citizenship were extended throughout the empire, in line with Stoic and Christian ideas. From AD 395 the Roman Empire was permanently divided into eastern and western halves. In the east, the Byzantine Empire remained in existence until 1453, when it finally fell victim to the expanding Ottoman (Turkish) Empire. The Roman Empire in the west collapsed in AD 476, but the imperial ideal was revived by the Frankish ruler Charlemagne, who was crowned emperor by

The imperialist powers (left to right) England, Germany, Russia, France, and Japan greedily divide China into spheres of influence in this satirical cartoon from a French journal of 1898. In the background a Chinese mandarin is powerless to prevent the slicing of the pie.

the pope in 800. This event is sometimes taken as the founding of the Holy Roman Empire, but the imperial coronation (962) of the German King Otto I marks the beginning of that entity as a continuing institution. The Holy Roman Empire survived until 1806, although it was a weak confederation for much of the time.

In 16th-century Europe, the centralization of political power in the hands of absolute monarchs was accompanied by the growth of a new social class, the bourgeoisie, or merchant class, and by the quest of European explorers for precious metals and other trade goods in the New World and the Orient. MERCANTILISM, seapower, and the establishment of powerful national armies provided impetus for a new wave of imperialism both within continental Europe and far beyond its boundaries. The Italian diplomat and political thinker Nicolò Machiavelli, writing at the beginning of the 16th century, interpreted such expansion as a natural expression of human aggression; the pursuit of power and glory, he believed, is an instinctual and inevitable drive.

The term *imperialism* is most commonly identified with 19th-century colonialism and the carving of the globe into "spheres of influence" by the European powers. One of the leading figures of 19th-century imperialism was the British financier and South African statesman Cecil Rhodes. Colonies in Asia and Africa supplied cheap labor, raw materials, and ready markets for European manufacturing, spurred on by the Industrial Revolution. They also enhanced the image of European powers; much of France's empire, for example, was acquired after its defeat by Germany in 1870. Imperialism was also linked to concepts of racial and moral supremacy, rationalized as "the White Man's Burden"—the so-called duty to bring civilization to backward peoples. In the Western Hemisphere, much of Latin America came under the sway of commercial and financial interests in the United States.

Economic imperialism, as this type of expansion is called, was first criticized severely by John A. Hobson, who viewed it as the attempt of the capitalist classes in industrial nations to achieve economic gain. Vladimir Ilich Lenin later elaborated this theory, as did subsequent Marxists. Marxist theory maintained that imperialism leading to war was the inevitable and final result of economic competition. A necessary corollary of the Marxist theory explained imperialism as a temporary phenomenon that characterized relations among capitalist states and that would be superseded by a communist world order. Marxist theory, however, fails to account for imperialism before the existence of capitalism as well as for those imperial policies that the Soviet Union subsequently pursued.

Since World War II imperialism has taken a new form. The old empires no longer exist; the former colonies have become independent states, often after prolonged national liberation struggles. The United States and the USSR have competed for

influence over these new nations, usually through economic and military aid to their governments. Direct military intervention is usually a last resort; certain prominent examples include American intervention in Vietnam and the Dominican Republic; Soviet use of Cuban troops in Africa; and the Soviet invasions of Hungary and Czechoslovakia to maintain its political hegemony in those countries. Britain and France also continue to exert economic influence over some of their former colonies in Africa, and occasionally this influence is supported by military intervention. Less developed countries decry modern economic imperialism (called neoimperialism), asserting that it seriously hampers their efforts towards economic growth and independence.   MARC SCHEINMAN

Bibliography: Boulding, Kenneth, and Mukerjee, Tapan, eds., *Economic Imperialism* (1972); Hobson, John Atkinson, *Imperialism: A Study*, 3d ed. (1948; repr. 1965); Lichtheim, George, *Imperialism* (1971); Schumpeter, Joseph, *Imperialism and Social Classes* (1919; repr. 1960); Winks, Robin W., ed., *Age of Imperialism* (1969); Wright, Harrison M., ed., *The "New Imperialism": Analysis of Late Nineteenth-Century Expansion*, 2d ed. (1976).

See also: BRITISH EMPIRE; COLONIALISM; EMPIRE; FRENCH EMPIRE.

impetigo   [im-puh-ty′-goh]

Impetigo is a skin infection that occurs predominantly in children. The causative pathogens are streptococci and staphylococci. The arms and face are most susceptible to impetigo; the legs are most susceptible to an ulcerative form, ecthyma. Both forms may follow a break in the skin or occur secondarily to DERMATITIS, insect bites, and fungus infections. The lesions progress to oozing and then become crusted. Itching is common and scratching can spread the infection. Systemic antibiotics should effect a prompt recovery.

Importance of Being Earnest, The

The Importance of Being Earnest (1895; published 1899), by Oscar WILDE, is considered by some critics the greatest comedy of modern times. A mad, witty farce peppered with brilliant epigrams, *The Importance of Being Earnest* both parodies the well-made play and satirizes Victorian earnestness. The slight and somewhat ridiculous plot hinges on mistaken identities and secrets. Two playboys, Algernon Moncrieff and Jack Worthing, court two young ladies, Cecily Cardew and Gwendolen Fairfax. The success of both suits hinges on Jack's being named Ernest—the name by which, in fact, he ultimately turns out to have been christened. Lady Bracknell and the governess Miss Prism are among the other foolish but memorable characters.   MYRON MATLAW

Bibliography: Eriksen, Donald, *Oscar Wilde* (1977); Sullivan, Kevin, *Oscar Wilde* (1972); Symons, Arthur, *Study of Oscar Wilde* (1930).

impotence

Impotence, or "erectile dysfunction," is a male's inability to attain a sufficiently strong erection to enable him satisfactorily to engage in sexual intercourse. Many males experience occasional episodes of impotence due to factors such as fatigue, distress, or the effects of excessive alcoholic intake. While organic or physiological factors may cause impotence, emotional or psychogenic factors are more common.

Primary impotence is the case in which the male has never maintained an erection of long enough duration to engage in sexual intercourse. Secondary impotence is the case in which a previously potent male loses his ability to maintain an erection for sexual intercourse. Fear of failure and performance anxiety frequently are negative psychological sources that underlie impotence.   STEPHEN P. McCARY

Bibliography: Hastings, Donald W., *Impotence and Frigidity* (1963); Kaplan, H. S., *The New Sex Therapy: Active Treatment of Sexual Dysfunctions* (1974); Masters, W. H., and Johnson, V. E., *Human Sexual Inadequacy* (1970); McCary, J. L., *McCary's Human Sexuality* (1978).

impressionism   (art)

Impressionism, the leading development in French painting in the later 19th century and a reaction against both the aca-

(Above left) Woman in White on the Beach at Trouville *(1869)* is typical of Eugène Boudin's many evocations of wind, clouds, and water. His pupil, Claude Monet, adopted Boudin's practice of painting in the open air. (Musée des Beaux-Arts, Le Havre.)

(Above right) The Bridge at Narmi *(1826)* is characteristic of the scenes that Camille Corot painted directly from nature. No landscape painter before Corot had achieved such a variety of effects solely through the study of light, and the impressionists owed much to his example. (Louvre, Paris.)

(Right) Théodore Rousseau's Landscape after the Rain *(c.1840)* portrays a magnificent but fleeting effect of light. As the leader of the Barbizon school, Rousseau did much to extend the tradition of 19th-century naturalism toward the impressionist study of color and atmosphere. (Narodni Galerie, Prague.)

(Left) Impression: Sunrise *(1872)*, by Claude Monet, first shown in 1874, caused a critic to sneer: ". . . since I am impressed it must contain some sort of impression." Although coined as a derogatory term, impressionism is an appropriate description of Monet's technique, which reduces solid forms to areas of pure color that dissolve into the single sensation of a glowing, hazy sunrise. In Monet's quest for a means to portray the experience of light, color, not form, was the primary medium of expression. (Musée Marmottan, Paris.)

In the 1890s, Monet's experiments with light led him to produce several series of paintings of the same subject seen under various atmospheric conditions. He exhibited 15 paintings of hayricks in 1891 and 6 studies of poplar trees in 1892. He rented (1892) a room overlooking Rouen Cathedral and began to study the effect of light on the west facade. These two canvases (1894) depict the building at noon (left) and at sunset (below). (Louvre, Paris.)

(Below) Unlike other impressionists, Auguste Renoir did not confine himself to painting landscapes. The Box (1874) brings impressionist traits of dissolved light to a subject that might have attracted an 18th-century baroque master. (Courtauld Institute Galleries, London.)

(Right) After experimenting with pointilism, Camille Pissarro returned in his later work to the impressionist style he had helped establish. Boulevard Montmartre (1897), portraying that Paris street on an overcast day, displays his characteristic use of controlled color tonality to evoke atmosphere. (Hermitage, Leningrad.)

In his later work, such as
Landscape with a Viaduct
(c.1895) at right, Paul Cézanne
invested his subjects with an
element of geometric design that
has often been regarded as a
foreshadowing of abstract art.
Although his membership of the
impressionist group is sometimes
forgotten, it was from Camille
Pissarro and his colleagues that
Cézanne learned to achieve
naturalistic immediacy by
painting directly from nature.
Living a hermitlike existence in
the town of Aix-en-Provence,
Cézanne constantly returned to
the task of portraying natural
objects, shaping the forms and
colors of reality to his unique
perception—as in Still Life with a
Curtain (1898-99) below.
(Hermitage, Leningrad.)

(Bottom) Alfred Sisley's
landscapes are among the most
serene of impressionist works.
Flood at the Port of Marly (1876)
is a masterly treatment of the
subtle tones of cloud and water.
(Musée de l'Impressionisme, Paris.)

(Above) Ballerina Posing for a Photograph (c.1879), one of Edgar
Degas's series of dancers, exemplifies the linearity and distinct form
that distinguishes his work from that of the other impressionists, as his
treatment of interiors contrasts with the landscapes preferred by the
other members of the movement. Degas captured the motion of his
subjects with bold color and perspective. (Poesjkinmuseum, Moscow.)

(Left) *Paul Gauguin's* Rocks by the Sea *(1886) is typical of his early work, in which his handling of light, color, and atmosphere reflects the work of the early impressionists. Following the last impressionist exhibition in 1886, Gauguin, during a sojourn in Brittany, developed the expressive use of color that characterizes his later work. He was one of the major figures of the postimpressionist movement. (Kunstmuseum, Göteborg, Sweden.)*

(Below) Van Gogh Painting Sunflowers *(1888) is characteristic of Gauguin's mature style, in which increasingly abstract representations of nature are expressed in blocks of flat color. By fragmenting the natural world into planes, contours, and angles, Gauguin became a seminal figure in the development of modern art, exerting an influence on later artists, such as Matisse and Kandinsky. (Van Gogh Museum, Amsterdam.)*

(Above) *In 1877, Mary Cassatt, a Pennsylvania-born American living in Paris, was invited by Edgar Degas to exhibit her paintings with the group later called the impressionists.* The Box at the Opera *(1880), with its informal pose and asymmetric composition, is characteristic of her lifelong interest in social scenes and reveals her debt to the style of Degas. (Museum of Fine Arts, Boston.)*

(Right) *Berthe Morisot was the only woman painter to show her work at the first impressionist exhibition in 1874.* The Butterfly Chase *(1874), a lyrical, sunlit scene, reveals her admiration for the later landscapes of Corot. Morisot became Édouard Manet's sister-in-law and encouraged him to paint outdoors. (Musée de l'Impressionisme, Paris).*

(Left) *Édouard Manet's* Bar at the Folies Bergère *(1881–82) is a masterpiece of impressionist naturalism. Muted reflections and a wealth of closely observed detail soften Manet's characteristic aloofness. (Courtauld Institute Galleries, London).*

(Below) *Georges Seurat's* The Models *(1887–88) epitomizes the "scientific impressionism" known as pointilism, divisionism, or neoimpressionism. Tiny dots of pigment both intensify and diffuse light to create shimmering mosaics of color. (Merion, Barnes Foundation, Pa.)*

(Bottom) *Vincent van Gogh's* Small House of Vincent at Arles *(1888) exemplifies the vigorous rhythm, brilliant color, and expressive power characteristic of his late work. Van Gogh is one of the greatest artists of the postimpressionist period. (Stedelijk Museum, Amsterdam.)*

(Above) *Whereas Monet had approached impressionism from his studies of nature, Manet's early painting owed much to his interest both in the flat perspectives of Japanese woodcuts and in the portraiture of Diego Velásquez. The* Balcony *(1868) resolved these disparate influences in its coolly elegant use of stark silhouette, large areas of color, and sharply contrasted tones. This painting, one of those for which Berthe Morisot posed, reveals the influence of Spanish art on Manet's style and composition. (Louvre, Paris.)*

demic tradition and romanticism, refers principally to the work of Claude MONET, Pierre Auguste RENOIR, and other artists associated with them, such as Camille PISSARRO and Alfred SISLEY, who shared a common approach to the rendering of outdoor subjects. Impressionism also refers to the work of artists who participated in a series of group exhibitions in Paris, the first and most famous of which was held from April 15 to May 15, 1874, at the studio of the photographer NADAR. The artists represented at the exhibition, or in the succeeding ones held by the group between 1876 and 1886, included Paul CÉZANNE, Edgar DEGAS, Jean Baptiste Armand GUILLAUMIN, Berthe MORISOT, and, after 1879, Paul GAUGUIN and the American artist Mary CASSATT.

The term *impressionism* was derived from a painting by Claude Monet—*Impression: Sunrise* (1872; Musée Marmottan, Paris), a view of the port of Le Havre in the mist—and was coined for the group by the unfriendly critic Louis Leroy. Monet probably intended the title to refer to the sketchy, unfinished look of the work, similar to receiving an impression of something on the basis of an exposure that is partially obscured and incomplete in its detail. The term, however, was quickly taken up by sympathetic critics, who used it in an alternative sense to mean the impression stamped on the senses by a visual experience that is rapid and transitory, associated with a particular moment in time. Monet, Renoir, Pissarro, and Sisley were impressionists in the latter sense; beginning in the later 1860s and culminating in 1872–75, they chose to paint outdoors (*en plein air*), recording the rapidly changing conditions of light and atmosphere as well as their individual sensations before nature. They used high-key colors and a variety of brushstrokes, which allowed them to be responsive both to the material character and texture of the object in nature and to the impact of light on its surfaces.

If the term *impressionism* is used to indicate a concern for contemporary subject matter of an informal and pleasurable kind—especially aspects of the social life of Paris and its environs—and an accompanying technique and organization that gives an impression of casualness or spontaneity, then it includes not only the work of Degas and Morisot, but also that of Édouard MANET. He did not exhibit with the group, but works such as his *Déjeuner sur l'herbe* (1863; Louvre, Paris) had an important influence on the younger painters during the 1860s. During the early 1870s, Manet was on friendly terms with the impressionists and adopted some of the same outdoor subjects.

Finally, when impressionism is extended to cover the early work of Gauguin and Cassatt, it reflects an influence of impressionism on a slightly younger group of artists, in their color range, brushwork, and approach to nature.

By the early 1880s the feeling of cohesiveness that had originally brought the impressionists together had begun to dissolve under the pressure of factions and rivalries. The sense of a shared approach to nature among the landscape painters had also dissolved by then, so that each artist increasingly took his own individual direction. At the same time, impressionism was beginning to have a tremendous impact, both on French painting generally and also on the art of other countries; this continued well into the 20th century. Either directly or through the intermediacy of the developments of the 1880s, such as NEOIMPRESSIONISM and POSTIMPRESSIONISM, impressionism influenced modern art in such fundamental features as a loosening up of brushwork, which abolished finally the traditional distinction between the finished painting and the preliminary sketch or study; a concern for the two-dimensional surface of a painting, which is defined by the patterns and feeling of movement of the paint on the ground; and a use of pure, bright colors, often taken directly from the tube. Concurrently, the members of the original group were extending in new and highly personal directions their original commitments as impressionists and their particular pictorial concerns. These developments in the latter part of their careers do not form part of impressionism, but represent a logical outgrowth, a carrying of its interests into new dimensions of technique and content.

MARK ROSKILL

Bibliography: Bazin, Germain, *French Impressionists Painting in the Louvre*, trans. by S. Cunliff-Owen (1958); Blunden, Maria and Godfrey, *Impressionists and Impressionism*, trans. by James Emmons (1972); Bowness, Alan, *Impressionists and Post-Impressionists* (1965); Dayez-Distel, Anne, et al., *Impressionism: A Centenary Exhibition* (1974); Dustan, Bernard, *Painting Methods of the Impressionists* (1976); Kelder, Diane, *The French Impressionists and Their Century* (1970); Leymarie, Jean, *Impressionism*, 2 vols., trans. by James Emmons (1955); Mathey, François, *The Impressionists*, trans. by Jean Steinberg (1961); Nochlin, Linda, *Impressionism and Post-Impressionism, 1874–1904: Sources and Documents in the History of Art* (1966); Pool, Phoebe, *Impressionism* (1967); Rewald, John, *The History of Impressionism*, 4th rev. ed. (1973).

impressionism   (music)

Impressionism, a term originally applied to a style of French painting, refers in music to a style introduced by Claude DEBUSSY in the 1890s. The essential characteristic of an impressionist composer is his desire to evoke moods. Although it differs from the romantic composer's desire to express feelings or to illustrate a story, impressionism is not far removed from PROGRAM MUSIC, for it too usually depends upon a title that will suggest the desired mood or atmosphere.

A composition in the impressionist style typically uses short melodic fragments or motives, and repeats them in whatever order enhances the desired mood. The motives often consist of patterns derived from pentatonic (5-tone) or whole-tone scales, as opposed to the standard major and minor scales. The impressionist composer likes to use 7th or 9th chords or chromatically altered chords, allowing them to move in parallel lines and leaving dissonances unresolved. The composer thus avoids the effect of tension-and-release found at cadence points in earlier music and establishes instead an elusive, indistinct musical structure. In impressionist piano music blurred harmonies produced by the use of the damper pedal are combined with the elements described above to create the veiled impressions on which the style depends.

Notable examples of musical impressionism include Debussy's *Prelude to the Afternoon of a Faun* (1894), the three *Nocturnes* for orchestra (1899), the opera *Pelléas et Mélisande* (1902), the orchestral suite *La Mer* (1905), and several of the *Préludes* (1910–13) for piano. Another leading impressionist composer was Maurice RAVEL.   HOMER ULRICH

Bibliography: Austin, William W., *Music in the Twentieth Century* (1966); Grout, Donald J., *A History of Western Music*, rev. ed. (1973); Hill, Edward B., *Modern French Music* (1924; repr. 1969); Palmer, Christopher, *Impressionism in Music* (1973).

imprinting

Through the process of imprinting, an instinctive behavior pattern, the young of a species rapidly learn to recognize and follow a member of their own species, typically the mother, or another object. This phenomenon takes place early in life, within a prescribed period; if the typical object of attachment (the mother) is not present within this period, the responses are oriented toward another object, usually a living organism.

Certain birds, such as ducks, geese, chickens, and turkeys, are precocial, meaning that they are able to leave the nest soon after they are hatched. By INSTINCT they begin to follow the first object they see, most often the mother, and they continue to do so until they are almost adults. If the mother is absent during the critical period for imprinting, the chicks will follow almost any conspicuous object, such as a decoy or a human being. The variety of objects that chicks are willing to follow is extensive, although not all objects are equally effective. For example, an adult duck is more effective as an object of attachment than is another duckling. The "following" behavior is more likely to occur if exposure to the moving object occurs within some relatively restricted time period. Ducks have an imprinting period only hours in length, with peak effectiveness about 13–16 hours after hatching. The range of new objects that are capable of eliciting the following response narrows toward the end of this period until only those objects previously experienced are recognized and followed. Imprinting, which involves species or object recognition, takes place only during this brief critical period.

The Austrian ethologist Konrad Lorenz used the term imprinting *to describe the way in which certain newly hatched birds follow the first moving object—usually the mother—they see. These greylag goslings were imprinted on Lorenz, now their mother substitute.*

Imprinting is considered to be the basis for a long-lasting dependence on the mother. Some animals, such as sheep, separate themselves from the rest of the herd when they deliver their young; this separation ensures that the infant will imprint on its mother rather than on another member of the flock. The attachment persists long after the critical period is over.

If the infant becomes attached to an artificial or unnatural object during this critical time, it may not be able to respond to its own mother at a later period. For example, if a young duckling becomes imprinted to an artificial object, such as a decoy, it will later reject the natural maternal attentions of a brood duck. Imprinting is not limited to visual stimuli; vocal sounds also have proved effective.

Imprinting begins after the newborn animal can move about. Attachment is weak if the object that the young follow does not move. The sensitive period possibly ends either with the natural loss of the following tendency because of maturation or with the development of fear responses to strong stimuli as discrimination improves. Human babies, when they are several months old, often exhibit such fear responses to strangers.

A newborn learns quickly what is predictable and stable in the environment and what is unpredictable or novel. When it learns to recognize physical properties of the objects it encounters—such as size, shape, and permanence—it can separate the familiar from the strange. Being in familiar surroundings is pleasant and comforting to the infant.

Konrad LORENZ, the Nobel laureate who studied imprinting extensively, described it as distinct from ordinary learning because imprinting can take place only during a narrowly defined period of the individual's life whereas learning is a lifelong process. He noted that once imprinted on a substitute object such as a person, the animal always responds to it as it would to another of its own species; in other words, imprinting is irreversible. Finally, Lorenz found that imprinting does not depend, as ordinary learning does, on the effects of reinforcement through rewards and punishments, and therefore it does not follow the expected pattern of ordinary learned behavior.

Contrary to Lorenz's assertion, other studies have demonstrated that the irreversibility of imprinting does not always apply. Chicks, for example, lose the following response after prolonged habituation to an artificial stimulus. Mallards that were strongly imprinted on a box ceased to follow it within ten days; coots ceased to follow an imprinted object after they became juveniles. The following response is maintained only if it proves rewarding to the young.

Lorenz has also demonstrated the possibility that sexual selectivity is learned during imprinting. When birds such as jackdaws are imprinted on a human being, at maturity they display sexually instinctive behavior toward humans other than the imprinted person. This may possibly be the way that an animal chooses members of the same species other than its parents with which to reproduce.   ARTHUR J. RIOPELLE

Bibliography: Hess, Eckhard H., *Imprinting: Early Experience and the Developmental Psychobiology of Attachment* (1973); Nevin, John, ed., *The Study of Behavior: Learning, Motivation, Emotion and Instinct* (1973); Sluckin, Wladyslaw, *Early Learning in Man and Animal* (1970) and *Imprinting and Early Learning* (1965).

improvisational and experimental theater

Improvisational and experimental theater can be traced back at least as far as the commedia dell'arte productions in 16th-century Italy, though elements of improvisation no doubt occurred in primitive rain dances centuries earlier. One of the greatest experimenters of the 20th century was the Russian director Vsevolod MEYERHOLD, originally one of Stanislavsky's colleagues; he looked for innovative scenic effects, introduced circus elements, and formulated a new approach to theatrical performance that he called biomechanics. Like Meyerhold, the German Bauhaus artists in the 1920s were entranced with the image of the machine.

The French actor Antonin ARTAUD proclaimed an irrational theater, a theater of dreams and of spectacle that came to be known as the theater of cruelty. Artaud and Jerzy GROTOWSKI have been two of the most influential forces on younger experimenters. Grotowski's emphasis on the performer as a physical being, as exemplified in the work of his POLISH LABORATORY THEATER, has sown seeds throughout Western Europe and also influenced such American groups as the LIVING THEATRE, the Open Theater, the Firehouse Theater, the Performance Group, and the Manhattan Project.   ARTHUR SAINER

Bibliography: Croyden, Margaret, *Lunatics, Lovers and Poets: The Contemporary Experimental Theatre* (1974); Roose-Evans, James, *Experimental Theatre: From Stanislavsky to Today*, rev. ed. (1974).

impulse, specific: see SPECIFIC IMPULSE.

Imru' al-Qais   [im'-ruhl-kays]

Considered the greatest pre-Islamic Arabic poet, Imru' al-Qais ibn Hujr al-Kindi, fl. AD c.540, used personal love experiences and descriptive detail to bring to life the stereotyped genre of the qasidah (ode). When his father, Hujr, king of the Banu Kinda, was assassinated, Imru' al-Qais expressed his grief in moving poetry and forswore wine and love until he had taken revenge on the murderers.   ILSE LICHTENSTADTER

Bibliography: Lichtenstadter, Ilse, *Introduction to Classical Arabic Literature* (1974); Najib, Ullah, *Islamic Literature* (1963); Nicholson, Reynold A., *A Literary History of the Arabs* (1907; repr. 1969).

Inca   [ink'-uh]

The Incas were the rulers of the largest native empire of the Americas. Near the end of the 14th century the empire began to expand from its initial base in the CUZCO region of the southern Andes mountains of South America. It ended abruptly with the Spanish invasion led by Francisco PIZARRO in 1532. At the time of its demise the empire controlled an estimated 12 million people in much of what is now Peru and Ecuador as well as in large parts of Chile, Bolivia, and Argentina.

INCA EMPIRE

The Incas called their land *Tawantinsuyu,* which in QUECHUA, the Inca language, means the "four parts." A land of markedly diverse terrain and climate, it included a long coastal desert strip, broken by rich irrigated valleys; the high peaks and deep fertile valleys of the Andes; and the mountainous edges of the tropical forest to the east. The term *Inca* refers to the ruler himself as well as to the people of the valley of Cuzco, the capital of the empire. It is sometimes used to refer to all of the peoples included within Tawantinsuyu, but this is not strictly correct. Most of the dozens of smaller local kingdoms retained their identities even though politically and economi-

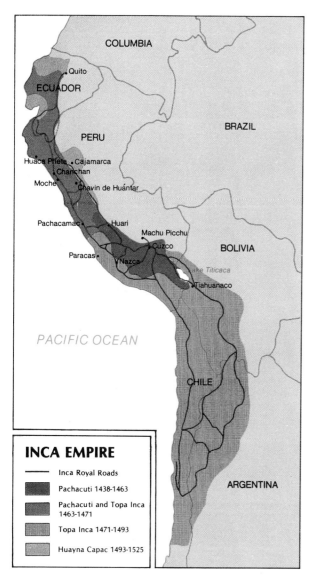

INCA EMPIRE

— Inca Royal Roads

▓ Pachacuti 1438-1463

▓ Pachacuti and Topa Inca 1463-1471

▓ Topa Inca 1471-1493

▓ Huayna Capac 1493-1525

(Above) *Shaded areas indicate the expansion of the Inca empire's borders under a progression of rulers between 1438 and 1525. Also located are the major centers of Inca culture and the sophisticated network of roads, called* capac nan, *that linked them.*

counts set down by the Spanish, the empire achieved about two-thirds of its final size under Pachacuti. Although Pachacuti's reign was a long one, the conquest was achieved extremely rapidly considering the limited means of transportation and communication available to the Incas. The wheel was not employed, and the horse did not exist here.

The expansion was achieved in part as the result of a program of conquests by the Inca armies. The battles of conquest were frequently brutal invasions of neighboring territories by which strong resistance was crushed. Not all of the groups were brought into the realm by direct military action, however. Some joined in alliances with the Incas as the result of peaceful overtures from the expanding state. Others joined out of fear that military intervention would result if an invitation to peaceful alliance were rejected.

About 1470 the Incas captured the rich and powerful CHIMU kingdom on the north coast of what is now Peru. With that major conquest won, little remained to challenge Inca expansion throughout what then constituted the "civilized world" of South America. Pachacuti's sons helped to complete the conquests. The heir Topa Inca (r. 1471-93) pressed on to the northern border of present-day Ecuador before ascending the throne. During his reign the south coast of Peru was conquered (1476), as was northern Chile, much of northwestern Argentina, and a portion of the Bolivian plateau. In parts of this vast territory, notably along the south coast of Peru, the price of conquest was high; great losses on both sides and the virtual extinction of local groups resulted. In addition, rebellions that sprang up periodically among previously conquered peoples had to be quelled.

In the last years before the Spanish invasion the Incas were still expanding in the north. HUAYNA CAPAC (r. 1493-1527), father of the last Inca ruler ATAHUALPA, was ruling the empire from his northern outpost in QUITO at his death in 1527.

Collapse of the Empire. It is theorized that, though still expanding when the Spanish arrived, the Inca empire was approaching a series of geopolitical limits that would preclude further expansion. Inca rule was predicated on a relatively stable sedentary life that provided both a system for political control and the basis around which the production of the goods needed to sustain the state could be organized. Inca incursion into the eastern jungles and other lightly populated areas was never successful; the effort required to exert control was too great, and the resources were not sufficiently concentrated to be easily mobilized.

The death of Huayna Capac plunged the Inca state into civil war. No fixed system for determining the succession of rulers appears to have been set up. Atahualpa, who had been with his father in the north, claimed that Huayna Capac had

(Below) *Atahualpa (left) and his brother Huáscar (right), the sons of Lord Inca Huayna Capac, plunged the empire into a bloody civil war. Atahualpa, an experienced military leader, vanquished Huáscar but was himself overthrown in 1532 by the Spanish conquistador Pizarro.*

cally subject to the Incas. Quechua was the official language and was spoken in most of the realm by the time the Spanish arrived, but at least 20 local languages persisted in various parts of the empire.

Origins. The early period of the empire is shrouded in mystery. An official version of early Incan history was told to the Spanish invaders, but it is difficult to separate actual historical events from the myth and legends with which they were mixed. The Inca empire probably started out as a small kingdom, similar to many others in the Andes during the 14th century. A powerful state centered at HUARI, in the vicinity of what is now Ayacucho, Peru, and well to the north of Cuzco, had apparently controlled the area several centuries earlier, but by the 10th century small feuding kingdoms dominated the scene. The reasons for the Incas' earliest triumphs over their neighbors are impossible to discern from existing sources. It is not known for certain whether MANCO CAPAC, listed as the founding ruler, was a historical personage.

Territorial Expansion. The Incas began their remarkable territorial expansion under PACHACUTI (r. 438-71). According to ac-

The Lord Inca Atahualpa (center) was unsuccessful in his attempt to evade being captured by the Spanish near Cajamarca. Although the Inca's subjects paid a ransom in gold and silver for his freedom, Atahualpa was put to death in 1533.

decided to divide the kingdom, setting up a new northern capital at Quito that Atahualpa would rule. His brother Huáscar claimed from Cuzco to be the legitimate ruler of the entire realm. Atahualpa finally won the bloody war and was on his way to Cuzco in 1532 to claim the whole kingdom when the Spanish conquistador Francisco Pizarro arrived. The Incas allowed Pizarro and a contingent of about 150 soldiers to enter the regional capital at Cajamarca, where Atahualpa and his army were camped. The Spaniards were able to take the Inca ruler captive and assured the collapse of the empire.

INCA CULTURE

The sketchy 16th-century written accounts of the Incas do not provide a very complete understanding of the economic and political organization of their state. It is clear, however, that the principles of Inca economics and politics were derived from old Andean traditions and were very different from European ones.

State Organization. The Inca state was not a monolith under the absolute control of its ruler. It was an amalgam of dozens, if not hundreds, of different political, ethnic, and even linguistic groups. In order to maintain unity within the empire, an attempt was made to introduce uniform organizational and administrative procedures to the realm. This process, however, was far from complete in 1532, and administrative practices varied greatly from one part of the empire to another. In some places members of the Inca elite came from Cuzco to exercise direct control over local peoples; in others the pre-Inca scheme of leadership was left relatively intact and a form of indirect rule was pursued. The threat of military force was probably always an important element in the control of the hinterlands.

An unusual characteristic of the Inca state was its ability to move people about the empire as "colonists" far from their homes. This custom of internal colonization allowed the Incas to place loyal groups in regions that were difficult to control. The practice also appears to have had economic aims in some cases; people could be relocated to develop new lands, new mines, or other resources. This use of colonists to exploit the Andean landscape was an old tradition that the Incas merely expanded to a state scale.

Politics and economics were not really separate for the Incas. The role of markets was very limited, and the exchange of many products was carried out through political channels. The exchanges were seen as gifts and favors, and purely economic value was not independent of the social and political positions of the people between whom goods and services passed. Leaders maintained their power by providing gifts of luxury goods and elaborate entertainment. The people re-

These drawings of officials in the Inca bureaucracy appear in Felipe Huaman Poma de Ayala's illustrated history of the Inca empire, which also includes detailed information regarding the Spanish conquest and subjugation of the Incas. A translation of Ayala's text, giving the position or describing the duties of these officials, appears at the bottom of each illustration. (Royal Library, Copenhagen.)

The palace mayor in Hanan Cuzco

The grand alguazil in Hurin Cuzco

The provincial corregidor

The provincial administrator

The royal courier (Hatun Chasqui)

The inspector of the roads

The inspector of the bridges

The secretary of the Inca

The traveling inspector of the Empire

The Tahuantinsuyu supreme council

(Below) *This 16th-century* kero, *a large wooden goblet used in Inca religious ceremonies, is decorated with the face of an* Orejon, *or Inca noble. The ritual beaker is also incised with geometric patterns and painted with mastic, a colored resin obtained from sumac trees.*

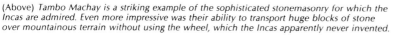

(Above) *Tambo Machay is a striking example of the sophisticated stonemasonry for which the Incas are admired. Even more impressive was their ability to transport huge blocks of stone over mountainous terrain without using the wheel, which the Incas apparently never invented.*

turned the favors by providing their leaders with labor. Such labor provided the Inca state with its "tax" revenues. A census of the male population was held regularly in connection with labor conscription.

Perhaps the greatest achievement of the Incas lay in their efficient mobilization and organization of the state's labor force into armies of conquest, a class of bureaucrats, and attendants for the ruling class. Of greater long-term importance, however, was the planning and execution of construction projects that increased production and improved the management of resources. Most of the technologies used by the Incas were improvements on innovations dating from several centuries earlier, but the Incas wedded their organizational skills to these existing techniques and produced a series of remarkable public works.

Architecture. The Incas developed a highly functional style of public architecture distinguished above all by its superior engineering techniques and fine stone masonry. The plan of their cities was based on a system of broad avenues intersected by smaller streets that converge on an open square lined by state buildings and temples. Structures were usually single-storied, with perfectly bonded joints of cut stone, although adobe bricks and plaster were commonly used in the coastal lowlands. For building large monuments such as the great fortress of SACSAHUAMAN near Cuzco, massive polygonal blocks were fitted together with extraordinary precision. In mountainous regions, as at the spectacularly situated Andean citadel of MACHU PICCHU, Inca architecture often reflects ingenious adaptations to the surrounding land forms. (See PRE COLUMBIAN ART AND ARCHITECTURE.)

Road System. Approximately 20,000 km (12,000 mi) of Inca roads constituted a transportation network rivaled only by that of the Romans in the pre-industrial world. Since the Incas did not utilize the wheel, the road system did not serve vehicular traffic, only pedestrians and the llamas they used to carry cargo. Levees were constructed across swamps in many areas, steps were carved into hillsides, and bridges of several types were built across rivers and streams. Two so-called royal roads were built, by which the rulers could travel the length of the empire—one near the coast and one through the An-

dean highland. These roads were fed by many lateral routes. As important as the roads themselves were the administrative and service centers that were built along them. On principal roads a way station was located at the end of each day's travel so that travelers could rest and get fresh supplies. On parts of the highland road, at the Peruvian sites of Tambo Colorado in the Pisco valley and at Huanuco Viejo, near modern Huanuco, several enormous administrative centers with more than 3,000 buildings each were constructed to house the bureaucracy, state manufacturing and storage facilities, and related activities.

Agricultural Production. Increases in agricultural production were achieved through the construction of large-scale terracing and irrigation systems. Many highland valleys—most notably the Urubamba, near Cuzco—were completely reshaped with terraces. By converting steep slopes to flat fields, terraces substantially increased the amount of tillable land. In warm, dry valleys irrigation systems were built into the terraces, bringing these valuable lands into production. Maize grew well in such warm areas, and maize and the beer made from it were luxury foods served by the state on ceremonial occasions. The increased production of these and other foods was important in giving the state access to an ever-increasing labor surplus, in turn leading to more craft specialization. Irrigation systems were especially important in the coastal desert regions of the empire, but most of the systems there were built long before the Incas had conquered the region.

Storage and Recordkeeping. Storage was another technological and organizational achievement of the Incas that enabled them to maintain a stable food supply in spite of a climate that resulted in frequent crop failures, especially in the highlands. Some of the administrative centers along the roads had food storage facilities that held as much as a million bushels of grains and tubers. Some of the thousands of storehouses throughout the realm had specialized ventilation systems, and many were placed at high altitudes to take advantage of the cool temperatures that extended storage life.

The Incas did not have writing as we know it. But the *quipu*—a recording device by which numbers were represented in the form of knotted strings—was developed to considerable complexity. The Inca numerical system employed a base of ten. *Quipu* frequently had hundreds of strings in different colors, enabling the Incas to keep accurate account of the goods in their storehouses, census and manpower figures for various parts of the realm, and other information.

Religion. The state religion centered on the worship of the Sun. The Inca emperors were believed descended from the Sun god and were worshiped as divine beings. Gold, the symbol of the Sun god, was extensively mined for use by the rulers and members of the elite, not as a means of exchange but principally for decorative and ritual purposes.

Religion permeated the entire political structure. From the Temple of the Sun in the center of Cuzco imaginary lines ran to shrines (*huacas*) in and around the city that were identified with different social groups. Religious practices included the consultation of oracles, the offering of sacrifices, religious trances, and public confessions. An annual cycle of religious festivals was regulated by the extremely accurate Inca calendar, as was the agricultural year. In this and other respects, Inca culture strongly resembled certain cultures of MESOAMERICA, such as the AZTECS and the MAYAS.

AFTERMATH OF SPANISH CONQUEST
After the Spanish captured and killed Atahualpa, the decline of the Inca state was swift. Although resistance to the invaders continued in several places, effective native rule ceased immediately, and the fabric of the state quickly disintegrated.

Manco Inca, a half brother and enemy of Atahualpa who had collaborated with the Spanish, became a puppet ruler. He had no real power, however, and was abused by the Europeans. In 1536 he left Cuzco for Vitcos, on the edge of the jungle, where he set up a retreat inaccessible to the Spanish. There he tried to maintain the customs of the Incas and to set up a base for reconquest. In spite of some military successes and near-successes, Manco's aim was not to be achieved. After his death his son, Sayri Tupac, negotiated capitulation in exchange for personal concessions and returned to Cuzco in 1558. Resistance continued under other Inca descendants, ending in 1572 with the execution of Tupac Amaru.

Some of the Inca regional capitals along the roads were converted to Spanish towns; others were abandoned within a few years of the arrival of the Spanish. The colonial governments that replaced Tawantinsuyu were very different from that of the Incas, and much of the native population was reduced to servitude. It is easier, however, to topple a government than to alter the customs and traditions of a people. The Quechua language is today spoken by millions of Indians in the Andes region. Many native customs continued during centuries of European domination, especially in isolated parts of the Andes, and some are still maintained.   CRAIG MORRIS

Bibliography: Baudin, Louis, *Daily Life in Peru under the Last Incas*, trans. by Winifred Bradford (1961); Bingham, Hiram, *Lost City of the Incas* (1948; repr. 1969); Hemming, John, *The Conquest of the Incas* (1970); Lumbreras, Luis G. *The Peoples and Cultures of Ancient Peru*, trans. by Betty Meggers (1974); Markham, Sir Clements R., *The Incas of Peru*, 2d ed. (1912; repr. 1969); Mason, J. Alden, *Ancient Civilizations of Peru*, rev. ed. (1968); Métraux, Alfred, *The History of the Incas*, trans. by George Ordish (1969); Moore, S. F., *Power and Property in Inca Peru* (1958); Prescott, William H., *History of the Conquest of Peru*, 2 vols. (1847; repr. 1942); Rowe, John H., "Inca Culture at the Time of the Spanish Conquest" in Steward, Julian H., ed., *The Handbook of South American Indians*, vol. 2 (1946); Von Hagen, Victor W., ed., *The Incas of Pedro de Cieza de León* (1976).

incandescent lamp   [in-kan-des'-ent]

The incandescent LAMP is a device for producing light by passing an electric current through a metallic filament, thereby heating the filament to a high temperature. The filament is placed inside an evacuated bulb, which is attached to the lamp base.

Although light is desired in the visible spectrum, quantities of infrared and some ultraviolet are also produced, decreasing the luminous efficiency. The efficiency, in lumens per watt, may be increased by raising the temperature of the filament, since more of the output energy is transferred from the infrared to the visible spectrum. The first lamps, produced in 1880

by Thomas EDISON, used carbonized strips of bamboo for the filament; since carbon has a high melting point—3,598° C (6,510° F)—it evaporates or sublimates from the solid phase much below this temperature, and early carbon lamps had to be operated at a lower temperature to prolong their life. Osmium, with a melting point at 2,700° C (4,890° F), and tantalum, with a melting point at 2,900° C (5,250° F), were later used for filaments, but ductile tungsten superseded these metals when it became available in 1912. Since tungsten melts only at 3,382° C (6,120° F), it operates at a higher temperature and emits a much whiter light.

Tungsten for filaments is formed into coils to concentrate the radiating surface. The luminous efficiency is about 22 lumens per watt, although short-life photoflood lamps reach 35.8 lumens per watt. Vaporization of tungsten causes blackening of the bulb, and inert gas is added to most lamps to reduce this evaporation. A variety of bulb shapes is used, with clear, colored, or frosted glass to reduce glare. Reflective material and lenses can be added for beam control.

J. D. RYDER

Bibliography: American Institute of Physics, *Incandescent Lamp* (1975); Cox, James, *A Century of Light* (1978); Henderson, S. T., and Marsden, A. M., eds., *Lamps and Lighting*, 2d ed. (1972).

incarnation

Incarnation denotes the embodiment of a deity in human form. The idea occurs frequently in mythology. In ancient times, certain people, especially kings and priests, were often believed to be divinities. In Hinduism, VISHNU is believed to have taken nine incarnations, or AVATARS. For Christians, the incarnation is a central dogma referring to the belief that the eternal son of God, the second person of the Trinity, became man in the person of JESUS CHRIST. The incarnation was defined as a doctrine only after long struggles by early church councils. The Council of Nicaea (325) defined the deity of Christ against ARIANISM; the Council of Constantinople (381) defined the full humanity of the incarnate Christ against APOLLINARIANISM; the Council of Ephesus (431) defined the unity of Christ's person against NESTORIANISM; and the Council of Chalcedon (451) defined the two natures of Christ, divine and human, against EUTYCHES.   REGINALD H. FULLER

Bibliography: Hick, John, ed., *The Myth of God Incarnate* (1977); Robinson, J. A. T., *The Human Face of God* (1973).

incense cedar   [in'-sens see'-dur]

Incense cedar, *Libocedrus decurrens*, in the cypress family, Cupressaceae, is an evergreen tree with cinnamon red bark, found in the forests of the Pacific coast of the U.S. It prefers moist habitats and tolerates shade. The close-grained, reddish wood is durable and is used to make posts, shingles, ties, and lead pencils. Incense cedar contains thymoquinone, which may cause contact dermatitis.   DIANNE FAHSELT

incest   [in'-sest]

Incest is prohibited sexual relations between members of the same KINSHIP group. It is almost universally proscribed between unmarried members of the NUCLEAR FAMILY (between siblings or between parents and children). In many cultures the definition of incest includes other relatives also, although which ones varies from society to society.

Most social scientists believe that the primary purpose of the prohibition, often called the incest TABOO, is to protect the nuclear family from the consequences of sexual rivalry and jealousy. The taboo is linked with the rule of EXOGAMY, which requires marriage outside of one's family. Besides reinforcing the incest prohibition, this rule prevents families from becoming culturally ingrown and encapsulated through perpetual ENDOGAMY, or marriage within specified segments of a society. Marriage to relatives outside the nuclear family is common in a number of cultures, however, and it is no longer widely believed that the incest prohibition serves principally to guard against inbreeding as a negative biological consequence of incest.

Some societies permit explicit, rare exceptions to the incest prohibition for cultural reasons. Such exceptions have included brother-sister marriage among the royal families in ancient Egypt, among the INCA, and in traditional Hawaiian society. Unpermitted violations of the incest prohibition occur with varying frequency in all societies.   JAMES LOWELL GIBBS, JR.

Bibliography: Maisch, Herbert, *Incest*, ed. by Fernando Henriques, trans., by Colin Bearne (1973); Master, R. E., *Patterns of Incest* (1963); Weinberg, S. K., *Incest Behavior*, 4th ed. (1966).

Inchon   [in-chahn]

Inchon (Chemulpo), a city on the Yellow Sea approximately 30 km (20 mi) from Seoul, is South Korea's most important port. It has a population of 799,982 (1975). Inchon's industries include shipping, iron and steel mills, chemical plants, a petroleum refinery, fisheries, and lumber and textile mills. Salt is manufactured on nearby tidal flats. Opened to international trade in 1883, Inchon was occupied by the Japanese from 1905 to 1945. During the KOREAN WAR, United Nations troops landed there on Sept. 15, 1950, and successfully halted the North Korean advance into the south.

inchworm

The inchworm, or measuring worm, is the larva of any member of the moth family Geometridae (from the Greek "earth measurer"). The legs and prolegs are only at the front and hind ends of the larvae's slender bodies, so that crawling is accomplished by pulling the hind end forward and then extending the front in a series of vertical loops. Many species, for protection, strongly resemble twigs, and some cause serious damage to the trees they feed on.   ALEXANDER B. KLOTS

incinerator   [in-sin'-ur-ayt-ur]

The incinerator is a device used to burn waste material. It may be composed of a single combustion chamber, or of multiple chambers that provide for more efficient combustion of wastes and less air pollution. HEAT EXCHANGERS such as a water wall can use the incinerator heat to produce steam. Fluidized beds burn wastes in a bed of sand suspended in air and can produce clean, high-pressure gases suitable to drive gas turbines and generate electricity.

As concern about air pollution increased in the 1960s, the use of incinerators decreased, but as techniques for air-pollution control have advanced, as urban land available for landfill disposal has decreased, and as energy costs have risen, more communities again are using incinerators not only for waste disposal, but also to produce steam useful for heating and even for electricity.   JOHN RANDOLPH

inclinometer   [in-klin-ahm'-uht-ur]

The inclinometer is a mechanical instrument composed of a vertical divided circle and a magnetic needle, freely suspended from a horizontal pivot. With careful adjustment, the instrument measures the dip or inclination of the Earth's magnetic field to the local horizontal. The instrument can also compare the altitude of an aircraft relative to the horizon.   DOUGLAS M. CONSIDINE

income, national

National income may be defined broadly as the sum of all the incomes in an economy resulting from the production of goods and services in any given year. Estimates of the national income accounts help to provide a general picture of the operation of the economic system; they show the total value of goods and services produced within the economy and the amounts of the national income that are consumed, saved, and invested. National income accounts also show the interrelationship of households, government, and INTERNATIONAL TRADE within the national economy. This is done by dividing the economy into four sectors, each with its own income and expenditure accounts: (1) producers, (2) households, (3) government, and (4) the foreign sector. Each of

these sectors represents a group of transactors—buyers and sellers; the account of each sector shows the transactors' receipts of income on the right side and their outlays and saving on the left. Every outlay by one sector is received by some other sector, and so the accounts show how the sectors are linked together.

The Production Sector. The activity of the production sector is shown in the gross national income and product account (table 1). The right side of this account records the receipts from expenditures on goods and services (GROSS NATIONAL PRODUCT at market prices) that are received by producers, and the left side of the account shows how producers distribute these receipts.

TABLE 1: 1978 U.S. GROSS NATIONAL INCOME AND PRODUCT ACCOUNT
(billions of dollars)

Wages and salaries	1,101	Personal consumption expenditures	1,340
Wage and salary supplements	200	Government purchases of goods and services	434
Proprietor and rental income	137	Gross private domestic investment	346
Net interest paid	106		
Corporate profits	160	Net export of goods and services	−12
		Exports	205
National Income (factor cost)	**1,704**	Imports	217
Indirect taxes	178		
Business transfer payments	11		
Statistical error	2		
Subsidies	−4		
Net National Product (market prices)	**1,891**		
Capital consumption allowances	217		
Gross National Income (market prices)	**2,107**	**Gross National Income (market prices)**	**2,108**

The U.S. government publishes gross national income and product account statistics that provide considerable detail on each of the items shown in table 1. On the expenditure side, personal consumption expenditures are broken down into detailed categories such as food, clothing, housing, transportation, personal services, and so on. Government purchases include two categories: (1) goods purchased from business (defense equipment, agricultural commodities, office supplies, and so on) and (2) wages paid to government employees. Gross private domestic investment represents investments in plant and equipment, construction of residential and commercial buildings, and the net accumulation of inventories. Finally, exports and imports include not only commodities, but also purchases of services (such as freight and insurance) and payments of property income (such as dividends to and from abroad). Thus, the gross national product measures the value of the output produced by the residents of a nation, including the profits from property that they own abroad. For some purposes, however, it may be desirable to measure the output produced within the geographical area of the nation, irrespective of whether the profits belong to residents or foreign investors. This concept is called gross domestic product. Although it is not used by the United States, it is in general use by other countries.

On the left side of the account, a distinction is made between national income, net national product, and gross national income. National income includes all payments made by producers for the use of labor and capital. These payments, which include such things as wages, interest, and profits, are referred to as factor costs. In the case of interest, only the amount of interest paid by producers that exceeds what they receive is included as net interest. The national income is valued in terms of production costs, not market prices. To convert the valuation to market prices, it is necessary to add indirect taxes (sales, excise, and property taxes), which are paid to the government, and business transfer payments, which consist of such things as charitable contributions given by business and consumer bad debts. This concept is called net national product at market prices. It is still, however, not equal to gross national product at market prices because it excludes the capital consumption allowances that producers set aside out of their total revenues to compensate for the depreciation of their plant and equipment. It is therefore necessary to add these capital consumption allowances to net national product to arrive at gross national income, which must equal gross national product.

The Household Sector. For the household sector a personal income account is drawn up that shows (1) the income households receive (on the right side) and (2) their outlays and saving (on the left). This account is shown in table 2.

TABLE 2: U.S. PERSONAL INCOME ACCOUNT FOR 1978
(billions of dollars)

Personal tax payments	256	Wages and salaries	1,101
		Other labor income	106
Disposable Income	**1,452**	Proprietor and rental income	137
		Dividends	49
Personal consumption expenditure	1,340		
Interest paid by households	34	Interest received by households	159
Personal savings	77	Transfer payments from government & business	226
		Personal contributions to social insurance	−70
Personal Outlays and Savings	**1,708**	**Personal Income**	**1,708**

Households receive payments from producers, as has already been shown in the gross national income and product account. In addition, they receive transfer payments from the government in the form of social security benefits, welfare, and unemployment payments. The total of all income received is personal income. In terms of outlays, households pay taxes to the government; their personal income minus taxes is their disposable income. From this they make consumption expenditures and pay interest on consumer debt. Finally, the income left over after taxes, spending, and interest payments is personal saving.

The Government Sector. The account for the government sector (table 3) shows for federal, state, and local governments (1) the revenue they receive, on the right side, plus (2) their spending and (3) the resulting surplus or deficit, both on the left. Government revenue comes from the taxes paid by producers and households. Government spending consists of goods and services purchased from producers, and transfer and interest payments. Most of these transactions have already been recorded in the gross national income and product account or in the personal income account.

The Foreign Sector. The foreign sector account (table 4) is quite simply the payments to foreigners and receipts from foreigners. Net foreign investment is the balancing item in the account. A negative net foreign investment indicates that foreigners are on balance lending money to the United States.

Savings and Investment Account. Finally, the various saving and investment items that appeared in each of the sector accounts can be brought together to show the gross saving and investment in the economy, as is done in table 5. Because each of the saving items was determined residually, and because all entries appear twice in the accounts, saving and investment in the national accounts will always, by definition, be equal. (See SAVING AND INVESTMENT.)

Real Gross National Product. Although the national income accounts for each year represent the values of transactions in current prices, it is also useful to present the figures in terms of prices of a single year in order to show the change in the quantity of goods and services produced and consumed. Table 6 shows the expenditures on gross national product in 1972 prices for a selected period of years.

RICHARD RUGGLES

TABLE 3: U.S. GOVERNMENT RECEIPTS AND OUTLAY ACCOUNT FOR 1978
(billions of dollars)

Government purchases of goods and services	434	Corporate profits taxes	84
Interest paid to producers and households	49	Social insurance contributions	164.4
Interest paid to abroad	9	Indirect taxes	178
Interest received	−30	Personal tax payments	256
Transfer payments to households	215	Federal grants-in-aid (to state and local governments)	77
Transfer payments to abroad	3		
Federal grants-in-aid (to state and local governments)	77		
Subsidies	4		
Surplus (+) or deficit (−)	−1.6		
Government Outlays and Surplus	**759.4**	**Government Revenue**	**759.4**

TABLE 4: U.S. FOREIGN-SECTOR ACCOUNT FOR 1978
(billions of dollars)

Exports	205	Imports	217
		Government transfers paid to abroad	4
		Government interest paid to abroad	9
		Net foreign investment	−25
Receipts from Foreigners	**205**	**Payments to Foreigners**	**205**

TABLE 5: U.S. SAVING AND INVESTMENT ACCOUNT FOR 1978
(billions of dollars)

Gross private domestic investment	345.6	Undistributed corporate profits	26.3
Net foreign investment	−25.2	Capital consumption	216.9
		Personal saving	76.9
		Government surplus (+) or deficit (−)	−1.6
		Statistical error	1.9
Gross Investment	**320.4**	**Gross Savings**	**320.4**

TABLE 6: U.S. GNP IN CONSTANT DOLLARS
(billions of dollars)

Expenditures	1947	1967	1974	1976	1978
Personal consumption	306	603	761	821	892
Government purchases of goods and services	75	248	258	264	275
Gross private domestic investment	70	152	184	165	211
Exports	30	54	93	96	107
Minus: Imports	14	51	77	80	99
Gross National Product	**467**	**1,006**	**1,219**	**1,266**	**1,386**

Bibliography: Bailey, M. J., *National Income and the Price Level*, 2d ed. (1971); Dahlberg, Arthur O., *National Income Visualized* (1956); Kendrick, John W., *Economic Accounts and Their Uses* (1972); Ruggles, N. D. and Richard, *The Design of Economic Accounts* (1970); Schultze, Charles L., *National Income Analysis*, 3d ed. (1971); Studenski, Paul, *The Income of Nations* (1958); United States Department of Commerce, "The Economic Accounts of the United States," *Survey of Current Business*, July 1971; United States Department of Commerce, "The National Income and Product Accounts of the United States: Revised Estimates, 1929-74," *Survey of Current Business*, January 1976.

income tax

The income tax is a tax levied on the net incomes of individuals, families, and corporations. Historically, it is a relatively new form of TAXATION. Only in modern times have national governments begun to tax money incomes on a large scale. Great Britain, the first nation to levy (1799-1816) an income tax of any significance, established a permanent one in 1874. Several other countries began to levy income taxes in the late 19th century. In the United States before World War I the federal government depended primarily on customs duties and excise taxes for its revenues. A national income tax was adopted for the first time in the United States during the years 1861-72, although some states had imposed taxes on income at various times since 1789. The road to an accepted national income tax in the United States, however, was not an easy one. In *Collector* v. *Day* (1870), for example, the Supreme Court held that although an income tax was valid, on the basis of the 10th Amendment it could not be levied against the salaries of state officials, a ruling that was not overturned until 1939. In POLLOCK V. FARMERS' LOAN AND TRUST Co. (1895), however, a uniform national income tax was declared unconstitutional. In 1909, Congress, through the Corporation Tax Act of 1909, began to tax the income of corporations, and in 1913 the ratification of the 16TH AMENDMENT to the U.S. Constitution enabled Congress to institute the personal income tax.

For many years the personal income tax was low (top rate of 6%) and fell mainly on those in the higher income brackets. During World War II the need for additional government revenues brought a lowering of exemptions and increases in rates; by the end of the war, the exemption for a single person had been lowered to $500, and the rates increased to a minimum of 23% of taxable income and a maximum of 94%. The burden was reduced after the war, but the income tax remained the primary source of federal revenues; in 1977, for example, corporation and personal income taxes provided 60% of federal revenues. By 1980 most states and some cities also had personal income taxes.

THE PERSONAL INCOME TAX

The personal income tax seems to be inescapable in an age of big government. It is a relatively efficient way of raising large amounts of revenue; it is widely accepted as the fairest kind of tax in that it is based on the ability to pay; and it can be adjusted to a person's individual circumstances such as family size. Tax experts generally agree on the first and last of these propositions, but they disagree as to whether the U.S. income tax in its present form is as fair as it might be.

Fairness. One criterion of fairness is that people with equal incomes and living in the same circumstances pay the same amount of tax and that those with higher incomes pay more. If one taxpayer is single with no dependents and another is supporting a family, fairness dictates a lower tax on the second person's income. Differences in family size are allowed for in the U.S. system by reducing taxable income by a certain amount for each dependent. Other allowances are made for differences in medical expenses, state and local taxes, and interest payments.

A recurrent question is how to tax husbands and wives when both of them work. If in one household all the income is earned by the husband, and in another both husband and wife work, fairness dictates that both households be taxed on their total incomes. Individuals who are married, however, may pay higher taxes than those who live together unmarried, a practice that critics say discriminates against marriage. The U.S. income tax allows married taxpayers to choose between filing separate returns or joint returns, but this practice has the drawback of permitting households with income from investments to divide their holdings so as to reduce their tax on such incomes.

Advantages of Homeowners. Congress has used the income tax law as a means to encourage home ownership. Taxpayers who own their homes are given substantial advantages over those who rent their homes. They are allowed many deductions from their taxable incomes, including the interest paid on their mortgages, as well as state and local real estate taxes. For a taxpayer in the 30% tax bracket, every hundred dollars deducted from taxable income means a saving of $30 in taxes. Many homeowners in the late 1970s had deductions of $1,000

or more. In addition, when a homeowner sells a house and within 18 months buys another costing as much or more, he or she does not have to pay a tax on the profit made on the first house (although this gain may affect the taxes on profits realized by the sale of the second house). In addition, a 1978 law allows a homeowner over 55 years old, once in a lifetime, to pay no tax on profits—up to $100,000—from the sale of a residence. The preferential treatment given homeowners has had far-reaching effects on the U.S. economy, some of them unforeseen; among other things, it has encouraged people to move from cities to suburbs, seriously weakening the tax base of American cities.

Other Deductions. The U.S. income tax law also seeks to encourage contributions to religious, charitable, educational, and cultural organizations by allowing the taxpayer to deduct these from taxable income. It also permits states and municipalities to issue tax-free bonds, enabling them to raise money at lower rates of interest than those prevailing in the money market.

Tax Loopholes. Wealthy taxpayers, and some not so wealthy, have found ingenious ways of avoiding or minimizing income taxes. A classic example was that of a widow who invested her husband's estate of $56 million in tax-exempt state and municipal bonds. Although such bonds paid very low interest rates at the time, she was left with a tax-free income of about $2 million a year. In the 1970s many wealthy people invested in oil and gas drilling projects or cattle-breeding enterprises and were allowed to write off some of their income under provisions of the corporation income tax law. Another well-publicized device has been the business expense account; this device enabled executives to treat personal expenses such as vacations and entertainment as expenses of doing business, which were deductible from their corporations' taxable income. Many persons in middle-income brackets found that if they owned rental properties they could deduct the value of the buildings from their taxable incomes over a period of years and also deduct the taxes and maintenance costs.

Efforts to close the loopholes in the federal income tax law are perennial but never completely successful. Some of the loopholes exist because Congress has sought to make the income tax more equitable or to further certain social policies. For example, the interest on state and municipal bonds is exempted from taxation in order to make it easier for those governments to obtain capital funds. Oil and gas companies are given special treatment because their properties are subject to depletion. Profits from the sale of property (capital gains) are taxed at lower rates than other forms of income in order to encourage business investment.

THE CORPORATION INCOME TAX

Corporations in the United States pay a flat-rate income tax on profits above a minimum amount (in 1979, the rate was 45% of net income over $50,000). The definition of profit or net income for the purposes of taxation imposes complex accounting problems, since the law allows companies to deduct various expenses from income before taxes. A major deduction is that allowed for the depreciation of plant and equipment, which have to be replaced as they wear out. In some cases, companies are allowed accelerated depreciation, which enables them to write off the cost of plant and equipment at a faster rate. Certain types of new investment, such as machinery and equipment, may allow credits to be applied against the income tax liability in order to encourage companies to expand. Most industrial countries make provisions of this kind in their corporation income taxes to encourage business investment, particularly during recessions.

The Issue of Double Taxation. The taxation of profits in the United States is often criticized because stockholders are taxed twice—first (as owners of the corporation) when the corporation pays business taxes and second on income distributed to them in the form of dividends. The critics argue that such "double taxation" discourages investment in private industry. Some countries have tried to integrate the corporation and personal income taxes to reduce or eliminate double taxation. One method is to tax corporations only on those profits that are not distributed to stockholders. Another is to allow stockholders to deduct corporation income taxes from the taxes they would otherwise pay on their dividend income.

Who Pays? Some critics of the corporation income tax argue that it is paid not by corporations but by consumers in the form of higher prices. To the extent that corporations are able to shift the tax to consumers, this factor contradicts the ability-to-pay criterion of fairness; it then resembles a sales tax, falling equally on rich and poor. Traditionally, however, economic theory has held that a tax on profits cannot be shifted to consumers and is a tax on the owners of capital. No conclusive evidence exists in favor of either viewpoint.

INFLATION AND THE INCOME TAX

The high rates of inflation in the 1970s tended to increase effective income taxes on most persons. As wages and salaries rose, taxpayers found themselves in higher tax brackets, requiring them to pay higher tax rates on their income even though the cost of living had risen. Inflation also had the effect of reducing the real value of exemptions and deductions. For U.S. taxpayers as a body, an increase in prices of 10% meant an increase of almost 15% in taxes paid.

The effect of inflation is thus to increase the share of the national income going to the government. The impact becomes more severe as inflation continues unless corresponding changes are made in the tax rates. Some countries, including Canada, have dealt with the problem by "indexing" their income taxes—linking tax rates, exemptions, and deductions to changes in the general price level. Opponents of indexing argue that it removes a fiscal brake on inflation, because higher tax rates help to discourage consumer purchases.

Congress has, in effect, adopted a crude form of indexing by legislating lower taxes on a year-to-year basis. The Revenue Act of 1978 raised the personal exemption for each taxpayer from $750 to $1,000 and reduced tax rates for each income bracket. It also provided for fewer, wider income tax brackets so that higher earnings would not push taxpayers into higher brackets so quickly. In the United States (and in other countries) popular pressure grew in the late 1970s to reduce taxes. Proposition 13—a 1978 California referendum on property tax reduction—spurred what has been called a nationwide tax revolt; in 1979, 18 states reduced income taxes.

THE NEGATIVE INCOME TAX

A number of economists, conservatives as well as liberals, have proposed using the income tax system to replace the complex system of payments made to low-income persons on welfare. Just as households above a certain income level pay income taxes to the government, so those below a certain level would receive negative tax payments from the government. As a family's income increased, it would receive smaller payments until, at a certain break-even point, the family would receive nothing. One theoretical advantage of the negative income tax is that it would provide its recipients with more incentive to work than those presently on the welfare rolls have. For the welfare recipient, taking a job usually means losing all or most welfare benefits; under the graduated system of the negative income tax, however, the benefits would be adjusted to the recipient's earned income to guarantee a minimum family income. President Richard Nixon sent a negative income tax proposal to Congress in 1969, but it was not enacted. Some opponents argued that it would tend to decrease the incentive of able-bodied people to work in order to add to their family incomes. Studies made of families in New Jersey and Pennsylvania have shown that this criticism contains some truth; wives in low-income families were less inclined to work if their husbands' wages were supplemented by an income guarantee from the government, and in some cases the men worked fewer hours than they otherwise would have.   DOUGLAS M. BROWN

Bibliography: Boskin, Michael, ed., *Federal Tax Reform: Myths and Realities* (1978); Carson, Gerald, *The Golden Egg* (1977); Goode, Richard, *The Individual Income Tax* (1976); Larson, Martin A., *Tax Revolt: U.S.A.!* (1973); Lasser Tax Institute, *Lasser's Your Income Tax* (annual); McCarthy, Clarence F., *The Federal Income Tax: Its Sources and Applications* (1977); Pechman, Joseph, *Federal Tax Policy*, 3d ed. (1977); Raby, William L., *Income Tax and Business Decisions*, 4th ed. (1978); Sabine, B. E., *A History of Income Tax* (1966).

incomes policy

An incomes policy is a governmental effort to restrain INFLATION by setting limits on wage and price increases. Such a policy is usually based on an agreement by employers and labor unions to observe certain guidelines. Wage or price changes that do not exceed the guidelines are presumed to be noninflationary. The government also attempts to limit the expansion of money and credit. Actually, most incomes policies have been designed to limit the growth of inflation rather than wholly eliminate it. Thus, under President Richard Nixon's price and wage controls of the early 1970s, wages were permitted to rise by 5.5%—more than was compatible with price increases. One argument for an incomes policy is that it decreases the need for other measures, such as stringent monetary controls, that might lead to recession and unemployment.

Bibliography: Parkin, Michael, and Summer, Michael T., eds., *Incomes Policy and Inflation* (1974); Ross, M. H., *Income: Analysis and Policy*, 2d ed. (1968); Schiff, Eric, *Incomes Policies Abroad, Part One: United Kingdom, Sweden, the Netherlands, Canada* (1971) and *Part Two: France, West Germany, Austria, Denmark* (1972).

incompetence   [in-kahm'-puh-tens]

Incompetence, in law, is an inability, incapacity, or lack of qualification to perform an act or duty. The term applies to situations such as a person's ability to function normally, a judge's legal qualification to hear a case, and a witness's legal ability to testify, as well as to the admissibility of evidence in a judicial proceeding.

When persons are unable to understand the nature of their acts, they are considered legally incompetent. A person may be incompetent with regard to one function (such as making a will) or to many functions. If a person is unable to perform daily activities at a minimal level of proficiency, a court may appoint a guardian to oversee the incompetent's affairs or commit the person to an appropriate institution. If an incompetent makes a will or enters into a contract, a court can declare it invalid.

Judges are considered incompetent to hear cases over which they have no proper legal jurisdiction or in which they have a vested interest. Witnesses are incompetent to testify if they cannot properly recollect or communicate or if they do not have relevant knowledge. Witnesses are normally not considered competent to express opinions, as distinct from recollections and observations, unless they are trained experts in the subject being considered. Evidence may be held legally incompetent for a number of reasons; it may, for example, be irrelevant or involve hearsay or improper opinion.

incubus   [in'-kue-buhs]

In medieval folklore, an incubus was an evil male spirit that haunted sleeping women; it was thought to father demons and witches. The corresponding female spirit, called a succubus, seduced sleeping men. Today the word *incubus* is used to describe an oppressive person or thing. It also refers to nightmares, once believed to be caused by evil spirits.

incunabula   [in-kue-nab'-ue-luh]

A term in PRINTING or publishing, *incunabula* derives from the Latin for "swaddling clothes." An incunabulum, or incunable, is any BOOK, pamphlet, or broadside printed during the 15th century—the beginning of the European printing industry.

Johann GUTENBERG first used movable type in about the year 1450; by the end of the century, presses had been established in over 200 communities, and as many as 40,000 different items had been printed. Books usually appeared as quartos bound between wooden boards and decorated copiously with woodcuts. Print runs were small, averaging less than 500, with some notable exceptions. Thomas à Kempis's *Imitation of Christ* (1471), for instance, ran to almost 100 editions by 1500. The vernacular had gained ground by that time, but most 15th-century productions were religious works in Latin, the most famous specimen being the 1455 GUTENBERG BIBLE.

Although German firms remained dominant throughout the period, Venice alone boasted 150 presses, and such printers as William CAXTON in England and Aldus MANUTIUS in Venice had a wide influence. Owners functioned as typecutters, publishers, and booksellers as well as printers.

Many incunabula were destroyed during the Reformation and Counter-Reformation, so the value of surviving copies is high. Most of these are housed in libraries and museums; the British Museum Library and the Bibliothèque Nationale have two of the largest collections outside of Germany.

Bibliography: Buhler, Curt F., *The Fifteenth-Century Book* (1960); Stillwell, Margaret B., *Incunabula and Americana: 1450-1800*, (1930; repr. 1968).

indefinite integral: see INTEGRAL CALCULUS.

Independence

Independence, a city in western Missouri, is the seat of Jackson County. It has a population of 709,700 (1979 est.). Set in an agricultural area that grows wheat, corn, and potatoes, Independence is a commercial and industrial center. Its manufactures include petroleum products, farm and industrial machinery, food products, munitions, and construction materials. There are also several printing and publishing firms. Harry S. Truman was a long-time resident of Independence and is buried on the grounds of the Harry S. Truman Library and Museum, where his papers are kept. Independence is also the world headquarters of the Reorganized Church of Jesus Christ of Latter-Day Saints (a branch of Mormonism).

Settled in 1825, the community was the starting point for pioneers following the Santa Fe, Oregon, or California trails. Mormons settled here briefly (1831) but were not welcomed. During the Civil War, Confederate forces held the town twice, each time for only one day.

Independence Day

Independence Day, July 4, the most important national holiday in the United States, celebrates the adoption of the DECLARATION OF INDEPENDENCE by the Second CONTINENTAL CONGRESS on July 4, 1776. Massachusetts delegate John ADAMS wrote his wife, Abigail, that the day "ought to be solemnized with pomp and parade, with shows, games and sports, guns, bells, bonfires, and illuminations from this time forward for evermore." His prescription has been followed to the letter. The day has always been the occasion for the pomp of parades and patriotic speeches, and for every variety of noisy jubilation. In fact, the firing of cannons and fireworks caused so many injuries that by the early 1900s, ordinances forbidding private pyrotechnics were passed in many cities. Today Fourth of July fireworks are largely handled by professionals, although Adams's "shows, games, and sports" are still abundantly in evidence.

Bibliography: Dupuy, Trevor N., ed., *Holidays: Days of Significance for All Americans* (1965); Krythe, Maymie R., *All About American Holidays* (1962); Myers, Robert J., and Hallmark Cards Editors, *Celebrations: The Complete Book of American Holidays* (1972).

Independence Hall

Designated the State House (and before that the Provincehall) of Pennsylvania, Independence Hall in Philadelphia is an excellent example of colonial Georgian public architecture. The building was designed primarily by Edmund Woolley (1696-1771), a master carpenter, and by Andrew Hamilton (c.1676-1741), a lawyer. Constructed in brick (1730-48), it was adorned with a wooden tower and steeple (1750-53), which soon rotted and was removed in 1781. Robert MILLS removed the building's existing wings and arcades and replaced them with office wings (1813-15; demolished 1896-98). In 1828 the proportions of the building were altered by William STRICKLAND's rebuilding of the tower and steeple in the large-scale, blocky forms now visible. Various restorations of the building undertaken in the 1920s—and again in the 1950s and '60s, when it came under the National Park Service—have returned it to a pristine state.   ANN VAN ZANTEN

Bibliography: Morrison, Hugh, *Early American Architecture* (1952; repr. 1974); Tatum, George B., *Penn's Great Town: 250 Years of Philadelphia Architecture Illustrated in Prints and Drawings* (1961).

See also: COLONIAL STYLES IN NORTH AMERICA; GEORGIAN STYLE.

Independent Treasury System

The Independent Treasury System was established in 1840 by an act of the U. S. Congress that withdrew all federal funds from state-chartered, private banks and placed them in government depositories located in major cities throughout the country. It was one of the most controversial measures of President Martin VAN BUREN's administration.

Intended to separate the banking system from the administration of the government's finances, the act was both a response to the bank failures that followed the Panic of 1837 and a reflection of the suspicion of banking and speculation harbored by hard-money Jacksonians. By depriving banks of federal deposits, the Independent Treasury System denied bankers the opportunity to use public funds as a basis for making loans and issuing notes.

The act was opposed not only by Whigs, but also by conservative Democrats allied to state banking interests. Repealed in 1841 during the administration of Whig President John TYLER, the Independent Treasury Act was reenacted under President Polk in 1846 and remained in force until the passage of the National Bank Act of 1863.   ALFRED A. CAVE

Bibliography: Kinley, David, *The Independent Treasury of the United States* (1910; repr. 1970).

See also: BANKING SYSTEM.

Index

The Index Librorum Prohibitorum (Index of Forbidden Books) was a list formerly issued by the Roman Catholic church of published works that church members were forbidden to read without specific permission from a qualified person, usually the bishop acting through a priest-delegate.

The first official listing of forbidden books was promulgated (405) by Pope Innocent I, but a decree issued by Pope Gelasius (c.496) has been referred to as the first formal index. The condemnation of specific works continued through subsequent centuries. At the Council of Trent (1545-63; see TRENT, COUNCIL OF) it was decreed that certain books could not be used for liturgical celebrations and even that no book on a religious subject could be published without the approval of ecclesiastical authorities. In 1559 the Congregation of the INQUISITION produced a long list of forbidden books, which Pope Paul IV accepted and published as an *index* (the first time the word itself was used to describe a listing of unacceptable literature). The Index went through several revisions in succeeding pontificates. Pope Leo XIII presided (1897) over the final major revision of the Index (which included, for example, all the works of the philosophers Thomas Hobbes and David Hume).

The effectiveness and appropriateness of the Index was re-evaluated at the Second VATICAN COUNCIL (1962-65). Within a few months of the final adjournment of the council in December 1965, the Congregation for the Doctrine of the Faith (formerly the Holy Office, and before that the Congregation of the Inquisition) announced the abolition of the Index.   RICHARD P. MCBRIEN

index

An index is a list of the subjects or topics contained in a book, magazine, computerized data base, collection of audiovisual materials, encyclopedia, or other compilation of recorded information. Index entries have two parts: a heading and a locator. Index headings identify the subjects, usually in a word or phrase describing them, and are arranged in a predetermined filing order (usually alphabetic). Index locators tell where the subjects are discussed in the material that has been indexed. In back-of-the-book indexes the locators are usually page numbers. All indexes should also have a system of cross references. These are usually of two types: *see also* references that lead from one heading to related headings, and *see* references that lead from a heading with no locators to headings that do have locators.

The goal of an index is to provide quick, easy, and unambiguous access to the information in the material that has been indexed. An index enables users to be selective in the information they read and helps them find the particular item they want without having to read all the other items in the collection. Even though information on a specific topic may be scattered throughout the indexed material, the index should bring together all the locators for the topic. Equally important, a good index should not lead the user to irrelevant information.

Many kinds of indexes are used. Some indexes are limited to individual books or periodicals. Others, such as the *Readers' Guide to Periodical Literature*, the *Book Review Index*, or the *Index to One-Act Plays*, are limited to one kind of publication. Still other indexes, such as the *Engineering Index* or the *Environment Index*, are limited to one subject area but cover all forms of publication affecting that area. Other printed indexes, such as the *Bulletin of the Public Affairs Information Service* and the *Social Sciences Index*, are produced by computer manipulation and computer typesetting. Today, many indexes, such as the *Science Citation Index* or the BASIC index to *Biological Abstracts*, would be impractical if not impossible to compile without the aid of the computer. Computer-stored indexes to computer-stored data also exist, such as the one maintained by the *New York Times* for its Information Bank.

The methods used to prepare indexes also vary widely. With analytical subject indexes, the indexer chooses the indexable concepts from the text and then makes index entries for them; by contrast, with word indexes, a computer is programmed to turn each word in a title or an abstract into an index entry; little or no attention is paid to the resulting problems of ambiguous terminology, of synonyms, or of the consequent scattering of information throughout the index. With precoordinate indexes, such as back-of-the-book indexes, the relationships among concepts in the text are established by the indexer at the time of indexing; on the other hand, with postcoordinate indexes (primarily computerized indexes), although the indexer identifies each concept in the text, the user must establish the relationships among the concepts when consulting the index. All indexes, however, have the common purpose of pointing to the place or places where information on a subject can be found.

Experts disagree as to when the first index was prepared. Some say that the Alexandrian Library in Egypt maintained indexes to the papyrus rolls in its collections from the 3d century BC; others say that the earliest index was created in medieval times. In modern times, as the number of books, periodicals, computerized data bases, and other such packages of recorded information continues to grow, and more and more bodies of computer-stored information come into existence, indexes have become increasingly important.

The Society of Indexers in Great Britain and the American Society of Indexers in the United States have been established to improve standards of indexing and to encourage education in the field.　　　　　　　　　　　　　BARBARA M. PRESCHEL

Bibliography: Borko, Harold, and Bernier, Charles L., *Indexing Concepts and Methods* (1978); Sheehy, Eugene Paul, *Guide to Reference Books*, 9th ed. (1976); Wheeler, Martha Thorne, *Indexing: Principles, Rules and Examples* (1957).

index fossil:　　see FOSSIL RECORD.

index of refraction

The index of refraction, or refractive index, n, of a substance is a measure of the extent that light is bent as it passes through the substance. It can be determined by measuring the angles of incidence (i) and refraction (r) of a beam of light; $n = \sin i / \sin r$. The index of refraction is also the ratio of the speed of light in a vacuum (c) to its speed in the substance (v), so that $n = c/v$.

The index of refraction of a medium is slightly different for each color. Measurements are normally taken using the yellow light of a sodium source. If a mixture of wavelengths, such as ordinary white light, is refracted by the medium, the paths of each wavelength will be refracted to a slightly different angle, and the original beam will appear colored. This process is known as dispersion. The greater the index of refraction, the higher the dispersion. The relatively high index of refraction of diamond accounts for its vivid display of color. The gemstone titania (rutile, titanium dioxide) has an even higher index of refraction than diamond and is thus more brilliant.　　　　　　　　　　　　　　　MARK S. VOGEL

India

India, the world's second most populous nation (after China) and the seventh largest in area, is located in South Asia on the Indian subcontinent. It is about 3,000 km (1,875 mi) wide and has, because of its peninsular shape, a shoreline of about 7,000 km (4,400 mi) along the Bay of Bengal on the east and the Arabian Sea on the west. The land frontier of about 5,700 km (3,600 mi) is shared with Pakistan and a small strip of Afghanistan on the west; by Tibet, Nepal, and Bhutan on the north; and by Bangladesh and Burma on the east. India's eighth neighbor is the island nation of Sri Lanka, located off the southern tip of the peninsula. Northeast India is virtually isolated from the rest of the nation by Bangladesh. Also part of India are the LACCADIVE ISLANDS (Lakshadweep) off the

INDIA

Official Name: Republic of India
Capital: New Delhi (1975 est. pop., 301,801)
Largest City: Bombay (1975 est. pop., 5,970,575)
Area: 3,275,198 km² (1,264,555 mi²)
Elevation: *Highest*—Nanda Devi 7,817 m (25,645 ft); *lowest*—sea level, along the Indian Ocean and Arabian Sea coasts
Population: 667,907,000 (1979 est.). *Distribution*— 20% urban, 80% rural; *density,* 204 persons per km² (528 per mi²); *annual rate of increase* (1970–77), 2.2%
Principal Languages: Hindi, English, Assamese, Bengali, Gujarti, Kannanda, Kashmiri, Malayalam, Marathi, Oriya, Punjabi, Sanskrit, Sindhi, Tamil, Telugu, Urdu (all official)
Principal Religions: Hinduism, Islam, Christianity, Sikhism, Jainism
Principal Products: *Agriculture*—rice, wheat, sugarcane, cotton, jute, sorghum, maize, millet, cattle, sheep and goats, buffalo. *Manufacturing and industry*—textiles, metal products, food products, machinery, transportation equipment, fertilizer, oil refining, engineering, cement, steel, aluminum. *Mining*—phosphates, chromium, magnesite, coal, iron graphite, pyrite, zinc, copper, asbestos, bauxite, limestone.
Railroads: 61,313 km/38,075 mi (1977)
Roads: 415,250 km/257,870 mi (1977 paved)
Currency: 1 rupee = 100 paisa

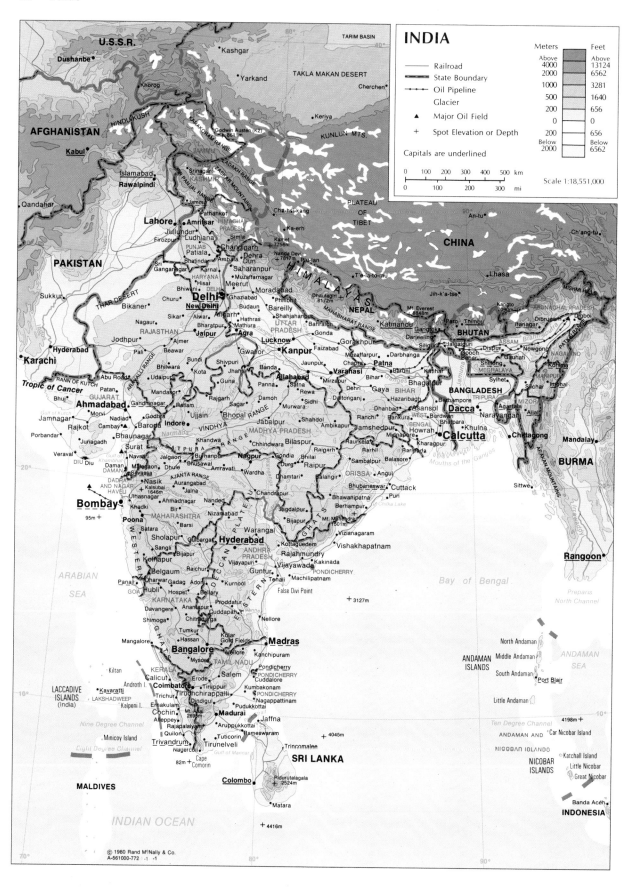

INDIA

	Meters	Feet
—— Railroad	Above 4000	Above 13124
▬▬▬▬ State Boundary	2000	6562
•—•—• Oil Pipeline	1000	3281
Glacier	500	1640
▲ Major Oil Field	200	656
+ Spot Elevation or Depth	0	0
	200	656
Capitals are underlined	Below 2000	Below 6562

0   100   200   300   400   500 km
0   100   200   300 mi

Scale 1:18,551,000

© 1980 Rand McNally & Co.
A-561000-772 -1 -1

(Left) *Darjeeling, in the state of West Bengal near India's border with Nepal, is world famous for the high-grade tea cultivated on the surrounding mountainsides. In 1835, British colonial authorities purchased Darjeeling from the Raja of Sikkim and used it as a rest and recreation area for British soldiers stationed in Bengal.*

(Below) *Pilgrims immerse themselves in the waters of the Ganges River as a rite of purification. The Ganges, which flows across the plains of northern India, has for thousands of years been revered as a holy river by followers of the Hindu religion.*

western coast and the ANDAMAN and NICOBAR islands, located in the eastern portion of the Bay of Bengal.

India and Bharat are both official names. The early settlers called their land "Bharat Varsha" or "Bharat," and during medieval times it was known as "Hind." The name India, which derives from the Indus River and was used by the ancient Greeks and Persians, came into wide usage during the colonial period.

Indian culture is of great antiquity. The earliest Indian civilization grew up in the Indus Valley from 4000 to 2500 BC. Beginning about 1500 BC Aryan invaders entered India from the northwest and intermingled with the local Dravidian population. The foundations of Indian society, including Hinduism and the caste system, were established from these two groups. Buddhism and Jainism also began in ancient India. The culture was subject to strong Islamic influences beginning in the medieval period and continuing under the Mogul Empire (established 1526). After 1750 the subcontinent was absorbed piecemeal into the British Empire, the local princes and rulers retaining much of their autonomy.

India gained its independence from the British on Aug. 15, 1947, at which time two predominantly Muslim regions in the northwestern and northeastern corners of the subcontinent became the separate state of Pakistan. The modern country of India is a union of 22 states—ANDHRA PRADESH, ASSAM, BIHAR, GUJARAT, HARYANA, HIMACHAL PRADESH, Jammu and Kashmir (see KASHMIR), KARNATAKA, KERALA, MADHYA PRADESH, MAHARASHTRA, MANIPUR, MEGHALAYA, NAGALAND, ORISSA, PUNJAB, RAJASTHAN, SIKKIM, TAMIL NADU, TRIPURA, UTTAR PRADESH, WEST BENGAL—and 9 union territories—GOA, DAMAN AND DIU, PONDICHERRY, Andaman and Nicobar Islands, Arunachal Pradesh, Chandigarh, Dadra and Nagar Haveli, Delhi, Lakshadweep (Laccadive Islands), and Mizoram. In 1956 the map of India was largely redrawn as provisions were made for reorganization of the states along linguistic lines, with the goal of preserving regional cultures and aspirations. A policy of "democratic decentralization" provides the states with a large measure of self-government.

Today India has one of the largest national industrial sectors in the world. Because the huge population is growing more rapidly than the economy, however, the primarily rural population of this huge, developing nation has one of the world's lowest per-capita incomes. Despite the accompanying social and political stresses, and despite a brief period of authoritarian rule (1975-77) under Prime Minister Indira Gandhi, India remains the world's largest democracy.

LAND

India can be divided into three main topographic regions; the Himalayan mountain system, on the north; the Northern Plains, drained by the Indus, Ganges, and Brahmaputra rivers in north-central India; and Peninsular India, in the south.

The HIMALAYAS form parts of India's borders with Pakistan, Afghanistan, and Tibet in the west and with Nepal, Bhutan, and Tibet in the east. The region is topographically complex and divided into prominent elongated valleys and mountain ranges. The highest mountains are in the KARAKORAM RANGE, where more than 30 other peaks rise above 7,300 m (24,000 ft). South of the Karakoram are the Great Himalayas, a range with extensive areas over 5,500 m (18,000 ft); sandwiched between the two major ranges is the narrow valley of the Upper Indus River. Southwest of the Great Himalayas and between them and the lower front ranges of the mountain system is the 160-km (100-mi) long Vale of Kashmir, which is located on the upper Jhelum River and focuses on the town of SRINAGAR. To the east, the mountains form most of Sikkim and the union territory of Arunachal Pradesh.

The Northern Plains are part of a vast lowland extending across the subcontinent from Pakistan in the west to Bangladesh (formerly East Pakistan) in the east. The plains are bordered on the north by the foothills of the Himalayas; south of the Bramaputra basin are the Khasi Hills and Shillong Plateau;

and south of the Indo-Gangetic Plain rise the uplands of Peninsular India. In India, this lowland has a length of about 1,600 km (1,000 mi) from east to west and a width of about 320 km (200 mi). It is drained in the west by the Beas and Sutlej rivers, which are tributaries of the Indus; in the east by the Brahmaputra; and in the rest of India by the Ganges and its many tributaries and distributaries. The Northern Plains are floored by alluvial deposits derived mainly from the Himalayas and deposited over the lowland by the major rivers.

Peninsular India is geologically the oldest part of India. Ancient crystalline and metamorphic rocks underlie most of the region, but basaltic lavas (igneous rocks) cover parts of the DECCAN PLATEAU. Topographically, the surface of the peninsula is tilted down toward the east and north, forming a belt of prominent uplands along the western edge. These uplands, reaching more than 2,500 m (8,000 ft), include the Western Ghats (see GHATS) and the Nilgiri Hills. The northern edge of the peninsula, although lower, is also prominent and rises south of the Northern Plains to form the Aravalli Range in the west and the jungle-covered Chota Nagpur Plateau in the east. Only a very narrow coastal plain lies between the Western Ghats and the Arabian Sea; more extensive plains, including the deltas of the Cauveri, Krishna, Mahanadi, and Damodar rivers, line the east coast.

Soils. The four principal soil types in India are mountain (or immature) soils, alluvial soils, regur soils, and red soils. Mountain soils are found in upland areas too steep for regular soil development; they range in texture from sandy in the drier Aravallis to clays in the wetter Himalayas. Alluvial soils cover the broad floodplains of the Indo-Gangetic valley and the Brahmaputra basin, the smaller river valleys and deltas of the peninsula, and the coastal lowlands; these soils, ranging from sandy loams to clays, are generally fertile, but are sometimes saline when improperly irrigated. The regur soils are rich, fertile black soils found in the sections of the peninsula covered with basaltic lavas and also in some eastern and southern regions. Red soils, which cover most of the peninsula, are less fertile, as are patches of nutrient-deficient lateritic soils.

Climate. The Rajasthan Desert in northwestern India has a semiarid climate, but the majority of India has a tropical monsoonal climate associated with a wind reversal between summer and winter. In summer low-pressure areas develop over the subcontinent as the land heats up, and summer monsoon winds are drawn onto the land from the surrounding seas. These moisture-laden winds release heavy rainfall when they reach the coast or are forced to rise over mountains; summers (mid-June to mid-September) are accordingly wet and hot, with temperatures between 27° and 32° C (81°

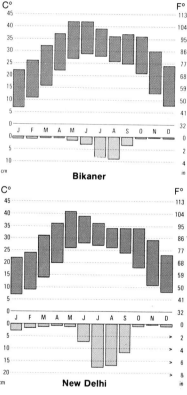

Bars indicate monthly ranges of temperatures (red) and precipitation (blue) for six cities in India. Much of the country experiences a tropical wet-dry climate, including New Delhi, the nation's capital, in north central India; Darjeeling, located in the northeast in the foothills of the Himalayas; Calcutta, India's largest city, located on the east central coast; and Madras, a port situated on the Coromandel Coast in the south. Cochin, a seaport near the southeastern tip of the subcontinent, has a monsoon climate. Because of its location in the Thar Desert of the northwest, Bikaner experiences a steppe climate.

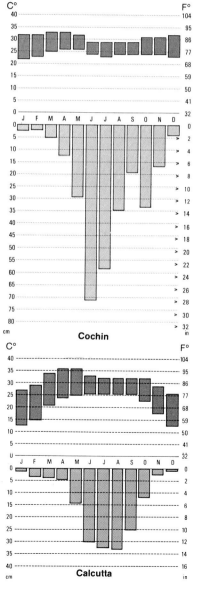

Kovalam is located near Trivandrum, Kerala, on the southwest coast of India. The climatic conditions of India's southern coastal regions yield fertile agricultural land and lush vegetation. The area is especially known for its coconut groves and spice gardens.

and 90° F). In winter high pressures build over the land; winds then blow predominantly from the land to the sea, and winter in India (mid-December to mid-March) is predominantly dry and cool, with temperatures averaging 21° C (70° F). Two transitional seasons occur before and after the summer rains. A hot and dry pre-monsoonal season lasts from mid-March to mid-June and is associated with temperatures between 38° and 43° C (100° and 110° F). A post-monsoonal season occurs as the monsoons retreat (mid-September to mid-December) and is associated with light and sporadic rainfall and temperatures around 25° C (77° F). Cooler, more temperate conditions prevail in the Himalayas and decrease with altitude.

Precipitation ranges from almost zero in the THAR desert to 10,870 mm (428 in) annually in the Shillong Plateau, which is one of the wettest places in the world. Rainfall is generally heaviest in coastal and highland areas and diminishes inland. Amounts vary widely from year to year, especially in inland areas, and dry years often cause widespread crop failures. Crop damage may also occur on a smaller scale in parts of eastern India when "nor-westers" and Bay of Bengal cyclones strike the land, most often in May and early June, in the form of tornadoes, whirlwinds, hailstorms, and heavy downpours.

Drainage. The principal river in India is the GANGES (Ganga), which rises in the Himalayas and flows across the Northern Plains in a broad, meandering course to reach the sea at the Bay of Bengal. Most of the Ganges reaches the sea through multiple distributaries in Bangladesh; its principal distributary in India is the Hooghly River, which flows through Calcutta. The major tributaries of the Ganges are the BRAHMAPUTRA, which joins the Ganges near its mouth in Bangladesh, and the YAMUNA, Gogra, Gandak, and Kosi rivers. In northern India the major drainage basin is that of the INDUS River; although most of this basin lies in Pakistan, the headwaters of the Indus and two of its major tributaries, the SUTLEJ and the Beas, are partly in India and are used heavily for irrigation. The principal rivers of Peninsular India are the Chambal, Son, Mahanadi, Godavary, Krishna, Cauveri, Narmada, and Tapi. Principal lakes include the Chilka, Kolleru, Pulicat, Lonar, Pushkar, and Wular. A coastal swamp, the Sundarban, fringes the Ganges delta. The Rann of KUTCH is a saline swamp in northwestern India and southern Pakistan, off the Arabian Sea coast.

The annual regime of river flow in India is controlled by climatic conditions. Rivers flowing from the Himalayas experience two high-water seasons, one in early summer caused by snow melt in the mountains, and one in late summer caused by runoff from monsoonal rains. Other rivers experience high waters only during the monsoon, followed by periods of diminished flow, when many of the smaller rivers run dry. To counteract this marked periodicity of river flow, groundwater wells and tube wells are widely used for irrigation in the Northern Plains and peninsular delta regions; and many dams have been built on the major rivers to regulate river flow and distribute water for an intricate system of irrigation canals.

Vegetation and Animal Life. Seven vegetation regions are found in continental India, although the natural cover has been modified by several millennia of human occupation. In the western Himalayas vegetation changes with altitude from temperate deciduous forests at low elevations through coniferous forests to Alpine vegetation above the treeline. The eastern Himalayas have more extensive deciduous forest cover. In northeastern India, east of Bangladesh, vegetation cover ranges from tropical evergreen in the wet lowlands to temperate deciduous forest in drier and cooler areas. The semiarid Punjab-Rajasthan-Gujarat region mainly supports scrub vegetation cover. In the heavily cultivated Ganges Plain, islands of deciduous trees and tuft grasses remain among the agricultural fields. The peninsular uplands support tropical monsoonal deciduous and scrub forest, while the wetter slopes of the Western Ghats support a tropical monsoonal deciduous forest, with an evergreen cover in some areas.

India's fauna includes about 500 species of mammals and more than 2,000 species of birds. The elephant, Indian bison, rhinoceros, and tiger live mainly in the wet, forested regions; the Himalayan markhor (ibex) and lion live in the Gir forest. Seven national parks, 135 wild life sanctuaries, and 24 zoological parks are concerned with conservation of wildlife.

Resources. India has a rich and varied mineral-resource base. Coal and iron ore are abundant and located close to each other in the Chota Nagpur Plateau in the eastern peninsula. Manganese, lignite, copper, bauxite, kyanite, fire clays, mica, and limestone are found in large quantities. Petroleum occurs offshore from Bombay and in Assam and Gujarat, but is not present in large amounts.

India also has vast land resources. Of the total land area, 20.5% is under forest; 41.6% is sown with crops; 7.6% is left fallow; 3.9% is in permanent pasture; and 1.5% supports permanent crops such as tea and fruit trees. Irrigation is of great importance to Indian farmers. India has the potential to irrigate 1.07 million km² (410,000 mi²), but only 42% of this land is currently irrigated. Canals from the major rivers provide water to 40.9% of the irrigated area; wells provide water for 40.7%; and tanks provide water to 11.4%.

PEOPLE

India has one of the world's most diverse populations. Historically, one race after another settled in India, and each successive wave usually drove the earlier settlers into forested highlands and extended their own area. The earliest occupants came from South Asia and Australia, and the subsequent migrations were from the northwestern Asian mainland. In this process a good deal of racial intermingling occurred. The Negritos including ANDAMANESE, the earliest occupants, now form small enclaves in Bihar and Kerala. The Mediterranean type has contributed most to the physical features. The Alpine element is more to be seen, although in a mixed form, in Gujarat, Maharashtra and Tamil Nadu. The proto-Nordic ARYANS moved first into the Indo-Gangetic lowland, and subsequently, highly mixed with other groups, into the peninsula. The Oriental PATHAN peoples are found in the northwestern Himalayas and Mongoloids in the northeastern Himalayas. Today, however, except for isolated tribal groups, it is difficult to identify any regional group based on purely ethnic or racial criteria; India's peoples are, therefore, generally classified according to language.

Languages. About 200 different languages are spoken in India, and an appreciation of the linguistic divisions provides a key to better understanding of the nation. Four principal language groups are recognized, of which the Aryan and the Dravidian are the most important. The Aryan linguistic group (see INDO-IRANIAN languages), which is to some extent associated with

(Left) *A crowd watches as students march along the Rajpath (or Kingsway), a major thoroughfare in New Delhi, the capital of India. The ceremonies mark the observance of Republic Day, a holiday celebrating the adoption of India's constitution, which established the nation as a democratic republic in 1950.*

the proto-Nordic peoples, includes Assamese, Bengali, Gujarati, Hindi, Kashmiri, Marathi, Oriya, Punjabi, and Urdu , which are spoken mainly in northern parts of the peninsula. The DRAVIDIAN LANGUAGE group includes Kannada, Malayalam, Tamil, and Telugu, which are spoken in the southern parts of the peninsula. The SINO-TIBETAN—including Manipuri—and Austro-Asiatic (see SOUTHEAST ASIAN LANGUAGES)—including Munda, Khasi, and Nicobari—linguistic groups are confined to small regions in northeastern India and the central and northeastern peninsular highlands. Interaction among the different Indian languages has occurred throughout the long human occupance of the region.

Hindi and English are both official languages; in addition, 14 other languages have received official recognition in the constitution: Assamese, Bengali, Gujarati, Kannada, Kashmiri, Malayalam, Marathi, Oriya, Punjabi, Sanskrit, Sindhi, Tamil, Telugu, and Urdu. Many other languages are spoken by smaller groups and are either regional variations or dialects; Sanskrit, claimed in the 1971 census as the language of 2,212 persons, provides the root for many of the Indian languages, but it is no longer a spoken language.

Religion. India was the birthplace of HINDUISM, BUDDHISM, JAINISM, and Sikhism (see SIKHS). Today, as a secular state, India has no official religion, and religious toleration is guaranteed under the constitution. Hindus constitute about 83% of the population, Muslims 11%, Christians 3%, Sikhs 2%, and Buddhists (mostly adherents of TIBETAN BUDDHISM) and Jains each less than 1%. Except for regional concentrations of Sikhs in the Punjab, Christians in Nagaland, and PARSIS (who practice ZOROASTRIANISM and number about 200,000) in the Bombay area, there is no marked regional distribution of religious groups.

The CASTE system, a set of social and occupational classes into which individuals are born, is an important facet of Hinduism and thus is a dominant feature of Indian life. Today the government is attempting to eliminate castes, but caste consciousness remains important in Indian politics. Harijans, the lowest caste, traditionally called UNTOUCHABLES, who constitute 15% of the population, and tribes, who constitute 7%, are given special protection by the central government.

Demography. India's population, the second largest in the world (after China), increased from 238,400,000 in 1901 to 548,200,000 in 1971 and stood at 667,907,000 in 1979. This enormous and rapid increase in population results from a

A throng of more than half a million people crowd into the streets of Calcutta after attending a political rally staged in the Maidan, a vast park. Calcutta, India's largest city and a primary industrial center, is also the capital of West Bengal state.

Bombay, on the Arabian Sea, is India's second largest city and the capital of Maharashtra state. Bombay has become a leading textile center because of its transportation facilities and its proximity to the major cotton-growing regions of western India.

crude birthrate that has remained high over the years at 45.3 per 1,000 and a death rate that has fallen to 16.9 per 1,000 (1973–75) from 36 per 1,000 in 1921. It is estimated that the population now increases by about 13 million people per year. The average life expectancy is 47.1 years for men and 45.6 years for women. The average population density is 204 per km² (528 per mi²), according to the 1971 census, but regional variations range from a high of about 504 per km² (1,305 per mi²) in densely populated Kerala to 6 per km² (16 per mi²) in sparsely populated Arunachal Pradesh. About 80% of the population is rural, living in 575,936 villages; 20% is urban, living in 2,643 towns and cities. The largest cities are CALCUTTA, Greater BOMBAY, NEW DELHI, MADRAS, HYDERABAD, AHMADABAD, BANGALORE, KANPUR, and POONA, all with more than 1 million inhabitants.

Education and Health. Education is the concurrent responsibility of the national and state governments, with the national government laying down policy directions and the states implementing them. The system of education comprises primary, secondary (with vocational and technical courses), and collegiate institutions. Primary education is free and compulsory, with 84% of the 6 to 11 year age group attending school in 1973–74. Literacy has risen from 17% in 1950–51 to 29% in 1971; in that year 39% of all men and 19% of all women were literate. Literacy is generally higher in urban areas.

In general the state governments provide health care facilities, and the national government sponsors and finances programs dealing with epidemic diseases and diseases resulting from nutritional deficiencies. In 1976 hospital beds numbered about 300,000 and doctors, 209,300. Family planning, with an emphasis on birth control, was officially encouraged for many years as the government attempted to lower the birthrate to 25 per 1,000. During the late 1970s, however, the government health program no longer emphasized birth control as heavily. Western medicine serves a large part of the country, but indigenous healing systems and homeopathy are also used.

The Arts. Independence has been accompanied by a vigorous promotion of the arts. In the visual arts a revival of Indian folk painting has occurred, along with new interest in the traditions of the Ajanta-Ellora, Rajasthan, Deccani, Mogul, and Kangra schools of painting. Architecture and sculpture, building on their magnificent ancient and medieval traditions in India, are finding new expressions as Western influences are combined with the old. Traditional handicrafts, like the textiles, wood- and ivory-carving, metalware, and pottery sought by 18th-century European traders, are being revived for the export market. For a historic survey of Indian arts, see INDIAN ART AND ARCHITECTURE.

In the performing arts a vigorous strengthening of classical Hindustani and Karnatic music has occurred, and many regional dance forms, such as BHARATA NATYAM and KATHAK, have received new recognition (see INDIAN MUSIC). Modern Indian theater stresses regional languages and experiments with new themes and forms; it often emphasizes the stress of modern living and the influence of Western traditions. A strong revival of folk music, dance, and drama has paralleled a rise in the popularity of Western music and dance forms, radio, and television. Perhaps the most popular art form today is motion pictures. Today India has the world's largest filmmaking industry, centered at Bombay and Madras.

ECONOMIC ACTIVITY
From independence until 1977 the economy was developed in accordance with five-year plans. Under these plans, a diversified, modern, industrial economy, with a large measure of state control, began to be developed in place of the colonial economy left by the British. Economic gains have been large, and today India is the world's tenth most industrialized nation in terms of output. However, economic gains have been largely nullified by the continuing growth of the population, and India still faces major social and economic problems in feeding and providing employment for such a large population.

Manufacturing and Mining. About 10% of the total labor force is employed in manufacturing, which contributes about 15% of the national income. Since the 1950s, India's development plans have stressed increased output in steel, engineering, and chemical industries, with concomitant support from mining; these, together with the large textile industry developed under the British, are today the principal manufacturing activities. In 1976 engineering industries contributed 29% of industrial production by value; India produced about 6.3 million metric tons (7 million U.S. tons) of steel, more than double the steel output of 1960. Principal steel and engineering centers are Asansol, Jamshedpur, Bhilai, Durgapur, and Raurkela, in the Chota Nagpur Plateau; and Bhadravati, in the southern peninsula. Chemicals and petrochemicals are produced in the greater Calcutta and Bombay areas, and India is Asia's third largest producer, in terms of output, of chemicals and chemical fertilizers. The textile industry is more dispersed, with factories and handlooms throughout India; India ranks third in the world in output of cotton yarn and fabric.

The most important minerals produced are coal and iron ore. India possesses rich iron-ore deposits in Bihar, Orissa, and West Bengal, and large coal reserves are located nearby. Manganese and limestone, also used in the steel-making process, are abundant, as are lead, copper, and bauxite.

Power. About 26% of all energy in India is derived from coal, 49% from petroleum, and 25% from electricity. More than 99.6 billion kW h of electricity were produced in 1977, of which hydroelectric power plants provided 39%, thermal power plants fueled by coal and petroleum 58%, and nuclear power plants 3%. In 1975, 29% of the villages were electrified. India has small petroleum deposits, some of them located offshore from Bombay, which came into production in 1975; the nation is increasing coal output and the construction of nuclear power plants in an effort to offset the inflationary impact of rapidly rising international petroleum prices.

Agriculture. India remains predominantly an agricultural nation. Landlordism was abolished in the 1950s, and small, owner-operated farms are the mainstay of Indian farming. About 70% of the labor force is employed in agriculture, and farming accounts for about 47% of the national income. About 55% of the total land area is cultivated, and many areas support two crops a year. The principal *kharif* (summer mon-

The Durgapur steel mill, in West Bengal, one of three government-operated mills proposed for construction in 1954, began operation in 1962. Since India achieved independence in 1947, an increase in the output of steel has been a priority of the nation's economic planners. By 1977, India's annual production of steel had risen to 7 million metric tons.

soonal) crops are rice, which is grown on 24% of the cultivated land, and millet, grown on 21%. The leading *rabi* (winter) crops are wheat, grown on 11% of the cultivated land, and pulses, which occupy 14%. India ranks fourth in world wheat production and second in rice, millet, and pulse production. The principal cash crops are cotton, grown widely as *kharif* crops on 5% of the cultivated land; jute, grown mainly in hot and humid areas, especially the Ganges Delta and the western coastal plain; tea, raised on plantations in the hills of Assam, West Bengal, Tamil Nadu, Kerala, and Karnataka; oil seeds; sugarcane; tobacco; spices; fruits; and rubber. India ranks first among the world's nations in production of tea and sugarcane; second in output of jute; and third in cotton production. Livestock, especially cattle, are numerous, reflecting the revered status of the cow in Hinduism. India is the leading Asian producer of milk, butter, and animal hides, although many cows are of poor quality and are a strain on the rural'economy in times of famine.

The improved seed strains used in the GREEN REVOLUTION to raise crop yields in Japan, China, Cuba, Taiwan, and other countries with a large population to feed, have also raised yields in India dramatically where used (in Punjab Haryana

and the peninsular deltas). Similarly, increased use of irrigation, chemical fertilizers, and pesticides with which the new seed strains are at their best, have also been shown effective in raising farm productivity. However, extending the benefits of the new farming methods is difficult because many farmers are too poor to buy the new seed strains and other supplies needed for increased yields. Often, the small size of their farms (the average is 2.6 ha/5.8 acres) and exhausted soils limit their ability to save the capital needed to raise them from subsistence to commercial farmers. Other conditions retarding farm modernization include the existence of a large, landless, and often unemployed labor force that must be supported in rural areas.

Forestry and Fishing. Forestry and fishing account for only 1.2% and 0.8% of the national income, but are locally important in some states. Forests occupy about 23% of the total land area but are not accessible for commercial development. The government is currently attempting to increase the forested area to 33.3% and improve lumber output. Fishing is locally important in Kerala and in some deltaic areas. Fish production has tripled since 1947 because of mechanization, introduction of deep-sea fishing vessels, and better preserva-

(Left) *Rice, the most important food crop of India, covers almost half of Bihar's northern alluvial plain. Although the Indian government has encouraged the modernization of agriculture, change has been slow and traditional farming methods are still common.*

(Right) *India is among the world's leading exporters of tea, and the state of Assam supplies almost half of the country's production. Tea leaves are picked by hand every 1 to 2 weeks to ensure a uniform crop.*

tion and marketing techniques. India is now fourth in Asia and eighth in the world in total fish production. Marine products account for 66% of the total catch, and inland fisheries (mainly from deltaic regions) for 34%.

Transportation. In 1973–74 the volume of railroad passenger and freight traffic was about double by that of 1950–51. In 1975 the total length of roads was three times greater than in 1950–51, and traffic on the roads was ten times greater in terms of passenger-kilometers traveled and six times greater in terms of cargo. Inland navigable waterways, which are primarily confined to deltaic regions, total 14,150 km (8,844 mi). Air services now reach most large cities, and Air India, which is government-owned, is a regularly scheduled international airline.

Trade. The total value of exports in 1975–76 was more than four times larger than it was a decade earlier and reflected the attempt to change from a colonial pattern of trade in agricultural commodities and raw materials with Great Britain to a diversification of export products and trading partners. The principal exports are cotton products; iron ore; jute and jute products; coffee; engineering, electrical, and leather goods; handicrafts; and chemical products. The principal imports are machinery, petroleum, chemicals, cereals, copper, and zinc. The major trading partners are the United States, Great Britain, USSR, Japan, and Iran. In most years the value of imports usually exceeds the value of exports, the adverse balance of trade resulting from the requirements of a developing economy and occasional crop failure.

GOVERNMENT

Under the constitution of 1950, India is a sovereign democratic republic, with membership in the Commonwealth of Nations and a two-house parliamentary form of government to which members are elected by universal adult (aged 21 and over) suffrage.

Executive authority is vested in the president and is exercised by him on the advice of the prime minister and council of ministers, who are responsible to parliament. The parliament consists of the Rajya Sabha (Council of States) and the Lok Sabha (House of the People). The Rajya Sabha is an indirectly elected permanent body, from which one-third of the members retire every second year. The Lok Sabha is a directly elected body, which sits for 6 years unless dissolved sooner.

The system of state government closely resembles that of the federal government. The governor of each state is appointed by the president, and the chief minister and council of the state serve in an executive capacity and are responsible to an elected state legislature. Seven states have a bicameral legislature, and the remainder a unicameral legislature. India's politics have long been dominated by the INDIAN NATIONAL CONGRESS which, after its founding in 1885, led the fight for independence. In 1969 the Congress party split into two factions, a conservative branch and a liberal branch. The latter, led by Indira GANDHI, continued to be the ruling party until 1977, when, after a period of emergency rule, it was defeated in the national elections by the Janata party, a coalition of several parties. In January 1980, however, Mrs. Gandhi and the Congress party were returned to power.

HISTORY SINCE 1947

The history of the modern state of India begins on Aug. 15, 1947, when British India was partitioned along mainly religious lines to form the primarily Hindu nation of India and the primarily Muslim country divided into East and West Pakistan. (For the history of the Indian subcontinent prior to 1947, see INDIA, HISTORY OF.) In India, Jawaharlal NEHRU, leader of the Congress party, became the first prime minister. The newly independent country struggled to organize itself under the constitution and to integrate into one national system hundreds of separate princely states that had existed under the British. The Partition of the subcontinent resulted in a massive migration of Hindus from Pakistan into India and Muslims from India into Pakistan. This movement of perhaps as many as 16 million people was accompanied by much violence; it is estimated that 1 million casualties occurred. During this period of upheaval, Mahatma GANDHI, India's revered pacifist leader of the independence movement, was assassinated (Jan. 30, 1948). Partition also led to warfare between Pakistan and India over the princely state of Kashmir, where a Hindu prince ruled over the largely Muslim population. A cease-fire was declared in 1949 (see INDIA-PAKISTAN WARS).

Despite these setbacks, however, the Nehru era (1947–64) brought stability to India's democratic institutions and saw the inauguration of India as a republic on Jan. 26, 1950. The princely state of Hyderabad was incorporated into India in 1948, and in 1962 the former Portuguese territories of Goa, Daman, and Diu and the former French territories of Pondicherry, Karikal, Mahe, and Yanam were annexed. Improvements were made in agriculture, irrigation, power, mineral development, industrial growth, and transportation; but social

Since Indian independence in 1947, politics has been dominated by Jawaharlal Nehru (left) and by his daughter, Indira Gandhi (right). Nehru served as prime minister from 1947 until 1964, a period marked by territorial disputes between India and neighboring Pakistan and China. Indira Gandhi became prime minister in 1966. During her tenure, India waged (1971) a successful war against Pakistan to secure the independence of Bangladesh; Gandhi's domestic program increased government planning and was one factor in her imposition of a state of emergency in 1975.

unrest grew as the income gap widened between the 10% of the population who accounted for 40% of all household income and the vast majority who remained poor and often without employment. These social and economic problems, exacerbated by unsolved caste problems, led to the growth of new political parties challenging Congress: the CPI (Communist party of India), the CPM (Communist party Marxists), and the extremist Naxalites (Maoists).

Nehru died in May 1964 and was succeeded by Lal Bahadur SHASTRI as prime minister. A second war with Pakistan over Kashmir erupted in 1965 and was ended by a peace treaty in 1966. On the death of Shastri in 1966, Nehru's daughter, Indira Gandhi, succeeded as prime minister. During Mrs. Gandhi's 11 years in office (1966–77) major gains were made in agricultural production, and irrigation and power facilities were expanded; domestic sources of natural gas and petroleum were discovered and developed; and diversified industrial development established India as the world's tenth most industrialized nation. In 1971, India also entered the civil war between East and West Pakistan, helping to establish the independence of Bangladesh. In 1975, Sikkim was integrated into the Indian nation.

Social unrest, however, continued to grow in the face of unsolved economic and social problems. Political opposition to Mrs. Gandhi's policies also mounted, and in 1969 the ruling Congress party split into a moderate wing supporting Gandhi and a dissident right wing. Separatist movements were curbed by the government to prevent further fragmentation of the national system, and government control of the economy was strengthened by nationalization of major banks in 1969, of general insurance in 1970, and of the coal and other industries in 1973.

Mrs. Gandhi survived the opposition within the Congress party and, forming a new political alignment, was returned to power in the 1971 elections. However, in the face of continuing opposition by such leaders as Jayaprakash NARAYAN, mounting political agitation, riots, strikes, and demands for Mrs. Gandhi's resignation, President Fakhruddin Ali Ahmed, on the advice of the prime minister, proclaimed a state of emergency on June 26, 1975 on the grounds that the security of India was threatened by internal disturbances. During the emergency, Mrs. Gandhi's political opponents were arrested and detained, and the constitution was amended to limit personal freedom and the powers of the courts. A 20-point program to deal with economic problems was announced.

The emergency was revoked in March 1977 and elections were held. A coalition of political parties opposed to Mrs. Gandhi, called the Janata party, won an absolute majority of seats in the Lok Sabha. Mrs. Gandhi resigned, and Morarji DESAI became the new prime minister. President Ahmed died the same year, and in August 1977 Neelam Sanjiva Reddy was elected president. Desai improved relations with Nepal, signed a pact with Bangladesh ending the 25-year-long dispute over India's diversion of the Ganges, and discontinued the fifth five-year plan in favor of year-to-year planning. In July 1979 Desai resigned, and Charan Singh served briefly as prime minister before resigning on August 20. Singh headed a caretaker government until elections in January 1980 returned Mrs. Gandhi and the Congress party to power.

C. D. DESHPANDE

Bibliography:

GENERAL: Basham, A. L., ed., *A Cultural History of India* (1975); Griffiths, Percival, *Modern India*, 4th ed. (1965); Mehta, Ved, *A Portrait of India* (1970).
GEOGRAPHY, LAND, AND PEOPLES: Houlton, M. L., *India: Land, People and Culture* (1974); Majumdar, D. N., *Races and Cultures of India*, 4th ed. (1961; repr. 1973); Spate, O. H. K., *India and Pakistan: A General and Regional Geography*, 3d ed. (1967); Weiner, Myron, *Sons of the Soil: Migration and Ethnic Conflict in India* (1978).
GOVERNMENT AND POLITICS: Austin, Granville, *The Indian Constitution: Cornerstone of a Nation* (1972); Eldersveld, Samuel J., and Ahmed, Bashiruddin, *Citizens and Mass Political Behavior in India* (1978); Gupta, D. C., *Indian Government and Politics* (1976); Hardgrave, Robert L., *India: Government and Politics in a Developing Nation*, 2d ed. (1975); Hiro, Dilip, *Inside India Today* (1977); Mehta, Ved, *The New India* (1978); Robb, Peter, *The Government of India and Reform* (1977).
ECONOMICS: Bhagwati, Jagdish N., *India's Economic Policy and Performance* (1975); Frankel, Francine R., *India's Green Revolution* (1971); Mellor, John W., *The New Economics of Growth: A Strategy for India and the Developing World* (1976); Veit, Lawrence, *India's Second Revolution* (1976).
MODERN HISTORY: Brown, W. Norman, *The United States and India, Pakistan, Bangladesh*, 3d ed. (1972); Spear, Percival, *India: A Modern History* (1972); Tharyan, P., *India: The Critical Decade After Nehru* (1975); Webster, John C., *History and Contemporary India* (1972); Wolpert, Stanley, *A New History of India* (1977).

India, history of

Over the millennia various invasions have added great diversity and complexity to the cultures of the Indian subcontinent; yet many ancient and unique features have remained recognizable throughout its history. Diversity is particularly evident in the 20th-century political division of the subcontinent into three nations: India (Bharat), Pakistan, and Bangladesh. However, the gradual incorporation of various cultural elements into its own complex civilization has been a continuing feature of India's history.

ANCIENT INDIA

Because the Indian subcontinent is one of great geographical diversity, it is not surprising that at least two distinct cultures developed in ancient India. Archaeological evidence suggests that humans first migrated to the subcontinent between 400,000 and 200,000 years ago. Some of these primitive peoples had probably crossed the Hindu Kush Mountains into the area that is now northern Pakistan. Other peoples had possibly sailed to southern India from eastern Africa.

Indus Civilization. One of the world's oldest and greatest civilizations took shape between about 3000 and 2500 BC in the valley of the Indus River, from which the name of the Indian subcontinent is taken. Sites of this INDUS CIVILIZATION at Harappa and Mohenjo-daro—both in present-day Pakistan—have been extensively excavated; other sites have been uncovered in India as far east as the cities of Simla and Bikaner and as far south as the Kathiawar Peninsula and the coast of the Gujarat region. The Indus, or Harappa, civilization, one of the most advanced of ancient times, was similar in many ways to contemporary cultures in Mesopotamia. Harappans lived in towns with two- and three-story brick houses, and well laid out streets and drainage systems; they employed tools of copper, bronze, and stone; they wore clothing of cotton; and they used rather sophisticated pottery and other kinds of cooking and serving utensils. Harappa script, which appears on innumerable seals and art works, has not yet been deciphered.

Aryan Culture. Harappa culture thrived until about 1500 BC, when the Indus Valley was overrun by ARYAN invaders from the Iranian plateau. The seminomadic Aryans spoke an archaic form of Sanskrit (see INDO-IRANIAN LANGUAGES) and left no remains of cities, burials, arts, or crafts. What is known about the Aryans has been passed down through religious texts—the VEDAS, especially the *Rig Veda* ("Verses of Knowledge"). Originally transmitted orally, the Vedas describe a highly ritualistic worship with innumerable deities, a rich my-

This square stamp is representative of the type found at Mohenjo-daro, a city of the Indus civilization (fl. 2500–1500 BC). The stamp may have been used by merchants to identify their wares. The pictographic script that appears on many seals remains undeciphered.

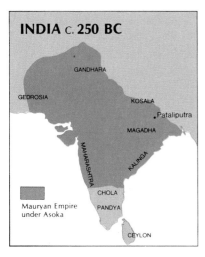

INDIA c. 250 BC

GANDHARA
GEDROSIA
KOSALA
•Pataliputra
MAGADHA
MAHARASHTRA
KALINGA
CHOLA
PANDYA
CEYLON

Mauryan Empire under Asoka

(Left) *This map illustrates India's Mauryan Empire at its height, under the ruler Asoka (r. 273–232 BC). Considered India's first great empire, it declined after Asoka's death.*

(Right) *The design of this 1st-century BC Buddhist stupa, or shrine, at Sanchi was influenced by the architectural style developed during the reign of Asoka, who advocated the spread of Buddhism.*

thology, and an elaborate fire sacrifice. They also mention the system of *varnas*, or classes, from which evolved the CASTE system. The four *varnas* were the Brahmans (see BRAHMIN), or priests; the Kshatriya, political rulers or warriors; Vaishya, traders and cultivators; and Shudra, artisans. The Vedas and the caste system remain central to the Indian socioreligious system, HINDUISM. Thus the Aryans gave to India many of its basic institutions and cultural habits.

Early Cultural Cleavages. According to one theory, the Aryans, a warlike people who rode on horseback, pushed southward many of northern India's darker-skinned and shorter inhabitants, whom they called *dasas*. This theory, yet to be proven, is sometimes used to explain the origins of the division between the Aryan linguistic groups in the North and the DRAVIDIAN LANGUAGES of the South. Some modern southern separatists have claimed that the Dravidian speakers predate the Aryan invaders, but there is not yet sufficient linguistic evidence to date the arrival of Dravidian speakers in southern India. Cultural distinctions between North and South remain, however, in modern India.

Aryan religious texts indicate that the Aryans viewed themselves as racially and culturally superior and despised the *dasas*. In the north, the area of Aryan dominance, the name *dasa* eventually came to mean "slave" or "bondsman." The *dasas* probably performed many of the unpleasant but necessary tasks in the segmented society that was developing under Aryan influence.

Challenges to Brahman Ascendancy. Over the centuries pre-Aryan and Aryan cultures gradually fused in northern India as the Aryans expanded slowly eastward into the Gangetic plain, where the second of ancient India's great urban civilizations developed. Such cities as PATALIPUTRA (near modern Patna), Kasi (modern VARANASI), and Ajodhya rose in importance. In the Bihar region in the 6th century BC a wealthy merchant class (largely Vaishyas) began to support speculation challenging orthodox beliefs. For example, that era's UPANISHADS (scriptural texts that were part of the Vedas but attempted to go beyond them) began to challenge the traditional authority of the Brahmans. In the northeast, where Aryan influence was relatively weak, the religious systems known as JAINISM and BUDDHISM were founded around 500 BC. Both were widely supported by the merchant and landowning aristocracies of eastern India, and both can be viewed in part as revolts against Brahmanism.

Maurya and Gupta Periods. In 326 BC, ALEXANDER THE GREAT, with his Macedonian army, invaded the Indus Valley. The subcontinent was still politically fragmented, and no Indian ruler was able to assemble an elephant and infantry force powerful enough to stop Alexander's armies. It was, rather, the vastness of the subcontinent and the discontent of his troops that convinced the Macedonian king to retreat.

In c.321 BC, shortly after Alexander's invasion, the great king CHANDRAGUPTA MAURYA (founder of the MAURYA dynasty) es-

tablished India's first large empire, centered at Pataliputra. His grandson ASOKA ruled an empire that extended to the south of central India's Deccan Plateau and west into Baluchistan and modern Afghanistan; in the east it included the state of Kalinga, which he had conquered c.261. Asoka also attempted to create a state religion incorporating Buddhism and other faiths as well as Hinduism. A convert to Buddhism, he sent Buddhist missionaries abroad and is credited with elevating Buddhism to a world religion (although eventually it waned as a separate belief system within India). Soon after Asoka's death (232 BC) his empire was reduced to the state of Magadha, although the dynasty survived until c.185 BC.

Under the Mauryas and succeeding dynasties, for a period of about 800 years, India evolved a civilization that still remains fairly intact. The institution of caste was solidly implanted, and Hindu philosophy and legal codes were developed.

The era of the GUPTA dynasty (AD c.320–c.540) is generally considered to be ancient India's classic period. Indic architecture, sculpture, painting, dance, and music flourished. Despite classical standards, however, many variations also came into being, primarily because of the numerous invasions of India by peoples from central Asia, but also because of the assimilation of elements of indigenous movements such as Buddhism.

MEDIEVAL INDIA

After the brilliance of the Gupta dynasty, India entered its medieval period, becoming divided politically into a number of small kingdoms. Scholasticism replaced scholarship, religion became highly ritualistic, and the arts generally turned from creativity to commentary and dialectic. This period,

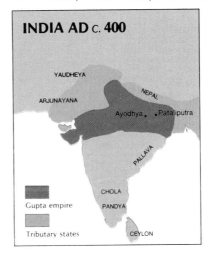

INDIA AD c. 400

YAUDHEYA
ARJUNAYANA
NEPAL
Ayodhya• •Pataliputra
PALLAVA
CHOLA
PANDYA
CEYLON

Gupta empire

Tributary states

This map shows India during the Gupta Empire under the reign of Chandragupta II (r. c.380–414), who expanded his family's kingdom into a vast domain that included most of northern India. During the reign of the Guptas—recognized as India's classical period—northern India was economically prosperous and the arts flourished. The political power of the Gupta dynasty waned during the 5th century.

which was characterized by many invasions and large-scale migrations from the northwest, was one of relative isolation from the more advanced civilizations of the Arabs and Chinese. It continued until the founding of the Mogul Empire in the 16th century.

Among the smaller states that appeared in India in the confusion of the 7th, 8th, and 9th centuries were the military aristocracies of the RAJPUTS in northern and central India. Ra-

INDIA c. 1690

Kabul
Lahore
Delhi
Agra
Patna
RAJPUTS
MARATHAS
Goa
(Portuguese)
Madras
(British)
Pondichéry
(French)
GOLCONDA
Mogul Empire
CEYLON

(Left) The vast Mogul Empire expanded to include the entire Indian subcontinent except for the southern tip. At the same time that the Moguls, a Muslim people, were gaining imperial control, European merchants were establishing trading settlements along the coasts of India. Under Akbar, the greatest Mogul ruler, Hindu and Muslim motifs were combined in the Indian arts, and a uniform structure of government was established.

cially, culturally, and linguistically distinct Dravidian kingdoms also flourished in southern India, where they are known to have existed from at least the 1st century BC. Most prominent were the kingdom of the Andhras, located in the areas around present-day Hyderabad, and the Tamil states of the Pandyas at the southern tip of the Indian peninsula; the Cholas, in the region that is now Madras; and the Cheras, who controlled the southwestern coast. From these local kingdoms many Indian ideas and practices spread to Indonesia and other parts of Southeast Asia. The Pallava dynasty, which sponsored limited colonization throughout the area and played a dominant role in southeast India from the 6th to the 8th century, although of uncertain genealogy, was most likely Brahman and northern Indian in origin. Through the Pallavas, who were patrons of the arts, elements of Indo-Aryan Sanskritic culture were widely introduced into southern India.

Despite the fundamental unity of Indic civilization, political diversity was the rule during the medieval period. Units of government were of all sizes and types. Boundaries were constantly in flux, with kings and maharajas usually unwilling to band together even in federal arrangements. Small personal kingdoms were frequently overturned, and newly victorious rajas were able to make quick deals with village kin leaders. A tradition of relative autonomy for villages—governed largely through kinship groups and paying tribute to rulers of regional kingdoms—helped preserve much of the stability that might otherwise have been lost in the confusion of changing boundaries and sovereigns.

Cultural unity was encouraged by shrines and pilgrimage sites throughout the subcontinent, by a great body of Sanskrit oral tradition and myth, and by cooperation between Brahman religious and political leaders. The ability of Hinduism to accommodate new peoples and ideas without conceding anything fundamental to them also helped to promote civilizational continuity.

ISLAMIC INFLUENCE

Islam first entered the Indian subcontinent in AD 711, when a young Arabian general, Muhammad ibn Qasim, fought his way into the Indus Valley. The state of Sind was added to the Arab caliphate and its people converted to Islam, but it did not serve as the springboard for a Muslim advance deeper into India. In the 9th and 10th centuries, Arab traders began to convert many Hindus in port cities along the southwest coast. Cultural influences were transmitted in both directions. Baghdad scholars were especially intrigued by Indian mathematics, astronomy, and other natural sciences.

The chief Muslim conquerors of India were not Arabs,

(Left) Akbar, third emperor of the Mogul dynasty, conducted military campaigns to extend his control of India. This 17th-century painting portrays his bloody seige of Chitor, a Rajput fortress.

(Right) A 17th-century portrait depicts Akbar's son, Emperor Jahangir. Jahangir allowed his favorite wife, Nur Jahan, and her Persian relatives to control the government. He himself encouraged the introduction of Persian elements and a new refinement into Indian art and architecture.

(Left) *This Indian painting shows a British officer riding an elephant amid an entourage of Indians during the time when India was governed by the British East India Company. The map (below) shows the gradual British annexation of Indian territories. British expansionist policies and insensitivity to Indian traditions were major causes of the Indian Mutiny of 1857-58. After this revolt was suppressed, the British crown assumed governmental control from the East India Company.*

however, but central Asian converts to Islam—Turks, Afghans, Persians, and Mongols—who began to enter the subcontinent around 1000. From Ghazni, a center of Persian culture controlled by Turkish tribes in the area that is now Afghanistan, MAHMUD OF GHAZNI led (998-1030) a series of raids into the Punjab region. Mahmud's tactics of massacre, pillage, and destruction secured for the Muslims a gateway into the Indian subcontinent. The Muslims eventually converted many low-caste Hindus and Buddhists—particularly in Bengal and other eastern areas—as they pushed across India. Many converts hoped that they would become part of a more egalitarian society and gain the protection of the powerful armies of the invaders.

The Delhi Sultanate. The first Muslim empire based in India was established in Delhi in 1206 by Qutb-ud-Din Aybak (d. 1210). This DELHI SULTANATE, a constantly expanding and contracting empire, was ruled by a line of 34 succeeding sultans. The history of the sultanate was filled with bloodshed, tyranny, and treachery; it was divided among five dynasties (the "Slave" kings, the Khaljis, the Tughluqs, the Sayyids, and the Lodis). During the Tughluq dynasty, TIMUR, the great conqueror from Samarkand, desolated (1398-99) the entire sultanate. Under the Lodi kingdom, which endured until 1526, the Delhi Sultanate stretched from the Punjab in the west to the Bihar region in the east.

Mogul Empire. The first ruler of the MOGUL dynasty was BABUR, who claimed the subcontinent as his right of inheritance because of the conquest of Delhi by his ancestor Timur. Babur (r. 1526-30) was a highly cultured man from Persia who disliked many facets of Indian life but nonetheless established the most glorious empire in India's history. Babur's son HUMAYUN reigned from 1530 to 1540 and again in 1555-56 despite the challenge mounted by the Afghan SHER SHAH, who ruled north India for five years.

Until 1707 a series of able emperors expanded and added to the glory of the Moguls, each in his own way. The greatest of the Moguls was AKBAR (r. 1556-1605), who built the administrative machinery that forms the basis for many present-day practices in India. A tolerant man, Akbar abolished a discriminatory tax on Hindus and did much to combine Hindu and Muslim motifs in palace architecture, art, literature, and music.

Akbar's son and successor, JAHANGIR, was a heavy drinker who reveled in luxurious living, as did Jahangir's son SHAH JAHAN. Best known for his great building program, which culminated in the TAJ MAHAL, Shah Jahan was also instrumental in extending the Mogul Empire to the Deccan Plateau. Both Shah Jahan and his son and successor AURANGZEB were much less tolerant of Hindus than their predecessors had been. Af-

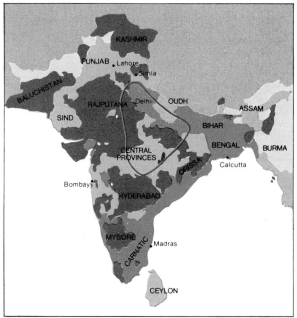

INDIA UNDER BRITISH RULE

British possessions 1805		Dependent Indian states by 1914
British acquisitions by 1858		Area of Mutiny 1857
British acquisitions by 1914		

ter the death (1707) of Aurangzeb, the Mogul Empire disintegrated quickly, although ineffective rulers remained on the throne at Delhi until 1858.

EUROPEAN INFLUENCE

Extensive European contact with India began in 1498 when Vasco da GAMA, a Portuguese navigator, landed with three small ships at Calicut, on the southwest coast. Both the Portuguese and the Dutch attempted to colonize India during the 16th century, but neither proved strong enough to maintain the naval presence necessary to rival the British and French. The Portuguese, who were further handicapped by their

Robert Clive, a leading military strategist of the British East India Company, ensured British dominance in India through his victorious campaigns against the French. Clive achieved his greatest conquest at the Battle of Plassey (1757), when he defeated the provincial forces of a Mogul ruler. Appointed governor of Bengal, he introduced several administrative reforms but was later accused of peculation in office.

heavy-handed policy of trying to convert Indians to Christianity by force, ended up with only a few small outposts in India, the most prominent of these being Goa on the western coast (see GOA, DAMAN, AND DIU). The more tolerant Dutch concentrated on building a trading monopoly, through their Dutch East India Company (see EAST INDIA COMPANY, DUTCH). By the mid-17th century, however, they had turned their attention almost exclusively toward Indonesia.

The British empire in India was established by a private trading firm, the East India Company (founded 1600; see EAST INDIA COMPANY, BRITISH), which governed with the consent of Parliament until 1858. The company bought a strip of sandy beach at Madras in 1639, acquired a lease to the port of Bombay from King Charles II in 1668, and in 1690 secured from the Mogul emperor Aurangzeb permission to build a settlement on a muddy flatland that eventually became Calcutta. At each of these three so-called presidency cities the company erected a fort, known as a factory, from which the British conducted their trading activities.

The French got off to a slow start in their attempt to build a trading empire in India. The government-run French East India Company (established in 1664; see EAST INDIA COMPANY, FRENCH) never succeeded in fostering a trade volume comparable to that of the British. In the 18th century both Britain and France sought to protect their trading interests by allying with native princes to fill the growing power vacuums created as the Mogul Empire disintegrated. As part of the War of the AUSTRIAN SUCCESSION, the two European powers came into conflict in India in 1746, when the French, under the aggressive leadership of Joseph François DUPLEIX, seized Madras. However, in 1761, during the SEVEN YEARS' WAR, the French surrendered their territory of PONDICHERRY to the British, and after the 1763 peace treaty the French retained only a few trading centers in India. The British were able to defeat the French largely because the British East India Company had a better navy, greater flexibility, and more reliable funding than the French East India Company.

The hero of Britain's battles against the French, Robert CLIVE, was a military adventurer who had started as a teenage clerk with the East India Company in the 1740s. Clive's greatest triumph came at the Battle of Plassey (1757), when he and 950 other Europeans combined with some 2,000 Indian soldiers (sepoys) to defeat a force of more than 50,000 led by a degenerate local Mogul nawab (provincial governor). Victory at Plassey led to effective political control over the vast riches of the Ganges Valley in 1765, when the nawab surrendered to Clive the right to collect land revenue for most of eastern India.

Some of the directors of the East India Company initially demurred at the prospect of governing the eastern region,

Bengal, preferring to set up puppet princes to administer the area while they exploited its wealth for their own private gain. To counter the growing corruption within the company and to reform the governance of India, Parliament passed the Regulating Act of 1773. Warren HASTINGS, governor of Bengal in 1772–73, helped to lay the administrative foundations for British rule under the provisions of this act. As India's first governor-general (1773–85), Hastings consolidated many of Clive's territorial gains. He attempted to assert the British right to interfere in the affairs of the MARATHAS, who became the leading rivals to the British after the virtual collapse of the Mogul Empire. He successfully met the challenge presented by the state of Mysore and its leaders HYDER ALI and his son TIPPU SULTAN in the early 1780s. Hastings was later tried before Parliament for high crimes and misdemeanors during his administration. He was eventually acquitted (1795), but his lengthy trial was an important factor leading to a genuine attempt by the company to put its house in order.

BRITISH INDIA

Lord CORNWALLIS, governor-general of India from 1786 to 1793, established the administrative, legal, and land-revenue codes that made British rule possible. Cornwallis separated the administrative and commercial functions of the company, organized a prestigious civil service, raised salaries to the point where irregular profits were unnecessary, and established disciplinary measures that made it possible to curb private trade by company employees.

Because of his belief that considerable corruption stemmed from contact with Indians, Cornwallis excluded people of Indian origin from higher posts of government. This policy led, during the 19th century, to a widening socioeconomic gap between the British and their Indian subjects, with British settlements taking on the character of prosperous English towns in the midst of increasingly squalid Indian slums. Indian poverty was encouraged by a rapid spurt in population growth that followed the establishment of peace and the adoption of public health measures throughout the subcontinent. British unwillingness to allow large-scale industrialization in India further intensified poverty. (The British preferred a subordinate economic role for their colonies within the British imperial system—a system that helped Britain to become an industrialized world power).

Lord WELLESLEY, governor-general from 1798 to 1805, launched a policy of expansion, which culminated in the mid-19th century—when the East India Company controlled more than three-fifths of India with the remaining two-fifths being run by 562 local princes who were clearly subordinates of the British raj (government). Coupled with British policies of expansionism and exclusivity, British insensitivity to Indian traditions and religious practices helped to increase tensions. Among the Indian elites resentment of British rule grew, especially during the regime (1848–56) of Lord DALHOUSIE, who attempted to modernize and westernize India. In 1857 many traditional groups, largely in north India, revolted, led by mutineers in the army. This violent and brutal INDIAN MUTINY, or Sepoy Rebellion, was put down by the British in 1858. As a direct result of the revolt, the crown took over most of the functions of the British East India Company. The revolt also intensified widespread feelings of distrust between the Indians and the British. Such feelings deepened as both Indian poverty and British wealth became magnified during the next century.

THE INDIAN NATIONALIST MOVEMENT

Indian nationalist sentiments found expression early in the 19th century in the writings of Rammohun ROY, a religious reformer, who hoped that a modern state of India would combine the best of both Hindu and western cultures. The first organizations attempting to reform British rule were also formed early in the century. In 1885 they were welded together in the INDIAN NATIONAL CONGRESS by a retired British civil servant, Allan Octavian Hume (1829–1912), and a number of prominent Bengali leaders.

The Congress was originally an elitist and moderate constitutional lobby, advocating such reforms as more seats for Indians in the legislatures and more schools. Early in the 20th

(Left) *Early in the 20th century Indian nationalist groups engaged in various campaigns to reform British rule. An extreme militant faction was responsible for this 1913 bombing attempt on the life of British viceroy Lord Harding.*

(Below) *The photograph shows Indian political leaders Jawaharlal Nehru and Mahatma Gandhi at the Indian National Congress (1942) that adopted the "Quit India" resolution.*

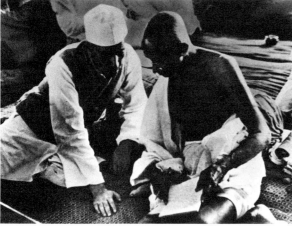

century the British made some attempts to meet its demands by widening Indian political participation. However, the extreme wing of the Congress increasingly demanded *swaraj* (complete independence). By 1907 the organization had split into a moderate group led by Gopal Krishna Gokhale (1866–1915) and a militant faction under Bal Gangadhar TILAK. At about the same time (1906) Muslim leaders, dissatisfied with Hindu dominance of the Congress, formed their own nationalist organization, the MUSLIM LEAGUE.

Although India's various nationalist groups united temporarily in 1916 in support of Britain's World War I effort, the increasingly dominant militants were disappointed in Britain's gradual approach to its professed goal of eventual self-rule for India. British prestige fell precipitously in 1919 with the passage of laws restricting political activity and with the massacre of Indian civilians by British troops at AMRITSAR. During the 1920s the Congress acquired a mass base, the support of prominent Indians, and increasing militancy under the leadership of Mahatma GANDHI, who introduced the highly successful techniques of passive resistance (*satyagraha*) and civil disobedience. During the 1920s, however, Muslims staged a large-scale withdrawal from the Congress. By the end of the decade, Muslim leaders such as Muhammad IQBAL were proposing the creation of a separate Muslim state.

During World War II the Muslims, led by Muhammad Ali JINNAH and now demanding their own independent state (Pakistan), supported the British. The Congress, however, insisted that Britain leave India. When Indians refused to cooperate in repelling the Japanese attack on the subcontinent in

1942, Britain arrested many leaders and outlawed the Congress. A group of extreme anti-British Indian nationalists led by Subhas Chandra BOSE even fought on the Japanese side in Burma and India.

At the end of the war Britain agreed to self-rule for India. However, in the 1946 elections the Muslim League won most of the Muslim vote, and Gandhi was unsuccessful in preventing the partition of the subcontinent into Muslim and Hindu states. In August 1947, India and Pakistan achieved independence. Five months later Gandhi was assassinated by a Hindu fanatic. The task of governing India fell to its first prime minister, Jawaharlal NEHRU. Jinnah became governor-general of the Muslim nation of Pakistan, which was then comprised of two separate territories, East and West Pakistan.

For the history of the Indian subcontinent since independence, see BANGLADESH, INDIA, and PAKISTAN.

MARCUS FRANDA AND VONETTA J. FRANDA

Bibliography: Allan, John, et al., *The Cambridge Shorter History of India* (1964); Basham, A. L., *The Wonder That Was India*, 3d ed. (1967); Edwardes, Michael, *British India, 1772–1947* (1968); Gascoigne, Bamber, *The Great Moghuls* (1971); Lamb, Beatrice P., *India: A World in Transition*, 4th ed. (1975); Majumdar, Ramesh C., *Ancient India*, 2d ed. (1964); Majumdar, Ramesh C., et al., *An Advanced History of India*, 3d ed. (1973); Smith, Vincent A., *The Oxford History of India*, 3d ed. (1968); Spear, T. G. P., *India*, rev. ed. (1972); Thapar, Romila, *A History of India* (1966); Wolpert, Stanley A., *A New History of India* (1977).

See also: INDIAN ART AND ARCHITECTURE; INDIAN LITERATURE; INDIAN MUSIC.

India-Pakistan Wars

INDIA and PAKISTAN have fought three major wars with each other since the partition of the Indian subcontinent in 1947.

The first conflict was over KASHMIR in 1947–49. With independence and partition, the subcontinent's numerous princely states faced the choice of joining either Hindu India or Muslim Pakistan. Contiguous to both India and West Pakistan, Kashmir was ruled by a Hindu prince, but the majority of its population was Muslim. In 1947, Pakistani tribesmen invaded the state in support of an uprising by Muslim peasants. The maharaja fled to Delhi, where he signed papers giving Kashmir to India. Indian troops were then flown in to defend the former princely state, bringing the Pakistani army into the fray. Fighting continued in Kashmir until a United Nations commission arranged a truce in January 1949. Kashmir was then divided along the cease-fire line, with India holding about two-thirds and Pakistan the remainder. India referred the case to the UN Security Council, which has heard conflicting claims intermittently ever since; periodic fighting has broken the uneasy peace.

In April 1965 sharp fighting broke out in the Rann of Kutch, on the border between West Pakistan and India, and later spread to Kashmir and to the Punjab. India charged that Pakistani infiltrators were again invading Kashmir while Pakistan claimed that the invaders were Kashmiri freedom fighters. India seized army posts on the Pakistan side of their common border in Kashmir; Pakistan countered with tanks secured as military aid from the United States; and India dispatched planes to destroy the tanks. When Pakistan unleashed its air force—trained by the United States—and each side launched a large-scale land invasion of the other's territory in September 1965, the United Nations again intervened to bring about a cease-fire. Direct confrontation between the troops ended in January 1966, shortly after an agreement between India and Pakistan had been reached at Tashkent, USSR, through Soviet mediation.

Although neither the 1948 nor the 1965 war was conclusive, India demonstrated unquestioned military superiority over Pakistan in the third war, which took place in December 1971. At that time India intervened in the civil war that had erupted between West and East Pakistan, facilitating the secession of the latter, which became the independent state of Bangladesh. The Pakistani army and air force were severely crippled in this war. Most defense analysts have since concluded that the truncated Pakistan no longer has the population base to support an army powerful enough to cope with the Indian armed forces, which number more than 1,000,000 (constituting the world's fourth largest military force).

MARCUS FRANDA AND VONETTA J. FRANDA

Bibliography: Barnds, W. J., *India, Pakistan, and the Great Powers* (1972); Lamb, Alastair, *Crisis in Kashmir, 1947-1966* (1966); Siddiqui, Kalim, *Conflict, Crisis, and War in Pakistan* (1972).

Indian Affairs, Bureau of

The Bureau of Indian Affairs (BIA), formerly known as the Office of Indian Affairs, the Indian Department, and the Indian Service, is an agency of the U.S. Department of the Interior set up to handle Indian affairs in the nation. It is directed by the Interior Department's assistant secretary of Indian affairs, who is appointed by the president. The BIA has eight area offices that supervise its programs on reservations and in other Indian communities. Education, social services, law enforcement, mineral and water rights, and land leasing are important caretaking responsibilities assumed by the BIA on some reservations. On other reservations, these functions are now entirely or in part administered by tribal governments. The BIA also sponsors job training for reservation Indians wishing to relocate in cities.

The bureau, created (1824) within the War Department, was transferred by Congress to the newly created Department of the Interior in 1849. When Indian lands west of the Mississippi were opened for white settlement in the 1850s, the bureau set aside Indian reservations and established treaties with individual tribal nations. Native Americans, however, had little or no voice in the early formulation of BIA policy and for much of its history the bureau did little to protect Indian interests. In the 1950s the governmental policy calling for termination of special services of the BIA to specific tribes was opposed by most Indians. The AMERICAN INDIAN MOVEMENT and other Indian-rights groups staged protests against the bureau in the 1970s and demanded that it become more responsive to the needs of native Americans. BEA MEDICINE

Bibliography: Brophy, William, and Aberle, Sophie, eds., *The Indian* (1966); Taylor, Theodore, *The States and Their Indian Citizens* (1972).

See also: INDIANS, AMERICAN.

Indian art and architecture

The artistic tradition of India is one of the oldest and richest in the world. Beginning with prehistoric rock paintings, which are believed to go back to the 6th millennium BC, and finding expression in a vigorous school of modern art, the tradition spans about 8,000 years and has produced a large and varied artistic output. It comprises masterpieces in all major artistic media, such as architecture, sculpture, painting, metal work, textiles, and ceramics. The true genius of the Indian artists has manifested itself most fully in sculpture, however. The outstanding works of classical GUPTA and medieval sculpture are rightly regarded as supreme achievements of world art. Unlike much of the great art of the Western world, they are the work of anonymous artisans who produced them not for their own fame or self-expression but in the service of religion at the request of kings and priests. Art created for purely aesthetic purposes only came into being in modern times under European influence and was alien to traditional Indian society.

The most important influences on traditional Indian art were the religious ideas and institutions that inspired it. As in other artistic traditions of the East, religion played an important role in the development of Indian art, but perhaps nowhere else has there been a richer and more varied spiritual heritage. The three major influences were BUDDHISM, HINDUISM, and ISLAM, but other cults such as JAINISM, TANTRA, and primitive fertility cults also played an important role. Although little is known about the religious beliefs of prehistoric India and the INDUS CIVILIZATION, it can be safely assumed that this art too served largely religious purposes. As stated in an ancient text, it is only with the help of images that the gods and goddesses can be visualized; it is for this reason that icons have played such an important part in religious worship in India.

This limestone bust, dating from the 3d millennium BC, was found at Mohenjo-daro, one of the great centers of the ancient civilization that flourished in the Indus Valley from about 2500 to 1500 BC. This bust, identified as either a high priest or an official, is one of the many small artifacts found in the Indus Valley that resembles those of ancient Mesopotamia. (National Museum of Pakistan, Karachi.)

The other major influence was the extensive patronage of the arts by the various rulers and dynasties that controlled India throughout its history. The Mauryan emperor ASOKA and the Kushan ruler Kanishka played a major role in the creation of Buddhist art, just as the Hindu kings sponsored the great temples of medieval times and the Mogul rulers commissioned the splendid palaces, mosques, and tombs of the Islamic period. It is doubtful that without this encouragement and support many of these magnificent artistic monuments would have come into being.

Art of the Indus Civilization. The earliest artistic tradition developed in the Indus Valley, with its centers in Mohenjo-daro and Harappa both located in present-day Pakistan. The Indus civilization flourished between about 2500 and 1500 BC. Its most notable artistic achievements are the numerous sculptures that, although small in scale, often display superb craftsmanship. They usually represent human figures or animals and were probably religious in character. Remarkable artifacts

A sandstone capital from Sarnath, where the Buddha first preached, displays the iconographical elements typical of early Buddhist art. Erected during the reign of the Mauryan emperor Asoka (272-232 BC), this lotus-shaped capital features four lions. At one time it supported an immense stone wheel that was representative of the Wheel of Law and that was reflected in the smaller wheel appearing on the plinth. (Archaeological Museum, Sarnath, India.)

(Right) *The caves of Ajanta in west central India are temples and chambers carved out of rock, containing some of the finest examples of Buddhist painting and sculpture. Much of this work was executed during the Gupta period (AD c.300-600), marking the culmination of India's Buddhist art.*

(Below) *A wall painting (AD c.600) from a vihara, or monk's cell, in Cave II at Ajanta, expresses in its animated gesture, serene expression, and graceful proportion the spirituality and compassion of the Buddha in a romantic style. Delicate shading, imparting a new plasticity to figural representation, was developed during the middle Gupta period.*

from Mohenjo-daro include the lithe, gracefully posed copper figure of a dancing girl (National Museum, New Delhi) and the more hieratic alabaster bust of a king-priest (National Museum of Pakistan, Karachi). Other outstanding works are the engraved seals with animals and inscriptions in a yet unidentified language that are carved in low relief from steatite. These small-scale art objects resemble seals found in ancient Mesopotamia, which suggests possible connections between the art of the Indus Valley and Sumer; some scholars have referred to this early art as Indo-Sumerian. At the same time, however, other features of the Indus seals are typically Indian and foreshadow iconographic themes and artistic motifs that later figure prominently in Hindu art; these include the sacred animals, the mother goddess, and the cult of the phallus. Particularly striking is the representation of a horned god surrounded by animals, found on one of the Harappan seals (National Museum of Pakistan, Karachi); this image anticipates the representation of Shiva as the lord of the animals that recurs in later Hindu art.

Early Buddhist Art. During the middle of the 2d millennium BC, India was invaded by ARYAN nomads who destroyed Mohenjo-daro and Harappa and brought an end to the Indus civilization. Having no artistic tradition of their own, it is unlikely that these invaders produced any distinctive art, although Vedic texts refer to palaces decorated with paintings and wood carvings. The resurgence of Indian art did not occur until the 3d century BC under the powerful emperor Asoka the Great of the MAURYA dynasty (321-184 BC), which had its center in PATALIPUTRA (present-day Patna). Most of the art of this age is Buddhist, and, technically and aesthetically, it owes much to Achaemenid Persia. Among the most important artistic monuments of this age are the great pillars topped with enormous lotus capitals and lions, of which the best-preserved example is at Lauriya Nandangarh in northern India, dated 242 BC. Other important examples of early Buddhist art are the sensually modeled sculptures of Yakshi (female) and Yaksha (male), deities associated with fertility and wealth, and the great STUPA shrine-mounds such as those at BHARHUT and SANCHI, surrounded by ornately carved gateways and railings.

In this early art the Buddha is merely symbolized by a wheel, a lotus flower, or by his throne. Not until the Kushan period (AD c.50-250) was the historic Buddha represented in human form. The inspiration for this came from the late classical art of ancient Greece. The art of Kushan India, often referred to as Greco-Buddhist art, had two great centers: in the GANDHARA province of northwestern India, where the Western influence was more marked, and at Mathura in central India, where a more truly Indian artistic style evolved. An important school of Buddhist sculpture also existed in the south at AMARAVATI.

Art of the Gupta Period. The culmination of the Buddhist phase of Indian art occurred during the Gupta period (AD c.300-600), often called the classical period of Indian art. Unfortunately almost nothing remains of the great temples and magnificent palaces of this period; the rock-cut cave temples at AJANTA, however, preserve a wealth of fresco-type

This 7th-century relief of Shiva as Kala-bhairava, from Cave 29 at Ellora, typifies the vitality of the sculpture in the round that is characteristic of the Hindu medieval period. Ellora features some of the finest examples of Hindu art and architecture in India.

Erotic art, such as this 11th-century relief from the Chitragupta temple at Khajuraho, was a salient feature of the Hindu medieval period. Physical ecstasy, providing momentary mystical union, is represented by many mithunas, or erotic couples, throughout India.

wall paintings and sculptures dating from this age. The images of the Buddha and Bodhisattvas (Buddhas of the future) give moving expression to the spiritual ideas of the Buddhist faith and show an artistic mastery and sophistication not present before that time.

Although the bulk of Gupta art was devoted to the worship of the Buddhist deities, other works were devoted to Hinduism, which had experienced a marked revival and was to replace Buddhism entirely by the end of this period. Outstanding among these early Hindu artistic monuments is the Vishnu temple at Deogarh, with its impressive relief carvings. Also important in the evolution of later Hindu architecture are the temples at Aihole, which are among the earliest surviving religious edifices in India, and the rock-cut temples at Badami, both sponsored by the Chalukya dynasty (AD 550–642), which ruled the Deccan. It was in Buddhist art, however, that the Gupta period found its richest and artistically most important manifestation.

Hindu Medieval Art. Although Buddhist art continued to be produced in Bengal under the Pala dynasty (c.750–1100) and in Afghanistan, the dominant art of the medieval period of Indian history was Hindu in character. Beginning in the 7th century and lasting, at least in the south, to the 17th century, Hindu art represents one of the great highpoints in Indian and in world art. The magnificent rock carvings in the Shiva temple at ELEPHANTA in the Bay of Bombay and the great Kailasa temple at ELLORA are an impressive embodiment of the ideals of Hinduism and are among the greatest masterpieces ever created by Indian artists. Another outstanding group of Hindu monuments from the early medieval period are found at MAHABALIPURAM, not far from Madras, where magnificent relief carvings and beautiful temples were created during the 7th and 8th centuries under the patronage of the Pallava dynasty (c.325–750).

This artistic development peaked about AD 1000 when huge temple complexes with towering *sikkharas* (spires) and elabo-

(Above) A bronze of Shiva as Nataraja, the Lord of the Dance, dating from the 12th to the 13th century, exemplifies the sculptural mastery of southern India during the Chola dynasty (970-1229). (Right) The exquisite Taj Mahal (begun 1628) exemplifies the architecture that was produced under Islamic influence, which reached its highest expression under the Moguls.

This miniature (1770) of Vishnu and his beloved on the back of his mount Garuda displays the brilliant and symbolic color characteristic of Rajput painting. Rajput painting frequently depicted scenes from Hindu tradition. (Victoria and Albert Museum, London.)

rate sculptural decorations were erected all over India. The finest of these are at KHAJURAHO, in north central India, with its sensuous carvings of loving couples often shown in ecstatic embrace, symbolizing the union between the soul and the deity. The largest group of such temples is at BHUBANESH-WAR in Orissa, where no less than 1,000 sanctuaries were erected during this period. The most immense and ambitious of these temples is the Surya temple at KONARAK, also in Orissa; the entire edifice takes the form of the giant horsedrawn sacred chariot associated with Surya the sun god, to whom the temple is dedicated. This colossal structure, begun c.1240, was never completed, and by the end of the 13th century the Muslim conquest put an end to Hindu art in northern India.

In the south, however, Hindu art continued to flourish. Although the finest southern monuments were from the earlier periods, such as the great temple at Tanjore built (AD c.1000) under the Chola dynasty (970–1229), major temple complexes, notably that at Madura in the extreme south, date from the 17th century. The huge gateways, or *gopurams*, that are covered with innumerable carvings representing the gods and goddesses and the multitude of sacred beings of the Hindu pantheon are a distinctive feature of 17th-century Madura-style architecture. The other great artistic achievement of southern India is represented in the often voluptuously shaped bronze images of Hindu deities, which are among the finest Indian sculptures ever produced. Cast in the *cire perdue*, or LOST-WAX PROCESS, they are masterpieces of the metalworkers craft and exemplify Hindu art at its best. Those made under the Chola dynasty between the 10th and 13th centuries are considered outstanding, with powerful representation of SHIVA as Nataraja, the Lord of Dance, symbolizing the entire drama of the cosmos.

Islamic Art of India. A very different artistic tradition, largely based on Persian and Turkish prototypes, came into existence during the 12th century, when much of northern India was conquered by Muslim invaders. Because Islam forbade the making of images, sculpture—which had been the dominant art form—declined, and architecture became the most important form of artistic expression. The first of the great edifices devoted to this faith was the Quwwat ul-Islam, or Might of Islam MOSQUE, erected (AD 1199) on the site of a Hindu temple in Delhi. Its most impressive remaining structure is the QUTB MINAR, a tall MINARET from which the hour of prayer was proclaimed. Other outstanding early Islamic buildings are the tombs of the great Muslim rulers, such as that of Ghiyas uddin Tughlag Shah in Delhi.

The culmination of Indo-Islamic art, however, occurred under the Mogul dynasty (see MOGULS), which came to power during the 16th century and ruled much of India until the British took control. It was under Mogul patronage that such architectural masterpieces as the TAJ MAHAL (begun 1628) in Agra and the great Friday mosque in Delhi were erected. The most extensive architectural remain of this age is FATEHPUR SIKRI, a city erected (1573–80) by the emperor AKBAR and abandoned after only 15 years. Other forms of artistic expression that flourished under the Moguls were miniature painting and decorative arts, notably the making of carpets, textiles, and metalwork as well as wood, ivory, and jade carving. (See MOGUL ART AND ARCHITECTURE.)

Indian Miniature Painting. The last great outburst of traditional Indian art took the shape of miniature painting, an art form that had existed in India for many centuries. The earliest of these pictorial compositions date from the 11th century and appeared in the form of palm leaf manuscripts illuminated with scenes from Buddhist texts. Another school of miniature painting, dating from a somewhat later period, was Jain in inspiration and flourished in the Gujarat region of western India. A third miniature tradition existed at the Mogul courts; its style was far more realistic and depicted secular

The Malwa style of Rajput painting, exemplified by this late-17th-century scene of Krishna surrounded by maidens, is characterized by angularity, flat composition, and rich color. The life of Krishna was frequently represented. (National Museum of India, New Delhi.)

themes. This court tradition was largely derived from Persian sources and was introduced by the Turkish and Mogul conquerors.

Out of these various traditions evolved a new school of painting known as Rajput, because its most important centers were in Rajputana (central India). Rajput painting flourished from about 1500 to 1800. The subjects were largely Hindu; frequently illustrated were scenes from the life of the divine cowherd KRISHNA and his love for Radha. Other favorite subjects were legendary epics and the ragamalas, or musical modes. Although small in size, these pictures, executed in opaque pigments on paper, are powerful evocations of the mood of the theme represented; they often display striking combinations of warm, vibrant colors, which frequently carry symbolic value. Another great style of miniature painting, called the Pahari school, was centered in the foothills of the

Himalayas. Here, in the courts of the local Hindu rulers, a style flourished that combined elements of Rajput painting with others taken from the Mogul tradition. This school, at its best during the 18th century, continued to flourish until the middle of the 19th century.

Indian Art of the Modern Period. By the end of the 18th century both the Hindu and Mogul artistic traditions had spent themselves. By about 1850 even the Pahari school had lost its vitality. At the same time European art and artistic ideas had been introduced into India by the British, and Western-style art schools were founded in the major cities in order to, as the British officials thought, elevate the taste of the nation. Indian painters painted in watercolors and oils, using modeling in light and shade and scientific perspective in imitation of contemporary English painting. Only on a folk level did traditional Indian art continue in the rural villages.

The first person to foster an integration of Indian traditions with Western styles of painting was an Englishman, E. B. Havell (1861–1934). As head of the Calcutta School of Art, he decided to base the instruction on traditional Indian models, notably the wall paintings at Ajanta and the Mogul miniatures. Although his attempts at reviving the older schools did not succeed, his ideas and writings were of great influence and helped spur the rebirth of Indian art during the 20th century. Basing their art on modern Western art and Indian folk art, such painters as Amrita Sher-Gil, Jamini Roy, and M. F. Husain have produced works of beauty and power that combine truly Indian qualities with the ideals of modern art. Since independence, newer and more avant-garde artistic tendencies have flourished in India and neighboring countries of the Indian subcontinent. In much of this more recent work a more abstract artistic idiom is used, which nonetheless preserves much of the traditional Indian aesthetic sensibility.

HUGO MUNSTERBERG

Bibliography: Archer, W. G., *Indian Painting* (1957); Bussagli, Mario, and Sivaramamurti, C., *5,000 Years of the Art of India* (1962); Coomaraswamy, A. K., *History of Indian and Indonesian Art* (1927; repr. 1965); Craven, Roy C., *A Concise History of Indian Art* (1975); Goetz, Hermann, *The Art of India*, 12th ed. (1964); Kramrisch, Stella, *The Art of India*, 3d ed. (1965); Mooherjee, Ajit, *The Arts of India* (1966); Rowland, Benjamin, *The Art and Architecture of India*, 3d ed. (1967); Welch, Stuart C., *Imperial Mughal Painting* (1978) and *Room for Wonder: Indian Painting During the British Period, 1760–1880* (1978); Zimmer, Heinrich, *The Art of Indian Asia*, 2d ed. (1955).

Indian languages, American

At the time of first European contact, probably close to 1,000 American Indian languages were spoken in North, Central, and South America. Although the number of languages in daily use has steadily declined because of persecution and pressures on the Indians to adopt Western languages and culture, well over 700 different American Indian—or, as they are sometimes called, Amerindian—languages are spoken today.

SCIENTIFIC STUDY

American Indian languages have long been a source of fascination for scholars and laymen alike. The only transcriptions of many now-extinct languages were made by interested soldiers and explorers untrained in phonetic science; in areas of Spanish domination, the careful records of Catholic missionaries provide invaluable documentation of the way indigenous languages were spoken as long as 400 years ago.

In the United States, many of the most famous linguists of the early 20th century—among them Leonard BLOOMFIELD, Franz BOAS, and Edward SAPIR—transcribed and analyzed North American Indian languages. Many descriptions of Indian languages are important in the literature of the linguistic school known as American structuralism.

Today interest in American Indian languages is increasing, and Americanists, as those who study the languages are called, now hold regular scientific meetings and congresses to report on their investigations. Current research on the native languages of the Americas is published in several periodicals, notably the *International Journal of American Linguistics*.

ORIGINS AND CLASSIFICATION

Most scholars believe that the aboriginal inhabitants of North,

Central, and South America migrated from Asia many thousands of years ago. Acceptance of this theory has led some to hypothesize that all Indian languages are genetically related—that is, that all of them can be traced back to one remote ancestor language. The great diversity of Indian languages, however, has thus far prevented proof of common origin, and most Americanists accept more conservative classifications of the languages into various distinct groups.

American Indian Historical Linguistics. Few American Indian languages have more than 100 years of written history; therefore, comparative linguists must use quite recent recordings of native speakers' pronunciations. Following the traditional principles of historical linguistics, words from Indian languages believed to be related are subjected to minute comparison, in a search for regular correspondences of sound and meaning. Regularity is the key; for instance, while Luiseño *paa-la*, Papago *wa-*, and Aztec *a-tl*, all meaning "water," do not immediately appear similar, the words are seen to be cognate (derived from the same word in the ancestor language) when other sets such as Luiseño *pe-t*, Papago *woog*, and Aztec *o-tli*, all meaning "road," are considered—Luiseño initial *p* and Papago initial *w* regularly correspond to the lack of any initial consonant sound in Aztec. When such correspondences are discovered, the languages being compared are judged to have a historical connection, either genetic—because of descent from a common ancestor—or through language contact, and the subsequent "borrowing" of words. As genetic relationships are discovered, languages are classified into families, which then are often compared themselves. Related families can be classified in turn into larger groups called phyla (singular, phylum) or stocks, or into even broader groupings known as macrophyla or superstocks.

On the basis of the Luiseño, Papago, and Aztec words cited above, linguists have proposed the reconstruction of initial *p* sounds in the words for "water" and "road" in the Proto-Uto-Aztecan ancestor of the three languages in question. The sound systems and vocabulary of a number of different American Indian language families have been partially reconstructed by linguists. Comparison of the reconstructed proto-languages leads to more informed conjecture about earlier connections between the ancestor languages and the peoples who spoke them and may eventually lend support to the theory that all the American Indian languages have a common origin.

Language Names. American Indian language names often seem confusing. Some names are chosen politically rather than linguistically. For instance, Chickasaw and Choctaw are mutually intelligible Muskogean languages, but are traditionally treated as separate because the tribes who use them are different. Many American Indian groups do not have a special name for themselves, but may call themselves simply "people"; language names sometimes translate as "my language." Often Indian groups come to be known by a foreign term, such as the English names Dogrib and Yellowknife given to Athabascan tribes in the Northwest, or the naming of most coastal Californian languages for the nearest Spanish mission (Luiseño was the Uto-Aztecan language spoken around Mission San Luis Rey, for example, and the Chumash language Obispeño was named for Mission San Luis Obispo). Some such designations, occasionally derogatory, originated with other Indians—like Chemehuevi, from Mojave *ʔači im-uueev-i*, "they work with fish," or Comanche, from Southern Paiute *kɨmantsɨ*, "stranger."

In some cases the same name has been used for two or more distinct languages. For instance, there are two languages in Central America called "Chontal," one Hokan and one Mayan.

The names of linguistic families and stocks are usually coined by linguists, often by adding -*an* to the name of a representative language. The Yuman family, for example, is named for the language Yuma.

North American Languages. Perhaps 300 languages were spoken in North America when the first Europeans arrived, and it is estimated that 200 are still spoken by some 300,000 persons. The American explorer and ethnologist John Wesley POWELL presented the first general classification of the languages north of Mexico in 1891, dividing them into 58 families. A number of scholars have subsequently suggested the arrangement of Powell's families into phyla, with the most influential classification credited to Edward Sapir. C. F. and F. M. Voegelin introduced the standard modern classification of American Indian languages in 1964–65, grouping most of the languages of the United States and Canada into seven macrophyla, with a few families and language isolates left unclassified. The outline of this classification is generally accepted, though some parts of it—particularly Hokan and Macro-Penutian—are still controversial.

One phylum, American Arctic-Paleosiberian, includes both Eskimo-Aleut, spoken from Alaska to Greenland, and the Chukchi-Kamchatkan family of Siberia. This phylum is the only American language family to have an accepted connection with a non-American language group.

Central American Languages. Of course language boundaries and political boundaries do not coincide. The Hokan and Aztec-Tanoan phyla of North America also include a number of Central or Meso-American languages, and it has been suggested that other Central American groups may be part of the North American phylum Macro-Penutian. An alternative proposal is a Central American Macro-Mayan stock with connections in South America. Recent estimates place the number of Central American Indian languages at about 70, with at least 3,000,000 speakers.

South American Languages. Linguistic diversity is greatest in South America, where many languages spoken in remote jungle and mountain regions remain unrecorded and unclassified. There are probably over 500 different languages still spoken, with more than 11,000,000 speakers. The various dialects of Quechua alone have 5,000,000 speakers.

Broader classifications of the more than 80 South American language families have been proposed by Joseph Greenberg, Cestmir Loukotka, and others. Greenberg—whose suggestions were followed in the later Voegelin classification—named just three South American genetic groups, with Macro-Chibchan opposed to Andean-Equatorial, plus other smaller families, and Ge-Pano-Carib. Because these macrophyla have not as yet been documented with lists of cognate sets, they are not accepted by all specialists.

GRAMMATICAL STRUCTURE

The grammatical structure—phonology, or sound system; morphology, or word structure; and syntax, or sentence structure—of American Indian languages varies considerably, but none of the languages can be called primitive. Their organization and means of expression make them as sophisticated as English and other familiar European languages.

Phonology. Though some Indian languages have a simple phonological structure (the Arawakan language Campa, for instance, has only 17 contrastive speech sounds, or phonemes), the phonology of others is very complex. Certain sounds, many of which are articulated toward the back of the vocal tract, have been cited as characteristic of the American languages, but none of these occur in all the languages. The glottal stop, made by briefly closing the vocal cords, as in the middle of the English word *uh-oh*, is a common sound (written ?). Many languages of western America, from north to south, have glottalized consonants, made with a glottal stop produced simultaneously with another consonant sound. For instance, Navajo *ts'in*, meaning "bone," has a glottalized *ts* sound (represented by *ts'*), while *tsin*, "tree," has a plain *ts*. Another common sound is a back *k* sound, normally written *q*, that is articulated not at the velum, as is English *k*, but rather in the postvelar or uvular region. Many languages contrast *k* and *q* in words like Cahuilla (Uto-Aztecan) *neki?*, "my house," beside *neqi?*, "by myself."

Vowel systems also vary considerably. Quite a few American Indian languages have nasalized vowels, like those used in French. For instance, Chickasaw *iyimmi*, "he thinks," is distinct from *ĩyimmi*, "he believes him," with nasalization represented by the tilde (˜) over the *i*. The use of tonal or pitch accent systems (as in Chinese) to differentiate words is more common in the Americas than the use of contrastive stress (as

found, for example, in English *impórt*, verb, beside *ímport*, noun). In the majority of American Indian languages, each syllable receives equal stress.

Morphology and Syntax. The most commonly cited trait of American Indian languages is polysynthesis—the expression of complicated ideas within a single word with many separate meaningful elements. The use of verbs with attached subject and object indicators (very often prefixes) is common; in many languages adverbial and other elements may also be attached to the verb, as in Cahuilla *pe-n-taxmu-max-llew-vičuqa?*, literally "him-I-sing-for-go-want-past," which means "I wanted to go sing for him," or in Mojave (Yuman) *ny-m-iyuu-mot-nti-e*, literally "me-you-see-negative-again-future," which means "you won't see me again."

Many languages use unmarked verbs for the third person. Thus Chickasaw *hiła* can mean either "dance" or "he dances." Possessive and locational indicators are often attached to nouns, as in Yup'ik Eskimo *aŋya-a-ni*, literally "boat-his-in," which means "in his boat." As in most Indo-European languages, male/female gender distinction is quite uncommon; but many Indian languages make a grammatically comparable distinction between animate, or living, and inanimate nouns. Alienable possession or ownership is often indicated differently from inalienable possession—as of kinship terms and body parts. Reduplication—the doubling of all or part of a word, usually to indicate plurality or intensity—is used in many languages, as in Barbareño Chumash *ma?*, "jackrabbit," *ma?ma?*, "jackrabbits."

The arrangement of words into sentences also varies from language to language. While the most common basic word order is subject-object-verb, subject-verb-object is frequently used, and some languages employ the rarer word orders verb-subject-object, verb-object-subject, and object-verb-subject.

Many American Indian languages make use of special syntactic patterns to differentiate several third-person participants in a sentence. Obviation (in the Algonquian languages) and the use of the so-called fourth person (in Athabascan) allow one participant to be coded as more important or interesting than another. Switch-reference is the name given to an unusual grammatical device found almost exclusively in the Americas; it allows the speaker to specify whether the subject of one clause is the same as or different from the subject of another clause. The English sentence *he knows he's fat* is ambiguous; if the first *he* is known to refer to Tom, for instance, the sentence has one meaning if the second *he* also refers to Tom ("Tom is fat and he knows it") and another if the second *he* refers to, say, Bill ("Bill is fat and Tom knows it"). Although the Mojave sentences *isay-k suupaw-pč* (fat—same know—perfective) and *isay-m suupaw-pč* (fat—different know—perfective) both translate as "he knows he's fat," they are not ambiguous: the first implies that the knower is fat, while the second means that someone else is.

The Whorf Hypothesis. Because of different cultural needs, American Indian vocabulary structure varies greatly, and some of the semantic concepts and sentence patterns often seem unfamiliar to those who have not grown up speaking the languages. The American linguist Benjamin Lee WHORF argued that the differences in semantic and syntactic organization of languages as diverse as English and Hopi were indicative of differences in thought processes as well. This theory, the so-called Whorf hypothesis, that language structure reflects cognitive structure, has yet to win widespread acceptance.

LANGUAGE CONTACT

Unrelated languages whose speakers are in daily contact often come to share various grammatical traits, which can then be called areal features of the region. In the Pacific Northwest, for instance, several genetic groups are represented, but the complex phonologies of the different languages are strikingly similar. In South America many languages of the Tupian family have nasalization as an attribute, not just of vowels or consonants but of whole syllables, and this feature has been borrowed by some unrelated neighboring languages.

The study of loanwords can reveal something of the prior history of a linguistic group. Many Alaskan languages and some as far south as California have Russian loans, for in-

TABLE 1: AMERICAN INDIAN LANGUAGES NORTH OF MEXICO*

1. American Arctic-Paleosiberian
Eskimo-Aleut
Chuckchi-Kamchatkan

2. Na-Dené
Athabascan (Apache, Beaver, Carrier, Chippewyan, Denaina, Dogrib, Hare, Hupa, Koyukon, Kutchin, Mattole†, Navajo, Sarsi, Slave, Tolowa, Yellowknife, etc.)
Tlingit
Haida

3. Macro-Algonkian
Algonquian (Arapaho, Blackfoot, Cheyenne, Cree, Delaware, Fox, Kickapoo, Menominee, Micmac, Montagnais, Ojibwa, Passamaquoddy-Malecite, Penobscot, Potawatomi, Shawnee, etc.)
Yurok
Wiyot
Muskogean (Alabama, Chickasaw, Choctaw, Creek, Hitchiti, Koasati, Mikasuki, Seminole)
Natchez†
Atakapa†
Chitimacha†
Tunica†
Tonkawa

4. Macro-Siouan
Siouan (Biloxi†, Crow, Dakota [Sioux], Hidatsa, Kansa, Ofo†, Omaha, Osage, Ponca, Quapaw, Tutelo†, Winnebago)
Catawba†
Iroquoian (Cayuga, Cherokee, Mohawk, Onandaga, Oneida, Seneca, Tuscarora, Wyandot [Huron]†)
Caddoan (Arikara, Caddo, Pawnee, Wichita)
Yuchi

5. Hokan (see also Table II-1)
Yuman (Cocopa, Diegueñno, Havasupai, Maricopa, Mojave, Walapai, Yavapai, Yuma)
Pomo (several languages)
Palaihnihan (Achomawi, Atsugewi)
Shastan
Yanan†
Chimariko†
Washo
Esselen†
Salinan†
Karok
Chumashan (several languages)†
Comecrudan†
Coahuiltecan†

6. Macro-Penutian (see also Table II-5)
Yokutsan
Maiduan
Wintun (Nomlaki, Patwin, Wintu)
Miwok-Costanoan (several languages)
Klamath-Modoc
Sahaptian (Nez Percé, Sahaptin, Yakima)
Cayuse†
Molale†
Coos
Yakonan (Alsea, Siuslaw, Umpqua)†
Takelma†
Kalapuya
Chinookan
Tsimshian
Zuni

7. Aztec-Tanoan (see also Table II-2)
Kiowa-Tanoan (Tewa, Tiwa, Towa, Kiowa)
Uto-Aztecan (Bannock, Cahuilla, Chemehuevi-Southern Paiute, Comanche, Cupeño, Hopi, Kawaiisu, Luiseño, Mono, Northern Paiute, Panamint, Pima-Papago, Serrano, Shoshoni, Tubatulabal, Ute, Yaqui, etc.)

Unclassified Languages of North America
Kersan
Yukian (Yuki, Wappo)
Beothuk†
Kutenai
Karankawa†
Chimakuan (Quileute, Chemakum†)
Salish (Bella Coola, Coeur d'Alene, Comox, Flathead, Kalispel, Lilloet, Lower Chehalis, Pend d'Oreille, Shushwap, Squamish, Thompson, Tilamook, Upper Chehalis, etc.)
Wakashan (Bella Bella, Kwakwala [Kwakiutl], Makah, Nitinat, Nootka, etc.)
Timucua†

---

* Phyla are numbered, with families listed and representative languages in parentheses. Some families are isolates consisting of only one language.
† Extinct language or family.

TABLE 2: CENTRAL AMERICAN LANGUAGE GROUPS*

1. Hokan (See also Table I-5)
Yuman (Diegueño, Paipai, Kiliwa)
Seri
Tequistlatec Chontal
Jicaque

2. Aztec-Tanoan (see also Table I-7)
Uto-Aztecan (Aztec [Nahuatl-Nahuat-Nhual], Cora, Guarijio, Huichol, Lower Pima, Mayo, Opatat, Papago, Tarahumara, Tepecano, Tepehuán, Yaqui, etc.)

3. Oto-Manguean
Oto-Pamean (Chichimec, Mazahua, Pame, Otomí, etc.)
Popolucan (Mazatec, Popoloc, etc.)
Mixtecan (Amuzgo, Mixtec, Trique, etc.)
Zapotecan (Chatino, Papabuco, Zapotec, etc.)
Chimantecan
Manguean (Chiapanec, Mangue, etc.)†

4. Macro-Penutian (see also Table I-6)*
Huave
Mixe-Zoque (Mixe, Sierra Popoluca, Tapachultect, Zoque, etc.)
Totonacan (Tepehua, Totonac)
Mayan (Aguacatec, Chol, Chontal [Yocotán], Chuj, Huastec, Ixil, Jacaltec, Kekchí, Mam, Quiché, Tojolabal, Tzeltal, Tzotzil, Yucatec [Maya], etc.)

5. Macro-Chibchan (see also Table III-1)
Xinca
Lencan (Lencat, Chilanga)
Paya
Misumalpan (Matagalpa, Mosquito, Sumo)

Other Central American Linguistic Groups
Cuitlatec†
Subtiabat-Tlapanec
Tarascan

---

* Phyla are numbered, with families listed and representative languages in parentheses. This classification is more controversial than most.
† Extinct language or family.

TABLE 3: SELECTED SOUTH AMERICAN LANGUAGE GROUPS

A. Major Language Families and Stocks (representative languages)

1. Macro-Chibchan (see also Table II-6) (Andaqui, Chibchat, Colorado, Cuna, Esmeraldat, Guaymí, Mocoa, Move, Páez, Quitot, Waica, Warao, etc.)

2. Quechumaran (Quechua, Aymara)

3. Macro-Tucanoan (Amaguajet, Carapana, Macuna, Pamöá, Siona, Tucano, Tuyuca, Waikina, etc.)

4. Arawakan (Amarizana, Amuesha, Araikút, Arauat, Arawak, Bauré, Campa, Goajiro, Ipuriná, Island Carib, Machiguenga, Mojo, Morique, Tainot, etc.)

5. Tupian (Ariquemt, Curuayat, Guaraní, Guarategayat, Kaiwá, Mundurukú, Oyampi-Emerillont, Puruborá, Tupinambá, Yuruna, etc.)

6. Macro-Ge (Bororo, Caingang, Coroadot, Fulniót, Jeico, Malalít, Maxakalí, Purí, Xokleng, etc.)

7. Macro-Pano-Tacanan (Amahuaca, Caripuna, Marinahua, Mosetent, Pano, Tacana, Tehuelchet, Yuracare, etc.)

9. Macro-Carib (Acawai, Apiacá, Carare, Caribe, Carif, Chocó, Palmellat, Pimenteirat, Hixkaryana, Waica, Yaruma, etc.)

B. Additional South American Language Families
Alacalufan, Araucanian, or Mapuche, Auaque, Caliana, Candoshi, Canichana, Canoe, Cariri, Catacaot, Catuquina, Cayuvava, Chiquito, Cofán, Cullit, Cunza, Guahiboan, Guaycurú-Charruan, Huarpeant, Kukurat, Lulean, Mascoy, Mataco, Mobima, Munichi, Otomaco-Taparitat, Puelche, Puinave-Maku, Salivan, Sect, Simacu, Tarumat, Timotet, Trumai, Tuyoneiri, Yaghant, Yurít, Zamuco, Záparo, etc.

---

† Extinct language or family.

stance, dating from the time of extensive trade with Russia, and borrowings from Spanish are common in California, the Southwest, and, of course, Latin America. Borrowed words are often changed to fit the structure of the borrowing language—Spanish *cabállo*, "horse," was borrowed into Tübatulabal (Uto-Aztecan) as *kawaayúʔ*, for instance, because all Tübatulabal words have final stress and the language has no bilabial *v* or *b* sound. Many Indian words have in turn been borrowed into English and Spanish. The words *moccasin, squash, squaw,* and *toboggan*, like the majority of Indian loans into English, are from Algonquian languages; *chocolate*, from Aztec, *tobacco*, from Carib, and *condor*, from Quechua, are examples of words that were borrowed into Spanish first, and then into English. The names of thousands of places throughout the Americas are of Indian origin.

WRITING SYSTEMS
The Mayan hieroglyphic system, which has not yet been completely deciphered, was the only well-developed writing system in use in the Americas before European contact, although a number of the Central American civilizations and the Quechua used pictographic systems, primarily for religious purposes, and other groups made nonlinguistic petroglyphs. Most Indian writing systems now in use were developed by linguists or missionaries, but one exception is the syllabary devised by the Cherokee SEQUOYA, which is still used for writing the Iroquoian language. The majority of Indian languages, however, do not yet have standard orthographies.

THE FUTURE OF AMERICAN INDIAN LANGUAGES
Many American Indian languages have few speakers and are in danger of extinction, but some are increasing in both influence and number of speakers. Two nations, Greenland and Paraguay, use American Indian languages—Greenlandic Eskimo and the Tupian language Guaraní—officially. In several places, elementary instruction has begun to be offered in Indian languages; for Navajo, even college-level instruction is available. The recent resurgence of interest by North American Indians in their cultural heritage has led to more extensive training of native American linguists and to programs of instruction in Indian languages for older children and adults. Such heightened interest may lead to the preservation of some of the threatened languages.   PAMELA MUNRO

Bibliography: Boas, Franz, *Race, Language and Culture* (1940); Driver, Harold E., *Indians of North America,* 2d ed. (1969); Loukotka, Cestmir, *Classification of South American Indian Languages* (1968); Matteson, Esther, et al., *Comparative Studies in Amerindian Languages* (1972); Spencer, R. F., et al., *The Native Americans,* 2d ed. (1977); Voegelin, C. F. and F. M., *Map of North American Indian Languages* (1966); Whorf, Benjamin L., *Language, Thought and Reality* (1956).

Indian literature

The Indian Constitution recognizes 14 official languages. Each has its regional literature, but all owe a debt to a classical culture in Sanskrit (see INDO-IRANIAN LANGUAGES).

Sanskrit literature has its origins in an oral tradition that produced the Vedic holy texts (see HINDUISM) some time after 1500 BC. These homilies and hymns gave rise to many commentaries, the most famous of which are the UPANISHADS.

Oral history, legend, and moral tales were later fused into the two great books of Hindu tradition, the MAHABHARATA and the RAMAYANA, which have since been used as the sources for countless literary works. Other major additions to Sanskrit literature are the *Puranas* (400 BC–AD 1400; Eng. trans., 1970) and the *Pancatantra* (AD *c.*450; Eng. trans., 1924).

Beginning about 400 BC, when PANINI produced his Sanskrit grammar, there was an outpouring of literature that sought to systematize all learning in the form of laws for the arts and sciences, called *shastras,* as well as devotional, epic, and lyric poetry and stylized drama treating either traditional heroic themes or invented plots often set in the Gupta cities of the 4th and 5th century AD.

During the peak of classical poetry (7th century AD) major writers such as BHARTRIHARI, Mayura (fl. AD *c.*750), and Subhandu (fl. AD *c.*75) emerged. KALIDASA, a poet of note, is better known for his play SHAKUNTALA. Other notable playwrights include Bhasa (fl. AD *c.*200) and BHAVABHUTI. Treatises on government, law, and love include *Arthashastra, Dharmashastra* and *Kamasutra,* the last by Vatsayana (AD *c.*400).

The stone inscriptions of the Emperor Ashoka, made in 269 BC, showed that Sanskrit was then changing internally and losing its position as the sole vehicle of cultured expression. This change was reflected in the introduction by Buddhists of the Pali language as a lingua franca common to many regions. The Theravada canon, the *Tripitaka* (5th century BC), and *The Jataka Tales* and the *Dhammapada* (both 1st century AD) are the major Pali texts.

By the second century AD several dialects known collectively as Prakrits were being used in literature. This development was especially notable in Sanskrit drama, where characters below the rank of royalty and priesthood often spoke in Prakrits. By AD 1000 these languages had evolved to the point of being recognizable as the forerunners of modern regional tongues. Sanskrit scholars of that time saw them as evidence of a cultural decline and labeled them *Apabhramsa* ("decadence").

During the Middle Ages Sanskrit was used only in religious contexts by the priesthood. Bengali, Marathi, and old Gujarati were among the first Northern languages to emerge as literary vehicles. A major figure of this period was the poet Amir Khusrou (1253-1325), who included Hindi verses among his Persian writings. In the south under the expanding Chola Empire (10th–13th centuries) the Kannada, Malayalam, and Telugu languages achieved a literary status previously held only by classical literature written in TAMIL. The best-known work of this tradition is perhaps an anthology of love lyrics, *Kuruntokai* (AD *c.*750). Tamil and, later, Telugu writing exercised a lasting influence on literature in the south, both through its courtly and mystical verse and through its many versions of Sanskrit sacred texts.

In the 7th century two devotional sects emerged in southern India and initiated the BHAKTI Hindu revival. This was a mystical, personalized mode of worship that focused on the figures of Radha-Krishna and Rama-Sita and produced an abundance of poet-saints of both sexes, philosophers and hagiographers, all of whom wrote in the vernacular. The movement spread throughout India and reached its zenith in the 16th century. Major works of the period include the *Gita-gouinda* (*c.*1180; Eng. trans., 1940) of Jayadsua (12th century) and the *Iramavataram* (*c.*1200; Eng. trans., 1961) by Kampan (*c.*1180-1250).

In the latter part of the Middle Ages the courts of the Mogul Emperors (see MOGULS) produced Perso-Arabic writing, which inspired a literature in Urdu. The major artistic form was the *ghazal,* a stylized form of lyrical folk song, and notable exponents of the form include Muhammed Quli Qutb Shah (*c.*1550-1611), Vali (1668-1744), Sauda (1707-1781) and Mir (1723-1810). Mir's protégé, Ghalib (1797-1869), carried the tradition into the 19th century.

The beginnings of modern Indian literature can be traced to the establishment of civil service training schools and printing presses early in the 19th century. While vernacular language and culture was taught to British colonial officials, an awareness of an Indian heritage as well as new Western literary and philosophical writing produced a cultural renaissance. In 1835, Thomas Babington Macaulay, then an advisor to the British government on Indian affairs, scornfully dismissed the entire Indian literary heritage, thereby inspiring a reaction in favor of Indian literary works and the vernacular among Indians. Macaulay established English-language schooling for Indians; consequently, English became a major tool for political polemic and social reform, as well as for literary expression, and its literature began to shape vernacular writing. Pioneers such as Raja Rammohan Roy (1772-1833), Mahavir Prasad Dvivedy (1864-1938), and Arunacala Kavi (fl. *c.*1780) developed a utilitarian prose style, whereas Michael Madhusudan Dutt (1824-73) and Jayashankar Prasad (1889-1937) introduced blank verse and the sonnet into Indian poetry. Madhusudan Dutt wrote the first plays modeled on Western drama and Sir Rabindranath TAGORE introduced the short story to vernacular writing in India. The novel was pioneered in India by such writers as Bankim Chandra CHATTERJEE and Hari Narayan Apte (1864-1919). The major poets of the period include Laksminath Bezbarua (1868-1938) and Mohammed Iqbal (*c.*1876-1938).

Twentieth-century writing has kept alive the sentimental romanticism of the 19th century. The social realism of earlier works developed first under the influence of nationalist leaders such as Mahatma Gandhi and later under Marxist ideology. Reaction to the figureheads of the Indian "renaissance" led to experimentation with surrealism, symbolism, and the style of Ezra Pound and T. S. Eliot. Contemporary writing seems to demonstrate a general trend toward introspection, an interest in psychology, and experimentation with new forms of writing within a general existentialist framework.

Writing in English is viewed with mixed feelings in post-Independence India but is well established nevertheless. Pioneers in this field included Michael (1824–73) and Sudhindranath (1901–60) Dutt, Tagore, and Sri AUROBINDO. Sarojini NAIDU achieved fame both as a poet in English and a patriot. Some leading contemporary figures in Anglo-Indian poetry are Nissim Ezekiel (b. 1921), P. Lal (b. 1929), Pritish Nandy (b. 1947), Kamala Das (b. 1934), and A. K. Ramanujan (b. 1929). Outstanding writers of fiction include R. K. NARAYAN and Ruth Prawer JHABVALA.

Nonfiction of political and journalistic origin includes Nirad C. Chaudhuri's *The Autobiography of an Unknown Indian* (1951), Gandhi's *An Autobiography,* Jawaharlal Nehru's *The Discovery of India* (1946), and works by Jayaprakash Narayan, Ved Mehta, and M. N. Roy.

Bibliography: Basham, A. L., *The Wonder That Was India,* 3d ed. (1968); Clark, T. W., ed., *The Novel in India* (1970); Dimock, Edward, ed., *The Literature of India* (1974); Kripalani, Krishna, *Modern Indian Literature* (1971); Lal, P., *The Concept of an Indian Literature* (1973); Mukherjee, Meenakshi, *The Twice Born Fiction: Themes and Techniques of the Indian Novel in English,* rev. ed. (1974); Williams, Haydn M., ed., *Studies in Modern Indian Fiction in English,* 2 vols. (1975); Winternitz, Maurice, *A History of Indian Literature,* 2 vols., 2d ed. (1972; repr. 1978).

Indian music

Indian music encompasses some of the richest, most remarkable musical traditions of the world. India's musical history begins in the second millennium BC with the advent of the Vedic period. The *Samaveda,* one of the sacred four Vedas ("four books of knowledge"), comprises the world's oldest notated melodies. These hymns have been passed down through oral tradition since that early period. Beginning with the second century AD, complicated theoretical systems developed, and the important RAGA principle was established. In the 11th and 12th centuries AD, Islamic influences were felt in India as the result of the invasions from the northwest. This

The tambura (top left) is the classical drone lute of northern India. Between 1.2 and 1.5 m (4 and 5 ft) long, it has a large gourd at the bottom of its unfretted neck. The player plucks the 4 strings with one finger of the right hand and adjusts the pitch by moving the tambura's ivory bridge. The sarod (top center) and the shahnai (bottom center) are northern Indian melody instruments. The sarod has 6 playing strings, 13 rhythmic strings, and an unfretted keyboard. The shahnai is a double-reed wind instrument that is made of wood and has a brass horn at the end. The tablas (drums, bottom left) and the bin are typical instruments of central and northern India. The tabla proper is made from a hollow log. The bayan, the second drum of the pair, is made of metal and is played with the left hand. The bin (top right) is a tubular zither with 2 gourd resonators, 4 melody strings on the fingerboard, and 3 drone strings on the side of the fingerboard. The strings are plucked by crystal plectra worn on the player's index and middle fingers. The mridanga (bottom right) is a barrel-shaped wooden drum from southern India.

The sitar, with tabla and tambura, form the Indian classical ensemble. A north Indian melody instrument, the sitar has playing strings that run over arched metal frets into a pegbox; sympathetic strings in the troughed neck run under the frets to lateral pegs.

intrusion undoubtedly brought about the division, about 1200, of Indian music into northern and southern systems, a separation that has continued to the present day.

Numerous differences exist between the music of the north and the south, but the regions have in common the two fundamental characteristics of Indian art music, the *raga* and the *tala*. In general, *raga* concerns melody and *tala* rhythm.

The Raga. A *raga* is identified by specific tonal material consisting of a particular combination of musical phrases that gives it its distinctive melodic character. The number of tones it possesses is fixed; these pitches—some more important than others—can often be presented in the form of ascending and descending scales. Many *ragas* are associated with certain standard musical phrases. It is this trait that most closely ties the *raga* concept to the ancient *Samaveda*. Many of these standard phrases are so well known that the informed listener is able to tell immediately which *raga* is being performed. Regardless of whether the *raga* performance is vocal or instrumental, a drone (a sustained tone of fixed pitch) is invariably heard in the background. The drone instrument is usually the *tambura*, which has a long neck and four strings tuned to the basic tones of the *raga*. Magical powers are attributed to some *ragas*, especially when they are performed faultlessly. Moreover, many *ragas* should be performed only at certain times of the day or night or during specific periods of the year. A number of *ragas* express certain moods or emotions, and some are believed to personify gods, ascetics, or devotees.

The Tala. The other basic element of Indian art music, the *tala*, is a rhythmic cycle containing a fixed number of beats. *Talas* give the rhythmic foundation of the melodic structure and are performed on drums. The sequence of beats serves as a framework on which the drummer plays rhythmic patterns associated with a particular *tala*. Once the drummer starts performing, he plays one cycle after another, often repeating the sequence of beats more than a hundred times in a single performance. The *tala* is divided into subsections, which can be equal or unequal in length. As a rule, the first beat of a section receives an accent. The most important accent occurs on the very first beat of the *tala* cycle; at this point the soloist sings or plays an important tone of the *raga*, and the drummer accents this with an appropriate drum stroke.

The North. The *raga* and *tala* are realized within distinctive musical forms. Although a number of these are prevalent in both north and south India, the major types of each region have certain traits in common. The northern classical music (Hindustani music) usually opens with a prelude, the *alap*. Here only the soloist and the drone instrument are heard; the

drum is silent, and the rhythm is free (there is no *tala*). The purpose of the *alap* is to explore the essential features of the *raga*—the important tones and the characteristic phrases—and to establish the appropriate mood. After the *alap* a short song is sung or played, and here the drum enters for the first time with the *tala*. The rest of the performance varies, depending on which formal type is being employed. But usually a great deal of improvisation is interspersed with recurring material from the song. The speed gradually increases, often leading to a rousing, extremely quick conclusion. In the north the chief melody instruments are the SITAR, a stringed instrument with a body usually made of a gourd split approximately in half, a fingerboard about 1 m (3 ft) long, and seven main strings; the *sarod*, a stringed instrument about 1 m (3 ft) long, made of wood, with a metal fingerboard and six main strings; the *shahnai*, a double-reed wind instrument about 0.6 m (2 ft) long with seven finger holes; and the *sarangi*, a bowed stringed instrument used both for solo playing and for accompanying vocal music. The most common drum in the north is the *tabla*, which is actually two small drums, each having a single head (membrane).

The South. The music of southern India (called Carnatic music, after a region in the south) is also based on the concepts of *raga* and *tala*, but the style of singing and playing and the musical forms are different from those of the north. South Indian music is often dancelike in character. Southern *ragas* are not equivalent to those of the north, and the manner of performing them is characterized by much ornamentation. The *talas* also are different, and they are performed on a different kind of drum—the *mridanga*, a cylindrical barrel drum about 0.6 m (2 ft) long with two heads. The principal southern forms begin with a rhythmically free introduction called *alapana*, which is followed by three main sections: *pallavi*, *anupallavi*, and *carana*. The *pallavi* melody serves as a refrain throughout, intermingled with a great deal of melodic and rhythmic elaboration and improvisation. The major melody instruments of the south are the *vina*, a stringed instrument similar in shape to the sitar of the north; the *venu*, a wooden transverse flute; the *nagasvaram*, an outdoor double-reed wind instrument with a conical bore, flared bell, and seven finger holes; and the Western violin.   WAYNE HOWARD

Bibliography: Daniélou, Alain, *Northern Indian Music*, 2 vols. (new ed., 1969); Goswami, O., *The Story of Indian Music* (1957); Holroyd, Peggy, *The Music of India* (1972); Howard, Wayne, *Sāmavedic Chant* (1977); Jairazbhoy, N. A., *The Rāgas of North Indian Music* (1971); Kaufmann, Walter, *The Rāgas of North India* (1968) and *The Rāgas of South India* (1975); Massey, Reginald and Jamila, *The Music of India* (1977); Krishnaswamy, S., *Musical Instruments of India* (1965); Nijenhuis, Emmie te, *Indian Music, History and Structure* (1974); Popley, H. A., *The Music of India*, 3d ed. (1970); Sambamoorthy, P., *South Indian Music*, 6 vols. (1963–69); Shankar, Ravi, *My Music, My Life* (1968); Wade, Bonnie, *Music in India: The Classical Traditions* (1979).

Indian Mutiny

The revolt called the Indian Mutiny, or the Sepoy Rebellion, is referred to by many Indians as their first war of independence. It was initiated in Meerut on May 10, 1857, by Indian troops (sepoys) of the British Indian Army. The insurrection was triggered when the British introduced new rifle cartridges rumored to be greased with oil made from the fat of animals—and the fat of sacred cows was taboo to Hindus while Muslims were repelled by pig fat. The revolt soon spread to large sectors of the civilian population and became extremely violent. In Meerut the sepoys killed every European that they found, and another massacre occurred at Cawnpore (KANPUR). British suppression of the mutiny quickly became barbaric.

The greased cartridges were only one factor leading to the revolt. The land policies of Lord DALHOUSIE, who served as governor-general from 1848 to 1856, and of his successor, Lord Canning, and their attempts to modernize and westernize India caused resentment. The British were insensitive to Indian religious practices; many of their social reforms, such as the abolition of child marriage and the banning of self-immolation of widows (SUTTEE), had disturbed Indian traditionalists. A regulation of 1856 requiring soldiers to serve overseas if needed (thus losing CASTE) intensified sepoy hostility toward the British. In addition, many discontented elements in northern India—dispossessed princes, unemployed soldiers, and people who had lost land rights—joined the revolt. Southern India was untouched by the mutiny, however, and the Sikh soldiers of the Punjab area remained loyal to the British throughout.

The rebel troops captured Delhi and proclaimed the aged Mogul emperor Bahadur Shah II emperor of all India. No strong national leadership emerged, however, and the mutiny was quenched in March 1858, although sporadic fighting and guerrilla sorties continued until late that year in northern and central India. In August 1858 the British crown assumed control of India from the East India Company (see EAST INDIA COMPANY, BRITISH), and in 1877 Queen Victoria was crowned empress of India. The mutiny played a pivotal role in Anglo-Indian history. The British afterward became cautious and defensive about their empire, while many Indians remained bitter and would never trust their rulers again.

MARCUS FRANDA AND VONETTA J. FRANDA

Bibliography: Collier, Richard, *The Great Indian Mutiny* (1963); Embree, Ainslie T., ed., *1857 in India: Mutiny or War of Independence* (1963); Hibbert, Christopher, *The Great Mutiny: India, 1857* (1978); Joshi, P. C., ed., *Rebellion: 1857* (1957); Sen, Surendra N., *Eighteen Fifty-Seven* (1957).

Indian National Congress

The Indian National Congress, a leading organization in India's independence movement, was the dominant political party in independent India for 30 years. Founded (1885) in Bombay, it sent petitions to the British government requesting a larger political role for Indians. In 1907 the Congress split, its moderate wing seeking eventual dominion status, while its radicals demanded immediate self-rule.

The Congress reunited in support of the British during World War I but was disappointed soon after the war when Britain restricted political activity in India. Under the leadership of Mahatma GANDHI the Congress demanded *purna swaraj* ("complete independence") and waged periodic campaigns of nonviolent civil disobedience. Although leaders of the organization were imprisoned several times, Britain made some concessions in the 1930s. During World War II the Congress was suppressed when it refused to support Britain. By this time, however, it had proved the strength of its popular support, and Britain granted (1947) independence to India following the war. The predominately Hindu Congress reluctantly accepted the creation of Pakistan as a separate Muslim nation.

After independence the Congress party, led by Jawaharlal NEHRU and later by his daughter, Indira GANDHI, dominated Indian politics; its policies were largely socialistic. In 1969 the Congress split, forming the New Congress party, led by prime minister Indira Gandhi, and the more conservative Old Congress party of Morarji DESAI. The former won the 1971 elections, but the increasingly repressive policies of Indira Gandhi led to its downfall. The Janata party, a coalition that included the Old Congress party, won the 1977 election. In 1978 the New Congress party was split when Gandhi established her own Congress party, which won power in the 1980 election.

Bibliography: Andrews, Charles F., and Mookerjee, Girija K., *The Rise and Growth of the Congress in India 1832-1920*, 2d ed. (1967); Chatterjee, Basant Kumar, *The Congress Splits* (1970); Ghose, Sankar, *The Indian National Congress* (1975); Weiner, Myron, *Party Building in a New Nation: the Indian National Congress* (1967).

See also: INDIA; INDIA, HISTORY OF.

Indian Ocean

The Indian Ocean is the third largest body of water in the world, covering about 20% of the Earth's water surface. It is bounded on the north by southern Asia; on the west by the Arabian Peninsula and Africa; on the east by the Malay Peninsula, the Sunda Islands, and Australia; and on the south by Antarctica. It is separated from the Atlantic Ocean by the 20° east meridian south of Africa, and from the Pacific by the 147° east meridian. The northernmost extent of the Indian Ocean is approximately 30° north latitude in the Persian Gulf.

The ocean is nearly 10,000 km (6,200 mi) wide at the southern tips of Africa and Australia; its area is 73,556,000 km² (28,400,000 mi²), including the RED SEA and the PERSIAN GULF. The ocean's volume is estimated to be 292,131,000 km³ (70,086,000 mi³).

Small islands dot the continental rims. Island nations within the ocean are Madagascar (formerly Malagasy Republic), the world's fourth largest island; Comoros; Seychelles; Maldives; Mauritius; and Sri Lanka. Indonesia borders it.

The ocean's importance as a transit route between Asia and Africa has made it a scene of conflict. Because of its size, however, no one nation had successfully dominated until the early 1800s when Britain controlled much of the surrounding land. Its strategic importance far outweighs the economic value of its minerals or marine life.

ENVIRONMENT
The African, Indian, and Antarctic crustal plates converge in the Indian Ocean. Their junctures are marked by branches of the MID-OCEANIC RIDGE forming an inverted Y, with the stem running south from the edge of the continental shelf near Bombay, India. The eastern, western, and southern basins thus formed are subdivided into smaller basins by ridges. The ocean's continental shelves are narrow, averaging 200 km (125 mi) in width. An exception is found off Australia's western coast, where the shelf width exceeds 1,000 km (600 mi). The average depth of the ocean is 3,890 m (12,760 ft). Its deepest point, in the Java Trench, is estimated to be 7,450 m (24,442 ft). North of 50° south latitude, 86% of the main basin is covered by pelagic sediments, of which more than one-half is globigerina ooze. The remaining 14% is layered with terrigenous sediments. Glacial outwash dominates the extreme southern latitudes.

Climate. The climate north of the equator is affected by a MONSOON wind system. Strong northeast winds blow from October until April; from May until October south and west winds prevail. In the ARABIAN SEA the violent monsoon brings rain to the Indian subcontinent. In the southern hemisphere the winds generally are milder, but summer storms near Mauritius can be severe. When the monsoon winds change, cyclones sometimes strike the shores of the Arabian Sea and the Bay of Bengal (see BENGAL, BAY OF).

Hydrology. Among the few large rivers flowing into the Indian Ocean are the Zambezi, Shatt-al-Arab, Indus, Ganges, Brahmaputra, and Irrawaddy. Currents are largely controlled by the monsoon. Two large circular currents, one in the northern hemisphere flowing clockwise and one south of the equator moving counterclockwise, constitute the dominant flow pattern. During the winter monsoon, however, currents in the north are reversed. Deepwater circulation is controlled primarily by inflows from the Atlantic Ocean, the Red Sea, and Antarctic currents. (See OCEAN CURRENTS.) North of 20° south latitude the minimum surface temperature is 22° C (72° F), exceeding 28° C (82° F) to the east. Southward of 40° south latitude, temperatures drop quickly. Surface water salinity ranges from 32 to 37 parts per 1,000, the highest occurring in the Arabian Sea and in a belt between southern Africa and southwestern Australia. Pack ice and icebergs are found throughout the year south of about 65° south latitude. The average northern limit of icebergs is 45° south latitude.

Economy. The warmth of the Indian Ocean keeps phytoplankton production low, except along the northern fringes and in a few scattered spots elsewhere; life in the ocean is thus limited. Fishing is confined to subsistence levels. The ocean's most important function has been that of trade transport. Europeans, following the ancient seafarers, had crossed its waters to reach the East and returned with silks, rugs, tea, and spices. The Indian Ocean is also noted for its role in the shipment of petroleum from Southeast Asia to the West. Petroleum is the most significant mineral of the area, extracted primarily on the Persian Gulf.

HISTORY
The earliest known civilizations, in the valleys of the Nile, Euphrates, Tigris, and Indus rivers and in Southeast Asia, have

developed near the Indian Ocean. During Egypt's 1st dynasty (*c.*3000 BC), sailors were sent out onto its waters, journeying to Punt, thought to be part of present-day Somalia. Returning ships brought gold and slaves. Phoenicians of the 3d millennium BC may have entered the area, but no settlements resulted. Marco POLO (*c.*1254–1324) is thought to have returned from the Far East by way of the Strait of Malacca (see MALACCA, STRAIT OF). Vasco da GAMA rounded the Cape of Good Hope in 1497 and sailed to India, the first European to do so.

The ancient peoples who lived along the ocean each tried unsuccessfully to control its commercial routes. Portugal attempted to achieve preeminence for more than a century but

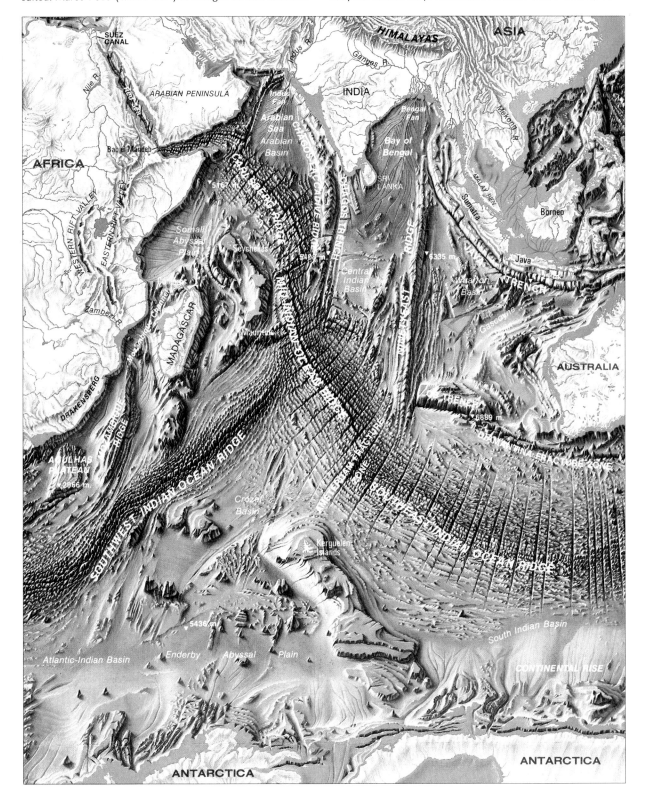

was thwarted in the mid-1600s. The Dutch East India Company (1602–1798) sought control of trade with the East across the Indian Ocean. France and Britain established trade companies for the area, but Britain became the principal power. After 1815 it dominated the area.

The opening of the Suez Canal in 1869 revived European interest in the East, but no nation was successful in establishing trade dominance. Since World War II the United Kingdom has withdrawn from the area, to be only partially replaced by India, the USSR, and the United States. The last two have tried to establish hegemony by negotiating for naval base sites. Developing countries bordering the ocean, however, seek to have it made a "zone of peace" so that they may use its shipping lanes freely.   MARTIN IRA GLASSNER

Bibliography: Adie, Ian W., *Oil, Politics and Sea Power: The Indian Ocean Vortex* (1975); Amirie, Abbas, ed., *The Persian Gulf and Indian Ocean in International Politics* (1975); Cousteau, Jacques-Yves, and Diole, Philippe, *Life and Death in a Coral Sea* (1971); Cubitt, Gerald, *Islands of the Indian Ocean* (1975); Ostheimer, John M., ed., *The Politics of the Western Indian Ocean Islands* (1975); Sverdrup, H. U., et al., *The Oceans: Their Physics, Chemistry and General Biology* (1942); Toussaint, Auguste, *The History of the Indian Ocean*, trans. by June Guicharnaud (1966); Vali, Ferenc, *The Politics of the Indian Ocean Region: The Balances of Power* (1976).

Indian paintbrush

Indian paintbrush is the common name for some members of the plant genus *Castilleja* in the figwort family, Scrophulariaceae. The flowers are mostly greenish with brilliant purple, red, or yellow spikelike racemes, giving the appearance of a dipped brush. *C. coccinea*, also called scarlet paintbrush, which is native to deep meadows, is the state flower of Wyoming. *C. californica* is the gaudy red Indian paintbrush of the West Coast of the United States.   CHARLES L. WILSON

Indian pipe

Indian pipe, or corpse plant, *Monotropa uniflora*, is a saprophytic, perennial herb in the wintergreen family, Pyrolaceae. The entire plant is usually pure white, or sometimes pale pinkish, with large nodding flowers borne singly, and simple, scalelike leaves. In the 19th century, juice from the plant was applied to sore eyes as a domestic remedy.   DIANNE FAHSELT

Indian Reorganization Act

The Indian Reorganization Act, a major reform of U.S. policy toward American Indians, was enacted by Congress on June 18, 1934 as a result of a decade of criticism of conditions on the reservations. It forbade the further allotment of tribal lands to individual Indians, authorized the purchase of additional lands for Indians, created a revolving-credit fund to be used for tribal enterprises, encouraged Indian groups to adopt written constitutions providing for limited self-government, gave Indians preference for positions in the Bureau of INDIAN AFFAIRS, and invoked strict conservation practices on Indian lands. The act, also known as the Wheeler-Howard Act, has been criticized by some Indians who charge that tribal constitutions created under the act are too restrictive of tribal sovereignty.   LAWRENCE C. KELLY

Indian schools, American

The U.S. government, through the Bureau of Indian Affairs, provides funds for the education of Indian children living on Indian-owned or restricted trust lands. In 1978 and 1979 the bureau operated 221 federal boarding and day schools for 40,781 children and 15 dormitories for 2,186 children attending public schools. The bureau also paid part of the costs for two-thirds of the Indian students attending public schools in states where bureau aid is still required. In recent years the total number of Indian children between the ages of 5 and 18 who attend school has increased substantially: in 1976 there were 216,168 Indian students, as compared with 178,476 in 1969. The government program, which includes adult education and various forms of aid to higher education, applies to natives of Alaska, that is, Indians, Eskimos, and Aleuts, and to

children of one-quarter degree or more of Indian blood. California, Idaho, Michigan, Minnesota, Nebraska, Oregon, Texas, Washington, and Wisconsin are responsible for the education of their Indian children. The famous all-around athlete Jim Thorpe, who was of Sauk and Fox descent, attended the Haskell Indian School, now Haskell Indian Junior College, in Lawrence, Kans., and began his football career at the Carlisle Indian School in Carlisle, Pa.

Bibliography: Adams, Evelyn C., *American Indian Education: Government Schools and Economic Progress* (1946; repr. 1971); Fischbacher, Theodore, *A Study of the Role of the Federal Government in the Education of the American Indian* (1967; repr. 1974); Fuchs, Estelle, and Havighurst, Robert J., *To Live On This Earth: American Indian Education* (1972); Jones, Louis T., *Amerindian Education* (1972); Szasz, Margaret, *Education and the American Indian: The Road to Self-determination, 1928–1973*, 2d ed. (1977).

Indian Territory

The term *Indian Territory* was originally applied vaguely to huge areas of the western United States occupied by the American Indians. Laws passed in the 1830s, however, most notably the Indian Removal Act (1830) and the Indian Intercourse Act (1834), defined Indian Territory as the area of present-day Oklahoma, Kansas, Nebraska, and the Dakotas to which Indian tribes were then being forcibly moved. By creating the territories of Kansas and Nebraska, the KANSAS-NEBRASKA ACT (1854) further limited the area to the territory of the FIVE CIVILIZED TRIBES in present-day Oklahoma. Because they had allied themselves with the Confederacy, these tribes were forced by new treaties negotiated in 1866 to relinquish the western half of their territory, which became part of the Oklahoma Territory. In 1907 the remaining Indian Territory was absorbed with the Oklahoma Territory into the new state of Oklahoma.   LAWRENCE C. KELLY

Bibliography: Debo, Angie, *A History of the Indians of the United States* (1970).

Indian treaties

The practice of concluding treaties with the American Indians was initiated in the colonial period by the British, who employed them especially after the British victory in the French and Indian War (1754–63). During the American Revolution, the U.S. government adopted the treaty system, signing its first treaty with the Delawares in 1778.

The major purposes of such treaties were to obtain land cessions from the tribes, to determine boundaries between Indian and white lands, and to regulate trade. By adopting the treaty system, the British and U.S. governments recognized the prior ownership of land by Indian tribes and in effect also acknowledged their strength and their status as independent nations. The most important of the early treaties were those of Fort Stanwix (1768 and 1784), by which the IROQUOIS LEAGUE ceded rights in the trans-Appalachian country, and the Treaty of Greenville (1795), by which 12 northern tribes surrendered the southeastern corner of the NORTHWEST TERRITORY to the United States.

By 1815 most of the Indians north of the Ohio River had been subdued and sentiment was strong to force all Indians to settle west of the Mississippi River. Although treaties to effect this end were formally negotiated, coercion, bribery, and the use of alcohol became commonplace in wringing favorable terms from reluctant tribal leaders. In the case of *Cherokee Nation* v. *The State of Georgia* (1831), the U.S. Supreme Court ruled that the Indians were no longer to be regarded as independent nations but rather as "dependent domestic nations," subject to regulation by the federal government. From that time until 1871 treaties became mere formalities in which terms were usually dictated by the government. Congress frequently enacted laws conflicting with the provisions of Indian treaties, and the whites frequently violated their terms, thus provoking many of the INDIAN WARS of the 19th century.

In 1871 the use of treaties was terminated by Congress, and Indians were thereafter governed by congressional legislation,

Benjamin West's *Penn's Treaty with the Indians* commemorates William Penn's exceptional peace initiatives, concluded shortly after his arrival in America in 1682. Penn's settlement with the Delaware Indians, which included payment for Indian lands, and his efforts to ensure fair treatment established a peace that lasted about 70 years. (1771; Pennsylvania Academy of Fine Arts, Philadelphia.)

executive orders, or executive agreements. On Aug. 13, 1946, in recognition of past injustices, Congress created the Indian Claims Commission to adjudicate all Indian land claims concerning noncompliance with treaties. By 1968 more than $216 million had been paid in awards to the tribes.

LAWRENCE C. KELLY

Bibliography: Cohen, Felix S., *Handbook of Federal Indian Law* (1942; repr. 1974); Deloria, Vine, *Behind the Trail of Broken Treaties* (1974); Kappler, Charles J., ed., *Indian Affairs: Laws and Treaties*, 5 vols. (1941; repr. 1977); Washburn, Wilcomb E., *Red Man's Land/White Man's Law* (1971).

Indian universities: see SOUTH ASIAN UNIVERSITIES.

Indian Wars

The Indian Wars in the area of the present-day United States began in 1540 when the conquistadors of Francisco Vázquez de CORONADO clashed with ZUÑI warriors of the pueblo of Hawikuh. The wars ended three and one-half centuries later, in 1890, when U.S. cavalry troops almost wiped out Big Foot's (1825?–90) band of SIOUX at WOUNDED KNEE. These two events and the numerous clashes in between were part of the continuing struggle for possession of North America. Warfare was but one instrument of conquest; diplomacy, trade, disease, and assimilation also played significant roles. Warfare, however, was a constant theme, one central to understanding the conquest of the continent.

Colonial Indian Wars. Almost continuous Indian warfare marked the colonial experience in North America. Spain established outposts in the area of the Rio Grande early in the 17th century with a major aim of converting the PUEBLO tribes to Christianity, a program severely retarded by the Pueblo Rebellion of 1680, which drove all Spaniards from the province for 12 years. In the East, English settlers also provoked uprisings as they began to spread inland from the Atlantic Coast. A bloody outbreak in Virginia in 1622 was followed by the PEQUOT WAR in New England in 1636–37. In most of the English colonies sporadic fighting alternated with full-scale war for a century and a half. One of the most violent conflicts was KING PHILIP'S WAR of 1675–76 in New England.

Moreover, in the imperial contest between Britain and France, each power incited and led Indian allies against the other. By the middle of the 18th century this struggle had spread beyond the Appalachian Mountains to the Great Lakes region and had become preeminently Indian warfare. Although the French enjoyed many advantages in the FRENCH AND INDIAN WAR of 1754–63, England finally prevailed. England's hold on the Great Lakes region was almost broken in

1763 with the outbreak of PONTIAC'S REBELLION. An alliance of Ottawa and other tribes stormed Detroit. The garrison held, however, and the so-called conspiracy of Pontiac collapsed. In that same year England forbade all white settlement beyond the Appalachians.

The Woodlands Wars of the Eastern United States. In the American Revolution the British, as the French had done earlier, made extensive use of Indians to fight the colonists. After the war settlers pushed west of the mountains, and new fighting erupted. North of the Ohio River, in 1790 and 1791, LITTLE TURTLE led warriors of the MIAMI, SHAWNEE, and other tribes to victories over American troops before the Indians were crushed by Gen. "Mad Anthony" WAYNE in the Battle of FALLEN TIMBERS in 1794. The Shawnee chief, TECUMSEH, carried on, striving to forge a grand alliance of tribes west of the mountains. His dream was shattered by Indiana's Governor William Henry HARRISON at the Battle of TIPPECANOE in 1811. Tecumseh himself fell in battle during the WAR OF 1812, in which Indians once again aided the British. In the South, Indian resistance collapsed after Gen. Andrew JACKSON smashed

The Jamestown Massacre of 1622, a surprise attack by the Powhatan Confederacy, began the intermittent warfare that was to disturb the Virginia colony for more than 20 years. Provoked by expropriation of Indian lands, the confederacy attacked and killed nearly 350 settlers.

This cartoon from the revolutionary war period depicts the Indian as henchman to the British. Although some Indians sided with the patriots, many tribes in the frontier regions fought bitterly against the colonists, often receiving British arms and encouragement.

the CREEKS in 1814 at the Battle of Horseshoe Bend, located in present-day Alabama.

In the three decades following the War of 1812 the U.S. government evolved a policy of moving eastern tribes to new homes west of the Mississippi River in order to clear the way for white settlement. For the most part, Indian removal was accomplished by nonviolent though coercive measures. Notable exceptions were Florida's SEMINOLE WARS (1817–18, 1835–42, 1856–58) and the brief BLACK HAWK WAR (1832) in Illinois and present-day Wisconsin.

The Later Indian Wars in the Western United States. In the mid-19th century the wars spread from the eastern woodlands to the plains, mountains, and deserts of the Trans-Mississippi West. The territorial acquisitions of the 1840s brought new tribes within the limits of the United States and, with the discovery of gold in California (1848) shattered the hope for a "Permanent Indian Frontier" along the eastern edge of the Great Plains. For four decades, as new mineral strikes and other economic opportunities pulled the frontier of settle-

ment westward, armed force alternated with negotiation until, one after another, the tribes had been brought under subjection.

At first the objective of U.S. military policy was to keep the travel routes open and protect the settled areas. A system of military posts developed in response to the threat as Indian raiders, their tribal ranges invaded, attacked both travelers and settlers. In the 1850s military forces defeated rebelling tribes in the Pacific Northwest, fought the first skirmishes with the Sioux and CHEYENNE of the Great Plains, and contended indecisively with KIOWA and COMANCHE raiders along the Texas frontier and APACHE raiders in the Southwest.

The Civil War diverted white energies momentarily, but the mobilization of volunteer armies soon enabled the federal government to field greater strength than ever. Between 1861 and 1865 volunteer forces conquered the NAVAJOS of the Southwest and fought with the Great Plains tribes. The Minnesota Sioux outbreak of 1862 took the lives of about 800 settlers amid scenes of savagery. At Sand Creek, in Colorado Territory, volunteer troops in 1864 perpetrated barbarities on BLACK KETTLE's Cheyennes rivaling those of the Sioux in Minnesota (see SAND CREEK MASSACRE).

Heavy fighting continued into the postwar years, highlighted by the Fetterman Massacre of 1866, when a detachment from Fort Phil Kearny, Wyo., was ambushed on the BOZEMAN TRAIL and wiped out. A new government policy of "conquest by kindness" ultimately flowered in President Ulysses S. Grant's "Peace Policy," however.

In a series of treaties in the late 1860s representatives of many western tribes promised to settle their people on reservations. The Peace Policy did not, however, bring peace. The wars that followed were fought to force tribes onto reservations they had supposedly already accepted or to return them to reservations that they had fled once they discovered the harsh realities of life there.

The most spectacular of these conflicts were those with the Sioux and Cheyennes of the northern Plains from 1876

(Opposite page) The maps indicate sites of major confrontations between Indians and the European and American settlers who swept westward across the continent between 1622 and 1890. Also shown are original Indian lands and reservations to which tribes were removed.

(Below) The Battle of the Little Bighorn, or Custer's Last Stand, was depicted by the Sioux veteran Kicking Bear more than 20 years after the battle, at the request of the artist Frederic Remington. The long-haired, mustachioed Custer (left center) appears with the deceased, whose departing spirits are outlined. The central standing group includes the artist. (c.1898; Southwest Museum, Los Angeles.)

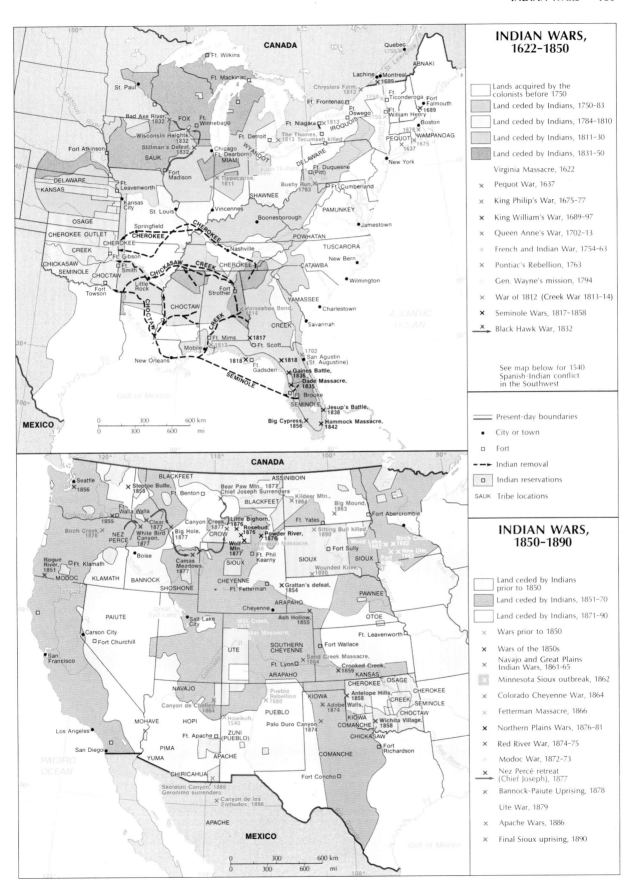

INDIAN WARS, 1622–1850

- ☐ Lands acquired by the colonists before 1750
- Land ceded by Indians, 1750–83
- Land ceded by Indians, 1784–1810
- Land ceded by Indians, 1811–30
- Land ceded by Indians, 1831–50

Virginia Massacre, 1622
× Pequot War, 1637
× King Philip's War, 1675–77
× King William's War, 1689–97
× Queen Anne's War, 1702–13
× French and Indian War, 1754–63
× Pontiac's Rebellion, 1763
× Gen. Wayne's mission, 1794
× War of 1812 (Creek War 1813–14)
× Seminole Wars, 1817–1858
× Black Hawk War, 1832

See map below for 1540 Spanish-Indian conflict in the Southwest

- Present-day boundaries
- • City or town
- ☐ Fort
- - - ► Indian removal
- ☐ Indian reservations
- SAUK Tribe locations

INDIAN WARS, 1850–1890

- ☐ Land ceded by Indians prior to 1850
- Land ceded by Indians, 1851–70
- Land ceded by Indians, 1871–90

× Wars prior to 1850
× Wars of the 1850s
× Navajo and Great Plains Indian Wars, 1861–65
⊠ Minnesota Sioux outbreak, 1862
× Colorado Cheyenne War, 1864
× Fetterman Massacre, 1866
× Northern Plains Wars, 1876–81
× Red River War, 1874–75
× Modoc War, 1872–73
→ Nez Percé retreat (Chief Joseph), 1877
× Bannock-Paiute Uprising, 1878
× Ute War, 1879
× Apache Wars, 1886
× Final Sioux uprising, 1890

through 1881, notably the now legendary Custer's Last Stand—the Battle of Little Bighorn (see LITTLE BIGHORN, BATTLE OF THE), in which more than 200 men under Gen. George A. CUSTER perished on June 25, 1876. Sioux and Cheyenne resistance ended with the surrender of the Sioux chief, SITTING BULL, in 1881. The Red River War of 1874-75 finally brought peace to the southern Plains and Texas as Kiowas, Comanches, Cheyennes, and ARAPAHOES accepted life on reservations. Other encounters were the MODOC war of 1872-73, in the California lava beds; the dramatic flight (1877) of Chief JOSEPH and the NEZ PERCÉ from Idaho across more than 1,500 miles of the American Northwest, almost to Canada; the Bannock-Paiute uprising of 1878 in Idaho and Oregon; and the UTE outbreak of 1879 in western Colorado. The long and bloody Apache wars of New Mexico and Arizona closed in 1886 when GERONIMO surrendered for the last time. Wounded Knee, the tragic clash of reservation Sioux with U.S. troops in 1890, marked the end of the Indian Wars—in the very year that the U.S. Census recorded the disappearance of a frontier of settlement. ROBERT M. UTLEY

Bibliography: Andrist, Ralph K., *The Long Death: The Last Days of the Plains Indian* (1964); McLeod, William C., *The American Indian Frontier* (1928); Prucha, Francis Paul, *The Sword of the Republic: The United States Army on the Frontier, 1783-1846* (1969); Utley, Robert M., *Frontiersmen in Blue: The United States Army and the Indian, 1848-65* (1967) and *Frontier Regulars: The United States Army and the Indian, 1866-91* (1973); Utley, Robert M., and Washburn, Wilcomb, *The American Heritage History of the Indian Wars* (1977).

See also: FRONTIER; INDIAN TREATIES; INDIANS, AMERICAN.

Indiana

One of five eastern north-central states, Indiana is bordered on the west by Illinois, on the north by Michigan and Lake Michigan, and on the east by Ohio. The Ohio River follows Indiana's southern border with Kentucky. The state is rectangular in shape, and its capital, Indianapolis, lies near its center. Indiana has an extreme length of 451 km (280 mi) and a breadth of 257 km (160 mi), giving it an area that makes it the 38th largest state.

Indiana was once part of the Northwest Territory; it became a state in 1816. Its name recalls the inhabitants at the time of first colonial exploration in 1679. The nickname, "Hoosier State" is thought to be derived from the pioneers' greeting to strangers, "Who's yere?"

Indiana has a large, accessible market, and it is located near several large metropolitan areas in neighboring states. Its Great Lakes and Ohio River ports, along with a network of major highways, provide Indiana with access to much of the nation.

LAND AND RESOURCES

Indiana has three distinct natural regions: the northern lakes, the central plains, and the southern hills and valleys. The sand dunes along Lake Michigan are considered by many to be the most scenic feature of the northern region. The central plains are flat or gently rolling, but tributaries of the Wabash River have dissected the western part of the state, creating hills and valleys. The southern hills are primarily limestone. Weathering has resulted in the formation of caves, sinkholes, underground streams, and mineral springs. Along the Ohio River, the bluffs are rugged and scenic.

All of Indiana except the south central portion was glaciated. Deposits of clay, sand, gravel, and boulders filled the preglacial valleys, and deep and fertile soils, primarily gray brown podzols, have developed. Under the till is stratified limestone, shale, and sandstone.

Drainage. Streams flowing to the Gulf of Mexico drain 97% of Indiana. The WABASH RIVER originates in west central Ohio, crosses central Indiana, and then flows southward into the OHIO RIVER, draining about two-thirds of the state. Through the lower one-third of its course, it follows the boundary between Indiana and Illinois. The principal tributary of the Wabash is the White River. The Whitewater River drains southeastern Indiana into the Ohio, while the Kankakee drains much of northwest Indiana. The Saint Joseph River, in northern Indiana, flows into Lake Michigan.

INDIANA

Capital and Largest City: Indianapolis (1979 est. pop., 706,000)

Population: 5,334,300 (1979 est.). *Distribution*—64.9% urban, 35.1% rural; *density*, 57 per km² (147 per mi²); *increase* (1970-79), 2.7%; *population rank*, 12th

Area: 93,993 km² (36,291 mi²), including 502 km² (194 mi²) of inland water; *area rank*, 38th

Elevation: *Highest*—Wayne County, 383 m (1,257 ft); *lowest*—Pasey County, 98 m (320 ft)

Principal Products: *Manufacturing and industry*—electric and electronic equipment, plastics, transportation equipment, machinery, chemicals, food products, rubber. *Agriculture*—corn, soybeans, hogs, beef and dairy products, wheat, eggs, vegetables, turkeys, tobacco. *Mining*—coal, cement, limestone, petroleum, sand and gravel

Government: *State legislature*—50 senators, 100 representatives. *Representation in Congress*—2 U.S. senators, 11 U.S. representatives

Number of Counties: 92

Statehood: Dec. 11, 1816; the 19th state

State Nickname: The Hoosier State

State Bird: Cardinal

State Flower: Peony

State Tree: Tulip

State Motto: The Crossroads of America

Climate. Indiana's continental climate is characterized by hot, humid summers and cold winters. January mean temperatures range from 2° C (35° F) in Evansville to −4° C (25° F) in South Bend. July temperatures at the same locations are 26° C (78° F) and 23° C (73° F), respectively.

Major temperature variations are caused by differences in latitude, elevation, terrain, and—in winter—by the lake effect. Moisture is picked up from Lake Michigan by air masses moving across it. When the moisture-laden air is forced to rise over the cold land surface, it loses its ability to hold water vapor and thus deposits the state's largest amounts of snow near the lake.

The growing season varies from 160 days in the north to 178 days in the south. Annual precipitation averages 864 mm (34 in) in the north and 1,118 mm (44 in) along the Ohio River. Most precipitation is caused by polar air masses mixing with humid tropical air masses from the Gulf of Mexico.

Vegetation. About 20% of Indiana was originally covered with

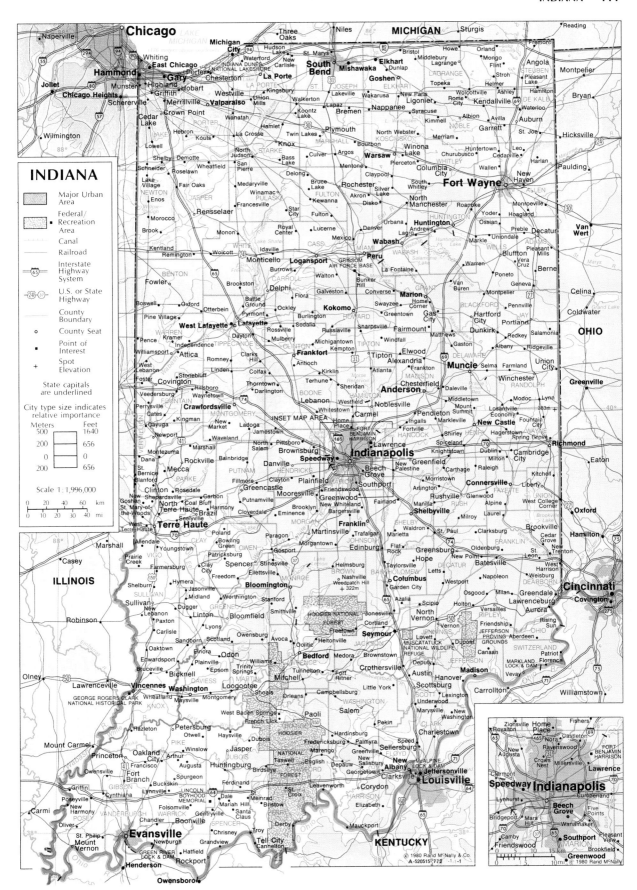

prairie grass. Dense mixed hardwood forests covered the rest of the state but were cleared for lumber and farming. Today less than 18% remains wooded. Of the 124 native tree species, the most abundant are sycamore, maple, and beech.

Wildlife. During the early years of settlement, wilderness life was threatened by commercial hunters and farmers, who cleared the land for agriculture. Bear, buffalo, deer, and wolves disappeared from the area. Smaller game species such as wild turkeys, prairie chickens, grouse, and pheasant were also threatened.

During the 1880s, Indiana pioneered in the enactment of environmental protection legislation. Deer, squirrel, and cottontail rabbit populations have been replenished; muskrat, opossum, raccoon, and fox have increased in number.

Resources. Bituminous coal, Indiana's most valuable mineral resource, lies under about 16,800 km² (6,500 mi²) of the state. Indiana is one of the ten leading coal-mining states. Oil and natural gas, extracted in eastern and southwestern Indiana, are refined near Fort Wayne, Indianapolis, and Mount Vernon. Sand and gravel are found in widely scattered areas. Gypsum and clay are also mined. Abundant groundwater is found in the sand and gravel deposits of glacial till.

PEOPLE

Among the 50 states, Indiana ranks 12th in population. Most of the early settlers came to Indiana from the South and were predominantly of English, Scottish, and Welsh extraction. Germans and Irish followed. Immigrants from Europe came to Indiana's cities during the period between the Civil War and the years immediately following World War I, lured by employment opportunities in the developing industries. As a result, Indiana's population grew steadily, and the state became more urbanized. Its largest cities, according to 1979 population estimates, are INDIANAPOLIS (706,000), FORT WAYNE (183,400), GARY (152,900), EVANSVILLE (130,100), and SOUTH BEND (109,300).

Nearly 75% of the state's population are Protestants. Roman Catholics constitute less than 15%, and Jews, less than 1%.

Education. Indiana's educational system developed gradually after the state was organized. The first kindergarten, trade school, and coeducational teaching system in the United States were founded in NEW HARMONY, Ind. Butler University (1849) was among the first institutions of higher learning to admit women.

Indiana has 28 colleges and universities. More than half of the college population attends the four state universities. For further information, see INDIANA, STATE UNIVERSITIES OF.

Culture. Cultural institutions include Clowes Hall in Indianapolis, home of a major symphony orchestra and theatrical touring companies. The Indianapolis Museum of Art houses collections of paintings, sculpture, graphics, ceramics, and silver.

A major sporting event is the Indianapolis 500 auto race, held annually on the Sunday preceding Memorial Day at Speedway. Basketball is the major sporting activity for most high schools and colleges, and the sport maintains a passionate following among the residents.

Indiana publishes 79 daily newspapers, including the Indianapolis *Star* and *News*, which have the largest circulations in the state. Commercial radio stations number 169, and commercial television stations, 20.

The state has produced several noted writers who used local themes in their works. Three are Theodore Dreiser; Edward Eggleston, author of *The Hoosier Schoolmaster;* and James Whitcomb Riley, the Hoosier poet. Indiana's songwriters include Cole Porter, Hoagy Carmichael, and Paul Dresser, composer of "On the Banks of the Wabash." Robert Indiana, born in New Castle, chose to use the name of his home state when he embarked on his career as an artist.

Columbus, Indiana (1979 est. pop., 28,900), is known for its many noteworthy buildings. In a program begun in 1957, city officials and community leaders commissioned world-famous architects, including Eero Saarinen and Harry Weese, to design buildings for the city. These structures, along with the city's pedestrian mall, have made Columbus an example of modern urban planning.

ECONOMY

The Calumet region in extreme northwestern Indiana is the

(Above) *A large paddlewheel ship on the Ohio River cruises past Madison, the seat of Jefferson County in southeastern Indiana. Founded in 1808, Madison developed into an important port until the 1820s, when it was superseded by Louisville and Cincinnati.*

(Left) *Indianapolis, the largest city of Indiana and the seat of Marion County, is located in the central portion of the state along the west fork of White River. The city, an important manufacturing center, has been Indiana's capital since 1825.*

dominant industrial center in the state. Its proximity to Chicago's market, combined with its Great Lakes location, has enabled the area to remain economically competitive. The northeast's proximity to the industrial centers of Detroit, Mich., and Toledo, Ohio, fosters economic growth in such cities as Elkhart and Fort Wayne.

Agriculture. Corn and soybeans are the state's most valuable cash crops. Wheat, oats, tobacco, hay, rye, apples, and peaches also contribute significantly to the economy. Indiana is among the nation's leading producers of spearmint and peppermint, both of which are grown in the rich muck soils of the northern lake region. Indiana is an extensively farmed state; more than 70% of the land is devoted to agriculture. It ranks eighth in the nation in value of farm products, recently estimated at $2.7 billion annually. During the 1800s, Indiana was a leading producer of hardwood lumber, but land clearing sharply reduced timber production.

Mining. Extraction of bituminous coal through strip mining takes place in the southwestern quarter of Indiana. The coal is shipped north to the Calumet region or south on the Ohio. Natural gas, once abundant in the eastern part of the state, has been virtually exhausted. Building stone is quarried in the south central region. The state produces 40% of the country's building limestone. Indiana limestone has been used for buildings such as the Empire State Building and The Pentagon.

Manufacturing. The major cities of the Calumet region—Gary, Hammond, East Chicago, and Whiting—produce iron, steel, and petroleum products. Other Indiana factories manufacture aluminum, auto parts, truck and bus bodies, cement, chemicals, brick, tile, and wood furniture. Indiana ranks first among the states in the production of pharmaceuticals and prefabricated homes and second in musical instruments.

Tourism. The state's forest land is well suited for outdoor recreation. Artificial lakes and reservoirs, primarily in central and southern Indiana, provide spawning areas for bass, bluegill, crappie, and catfish. Major fishing streams include the Kankakee, Tippecanoe, White, Wabash, Whitewater, Muscatatuck, Salomonie, and Blue rivers. It is estimated that more than 700,000 enthusiasts catch 17 million fish each year. Many fish are caught from lakes formed in abandoned strip mines.

The Indiana Dunes National Lakeshore attracts visitors to the state's northern water body. Brown County State Park is well known for its fall foliage and the artist colonies in its vicinity. Wyandotte Cave in Harrison County is one of the nation's largest. West Baden Springs near the Hoosier National Forest has mineral springs.

Indiana has 267 km² (103 mi²) of state forests, parks, and memorials. Most of the 26 state parks and 15 state forests are

(Above) *A massive ore freighter lies at berth in Gary as its cargo of iron ore is unloaded for use at the Gary Steel Works, one of the largest mills in the United States. A conveyor along the bridge above the freighter carries the ore from dockside to the mill.*

(Above) *Huge blocks of limestone await shipment at the P. M. & B. Limestone Company's quarry near Bedford, in Lawrence County. Indiana is one of the leading states in the production of limestone used for building.*

(Left) *Corn is harvested in Wayne County, near Indiana's border with Ohio. Indiana's most valuable cash crop is grain corn, that used for cattle feed, which annually accounts for more than $1.2 billion in farm revenue.*

Indiana Dunes National Lakeshore, occupying a strip of waterfront on the southern shore of Lake Michigan in Porter County, is famous for its sand beaches and shifting dunes. The area, which covers 3,371 hectares (8,330 acres) was created as a national lakeshore in 1972.

centered on a feature of natural or historical interest. Remains of a prehistoric Indian culture are preserved at Mounds State Park. Other tourist attractions include the earliest settlement by Europeans at Vincennes, Lincoln's boyhood home near Lincoln City, and the restored communal settlement at New Harmony.

Transportation. One of the first stagecoach routes, the NATIONAL ROAD, was constructed through Indiana soon after statehood. By 1840, steamboats and flatboats plied rivers and canals until the advent of the railroad. Today 10,460 km (6,500 mi) of railroad track and 147,570 km (91,700 mi) of highways cross Indiana. Five interstate routes serve the city of Indianapolis alone. Airlines fly to more than 200 airports in the state.

Water transportation is important near Lake Michigan and the Ohio River. Burns Harbor on Lake Michigan accommodates ocean liners, and barge traffic on the Ohio stops at the ports of Jeffersonville and Mount Vernon. Indiana's central location in the Midwest provides easy accessibility via multiple modes of transportation.

Energy. Most electrical energy is generated from coal. Indiana's total power development consists of a steam plant capacity of more than 8 million kilowatts, a hydroelectric capacity of 29,155 kW, and an internal combustion engine capacity of 26,363 kW.

GOVERNMENT

Structure. Indiana's original 1816 constitution was replaced in 1851 by its present one. Amendments to the constitution require approval by a majority of both general assembly houses in two consecutive legislatures and by a majority of voters.

The general assembly consists of 50 senators and 100 representatives. Senators are elected to four-year terms and representatives to two-year terms. The state supreme court consists of five judges, appointed by the governor. The judicial branch also maintains circuit, city, town, and justice of the peace courts.

All of Indiana's 92 counties, except for Marion County in Indianapolis, are governed by a board of county commissioners. Cities operate under a mayor-council form of government, while towns are governed by boards of trustees.   J. LEE GUERNSEY

Politics. Politics in Indiana is a closely knit operation, resistant to outside influences or national bureaucratic interferences. Independence has even been maintained despite the threat of losing federal funds. Representation in the federal legislature is not dominated by one political party. The governorship, too, has passed from one party to the other.

Two U.S. presidents have been closely associated with Indiana. William Henry HARRISON, victor in the Battle of Tippecanoe, had been a territorial governor of Indiana. He was elected president in 1840 as the candidate of the Whig party. His Republican grandson, Benjamin HARRISON, was an Indianapolis lawyer before his election to the presidency in 1888. The last major-party presidential candidate from Indiana was Wendell L. WILLKIE, who was defeated by Franklin D. Roosevelt in the election of 1940.

HISTORY

Archaeologists now recognize Indian village sites and constructions in Indiana as evidence of habitation by ancient MOUND BUILDERS. Mounds State Park in Madison County preserves some remnants of their past. Most spectacular of the archaeological finds is the Angel Mound site near Evansville. At least seven mounds have been identified within the Ohio River flood plain. The largest "beehive" has provided more than a million cataloged artifacts since its discovery in 1939. Centuries of habitation by the MIAMI, POTAWATAMI, DELAWARE, and KICKAPOO Indian tribes made little change in the natural environment of Indiana.

The first European exploration of present-day Indiana was in 1679 by Robert Cavelier, Sieur de LA SALLE, who attempted to establish French military domination over the Mississippi region. French Jesuit priests founded the first permanent European settlement, VINCENNES, in 1725. The French traders bargained for furs, and the Jesuits pursued their missionary work.

Even as late as 1800 most of what is now Indiana was recognized as Indian territory. The arrival of the colonists brought on a period of violence between the settlers and the Indian inhabitants. Friendly secessions from white occupied areas began in the late 1700s. The best known of the Indian land transfers was the New Purchase of 1818 that opened the bulk of Indiana to the whites.

Before statehood Indiana had several administrative centers. Vincennes became a French fort in 1732, about 50 years after colonial trading began. The British controlled Vincennes from 1763 until 1779, when George Rogers CLARK, financially aided by Governor Patrick Henry of Virginia, seized the fort for the Americans.

In 1784, Virginia relinquished its claim to the NORTHWEST TERRITORY. Indiana Territory was created in 1800 and included what was to become the states of Indiana, Illinois, and Wisconsin, along with parts of Michigan and Minnesota. Indiana's boundaries have changed little since it became a state.

The Battle of TIPPECANOE in 1811 effectively broke the power of Indian tribes in the territory. Indiana was admitted to the Union in 1816, the second state formed from the Northwest Territory. Corydon, the first state capital, was superseded in 1825 by Indianapolis, which had been designed as the seat of state government. Communities began to form in the territory as statehood approached. New Harmony along the Wabash was the site chosen for George Rapp's Harmony Society and by Robert OWEN for his cultural and scientific commune.

Indiana's first railroad was begun in 1834, connecting Indianapolis to the Ohio at Madison, the state's largest city in 1847. The rail line fostered economic growth and provided access to European markets for Indianapolis through the Mississippi River system. The National Road gave rise to numerous highway junctions that grew to become thriving communities.

Canal construction and railroad building left a permanent mark on state government. By publicly funding these projects, the state approached bankruptcy. State indebtedness was forbidden by the 1851 constitution. All governmental agencies are required to have balanced budgets at the end of each fiscal year.

One Confederate raid in 1863, led by General John Hunt MORGAN, was the only significant incident to take place in Indiana during the Civil War. The state backed the Union efforts despite the Southern origins of many residents. Abraham Lincoln had spent his boyhood in Spencer County, Ind., and many Hoosiers considered him a native son worthy of support.

Farming, mining, and forestry developed after the Civil War. One of the oldest industries in the state produced sandstone grinding wheels and honing stones. European immigrants to Indiana provided skills that diversified the industry of the state: glassmaking, furniture manufacturing, and brick and tile making. Laborers from the industrial centers of Europe settled in the Calumet region, lured there by employment opportunities in the steel mills and foundries.

Today, Indiana maintains a diverse economy. Although farming is declining in importance relative to industry, it remains a significant sector of the economic life of the state. The state's inland location makes adequate transportation critical. Despite protests by environmentalists, Burns Harbor—the Port of Indiana—was constructed on Lake Michigan to serve oceangoing vessels, thus underscoring the priority status given to commerce in the Indiana economy.

BENJAMIN MOULTON

Bibliography: Barnhart, John D., and Riker, Dorothy, *Indiana to 1816* (1971); Dreiser, Theodore, *A Hoosier Holiday* (1916; repr. 1974); Federal Writers' Project, *Indiana: A Guide to the Hoosier State* (1941); Havighurst, Walter, *The Heartland* (1962); Indiana State Chamber of Commerce, *Here Is Your Indiana Government* (1977); Kessler, James B., ed., *Empirical Studies of Indiana Politics* (1970); Leary, E. A., *The Nineteenth State*, rev. ed. (1967); Peckham, Howard H., *Indiana: A History* (1978); Phillips, Clifton J., *Indiana in Transition: The Emergence of an Industrial Commonwealth, 1880-1920* (1968); Thornbrough, Emma L., *Indiana in the Civil War Era, 1850-1880* (1965); Wilson, William E., *Indiana: A History* (1966).

Indiana, Robert

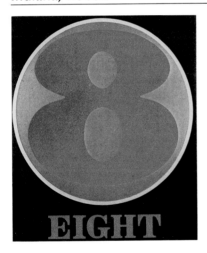

Robert Indiana's Eight *(1965) plays on the difference between the perception of verbal and numerical signs. Indiana's interest in the process of sign-making includes their means of reproduction as well as their formal patterns. (Stedelijk Museum, Amsterdam.)*

Robert Indiana, a leading American pop artist (see POP ART), was born Robert Clark in New Castle, Ind., Sept. 13, 1928, and later took the name of his home state. Having completed his education in 1954, he moved to New York. Indiana's early experiments with severely schematized form led in 1960 to his distinctive brand of pop painting, which combines stenciled lettering—*DIE* and *LOVE*—with clearly defined areas of bright color. Since the late 1960s he has expanded his *LOVE* theme to a series of sculptures, some of them monumental in size. Indiana has also designed sets and costumes for theatrical productions, most notably for the Santa Fe Opera's production (1976) of Virgil Thomson's *The Mother of Us All*, based on the life of Susan B. Anthony.

CARTER RATCLIFF

Bibliography: McCoubrey, John W., *Robert Indiana: An Introduction* (1968).

Indiana, state universities of

Indiana has four state universities, all of which are coeducational and offer undergraduate and graduate degrees. **Indiana University** (1820; enrollment: 31,890; library: 3,510,000 volumes), at Bloomington, has a college of arts and sciences and schools of education, business, law, and, at Indianapolis, the medical center, with divisions of nursing, dentistry, and medicine. The university is known for its programs in linguistics and foreign languages and for its archives on folklore. Other campuses are Kokomo (1965; enrollment: 2,480; library: 70,000); Northwest (1922; enrollment: 4,800; library: 115,000 volumes), at Gary; Southeast (1941; enrollment: 4,010; library: 115,000 volumes), at New Albany; and South Bend (1940; enrollment: 6,170; library: 190,000 volumes). The last two are commuter colleges. Purdue and Indiana universities have joint campuses at Fort Wayne (1974; enrollment: 9,425; library: 167,000 volumes) and Indianapolis (1969; enrollment: 21,700; library: 227,000 volumes), which has a medical center.

Purdue University (1869), a land-grant institution, has its main campus at West Lafayette (enrollment: 42,975; library: 1,265,000 volumes), with schools of engineering, pharmacy, and veterinary medicine; the Calumet campus (1948; enrollment: 7,000; library: 105,000 volumes) is at Hammond. **Ball State University** (1918; enrollment: 17,000; library: 790,000 volumes) is at Muncie. **Indiana State University** (1865) has campuses at Terre Haute (enrollment: 11,540; library: 651,000 volumes) and at Evansville (1965; enrollment: 2,925; library: 95,000 volumes), the university's commuter campus.

Indianapolis   [in-dee-uhn-ap'-uh-lis]

Indianapolis is the capital and largest city of Indiana. Located in the center of the state on the unnavigable White River, the city is the seat of Marion County and has a population of 706,000 (1979 est.). Since 1970 the city limits of Indianapolis have been coextensive with the boundaries of the county; however, four towns lying within the county (Beech Grove, Lawrence, Southport, and Speedway) do not participate in the combined city and county government, called "Unigov." Indianapolis has a January mean temperature of −1.7° C (29° F), and a July mean of 24° C (75° F). Annual precipitation averages 1,016 mm (40 in).

Indianapolis is the market center for the surrounding grain and livestock region and is an important trucking center along long-distance cargo routes. Transport and electrical equipment manufacturing dominates the economy of the city. Indianapolis produces more telephones than any other city in the United States.

The city's streets are laid out in a wheel pattern, with major arteries converging at Monument Circle, with an 87-m-high (285-ft) Soldiers and Sailors Monument. Mile Square, surrounding the monument, contains the state capitol (built 1878-88) and Market Square Arena.

The Indianapolis Motor Speedway with its annual Indianapolis 500 Auto Race is to the northwest. President Benjamin Harrison's home is to the north, and the fort bearing his name is in the northeastern part of the city. Butler University (1849) also lies north of Monument Circle.

Indianapolis was settled in 1820 and was designated the state capital in 1825, replacing Corydon. By 1827 the National Road had reached Indianapolis. In 1836 it was incorporated as a town and, in 1847, as a city. The first of its present five railroads arrived in 1847, linking the city by rail with markets to the east.

Indians, American

In 1492, when Christopher Columbus landed at the Caribbean island of Hispaniola, he believed that he had reached the East Indies. Consequently, he labeled the inhabitants of the island *Indians*, a misnomer still in general use referring to the indigenous peoples of North, Central, and South America. In 1735 the Swedish taxonomist Carolus Linnaeus gave formal biological recognition to the original inhabitants of the New World by labeling them the "American," or "red," race. Thus many

The physical traits of the indigenous peoples of North, Central, and South America vary widely within a basically homogeneous Mongoloid type. The Eskimo (left) more closely resembles the Mongoloid peoples of north Asia than does this Iowa tribesman (right) of the plains.

millions of humans, in 2,000 or more different cultures, came to be lumped together under totally inappropriate racial and cultural terms. These *native Americans* were neither "Indians" nor "red," nor could they easily be classified under a single cultural heading because of their great variety.

Earliest European impressions of native Americans had been of a strong, handsome people, neither inferior nor superior to Europeans. In the course of European settlement of the New World, however, Indians came to be considered different physically, inferior intellectually, and limited in cultural potential compared with their white conquerors. Extensive physical anthropological research, however, failed to find significant differences between native Americans and members of any other human population group.

Physical Characteristics. Physically, the native Americans encountered by early explorers, from the Arctic to the tip of South America, were more homogeneous than any other continental population. In skin color the Indians were yellow brown to ruddy brown, or "medium light" on a world color scale; thus they were probably no darker than, if as dark as, some of Columbus's sailors. Hair and eye color was uniformly dark; reports of "white" or blue-eyed native Americans referred either to albinos or to offspring resulting from early miscegenation. Head hair was coarse and capable of growth to the ground; body hair and beard were scant. In all these respects the physical characteristics of native Americans reflect their ancient north Asian ancestry.

Native Americans vary greatly in body size, but their average height is about that of the human species as a whole: 1 m 62 cm to 1 m 66 cm (5 ft 4 in to 5 ft 6 in) for males; about 10 cm (4 in) shorter for females. Certain native-American groups of northeast North America, of portions of the American Southwest including Baja California, and of southern South America tend to be taller than average. Lips and noses vary markedly among individuals and groups of native Americans. Most possess relatively large faces, high cheekbones, and weak chin development.

Blood group O is the most common type among native Americans; types A and B appear to have been absent in pre-Columbian South America. In North America type A[1] reaches its highest percentage of any world population among the Blackfoot of Alberta and Montana, and type M, its world high among the Sarci, Naskapi, and other northern North American peoples. Rh negative was probably absent in the New World.

Origins and Population Estimates. The ancestors of the native American people entered America from Asia more than

(Above) *This pre-Inca pottery vase of a warrior, dating from* AD 600–800, *illustrates the highly developed plastic art characteristic of the civilizations of pre-Columbian South America. (British Museum, London.)*

(Left) *A woman from the Yamana, or Yaghan, tribe of Tierra del Fuego appears in a painting (c.1769) by Alexander Buchan. The Yamana were the southernmost tribe of the Western Hemisphere. (British Museum, London.)*

20,000 years ago. Some archaeologists have suggested that this migration began much earlier—by at least 40,000 years ago. The first Americans passed into the New World by way of the BERING LAND BRIDGE, an expanse of dry land that connected Siberia and Alaska during late Pleistocene times. Archaeological findings indicate that foragers and hunters were dispersed throughout North America by 17,000 years ago and had passed through to the tip of South America by 12,000 years ago. (See NORTH AMERICAN ARCHAEOLOGY.)

Little agreement exists among anthropologists on the number of people inhabiting the New World on the eve of its discovery by Europeans. Estimates have ranged from a low of 8.4 million to a high of perhaps 112 million. An error of only

(Above) *Councils, such as the one portrayed in this painting by Seth Eastman, determined tribal policy through extensive debate; consequently, oratory was a highly developed art among many native-American groups. Among the league of Iroquois tribes the position of chief, an elective office, could be held by either a man or a woman. (Thomas Gilcrease Institute of American History and Art, Tulsa, Okla.)*

(Right) *The village of Secoton is portrayed in this watercolor (c.1585) by an early Virginia colonist, John White. The houses are typical of those used by many Eastern seaboard peoples. Fields of maize and a communal dining area, among other features, are labeled.*

50% in estimate would be remarkable, considering the scarcity and frequent distortions to be found in early records and the unknown impact of new diseases. Scholars supporting the higher estimate have contended that new diseases (smallpox, measles, diphtheria, whooping cough, influenza, and possibly yellow fever and malaria) introduced into America through contact with newcomers may have been responsible for upward of 80 million deaths.

It is, however, certain that for centuries after European contact, native-American populations suffered rapid decline. Only in the 20th century has the number of Indians in most countries of the Americas begun to increase, partly as the result of a declining rate of infant mortality.

Native-American Contributions to World Culture. Discovery of the New World brought about a revitalization of European culture, which would lead to the Industrial Revolution and the pursuit of raw materials and markets, which in turn would lead to worldwide European colonialism on a grand scale. The Americas' contributions to world culture included tobacco, rubber, a new form of cotton, hundreds of new plants of medicinal value, turkeys, toboggans, moccasins, snowshoes, and numerous material items of lesser significance. The domestication of previously unknown food plants, however, was perhaps the greatest of native American contributions to the Old World: of the hundreds of plant species the Indians cultivated, more than 50 are now of major significance worldwide. Maize ("Indian corn"), beans, potatoes, manioc (cassava or yucca), and sweet potatoes have become staple foodstuffs of people on all continents. Tomatoes, chili peppers, cacao, pineapples, squashes, artichokes, cashews, and maple sugar are other important plants first cultivated by native Americans.

TRADITIONAL CULTURE OF THE NATIVE AMERICAN

The history of native-American culture is sometimes divided into pre-Columbian and post-Columbian eras. Although literally meaning the periods before and after the arrival of Columbus, this chronological division is generally used to refer to the periods before and after European conquest of Indian lands. The term *pre-Columbian* is especially used in referring to cultures of the first regions to be dominated by Europeans—namely, the Caribbean area, Mexico, and Peru. Most areas of the Americas came under foreign control at a much

(Below) *This European engraving (1582) of Cuzco, the Inca capital, illustrates the magnificent organization of the Inca civilization. The Inca empire was the largest, most powerful, and most advanced state in South America. (British Museum, London.)*

later date, although the European presence elsewhere on the continent often affected a given area long before its actual settlement by Europeans. This sequence was especially the case in the forest regions of North America, where a European-organized fur trade flourished, and in the Great Plains, where the European introduction of the horse completely disrupted the way of life of indigenous Plains dwellers.

Social and Political Units. By far the greatest number of societies inhabiting the greatest extent of terrain in the New World before European contact consisted of nomadic bands of from 20 to 50 people who subsisted by collecting wild plant and animal foods. The culture of these simple foragers was in general characterized by a simple technology; by a system of dispersed settlement based on seasonal occupation of sites located near food resources; by consensual leadership exercised by older persons, usually males; and by weak commitment to precise territories. These band-level societies were generally peaceful most of the time.

By about 9,000 years ago certain native-American peoples had begun to domesticate plants to supplement food that was foraged. By the time of European contact maize, beans, and squash, supplemented locally by manioc, potatoes, and highland grains such as quinoa, were in wide use in areas where they could be grown. Simple slash-and-burn cultivation of such crops without the use of irrigation or other more-advanced techniques was usually undertaken on small patches of land; vegetation had to be cleared and burned before the seeds were planted by means of either a digging stick or a hoe, the two basic American horticultural tools.

Horticultural groups generally lived in tribes of about 100 to 1,000 or more members; these tribes tended to build relatively permanent houses and villages, usually with village leaders associated with lineage or clan organizations. Such tribal societies often had craft specialists and substantial inventories of material items for utilitarian or ritual use. Feuds, raids, and wars between tribes occurred often, in part because of the capacity of tribes to expand into new territories and their attendant inability to predict the intent of unfamiliar neighbors; wars were often waged for revenge or to preempt anticipated raids.

Only in Mexico, Central America, and the central Andes (collectively referred to as *Nuclear America* by anthropologists) did cultures possessing cultivation techniques—including irrigation, terracing, and fertilizing—develop sufficient surpluses to permit the formation of towns and cities. The Aztecs, Incas, and Maya attained the highest level of sociopolitical development in pre-Columbian America, characterized by chiefdoms or states with thousands to millions of citizens organized into hierarchical castes and classes. Other features of Nuclear American civilization included priest-idol-temple complexes; markets to facilitate redistribution of goods and wealth; and means to unify the labor force for public ends, including military service. War was often the focus of life. Absolutist kings, nobility of great privilege, complex state architecture for religious and civil purposes, and predatory military expansionism all mark the Nuclear American civilization as a functional equivalent of that which appeared in the Near East and from which European culture was derived.

Kin Groups. The vast majority of native-American societies were organized on the basis of kinship; only in Nuclear America and adjacent areas did nonkinship sodalities and social stratification become important. Lineages and clans existed in many culture areas of the Americas, particularly in the Eastern Woodlands of North America, among western Pueblo groups, and in Amazonia. Division of societies into reciprocating halves (moieties) for ceremonial, marriage, or competitive purposes was common.

Marriage for women usually took place in early adolescence, soon after the first menstruation and often to older men. Premarital sexuality was usually allowed and occasionally made all but mandatory; some societies, however, such as the Cheyenne of the Great Plains, prized chastity for all the unmarried. Adultery was often harshly punished.

The incest taboo prohibited sex and marriage between close relatives and, not infrequently, between any relatives.

Cultivation, at first only supplemental to the native-American diet, came to equal hunting and gathering as means of obtaining food for many tribes. Maize, beans, and squash were among the many plants cultivated by the horticultural peoples of the Southeast.

Many societies practiced marriage with cross-cousins, usually in association with lineage or clan organizations. Marriage to a brother's widow (levirate) and to a sister's husband (sororate) were common customs.

Most native-American cultures encouraged men to have two or more wives (polygyny), although most men had but one. Residence after marriage was usually with the family of the husband, but residence with the family of the wife commonly occurred in eastern North America, in the American Southwest, and in the Caribbean. Inheritance usually correlated with the postmarital residence patterns.

Diet and Subsistence Methods. Most native-American cultures traditionally relied upon the harvest of wild plant foods for their basic subsistence. Few groups did more than merely supplement plant foods with animal products; some excep-

Fish were another source of staple food for many native Americans. This painting (1585) by a Virginia colonist, John White, illustrates some methods used in fishing near Roanoke Island. Spears, nets, rakes, and weirs, among other devices, were employed.

Scouts disguised under wolfskins prepare to attack a buffalo herd in this painting (1832–33) by George Catlin. Buffalo products contributed greatly to the livelihood of the peoples of the Great Plains, providing food, clothing, and shelter. (National Collection of Fine Arts, Washington, D.C.)

tions were the Inuit (Eskimo) and various subarctic peoples and coastal shellfish gatherers. Among the most important wild plant foods in North America were acorns, pine, walnut, hickory, and other nuts; grass and plant seeds (including amaranthus, pigweed, sunflower, and salvias); roots and bulbs (onion, Indian potato, camas, and cattail); dozens of kinds of fruits and berries; and wild rice. Desert regions of the Americas provided aloes, opuntias, and many other xerophytic plant foods. In South America palms provided fruits and nuts as well as hearts, shafts, pith, and beer. Other South American plant foods included algarroba pods, chanar fruit, and mistol seeds, as well as wild rice in swampy areas such as the upper Paraguay River. Many plant foods required complex processing in order to remove harmful substances (such as tannin from acorns or prussic acid from bitter manioc).

The most widely available animal food was shellfish, as evidenced by the remains of huge shell heaps found by archaeologists on river banks and seacoasts throughout the hemisphere. Most foragers ate larger quantities of small animal life (insects, larvae, worms, snakes, bird eggs, and rodents) than they did the more desirable but rarer large animals. In South America the primary large game were members of the camel family (llama, alpaca, guanaco, and vicuna) as well as peccaries, tapirs, monkeys, iguanas, anteaters, cats, alligators, crocodiles, and freshwater and saltwater mammals. Two or more species of deer, common in parts of South America, were the most widely hunted large game animals in North America. Also in North America were sizable regional herds of bison and caribou; smaller local herds of wapiti elk, pronghorn antelope, and mountain sheep and goats; as well as black and brown bears, badgers, raccoons, opossums, coatimundis, wolverines, and a host of other game animals.

Freshwater and saltwater fish, especially the anadromous varieties—such as salmon, alewives, steelhead trout, and striped bass—provided abundant food for peoples along the northern coasts of North America and in Amazonia. Fish were hooked; netted; trapped; or poisoned with over 50 different plant poisons, mainly in South America. Birds also served as a source of food, particularly for peoples located on land along the migratory flyways and in winter haunts and summer rookeries.

For most Indian cultures foraging enabled the population to survive in most years, to thrive in some, but in others to experience severe privation and even starvation. Bad years—particularly two or more occurring consecutively—effectively limited the population growth of most native-American societies. Marked population increases occurred in parts of Nuclear America, however, where plants had begun to be domesticated about 9,000 years ago.

By 1492 many Nuclear American peoples had become almost entirely reliant on cultivation. Hundreds of species of plants were domesticated for use not only as foods, but also as raw materials (such as pima cotton), as poisons, and as hallucinogens and stimulants. Domesticated plants and agricultural techniques gradually spread to other parts of the Americas, although most other New World cultivators, such as those in the tropical forest of South America and in the Southeast and Southwest of North America, continued to supplement cultivation with ancient food-collecting techniques.

Hallucinogens and Stimulants. Tobacco was the most widely cultivated plant in native America, grown by some foragers who grew nothing else. It was used mainly by men in ceremonial settings by smoking, chewing, sniffing, or in enemas. Jimson weed was the next most available drug in North America; it was used mainly in the West—especially in California. In Mexico and Central America peyote, mescal bean, the mushroom called teonanácatl, and a seed called ololiuqui were used. Coca, the source of cocaine, was grown in the eastern Andes, where the leaves are still chewed by the Indians. In Amazonia numerous hallucinogenic plants were known.

Before the introduction of the distillation process, only beers and wines were known in the Americas. The principal types were maize beer and alcoholic beverages fermented from manioc, agave, sotol, mesquite beans, saguaro fruit, persimmons, and sea grapes.

Hunting, Planting, and Cooking Technology. Several varieties of bows and arrows were the commonest hunting implements; thrusting lances, harpoons, atlatls (throwing darts), clubs, bolas, and slings were also used. Blowguns with poisoned darts were used in eastern North America, the Caribbean, and Amazonia. Poisoned arrows were widely used in

A portrait of Chief Tishcohan of the Delaware, or Lenni Lenape, tribe shows him wearing a tobacco pouch. Tobacco, indigenous to the Americas, was widely used by native Americans in rituals and ceremonies. (Historical Society of Pennsylvania, Philadelphia.)

the tropical rain forests of South America. Woven nets, deadfalls, nooses, and dogs were also employed in the hunt.

Farmers cleared fields either by chopping trees with stone axes or by girdling trees and burning them. Sharpened sticks, simple hoes, and human labor were the means of planting. In Nuclear America complex irrigation works (with ditches and dams), terraces, and urine, potash, and guano fertilizers were developed.

Foods were prepared by boiling, roasting, broiling, or baking in preheated earth ovens. The addition of hot rocks to water and food that had been placed in either watertight baskets or stone vessels was another widely practiced cooking method ("stone boiling"). Foods were preserved by drying, smoking, salting, or packing in containers with animal lard (PEMMICAN); in Arctic and subarctic areas foods were simply frozen in permafrost. Salt was an important item sought in trade, especially by horticultural people.

Housing and Architecture. For shelter simple foragers generally used brush windscreens or small, portable tepees, tents, or wigwams of poles, bark, or hides. Semisubterranean pit houses served as traditional dwellings for various Arctic and subarctic peoples. Rectangular single- or multiple-family dwellings constructed of posts and beams were used by culti-

These Arizona cliff dwellings, known as Montezuma's Castle National Monument, are typical of the complex settlements built on the mesas and into the canyons of the Southwest by the Anasazi, a highly advanced agricultural people, possible ancestors of the Pueblos.

vators in North and South America. Large rectangular structures "longhouses" housing entire lineages or tribes were built in Amazonia and among some tribes of northeastern North America. In the American Southwest multistory apartment houses in the form of pueblos made of stone, mud, and beams were made by the ANASAZI, possible ancestors of the Pueblo peoples.

Temple and burial mounds were built widely in Nuclear America and in the Eastern Woodlands and the southwest of North America. East of the Mississippi River are the remains of an estimated 100,000 mounds, ranging from a few feet in height to that at CAHOKIA (in Missouri), with its base of 6.5 ha (16 acres) and a height of 30 m (98 ft). The most spectacular monuments of pre-Columbian American architecture are found in Nuclear America, where entire cities with pyramids,

(Above) *Wigwams, such as those seen in this painting by Frederick Verner, were the characteristic dwellings of native Americans of the Northeast. Wigwams, usually permanent, were built by covering poles with bark, mats, reeds, or hides. (Glenbow Foundation, Calgary, Alberta.)*

(Right) *The partially sunken earth lodges of the Mandan of the northern plains, seen here in an engraving by Karl Bodmer, were large enough to house several families and their animals. These domical structures were supported by timber frames and were covered with sod for insulation. (New York Public Library, Rare Book Division.)*

This 1835 portrait of Keokuk, chief of the Sauk and the Fox, was painted by the American artist George Catlin. The elaborate costume of Chief Keokuk, which includes ornaments and skins, specifically reflects the social status of the wearer. (National Collection of Fine Arts, Washington, D.C.)

The Pyramid and Temple of Inscriptions at the ancient Mayan city of Palenque, in southern Mexico, is representative of the architectural achievement of the classic period (AD 250-950) in Mayan culture. The temple is particularly important for its hieroglyphic tablets.

temples, palaces, convents, civic buildings, and astronomical observatories were built in great splendor.

Clothing and Personal Adornment. Little clothing other than loincloths, draped hides or cloth mantles, and headgear was worn by most native Americans except in Nuclear America and in the extreme north. Before needles became available through trade, only the Eskimo and their neighbors possessed tailored clothing. Tanned deer hide (buckskin), bison hide, and the furs of small animals were common clothing materials in North America. Feathers, bark, and various wild-plant materials were also commonly used, especially in the Pacific Northwest and California. Woven cotton cloth was the dominant material in the American Southwest and in much of Mesoamerica, where costumes often reflected social status. Many tribes in North America wore MOCCASINS to protect

their feet; sandals made of plant fibers were also common in the Great Basin and the Southwest. Hide sandals made from dehaired skins were worn in Mesoamerica and in parts of South America.

Body painting and tattooing; head and tooth deformation; lip, ear, and nose plugs or rings; and bracelets, arm bands, necklaces, and head ornaments were traditionally used by many groups to enhance beauty or to indicate status.

Metallurgy, Craft, and the Arts. Beginning as early as 3000 BC raw copper was worked by simple hammering for use as weapons or as ritual objects; this process was widely practiced, particularly in the Great Lakes region of North America. By AD 500 gold, copper, and silver were being smelted and cast, soldered, gilded, and alloyed in Ecuador and elsewhere in Nuclear America; objects of copper combined with lead also appeared about this time in Mexico. Bronze was apparently in use in Bolivia by about AD 1100, but native Americans had not discovered the use of iron before European contact.

Throughout the Americas native artisans traditionally embellished tools, containers, houses, and sometimes even the

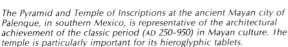

(Left) This intricately crafted gold ceremonial knife, decorated with turquoise, dates from the 14th or 15th century, when the Inca empire was emerging in the Andean highlands. The Inca achieved technical mastery in metallurgy in their use of hammered metals and innovative soldering techniques. (Below) The elaborate, highly stylized craftwork typical of the Aztec artisans of Mexico is exemplified in this shield, where a prairie wolf is depicted in a colorful featherwork mosaic.

American Indian pottery of the Southwest has a distinctive history. This pottery jug fashioned in the shape of an owl is an artifact of the Zuñi, who live in Arizona and New Mexico. The mythology of the Indians permeates their traditional artwork; animal figures such as the one depicted here are often regarded as animistic religious objects as well as decorative or utilitarian pieces.

This turquoise mosaic mask represents Quetzalcóatl, one of the major deities of ancient Mexican religion. Worship of the feathered serpent god was adopted from the Toltec by the Aztec peoples, who associated Quetzalcóatl with death and resurrection and revered him as the god of civilization.

human body with artistic designs and decorations. Local traditions of painting, sculpture, pottery, jewelry, tapestry weaving, and architectural decoration were well developed in various parts of North America. (See INDIANS OF NORTH AMERICA, ART OF THE.)

In Nuclear America libraries of the Aztecs, Incas, and Maya contained thousands of illustrated books (called codices) with accumulated thought and knowledge about ancient ways. The invading Spaniards systematically destroyed these manuscripts, which they thought to be works of the devil. Working on walls, in the round on solid stone, in bas-relief, and with semiprecious stones (jade, turquoise, serpentine, amber, and others), artists of these and other pre-Columbian cultures produced items of both representational and abstract art ranking with the finest human productions anywhere. (See PRE-COLUMBIAN ART AND ARCHITECTURE.)

Traditional native-American music tended to be highly rhythmic and monophonic and was usually played and sung by men for either ritual or social occasions. Harmony was absent, and most scales were pentatonic. Lyrics generally had symbolic but not morphemic meaning, and most songs lasted less than three minutes. Indian musical instruments included drums, rattles, clappers, and sticks and other percussive devices, along with flutes, whistles, and shell trumpets. (See IN-

DIANS OF NORTH AMERICA, MUSIC AND DANCE OF THE.)

Politics and Warfare. The political complexity of most native-American societies was generally in direct relation to the mode of food production: foragers rarely had more leadership than a headman, a person respected but with little real power. Simple cultivators and, following European contact, many foraging peoples—particularly those who became horse nomads—elevated successful war leaders and SHAMANS (part-time religious leaders) to posts of power during war.

True central government was found only in Nuclear America and adjacent areas, where privileged chiefs or kings, noble councilmen, and priests, supported by armed militia, possessed absolute power over thousands of people. War was a frequent activity in the complex political societies of Mesoamerica and the Andes. Highly organized armies of tens of thousands massed and moved under central leadership unknown elsewhere in the Americas.

Foragers were characterized by a relative peacefulness made possible by low population density, close kinship ties to neighboring peoples, and patterns of resource use that aided in avoiding conflict. Feuds did erupt over sexual jealousies and accusations of witchcraft, but these feuds usually involved only a few people and were of short duration. Simple cultivators and horse nomads, on the other hand, with an investment in fields, in stored foods, or in herds, engaged in frequent and often bloody conflict. Various peoples on the Great Plains, on the Pampas, in Amazonia, and in the Eastern Woodlands of North America for a time became as warlike as any group ever known: they were at war at all times with all people with whom they did not have an immediate alliance.

Religion and the Supernatural. The traditional way of life of native Americans was characterized by beliefs and practices stemming from an acceptance of a universe controlled by supernatural beings and forces, with humans, at most, as junior partners. All cultures had beliefs in souls; in animistic spirits that occupied natural objects (rocks, trees, unusual landforms, bodies of water, or lightning); in powerful, distant, usually diffuse creator beings; and, often, in numbers of other, more-immediate godlike beings.

In most cultures the supernaturals of greatest importance were the good and evil spirits capable of influencing the outcome of hunts, gambling, fights, the pursuit of love partners, the search for health, and other human strivings. These spirits might inhabit dark places, such as caves or forests, deep canyons, high mountains, beasts, or even other people. In order

In this 1847 painting the Canadian artist Paul Kane recorded his experience at a medicine-man mask dance held by Clallam Indians on Vancouver Island. The Clallam believe that supernatural forces of good and evil influence health and other physical phenomena. The tribal ritual depicted here is typical of the healing rite performed by these physician-priests, who are called on to exorcise evil and ensure protection from further harm.

for a native American to succeed in life a constant balance had to be maintained between the spirit forces and human needs, a balance made difficult by the presence of evil spirits. The souls of the dead (ghosts) were often believed to be the most malignant of spirits.

Most native-American cultures possessed beliefs in a diffuse supernatural power anthropologists call MANA. This power was sought through ceremonies, vision quests, self-privation or mutilation, drugged states or dreams, or control of powerful natural entities who could then lend power, or "medicine." Most native Americans believed that many animals and natural objects possessed this power and if violated

by humans might cause pimples, ill health, painful menstruation, accidents, bad luck, or even death. Taboos surrounded many commonplace events: birth, puberty, sexual relations, war, and hunting all required constant precautions.

Ceremonies. All native-American cultures possessed supernatural techniques with which to face most of life's unpredictable events. To effect cures part-time religious leaders, shamans, were usually consulted. They massaged, danced, sang, smoked tobacco, or took drugs in order, with the aid of spirit helpers, to search out the cause of ailment, generally considered to be the result of either the loss of the soul or the intrusion of a foreign object. The source of the illness was almost always believed to be witchcraft, despite the fact that in practically no native-American cultures were there individuals who attempted to practice sorcery to harm others.

Other than those associated with curing, rites were of passage (birth, puberty, marriage, death); of crisis associated with war, rain, and other natural phenomena; or of maintenance (propitiation of the sun, moon, animals, and other forces) designed to assure harmony among humans and all other elements in the universe. At death the possessions of the deceased were sometimes given away or destroyed, names forgotten, and all verbal references to the person's existence terminated. In Nuclear America and in some adjoining areas, where ancestor worship was practiced, ceremonies accompanying death were aimed at maintaining ties with the now-powerful departed.

Priests served as interpreters and intermediaries in Nuclear America's rich ceremonial complex. Public ceremonies, often conducted on top of temple-pyramids or in elaborate public buildings, were designed to provide continuing power to the leaders of the chiefdoms and states. Priests were usually drawn from the upper classes, were well educated, and served as custodians not only for formal theology and ritual but also as scholars, engineers, and scientists. Up until the time of the Spanish conquest, priests were in possession of the most advanced and esoteric forms of knowledge associated with the ancient traditions of civilization developed in Nuclear America. As a class they were routinely slaughtered by the Spanish.

Language. Over 2,000 separate languages were spoken by native-American peoples at the time of European contact. Approximately 1,400 of these existed in South America, and roughly 200 were spoken in the territory constituting present-day California. All American languages possessed complete

The customs and rituals of numerous American Indian tribes were captured in the paintings of the 19th-century American artist George Catlin. (Above) In Catlin's Medicine Man (1832), the magical clothing of a Blackfoot shaman includes a bearskin mask. The various animal skins worn by the shaman have animistic qualities intended to enhance his power to heal.

(Right) Catlin's Scalp Dance (1835–37) portrays a victory celebration of the Teton Sioux, the most populous of the seven Sioux tribes.

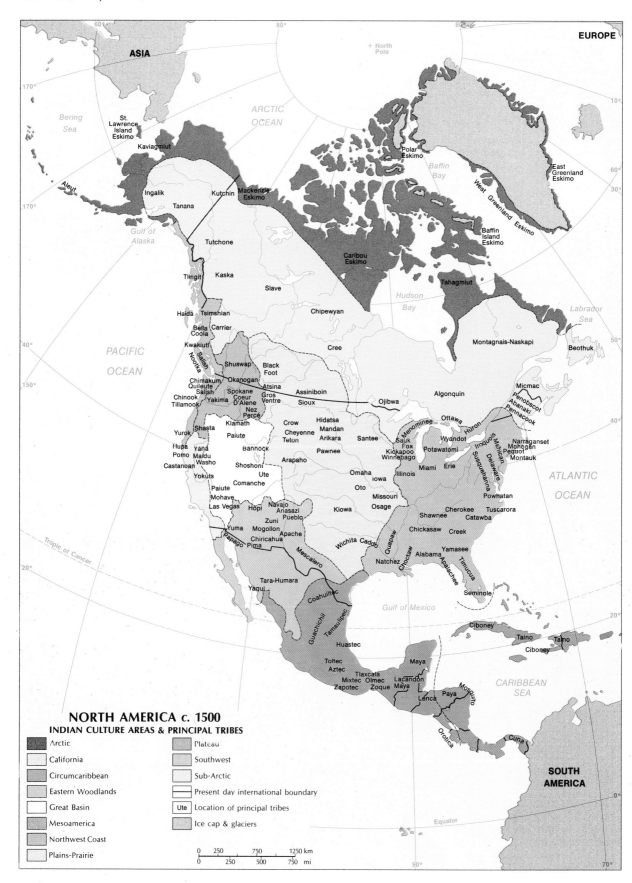

NORTH AMERICA c. 1500
INDIAN CULTURE AREAS & PRINCIPAL TRIBES

- Arctic
- California
- Circumcaribbean
- Eastern Woodlands
- Great Basin
- Mesoamerica
- Northwest Coast
- Plains-Prairie
- Plateau
- Southwest
- Sub-Arctic
- Present day international boundary
- Ute — Location of principal tribes
- Ice cap & glaciers

0 250 750 1250 km
0 250 500 750 mi

sound-signaling systems (phonemes), thousands of meaning units (morphemes), and ordering systems for utterances (syntax). Only in pre-Columbian Mexico did hieroglyphic writing develop; nowhere in the Americas had phonetic-phonemic writing been invented before European contact.

Few people who are not native Americans have ever mastered Indian languages, in part because of their difficult sounds and unfamiliar grammar systems. No feature of native-American languages, however, is without parallel in languages elsewhere. Except for the Eskimo-Aleut language, which belongs to Chukotan, a northeast-Siberian language family, no definite ties have been established between American languages and Old World languages. Efforts continue to group the numerous American languages into families of related languages. In 1891, John Wesley POWELL proposed 57 language families for North America. D. G. Brinton, at about the same time, estimated 60 families for South America. Linguists have reduced the number of apparently unrelated language families in North America to about a dozen and as few as four for South America. (See INDIAN LANGUAGES, AMERICAN.)

Today 500 or so of America's native languages are spoken. In Paraguay, 95 percent of the people speak Guaraní, where it is the colegal language; native-American languages are also spoken widely in Peru (Quechua) and Greenland (Inuit). The Navajo represent the largest group north of Mexico to speak a native-American language. Navajo, along with 200 or more other native-American languages, now may be phonemically written. Many national governments are impatient with speakers of Indian languages, however, and civil administrators, teachers, and missionaries have often contributed to making European languages dominant among native-American peoples. It is highly probable that before long the number of Indian languages still being spoken will diminish to a handful.

MAJOR CULTURE AREAS OF NATIVE AMERICA

The original Americans came from northeast Asia tens of thousands of years ago. Southeast Asians may have reached the northwestern shore of South America (Valdivia, Ecuador) about 3600 BC; Vikings established a limited number of settlements on Newfoundland about AD 1000. Experts agree, however, that native-American culture developed indigenously, and efforts to trace its origin to these or other outside sources have been proved unsuccessful.

The earliest Americans encountered a bounty of plant and animal foods. Hundreds of animal species, many large and numerous, were hunted vigorously. The remains of these animals, occasionally associated with stone tools—as at Folsom, N.Mex. (see FOLSOM CULTURE)—provide the best evidence of

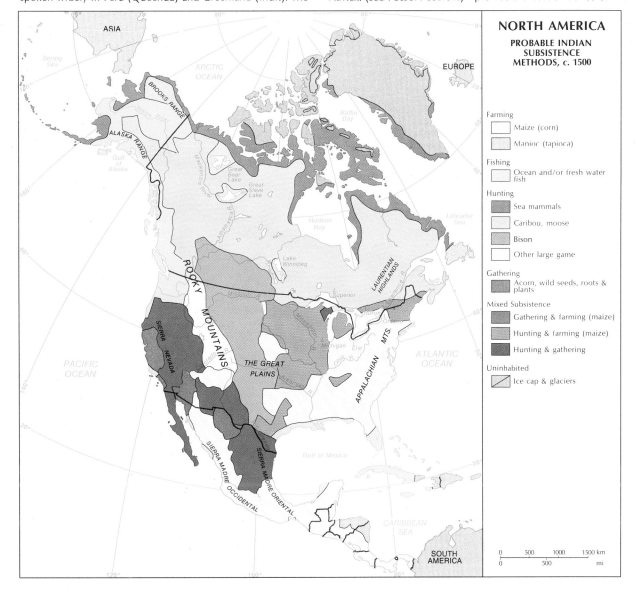

NORTH AMERICA

PROBABLE INDIAN
SUBSISTENCE
METHODS, c. 1500

Farming
- Maize (corn)
- Manioc (tapioca)

Fishing
- Ocean and/or fresh water fish

Hunting
- Sea mammals
- Caribou, moose
- Bison
- Other large game

Gathering
- Acorn, wild seeds, roots & plants

Mixed Subsistence
- Gathering & farming (maize)
- Hunting & farming (maize)
- Hunting & gathering

Uninhabited
- Ice cap & glaciers

This early-19th-century engraving portrays Eskimo of Melville Peninsula, in the Canadian Northwest Territories, constructing an igloo. Commonly used in winter as a temporary shelter, the igloo is made from blocks of snow; permanent dwellings are made from sod and stone.

The Cree chief "Man Who Gives the War Whoop" is depicted in this 1848 portrait by Paul Kane. The Cree belong to the Subarctic cultural group of Algonquian-speaking Indians from eastern Canada.

paleo-Indian culture in the Americas. About 10,000 years ago more than 50 large game species began to become extinct. Their disappearance is attributed by some archaeologists to human hunting and by others primarily to climatic change. As available game diminished, humans came to rely more on local resources, particularly plant foods, for their subsistence. New food-processing tools—the mano and metate, mortar and pestle, and others—made new foods available, and gradually a pattern of regional adaptations developed that would characterize portions of native America until the arrival of European and American settlers. North America has been divided into the following major culture areas: the Arctic, Subarctic, Northwest Coast and Interior Plateau, Great Basin, Great Plains, Eastern Woodlands, and Southwest. The major culture areas of Latin America are Mesoamerica, the Caribbean and North Andes, the Central and South Andes, the Tropical Forest, and the Marginal Areas of South America.

Arctic and Subarctic Hunters and Fishers. The Arctic culture area comprises the longest continuous stretch of terrain occupied by any common culture and language group on Earth: it extends from southern Alaska into northeast Siberia and around the northern rim of North America to eastern Greenland. Two primary native-American groups are found in this region: the Inuit (Eskimo) and the ALEUTS of the Aleutian Islands. For a discussion of the traditional way of life of the Arctic culture area, see ESKIMO.

The Subarctic culture area includes all of Canada, except the Northwest Coast and the Arctic margin, and south to where cultivable lands and the Great Plains begin. This cold, wet region of forests and tundra provided a harsh climate for human survival. Heavy rains in the summer, deep snows in the winter, as well as endless chains of rivers, lakes, swamps, and muskeg (waterlogged land), traditionally prohibited travel except by canoe or toboggan or with snowshoes. The hundreds of independent local groups can be divided into two major linguistic blocks: the Athabascan speakers of western Canada and interior Alaska (CARRIER, INGALIK, Dogrib, Han, Hare, Koyukon, Kutchin, Mountain, Slave, Tanaina, Yellowknife, and others) and the Algonquian speakers of eastern Canada (CREE, MICMAC, OJIBWA, Malecite, Montagnais, and others).

Vast migrating herds of caribou were hunted by most Subarctic peoples and along with other game (moose, bear, and deer) and fish provided a largely protein diet. Residence was in small groups, usually in hide or bark-covered tepees or wigwams that could be easily moved. Family heads were usually the leaders; although great suspicion of one's neighbors was common, interband conflict was slight.

Religion was essentially informal, with few widely held beliefs except those concerned with guardian spirits or witchcraft. Many people, particularly among the Algonquian speakers, believed that the forests harbored windigos, 9-m-tall (30-ft) monsters who could turn humans into cannibals. Menstrual taboos were as strong among the northern Athabascans as among any known culture.

The eastern Subarctic, especially the Great Lakes region, was disrupted by the fur trade in the 16th and 17th centuries. The possession of guns gave power to the Cree, Ojibwa, and others, some of whom moved to the Great Plains to hunt bison. In the eastern and central Subarctic little of the ancient way of life remained after about 1700. In western Canada and interior Alaska many bands were left relatively undisturbed until well into the 19th century, but disease, alcohol, trading posts, missions, and other manifestations of Western influence have since brought cultural dissolution.

Northwest-Coast Fishermen. The Pacific rim of northwestern North America and the plateau drained by the Columbia and Fraser rivers formed a uniquely hospitable niche for its native-American inhabitants because of salmon-spawning streams throughout, draining into the north Pacific. From

The Micmac of the Canadian Maritime Provinces were one of the first Indian tribes encountered by early explorers. This anonymous 19th-century painting shows the influence of European traders in the Indians' possession of rifles and other firearms.

The Kwakiutl of northern Vancouver Island and adjacent British Columbia exhibited a way of life typical of Northwest Coast tribes. Heavily dependent on the sea for their livelihood, they moved seasonally from one permanent settlement to another, building rectangular, multifamily homes just above the shoreline. The Kwakiutl's efficient dugout canoes varied according to function. Clothing, made of the soft inner bark of cedar trees, was often trimmed with fur to designate rank. Their renowned artwork includes totem poles, representing the crest or symbol awarded an ancestor by a spirit.

north to south important groups were the TLINGIT, HAIDA, TSIMSHIAN, KWAKIUTL, NOOTKA, SALISH, HUPA, YUROK, and Karok. Most languages spoken in the Northwest Coast culture area are of Athabascan, Penutian, or Mosan linguistic stock.

Several species of salmon endowed the region with an abundant annual harvest. Candlefish, herring, halibut, and other fish; sea lions and whales; and mussels, clams, and oysters were available from the sea. The land, too, was generous: caribou, moose, mountain sheep and goats, deer, and a wealth of small animals combined with numerous roots and berries to provide a rich and varied diet.

Villages traditionally consisted of 100 or more related people, usually politically independent of all other such groups. Great variation in kinship patterns existed, but one feature was common to all: each village ranked its members according to their closeness to the headperson or chief. Only war captives and debt victims, who formed an outcast or slave category, were excluded from this strictly hierarchical ranking system.

Great emphasis was placed on individual and group wealth, measured by the enumeration of possessions such as cedar-bark blankets, dentalium shells, dried fish and fish oil, dugout canoes, coppers (native copper hammered into a shield, named, and ascribed a set value), ownership of resources, and slaves. Wealth was exchanged on a number of occasions in reciprocal POTLATCH, or gift-giving sessions between parents and children, between relatives, and even between competitors or enemies. In the latter case, a potlatch recipient had to return within a stipulated time goods equivalent to those given but with high interest; if unable to do so, the recipient and all relatives whose goods were involved could be economically and socially ruined. Intertribal conflict, characteristic of the 19th century, was probably less frequent earlier. Disputes over territory, valued resources, or succession to high rank might involve bloody conflict but could also be resolved by paying indemnities.

Religious practices, based mainly on faith in mythical ancestors, often took on dramatic flair in public dramas involving spirit quests and encounters. Highly stylized representations of these ancestors were everywhere, not only on TOTEM poles but also on house facades, boat prows, masks, bones, and blankets.

The Northwest Coast area, first visited (1741) by Vitus Bering, was later frequented by at least 100 foreign ships be-

(Below) A delicately carved wood sculpture of a Haida woman exhibits the artistic skill of this coastal British Columbian tribe. (Pitt-Rivers Museum, Oxford, England.)

(Above) This mid-19th-century painting portrays Northwest Coast Indians fishing on the Columbia River. Heavily reliant on salmon for subsistence, many groups would begin the fishing season with propitiatory rites to the spirit of the fish. (Royal Ontario Museum, Toronto.)

(Above) *George Catlin's painting (1834) of a Comanche village shows women preparing bison hides, the chief material used for both clothing and shelter. Greatly skilled in warfare and horsemanship, the Comanche were among the most feared of the Great Basin Indians. (Smithsonian Institution, Washington, D.C.)* (Right) *Washakie, a chief of the Wyoming Shoshoni, consistently offered friendship and aid to peaceful settlers.*

tween 1774 and 1794. Disease, guns, conflict, and alcohol took a rapid toll. During these same years the decorative art for which the region is world renowned reached its greatest elaboration. By the end of the 19th century the traditional economy and culture was increasingly undermined, but the people remained on or near their ancient lands. Many, now working in forestry, have attempted to restore portions of their ancient life; there is also a strong resurgence in arts-and-crafts production.

Interior-Plateau Foragers. The Interior-Plateau culture area, located east of the Northwest Coast to the Rocky Mountains, was a high, relatively well watered, wooded region peopled by numerous small groups of peaceful, foraging village dwellers. Some of the best-known Interior-Plateau tribes are the FLATHEAD, KUTENAI, NEZ PERCÉ, OKANOGAN, SHUSWAP, SPOKAN, YAKIMA, Coeur d'Alene, Lillooet, Thompson, and Umatilla. They subsisted on an abundance of game, fruits, and salmon harvested from the upper reaches of the Columbia and Fraser rivers and culturally resembled their Northwest Coast, Great Basin, and California neighbors. The languages of most groups were of Mosan or Penutian linguistic stock.

After horses reached the Umatilla in about 1740 and then spread northward, many plateau peoples began to participate in the great bison hunts. Fur trappers arrived during the early 19th century, followed by missionaries and tens of thousands of pioneers. Disease and bloody conflict led to loss of life, culture, and land; by 1860 little remained of the traditional Plateau way of life.

Great Basin Desert Foragers. Southwest of the Interior Plateau was a vast, dry, upland expanse of mountains and basins with interior drainage and sharp extremes of temperature occurring in winter and summer. Major groups included the CO-MANCHE, KLAMATH, PAIUTE, SHOSHONI, UTE, WASHO, Panamint, and others. Nearly all spoke Numic (Shoshonean) languages.

Small foraging bands, sometimes a single family in size, spread over the inhospitable land with population densities as low as 1 person per 130 km² (50 mi²). Summer foods included seeds, roots, berries, cactus fruits, and pine nuts; ants, locusts, snakes, lizards, and rodents (particularly mice and rabbits); along with occasional pronghorns and deer. Coyotes were not eaten because they were believed to be endowed with supernatural power. In winter, foods were minimally available; stored summer foods were relied upon, and the threat of starvation was ever present.

Brief periods of plenty and the barren winter months were times when people traditionally grouped together in larger bands, usually composed of bilaterally related people. Leadership was informal and in the hands of respected elders, usu-

ally males. Interband conflict, although rare, occasionally occurred as the result of witchcraft accusations or rivalry over females. Little existed in the way of formal religion. Powerful spirits could be known through dreams or visions; such associations were believed to bring with them the power not only to cure but also to hunt pronghorns or to gamble.

After obtaining horses in about 1680, the Ute helped to spread them north to the Comanche and to other Great Basin peoples. Thereafter, many Basin societies took to the Great Plains in pursuit of the bison herds. In 1805, Lewis and Clark became the first white explorers to cross the Great Basin; later pioneers, who used to call the Basin Indians "diggers" because they dug for roots, freely dispossessed these impoverished peoples of their lives and land. Basin culture, based upon the narrowest margins of survival, quickly succumbed.

California Foragers. The California culture area covers approximately the extent of the present state minus the southeast section along the Colorado River. Among its aboriginal population, estimated at more than 200,000 people, more than 200 independent dialects existed. Prominent groups included the MODOC, POMO, YANA, Chumash, Costano, Maidu, Miwok, Patwin, Salinan, Wintun, Yokuts, Yuki, and the so-called Mis-

California Indians at the mission of San Jose de Guadalupe were portrayed during the early 19th century. Forced onto missions by the Spaniards and brutalized by settlers during the 1850s, the tribes were nearly eliminated by 1900. (1806; Oakland Museum, Calif.)

sion Indians: Cahuilla, Diegueño, Gabrileño, Luiseño, and Serrano.

All Californians were primarily foragers who relied heavily upon acorns, grass seeds, cattails, and other plant foods. Shellfish and fish were important along the coast, as were deer, wapiti, bears, rabbits, and other animals in the interior. The single village (tribelet) of 100 or more people, bounded by its own dialect, was often the largest unit of political integration. Exogamous moieties were common, thus permitting village endogamy. In the south localized patrilineages were the common residence type.

Headmanship, inherited in some groups, served to organize social and ceremonial life but carried little political power. Organized conflict between villages was rare. Curing ceremonies were frequently held; drug cults and male puberty ceremonies were especially important.

Juan Rodríguez Cabrillo first explored California in 1542, followed by hundreds of boats whose impact on the native inhabitants remains unclear. The first California mission was established in 1769; within about 100 years most Mission Indians were gone. When hordes of Americans arrived in Califor-

Former foragers and farmers spent the summers based in encampments of dozens of portable tepees arranged in large circles for the purpose of bison hunting on an intensive scale. Here public ceremonials, particularly the SUN DANCE ritual, served to unite groups in common purpose. Individual power, first sought through the vision quest accompanied by self-mutilation and severe privation, was furthered by participation in raids and the counting of war honors (coups) against enemies. Warrior societies grew to be the primary war-making bodies; occasionally, they also served to police some of the large encampments. Individuals joined the societies as young men and then proved themselves by counting coups (SCALPING, stealing horses, killing, or touching a dead enemy) against enemies or by performing an act of conspicuous bravery. Success in raids (usually carried out by fewer than a dozen men), possession of many horses, and power obtained through visions or in the Sun dance served to bestow high rank on the Plains Indian and his family.

Plains culture was in full flower in the 18th and early 19th centuries. With the introduction of guns and the westward movement of trappers and pioneers, the fate of the bison and

(Below left) *George Catlin's* Buffalo Chase *(1832–33) dramatizes a Hidatsa buffalo hunt, which allegedly eliminated the substantial herd in a matter of minutes. The hunt, crucial to the survival of many Plains tribes, was often supervised by special warrior societies. (National Collection of Fine Arts, Washington, D.C.) (Right)* Rain-in-the-Face, *a Hunkpapa Sioux chief, was one of the leading warriors in the defeat of General Custer at Little Bighorn. His fierce resistance to white settlement on Sioux lands was well known and feared.*

nia during the Gold Rush of 1849, many Indians were ruthlessly overrun and often wantonly massacred. By 1900 fewer than 15,000 survived, and native-American cultural traditions were largely destroyed.

Plains-Prairie Bison Hunters. From the Rocky Mountains to the Mississippi River, from southern Canada to the Gulf of Mexico, the Great Plains formed the vast, undulating, sod-covered home of one of the world's great animal populations—the 60 million or more bison (American, *buffalo*) that migrated seasonally in huge herds. Three dozen or more tribes made use of the Great Plains in the early historic period (*c.*1700–1850), including the ARAPAHO, ARIKARA, BLACKFOOT, CHEYENNE, CROW, HIDATSA, IOWA, MANDAN, OSAGE, PAWNEE, SIOUX, WICHITA, Kiowa-Apache, Plains Cree, and Sarci.

The Great Plains had been occupied for thousands of years by pedestrian nomads who foraged a living in its river bottoms and developed various methods of exploiting its bison herds. More than a thousand years ago peoples of the Eastern Woodlands cultural tradition established farming villages along the western tributaries of the Mississippi River. After 1600, when horses were introduced by European settlers, and by 1700, when horses became available throughout the Great Plains, the area became a melting pot of former sedentary peoples intruded upon and sometimes displaced by mounted hunter-warriors from neighboring areas.

(Below) *A fallen Mandan Indian scalps his assailant in this Catlin sketch (1835–37). The trophies of war, including the war bonnets, weapons, and horses of the enemy, brought great honor to the conqueror. (National Collection of Fine Arts, Washington, D.C.)*

(Above) *Great Serpent Mound in southern Ohio, one of many effigy mounds in the midwestern United States, is believed to have been built by an Indian culture that flourished between about 1000 BC and AD 1100. The 400-m-long (1,312-ft) structure's purpose is unknown.*

Eastern Woodlands Cultivators. Many Indian cultures flourished in the great forests of the Eastern Woodlands culture area, which stretched from the Mississippi River to the Atlantic Ocean and from southern Canada to the Gulf of Mexico. Coniferous in its northern and southern portions, this abundantly watered, often humid region was covered in its midportion by 50 or more different species of deciduous hardwood.

The peoples of this area were descended from an ancient cultural tradition that culminated in the construction of more than 100,000 earthwork mounds and walled towns of up to 30,000 inhabitants (see MOUND BUILDERS). These mound-building cultures possessed priest-temple-idol complexes and a highly stratified set of classes and castes, all of which were in part derived from the high cultures of Mesoamerica. The northeastern subsection of the woodlands did not experience the full impact of cultural elements from this southern influence, but the southeastern portion of the woodlands is considered by some scholars to be a northern hinterland, or Chimeca, of Mesoamerican culture.

The Northeast subsection was peopled by numerous societies that can be classified into two principal divisions: Iroquoian speakers, including the CAYUGA, ERIE, HURON, MOHAWK, ONEIDA, ONONDAGA, SENECA, TUSCARORA, and Neutral; and Algonquian speakers, including the DELAWARE, FOX, ILLI-

(Left) *The Algonquian village of Pomeioc, in North Carolina, was portrayed in 1585 by John White, a member of the first colonizing expedition to Virginia. (British Museum, London.) (Below) Zacherie Vincent, a Huron brave, painted this self-portrait. (Musée du Séminaire de Québec.)*

Plains culture was, however, soon sealed. By 1880 bison no longer existed in sufficient numbers to permit the summer hunts, tribes were being shunted to reservations, and the Great Plains culture was essentially destroyed. The often-fierce and bloody conflicts between Plains Indians and whites culminated in 1890, when a group of Sioux followers of the revivalistic GHOST DANCE movement encountered cavalry units at WOUNDED KNEE, S.Dak., where nearly 300 native Americans, mainly women and children, were massacred by the 7th Cavalry, Gen. George Armstrong Custer's former unit.

Although the resistance of the Plains peoples was eventually broken, many of the most powerful tribes escaped being driven outside their own territories. Although on the reservations they had little or no opportunity to maintain their traditional way of life, certain aspects of Plains culture have nevertheless been preserved although in adjusted form. Indian activism in the 1970s was especially strong among the former Plains dwellers. Wounded Knee again became a symbol of native-American protest when in 1973 it was occupied by the militant AMERICAN INDIAN MOVEMENT (AIM).

NOIS, KICKAPOO, MAHICAN, MASSACHUSET, MENOMINEE, MIAMI, MOHEGAN, OTTAWA, PEQUOT, SAUK, SHAWNEE, Shinnecock, and Wampanoag.

Cold weather and a short growing season in the Northeast and around the Great Lakes tended to limit horticulture and force heavy dependence on wild foods. Where available, fish, game, maple syrup, and wild rice were all important food sources. Among cultivators men generally cleared the fields, and women did most of the farming.

The Iroquoian-speaking peoples were organized into matrilineal villages, each governed by a council; women played a prominent role in village leadership. The Iroquois were intensely committed to raids, warfare, and the taking of captives, with torture and cannibalism inflicted upon the noblest male captives. Sometime during the 16th century the five tribes (Cayuga, Mohawk, Onondaga, Oneida, and Seneca, later joined by the Tuscarora) united into the powerful IROQUOIS LEAGUE, a military and political presence that held the balance of power in North America until the end of the 18th century.

Along the eastern seaboard, extending north and west to the Great Lakes, were the Algonquian-speaking peoples. They lived in small, semisedentary villages, except for the Pamlico, Powhatan, and others along the south Atlantic coast, who were strongly influenced by their southeastern neighbors. Horticultural activities were less developed along the coast, where foraging was usually excellent. Group leadership was generally weak, territory ill defined, and political organization similar to that of tribelets elsewhere. Algonquian groups were among the first native North Americans to suffer destruction at the hands of Europeans; the cultures of many effectively ended before the 18th century began.

In the Southeast prominent groups included the ALABAMA, CADDO, CHEROKEE, CHICKASAW, CHOCTAW, CREEK, NATCHEZ, QUAPAW, SEMINOLE, Biloxi, Chitimacha, Timucua, and Tunica. Many of these peoples achieved the most advanced cultural development north of Mesoamerica, by which their cultures were strongly influenced. Productive horticulture engaged in by both men and women and supplemented by abundant products of the forests provided the basis for large-scale settlements and political forms characteristic of chiefdoms. Villages with hundreds of inhabitants were palisaded against attack; inside they contained mounds on which were temples with perpetually burning fires, as well as residences of the highly ranked. Chiefs and kings possessed absolute political

foragers of the Southwest, who occupied either matrilineally or patrilineally organized settlements within a given range of territory. Raids against settled farmers in adjacent areas were common.

Maize cultivation first appeared north of Mexico in the Southwest, probably by about 200–100 BC. Introduced by the HOHOKAM, an ancient culture centered in southern Arizona, agriculture was also practiced by the ANASAZI, ancestors of the present-day Pueblo peoples, from AD 400 to 1300. When Spaniards visited the Southwest in 1540 the irrigation works, ball courts, and settlements of the Hohokam had fallen into disuse. The Pima and Papago, believed to be their descendants, lived in small, semiindependent patrilineage villages and were frequently at war with Apache bands.

The Pueblo people inhabited perhaps 90 independent villages in 1540, which ranged along the Rio Grande in northern New Mexico and northeast Arizona. As village-dwelling cultivators they constructed multistory apartment houses focused around subterranean religious rooms (kivas). Political power was vested in religious organizations, and each member of Pueblo society took part in the intense ceremonial cycle that filled each year. Warrior societies existed in each village, but they were primarily oriented toward defensive actions.

The Apache-Navajo, speakers of Athabascan languages

(Left) *Hopi Indian priests are shown with poisonous snakes gripped between their teeth in the annual snake ceremony, a dramatic rain dance and fertility rite. The ritually bathed snakes are kept from striking by the adroit use of a feathered wand, thought to stupefy the reptiles. The snakes are sprinkled with cornmeal before they are released to intercede with the rain spirit.*

(Below) *Contemporary Navajo Indians, members of the largest native-American group in the United States, raise livestock on their arid reservation lands in the American Southwest.*

power over their noble or commoner subjects and in some cases commanded a dozen or more villages. Raids and wars took place primarily to obtain wealth and honor but also to secure captives for slavery, sacrifice, and group cannibalism.

Disease and the effects of war destroyed many of these peoples before any but the most superficial accounts were written by European explorers and settlers. Nearly all groups to survive the period of exploration and colonization were forced by the U.S. government to move west to INDIAN TERRITORY (present-day Oklahoma) during the early 19th century.

Southwest Cultivators and Foragers. The Southwest culture area is a hot, arid region of mountains and intervening basins within which oases are often located. It comprises present-day Arizona, New Mexico, and portions of adjoining states and northwest Mexico. The Southwest was the homeland both of foraging peoples—including the APACHE, Havasupai, Seri, Walapai, and Yavapai—and of horticultural peoples—such as the MOJAVE, NAVAJO, PAPAGO, PIMA, PUEBLO peoples (including the HOPI and ZUÑI), YAQUI, YUMA, Cocopa, and Opata. In spite of its arid conditions the region provided substantial quantities of wild food, both plant and animal, for the

CARIBBEAN SEA

ATLANTIC OCEAN

CIRCUMCARIBBEAN

CENTRAL AMERICA

CIRCUMCARIBBEAN

NORTHERN ANDES

Equator

CENTRAL ANDES

PACIFIC OCEAN

Tropic of Capricorn

SOUTHERN ANDES

Falkland Is.
(uninhabited)

SOUTH AMERICA c. 1500
INDIAN CULTURE AREAS & PRINCIPAL TRIBES

- Tropical Forest
- Central & Southern Andes
- Chilean Archipelago
- Circumcaribbean & Northern Andes
- Marginal Forest Areas
- Patagonia/Pampas
- Tropical Aquatic
- Mura Principal Indian tribes
- Present day international boundary

0   500   1000 km
0   250   500   mi

closely related to those of northwest Canada, appear to have arrived in the Southwest less than 1,000 years ago. There they acquired semisedentary residence patterns, horticulture, and many cultural items borrowed from the region's more ancient inhabitants, probably the Pueblo.

From 1589 on, Spanish priests and settlers sought to control the Southwest; in 1680 the Pueblo people under POPÉ drove them out only to see them return in greater force. The Apacheans and others successfully fought off Spanish domination but later succumbed to the U.S. Army after the annexation of the Southwest in the 1840s. GERONIMO, the last Apache headman to resist, surrendered in 1886. Today the Navajo, the largest surviving body of Apacheans, constitute the largest native-American group in the United States. They and their Pueblo neighbors, the Hopi, are generally considered to possess the best-preserved traditional cultures in North America.

Mesoamerican Agriculturalists. The Mesoamerican culture area occupies present-day Guatemala, Belize, part of Honduras, and central Mexico southeast to the Yucatán Peninsula. The most famous Mesoamerican cultures were those of the MAYA and the AZTEC, but many other groups existed here also, including the HUASTEC, LENCA, MIXTEC, OLMEC, TARASCAN, ZAPOTEC, Chontal, Chorti, Jicaque, Mixe, Otomi, Totonac, Zacatec, Zoque, and others.

Cultivation of 100 or more plant species, particularly maize, beans, and squash, provided substantial food throughout this region for more than 3,000 years. Mesoamerican civilizations developed hieroglyphic writing, bark-paper books, and maps; positional mathematics and the zero concept; astronomical observatories, a highly accurate calendar, and the ability to predict eclipses; elaborate civic-ceremonial centers; and highly stratified societies with absolutist rulers.

In 1519, Hernán Cortés began his attack on the Aztecs and defeated them completely by 1521. Conquest of the Maya proved more difficult but was successful by the middle of the 16th century.

Today the Maya and other Mesoamerican groups constitute the largest Indian population of the Americas. They are chiefly subsistence farmers living in small villages, although extensive urbanization has occurred among the Indians of Mexico. Their lives are permeated by Roman Catholicism heavily mixed with native-American beliefs and ritual practices.

Circumcaribbean and North Andean Agriculturalists. The islands of the Caribbean, together with Colombia and northern Ecuador, form a zone of great climatic variation, ranging from rain forest to temperate highlands and arid desert. Two types of chiefdom traditionally existed in this culture area: those

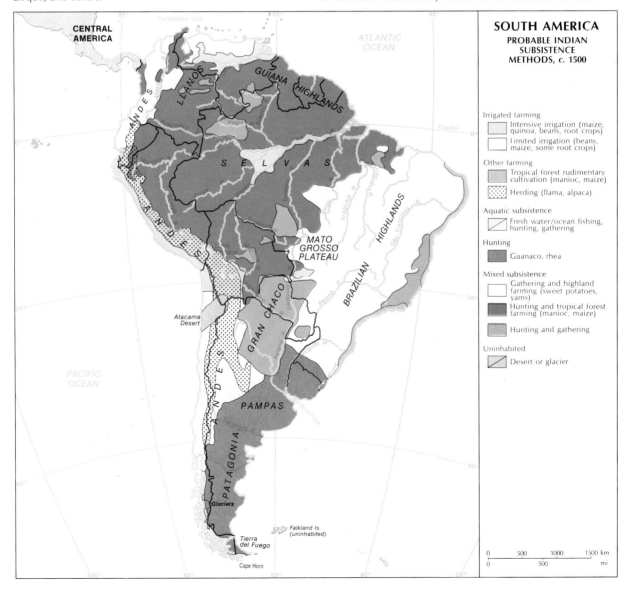

SOUTH AMERICA
PROBABLE INDIAN
SUBSISTENCE
METHODS, c. 1500

Irrigated farming
  Intensive irrigation (maize, quinoa, beans, root crops)
  limited irrigation (beans, maize, some root crops)

Other farming
  Tropical forest rudimentary cultivation (manioc, maize)
  Herding (llama, alpaca)

Aquatic subsistence
  Fresh water/ocean fishing, hunting, gathering

Hunting
  Guanaco, rhea

Mixed subsistence
  Gathering and highland farming (sweet potatoes, yams)
  Hunting and tropical forest farming (manioc, maize)
  Hunting and gathering

Uninhabited
  Desert or glacier

(Below) *This ceramic figure, from Veracruz, Mexico, dates from AD c.600–900, the late Classic period of pre-Columbian art. (Metropolitan Museum of Art, New York.)*

(Above) *Envoys of the Aztec emperor Montezuma presented gifts to Hernán Cortés, a Spanish conquistador, on his arrival in Mexico in 1519. Although Montezuma had dispatched envoys to report on the Spaniard's activities, Cortés rallied several rebellious subject tribes against Montezuma and in 1521 sacked the Aztec capital Tenochtitlán.*

which were politically organized—including the ARAWAK, Calamari, Cenú, Mompox, Quimbaya, and Tolú—and those which were feudally organized—as were the CHIBCHA and Nicarao societies.

Intensive farming with irrigation and terracing produced surpluses in the lowlands of sweet potatoes, maize, sweet manioc, beans, peanuts, pineapples, avocados, and papayas and in the highlands of quinoa, achira, auyama, and potatoes. Villages and towns of 1,000 to 3,000 people, with both matrilineages and patrilineages, were stratified into classes of chiefs, nobles, and commoners, with captives forming a slave class. Rank was partially hereditary, but a degree of mobility was permitted to the wealthy or to successful warriors. War was frequent and often either aimed at the capture of women as concubines and household workers or conducted as a search for sacrificial victims. Priests were associated with idols and temples; in some groups the chief was the high priest.

After European contact these small chiefdoms came under direct assault during the white man's search for gold and slaves. Few of the millions of native Mesoamerican inhabitants survived the first 50 years. Today only a few of the indigenous groups remain, among them the CARIB, CUNA, and Mosquito.

Central and South Andean Agriculturalists. The Central Andean culture area occupied the Andes and the western coast of South America from southern Colombia and Peru to central Chile. This area coincides with the ancient and powerful Inca empire, which fell to Francisco Pizarro and the Spanish conquistadors in 1532 (see INCA). Today the largest Indian population in all of South America lives in this region.

A subgroup within this culture area is formed by the indigenous peoples (the Atacameños and Diaguita) of the Atacama Desert and those (the ARAUCANIANS) of the central valley of Chile. The people of the Atacama traditionally shared many cultural features with the central Andeans but because of the scarcity of water did not develop large communities or elaborate political and religious features. The Araucanians farmed the central valley of Chile south to the Chiloe Islands. They lived in linked hamlets that sometimes joined together in time of conflict. The southern Araucanians, especially the Huilliche and Mapuche, resisted the Spanish until the end of the 19th century. More than 200,000 Araucanians remain today on scattered reservations.

Tropical Forest Culture Area. Hundreds of small horticultural

cultures traditionally occupied tracts of rain forest in Amazonia and in scattered regions in the Antilles and in Central America. Tribes of this culture area included the GUARANÍ MUNDURUCÚ, TUPÍ, Amanayé, Carajá, Guajá, Maué, Mojo, Mura, Nambicuara, Siriono, Tapirapé, and Tenetehara. The heavy rainfall of this area tends to leach nutrients from the soil, therefore horticultural societies had to shift fields constantly, and in the process these societies often shifted their entire villages.

Slash-and-burn cultivation of sweet potatoes, sweet and bitter manioc, yams, maize, beans, peanuts, and various types of palms provided a protein-deficient though often abundant supply of food. (More recently, plantains, a type of banana,

These girls from Cuzco, Peru, are descendants of the Incas, founders of an Indian empire that stretched along South America's Pacific coast from Ecuador to central Chile. Like the Aztecs and the Toltecs of Central America, the Incas were subjugated by Spanish colonizers.

were introduced from Asia.) The primary sources of protein were fish, turtles, and turtle eggs, supplemented by meat from a great variety of scarce game, including deer, peccaries, tapirs, monkeys, armadillos, anteaters, sloths, pacas, capybaras, birds, manatees, and cayman.

Villages generally were small (100–1,000 people) and the population density low (averaging 1.3–2.6 persons per km²/0.5–1.0 per mi²), and the village was often the largest unit of political integration. Patrilineages, except in the Guianas and the Lesser Antilles, were the predominant form of social affiliation, although clans existed in some of the larger villages. In small societies leadership was exerted by the male elder; in larger groups shamans sometimes gained power through intimidation. Incipient class structures existed among some of the upper-Amazon societies.

The shaman led puberty, harvest, and death ceremonies, all of which were highly elaborated in the Tropical Forest culture area. Many men became shamans through the use of powerful hallucinogenic drugs. Puberty ceremonies for both males and females often involved whipping, scarification, and the use of drugs. Death ceremonialism in various cultures included burial, reburial, and cremation (sometimes followed by ritual consumption of the ashes in beer), as well as funerary cannibalism. Spirits of the bush and rivers were thought to be malignant and to be avoided.

Feuds and raids were a way of life for most Tropical Forest peoples and were conducted for revenge, for captives, or simply out of fear of the intentions of the enemy. Tropical Forest populations declined quickly after contact with European culture—through the spread of disease and new weapons for intergroup conflict (iron knives, axes, guns) and as a result of extermination by European slavers (*bandeirantes*) and explorers. Nevertheless, the traditional culture of some groups still survives in the most remote corners of the rain forest.

Nomadic Foragers and Hunters of South America. Small, scattered groups of nomadic foragers and hunters traditionally occupied isolated parts of eastern and southern South America. Their cultures represented survivals of earlier, preagricultural adaptations to environmental conditions in which cultivation was not possible. These societies have been classified into the following principal groups: the shellfish gatherers of the archipelagoes of southern Chile; nomadic hunting bands of the pampas of PATAGONIA; forest hunter-gatherers of the CHACO, the eastern Brazil highlands, and other scattered areas; and tropical aquatic nomads along certain rivers and swampy areas who traveled by means of the dugout canoe.

These groups had the lowest population density of any South American culture area and possessed only simple band organization. All shared the characteristic of low food pro-

(Left) *A family of Araucanian Indians is portrayed against a background of Andean peaks. These peoples of southern Chile, organized as a loose confederacy of farming tribes, successfully defended their independence against the same 16th-century Spanish conquistadors who had subjugated the Incan Empire. Araucanians successfully maintained their traditional way of life until late in the 19th century, when the Chilean government forced them to settle on reservations in less desirable portions of the country.*

(Above) *Two Indians of the Amazonian rain forest remove poison-tipped arrows from the body of a freshly killed tapir. The scene is based on sketches and accounts of the Orinoco River expedition made by Alexander von Humboldt and Aimé Bonpland at the beginning of the 19th century.*

(Left) *The diversity of clothing worn by the various Indian tribes native to Patagonia, located at the southern extreme of South America, is displayed in a French text that was published in 1835.*

Portuguese sailors from the expedition led by Amerigo Vespucci, which sailed along the Atlantic seaboard of Brazil, Uruguay, and Argentina during the early 16th century, overwhelmed a fierce coastal tribe of Indians that opposed their landing. (British Museum, London.)

ductivity exploited by a relatively simple technology. Religion consisted of life-crisis rites, shamanism, and a belief in spirits. Feuds and raids were rare; survival for many of these societies was dependent on avoiding their more powerful, warlike neighbors. After the early Spanish explorers brought horses into the South American plains, some of the pedestrian nomads of Patagonia became gauchos (cowboys). However, most of the nomadic societies were too small and independent to serve Europeans, and many were exterminated or died out from newly introduced diseases soon after contact with Europeans.

EARLY IMPACT OF EUROPEAN CONTACT

In Latin America many Indian populations succumbed completely when faced with European domination. Others were enslaved on plantations, where they intermingled with African slaves and survived mixed in race and culture. Other Indian peoples, however, particularly throughout the densely inhabited centers of Nuclear America, gradually entered into the economic, religious, and social life of their conquerors and became the lowest class or caste of the colonial society. Some ancient Indian communities in Mexico, Guatemala, and the Andean countries resisted domination and have managed to survive into the 20th century in ethnic enclaves that constitute what has been called a corporate peasantry.

The first Spaniards came to the New World on a quest for gold and adventure. Often they intermarried with the indigenous peoples, producing in Latin America a large, mixed class called MESTIZOS. In Canada the first French explorers were mostly trappers and traders; they, too, often intermarried with the Indians, and they maintained generally friendly relations based on cooperation and trade partnership with the Indians.

In contrast with these other European groups, the earliest Anglo-Americans generally came to North America with their families in order to set up colonies; most of them were seeking, above all, to settle the land. Because virtually all of North America was already in use by the indigenous inhabitants, conflict was inevitable. The Dutch and British began early a policy of buying land, a practice never understood by the native-American sellers, who generally believed that they were granting the newcomers rights to use rather than to own the lands occupied by the Indians.

(Above) Like most groups of Europeans who colonized North America, the Swedish pioneers who settled along the Delaware River near present-day Wilmington during the 17th century were able to establish their colony only by maintaining amicable relations with local Indian tribes.

(Left) A sketch by Alfred Jacob Miller, titled Migration of the Pawnees, portrays a group of nomadic Plains Indians leaving their main encampment in search of more productive hunting grounds. (Yale University Library.)

After the American colonists won their independence from Great Britain, the U.S. government continued the British practice of treating the tribes as sovereign nations; between 1778 and 1871, when the policy was ended, a total of 389 treaties had been signed and ratified (see INDIAN TREATIES). Nonetheless, many of these treaties were relentlessly broken in the 19th century as large numbers of white settlers moved into Indian lands. In addition, beginning about 1815, federal policy supported the forced removal of Indians from their traditional territories to isolated reserved areas that were administered as trusts by the U.S. government. Between 1830 and 1840 more than 70,000 highly acculturated southeastern peoples (including the Cherokee, Choctaw, Creek, and other members of the so-called FIVE CIVILIZED TRIBES) were removed to the newly established Indian Territory in Oklahoma, land already in use by other native-American peoples.

Many Indians fought bitterly against their forced resettlement on reservations (see INDIAN WARS). By the mid-1800s, as white settlers pushed westward to the Pacific Ocean, tragedy after tragedy was visited upon Indians of the Great Plains and the Far West. The doctrine of manifest destiny fueled the frontier peoples to hostile actions against even peaceful peoples, and massive slaughter of men, women, and children sometimes resulted. The spread of disease also contributed to the defeat of the Indians and the suppression of their traditional way of life. Only in the American Southwest did ancient cultures such as the Hopi, Zuñi, and Navajo manage to insulate themselves against the white man's unrelenting hunger for land, which destroyed many native-American cultures throughout the continent.

INDIANS IN THE 20TH CENTURY

In 20th-century America no single definition of precisely who is an Indian exists. To be eligible for federal Indian aid in the United States, a person must live on or near a federal reservation or be of Eskimo or Aleut descent. Persons who are listed on the rosters of state reservations or who can prove one-fourth or more Indian ancestry are generally accepted as Indians by the U.S. government. In the eastern United States some groups with mixed ancestry (such as the Lumbee of North Carolina) have claimed Indian status but have not always been granted it by the federal government.

Canada recognizes "status," or treaty, Indians (those who belong to a band with a treaty with the government) and "nonstatus," or nontreaty, Indians (those who are clearly of Indian descent but who do not have treaties—for example, the Indians of the Maritimes or the Iroquois of Brantford, Ontario). People in these categories may or may not be of unmixed Indian ancestry, but they enjoy all the rights that the government grants to Indian peoples. In some parts of Canada, primarily in Quebec Province but also elsewhere, métis (persons of Indian and white ancestry) are accorded no special privileges under the law.

In Latin America cultural style rather than physical type or even ancestry is generally the criterion that determines whether one is deemed an Indian. Individuals or groups who speak Indian languages, wear Indian clothes, and participate in Indian cultural activities are identified as Indians. Many members of the Spanish-speaking mestizo class are genetically little different from persons classified as *indio*.

In the United States. In 1980 an estimated 1.2 million Indians, including Eskimos and Aleuts, lived in the United States. The native-American population is growing at 3.5% per year. Most native Americans live west of the Mississippi River, especially in the states of Oklahoma, New Mexico, Arizona, South Dakota, and California. In 1977 approximately 650,000 people lived on some 285 state or federal reservations. In 1976 the total land held in trust by the federal government and administered by the Bureau of Indian Affairs—an agency of the Interior Department (see INDIAN AFFAIRS, BUREAU OF)—was slightly more than 51 million acres. In 1978 the total government expenditure from all agencies for native-American affairs was estimated at $1.7 billion.

During the 19th and early 20th centuries the governmental policies toward Indians were disastrous from the point of view of the Indian. In 1887 the Dawes Act, also called the General Allotment Act, authorized the breaking up of tribal lands into small property units of 16 to 65 ha (40 to 160 acres), to be given to individual Indians. This action, supposedly aimed at encouraging the Indians to become farmers, led instead to the widespread sale of tribal lands to whites. By 1934, when the Wheeler-Howard INDIAN REORGANIZATION ACT overturned the General Allotment Act, the land owned by Indians had dropped from about 63 million ha (155 million acres) in 1887 to about 19 million ha (47 million acres). The new legislation restored tribal ownership of reservation lands. It also provided reservation Indians with self-government on a limited scale and partnership with the BIA in the development of land and resource management and other programs. In 1946 the Indian Claims Commission was established to settle claims of Indian groups that could prove loss of lands due to past governmental malfeasance. The commission received more than 600 claims and has so far awarded more than 1 billion dollars.

In another federal policy shift during the 1950s, Congress called for the termination of special federal programs and trust relationships with Indians. It was hoped that this policy would hasten the assimilation of Indians into the larger white society. For the Menominee of Wisconsin, the Klamath of Oregon, and a number of other tribes whose trust status was ended, termination took place too quickly and without the

(Above) *Corpses of Sioux lie about the ruins of their camp at Wounded Knee, S.Dak., in 1890, after a brief, one-sided battle with the U.S. 7th Cavalry. The outnumbered and surrounded Indians were massacred after a Sioux wounded a soldier while the tribe surrendered.*

(Left) *During the 1970s, various alliances of American Indians pressed for the return of their ancestral lands, using both legal means and the tactics of civil disobedience to achieve their goals. Their efforts have met with some successes in New Mexico, Maine, and Alaska.*

necessary preparation for independence, and economic disaster followed. The government abandoned the termination policy by the mid-1960s, following its widespread opposition by both Indians and non-Indians.

In the 1970s, partially stimulated by militant Indians of the American Indian Movement and the writings of Vine Deloria and others, many native-American groups have been more forceful in searching for their rights. Although a federal act of 1790—the Indian Trade and Intercourse Act—had prohibited sale of Indian lands without prior federal approval, vast sections of the eastern United States passed from Indian control after that time. Today many native peoples are seeking substantial recompense for these losses. In the late 1970s the Narragansett, the Dakota, the Oneida, and other Indian peoples received favorable claims decisions. In the Pacific Northwest native-American fishermen have been upheld by the Supreme Court in their claim to half of the fish in Puget Sound. In the Southwest the Apache, Paiute, Pima, and others are pressing their legal claims to the increasingly valuable water rights in the region. Various western Indian groups, who control perhaps one-third of the total U.S. coal reserves, have formed a committee to ensure equitable treatment when the coal is mined.

Many Indian reservations are unable to provide their growing numbers of people with an adequate standard of living or means of employment. On reservations nearly 50% of the population does not graduate from high school; unemployment runs at 40% or higher; birth and death rates are high; and suicides occur at twice the national rate. Since the 1950s the BIA has supported a relocation program for native people choosing to move to cities; more than 200,000 have relocated. Eighty thousand Indians live in Los Angeles, with 25,000 or more in Minneapolis, Minn., San Francisco, and Chicago; smaller groups are found in most major American cities. Most relocated Indians lack skills useful in urban areas, and many escape reservation poverty only to find urban poverty. Alcoholism and crime rates are extremely high among Indian communities in cities and on reservations, and most Indians are socioeconomically impoverished.

Despite the present bleak picture, the future appears hopeful. Indians themselves are assuming greater control of their own destiny, and old rivalries and enmities are being put aside in pursuit of the common good. The BIA (of which two-thirds of the staff is now Indian) is becoming more effective than it was previously in articulating Indian goals. Tens of thousands of Indians are seeking higher education, often beginning with community colleges on their own lands.

In Canada. When Europeans first arrived, Canada had an indigenous population estimated at 200,000. Today the population of Canadian Indians numbers more than 280,000, and this figure is growing. In 1975 there were 561 separate Indian bands located on more than 2,300 reservations ranging in size from a few acres to more than 1,300 km² (500 mi²).

The office of superintendent for Indian affairs in Canada was first established by the British in 1755. In 1860 control of Indian affairs passed to the Canadian government, and in 1880 a Department of Indian Affairs was established, now a part of the Department of Indian Affairs and Northern Development. The primary function of the department is to aid in maintenance of the bands and to encourage full and free participation in national affairs. All effective Indian legislation in Canada is contained in the Indian Act of 1951. All Indians are citizens of Canada; are free to elect band chiefs and councils; may leave reserves at any time; and may participate, with representatives of the department, in running their own social and economic affairs. Indians may choose to give up band rights, become "enfranchised," and then obtain their share of any funds due the band.

About 35% of Canada's Indians live in urban centers: Vancouver, Winnipeg, and Toronto each have Indian populations of more than 20,000. Many of these are "nonstatus" people who suffer the same effects of economic and social poverty characteristic of urban Indian communities in the United States.

Canadian Indians historically have faced strong assimilatory pressure, which many are now resisting. Tens of thousands of "nonstatus" Indians have no significant land with which to affiliate and are seeking redress of their early land losses. Throughout the northern reaches of the country, hydroelectric power development and the search for and exploitation of mineral resources have threatened some native peoples with displacement from their lands.

In Latin America. Today 16 countries in Latin America have sizable Indian populations. Indians are estimated to number 19 million in Mexico; 7 million in Peru; and over 3 million each in Bolivia and Ecuador. Central America, Venezuela, Colombia, the Guianas, Chile, and Argentina each have several hundred thousand Indians; Brazil, Uruguay, and Paraguay each have 100,000 or fewer.

Throughout Latin America, Indians constitute the poorest segment of the population. Their values and customs are rejected in favor of those of the Spanish-speaking white or mestizo social classes. As a result, many Indians have chosen to join the non-Indian population through cultural assimilation. This is especially true in urban, plantation, and agribusiness areas. On the frontiers of expansion, in Ecuador, Peru, Venezuela, and Brazil, many of the remaining tribal Indians have suffered persecution and displacement at the hands of large landowners and mining and forestry enterprises.

ROGER C. OWEN

Bibliography: Berkhofer, Robert F., *The White Man's Indian: Images of the American Indian from Columbus to the Present* (1978); Deloria, Vine, Jr., *Custer Died for Your Sins: An Indian Manifesto* (1969); Denevan, William M., *The Native Population of the Americas in 1492* (1976); Driver, Harold E., *Indians of North America*, rev. 2d ed. (1969); Farb, Peter, *Man's Rise to Civilization: The Cultural Ascent of the Indians of North America*, rev. 2d ed. (1978); Jennings, Jesse D., ed., *Ancient Native Americans* (1978); Josephy, Alvin, *The Indian Heritage of America* (1968); Price, John A., *Native Studies: American and Canadian Indians* (1978); Spencer, Robert F., and Jennings, Jesse D., et al., *The Native Americans: Ethnology and Backgrounds of the North American Indians*, 2d ed. (1977); Steward, Julian H., ed., *The Handbook of South American Indians*, 7 vols. (1946–59); Steward, Julian H., and Faron, Louis C., *Native Peoples of South America* (1959); Sturtevant, William C., ed., *Handbook of North American Indians*, 20 vols. (1978–); Underhill, Ruth M., *Red Man's Religion: Beliefs and Practices of the Indians North of Mexico* (1965); Wauchope, Robert, ed., *Handbook of Middle American Indians*, 16 vols. (1964–76).

Indians of North America, art of the

North American Indian art includes many distinct traditions developed by native American peoples throughout the continent. In spite of great diversity among the traditional cultures of native American populations, several key concepts underlie the artistic expression of most groups. Primary among these is the assumption that art was to serve social purposes. It was to be used in religious and other rituals; it proclaimed class, rank, and political status; it was wealth; and it signified group solidarity. All native American societies had well-defined aesthetic systems, and for art to function properly, it had to conform to that society's particular set of visual principles. Some Indian groups supported professional artists. Distinctions between fine and applied art did not exist, however. Artistic innovations and individual expression were limited by the need to communicate, for above all, art was a mode of communication.

Art objects were traditionally made from a rich variety of natural products found in the environment, ranging from shell, bone, feather, and animal skin to wood, stone, clay, colored minerals, and vegetable fibers. These materials were variously carved, abraded, engraved, modeled, baked, painted, woven, tied, twined, and braided. Later, materials of European manufacture such as glass beads and machine-made cloth were also used. Raw materials and finished art objects were sometimes traded over long distances.

Traditional styles of North American Indian art can be broadly classified according to the following culture areas, although wide variations have occurred over time and among the various local groups of each region.

Arctic Art. The Arctic culture area corresponds to the geographic zone inhabited by the ESKIMO. A sequence of prehis-

This soapstone carving of a hunter in combat with an ivory-toothed bear is representative of the stylistic refinement in modern Eskimo art, with its sense of movement and life. Skilled Eskimo artisans typically work in bone, ivory, or stone. (Winnipeg Art Gallery, Manitoba, Canada.)

toric Eskimo art that began about 2,000 years ago can be traced in the Bering Sea region (see OKVIK); another tradition, possibly older, has been identified with the Dorset culture of central and eastern Canada. Some ancient carved wooden objects have survived, but most remaining examples of prehistoric Eskimo art are fashioned of walrus ivory, bone, antler, or stone. Carving and engraving were the principal techniques used in prehistoric times. The finely worked carvings often exhibit markedly sculptural qualities of execution, despite their tiny scale (many are small enough to be hidden in a closed hand).

Utilitarian objects such as ivory harpoon heads and other tools were often engraved or enhanced by other forms of decorative carving, but many Eskimo sculptures have no obvious use. Game animals were favorite subjects; small animal carvings with bored holes may have been used as hunting charms tied to weapons or clothing. Other carvings of skeletonized animals, groups of human heads, or monster forms may have been the paraphernalia of shamans. The 19th-century painted wooden ritual masks of the southern Alaskan Eskimo, prized by collectors of ethnographic art, are exceptionally imaginative in their lively anthropomorphic shapes and incorporation of diverse materials.

Northwest Coast. The Northwest Coast art tradition is shared by a number of different peoples living along a narrow strip of land facing the Pacific Ocean between southern Alaska and the Columbia River valley. The distinctive and elaborate tradition associated with this region is hundreds of years old and can be subdivided into two major styles. The northern style—associated primarily with HAIDA, TSIMSHIAN, and TLINGIT peoples—is characterized by precise, intellectualized art forms, often displaying great refinement and intricacy of execution. The southern style—identified with the BELLA COOLA of British Columbia and the KWAKIUTL and NOOTKA of Vancouver Island—is by contrast robust and dramatic in its use of strong colors and powerful designs.

In both of these areas art objects traditionally were used to identify rank and were displayed as symbols of wealth and status. Monumental TOTEM poles, painted house posts and other architectural forms, canoe ornaments, feasting dishes, ceremonial dance hats and dance masks, helmets, and textiles are among the display objects that were made by professional artists throughout the region. Ritual paraphernalia, tools, and household articles were also made as works of art. The subject matter of most Northwest Coast art was traditionally heraldic and chosen according to the wishes of the patron. Images were generally portrayed in curvilinear, highly conventionalized and bilaterally symmetrical modes, with great emphasis on the textural qualities of the material. In addition to wood and cedar bark from the immense forests of the Northwest, native art materials included shell, horn, and stone, the wool of mountain goats, and dog hair, of which the Tlingit Chilkat blankets (actually capes denoting tribal rank) are woven. Copper sheets, glass beads, and machine-made cloth later obtained from Europeans were also worked by native artists.

Large carved totem poles, such as these of the Kitwancool of British Columbia, are commonly found in the villages of Northwest Coast Indians. Considered magical, the carvings document the lineage and social position of the patron who commissioned them.

California and Basin-Plateau Art. Farther south, among the Indian tribes of California, several artistic traditions flourished, in particular basketry-related arts. Twined baskets and featherwork are characteristic of northern groups such as the HUPA and YUROK, who are noted for their watertight basketry decorated with geometric patterns woven in a variety of twining techniques. In central California, the Chumash made small steatite animal carvings, fine coiled baskets, and magnificent, multicolored pictographic designs on the walls of caves. Other central and southern California people, notably the POMO and Diegueño, produced coiled and twined baskets of great complexity and beauty.

The Plateau and Great Basin culture areas are situated inland between the Rocky Mountains on the east and the Cascades and Northern Sierras on the west. Parts of this region were influenced by traditions of the Plains culture area during

This painted eagle mask, carved in wood, symbolizes totem ancestry. It was crafted by the Kwakiutl of British Columbia. When opened, the wings of the eagle reveal a human face.

The basket-making expertise of the Pomo of northern California, developed since prehistoric times, is exemplified in this spiral-design basket by the 20th-century artist Mary Benson. (Museum of the American Indian, New York City.)

the 19th century. Tribes of the sparsely settled Basin area produced lightweight basketry containers to hold the wild foods and seeds that were their sustenance. Handsomely styled baskets made in modern times by PAIUTE, WASHO, and other Basin people continue the age-old traditions developed by particular tribes of the region.

Greater variety existed in the arts of the Plateau area, where village dwellers such as the KLAMATH and Washo traditionally made hieratic, strictly frontal wooden statues. Baskets and costume arts using varied decorative techniques were made by many plateau groups; some, such as the NEZ PERCÉ, wove soft carrying bags. The beadwork of the SHOSHONI was strongly derivative of Plains designs. Rock art of great antiquity is found throughout the intermontane zone, and immense stone alignments forming patterns that often can be read from the air are located in the Basin.

Art of the Southwest. The Southwest culture area extends over present-day Arizona, New Mexico, southern Colorado, and southern Utah. Coiled baskets made at least 2,000 years ago mark the beginning of decorative traditions that continue to flourish among native American artists today.

Pottery decorated with painted motifs was made by HOHO-KAM villagers of southern Arizona after about AD 200. Within a short time painted pottery became the dominant art form throughout the region. Many varieties were made by other farming groups, among them the ANASAZI and Mogollon, ancestors of today's PUEBLO peoples. Mimbres artists of southwestern New Mexico made remarkable figurative paintings on pottery in the period from about 1000 to 1150, but much painted pottery of the Southwest was nonfigurative and depended on complex linear patterns for its striking appearance. Other domestic Pueblo arts include basketry, textile weaving, and shell and turquoise jewelry. Stone and wood sculpture, masks, including those used by KACHINA dancers, and impressive dry-fresco mural paintings in the underground chambers known as KIVAS are among the many traditional ritual arts. From dry materials such as sand, ocher, and finely ground leaves and flower petals, the Pueblos also created sand paintings for their kivas.

(Above) A Navajo artist creates a sand painting by trickling finely ground sand and mineral pigments through his fingers. The finished painting is an integral part of healing rituals, in which the power of its symbols is believed to cure an ailing person. The art of sandpainting, borrowed from the neighboring Pueblos, was refined by the Navajo.

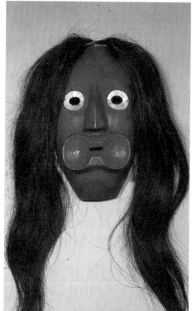

(Left) This carved wood mask represents the work of the Iroquois False Face Society. With their hideous and distorted features, the masks, symbolizing patron spirits, are designed to ward off evil spirits. (British Museum, London.)

The nonfigurative linear decorations of this Anasazi pitcher are derived from earlier basket-making designs. The Anasazi, of the American Southwest, developed a distinctive firing technique that yielded vivid black-on-white colors on their ceramic works. (Milwaukee Public Museum, Wisconsin.)

The non-Pueblo NAVAJO people further elaborated the sand painting techniques learned from their Pueblo neighbors. They developed the symbolic configurations of their sand paintings in conjunction with the many chants used in traditional Navajo curative rites. The Navajo also developed rich styles of textile weaving and from about 1850 on have produced beautiful silver and turquoise jewelry. Other non-Pueblo southwesterners, including the PAPAGO and PIMA of southern Arizona and several bands of Apache, are famous for their coiled basketry.

Northeast, Southeast, and Subarctic Art. Small stone carvings of great subtlety were made 4,500 years ago in the Eastern Woodlands culture area, which covers much of what is now the northeastern United States. Beginning about 1000 BC people of the Adena culture built great mounds in the Ohio Valley and produced carved-stone pipes and engraved tablets associated with complicated burial rites. From about 300 BC to AD 500, artists of the Hopewell tradition built earthwork and effigy mounds, sculpted naturalistic figures in clay and on stone pipes, and cut out ornaments of sheet copper and of mica.

After about 700, a vigorous tradition of stone, wood, and pottery sculpture is associated with the Mississippian mound-building cultures in the South (see MOUND BUILDERS). Carved-stone effigy pipes and masks of shell and wood are among the ritual objects that have survived. Suggestions of these early traditions are still discernible in historic-period Indian arts that incorporate glass beads, trade cloth, and new ideas introduced through European contact. The SEMINOLE and some other native Americans of the Southeast today produce distinctive basketry articles and cotton-cloth garments ornamented with colorful appliqué.

Articles of traditional Iroquoian culture include WAMPUM belts, composed of shell beadwork, and powerfully expressive carved masks used in religious ceremonies of the False Face Society. Silk appliqué, quillwork colored with vegetable dyes, floral beaded designs, and small containers of birchbark were traditionally made by Algonquian tribes from around the Great Lakes, such as the CREE, HURON, OJIBWA, POTAWATOMI, and WINNEBAGO. Farther north a hostile environment kept populations small and scattered, and art was simpler. Subarctic art forms often appear to have been derived from traditions of their Plains, Woodlands, or Eskimo neighbors and later translated into a vigorous local idiom.

Plains. The region between the Mississippi and the Rockies was sparsely settled, and the village-dwelling agriculturalists who lived along river valleys there made Woodland-style art objects. A Plains art tradition developed only after the European presence in the New World introduced the horse, the fur trade, and the forced westward movement of many native American groups. By about 1800 the Plains was a melting pot of displaced tribes, who invented a vigorous art style there within a remarkably short time. Prominent Plains art producers included the BLACKFOOT, CHEYENNE, CROW, KIOWA, PAWNEE, and SIOUX. Art produced by women traditionally was geomet-

ric, angular, and nonfigurative. Most of it was painted or embroidered with porcupine quills, and later with glass trade beads, onto garments, moccasins, horsetrappings, parfleches (envelope-shaped satchels), and other utilitarian articles. Art produced by men was figurative, with much of it painted on robes, shields, and tepee covers. Some subjects were of mystic visions; others represented actual events experienced by the artist or significant to the history of the group. After about 1830 pictorial art became increasingly realistic. By mid-century many historical pictures were made on paper or muslin with European media such as ink, and after 1875 some imprisoned Plains warriors painted nostalgic pictures of traditional life in earlier times. These depictions represent the climax of the first Pan-Indian art tradition.

North American Indian Art Today. The manufacture of art for domestic use ended in most native American communities when machine-made products replaced many indigenously made utilitarian ones. Art production for native religious and social institutions also ended wherever these were replaced by alien ones. Traditional art for religious and social ritual has been continuously produced, however, in the Southwest, where such traditional household arts as basketry, textile weaving, and pottery also became cash-producing craft industries in the 19th and 20th centuries. Ritual art production was revived during the mid-20th century among peoples of the Northwest Coast, where a high-level craft industry has long flourished. Some tribal ceremonials have also been revived among Plains peoples in recent years, and an impressive array of Pan-Indian religious and social rituals has encouraged the creation of new art traditions. Craft production has similarly become important to the economy of the Canadian and Alaskan Eskimo, who have developed distinctive styles of printmaking and soapstone sculpture.   J. J. BRODY

Bibliography: Berlant, Anthony, and Kahlenberg, Mary Hunt, *Walk in Beauty* (1977); Brody, J. J., *Indian Painters and White Patrons* (1971) and *Mimbres Painted Pottery* (1977); de Laguna, Frederica, Carpenter, Edmund, and Stone, Peter, *The Far North: 2,000 Years of American Eskimo and Indian Art* (1973); Dockstader, Frederick, *Indian Art in America* (1961); Douglas, F. H., and d'Harnoncourt, Rene, *Indian Art of the United States* (1941; repr. 1970); Ewers, J. C., *Plains Indian Painting: A Description of Aboriginal American Art* (1939; repr. 1977); Feder, Norman, *American Indian Art* (1971); Highwater, Jamake, *Song from the Earth: American Indian Painting* (1976); Holm, Bill, *Northwest Coast Indian Art: An Analysis of Form* (1965); Mason, Otis T., *Aboriginal American Indian Basketry* (1904; repr. 1976); Walker Art Center, *American Indian Art: Form and Tradition* (1972).

Indians of North America, music and dance of the

The earliest known inhabitants of North America were a highly music-and-dance-oriented people who responded to their environment by creating a vast repertoire of unwritten songs and dances long before the arrival of the Europeans. These songs and dances were transmitted orally from generation to generation down to the present day. The descendants of those early tribal musicians continue to create and perform their unique art in the many ceremonials and rituals as well as public fairs and powwows that take place annually throughout the continental United States, Canada, and Alaska. Although many native Americans have been assimilated into modern society, several tribal groups are making serious efforts to preserve their traditional cultures.

From the end of the Civil War to 1889, the year of the Wounded Knee massacre, the temper of the times discouraged sympathetic understanding or wide dissemination of Indian music and dance beyond tribal circles. Since then, however, frequent cross-cultural contacts between Indians and non-Indians, aided by modern travel and communications, have exerted a definite influence on the older forms of tribal music and dance. Nevertheless, each regional and geographic cultural area has retained its own identity just as, in most instances, the identity of each tribe has been tenaciously retained. If a song or dance is "borrowed," it is immediately suspected or recognized by the tribal music masters as com-

The Cheyenne developed a distinctive art form by decorating animal hides with dyed porcupine quills or colored glass beads. The glass beads sewn on this leather waistcoat, dating from about 1900, illustrate Indians on horseback in a typical scene from Plains life. Histories of the owner's exploits were often portrayed on the leather hides.

The Sioux decorated their homes and personal objects, exemplified here by a decorated Sioux water pouch (right) and a parfleche (left), a bag used to carry food.

Percussive instruments, such as this gourd rattle, are an integral part of American Indian music and are frequently the only accompaniment. Gourd rattles, which are always shaken, never worn, traditionally contained pebbles or organic material, such as seeds, kernels, or grain. Animal rattles, comprising hooves, nails, skins, or turtle shells, were usually worn and served an invocational or evocative purpose.

ing from a specific cultural area, such as the Eastern Woodlands territory, the Great Plains, the Southwest, California and the Pacific Northwest, the Great Basin and Plateau, or Alaska and the Arctic Circle.

MUSIC

The music of the North American Indians is primarily vocal-monodic (single melodic line). All songs, both melody and words, have been and continue to be composed by individuals and "head singers," either male or female. Some songs are conceived during visionary or dreamlike states, while others are consciously created for special functions. Extemporization is rare. Musical notation is nonexistent in the traditional culture, although isolated instances of mnemonic music aids have been found. Although there is free use of microtones (intervals smaller than a semitone), melodies are based predominantly on the pentatonic (5-tone) and modal scales with intervals of the fourth and fifth being the most common. Some Indian music is strongly rhythmic, some predominantly

melodic; sometimes whole words are sung, sometimes only syllables. Likewise, some dances are energetic and agitated, while others are placid and sedate. Occasionally, music and dancing are used merely for personal exposure in a public performance before an invited audience. Nearly always, however, dance is accompanied by vocal music and some kind of percussive instruments.

European forms of harmony and counterpoint are absent, although instances of incidental harmony do occur. Accompaniment is mainly percussive: drums with animal-skin heads and rattles, shakers, and scrapers made of various materials such as deer hooves, seashells, bird beaks, animal horns, and so on. Flutes, whistles, and some stringed instruments are also used. All music is functional and accompanies specific activities such as dance, work, games, prayer, harvesting, healing, hunting, whaling, burial ceremonies, etc. Chants may contain many vocables or nontranslatable vocal sounds and may have either elaborate or simple language and narrative content. Vocables generally derive from the respective languages of the more than 200 tribal groups. Metric values are primarily in common meter, seldom irregular, but combinations of meters do occur.

Many attempts have been made to codify the formal structures of Indian songs, which appear to be rigidly composed within the context of their respective functions. For example, the war dance songs of the Plains Indians generally have a descending contour with an introduction followed by variations of A—as in the formula AA' BA' CA'—ending with a "tail-dance" section that reiterates part of the principal section. These seemingly simple chants are of such variety, however, that it is virtually impossible to isolate hard and fast rules for their composition due to language differences among the various tribal cultures, the differences in stylistic coloration among the individual singers, and the regionalism and variety of dance styles.

While traditional forms of tribal music retain their melodic and historical links with the past through oral transmission, the increasing availability of sound recordings and ethnomusicological documentation of Indian chants has increased the musical skills and expanded the repertoire of the tribal songmakers. Moreover, in Missouri, Colorado, Arkansas, and other border areas, there are non-Indian folklorists who perform Indian dances and songs in the Indian style. Also, far afield, in Europe (Germany, France, Finland) there are non-Indian clubs of American Indian aficionados who present their folklore programs with full regalia.

Other forms of North American Indian music familiar to

An Ojibwa (Chippewa) snowshoe dance celebrates the season's first snowfall in this painting (c.1835) by George Catlin. A single-file circling dance could be free form or rigid form. (Smithsonian Institution, Washington, D.C.)

the public through the concert hall, the cinema, and popular music are often, at best, quasi-romantic, pseudoethnic versions of Western music that do not reflect the true spirit of Indian music. Antonín Dvořák's prophecy that America should have a national music based on North American Indian songs will be fulfilled only when our creative artists repudiate the old clichés and seek more valid art forms inspired by an understanding and love of Indian music.

North American Indian music has undergone a transmutation of values in the oral-to-written process, the results of which have been intended for non-Indian audiences; tribal music has remained in its pristine state only where the Indians have remained on the periphery of American society. This will not always be the case, however, as this music comes to be understood and felt deeply by an ever-growing audience receptive to its unique artistic value. The use of Indian elements in today's performing arts can be a revitalizing factor in American music and music education. An excellent example of a successful ensemble is the American Indian Creative Percussion Ensemble, which performed at the National Folk Festival, Vienna, Va., to wide acclaim; the work performed was *Cacega Ayuwipi*, a tour de force for 45 Indian instruments together with standard Western percussion. Although the players donned tribal dress, the techniques used were contemporary and exemplified the best of North American Indian and Western traditions. Another group, the E-Yah-Pah-Hah Indian Chanters, was a development of the first bicultural music education program of the Bureau of Indian Affairs: it featured Indian songs, poetry, and mime within the framework of a modern choir. Also, the initial performance of the first all-Indian halftime marching band at an American football game took place at RFK Stadium in Washington, D.C., in 1977; and 150 young Indian musicians from 80 tribes and 30 states performed a pageant called "American Indian Heroes, History and Heritage."

DANCE

All forms of Indian dance are graceful; the movements appear to correspond with the dancers' concept of oneness with the earth and the natural environment. These are not merely leg dances but whole-body, whole-soul forms of kinetic expression that coordinate with and extend the meaning of the music and songs.

Dance styles vary; they include (1) *individual free-form* dances, wherein each individual is at liberty to select his or her own movements within accepted and traditional limits (examples: Plains Indian war dances, once performed prior to and after battle, that have evolved into the contest powwow dances or "fancy" dances of today; the Pacific Northwest drama-story dances, in which the dancers wear elaborate, carved masks; the Potlatch stick dances of interior-Alaska Athabascan groups; the Southwest Yaqui Pascolas-deer dances, and various Pueblo Koshare dances of Hopi, Tewa, Tiwa, and Southwest groups); (2) *group free-form* dances, wherein each individual selects his movements and follows a leader (examples: East Woodland Iroquois long-house dances, in which a single file of male dancers performs around one or more singers seated in the middle of the room; Southwest Apache Gan, or mountain spirit, dances, wherein male dancers follow a leader around a fire while a group of male singers stands aside and accompanies with songs); and (3) *group rigid-form* dances, wherein each individual must adhere to uniform dance steps, movements, and formations in a choreographed fashion (examples: the special religious rituals of the Southwest Pueblo Indians, in which as many as 200 dancers, male and female, perform in formations to the accompaniment of 150 male singers and one or more drummers; the Eskimo mime dances with multiple drummers and singers and a line of female dancers; the Eastern Woodlands stomp dances, in which a leading dancer calls out a chant to be echoed by the following line of dancers, male and female, all doing a shuffle step around a wood fire, each dance sequence lasting 20 to 45 minutes during a night of festivities from sundown to dawn; and the powwow social dance known as the "two-step," in which male-female couples follow a lead couple around the dance arena, taking two steps forward and one step back,

while the singers are seated around a big drum). Generally, social dances of all tribes are in the last category.

In the older traditional styles, female dancers were not allowed to be as energetic as the male dancers—for example, the old-style Plains Indian war dance, in which the female remained standing in one spot, keeping time to the music while the male dancer moved around the arena. This has changed, however, to allow more freedom in the modern powwow. Generally, the female Indian dancer's movements are subordinate to those of the male, although isolated instances of all-female dances do exist (examples: the East Woodlands Penobscot pine cone dance—group free-form—in which two concentric circles intertwine around a group of male singers seated at a big drum; the Apache girls' puberty rite—individual free-form—with one to three male singers; the Northwest Yakima butterfly dance—individual free-form; the Plateau region Colville swan dance; the Alaska Eskimo mime dance; the Eastern Woodlands sac and fox swan dance; the Plain Caddo turkey dance; the Southwest Pima basket dance; and the Plains Kiowa scalp dance—all group rigid forms.

Couple dances with and without hand contact are fairly common in the larger tribal groups and powwows and may serve exclusively social purposes or may be solely ceremonial (examples: the Eastern Woodlands Iroquois rabbit dance; the Penobscot and Passamaquoddy couple dances; various stomp dances of the Cherokee, Creek, Seminole, Shawnee, Eucha, and Quapaw; the Choctaw wedding and Muskogee dance; the Plains powwow two-step; the Ute bear dance; the Southwest Pueblo corn dances; the Navajo and Apache social dances, and many others).

In the culturally rich Southwest a fairly common sight at special ceremonials is the line of dancers, all males, each holding gourd rattles, singing to their own accompaniment. Many of these religious society dances are only partially exposed to the public, if at all, while viewers are prohibited from taking photos or making sketches without prior approval from tribal officials. Masked dances are especially restrictive in that they are done by specially initiated performers, and the music may not be recorded (the Zuni Shalako dances, performed in December; the Hopi Niman Kachina dances, performed in July; the Kiva dances, performed year-round;

The corn dance of the southwestern Pueblo Indians is held during spring and summer to ensure a good corn harvest. Here, members of the Santa Clara Pueblo in New Mexico are shown performing with the dance's characteristic gourd rattles and evergreen branches.

the Navajo Yeibichai dances, performed in winter; and healing ceremonies and masked dances of other culture areas).

Dance paraphernalia and attire varies widely; some examples are: simple street clothing, as in East Woodlands stomp dances and social dances; special sash and beads, as in Plains Indian gourd dances; highly elaborate, ornate, head-to-toe special clothing, as in the Shalako dances, in which the dancer is completely hidden by the costume; a headpiece of deer tail and porcupine quills, a velvet shirt, silver armbands, leggings of broadcloth, beaded moccasins, bells, and beaded garters, as in the events of the Plains Indians Osage War Dance Society; war-dance feather outfits of the Crow, Blackfeet, Sioux, Cheyenne, Nez Percé, Cree, Arapahoe; kilts, leg rattles, spruce branches, headpieces of imitation animal heads or real buffalo skin, as found in the Southwest; or simply the fur parkas worn by the Eskimo in Alaska. Generally, the male dance costume is more colorful than that of the female, although in California the women wear ornate abalone shells, feathers, and woven basket hats.

LOUIS W. BALLARD
(HUNKA-NO-ZHE)

Bibliography: Ballard, Louis W., *The American Indian Sings*, books 1-2 (1970), *Music of North American Indians* (1975), and *My Music Reaches to the Sky* (1973); Burlin, Natalie, *The Indians' Book* (1968); Densmore, Frances, *The American Indians and Their Music* (1926; repr. 1975) and several books on the music of individual tribes (1910-57); Highwater, Jamake, *Ritual of the Wind: American Indian Ceremonies, Music and Dances* (1977); Nettl, Bruno, *North American Indian Styles* (1954); Powers, William K., *Indian Dancing and Costumes* (1966).

indicator

An indicator is a chemical substance that, by being able to change color, provides visual evidence of the nature of the chemical system in which it is placed. Most indicators are complicated organic molecules that exist in two different colored forms (sometimes one form is colorless) in different chemical environments, such as acidic or basic solutions.

Indicators are used mainly to signal the completion of TITRATIONS, usually by changing color at the endpoint, which is when sufficient titrant has been added to react with all the substance being analyzed in the sample solution. Ordinarily, the tiny amount of intensely colored indicator needed to impart a distinct color consumes a negligibly small volume of titrant when the color changes at the endpoint.

COMMON ACID-BASE INDICATORS

Indicator	Approximate pH Range	Color Change
Methyl green	0.2-1.8	Yellow to blue
Thymol blue	1.2-2.8	Red to yellow
Bromophenol blue	3.0-4.6	Yellow to blue
Methyl orange	3.2-4.4	Red to yellow
Methyl red	4.8-6.0	Red to yellow
Alizarin	5.6-7.2	Yellow to red
Bromothymol blue	6.0-7.6	Yellow to blue
Neutral red	6.8-8.0	Red to amber
Metacresol purple	7.4-9.0	Yellow to purple
Phenolphthalein	8.2-10.0	Colorless to pink
Alizarin yellow R	10.1-12.0	Yellow to red

Most indicators can be classified according to their color change mechanisms or kinds of titrations for which they are applicable. Acid-base indicators respond to changes in hydrogen ion concentration (see pH), oxidation-reduction indicators to changes in oxidizing strength (potential), and metallochromic indicators (for complexation titrations) to changes in free metal ion concentration. Indicators for precipitation titrations function by adsorbing on a precipitate surface or by forming a (colored) precipitate or colored metal complex. Occasionally, a titrant or analyte such as potassium permanganate is highly colored and serves as its own indicator. Fluorescent indicators are useful in titrating turbid or highly colored solutions.

LAURANCE A. KNECHT

Bibliography: *CRC Handbook of Chemistry and Physics, 1977-78*, 58th ed. (1977).

indictment [in-dyt'-ment]

An indictment in criminal law is a formal, written accusation made by a GRAND JURY, charging someone with committing a crime. A bill of indictment is drafted by a public PROSECUTING ATTORNEY and submitted to a grand jury for its approval. Usually the prosecutor produces witnesses and evidence to support the charges, although the grand jury may conduct its own investigation. If, by a majority vote, it finds sufficient evidence to warrant a trial, the grand jury returns a true bill endorsing the bill of indictment. The indictment must, through a bill of particulars, sufficiently apprise the accused of the offense charged so that he or she can adequately prepare a defense. A grand jury may also make a formal accusation, or "presentment," without indictment by a public prosecutor; an accusation made by the prosecutor without a grand jury is called an information. The 5TH AMENDMENT to the U.S. Constitution requires presentment or indictment for serious federal crimes, whereas information may be used by state courts (see HURTADO V. CALIFORNIA).

indigestion

Indigestion, or dyspepsia, commonly refers to general abdominal discomfort during and after meals and may be the result of specific diseases of the stomach or the intestines. The most frequently occurring symptoms are diarrhea, heartburn, abdominal cramps and pain, gas distress, and nausea. Some common causes of indigestion in the stomach include swallowing air in large amounts and ulcers. In the intestine, indigestion can arise from colitis, viral or bacterial infections, and chronic inflammation. Other causes include gallstones, malignant growths, and emotional tension. A physician should be consulted when the indigestion is persistent.

indigo [in'-di-goh]

Indigo is a blue vat DYE important in dyeing cotton. Until a synthetic indigo was developed, the dye was obtained by fermenting leaves of various species of the tropical leguminous plant *Indigofera*. Indigo was used in India and Egypt long before the time of Christ; Marco Polo described its manufacture in the 13th century. Brought to Europe in the 16th century by the Portuguese, Dutch, and English, indigo was introduced into South Carolina where it became (mid-18th century) the staple crop of the colony. Exports to England reached 453,000 kg (1,000,000 lb) a year in colonial times. (The English later imported better and cheaper indigo from East India, and rice and cotton replaced *Indigofera* as a cash crop in South Carolina.) During the 18th and 19th centuries indigo was the most widely used dye in the United States.

The production of natural indigo requires 400 units of plant material to produce 1 unit of dye. The first synthetic indigo was produced by Adolf von BAEYER in 1880, and today nearly all the world's production is of synthetic rather than natural indigo. In order to make the dye soluble for dyeing cotton, it must first be treated with alkali and a chemical reducing agent. It is then applied to the fabric in a dye bath. After dyeing, the blue in the fabric is made permanent by oxidizing—exposing it to the air.

ISABEL B. WINGATE

Bibliography: Gerber, F., *Indigo and the Antiquity of Dyeing* (1977).

indium [in'-dee-uhm]

Indium is a relatively uncommon metallic element used in engine-bearing coatings, low-melting alloys, and solid-state electronics. Its chemical symbol is In, atomic number 49, and atomic weight 114.82. It belongs to group IIIA in the periodic table, along with boron, aluminum, gallium, and thallium. Ferdinand Reich and H. T. Richter first isolated the element in 1863 at the Freiberg School of Mines in Germany. The name is derived from the intense indigo blue color that indium salts impart to flames; the element's presence still is detected by this method.

Indium is most commonly found in nature associated chemically in low concentration with sulfide minerals of zinc and lead. The average abundance of the element in the

Earth's crust is about 0.1 ppm. Pure indium is a highly lustrous, silver white metal (m.p. 156.17° C, b.p. 2,070° C, density 7.31 g/ml) and is soft and easily deformed under pressure. The metal is a weak reducing agent comparable to copper.

Indium forms salts in the +1 and +3 oxidation states; compounds of the formula type "InCl$_2$" are really mixed In(I) In(III) salts, In(InCl$_4$). The toxicity of most indium compounds is very low. High cost restricts the use of indium and its compounds to special applications.   PHILIP C. KELLER

Bibliography: Cotton, Frank A., and Wilkinson, Geoffrey, *Basic Inorganic Chemistry* (1976); Hampel, C. A., ed., *The Encyclopedia of the Chemical Elements* (1968).

Indo-European languages

The Indo-European languages, spoken today on every continent and by fully half the world's population, all descend from the speech of a single tribe that lived about 5 or 6 thousand years ago in Europe or western Asia. The surviving branches of Indo-European, the name given to the original prehistoric language, are: INDO-IRANIAN, from which descend Bengali, Hindi, Persian, and several other modern languages; BALTIC, which includes modern Lithuanian and Latvian; SLAVIC, including, among others, Russian, Polish, Czech, and Bulgarian; ARMENIAN; Albanian; GREEK; CELTIC, which includes Irish Gaelic, Scottish Gaelic, Welsh, and Breton; Italic or Romance, including LATIN and its descendants Italian, French, Spanish, Portuguese, and Romanian; and GERMANIC, which includes German, Dutch, English, and the Scandinavian languages. At least two branches of Indo-European have died out, Anatolian and Tocharian (see LANGUAGES, EXTINCT).

The oldest written remnants of any Indo-European language date from the 17th century BC; they are in Hittite, a representative of the Anatolian branch. Records of Mycenaean, an early form of Greek, in the writing system known as LINEAR B, are nearly as old. Much Sanskrit and classical Greek also survive from well before the Christian era. Comparison of these and other languages reveals that Indo-European was a highly inflected language. Nouns, for example, were declined into eight different cases, of which Latin has preserved six, and Greek, five. The nouns of present-day English, however, have only two cases: either no inflection or the possessive with final s. Indo-European verbs were conjugated for person, number, voice, tense, mood, and aspect.

Apparently the Indo-Europeans had not invented the wheel, since their reconstructed language has no word for it. Their language did include words for the numbers 1 through 10 and for the number 100, but probably nothing in between. They had a word for copper, perhaps one for bronze, but no word for iron; nor did they have a term for sea or ocean, which suggests that the original tribe lived inland. They had words for the domestic animals sheep, pig, cow, horse, and dog, as well as for the wolf and bear. They also had a name for snow.

Until nearly the end of the 18th century AD, false premises such as the belief that Latin was a corrupt form of Greek prevented anyone from deducing the true relationship among the languages of Europe and Asia. In 1786, however, Sir William JONES, newly arrived in India, suggested that Sanskrit, Greek, and Latin, as well as Germanic and Celtic, descended from an earlier, extinct language; and 30 years later Franz BOPP systematically demonstrated this relationship. Someday it may be equally clear that Indo-European shares a common source with one or more of the many other language families of the world. Semitic (see AFROASIATIC LANGUAGES) and Uralic (see URAL-ALTAIC LANGUAGES) are good candidates for such an affiliation, but so far the evidence is inconclusive.

                                                    DAVID YERKES

Bibliography: Benveniste, Émile, *Indo-European Language and Society*, trans. by Elizabeth Palmer (1973); Lockwood, W. B., *A Panorama of Indo-European Languages* (1972); Pederson, Holger, *The Discovery of Language: Linguistic Science in the Nineteenth Century*, trans. by John Spargo (1959); Thieme, Paul, "The Indo-European Language," *Scientific American*, October 1958; Watkins, Calvert, "Indo-European and the Indo-Europeans," in *The American Heritage Dictionary* (1969).

Indo-Iranian languages   [ir-ayn'-ee-uhn]

Indo-Iranian, or Aryan, is a branch of the Indo-European family of languages. Indo-Iranian itself has three coordinate branches: Indo-Aryan, or Indic, consisting of languages spoken in India, Pakistan, Bangladesh, Nepal, and Sri Lanka by about 450 million people; Iranian, spoken in Iran, Iraq, Afghanistan, Pakistan, Turkey, and the southern USSR by about 50 million people; and Kafiri, or Nuristani, of the Hindu Kush region, spoken by an estimated 100 thousand people. Among the other Indo-European branches, Indo-Iranian shows the closest affinities with BALTIC and SLAVIC—sometimes grouped together as Balto-Slavonic. Indo-Iranian's ancestral home is traced to the southern USSR, with outposts as far west as Hungary, where Ossetic was spoken. Romany, the language of the Gypsies, is descended from Indic.

Indic. Vedic (c.1200 BC) and the later Classical Sanskrit (see AFROASIATIC LANGUAGES) together constitute Old Indic. Middle Indic extends from Prakrit (c.450 BC) and Apabhramsa (AD c.250) to about the year 1000, when it gave way to the scores of Modern Indic languages, notably Hindi, Urdu, Bhihari, Rajastani, Bengali, Assamese, Oriya, Sindhi, Nepali, Pahari, Kashmiri, Punjabi, Gujarati, Marathi, Konkani, Maldivian, and Sinhalese. The canonical literatures of Hinduism, Buddhism, and Jainism are written in Sanskrit and Prakrit, and the literary use of Sanskrit continues to the present day. Pali, Ardhamagadhi, Maharashtri, and Paisaci are some of the more important Prakrit dialects.

Sanskrit is a highly inflected language, with elaborate noun, adjective, and verb morphologies. Nouns and adjectives are declined into three genders, three numbers, and eight cases. Verb conjugations include the present, future, aorist, perfect, imperfect, and pluperfect tenses, in the indicative and five other moods, with active, middle, and passive voices. Sanskrit also has compounds, participles, and verbal nouns. Much of this complexity is absent, however, from the various present-day descendants of Sanskrit. Although Marathi and Konkani retain three grammatical genders, Hindi has only masculine and feminine, and Bengali, Assamese, and Oriya do not distinguish gender at all. Dual number—the grammatical number denoting two—has been lost, and most Modern Indic languages distinguish only two cases, the nominative and oblique. The verb stem has become so regularized that tenses often must be indicated periphrastically. The simplified case system has led to subject-object-verb being the normal word order, except in Kashmiri, where the object follows the verb.

Most Indic languages are written in the Devanagari script, which has been traced to North Semitic. Urdu, Sindhi, Kashmiri, and Punjabi also employ the Arabic alphabet (see ARABIC LANGUAGE). Usually, a one-to-one correspondence is maintained between the Devanagari letters and the sounds they represent. Diacritical marks indicate noninitial vowels.

Iranian. Ancient Iranian (600–300 BC) comprises Avestan, the language of Zoroastrian religious tradition, and Old Persian, the language of the Achaemenid rulers. Pahlavi, Manichaean, and Inscriptional Middle Persian constitute one branch of Middle Iranian (300 BC–AD 950), and Parthian, Sogdian, and Saka—including the Khotanese of Buddhist literature—constitute another. In addition to Persian or Farsi, Pashto, Tadzhik, Ossetic, Kurdish, and Baluchi, all of which have literary traditions, Modern Iranian includes many lesser-known languages, such as Wakhi, Yaghnobi, and Shugni. Unlike Indic, however, Iranian lacks lineal continuity from one stage to another.

The phonology and, to a lesser extent, the morphology of Vedic Sanskrit and Ancient Iranian are almost identical. As with Sanskrit, simplification and loss of inflection has meant that the flexible word order of Ancient Iranian has had to give way to the rigid word orders found in Modern Iranian languages. Indo-European diphthongs were simplified in Indic, but not in Iranian.

CUNEIFORM syllabary, Aramaic, Pahlavi, Greek, and Brahmi scripts have all been used at different times for the Iranian languages. Now, however, the Arabic alphabet, of Aramaic origin, generally prevails.

Kafiri. The identification of Kafiri as a third branch of Indo-

Iranian is somewhat uncertain. Kafiri was once grouped with Kashmiri, Shina, Indus Kohistani, and Khowar as a Dardic language, descended from Paisaci, the Prakrit dialect of northwestern India. Despite many lexical similarities, it is now realized that Kafiri maintains certain archaic phonological features no longer found in either Indic or Iranian.

R. RADHAKRISHNAN

Bibliography: Bloch, Jules, *Indo-Aryan, from the Vedas to Modern Times,* trans. by Alfred Master, rev. ed. (1965); Boyle, John A., *The Grammar of Modern Persian* (1966); Burrow, Thomas, *The Sanskrit Language,* 2d ed. (1965); Chatterji, S. K., *Indo-Aryan and Hindi,* 2d ed. (1960); Ghatage, A. M., *Historical Linguistics and Indo-Aryan Languages* (1962); Gray, Louis H., *Indo-Iranian Phonology* (1902; repr. 1965); Kent, Roland G., *Old Persian* (1950); Rastorgueva, V. S., *A Short Sketch of the Grammar of Persian,* trans. by Steven P. Hill (1964); Sebeok, Thomas A., ed., *Linguistics in South Asia* (1969).

Indochina [in-doh-chy′-nuh]

Indochina (French: Indochine) was the name given to France's former dependency in Southeast Asia, an area comprising the present-day states of KAMPUCHEA, LAOS, and VIETNAM. French rule was established between 1862 and 1893. In 1887 the French created the Union of Indochina, a federation of the colony of COCHIN CHINA (southern Vietnam) and the protectorates of ANNAM (central Vietnam), TONKIN (northern Vietnam), and Cambodia (Kampuchea); the protectorate of Laos was added in 1893. French rule was interrupted by Japanese incursions during World War II. After the war France agreed to grant self-government to Vietnam, Laos, and Cambodia within the FRENCH UNION. The Vietnamese nationalists rejected this arrangement, and prolonged bitter fighting culminated in the French defeat (1954) at DIEN BIEN PHU. France withdrew from Indochina in accordance with the terms of the GENEVA CONFERENCE of 1954.

Indochina War: see VIETNAM WAR.

Indonesia [in-doh-nee′-zhuh]

The Republic of Indonesia is located in Southeast Asia on an archipelago of more than 3,000 islands astride the equator. SUMATRA, the westernmost major island, lies south of Burma, while IRIAN JAYA on the island of NEW GUINEA is the country's eastern extreme. The total area of all the islands approximates that of Mexico. The islands command vital sea routes between Australia, Europe, and the Asian mainland and are the principal link between the Indian and Pacific oceans. The islands lie within the Java (see JAVA SEA), Flores, Banda, and Molucca seas, and are interrupted by the Strait of MALACCA, SUNDA STRAIT, and MAKASAR STRAIT. Traders, immigrants, cultural ideas, and technologies reaching Indonesia have resulted in great internal diversity. Indonesia, formerly part of the Netherlands East Indies, proclaimed its independence on Aug. 17, 1945, after more than 300 years of Dutch control.

LAND AND RESOURCES

Territories on five islands make up 90% of Indonesia. The largest territory, Kalimantan, occupies the southern two-thirds of the island of BORNEO and comprises 28% of Indonesia's total area. Second in size is the island of Sumatra (Sumatera), with 24% of the total area. Irian Jaya, which occupies the western half of New Guinea, forms 22% of the country; SULAWESI (Celebes), 10%; and the islands of JAVA and Madura—inhabited by 64% of the population—only 7%. Notable small islands include BALI, TIMOR, Lombok, and Sumba of the Lesser SUNDA ISLANDS, and Halmahera, Buru, Seram, and Ambon, parts of the MOLUCCAS (formerly known as the Spice Islands).

High mountains, some of them volcanic, extend the length of the archipelago. On Irian Jaya, Indonesia's highest mountain, Jaya, reaches 5,030 m (16,495 ft). High mountains also form the southern edge of Sumatra. They continue across the Sunda Strait, where the famous volcano KRAKATOA is located, and into Java, where they rise to 3,676 m (12,060 ft) in Semeru. On Sulawesi, the mountains rise to 3,455 m (11,335 ft) in Rantekombolo. Extensive, swampy lowlands characterize the eastern half of Sumatra, southern Kalimantan, and southeastern Irian Jaya.

INDONESIA

Official Name: Republic of Indonesia
Capital and Largest City: Jakarta (1975 est. pop., 4,810,531)
Area: 1,919,494 km² (740,925 mi²)
Elevation: *Highest*—Jaya, 5,030 m (16,495 ft); *lowest*—sea level, along coasts
Population: 145,958,000 (1979 est.). *Distribution*—19% urban, 81% rural; *density,* 76 persons per km² (197 per mi²); *annual rate of increase* (1970-76), 2.6%
Principal Languages: Bahasa Indonesia, various Malayo-Polynesian languages, English
Principal Religions: Islam, Christianity, Hinduism
Principal Products: *Agriculture*—rice, rubber, copra, tea and coffee, sugarcane, palm oil, cassava, tobacco, timber. *Manufacturing and industry*—textiles, food processing, tires, petroleum and sugar refining, cement. *Mining*—petroleum and natural gas, tin, bauxite, nickel
Railroads: 7,891 km/4,900 mi (1974)
Roads: 21,000 km/12,600 mi (1974 paved)
Currency: 1 Rupiah = 100 sen

Soils. As in many rainy, tropical areas, the soils are predominantly infertile in Indonesia because of leaching. The most productive are those on Java and adjacent islands. Soil nutrients there are replenished by frequent volcanic eruptions, and the lavas' alkalinity is conducive to plant growth.
Climate. Most islands are hot and humid throughout the year. Rain falls primarily from December to March, when the winter monsoon dominates, blowing from the Asian mainland. Only western Java and the Lesser Sunda Islands have a dry season, from June to September, when dry winds blow from the interior of Australia's deserts. Temperatures in coastal areas range from 24° C to 28° C (75° F to 85° F), while mountains are cooler. The average annual rainfall varies from 3,040 mm (120 in) in Sumatra, Kalimantan, and Irian Jaya to 1,015 mm (40 in) in the Lesser Sundas.
Drainage. Rivers are numerous, short, and important for irrigation. The longest is the Mamberamo, on Irian Jaya, navigable for 160 km (100 mi). Lake Toba (1,300 km²/ 502 mi²), in the Barisan Mountains of northern Sumatra, was formed within the world's largest caldera of a volcano.
Vegetation and Animal Life. Tropical rain forest covers most of the islands; this is characterized by a dense overhead canopy of trees, an abundance of tree species, and numerous lianas (vines), along with ferns, orchids, and other epiphytes. The monsoon forests are composed primarily of stands of bamboo with a seasonal fall of leaves. Indonesia's animals have an Asian affinity in the west and an Australian relationship in the east, suggesting the past existence of land bridges between the islands and the two continents. In the Lesser Sundas, the island of Komodo is the last protected habitation for the Komodo dragon, the world's largest lizard.
Resources. Indonesia is potentially rich in mineral resources. The most important is crude petroleum—with associated deposits of natural gas—extracted in eastern Sumatra and Kalimantan. Tin ores are found on a number of islands, as well as deposits of bauxite, nickel, and coal. Large reserves of low-grade iron ore have been reported, but no production has begun.

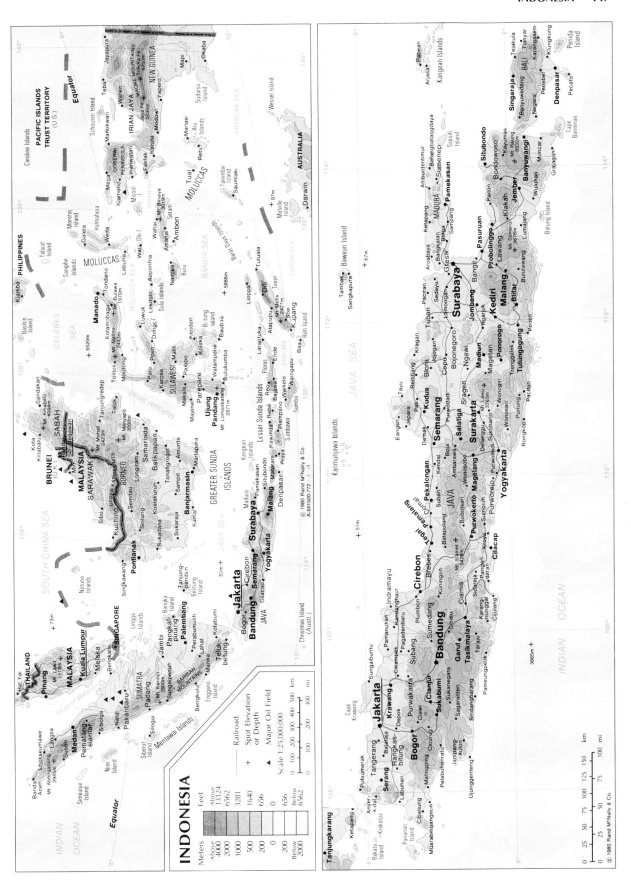

INDONESIA

Meters	Feet	
Above 4000	Above 13124	
2000	6562	
1000	3281	
500	1640	
200	656	
0	0	
200	656	Below
Below 2000	6562	

Railroad

+ 2985m Spot Elevation or Depth

▲ Major Oil Field

Scale 1:25,000,000

© 1980 Rand McNally & Co.
A-561500-772 -1 -1

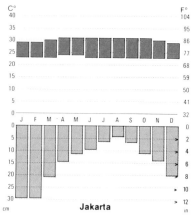

Jakarta

(Above) *Bars indicate monthly ranges of temperatures* (red) *and precipitation* (blue) *of Jakarta, the capital and largest city of Indonesia. Located on the island of Java, the city has a tropical wet climate with constant temperatures and high precipitation.*

(Left) *Rice terraces on the island of Bali mark the location of the small rural settlements of the mountainous interior. More than 60% of Indonesia's labor force earns its living through agriculture, with the majority on Java, Madura, and Bali.*

PEOPLE

Indonesia has one of the most ethnically diverse populations in the world. More than 300 distinct groups are recognized. The largest is the Javanese, who constitute 40–50% of the total population and form the majority on densely populated Java. Sundanese in western Java make up about 15% of the total population, and the Madurese, on Madura, an estimated 5–10%. Smaller, but regionally important, ethnic peoples include the BALINESE, BATAK, DAYAK, PAPUANS, ACEHNESE (Achinese), and Toraja. The largest nonindigenous group is the Chinese, constituting about 3% of the total population and living mainly on Java and Sumatra.

Language. The official language is Bahasa Indonesia (Indonesian), which evolved from Pasar Malay, a dialect widely spoken on Sumatra and used by traders in the islands. In addition, about 200 languages, most of Malayo-Polynesian origin, are spoken locally, including Javanese, Sundanese, Madurese, and Balinese.

Religion. Islam is the dominant religion in Indonesia today and is practiced by an estimated 90% of the population. Hinduism, widespread in the archipelago before the 14th century, is now the religion of 3% of the population, mostly on Bali. About 5% are Christian, primarily Protestant; and 2–3%, mostly Chinese, follow Buddhist-Taoist teachings.

Demography. Indonesia is the world's fifth most populous nation. The country continues to grow rapidly, adding 2,000,000 persons annually. About 64% of the population is crowded onto the island of Java, where the density exceeds 600 persons per km² (1,550 per mi²), among the highest in the world. Other islands, by contrast, are sparsely populated. The rapid growth rate results from a birthrate that continues to be one of the highest in Asia, 43 per 1,000, while the death rate has been reduced to 17 per 1,000. The largest cities are JAKARTA (the capital), BANDUNG, SURABAYA, Malang, Surakarta, and Yogyakarta, all on Java.

Education and Health. Education is free and compulsory between the ages of 8 and 14, but because 45% of the population is under the age of 15, facilities are severely strained. About 60% of the population is literate. The University of Indonesia (1950) at Jakarta and 50 other institutions provide higher education opportunities. (See SOUTHEAST ASIAN UNIVERSITIES.) Health facilities are limited; a severe shortage of doctors and nurses developed after the departure of the Dutch in the 1950s. Statistically, one doctor is available for approxi-

mately every 21,000 inhabitants, but because at least 40% of the physicians are concentrated in Jakarta, many rural areas are grossly underserved. The infant mortality rate is high—137 per 1,000 live births. Malaria and tuberculosis are still common, but the incidence of cholera, hepatitis, and typhoid fever has been reduced.

The Arts. The Javanese are famous for BATIK, a cloth widely used for sarongs. It is imprinted with intricate, elaborate designs by waxing and dyeing fabric. Indonesia is also known for SHADOW PLAYS, a popular art form used to instill moral values and for social comment. The Museum of Indonesian Culture in Jakarta houses an extensive collection of early Indonesian ceramics. (See also SOUTHEAST ASIAN ART AND ARCHITECTURE.)

ECONOMIC ACTIVITY

Indonesia's traditional subsistence and trading economy was altered radically under the rule of the Dutch. Export crops were emphasized, and for many years their growth was mandatory. A state-dominated, centralized economic system was developed after independence, but it was replaced in 1969 by the "New Order" of President Suharto and a return to a mainly free-enterprise system.

Mining and Manufacturing. Mining employs less than 1% of the labor force but accounts for 21% of the gross national product. The principal mineral is petroleum, which accounts for 70% of all export earnings; associated natural gas deposits are beginning to be worked, and liquefied gas is being exported. Most petroleum is produced in eastern Sumatra and Kalimantan, but new fields have been located off Java and northern Sumatra. Pertamina, the state oil company, became bankrupt in 1976 because of unsound contracts for petroleum tankers and general mismanagement. As a result, Indonesia, a member of the ORGANIZATION OF PETROLEUM EXPORTING COUNTRIES, has not been able to gain much by rising petroleum prices.

Tin is abundant on the islands of Bangka, Belitung, and Singkep, and Indonesia ranks third in the non-Communist world in tin production. Bauxite is mined on the island of Bintan, and nickel on Sulawesi.

Manufacturing and handicrafts employ slightly over 7% of the labor force and account for 11% of the gross national product. Most manufacturing establishments are on Java, where Jakarta and Surabaya are the leading industrial centers. Only about 25% of total manufacturing occurs on Sumatra,

Some of the landscape of Djawa Timur (East Java), one of the three major provinces of Java, is covered with craters as a result of intense volcanic activity. Lying between Sumatra and Bali, Java is the fourth largest island of the Indonesian archipelago.

After a Balinese funeral procession the deceased is cremated in accordance with Hindu tradition. When most of the Indonesian islands came under Islamic rule during the 16th century, Bali resisted the invaders and remains the nation's center of Hindu culture.

and very little on other islands. Textiles are the chief manufactured item. Other manufacturing activities include automobile assembly and the production of tires and chemical fertilizers.

Energy. Power facilities are state owned and presently inadequate. In 1976 the installed capacity was 1,100,000 kW, of which 450,000 was from hydroelectric plants. Additional hydroelectric power projects have been planned.

Agriculture. Agriculture continues to be the mainstay of the Indonesian economy, employing about 61% of the total labor force. The traditional systems have been superseded in most cases by highly intensive production methods. Indonesia's government was an early proponent of the GREEN REVOLUTION, and encouraged multiple plantings of high-yield rice on terraced lands. This, coupled with lowered birthrates, was to move the country toward agricultural self-sufficiency. Expectations have not been met, however, and Indonesia has become the world's largest rice importer. Insect pests and erosional floods have been blamed for the shortage. Because the mountain slopes have been stripped of trees used for firewood, the heavy rains wash away the soil and flood the terraces. Efforts have been made to encourage the efficient planting of mountain-grown crops such as cassava (manioc), tea, and coffee. Other cash crops grown are tobacco, sugarcane, copra, cacao, and spices. Palm oil and rubber are exported in quantity.

Forestry and Fishing. Indonesia has abundant forests, and lumber—especially teak—is now the leading nonpetroleum export. Fish are locally important, but commercial fishing, despite the vast potential of the surrounding seas, is largely undeveloped.

Transportation. Java is the only island with a well-developed transportation network, but many roads are unpaved and poorly maintained. On Sumatra, only major cities are served by highways and rail lines. Travel on other islands is mainly by sea and dirt tracks. Air transportation linking the islands is provided by Garuda National Airways. Tanjungpriok, the port for Jakarta, is the nation's principal port. Communications are state controlled.

Trade. Indonesia's principal trading partners are Japan and the United States. The country exports crude petroleum and petroleum products, lumber, rubber, and palm oil. Its principal imports are rice, machinery, and fertilizers.

GOVERNMENT

The constitution of August 1945 was restored on July 5, 1959, in place of two provisional constitutions that had been adopted in 1950. Executive power is vested in the president, who is elected by the People's Consultative Assembly (MPR) for a 5-year term, and in the president's appointed cabinet. Legislative power rests with the 460-member Council of Representatives, but in effect the president rules by decree. Governors and regents appointed by the central government administer local government for 27 provinces and 281 regencies.

HISTORY

Indonesia is thought to have been settled mainly by peoples from Malaya and Oceania, and the area was dominated from the 3d to the 13th century by the Hindu and Buddhist Indianized kingdoms of the SRIVIJAYA EMPIRE, Mataram, Sailendra, Kediri, and the MAJAPAHIT EMPIRE. Islamic influences, brought by Arabic and other traders in the 14th and 15th centuries, replaced the Indian religions in most areas except Bali. From 1602 until 1798 most of the islands were controlled by the Dutch East India Company (see EAST INDIA COMPANY, DUTCH), and from 1816 to 1949, Indonesia was regarded as a colony of the Netherlands. During World War II, Japan occupied the islands and encouraged many Indonesians in their quest for independence.

On Aug. 17, 1945, Indonesian nationalists led by SUKARNO and Muhammad Hatta proclaimed the nation independent. On Dec. 27, 1949, after much dispute, the Netherlands transferred sovereignty to the new nation. West Irian became part of Indonesia in 1963, and was renamed Irian Jaya in 1973. On July 17, 1976, the former Portuguese territory of East Timor was annexed.

Sukarno was Indonesia's first president. He ruled from 1945 to 1965, backed by the military and supported by the Asian Communist nations. During these years, the economy declined, and Indonesia's continually closer ties with the Com-

Jakarta, located on the northwestern coast of Java, is the capital and largest city of Indonesia. A port city and industrial and administrative center, Jakarta has experienced rapid growth since the country's independence in 1949. The city's architecture blends 17th-century churches, canals, and drawbridges built by the Portuguese and Dutch with modern structures built during this century.

munist bloc stifled assistance from Western nations. At the end of September 1965, an attempted Communist coup led to an anti-Communist takeover of the government by the military under General SUHARTO. An estimated 250,000 were killed in the fighting. Sukarno continued temporarily as president, but de facto control of the nation was transferred to Suharto, who became acting president in March 1967.

Under Suharto, Indonesia began to look to the West for economic assistance, while attempting to gain the internal stability that would encourage foreign investment. The Inter-Governmental Group on Indonesia (IGGI) was formed in 1966 by 12 nations to assist in Indonesia's economic development. After withdrawing from the United Nations in 1965, Indonesia rejoined that international body in 1966. Indonesia also became a charter member of the Association of Southeast Asian Nations, founded in 1967. Raids against Malaysia, initiated by Sukarno in 1964, were ended by Suharto. Elections, held in 1968 for the first time in 13 years, gave Suharto the presidency. He was reelected in 1973 and 1978, supported by his GOLKAR political party. In 1969, REPELITA I, the First Five-Year Plan, was inaugurated. With U.S. assistance, Indonesia set up priorities in economic policy to make the country

more self-sufficient. This first attempt at central planning was followed by REPELITA II, in effect from 1974 to 1979, which focused on the improvement of agricultural methods at home. Both plans recommended the retention of foreign investments and technology in mining and petroleum exploration, the two most critical areas of the Indonesian economy.

THOMAS R. LEINBACH

Bibliography: American University, *Area Handbook for Indonesia*, rev. ed. (1975); Brackman, Arnold C., *The Communist Collapse in Indonesia* (1969); Crouch, Harold, *The Army and Politics in Indonesia* (1978); Fryer, D. W., and Jackson, James C., *Indonesia* (1977); Holt, Claire, et al., *Culture and Politics in Indonesia* (1972); Kosut, Hal, ed., *Indonesia: The Sukarno Years* (1967); Peacock, James L., *Indonesia: An Anthropological Perspective* (1973); Sievers, Allen M., *The Mystical World of Indonesia* (1974); Smith, Datus C., *The Land and People of Indonesia*, rev. ed. (1968); Wolf, Charles, *The Indonesian Story* (1948; repr. 1973).

Indore [in-dor']

Indore is the largest city in Madhya Pradesh state in west central India. It is situated 558 m (1,830 ft) above sea level, at the confluence of the Khan and Saraswati rivers. Its population is 572,622 (1971). The city is the major rail and road hub of Madhya Pradesh state. Cotton textiles are the city's major product, but iron and steel, chemicals, and machinery are also manufactured there. Indore University was established in 1964.

Indore, founded as a trade market in 1715, grew under the Holkar dynasty (1733–1818); their palace still stands in the main square. The city became the capital of the Indore princely state in 1818. Between 1948 and 1956, Indore served as the summer capital of the former Madhya Bharat state.

ASHOK K. DUTT

indri

The indri is an arboreal, lemurlike primate, *Indri indri*, formerly found in the rain forests along the eastern coast of Madagascar from sea level to mountain heights of nearly 1,800 m (6,000 ft), but now largely confined to a small area in the central coastal region. Its numbers are steadily dwindling due to habitat destruction (deforestation) by humans. The indri is a member of the family Indriidae, which also contains three other living species; the avahi, or woolly indri, *Avahi*, and two species of sifakas, *Propithecus*, all native to Madagascar. The indri stands about 70 cm (2.5 ft) tall and has a narrow, nearly hairless muzzle, very long hind legs, and a stumpy, 5-cm (2-in) tail. Its coat is dense and silky and variable in pattern but often is black on the head, shoulders, back, upper arms, front of the thighs, and hands and feet, and white, gray, or pale red on the rump, the back of the legs, and the lower arms.

Indris are diurnal and feed on leaves, fruit, and flowers. They may live singly or, more commonly, in small family groups of 2 to 5 individuals. It is thought that they produce a

Canals in the city of Banjarmasin are a major transportation system of the capital and principal seaport of South Borneo province. Located about 16 km (10 mi) from the Java Sea, on the delta of the Martapura and Barito rivers, the city has been built behind dikes on pilings.

The largest of all lemurlike animals, the indri, I. indri, is almost exclusively arboreal, rarely descending from the trees. Its hands, six times as long as they are wide, are adapted for grasping branches.

single young after a gestation period of about 60 days. The indri has a laryngeal air sac, or throat pouch, and is able to produce very loud doglike howls, often uttered in chorus throughout the forest.

The avahi, *A. laniger*, sometimes known as the woolly lemur, is a nocturnal, arboreal, and usually solitary animal of the rain forest, where it feeds on leaves, buds, and bark. It has a thick, woolly, gray brown fur and is about 40 cm (16 in) long, plus a thickly furred tail about as long as the body. It is thought to produce a single young after a gestation period of 4 to 5 months.

EDWIN E. ROSENBLUM

inductance

Inductance is a property of an electrical circuit in which an electromotive force (emf) is induced (see ELECTROMAGNETIC INDUCTION) by a change in current; the current change may occur either in the circuit itself or in a nearby circuit. The symbol for inductance is *L*; it is measured in units of henrys, named for Joseph Henry.

Inductance results from the interaction of the magnetic field, established by the current, with the charges inside the conductor. Inductance can be increased by winding wire into a coil to strengthen the interaction. According to LENZ'S LAW, if a changing current flows through the inductance coil, or INDUCTOR, an emf is induced which opposes the *change* in the current flow. Thus, a drop in the current induces an emf in the same direction as the current, supporting the original current; if the current increases, the induced emf acts in the opposite direction, opposing it.

If a single coil is involved, the phenomena is known as self-inductance. Two nearby coils can be linked by mutual inductance, as in a TRANSFORMER.

induction

Induction is a major kind of reasoning process in which a conclusion is drawn from particular cases. It is usually contrasted with deduction, the reasoning process in which the conclusion logically follows from the premises, and in which the conclusion has to be true if the premises are true. In inductive reasoning, on the contrary, there is no logical movement from premises to conclusion. The premises constitute

good reasons for accepting the conclusion. The premises in inductive reasoning are usually based on facts or observations. There is always a possibility, though, that the premises may be true while the conclusion is false, since there is not necessarily a logical relationship between premises and conclusion. For example, a child growing up in a community where only English is spoken may wrongly conclude by induction that everyone in the world speaks English.

Inductive reasoning plays a very important role in our acquisition of knowledge about the world. Practically all our scientific and practical knowledge is based on induction. Past experience is used as the basis for generalizing about future experience. David HUME pointed out what is now called the problem of induction, namely, that the results of the inductive processes are always in doubt, because one cannot justify the movement to the conclusion, and the conclusion can turn out to be false. There has been a great deal of work in the last 200 years in the philosophy of science to find some solution to Hume's analysis—some way of justifying inductive procedures. This type of study continues because, Hume's arguments notwithstanding, we live according to inductive reasoning, which is essential to science, law, and other fields of knowledge.

What is called mathematical induction is actually not a form of induction at all; rather, it is a special kind of deductive mathematical reasoning process (see INDUCTION, MATHEMATICAL).

RICHARD H. POPKIN

Bibliography: Broad, C. D., *Induction, Probability and Causation* (1969); Cohen, Laurence J., *The Implications of Induction* (1970); Harrod, Roy, *Foundations of Inductive Logic* (1956; repr. 1974); Toulmin, Stephen, *The Uses of Arguement* (1958).

induction, electromagnetic: see

ELECTROMAGNETIC INDUCTION.

induction, mathematical

Mathematical induction is a special technique used to prove any proposition that involves the positive integers *n*. The theorem of mathematical induction states that if a proposition is correct for $n = 1$, and if it is true for $n = k + 1$ whenever it is true for an arbitrary positive integer *k*, then the proposition is true for all positive integers *n*. This theorem is basic to the study of algebra.

An example is the proof of the equation $1 + 3 + 5 \ldots + (2n - 1) = n^2$. For $n = 1$, the equation reduces to $1 = 1$, which is obviously true. The next step is to see if the equation is true for $n = k + 1$ when it is assumed to be true for $n = k$. Making the substitution $n = k + 1$ yields the expression $1 + 3 + 5 + \ldots + (2k - 1) + [2(k + 1) - 1] = (k + 1)^2$. This simplifies to $n = k$, which is assumed true, so the original expression must also be true.

Note that a mathematical PROOF carried out by mathematical induction uses a deductive method of proof and is thus actually a form of DEDUCTION. It does not use the logical technique of INDUCTION (inductive logic).

Bibliography: Leithold, Louis, *College Algebra* (1975); Richardson, Moses, and Richardson, Leonard F., *College Algebra*, 4th ed. (1973).

inductor

An inductor is an electrical component that opposes any change in an electrical current. Also known as a coil or choke, it is composed of a coil of wire wound around a supporting core that may be magnetic or nonmagnetic. When a current running through the coil increases or decreases, the magnetic field around the coil also increases or decreases, generating (because of ELECTROMAGNETIC INDUCTION) a current in the coil opposing the original current. Because of this property, known as INDUCTANCE, an inductor is often used in an AC-to-DC power-supply filter circuit to reduce the fluctuations and smooth the current.

Another important application is in a fluorescent light circuit, in which a voltage of several hundred volts is required to cause the initial current, and a much lower voltage is needed to keep the lamp lighted. A type of inductor known as a ballast serves both needs. In the preheat type of fluorescent lamp, a starter is in series with the lamp filaments and the ballast. This starter opens a few seconds after the lamp is turned on, interrupting current through the ballast. The collapse of the magnetic field induces a high voltage in the inductor, which lights the lamp. The voltage across the lamp decreases, and the excess voltage is dropped across the ballast because of its inductive reactance (opposition to AC current due to inductance).

Because of the good magnetic properties of iron, the inductance of iron-core coils can be as high as 50-100 henries (H). Such coils are generally used at low frequencies, such as 60 or 400 Hz. Iron-core coils, however, can also be used with DC, as in the ignition system of an automobile, in which two coils are wound on the same core. The primary is composed of several hundred turns of heavy wire and is connected to the 12-V DC supply through a set of points or a transistor switch. The secondary coil is composed of several thousand turns that produce 20 to 40 kV for the spark plugs when the primary side is interrupted. Such an arrangement of inductors is called an induction coil, although it is actually a TRANSFORMER.

High-frequency air-core inductors are wound on a fiber, ceramic, or plastic nonmagnetic core. Their inductances may be only a few microhenries (μH) or millihenries (mH) and are used primarily in communication equipment. In radio amplifiers the output from one stage may be inductively coupled to the next stage by two coils wound on the same core. Often, the degree of coupling may be varied by using a powdered-iron movable slug within the core. This varies the inductance and the tuning or alignment of the radio.

Since an inductor has no effect on DC (except its resistance), it is often used in the ignition coil's high-voltage lead as a radio-frequency choke to block radio interference resulting from an automobile's ignition system.   ALLEN MOTTERSHEAD

Bibliography: Shrader, Robert L., *Electronic Communication*, 3d ed. (1975).

indulgences   [in-duhl'-jen-sez]

In the Roman Catholic church, an indulgence is the remission of the punishment that remains due for SIN after sacramental absolution. This remission, which is granted by ecclesiastical authority, applies only to temporal punishment (in this world or in PURGATORY) and is, therefore, to be distinguished from divine forgiveness.

The system of indulgences, which developed out of the penitential discipline of the early church, became, in the medieval period, a means by which punishments for breaches of church discipline were commuted for proportionate fines. This practice was so general that the sale of indulgences was an important source of church revenue. The proceeds were used for many worthy purposes, such as the maintenance of religious orders and the building of churches. But the system was also subject to much abuse. This led to the protest of Martin LUTHER, whose 95 theses against the misuse of indulgences (1517) precipitated the REFORMATION in Germany. At the Council of Trent (see TRENT, COUNCIL OF) the Roman Catholic church reformed the system, which was continued only under carefully controlled conditions. A decree of Pope Pius V (1567) finally prohibited the sale of indulgences.
CHARLES W. RANSON

Indus   [in'-duhs]

The Indus River, one of South Asia's longest rivers, flows for 2,900 km (1,800 mi) from its source in Tibet through northern India and then for most of its course through Pakistan. Its drainage basin covers 1,165,500 km² (450,000 mi²). Its waters irrigate the arid PUNJAB plain, making it Pakistan's most productive agricultural region, with wheat, corn, rice, millet, dates, and other fruits grown. Large dams have been constructed by both Pakistan and India, providing water for irrigation and hydroelectric power. Tarbela Dam, completed in 1974, is the world's largest earth-fill dam.

INDUS RIVER

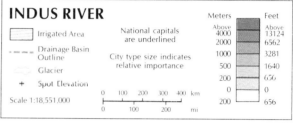

	Meters	Feet
	Above	Above
	4000	13124
	2000	6562
	1000	3281
	500	1640
	200	656
	0	0
	200	656

Irrigated Area

Drainage Basin Outline

Glacier

+ Spot Elevation

National capitals are underlined

City type size indicates relative importance

Scale 1:18,551,000

0   100   200   300   400   km

0   100   200   mi

Temperatures in the Indus Valley range from below 0° C (32° F) in the north in January to a maximum of 38° C (100° F) in the desert areas of Sind and Punjab in July. Rainfall varies between 127 and 508 mm (5 and 20 in). The river's source is the meltwater and streams of the Himalayas and the Karakoram Range. The Indus flows northwestward through the mountainous Indian state of Jammu and Kashmir. In its upper reaches the river is a turbulent, unnavigable stream, which is especially flood-prone between June and September. Its course then turns south, entering Pakistan, and as it leaves the mountains for the arid Punjab plain it becomes broad and silt-laden. Here it receives its major tributary, the Punjab, with that river's five tributaries, the SUTLEJ, Chenab, Jhelum, Ravi, and Beas rivers. The river delta begins at Tatta, about 110 km (70 mi) from the Arabian Sea coast; the river splits into several channels here, each emptying into the sea at a different place.

The Indus Valley fostered human settlement more than 70,000 years ago. Harappa and Mohenjo-daro, the great cities of the INDUS CIVILIZATION, were built along the river around 2500 BC. Until the British period the Indus formed the frontier of India. Use of the river's water has been a source of dispute between India and Pakistan during recent years.

Indus civilization

The Indus civilization, an ancient civilization in South Asia, existed from about 2700 to 1750 BC. It is sometimes referred to as the Harappan civilization, named for the site of Harappa, one of its major centers. Geographically one of the most extensive early civilizations of the Old World, it stretched from north of the Hindu Kush down the entire length of the Indus and beyond into peninsular India; in the west, outposts that extended almost to the present-day Iranian-Pakistani border have been found along the inhospitable Makran coast. Unlike the ancient Sumerian and Egyptian civilizations, which were largely restricted to river valleys and their alluvial plains, remains of the Indus civilization have been found in diverse environmental settings. Its settlements were, however, remarkably similar in layout and material culture.

Origins. Because its script remains undeciphered, the Indus civilization is known only from archaeological evidence. Its origins traditionally were viewed as the result of the diffusion of farming and technology from more advanced cultures in Mesopotamia and on the Iranian plateau to Baluchistan and ultimately to the Indus Valley. Today this theory is seen as largely incorrect. Knowledge about early plant and animal domestication in lands east of the Iranian plateau is still obscure, but the results of excavations at the important site of Mehrgarh, at the foot of the Bolan Pass, indicate that large settlements may have existed as early as the 7th millennium BC.

Two thousand or more years later sites in eastern Baluchistan and the Indus Valley were larger and more numerous; at some, like Kot Diji on the east bank of the Indus, archaeologists have found various distinctive ceramic objects, such as terra-cotta toy carts. From this evidence archaeologists speculate that there took place an early, or pre-Harappan, spread of culture from the Punjab south to the Arabian Sea. Scholars differ as to whether or not these early settlements evolved directly into the urban communities of the mature Indus civilization, but it is clear from archaeological research that by the

The map below illustrates the extent and major cities of the Indus civilization, which existed from about 2700 to 1750 BC in ancient India. The Indus culture, now represented by nearly 70 sites, extended for more than half a million square miles in northwestern India.

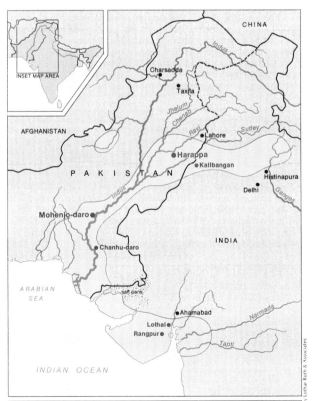

INDUS CIVILIZATION

Area of civilization
c. 2700 to 1750 B.C.

——— Modern boundaries

Major centers of civilization

| 0 | km | 500 |
| 0 | mi | 300 |

late 4th millennium (c.3200 BC) large villages were being formed along the entire course of the Indus River.

Major Centers. The famous cities of the mature Indus civilization were discovered accidentally in the mid-19th century during the construction of a railroad by British engineers. Although it was correctly surmised at that time that antiquities from Harappa predated the historical period, true archaeological excavations were not begun until the 1920s. During that decade the so-called twin capitals of Indus civilization, Mohenjo-daro and Harappa, were excavated under the direction of Sir John MARSHALL; other important settlements were surveyed by Sir Aurel STEIN and N. G. Majumdar. The existence of a great civilization roughly contemporaneous with that of Sumer and of ancient Egypt soon was confirmed. Hundreds of smaller settlements have since been discovered. Recent archaeological investigation has been concentrated on documenting the beginnings of urban life in the area, and a variety of different types of sites have been excavated, including fishing villages, trading outposts, and what may have been a port (see LOTHAL).

One of the most important centers of Indus civilization was Mohenjo-daro, situated along the west bank of the Indus River, about 320 km (200 mi) north of Karachi, Pakistan. Like most cities of the Indus civilization, it consisted of two major areas of occupation: a high citadel to the west and a lower city of domestic dwellings to the east. Careful urban planning is evident in the neat arrangement of the major buildings contained in the citadel, including the placement of a large granary and water tank or bath at right angles to one another. The lower city, which was tightly packed with residential units, was also constructed on a grid pattern consisting of a number of blocks separated by major cross streets. Baked-brick houses faced the street, and domestic life was centered around an enclosed courtyard. Sanitation was provided through an extensive system of covered drains running the length of the main streets and connected by chutes with most residences.

Other important centers include the almost identical city of Harappa, located 640 km (400 mi) northeast of Mohenjo-daro, in the Punjab of India, and the nearby but smaller site of Kalibangan, situated farther east along the banks of the now extinct Ghaggar-Hakra River. Both sites follow the familiar plan of a small, high citadel to the west and a lower city to the east, with the streets arranged in a rectilinear grid pattern. Immediately north of the heavily fortified citadel at Harappa, two sets of barracklike dwellings for laborers were excavated alongside enormous granaries for the city's food supply. At Kalibangan excavation has revealed a pre-Harappan settlement that underwent drastic change when the site was incorporated into the expanding Indus civilization. Southwest of Kalibangan along the same bed of the ancient Ghaggar-Hakra River, several more cities have been discovered, indicating that at the height of the Indus civilization multiple regional centers may have been built according to a standard plan.

Aspects of Indus Culture. The Indus people supported themselves by irrigation-based agriculture. They grew domesticated rice, wheat, and barley, and they may have cultivated dates and cotton. Among the first people in the world known to have kept chickens, they also had dogs, buffalo, and humped cattle. They may also have domesticated pigs, horses, camels, and, possibly, elephants.

Archaeologists have long commented on the uniformity and standardization of the material remains of the Indus civilization. Except in outposts along the Makran coast and in its most remote colonies, Indus cities were all built of baked-brick blocks with a standard proportion of length to width to thickness of 4:2:1. Pottery forms and designs were also remarkably similar throughout the vast area encompassed by the Indus civilization. Few large works of art or pieces of statuary have been discovered, except for several notable examples from Mohenjo-daro and Harappa (see INDIAN ART AND ARCHITECTURE). Spears, knives, and other objects of copper and bronze have been found, but most are of rather poor quality.

The most developed craft appears to have been the carving and drilling of square stamp seals that depict various domes-

Excavations at Mohenjo-daro, one of the major centers of Indus civilization, have yielded rich archaeological finds. (Below) A terra-cotta statue of a female figure driving an oxcart exemplifies the skills of Indus Valley artisans. (Right) The Great Bath at Mohenjo-daro comprised bathing and robing rooms around a pool and courtyard.

tic animals, such as humped bulls, rhinoceroses, and elephants. These seals, numbering in the thousands, are the major source of writings in the pictographic Indus script. Attempts to decipher these symbols have so far been unsuccessful, largely because no major inscriptions have been discovered. This lack of evidence has forced some scholars to conclude that the characters do not represent writing in the same sense as Sumerian CUNEIFORM or Egyptian HIEROGLYPHICS; instead, they may symbolize elaborate heraldic devices or standards that served to identify families and their properties from others. Three seals from Mohenjo-daro show a seated horned deity surrounded by wild animals, an image that may foreshadow the portrayal of the Hindu god SHIVA in his aspect of *Pasupati*, the Lord of Beasts. The apparent cult of the bull and the emphasis on washing, or ablutions, that are suggested by the material remains raise the fascinating if unanswerable question of the influence of this early pre-Aryan civilization on Hindu practices in historic India.

Decline of Indus Civilization. The Indus civilization appears to have declined rapidly in the early 2d millennium BC. The archaeological evidence indicates that the efficient urban administration of Mohenjo-daro had deteriorated by c.1750 BC, when the construction of houses markedly declined. Evidence has also been discovered of intermittent and devastating floods from this time, and, intriguingly, the remains of 38 corpses were found apparently left unburied in lanes and houses of the latest level of occupation.

Some scholars have postulated a final massacre, possibly by conquering ARYAN peoples whose epics refer to their conquest of walled cities. Others have attributed the decline to an ecological catastrophe that created violent and recurrent flooding along the southern course of the Indus. Still others suggest that the Indus civilization may have overextended itself, resulting in its collapse under the combined onslaught of natural disasters and barbarian incursions.　　PHILIP L. KOHL

Small soapstone stamps, such as this one, were found in great profusion at Mohenjo-daro and throughout the Indus Valley. The seals, which were probably used by merchants to identify their goods, portray indigenous animals. Their pictographic signs, which represent Indian civilization's earliest writing, remain undeciphered.

Bibliography: Allchin, Bridget and Raymond, *The Birth of Indian Civilization* (1968); Fairservis, Walter A., Jr., *Roots of Ancient India*, 2d rev. ed. (1975); Piggott, Stuart, *Prehistoric India to 1000 BC* (1950); Sankalia, Hasmukhal, *The Prehistory and the Protohistory of the Indus Civilization* (1974) and *The Prehistory of India* (1977); Wheeler, Sir Mortimer, *Civilization of the Indus Valley and Beyond* (1966) and *The Indus Civilization*, 3d ed. (1968).

industrial archaeology

Industrial archaeology is the organized study of the physical remains of past industries, especially of the last 200 years. A subfield of ARCHAEOLOGY, it uses systematic fieldwork, supplemented by historical records, to survey, record, and in some cases, preserve industrial artifacts, especially those associated with the technological developments of the INDUSTRIAL REVOLUTION.

During the past 25 years this relatively new subdiscipline has investigated the archaeology of coal and metals, including mining and smelting; natural energy sources such as windmills, waterwheels, and steam engines; manufacturing industries such as textiles, pottery and glass, food preparation, brewing and distilling; means of transportation, including roads, bridges, canals, and railways; building materials such as quarries, brickworks, and sawmills; agricultural history; housing for industrial workers; public utilities, including electricity, gas, water, and communications systems; and the industry of recreation such as resorts, spas, and cinemas.

Faced with the rapid destruction of old technologies, industrial archaeologists attempt to salvage and evaluate information in the context of social and technological history. Although the term *industrial archaeology* was not introduced until the 1950s in Britain, the field has existed since the British astronomer Isaac Fletcher documented the archaeology of the West Cumberland coal trade in the late 19th century.

ELAINE J. SCHECHTER

Bibliography: Bracegirdle, Brian, *The Archaeology of the Industrial Revolution* (1973); Buchanan, R. Angus, *Industrial Archaeology in Britain* (1972); Hudson, Kenneth, *Industrial Archaeology: An Introduction*, 2d. ed. (1966); Major, J. Kenneth, *Fieldwork in Industrial Archaeology* (1975); Raistrick, Arthur, *Industrial Archaeology: An Historical Survey* (1972).

industrial arts programs

Industrial arts programs, offered in all grades at school, are designed to help children attain a general and practical understanding and knowledge of how things work, the materials they are made of, and the tools that are used in their construction. The programs explore aspects of technology such as communications, power, and manufacturing. Industrial arts programs train students not for vocations but for knowledge of how to apply practical learning to everyday situations. Educational pioneers and leaders such as John Amos COMENIUS, Maria MONTESSORI, and Johann Heinrich PESTALOZZI encouraged children to work with various materials and tools. John

DEWEY believed that manual creativity fostered both intellectual and creative development.

From kindergarten through grade six, children learn to use simple materials and machine and hand tools. Demonstrations and experiments with materials like clay, textiles, and wood are usually conducted in the classroom. At the secondary level firsthand and more sophisticated learning experiences offer students the opportunity to develop their creative or mechanical talents by using and experimenting with tools, materials, machines, and processes in the actual design, construction, and evaluation of industrial arts projects. Courses are given in such areas as electronics, metalworking, photography, woodworking, textiles, and mechanical drawing.

About 215 American colleges and institutions offer bachelor's degrees in industrial arts; 154 offer master's degrees and 27 offer doctoral degrees in the field.

Bibliography: Barlow, Melvin L., *A History of Industrial Education in the United States* (1967); Miller, W. R., and Boyd, T. Gardner, *Teaching Elementary Industrial Arts* (1970).

industrial design

The term *industrial design* was first used in the mid-19th century to refer not only to the design of objects for mass production by industrial methods (which is its modern definition) but also to describe designs for fine wares produced in limited quantities by handcraft methods. This distinction between artistic and commercial design shaped the history of industrial design theory from its origin until the end of World War I.

Theorists of the 1850s were alarmed by what they felt were the declining aesthetic standards of mass-produced objects of everyday use and sought to improve industrial design by reforming the education of artists and designers. As early as 1835, a committee on arts and manufactures was set up in London to investigate the poor performance of British exports in industrial markets dependent on design, such as textiles, ceramics, glass, metalwork, and furniture; in 1836 the Government School of Design was opened at Somerset House. After the Great CRYSTAL PALACE Exhibition (1851), a newly reorganized school of design was established in combination with a museum that later became the Victoria and Albert Museum in South Kensington, London. This example was soon followed in Europe and the United States; between 1850 and 1900 new design schools were founded in England, France, and Germany.

The remarkable improvement in British industrial designs shown at the London international exhibition of 1862 did much to encourage the foundation of schools of applied art elsewhere. During the 1860s, French government schools of design were reformed, and the Central Union of Fine Arts Applied to Industry in Paris sponsored competitions in 1865 and 1869 for the design of industrial products. In 1867 a school of design was added to the Austrian Museum for Art and Industry in Vienna, and in the following year a combined design school and museum opened in Berlin.

The strongest arguments for reform and quality in design continued to come from England, where the work and writings of William MORRIS helped reestablish values of artistic craftsmanship in utilitarian objects. Morris, who has been called the father of modern design, revived handcraft methods for the objects produced by his firm from 1861 and, as craftsman and designer, rejected machine production. As a result, his products were expensive and limited in quantity despite Morris's own interest in making inexpensive products of high quality. At the end of the 19th century, however, a few progressive architects in Austria, the United States, and Belgium argued that machines could be used to produce fine products. Adolf LOOS, Louis SULLIVAN, Henri VAN DE VELDE, Otto WAGNER, and Frank Lloyd WRIGHT advocated the use of modern materials like iron, steel, aluminum, and cement in simple, even severe forms that reflected a new aesthetic. The ideas of these architects flourished in Germany, where modern industrial design theory was first realized in practice. By 1898, Peter BEHRENS was designing prototype flasks for mass production, and in 1907 he became designer to AEG, a large electrical combine. Behrens's first works for AEG in 1907-08 included street lamps whose simple geometrical forms and plain surfaces sharply contrasted with the historicizing and heavily ornamented styles of the later 19th century. At about the same time the Deutsche Werkstätten in Dresden employed Richard Rieimerschmid and Bruno Paul to design furniture for mass production; it was described in the firm's trade catalog as a "style of furniture developed from the spirit of the machine." In 1907 the superintendent of the Prussian Board of Trade for Schools of Arts and Crafts, Hermann Muthesius, publicly called for the creation of a new machine style, "abstaining from outward decoration, and with shapes completely dictated by the purposes which they are meant to serve." In the same year Muthesius inspired the formation in Munich of the Deutscher Werkbund, an association of representatives of "art, industry, crafts and trades, combining all efforts towards high quality in industrial work."

The ideals of William Morris and the reality of mass production were first synthesized by Walter GROPIUS, who insisted that standards of design could be raised only if the craftsmen were involved in machine production. For Gropius, industrial design was a union of the craftsman's art and technology. In 1919, Gropius became director of the Staatliches BAUHAUS (the State School of Building) in Weimar, a combined academy of art and school of arts and crafts. Through the work of Gropius and his faculty the Bauhaus became internationally famous, establishing the principles and forms that have dominated industrial design in the 20th century. Gropius's program trained craftsmen to create prototypes for industry and to develop standardized, inexpensive products of high quality for a wide popular market. From the Bauhaus emerged a new industrial aesthetic, conceived to express the nature of industrial materials and to reveal rather than disguise the process by which objects were formed in a new style—spare, clean, devoid of ornament, and geometrical in form. There Marcel BREUER first experimented with metal furniture, inspired by the curved metal tubing of his bicycle handlebars. In 1926 his colleague Ludwig MIES VAN DER ROHE devised one of the classics of modern industrial design, a cantilevered chair of chromium-plated tubular steel. The strength of the tubular metal allowed the designer to discard the traditional four legs and cantilever his chair on only two supports.

The ideas of the Bauhaus have continued to influence the training of industrial designers and the design of objects of everyday use. Many designs of the 1920s have remained in contemporary production, but after World War II new materials and processes were developed in Italy, France, Scandinavia, and the United States that relaxed the aggressive precision and rational purity of the Bauhaus's machine style. Designers such as Alvar AALTO, Charles EAMES, Arne JACOBSEN, and Eero SAARINEN have produced enduringly popular designs for furniture and other domestic articles that have made innovative use of wood, plastic, metal, and glass.

Industrial Design in the United States. Although the Europeans involved in industrial design were primarily artists and architects, in the United States the field became the profession of a group of people who were, for the most part, specialists in sales promotion; that is, they were originally concerned with product-packaging and advertising design as a means of increasing sales. During the Depression of the 1930s such innovative designers as Norman BEL GEDDES, Henry DREYFUSS, Raymond LOEWY, and Walter TEAGUE were employed by industry to "streamline" consumer products. The success of these men—who have left their mark on objects as diverse as the refrigerator, camera, automobile, and airplane—stimulated the establishment of corporate design staffs in most major industries and introduced industrial design as a degree program at universities and schools of art. American designers eventually drew both on the earlier European theories of the aesthetics of mass-produced objects and on the engineering technologies used in the development of new processes and materials. Industrial designers are currently involved in the design of whole systems as well as separate products and work with industrial and systems engineers to design units of enormous complexity such as space stations, mass-transit systems, or inner city reconstructions.

Bibliography: Carrington, Noel, *Industrial Design in Britain* (1976); Dreyfuss, Henry, *Designing for People*, rev. ed. (1967); Ferekee, Ann, *A History of Design from the Victorian Era to the Present* (1970); Pevsner, Nikolaus, *Pioneers of Modern Design* (1949); Papanek, Victor, *Design for the Real World: Human Ecology and Social Change* (1971); Pye, David, *The Nature and Art of Workmanship* (1968); Read, Herbert, *Art and Industry: The Principles of Industrial Design* (1945).

industrial engineering

Industrial engineering, a branch both of engineering and of industrial management, is primarily concerned with the analysis of the processes of production and the design of methods for making them more efficient. An analysis of production process might include the selection of tools and materials and the design of the sequence of production operations. The industrial engineer may also design plant facilities, establish work standards through time and motion studies, develop wage scales based on an analysis of required job skill levels, and determine quality-control procedures.

Bibliography: Turner, Wayne C., et al., *Introduction to Industrial and Systems Engineering* (1978).

industrial management

Industrial management is concerned with the management of manufacturing enterprises. In its broadest sense, the term includes such specialized areas of management responsibility as INDUSTRIAL RELATIONS, MARKETING, and production management. A more narrow definition, however, restricts the area of industrial management to the management of production processes.

A production process is a process that transforms an input of capital, labor, and raw materials into a physical product. The primary objective of industrial management is to perform this transformation as efficiently as possible.

Development of Concepts of Industrial Management. Many of the essential concepts of industrial management must have been familiar to the ancient Egyptians, Chinese, Romans, and Incas, as they could not have built such gigantic works as the pyramids, the Great Wall, the aqueducts, or the magnificent public works and temples of South America without using organizational principles similar to those used in any modern industrial enterprise. The first formal discussion of the economics of the production process, however, appeared only in 1776, in Adam Smith's classic work, WEALTH OF NATIONS. Smith noted the advantages of division of labor and specialization as a basis for an efficient production system. This concept contrasted sharply with the model of the artisan of the Middle Ages who performed every task required in the making of a product.

Another early contributor to the field of industrial management was Charles BABBAGE, who published *On the Economy of Machinery and Manufactures* in 1832. Babbage agreed with Smith that the division of labor would lead to higher productivity, and he suggested that the skill levels required for each job should be used to determine the appropriate wage payment and that this practice would result in lower total costs. He discussed the general concepts of TIME AND MOTION STUDY and advocated the use of the scientific method in the analysis of business problems.

Although Smith, Babbage, and others provided the basic concepts of industrial management, Frederick W. TAYLOR must be given credit for their popularization. Taylor promoted the idea of scientific management: that observation, measurement, classification, and the principles derived from these empirical studies should be applied to all managerial problems; that the methods by which work was accomplished should be determined by management through the same kind of investigation; and that workers should be "scientifically" selected, trained, and developed. Several fields of management evolved from his philosophy, including time and motion study, personnel management and industrial relations,

and the managerial functions of planning and control.

The concept of division of labor was carried to its logical extreme in 1913 by a technological innovation—the use of a moving ASSEMBLY LINE to manufacture Ford automobiles. Although Henry Ford's innovation has greatly improved productivity, critics argue that the assembly line dehumanizes employees by treating them as parts of a large machine. More recently efforts have been made to enrich factory work by making it more varied, more complex, and more challenging for workers. The objective is to identify jobs that can be done efficiently by employees and at the same time provide sufficient challenge and satisfaction to encourage high morale.

Mathematical Methods and Models. Another significant development in the early 1900s was the use of mathematical models to analyze common problems in industrial management. In 1915, F. W. Harris developed the first mathematical formula that could be used to determine an economical method for maintaining inventories. In 1931, Walter Shewhart demonstrated that statistical methods could be used to reduce the costs of the operations involved in quality control of products.

This trend accelerated during World War II, when large mathematical models were developed to analyze resource allocation, production scheduling, and logistics problems. The development of electronic computers greatly facilitated the computations required to analyze these large mathematical models. Mathematical modeling provided the basis for the development of the field of OPERATIONS RESEARCH that now provides many of the analytical tools used in MANAGEMENT SCIENCE.

Virtually every aspect of industrial management has been affected by the use of mathematical analysis. A mathematical modeling approach known as linear programming has been applied to the problem of scheduling and allocating resources in many production systems. The complex series of decisions that determine the mix of gasolines, chemicals, and oils produced by large refineries are commonly made with the use of a linear programming model. Theories that were developed to explain the statistical behavior of waiting lines (QUEUING THEORY) were applied first to problems in the telephone industry and later to the design of production lines, toll booths, bank service areas, and post offices.

Industrial management has helped enhance the standard of living in modern society, but is confronted by many challenges. The field has been criticized for contributing to serious environmental and social problems because of its narrow definition of the notion of an efficient production process. Efforts are currently under way to enlarge the concept of efficiency to include the costs of pollution control and the social impacts of production as well as the costs of raw materials, capital, and labor.   JAMES S. DYER

Bibliography: Bethel, Lawrence L., *Industrial Organization and Management*, 5th ed. (1971); Buffa, Elwood S., *Modern Production Management*, 5th ed. (1977); Chandler, Alfred D., *The Visible Hand: The Managerial Revolution in American Business* (1977); Markland, Robert E., *Major Topics in Management Science* (1979); Rue, Leslie, and Byars, Lloyd L., *Management: Theory and Application* (1977); Taylor, Frederick W., *The Principles of Scientific Management* (1911; repr. 1967); Wren, Daniel A., *Evolution of Management Thought*, 2d ed. (1979).

industrial park

An industrial park is a real estate development designed for industrial use and located outside the main residential area of a city. The developer provides essential services such as utilities as well as a controlled environment. Many parks specialize in certain types of industry, such as warehousing or office work. They may lease buildings and sites or sell lots for occupants to develop by themselves. State and municipal governments in the United States have encouraged industrial parks as a way of attracting new industry, often helping to finance them with low-interest bond issues.

industrial psychology

Industrial and organizational psychology is the field of applied psychology that studies the behavior of persons in organizational work settings. Its areas of concern are personnel selection; the mapping of organizational processes; training; improvement of employee morale and working conditions; and improvement of both individual and group productivity. HUMAN FACTORS ENGINEERING and consumer psychology, once areas of industrial psychology, are now often considered fields in their own right.

Two contrasting aims can be identified in industrial psychology. On the one hand, its focus on modifying equipment, work settings, and people to maximize productivity seems to serve the technological process itself. On the other hand, its focus on the individual rights and satisfactions of employees seems to serve the cause of humanistic processes. As C. Argyris said (1976): "In some cases the industrial psychologist may be seen as a genuine link to the top. In other cases, they are seen as the Gestapo."

History. Industrial psychology originated in the United States in the early 1900s. Walter Dill Scott first applied psychology to advertising and the selection of salesmen in 1901. F. W. TAYLOR and Frank and Lillian GILBRETH pioneered (1911) techniques that came to be known as TIME AND MOTION STUDY. These methods utilized systematic procedures for recording and analyzing movements of employees as they performed their jobs for the purpose of suggesting more efficient—and therefore more productive—ways of carrying out the jobs. The translation (1913) of Hugo Münsterburg's *Psychology and Industrial Efficiency* from German into English gave early impetus to the new field, but the major impetus occurred as a result of psychologists' efforts during World War I. During the brief span of two years (1917-18), 1,726,966 men were tested. Job specifications were written, job-knowledge tests invented, officer rating forms devised, and training and psychological counseling programs undertaken.

The HAWTHORNE STUDIES of assembly-line workers, begun in 1925, marked the first serious recognition of the role of human relations as an important factor in the interplay between people and organizations. The Depression of the 1930s saw widespread development of vocational guidance and counseling as a result of research carried out under the leadership of D. G. Paterson at the University of Minnesota's Employment Stabilization Research Institute. In World War II psychological methodology was employed to an unprecedented degree in selection and training, especially in the selection and training of air crews. Many new measurement methods and techniques of test development and performance analysis grew out of the rapid advances made during World War II. Following the war the American Psychological Association formally recognized industrial psychology as a field by creating (1945) a Division of Industrial and Business Psychology, since retitled the Division of Industrial and Organizational Psychology. In the following decades ever-increasing use has been made of industrial psychology in American industrial and business organizations for personnel selection, training, management assessment, human relations, communication, and counseling. Contemporary industrial psychology is far more advanced in theory, research, and application in the United States than in any other country.

Some Areas of Concern. Industrial psychologists study worker motivation and morale, reward systems, communication processes, and working conditions as factors which may affect productivity and worker satisfaction. Many variations of Victor Vroom's expectancy theory—that performance and satisfaction are functions of employee expectancies and values—have received considerable theoretical and research attention.

Personnel selection is associated mainly with testing (see PSYCHOLOGICAL MEASUREMENT). Psychologists have developed sophisticated methods for analyzing jobs according to what employees must do to carry them out successfully. From such analyses tests have been developed that are helpful in evaluating individuals' qualifications for doing different jobs. Selection and job placement in an organization should meet criteria discovered in the job analysis, and should also contribute positively to each individual's own vocational fulfillment. These objectives may not always be compatible, however. It is the job of the industrial psychologist to seek, in as many ways

as possible, to make them compatible. Psychological testing has sometimes been criticized for discriminating unfairly against minority groups and the economically disadvantaged. Professional guidelines have been formulated by the American Psychological Association and by government agencies to aid users in making fair and proper use of such tests.

Investigation of the efficiency of organizational processes has led to the identification of different types of organizational structures with their resultant climates of attitude and behavior. Key factors in organizational theory are COMMUNICATION, LEADERSHIP, and the placement of authority. D. McGregor articulated two opposing theories, "theory X" and "theory Y." Theory X holds that an individual dislikes work, must be coerced to work, and wishes to avoid responsibility by being told what to do and how to do it. Theory Y, in contrast, maintains that working is natural, that most people like to take responsibility, express creativity, or in general work toward a goal. Participative management is based on premises like those of theory Y. Other theories of management have been offered by R. R. Blake and J. S. Mouton, C. Argyris, F. Herzberg, F. Fiedler, Victor Vroom, E. Lawler, L. Porter, Peter Drucker, and many other researchers.

New Directions. Industrial psychology has been accused of a certain stasis. Little work has been done, for instance, in studying the impact of labor unions, unethical behavior such as bribes and thefts, or alcoholism and drug abuse as related to job pressures. Nevertheless, with the ubiquitousness of industrial psychologists in large American concerns—and the growing attention paid by industrial psychologists and others to job enrichment, environmental problems such as pollution and depletion of natural resources, and even the desirability of economic growth—industrial and organizational psychology has unlimited potential for further development.

REVIEWED BY MARVIN D. DUNNETTE

Bibliography: Argyris, Chris, *Integrating the Individual and the Organization* (1964); Blum, Milton L., and Naylor, James C., *Industrial Psychology: Its Theoretical and Social Foundations* (1968); Dunnette, Marvin D., ed., *Handbook of Industrial and Organizational Psychology* (1976); Gilmer, Beverly von Haller, and Deci, Edward L., *Industrial and Organizational Psychology*, 4th ed. (1977); Maier, Norman R. F., *Psychology in Industrial Organizations*, 4th ed. (1973); Miner, John B., *Personnel Psychology* (1969); Vroom, Victor, and Yetton, Philip, *Leadership and Decision Making* (1973).

industrial relations

The field of industrial relations concerns the formal relations between employers and their employees and generally encompasses the work of personnel specialists, industrial engineers, psychologists, and labor-relations experts. In a large company the following activities may be considered industrial relations functions: recruiting and selecting new employees and developing the terms and conditions of employment; classifying jobs and occupations; negotiating with unions; implementing government regulations that affect the work force; and instituting training programs.

Selecting and Evaluating Workers. When a company seeks to fill a vacant job, it may advertise the opening, promote someone from within, or ask an outside EMPLOYMENT AGENCY to send applicants. After interviewing, checking references, and perhaps administering a battery of tests, the company selects an employee from among the applicants. The new worker will usually require some training, which may consist of on-the-job learning or formal instruction. Large companies find it necessary to develop ways of formally evaluating the performance of workers; they usually devise objective standards for measuring the quality and quantity of work and consider those in addition to the supervisors' impressions.

The aspects of industrial relations described above constitute what is usually called personnel administration or personnel management. Much of this work requires a knowledge of INDUSTRIAL PSYCHOLOGY, PSYCHOLOGICAL MEASUREMENT, and STATISTICS. Employers are increasingly concerned with the psychological aspects of work, as research shows that employees who obtain satisfaction from their jobs are more productive.

Incentive Systems. Most workers are paid by the hour or by the day. In some industries, however, the work speed can be controlled by the individual, and payment is based on "piece rates." The simplest type of piece rate is a specific amount of money for each item produced, but most incentive systems are more complex. For example, an employee may receive a standard base rate plus additional pay for items produced over a given minimum. The rate of extra pay may vary, increasing with each subsequent item produced. Or the worker may receive a bonus for the amount of time saved in performing a task. Developing a satisfactory incentive system requires that experts trained in INDUSTRIAL ENGINEERING determine what workers can reasonably be expected to produce and what can be considered equitable rates of pay for producing different amounts.

Collective Bargaining. When a company has been organized by a union, an additional dimension is introduced to industrial relations. The terms and conditions of employment—wages, hours, holidays, vacations—are determined in negotiations between the union and the employer and are set down in a formal contract (see LABOR UNION). In addition, the union-management contract provides channels through which workers who feel their rights have been violated may seek redress. A worker's grievance will be reviewed by increasingly higher levels of management in an effort to reach a solution (see GRIEVANCE PROCEDURE). If the union and management cannot resolve the problem, it may be referred to a neutral third party for arbitration (see ARBITRATION, labor-management and commercial). Some companies have a separate industrial relations department responsible for negotiating and administering collective bargaining agreements with unions.   JAMES W. ROBINSON

Bibliography: Barkin, Solomon, ed., *Worker Militancy and Its Consequences, 1965-75: New Directions in Western Industrial Relations* (1975); Burgess, Keith, *The Origins of British Industrial Relations* (1975); Robinson, James W., et al., eds., *Introduction to Labor* (1975); Rowan, Richard L., ed., *Readings in Labor Economics and Labor Relations*, 3d ed. (1976); Sloane, A. A., and Whitney, F., *Labor Relations*, 3d ed. (1977); Yoder, Dale, *Personnel Management and Industrial Relations*, 6th ed. (1970).

Industrial Revolution

The term *Industrial Revolution* describes the historical transformation of traditional into modern societies by industrialization of the economy. The main defining feature of the revolution was a dramatic increase in per capita production that was made possible by the mechanization of manufacturing and other processes that were carried out in factories (see FACTORY SYSTEM). Its main social impact was that it changed an agrarian into an urban industrial society. The historical term *Industrial Revolution* can be applied to specific countries and periods of the past, but the process known as industrialization is still going on, particularly in developing countries. Since industrialization makes possible long-term increases in production and income, economists seeking to create in developing countries a process similar to the one that first occurred by accident in 18th-century Britain have carefully studied the Industrial Revolution.

THE REVOLUTION IN GREAT BRITAIN

Historians disagree on the exact causes of Britain's Industrial Revolution, which may be viewed as stemming from a variety of related and coincidental factors.

Britain's Advantages. Britain had certain natural advantages that help to explain why the Industrial Revolution began there. It was richly endowed with coal and iron ore, easily navigable waterways, and easily negotiated coasts. It was favorably placed at the crossroads of international trade, and internal trade was stimulated by the absence of domestic tariffs in what was, after the union of England and Scotland in 1707, the largest free-trade area in Europe. Political liberty was guaranteed, and a relatively open social structure made upward social mobility common, thus giving an incentive to the accumulation of wealth. The principles of the Protestant NONCONFORMISTS, who were to form the backbone of the new middle class, encouraged industry and thrift. New knowledge, especially in science, was freely disseminated, breeding an in-

ventiveness and a willingness to accept change. In short, 18th-century British society provided the framework within which could interact the effects of five fundamental sorts of change—in agriculture, population, technology, commerce, and transportation.

The Agrarian and Demographic Revolutions. Industrialization usually goes hand in hand with agrarian reform if for no other reason than that an agrarian revolution allows a relatively small agrarian labor force to feed a larger manufacturing work force. In Britain the revolution in land use even more than improved technology dramatically increased agricultural production. The ENCLOSURE movement of the 18th century increased the efficiency of farm lands as common pastures and fields were replaced by more compact and easily farmed private holdings. Farmers were thus motivated to experiment with new forms of husbandry—notably root crop rotation and convertibility between cultivated and pasture land—that increased productivity.

The stimulus to these agrarian changes was the increased demand for food generated by a demographic revolution—Britain's population nearly doubled in the 18th century and doubled again by 1850. Population growth tends to retard economic development in a modern developing country, but Britain was a wealthy country with a standard of living well above subsistence; thus the population explosion from 1750 on enlarged the effective demand for consumption and had a beneficial effect on economic development.

The Technological Revolution. Because British entrepreneurs were unable to meet the increased demand for goods by tra-

(Above) *The coal mines of the English Midlands provided plentiful fuel for rapid industrial development during the 18th century. Among the earliest technological inventions was the Newcomen steam engine (center), used for more than 50 years to pump water from mines.*

(Below) *Manchester spinning factories of the mid-19th century used steam-powered machines to produce the cotton thread demanded by Britain's mechanized weaving industry. The innovations that revolutionized textile production took place between 1760 and 1850.*

A detail from John Ferguson Weir's Forging the Shaft: A Welding Heat dramatizes the shaping of a massive steel shaft. The development in 1856 of the Bessemer process, the first low-cost method of producing steel, gave great impetus to heavy industry in both the United States and Great Britain. (Metropolitan Museum of Art, New York City.)

ditional methods of production, the domestic handicraft system of manufacture gave way beginning in the late 18th century to factory-based mechanization. Bottlenecks in production led to a search for new methods, and technical innovation was as much a response to market conditions as a primary cause of industrialization.

The cotton textile industry was the first to be fully mechanized. The crucial inventions were John KAY's flying shuttle (invented in 1733 but not widely used until the 1760s), James HARGREAVES's spinning jenny (1765), Richard ARKWRIGHT's water frame (1769), Samuel CROMPTON's mule (1779), and Edmund CARTWRIGHT's machine LOOM (1785, but delayed in its general use).

The first factories were driven by water, but James WATT's improved Newcomen STEAM ENGINE (1769; especially his "sun and planet" adaptation converting linear into circular motion) made steam-driven machinery and modern factories possible from the 1780s. This use of steam power led, in turn, to increased demand for coal and iron. Each development spawned new technological breakthroughs, as, for example, Sir Henry BESSEMER's process for making steel (1856). Other industries such as chemicals and mining and the engineering professions also developed rapidly.

Capital, Commerce, and Transportation. Every inventor needed an entrepreneur with the capital and the vision to exploit innovation, and British industrialization was financed almost wholly by domestic capital. The accumulation of capital from land and overseas trade was a long-term process in which the propensity to save was crucial; thus the emergence of banking and insurance services oiled the wheels of a market economy.

Similarly, for the market to respond to demand, an adequate transport system was essential, and in the 18th century, British roads were improved for the first time since the Romans had withdrawn. Even more important, in the last quarter of the century a burst of CANAL building enabled raw materials to reach the factory quickly and cheaply and allowed finished goods to supply an even larger market. From 1830 on, the development of steam-driven LOCOMOTIVES brought the advent of RAILROADS, extending the transportation network.

The net effect of all these changes was a dramatic increase in production; during the 19th century the gross national product per capita in Britain increased an unprecedented 400 percent in real terms.

THE SPREAD OF INDUSTRIALIZATION

Until well after 1850, Britain dominated the international economy. Britain itself, however, sowed the seeds of industrialization elsewhere by exporting knowledge, engineers, entrepreneurs, and, above all, capital.

Europe. In continental Europe, Belgium, rich in iron and coal, was first to embark on industrialization in the 1820s, and by the 1830s the French Industrial Revolution had begun. Prussia, much richer in essential minerals than France, developed rapidly from the 1840s; by the time of German unification in 1871, Germany was a powerful industrial nation. Perhaps the most important British innovation to be exported was the railroads, because those countries that industrialized most rapidly were those that established an extensive rail network—Belgium, Germany, and the United States.

The United States. American society was an ideal vehicle for industrialization. The Puritan ethic and a belief in free enterprise fostered technological innovation and economic growth, and the country had enormous natural resources. In the late 18th century Samuel SLATER, a textile worker from England, copied Arkwright's machine designs and opened a cotton mill in Rhode Island. Under the leadership of such entrepreneurs as Francis Cabot LOWELL, the New England TEXTILE INDUSTRY continued to develop. The supply of cotton fiber for the textile mills was vastly increased by Eli WHITNEY's invention (1793) of the COTTON GIN. Another major mechanical innovation in crop harvesting was Cyrus McCORMICK's reaper (1831). Labor-saving devices such as these freed workers to enter the factories, which also drew upon immigrant labor.

Aided by the spread of the transportation network, the boom period in American industrialization came in the second half of the 19th century. By the turn of the century the United States had overtaken Britain in the output of iron and coal and the consumption of raw cotton. Britain, with its older plants and equipment, faced increasing economic competition from other countries and lagged behind, particularly in the newer chemical and electrical industries; the former was led by Germany and the latter by the United States. In the 20th century the United States also dominated the new automobile industry, which Henry Ford (see FORD family) revolutionized by introducing a system of coordinated ASSEMBLY-LINE operations. Ford's success led to the widespread adoption of MASS PRODUCTION techniques in industry.

Elsewhere. By 1914 other European countries such as Italy and the Netherlands had begun to industrialize, and the process had spread to Japan. There, rapid industrialization made a small island people a world power, just as it had done for the British.

The Industrial Revolution in Russia had started well before 1914, but economic development was halted by World War I and the 1917 Bolshevik Revolution. When Soviet industrialization resumed about 1930, it was no longer a response to market forces but a planned economic development by the Communist state. The Soviet Industrial Revolution involved state investment in plant, machinery, and heavy industrial goods and a restriction on consumption of consumer goods. From the 1950s, Communist China also embarked on a planned Industrial Revolution, seeking to accomplish in a decade what had taken Britain a century.

SOCIAL EFFECTS

The social effects of industrialization may be summed up as short-term misery for long-term gain. Factory labor was often more disciplined, tedious, and dangerous than work in agriculture or domestic industry. It exploited women and, until the introduction of child labor laws in most countries by the early 20th century, children. It also rendered many skills obsolete and made workers dependent upon fluctuating market forces. People often felt that they had less control over their destiny as machines, although created by humans, seemed to become their masters.

At the same time, life in the 19th-century city was unpleasant. The environment was often polluted with filth and smoke, and housing conditions were crowded and unsanitary. Basic amenities such as water supply and sewage disposal were deficient, and as a result disease and death rates were high. So common were these conditions that critics sometimes claimed all industrial cities were the same, whatever the country. Manchester, Lille, Essen, and Pittsburgh all fit the image of Coketown, which Charles Dickens created in *Hard Times*.

In fact, however, each city had its distinctive features, and the conditions in them were not as uniformly bad as is often asserted. Two developments improved conditions. First, both national and local governments, perhaps fearful of social revolution, began to introduce ameliorative measures such as factory legislation, sanitary provisions, and social welfare programs. Second, the workers themselves often found ways to improve their working and living conditions. Cities were places of opportunity and personal development in ways that had never been possible in the closed, static rural society. Karl MARX and Friedrich ENGELS argued that only through industrialization could workers develop their social and political consciousness. Finding strength through common experience, workers developed labor unions and political organizations to protect their interests and achieve a greater share of the profits of industry. For all its ill effects the Industrial Revolution solved the problem of the poverty trap described by Thomas MALTHUS in *An Essay on the Principle of Population* (1798)—the cycle of low income, low consumption, low demand, and low production.   DEREK FRASER

Bibliography: Ashton, T. S., *The Industrial Revolution, 1760-1830* (1964); Deane, Phyllis, *The First Industrial Revolution* (1966); Hartwell, R. M., *The Industrial Revolution and Economic Growth* (1971); Henderson, W. O., *The Industrial Revolution in Europe* (1968); Hobsbawm, E. J., *Industry and Empire* (1968); Humphreys, Mary B., et al., *The Industrial Revolution*, 3d ed. (1976); Landes, D. S., *The Unbound Prometheus* (1969); Osborne, J. W., *The Silent Revolution: The Industrial Revolution in England as a Source of Cultural Change* (1970); Stearns, P. N., ed., *The Impact of the Industrial Revolution* (1972); Temin, Peter, *Causal Factors in American Economic Growth in the 19th Century* (1975); Thompson, Allan, *The Dynamics of the Industrial Revolution* (1973).

industrial training programs: see VOCATIONAL EDUCATION.

industrial union

An industrial union is a LABOR UNION that admits as members all employees of a given firm or industry regardless of their jobs or skills. In the United States industrial unions began to develop in the first decade of the 20th century, although the KNIGHTS OF LABOR (1869-1900) was an important forerunner. Early leaders were often political radicals, associated with such groups as the Industrial Workers of the World. In the 1930s industrial unions were organized in mass-production industries, such as steel, automobiles, and textiles, under the leadership of John L. LEWIS. They formed a national association called the Congress of Industrial Organizations (CIO). The CIO and the older, more traditional American Federation

of Labor (AFL) merged in 1955 to form the AMERICAN FEDERATION OF LABOR AND CONGRESS OF INDUSTRIAL ORGANIZATIONS.

Bibliography: DeCaux, Len, *Labor Radical* (1970); Fink, Gary M., *Labor Unions* (1977); Galenson, Walter, *The CIO Challenge to the AFL: A History of the American Labor Movement, 1935-1941* (1960); Goldberg, Arthur, *AFL-CIO: Labor United* (1956; repr. 1964); Jacobs, Paul, *The State of the Unions* (1963); Livesay, Harold, *Samuel Gompers and Organized Labor in America* (1978); Taft, Philip, *Organized Labor in American History* (1964).

Industrial Workers of the World

The Industrial Workers of the World, a revolutionary socialist industrial union, was formed in 1905 by the Western Federation of Miners and a number of other labor organizations. Its early leaders included Eugene DEBS and Daniel DE LEON. In 1908, Debs and the WFM withdrew and De Leon was forced out; leadership passed to Vincent St. John and William HAYWOOD. The Wobblies, as they were called, preached permanent class warfare against employers. As adherents of the doctrine of SYNDICALISM, they held that, ultimately, after a general strike, capitalism would be replaced by industrial democracy.

During 1909-11 the IWW tried to organize unskilled and migratory workers into industrial unions but met with strong repression by vigilantes, police, and federal troops. It had some success in textile workers' strikes in Lawrence, Mass. (1912), and Paterson, N.J. (1913); but created no lasting organization. From 1915 to 1918, during the prosperity of World War I, the Wobblies organized blacks, metal miners, lumberjacks, dock workers, and agricultural laborers. Employers and their local allies, however, took strong countermeasures. Arizona strikers were deported into the desert; in Butte, Mont., IWW organizer Frank Little was abducted and lynched. Another IWW organizer, the folk-song writer Joe HILL, was convicted of murder on circumstantial evidence and executed (1915) in Salt Lake City; he was subsequently celebrated as a martyr in the radical labor movement. The U.S. Department of Justice arrested over 200 IWW leaders in 1917 and prosecuted them for interfering with the war effort and for spreading antiwar propaganda. After the war the remnants of the IWW leadership were scattered in the repressive atmosphere of the "red scare." By the mid-1920s, the Wobblies had even lost touch with American radicalism.   FRED GREENBAUM

Bibliography: Brissenden, Paul, *The IWW* (1920; repr. 1958); Dubofsky, Melvin, *We Shall Be All: Industrial Workers of the World* (1967); Foner, Philip, *History of the Labor Movement in the United States*, 4 vols. (1947); Gambs, J. S., *The Decline of the I.W.W.* (1932; repr. 1966); Renshaw, Patrick, *The Wobblies* (1967).

Indy, Vincent d'   [dan-dee', van-sahn']

The French composer Vincent d'Indy, b. Mar. 27, 1855, d. Dec. 1, 1931, is perhaps best known today for his Symphony on a French Mountain Air (1887) for piano and orchestra and also as the leading disciple of César Franck. He studied privately (1862-70) with several teachers in Paris, served in the Garde Mobile during the Franco-Prussian War, then studied composition and organ with Franck. D'Indy was an enthusiastic Wagnerite—he first met Wagner in 1873—and he visited Germany frequently. In 1894 he became one of the founders of the Schola Cantorum in Paris and saw it develop into one of the foremost music schools in the world. He traveled widely as a conductor of his own works, visiting Spain (1897), Russia (1903 and 1907), and the United States (1905 and 1921).

As Franck's most celebrated pupil, d'Indy maintained his teacher's tradition—particularly in his use of cyclical form, in which thematic material reappears in successive movements of a large composition. Plainsong elements and baroque polyphony are used also, giving his music an air of severity and reserve. His best-known works include three symphonies, the symphonic variations *Istar* (1897), and an opera (*Fervaal*, 1897). He also wrote chamber music, smaller orchestral pieces, many songs, and choral works.   HOMER ULRICH

Bibliography: Davies, Laurence, *César Franck and His Circle* (1970); Demuth, Norman, *Vincent d'Indy* (1951; repr. 1974).

inequality

An inequality is a statement between two real numbers that indicates that one of the two numbers is less than the other number or, what is equivalent, that one number is greater than the other number. If a statement is true for all values of a variable, or if there is no variable in the statement, then the statement is called an absolute, or unconditional, inequality; for example, $x^2 + 1 > 0$ or $1 < 2$. A conditional inequality is true for only certain values of a variable (see below). If the real numbers are represented on a number line, it can be said that a is less than b; this is written as $a < b$ if the point corresponding to a on the number line is to the left of the point corresponding to b. In the figure, for example, $-2 < -1$, $-\frac{1}{2} < 0$, $0 < \frac{1}{4}$, and $\frac{7}{4} < 2$. Algebraically, it can be said that $a < b$ if $b - a$ is a positive number.

number line

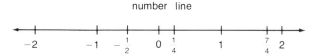

To say that a is less than b (written $a < b$) is equivalent to saying that b is greater than a (written $b > a$). That is, $b < a$ if and only if $a > b$.

Inequalities have the following basic properties: for a, b, and c real numbers,

(1) if $a < b$ and $b < c$, then $a < c$
(2) if $a < b$, then $a + c < b + c$
(3) if $a < b$ and $c > 0$, then $a \cdot c < b \cdot c$
(4) if $a < b$ and $c < 0$, then $a \cdot c > b \cdot c$

Note that property (4) starts with $a < b$ and ends with $a \cdot c > b \cdot c$. Passage from "$<$" to "$>$" (or vice versa) is called a reversal of the sense (or direction or sign) of an inequality.

Another set of properties can be obtained by replacing the symbol "$<$" by "$>$," and vice versa, throughout (except for $c > 0$ and $c < 0$, which are not changed). For example, carrying out this replacement in property (4) yields the property: if $a > b$ and $b > c$, then $a > c$. As a numerical example, if $4 > 2$ and $2 < -1$, then $4 > -1$.

A conditional inequality is one that involves a variable and is true for only certain values of the variable, for example, $2x + 5 < 7$. The properties of inequalities can be used to solve the inequality, that is, to find the value or values of the variable for which the inequality is true.

$$2x + 5 < 7$$
$$(2x + 5) + (-5) < 7 + (-5) \quad \text{by property (2)}$$
$$2x < 2$$
$$\tfrac{1}{2}(2x) < (1/2)(2) \quad \text{by property (3)}$$
$$x < 1$$

The notation $a \le b$ means that $a < b$ or $a = b$ and is read "a is less than or equal to b." Similarly, $a \ge b$ means $a > b$ or $a = b$.   ROY DUBISCH

Bibliography: Beckenbach, E. F., and Bellman, R., *An Introduction to Inequalities* (1961).

inert gases   [in-urt']

The inert, or noble, gases are a family of gaseous elements that comprise group O of the periodic table. Their physical and chemical properties are closely related. The inert gases and their atomic numbers are helium (2), neon (10), argon (18), krypton (36), xenon (54), and radon (86). Together they constitute just under 1%, by volume, of the atmosphere near the Earth's surface. The terms *inert* and *noble* are derived from the extreme reluctance of these gases to chemically combine with other elements. This chemical stability is caused by the existence of eight electrons (two for helium) in the outermost shell of each noble gas atom. Most other chemical elements, when they react with one another, do so in order to achieve this stable octet electron configuration either by losing electrons to their reacting partners or by gain-

ing electrons from them. Because the noble gases already have the stable electron configuration, they are relatively inert.

The chemical and physical properties of the noble gases within the group can be closely correlated with the atomic number of each member. Their boiling points decrease sequentially from radon, which has the highest, $-61.9°$ C, to helium, with the lowest, $-269.0°$ C. Similarly, the melting points range from $-71.0°$ C for radon to $-248.7°$ C for neon. Helium solidifies below $-272.1°$ C only if a pressure of 25 atmospheres is applied.

The ability to form chemical compounds with other elements increases with atomic number. Xenon forms numerous compounds that are stable at room temperature and atmospheric pressure.

Some of the compounds created since 1962 are XeF_2, XeF_4, and XeO_3. Krypton forms KrF_2 and KrF_4, which are stable only at low temperatures.

Because helium is lighter than air and nonflammable, it is used to fill balloons and dirigibles. Helium is less soluble in the human bloodstream than nitrogen and is therefore mixed with oxygen to provide a breathing mixture for deep-sea divers. Nitrogen in the blood can cause a disease called the bends.

Many electrical conductors, when cooled to liquid helium temperatures, become superconducting; that is, they lose all their electrical resistance. Liquid helium is used in superconducting cables having extremely low power losses and is standard in many laboratories where experimentation requires temperatures below $-269°$ C (see CRYOGENICS).

Neon is used in vapor lamps, signs, and helium-neon lasers. Argon is a filler in electric light bulbs and an oxidation inhibitor in shielded arc-welding and is used wherever inert atmospheres are desirable. A radioactive isotope of krypton, krypton 85, is used in the detection of gas leaks. Xenon is used in certain specialized vapor lamps. Radon, which apparently appears in water wells shortly before earthquakes, may eventually provide a means of earthquake prediction.

RICHARD M. NEUMANN

Bibliography: Asimov, Isaac, *The Noble Gases* (1966); Holloway, J. H., *Noble-Gas Chemistry* (1968).

inertia   [in-ur'-shuh]

The inertia of a body is its tendency to resist acceleration, or change in its motion. The MASS of a body is a quantitative measure of its inertia. Thus, a very massive object, such as a steamship, requires a significant force acting for considerable time in order to bring it either to a stop or up to speed, and a relatively light object such as a table-tennis ball requires little effort to sharply change its motion.   CHARLES E. SMITH

Bibliography: Resnick, Robert, and Halliday, David, *Physics*, 3d ed. (1977).

See also: LAWS OF MOTION; MOMENTUM; MOTION, PLANAR.

inertial guidance system: see GUIDANCE AND CONTROL SYSTEMS.

infallibility

Infallibility means, literally, immunity from error. In Christian theology, the term is applied to the whole CHURCH, which, it is believed by many Christians, cannot err in its teaching of revealed truth because it is aided by the HOLY SPIRIT.

Christians disagree, however, about how infallibility can be recognized. Some accept as infallible those doctrines universally taught and believed from antiquity. Others recognize as infallible the doctrinal decisions of the ecumenical councils (see COUNCIL, ECUMENICAL).

Roman Catholics believe that the pope can make infallible definitions on faith or morals when he speaks *ex cathedra*, that is, as head of the church, and when he has the clear intention of binding the whole church to accept as dogma whatever he is defining. Papal infallibility was formally defined at the First VATICAN COUNCIL (1870). The doctrine was reaffirmed at the Second Vatican Council (1962-65), which also stressed that the entire body of bishops in union with the pope teach infallibly when all concur in a single viewpoint on matters of faith and morals.

RICHARD P. MCBRIEN

Bibliography: Kirvan, John, ed., *The Infallibility Debate* (1971); Küng, Hans, *Infallible? An Inquiry* (1971).

infancy

Infancy is the period of human life that begins at birth and ends with the onset of language. The subject of this article is thus the first 1 to 2 years of human life. Although this is a short period, recent research confirms the long-held belief that the first two years of life are the most important two years of life. What the baby *does* learn about the physical and social worlds apparently determines what the child and the adult *can* learn. Experiences in infancy thus have a more profound effect than later experiences.

THE WORLD OF THE NEWBORN BABY

A newborn baby seems a small and helpless creature, only 50 cm (20 in) long and weighing 3,200 g (7 lb), on the average. This tiny frame, however, conceals an amazing perceptual and intellectual capacity, as well as some surprisingly precise motor abilities. For instance, babies less than a week old will imitate other people. If someone sticks out his or her tongue at the baby, within a fairly short time the baby will begin to stick out his or her tongue in return. If the other person switches to fluttering his or her eyelashes, the baby will flutter his or her eyelashes back; and if the adult opens and closes his or her mouth, for example, the baby will return this behavior in synchrony. Of course, the baby will also perform such actions spontaneously, but he or she does so to a greater extent if an adult model is present. Furthermore, the newborn seems to enjoy the game.

The perceptual discriminations involved in those simple actions are of a high order. The baby must detect the event to imitate from the whole pattern of stimulation that is before him or her. The infant must understand that the tongue seen in someone else's face is matched by the tongue the infant can feel in his or her own mouth, a tongue he or she has never seen; and the baby must have precise enough motor control to make the required movements.

Another social behavior, interactional synchrony, is related. Interactional synchrony is the accompaniment of conversation with very precise motor movements; each participant moves in synchrony with the movements of the other and with the flow of speech. The movements of speaker and listener begin and change at changes in speech: at the beginnings and ends of words, for example. It is difficult for an *adult* to detect the beginnings and ends of words in a language with which he or she is unfamiliar. Babies, who know no language at all, nevertheless demonstrate interactional synchrony, moving precisely in time with the breaks in adult speech; and they can do so with any language.

Newborn babies also show the ability to pick up information about the physical world. They will defend themselves against approaching objects that would hit them in the face, while ignoring approaching objects that would miss them. Babies can also localize sounds, turning their eyes toward the source of a sound. This behavior may be a demonstration of intersensory coordination—in this case, the knowledge that sounds have sources that can be seen; or it may indicate a lack of differentiation in the perceptual system of the newborn.

Newborns have a small repertoire of nonsocial motor abilities. They can move their heads and eyes in a coordinated fashion; they can suck; they may also, if correctly supported, show walking movements and reaching movements (reaching movements normally disappear between 1 and 2 months of age).

In addition, newborns have a conspicuous ability to learn. They are particularly adept at learning what goes with what. One authority even suggests that the newborn can learn more efficiently while still a newborn than he or she will *ever* be able to learn at a later age. A baby only 10 days old recognizes his or her mother's face and his or her mother's voice and knows that the face goes with the voice. This learning has been demonstrated in simple experiments with four different situations: (1) the mother looking at and talking to the baby; (2) an unfamiliar female looking at and talking to the baby; (3) the mother looking at and talking to the baby while the baby hears an unfamiliar female voice; and (4) an unfamiliar female looking at and talking to the baby while the baby hears the mother's voice. Ten-day-old babies like the first situation much more than the second; and the third and fourth situations produce aversive behavior and fussing.

PHYSICAL AND MOTOR DEVELOPMENT

As the baby grows in size and weight, the range and flexibility of his or her behavior increases. There is a great deal of controversy about the origin of newborn behavior. Do the abilities just "grow" as the child does, or is specific input required from the environment?

Both seem necessary. As an example consider smiling, which normally begins 46 weeks after the baby has been *conceived*. A child born after a pregnancy of the normal length of 40 weeks will begin to smile at the age of 6 weeks. A child born prematurely will not smile until a later age—for instance, if the pregnancy lasted only 32 weeks, the child will begin to smile at the age of 14 weeks. The extra environmental input received by the premature baby does not accelerate the appearance of smiling; growth or *maturation* is thus a primary determinant. It is not, however, the only determinant: in the absence of necessary environmental input the behavior will not appear. The "necessary input" seems to be some action of the baby's producing a fixed change in his or her environment, and this normally occurs when the parents play games with the baby. Machines that play games with the baby will also cause smiling to appear.

Other motor activities show a similar pattern, although some of them can be considerably accelerated. Walking can be made to appear about 6 months earlier than it normally would if newborn walking is practiced. The rate of motor development, while naturally a source of concern to parents, is not a good indicator of the rate of intellectual or social development.

COGNITIVE DEVELOPMENT

The cognitive changes that occur during infancy are—though less obvious—even more striking than changes in motor behavior. Cognitive changes are changes in both the child's rules for interpreting events and his or her rules for action. During infancy the child develops, in rudimentary form at least, most of the skills that distinguish human beings from other animals. The infant begins, however, from a basic set of rules that are very different from those he or she must develop.

Consider a set of skills generally referred to as object permanence. If a baby of 6 or 7 months sees a toy on a table, he or she may reach out to take it. If a cup is placed over the toy, the baby acts as if the toy no longer exists. In fact, when the cup is removed to reveal the toy, the baby will be astonished to see it again. This seemingly strange behavior is not due to lack of memory or inability to imagine unseen objects—the baby acts the same way if a transparent cup is used. If rather than using a cup to conceal the toy the room lights are switched off, leaving the baby in total darkness, he or she will be astonished but will eventually reach out for the object. So it appears that young babies cannot understand that one object can be inside another; in fact, babies apparently do not understand that two separate objects can be in *any* spatial relationship to one another. A baby who can remove a cup to get a toy may be confused if the cup is moved to a different place; an infant does not realize that an object in a container shares in all of the movements of the container. The baby will be at least a year old before he or she has mastered all of the complexities of these spatial relations.

Even after 12 months a baby has problems with spatial relations. If a baby of 12 months sees a toy placed in one of two cups—the cup on his or her right, for example—the baby will reach out to the cup on the right. If the baby is moved around the table to the opposite side, however, he or she will still reach out to the cup on the right. Babies do not seem to realize that a spatial relationship like "on the right" is only meaningful in relation to their own specific position (an error referred to as "egocentrism"). These kinds of errors normally disappear at about 18 months of age.

The rate of development of object permanence skills has proved to be a powerful predictor of later INTELLIGENCE. Perhaps more importantly, it has been shown that the rate of development of object permanence skills is highly susceptible to environmental influence, a result that has implications for theories of intelligence.

As well as the spatial skills embodied in object permanence tasks, babies learn a range of numerical and scientific skills. Young babies cannot count. If shown two arrays of candy—one with four pieces, one with five—the arrangement of pieces will be more important than the actual number in determining which one the baby chooses. By the age of 18 months this is no longer so: babies then can count at least up to 6. Similarly, by this age their learning has become much more "scientific" and babies frequently perform experiments of their own to determine how things work. Appropriate environmental opportunities are necessary if these numerical and scientific skills are to appear.

SOCIAL DEVELOPMENT

Infancy is also an important period for social development, and perhaps the critical period for SEXUAL DEVELOPMENT and the development of ATTACHMENT. During infancy the child learns what to expect from other people and what other people expect from him or her. What he or she expects will determine the baby's subsequent behavior with people; a baby who learns that people are nice will grow into a different adult from a baby who learns that people are nasty. In addition to learning general expectations, babies learn specific ways of communicating during infancy. The newborn is prepared to communicate with anyone. This readiness soon disappears, leaving a more developed communication system that is specific to a few people, such as the parents. Communication at this level is largely nonverbal. By about 9 months of age the baby first tries out verbal communication. "Language" at this point is entirely private—the baby does not use adult words but rather private words he or she produces himself or herself, words that sympathetic adults can nonetheless interpret. The replacement of such private words with public words marks the end of infancy.

THE ENVIRONMENT OF INFANCY

This article has emphasized the importance of the baby's environment in his or her development. Determining what exactly is an optimal environment is an ongoing preoccupation of many research workers. At present no prescription can be given. It is certain, however, that a happy, interested baby develops well.

Keeping a baby interested and happy requires changes in the baby's environment, the presentation of novel problems (though not in overwhelming number), and the presence of caring and communicating caretakers, who need not be the biological parents.   T. G. R. BOWER

Bibliography: Bower, T. G. R., *The Perceptual World of the Child* (1977) and *A Primer of Infant Development* (1977); Brazelton, T. B., *Infants and Mothers* (1969); Kagan, Jerome, et al., *Infancy: Its Place in Human Development* (1978); Macfarlane, Aidan, *The Psychology of Childbirth* (1977); Mahler, Margaret S., et al., *The Psychological Birth of the Human Infant* (1975); Ribble, Margaretha A., *Rights of Infants: Early Psychological Needs and Their Satisfaction*, 2d ed. (1965); Schaffer, H. R., *Mothering* (1977); Stern, Daniel, *The First Relationship* (1977); Stone, L. Joseph, *Behavior of the Newborn* (1978) and *The Infant's First Year* (1978).

See also: CHILD DEVELOPMENT.

infanticide   [in-fant'-uh-syd]

Infanticide (from the Latin for "child murder") is the act of killing an infant at birth. Traditionally found among the Australian Aborigines and the Eskimo, infanticide is known to have been practiced on every continent by many different peoples. Religious offerings of the newborn are referred to in

records of the ancient Egyptians, Greeks, and Romans. Sacrifice of the firstborn child was common among tribal groups in India until the 19th century.

Many anthropologists believe that infanticide was traditionally prevalent among some primitive peoples because, along with abortion, it served as a method of controlling population size. This control was especially important for groups living in a harsh environment in which the available food supply was severely limited. Often only female children were killed, especially in hunting societies (such as that of the Eskimo) or among groups in which warriors were especially valued. In certain societies sickly or deformed children were killed at birth. Where traditionally practiced, infanticide was a socially sanctioned act, dictated for the most part by survival needs of the group, a fact recognized and accepted by those who performed it.   CHARLES C. HUGHES

Bibliography: Kohl, Marvin, ed., *Infanticide and the Value of Life* (1978); Piers, Maria W., *Infanticide* (1978).

infantry

The infantry is that part of an army consisting of armed foot soldiers, as distinguished from cavalry, air, or sea forces. Since ancient times the infantryman has been the front line fighting soldier, bearing the brunt of offensive or defensive attack and suffering the greatest number of military casualties. Only during the feudal period and in nomad societies was the infantry's role insignificant.

Infantry appeared with the advent of organized societies in the 3d and 2d millennia BC. The most powerful early infantry were Greek and Roman foot soldiers who fought in compact groups while engaging their enemy with spear and sword. In China during the Warring States period infantry armies numbered in the hundreds of thousands. The defeat of the Roman infantry by barbarian cavalry in AD 378 heralded a thousand-year period during which infantry took second place to the cavalry.

It was not until guns began to replace swords and lances that the infantry again became the primary fighting unit. By the era of the standing or permanent army in the 17th century, foot soldiers were armed with musket and pike. The infantryman was meant to be a mindless brick in a human wall that advanced toward the enemy in a long line, firing all the while. This technique was perfected by FREDERICK II of Prussia in the mid-18th century. The method was most successful when troops had been continuously drilled and so disciplined that they could load and fire while advancing in precise formation regardless of battle conditions.

During the last of the FRENCH AND INDIAN WARS (1754-63), new tactics were borrowed from the Indians by the American colonists. Troops under British General James WOLFE included regiments of specially trained scouting and skirmishing units using flexible tactics that took advantage of any available concealment. These troops regularly overcame larger French units that continued to use the more rigid formations. The flexibility of these early American infantry soldiers has been continued through the infantry of today.

In the 19th century infantry tactics were forced to change to cope with new technology. As weapons became more accurate and effective, infantry had to spread out and dig in to make itself less vulnerable. By the time of the U.S. CIVIL WAR hand grenades, barbed wire, and repeating rifles made mass attacks ineffective. Troops began to attack in waves—one wave raking the opposing troops with fire while the next scrambled toward the enemy. In the 20th century, as weapons became more sophisticated, many expected the infantry to become obsolete. In spite of the many innovations in transportation, communication, and weapons, however, the foot soldier played a major role in the battles of World Wars I and II and in the Korean War, where the option of firing nuclear weapons was rejected in favor of the use of conventionally armed infantry.

Although the range of weapons available to present-day infantry is enormous, they still fight on foot. Troops and supplies, however, are likely to be transported to the battlefield

(Left to right) *The Roman legionnaire's short broadsword and* pilum, *a type of spear, helped Rome maintain supremacy. The increased range of the longbow enabled English archers to overwhelm the French at the Battle of Agincourt (1415), a decisive engagement of the Hundred Years' War. Standardized flintlock rifles, ammunition, and powder charges helped establish the disciplined Prussian army of Frederick the Great as the most effective fighting force of its time. The American doughboy of World War I, who turned the tide of victory in favor of the Allies, was equipped with the U.S. Model 1903 Springfield, a reliable bolt-action rifle that remained in limited use even during World War II. Modern American infantrymen use the U.S. M-16, an automatic/semiautomatic rifle with an effective range of 460 m (1,500 ft).*

by aircraft, ships, trucks, and armored personnel carriers. The helicopter, in particular, has been used extensively as the packhorse of the modern infantry.

Bibliography: Archer, Denis, ed., *Jane's Infantry Weapons* (annual); Ellacott, S. E., *Spearman to Minuteman* (1966); Foss, Christopher, *Infantry Weapons of the World* (1977); Montiosa, Lynn, *War Through the Ages*, 3d ed. (1960); Warner, Philip, *The Soldier: His Daily Life Through the Ages* (1975).

See also: MILITARY STRATEGY AND TACTICS.

infarction   [in-fark'-shuhn]

Infarction is the death, or necrosis, of a tissue resulting from obstruction of its blood supply, usually by a blood clot in an artery, as a result of atherosclerosis. The area of tissue death is called an infarct. When a blood clot blocks a brain artery, the result is a stroke; when one blocks a coronary artery supplying the heart muscle, the result is a heart attack, or coronary; and when one blocks a lung artery, the result may be pulmonary infarction.   PETER L. PETRAKIS

infectious diseases   [in-fek'-shohs]

All species of animals are afflicted with infections caused by a wide variety of organisms, from submicroscopic viruses to wormlike parasites. Infectious diseases range from the benign common cold to such fearsome conditions as BUBONIC PLAGUE and RABIES. Infections are usually characterized by several stages. First, the organism gains access to the patient, survives within the body, and multiplies. Next, the patient manifests symptoms of illness and, in some instances, sheds organisms that have the potential to infect other individuals. The patient may die or recover spontaneously, or the infection may respond to specific therapy. Often, there is a postinfection IMMUNITY, which results in resistance to infection by the same organism in the future.

Some infections have a quiescent, latent period that can be measured in years. Included in this group are those infections which cause chronic destruction of the brain. Certain viral infections in animals cause cancers. A viral etiology for human cancers has not been proved but seems likely for some tumors. Evidence has been found suggesting that patients may develop diabetes following viral invasion of the pancreas with resultant destruction of the insulin-producing islet cells.

Infectious diseases have strongly influenced the course of history on Earth. The Black Plague changed the entire social structure of medieval Europe. The decrease in number of the working class, which led to the final downfall of the feudal system, was partially caused by decimation of the population from the plague. The outcome of major military campaigns has been profoundly influenced by outbreaks of diseases such as DYSENTERY and TYPHUS. Infectious diseases have interfered with habitation and settlement of large areas of the world. MALARIA, YELLOW FEVER, and CHOLERA have played an important role in influencing the development of society in certain regions of the Earth.

AGENTS OF INFECTION

The organisms responsible for human infections are extremely variable. VIRUSES are simple life forms consisting of nucleic acid, encoding genetic information, and surface components of protein that enable them to enter cells. Unable to multiply outside of living host cells, they are completely dependent on these cells for their continued maintenance. Viruses utilize the metabolic machinery of the cell and have the ability to interfere with, or direct in an adverse fashion, the activities of the cell. MUMPS, MEASLES, GERMAN MEASLES, and CHICKEN POX are common childhood illnesses caused by viruses. The common cold is usually due to the rhinovirus. The "flu" or the "grippe" is caused by INFLUENZA viruses. HEPATITIS, an inflammation of the liver, may be the result of one of several viruses. Rabies, yellow fever, and Lassa fever are highly lethal viral diseases.

Rickettsiae, small microbes that usually grow inside host cells, have a more complicated structure and metabolic makeup than the viruses. Unlike viruses, they are susceptible to antibiotics. Rickettsial diseases are frequently transmitted by arthropods, and stages in the development of the pathogen often take place in ticks or lice. Examples of rickettsial diseases include ROCKY MOUNTAIN SPOTTED FEVER, Q FEVER, and typhus.

Mycoplasma and *Chlamydia* are bacterialike organisms that frequently grow inside cells. Their outer cell walls are less complex than those of bacteria. *Chlamydia* cause TRACHOMA (a scarring eye disease), certain types of urethritis (inflammation of the external urinary passage), and PSITTACOSIS (a pneumonia transmitted from birds to man). *Mycoplasma* are commonly associated with a relatively mild type of PNEUMONIA.

Nearly all objects in the environment, including plants and animals, are associated with large numbers of bacteria. These organisms can grow and multiply in water and on foods. Certain species can thrive on inorganic nutrients. Garden soil contains countless bacteria per gram, and these organisms are largely responsible for the fertility of the soil. Bacterial diseases are common and include such conditions as streptococcal pharyngitis ("strep throat"), pneumococcal pneumonia, and staphylococcal boils. DIPHTHERIA, GONORRHEA, TUBERCULOSIS, and SYPHILIS are also caused by bacteria. Bacterial diseases respond to treatment with antibiotics.

Fungi, commonly called yeasts or molds, are organisms that frequently grow as single cells (yeasts) and as long, branched filamentous structures (mycelia). Infections caused by these organisms are frequently chronic and slowly destructive. Cryptococcosis, histoplasmosis, and blastomycosis may involve the lung and brain tissue. FUNGUS DISEASES may be superficial, as illustrated by ringworm and thrush.

Parasites that commonly cause infections include protozoa and helminths, or worms. Malaria and amebiasis are protozoal diseases common in the tropics. SCHISTOSOMIASIS, which results in inflammation of the liver, and TRICHINOSIS, involving invasion of muscle and brain tissue, are examples of helminthic diseases. Ectoparasites, organisms that live on the surface of the body, may transmit infectious diseases. For example, lice may carry epidemic typhus, and ticks may be vectors for Rocky Mountain spotted fever (see PARASITIC DISEASES).

MICROBIAL VIRULENCE FACTORS

Infectious agents cause disease in the host by several mechanisms. Most typically, microbial virulence, or the potential to cause disease, involves the ability of the pathogen to gain access to the host by surviving on mucous membranes or by being ingested or inhaled. Pili, submicroscopic hairlike structures on the surface of some bacteria, allow them to attach themselves firmly. Next, there is multiplication of the organism on or in the host. The invading microbe must have the capability of avoiding or counteracting the normal protective mechanisms of the host. Capsules surround some bacteria, and these structures serve to prevent the microbes from being ingested and killed by defending phagocytic cells. Other bacteria produce toxins that can destroy phagocytes. Certain highly virulent organisms produce disease in a large percentage of people whom they contact, while other microorganisms produce illness in only a small percentage. When a nonimmune person encounters the influenza virus, the organisms are inhaled, multiply in respiratory cells, damage these cells, and cause disease. In contrast, certain organisms produce toxins, making the patient ill without actually being invaded by the microbes. *Clostridium botulinum*, a bacterium that grows in improperly preserved foods, produces a potent toxin that when ingested may cause BOTULISM, often leading to paralysis and death. Patients may die by ingesting products of this bacterium without actually being infected by the organism. Other organisms may produce a toxin only after infecting the patient. For example, certain strains of *Escherichia coli*, a common intestinal bacterium, produce a toxin when colonizing the intestine. This toxin, known as an enterotoxin, causes diarrhea. Infection with this organism has been shown to be the most common cause of diarrhea of travelers.

In some instances the host's own defenses against infection may be responsible for the damage. For example, infections caused by *Mycoplasma pneumoniae* may result in inflammation of the airways and lungs. When the microbes grow in the respiratory cells, they do not damage the cells. However, during the host's attempt to kill foreign invaders, the infected cells are attacked and destroyed by immune mechanisms.

HOST DEFENSE AGAINST INFECTION

Since human beings exist in a veritable sea of microbes, defense against microbial attack is important for survival of the species. The skin, mucous membranes (interior of the nose, mouth, vagina, rectum), and intestines are colonized by large numbers of bacteria. These organisms are called the normal flora. They are protective and form a barrier against invasion by foreign microbes due, in part, to the metabolic products of these organisms, which may be harmful to potential invaders. In addition, utilization of essential metabolites by the normal flora may "starve" pathogenic invaders. If the normal flora are destroyed by agents such as ANTIBIOTICS, infection may become more likely. The skin and skin secretions are an effective barrier to invasion by most microorganisms. Tears and saliva have intrinsic antibacterial activity. The respiratory tract is kept clean by coughing and sneezing and by the continuous upward movement of particle-trapping mucus, which is transported by the continuous beating of tiny fibrils, or cilia, of the respiratory lining cells. Once microorganisms invade body tissues, mechanisms come into play that strive to neutralize and destroy them. These defenses may be divided into two major groups: humoral and cellular (for example, phagocytic cells). The humoral (or fluid) mechanisms include the ANTIBODY and complement systems.

Antibodies. Antibodies are proteins produced by specialized white blood cells called lymphocytes. Antibodies have a strong chemical affinity for specific types of foreign biologic matter. ANTIGENS are components of foreign material (that is, microbes) that interact with antibodies. Thus, specific anti-influenza virus antibodies or specific antistaphylococcal antibodies may be present. The interaction of antibodies and components of microbes may serve to destroy, inactivate, or prevent the multiplication of microorganisms. In addition, when an antibody attaches to the surfaces of microorganisms, it makes these microbes more ingestible by phagocytic cells, which have the special role of engulfing and destroying invading microbes.

Complement. In addition to antibodies, another group of proteins circulates in the blood and body fluids, constituting the complement system. These proteins have the ability to destroy certain pathogens by interacting with them. This interaction may be promoted by antibodies or may take place in the absence of antibodies. Thus, blood serum from healthy individuals, lacking antibodies, will destroy many species of bacteria, and this additional means of protection may partially explain why most bacterial species are unable to cause disease in humans.

Lymphocytes. Lymphocytes have the ability to produce antibodies directed against specific foreign antigens to which they are exposed. This is the basis for prevention of disease by immunization. For example, patients may be infected with an attenuated, or weakened, strain of polio virus (see POLIOMYELITIS). The lymphocytes will then make antibodies against the polio virus, which will also be active against wild type, fully virulent organisms. Thus, when patients come in contact with these organisms, they do not become ill because they are now immune.

Inflammation. INFLAMMATION is the phenomenon by which the body responds to an irritant or to an infection. Small blood vessels dilate and leak fluid, producing swelling, redness, and warmth. In addition, phagocytic white blood cells enter the area, adhere to the lining of the blood vessels, and migrate out of the blood vessels into the tissue to attack microbial invaders. Fever, or elevation of the normal body temperature (37° C/98.6° F), is a common response to many infections. It is not clear whether fever aids the host in fighting infection. Fever results when a product of phagocytic cells known as endogenous pyrogens acts on a thermostatlike area (hypothalamus) of the brain to raise the body's "set point."

Phagocytic Cells. Three major types of phagocytic cells are involved in protecting human beings against infection. The polymorphonuclear neutrophil is a motile phagocytic cell that can engulf and destroy pathogens. Ingestion is more efficient when the pathogens have been coated with antibodies or complement or both. Neutrophils are the cells that constitute pus; they migrate to the site of trauma or infection in an attempt to destroy microbes. Macrophages are larger, slower-moving phagocytic cells that have the special capability of killing organisms that can survive ingestion by polymorphonuclear neutrophils. Thus, such organisms as *Mycobacterium tuberculosis* (the agent that causes tuberculosis) are not destroyed by polymorphonuclear neutrophils but are destroyed by macrophages. Macrophages are found in the liver, spleen, lungs, and bone marrow. The eosinophil is a cell that has special potential for killing multicellular microbes such as helminths. Patients with infections such as trichinosis caused by a helminth will frequently have high eosinophil count in the blood, and this is a clue to physicians as to the nature of the infection. Phagocytic cells kill organisms by engulfing them and enclosing them in a pouch called a phagosome. This pouch then becomes bathed with active metabolites of oxygen, including hydrogen peroxide and superoxide, and various enzymes found in the phagocytic cell. Most microbes are rapidly killed by these cells.

Immunity. Humans have a natural or inherent immunity to many infections. Intact barriers such as skin and mucous membrane secretions and normal function of the humoral and cellular systems help prevent infection. Recovery from infection most often results in acquired immunity. In addition to production of specific antibodies, the body may induce a state of cellular immunity whereby macrophages and certain types of lymphocytes that enhance macrophage function become able to destroy invaders more efficiently. Immunity may be passed from mother to fetus via the placenta, which serves as a bridge between maternal and fetal circulatory systems. Thus, newborn infants are protected against many infectious diseases for the first few months of life. Some evidence indicates that breast milk also contains antibodies that may be protective during this early period. Many childhood illnesses seem to be most common and most serious between the ages of 6 months and 6 years, when maternal immunity wanes and acquired immunity has not yet become effective.

ROUTES AND MODES OF INFECTION

Respiratory Route. Pathogenic organisms may be inhaled. This mechanism by which infection is spread is especially significant in many respiratory diseases and is responsible for large epidemic outbreaks. Viral influenza is spread by tiny, airborne particles that can reach the lower airways of the lungs. Tuberculosis, smallpox, and measles are spread by contamination of the air by infected patients. In contrast, fungal diseases such as histoplasmosis and coccidioidomycosis are acquired by inhaling infectious particles derived from soil harboring the organisms.

Gastrointestinal Route. Infections may be acquired by ingestion of the causative organism. Infectious hepatitis, poliomyelitis, and typhoid fever are transmitted by this means. The infecting dose varies from disease to disease. In some conditions as few as one or two organisms can initiate infection, whereas in others as many as 1 million organisms may be required. Certain features of the person encountering the organisms may potentiate their effects. For example, in patients ingesting *Salmonella typhi*, the causative organism of typhoid fever, who have a lack of acid production in their stomachs, many fewer organisms may be required to infect these persons than those who have normal acid production. Stomach acid is an important host defense because it can kill these microbes.

Direct Contact. Mucous membranes may be a portal of entry for many infections. The venereal diseases gonorrhea and syphilis are transmitted by direct contact of mucous membrane to mucous membrane. This may involve penis, vagina, urethra, mouth, or anus. The causative organisms lack the ability to penetrate and attack intact skin, but can infect via mucous membranes.

Although the skin is an impenetrable barrier for most infections, certain organisms may break through. For example, staphylococci may cause boils on skin that is normal or has only a trivial irritation. The streptococcus may cause cellulitis (a spreading inflammation) or IMPETIGO (a crusting lesion) on skin that is intact.

Mother to Child. It is possible for a fetus to become infected while in the uterus. Therefore, infections that the mother acquires during pregnancy may damage the fetus. Some of the most dangerous of these include rubella (German measles), cytomegalovirus disease, and toxoplasmosis. All these conditions produce mild disease in the pregnant woman but may result in devastating damage to the developing fetus. In addition, infants may be infected at birth during passage through an infected birth canal. This can result in congenital (present since the time of birth) gonorrhea, syphilis, herpes viral infections, or streptococcal infections.

RELATIONSHIP OF ENVIRONMENT TO INFECTION

The ecology of infection is complex and involves interactions with climate, food and water supply, arthropod vectors, animal contacts, and other human beings. Many of the great scourges of humankind, such as tuberculosis, cholera, malaria, and typhoid fever, were markedly decreased in incidence by changes in the environment. These changes anteceded development of effective vaccines and therapeutic agents. The greatest danger to *Homo sapiens*, regarding the spread of infection, are other *Homo sapiens*.

Organisms may spread from one person to another by direct contact, by the airborne route, or by oral ingestion of contaminated food or water. Food and water supplies may become contaminated with microbes derived from humans or animals or from the environment. For example, unpasteurized milk may serve to transmit disease if it is contaminated with organisms from an infected cow (for example, brucellosis) or from an infected dairy person (for example, streptococci emanating from a skin lesion). In some instances the microbe may actually grow and multiply on the food, increasing the efficiency of transmission.

Density of population directly affects the spread of certain communicable diseases. Major epidemics have occurred in boarding schools and military barrack populations where contact is close. When people are confined to enclosed places, airborne pathogens tend to spread more readily. Thus, the peaks of respiratory diseases such as influenza and pneumonia are the fall, winter, and early spring months in temperate climates. Patients interacting with domestic or wild animals may have special problems with infections related to pathogens that are harbored by animal species. For example, butchers and meat packers have the highest incidence of brucellosis, a bacterial infection of liver, spleen, and bones. Hunters may contract TULAREMIA, a bacterial infection of rabbits that can be transmitted to humans through handling of pelts.

Insects are significant in the transmission of many infections. The malaria parasite is transmitted from one human to another, or from an animal to a human being, by the bite of the anopheles mosquito. Because this mosquito cannot survive in cold climates, malaria is not a problem in temperate countries. The tick vector of Rocky Mountain spotted fever requires bushy underbrush and a small mammal population to feed on for survival. Areas that do not have these conditions will not support the tick and are thus free of Rocky Mountain spotted fever. Schistosomiasis is a parasitic disease caused by an organism that spends part of its life cycle in a snail. If the snail does not have the proper water conditions to survive, the disease will not be found in that area.

THE IMPAIRED HOST

It is clear that some people are more susceptible to infections than others. Sometimes the cause of the increased susceptibility is obvious. A severely burned person, for example, lacks the normal protective features of intact skin and suffers from infections related to that fact. Patients with diseases that impair the function of protective white blood cells frequently have severe and fatal infections. For this reason, patients with leukemia (cancer of the white blood cells) frequently die of infections. In addition, drugs that interfere with normal host defenses may make the patient especially prone to infection. Patients receiving drugs that kill cancer cells frequently have suppressed phagocytic cell function because the drugs are known to also kill healthy cells. Severe malnutrition increases susceptibility to certain forms of infection. Recent evidence suggests that this vulnerability is due to impaired functioning of lymphocytes and macrophages.

RESPIRATORY INFECTIONS

The respiratory tract includes the nose, throat, bronchial tubes leading to the lungs, and the lungs. Closely associated with the system are the paranasal sinuses and the middle ear. The most common infections are viral infections of the upper respiratory tract, for example, the nose and the throat. The common cold, viral PHARYNGITIS, and BRONCHITIS are annoying, but rarely serious, illnesses. Occasionally, however, bacterial infections may supervene, and the illness may become more severe. Bacterial infections of the middle ear may, if untreated, result in loss of hearing. Infections of the sinuses occasionally lead to infection of the brain and surrounding structures. Streptococcal pharyngitis is of importance mainly because of the sequelae that may follow. Patients who suffer from untreated streptococcal disease may develop complications such as rheumatic fever (an inflammation of various organs, most prominently the heart valves) or inflammation of the kidneys (see COLD, COMMON).

More serious RESPIRATORY SYSTEM DISORDERS involve the lungs. Bacterial pneumonias, especially those caused by the pneumococcus and the staphylococcus, are common and serious diseases. Tuberculosis and the fungal diseases such as histoplasmosis and coccidioidomycosis may also involve the lungs. Infections of the lungs may damage tissue and cause chronic scarring and impairment of respiratory activity. In acute infections, death resulting from interference with normal gas exchange may occur. Patients with underlying lung diseases such as chronic bronchitis, an irritative condition associated with smoking and air pollution, are more susceptible to pulmonary infections.

GASTROINTESTINAL TRACT INFECTIONS

The processes of digestion and absorption of nutrients take place in the gastrointestinal tract. Major components of this system include the esophagus, stomach, intestines (small intestine and large bowel, or colon), and the organs of digestion, including the liver and pancreas. The symptoms of the most common GASTROINTESTINAL TRACT DISEASES include nausea, vomiting, and diarrhea. Disease may be caused by ingestion of a preformed toxin such as in some kinds of FOOD POISONING, or illness may be due to a true infection as in viral or bacterial gastroenteritis.

The most severe forms of gastroenteritis are those caused by bacteria. Shigella bacterial organisms cause bacillary dysentery, a fulminating form of diarrhea, which causes destruction of the lining of the bowel. Salmonella bacteria may cause gastroenteritis and at times invade the bloodstream, leading to infections in widespread areas of the body such as bone, liver, and blood vessels. Viral gastroenteritis is usually benign and self-limited, requiring no specific therapy. Various parasites that infect the gastrointestinal tract include protozoa such as *Entamoeba histolytica*, the cause of amebiasis, and *Giardia lamblia*, the cause of giardiasis. These two infections may be chronic and indolent and may mimic the signs and symptoms of noninfectious gastrointestinal diseases such as ulcerative colitis and regional enteritis.

The majority of patients who develop acute symptoms of diarrhea with or without nausea and vomiting have a self-limited disease that requires no therapy. The most common identifiable causes of this syndrome include viral gastroenteritis and toxin-producing strains of the common colon bacillus *Escherichia coli*.

Helminth, or worm, infections of the gastrointestinal tract range in severity from asymptomatic to those that may result in severe illness. Hookworms attach to the wall of the intestines and destroy red blood cells. A heavy infection may thus produce anemia. Large tapeworms in the gastrointestinal tract may induce illness by absorbing foodstuffs and vital nutrients.

Hepatitis, an inflammation of the liver, is most commonly caused by viruses. Hepatitis A, or infectious hepatitis, is a disease that is transmitted by direct fecal-oral contact. It is a common illness in young children and is usually benign. Hepatitis B, or serum hepatitis, is transmitted by exposure to contaminated blood or blood products and by direct intimate (often sexual) contact. It may be a more serious disease, especially in older patients. Blood donors are carefully screened for evidence of hepatitis B. Those who have evidence of prior viral infection are excluded from donating blood.

SKIN AND MUCOUS MEMBRANE INFECTIONS

Infection may primarily involve the skin and mucous membranes, or skin lesions may indicate infection elsewhere. The most common bacterial SKIN DISEASES include those caused by staphylococci, which tend to form boils (or pus-filled areas of inflammation), and streptococci, which result in a spreading area of skin inflammation. Measles, a systemic infection, is characterized by a generalized skin rash. Herpes simplex virus causes cold sores, and in impaired hosts, more widely spread lesions. Shingles, or herpes zoster, is an infection of the nerves supplying a specific area. The virus, identical to that which causes chicken pox, is thought to represent a reactivation of an old chicken pox infection. Diagnosis is usually easily made, because lesions characteristically cluster in a pattern representing the distribution of nerves on the surface of the skin. Parasites may invade the skin. For example, scabies is due to a small mite that burrows in the skin, causing intense itching and inflammation. The louse, which lays its eggs (nits) on hair, and ticks, which suck blood from the host, may transmit serious diseases. Fungal skin diseases, which are common and usually benign, include ringworm, athlete's foot, and thrush.

VENEREAL DISEASES

VENEREAL DISEASES are transmitted by sexual contact. Syphilis is caused by a spiral-shaped bacterium, a spirochete. This disease is especially dangerous because after initial infection of the genitals or mucous membranes it may become quiescent for years and then activate and cause damage to the nervous system or cardiovascular system. The chancre, a painless ulcer, is the most common initial lesion. Syphilis may be diagnosed by blood tests. Treatment with antibiotics is very effective. Gonorrhea is a common bacterial disease characterized by inflammation of the urethra. In females, inflammation of the fallopian tubes may result in abdominal pain, fever, and sterility. Gonorrhea is diagnosed by bacterial cultures. Antibiotic therapy is extremely effective. Sexually transmitted urethritis may also be caused by other microorganisms including *Chlamydia* and *Mycoplasma*. These diseases are relatively benign in adults. When transmitted to infants, however, these agents may cause eye infection and pneumonia. Herpes simplex type 2 is a virus that causes painful involvement of the genital area. This disease tends to wax and wane. There is at present no established effective therapy, but new drugs are being evaluated.

OTHER INFECTIONS

The brain and spinal cord may be directly involved in infection. Viral encephalitis damages the brain, and poliomyelitis is an infection of the spinal cord. The lining of the nervous system may be affected by meningitis due to bacteria, viruses, or fungi.

Bacterial infection of the urinary tract is common, especially in adult women. Antimicrobial therapy is effective unless there is a structural abnormality present. Infections of bone (osteomyelitis) and of joints (septic arthritis) may result in deformity and disability. Infective endocarditis is a serious infection of the valves inside the heart. In addition to antibiotic therapy, the involved heart valves may require surgical excision and replacement with artificial valves.

PREVENTION

Prevention is much more efficient than treating infectious diseases. Prevention may involve general improvements in sanitation and the nutritional state of the population or more specific maneuvers such as immunization. Toxoids, or altered toxins, are used to immunize against tetanus and diphtheria, two diseases where the major damage is done by the toxin rather than invasion by the microbe. Attenuated, or weakened, live viruses are used to immunize against poliomyelitis and rubella (German measles). Killed organisms or fractions of organisms are the immunizing agents for influenza and typhoid fever. The live virus vaccines usually give longer-lasting protection than killed vaccines. Immunization with a related virus (vaccinia, or cowpox virus) has been effective in eliminating smallpox as a threat to humans.

Patients who may spread highly contagious diseases to other patients may have to be isolated while they are undergoing treatment. Thus, before chemotherapy for tuberculosis was available, patients with this disease were separated from the rest of society in sanitoriums. Now, since therapy is so effective, these patients may be treated in general hospitals, or even in their own homes. Infections that may be acquired in a hospital can be eliminated or reduced by strict attention to cleanliness and avoidance of cross-contamination from one patient to another; from patients to hospital personnel; and from personnel to susceptible patients.

THERAPY OF INFECTIOUS DISEASES
Most infections are self-limited and require no therapy. However, appropriate therapy is effective in shortening the course of illness, reducing the risk of transmission to other patients, and in the case of severe infections, reducing mortality. No truly effective agents for the therapy of infection were available until the 1930s, when sulfonamides were developed. These agents interfere with steps in the metabolism of bacteria and are effective therapy for certain bacterial diseases. Penicillin, the first of the antibiotics, became available in the 1940s. Antibiotics are substances produced by microbes that act against other microbes. The useful antibiotics are relatively nontoxic to mammalian systems. Antibiotics have a specific spectrum of action, and thus some agents are more effective for certain infections. Commonly used antibiotics include the penicillins, tetracyclines, cephalosporins, and the aminoglycosides. In addition, several nonantibiotic drugs are effective against bacterial infections. Fungal infections will respond to chemotherapy, and recently drugs effective against a few viral infections have been developed. The vast majority of viral infections, however, remain unaffected by any known therapeutic agents. New antimicrobials are constantly being developed and tested. This research is important because microbes can develop resistance to established agents, and therapy of infections caused by these microbes with available antibiotics may become ineffective.

CURRENT RESEARCH
Although the major infectious scourges of mankind have been eliminated or reduced, the search for discoveries in infectious diseases is still of major importance. Infections continue to afflict millions of people each year and are still a significant cause of discomfort, severe illness, and death. New methods of prevention as well as therapy must be developed. As medical technology advances, large numbers of patients with severely impaired defenses as a result of such treatment are acquiring frequent and severe infections. If advances in the therapy of cancers and success in organ transplantation is to continue, better methods of preventing and treating infections in these patients is vital. Some of the chronic debilitating diseases that have been previously thought to be noninfectious may in fact be related to infectious organisms. Thus, such diverse conditions as diabetes mellitus and multiple sclerosis may be caused by infectious agents. The new science of genetic engineering may enable us to alter the properties of microbes so that they can serve as effective immunizing strains without causing disease. In addition, alterations in microbes may result in production of antibiotics that may be more active and less toxic than those previously available. A more complete understanding of normal host defenses allows us to manipulate these mechanisms in an effort to prevent, control, and treat infections.   GERALD LEE MANDELL, M.D.

Bibliography: Burnet, F. M., and White, D. O., *Natural History of Infectious Diseases* (1972); Cluff, L. E., and Johnson, J. E., *Clinical Concepts of Infectious Diseases*, 2d ed. (1978); Dowling, Harry F., *Fighting Infection* (1977); Hunter, G. W., et al., *Tropical Medicine* (1976); Krugman, Saul, *Infectious Diseases of Children*, 6th ed. (1977); Mandell, G. L., et al., eds., *Principles and Practice of Infectious Diseases* (1979); Rosebury, Theodore, *Microbes and Morals* (1971); Siegfried, Andre, *Routes of Contagion* (1960); Top, Franklin H., and Wehrle, Paul F., eds., *Communicable and Infectious Diseases* (1976); Youmans, G. P., et al., *The Biological and Clinical Basis of Infectious Diseases* (1975).

inference

In the science of statistics, inference is the process of using information from observed phenomena to derive conclusions about the underlying probability distribution of the observa-

tions (see DISTRIBUTION, statistics). Suppose a coin is known to have some unknown PROBABILITY p of coming up heads. (In most cases, p will not be ½ and the coin will be biased.) Assume that in a coin-tossing experiment, 70 heads were observed out of 100 tosses. Two typical problems of inference are (1) to decide whether or not the coin is biased and (2) to estimate the value of p. The first of these questions is an example of hypothesis testing: the NULL HYPOTHESIS that the coin is unbiased is being tested. The second question is a problem in estimation; it does not seek a simple yes or no answer, but rather an estimated value of a parameter of interest. In estimation, some measure of the precision of the estimate is also sought. This may take the form of the VARIANCE of the estimate in (hypothetical) repeated SAMPLING. Alternatively, instead of giving a point estimate and the variance, there are ways of giving a confidence interval. Such an interval, whose ends are computed from the data, will include the true value in some specified fraction of hypothetical repetitions.

GEOFFREY S. WATSON

Bibliography: Bickel, P. J., and Poksum, K. A., *Mathematical Statistics* (1977); De Finetti, Bruno, *Probability, Induction and Statistics* (1972).

inferiority complex: see COMPLEX (psychology).

infinitesimal [in-fin-i-tes′-i-mul]

An infinitesimal is a quantity that can be made arbitrarily small (close to zero). For example, the function $f(x) = 1/x$ can be made smaller than any preassigned positive number by making x sufficiently large. We express this idea by saying that the LIMIT of $1/x$ as x exceeds all bounds (or approaches infinity) is zero. Since CALCULUS and its two branches—DIFFERENTIAL CALCULUS and INTEGRAL CALCULUS—deal with limits and infinitesimal quantities, they are sometimes called infinitesimal calculus.   JOE K. SMITH

infinity [in-fin′-i-tee]

Infinity, as used in mathematics, denotes a quantity that increases without bound and is in contrast to a finite quantity. The word is often encountered in the study of LIMITS. For example, we can consider the limit of $1/x$ as x approaches infinity, that is, as x increases without bound. We use the symbol ∞ for the word *infinity* and write $\lim_{x \to \infty} 1/x$ where lim stands for "limit" and $\to$ means "approaches." Now, $1/x$ gets closer to 0 as x gets larger. As larger and larger values of x are taken, the quantity $1/x$ can be made arbitrarily close to 0; this means that $\lim 1 = 0$, which is read, "The limit of $1/x$ as x approaches infinity is zero."

Infinity is not a number; any number, no matter how large, is finite. The expression $\lim 1/x^2 = \infty$ means that, by taking x closer and closer to 0, $x \to 0$, the quantity $1/x^2$ can be made larger and larger without bound.

A set A is said to be an infinite set if there exists a subset of A (other than A itself) that can be put into one-to-one correspondence with A (see SET THEORY). For example, the set A of natural numbers (1, 2, 3, 4, . . .) is an infinite set because its subset B, consisting of the even numbers (2, 4, 6, 8, . . .), can be put into a one-to-one correspondence with A in the following way:

$$1 \text{ in } A \longleftrightarrow 2 \text{ in } B$$
$$2 \text{ in } A \longleftrightarrow 4 \text{ in } B$$
$$3 \text{ in } A \longleftrightarrow 6 \text{ in } B$$
$$. . .$$
$$n \text{ in } A \longleftrightarrow 2n \text{ in } B$$

This correspondence also indicates an aspect of infinity that seems paradoxical. Since each natural number is matched up with an even number, the infinity of even numbers is just as large as the infinity of natural numbers (odd and even)—there are just as many even numbers as there are natural numbers.

The method of comparing infinities by pairing the objects in different infinite collections was devised by Georg CANTOR. Using this method, he showed that there are different orders of infinity, which are represented by quantities called transfinite numbers. For example, there are more points on a line than there are natural numbers (positive integers), even though both quantities are infinite. A set in which the number of elements is the same as the number of natural numbers is called a countably infinite set. Such a countable infinity is the smallest order of infinity. ROY DUBISCH

Bibliography: Zippen, Leo, *Uses of Infinity* (1962).

inflammation

The process of inflammation occurs in response to an injury, such as a trauma or an infection, to the tissues of the body. The series of events that constitute inflammation are controlled by chemical mediators and cells and are vital to the protection of the organism. Despite the wide range of causative agents, the process of inflammation is basically the same in all organisms. Inflammation is characterized by four physical signs. Warmth, caused by increased local blood flow, is felt in areas such as the skin that are normally cooler than the rest of the body; redness results from persistent dilation of the small blood vessels in the injured area; swelling, or local edema, is due to increased permeability of blood vessels, which allows exudate (protein-rich fluid) to escape to the damaged tissue; and pain is believed to result from chemical substances such as serotonin or from tissue tension, as is present in the skin over a boil. Sometimes loss of function is included as a sign of inflammation.

In response to tissue insult, the following events take place in simple acute inflammation. The small blood vessels in the area dilate (vasodilation) after an initial contraction. Blood circulation, however, tends to slow down, and blood may even clot. Leukocytes move toward and adhere to the vessel wall, perhaps because of the sluggish flow of blood. The leukocytes, usually neutrophils, pass into the tissue and form an exudate with the preceding fluid exudate; the walls of the vessels lose their impermeability to protein, and the protein escapes with water. Loss of fluid can lead to sluggish blood flow and coagulation. Fibrinogen, a plasma protein, escapes to the tissue and is acted on by thrombin to form fibrin, resulting in strands of fibers covering the injured area. Gamma globulin, which contains antibodies, also enters the tissue and accelerates the ingestion and digestion of bacteria by phagocytes. Cells called granulocytes are capable of phagocytosis; of them, the basophils and the tissue mast cells are the major sources of mediators of inflammation. Neutrophils and eosinophils, other granulocytes, are attracted to the site of tissue damage where the former function through release of lysozymes and the latter may act to control allergic reactions. Monocytes, called macrophages in the tissue, have a role in antigen processing and phagocytosis. Lymphocytes play a role in antibody production and cell-mediated IMMUNITY, which is effected, in part, through mediators called lymphokines.

Chemical mediators are classified into two groups. The first group consists of proteins of high molecular weight that constitute the complement and interrelated enzyme systems. Complement, a factor necessary for antibody-mediated cell lysis (destruction), is a series of proteins activated by immune complexes or other initiating factors. It also modulates inflammation through its ability to increase capillary permeability, direct migration of cells to the tissue, and enhance the ingestion of cells by phagocytosis. The complement system interrelates with enzyme systems responsible for blood coagulation; the breakup of fibrin (fibrinolysis); and formation of kinins, or potent vasodilators.

The second group of mediators consists of low molecular weight chemical mediators such as histamine. These chemicals are released during allergic reactions and result in vasodilation, increased vessel permeability, and attraction of cells to the site of injury.

Treatment of inflammation is aimed at its cause. When the cause is unknown, anti-inflammatory drugs, such as cortisone and aspirin, are used. Cortisone must be carefully administered, because inflammation is part of the body's defense system and, thus, the cure may be more harmful than the affliction.

Chronic, or long-term, inflammation occurs in such diseases as tuberculosis, leprosy, syphilis, and rheumatoid arthritis. These diseases are caused by microorganisms, except rheumatoid arthritis, the cause of which is unknown but may involve an immune disturbance. DOROTHY SOGN, M.D.

Bibliography: Hurley, J. V., *Acute Inflammation* (1972); Movat, Henry Z., *Inflammation, Immunity and Hypersensitivity*, 2d ed. (1978).

inflation

Inflation is an increase in the general level of prices of goods and services in a particular economic system. The causes of inflation may vary widely. Some of the great historic inflations have followed wars, political instability, and economic breakdown, as, for example, in Germany and Russia after World War I, China after World War II, France in 1794–97, and the United States in 1777–80. Since World War II the industrialized and developing countries have all experienced a slow but persistent rise in prices (called creeping inflation). At certain times and in certain countries prices have risen at rates of 10% or even 20% per year. This increase is low when compared with the German hyperinflation of the early 1920s or with chronic inflation in Latin America, where increases of several hundred percent per year have occurred. In the United States prices rose at an average of about 1.7% per year during the period 1948–65, at 6% per year during 1966–78, and at a 13% yearly rate during the first half of 1979.

CAUSES OF INFLATION

Demand-Pull Inflation. Economists have distinguished several kinds of inflation. Demand-pull inflation occurs when the aggregate demand by consumers for goods and services exceeds the supply that the economy is capable of producing at a given time. Buyers in a sense bid prices up, but this does not lead to increased production because the economy is already producing at full or near-full capacity. Low unemployment may allow workers to raise wage demands because employers are not easily able to find lower-paid replacements.

Demand-pull inflation may occur for several reasons. After a war, for example, a sudden demand for products along with increased purchasing power can create inflation. This situation was the case in the United States after World War II when inflation soared to 14%. High government expenditures that add to incomes, particularly when the expenditures are not covered by taxes, result in inflation. The 35% increase in defense spending (without a tax increase) during the Vietnam War, for example, was a primary cause of the inflationary economy of the 1970s. In this case military-goods production could not satisfy consumer demand, and private sector demand was not decreased by greater taxes. Another cause of demand-pull inflation may be an increase in the total money supply beyond what is needed to buy the existing supply of goods and services; this situation may result from heavy borrowing by consumers and businesses, which is encouraged by low interest rates set by central bank policy; it may arise because of easy availability of credit that comes with the increased use of credit cards and other charge plans; it may also be caused by national budget deficits that may result in the government's essentially printing more money. Historically, money-supply expansion and resulting inflation has occurred with the discovery of new supplies of gold. Another cause of demand-pull inflation may be a sudden increase in foreign demand for a country's products (which also has the effect of reducing the supply of goods and services in that country and increasing the money supply).

Cost-Push Inflation. In cost-push inflation, also called the wage-price spiral, the inflationary pressure arises on the supply side of the market. Cost-push inflation has been regarded as the chief cause of inflation after the demand-pull inflation of the 1960s. Prices rise because of increasing costs, particularly costs of labor and materials. Some economists have pointed to labor unions as a major cause of inflation, arguing that many employers yield to union demands even when they consider such demands too high, preferring to pass on the higher costs to their customers rather than risking a strike. Other economists argue that the ultimate cause of cost-push

PRICE LEVELS IN SELECTED COUNTRIES 1948-79
(base index year is 1970)

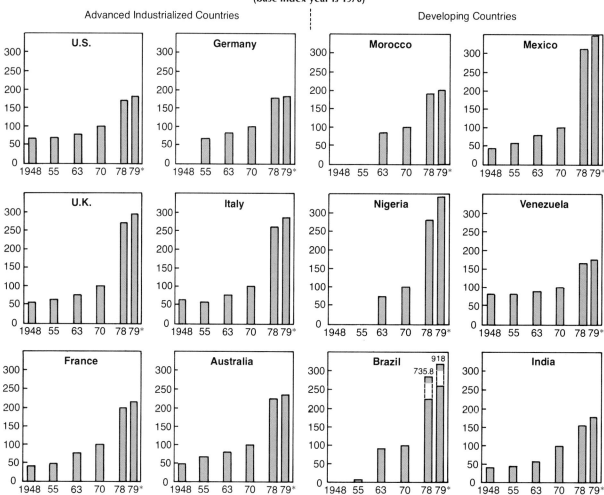

Advanced Industrialized Countries | Developing Countries

*Estimated

Adapted from IMF, International Financial Statistics

inflation is monetary because companies would not be able to pass on their higher costs to customers if governmental authorities were to keep the money supply under tight control.
Complex Causes of Inflation. Recently, more complex causes of inflation have been studied. Economists note that the rate of inflation depends not only on the present state of the economy but also on people's expectations about how much inflation will occur in the future. If unions and employers expect prices to continue to increase at, say, 5% per year, they are likely to agree on wage increases in excess of that amount. If bankers have similar expectations, they will charge rates of interest that are correspondingly higher than the expected rate of inflation. If consumers expect sustained inflation, they will begin to adopt a "buy now" attitude—increasing demand-pull inflation—instead of investing, saving, or decreasing their spending. To the extent that inflation is influenced by people's expectations, inflationary momentum will continue until people begin to expect lower inflation rates.

Another reason for cost-push inflation may lie in what economists call administered pricing. This term refers to prices that are controlled by firms—especially large firms dominating an industry—rather than by competition among firms. Companies that can freely administer prices are able to increase prices even when demand does not justify that course. These companies are less resistant to increased labor costs because they pass costs on to consumers and because these firms expect the government to keep demand high through expansionary (and inflationary) policies.

Productivity, or improvement in efficiency, also has an impact on inflation. If productivity declines, costs of production increase, prices increase to cover these costs, and labor demands higher wages in order to meet these costs. One of the more significant factors in decreased productivity has been the costs—estimated at over $100 billion a year—of GOVERNMENT REGULATION of job safety and the environment.

One reason that inflation has become a persistent problem for modern economies is that governments are larger and play a greater role in economic life than previously. Governments spend vast sums of money on national defense and general welfare programs, including social insurance and medical care. Most governments are committed to maintaining fairly high levels of employment—even at the risk of borrowing heavily—and avoiding the economic disasters of the past.

INFLATION DURING THE 1970s
In the early 1970s inflation persisted despite a serious slump in economic activity. Unemployment reached its highest levels since the 1930s, and, simultaneously, prices continued to soar. This situation sharply contradicted past experience, in which rising prices and higher employment tended to accompany one another (see PHILLIPS CURVE). Economists coined a new term for it: STAGFLATION (*stagnation* plus *inflation*). The expectation of continuing inflation seemed to be a cause of this inflation, but prices rose during the early 1970s for other reasons as well. Simultaneous international economic expansion led to global inflation. A worldwide grain shortage

caused an upsurge in food prices. In the United States this problem was made worse by large wheat deals in 1972 and 1975 between the United States and the Soviet Union. The increase in oil prices from about $2 per barrel to about $10 per barrel during 1973-74 by the Organization of Petroleum Exporting Countries raised costs for all oil and gas consumers. In the United States the president's Council of Economic Advisers estimated that higher oil and food prices accounted for about half of the 12% rise in the cost of living in 1974. Productivity also declined; during 1973-77 productivity in the United States grew at an average yearly increase of 1%, and during 1978, at 0.3%. (In contrast, productivity during 1955-65 grew at an average annual gain of 3.1% and during 1965-73, at 2.3%.)

Not everyone suffers equally from inflation. Workers in unionized industries can usually obtain cost-of-living increases. Retired prople living on social security and pensions may eventually receive adjustments. People who owe money may even profit from inflation because they can pay back their debts with money that has less purchasing power than the money they borrowed. Holders of fixed-interest savings accounts and those whose incomes do not keep up with inflation suffer most. Inflation has had a severe impact in many of the less-developed countries, which have had to pay rising prices for their imports from industrial countries while selling their raw materials and commodities at relatively low prices. During the 1970s some of these countries went heavily into debt.

SOLUTIONS TO INFLATION

There are many proposed solutions to inflation. During the 1970s the critical issue became how to solve the problem of rising inflation without generating unacceptable levels of unemployment and hardship.

Monetary theories of inflation hold that inflation can best be controlled by keeping the supply of money in proper relation to economic activity. The monetarists seek to control inflation by having the central bank (the FEDERAL RESERVE SYSTEM in the United States) impose tight controls on the money supply. Such controls have been adopted in recent years in the leading industrial countries. Critics of pure MONETARY POLICY agree that it can help to slow down inflation but argue that it may slow down the economy as well, thus leading to more unemployment.

To control excess economic demand, advocates of FISCAL POLICY call for reductions in government expenditures, tax cuts for business and tax increases for individuals, and reductions in budget deficit. This approach, however, while also potentially effective, may significantly reduce government spending on job programs and on other types of social policy. In addition, the taxation portion of the programs can be politically unpopular.

Another approach is an INCOMES POLICY to hold down increases of prices, profits, wages, and other types of income. The wage and price controls introduced by U.S. President Richard M. Nixon during 1971-73 is an example of this type of approach. Other forms of incomes policy include voluntary wage and price guidelines and tax-based incomes policy, also called real wage insurance (which rewards companies and workers for wage-increase restraints by reducing their taxes).

Other proposed solutions include energy conservation and self-sufficiency measures, large-scale dismantling of government regulations, and increased productivity through programs designed to reduce structural unemployment. Most economists agree that no single approach is sufficient to check inflation.   FRANCIS S. PIERCE

Bibliography: Bach, George Leland, *Inflation* (1958); Brown, Arthur Joseph, *The Great Inflation, 1939-1951* (1955); Flemming, J. S., *Inflation* (1976); Harriss, C. L., ed., *Inflation* (1975); Okun, Arthur M., *Inflation* (1970); Trevithick, J. A., *Inflation* (1977); Wilson, T., *Inflation* (1961).

influenza   [in-floo-en'-zuh]

Influenza is an infectious disease of the respiratory tract caused by the influenza virus. It is probably the last remaining pandemic (worldwide) infection of humans. Periodically, when new strains of influenza virus are introduced they spread rapidly all over the world, infecting millions of people and causing significant increases in mortality.

Although many different viral and nonviral respiratory and nonrespiratory illnesses are commonly called influenza or "flu" for lack of more exact diagnosis, influenza is an infectious respiratory disease caused by a specific virus of the genus *Orthomyxovirus*. The disease, which generally lasts 3-7 days, is characterized by fever, cough, and considerable muscle aching (myalgia) and is sometimes complicated by secondary bacterial pneumonia. Flu starts abruptly, usually with a fever up to 39.4° C (103° F) in adults and higher in children. The illness may be followed by a period of weakness and depression.

Bed rest, aspirin, and plenty of fluids constitute the best treatment. However, flu victims 50 years old or above may be given antibiotics to prevent pneumonia. Persistent fever or worsening symptoms may indicate one of three types of the pneumonia form of influenza. The first is sudden, severe, and often fatal and is present from the onset of influenza; the second is less severe and appears a few days after the onset of influenza; and the third, also less severe, appears after apparent recovery.

FLU PREVENTION

An attack of influenza produces a temporary immunity, but unfortunately the protection is against only the type of virus causing the influenza. The disease is produced by any one of three types (A, B, and C), with many strains. Vaccines have been developed that have been found to be 70 to 90 percent effective for at least 6 months against either A or B types. Vaccination is especially important for older people, patients with cardiac or respiratory diseases, and pregnant women. Periodically, influenza viruses change their character slightly, and each change requires a different vaccine. Thus, routine annual vaccination is not recommended, except when a new and virulent strain appears and for the high-risk groups mentioned above. Investigation is under way to characterize virus strains prevalent in animals and to determine which of these might be the source of future pandemics.

EPIDEMIOLOGY

The name *influenza* derives from an observation made over 400 years ago that epidemics of cough and fever occurred more frequently at certain times of the year. At the time, the conclusion was drawn that such epidemics occurred under the influence of particular constellations of planets. Even today, the seasonal factors in influenza remain poorly understood. In north temperate zones influenza epidemics generally begin late in December and usually end by the end of March. Although chilling and low humidity may play a role in the seasonal incidence in such areas, seasonal differences in the incidence of influenza have also been observed in tropical areas. The incidence of infection is highest among school-age children, partly because of their lack of previous exposure to antigenically related strains. Infection is probably transmitted as a small-particle aerosol. A high proportion of infected individuals do not develop symptoms but are probably capable of transmitting infection to others.

PANDEMIC INFLUENZA

Every 10 years or so, influenza pandemics have been caused by new strains of type-A virus. Epidemics, or regional outbreaks, have appeared every 2 to 3 years for influenza A and 4 to 5 years for influenza B. The pandemic of 1918-19 is estimated to have killed 21 to 22 million people throughout the world. More than 500,000 deaths were recorded in the United States. Death from influenza in the U.S. armed forces in 1918 amounted to about 80 percent of the total number of battle deaths during World War I.

Changes in influenza A virus have been responsible for such worldwide outbreaks as the so called Asian flu (1957) and Hong Kong flu (1968). The most prevalent strains today are known as A-Texas and A-Victoria. Two characteristics, called antigens, are so different in these strains from those of previous strains that many people have little or no immunity. The two antigens are H (hemagglutinin) and N (neuraminidase). H is a protein on the surface of the virus that causes the virus to attach itself to a cell. After infection, antibodies to the H molecule are formed, preventing infection by the same influenza virus. The N antigen is an enzyme on the surfaces of the virus that may facilitate the spread of the virus from cell to cell.

In the fall of 1918, J. S. Koen, a veterinarian, reported that a new disease that had appeared in pigs in the Middle West was strikingly similar to and coincident with human influenza in farm families. In 1928 the American virologist Richard Slope began intensive study of SWINE FLU and later demonstrated that it was primarily caused by a virus similar to the one responsible for the 1918 pandemic. Because of the dreaded experience of the 1918 pandemic, U.S. public health officials were apprehensive when another outbreak of influenza, apparently involving a similar strain of swine-influenza-like virus, appeared at Fort Dix, N.J., in January 1976. The U.S. government decided by late March to sponsor production of sufficient swine-flu vaccine to innoculate the entire U.S. population. Some scientists criticized this policy on the grounds that evidence was insufficient to indicate a major new influenza virus. After several months and following an outbreak of Guillain-Barré syndrome (a nerve disorder) among recipients of the vaccine, the mass vaccination program was suspended.

ORIGIN OF THE PANDEMIC STRAINS

Currently, the origin of the pandemic strains of the virus in humans cannot be explained satisfactorily. At one time the new H and N antigens were thought to arise by a series of mutations, but no evidence for this theory was ever found. Recent evidence does indicate, however, that fresh pandemics may come from an influenza virus that normally infects animals but also infects humans under exceptionally favorable conditions. They may also arise from a hybridization of an animal strain and a human strain. The vast reservoir of influenza-virus strains may therefore present a continuing and ineradicable threat to humans.   JAMES L. SCHULMAN

Bibliography: Beveridge, W. I. B., *Influenza: The Last Great Plague* (1977); Kilbourne, E. D., ed., *The Influenza Viruses and Influenza* (1975).

information science

Information science is the study of the ways in which organisms process information. It embraces such disparate topics as the means of genetic information processing in cells, the individual's use of information concerning the environment, and the methods of human learning and information generation. The dominant emphasis of information science today, however, is the last of these: human information processing at the conscious level. Information science integrates parts of other disciplines, such as biology, physics, computer science, sociology, psychology, and librarianship, insofar as they involve human information processing.

It is common to speak of the present as the Information Age, or to refer to the information explosion. About 50 percent of all workers in the United States today are in some way involved in information processing. Many people do not receive the right information at the right time, however, because they are not aware the information exists, because they do not know where to look for it, or because it is buried in a mass of extraneous information and is difficult to find.

Uses of Information Science. In the theoretical sense, information science tries to increase understanding of the ways in which information is generated, stored, made available, and used. In the practical sense it undertakes specific actions to try to improve these same functions of information science. The information scientist may consider alternative means of making information available, as by INDEXING, to determine which means work most satisfactorily, or the scientist may devise tools and methods for improving the transfer of information. One of the earliest of these tools was Keyword in Context (KWIC) indexing, first introduced in 1959 and developed by Hans Peter Luhn and his colleagues at IBM. In a KWIC index, the computer is used to generate entries from title words, saving the time and cost of human indexing but losing the benefits of human understanding of the document. In Selective Dissemination of Information (SDI) a list, or profile, of topics of continuing interest to a user is prepared. This is then compared to the index terms of particular documents in the current literature on an ongoing basis, and the user is notified of those that match the profile.

The concept on which these and other new methods of disseminating information depend is that of the data base, which is a body of information, usually computer-stored, that can be searched and manipulated for a variety of needs. Data bases have grown out of computer-based publishing, in which the material is keyboarded for computer typesetting; once this process is completed, the information can be reused for other purposes. These data bases are of two main varieties: bibliographic and numeric. Bibliographic data bases are usually spinoffs from printed abstracting and indexing services, and are searched for similar needs in libraries and other organizations. A user usually works with a searcher to phrase a request to produce the needed information. Millions of bibliographic citations can be searched simultaneously, with retrieval of only those that match the search request.

Numeric data bases are much more varied, consisting of any sort of data an organization has found it needs. While some of these are publicly available, far more are reserved by their owners for their private use. A sophisticated data base technology based on magnetic tapes, drums, and disks has developed for INFORMATION STORAGE AND RETRIEVAL, and for DATA PROCESSING. When large quantities of information on printed pages must be stored, microforms are usually used (see MICROFILM). These permit maintenance of a vast number of documents in a very small space.

Future Techniques. A number of factors are coalescing today to make information science quite different in the future. Computer conferencing uses sophisticated computer networks to permit interchange of a great variety of computer conferencing messages among users. Although still experimental, computer conferencing shows promise of rapid development and may lead to the integration of all current processes of generation, storage, and transfer of information. Advances in communication technology may produce the "global village" envisioned by Marshall McLuhan—or they may instead lead to greater isolation.

In the future, a researcher who is engaged in experimental work and needs the advice of colleagues in other locations may go to a computer terminal and send a message concerning the work in progress. The colleagues, at their own terminals, would receive the message, and reply at their convenience. This dialogue could continue for some time, until the researcher's work was completed, whereupon a report would be prepared at the same terminal and transmitted by computer to the editor of a journal, to be considered for publication. After the editor receives it, he or she would transmit it to reviewers who would judge its publication worthiness and send their comments back to the editor, who would synthesize them for the author. After revising the paper, the author would retransmit it; the editor would then arrange for it to go through composition and publication in the journal. At the same time the paper would go to the abstracting and indexing services that covered it in their publications.

A scenario such as this one is technically possible at present; all these steps can be carried out at electronic speeds on the basis of only one keyboarding. Omission of the final step of paper publication is also possible, with substitution of direct transmission, as in SDI, to workers who have registered an interest in the topic of the paper.

These technologies will also affect daily life. Libraries are becoming access points for information, not just repositories for books. A person may telephone or go to the library to locate information on community agencies and services, on jobs, on the stock market, or any other need. If the library does not possess the information, it is likely to have network connections with other libraries or agencies that do. The potential of accessing information resources by means of computer terminals within the home is growing rapidly. Various systems that permit viewers to have interactive access to data bases via their television sets are being market tested. They include QUBE in the United States and Prestel in Great Britain. Viewers can call for information on the weather, the price of a stock or of grocery items, consumer information, or any other information that a provider wishes to make available.   JESSICA L. HARRIS

Bibliography: Artandi, Susan, *An Introduction to Computers in Information Science*, 2d ed. (1972); Becker, Joseph, *First Book of Information Science* (1973); Elias, Arthur W., ed., *Key Papers in Information Science* (1971); Hammer, Donald P., ed., *The Information Age: Its Development, Its Impact* (1976); Kent, Allen, et al., *Encyclopedia of Library and Information Science*, 25 vols. to date (1968-75); Lancaster, F. Wilfred, and Fayem, Emily G., *Information Retrieval On-Line* (1973); Rowley, J. E., and Turner, C. M., *The Dissemination of Information* (1978); Saracevic, Tefko, *Introduction to Information Science* (1970).

information storage and retrieval

In modern society the task of the storage and retrieval of vast amounts of information has been taken over almost entirely by COMPUTER systems. No longer a tool exclusively for mathematical computation, the computer now handles large collections of information called data bases. Government agencies such as the Internal Revenue Service, the Social Security Administration, and the National Crime Information Center maintain data bases, as do private industry (personnel records) and other organizations (medical records, credit records). Computer access to such stored information raises questions of great importance to modern society: How accurate is the information, and how can inaccuracies be corrected? Who has access to the information? How is improper or illegal access prevented? These questions are currently under study by computer scientists, lawmakers, and those with an interest in data bases.

Information is stored on various media by means of devices interfaced to computers. This storage is considered secondary, as opposed to the primary, internal COMPUTER MEMORY. Secondary memory has greater capacity than primary, but access is slower. Computer access to secondary memory may take time on the order of several thousandths of a second up to several seconds. This speed is in contrast to primary memory access times of less than one-millionth of a second.

Memory hierarchies extend to a tertiary, or archival, level with capacity for trillions of bits of information. An 8-million-word encyclopedia such as the *Academic American Encyclopedia* contains about 400 million bits of information (8 million words × 6 characters per word × 8 bits per character). A trillion-bit storage can store 2,500 times as much information as there is in such an encyclopedia, all of it directly accessible to the computer.

COMMON STORAGE DEVICES

Secondary memory devices include drums, disks, and magnetic tape. Each of these uses the property of magnetic material that allows particles to be oriented, or polarized, in one of two directions. The direction of polarization is used to record signals that can be interpreted as bits with binary number system values of zero or one.

Drums and disks are shaped differently but have many other properties in common. Drums are shaped like a drum, or cylinder, with the recording material wrapped around the outside. Information is recorded in individual tracks which form circles around the drum. Several hundred tracks lie adjacent to each other along its length. Disks are shaped like a disk, or phonograph record, with the recording material on the flat surfaces. Information is recorded in individual, concentric circle tracks. Several hundred tracks may be on each surface. More than one disk can be packaged together to form a unit with more than two surfaces.

Both drums and disks have read/write heads similar to the play and record heads on TAPE RECORDERS used for sound recording. Rotation of the recording medium causes the information storage tracks to pass under the heads for both devices. Heads are positioned on selected tracks, to access-selected information, by mechanical or electronic means. Both of these devices keep the recording surface in constant

rotational motion when they are on-line (actively interfaced) to the computer. This procedure eliminates the time delay of waiting for a device to reach operational speed.

Disks are by far the more predominant of the two devices. Both are used to store information that needs to be readily accessible to the computer, but either exceeds the capacity of primary memory or is used so infrequently that it does not merit being maintained in internal memory.

Magnetic tape units record digital signals on reels or cassettes of magnetic tape. Information is recorded in parallel tracks that run the length of the tape. Spinning the reels causes the tape to move from the supply reel, past the read/write heads, onto the take-up reel. Common tape drives have seven or nine parallel tracks across the tape so that at one recording position along the tape length, a character (such as a letter or number) of information may be stored. Storage capacity is determined by the total length of the tape and by the recording density in characters per inch. Typical values of length are 2,400 ft (230 m) with densities of 1,600 characters per in (630 characters per cm). Not all of the length is usable, however, since recording methods require certain unused areas. Tapes may be dismounted from tape drives and stored in libraries, which may hold essentially unlimited amounts of information. Tapes in a manually maintained library are not directly accessible from the computer. A computer operator must find the desired tape and mount it on a tape drive.

Information is recorded from the beginning of a tape towards the end in sequential fashion. To retrieve selected information it is necessary to wind or rewind the tape to the place where the information was recorded. This form of access, known as sequential access, requires examination of recorded information in the order (or reverse order) that it was recorded.

NEW DEVELOPMENTS

Newer storage devices are being developed out of electronic technology rather than the electromechanical technology of rotating or spinning devices. Bubble memories in which microscopic bubble patterns are formed on wafers of garnet crystals have recently become commercially available. These use the presence or absence of magnetic domains to represent the binary values zero and one. Similarly, charged couple devices (CCD) utilize the presence or absence of electronic charges to store information. Both devices are sometimes called electronic disks because they store information in patterns that make it accessible in a cyclic fashion, much like disk storage. Electronic disks have a significant advantage, however. Since there is no mechanical motion, the cycling may be stopped when the next needed storage area is available at the input/output (I/O) port. Rotating devices must keep moving past the desired storage area if the system is not yet ready for the actual I/O operation. Waiting for the area to reappear can cause large time delays, compared to computation times.

Another new technology is the electron beam accessed memory (EBAM). This may become the fastest of the secondary memory devices, but it is not as well developed or readily available as bubble and CCD memories. The EBAM stores information by using an electronic beam to charge a small area on a silicon dioxide plane.

ARCHIVAL STORAGE

Archival storage is the third level in the memory hierarchy. Archival storage devices are intended to hold information that is infrequently accessed but extensive in quantity. The devices are slow but have great capacity. The most successful devices in this category use magnetic tape. A straightforward system is simply an automation of the conventional tape library. Reels of tape stored in racks are electromechanically selected, moved to one of several tape drives, and mounted. If the tape to be selected can be specified in a program, then the system is fully automated. There is no need for a person to walk through the library, select, and manually mount the tape. Automatic dismounting and replacing of the tape in its rack is also supplied. An alternative tape system operates in a similar manner but uses a newly designed tape cartridge rather than standard reels.

Other mass memory technologies in various stages of research or development use videotape, holograms, laser beam recording, or optical techniques.

SOFTWARE CONSIDERATIONS

Information storage and retrieval involves more than hardware devices and storage media alone. To make the physical equipment readily usable it is necessary to provide SOFTWARE (programs) routines or systems. If the information exists as a data base, operations associated with it are to add information, to change existing information, to delete information, and to retrieve items of interest.

Large data bases employ data managers who maintain the data base for users. The need for powerful retrieval methods while maintaining strict security against unauthorized access gives rise to the need for complex software. Users inevitably want to retrieve information in different ways from the way it is stored. For example, because of the way information is stored in a phone book, it is easy to find a phone number if the name is known. A complex software system would make it equally easy to reverse the process and find the name if the phone number is known.

Information storage and retrieval is an active area of computer-related work both for hardware devices and for software systems.

EDWARD W. DAVIS

Bibliography: Artandi, Susan, *An Introduction to Computers in Information Science*, 2d ed. (1972); Becker, Joseph, and Hayes, M., *Information Storage and Retrieval* (1963); Burch, John G., and Hod, Nathan, *Information Systems* (1975); Couger, J. Daniel, and McFadden, Fred, *Introduction to Computer-Based Information Systems* (1975); Kruzas, Anthony, ed., *Encyclopedia of Information Systems and Services*, 3d ed. (1978); Martin, E. W., and Perkins, William, *Computers and Information Systems: An Introduction* (1973); Sharp, John, *Some Fundamentals of Information Retrieval* (1965).

See also: DATA PROCESSING; INPUT-OUTPUT DEVICES.

information theory

Information theory, also called the theory of communication, is a branch of PROBABILITY theory that has been developed to provide a measure of the flow of information from an information source to a destination. It also supplies a measure of the channel capacity of a communications medium such as a telephone wire and shows the optimal coding procedures for communication. Although originally concerned with telephone networks, the theory has a wider application to any communication process, even as simple as one human being talking to another. It may also be viewed as a branch of CYBERNETICS, the science of control and communication, and it has strong associations with control engineering, theories of learning, and the physiology of the nervous system.

Information theory was developed to a great extent at the Bell Telephone Company laboratories in New Jersey under the auspices of Claude SHANNON in the 1940s and '50s. Many other versions of the theory have been suggested, notably by D. M. MacKay and Dennis GABOR.

Principles. The principal features involved in information theory are a source of information that is encoded and transmitted on a channel to a receiver, where it is decoded.

There are two versions of information theory, one for continuous and the other for discrete information systems. The first theory is concerned with the wavelength, amplitude, and frequency of communications signals, and the second with the stochastic (random) processes associated with the theory of AUTOMATA. The discrete theory applies to a larger range of applications and was developed for both noiseless and noisy channels. A noisy channel contains unwanted signals and requires a filter to take a copy of the transmitted message and compare it to the message received.

Entropy—the Measure of Information. The Shannon-Weaver measure of information is given by the formula $H = -\Sigma P_i \log_2 P_i$, where the amount of information H is called the entropy (a term borrowed from thermodynamics, where it means a tendency toward randomness or disorder), P_i is the probability of a message being sent, and the minus sign and the LOGARITHM to base 2 are convenient in providing a simple and positive measure of information. The applica-

tion of the formula can be illustrated by considering four horses A, B, C, and D running in a race where they are all joint favorites, so that any one horse has one chance in four of winning. The application of the formula for H gives $H = \frac{1}{4} \log 4 + \frac{1}{4} \log 4 + \frac{1}{4} \log 4 + \frac{1}{4} \log 4$, which works as $\frac{1}{2} + \frac{1}{2} + \frac{1}{2} + \frac{1}{2}$, which equals 2, because $\log_2 4 = 2$. This result means that the average amount of information in this situation is worth 2 bits, where "bits" is a contraction of binary digits: 2 binary digits would be needed to encode the message "A has won" where the conversion from the usual decimal code to BINARY NUMBER code is $0 = 0$, $1 = 1$, $2 = 10$, $3 = 11$, $4 = 100$, $5 = 101$, $6 = 110$, $7 = 111$, $8 = 1000$, and so on. Thus horse A might be represented in binary code by 0, B by 01, C by 10, and D by 11.

Since the horses would not normally all have the same odds, the resultant value of H depends upon the actual odds, and the amount of information passed by any one message (e.g., A has won) would depend upon the odds (the associated probability). This means that when the horse with the longest odds wins, the message supplies more information than when a favorite wins. In general this means that the more unlikely the event described, the more information is contained in the message. In the limiting case, a message passing information to a destination about something already known contains no information. Similarly the maximum information for the system as a whole occurs when maximum uncertainty occurs, which happens when all the probabilities are equal, as in the example of a four-horse race.

Channel Capacity. The measure of the channel capacity of an information system is best illustrated where the probabilities again are equal. Given a set of 16 horses A, B . . . , P, each carrying 4 bits of information, then the channel capacity is $4n$ bits per second, where the channel is capable of transmitting n symbols per second; this becomes slightly more complicated when the probabilities are not all the same. The encoding of messages now requires a suitable procedure. It requires punctuation, as in the case of a "pause" in Morse code, or alternatively, all the words must be of fixed length. Furthermore, to achieve an optimal code, there are certain procedures that are all based on the principle that the most frequently occurring words (or letters) should be coded with the symbol of shortest duration. Thus e (the most frequently occurring letter in English) would be 1 in binary code, whereas the letter x might be 26 (11010 in binary).

Applications. More complicated theorems for continuous and discrete systems, with or without noise, make up the mathematical theory of information. The discrete theory can generate letter sequences and word sequences that can approximate ordinary English. A Markov net is a stochastic process that deals with conditional probabilities. For example, the probability of q being followed by u in an English word is very nearly 1 (certainty); one can also work out the probabilities for all letters and all words: for instance, the probability of "the" being followed by "the" is very nearly 0 (impossible). Information theory is thus an important tool in the analysis of language or of any sequence of events—and its encoding, transmission, reception, and decoding. Such methods have been used to describe learning from the point of view of the learner, where the source is one where some pattern of events occurs (in the case of human learning, this is often nature or life).

The theory of information has also been used in some models of the brain, where the thoughts and beliefs (some configuration of neurons) are the source; they are encoded in neural language, translated into a natural language such as English, and decoded by the hearer into his or her own thoughts. There is also a semantic of information, so far little developed, which deals with meaning, as opposed to uncertainty of information.

F. H. GEORGE

Bibliography: Ash, R. B., *Information Theory* (1965); Bendat, Julius S., *Principles and Applications of Random Noise Theory* (1958; repr. 1978); Clark, F., *Information Processing* (1970); Guiascu, Silviu, *Information Theory with New Applications* (1977); Haber, Fred, *An Introduction to Information and Communication Theory* (1974); Kullback, Solomon, *Information Theory and Statistics* (1974); Littlejohn, Stephen,

Theories of Human Communication (1978); MacKay, Donald, *Information, Mechanism and Meaning* (1970); Meetham, A. R., *Encyclopedia of Linguistics, Information and Control* (1969); Rosie, A. M., *Information and Communication Theory*, 2d ed. (1973).

infrared astronomy   [in-fruh-red']

Infrared astronomy is the branch of astronomy that studies radiation from celestial bodies at infrared wavelengths, which are longer than optical wavelengths and shorter than radio wavelengths. The infrared spectral region can be arbitrarily divided into two regions: the photographic infrared, which covers the wavelengths from 7,000 to 11,000 angstroms, and the far infrared, which ranges from 1.1–330 microns, where one angstrom (Å) is 10^{-10} m and one micron is 10,000 Å. Although William Herschel detected infrared radiation in the Sun's spectrum in the late 1700s, instruments necessary for a study of the entire infrared region did not become available until the second half of the 20th century.

Conventional astronomical tools such as the photographic plate (see ASTROPHOTOGRAPHY) and the photoelectric photometer (see PHOTOMETRY) are used to make observations in the photographic infrared. Beyond this region, a lack of suitable detectors rendered infrared work extremely difficult prior to about 1960. The devices used to study wavelengths greater than 1.1 microns are based on various types of photoconductive solid-state detectors that, when exposed to light, change their electrical conductivity proportional to the intensity of the incident radiation and produce a measurable change in electric current.

Lead sulfide (PbS) cells sensitive to radiation from 1.1 to 4 microns were first used to measure celestial sources in the early 1950s; it was not, however, until the 1960s that the PbS detector was more than a novelty. By the late 1960s, PbS cells were in widespread use as infrared detectors. To observe longer wavelengths, detectors composed of the semiconductor germanium doped with other materials are used. Sensitivity to various wavelength regions depends on the doping material used. In astronomical applications, all infrared detectors require cooling to be effective. The PbS cell must be cooled to 77 K ($-196°$ C), a temperature relatively easy to achieve, while other cells require the use of elaborate cryogenic equipment to cool the equipment to even lower temperatures.

The infrared astronomer is faced with a serious problem because water and carbon dioxide molecules in the atmosphere strongly absorb infrared radiation at many wavelengths. Ground-based astronomers are able to observe only in the gaps between the molecular absorption bands, known as atmospheric windows. To optimize observing conditions, ground-based infrared observatories are constructed at very high and dry locations. Two of the best infrared sites in the world are located in Wyoming and on the 3,270-m (14,000-ft) Hawaiian volcano Mauna Kea. To observe infrared wavelengths between 40 and 330 microns, astronomers use high-flying jets, rockets, balloons, and satellites to get above the atmosphere.

Although it is possible to make infrared observations with the detectors attached to conventional reflecting telescopes, infrared astronomy has benefited from the construction of large telescopes specifically designed for use at infrared wavelengths. An important attribute of these instruments is their ability to alternately measure the infrared source and the sky background in rapid succession. Without the subtraction of the background radiation, most infrared observations would be hopelessly inaccurate.

During the formative years of infrared astronomy, astronomers conducted surveys in search of interesting objects that would merit future investigation. In 1969, Gerry Neugebauer and Robert B. Leighton published an infrared catalog containing 5,612 sources north of $-33°$ declination observed at 2.2 microns. A United States Air Force survey of 2,066 objects observed at 4, 11, and 20 microns was published in 1974. Because a star having the relatively cool surface temperature of 3,000 K will have a peak in its energy distribution at a wavelength of about 2 microns, it is not surprising that a large number of the infrared sources found in these surveys are cool stars. Many of the remaining objects show an unexpectedly large amount of infrared radiation, commonly referred to as an infrared excess. A number of them have proved to be of great importance to the understanding of both early and late stages of stellar evolution.

Infrared observations within the solar system have also produced interesting results. Prior to the lunar landings in the 1960s, infrared observations provided the data sufficient to correctly determine the existence and properties of lunar dust. Infrared observations of asteroids have recently permitted the accurate determinations of the diameters of these small bodies. Infrared observations indicate that Jupiter emits more radiation than it receives from the Sun, so that Jupiter, though not massive enough to become a star, may be undergoing a slow gravitational contraction that releases the excess of radiation observed.

The future of infrared astronomy lies in orbiting observatories, in the development of more sensitive detectors, and in relatively easy-to-use equipment that will permit high-resolution observations over the whole spectral region.

CYNTHIA E. IRVINE

Bibliography: Allen, David, *Infrared: The New Astronomy* (1975).

infrared radiation

Infrared radiation is the region of the electromagnetic spectrum between visible light and microwaves, containing radiation with wavelengths ranging from about 0.75 μ (1 micron equals 1 one-millionth of a meter) to about 1,000 μ (1 mm). These limits are arbitrary, because the characteristics of the radiation are unchanged on either side of the limits. The discovery of infrared radiation is attributed to Sir William Herschel who, in 1800, dispersed sunlight into its component colors with a prism and showed that most of the heat in the beam fell in the spectral region beyond the red, where no visible light existed. In 1847, Armand Fizeau and Jean Foucault of France showed that infrared radiation, although invisible, behaved similarly to light in its ability to produce interference effects.

Infrared radiation is generally associated with heat because heat is its most easily detected effect. Most materials, in fact, readily absorb infrared radiation in a wide range of wavelengths, which causes an increase in the temperatures of the materials. All objects with a temperature greater than absolute zero emit infrared energy, and even incandescent objects usually emit far more infrared energy than visible radiation; about 60% of the Sun's rays are infrared. Sources of infrared radiation other than hot, solid bodies include the emissions of electrical discharges in gases and the laser (see LASER AND MASER), which can emit highly monochromatic (single-wavelength) infrared radiation of extremely high radiant power.

Infrared radiation can be used to detect the temperature of a distant object and therefore has many temperature-sensing applications, such as in astronomy or in heat-seeking military missiles. Photographs taken by infrared radiation reveal information not detectable by visible light. In the laboratory, infrared spectroscopy is an important method for identifying unknown chemicals.

STEPHEN FLEISHMAN

Bibliography: Kruse, P. W., et al., *Elements of Infrared Technology* (1962); Smith, R. A., et al., *Detection and Measurement of Infrared Radiation* (1968).

See also: ELECTROMAGNETIC RADIATION.

Ingalik   [ing'-guh-lik]

The Ingalik Indians, the westernmost Athabascan-speakers of interior Alaska, traditionally occupied territory along the lower Yukon and the upper Kuskokwim rivers. They borrowed a number of culture traits from their Eskimo neighbors, in spite of the enmity traditionally prevalent between Athabascans and Eskimo. Intermarriage, however, was uncommon.

The Ingalik occupied small winter villages composed of earth-covered semisubterranean lodges with racks in front for storage of canoes and sleds, elevated caches for winter stores, separate smokehouses, and drying racks for salmon. In summer they lived in houses made of cottonwood or spruce bark. The *kashim* was the center of various social activities. Fishing was the major activity from spring until summer, with migratory waterfowl forming another summer food resource. In spring muskrats provided both food and peltries that, stitched together, formed robes and parkas. Caribou, moose, and occasionally bears were hunted on snowshoes but were not abundant. Shamanism conformed to Western Eskimo patterns, with the novice trained by an established practitioner. POTLATCH festivals with feasts and gift giving, masked dances, ceremonials for animal souls, and memorials for the dead were popular events in traditional Ingalik society, demonstrating the tribe's thorough adaptation to Western Eskimo culture. The remaining Ingalik population today is largely assimilated into white society.   PHILIP DRUCKER

Bibliography: Osgood, Cornelius, "Ingalik Material Culture," *Yale University Publications in Anthropology*, vol. 22 (1940), and "Ingalik Social Culture," *Yale University Publications in Anthropology*, vol. 53 (1958).

Inge, William   [inj]

A popular and highly respected playwright of the 1950s, William Inge, b. Independence, Kans., May 3, 1913, graduated (1935) from the University of Kansas. Inge specialized in simple, well-crafted dramas describing the yearnings, frustrations, and failures experienced by small-town midwesterners. His most successful plays were *Come Back, Little Sheba* (1950; film, 1953), the Pulitzer Prize-winning *Picnic* (1953; film, 1956), *Bus Stop* (1955; film, 1956), and *The Dark at the Top of the Stairs* (1957; film, 1960). Inge wrote little after his 1959 Broadway failure *A Loss of Roses* (filmed as *The Stripper*, 1963), and on June 10, 1973, committed suicide.

Bibliography: Shuman, R. Baird, *William Inge* (1965).

Inge, William Ralph

The English churchman William Ralph Inge, b. June 6, 1860, d. Feb. 26, 1954, became known as the "gloomy dean" while dean (1911–34) of Saint Paul's Cathedral in London. He was educated at Cambridge University, where he was later (1907–11) Lady Margaret professor of divinity. Inge's sympathies with Platonic spirituality were expressed in a series of theological and devotional writings, among them, *Christian Mysticism* (1899), *Personal Idealism and Mysticism* (1907), *The Philosophy of Plotinus* (1918), and *Outspoken Essays* (1919, 1922). His distinctive pessimism and provocative style made Inge a well-known churchman to his generation.

Bibliography: Helm, Robert M., *Gloomy Dean: The Thought of William Ralph Inge* (1962).

Ingemann, Bernhard Severin   [ing'-e-mahn, bairn'-hahrt sev'-uh-reen]

Bernhard Severin Ingemann, b. May 28, 1789, d. Feb. 24, 1862, was a Danish author whose historical novels earned him wide acclaim in his day. Set in medieval Denmark, they included *Waldemar, Surnamed Seir* (1826; Eng. trans., 1841), *The Childhood of King Erik Menved* (1828; Eng. trans., 1846), and *King Erik and the Outlaws* (1833; Eng. trans., 1843). He also wrote patriotic and religious poetry.

Ingersoll, Robert Green   [ing'-gur-sohl]

Robert Green Ingersoll, b. Dresden, N.Y., Aug. 11, 1833, d. July 21, 1899, was an American orator known as the Great Agnostic. Self-educated, he was admitted to the Illinois bar in 1854. After serving in the Union army during the Civil War, he was attorney general of Illinois (1867–69) and became a vigorous campaigner for Republican candidates. His most famous political address was the speech in which he nominated James G. Blaine, whom he called a "plumed knight," for president. At the 1876 Republican convention, Ingersoll's own political ambitions were thwarted by public disapproval of his attacks on religion, which he delivered from lecterns all over the country. Ingersoll symbolized the intellectual ferment that buffeted orthodox religion in late-19th-century America.

Bibliography: Cramer, C. H., *Royal Bob* (1952); Ingersoll, Robert G., *The Works of Robert G. Ingersoll*, ed. by Clinton P. Farrell, 12 vols. (1902); Larsen, Orvin, *American Infidel: Robert G. Ingersoll* (1962).

Ingrao, Pietro   [een-grah'-oh, pee-ay'-troh]

Pietro Ingrao, b. Mar. 30, 1915, was the first Italian Communist party leader to become president (1976) of Italy's Chamber of Deputies. Ingrao joined the party in 1940, and from 1947 to 1957 was editor in chief of the party's daily newspaper *l'Unità*. He was elected to the Chamber of Deputies in 1948.

Ingres, Jean Auguste Dominique   [ang'-gruh]

The major French painters of the first half of the 19th century were Eugène Delacroix and Ingres, who were then seen as leaders of the opposed styles of romanticism and neoclassicism. Jean Auguste Dominique Ingres, b. Aug. 29, 1780, d. Jan. 14, 1867, learned drawing from his father, who was a sculptor, before attending the Academy of Art in Toulouse from 1791. In 1797 he entered Jacques Louis DAVID's studio in Paris. He competed several times for the coveted Prix de Rome, finally winning it in 1801. Lack of government funds prevented him from going to Italy until 1806, but he remained there until 1824, supporting himself after his scholarship had ended by painting portraits.

The neoclassicism of Ingres's style was already apparent in the painting that won him the Prix de Rome, *The Ambassadors of Agamemnon Arriving at the Tent of Achilles* (1801;

Woman Bathing, also known as La Grande Baigneuse, painted by J. A. D. Ingres in 1808 during his residence at the French Academy in Rome, reveals his earlier training with Jacques Louis David in its austere linear composition and muted colors. (Louvre, Paris.)

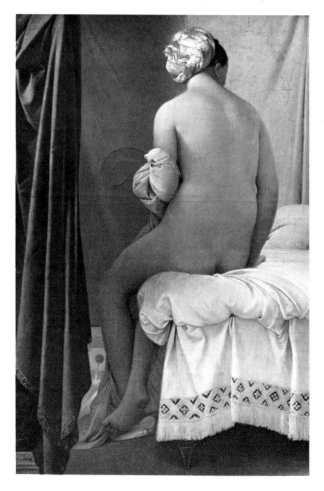

École des Beaux-Arts, Paris), which owes much to David's work. Ingres used ancient classical sculptures as source material for his figures, accentuating their contours. This stress on line, deriving ultimately from Greek art and Raphael, was an important part of Ingres's style, which he was to stress when instructing his pupils. Although classical antiquity often inspired Ingres, his iconic portrait of Napoleon (1806; Musée de l'Armée, Paris) was influenced by Byzantine art and Jan van Eyck.

While in Italy Ingres sent paintings to Paris for exhibition, but they were frequently attacked because of their unorthodox style. He rejected the influence of any artist after the 16th-century Italian painter Raphael, and vigorously defended his preference for classical art. In 1824 he returned to France to show his important religious painting *The Vow of Louis XIII* (1823; Montauban Cathedral, France), which met with a triumphant success and appealed to both neoclassical and romantic tastes. Ingres became famous: Charles X awarded him the Cross of the Legion of Honor; he was elected to the Academy of Fine Arts and opened a large, flourishing studio. He was to remain in Paris for the rest of his life, except for the period 1834–41, when he was Director of the French Academy in Rome.

He painted historical and religious subjects throughout his career and was also drawn to exotic Levantine subjects, notably a series of bathers (begun 1807), of which the most famous are the *Turkish Bath* (1859–63; Louvre, Paris) and *The Grand Odalisque* (1814; Louvre). Ingres also executed commissions for portraits, in which his meticulous method of painting captured details and textures with astounding verisimilitude. The polemical distinction between romantic and neoclassic, which Ingres himself did much to enforce, cannot be applied to his work dogmatically. His enormous canvas *The Dream of Ossian* (1813; Musée Ingres, Montauban), originally intended to decorate a palace in which Napoleon was expected to stay while in Rome, is thoroughly romantic in subject and style. The nonclassical enthusiasms of his time are reflected in his taste for Eastern subjects and historical romances.   KENNETH BENDINER

Bibliography: Friedlaender, Walter F., *David to Delacroix*, trans. by Robert Goldwater (1930; repr. 1952); Rosenblum, Robert, *Ingres* (1967); Wildenstein, Georges, *Ingres* (1954).

inheritance: see TRUST; WILL (LAW).

inheritance tax

An inheritance tax is a tax levied on a person (heir or legatee) who receives property upon the death of a benefactor. The tax is assessed after the total property has been divided among all the heirs. It differs from an estate tax, which is placed on the deceased's estate before the estate is divided. The U.S. government has taxed estates (since 1916) but does not have an inheritance tax. Most states, however, have an inheritance tax, an estate tax, or both. A state inheritance tax is usually paid by the executor of a deceased's estate. The executor withholds an assessed amount from the heirs or establishes a claim against the heirs who are responsible for paying the tax.

Inheritance taxes are usually progressive—that is, the tax rate increases with the amount of the inheritance. Federal estate tax rates are also progressive, ranging from 3 percent on the first $5,000 over $60,000 to 77 percent on estates over $10 million. Estates of $60,000 or less are not taxed, and an estate passing to a spouse is exempt up to half the total amount.

Some persons give much of their property away before they die, allowing their future heirs to avoid paying inheritance and estate taxes. Although federal and state gift taxes are designed to discourage avoidance of inheritance and estate taxes by the wealthy, these taxes have proved largely ineffectual for this purpose because of their lower rates.

Bibliography: Wagner, Richard E., *Death and Taxes: Some Perspectives on Inheritance, Inequality, and Progressive Taxation* (1973); West, Max, *Inheritance Tax*, 2d ed. (1908; repr. 1971).

inhibitor

A chemical substance that slows down or retards a chemical reaction is called an inhibitor. This type of substance, a form of catalyst, plays an important role in decreasing the rate of a reaction in industrial chemistry or in chemical research. One important class of inhibitors is ANTIOXIDANTS, which are used to prevent organic compounds from deteriorating. An inhibitor may also prevent a chemical CHAIN REACTION from taking place by combining with the chemical agents that perpetuate the chain. For example, the "knocking" that occurs in a gasoline engine results from a chain reaction; tetraethyl lead is added to gasoline to stop or break this reaction.

WILLIAM H. NYCE

Initial Teaching Alphabet

The Initial Teaching Alphabet is a special alphabet designed by Sir James Pitman, a British educator, in collaboration with C. N. Fellowes and D. H. J. Schenck, to simplify the first steps in learning to read. It consists of 44 letters, omitting the *q* and *x* and adding 20 characters for sounds that require more than one letter in English, such as "oo." Texts can then be written phonetically.

The Initial Teaching Alphabet is only one of several special alphabets, but it is used extensively. Research in the early 1960s indicated that children using it learned to read more quickly and with better comprehension. Within a decade more than 700 books were published in it.

Bibliography: Downing, John A., *The Initial Teaching Alphabet Explained and Illustrated* (1964) and *Evaluating the Initial Alphabet* (1967); Pitman, Sir James, and St. John, John, *Alphabets and Reading: The Initial Teaching Alphabet* (1969).

See also: READING EDUCATION.

initiative: see REFERENDUM AND INITIATIVE.

injunction

An injunction is a court decree granted by a judge requiring a person to act or cease to act in a specific way. Injunctions are of two kinds: prohibitory and mandatory. Prohibitory injunctions forbid certain acts or activities; mandatory injunctions require that certain acts or activities be undertaken. If an injunction is defied, a judge may cite the offender for CONTEMPT.

Injunctions may be preliminary or permanent. A preliminary (also temporary or interlocutory) injunction is awarded when a court is convinced that such an injunction is necessary to prevent irreparable damage to the party seeking it. This injunction remains in force until the issue has been settled by a court decision or until a specified, limited period of time has elapsed. A temporary restraining order is a type of preliminary injunction in which only the party seeking the order is heard by a court. Such an injunction is limited in its duration and is often replaced by a regular temporary injunction as soon as both parties are present in court. A permanent, or final, injunction is granted at the conclusion of the lawsuit.

Injunctions are governed by the common-law principles of EQUITY. These principles apply to situations in which legal remedies are considered inadequate, as in labor-management disputes and issues involving governmental regulation. Because an injunction can be obtained quickly—as opposed to litigation, which is time-consuming—it is an effective way to enforce regulatory statutes. Injunctions were frequently used against labor unions until the Federal Anti-Injunction Act (Norris-LaGuardia Act) of 1932. The LABOR-MANAGEMENT RELATIONS ACT (Taft-Hartley Act) of 1947 and the LABOR-MANAGEMENT REPORTING AND DISCLOSURE ACT (Lendrum-Griffin Act) of 1959 provided for the use of injunctions under certain conditions.

ink

Inks are paintlike fluids and pastes used for writing and printing. The use of colored fluids for drawing characters on parchment, hide, or cloth was common in ancient Egypt and China at least as early as 2000 BC. Ancient writings that are still preserved often used inks based on lampblack (carbon black), a finely ground pigment dispersed in water or oil, and sometimes stabilized with a vegetable gum or glue. Modern India inks, which are noted for their intensity and permanence, are similarly composed. Carbon black provides excellent opacity and is not affected by moisture or light. Other inks were made from indigo; from the galls of oak and nut trees; from tannin; and from the inky fluids secreted by octopus, cuttlefish, and squid.

Writing Inks. Most fountain pen inks employ solutions of water-soluble dyes, which can be washed out but which have relatively poor light and moisture resistance. Soft-tip PENS also use soluble dyes, which are dissolved in alcohol solvents to prevent the tips from drying or clogging. Ball-point inks are considerably heavier in consistency and are mixtures of oils, polymers, dyes, and solvents; they are designed to provide a continuous delivery of ink to a variety of surfaces and to dry instantaneously.

Printing Inks. Inks employed in PRINTING are prepared from natural and synthetic film-forming resins and generally use pigments rather than dyes to provide color. Early letterpress printing used inks composed of varnish, linseed oil, and carbon black. Modern letterpress inks must have sufficient consistency to adhere to the raised portion of the plate. The composition of resin, pigment or dye, and solvent depends on the method of drying the ink—whether by heat, by the absorption of the solvents into the paper, or by precipitating the ink through the steam-removal of the solvent.

Lithographic, flexographic, and gravure inks are deposited from etched, molded, or raised printing plates. Since the LITHOGRAPHY process uses water-saturated plates, the inks must be incapable of mixing the water and are usually linseed-oil based. Flexographic printing deposits ink from molded rubber plates, which can be used for printing almost any surface, including cloth, plaster, and foil. Special solvents in the inks evaporate rapidly or are absorbed quickly into the printed surface. Gravure printing on high-speed presses uses inks that dry almost instantaneously.

SILK-SCREEN PRINTING requires a relatively thick, viscous ink because it involves the forcing of ink through small holes in a screen or fabric.

Many specialty inks have been developed for special purposes. Industrial packaging requires inks that are resistant to scuffing or that have a high gloss. Fluorescent inks are now available for use on labels and packages and for printing maps that will be read at night. Magnetic inks use pigments that can be magnetized so the characters can be read by computers.   JOHN J. OBERLE

Bibliography: Carvalho, David N., *Forty Centuries of Ink, or a Chronological Narrative Concerning Ink and Its Backgrounds* (1904; 1971); Davids, Thaddeus, *The History of Ink, Including Its Etymology, Chemistry and Bibliography* (1977); Wells, Andrew M., *Printing Inks—Recent Developments* (1976).

See also: PAINT AND VARNISH.

Inland Sea

The Inland Sea (Japanese: Seto-naikai) of Japan is a body of water surrounded by the major islands of HONSHU, KYUSHU, and SHIKOKU. Covering approximately 9,480 km² (3,660 mi²), it is about 385 km (240 mi) long and ranges between 6 and 58 km (4 and 36 mi) in width. It is linked to the Pacific Ocean by the Akashi, Naruto, and Bungo straits, and to the Sea of Japan through the narrow Strait of Shimonoseki. The mountainous islands that enclose it offer protection from winds, making the waters unusually calm. The sea is shallow, and at no point does the depth exceed 150 m (492 ft). Dotting the waters are approximately 950 islands ranging from small, rocky outcrops to the largest, Awaji-shima, which has an area of 590 km² (228 mi²) and is located at the sea's eastern end. The many natural harbors on the sea's shoreline include HIROSHIMA, KOBE, a deepwater port, and OSAKA. Fishing is an important economic activity of the area; oyster dredging is pur-

sued in Hiroshima Bay. The shoreline is heavily industrialized, yet the area is noted for its scenic beauty, including that of the Inland Sea National Park.

Inn River

The Inn River, a major tributary of the DANUBE, is 515 km (320 mi) long. It rises in Lake Lughino in east central Switzerland and flows northeast along the Engadin Valley, through the Bavarian Alps of western Austria and southeastern West Germany, to join the Danube River at Passau. It drains an area of about 25,900 km² (10,000 mi²) and supplies much hydroelectric power. The river is part of the Austria-West Germany border. INNSBRUCK is on its course.

innate ideas

Innate ideas are ideas or functions originating in the mind apart from sense experience. Different theories of innate ideas have appeared over the centuries. PLATO believed that people developed understanding in a previous life but were born into their present life in a condition resembling forgetfulness. All learning, according to this theory, is remembering what one once knew explicitly and still somehow knows despite having forgotten it.

For the Stoics, all people have certain "common notions" that are the roots of science and morality prior to any sense experience. Saint AUGUSTINE adapted the Platonic remembrance theory and spoke of a nonsensory source of knowledge in a divine illumination. Saint BONAVENTURE and his disciples repeated this doctrine. In the 17th century, René DESCARTES taught that ideas such as God, the soul, and even geometrical axioms, are innate, having been implanted by God. Variations on this are found among Cartesian and rationalist thinkers in the next century.

What may be regarded an an innate-ideas doctrine is also present in the writings of Immanuel KANT, for whom space and time, "the categories" of understanding, and the "pure ideas" of God, the soul, and the world, all derived from the structure of the knower prior to sensation. For Kant, as for others accepting innate ideas, morality is not rooted so much in experience as in common forms or rules possessed by everyone anterior to any experience.   JOHN P. DOYLE

Bibliography: Stich, Stephen P., ed., *Innate Ideas* (1975).

inner city

The inner city—that part of a city embracing the central business district and the immediately surrounding area of housing, commerce, and industry—stands today as a monument to technological prowess. The inner city represents what is powerful and awesome in industrial culture. The skyscrapers, the maze of subways, the intricate webs of commerce and industry, and the complex networks of transportation and communication that make them possible—all reach their zenith in the inner city. In an age of space exploration and nuclear fission, one tends to forget the amazing accomplishments represented by so ordinary a thing as a sewer system or the communications tunnels. One also forgets because the inner city no longer holds much glamour for Americans, and has experienced recent decay. It is a study in sharp contrasts: a tribute to technical virtuosity and, at the same time, to shortsightedness.

Through much of the 19th and 20th centuries the inner cities of America were dynamic and growing. As the economy and population grew, and as transportation technology evolved faster and cheaper means of moving goods and people, the United States became increasingly a nation of city dwellers. By 1920 fewer than half of all Americans lived in rural areas. In the 1950s, after decades of expansion, the inner cities began losing population to the suburbs and smaller outlying areas existing around the inner city's periphery. In 1970 nearly three-quarters of all Americans lived in urban areas, but only about 30 percent lived in the inner city.

In its heyday, the inner city was home to an incredible variety of people and activities. Luxurious apartments and penthouses were located there, as well as the most squalid tenements; such extremes excited the imaginations of many and horrified others. The inner city was a battleground of contrary values and juxtaposed ways of life.

Much of the flavor of the inner city has come from the waves of immigrants, first from Ireland in the 1830s and then, at intervals, from Germany, Italy, Central and Eastern Europe, Asia, and the Jewish ghettos of Russia. Each group tended to concentrate in a particular area, giving the inner city a mosaic quality. This mosaic of groups, often struggling with one another over scarce jobs and housing, has given urban politics a distinctive character that still endures.

The inner city has also been the scene of economic change. Economic activity involved the process of centralization, moving from the home, to the small factory, and to ever larger factories. The inner city came to epitomize centralization with its fabled department stores, corporate headquarters, and banks; and nearby—if not directly in the center—the great factories produced the steel, rubber, and chemicals that became the industrial trademarks of the United States.

As people drifted away from an involvement with their ethnic pasts, inner-city neighborhoods grew less and less attractive. World War II veterans were encouraged to attend college and did so in record numbers; afterwards many found jobs in new, rapidly expanding industries ouside the inner city. Federally guaranteed mortgages for veterans also helped spur new residential construction, most of which was located in the suburbs. Major inner-city stores followed customers and located in suburban shopping malls. As a result of the general exodus, fewer business dollars were spent in the inner city, and city tax revenues shrank.

Industrial expansion took new forms as well. New factories were easier and cheaper to build in the country; as the old factories of the inner cities became outmoded, this consideration became overwhelming. In addition, the tax structure often made it cheaper to build new factories than to renovate old ones. Corporate headquarters also were attracted to less densely settled areas.

While tax revenues dropped, the need for services rose. A greater proportion of the inner city's residents now are either elderly or very young, and both groups require more services. As the white middle class left for new homes and jobs around the periphery, the inner-city population became more and more the home of blacks and Hispanics. These groups, like earlier ethnic groups, came to the inner city in search of jobs and expanded cultural opportunities; but the economy that greeted the earlier immigrants had need of unskilled workers. Unskilled labor is no longer in such high demand and, in any case, the inner city is no longer the place where new jobs are being created. Thus, to compound matters still more, a growing proportion of the inner city's residents are poor and unemployed, increasing still further the need for social services. The inner city, once a place of promise and optimism, is increasingly a place of despair.

Many of the nation's largest cities are near bankruptcy or have been so in recent years. New York City, the nation's largest city, is by no means alone in this regard. Most cities have been forced to cut back on hospital services and police and fire protection. Occasionally an inner-city school will close during the school year because funds have run out.

Three kinds of attempts have been made toward reversing the fate of the inner city. First, urban renewal programs have financed major inner-city construction in an attempt to make the inner city attractive once more to the middle class; but the net effect has been to displace the poor rather than to attract new city dwellers. The second kind of action has been returning federal and state tax revenues to cities. And finally, numerous programs, including federally guaranteed loans and tax incentives, have encouraged merchants and industry to relocate or stay in the inner city. To date, these approaches have had little dramatic effect: they have at best helped avert disaster. Most urban planners now agree that major new efforts will be needed, including innovative mass transit and massive job creation, if the inner city is once again going to encourage and inspire its residents.   JAN E. DIZARD

Bibliography: Alcaly, Roger, and Mermelstein, David, *The Fiscal Crisis of American Cities* (1977); Banfield, Edward C., *The Unheavenly City Revisited* (1974); Hoag, Edwin, *American Cities* (1969); Jacobs, Jane, *The Death and Life of Great American Cities* (1961); Lewis, M., *Urban America* (1973); Murphy, R. E., *The American City*, 2d ed. (1974); Weaver, R. C., *Dilemmas of Urban America* (1966); Wilson, J. Q., ed., *The Metropolitan Enigma*, rev. ed. (1967; repr. 1968).

Inner Mongolia

Inner Mongolia is an autonomous region of northern China, bounded on the north by the Mongolian People's Republic and the USSR. The area is 1,191,400 km² (460,000 mi²), and the population, in which Chinese outnumber the indigenous MONGOLS, is 8 million (1976 est.). Huhehot is the capital. Inner Mongolia has long, cold winters and short, mild summers; most of the region is steppe or desert. The main occupation is livestock raising, but some farming (especially wheat) is possible in oases and areas irrigated with water from the Hwang Ho (Yellow River), which flows through the region. The Inner Mongolian Autonomous Region was the first self-governing entity established by the Chinese communist government in 1947.   JOHN E. MacDONALD

inner product: see VECTOR ANALYSIS.

inner speech

Inner speech, a kind of silent talking to oneself, is a central issue in the problem of the relation between thought and language. John WATSON, a spokesman for BEHAVIORISM, maintained that thought is merely subvocal speech—overt speech grown very small. The Russian psychologist Lev Vygotsky, in opposition to behaviorism, held that the mind evolves to reflect social reality. The process of trying to communicate with others, according to this theory, results in the development of word meanings that then form the structure of consciousness. Inner speech cannot exist without social interaction. In a gradual developmental process, symbols, first used in COMMUNICATION, are turned inward to regulate behavior in the interests of social cooperation. On this account, in early childhood (ages four to five years) impulses cannot be controlled linguistically. The theory is currently being tested and employed in studies of the development of language and of its relation to thought.   JOHN McLEISH

Bibliography: Luria, Aleksandr, *Cognitive Development, Its Cultural and Social Foundations* (1976); Piaget, Jean, *Language and Thought in the Child*, 3d ed. (1959); Vygotsky, Lev, *Thought and Language* (1962).

See also: PSYCHOLINGUISTICS.

Innes, Michael   [in'-is]

John Innes Mackintosh Stewart, b. Sept. 30, 1906, a reader emeritus at Oxford University, is known principally for a series of popular detective novels written under the pseudonym Michael Innes. His critical works on Kipling, Conrad, and Hardy, published under the name Stewart, are well regarded by his academic peers, but a much wider audience has responded to such stylish, allusive thrillers as *A Night of Errors* (1948), *The Long Farewell* (1958), and *Death at the Chase* (1970). Novels published under his own name include *An Acre of Grass* (1965) and *The Gaudy* (1974). Stewart's major scholarly contribution is *Eight Modern Writers* (1963), volume 12 of *The Oxford History of English Literature*.

Inness, George   [in'-is]

Widely regarded as the greatest American landscapist of the 19th century, George Inness, b. Newburgh, N.Y., May 1, 1825, d. Aug. 3, 1894, brought the influence of the French BARBIZON SCHOOL to the United States; later, he developed a style that was uniquely his own.

Inness showed artistic promise as a child and was largely self-taught. His early paintings were influenced by the HUDSON RIVER SCHOOL; *The Old Mill* (1849; Art Institute of Chicago) is typical. In 1854, during one of several visits to Europe, Inness studied the Barbizon painters—especially Jean

In The Lackawanna Valley (1855) George Inness transformed a commission from a railroad into an original work of art by subordinating detail to a broad panoramic view. Inness's rendering of distance and atmosphere raised his art above the pedestrian realism of 19th-century landscape painting. (National Gallery, Washington, D.C.)

COROT and Théodore ROUSSEAU, whom he imitated for a time—and the work of Claude Lorrain and Nicolas Poussin. His art began to show a breadth and grandeur that contrasted sharply with the literalism and "picturesqueness" plaguing the work of many of his contemporaries. *Peace and Plenty* (1968; Metropolitan Museum, New York City) reflects this trend away from literal detail and toward more generalized form, a focus on atmosphere and color, and greater expressiveness.

In 1870, Inness returned to Europe, where he studied for 4 years. During the middle period of his career (until c.1884), his paintings were characterized by a freer brushwork, an increasing interest in the possibilities of color, and less emphasis on detail, as seen in *Coming Storm* (c.1880; Addison Gallery of American Art, Andover, Mass.).

Inness's last period, from about 1884, is regarded by some as his finest; it was probably influenced by his immersion, about 1865, in Swedenborgian mysticism. The paintings of this period are semiabstract masses of color, whose dematerialized subjects are seemingly enveloped in ghostly mists. The settings of works such as *Home of the Heron* (1893; Art Institute of Chicago) are intimate and undramatic, sometimes peopled by solitary, brooding figures, and reflect an intensely personal and mystical vision of nature.   ABRAHAM A. DAVIDSON

Bibliography: Cikovsky, Nicolai, Jr., *The Life and Work of George Inness* (1965; repr. 1977); Davidson, Abraham A., *The Eccentrics and Other American Visionary Painters* (1978); Inness, George, Jr., *Life, Art and Letters of George Inness* (1917; repr. 1969); Ireland, LeRoy, *The Works of George Inness, An Illustrated Catalogue Raisonné* (1965); McCausland, Elizabeth, *George Inness* (1946; repr. 1977); Werner, Alfred, *Inness Landscapes* (1973).

Innocent III, Pope

Innocent III, b. c.1160, d. July 16, 1216, was pope from 1198 to 1216; during his pontificate, the PAPACY reached the height of its political power. Named Lotario de'Segni, he was born of a noble family and educated at Paris and Bologna where he studied theology and canon law. He served in the court of his uncle, Pope Celestine III, who appointed him cardinal in 1190. At this time he had already formulated his own theory of papal power, holding that secular rulers must be subject to the pope just as the body must be subject to the spirit. The youngest cardinal of his day, he was elected pope on the very day that Celestine died.

From the beginning of his pontificate, Innocent was in-

volved in imperial affairs. After Constance of Sicily, widow of Holy Roman Emperor HENRY VI, accepted papal sovereignty over Sicily, Innocent recognized (1198) her son, the future Holy Roman Emperor FREDERICK II, as king of Sicily. When Constance died the same year, Innocent became regent for the infant Frederick. Although he crowned OTTO IV emperor in 1209, he soon shifted his support to young Frederick, who became German king in 1212.

Innocent was equally successful in developing the claims of the papal authority over other nations. In England he intervened in the disputed appointment of the archbishop of Canterbury and procured the election of Stephen LANGTON. When King JOHN refused to allow the pope's appointee, Innocent placed (1208) England under interdict (in effect, banning church services). John finally yielded (1213) and became a papal vassal. In France, Innocent forced (1210) PHILIP II to obey canon law on the question of his divorce from his wife, Ingeborg of Denmark. The pope also made his authority felt in Spain, intervening in the marital affairs of Peter II of Aragon and Alfonso IX of León.

Innocent was instrumental in organizing the Fourth CRUSADE, but was unable to prevent its diversion to capture Constantinople in 1204. He also extended the crusade idea to the suppression of the ALBIGENSES and procured a war against them that lasted long after his death. At the end of 1215, he called the Fourth LATERAN COUNCIL, the culminating event of

Pope Innocent III (r. 1198-1216), depicted in a 13th-century mosaic, brought the medieval papacy to the height of its political influence through his diplomatic activity. He sponsored the work of Saint Dominic, launched the Albigensian Crusade, and called the Fourth Lateran Council near the close of his pontificate.

his pontificate. Among his many works, *De contemptu mundi* (On the Contempt of the World) was a popular ascetical treatise, written before he was elected pope. DAVID HARRY MILLER

Bibliography: Barraclough, Geoffrey, *The Medieval Papacy* (1968); Clayton, J., *Pope Innocent III and His Times* (1941); Packard, S. R., *Europe and the Church under Innocent III*, rev. ed. (1968); Smith, C. E., *Innocent III, Church Defender* (1951; repr. 1971); Ullmann, Walter, *The Growth of Papal Government in the Middle Ages*, 2d ed. (1962).

Innocent IV, Pope

Innocent IV, b. *c.*1200, d. Dec. 7, 1254, was pope from 1243 to 1254. His name was Sinibaldo Fieschi. Because of his belief in the universal authority of the PAPACY, he was engaged in a constant struggle for power with Holy Roman Emperor FREDERICK II. Following his election, Innocent tried to negotiate with Frederick but was forced to flee (1244) to France. From 1244 to 1251 the papal court was at Lyon. In April 1245, Innocent condemned the emperor and summoned him to appear before the Council of Lyon (see LYON, COUNCILS OF). Since Frederick refused to appear, he was convicted in absentia and declared deposed; the pope then tried to secure the election of a new emperor. Innocent continued to interfere in the affairs of the empire under Frederick's successors. The papal bull *Ad extirpanda*, which he issued in 1252, justified the use of torture by the Inquisition. DAVID HARRY MILLER

Bibliography: Ullmann, Walter, *The Growth of Papal Government in the Middle Ages* (1962); Waley, D. P., *The Papal State in the Thirteenth Century* (1961).

Innocent XI, Pope

Innocent XI, b. May 19, 1611, d. Aug. 12, 1689, was pope from 1676 to 1689. His name was Benedetto Odescalchi. His pontificate was dominated by a constant struggle against LOUIS XIV of France, who had tried twice to prevent his election (in 1669 and again in 1676). In 1682, a synod convoked by Louis issued the Gallican Articles (see GALLICANISM), which called for restrictions on papal authority. Innocent condemned the articles and refused to invest as bishops any of the clergy who supported them. He encouraged reforms in the church and was notable for his piety, generosity, and freedom from nepotism. He sympathized with JANSENISM but condemned QUIETISM in the bull *Coelestis Pastor* (1687). He was beatified by Pope Pius XII in 1956. Feast day: Aug. 13.

Innocent XII, Pope

Innocent XII, b. Mar. 13, 1615, d. Sept. 27, 1700, was pope from 1691 to 1700. His name was Antonio Pignatelli. He persuaded LOUIS XIV of France to disavow (1693) the Gallican Articles of 1682 (see GALLICANISM); in return he extended Louis's right to administer vacant French sees. Innocent's pontificate was noted for church reform. His bull *Romanum decet Pontificem* (1692) decisively ended nepotism in church appointments.

Inns of Court

The Inns of Court, in London, are private associations that supervise legal education and control admission to the bar in Great Britain. The inns developed early in the 14th century in response to a growing interest in the teaching of common law. The four inns are the Inner Temple, Middle Temple, Lincoln's Inn, and Gray's Inn. Those seeking admittance to the bar must enroll in an inn for a period of "pupillage," as well as pass an examination. Similar but less important societies called Inns of Chancery went out of existence in the 19th century.

Bibliography: Blackham, Robert J., *The Story of the Temple: Gray's and Lincoln's Inn* (1920); Daniell, Timothy, *Inns of Court* (1971); Prest, Wilfrid R., *Some Aspects of the Inns of Court, 1590-1640* (1972).

Innsbruck [inz′-bruk]

Innsbruck is the capital of TYROL province in western Austria. Its population is 115,197 (1971). Located in the eastern Alps at an altitude of 574 m (1,883 ft), it is an important tourist and winter sports resort and hosted the 1964 and 1976 Winter Olympics. The city is also a rail and market center and manufactures textiles. The bridge over the River Inn, which gives the city its name, made Innsbruck an important point on the trade routes to Germany from Italy and Switzerland in the 12th century. Originally belonging to the counts of Andech, it passed to the Habsburgs in 1363, and became the ducal residence in 1420. Innsbruck has many notable medieval buildings, including the 16th-century Franciscan Hofkirche (church) and the Fürstenburg, a 15th-century castle with a famous copper-roofed balcony.

inoculation: see VACCINATION.

İnönü, İsmet [ee-nu-noo′, is-met′]

The Turkish statesman and career military officer İsmet İnönü, b. Sept. 24, 1884, d. Dec. 25, 1973, became the principal lieutenant of Kemal ATATÜRK in the post-World War I struggle for Turkish independence. İnönü was the Turkish representative at the Lausanne Conference (see LAUSANNE, TREATY OF), which overturned the wartime settlement and established the Turkish Republic in 1923. He was twice prime minister (1923-24, 1925-37) during Atatürk's presidency. As president (1938-50), İnönü kept Turkey neutral during World War II and prepared the country for democratic elections, which resulted (1950) in the removal of İnönü and his Republican People's party (RPP) from power. He then led the opposition to the Democratic party's regime until its overthrow by coup in 1960. Prime minister again from 1964 to 1965, İnönü was ousted as RPP leader in 1972. STANFORD J. SHAW

inorganic chemistry

The field of inorganic chemistry deals with the properties and behavior of all the elements and their compounds, with the exception of all but a few compounds of carbon. The field that studies most carbon compounds is organic chemistry.

Inorganic chemistry has its historical roots in the study of natural minerals and other nonliving matter. The extraction and discovery of the chemical elements from their ores inevitably led to the investigation of their chemical behavior in their own right and to the discovery of new inorganic compounds. The vast majority of inorganic substances known today do not occur naturally; rather, they are products of laboratory synthesis. Modern inorganic chemistry is a large, diverse field with many subdivisions that overlap with organic chemistry, biochemistry, metallurgy, mineralogy, solid state physics, and atomic and molecular theory.

Organic and Inorganic Compounds. The separation of chemical substances into organic and inorganic matter is based on the notion that "organic" carbon compounds can be produced only by living organisms. This misconception was dispelled in 1828 when the German chemist Friedrich Woehler converted ammonium cyanate (NH_4NCO) to urea (H_2NCONH_2). It was the first transformation of an inorganic substance into a natural, organic metabolism product of many organisms. Unfortunately, these terms are still in use.

Inorganic compounds form many types of chemical bonds not found in the chemistry of organic materials. Carbon forms covalent bonds exclusively, using its four valence electrons. This gives rise to a limited set of single and multiple bonds that connect carbon atoms with themselves and with hydrogen, oxygen, nitrogen, and a few other elements. The chemist who is familiar with the fundamental types of bonds is thereby equipped to deal rationally with organic compounds, of which several million are known. The greater variety of bonds found among inorganic substances results from the range of possible combinations of the more than 100 elements. In addition to the special bonding of metals and alloys, which allows the conduction of electricity and the ionic bonding of inorganic salts, many elements can form covalent bonds of a type that differs from those of carbon. An example of this is a family of transition metal compounds in which pairs of metal atoms are linked by quadruple bonds.

Many areas of research exist in modern inorganic chemistry, and every chemical element is being investigated. Research is divided into three major divisions: nonmetallic, solid-state, and metallic chemistry. Within the first two divisions are subdivisions involving compounds of the elements that are bonded to carbon.

Nonmetallic Chemistry. Until recently, the noble gases were believed to be completely inert, or unreactive. The first true compound of a noble gas was discovered by Neil Bartlett in 1962. Research in the field has been active since that time, and today a relatively great number of compounds of krypton, xenon, and radon are known. These compounds have already been applied in synthesis and analysis.

Fluorine is a reactive and hazardous element. Various fluorine compounds—for example, Teflon and Freon—are exceptional for their inertness or for their extraordinary reactivity (derivatives with oxygen, chlorine, and bromine). Both types of material are widely used as corrosion-resistant coating or high-energy fuel oxidizers.

Compounds of silicon are the basis of the mineral world. About 95 percent of the material in the Earth's crust contains silicon; thus, there is great interest in this chemistry and in developing new ceramic materials. Organic compounds of silicon are also important; best known are the silicones.

Boron is the only nonmetal that has more valence orbitals than valence electrons. This allows it to form unique electron-deficient bonds with itself and certain other elements, thus giving rise to covalent, molecular substances which have intrigued chemists for decades. Boron chemistry is so diverse that it has the potential of rivaling the chemistry of carbon.

Solid-State Chemistry. The solid-state revolution in electronics is the direct result of the perfecting of chemical techniques for producing silicon and germanium that is extemely pure, and for the introduction of trace levels of other elements, to alter the electrical properties of these substances. The chemistry and physics of silicon and germanium is important in synthesizing new semiconductors such as the compound gallium arsenide.

The synthesis of new ceramic solids having special properties is of constantly growing importance. This includes new types of glass with special transmission or absorption characteristics; materials of high mechanical strength and resistance, for use at extremely high temperatures; and new solids with electromagnetic properties useful for solid-state electronic devices and computer memories.

Metallic Chemistry. TRANSITION ELEMENTS form a remarkable variety of interesting and useful substances called COORDINATION COMPOUNDS. These are molecules composed of one or more metal atoms surrounded by a group of electron pair donor molecules called ligands. The chemical and physical properties of the entire complex are profoundly influenced by the identity, structure, and geometrical orientation of the ligands about the metal center. Ligand field theory is the general theory that is being developed to explain the detailed chemical, structural, electronic, and magnetic properties of coordination compounds. Great interest has been shown in synthesizing new transition metal compounds and in further developing the ligand field theory.

Although catalysts are employed throughout chemistry in countless ways, scientists have yet to fully understand how they work. Most catalysts are transition metal compounds; unraveling the secret of their operation lies in developing a deeper understanding of metal-ligand interaction.

A challenging new area in inorganic chemistry is that of understanding the role of transition metals in the biochemical catalysts called enzymes. Enzymes are the highly complex organic molecules that control the chemistry of living cells. In many cases, the active catalytic site in an enzyme is the point at which a transition metal such as iron, molybdenum, or zinc is bound to the molecule.   PHILIP KELLER

Bibliography: Cotton, Frank A., and Wilkinson, Geoffrey, *Basic Inorganic Chemistry* (1976); Laidler, K. L., and Ford-Smith, M. H., *The Chemical Elements* (1970); Pauling, Linus, *General Chemistry*, 3d ed. (1970).

See also: INERT GASES; PERIODIC TABLE.

Inouye, Daniel K.   [ee-noh′-way]

Daniel Ken Inouye, b. Honolulu, Sept. 7, 1924, became U.S. senator from Hawaii in 1963. A Democrat, he was chairman of the Senate Select Committee on Intelligence (1976-77) and one of 7 members of the Senate Select Committee to investigate the Watergate affair. Previously he had served (1954-59) in the Hawaii legislature.

Bibliography: Inouye, Daniel K., and Elliot, Lawrence, *Journey to Washington* (1967).

input-output analysis

Input-output analysis is a system for comparing the flow of goods and services among different industries and sectors of an economy. The output of one industry, for example, coal, becomes the input of other industries, such as the steel and electric power industries; the outputs of these industries in turn become inputs for other industries. Input-output analysis is useful in determining how a change in the output of one industry will affect other industries. For example, before beginning a program of road building, a government would want to know how the program will affect key industries such as the cement, steel, and machinery industries and the industries that supply them. These effects can be determined from an input-output grid showing how each industry draws its inputs from the outputs of other industries.

Input-output analysis was developed principally by Wassily LEONTIEF of Harvard University, who received (1973) a Nobel Prize for economics for his work. Several governments, including the United States and the USSR, have established national input-output tables. One drawback to input-output analysis is that it usually assumes constant proportions among the different inputs and outputs, while in reality these are subject to change.

Bibliography: Leontief, Wassily, *Input-Output Economics* (1966).

input-output devices

Devices that provide for the movement of information between the CENTRAL PROCESSING UNIT of a COMPUTER system and the external world are called input/output devices, or simply I/O devices. They are extremely important because every computer functions by accepting input and producing output. Input is the control information (programs and commands) that directs computing activities; it also includes the data information (digital numbers, characters, or pictures) that is manipulated by the computing activities. Output is information produced as a result of computing activities.

Because of the wide variety of forms of information, many types of I/O devices are used. They may be characterized according to the information medium, the hardware technology, the speed of information transfer, and the amount or capacity of information involved. Many devices support the movement of information between a storage medium and processor. Others support communication between the computer system and the external world of noncomputer devices.

Storage-oriented devices store information in computer-readable form. Information is placed in storage with the intent of later inputting the same information for further processing. Nonstorage devices are used when it is not necessary to move the same information both into and out of the computer. The information is transformed by the devices from a computer-readable form to a form readable by a person or another machine.

Nonstorage-Oriented Devices. Typical devices that are not oriented toward machine-readable storage are computer terminals, printers, graphics and image displays, plotters, computer output microfilm (COM), optical scanners, and converters between analog and digital information.

COMPUTER TERMINALS may support the input of character information via a keyboard (see also KEY PUNCH), or the output of characters on paper or on a cathode ray tube (CRT) screen similar to television. Printers prepare paper output of character information at high speed.

Graphics and image displays present pictorial information

and are becoming increasingly important. Graphs may be formed from dots or lines. Pictures are represented in a computer in a digitized form where a picture is composed of many small parts called picture elements, or pixels. The value given to a pixel corresponds to the intensity of the picture at that point. For color pictures the pixels have components for each of the three primary colors, red, blue, and green. A picture is displayed on a CRT by illuminating the screen proportional to pixel values. This arrangement is similar to the formation of color television pictures, although television is an analog device. Plotters and computer-output microfilm devices produce graphical output on paper or film.

Optical scanners are input devices that read intensities of reflected light. They are used commercially to read standard product code bars on retail merchandise for input to computers. The computer then computes sales price, updates inventory records, prepares purchase orders, and performs a variety of other tasks. ANALOG-TO-DIGITAL CONVERTERS and digital-to-analog converters enable communication between digital computers and analog devices.

Storage-Oriented Devices. Examples of storage-oriented devices, listed from fastest to slowest speed of information transfer, are drums, disks, magnetic tape drives, card readers and punches, and paper tape readers and punches. The first three devices use magnetic surfaces or tape as the storage medium, and the remainder employ punched holes. (See also INFORMATION STORAGE AND RETRIEVAL.) Devices for special purposes also exist; particularly important in computer networks are those devices that provide communication between computers.

Interfacing I/O Devices to Computers. The set of problems associated with the interaction between two dissimilar systems, such as the computer and an I/O device, is known as interfacing. On the computer side of an I/O operation, the information is in a binary digital form. Numbers are in binary or a binary encoding of decimal. Characters are encoded in binary. Pictures are made up of binary pixels. All I/O operations move binary information between the computer and an I/O device. Output devices have the responsibility of changing the binary information into the output form: that is, to characters on a CRT or piece of paper, points and lines on the various picture-oriented devices, analog voltage signals, magnetic polarizations on drums, disk, and magnetic tape, and holes in cards and paper tape. Input devices have the responsibility of changing input form into binary. Examples of input forms are keystrokes, light intensities, analog signals, magnetic polarizations, and holes.

To provide some standardization of interfaces for the many types of I/O devices and to increase efficiency of I/O operations, I/O channels have been developed. A channel exists between the computer and perhaps several devices so that the specializations of each device are isolated. Channels provide a direct path between various devices and the COMPUTER MEMORY. This feature is known as direct memory access (DMA). Channels are programmable and operate independently of the processor, once started, thus allowing I/O to take place simultaneously with computation.

All hardware I/O devices require SOFTWARE support for the transfer of information in the computer.

The improvement of existing I/O devices in terms of speed, capacity, accuracy, and reliability, makes I/O technology a fast-changing field. In addition, sophisticated forms of I/O, such as voice, visual, and tactile communication, are being pursued.   EDWARD W. DAVIS

Bibliography: Artandi, Susan, *An Introduction to Computers in Information Science* (1972); Crowley, Thomas, *Understanding Computers* (1967); Kurzas, Anthony, ed., *Encyclopedia of Information Systems and Services*, 3d ed. (1978); Martin, E. W., and Perkins, William, *Computers and Information Systems: An Introduction* (1973).

inquest   [in'-kwest]

An inquest is an inquiry made by a group of persons appointed by the law. The term usually applies to a jury conducting a legal investigation of evidence. Such investigations include those made by grand juries, CORONER's juries, and sur-

rogate's courts. A GRAND JURY may initiate its own investigation or review indictments brought to it by a public prosecutor. A coroner's jury identifies victims of death by unnatural causes and decides how, where, and when the victim died. A surrogate's court inquires into the circumstances of a will offered for probate.

Inquisition   [in-kwi-zish'-uhn]

The Inquisition was a medieval church court instituted to seek out and prosecute heretics. The term is applied to the institution itself, which was episcopal or papal, regional or local; to the personnel of the tribunal; and to the judicial procedure followed by the court. Notoriously harsh in its procedures, the Inquisition was defended during the Middle Ages by appeal to biblical practices and to the church father Saint AUGUSTINE, who had interpreted Luke 14:23 as endorsing the use of force against heretics.

Development and Institution. Problems with sects like the ALBIGENSES (Cathari) and WALDENSES in the 12th century first led to the episcopal Inquisition. Often at the instigation of secular rulers, bishops were urged to investigate and deal locally with heretics, since they were seen as a threat to both the ecclesiastical and the social order. Papal documents as well as the Second, Third, and Fourth LATERAN COUNCILS (1139, 1179, 1215) prescribed imprisonment and confiscation of property as punishment for heresy and threatened to excommunicate princes who failed to punish heretics.

This painting portrays the culminating ceremony of the Inquisition: the sermo generalis, *or* auto-da-fé; *the accused are seen being sentenced (left), awaiting punishment (center), and at the stake (right). A procession, mass, and sermon preceded the sentencing. Those who refused to recant were delivered to the secular authorities for implementation of the death penalty. (Prado, Madrid.)*

The papal Inquisition was formally instituted by Pope GREG-ORY IX in 1231. Following a law of Holy Roman Emperor FREDERICK II, enacted for Lombardy in 1224 and extended to the entire empire in 1232, Gregory ordered convicted heretics to be seized by the secular authorities and burned. Like Frederick, Gregory also mandated that heretics be sought out and tried before a church court. For this purpose, he first appointed special inquisitors (for example, Conrad of Marburg in Germany and Robert le Bougre in Burgundy) and later entrusted the task to members of the newly established DOMINICAN and FRANCISCAN orders of friars. The independent authority of the inquisitors was a frequent cause of friction with the local clergy and bishops.

Procedures. During the 13th century, the typical procedure began with the arrival of the inquisitors in a specific locality. A period of grace was proclaimed for penitent heretics, after which time denunciations were accepted from anyone, even criminals and other heretics. Two informants whose identity was unknown to the victim were usually sufficient for a charge. The court then summoned the suspect, conducted an interrogation, and tried to obtain the confession that was necessary for conviction. In order to do this, assisting secular authorities frequently applied physical torture. This practice probably started in Italy under the impact of rediscovered Roman civil law and made use of such painful procedures as stretching of limbs on the rack, burning with live coals, squeezing of fingers and toes, or the strappado, a vertical rack.

At the beginning of the interrogation, which was recorded summarily in Latin by a clerk, suspects and witnesses had to swear under oath that they would reveal everything. Unwillingness to take the oath was interpreted as a sign of adherence to heresy. If a person confessed and was willing to submit, the judges prescribed minor penances like flogging, fasts, prayers, pilgrimages, or fines. In more severe cases the wearing of a yellow "cross of infamy," with its resulting social ostracism, or imprisonment could be imposed. Denial of the charges without counterproof, obstinate refusal to confess, and persistence in the heresy resulted in the most severe punishments: life imprisonment or execution accompanied by total confiscation of property. Since the church was not permitted to shed blood, the sentenced heretic was surrendered to the secular authorities for execution, usually by burning at

This woodcut from John Foxe's Book of Martyrs *(1554) illustrates the means employed by some inquisitors to elicit confessions of heresy. Although inquisitors often used torture, this practice was not as prevalent as some contemporary accounts indicate.*

the stake. When the Inquisition had completed its investigations, the sentences were pronounced in a solemn ceremony, known as the *sermo generalis* ("general address") or, in Spain, as the *auto-da-fé* ("act of faith"), attended by local dignitaries, clergy, and townspeople. Here the penitents abjured their errors and received their penalties; obstinate heretics were solemnly cursed and handed over to be burned immediately in public.

Several inquisitors' manuals have survived, among them those of Bernard Gui and Nicolas Eymeric. Other sources include checklists of standard questions and numerous official minutes of local inquisitions. Some of these materials have been published, but most exist in manuscript only.

The first inquisitors worked in central Europe (Germany, northern Italy, eastern France). Later centers of the Inquisition were established in the Mediterranean regions, especially southern France, Italy, Portugal, and Spain. The tribunal was used in England to suppress the LOLLARDS (followers of the 14th-century reformer John WYCLIFFE). Queen Mary I of England (r. 1553–58) used the tribunal in her effort to reverse the Protestant REFORMATION. The Inquisition's long survival can be attributed to the early inclusion of offenses other than heresy: sorcery, alchemy, blasphemy, sexual aberration, and infanticide. The number of witches and sorcerers burned after the late 15th century appears to have been far greater than that of heretics.

Spanish Inquisition. The Inquisition underwent special development in Portugal and Spain and their colonies. At the insistence of Ferdinand II of Aragon and Isabella I of Castile, Pope SIXTUS IV endorsed (1483) the creation of an independent Spanish Inquisition presided over by a high council and grand inquisitor. Legend has made the first grand inquisitor, Tomás de TORQUEMADA, a symbol of ultimate cruelty, bigotry, intolerance, and religious fanaticism. The truth is that the Spanish Inquisition was particularly severe, strict, and efficient because of its strong ties with the crown. Its major targets were the Marranos (converts from Judaism) and Moriscos (converts from Islam), many of whom were suspected of secretly adhering to their original faiths. During the 16th century, Protestants and Alumbrados (Spanish mystics) seemed to be the major danger. Often serving political ends, the inquisitors also exercised their dreaded functions among the converted Indian populations of the Spanish colonies in America. The Inquisition was finally suppressed in Spain in 1834 and in Portugal in 1821.

Roman Inquisition. At the time of the Reformation, Pope PAUL III created a cardinals' commission at the curia as the final court of appeal in matters of heresy. This Roman Inquisition was solidified (1588) by SIXTUS V into the Congregation of the Roman and Universal Inquisition, also known as the Holy Office, whose task was to watch over the correct doctrine of faith and morals for the whole Roman Catholic church. Reorganized in 1908 under the simpler title Congregation of the Holy Office, it was redefined by Pope PAUL VI in 1965 as the Congregation for the Doctrine of the Faith, with the more positive task of furthering right doctrine rather than censuring heresy.

Conclusion. Among the innumerable victims of the Inquisition were such famous people as the philosopher Giordano BRUNO, GALILEO, JOAN OF ARC, and the religious order of knights called the TEMPLARS. The institution and its excesses have been an embarrassment to many modern Christians. In anti-Catholic and antireligious polemics since the Enlightenment (for example, Voltaire's *Candide*), the Inquisition has been cited as a prime example of what is thought to be the barbarism of the Middle Ages. In its day there was some popular sympathy for the Inquisition. Some saw it as a political and economic tool, others, as a necessary defense for religious belief. Nevertheless, despite all efforts at understanding the institution in the light of social, political, religious, and ideological factors, today the Inquisition is generally admitted to belong to the darker side of Christian history.

KARLFRIED FROEHLICH

Bibliography: Coulton, George G., *The Inquisition* (1929; repr. 1974); Hauben, Paul J., ed., *The Spanish Inquisition* (1969); Kamen, Henry A.,

The Spanish Inquisition (1965); Langdon-Davies, John, The Spanish Inquisition (1938; repr. 1964); Lea, Henry C., A History of the Inquisition in the Middle Ages, 3 vols. (1888; repr. 1958); Le Roy Ladurie, Emmanuel, Montaillou: The Promised Land of Error, trans. by Barbara Bray (1978); O'Brien, John A., The Inquisition (1973); Roth, Cecil, The Spanish Inquisition (1938; repr. 1964); Wakefield, Walter L., Heresy, Crusade, and Inquisition in Southern France, 1100-1250 (1974).

inquisitorial procedure: see ADVERSARY PROCEDURE.

insanity, legal

Insanity, in law, is a mental defect or disorder sufficient to prevent a person from knowing the difference between right and wrong conduct or from understanding the nature of his or her actions.

In criminal law, insanity is a defense against responsibility for a crime. Anglo-American common law has traditionally assumed that punishment for criminal behavior is applicable only to those who can make moral choices and who have the ability to conform their behavior to the dictates of law. The first modern test of insanity, still applicable in many jurisdictions, was the M'Naghten rule (1843). It held that a person was insane if he or she had such a defect of reason at the time of committing a criminal act that he or she did not know the nature and quality of the act or was unable to distinguish between right and wrong. Some jurisdictions have added the "irresistible impulse" test to the M'Naghten test. This labels as insane those who know the difference between right and wrong but cannot control their behavior because of mental disorder. More than half the states now accept the test promulgated by the American Law Institute. It defines a criminal as insane "if at the time of such conduct as a result of mental disease or defect he lacks substantial capacity either to appreciate the criminality (wrongfulness) of his conduct or to conform his conduct to the requirements of law." The concept of legal insanity has been controversial; courtroom methods of establishing legal insanity, definitions of insanity, and ways of coping with those acquitted on grounds of insanity have been strongly criticized.

Another application of the concept of insanity in criminal law is the notion that a person must be sane to stand trial. This test differs from those used to determine criminal responsibility. Defendants must be able to understand the nature of the proceedings against them and to assist in their own defense.

Bibliography: Allen, Richard C., et al., eds., Readings in Law and Psychiatry, rev. ed. (1975); Biggs, John, The Guilty Mind: Psychiatry and the Law of Homicide (1967); Fingarette, Herbert, The Meaning of Criminal Insanity (1972); Morris, Grant H., The Insanity Defense (1975); Szasz, Thomas, Law, Liberty, and Psychiatry (1963).

inscription

Inscription is writing in the form of letters, words, or other conventional symbols cut into a permanent material for the purpose of conveying and preserving information. The earliest writings probably appeared in the form of inscription, which later gave rise to the related art of CALLIGRAPHY, or fine writing on perishable materials such as papyrus, parchment, and paper. The origins of writing and the evolution of alphabetic systems can be traced through epigraphy, the study of ancient inscriptions (see WRITING SYSTEMS, EVOLUTION OF).

Ancient inscriptions appear on diverse types of hard material, including marble, crystalline limestone, and other varieties of stone; metals such as bronze, gold, and silver; and bone, ivory, clay, and wood—although few examples of the last have survived. The inscribers's tools have varied, depending on the surface used; common implements include the chisel, often formed with a square blade; a stylus, with one end blunt and the other pointed, for impressing inscriptions into clay before firing; and a punch or pointed hammer, when hard stone is being worked.

Throughout history inscriptions have been executed on temples or churches, civic buildings, monuments, tombs, statues, vases, and coins; sometimes the text is accompanied by

Epigraphy, the study of inscriptions, is an important ancillary discipline in the study of ancient cultures. Latin inscriptions frequently appear on Gallic effigies and monuments. This monument, found at Cologne, Germany, dates from the Gallo-Roman period. It is dedicated to the triad of Celtic goddesses known collectively as the Matronae.

pictorial reliefs. Inscriptions have frequently been used for public announcements or administrative documents recording political and religious decrees, law codes, public and private contracts, treaties and other matters of state, dedications, benefactions, and honors. As such, they serve as an invaluable source of historical information, both social and political. Modern inscriptions are most often found on building facades, cornerstones, and tombstones, on which occurs the oldest continuous use of inscription.

Inscriptions are generally composed primarily of alphabetic or phonetic symbols. Often they also contain numerals. Initials or abbreviations were used but not commonly until the advent of Roman inscriptions; certain Latin styles were composed entirely of such formulas. Late Greek and Latin inscriptions also sometimes include monograms. These appear frequently, often in forms that are difficult to interpret, in the inscriptions of the Early Christian and Byzantine periods.

Some form of punctuation is generally found within inscriptions because words are seldom separated by spaces. In Greek inscriptions a vertical line, a dot, or a series of dots marks the end of a sentence, phrase, or word. Roman inscriptions use a single dot for such distinctions. In Christian inscriptions the beginning of the text is indicated by a cross whereas a leaf or other symbol signifies the end. The direction of inscriptions also varies, from vertical arrangements to horizontal sequences to placements in patterns. Semitic inscriptions, including those of the Phoenicians, read from right to left, as do the earliest Greek inscriptions. The left-to-right direction was not standardized by the Greeks until the 5th century BC; it was later adopted by the Romans and consequently by all the European languages.

Early Inscription. The history of Western inscription began in Mesopotamia, where in about 4000 BC the Sumerians developed CUNEIFORM. This writing system consists of characters made with wedge-shaped strokes impressed into clay, brick, or stone. By the 2d millennium BC an alphabet of 29 cuneiform signs was in use at ancient UGARIT; these signs closely resemble Hebrew and Phoenician letters. Many thousand tablets and fragments inscribed in Sumerian from the first half of the 2d millennium BC exist, a number of them excavated at NIPPUR. Cuneiform inscriptions have also been discovered at AMARNA, BOĞAZKÖY, EBLA, LAGASH, NINEVEH, SUSA, and URUK. Cuneiform was also the system used by the HITTITES at Elam; Old Persian, the writing of the ACHAEMENIDS, was a revised form of cuneiform writing. The famous BEHISTUN inscriptions of Darius I, dated c.500 BC, exemplify Achaemenid script; with the conquest of these regions by Alexander the Great, Greek became the dominant inscribed language.

Egyptian inscriptions in the form of HIEROGLYPHIC writing date from the 1st dynasty (4th millennium BC). The system of inscription established then continued in use with only minor modifications until the time of the Romans. A fine example of the Egyptian style is preserved in the form of rock inscriptions at THEBES. Another renowned epigraphical monument is the ROSETTA STONE, discovered in 1799. This basalt tablet, dated 196 BC, was inscribed in three languages: ancient Egyptian hieroglyphs, demotic (an Egyptian cursive script), and Greek. By studying the royal names enclosed in cartouches (oval frames) and comparing the inscriptions, J. F. CHAMPOLLION was able to assign phonetic values to some of the hieroglyphs and eventually to the entire system.

On the Aegean island of Crete an independent hieroglyphic system existed, replaced in the beginning of the Middle Minoan period (1750–1450 BC) by a linear script, read from left to right, which developed into the script known as Linear A; this in turn was followed by another script, designated LINEAR B. Thousands of examples of these scripts inscribed on tablets, ranging in date from c.3000 BC to the fall of Knossos (c.1400 BC), have been excavated at sites on Crete and on the Greek mainland.

Phoenician inscriptions date from c.1000 BC; the Phoenician alphabet, adapted and modified by the Greeks at an uncertain date, remained in use until the 3d century BC. The earliest Greek inscriptions date from the 7th century BC. At first each Greek state had its own alphabet, but in 403 BC, under the archon Euclides, the Ionian alphabet—still used for Greek capital letters—was officially adopted by Athens and soon spread throughout Greece. The art of inscription flourished, evidenced by the innumerable writings found on vases, coins, statues, votive offerings, and relief panels. Records of temple expenditures, decrees, bookkeeping accounts, ostraca (sherds of pottery used for voting), lists of citizens, and annals were also inscribed, notable examples being the exquisitely carved Parian Chronicle from Paros and the Gortyna code of property laws, executed during the 5th century BC. An unusual example of early Greek inscription appears in the form of graffiti scratched (c.590 BC) by Greek mercenaries on the legs of the colossal statues of Abu Simbel in Egypt.

Latin Inscription. From the Greek alphabet were derived various local Italic alphabets, including that of the Etruscans and that of the Chalcidean colony of Cumae, on which the Roman alphabet was based. The Roman inscriptional style, in wide use from the 3d century BC, persists in essentially the same form to the present day. The influence of Latin inscription extended throughout the Roman Empire. In Gaul, concurrent with Latin inscriptions of the late republic, a form of Celtic inscription appeared, based on Greek letters. Later, during the Christian period, Celtic inscriptions were written in ogham, one of the Irish runic languages. This writing was alphabetical and apparently an independent invention, based on arbitrary symbols much like a Morse code. The Germanic runes, much used in the same region, were derived from the Greek or Latin alphabets.

Early Christian stoneworkers adapted the old forms of Latin inscription, first in the CATACOMBS and later in the churches. Modern monumental inscriptions continue the tradition, modified by a series of classical revivals, especially by the Renaissance. The custom of placing Latin and Greek inscriptions on buildings and monuments endures, with these two classical languages still considered the appropriate languages for religious, public, and private epigraphical documents.

Non-Western Traditons. Important epigraphic traditions of the New World include the hieroglyphic inscriptions on stone monuments (stelae) of the AZTEC, MAYA, and TOLTEC cultures (see PRE-COLUMBIAN ART AND ARCHITECTURE) as well as the enigmatic rock inscriptions of EASTER ISLAND. In China the earliest known inscriptions were executed on bronze vessels and ORACLE BONES of the Shang dynasty (c.1600–1027 BC; see CHINESE ART AND ARCHITECTURE). After the Chinese invention of paper in about AD 100, inscription was relegated to a lesser role. At Harappa and Mohenjo-daro, two major sites of the INDUS CIVILIZATION, low-relief inscriptions made on steatite seals dated from c.2500 BC. An important inscription from the early Buddhist period in India is the Prakrit of ASOKA, dated 3d century BC.   LILLY WEI

Bibliography: Frimmer, Steven, Stones That Spoke and Other Clues to the Decipherment of Lost Languages (1969); Matson, Esther, A Book of Inscriptions (1914; repr. 1977); Pope, Maurice, The Story of Archaeological Decipherment: From Egyptian Hieroglyphic to Linear B (1975); Woodhead, A. G., The Study of Greek Inscriptions (1959).

insect

Insects are members of the phylum Arthropoda (see ARTHROPOD), class Insecta, the largest and most diverse class in the animal kingdom. The number of described insect species is estimated to be 750,000 and the actual number of living species is perhaps 3 million. Even at 750,000 species, however, insects outnumber all other plant and animal groups.

Insects have three body divisions—head, thorax, and abdomen—and six legs borne on the thorax as an adult. Many insects possess wings as adults. Because of their small size, ability to fly, rapid reproductive rate, and external skeleton (exoskeleton), insects are highly successful animals that have thoroughly exploited every habitat in the biosphere except the polar ice caps. The exoskeleton is coated with a waxy layer that helps insects conserve body moisture. The small size of insects aids in their dispersal to more favorable habitats. Thrips and aphids are carried by frontal systems for long distances. Small insects have been collected by airplane at 3,000 m (10,000 ft). Migratory butterflies and locusts may fly hundreds of kilometers in a few weeks.

Their rapid rate of development allows insects to respond fairly precisely, genetically speaking, to changes in the environment. That is, most insects mature in a year or less, and many insects have several generations each year. Because most individual insects are either male or female, recombination of genetic material takes place with each generation and allows NATURAL SELECTION to shape the genetic course of a species.

Insects display almost every color, from drab, dull browns, and black to iridescent blues, reds and purples, or the metallic greens, blues, yellows, and reds of some WASPS and BEES. Size varies from tiny mymarid wasps less than 1 mm (.04 in) long to huge beetles or slender walking sticks up to 30 cm (12 in) long. Shape is equally variable. For example, legs may be adapted for walking, jumping, running, clinging to hairs, swimming, spinning silk, carrying pollen, hearing, or smelling, or they may be absent. Almost any aspect of insects is usually predictable within related groups but is highly variable among the orders.

STRUCTURE AND FUNCTION

Insects usually have a clearly defined head, thorax, and abdomen. The head bears antennae, eyes, and mouthparts; the thorax bears legs and wings; and the abdomen has various styli, cerci (antennalike sensory organs), and the genital apparatus. Most insects have a pair of relatively large compound eyes on the head as well as two or three simple eyes (ocelli) on top of the head. Food is chewed by the mandibles while it is held, sensed, and manipulated by the maxillae. Salivary glands generally open on or near the middle of the hypopharynx. The masticated food is directed through the preoral cavity, surrounded by the labrum, mandibles, maxillae, and hypopharynx, into the mouth. In the Hemiptera—fleas, flies, lice, and thrips—the mouthparts are modified into piercing stylets. Host plants or animals are pierced by the stylets, and juices are sucked up by the insect.

The thorax is the middle body region of an insect from which the legs and wings originate. The thorax is joined to the head by the neck and to the abdomen. The thorax is divided into the prothorax, mesothorax, and metathorax. Each segment typically bears one pair of legs and the last two segments bear the wings.

The legs of insects are divided by joints into six segments: the coxa (next to the body), trochanter, femur, tibia, pretar-

The external anatomy of a female grasshopper is representative of the majority of insects. The elongated body is bilaterally symmetrical, segmented, and covered by a hard exoskeleton; it is divided into three regions: head, thorax, and abdomen. The head bears both compound and simple eyes, antennae, and mouthparts. The thorax is divided into three segments; each bears a pair of jointed legs, and the last two each have a pair of wings. The abdomen has spiracles, or breathing pores, and the external parts of the reproductive organs. Some grasshoppers also have tympana—oval eardrums—located on the abdomen.

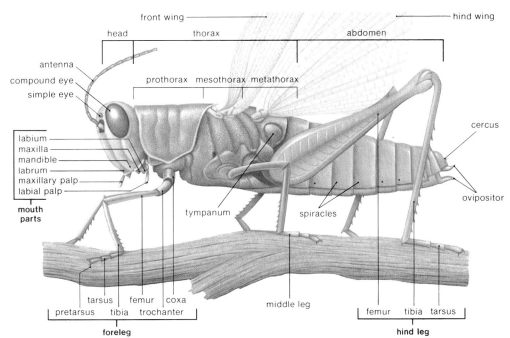

The internal structure of a female grasshopper, like that of most insects, includes a respiratory system (top) composed of spiracles, or breathing pores, and tracheae, a network of tubes that carry oxygen throughout the body. The circulatory system is open; blood is pumped from the heart to the aorta and then flows through the body back to the heart. The brain, ganglia, and nerve cords comprise the nervous system. Food enters the digestive system (bottom) through the mouth, mixes with saliva, and then passes into the esophagus, crop, and stomach; wastes are eliminated through the anus. Reproductive organs include two ovaries and a system of oviducts.

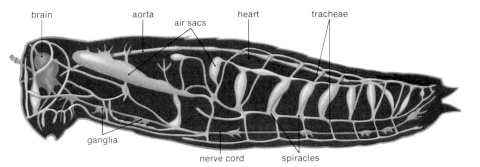

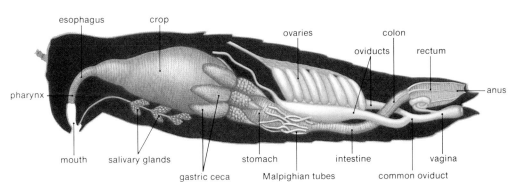

sus, and tarsus or foot. The legs of insects often have secondary functions which may affect leg size and shape dramatically. A common secondary function of legs in males is that of holding the female during mating. Except when thickened and tough, the wings of insects often have veins, or hardened tubes that strengthen the wing. Wing venation is important to the classification of insects.

The abdomen is composed of 11 or fewer segments. The last few abdominal segments are often associated with the external portions of the reproductive organs and with them are called the terminalia. The terminalia in female insects are often modified into an elaborate egg placer (ovipositor) which in the bees and wasps has been modified into a stinger.

The integument, or skin, of insects is particularly important because of its flexibility, its waterproof quality, and its hardness. The integument is formed by three layers: the basement membrane (connective tissue, which forms the innermost layer), the epidermis (a cellular layer just above the basement membrane, which secretes the cuticle), and the cuticle (the exoskeleton of the insect, which also lines the fore and hind gut). The cuticle consists largely of protein and of chitin (a substance closely related to the cellulose of plants). Cuticle is not extensible; growth is possible only until the wrinkles are smoothed out of the cuticulin. Then, an insect must molt (shed) to resume growth. In the abdomen, thorax, and head, invaginations of the integument into the body cavity give insects the equivalent of an internal skeleton in these areas of high mechanical stress.

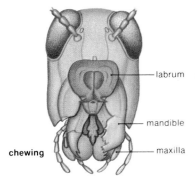

chewing

Insect mouthparts are classified in two broad categories: chewing, or mandibulate, and sucking, or haustellate. The grasshopper has chewing mouthparts; it bites its food and then chews by moving its mandibles sideways.

labrum

mandible

maxilla

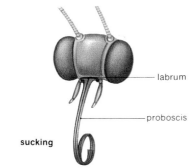

sucking

The sucking mouthparts of the butterfly include a proboscis—a long, tubelike structure formed from parts of the maxillae. The proboscis is coiled when not in use; when uncoiled by blood pressure, the butterfly uses it to suck or siphon liquids.

labrum

proboscis

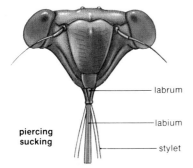

piercing sucking

In the cicada, the labium, or lower lip, is modified into a grooved beak that encloses four stylets—long, needlelike structures formed from the mandibles and maxillae. The cicada uses the stylets to pierce plant tissue and then suck the juices.

labrum

labium

stylet

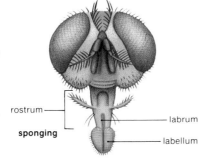

sponging

The sponging mouthparts of a housefly are suspended from a rostrum, or snout. The mandibles and maxillae are absent; the labium is modified into a tube that ends in two labella—soft, grooved, oval lobes that the fly uses to lap up liquid.

rostrum

labrum

labellum

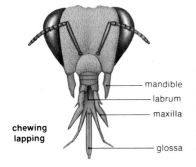

chewing lapping

The honey bee has modified chewing mouthparts described as chewing-sucking. The labium is modified into a tonguelike glossa. The bee can bite into a flower and then suck or lap the nectar with its glossa.

mandible

labrum

maxilla

glossa

Circulatory System and Breathing. The heart is a series of pumping chambers with an upper tube having openings along the side; the tube allows a colorless blood to be moved forward by a wave of contraction. Blood bathes the internal organs and is only partially enclosed by an upper diaphragm. Because insects are cold blooded, pulse rate may range from 140 per minute in an active insect to 1 per hour in chilled insects. Insects usually breathe by taking in air through a series of holes (spiracles) along the thorax and abdomen. Leading from the spiracles are tubes (tracheae) which interconnect to form a tracheal system.

Feeding and Digestion. Insects obtain food by a variety of methods, including biting, lapping, and sucking. Butterflies have a coiled proboscis that can straighten out and be thrust into a flower to suck out nectar. Honeybees lap nectar with their tongues. Bumblebees are equipped for both lapping and biting and are able to chew their way into a flower to reach nectar. Beetles, wasps, and ants have powerful biting mouthpieces. Some beetles are capable of chewing through lead or zinc. All insect jaws work at right angles; they are hinged at the sides of the head and bite inward, from side to side.

Carnivorous insects such as the praying mantis catch and chew their prey. Some wasps, by contrast, paralyze their prey with venomous stings, lay their eggs in the bodies, and provide a living food supply for their young. The ichneumon fly deposits its eggs in the tissues of newly hatched insects and produces tiny, ravenous larvae that begin to devour their host. Termites are able to digest and receive nourishment from wood because tiny protozoans within their digestive system "predigest" the cellulose in the wood.

The digestive system in insects is essentially a tube that begins with the mouth and is divided into a pharynx; esophagus; crop, stomach, or midgut, and intestine, or hind gut; colon; and rectum. The midgut has glandular outgrowths called the gastric ceca, which secrete digestive juices. The Malpighian tubes remove nitrogenous waste from the blood. Each blind tube empties into the hind gut at its junction with the stomach. The principal end product is nonsoluble uric acid, which is passed out with the feces.

SENSE ORGANS AND NERVOUS SYSTEM

Insects orient to the environment by means of touch and stretch receptors in the integument. Auditory receptors are usually stretch-type receptors associated with an "eardrum" (tympanum). Unlike other animals, insects have light receptors, or eyes, that can neither be turned nor moved and are usually fitted together into a pair of compound eyes. A compound eye may contain a honeycomb of as many as 28,000 lenses, like that found in the large dragonfly. Each lens serves as a basic unit, or ommatidium. The images from each ommatidium are somehow interpreted together in the insect's brain, but it is not known what the insect sees. In addition, many insects have two or three simple eyes, called ocelli, and these probably can only distinguish light from dark.

Most insects detect odors through olfactory receptors often found on the antennae and in the mouthparts and feet. Beetles that feed on carrion can scent a carcass for many kilometers, but if their antennae are damaged they cannot detect the carrion from a few meters away. Ants leave trails of odorous chemicals (pheromones) that can be recognized by others in the same colony, even when the scent leads through a maze of crossing trails left by ants of other colonies. The antennae are also sensitive to sound waves, or vibrations of air molecules, by means of special structures called Johnston's organs situated on the antennae. Katydids and crickets have ears in the form of sensitive hairs on the front legs.

The nervous system in insects primarily consists of paired nerve masses (ganglia) resembling a ladder lying on the lower inner surface of the body. In the head there is a ganglion (cluster of nerve cells). Nerves connect the cerebral ganglion with the nerve masses in the body, which control muscles and direct the endocrine system to release hormones.

Growth and development in insects is largely regulated by hormones secreted by the brain. Hormones may be liberated in the blood to keep the insect actively growing or may be directed to specific endocrine glands via the connective nerve

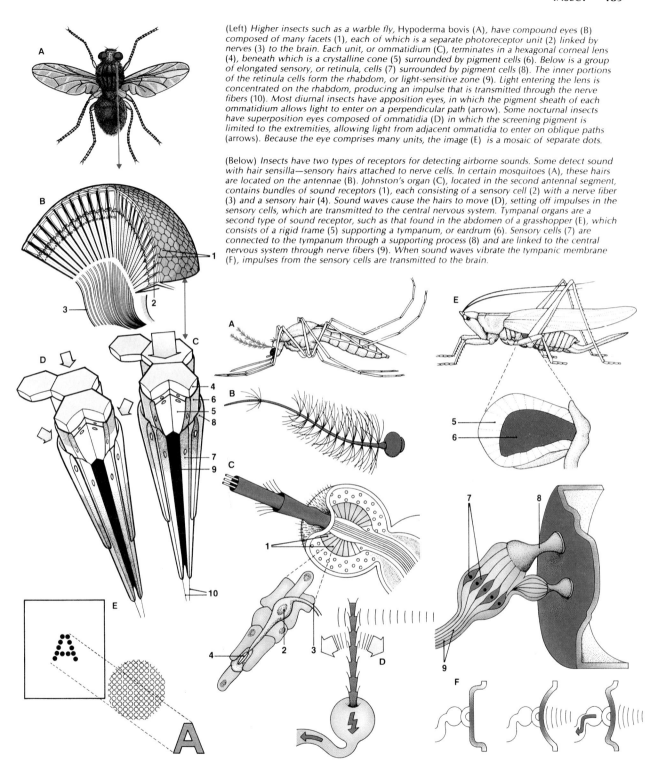

(Left) *Higher insects such as a warble fly,* Hypoderma bovis *(A), have compound eyes (B) composed of many facets (1), each of which is a separate photoreceptor unit (2) linked by nerves (3) to the brain. Each unit, or ommatidium (C), terminates in a hexagonal corneal lens (4), beneath which is a crystalline cone (5) surrounded by pigment cells (6). Below is a group of elongated sensory, or retinula, cells (7) surrounded by pigment cells (8). The inner portions of the retinula cells form the rhabdom, or light-sensitive zone (9). Light entering the lens is concentrated on the rhabdom, producing an impulse that is transmitted through the nerve fibers (10). Most diurnal insects have apposition eyes, in which the pigment sheath of each ommatidium allows light to enter on a perpendicular path (arrow). Some nocturnal insects have superposition eyes composed of ommatidia (D) in which the screening pigment is limited to the extremities, allowing light from adjacent ommatidia to enter on oblique paths (arrows). Because the eye comprises many units, the image (E) is a mosaic of separate dots.*

(Below) *Insects have two types of receptors for detecting airborne sounds. Some detect sound with hair sensilla—sensory hairs attached to nerve cells. In certain mosquitoes (A), these hairs are located on the antennae (B). Johnston's organ (C), located in the second antennal segment, contains bundles of sound receptors (1), each consisting of a sensory cell (2) with a nerve fiber (3) and a sensory hair (4). Sound waves cause the hairs to move (D), setting off impulses in the sensory cells, which are transmitted to the central nervous system. Tympanal organs are a second type of sound receptor, such as that found in the abdomen of a grasshopper (E), which consists of a rigid frame (5) supporting a tympanum, or eardrum (6). Sensory cells (7) are connected to the tympanum through a supporting process (8) and are linked to the central nervous system through nerve fibers (9). When sound waves vibrate the tympanic membrane (F), impulses from the sensory cells are transmitted to the brain.*

to control molting, heart beat, sugar content of the blood, juvenile characteristics, and egg production.

LIFE CYCLE

The reproduction system of insects consists of a pair of gonads (testes or ovaries) connected to a median duct, which opens at a gonopore. During copulation the male introduces sperm into a copulatory aperture, where it is stored in the female's spermatheca. As an egg matures, it slides into the median oviduct, where it is fertilized by the sperm. When the

egg is laid, it may be glued to the substrate or covered with a protective secretion that originated from the accessory glands.

Almost 85 percent of insect species develop by a process of complete METAMORPHOSIS, which is a series of successive stages that do not resemble one another. The remainder, except for less than 1 percent, undergo incomplete metamorphosis, where changes are not extreme. The life cycle of an insect usually starts with the placement of an egg on a substrate, the development of an immature form through succes-

Cicadas are known for the characteristic loud, high-pitched sounds produced by males with a pair of tymbals—ribbed, platelike organs on the abdomen. Eggs are laid in trees; when they hatch, the nymphs burrow into the ground and feed on sap sucked from roots (left). They remain underground until just before the final molt; for Magicicada septendecim of eastern North America, this period lasts 17 years. The nymph then crawls out of the soil, climbs a tree and digs its claws into the bark, and finally molts into a fully winged adult (right).

In most insects, such as the cockroach, reproduction is sexual. Male reproductive organs (A) include the testes (1), which produce sperm that is stored in the seminal vesicles (2), and the accessory glands (3), which coat the sperm with a hard capsule, or spermatophore. Female reproductive organs (B) include the ovaries (4), which produce eggs that are discharged through the oviducts (5). After copulation (C) sperm is stored in the female's spermatheca (6) until it fertilizes the eggs, which are then protected by a coating from the accessory glands (7).

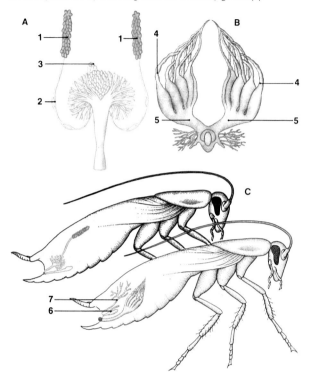

sive molts, and then the emergence of the adult stage at the last molt. Adult insects usually mate, feed, and then lay eggs. Some insects give birth to live young (an aphid may produce more than 175 young). Some female termites lay 2,000 to 3,000 eggs per day and may live 15 to 50 years. Eggs may be variously shaped and covered by scales or secretions.

Immature insects are called nymphs, naiads, or larvae. Nymphs develop gradually and resemble their adult stage. Naiads develop gradually but are aquatic. Larvae generally do not resemble the adult stage, and they develop through a pupal stage, usually nonmotile, often in a cocoon. Larvae often live in a habitat different from that of the adult and feed on different resources. Larvae have been named on the basis of form and function. Caterpillars, grubs, and maggots are immature stages of moths, beetles, and flies, respectively. Pupae have also been categorized by form (see PUPA). Obtect pupae have all the limbs and wings seemingly "glued down" to the body. Exarate pupae have the wings and legs standing out from the body. Coarctate pupae are exarate fly pupae that are formed inside the last larval integument (puparium). Certain cicadas develop for seventeen years.

Care of the eggs and the young by insects ranges from the practice of walking sticks, in which eggs are scattered indiscriminately, to that of earwigs, lace bugs, and certain sawflies, in which the mother broods over the eggs and young nymphs or larvae. Ant, wasp, and bee queens rear the first brood of workers by themselves.

Probably the most fascinating life history in the class Insecta is that of a beetle, Micromalthus debilis. One of the immature stages is capable of laying an egg or giving birth to

Most insects develop by metamorphosis, or changing form. Primitive insects, such as the grasshopper, undergo incomplete metamorphosis, in which changes are gradual. The nymph, or larva, resembles a wingless adult; it molts several times, emerging from the final molt as an adult. The large majority of insects, however, undergo complete metamorphosis. Higher insects such as the butterfly hatch into wormlike larvae that molt several times without change in form, then molt into pupae—a quiescent stage—and finally emerge as adults.

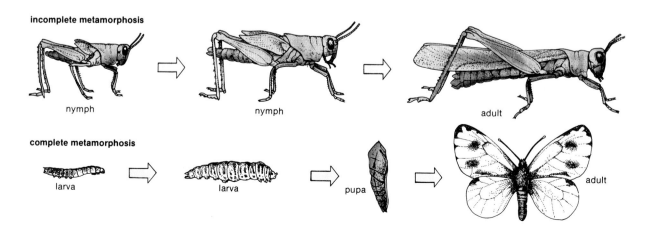

incomplete metamorphosis

nymph   nymph   adult

complete metamorphosis

larva   larva   pupa   adult

The stag beetles, family Lucanidae, are named for the elongated jaws, or mandibles, of the males—in some species over half as long as the body—which resemble the antlers of a stag. The mandibles are used both in fighting and for holding the female during copulation.

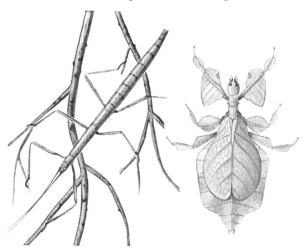

Leafcutting ants, Atta, cut pieces of leaves and transport them to their nest, where they feed on fungi that grows on the leaves. The larger worker ant is carrying the leaf while the smaller worker guards against parasitic flies that may attempt to lay their eggs on the leaf's surface.

The bodies of stick insects, Carausius, and leaf insects, Phyllium, mimic parts of the plants on which they live, providing an effective form of camouflage. During the day these insects hang motionless and are all but undetectable against their surroundings.

live larvae. If the egg hatches, the resulting larva devours its mother larva and develops into a male beetle. Larvae that are born live can either develop into female beetles or reproduce as larvae. The offspring of adult *Micromalthus* beetles are unknown. The adult beetles are thought to be sterile.

BEHAVIOR

Insect behavior, for the most part, is hereditary, and responses to stimuli are mostly automatic or instinctive. Direct responses (moving toward or away from the stimuli) may be made in reaction to light, temperature, water, contact, gravity, or currents of air or water. Often a response to a stimulus can be modified by other stimuli, as well as by the insect's physiology, food, and state of development. Some behavior involves a series of different acts. Such complex behavior includes nest building and mating. While this behavior may appear intelligent, it is usually found to be instinctive. However, since insects can be taught to modify their behavior, it is believed that they have a limited capacity to learn. Examples include the ant that can learn a maze and the honey bee that finds its way home by recognizing landmarks.

Social Behavior. Many insects occur in groups, each group differing in the factors that bring the individuals together. Often the aggregation results from a mutual attraction to the same stimulus such as food supply. Ants, termites, and some bees live in more integrated groups, called societies. The insect society works as a unit despite the large number of individuals. One distinct feature is the division of labor, with coordination of the activities of each individual with great efficiency.

Auditory Behavior. Sound plays an important role in insect behavior. Only a few sounds produced by insects are heard by humans, because these sounds are either too low or too high pitched. Sound is produced in several ways. Rubbing one body part against another, called stridulation, may involve almost any part of the body, in various species. Some insects vibrate special membranes called tymbols, as in the leafhoppers. A few insects will strike a part of their body on the substrate, for example, some grasshoppers use their feet.

Many insects produce sound on a continuous basis during

The wings (A) of flying insects such as the honey bee, Apis mellifera *(B), are membranous outgrowths of the body wall strengthened by longitudinal veins (1) and cross veins (2). The wings are moved indirectly by muscles that alter the shape of the thorax (cross sections). Elevation (C) of the wings is produced by contraction of the vertical muscles (3); contraction of the longitudinal muscles (4) produces downward movement (D). During flight, complex wing movements follow a figure-8 path (5).*

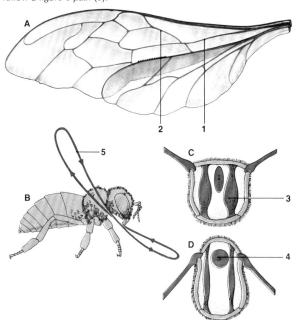

The more than 750,000 species of insects are classified in 23 to 32 different orders (according to different authorities) on the basis of various characteristics that include presence or absence of wings, structure and position of mouthparts, type of wings and pattern of wing venation, and type of metamorphosis. Among the more primitive insects are the Collembola (springtails), wingless insects that do not metamorphose. The Odonata (dragonflies and damselflies) undergo incomplete metamorphosis and have wings that do not fold. Katydids and other Orthoptera have folding wings. The highest orders, including the Diptera (true flies) and Lepidoptera (butterflies and moths) have folding wings and undergo complete metamorphosis.

katydid
Orthoptera

lacewing
Neuroptera

flea
Siphonaptera

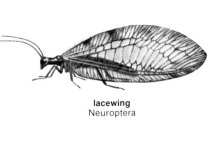

earwig
Dermaptera

bee
Hymenoptera

butterfly
Lepidoptera

springtail
Collembola

house fly
Diptera

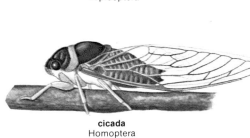

cicada
Homoptera

spider
Embioptera

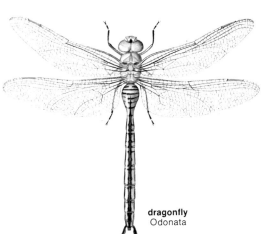

scorpion
Hemiptera

dragonfly
Odonata

beetle
Coleoptera

certain periods; they are said to sing. The rhythmic features of insect songs are affected by such factors as temperature, chirp rate, and pulse rate. The principal role played by sound is in mating. Because songs of singing insects are different and because females will respond only to songs of their species, song plays a role in species isolation and evolution.

Defenses. Most insects try to escape when threatened and some insects "play dead," for example, some beetles fall to the ground after folding up their legs, giving the appearance of a clump of dirt. Many insects use shelters ranging from burrows in the ground to elaborate shelters constructed of various materials. Insects also employ camouflage. (See also MIMICRY.) Many are so colored that they blend into their background, such as moths colored like the bark of trees. Some insects bear a close resemblance to objects in the environment, such as inchworms, which resemble twigs. Other insects will cover themselves with debris or excrement. Chemical defenses often involve distasteful body secretions, repellent secretions, or poisonous injection into an attacker. The use of the sting is probably the most effective and often a severe method. The only stinging insects are Hymenoptera (bees, wasps, and some ants).

Flight. Although most insects fly, their weight-to-wing ratio in theory is not advantageous to flight. They build up enough energy so that speed of the wing-beat makes up for the theoretical lack of lifting power. The vibrating insect wing actually follows a figure 8 or ellipsoid path. The effect is the same as a propeller going round and round, and the insect is drawn forward by a stream of air directed downward and backward.

Insects may vibrate their wings at speeds of up to 600 to 1,000 complete beats per second, which is about 20 times faster than the wing beats of any bird. Insects move their wings by a combination of forces: the action of the flight muscles, which attach the wings to the thorax, and the build-up of forces in the thorax itself, which acts as if it contained a spring. Each contraction of the wing muscles compresses the thoracic box, which then springs back and thus helps in powering the next wing stroke.

EVOLUTION AND CLASSIFICATION

Insects are thought to have evolved from a centipedelike class of terrestrial arthropods (class Symphyla) at least as far back as the Devonian Period, more than 350 million years ago. Others believe that both the insects and the symphylans evolved from a common ancestral group called the Protosymphyla. All available evidence indicates that these first insects were wingless and not very different from those now included in the order Thysanura: the bristletails and silverfish common in houses. During the next 100 million years a great diversity of insects occurred over the land and winged insects appeared, representing the first animals to fly.

The known living species of insects may be divided into 23 to 32 orders, depending on the authority cited. The most convenient classification, however, may be according to evolutionary grades, each representing adaptations to a wide range of environments. At the lowest level, therefore, are the primitive wingless insects such as silverfish and springtails (Collembola). The Collembola are the earliest fossil insects known and are now among the most abundant of all insects.

The higher orders of insects have wings and are divided into two major groups: Palaeoptera, or "ancient wings," and Neoptera, which are the greater number of present-day insects. Palaeoptera are the most primitive winged species and cannot fold the wings over the abdomen when at rest. They contain two surviving orders: dragonflies (Odonata) and mayflies (Ephemeroptera). They are excellent flyers but need large open spaces to maneuver in with their spread wings.

Neoptera do possess a wing-flexing, or folding, mechanism and can crawl into small spaces. Many orders of Neoptera have this ability, including Orthoptera (GRASSHOPPERS and CRICKETS) and Isoptera (TERMITES).

The highest evolutionary grade includes those insects that undergo complete metamorphosis as well as fold their wings. Insects that undergo complete metamorphosis often emerge from the egg as wormlike larvae that change first into a pupa, often encased in a cocoon, before emerging as an adult. This group includes the most diverse and successful of all insects: beetles (Coleoptera); butterflies and moths (Lepidoptera); flies (Diptera); fleas (Siphonaptera, which have become wingless); and the bees, wasps, and ants (Hymenoptera).

Some bees and wasps and all ants have developed a highly organized social life, with differentiation of members of the community into castes with different duties. Evolution has also resulted in elaborate means of communication by pheromones or gestures (see ANIMAL COMMUNICATION) and highly engineered nest structures that even contain means for controlling temperature and humidity.

INSECTS AND HUMANS

The science concerned with insects is called entomology, which involves the description, classification, and evolution of insects, and research studies such as insect metabolism, behavior, genetics, and ecology. The fruit fly has long been a preferred experimental animal for research in basic genetics and has permitted discoveries that also apply to humans, other animals, and plants.

Entomological research is also concerned with improving knowledge of those insects that are helpful or harmful to humans. Pollination by insects is essential for many crops, especially fruit. Bees are the most important pollinators and also make honey, one of the oldest crops developed by humans. Other products derived from insects include beeswax, used in polishes, and silk from the cocoons of the silkworm moth.

Other insects, such as locusts and boll weevils, may destroy crops and stored products. Millions of locusts periodically swarm across parts of Africa and eat everything green in their path. The boll weevil, which is a tiny brown beetle, destroys millions of dollars worth of cotton annually in the United States. The gypsy moths defoliate a wide variety of orchard and forest trees. Much entomological research is directed at devising methods for controlling these pests.

Many insects carry diseases fatal to humans and livestock. The science concerned with preventing such diseases is called medical entomology. Some of the diseases include sleeping sickness, bubonic plague, malaria, typhoid fever, dysentery, and cholera.

Thus, although crops, houses, clothes, and even health may be damaged by insects, some benefits may be found in pollination and in the fascination of observing the fantastic variation in form, color, and size of insects. JAMES R. BAKER

Bibliography: Borror, D. J., et al., *An Introduction to the Study of Insects*, 4th ed. (1976); Elzinga, Richard, *Fundamentals of Entomology* (1978); Klots, Alexander and Elsie, *Living Insects of the World* (1975); Rainey, R. C., ed., *Insect Flight* (1976); Saunders, D. S., *Insect Clocks* (1976); Swann, Ralph B., *The Common Insects of North America* (1972); Tweedie, Michael, *An Atlas of Insects* (1974) and *Insect Life* (1977); Wigglesworth, Vincent B., *The Life of Insects* (1964); Wilson, Edward O., *The Insect Societies* (1971).

insecticide: see PESTICIDES.

insectivore [in-sek'-ti-vor]

Insectivores, which means "insect-eaters," are members of the mammalian order Insectivora. The order includes 8 living families, 63 genera, and about 400 species, of which about 300 are shrews. Other species among the insectivores are moles, tenrecs, hedgehogs, desmans, gymnures, and solenodons. The insectivores include the smallest of all mammals, Savi's pygmy shrew, *Suncus etruscus*, which may measure only 60 mm (2.4 in) including the tail, and weigh as little as 1.5 g (0.05 oz). The largest insectivore has 5 clawed toes. The snout is long and narrow, useful for poking into insects' nests. The typical coat is short, thick fur, or sometimes spines. The eyes are extremely small and sometimes have no external opening. The ears are tiny. Insectivores inhabit all parts of the world with the exception of Antarctica, Greenland, Australia, and most of South America. They are useful to humans because of their great consumption of insects, most of which are considered pests. Many insectivores, especially hedgehogs, moles, and shrews, also eat invertebrates, such as worms, and some small vertebrates. EVERETT SENTMAN

Bibliography: Ripper, Charles L., *Moles and Shrews* (1975).

inselberg [in'-sul-burg]

An inselberg ("island mountain" in German) is an isolated mountain left behind after the erosion of surrounding material. Usually rising abruptly from a monotonously flat plain, it is typically found in arid tropical regions and was first described in such a region in Africa. Inselbergs are common in the BASIN AND RANGE PROVINCE of the United States, where they protrude above the gently sloping erosional plain that surrounds many of the block mountains of the area. An analogous landform in temperate climates is the MONADNOCK.

JOHN A. SHIMER

insolation

Insolation is a general term for the solar radiation received at the Earth's surface. It is a major radiation input for the microclimatic energy budget (see GROUND TEMPERATURE; MICROCLIMATE).

The term is sometimes used specifically for the rate of direct-beam solar radiation (total solar radiation minus the diffused or scattered portion) incident on a horizontal plane above or below the atmosphere. In the former case, the rate can be analytically determined by using the Sun's energy output, the varying Earth-Sun distance, the latitude, the season, and the time of day for any particular point on Earth. In the latter case, the transmission of the solar radiation from space through the atmosphere has to be computed, a problem only partially solved.

WERNER H. TERJUNG

Bibliography: Kondratyev, K. Ya., *Radiation in the Atmosphere* (1969).

insomnia: see SLEEP.

Inspector General, The

The Inspector General (1836; Eng. trans., 1892), a comic drama by Nikolai Gogol, is considered Gogol's most expertly crafted play and has become a staple of Western stage literature. The action takes place in a Russian provincial town whose officials mistake a new arrival for an imperial inspector general assigned to investigate corruption. The officials set about impressing, entertaining, and bribing the visitor (Khlestakov), who happily makes the most of his false identity and escapes with his gains just before the real inspector general appears. Because it ridiculed petty officialdom and, by extension, contemporary Russian society, the play raised a storm of criticism from conservative elements at its first performance in Saint Petersburg.

installment plan

The installment plan is a method of buying goods on credit and making payments for them over a period of time. In Great Britain the practice is called hire purchase. In the United States most durable goods can be bought this way. About one-fourth of all retail sales are made on the installment plan.

Installment buying is only one method of borrowing money and paying it back over a period of time. Other forms of credit include CREDIT CARDS, home MORTGAGES, bank loans, and charge accounts. In 1977 consumer installment credit in the United States was close to $217 billion.

A customer who buys on the installment plan does not usually gain title to the goods until they are paid for. If the buyer defaults on payments the seller can repossess the goods and sell them to someone else; the first buyer is entitled to receive his or her money back minus depreciation. The installment contract may also give the seller the right to collect payments from the buyer's employer—to garnishee wages (see ATTACHMENT LAW).

Because the installment purchaser is in effect borrowing money to make the purchase, the buyer must pay interest on the loan. The Consumer Credit Protection Act of 1968 requires installment sellers to make the finance charge and the annual rate of interest clear to borrowers.

Bibliography: Cohen, Jerome B., *Personal Finance*, 5th ed. (1975); Donaldson, Elvin F., et al., *Personal Finance*, 6th ed. (1977).

instant camera and photography: see CAMERA.

instant replay: see VIDEO RECORDING.

instinct

Instinct is inherited, unlearned ANIMAL BEHAVIOR that is typical to each species. Instinct is prominent in aggression, courtship, and mating, and in various social behaviors, although learning, maturation, growth, or circumstance can modify the behavior. Human behavior is mostly a product of learning, whereas the behavior of a moth, a snail, or a bird mainly depends on instinct. A species can be characterized and perhaps identified by its behavior patterns as distinctively as by its anatomy. For example, almost all birds drink by scooping water into their bills and lifting their heads, letting the water trickle down their throats. Pigeons, however, which are anatomically like other birds, are among a few bird species that pump, not scoop, their drinking water. Different species of spiders can be identified by the webs they spin. Such behavioral traits are especially useful for distinguishing closely related groups.

Instinctive Patterns. Behaviors that are most instinctive include reproduction, concealment, defense, escape, threats or warnings, and aggression, all of which are essential to the survival of the species.

A species' instinctive behaviors appear similar in form: chickens and turkeys seek a high place to roost at night, cats stalk prey in a characteristic manner, and dogs mark their territories in a species-specific method. Typical behavior patterns appear even in animals that are raised isolated from other members of their own species, a situation in which learning by observation, imitation, or instruction cannot occur. Many, but not all, birds sing the songs of their conspecifics (other members of their species) even though they are removed from the nest before hatching and are raised in a quiet room. Others sing a simplified version of the species' song.

The term *instinct* is usually restricted to relatively complex acts, depending on the capabilities of the animal, and excludes simple reflexes such as the eyeblink and knee jerk, which are externally rather than internally provoked and which involve simple muscle groups. An example of complex instinctive behavior is nest building, which involves a great many different motions. Specific instincts have probably evolved through countless generations, as they are characteristic of particular species. They are part of the species' adaptive equipment, most likely to preserve the species.

MIGRATION AND REPRODUCTION

ANIMAL MIGRATION and COURTSHIP AND MATING are instinctive behaviors. Many animals travel great distances to particular locations where they engage in courting, mating, or caring for their young. Salmon arduously return to the river of their origin in order to reproduce; males and females of many mountain animals normally live in separate groups, but during mating season both sexes migrate to certain valleys and intermingle.

Mating rituals tend to be highly stylized for a given species. Because of this specificity, no mistakes are made in the meaning of the message or of the intent of the signaler. Moreover, messages announcing the receptivity of a female are usually interpretable only by members of the same species. Several kinds of fireflies can occupy the same yard without interbreeding, because each uses its own specific flashing pattern to notify others of its intent, and each responds only to its species' particular pattern. Whereas reproduction signals must be species-specific to maintain reproductive isolation, one species' alarm call can be understood by members of other species.

Although the most dramatic instinctive behavior relates to reproduction, instincts have a role in other aspects of animal life. Nestlings gape when a parent bird arrives at the nest; the highly colored throat pattern is a strong stimulus for the parent to stuff food into the beaks of the young. The young of mouthbreeder fish always swim toward the mother's mouth, which is opened at the first sign of danger to admit the

Each species of firefly has a characteristic mating signal, determined by the male's rate of flashing and the interval at which the female responds. In swallows and other birds the parents' feeding response is triggered by markings in the chicks' mouths and throats.
Mouthbreeder fish such as cichlids protect their young in their mouths, even though the fry may resemble small fish common to the parents' diets. The carrion crow will modify its instinctive nest-building behavior and use artificial materials if grass and twigs are unavailable.

young inside. The social organizations of species represent a kind of collective instinct that, although highly complex and adaptable, is similar enough for individuals of a species to act cooperatively, such as during hunting raids or forays to expand territory. Red-wing males rise to attack a crow who flies over their territory during spring. Many species fly in formations, and some fishes school in characteristic arrangements.

Although instinctive behaviors are predictable, higher animals still can adapt to varying circumstances. Animals such as the fox hunt over great distances to seek widely dispersed prey. When confined to zoos, these animals develop trotting circuits about the cage, wearing down the ground in paths. Crows collect shiny manufactured objects for nest building when natural material is unavailable.

The role of the concept of instincts in understanding and in theorizing about human and animal behavior has long been debated. Calling a certain type of behavior instinctive may only label it, not explain it, and labeling it may deter its being studied. The proper viewpoint would suggest that as few instincts be postulated as is necessary.   ARTHUR J. RIOPELLE

Bibliography: Ardrey, Robert, *The Territorial Imperative* (1966); Birney, Robert C., and Teevan, Richard C., *Instinct* (1961); Hinde, Robert A., *Animal Behavior: A Synthesis of Ethology and Comparative Psychology*, 2d ed. (1970); Marler, Peter R., and Hamilton, William J., *Mechanisms of Animal Behavior* (1966); Scott, John P., *Animal Behavior*, rev. ed. (1972); Schiller, Claire, *Instinctive Behavior: The Development of a Modern Concept* (1957); Tinbergen, Nikolaas, *The Study of Instinct* (1975).

Institute for Advanced Study

Founded in 1930, the Institute for Advanced Study in Princeton, N.J., provides research facilities to approximately 150 visiting American and foreign scholars who spend a term or a year or more on advanced study and work on academic projects. A staff of 24 faculty members in four schools (mathematics, natural sciences, social science, and historical studies) work with the visiting members. The institute offers no courses or degrees and provides no laboratories. Princeton University's library is available to institute members and faculty. The institute was endowed by Louis Bamberger, a department-store owner, and its first president was Abraham FLEXNER.

Institut de France   [een-stee-tue' duh frahns]

Established in Paris in 1795 to replace learned societies closed by the French Revolution, the Institut de France is the highest cultural center for science, learning, and the arts in France. After 19th-century reforms, it came to consist of five academies: The ACADÉMIE FRANÇAISE (1635, the French language academy), the ACADÉMIE DES SCIENCES (1666), the Académie des Inscriptions et Belles-Lettres (1663, for history and archaeology), the Académie des Beaux-Arts (1648), and the Académie des Sciences Morales et Politiques (1795). Membership in each academy is limited to a small, distinguished group of persons, and vacancies are filled by election.

Institute of Journalists

The oldest professional organization of journalists in Great Britain, the Institute of Journalists was founded in 1884 and was chartered by the crown in 1890. Although it is recognized officially as a trade union, its stated policy is more to protect individual rights than to promote unionism. Its major competitor is the National Union of Journalists.

CHRISTOPHER G. TRUMP

Institute of Navigation

The Institute of Navigation was founded in 1945 by Samuel Herrick and Captain P. V. H. Weems in order to establish a common meeting ground for individuals who are professionally concerned with land, sea, air, and (later) space navigation. The institute currently has about 3,000 members and a staff of two with headquarters in Washington, D.C. It publishes the quarterly *Navigation*, the biannual *Proceedings*, and holds annual conventions.

institution, social

An *institution*, as social scientists use the term, is a significant and persistent element in human society that fulfills certain basic needs both of individuals and of society as a whole. Marriage and inheritance are examples of institutions as defined this way. Marriage unites the biological drives of individuals with the social imperative of producing and caring for children. Inheritance provides for the transmission of property from one generation to another. Other institutions include laws, education, and religion, which exist in various forms in all societies and cultures. In this sense an institution represents a social NORM or pattern of behavior, approved by society, which individuals are expected to conform to.

The term is also used to mean an association or group that is organized to carry out a pattern of social behavior. The family, church, and government are often called social institutions. Recent writers prefer to distinguish institutions as social norms (marriage, religion) from social structures (the family, the church) established to administer those norms.

Bibliography: Durkheim, Emile, *Emile Durkheim on Institutional Analysis*, ed. by Mark Traugott (1978).

instrumentation

Although an instrument, broadly defined, includes anything that performs or facilitates an action, in practice an important distinction is made between general instruments, which might range from a wheelbarrow to a scalpel, and scientific instruments. This article will deal with the latter category.

Scientific instruments may be divided into four broad classes according to their use: (1) instruments used in everyday life that depend on scientific or mathematical principles in their operation, including SUNDIALS, CAMERAS, SPEEDOMETERS, CLOCKS, and electrical gadgets; (2) devices employed by scientific practitioners to assist in the examination of natural phenomena, such as the astronomical TELESCOPE, MICROSCOPE, SPECTROSCOPE, and particle DETECTOR; (3) apparatus employed to produce phenomena for laboratory examination, including most chemical apparatus and demonstration apparatus; and (4) CALCULATORS, whose purpose is to facilitate mathematical operations at a simple or advanced level. Historically these four groups have always overlapped.

The history of instrumentation may be seen as the development of specialized instruments for specific tasks in response to refinements of scientific theory requiring greater precision in MEASUREMENT or the isolation of some particular phenomenon. The intimate relation between instrumentation and the generation and testing of scientific theories has always been apparent to the productive scientist. Between the scholar and the craftsman there has always been a close connection, so close that in every period of history examples can be found of the two roles combined by the same person, whether it be the 14th-century mathematician and horologist Richard of Wallingford, the 17th-century physicist, microscopist, and mechanician Robert Hooke, or the 20th-century bacteriologist Alexander Fleming, who discovered penicillin.

EARLY DEVELOPMENT OF PRACTICAL INSTRUMENTS

The earliest scientific instruments were astronomical and were concerned with timekeeping. In Megalithic times the movement of the Sun or Moon in relation to fixed landmarks was deliberately utilized to mark recurrent seasonal points or to aid the counting of the number of moons required to elapse between two events, such as harvesting and sowing. The ancient stone alignment at STONEHENGE and CARNAC may be considered the forerunners of the more elaborate mechanical instruments later used in astronomy and other sciences.

Another early instrument related to the measurement of time was the gnomon, an object set vertically that could be used as a seasonal indicator by the change in the minimum length of the shadow cast by the Sun. Known in ancient Mesopotamia, and apparently transmitted to the Greeks, the gnomon was an important instrument for astronomical operations throughout the Middle Ages and Renaissance. That it could also be used to indicate the time of day by the change

in the length of its shadow was known from an early date, and by the 1st century AD it had been recognized that if the gnomon was inclined so as to lie parallel with the Earth's axis it would mark 24 hours that were equal in length with one another. This recognition was of fundamental importance for the subsequent development of sundials.

The development of geometry in the Hellenistic world made possible the development of a much wider range of instruments. Of these perhaps the most important was the ASTROLABE, which combined the functions of analog computer, observational instrument, and time-finder. Developing steadily throughout the following centuries, it was transmitted from Greece to the Islamic world and to Western Europe, where it remained in use until the end of the 17th century. In the Islamic world it retained its usefulness until comparatively recent times.

As a portable instrument for finding the time, the astrolabe was complemented by a range of portable sundials. These devices, which also originated in the Hellenistic world, slowly increased in number (especially after the invention of the magnetic COMPASS, which made portable direction dials possible) during the Middle Ages. The growth of instrument making as an independent manufacturing and retail trade from the 16th to the 18th century led practitioners to develop novel forms of sundials to increase both their reputation and trade. The growing popularity of domestic clocks in this period produced a demand for easily used sundials in order to check and set them. It was not until the electric telegraph, national systems of time distribution, and radio signals that the sundial became irrelevant.

Of fundamental importance to the development of ancient instruments was the growth of a tradition of mechanical technology at Alexandria from the 3d century BC to the 1st century AD, associated with the names of Ctesibos, Philo, Hero, and Archimedes. This technology produced interesting gadgets, many of which employed automated figures and were controlled by water, strings, and levers. A parallel development produced geared or mechanical models of the planetary system, an example of which has survived in the remarkable Antikythera machine. Transmitted to China and to the Islamic world, this technology gave rise to a series of outstanding, complicated, water-driven astronomical models and clocks with hour sounding and automated figures.

Although direct contact between the West and this tradition was limited, some transmission did take place, and with the independent invention in Europe of an escapement to regulate weight-driven machines, the attempt to produce automatic, astronomical models was given fresh vigor. The subsequent investigations into gearing and gear ratios for the production of accurate astronomical clocks and models was a major factor in the development of industrial machinery in the West, because the clock and instrument makers who built these elaborate devices provided a reservoir of skills not only for making other kinds of clockwork instruments such as ships logs and timing mechanisms, but also for much of the early industrial machinery.

The range of instrumentation available to the medieval West was not large. For the mechanical operations of arithmetic some aid was offered by the ABACUS, while simple forms of PROTRACTORS, levels, dividers, and set squares were available to the surveyor, the mason, and the geometer.

DEVELOPMENT OF LABORATORY INSTRUMENTS

Little is known about the only substantial group of medieval laboratory apparatus, the glass and earthenware utensils of the alchemist (see ALCHEMY) and the apothecary. Beginning in the late 16th and 17th centuries, under the impact of new scientific theories, systematic attempts were made to investigate nature, and to quantify these investigations through accurate measurements. New devices were developed and adapted to increasingly specialized tasks. New instruments stimulated new theories and vice versa. Thus the investigations of Evangelista Torricelli into air pressure led to the invention of the BAROMETER, which immediately made possible a wide new field of investigation into meteorological phenomena.

The most important developments during the scientific

revolution of the 17th and 18th centuries were the invention of optical instruments such as the telescope and microscope, electrical research instruments such as the LEYDEN JAR and electroscope, and research into the pendulum (1610–80). Machines for calculation were also developed from the 17th century onwards. Some, such as Samuel Morland's and Blaise Pascal's devices, employed mechanical principles; others, such as Napier's bones, depended on inspection only. Both the SLIDE RULE and the sector appeared in the early 17th century, the former being comparatively rare (except as an instrument of gauging) until the late 18th century, when it gradually replaced the sector. For accurate measurement the MICROMETER and the VERNIER scale were both of the first importance.

With increasing specialization, instruments began to appear in dozens of different forms, with different calibrations or shapes to fulfill different tasks. The 18th century saw the steady development of more specialized forms of instruments sharing common principles, rather than the invention of entirely new classes of instruments. The 19th century saw an enormous proliferation of instruments, including the introduction of those based on electromagnetism, such as the GALVANOMETER, AMMETER, and VOLTMETER. Not until the appearance of X-ray, radio, and nuclear instrumentation were innovations made that compared in importance to the appearance of optical, electrical, and electromagnetic apparatus.   A. J. TURNER

Bibliography: Adler, Irving, The Changing Tools of Science, rev. ed. (1973); Bedini, Silvio A., Thinkers and Tinkers (1975); Daumas, Maurice, Scientific Instruments of the 17th and 18th Centuries, trans. by Mary Holbrook (1972); Michel, Henri, Scientific Instruments in Art and History (1967); Pacey, Arnold, The Maze of Ingenuity (1976); Wynter, Harriet, and Turner, Anthony, Scientific Instruments (1975).

See also: LABORATORY TECHNOLOGY; MEDICAL INSTRUMENTATION; METEOROLOGICAL INSTRUMENTATION; OCEANOGRAPHIC INSTRUMENTATION.

insulating materials

Materials that are poor conductors of heat are considered thermal insulators. They include mineral wool, vegetable fibers, glass fibers, cork, and foamed plastics. Aluminum, copper, and steel, by contrast, are excellent conductors of heat. Concrete, brick masonry, and stone have lower conductives.

The transfer of heat by conduction (see HEAT AND HEAT TRANSFER) is resisted by all materials in direct proportion to their thickness, but construction techniques, weight factors, and economics limit the thickness of solid insulation employed in buildings. Moving air transfers heat by a process known as convection. Still air, however, is an excellent insulating medium. A 2-cm (¾-in) enclosed air space has a better insulating value than 10 cm (4 in) of solid concrete. Materials of pressed fibrous materials have good insulating qualities because they entrap numerous pockets of still air.

Materials that reflect heat into adjacent air spaces insulate by a different principle. Polished aluminum foil will reflect up to 95% of the heat that reaches its surface. Such reflective insulation must be adjacent to a 2-cm (¾-in) air space to be effective. Cane fiber, wood fiber, mineral wool, or glass, pressed into boards, may be covered with aluminum foil to serve as both rigid insulating material and a reflective insulation. Loose fibers of mineral wool or glass fibers enclosed in a tough paper covering form flexible insulating batts or blankets. These same materials may be blown between framing members to form heat barriers. Foamed plastic boards formed of plastics such as polyurethane or polystyrene are also used as insulation. A recent technique is to add chemicals to granular or liquid plastic, causing it to foam in place and thus to fill all voids between structural framing with an efficient insulating material.

The effectiveness of a given type and thickness of insulating material is expressed by its R-value. Building codes often specify certain minimum standards for insulation in new construction. Typical modern requirements for a single-family dwelling in a climate where winter temperatures fall to −18° C (0° F) might be R-11 for walls (equivalent to 9 cm/3½ in of glass fiber batts) and R-19 for ceilings (15 cm/6 in of glass fiber batts).   DON A. WATSON

insulator

An insulator is a substance that is a very poor conductor of heat or electricity. A material that is a poor conductor of heat generally is also a poor conductor of electricity, since both phenomena largely depend on the transport of energy by electrons. A conductor has many free electrons (roughly one per atom), which are free to move throughout the material, while in an insulator essentially all the electrons are bound to the atoms.

The distinction between conductors and insulators, although not absolute, is dramatic. It may be expressed in terms of the resistivity, which is the resistance in ohms of a piece of material 1 cm long, with cross-sectional area 1 cm. The difference between the resistivity of copper, an excellent conductor, and that of glass, a typical insulator, is over 10^{20}, or 100 billion billion.

RESISTIVITY OF SELECTED MATERIALS

Material	Resistivity, ohm-cm
Conductors:	
Silver	1.59×10^{-6}
Copper (hard drawn)	1.77×10^{-6}
Gold	2.44×10^{-6}
Insulators:	
Ivory	2×10^{8}
Glass	9×10^{13}
Mica	9×10^{15}
Quartz (fused)	7.5×10^{19}

Intermediate between conductors and insulators are SEMICONDUCTORS, which can have resistivities of the order 1 ohm-cm. These include substances such as germanium and silicon. Impurities strongly alter the conducting properties of such materials. For example, the addition of boron to pure silicon in the ratio of 1:100,000 increases the conductivity a thousandfold at room temperature.

The origin of the vastly different conductivity properties of materials can be explained by the band theory of solids. In a solid there are certain continuous bands of energy states that electrons can occupy, separated by forbidden bands or gaps. Conduction will take place if electrons partially fill an energy band, the conduction band. They are then free to travel throughout the solid.

In an insulator the valence (outer) electrons completely occupy the so-called valence band, which is separated by a large energy gap from the higher energy conduction band. The electrons in the valence band, which is filled, cannot respond to an external field, since to do so would require them to occupy other states of motion that are already occupied. (No two electrons can occupy the same quantum state, by the Pauli EXCLUSION PRINCIPLE.) Nor can the electrons jump the large gap into the empty conduction band except at high temperature, when the electrons can be thermally excited to higher levels, or if imperfections or impurities are present.

A semiconductor also has a filled valence band, but a rather narrow energy gap separates it from the conduction band, so that a significant number of electrons are thermally excited to the conduction band even at room temperatures. A conductor, on the other hand, always has a partially filled conduction band even at absolute zero, so there are always electrons free to respond to electrical or thermal differences.

KIMBALL A. MILTON

Bibliography: Saccoma, Frank, Insulators, Just Insulators (1967); Schroeder, Bill, Eight Hundred Insulators (1971); Sillars, R. W., Electrical Insulating Materials and Their Application (1974).

insulin   [in′-suh-lin]

Insulin is a HORMONE produced in all vertebrates by beta cells of the islets of Langerhans in the PANCREAS. Insulin regulates the level and utilization of blood sugar and affects RNA and PROTEIN SYNTHESIS, as well as the METABOLISM and storage of fats. Specifically, it controls the absorption of glucose—an energy source of the body—by cells. Low levels of insulin result in increased levels of blood sugar, which causes the disease DIABETES MELLITUS, which is characterized by excessive urination, acidosis, and vascular degeneration. High levels of insulin, or hyperinsulinism, result in lowered blood sugar levels, the symptoms of which are dizziness, weakness, and coma.

Insulin is a protein consisting of 51 amino acid residues, 30 of which comprise one polypeptide chain and 21 of which comprise a second chain. The two chains are linked by two disulfide bridges. Insulin was first isolated in 1921 by Frederick G. Banting and Charles H. Best, Canadian biochemists. It was the first protein to be characterized by its amino acid sequence—in research done in 1955 by Frederick Sanger, a British biochemist—and the entire structure was characterized in 1969. In 1966 insulin was synthesized independently by the American biochemist Michael Katsoyannis and by scientists in the People's Republic of China. Most recently, research has been directed toward producing quantities of insulin by means of the recombinant DNA techniques of genetic engineering. Insulin that has been derived from animal pancreases is administered to diabetic patients in order to control their disease.

Bibliography: Krahl, Maurice E., *The Action of Insulin on Cells* (1961); Kutsky, Roman J., *Handbook of Vitamins and Hormones* (1973); Rieser, P., *Insulin, Membranes and Metabolism* (1967); Sawin, Clark T., *Hormones: Endocrine Physiology* (1969).

See also: ENDOCRINE SYSTEM; ENDOCRINE SYSTEM, DISEASES OF THE.

Insull, Samuel   [in'-sul]

American financier Samuel Insull, b. England, Nov. 11, 1859, d. July 16, 1938, acquired an enormous public utilities empire that was forced into receivership in 1932. Insull immigrated to the United States in 1881 to work as private secretary to Thomas Edison. By 1892 he was president of the Chicago Edison Company, which he built into a mammoth pyramid of electrical power companies throughout the Middle West, controlled through holding companies. In 1932, Insull moved to Europe to escape prosecution. Extradited to the United States in 1934, he was tried separately on charges of mail fraud, violation of federal bankruptcy laws, and embezzlement, but was acquitted each time.

Bibliography: McDonald, Forrest, *Insull* (1962); Ramsay, Marion L., *Pyramids of Power* (1937; repr. 1975).

insurance

Insurance is a systematic means of dealing with financial risk. It enables people to substitute certainty for uncertainty with respect to losses resulting from accidents and other unforeseeable events. While an individual cannot be certain as to the likelihood, for example, that his or her house will burn down, it is possible to predict with a fair degree of accuracy the losses among the population as a whole that will occur from fire. The person buying insurance agrees to share these losses with others. The insurance company determines its premiums—specified individual payments—by estimating through actuarial techniques what the losses will be among those to whom it sells policies, based on the law of averages and past experience with a similar segment of the population. Policyholders are thus able to exchange the risk of a loss, which may far exceed their ability to pay, for a small, certain cost that is well within their means. The principle underlying fire insurance can be applied to the risk that an individual's car may be damaged, or that heavy medical expenses may be incurred, or that a person may die in a certain year.

INSURABLE RISKS

Not all risks can be insured. An insurable risk is one that is distributed over a large population, involving a loss that is definite but cannot be foreseen. The insured objects cannot be exposed to risks that are likely to provide loss to many policyholders at the same time, such as houses in a flood plain, because no insurance company can afford such losses unless it charges an exorbitant premium.

Risks are generally classified into three broad groups: personal risks, property risks, and liability risks.

Personal Risks. Risks involving the life of the insured person are called personal risks. They include risks of loss from medical expenses, loss of income while a person is unable to work, the cost of dying (and the cost of supporting a family whose breadwinner has died), and the costs of old age. Personal risks are covered by health insurance, accident insurance, and life insurance.

Property Risks. Losses associated with property include loss of the property itself—a house, a car, or business and industrial property—and loss of income when property is destroyed or damaged. When a drycleaning store catches fire, the owner loses not only the premises but the means of earning an income. Associated losses may include the cost of living in rented quarters while the home is being restored.

Liability Risks. Large losses may occur from claims made by other persons through legal action. A physician may be sued for hundreds of thousands of dollars if a patient dies. An automobile owner may be required to pay for the medical bills of others injured by the car he or she owns, even when driven by someone else. Juries have been known to award damages of millions of dollars to victims of hospital or airline accidents. Such claims, arising under the law of LIABILITY, cover events for which a person is held responsible because of certain acts or omissions. The most common type of liability risk is that of NEGLIGENCE, or failure to take precautions against danger to others. If a homeowner with a backyard swimming pool leaves the gate open and unwatched, and a child in the neighborhood falls in and drowns, the owner may be charged with negligence.

Liability may also arise under contract. An employer is liable for the acts of employees or for failure to carry out agreements with other business firms.

KINDS OF INSURANCE

In the United States insurance is written by government agencies as well as by private companies. Government insurance is, for the most part, intended to supplement private insurance or to cover persons who could not otherwise afford it. Most adults acquire insurance from both sources.

Government Insurance. Federal and state governments offer many kinds of insurance programs, some voluntary and some compulsory. The best known of the latter is SOCIAL SECURITY, which provides old-age, survivors, and disability and health benefits. Associated with Social Security are the MEDICARE and MEDICAID insurance programs. State governments administer the system of UNEMPLOYMENT INSURANCE. Federal insurance programs also include life insurance for military personnel, insurance for railroad workers and retired government employees, insurance on bank deposits, mortgage insurance, and crop insurance for farmers.

Private Insurance. The business of private insurance has four main branches: LIFE INSURANCE, accident and HEALTH INSURANCE, FIRE INSURANCE and PROPERTY INSURANCE, and casualty insurance (see LIABILITY INSURANCE). Many companies write policies in more than one of these branches, so that for practical purposes the industry comprises life insurance companies and nonlife insurance companies.

Life insurance companies write three basic types of policies: life insurance, ANNUITIES, and health insurance. Because life insurance includes an element of saving by which the insured person acquires a personal estate, the assets of life insurance companies are very large; in 1974, U.S. life insurance companies had assets of more than $263 billion.

Other insurance companies write policies covering property, health, liability, and surety. The last is often called bonding; it provides a financial guarantee of an employee's honesty or a builder's performance of a contract. In 1970, U.S. property and liability insurance companies had assets of more than $97 billion.

Specialized Coverages. Many specialized fields exist in private insurance. So-called marine insurance is primarily transportation insurance, covering goods in transit by sea, land, or air. Some marine policies also cover certain types of personal property such as yachts and motorboats.

Title insurance, sold by title companies, covers purchasers of real estate against losses from defects in the title to their property. Homeowners purchase title insurance to protect themselves against mistakes by title searchers.

Boiler and machinery insurance is written by companies that inspect boilers, motors, and other machinery for defects.

Multiple-line insurance has been developed in recent decades to enable companies to cover many different perils in one insurance policy instead of writing several different policies. The so-called homeowners insurance policy, for example, protects the owner of a residence against losses from fire, theft, personal liability, physical damage to the property of others, and various other perils.

THE INSURANCE CONTRACT

The insurance contract is a legal instrument setting forth the promises, terms, and conditions of the policy. Contracts have four parts: the declaration, the insuring agreement, exclusions, and conditions. Usually there are riders or endorsements that modify one or more of the basic parts.

The Declaration. On the first page of the contract is a statement giving information about the insurance company, the person or firm being insured, the term for which the contract will run, the amount of the insurance, the premium, and warranties or promises made by the insured.

The Insuring Agreement. The coverages provided by the policy are described in the insuring agreement. Sometimes it also defines terms used in the contract.

Exclusions. Every insurance contract states specifically what situations are not covered by the policy. Exclusions are necessary in order to eliminate coverage that is not needed by most policyholders and to exclude perils that the insurer does not want to cover or that cannot be insured against. Life insurance contracts, for example, usually exclude death by suicide if the insured takes his or her own life within one or two years—to prevent obvious abuse by persons planning suicide. Homeowners policies usually exclude damage from war and flood, automobile liability, and claims that would be paid under workers' compensation laws.

Conditions. The largest part of the printed policy describes the duties of the parties to the contract. They include the obligations of the insured person in the event of a loss, the time limit for paying claims, the period of time in which the insured can take legal action against the insurer, and penalties for fraud.

Endorsements and Riders. Because most insurance policy forms are printed and standardized, they need to be adapted to the requirements of the particular person being insured. A fire insurance contract consists of a standard form with a description (endorsement) of the insured property attached to it. A completed insurance contract may be changed after the coverage or terms.

HISTORY OF INSURANCE

The basic notion of insurance was obvious to humankind at a very early stage in social development. Records of the insurance practice survive from ancient Babylonia, when traveling merchants insured their caravans against loss from thieves or brigands. Marine insurance may be the oldest form of insurance. It existed in ancient Greece, where bottomry contracts made by shipowners included premiums insuring them against loss.

Modern insurance practices date back to the 14th century, when marine insurance policies were written in Genoa and other European maritime cities. The coffeehouses of London were the seat of English underwriters (policies were signed at the bottom of the contract—individuals who signed there were called underwriters); the best known of them was Edward Lloyd's on Tower Street, the forerunner of LLOYD'S OF LONDON. The London fire of 1666 inspired the first fire insurance company, run by Dr. Nicholas Barbon. The first life insurance contract was drawn up in England, and life insurance companies, aided by Edmond Halley and Joseph Dodson's mortality tables, flourished in 18th-century London, among them the Society for the Equitable Assurance of Lives and Survivorships, which still exists.

American insurance companies were formed before the Revolution. The first mutual fire insurer, for example, was the Philadelphia Contributorship for the Insurance of Houses

from Loss of Fire, organized in 1752 and still existing today. Marine and property insurance were the dominant fields until the 19th century, when life insurance companies began to be organized on a wide scale. In the 20th century life insurance enjoyed an enormous growth; the total value of life insurance policies in force in 1969 was 100 times the value in 1909.

Flood Insurance. The consumer movement of the 1960s and '70s brought a number of proposals for reforms in the insurance industry. The National Flood Insurance Act (Title XIII of the Housing and Urban Development Act of 1968) provided for government-subsidized flood insurance on residences and small business properties in areas subject to flood. The flood insurance is sold by private companies in cooperation with the Federal Insurance Administration. Communities that wish to become eligible must take measures to reduce the hazard of flood damage. The legislation removed floods from the category of uninsurable perils for large numbers of property owners.

No-Fault Automobile Insurance. The high cost of automobile liability insurance and the delays and inequities in establishing that one of the parties to an accident was negligent have brought proposals for NO-FAULT INSURANCE. The essential principle of these proposals is that the victims of an accident are to be compensated for medical expenses and income losses by their own insurance companies, regardless of who is at fault. They cannot claim large damages for pain and suffering except when there is serious injury or loss of life. A number of states have passed some form of no-fault insurance law, but early experience indicated that the cost of insurance was not substantially reduced.   ROBERT S. CLINE

Bibliography: Bickelhaupt, David L., *General Insurance*, 9th ed. (1974); Chernick, Vladimir P., *The Consumer's Guide to Insurance Buying* (1970); Davids, Lewis E., *Dictionary of Insurance*, 5th ed. (1977); Greene, Mark R., *Risk and Insurance*, 4th ed. (1977); Huebner, S. S., *Property and Liability Insurance*, 2d ed. (1976); Kimball, Spencer L., and Deneberg, Herbert S., *Insurance, Government and Social Policy* (1969); Mehr, R., and Cammack, E., *Principles of Insurance*, 6th ed. (1976).

intaglio   (art)   [in-tal'-ee-oh]

The term *intaglio*, derived from the Italian *intagliare*, "to engrave or cut," refers to an incised carving or engraving depressed below the surface of the material. The word is most often used in reference to engraved gems that, when pressed into softened wax, yielded an image in relief that could be used as a seal for documents. Intaglios have been valued as an art form since the Roman Empire.

The technique of engraving hard stones was known as early as about 4000 BC in Mesopotamia, but the style of typical intaglios was evolved by the ancient Greeks. Intaglio carving was widely practiced in Roman times; it was revived during the Renaissance and the 18th and 19th centuries.   BETTY ELZEA

Bibliography: Sutherland, Beth B., *The Romance of Seals and Engraved Gems* (1965).

intaglio   (printing)

Intaglio is the general term for a PRINTING process in which the printing surface is recessed below the nonprinting surface on the plate. (This is in contrast to letterpress, in which the image is raised, and planographic methods such as offset lithography, in which the printing and nonprinting areas are essentially on the same level.) The two basic types of intaglio are *line intaglio* and *gravure*.

Line intaglio can be further divided into ENGRAVING and ETCHING. In engraving, the design to be printed is cut directly into a metal surface by the engraver. In etching, an acid-resistant coating is first applied to the metal. Next, some of this coating is selectively scratched away to form a design. The design is then cut, or etched, into the plate by immersing the plate in an acid solution. In addition to being a fine arts technique, engraving is used as a printing process. Copperplate engraving was once a widely used illustration process, but it has generally been replaced by PHOTOENGRAVING. Steel-die engraving is still used extensively for printing money, stocks, and postage stamps. Copper plates and steel dies are produced manually, mechanically, or photomechanically.

Gravure is a special type of intaglio process in which the printing surface is divided, by means of a screen, into a series of cells etched below the plate surface. The printing surface may be formed in various ways, each of which differs in the method of producing the acid-resistant coating, but in all cases the final step consists of etching the plate to produce cells of varying depth. Sheet-fed and web-fed presses may be used in gravure. Web-fed presses can operate at high speeds because they have the plate wrapped around a cylinder; they are, therefore, called cylindrical, or rotary, presses, and such a printing process is called ROTOGRAVURE.

In the gravure printing process the plate is mounted on the press. A very fluid ink is applied to the plate, after which excess ink is scraped off with a steel doctor blade, and paper is then pressed against the plate in order to transfer the ink from the plate's cellular depressions onto the paper. The gravure process is capable of producing high-quality printing, but because of the expense of the plates, the process is used mainly for long printing runs.　　　MICHAEL H. BRUNO

Bibliography: Bannister, Manly, *Etching and Other Intaglio Techniques* (1969); Hague, Clifford W., *Printing and Allied Graphic Arts* (1957); Ross, John, and Romano, Clare, *The Complete Intaglio Print* (1974); Strauss, Victor, *The Printing Industry* (1967).

integer   [in'-tuh-jur]

The integers are all the positive and negative whole NUMBERS and ZERO (. . . , -4, -3, -2, -1, 0, 1, 2, 3, 4, . . .). The sum of two integers is an integer, and the product of two integers is also an integer. If a is any integer, then $0 + a = a$ and $a \times 1 = a$.

integral calculus   [in'-tuh-grul kal'-kue-luhs]

Integral calculus is a branch of mathematics in which a whole is calculated by (1) dividing the whole into n parts that are all relatively easily approximated, (2) taking the sum of the n approximations, and (3) improving the approximation to the whole to any desired degree of accuracy by increasing the number of elements summed. A related problem is the determination of a function when its rate of change, or *derivative*, is known. Integral calculus is closely related to DIFFERENTIAL CALCULUS; the two are briefly treated, related, and contrasted in CALCULUS. The strategy of evaluating a sum of elements is useful in many applications, including the calculation of plane areas, surface areas, and volumes.

INTRODUCTORY ILLUSTRATION

As an illustration, one may calculate the area A of the region $OPQR$ bounded by the graph of $y = 1 + x^2$, the coordinate axes, and the line $x = 1$ (see figure 1). Subdivide OP into n equal parts, each of length $\Delta x = 1/n$, by choosing subdivision points $x_0 = 0$, $x_1 = 1 (\Delta x)$, $x_2 = 2 (\Delta x)$, $x_3 = 3 (\Delta x)$, . . . , $x_n = n (\Delta x) = 1$. Subdivide $OPQR$ by drawing ordinates parallel to the y-axis at the subdivision points of OP. Then approximate each subdivision of $OPQR$ by the rectangle whose height is the right-hand ordinate. The sum of the areas of the n rectangles is

$$A_n = (1 + x_1^2)\Delta x + (1 + x_2^2)\Delta x + . . . + (1 + x_n^2)\Delta x =$$

$$\sum_{k=1}^{n} (1 + x_k^2)\Delta x = n\Delta x + (x_1^2 + x_2^2 + x_3^2 + . . . + x_n^2)\Delta x$$

taking heights at the subdivision points from $y = 1 + x^2$.
Since $x_k = k\Delta x$,

$$A_n = n\Delta x + (1^2\Delta x^2 + 2^2\Delta x^2 + 3^2\Delta x^2 + . . . + n^2\Delta x^2) \Delta x =$$

$$n\Delta x + (1^2 + 2^2 + 3^2 + . . . + n^2) (\Delta x)^3 = n\Delta x +$$

$$1/6 (n) (n + 1) (2n + 1) (\Delta x)^3$$

using the fact that $1^2 + 2^2 + 3^2 + . . . + n^2 = 1/6 (n)$ $(n + 1) (2n + 1)$, which can be established by mathematical induction. Now, because $\Delta x = 1/n$,

$$A_n = n\left(\frac{1}{n}\right) + \frac{1}{6} n(n + 1)(2n + 1)\frac{1}{n^3} = \frac{4}{3} + \left(\frac{1}{2} \cdot \frac{1}{n}\right) + \left(\frac{1}{6} \cdot \frac{1}{n^2}\right)$$

The quantity A_n is larger than A, but will approach A as n is chosen larger, or, as Δx approaches 0.

Thus, $A = \lim_{n \to \infty} A_n = 4/3$

GENERALIZATION

In general, one tries to compute a quantity Q defined for $a < x < b$ by (1) choosing subdivision points $a = x_0 < x_1 < x_2 < . . . < x_n = b$; (2) approximating to Q with $Q_n = f(x_1^*) (\Delta x)_1 + f (x_2^*) (\Delta x)_2 + . . . + f (x_n^*) (\Delta x)_n = \sum_{k=1}^{n} f(x_k^*) (\Delta x)_k$, where x_k^* is a point of the kth subdivision and $(\Delta x)_k = x_k - x_{k-1}$ is the length of the kth subdivision; and (3) taking n ever larger, so that all the subdivisions approach 0 and Q_n approaches Q:

$$Q = \lim_{\substack{n \to \infty \\ (\Delta x)_k \to 0}} Q_n = \lim_{\substack{n \to \infty \\ (\Delta x)_k \to 0}} \sum_{k=1}^{n} f(x_k^*) (\Delta x)_k$$

When the limit exists, one writes Q as a *definite integral*: $Q = \int_a^b f(x) \, dx$. In the above example of computing an area, for instance,

$$A = \int_0^1 (1 + x^2) \, dx$$

The limit required will exist for a wide variety of functions $f(x)$. In particular, if $f(x)$ is continuous at each point of $a \leq x \leq b$, then $\int_a^b f(x) \, dx$ will exist.

The area $OPQR$ bounded by $y = 1 + x^2$, the coordinate axes, and $x = 1$ can be calculated in a second way. Let $A (x)$ be the area of $OSTR$ (see figure 2). When $x = 0$, then $A (x) = 0$, and when $x = 1$, then $A (x)$ is the area $OPQR$. One can compute dA/dx by forming $A (x + \Delta x)$, $\Delta A = A (x + \Delta x) - A (x)$, $\Delta A/\Delta x$, and then $dA/dx = \lim_{\Delta x \to 0} \Delta A/\Delta x$.

Observe that $A (x + \Delta x)$ is $OUVR$, that ΔA is $SUVT$, and that $y \Delta x < \Delta A < (y + \Delta y) \Delta x$, $y < \Delta A/\Lambda x < y + \Delta y$, $dA/dx = \lim_{\Delta x \to 0} \Delta A/\Delta x = y = 1 + x^2$ because $\Delta y \to 0$ when $\Delta x \to 0$.

From a knowledge of derivatives one can guess that if $A (x) = x + (x^3/3) + C$, where C is any constant, then $dA/dx = 1 + x^2$ as required. But A must be 0 for $x = 0$, and hence $C = 0$; $A (x) = x + (x^3/3)$. The area of $OPQR$ is obtained by taking $x = 1$; $A (1) = 1 + (1^3/3) = 4/3$.

The fact that area $OPQR$ above is $\int_0^1 (1 + x^2) \, dx$ from the limit-of-a-sum point of view, and can also be found by looking for $A (x)$ with derivative $1 + x^2$, is an illustration of a more general theorem, the fundamental theorem of the inte-

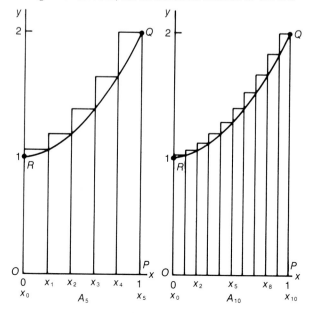

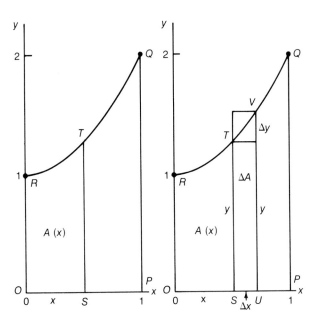

gral calculus: If $f(x)$ is continuous for $a < x < b$ and $d\phi/dx = f(x)$ for $a < x < b$, then

$$\int_a^b f(x) \ dx = \phi(b) - \phi(a)$$

In words, if $\phi(x)$ is an *antiderivative* for $f(x)$ for $a \le x \le b$, then the computation of $\int_a^b f(x) \ dx$ as a limit of a sum can be replaced by the evaluation of the difference $\phi(b) - \phi(a)$.

EVALUATION OF SPECIFIC INTEGRALS

The ability to evaluate specific integrals by using antiderivatives is developed by learning to recognize some antiderivatives, and then reducing other antiderivatives to those already known by using identities and several powerful theorems.

When one does not know an antiderivative function $\phi(x)$ such that $d\phi(x)/dx = f(x)$, one must approximate $\int_a^b f(x) \ dx$ to the desired degree of accuracy by using the summation point of view.   ABRAHAM SCHWARTZ

Bibliography: Courant, Richard, and John, Fritz, *Introduction to Calculus and Analysis*, 2 vols. (1974); Granville, Evelyn, et al., *Elements of the Differential and Integral Calculus*, rev. ed. (1962); Leithold, Louis, *The Calculus, with Analytic Geometry*, 3d ed. (1976); Schwartz, Abraham, *Calculus and Analytic Geometry*, 3d ed. (1974).

integrated circuit

An integrated circuit is an organized assembly of interconnected electronic components contained within the upper layer of a small, flat SEMICONDUCTOR chip measuring only a few millimeters on a side. Because the individual components that make up an integrated circuit, such as transistors, diodes, and resistors, are generally of microscopic size, hundreds or even thousands of components can be placed on a single chip.

The fabrication of an integrated circuit requires a complex series of steps. After the circuit to be integrated has been designed and tested, the entire circuit is drawn on a master transparency. The various components that require identical processing steps are then drawn on separate transparencies using the master as a guide.

The various overlays are then photographically reduced to the actual size of the integrated circuit chip, and arrays of up to a hundred or more patterns are formed on individual transparencies. The transparencies are then used to photographically reproduce a sequence of protective patterns on the surface of a circular wafer of silicon.

A series of production steps such as etching, heating, and diffusion of impurities into the silicon is carried out simultaneously on the unprotected silicon surface to produce the various regions of individual transistors, diodes, and resistors of each integrated circuit.

Finally, a network of aluminum interconnections is applied to the surface of the silicon to interconnect the various components. The silicon wafer is then separated into individual integrated circuits, which are tested and installed in protective plastic, ceramic, or metal packages.

Numerous kinds of integrated circuits have been developed by solid-state research laboratories. Most of these circuits can be categorized as analog, digital, or analog-digital, according to their function.

Analog integrated circuits generally respond to a variable incoming voltage by producing a correspondingly variable output voltage. Many analog integrated circuits, particularly audio-frequency amplifiers and operational amplifiers, are designed to produce an output voltage that is an amplified but faithful copy of the input voltage. These are called linear integrated circuits.

Analog integrated circuits are also used to generate time delays, produce both simple and complex waveforms, compare the phase relationship of two different electrical signals, and synthesize audible tones and electronic music. OPERA-

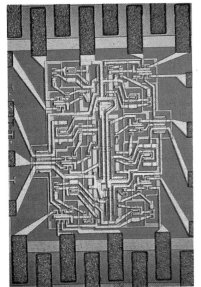

(Left) *The miniaturization and cost savings possible with integrated circuits are illustrated by this photomicrograph, in which several logic gate circuits are combined on a single small slice, or chip, of crystalline silicon.* (Below) *The first step in the mass production of an integrated circuit involves the drawing of the circuit design. The drawing is reduced photographically several hundred times to produce a final-size mask, or template, which is used to deposit the various components in correct position on a silicon chip.*

TIONAL AMPLIFIERS are used in applications ranging from monitoring the faint electrical impulses produced by living organisms to comparing the magnitude of two signals and indicating which is larger. They also serve as the fundamental building block of the electronic analog computer.

Digital integrated circuits are electronic logic circuits that count, compare, and otherwise process information in the form of on-off electrical pulses. This two-state operation means that the active components in a digital integrated circuit are either fully on or fully off at any given instant.

Recent advances in integrated-circuit manufacturing technology have led to the design of MICROPROCESSORS, inexpensive hand-held CALCULATORS, and digital watches.

FORREST M. MIMS III

Bibliography: Fitchen, Frank C., *Electronic Integrated Circuits and Systems* (1970); Hamilton, Douglas, and Howard, William, *Basic Integrated Circuits* (1975); *Scientific American*, special issue on microelectronics (September 1977); Wojslaw, Charles F., *Integrated Circuits: Theory and Applications* (1978).

See also: MICROELECTRONICS.

integration, racial

Racial integration may be defined as a condition in which the color of a person's skin has no important social consequence. In a racially integrated society, people associate freely, regardless of race. Cultural differences may persist, but these do not diminish any group's access to jobs, housing, the ballot box, or public services. In an integrated society no systematic discrimination exists against the members of a racial group.

Segregation is the opposite of integration. A segregated society is one in which members of different races rarely, if ever, come into contact with one another as equals. All aspects of daily life are separated, and contact between members of the races is regulated so that one race is always in a superior position to the other. Until only recently, racial segregation of blacks and whites was the prevailing practice in the United States. In the North, such segregation began well before the Civil War. Although never written into law, segregation was accomplished in informal custom and agreement, sometimes called de facto segregation. In the South states began passing laws (see JIM CROW LAWS) after the Civil War and Reconstruction era decreeing segregation of the races. Such segregation came to be known as de jure segregation.

Societies are seldom completely segregated or completely integrated. A wide range of possibilities exists between these extremes. In the United States today, for example, people of different races work side by side and ride buses together but often have little to do with one another in their private lives. Some authorities believe that desegregated activities will lead in the long run to expanding integration; increased contact between races on an equal basis will tend to reduce the suspicion and fear that underlie much racial hostility. This article reviews the progress along such a course in the United States with respect to the integration of blacks and whites.

THE STRUGGLE AGAINST SEGREGATION

Segregation, whether de facto or de jure, is discriminatory. Not only does segregation limit opportunities, but it is an insulting and degrading practice and has been opposed by black (and many white) people since its beginnings. Challenges to segregation have taken two general forms. One form was insistence on equal treatment through integration. An early leader of the integrationist movement in the United States was W. E. B. DU BOIS, a founder (1909) of the NATIONAL ASSOCIATION FOR THE ADVANCEMENT OF COLORED PEOPLE (NAACP). The other major challenge to segregation came from those who urged the establishment of independent black states or nations that would not be subservient to white people. An early leader of the BLACK NATIONALISM movement was Marcus GARVEY, who founded the Universal Negro Improvement Association in 1914. Both these positions are represented in black communities today.

The movement against segregation, particularly de jure segregation in the South, began to gather strength in the 1930s. Along with appeals to conscience, black leaders began to find economic leverage in all-black unions such as the Brotherhood of Sleeping Car Porters. At the beginning of World War II, threats of strikes by black unions led President Franklin D. Roosevelt to order an end to racial discrimination in defense plants. Continuing pressure brought an end, in 1944, to all-white primary elections in the South and won the passage in 1947 of the Fair Employment Practices Act that forbade discrimination in hiring on the basis of race or national origin. In 1948, President Harry S. Truman issued an order to desegregate the armed forces. In 1954 nearly three decades of grassroots militancy and patient legal strategy culminated in a Supreme Court decision declaring separate schools for blacks and whites unconstitutional. In BROWN V. BOARD OF EDUCATION OF TOPEKA, KANSAS, the Court ruled that its 1896 decision in PLESSY V. FERGUSON upholding "separate but equal" facilities was invalid and that segregation necessarily meant inequality. Finally, with the passage of the 1964 Civil Rights Act, the 1965 Voting Rights Act, and the 1968 Fair Housing Act, all de jure segregation was declared unlawful.

The dismantling of de jure segregation did not come about smoothly; its enactment required considerable agitation by both blacks and whites. An incident in Montgomery, Ala., in 1956 proved to be the start of one of the most important popular movements in U.S. history. Rosa Parks, a black working woman, refused to give up her seat in a bus and move to the section reserved for blacks. After the driver ordered her off the bus, the black community of Montgomery decided to boycott all public transportation. The boycott continued for months until Montgomery ended segregated seating on its buses. The protest spread to other cities and to other aspects of segregation. Dr. Martin Luther KING, Jr., a young black minister who had been drawn into the struggle in Montgomery, emerged as a leader of the movement against segregation and became, until his assassination in the spring of 1968, a powerful and charismatic figure in the fight for civil rights.

King was by no means alone. Thousands of boycotts, demonstrations, sit-ins, and marches occurred in those years as blacks and their sympathizers sought to overturn the laws protecting racial segregation. Though the demonstrators were usually well disciplined and nonviolent, they often met bitter opposition. Reports and photographs in the media of demonstrators being beaten by southern law enforcement officers or attacked with police dogs and fire hoses had a strong impact on national opinion. The courts and the federal government began to move in response to a growing popular indignation.

As integration progressed in the South, attention began to shift northward. Targets in the North, however, were more elusive. Segregation in the northern cities did not rest on laws so much as on attitudes, customs, and economic relationships. These were more difficult to confront with the tactics of nonviolent protest. Frustration and resentment grew in the black ghettos. In 1965 the Watts area of Los Angeles erupted into a riot that lasted for several days and left 34 dead. For three successive summers, outbursts of rebellion occurred in cities across the country. The most massive was the Detroit riot of 1967, which lasted nearly a week, took 40 lives, and destroyed property worth $250 million.

The passions and upheavals of the 1960s gave way in the 1970s to at least the appearance of calm. Protests have been rare for several years now as blacks and whites alike take stock of the gains of one of the most tumultuous periods in U.S. history.

PROGRESS AND PROSPECTS

By the end of the 1960s de jure segregation had been ended in all its aspects. The law was no longer an ally of those who believed that blacks are inferior to whites. The majority of whites said they no longer subscribed to such racist notions, and support for integration was steadily increasing. Blacks were now able to vote everywhere; they turned to the ballot box in large numbers, and by the late 1970s thousands of black elected officials were serving in municipal, county, state, and federal governments.

Many jobs traditionally reserved for whites were now open to blacks. During the 1960s and '70s the proportions of blacks in the professions and in managerial positions increased dramatically. Blacks accounted for more than 8% of the white-collar labor force in 1978. Although black earnings in 1978 were still only 62 percent of white earnings nationally, some important subgroups within the black population had incomes nearly equal to those of their white counterparts. For example, young blacks with a college education, and black women in general, had incomes roughly equal to those of their white counterparts. Outside the South, young black families in which both husband and wife worked were earning, on the average, as much as young white families in which both husband and wife worked.

Even though dramatic progress has been made, and even though by the end of the 1960s a clear majority of whites claimed to be in favor of integration, much remained unchanged. Residential segregation in the North was hardly less prevalent than it had been in the 1950s. Efforts to desegregate the schools by busing children to schools outside their neighborhoods had often encountered bitter resistance (see BUSING, SCHOOL). Even in schools that had been formally integrated, blacks and whites tended to pursue different programs that prevented them from having much contact with one another. And although the black middle class had increased considerably, the majority of blacks were still disproportionately poor. Unemployment hit blacks hardest, particularly black youth.

Moreover, a growing resistance appeared on the part of many whites to programs that attempted to go beyond merely forbidding discrimination. The opposition to busing could be seen as one example of this reluctance. Another was the opposition that arose in the 1970s to the federal government's policy of AFFIRMATIVE ACTION in employment and education. This policy put pressure on employers and educators to seek out minority applicants and, wherever feasible, give them preference in hiring and promotion and in admission to higher education. Proponents of the policy argued that it was necessary to compensate blacks and other minorities for the inequalities resulting from generations of segregation. Opponents argued that affirmative action was reverse discrimination and therefore in conflict with the principle of EQUAL OPPORTUNITY that was supposedly being upheld. Affirmative action was challenged, largely unsuccessfully, in the courts by whites who claimed that their rights had been violated by the preferential treatment given minorities (see UNIVERSITY OF CALIFORNIA V. BAKKE; UNITED STEELWORKERS OF AMERICA V. WEBER).

THE EXPERIENCE OF OTHER COUNTRIES
Racial problems are not, of course, confined to the United States. In Great Britain, for instance, a growing population of blacks and Asians, most emigrating from former colonies, experiences considerable de facto segregation. Racial disturbances have become commonplace, although on a smaller scale than those of the United States in the 1960s. Demands for an end to immigration have been voiced, and race has become one of the most volatile political issues in Great Britain.

Among Western countries with large proportions of blacks in their populations, only Cuba had come close to full integration. Since the revolution of 1959, enormous improvements have been made in race relations. Even in Cuba, however, complete integration and racial equality are far from accomplished facts.

The extreme segregation and resistance to change that characterizes the Republic of South Africa is a vivid example of one response to racial difference (see APARTHEID). Cuba's attempts to accomplish thorough racial integration are at the opposite end of the continuum of possibilities. On such a continuum, the United States has moved decisively away from the South African possibility, but still remains far behind the example of Cuba. At the very beginning of the present century, Du Bois wrote that "the problem of the Twentieth Century is the problem of the color line." Much must still be done so that the same cannot be said of the 21st century.   JAN DIZARD

Bibliography: Allen, Robert L., *Reluctant Reformers: Racism and Social Reform Movements in the United States* (1974); Bracy, John H., et al., *Black Nationalism in America* (1970); Edwards, T. B., ed., *School Desegregation in the North* (1968); Fancher, Betsy, *Voices from the South* (1970); Green, R. L., *Racial Crisis in American Education* (1969); Harris, Norene, et al., *The Integration of American Schools* (1975); Kluger, Richard, *Simple Justice* (1975); Konvitz, M. R., *A Century of Civil Rights* (1961; repr. 1967); Levitan, Sar, et al., *Still a Dream* (1975); Louis, Debbie, *And We Are Not Saved* (1970); Mitchell, J. P., *Race Riots in Black and White* (1970); Singh, Tarlok, *Towards an Integrated Society* (1969); Woodward, C. Vann, *The Strange Career of Jim Crow*, 3d ed. (1974).

intelligence

Intelligence refers to the all-around effectiveness of an individual's mental processes, particularly his or her comprehension; learning and recall; and thinking and reasoning capacities.

Because no one can observe or measure the mind as such, one can only infer a person's intelligence from his or her behavior in various situations. No consensus exists among psychologists on the definition of intelligence, or on the number of different factors of intelligence that can be tested.

Initially, intelligence was conceived of as innate brain power—that which distinguishes the more highly evolved animals from simpler organisms, and geniuses from average persons. Scientists now realize, however, that the development of intelligence, although partially determined by heredity, also depends on the stimulating or suppressing character of the environment in which an individual is reared.

Originally, intelligence was also conceived of as a unitary power or faculty of the mind. Experimental studies have shown, however, that intelligence includes numerous, partially distinguishable factors, such as verbal, spatial, memorizing, and reasoning abilities. Thus it is preferable to think of intelligence as a collection of a large number of highly varied, although overlapping, skills, rather than as a single faculty.

Jean PIAGET takes a different point of view altogether, emphasizing the development of children's mental skills through a series of stages of increasing complexity and rationality. Piaget explores the limitations and growth of young children's thinking, rather than merely measuring intelligence.

The earliest tests of intelligence were the Binet-Simon (1908) and the Stanford-Binet scales (see STANFORD-BINET TEST). These consist of short tasks that provide samples of intelligent thinking. They are administered orally and individually, and a child's score consists of the mental age level of the tasks he can accomplish. The ratio of mental to chronological age gives his intelligence quotient, or IQ. The Wechsler scales are also widely used for testing adults and children.

Group tests, consisting of printed problems that can be given to a group of people simultaneously, came into use in the U.S. Army in 1917; many similar tests have since been devised for educational and occupational purposes. These, too, usually yield IQs, where the average person, regardless of age, obtains a score of 100; the mentally defective may range down to IQ 40 or below, and the extremely intelligent up to 160 or above.

It is no longer claimed that the IQ remains constant over long periods of time. Tests of infant development are available; not until about age 5, however, do IQs begin to distinguish between those who are likely to show high, or low, intelligence as adults. From about age 12 measured intelligence is reasonably consistent with subsequent adult intelligence, although wide fluctuations with growth are still possible. Caution is necessary before using an IQ score to attempt to predict high or low achievement in school or daily life. School achievement depends at least as much on interest, home support, and the quality of instruction as it does on intelligence. Occupational success is even more a matter of personality, opportunity, and specialized talents. Nevertheless, the average IQs of persons in professional and managerial employment tend to be greater than the average for persons in unskilled jobs that make less demand on intellectual capacity.

Intelligence tests are currently under heavy fire regarding the extent to which they measure genetic or inherited ability as opposed to reflecting the type of upbringing, social background, and education of a person. The tests were originally devised with a view to measuring potential ability, free from the influence of wealth or privilege. At present, however, some critics argue that intelligence tests have become instruments for discriminating against lower-social-class or minority-group children. Careful research seems to support both points of view.

The reasonably close IQs of identical twins reared in different homes is taken to demonstrate genetic determinism. On the other hand, striking evidence indicates that children reared in highly deprived environments gain considerably when given more stimulating environments. The most effective type of stimulation seems to be provided by the mothers of such children through playing, talking, and interacting with their babies. Improvements in maternal and infant health and nutrition also play some part. This does not mean, however, that there is any easy recipe for training children to be more intelligent. Providing additional schooling, for example, may have no lasting effect; and coaching on intelligence tests may raise children's test scores without affecting their overall intellectual capabilities.

Intelligence tests, particularly of the group variety, do sometimes give misleading results that are often liable to be misinterpreted. These tests still have some predictive and diagnostic value, however, when administered and interpreted by trained experts who are aware of both hereditary and environmental influences.

PHILIP E. VERNON

Bibliography: Cronbach, Lee J., *Essentials of Psychological Testing*, 3d ed. (1970); Dobzhansky, Theodosius, *Genetic Diversity and Human Equality* (1973); Fincher, Jack, *Human Intelligence* (1976); Hunt, Joseph McVicker, *Intelligence and Experience* (1961); Jensen, Arthur, *Bias in Mental Testing* (1979); Kamin, Leon J., *The Science and Politics of I.Q.* (1974); Loehlin, John C., et al., *Race Differences in Intelligence* (1975); Piaget, Jean, *The Origins of Intelligence in Children*, trans. by Margaret Cook (1963); Resnick, Lauren B., ed., *The Nature of Intelligence* (1976); Vernon, Philip E., *Intelligence: Heredity and Environment* (1979).

intelligence, artificial: see ARTIFICIAL INTELLIGENCE.

intelligence gathering

Intelligence gathering is the overt and covert collection by a government of information about the plans or activities of other governments. Clandestine intelligence gathering, sometimes called espionage, has been used since earliest times, but now forms only a small portion of overall intelligence activities. Originally it consisted of sending a person—called a spy—to another country to collect information. Some intelligence was easily obtainable in marketplaces or coffee shops, but the more important information could usually be obtained only by surreptitious means.

The history of intelligence gathering is long and universal. In ancient times it was used in, among other places, Egypt, Syria-Palestine, Greece, and China. In England spying became so well organized under Elizabeth I's secretary of state Sir Francis WALSINGHAM that he was able to detect Spain's preparations for an attack on England by the Armada (1588). In Napoleonic France, minister of police Joseph FOUCHÉ developed what is regarded as the first modern system of political espionage. Two of the most famous espionage agents in history were the American national hero Nathan HALE, a spy during the Revolutionary War, and MATA HARI, a spy for Germany during World War I.

In modern times, especially since the technological developments of the second half of the 20th century, the work of the human agent has been greatly supplemented by the use of artificial devices, including spy satellites, high-powered cameras, and complex electronic equipment.

Modern Intelligence Gathering. The most important (and least reliable) form of intelligence gathering is political: the collection of information on what other countries are about to do. The knowledge of national intentions is usually known only by the highest officials and is therefore the most difficult to obtain. In some instances national intentions cannot be determined until a time of crisis; lacking such information, intelligence-gathering forces fall back on other indications such as those which might be gained from an intimate knowledge of the character of a leader.

The collection of military intelligence on the armed forces of the world is now accomplished more by technical means than by human agents. Space satellites are able to photograph in great detail everything on the surface of the land and sea over which they pass; communications satellites add further information by intercepting local radio signals, and ground sensors—or acoustic listening instruments—provide knowledge of the movements of troops and supplies. Space satellites obtain such reliable information that they have been accepted as one means of verifying that the Strategic Arms Limitation Treaties (SALT) are being observed by the United States and the USSR.

The modern work of intelligence gathering involves considerable research and analysis. Professional analysts evaluate the incoming flow of information—whether from newspaper, human agent, communications intercepts, or other technical means of collection—in terms of what is already known. The U.S. CENTRAL INTELLIGENCE AGENCY, for example, has made elaborate studies of the Soviet economy in order to determine how rapidly it is developing and how much of its resources are devoted to military purposes. The CIA also studies economic and political trends in other countries of strategic importance to the United States in an effort to provide national leaders with a basis for making policy decisions.

Covert Functions. The craft of intelligence can involve much more than the passive collection and processing of information. Counterintelligence, carried on by most intelligence agencies, is the effort to prevent or overcome infiltration by agents of other countries, particularly hostile ones, or to deceive foreign intelligence regarding the intentions of one's own government. During World War II, British counterintelligence contributed greatly to Allied success by misleading the Germans about Allied plans. After the war, U.S. counterintelligence uncovered espionage rings that were supplying information to the Soviet Union on atomic bomb research. The British scientist Klaus Fuchs was arrested (1949) and imprisoned for these activities; the Americans Julius and Ethel ROSENBERG were executed (1953) after conviction on related charges. Special sections of intelligence agencies sometimes get involved in activities that have little to do with intelligence, such as intervening in the affairs of other countries, which, for example, the CIA has done in Latin America and elsewhere. Such activities may include covert political or military warfare—influencing public opinion through the press, bribing political leaders, or even helping to overthrow governments.

Intelligence Organizations. The United States has a number of intelligence-gathering agencies. Chief among them is the Central Intelligence Agency, which was established in 1947. Other agencies include the NATIONAL SECURITY AGENCY—the largest and most secret agency—which is concerned mainly with communications, or "code-breaking"; the DEFENSE INTELLIGENCE AGENCY in the Pentagon; the Department of State's Bureau of Intelligence and Research; and the FEDERAL BUREAU OF INVESTIGATION, which deals mainly with domestic security matters.

Great Britain also has a number of intelligence agencies, the best known being the Secret Intelligence Service (MI-6), which deals with foreign intelligence and covert operations, and the Security Service (MI-5), which is concerned mainly with counterintelligence and undercover internal security. Other British services include the Defense Intelligence Staff and various foreign-office intelligence groups.

The Soviet Union's intelligence activities—the most extensive in the world—are centered in the KGB, or Committee on State Security, which combines foreign intelligence, counterintelligence, and internal security functions.

The intelligence services of Israel have acquired an impressive reputation in the Middle East and elsewhere. They include the Central Institute for Intelligence and Security, which resembles the CIA in its functions, and the counterintelligence agency Shin Bet.

The history of modern intelligence agencies offers many examples of their ingenuity. During World War II, British intelligence was able to gain advance information about German plans by cracking the German "Enigma" code through the use of a secret device called "Ultra" (see CRYPTOLOGY). The high-flying U-2 aircraft (see U-2) of the 1950s supplied the United States with accurate photographs of Soviet industrial and military strength. The same aircraft supplied information about the presence of Soviet missiles on Cuba, which led to the CUBAN MISSILE CRISIS of 1962. The PUEBLO INCIDENT of 1968, which resulted when the North Korean government captured a U.S. military vessel and imprisoned its crew, revealed the sophistication of U.S. electronic espionage. Soviet intelligence forces in 1967 were able to steal a NATO air-to-air missile, a brilliant coup. Intelligence agencies have also had their conspicuous failures. The CIA, for example, was heavily implicated in the 1961 BAY OF PIGS INVASION fiasco and in the late 1970s was criticized for failing to provide adequate intelligence on events in Iran. Since World War II, British intelligence has been embarrassed several times by the discovery of Soviet spies within the British intelligence apparatus; the most celebrated of these were Guy Burgess and Donald Maclean, who defected to the Soviet Union in 1951, and Harold (Kim) Philby, who followed in 1963. Defectors to the West from the Soviet Union and other Communist countries, on the other hand, have also included high-placed intelligence officials possessing invaluable information.

Spies are still employed by governments to obtain information that is not accessible in any other way. They may be traditional, specially trained agents; an increasing number of them, however, are diplomats and commercial officials. In February 1978, Canada expelled 11 Soviet diplomats and officials on the grounds that they had tried to penetrate the security apparatus of the ROYAL CANADIAN MOUNTED POLICE. In May 1978 the Federal Bureau of Investigation arrested two United Nations employees from the USSR on charges of stealing secrets about U.S. submarine defenses. In May 1978 an employee of the United States Information Service was convicted of passing documents to an agent of Vietnam.

LYMAN B. KIRKPATRICK

Bibliography: Cline, Ray S., *Secrets, Spies and Scholars* (1976); Dulles, Allen, *The Craft of Intelligence* (1963; repr. 1977); Kahn, David, *The Codebreakers* (1967); Jones, R. V., *The Wizard War* (1978); Kirkpatrick, Lyman, *The U.S. Intelligence Community* (1973); Marchetti, Victor, and Marks, John D., *The CIA and the Cult of Intelligence* (1974); Ransom, Harry Howe, *The Intelligence Establishment* (1970); Rositzke, Harry, *The CIA's Secret Operations* (1977).

intelligence quotient: see PSYCHOMETRICS.

Intelsat   [in'-tel-sat]

A giant 5-m-high (17-ft) Intelsat 4 communications satellite dwarfs the technicians working on the device during the final stages of its assembly and testing. To prevent contamination of sensitive electronic components by dust and dirt, all work was done in an air-conditioned room and all workers were required to wear dust-free clothes, smocks, and shoes.

INTELSAT SERIES

Satellite	Launch Date	Period (min)	Apogee km (mi)	Perigee km (mi)
Intelsat 1	Apr. 6, 1965	1436	36,373 (22,733)	34,797 (21,748)
Intelsat 2A	Oct. 26, 1966	730	36,822 (23,014)	3,341 (2,088)
Intelsat 2B	Jan. 11, 1967	1436	35,611 (22,257)	35,590 (22,244)
Intelsat 2C	Mar. 22, 1967	1436	35,606 (22,254)	35,594 (22,246)
Intelsat 2D	Sept. 27, 1967	1439	35,592 (22,245)	35,552 (22,220)
Intelsat 3 (F1)	Failure Sept. 18, 1968			
Intelsat 3 (F2)	Dec. 18, 1968	1436	35,611 (22,257)	35,590 (22,244)
Intelsat 3 (F3)	Feb. 5, 1969	1436	35,581 (22,238)	35,581 (22,238)
Intelsat 3 (F4)	May 21, 1969	1436	35,581 (22,238)	35,581 (22,238)
Intelsat 3 (F5)	Failure July 16, 1969			
Intelsat 3 (F6)	Jan. 15, 1970	1436	35,613 (22,258)	35,546 (22,216)
Intelsat 3 (F7)	Apr. 23, 1970	1436	35,598 (22,249)	35,571 (22,232)
Intelsat 3 (F8)	Failure July 23, 1970			
Intelsat 4 (F2)	Jan. 26, 1971	1436	36,139 (22,587)	35,594 (22,246)
Intelsat 4 (F3)	Dec. 20, 1971	1436	35,586 (22,241)	35,573 (22,233)
Intelsat 4 (F4)	Jan. 23, 1972	1436	35,797 (22,343)	35,784 (22,222)
Intelsat 4 (F5)	Jun. 13, 1972	1436	35,804 (22,234)	35,771 (22,214)
Intelsat 4 (F7)	Aug. 23, 1973	1436	35,788 (22,224)	35,779 (22,219)
Intelsat 4 (F8)	Nov. 21, 1974	1436	35,800 (22,232)	35,776 (22,217)
Intelsat 4 (F6)	Failure Feb. 20, 1975			
Intelsat 4 (F1)	May 22, 1975	1436	35,789 (22,225)	35,786 (22,223)
Intelsat 4A (F1)	Sept. 26, 1975	1436	35,819 (22,243)	35,752 (22,202)
Intelsat 4A (F2)	Jan. 29, 1976	1436	35,790 (22,225)	35,784 (22,222)
Intelsat 4A (F4)	May 26, 1977	1436	35,793 (22,227)	35,783 (22,221)
Intelsat 4a (F3)	Jan. 6, 1978			
Intelsat 4a (F6)	Mar. 31, 1978			

Intelsat (International Telecommunications Satellite) is a continuing series of commercial COMMUNICATIONS SATELLITES owned and operated by the multinational International Telecommunications Satellite consortium.

As the series developed from EARLY BIRD (Intelsat I, 1965), the spacecraft grew in size, weight, and capability. The four *Intelsat 2* satellites, made by Hughes Aircraft Company, were aluminum cylinders 142 cm (56 in) in diameter, 67 cm (26.5 in) in height, and 89 kg (196 lb) in weight. Electric power, supplied by 12,756 solar cells attached to the outer surface and nickel-cadmium batteries inside, provided 240 two-way voice channels as well as teletype, television, and facsimile communications.

The *Intelsat 3* series of eight satellites, manufactured by the TRW Corporation, were aluminum cylinders 142 cm (56 in) in diameter, 104 cm (41 in) in height, and 291 kg (642 lb) in weight. Their electric power of 130 W was supplied by 10,720 solar cells and nickel-cadmium batteries. The satellites had a design capacity of 1,200 telephone circuits or up to four television channels. The series represented a fivefold increase in communications capability over the *Intelsat 2* series.

The *Intelsat 4* series of eight satellites, made by Hughes, are aluminum cylinders 239 cm (94 in) in diameter, 282 cm (111 in) in height (without antennae), and 1,406 kg (3,100 lb) in weight. Their power (570 W) is provided from solar cells on the external surface and interior nickel-cadmium batteries. The six satellites in the Intelsat 4A series increased the telephone circuits from 6,000 to 9,000, or 12 color TV broadcasts. In all, the Intelsats 4 and 4A represent a fivefold increase in communications capability over the preceding series.

Intelsat 5, scheduled for launch in the early 1980s, will have a capacity of almost 12,000 telephone circuits or 2 TV channels.

The Intelsat series has proved the concept of satellites for communications purposes and has materially decreased the costs involved in intercontinental communications.

MITCHELL R. SHARPE

Bibliography: Edelson, Burton I., "Global Satellite Communications," *Scientific American,* February 1977; Martin, James, *Communications Satellite Systems* (1979); Pelton, Joseph N., *Global Communications Satellite Policy: INTELSAT, Politics, and Functionalism* (1974).

intendant   [in-ten'-dent]

The French intendants, originally temporary troubleshooters on specific royal missions, became the absolute monarchy's key regional administrators during the 17th and 18th centuries. In France, an intendant of justice, finance, and police presided over each *généralité* (local government district), and army intendants were civilian supervisors of the armies. In New France, on the other hand, a single intendant shared power with the governor and the bishop. Members of the judicial nobility (*noblesse de robe*) but with removable commissions, the intendants were more reliable than the hereditary officials in the PARLEMENTS and taxing bureaus they had to control.

Under Louis XIII and his minister Cardinal Richelieu, the intendants ruthlessly imposed justice and supervised tax collection. Overthrown by the rebellions known as the FRONDE (1648–53), they gradually reemerged under Louis XIV as information gatherers and then as superb local administrators. They were known under Louis XV and Louis XVI as the 30 tyrants because they seemed to control everything in the provinces, including towns, manufactures, roads, taxes, and police. The intendants were abolished by the French Revolution in 1789.

A. LLOYD MOOTE

Bibliography: Baxter, D. C., *Servants of the Sword: French Intendants of the Army, 1630-70* (1976); Gruder, Vivian R., *The Royal Provincial Intendants: A Governing Elite in 18th Century France* (1968).

Inter-American University of Puerto Rico

Established in 1912 by the United Presbyterian Church, Inter-American University of Puerto Rico (enrollment: 27,000; library: 330,000 volumes) is now a private independent institution for men and women whose main campus is in San Germán, Puerto Rico. There are branches at San Juan and at Santurce, which houses the School of Law. The university has seven regional colleges.

Inter-Parliamentary Union

The Inter-Parliamentary Union, founded in 1889, is an organization composed of members of parliaments throughout the world. Its purpose is to foster personal contacts among members of parliaments with the objective of promoting democratic institutions and international peace and cooperation. With headquarters in Geneva, Switzerland, the Union included in 1978 representatives from 72 countries, including the United States. It holds an annual Inter-Parliamentary Conference open to all members and operates the International Centre for Parliamentary Documentation, which gathers information on legislative assemblies.

interactions in physics: see FUNDAMENTAL INTERACTIONS.

Intercontinental Ballistic Missile: see BALLISTIC MISSILE.

interest

Interest is a sum of money paid for the use of another amount of money, called the principal. Banks and other financial institutions pay interest to savers for the use of money deposited in savings accounts; borrowers pay interest for the use of money loaned to them. Interest is sometimes referred to as "carrying charge," "finance charge," "time-price differential," "terms," and "credit charge." Interest is usually stated as a yearly rate or percentage of the principal involved. Thus a savings deposit may earn 6% interest a year, or the interest charge on a loan may be stated as 12% a year. Interest was regarded with disfavor from very early times. Aristotle labeled it an evil practice, a view that persisted through the Middle Ages; religious and secular laws prohibited interest, or usury as it was called. With the growth of commerce and the development of banks, usury came to be viewed merely as exorbitant interest, and governments began to set limits on interest rates.

SIMPLE AND COMPOUND INTEREST

Interest is calculated in two different ways: as simple interest and as compound interest. Simple interest means that the interest payment for the year is the principal amount multiplied by the interest rate; for example, the interest on $1,000 is $60 if the interest rate is 6%. Most borrowing, lending, and saving, however, uses compound interest. When compound interest is computed, the basic one-year period is divided into smaller periods, and the interest earned in each shorter period is added to the principal amount. Since the principal amount becomes larger throughout the year, the total amount of interest paid for the entire year is larger under compound interest than it would be if calculated by a simple interest rate.

Interest is usually compounded on a semiannual, quarterly, monthly, or daily basis, which means that earned interest is added to the principal at the end of every six months, every quarter, every month, or every day. For convenience, the interest rate is often stated as a nominal rate compounded at specified periods: 6% compounded monthly, for example. The effective rate, however, is higher than the nominal rate. The effective rate, or the rate actually paid, is illustrated in the following example using a $1,000 deposit that receives 6% interest (the nominal rate) compounded quarterly.

Principal (1st quarter)	$1,000.00	+ $15.00 interest (1st quarter)
Principal (2d quarter)	$1,015.00	+ $15.23 interest (2d quarter)
Principal (3d quarter)	$1,030.23	+ $15.45 interest (3d quarter)
Principal (4th quarter)	$1,045.68	+ $15.68 interest (4th quarter)
Principal (at the end of the year)	$1,061.36	$61.36 total interest for year = 6.136% of original ($1,000) principal.

The effective interest rate in this example is 6.136%. If the rate were 6% compounded *daily,* a principal sum of $1,000 would earn $61.83 in a year, and the effective rate would be 6.183%. The following formula may be used for calculating effective rate of interest:

$$E = \frac{P(1 + r)^n - P}{P} \times 100$$

where E = effective rate of interest; P = original principal; r = rate of interest per time period; and n = number of time periods. The effective rate, therefore, for $1,000 at 6% interest compounded quarterly is:

$$E = \frac{1000(1 + .015)^4 - 1000}{1000} \times 100 = 6.136\%$$

In some cases interest is discounted at the beginning of the loan period, meaning that it is deducted from the principal. On a discounted loan of $100 at 6%, the borrower receives only $94; thus paying $6 for the use of $94, or approximately 6.4% interest.

INTEREST AND THE ECONOMY

Individuals are very concerned with interest rates because the rates determine the amount they receive for saving or must pay for loans. The general level of interest rates is also an indicator of the health of the economy and is closely watched by financial institutions, governments, and monetary authorities. Most attention is focused upon the prime interest rate, or prime rate, which is the lowest commercial interest rate available at a given time. The prime rate is the rate that banks charge on loans to their most preferred customers. Other interest rates usually bear a fairly stable relation to the prime rate, and rise and fall as the prime rate rises and falls.

It is well known that interest rates change from time to time, sometimes from day to day. There is less agreement on exactly why and how the rates change. The demand and supply of loanable funds, the degree to which people want to hold cash rather than securities, the amount of money and money substitutes in the economic system, and the expectations of people are most often suggested as the major factors that determine the level of interest rates at any particular time. Fundamentally, interest rates depend on the ability to make a profit on borrowed money, on the willingness of lenders to defer their own use of money, and on such things as the risks involved and administrative costs in lending.

GOVERNMENT REGULATION

Because interest rates influence the level of economic activity by affecting the ease with which money may be borrowed and the incentive for saving, governments frequently regulate interest rates. In the United States, the federal government regulates interest rates indirectly through a variety of agencies. The most important of these is the FEDERAL RESERVE SYSTEM. The Federal Reserve influences interest rates by controlling the discount rate, which is the interest rate charged banks that borrow from the Federal Reserve banks; by setting reserve requirements, which fix the maximum ratio of loans to deposits for many commercial banks; and by controlling margin requirements, which stipulate the amounts that investors can borrow in order to buy or hold securities. Other federal agencies, or federally sponsored organizations active in the mortgage market, affect interest rates by buying and selling mortgages, by guaranteeing or insuring loans, and by making funds available to savings and loan associations and other lenders. Some of the more important of these institutions are the FEDERAL NATIONAL MORTGAGE ASSOCIATION (created and regulated by the government but now a privately owned corporation), the FEDERAL HOME LOAN BANK BOARD, the VETERANS ADMINISTRATION, the Federal Housing Administration, and the Government National Mortgage Association. Farm credit is affected by Federal Land Banks, Federal Intermediate Credit Banks, and Banks for Cooperatives, all of which are supervised by the FARM CREDIT ADMINISTRATION. Agencies that insure deposits in commercial banks, savings and loan associations, and credit unions also affect interest rates to an extent, by reducing the risk that depositors bear. The FEDERAL DEPOSIT INSURANCE CORPORATION, which insures savings deposits in commercial banks, is an example of such an organization.

The Board of Governors of the Federal Reserve System also administers the Truth-in-Lending Act, designed to inform borrowers about the cost of credit. The act, as embodied in Federal Reserve Regulation Z, requires that the total finance charge (which may include interest, insurance premiums, credit report fees, and other fees) and the annual percentage rate must be disclosed to the borrower before credit is extended. The act covers all credit used for personal, family, or agricultural purposes not exceeding $25,000, and all real-estate transactions by individuals or for agricultural uses. Most states have usury laws that specify the maximum interest rate that may be charged on loans or (sometimes) sales of merchandise in which payment is delayed. The usury rate varies from state to state.   WILLIAM W. CURTIS

Bibliography: Burger, Albert E., *The Money Supply Process* (1971); Cole, Robert H., *Consumer and Commercial Credit*, 5th ed. (1976); Gup, Benton E., *Financial Intermediaries* (1976); Guttentag, Jack M., and Cagan, Philip, eds., *Essays on Interest Rates* (1969).

interference

Interference is a phenomenon of LIGHT or any other type of wave in which two or more waves can combine to yield a resultant wave whose amplitude or intensity may be greater or less than the component waves. Interference has been demonstrated in all types of waves, including sound, microwaves, X rays, and water waves.

If two waves of the same type and the same frequency are combined so that the crest of one coincides with the trough of the other, they will completely cancel each other. This is destructive interference. Alternatively, the two waves could combine when their crests coincide; they would then interfere constructively and the resultant amplitude would be equal to the sum of the separate amplitudes.

White light is a mixture of frequencies, each associated with a different COLOR. When two or more beams of white light interfere, certain frequencies are removed by destructive interference and the resultant light is colored. This accounts for many of the striking natural color displays, such as the colors of oil slicks and the iridescence of mother-of-pearl.

The fate of the "cancelled" light should be noted. The term *destructive interference* is misleading, as no interference phenomenon results in the actual loss of light. A redistribution occurs, and the light missing from the regions of destructive interference is found in the regions of constructive interference. In cases where interference prevents the reflection of light, as will be discussed later, the light is either transmitted or absorbed by the medium. Thus, the conservation of energy principle holds.

Interference is such a characteristic property of waves (as opposed to a stream of particles) that any beam that exhibits interference is considered to be a wave phenomenon or to have a wavelike nature. When Clinton Davisson and Lester Germer showed in the 1920s that two ELECTRON beams could

Interference occurs when two or more wave disturbances travel in the same region of space. Two light waves (1, 2) of equal amplitude and wavelength with their peaks and troughs in phase, or in step, will combine to give a reinforced resultant wave (3) with double their amplitude (A). Two similar but slightly out-of-phase light waves (4, 5) will partially cancel each other and yield a resultant wave (6) of lower amplitude and brightness (B) than either original wave. Waves (7, 8) of opposite phase cancel each other, resulting in darkness (C).

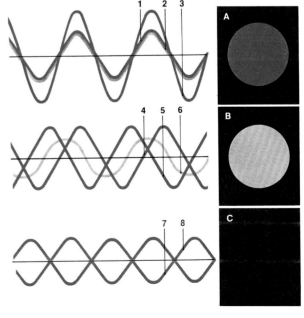

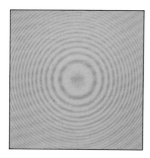

(Left) Newton's rings refer to concentric bright and dark rings produced by the interference of light rays reflected between a convex lens and a plane surface. (Below) To observe these rings (7), light passed through a lens (1) is reflected by a clear glass plate, or beam splitter (3), onto a convex lens (5) and glass plate (6). After multiple reflections between the lens and plate, the light rays (4) are returned and observed through a telescope eyepiece (2).

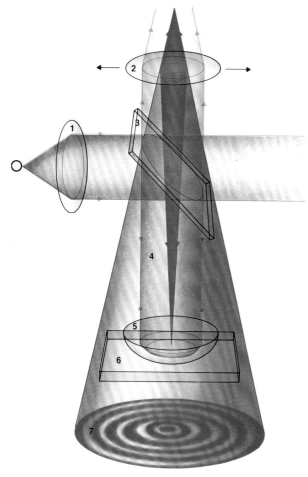

(Below) Newton's rings result (left) when an entering light ray is partially reflected at the bottom of the lens and partially reflected from the glass plate. These two reflected waves interfere when they meet. The reflected closes (right) annul each other at point X, forming a dark ring, but are reinforced at Y to yield a bright ring.

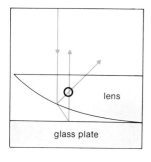

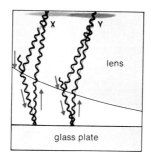

be made to interfere, this was not considered a contradiction of the principle; rather, it was taken as evidence of the wave-like behavior of atomic particles.

Phase Difference. When two waves interfere, the resultant depends on the difference in *phase* between the two waves. Waves originating from the same source may travel different distances before they are recombined; the number of wavelengths in the path difference determines the phase difference. For example, if the path taken by one wave differs in length from the other by exactly 0, 1, 2, 3, . . . wavelengths or any whole number of wavelengths, the waves will recombine *in phase*; that is, their peaks will coincide and they will constructively interfere. The phase difference is zero. If the difference in path lengths is ½, 1½, 2½, . . . wavelengths, the waves will be completely *out of phase* and will cancel each other. In this case the phase difference is half a wavelength. Intermediate values for phase differences will, of course, give resultants between these limits.

Phase is also indicated in analogy with a circle, with one full cycle of a wave being equivalent to 360° (or 2π radians). Waves that are completely out of phase, differing by half a wavelength, thus have a phase difference of 180° (π radians).

It is clear that a given path difference will result in a phase difference that depends on the wavelength of light. Thus, if an interference pattern is created using red light and the experiment is then repeated with blue light, the light and dark bands will have different locations and thicknesses.

Newton's Rings. Although interference effects may be commonly observed in nature, it was not until the 17th century that they were studied under controlled conditions. Robert HOOKE examined the colors in thin, transparent films of mica, in soap bubbles, and in layers of air between two sheets of glass. Hooke is attributed with the discovery of Newton's rings, the colored circles that form in the air layer between a convex lens and a flat sheet of glass on which the lens rests.

Isaac NEWTON's experiments on this effect became the foundation of Book Two of his *Opticks*. He was not able to correctly explain the cause of the rings. It is curious that these rings, which are one of the most striking demonstrations of the interference of light waves, should be credited to Newton, who was one of the chief proponents of the corpuscular (particlelike) nature of light.

Superposition Principle. Thomas YOUNG is generally considered to be the founder of the wave theory of light. Young discovered the interference principle in 1801 and calculated the wavelengths and frequencies of the visible spectrum. In 1802 he stated the important superposition principle that applies to all waves: when two waves travel simultaneously through the same medium, each behaves independently except at the region of crossing; there the waves are superimposed, and their effect may be greater or less than the effect of either alone.

Young demonstrated his theories with the now-famous double-slit experiment. (Although Young originally used sunlight passing through pinholes, the demonstration is best repeated by replacing the pinholes with slits and using a source of monochromatic light; that is, light of a single wavelength.) Light is allowed to pass through a narrow slit and then through a pair of closely-spaced slits to form an image on a screen. The two sets of light waves emerging from the double slit will interfere with each other, and the image will consist of evenly spaced light and dark bands, or fringes. Young correctly traced the origin of the fringes to the differences in the path lengths of the two sets of waves, meaning that some would arrive in phase to create the bright fringes, and others would arrive out of phase, leaving dark bands on the screen.

Interference by Division of the Wavefront. Young's double-slit apparatus produced interference by recombining light in which the original wavefront had been divided by the two slits. Other means were soon devised to accomplish this purpose. The biprism of Augustin FRESNEL is noteworthy because it answered the objections raised by Young's experiment, that is, that the fringes were actually a result of the light being modified in some complicated way by the edges of the slit. Fresnel used (1818) a thin, double prism to refract light from a single source into two overlapping beams. Such a biprism can easily be made from a microscope slide by slightly beveling half of one of the faces. Using the results of this experiment and others, Fresnel was able to do what Young had not—to derive a detailed mathematical analysis of most known optical phenomena (see also DIFFRACTION). There could now be no doubt that light is a wave.

Fresnel was also able to separate a single wavefront into two by using two mirrors slightly inclined to each other, creating an interference pattern in the region where the beams overlap. What is known as Lloyd's mirror involves a simpler arrangement: light is sent across the face of a mirror at a grazing angle, so that the reflected beam is nearly parallel to the direct beam. Again, interference occurs in the region where the beams overlap.

Coherent Light. In each of the above cases, the interfering beams of light were derived from a single source. Interference effects cannot be obtained using two separate light sources, such as two adjacent lamps, because light from any one source is not emitted as a continuous and uniform train of waves. Emission is in the form of a series of pulses of extremely short duration (less than a millionth of a second), and the phase relationships of light from two separate sources are completely random and change rapidly.

Coherency is a necessary condition for obtaining a steady-state interference pattern. Two wave sources that emit identical frequencies and maintain a constant phase relationship are said to be coherent. For light waves, coherency is conveniently achieved by dividing the light from a single source. The random phase changes that constantly occur in one beam are duplicated in the other. Interference of radio waves or microwaves, however, can be achieved easily using separate sources. The waves are generated by oscillators that emit signals approximating an infinite train of waves at a constant frequency, thus satisfying the coherency condition.

Interference by Amplitude Division. In addition to wavefront splitting, a beam of light may be divided, for interference purposes, by partial reflection. If light is incident on a lightly-silvered mirror, part of the light is reflected, while the remainder is transmitted. Each beam has a reduced amplitude. The two beams are sent in different directions and are then recombined with mirrors to give the interference. The interferometer is an important example of a device that operates by amplitude division (see also MICHELSON-MORLEY EXPERIMENT).

Interference by Multiple Reflections. Light incident on a thin, transparent medium such as a soap film or an oil slick over water can be reflected by both the upper and lower surfaces of the medium. In fact, light can be reflected several times within the medium before emerging. The interference of the reflected beams creates some of the most spectacular color effects seen in nature.

As noted earlier, the colors are the result of the nonreflection of certain components (frequencies) of white light according to the angle the surface makes with the observer's line of sight. Newton's rings are formed by this principle, as reflections from the lens-to-air surface interfere with those from the plate-to-air surface.

Nonreflecting Coatings. A simple and important application of interference principles is the coating of optical lenses and prisms used in cameras, binoculars, and other devices to render the surfaces nonreflective. This reduces the loss of light that could be reflected from the surfaces, as well as reducing the stray light that could reach the image and cause a loss of contrast. A thin film of a transparent substance is deposited on the lens, so that the thickness of this coating is equal to one-quarter of the average wavelength of visible light. Light reflected from the film-lens surface travels through the film twice, so its path is half a wavelength longer than the light reflected from the air-film surface. The two reflected beams interfere destructively, and therefore there is no reflection. The light is not destroyed; it is added to the transmitted light.

Destructive interference can only be complete for one wavelength, which is generally chosen to be in the middle of the spectrum (yellow). Reflection of neighboring wavelengths is suppressed but not eliminated. Because the

central part of the spectrum is not reflected by the film, coated lenses exhibit a purplish tint when seen by reflected light.

MARK S. VOGEL

Bibliography: Born, Max, and Wolf, Emil, *Principles of Optics*, 5th ed. (1975); Jenkins, Francis A., *Fundamentals of Optics*, ed. by Robert A. Fry, 4th ed. (1975); Steel, William H., *Interferometry* (1967); Waldron, Richard A., *Waves and Oscillations* (1964).

See also: STANDING WAVE; WAVES AND WAVE MOTION.

interferometer   [in-tur-fuh-rahm'-uh-tur]

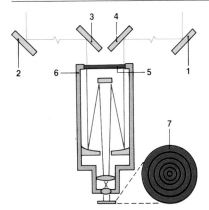

An interferometer can be used to calculate the angular diameter of a star. Light collected from a star by movable mirrors (1, 2) is directed by fixed mirrors (3, 4) through a filter (5) into a telescope (6). An interference pattern (7) results, which is related to the distance between the movable mirrors and the angular diameter of the star.

An interferometer is an instrument that allows a variety of precise measurements to be made through the interference patterns of light, sound, or radio waves. In the laboratory, the optical interferometer may be used to determine the thickness or refractive index of a material, and the acoustical interferometer can measure the velocity of sound in a gas or liquid. In optical astronomy the interferometer serves to determine the apparent diameter of stars. In radio astronomy the technique is used to obtain accurate measurements of the position of radio sources. The interferometer is also used in the study of stellar spectra.

The principle of the interferometer, first demonstrated by A. A. Michelson in 1881, is based on the phenomenon that waves can intensify or extinguish one another. If a beam of parallel rays is directed perpendicularly onto a plane, all the waves will be in phase on arrival. If the incoming rays at two different spots of the plane are converged to a single point along paths of equal length, the waves will intensify one another at that point. If the plane is not perpendicular to the beam, a phase difference is introduced through the difference in time of arrival, and an interference pattern is created at the focal point. Information can be extracted from this interference pattern.

In astronomy, for example, when the components of a double star are very close together, they cannot be separated with an ordinary telescope. Instead, two mirrors are used, spaced at a considerable distance apart and connected to a telescope. Each receives light from the star and reflects it toward the telescope, where it is finally assembled in a single focal point. Because the wavefront of the beam of one star makes a very small angle with that of the other, the two beams will not arrive simultaneously, and two interference patterns will be formed at the focus. By varying the distance between the mirrors, the intensity maxima of one image can be made to coincide with the minima of the other so that the interference pattern vanishes. This distance (D) is a function of the distance in arc (A) of the two stars and of the wavelength (λ) of the light concerned. When no interference pattern is observed, the size of angle a, in radians, becomes $\lambda/2D$. This method was first used in 1920 to separate the components of Capella, which were found to be 0.045 seconds of arc apart.

In the case of a single star, the two halves of the star's disk can be regarded as two half-disks whose centers constitute the centers of two light sources so that the star is seen artificially as double. When the interference vanishes, the diameter of the star is expressed by 1.22 λ/D. Michelson first measured the diameters of the moons of Jupiter by this method in 1890.

Modern interferometers allow angles smaller than 0.001 seconds of arc to be measured. The new technique of speckle interferometry makes use of the interference patterns from time exposures of 0.02 seconds or less.   STEVEN J. DICK

Bibliography: Brown, R. Hanbury, *The Intensity Interferometer: Its Application to Astronomy* (1974); Cook, A. H., *Interference of Electromagnetic Waves* (1971); Steel, William H., *Interferometry* (1967); Tolansky, Samuel, *An Introduction to Interferometry* (1955).

interferon   [in-tur-fir'-ahn]

An animal cell that is infected by a virus produces and releases the protein interferon into the bloodstream or intercellular fluid. Interferon induces healthy cells to manufacture another protein that inhibits the translation of viral ribonucleic acid (RNA) but permits normal translation of the host cell's RNA. As a result, interferon prevents the spread of viral infection throughout the body while allowing normal body function. Interferon thus holds great promise in fighting infections and possibly cancer. Because interferon is naturally produced only in human cells, production has yielded very little of the substance and at an extremely high cost. The first results from massive research efforts directed at synthesizing high yields of interferon were reported in January 1980. Using a technique of recombinant DNA research, researchers succeeded in producing interferon by splicing genes to modify bacteria. Large yields at relatively low cost would broaden research on interferon and permit its use with patients.

Interior, United States Department of the

The U.S. Department of the Interior, created in 1849 and described as "the custodian of the nation's natural resources," is a cabinet-level executive department. It administers conservation programs, manages fish and wildlife resources, operates national parks and historic sites, and is responsible for Indian and Alaskan Native Americans and for inhabitants of Pacific island territories under U.S. administration.

The department's 30 bureaus and offices are directed by the secretary of the interior, an undersecretary, and five assistant secretaries—one each for fish and wildlife and parks; energy and minerals; land and water resources; policy, budget, and administration; and congressional and legislative affairs. In 1978 the department had 83,696 employees and a budget of almost $4 billion.

Perhaps the best-known agency of the department is the NATIONAL PARK SERVICE, established in 1916. The Fish and Wildlife Service (1871) conducts research and conservation programs. The Bureau of Outdoor Recreation (1962) administers various federal laws concerning recreation, such as one for converting abandoned railroad property to recreational purposes. The UNITED STATES GEOLOGICAL SURVEY (1879) studies topography, geology, and mineral and water resources. The Bureau of Mines (1910) does research in mining technology and mineral resources. The Bonneville Power Administration (1937), the Alaska Power Administration (1967), the Southeastern Power Administration (1950), and the Southwestern Power Administration (1943) base their activities on the transmission and sale of power generated by federal dams and reservoirs. The Bureau of Indian Affairs (1824) is concerned with the education and advancement of Indians, Aleuts, and Eskimos (see INDIAN AFFAIRS, BUREAU OF). The Bureau of Reclamation (1902) works to reclaim arid and semiarid lands in 17 western states and Hawaii.

interior design

Interior design is the arrangement of interior space in public and domestic buildings to create a suitable and pleasant environment for living, working, and recreation using such elements as FURNITURE, decorative accessories, interior architectural components, color, and lighting. The arrangement of these elements may be determined by ARCHITECTURE, function,

historical style, geographical location and climate, human needs and customs, and personal preferences.

HISTORY OF INTERIOR DESIGN

Ancient Interior Design. Few examples of the domestic architecture, interior decoration, furnishings, and accessories of the ancient civilizations have survived. Egyptian tomb artifacts (c.3000–c.300 BC) have revealed that the luxurious homes of the Egyptian nobility contained fine wall decorations of MURAL PAINTING and painted reliefs. Furniture, usually made of wood, was often inlaid with ebony and ivory as well as decorated with gold and ENAMEL. Accessories included alabaster containers, glassware, pottery, and fine metalwork of bronze, silver, and gold (see GOLD AND SILVERWORK).

Modern knowledge of ancient Aegean and Greek domestic architecture and design has come principally through Greek vase paintings. The remains of brightly colored wall paintings were found at the enormous, labyrinthian palace at KNOSSOS (c.1700–1400 BC) in Crete. Although less luxurious, classical Greek decoration (beginning about the 6th century BC) was probably similar to that of the later Roman civilization. During the Hellenistic period (late 4th–2d century BC) the Greeks perfected the art of MOSAIC, which was used to decorate the floors and walls of fine homes.

Roman interior design of the 1st century AD has been preserved in the cities of POMPEII and HERCULANEUM. Elaborate wall painting and wall and floor mosaics were used to decorate the luxurious houses and villas of Pompeii, as seen in the Villa of the Mysteries (see MYSTERIES, VILLA OF THE).

Medieval Interior Design. Because of the unsettled conditions in the early medieval period following the fall of Rome in the 5th century, much of the interior design was not especially noteworthy, with the exception of those areas under the influence of the Byzantine and Islamic cultures. A majority of the people lived in small, rather primitive dwellings; only the nobility lived in fortified CASTLES and manor houses (see HOUSE, in Western architecture), which were designed for defense, not comfort. The most important room in the castle was the great hall, which functioned as a kitchen, dining hall,

The medieval Anglo-Saxon dwelling of a thane (a minor noble) was composed of a large communal hall housing both animals and people. The A-frame construction was based on two curved beams, or crucks, at either end of the building; rafters, supplemented by wattle-and-daub walls, gave internal support. The entire structure was covered by thatch. Inside, trestle tables and benches surrounded the central hearth. The high seat of the thane was placed at the north end of the hall. Private rooms might be located at either end of the building.

and even a bedroom. Medieval furniture was usually simple and heavy, with few articles beyond the essentials. The use of wall hangings and TAPESTRIES as a form of insulation became common during the Norman period (c.1020–c.1180).

In the later medieval and Gothic period (mid-12th to the 16th century) an increasing security led to greater luxury and comfort. The manor house became more important with the development of a larger number of rooms to serve specialized needs. Both furnishings and architectural details became more refined with more ornamentation, which reflected the Gothic style of architecture in its use of the pointed arch, stone and wood tracery, and STAINED GLASS. Wood paneling to give warmth to the room began to be used in late medieval interiors. In the 14th century the fireplace was moved from the center of the room to a wall.

Renaissance Design. Greatly influenced by classical architectural elements, furniture, and ornament, the interiors of the magnificent PALACES and VILLAS of Renaissance Italy (c.1420–1600) were designed with greater comfort, formality, grandeur, and luxury. Decoration became more elaborate with painted ceilings and the ornamentation of walls with fancy MOLDINGS, inlay, and mural painting. Furniture was monumental in size, and cabinetmakers often incorporated such architectural forms as the ACANTHUS, ARABESQUE, and the classical orders in their work. Panel paintings, sculpture, ceramics, fine metalwork, glassware, and tapestries were important elements in the decor. The FARNESE PALACE in Rome and the PALAZZO VECCHIO in Florence are outstanding examples of Italian Renaissance design.

The influence of the Renaissance style was felt throughout Europe; many great Italian artists, including Benvenuto CELLINI, LEONARDO DA VINCI, and Giacomo Barozzi da VIGNOLA, worked outside Italy. The great 16th-century *châteaux* (see CHÂTEAU) of BLOIS, CHAMBORD, CHENONCEAUX, and FONTAINEBLEAU were adaptations of Italian Renaissance design to French taste. The English Renaissance style, exemplified by the TUDOR STYLE, ELIZABETHAN STYLE, and JACOBEAN STYLE, was characterized by a combination of Gothic forms with a gradual introduction of Italian design.

Baroque Style. The baroque style emphasized elaborate ornament, large-scale interiors, opulence, and theatricality. Such Italian interiors as the DOGE'S PALACE in Venice and the PITTI PALACE in Florence reveal the marvelous carved and painted ceilings and walls typical of the baroque period (c.1600–1750). The reign (1643–1715) of Louis XIV (see STYLES OF LOUIS XIII–XVI), under the direction of such designers as Jean

The Tudor style is exemplified by the Great Hall of Hampton Court Palace, Middlesex, added (1531–36) to the original plan by Henry VIII and notable chiefly for its hammered beam ceiling. Tudor style shows the influence of Gothic and classical styles; the plan, resembling the medieval hall, and the vertical line reflect the Gothic. The work of Italian designers is discernible in the rich decoration.

BÉRAIN, André Charles BOULE, Robert de COTTE, Jules HARDOUIN-MANSART, Charles LE BRUN, and André LE NÔTRE, set a new standard of grandeur and elegance. The Château de VAUX-LE-VICOMTE and the Palace of VERSAILLES are important examples of the French baroque.

French interior design had great influence throughout Europe. Germany and Austria, in particular, developed a version of the baroque and rococo that is exemplified at SCHÖNBRUNN

The Double Cube Room in Wilton House, Salisbury, is one of the finest examples of a baroque interior. Designed by Inigo Jones, one of England's greatest architects, in the mid-17th century, the Double Cube Room is a classically proportioned setting for the Earl of Pembroke's collection of Van Dyke portraits. Jones introduced the Palladian style to England, initiating elegant and restrained interior and exterior architectural forms of classical proportion, design, and decoration.

The Oval Salon in the Palais Soubise, Paris, designed (1738-40) by Germain Boffrand for the Princesse de Soubise, reflects the smaller and more varied room size, informal air, and curvilinear line characteristic of the rococo style, which developed in France during the 18th century. Furniture, decoration, and architecture harmonized through rhythmically flowing curves and delicate coloring.

PALACE near Vienna and the WÜRZBURG RESIDENZ, designed by Johann Balthasar NEUMANN with frescoes by Giovanni Battista TIEPOLO. The baroque style was also prevalent in England in the designs of Inigo JONES—who introduced Palladian architecture (see Andrea PALLADIO) to Britain—Sir Christopher WREN, and Sir John VANBRUGH. Two important English baroque interiors are Vanbrugh's BLENHEIM PALACE and Jones's WHITEHALL PALACE, which also contains examples of Grinling GIBBONS's fine woodcarving. During the early 18th century the classical influence continued in the work of Colin CAMPBELL. The QUEEN ANNE STYLE of furniture and interior design was introduced at this time, also.

Rococo Style. The ROCOCO STYLE, developed in France during the reign (1715-74) of Louis XV, emphasized smaller-scale rooms, lighter furniture, the use of free-curved forms, and a more delicate color scheme. The influence of Oriental decoration was evident as increasing amounts of Chinese porcelain, lacquer, and other objects were imported. The rococo

Claude Nicolas Ledoux, one of the most gifted exponents of the neoclassical style in France, created (c.1780) this boudoir for Mme. de Sérilly, a favorite of Marie Antoinette. The grace, symmetry, and quiet grandeur of this room is characteristic of both Ledoux's work and neoclassical style in general, which received added impetus from the mid-18th-century discoveries at Herculaneum and Pompeii.

style was also prevalent in Germany, as is visible in the AMALIENBURG PAVILION, designed by François CUVILLIÉS, and the NYMPHENBURG PALACE, both near Munich.

Neoclassicism. The reign (1774-92) of Louis XVI was the age of French NEOCLASSICISM, characterized by a return to naturalism and simplicity, the use of straight lines and compass curves, and a revival of the classical orders of architecture, as seen at the PETIT TRIANON at Versailles. The archaeological discoveries being made in Greece and Italy, particularly Pompeii, were to play an important role in the development of style in architectural ornament and furniture design by such artisans as Georges JACOB and Jean Henri RIESENER. English decorative influence, especially the designs of Robert Adam, was also important.

Georgian Period. The 18th- and early-19th-century English GEORGIAN STYLE was extremely important in interior design. The early Georgian period was dominated by the classical influences of Richard Boyle, 3d earl of BURLINGTON, and William KENT and the baroque style of James GIBBS. The style was characterized by a growing neoclassicism and lighter proportions in architecture, ornament, and furniture. The most important figures in the later Georgian period were Robert ADAM and Sir William CHAMBERS. This was also the age of the great furniture designers Thomas CHIPPENDALE, George HEPPLEWHITE, and Thomas SHERATON, and the ceramics of Josiah WEDGWOOD. During the late Georgian period the neoclassical GREEK REVIVAL style became an important movement in both Britain and the United States. The English REGENCY STYLE of the late Georgian period was also predominantly neoclassical, although variations of many different architectural styles appeared; one example is John NASH's Oriental ROYAL PAVILION AT BRIGHTON. Furniture and accessories also revealed a great diversity in style.

Early American Style. Early American interior design (see COLONIAL STYLES IN NORTH AMERICA) in the 17th and 18th centuries was dominated more by simplicity and utility than by style. Furniture and accessories were predominantly copies of English designs adapted to American needs, tastes, and native materials, although Dutch, German, Swedish, and French influences were also evident. Fine furniture in the Chippendale tradition was produced by John GODDARD of Rhode Island and in Philadelphia. Native American FOLK ART and crafts were also important. The early 19th century reflected the continued influence of English design with the FEDERAL STYLE and the furniture designs of Duncan PHYFE and, later, John Henry BELTER.

Directoire Style. The austere DIRECTOIRE STYLE (1795-99), following the neoclassicism of Louis XVI in France, emphasized greater simplicity and the use of new decorative motifs reflecting the patriotic and republican sentiments of the post-Revolutionary period. Jacques Louis DAVID was the foremost arbiter of artistic taste at this time.

Empire Style. The early-19th-century French EMPIRE STYLE, under the artistic guidance of Pierre François Léonard FONTAINE and Charles PERCIER, combined the ornamental forms of classical antiquity with Egyptian motifs to create a majestic interior design corresponding to the reign (1804-15) of Napoleon I.

Biedermeier. The BIEDERMEIER movement was a style of painting, furniture, and interior design popular during the first half of the 19th century in Germany and Austria. It was characterized by solid, functional furniture and small-scale interiors.

Victorian Period. The eclectic, and cluttered, VICTORIAN STYLE was characterized by a wide diversity in styles of architecture, ornament, and furniture (see ECLECTICISM, art). The romantic GOTHIC REVIVAL, under the impetus of Augustus PUGIN and the PRE-RAPHAELITES, sought its inspiration in the design and forms of the Gothic period. William MORRIS's ARTS AND CRAFTS MOVEMENT of the second half of the 19th century advocated a return to high-quality craftsmanship in the decorative arts. The movement began as a reaction against the influx of mass-produced furniture and crafts after the Great Exhibition of 1851 at the CRYSTAL PALACE in London.

Art Nouveau. The ART NOUVEAU style was a movement in the decorative arts and architecture, popular about 1900 and characterized by rich, curvilinear forms and motifs taken from nature. The decorative glassware of Émile GALLÉ and Louis Com-

(Right) *The interior, exterior, furnishings, and decoration of Osterley House (1761–80), exemplified by the Eating Room, were created by Robert Adam, one of the most brilliant and influential Georgian designers of the late 18th century. Adam's work, distinguished by delicate color, understated ornamentation, and spaciousness, emulated classical styles in an original and inventive manner. Adam's use of color and meticulous attention to detail produced remarkable unity in his interior designs.*

(Below) *The designs of the Shakers, an American religious community flourishing during the late 18th and the 19th century, are noted for an austere, functional style and economy of material and space. Cupboards and drawers built into the walls eliminated the need for bulky chests and sideboards; pegs on the walls provided storage space for unneeded furniture. The spare quality of a Shaker interior is emphasized by the simple, linear forms of their furniture, designed to fulfill their function with a minimum of material.*

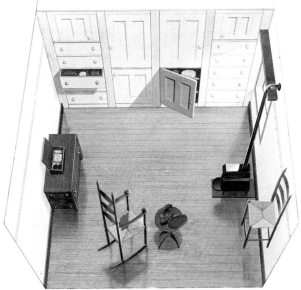

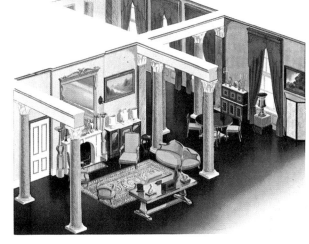

fort TIFFANY and the architecture of Hector GUIMARD, Victor HORTA, and Charles Rennie MACKINTOSH are typical.

Art Deco. ART DECO emerged about 1910 as a reaction to some of the excesses of the Art Nouveau style. Characterized by stylized geometric and natural ornamental forms, examples of the style can be found in the jewelry and fine glassware of René LALIQUE and in the architecture of the CHRYSLER BUILDING and RADIO CITY MUSIC HALL in New York City.

Modern Design. The Industrial Revolution, mass-production of furniture and accessories, the emergence in the 1920s of the INTERNATIONAL STYLE of architecture, and technological developments in architectural materials, construction, and engineering have greatly influenced modern interior design. Louis SULLIVAN's idea that "form follows function" was adopted by the German BAUHAUS under the leadership of Walter GROPIUS, who advocated a new style of design based on simplicity, geometric form, and truth to line, form, and function. The work of such European architects as Alvar AALTO, Marcel BREUER, Le CORBUSIER, and Ludwig MIES VAN DER ROHE has played an important part in establishing the principles of modern design. In such works as the ROBIE HOUSE (1909), Chicago, Frank Lloyd WRIGHT has been influential in the development of contemporary American design.

Osborne House, on the Isle of Wight, was designed (1745–46) by Thomas Cubitt for Queen Victoria as a country house. The drawing room at Osborne, adjacent to the dining room and billiard room, displays a typically Victorian confusion. The Victorian period was characterized by an eclectic assortment of architectural styles and furnishings, the latter profusely displayed in informal groupings.

The modern period has seen the breakdown of traditional room divisions and arrangement of space and the development of smaller, more efficient, and less elaborate houses. Furniture by such designers as Charles EAMES and Aalto has become simpler and more geometric in form; modular furnishings have created greater flexibility in room arrangement. Despite modern developments, however, the traditional and historical styles of design have remained popular. Interior design of the 20th century often combines traditional and modern elements to create a comfortable and pleasant environment to suit the modern life-style.

THE PROFESSION OF INTERIOR DESIGN

A professional interior designer is qualified by education and experience to identify, research, and creatively solve problems relative to the function and quality of the interiors of domestic and other buildings.

The decorator, a forerunner of the professional interior designer, was principally a cosmetician whose knowledge of design was confined primarily to color, scale, and balance and in some cases included the history of decorative periods. Their work was almost exclusively in the residential field. The contemporary professional interior designer has both a greater depth of knowledge and a broader scope of practice.

A designer's competency must include fundamental design, design analysis, and space planning and programming as well as a comprehensive understanding of fibers and finishes, new materials and production techniques, electrical technology, architecture, building codes and government regulations, product performance, and other data related to interior design. The scope of a designer's influence touches virtually every area of life, including low-cost housing, hospitals, schools, libraries, and other public buildings. In addition to designing homes, offices, restaurants, banks, hotels, recreational facilities, and stores, they also design facilities for the handicapped and the aged, churches, theaters, funeral homes, and resort areas. Far from the purely decorative practice of a few decades ago, the professional interior designer is often called on to improve specific conditions. Improving productivity and employee incentive in an office situation is a common assignment.

A knowledge of design history, architecture, and engineering has made the designer an important factor in HISTORIC PRESERVATION and restoration and in the growing practice of recycling homes and other buildings. The work of professional designers also influences life in the United States through their involvement in advertising, magazine and newspaper editorials, creating model rooms in retail stores and real estate promotions, and their work for museums, television, stage and movie sets, and in product design.

The myriad of design practices and careers produces a wide variety of work situations. The designer who works primarily in the residential field is generally an independent designer or one who works in a relatively small interior design studio. Another career alternative is offered by home furnishings and department stores, which have been replacing their decorator-salespeople with professional designers in the last 10 years. A contract designer, one involved in other than residential design, may work in his or her own firm, in an architect's office, in the design department of a large firm, or on the staff of a large corporation. Many manufacturers, including automotive firms, health products companies, and home furnishings producers, have interior designers on their staffs.

The group now called the American Society of Interior Designers (ASID), the largest organization of professional designers in the world, initiated (1971) the Foundation for Interior Design Education Research (FIDER) toward improving the quality of interior design education. FIDER's programs and dedication have been recognized by the U.S. government and by both the U.S. Office of Education and the Council of Postsecondary Accreditation. It is now the accrediting body for interior design programs in schools and universities throughout the United States. The ASID, the standard-bearer for the profession, demands a degree in a 3-, 4-, or 5-year interior design program, as well as substantial experience and the successful completion of the NCIDQ (National Council for Interior Design Qualification) examination, among other requirements for professional membership in the organization. Government legislation has been introduced in a number of states that would enforce legal registration or licensing based on stringent standards.

The growth from an undisciplined art to its current proficiency has taken place in a relatively short time. The stereotype of the flamboyant decorator of years ago still persists in many minds, and there is still an immense lack of public understanding of the skills and functions of the professional designer.   OLA M. PFEIFER

Bibliography: Friedmann, Arnold, *Interior Design* (1976); Grant, Ian, *Great Interiors* (1967); Greer, Michael, *Your Future in Interior Design* (1970); Harling, Robert, *Modern Furniture and Decoration* (1971); Pahlmann, William, *The Pahlmann Book of Interior Design*, 3d ed. (1968); Pegler, Martin, *Dictionary of Interior Design* (1966); Rogers, Meyric R.,

American Interior Design: The Traditions and Development of Domestic Design from Colonial Times to the Present (1947; repr. 1976); Savage, George, *A Concise History of Interior Decoration* (1966); Whiton, Sherrill, *Interior Design and Decoration*, 4th ed. (1974).

See also: BAROQUE ART AND ARCHITECTURE; BYZANTINE ART AND ARCHITECTURE; CHANDELIER; EGYPTIAN ART AND ARCHITECTURE; FRESCO PAINTING; GLASSWARE, DECORATIVE; GOTHIC ART AND ARCHITECTURE; GREEK ARCHITECTURE; GREEK ART; ISLAMIC ART AND ARCHITECTURE; MINOAN ART; MODERN ARCHITECTURE; POTTERY AND PORCELAIN; RENAISSANCE ART AND ARCHITECTURE; ROMAN ARCHITECTURE; ROMAN ART; ROMANESQUE ART AND ARCHITECTURE; RUGS AND CARPETS.

interior monologue: see NARRATIVE AND DRAMATIC DEVICES.

Interlaken   [in'-tur-lah-ken]

Interlaken (1970 pop., 4,735) is a resort town in Bern canton, central Switzerland. Situated between Lakes Brienz and Thun in the first range of the Bernese Alps, Interlaken is only a short distance from the JUNGFRAU peak. Tourism is the major industry. Originally the site of an Augustinian convent (founded 1130), Interlaken was virtually unknown until the 19th century, when interest in the Alps began to draw tourists to the area.

Interlingua: see LANGUAGES, ARTIFICIAL.

interlude

Interludes, from the Latin *interludium*, meaning "between the games," began in England as playlets of love and adultery that were performed by troupes of traveling actors at banquets and festivals. One of the earliest, the *Interludium de Clerico et Puella* (1290–1335), was a dialogue between a cleric and a girl. Similar playlets were common on the continent; called *entremeses* in Spain and *intermezzi* in Italy, they were performed with music between the acts of plays or operas.

From at least 1493 to the time of Elizabeth, the Players of the King's Interludes, *Lusores Regis*, performed at the English court and at festivals. In a continuation of the medieval fabliau tradition, interludes at first treated contemporary life candidly, but around 1500 they became moralities, often historical and satirical, in the works of John Redford, John Rastell, John Heywood, David Lindsay, John Skelton, and John Bale. Some of the satire contained in them was so offensive that interludes were banned by proclamation in 1533, the more political having lost their lightness and their aristocratic audience. Later, some became debating dialogues. The interludes of Nicholas Udall, considered the first comedies, were classical in structure and theatrical in style. The plays of Marlowe, Shakespeare, and Jonson were influenced by interludes, which they replaced in the Elizabethan theater.

HENRY F. SALERNO

Bibliography: Boas, Frederick, *An Introduction to Tudor Drama* (1933; repr. 1977); Craik, T. W., *The Tudor Interlude* (1958); Hopper, V. F., and Lahey, G. B., eds., *Medieval Mysteries, Moralities and Interludes* (1962); Pollard, A. W., *English Miracles, Moralities and Interludes* (1927); Reed, A. W., *Early Tudor Drama* (1926; repr. 1969); Rossiter, A. P., *English Drama from Early Times to the Elizabethans* (1950; repr. 1975); Schell, E. T., and Shucter, J. D., *English Morality Plays and Moral Interludes* (1969).

See also: MEDIEVAL DRAMA.

intermezzo   [in-tur-met'-soh]

The term *intermezzo* has two meanings: a character piece, generally for piano, such as those composed by Brahms and Schumann (the term is also occasionally applied to short movements in orchestral and chamber works); a theater piece, usually humorous, placed between the acts of a serious work. In opera the insertion of intermezzi between the acts of *opera seria* provided a relief from seriousness and gave rise to a new form, the *opera buffa*, that would exist independently of the serious works. The best known intermezzo of this type is Pergolesi's *La Serva Padrona* (1733).

ELWYN A. WIENANDT

intermolecular forces   [in-tur-muh-lek'-yoo-lur]

The three-dimensional shapes adopted by molecules, their ability to condense from gases to liquids, and their arrangement in solid crystal lattices are all controlled by weak intermolecular forces. These intermolecular interactions are termed *van der Waals forces*, in honor of Johannes van der Waals, and include hydrogen bonding, dipole-dipole attractions, and dispersion forces.

A very significant intermolecular force is the HYDROGEN BOND, which occurs between a hydrogen atom bound to an electronegative (or electron-attracting) atom and another such atom. Another intermolecular force is the dipole-dipole interaction that occurs between molecules having permanent DIPOLE moments. Dipole forces operate in solid iodine chloride, ICl, for example. Since chlorine is a more electronegative element than iodine, the bond in ICl is polar covalent (see CHEMICAL BOND) and may be written as ^+I—Cl^-. The molecules in solid ICl are so aligned that each chlorine atom of one molecule is adjacent to the iodine atom of a neighboring molecule. The attractions, shown by the dashed line $---$ ^-I—$Cl$$^+$$----$$^-I$—$Cl$$^+$$---$, are electrostatic but weaker than those which occur in ionic bonding. When a solid such as iodine chloride is heated, the I—Cl molecules rotate, the alignment disappears, and the dipolar attractions are disrupted. They still occur to some extent in the molten material but vanish altogether in gaseous ICl, in which the distance between adjacent molecules is too great for dipolar forces to operate.

Intermolecular attractive interactions also occur between nonpolar molecules. Although these are more difficult to envision, they must occur to explain why a nonpolar gas such as chlorine, Cl_2, can exist as a liquid or, at sufficiently low temperatures, as a solid. The attractive interactions here are called dispersion, or London, forces (after Fritz London) and are caused by temporary polarizations of the electron cloud in a molecule that interacts with neighboring molecules undergoing a similar polarization.

Dispersion forces are weaker than dipole-dipole interactions and can occur between molecules that have a permanent dipole moment. They are also disrupted by raising the temperature and do not occur in gases in which molecular motion is essentially random. In addition to polarizability, dispersion forces are also related to molecular size and shape. Small, compact molecules are generally less polarizable than larger molecules, and the physical properties of matter consisting of small, compact molecules (low boiling and melting points) reflect weaker intermolecular forces. Dispersion forces are the most common and significant of the van der Waals forces.

STEPHEN J. LIPARD

Bibliography: Daniels, F., and Alberty, R., *Physical Chemistry*, 4th ed. (1975); Rosenberg, R., *Principles of Physical Chemistry* (1977).

internal combustion engine

An internal-combustion ENGINE is a HEAT ENGINE that burns fuel and air inside a combustion chamber located within the engine proper. (Simply stated, a heat engine is an engine that converts heat energy to mechanical energy.) The internal-combustion engine should be distinguished from the external-combustion engine, for example, the STEAM ENGINE and the STIRLING ENGINE, which burns fuel outside the prime mover, that is, the device that actually produces mechanical motion. Both basic types produce hot, expanding gases, which may then be employed to move pistons, turn turbine rotors, or cause locomotion through the reaction principle as they escape through the nozzle.

Most people are familiar with the internal-combustion reciprocating engine, which is used to power most automobiles, boats, lawnmowers, and home generators. Based on the means of ignition, two types of internal-combustion reciprocating engines can be distinguished: spark-ignition engines and compression-ignition engines. In the former, a spark ignites a combustible mixture of air and fuel; in the latter, high compression raises the temperature of the air in the chamber and ignites the injected fuel without a spark. The diesel engine is a compression-ignition engine; such engines are discussed under DIESEL ENGINE. This article emphasizes the spark-ignition engine.

HISTORY

The invention and early development of internal-combustion engines is usually credited to three Germans. Nikolaus OTTO patented and built (1876) the first such engine; Karl BENZ built the first automobile to be powered by such an engine (1885); and Gottlieb DAIMLER designed the first high-speed internal-combustion engine (1885) and carburetor. Rudolf DIESEL invented a successful compression-ignition engine (the diesel engine) in 1892.

OPERATION

The operation of the internal-combustion reciprocating engine employs either a four-stroke cycle or a two-stroke cycle. (A stroke is one continuous movement of the piston within the cylinder.) In the four-stroke cycle, also known as the Otto cycle, the downward movement of a piston located within a cylinder creates a partial vacuum. Two VALVES located inside the combustion chamber are controlled by the motion of a camshaft connected to the crankshaft. The four strokes are called, in order of sequence, intake, compression, power, and exhaust. On the first stroke, the intake valve is opened while the exhaust valve is closed; atmospheric pressure forces a mixture of gas and air to fill the chamber. On the second stroke, the intake and exhaust valves are both closed as the piston starts upward. The mixture is compressed from normal atmospheric pressure (1 kg/cm^2, or 14.7 lb/in^2) to between 4.9 and 8.8 kg/cm^2 (70 and 125 lb/in^2). During the third stroke, the compressed mixture is ignited—either by compression ignition or by spark ignition. The heat produced by the combustion causes the gases to expand within the cylinder, thus forcing the piston downward. The piston's connecting rod transmits the power from the piston to the crankshaft. This assembly changes reciprocating—in other words, up-and-down or back-and-forth motion—to rotary motion. On the fourth stroke, the exhaust valve is opened so that the burned gases can escape as the piston moves upward; this prepares the cylinder for another cycle.

Internal-combustion spark-ignition engines having a two-stroke cycle combine intake and compression in a single first stroke and power and exhaust in a second stroke.

ENGINE SUBSYSTEMS

The internal-combustion reciprocating engine contains several subsystems: ignition, fuel, cooling, and exhaust systems. **Ignition System.** The IGNITION SYSTEM of a spark-ignition engine consists of the sparking device (the spark plug); the connecting wire from the plug to the distributor; and the distributor, which distributes the spark to the proper cylinder at the proper time. The distributor receives a high-energy spark from a coil, or magneto, that converts low-voltage energy to high-voltage energy.

Some new ignition systems employ transistorized circuitry, which is generally more efficient and less troublesome than the mechanical breaker-point system used in the past. Most ignition systems require an external electrical energy source in the form of a BATTERY or a magneto.

Fuel System. Spark-ignition engines require a means for mixing fuel and air. Generally, a device called the CARBURETOR is used for this purpose. The carburetor atomizes the fuel and air mixture. The mixture is then vaporized in the intake manifold before being drawn into the combustion chamber.

The ratio of fuel to air varies considerably with the engine operation. A carburetor is designed to automatically supply the proper ratio, even though the volume of air through the carburetor may increase by a factor of more than 100 as the engine accelerates from idle to high speed.

Starting System. Internal-combustion engines require some type of starting system. Small engines are generally started by pulling a starting rope or kicking a lever. Larger engines may use compressed air or an electric starting system. The latter includes a starter—a high-torque electric motor—to turn the crankshaft until the engine starts. Starting motors are extremely powerful for their size and are designed to utilize

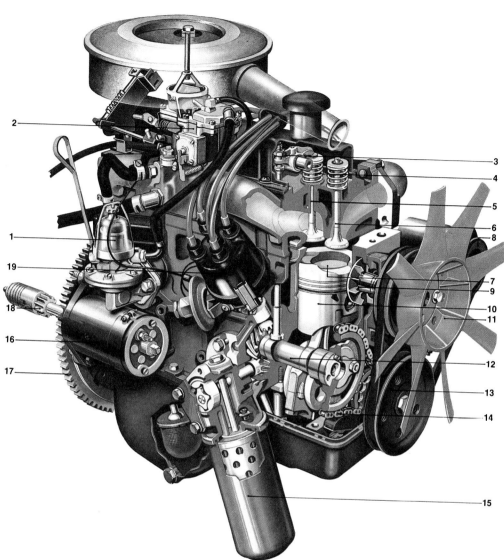

A four-cylinder overhead valve engine is used in most European and Japanese cars, as well as in some small American cars. Fuel drawn from a gasoline tank by a fuel pump (1) is fed to a carburetor (2), where it is vaporized, mixed with air, and passed through an inlet valve (5) into a cylinder (10). The valve is kept closed by a spring (4) until opened by the action of a pushrod and rocker arm (3) controlled by a camshaft (12). The camshaft also turns a distributor (19), which feeds electricity from a coil to spark plugs that ignite the fuel in each cylinder in sequence. The burning gases expand and force each piston (7) downward, rotating a crankshaft. A pulley (13) on the crankshaft drives a generator (8), cooling fan (11), and water pump (9) by means of a belt. The crankshaft also spins the camshaft via a timing chain (14) and drives an oil pump that circulates oil through a filter (15) and around moving engine parts. Exhaust gases are forced out of the exhaust valve (6) when the piston moves upward. The engine is started by an electric motor (16) that turns the flywheel (17) after engaging the gear (18).

high currents (200 to 300 amperes). The large starting currents can cause a battery to drain rapidly; for this reason a heavy-duty battery is usually used. Interrupting this connection is an electrical switch called a SOLENOID, which is activated by the low-voltage starting switch. In this way the ignition switch can be located away from the starter and yet still turn the starter on and off.

Cooling System. The COOLING SYSTEM is important because internal-combustion engines operate at high temperatures of combustion—spark-ignition engines at approximately 2,760° C (5,000° F) and diesel engines at even higher temperatures. If it were not for the cooling system, these high temperatures would damage and melt many parts of the engine. The cooling system essentially dissipates the heat of combustion in metal, water, or air and automatically regulates the temperature so that the engine can operate at its optimum temperature—about 93° C (200° F).

Air-cooled engines, popularly used to power small lawnmowers, chainsaws, power generators, and motorcycles, as well as small cars and airplanes, often require no moving parts, and therefore little or no maintenance, for the cooling system. The head, or uppermost part, of the cylinder and the cylinder block have fins cast into them; these fins increase the surface exposed to the surrounding air, allowing more heat to be radiated. Usually a cover or shroud channels the air flow over the fins. A fan is sometimes included if the engine is located away from a stream of fast-moving air.

Water-cooled engines have water jackets built into the engine block. These jackets surround the cylinders. Usually a centrifugal water pump is used to circulate the water continuously through the water jackets. In this way the high heat of combustion is drawn off the cylinder wall into the circulating water. The water must then be cooled in a radiator that transfers the heat energy of the water to the radiator's cooler surrounding fluid. The surrounding fluid can be air or water, depending on the application of the engine.

Exhaust System. Internal-combustion engines include an EXHAUST SYSTEM, which allows the hot exhaust gases to escape efficiently from the engine. In some small engines, if the noise is not too loud, the exhaust gases can exit directly into the atmosphere. Larger engines are noisier and require some type of muffler or sound deadener, usually a canister with an inner shell that breaks up the sound waves, dissipating their energy within the muffler before the exhaust gases are permitted to escape.

The power capacity of an engine depends on a number of characteristics, including the volume of the combustion chamber. The volume can be increased by increasing the size

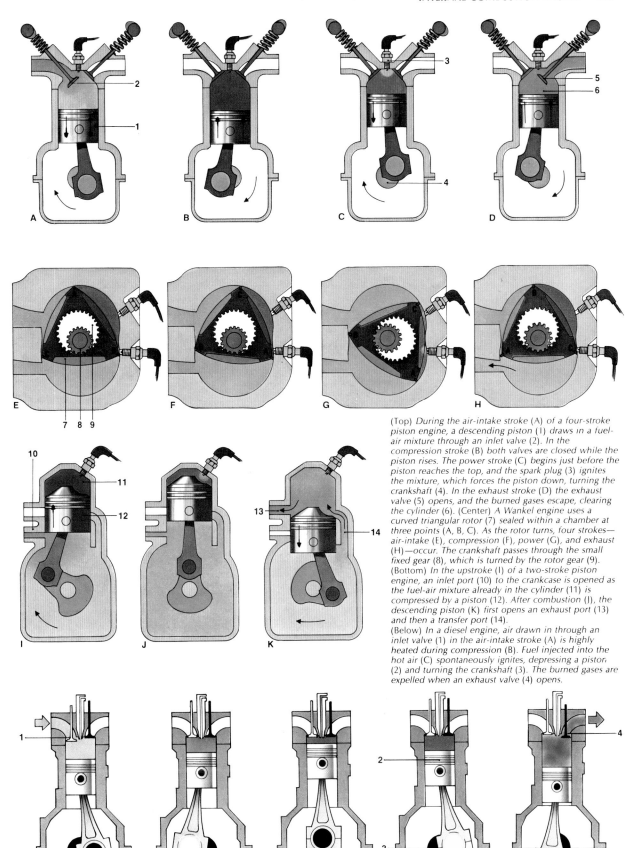

(Top) *During the air-intake stroke (A) of a four-stroke piston engine, a descending piston (1) draws in a fuel-air mixture through an inlet valve (2). In the compression stroke (B) both valves are closed while the piston rises. The power stroke (C) begins just before the piston reaches the top, and the spark plug (3) ignites the mixture, which forces the piston down, turning the crankshaft (4). In the exhaust stroke (D) the exhaust valve (5) opens, and the burned gases escape, clearing the cylinder (6). (Center) A Wankel engine uses a curved triangular rotor (7) sealed within a chamber at three points (A, B, C). As the rotor turns, four strokes—air-intake (E), compression (F), power (G), and exhaust (H)—occur. The crankshaft passes through the small fixed gear (8), which is turned by the rotor gear (9). (Bottom) In the upstroke (I) of a two-stroke piston engine, an inlet port (10) to the crankcase is opened as the fuel-air mixture already in the cylinder (11) is compressed by a piston (12). After combustion (J), the descending piston (K) first opens an exhaust port (13) and then a transfer port (14).*

(Below) In a diesel engine, air drawn in through an inlet valve (1) in the air-intake stroke (A) is highly heated during compression (B). Fuel injected into the hot air (C) spontaneously ignites, depressing a piston (2) and turning the crankshaft (3). The burned gases are expelled when an exhaust valve (4) opens.

of the piston and cylinder and by increasing the number of cylinders. The cylinder configuration, or arrangement of cylinders, can be straight, or in-line (one cylinder located behind the other); radial (cylinders located around a circle); in a V (cylinders located in a V configuration); or opposed (cylinders located opposite each other). Another type of internal-combustion engine, the WANKEL ENGINE, has no cylinders; it has a rotor that moves through a combustion chamber.

Transmission. An internal-combustion engine must also have some kind of TRANSMISSION system to control and direct the mechanical energy where it is needed; for example, in an automobile the energy must be directed to the driving wheels. Since these engines are not able to start under a load, a transmission system must be used to "disengage" the engine from the load during starting and then to apply the load when the engine reaches its operating speed.   JOSEPH W. DUFFY

Bibliography: Cummins, C. Lyle, *Internal Fire: The Internal Combustion Engine, 1673–1900* (1976); Lichty, Lester, *Combustion Engine Processes*, 7th ed. (1967); Obert, Edward F., *Internal Combustion Engines*, 3d ed. (1973); Rogowski, Augustus R., *Elements of Internal Combustion Engines* (1953); Taylor, Charles F., *The Internal-Combustion Engine in Theory and Practice*, 2 vols., 2d ed. (1977); Urquhart, David I., *The Internal Combustion Engine and How It Works* (1973).

internal medicine: see MEDICINE.

Internal Revenue Service

The U.S. government's tax collecting agency, the Internal Revenue Service, was created in 1862. However, it did not assume its present shape until the federal taxing power was sanctioned by the 16TH AMENDMENT (1913) and revenues increased enormously after World War II. The IRS, a division of the Department of the Treasury, administers all of the internal revenue laws except those relating to alcohol, tobacco, firearms, and explosives; its most important assignments are to collect personal and corporate INCOME TAXES, social security taxes, and excise, estate, and gift taxes.

The IRS seeks to obtain voluntary compliance with the tax laws as far as possible. To this end it stresses communication with taxpayers by providing assistance and information for those who need it, as well as enforcing the laws and regulations.

Most of the approximately 85,000 employees of the IRS work in field offices throughout the country. There are 7 regions, each headed by a regional commissioner, and 58 districts administered by district directors. Tax returns are processed in separate tax service centers. The national office in Washington, D.C., develops policies and supervises the field organization. The single commissioner of internal revenue is assisted by a deputy commissioner and eight assistant commissioners, each of whom is assigned certain functions such as collecting tax money, enforcing compliance with the laws, and issuing rulings and regulations. The chief counsel of the IRS is in charge of all legal actions.

When there is a dispute between a taxpayer and the agency, the taxpayer may take the case to the U.S. TAX COURT, then to a court of claims, and then to a U.S. district court. If not satisfied, a taxpayer may take an appeal to a U.S. court of appeals and, ultimately, to the Supreme Court.

Bibliography: Crockett, Joseph P., *The Federal Tax System of the United States* (1955); Schnepper, Jeff A., *Inside IRS* (1978).

International, Socialist

Socialist Internationals were a series of organizations formed by socialists and communists in the 19th and 20th centuries in order to coordinate attempts to achieve SOCIALISM or COMMUNISM.

The International Workingmen's Association, known as the First International, was founded Sept. 28, 1864, in London, and Karl MARX became its leader. Annual congresses of the International were attended by workers' representatives from 13 European countries and the United States. During the COMMUNE OF PARIS of 1871, the specter of the International aroused unwarranted anxiety in European governing circles.

Disputes between Marx and the anarchist Mikhail BAKUNIN over the structure of the International ended at the Hague Congress of 1872 with the expulsion of Bakunin and transfer of the General Council to New York. The First International was dissolved at the Philadelphia Conference in 1876.

The Second International, established July 14, 1889, at Paris, was a loose federation of trade unions and socialist parties. The Socialist Bureau at Brussels under Emile VANDERVELDE coordinated its activities. Among the leaders were August BEBEL, Friedrich ENGELS, and Karl KAUTSKY of Germany, Jean JAURÈS of France, and Georgy PLEKHANOV of Russia. The Second International passed resolutions opposing support for capitalist governments and attacking colonialism and war. But the member parties supported their national governments at the outbreak of war in 1914, and the Second International dissolved. After World War I a Third International was formed (1919) under the leadership of Vladimir Ilich LENIN and the Soviet government in Moscow. It was known as the Communist International, or COMINTERN, and lasted until 1943. Moderate socialists reconstituted (1919) the Second International, which in 1923 became the Labor and Socialist International and in 1951 the Socialist International. In 1979, with headquarters in London, it had 39 member parties from 35 countries. A Fourth International was founded (1938) by Leon TROTSKY in opposition to the Third International. It was never very successful and broke up in 1953. The SOCIALIST WORKERS' PARTY in the United States was its only active offshoot.

FREDERIC B. M. HOLLYDAY

Bibliography: Braunthal, Julius, *History of the International*, 2 vols. (1967); Derfler, Leslie, *Socialism since Marx: A Century of the European Left* (1973); Haupt, Georges, *Socialism and the Great War: The Collapse of the Second International* (1972); Joll, James, *The Second International, 1889–1914* (1974).

International Association of Machinists and Aerospace Workers

The International Association of Machinists and Aerospace Workers is a labor union within the American Federation of Labor–Congress of Industrial Organizations, consisting of air-transport and automotive mechanics and aerospace and railroad machinists. Founded in 1888, it was originally named the Order of United Machinists and Mechanical Engineers. The next year the union was renamed the National Association of Machinists. With new members joining the name was again changed to the International Association of Machinists (IAM; in 1964 "Aerospace Workers" was added). The Machinists affiliated with the AFL in 1895. Union morale and membership was hurt when the Committee of Industrial Organizations left the AFL in 1938 to form the Congress of Industrial Organizations. The IAM increased its organizing activities, bringing it into jurisdictional conflict with other unions. This conflict led to its withdrawal from the AFL, until 1951. In 1979 the IAM had a membership of 927,000 in 1,832 local unions.

Bibliography: Perlman, Mark, *Machinists: A New Study in American Trade Unionism* (1961).

International Association of Universities

The International Association of Universities, founded in 1950 and located in Paris, France, is an association of 705 universities in 115 countries. It promotes cooperation among universities and provides information in such areas as the equivalency of degrees and diplomas.

International Atomic Energy Agency

An autonomous intergovernmental agency of the United Nations, the International Atomic Energy Agency (IAEA) was founded in 1957 to promote the peaceful uses of atomic energy. The IAEA, headquartered in Vienna, meets annually in general conference to establish policy and organize programs for the exchange of information. It is authorized to buy and sell fissionable materials and to provide technical assistance to member states for use in agriculture, medicine, and other nonmilitary applications. The agency also sets standards and controls to ensure the peaceful use of atomic power and to safeguard public health. The Treaty on the Non-Proliferation of Nuclear Weapons (which came into force in 1970) requires that the signatories not possessing nuclear weapons conclude an agreement with the IAEA not to divert the use of nuclear fuel from peaceful to military purposes.

The agency consists of a secretariat with a director-general and a 34-member board of governors. In 1978 the IAEA had 110 members.

Bibliography: Sanders, Benjamin, *Safeguards against Nuclear Proliferation* (1975).

International Bank for Reconstruction and Development: see WORLD BANK.

International Bureau of Weights and Measures

The International Bureau of Weights and Measures, founded in 1875, establishes measurement scales of physical quantities, verifies national and high-precision standards and measurement scales, and improves the international system of units (SI). (See METRIC SYSTEM.) It has a staff of 50 at its headquarters in Sèvres, France. Its members are governments; 44 countries participate, including the United States.

International Civil Aviation Organization

The International Civil Aviation Organization (ICAO) was established on Apr. 4, 1947, after 26 nations had ratified the Convention of International Civil Aviation, a document drawn up at the International Civil Aviation Conference in Chicago in 1944. The organization has its headquarters in Montreal, Canada, and had 141 member nations as of Jan. 1, 1978. Its aims include the study of problems of international civil aviation, the establishment of international standards and regulations, and the fostering of the development and planning of international air transport. ICAO encourages the use of safety measures, uniform regulations for operation, and simpler procedures at national borders.   JOHN G. STOESSINGER

International Communications Agency

The International Communications Agency, with 8,900 employees and a budget of $413 million in 1979, is an independent agency of the executive branch of the U.S. government. It was created in 1977 through the merger of the U.S. Information Agency (founded in 1953) and the Bureau of Educational and Cultural Affairs of the Department of State. Its purpose is to spread information about the United States abroad, to inform the U.S. government about foreign opinion regarding the United States, and to arrange cultural and educational exchanges with foreign countries. The ICA maintains libraries, reading rooms, and information centers in more than 90 countries. Its largest component, the Voice of America, broadcasts in 36 languages.

International Confederation of Free Trade Unions

The International Confederation of Free Trade Unions (ICFTU) is a labor organization established in 1949 by unions from democratic countries. These unions had withdrawn from the WORLD FEDERATION OF TRADE UNIONS when it failed to reconcile Communist and non-Communist factions among its member countries. The ICFTU has its headquarters in Brussels and has regional offices in Africa, India, and Latin America. It holds educational conferences and, through its International Solidarity Fund, aids trade unionists in the developing countries. In 1978 the ICFTU had 119 affiliated organizations in 88 countries.

International Court of Justice

The International Court of Justice—or the World Court, as it is also called—is the principal judicial organ of the United Nations (UN). It is designed to play a judicial role within the UN system as well as to decide disputes between states. Its seat is in The Hague.

From the time of ancient Greece leaders of states have agreed, on occasion, to submit a dispute for settlement on the basis of law. Often these adjudications have taken the form of court procedure; these tribunals, however, have been ad hoc courts existing only for the dispute for which they were created and without the power to require states in conflict to come before them.

In the 19th century a popular peace movement, based primarily in the United States, began to press for the creation of a real and permanent international court as a way of resolving international disputes and preventing war. At a widely attended conference at The Hague in 1899, the Permanent Court of Arbitration was formed, which, despite its name, scarcely differed from the traditional ad hoc tribunals. Under the Covenant of the League of Nations a Permanent Court of International Justice was established (1921). It operated until 1945, rendering 32 judgments and 27 advisory opinions.

The Charter of the United Nations (1945) created a successor court, the International Court of Justice. It has 15 judges, each with a 9-year term; decisions are taken by majority. Judges are elected in the United Nations, in simultaneous polling in the Security Council and the General Assembly. Candidates' names are submitted by groups of national experts who are selected by their governments. No state may have more than one judge on the court, and a state that appears in litigation has the right to appoint an ad hoc judge, who participates only in that particular case. Judges may sit in cases in which their states appear, but they are expected to remove themselves when they have a personal interest or connection with a case.

The International Court has two types of jurisdiction—contentious and advisory. Contentious jurisdiction is available to states for their disputes; when exercised it results in a decision that is binding upon the parties and is theoretically enforceable, if necessary, through the UN Security Council. Advisory jurisdiction is available to international organizations that have received an authorization from the UN General Assembly; when exercised it results merely in an advisory opinion.

All members of the United Nations are automatically parties to the statute of the court. States not members of the United Nations may be permitted to sign the statute.

States may sign an optional clause agreeing to submit all or certain types of disputes to the court, or they may agree to submit a specific dispute to the court. Except for these voluntary submissions, the court cannot compel a state to submit to its jurisdiction.

The court has pronounced on a wide variety of international legal issues. Though it supposedly only applies international law expressed in treaties, custom, and general principles, the World Court makes law as well.

The court's most important contributions have involved the law of the sea, boundaries, nationality, human rights, treaties, arbitral procedure and, in its advisory opinions, what may be called international constitutional law. Its efforts in the security area, notably on the limitation of atmospheric nuclear-weapons testing, have failed.

The World Court is not a major factor in world politics and cannot be said to have been significant in the prevention of war or conflict. Its enforcement mechanisms are inadequate, and some judgments and opinions have been ignored. Yet many continue to believe that an expanded and more effective international court is indispensable to improved world order.   W. MICHAEL REISMAN

Bibliography: Gamble, John K., and Fischer, Dana, *The International Court of Justice* (1976); Hudson, Manley, *The Permanent Court of International Justice, 1920-1942* (1943; repr. 1972); Lauterpacht, Hersh, *The Development of International Law by the International Court* (1934; rev. ed., 1958); Rosenne, Shabtai, *The Law and Practice of the International Court*, 2 vols. (1965), and *The World Court* (1962); Reisman, W. M., *Nullity and Revision: The Review and Enforcement of International Judgments and Awards* (1971).

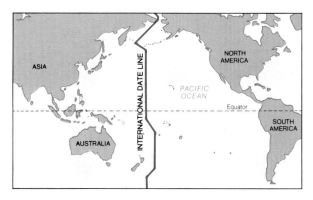

international date line

The international date line is an imaginary line that runs approximately along the 180° meridian in the Pacific Ocean. By an 1884 international agreement, the earth day is considered to begin immediately west of the line and ends immediately east of it. Therefore, the time zones on each side are 24 hours apart. Those who cross the line from west to east repeat one day, while those traveling the reverse course omit one. In the few places where the 180° meridian crosses land the international date line deviates so as not to disrupt the pattern of life within a political union.   ROBERT S. WEINER

International Development Association

The International Development Association, instituted in September 1960, is an affiliated organization of the International Bank for Reconstruction and Development (WORLD BANK). Its members must also be members of the World Bank (total membership stands at 120 countries). The IDA extends credit to developing nations on terms that are easier and more flexible than those of the Bank. IDA borrowers may repay their loans over a period of up to 50 years, with a service charge of less than one percent instead of interest. Loans are for the purpose of stimulating investment and economic development and for encouraging foreign trade. By mid-1978, IDA credits totaled $13.7 billion for 66 member countries.
                                        JOHN G. STOESSINGER

International Falls

International Falls (1975 est. pop., 6,200) is a city and port of entry in northern Minnesota. Situated on the Rainy River, opposite Fort Frances, Ontario, it is the seat of Koochiching County. The economy is based on tourism and lumbering. The 11-m (35-ft) falls of the river, for which the city is named, are now concealed under a dam and a reservoir. International Falls was settled in 1881.

International Finance Corporation

The International Finance Corporation (IFC) is a specialized agency of the UNITED NATIONS that is closely associated with the WORLD BANK. It was established in July 1956 to provide capital for private enterprise in its member countries, particularly less-developed countries. The IFC invests in private enterprise when sufficient private capital is unavailable. It also serves as a clearinghouse to bring together investment opportunities, foreign and domestic private capital, and experienced management. It is authorized to borrow from the World Bank and to sell its own bonds to the public. By mid-1977 the IFC had made loan commitments of $1.7 billion since its establishment. Headquartered in Washington, D.C., it had 105 members in 1978.   JOHN G. STOESSINGER

International Geophysical Year

The International Geophysical Year (1957-58) was an 18-month period of intense scientific exploration of the physical aspects of the Earth. Organized by the International Council of Scientific Unions, it coincided with a period of maximum solar activity (see SOLAR CYCLE). Thousands of scientists from 67 nations worked together, performing a variety of experiments and observations and sharing their results. During this period many new features of the Earth and its space environment were discovered, including the VAN ALLEN RADIATION BELTS. The first artificial satellites, SPUTNIK and EXPLORER, were launched as part of this program.   WILLIAM MENKE

Bibliography: Chapman, Sidney, *I. G. Y., Year of Discovery: The Story of the International Geophysical Year* (1959); Ross, Frank, *Partners in Science: A Survey of the International Geophysical Year* (1961).

See also: INTERNATIONAL YEARS OF THE QUIET SUN.

International Hydrological Decade

A resolution unanimously adopted in November 1964 by the General Conference of the United Nations Educational, Scientific and Cultural Organization (UNESCO) established the International Hydrological Decade (1965-74); 107 of UNESCO's 125 member states participated in it. The 10-year research program, which fostered study of the complex interrelations among various hydrological variables and of the increasing effects of human activity on water phenomena, aimed at providing each country with more complete assessments of its water resources and with better means of rationally using them. The IHD program encouraged collaboration in developing research techniques, in diffusing data, and in planning dams and other hydrological installations.

Bibliography: UNESCO, *Status and Trends of Research in Hydrology* (1972).

International Ice Patrol

The International Ice Patrol protects 117,000 km² (45,000 mi²) of North Atlantic shipping lanes from ICEBERGS during the danger season (March to July). Established in 1914 after the sinking (1912) of the *Titanic*, it is manned by the U.S. COAST GUARD, which uses airborne radar and information about ocean currents and the weather to predict the location of ice masses at 12-hour intervals. From 1946 to 1978 the average seasonal number of icebergs below the 48th parallel was about 300. The southernmost iceberg observed by the Patrol was at 36° north latitude, just north of Bermuda.

International Labor Organization

The International Labor Organization (ILO) was established on Apr. 11, 1919, by the Treaty of Versailles for the purpose of improving labor conditions and living standards among the world's workers. Its headquarters is in Geneva, Switzerland. In 1946 it became the first specialized agency of the UNITED NATIONS. The ILO recommends international standards for wages, hours of work, vacations, social insurance, and other issues affecting employees. It provides technical assistance in matters such as vocational training and management development. In 1969 the ILO was awarded the Nobel Peace Prize. In 1977 the ILO spent more than $48 million on technical assistance programs, primarily in less-developed countries.

The supreme deliberative body of the ILO is the annual International Labor Conference, which is attended by about 1,500 delegates, advisors, and observers. Each national delegation—there are 137 member nations—is composed of two government representatives, one employer representative, and one labor representative. They vote and speak independently. The ILO's executive council is the Governing Body, composed of government members from 28 countries plus 28 employer and worker members elected as individuals.

The United States withdrew from the ILO in 1977—severing a link dating from 1934—because of political attacks made in ILO meetings against Israel and U.S. policies in the Middle East. This withdrawal deprived the organization of a quarter of its annual budget of about $169 million.   JOHN G. STOESSINGER

Bibliography: Jenks, C. Wilfred, *Social Justice in the Law of Nations: The ILO Impact After Fifty Years* (1970); Landy, E. A., *The Effectiveness of International Supervision: Thirty Years of I.L.O. Experience* (1966); Morse, David A., *The Origin and Evolution of the ILO and Its Role in the World Community* (1969).

International Ladies' Garment Workers' Union

The International Ladies' Garment Workers' Union (ILGWU) is an industrial labor union representing workers in the women's garment industry. Established in 1900 in New York City, the ILGWU has been known for militancy and for progressive innovations such as developing (1910) a system of industry-wide bargaining with the use of arbitration to settle disputes. Factionalism in the 1920s nearly destroyed the union, but under David DUBINSKY, its president from 1932 to 1966, membership grew from 45,000 to more than 450,000. The ILGWU was one of the first U.S. unions to include fringe benefits such as health insurance and pensions in its contracts with employers. Membership in 1979 was 351,794, organized in 482 locals.

Bibliography: Lorwin, Lewis, *The Women's Garment Workers* (1924); Smuts, Robert W., *Women and Work in America* (1959); Stein, Leon, ed., *Out of the Sweatshop: The Struggle for Industrial Democracy* (1977).

international language: see LANGUAGES, ARTIFICIAL.

international law

International law has traditionally been defined as the body of rules governing relations between sovereign states. It is often called public international law to distinguish it from private international law, which concerns the transnational relations of individuals with one another and with states. Because of radical changes in the world, international lawyers have had to redefine international law as the institutions and processes governing matters of international concern and the norms or rules they produce. This definition allows for the law-creating part played by international organizations, multinational corporations, political parties, pressure groups, and even international gangs of terrorists, all of whose roles tend to erode the distinction between public and private international law. In addition, international law today is concerned with intranational matters—that is, those within states—such as HUMAN RIGHTS and investment by the citizens of one country in the economy of another.

In any community—local, national, or global—there is a constitutive process: a pattern of making decisions about how decisions will be made. Nationally, this process may produce a document—a constitution—or it may remain unwritten. Even when a document exists—be it the U.S. Constitution or the United Nations Charter—the process continues. The world constitutive process is one in which state elites, international officials of public and private organizations, corporate executives, interest- and pressure-group leaders, and individuals establish and maintain the basic structures for making key international decisions. The body of international law resulting from this constitutive process has to do with almost every area of international relations, including the recognition of states and their admission to international organizations; trade and foreign investment; diplomatic protection of nationals; nationality; war; human rights; boundaries; territorial acquisition; and the law of the oceans.

International law in the modern sense began to emerge with the growth of international trade and the development in the 14th and 15th centuries of the European state system. The increase in international trade contributed to growth and change in commercial and maritime laws. The growth in government-to-government relations—among the Italian city-states, for example—led to new developments in the laws of diplomacy. Italian, Spanish, and Anglo-Dutch schools of international lawyers arose to interpret and systematize these laws. One of the first jurists to produce a systematic treatise on international law was the Dutch philosopher Hugo GROTIUS, whose *De jure belli ac pacis* (On the Laws of War and Peace, 1625) was a blend of natural law and Roman law applied to the practices of the new national states. Other important early theorists of international law were Baron Samuel Von PUFENDORF, Francisco SUÁREZ, Emerich de VATTEL, Christian WOLFF, Cornelis van Bynkershoek (1673–1743), Alberico Gentili (1552–1608), and Richard Zouche (1590–1660).

During the 19th century the scope and ambition of international lawmakers began to broaden. In 1856 the Congress of Paris attempted the first significant codification of rules of maritime warfare. The Geneva and Hague Conferences of the late 19th and 20th centuries began to establish laws concerning the conduct of warfare. The League of Nations and the United Nations went further, attempting to outlaw military aggression. After World War II international law expanded into areas as diverse as war crimes, international economic cooperation and development, nuclear testing, deep-sea mining, and outer space.

SOURCES OF INTERNATIONAL LAW

Article 38 of the statute of the INTERNATIONAL COURT OF JUSTICE identifies three sources of international law: treaties, custom, and "general principles of law" common to civilized states.

Treaties and Resolutions. Treaties, or formal agreements between nations, are considered legally binding upon the parties concerned. To this formal means of lawmaking must now be added the work of international organizations, such as the United Nations (UN). Strictly speaking, these organizations have little or no formal lawmaking competence; in a number of leading decisions, however, the International Court of Justice has recognized the resolutions of the UN and other international organizations—as well as the decisions of international conferences—as important in the formation of international law.

Customary Law. Customary law consists of principles that are derived from actual behavior rather than from formal legislation, and the derivation can be subtle. For example, officials of State X may begin to police a belt of coastal waters that is 4 rather than 3 miles wide. Ships flying the flag of State Y defer to this new and hitherto unlawful assertion. Over time, a custom may form that State X is entitled to a 4-mile territorial sea. The custom may form even though officials of State Y protest the extension and direct their vessels not to honor it.

General Principles. The notion of "general principles" has caused controversy among legal writers. Although some principles have been widely recognized, such as *pacta sunt servanda* (agreements are to be honored by their signatories), some legal scholars feel that the use of "general principles" has been an invitation for courts to create law where none exists. In fact, the opinions of courts, together with the writings of legal scholars, are recognized as subsidiary sources of international law. They provide a basis for judicial decisions when no rules of customary law or treaty law apply.

Because of this proliferation of law-making institutions, it is often difficult to decide which rule is to prevail in international disputes or to gauge whether a particular rule or norm is becoming more important or is losing authority. In this respect international law is a more difficult field than its domestic counterpart.

THE EFFECTIVENESS OF INTERNATIONAL LAW

International law tends to be most effective when governments share an obvious and continuing interest in its maintenance. When the contours of common interest are less clear, or when governments have no common interest, international norms that may have survived from earlier periods are usually ineffective, and matters are likely to be settled by power.

The law of diplomacy has, on the whole, been one of the most successful and durable fields of international law. For centuries national leaders have depended on it for the security of their envoys. A body of law has grown up that guarantees rights and immunities to diplomats stationed in foreign countries and secures their premises and their lines of communication (these laws are now codified in the Vienna Convention of 1961). But as national leaders find other ways of communicating, their common support for diplomacy may wane. The increasing toleration of wiretapping and electronic espionage suggests that this area of international law may be decreasing in effectiveness.

The law of boundaries and territorial acquisition has enjoyed wide support among nations at certain times. An international system based on national territorial units obviously demands that the territorial integrity and political independence of states be respected. With the advent of the principle of self-determination as the ultimate claim for title to territory, however, even this comparatively sedate area of international law has changed radically.

For more than 300 years, the basic principles of the law of the seas were widely accepted and enforced. The oceans were considered a *res communis*, or common property, and not subject to appropriation. The freedoms of the oceans were available to all for reasonable use. With new technology and the growing demand for petroleum, minerals, and fish, the area of the *res communis* has decreased; more and more claims to certain parts of the oceans have been made and accepted, and the traditional public order of the oceans is being radically revised. (See SEAS, FREEDOM OF THE; TERRITORIAL WATERS.)

A basic function of the international system is maintaining minimum order. In the language of the UN Charter, "threats to the peace, breaches of the peace, and acts of aggression" are unlawful. In periods of world revolution, however, states will view differently what constitutes an acceptable system of minimum order. Since 1945 continuing violence has demonstrated, on the whole, the inability of international law to maintain minimum order; yet global war has been avoided.

The effectiveness or ineffectiveness of the international legal system is a function of the structure of the world community. Whereas national leaders often pay lip service to international principles, they actually demand full loyalty to their own national symbols. In time of crisis, when international law is most needed, these national loyalties receive even more emphasis. National politicians are most likely to support the principles of international law when to do so will yield short-term gains for their states, but even these commitments are fragile and may be abandoned when they no longer seem to serve national interests. In areas such as ARMS CONTROL, national security and international trade, governments are constantly negotiating, but the resulting agreements are often short-lived. In many other areas, however, international links and international law have grown closer and stronger. Whether this trend will continue is not clear. Certainly, for the foreseeable future, the effectiveness of international law will be sporadic.   W. MICHAEL REISMAN

Bibliography: Akehurst, Michael, *A Modern Introduction to International Law,* 3d ed. (1977); Brierly, James L., *Law of Nations: An Introduction to the International Law of Peace,* 6th ed. (1963); Brownlie, Ian, *Principles of Public International Law,* 2d ed. (1973); Corbett, Percy E., *The Growth of World Law* (1971); Higgins, Rosalyn, *Development of International Law through the Political Organs of the United Nations* (1963); Jessup, Philip C., *Transnational Law* (1956); Kaplan, Morton, and Katzenbach, Nicholas, *The Political Foundations of International Law* (1961); Lauterpacht, Hersh, *The Function of Law in the International Community* (1933; repr. 1966); McDougal, Myres S., *The Public Order of the Oceans* (1962); Nussbaum, Arthur, *A Concise History of the Law of Nations* (1954).

international longshoremen's unions

The International Longshoremen's Association (ILA), founded in 1892, became the major trade union representing longshoremen on the Atlantic and Pacific coasts. Harry BRIDGES led the West Coast dock workers out of the ILA in 1937, forming the International Longshoremen's and Warehousemen's Union (ILWU).

In 1953 the ILA was expelled from the American Federation of Labor for corruption, but it was readmitted in 1959. In 1979, with headquarters in New York and headed by Thomas W. Gleason, the ILA had 100,000 members in 350 locals.

ILWU staged a 134-day dock strike along the West Coast (1971-72), the longest in the nation's history. With headquarters in San Francisco and headed by James R. Herman, ILWU had 60,000 members in 76 locals in 1979.

Bibliography: Ball, Joseph H., *The Government-Subsidized Union Monopoly* (1966); Russell, Maud, *Men Along the Shore* (1966).

International Monetary Fund

The International Monetary Fund (IMF), a creation of the BRETTON WOODS CONFERENCE (1944), was established on Dec.

27, 1945, to promote international monetary cooperation and exchange stability. In 1978 the IMF had 132 member countries, of which two were Communist-governed.

Under the IMF's original rules, the members agreed not to alter the exchange value of their currencies beyond certain limits without prior consent by the IMF. Members who experienced BALANCE OF PAYMENTS difficulties could borrow foreign exchange from the IMF on condition that they follow approved antiinflationary and other policies to correct their difficulties. In the 1970s, however, the system of fixed EXCHANGE RATES gave way to floating rates, that is, to rates largely determined by supply and demand in international currency markets. In 1976 the IMF adopted new policies, which took effect in 1978, designed to help it control floating rates by exercising "firm surveillance" over exchange rates. Each member country pledged to "endeavor to direct its economic and financial policies toward the objective of fostering orderly economic growth with price stability."

To enable members to overcome shortages of foreign exchange, the IMF in 1969 established currency reserves called Special Drawing Rights, also known as "paper gold." Members may draw on these reserves in units known as SDRs. In 1974 the value of SDRs was no longer based on gold and was based instead on a weighted average of the values of the currencies of the 16 leading trading nations.

The IMF has a board of governors drawn from every member country, 20 executive directors, and a managing director who supervises its operations. Its headquarters is in Washington, D.C.   JOHN G. STOESSINGER

Bibliography: Grubel, Herbert G., *The International Monetary System: Efficiency and Practical Alternatives* (1970); Solomon, Robert, *The International Monetary System, 1945-1976* (1977); Tew, Brian, *The Evolution of the International Monetary System, 1945-1977* (1977).

International Press Institute

An association of publishers, editors, and news broadcasters, the International Press Institute seeks to safeguard freedom of the press and to promote responsible journalism. Founded in 1951, the organization has nearly 2,000 members in more than 60 countries. The group's headquarters are located in Zurich and London.

international relations: see FOREIGN POLICY.

international scientific associations: see SCIENTIFIC ASSOCIATIONS.

International Style   (architecture)

The International Style of architecture, which became the predominant form of commercial and public buildings all over

The Bauhaus (1926), in Dessau, embodies the ideals of International Style in its innovative use of space, material, and geometric form. It was designed by Walter Gropius, one of the leading advocates of the harmonious integration of technology and art in architecture.

the world in the 1950s and 1960s, was first conceived in Germany during the 1920s. Its most characteristic expression appeared in buildings both of the Staatliche BAUHAUS in Dessau (1926) by Walter GROPIUS and of the Weissenhof Housing Exhibition of the Deutscher Werkbund in Stuttgart (1927) by a group of architects under the leadership of Ludwig MIES VAN DER ROHE. The theories that informed the style were published by Walter Gropius in *Internationale Architecktur* (International Architecture, 1925), by Ludwig Hilberseimer in *Internationale neue Baukunst* (New International Architecture, 1927), and in 1932 by Henry-Russell HITCHCOCK and Philip JOHNSON in *The International Style* in conjunction with an exhibition at the Museum of Modern Art in New York City.

The influential characteristics of the International Style include asymmetrical composition, cubic interior spaces, steel girder and concrete construction, smooth exterior surfaces, and avoidance of applied ornament. Flat roofs and large glass windows arranged in horizontal bands are also preferred. For its originators, the style heralded the advent of a new social order, in which work and leisure could take place in well-lit, uncluttered surroundings. The work of LE CORBUSIER in France and of Alvar AALTO in Finland also played an important role in forming the style, which is now a commonplace of urban architecture. A typical New York City International Style structure is the Lever House office building (1950–52) by Skidmore, Owings, and Merrill.　　　　　　　　　RON WIEDENHOEFT

Bibliography: Banham, Reyner, *Theory and Design in the First Machine Age* (1960); Hatje, Gerd, *Encyclopedia of Modern Architecture* (1964); Hitchcock, Henry-Russell, and Johnson, Philip, *The International Style* (1932; repr. 1966).

International Style (art)

From approximately 1350 to 1430 much of the pictorial art of Europe manifested a remarkably homogenous style in which the spatial depth and compositional structure achieved by GIOTTO DI BONDONE and other 14th-century Italian painters were combined with the sinuous arabesques and elegant mannerisms of northern GOTHIC ART. This artistic synthesis, known as the International Style, was preeminently a courtly art. Its most famous patron, the duc de Berry, commissioned the LIMBOURG BROTHERS to execute a BOOK OF HOURS, the *Très Riches Heures* (*c.*1416; Musée Condé, Chantilly, France), the illuminated manuscript that best exemplifies the richness and elegance of the International Style. The International vogue spread throughout Europe, from the Court of Emperor Charles IV in Bohemia to the Hanseatic city of Hamburg—as well as to Italy, where GENTILE DA FABRIANO and Antonio PISANELLO kept it alive well into the 15th century. In the 1420s, however, the classical humanism of MASACCIO and the Flemish realism of Jan van EYCK introduced the era of RENAISSANCE ART, and the period of the International Style rapidly drew to its close.　　　　　　　　　WILLIAM M. HINKLE

Bibliography: Cuttler, C. D., *Northern Painting* (1968); Dupont, Jacques, and Gnudi, Cesare, *Gothic Painting* (1954); Verdier, Philippe, *The International Style: The Arts in Europe around 1400* (1962).

international trade

International trade is the exchange of goods and services among countries. Countries tend to specialize in the production and export of those goods and services that they can produce relatively cheaply and to import things that are produced more efficiently elsewhere.

WHY COUNTRIES TRADE
International trade enables countries to use their labor, capital, and other resources in the most productive way possible. In this way they can enjoy a larger quantity and variety of goods than if they did not trade with each other. The classical model of economics, however, holds that to realize the greatest possible gains from international specialization and trade, industries must be competitive, workers must be able to enter or leave occupations without difficulty, and government policies must encourage efficiency and promote competition.

The tendency of countries to specialize in the production and export of things that they can produce best and relatively

cheaply is called by economists the principle of comparative advantage. It is sometimes difficult, however, to explain why countries specialize in some products and not in others. The major reasons involve differences in factor endowments and in technology.

Factor Endowments. A country's factor endowments include its stocks of physical capital, human capital, workers, and natural resources. Physical capital consists of machinery, factories, highways, railways, harbors, and other equipment and facilities used in production. Human capital represents investment in the labor and management force through education, on-the-job training, and work experience. To understand what determines the kinds of products that a nation exports or imports, a first step is to compare its factor endowments with those elsewhere. Great Britain, for example, although highly industrialized, is deficient in agricultural products and raw materials. It sells manufactured goods and machinery abroad in order to pay for the needed factor endowments.

Technology. Technology refers to the methods of producing goods and services that determine efficiency in production. New technology, for instance, is most readily available in the advanced industrialized countries. These countries also have highly trained scientific personnel and workers with considerable production skill and experience. Moreover, the markets for products in these countries are very large, and income levels are substantial. All these advantages encourage larger firms to expand their operations and to seek the economies of mass production (also called economies of scale), enabling them to compete with foreign producers who lack such advantages. Comparison of the technological characteristics of nations' major producing sectors, therefore, will aid in understanding differences among them in exports and imports. Latin American countries, for example, rich in factor endowments, need to import manufactured goods.

PROTECTION
In addition to factor endowments and technology, government policies play an important role in shaping the structure of a country's trade. This is perhaps most obvious in the case of TARIFFS and quotas on imports and manipulation of EXCHANGE RATES. The government may also encourage exporters by subsidizing them. Subsidies can be direct, as when the government makes up the difference between lower foreign and higher domestic prices, or indirect, as when the government supports research and development activities by private firms.

One reason why governments adopt such policies is to shield domestic producers from foreign competition. Other reasons why governments introduce policies that interfere with FREE TRADE are: to increase the wages of certain groups of workers and their share of the national income; to bring monopoly power to bear in trade with other countries; to offset difficulties in domestic markets, particularly those in which workers are unemployed; to increase national self-sufficiency in time of war or other emergency; and to protect young industries until they have had time to mature. Protectionist policies have also been invoked in the face of dumping policies of other countries. Dumping occurs when a product is sold abroad at less than its domestic cost in order to take over a market or to eliminate a glut in the home market. The United States imposes special customs duties on dumped products in order to raise their prices. While each of these objectives may be reasonable from a given nation's point of view, economists have argued that restriction of trade may not be the best means to achieve the objectives. This is because policies affecting trade in such a way may have unintended side effects. First, consumers may be made worse off by having to pay higher prices for imports. Second, by protecting inefficient industries the policies may discourage a more productive use of a country's factor endowments. Third, the restriction of imports may injure the economies of other countries by reducing their exports, especially countries that are relatively poor and less developed. As other countries then begin to experience unemployment and diminished incomes, they become increasingly unable to import goods, a situation that may have a deleterious effect on the protectionist country. Most countries nevertheless maintain varied protectionist policies, principally as a result of special-interest political pressure.

HISTORY OF INTERNATIONAL TRADE

Trade among different peoples can be traced to prehistoric times. African, Arabian, and Asian caravans and Mediterranean and Indian Ocean maritime trade are well-known examples of early far-flung commercial transportation. World trade came to be dominated at various times by such groups as the Egyptians, Phoenicians, Greeks, Venetians, Spanish, Dutch, and British. The Crusades gave a significant impetus to European trade and voyages of exploration and discovery later expanded trade beyond the Mediterranean basin. The increasing political supremacy of the national states enabled them to supplant the commercial power of city trading blocs such as the HANSEATIC LEAGUE.

The major nations conducted trade from the 16th to the 18th century, mainly with their colonies, under principles of MERCANTILISM. The Industrial Revolution in the 19th century transformed the theory and practice of international commerce. Mercantile principles gave way to LAISSEZ-FAIRE and an emphasis on free trade. Mass production, technological advances in communication and transportation, and new, large business organizations such as commercial banking and insurance corporations extended world trade and stimulated the search for new markets—a search that in many instances resulted in national policies of COLONIALISM and IMPERIALISM.

The first half of the 20th century was a time of great disruption of world trade caused by World War I, the DEPRESSION OF THE 1930s, and World War II. In the 1930s in particular, inflation in European countries, protectionist policies, and the abandonment of the GOLD STANDARD by many countries were factors in the collapse of international trade. During World War II the BRETTON WOODS CONFERENCE (1944) was held to organize postwar international monetary and financial arrangements so that global commerce could be resumed cooperatively and with a minimum potential for further disruption. The creation (1945) of the INTERNATIONAL MONETARY FUND and the WORLD BANK was a result of this conference. The GENERAL AGREEMENT ON TARIFFS AND TRADE was established in 1948 and meets regularly to negotiate tariff reductions on the basis of the MOST-FAVORED-NATION STATUS. Regional trade blocs, called CUSTOMS UNIONS—for example, the EUROPEAN ECONOMIC COMMUNITY, the EUROPEAN FREE TRADE ASSOCIATION, the COUNCIL FOR MUTUAL ECONOMIC ASSISTANCE, and the LATIN AMERICAN FREE TRADE ASSOCIATION—were established to promote international trade, and therefore economic prosperity within certain areas of the world. In the 1970s the persistence of global inflation, the increasing commercial power of the ORGANIZATION OF PETROLEUM EXPORTING COUNTRIES, and the weakness of the dollar—used as the principal international standard of payment—have been major factors in the changing patterns of international trade.

PATTERNS OF TRADE

The trade of the United States is notable for its broad variety. U.S. exports include not only manufactured goods but food and raw materials as well. The composition of U.S. trade in 1978 was as follows:

	Exports	Imports
Food, raw materials, and ores	26%	15%
Petroleum and other fuels	4	30
Metals, chemicals, and other products	16	15
Manufactured goods	53	39

More than 40% of imports consisted of primary commodities and petroleum, and about the same percentage was represented by manufactured goods.

The composition of trade of the European Economic Community (EEC) in 1978 was:

	Exports	Imports
Food, raw materials, and ores	14%	23%
Petroleum and other fuels	6	18
Metals, chemicals, and other products	25	21
Manufactured goods	54	37

The total trade of the EEC countries was about three times that of the United States, but this included trade among the EEC members as well as their trade with nonmember countries. EEC exports consisted mainly of industrial products and manufactured goods. Their imports were heavily concentrated in natural resources products and industrial materials.

Some light can be thrown on world trade by comparing the advanced industrialized countries, shares of world exports with those of other countries. The advanced industrialized countries—primarily the United States, Canada, Western Europe, and Japan—accounted for 65% of world exports in 1978.

TOTAL WORLD EXPORTS

Advanced industrialized countries	66%
Less-developed countries	23
Communist countries	10

Exports From	To Advanced Industrialized Countries	To Less-Developed Countries	To Communist Countries
Advanced industrialized countries	71%	23%	5%
Less-developed countries	71	24	4
Communist countries	27	17	55

That these countries were each other's best customers is evident from the fact that 71% of their total exports went to each other. The less-developed countries, which export mainly primary commodities, accounted for 23% of total world trade in 1978. Of their total exports, 71% went to the advanced countries. The Communist countries accounted for 10% of world trade in 1978. These countries took only 5% of advanced-country exports and 4% of the exports of the less-developed countries. Some 55% of the Communist countries' exports went to one another.

The patterns of world trade suggest some of the important economic issues confronting the world today. The advanced industrialized countries are seeking to expand their mutual trade and to reduce their dependence on imported commodities, especially petroleum. The less-developed countries are trying to expand their exports, especially to the advanced countries that constitute their biggest markets. The Communist countries have been concerned mainly with using foreign trade to carry out government plans for economic development, and have not been heavy traders with capitalist countries.　　　　ROBERT M. STERN

Bibliography: Bhattacharya, A. K., *Foreign Trade and International Development* (1976); Chacholiades, M., *International Trade Theory and Policy*, 2d ed. (1978); Ellsworth, P. T., and Leith, J. C., *The International Economy*, 5th ed. (1975); Freeman, A. M., *International Trade* (1971); Green, R. T., and Lutz, J., *The United States and World Trade* (1979); Ingram, J. C., *International Economic Problems*, 2d ed. (1977); Kreinen, M. E., *International Economics*, 2d ed. (1975); Wexler, I., *Fundamentals of International Economics*, 2d ed. (1972).

International Trade Commission, U.S.

The U.S. International Trade Commission administers laws governing TARIFFS and international trade. It advises the president, Congress, and government agencies on tariff questions and on problems arising in trade negotiations with other countries. On petition, it investigates whether the import of a specified article is injuring a specific firm, a group of workers, or domestic industry in general to the extent that the president ought to take protective action. The commission also publishes tariff schedules and statistics of imports and exports. It is directed by 6 commissioners appointed by the president for terms of nine years, and it has 385 employees. Formerly known as the U.S. Tariff Commission, it was established by an act of Congress in 1916; its name was changed to its present form by the Trade Act of 1974.

Bibliography: Chachiliades, Miltiades, *International Trade Theory and Policy*, 2d ed. (1978); Green, Robert T., and Lutz, James, *The United States and World Trade: Changing Patterns and Dimensions* (1979); Monroe, Wilbur, *International Trade Policy in Transition* (1975).

International Typographical Union

The International Typographical Union, with headquarters in Colorado Springs, Colo., was founded at a national convention of typographers in Cincinnati, Ohio, in 1852 as the National Typographical Union, 37 years after the founding of the first regional typographer's union in the United States. By 1886, when the ITU joined the American Federation of Labor, it had 30,000 members. In 1912 the union began a two-party system internally. In the 1960s and '70s the introduction of modern typesetting machines was often resisted by the union, which feared for the job security of its members. It had 100,499 members in 581 locals in 1979.

Bibliography: Lipset, Seymour M., et al., *Union Democracy: The Internal Politics of the International Typographical Union* (1956).

International Years of the Quiet Sun

International Years of the Quiet Sun was a 2-year period (1964–65) of minimum solar activity (see SOLAR CYCLE) during which scientists from 71 countries or research organizations studied solar radiation and its effects on the Earth and its atmosphere. Half of the 2,000 stations set up were for meteorology, 265 studied geomagnetism, 109 the auroras, 58 airglow, 310 the ionosphere, 155 solar activity, and 117 cosmic radiation and geomagnetically trapped particles. Research ships made special cruises, instrumented aircraft flew special missions, and sounding rockets of many kinds were launched. These studies were a specialized sequel to the worldwide measurements obtained during the INTERNATIONAL GEOPHYSICAL YEAR, an 18-month period (1957–58) of maximum solar activity, and the 2-year period that followed.   ARNOLD COURT

Interplanetary Monitoring Platform: see IMP.

Interpol   [in'-tur-pohl]

Interpol (International Criminal Police Organization) is a mutual assistance organization of police forces. Founded in Vienna in 1923, it now has a membership of 126 countries. The United States has been a member since 1938. Yugoslavia and Romania are the only Communist countries that belong to the organization. Day-to-day operations are handled at the Paris (St. Cloud) headquarters by a 180-person staff, and major policy decisions are made at annual meetings of the general assembly of all members.

Each member nation maintains a domestic clearinghouse that processes data on international criminals and their activities, especially smuggling, counterfeiting, and trade in narcotics. Members cooperate by detaining suspects within their borders and by providing information on criminals, missing property, and unidentified bodies. Interpol has its own agents. They are not, however, permitted to pass freely from one country to another; arrests and investigations are the responsibility of each member country's own police force. Involvement in political, religious, military, or racial matters is strictly prohibited.

Bibliography: Forrest, A. J., *Interpol* (1955); Tullett, Tom, *Inside Interpol* (1965).

interpolation   [in-tur-puh-lay'-shun]

Interpolation is the process of determining the value of a FUNCTION between known values of the function. In mathematical notation, if $y_a = f(x_a)$ and $y_b = f(x_b)$ are known values of the function $y = f(x)$, interpolation is the process of determining $y_i = f(x_i)$, where $x_a < x_i < x_b$. A related process is that of extrapolation, finding $y_e = f(x_e)$, where x_e falls outside the interval between x_a and x_b. The process depends upon knowledge of the behavior of the function in the neighborhood of x_i or x_e. The simplest method, which is usually sufficiently accurate, is linear interpolation, in which it is assumed that the behavior of the function may be approximated by a straight line through the known points. In such a case, the points of interest define similar triangles and the following approximation holds:

$$\frac{y_i - y_a}{y_b - y_a} = \frac{x_i - x_a}{x_b - x_a}$$

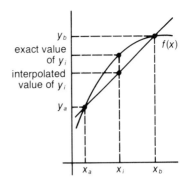

Since y_i is the only unknown, it can be determined from this equation. Interpolation is used to approximate intermediate values in MATHEMATICAL TABLES, especially tables of LOGARITHMS and trigonometric functions.   ALARIC MILLINGTON

Interpretation of Dreams, The

The Interpretation of Dreams (1900; Eng. trans., 1909) is a theoretical interpretation of DREAMS AND DREAMING by Sigmund FREUD. Freud believed that dreams are expressions of unfulfilled wishes and desires. Because such wishes often center on social taboos—particularly those concerning sex—their expression must be disguised; hence the frequent occurrence of symbols in dreams. To interpret such dream symbols Freud had to describe and analyze the workings of the subconscious and unconscious mind, and in so doing he created PSYCHOANALYSIS. Many psychologists, including Freud, consider *The Interpretation of Dreams* his masterwork.

intersection: see SET THEORY.

Interstate Commerce Commission

The U.S. Interstate Commerce Commission (ICC) regulates surface transportation among the states by trains, trucks, buses, boats, oil pipelines, and companies that carry freight or parcels. Its duties are defined by the Interstate Commerce Act of Feb. 4, 1887, and other laws regulating transportation. The 11 commissioners are appointed for 7-year terms by the president, who names one of them chairperson. The commissioners elect their own vice-chairperson annually. Most of the ICC's work centers on hearings concerning freight and passenger rates or operating rights, the bulk of the cases involving motor carriers.

Bibliography: Hoogenboom, Ari and Olive, *A History of the ICC from Panacea to Palliative* (1976).

See also: GOVERNMENT REGULATION.

Interstate Highway System

The Interstate Highway System, officially named the National System of Interstate and Defense Highways, is a network of multiple-lane, limited-access expressways that cover the United States. Authorized by the Federal Aid Highway Act of 1956, a 41,000-mi (65,981-km) system was to be completed by 1969 at a cost of $25 billion. The federal government was to pay 90% of this total and the states 10%. Escalating costs and additions to the system changed these figures to 42,758 mi (68,810 km) at an estimated $76 billion by 1974. The highways were designed to carry one-fifth of the nation's motor traffic, connect all states in the continental United States, and reach 90% of all U.S. cities with populations of 50,000 or more. Designs and standards of construction were based on estimates of the highest hourly traffic volume in 1975. Routes are designated by numbers—those running east-west by even, north-south by odd numbers.

interstellar matter

Interstellar matter is gas and dust existing between stars in a galaxy. Every atom that is not in a star in a particular galaxy

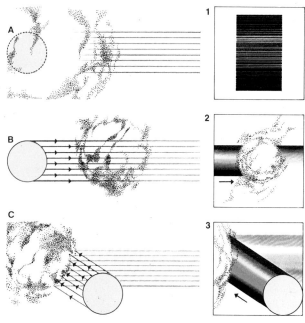

Large, visible clouds of gas and dust, called nebulae, are spread throughout the space between the stars. Nebulae are classified into three different types. An emission nebula (A) consists of gas near a very hot star that emits light as a result of fluorescence caused by ultraviolet radiation from the star. These emission nebulae have bright-line spectra (1) that are characteristic of the elements present in the excited gases. A dark or absorption nebula (B) occurs when dust in the clouds blocks out all or most of the light from stars or emission nebulae beyond (2). A reflection nebula (C) results when a dust cloud either reflects or scatters starlight (3).

can be considered as part of that galaxy's interstellar matter. The study of this matter is one of the most important branches of modern astrophysics.

Because interstellar matter is not as easy to see as stars, its existence was recognized only recently. By observing the spectrum of the Orion nebula, William Huggins found in 1864 that the nebula consists of luminous interstellar gas. In the early days of astronomical photography, E. E. Barnard recognized the existence of dark matter, now called interstellar dust, by its effect in absorbing the light of stars behind it. In 1904, Johannes F. Hartmann found an absorption line in the spectrum of the star δ Orionis, showing the interfering presence of nonluminous interstellar gas. He recognized that this line, caused by ionized calcium (Ca^+), did not arise in the star because it did not share the periodic changes in wavelength of all the other lines in the star's spectrum, caused by the changing velocity of its orbital motion. Large amounts of interstellar gas, composed mostly of atoms but also containing ions and molecules, are now known to be present in our galaxy. Interstellar dust also exists, although in a smaller amount than the gas, because hydrogen and helium, the two most abundant elements in the universe, form only transparent gases; hydrogen can form dust particles only when combined with less abundant elements such as carbon, nitrogen, oxygen, magnesium, silicon, and iron.

INTERSTELLAR MATTER IN OUR GALAXY

Nearly all the information about interstellar matter is obtained from studying its interaction with radiation through the emission, absorption, or scattering of light at optical, ultraviolet, infrared, and radio wavelengths. Atoms, molecules, and ions emit and absorb radiation at discrete wavelengths, causing spectral lines, and dust particles with sizes ranging from 10^{-4} cm to 10^{-6} cm emit and absorb radiation at all wavelengths, resulting in a continuous spectrum. Considerably larger particles the size of baseballs could be present in interstellar matter, but because they are much less effective per unit mass in emitting or absorbing radiation, they would be

essentially undetectable. On theoretical grounds, however, such large particles are thought not to exist.

The only indirect way of detecting the presence of interstellar matter, independently of its interaction with radiation, is by its gravitational effect on the motions of stars. Because all forms of mass have this same effect, interstellar matter and faint, low-luminosity stars are not easily distinguished by this method. The best estimate is that approximately 2 or 3 percent of the mass of our galaxy is interstellar matter, and the rest stars. Some galaxies contain much more interstellar matter than our galaxy; others contain much less.

Atoms, Ions, and Molecules. Interstellar matter in cool regions of space can be observed by the absorption lines it causes in the spectra of distant hot stars. Interstellar absorption lines usually cannot be observed in the spectra of cooler stars, because absorption lines of atoms and ions in the stars' atmospheres blend with the interstellar lines. The strongest interstellar absorption lines observed in the optical spectral region are those of Ca^+ and Na, and weaker lines are observed of Ti^+, Ca, Fe, and K. These are not the most abundant atoms and ions in interstellar space, but they are the most abundant atoms and ions that have interstellar absorption lines in the optical part of the spectrum accessible to Earthbound instruments. Because of the low density of interstellar matter—one atom per cm^3, or 10^{-24} g per cm^3—atomic, ionic, and molecular collisions are infrequent, and the interstellar atoms and ions are almost always in their ground level, the lowest electronic energy level. The only absorption lines that can be observed, therefore, are those which arise from ground levels, and Na and Ca^+ are the two most abundant interstellar substances that have lines from the ground level in the ordinary region.

Interstellar matter also is observed by the radiation it emits if it is heated or ionized. Hot stars emit large amounts of high-energy ultraviolet radiation. If a hot star is located in a cloud of interstellar matter, its ultraviolet radiation ionizes the nearby interstellar gas and transfers energy to it, causing the ionized gas to emit the characteristic emission-line spectrum of a galactic nebula with ionized hydrogen, known as an H II region.

Most abundant atoms and ions, such as H, O, O^+, C, and C^+, have their spectral lines in the ultraviolet spectral region. Ultraviolet radiation from hot stars can be measured using telescopes in rockets or artificial satellites above the Earth's atmospheres. The telescopes these orbiting observatories carry are small, and only a few of the brighter, nearer stars have been measured. These ultraviolet spectra, nevertheless, show the presence of many absorption lines including the interstellar absorption lines of molecular hydrogen (H_2). Previously, only the molecules CH, CN, and CH^+ were seen to have interstellar absorption lines in the ordinary optical region.

Even at the very low temperature (about 100 K) of typical neutral interstellar material, very low-lying energy levels are collisionally excited and radiate. Neutral hydrogen (H) has an excited hyperfine-structure level close above its ground level, which causes an emission line with a wavelength of 21 cm, in the radio-frequency spectral region. Observations of this line have provided information on the distribution and amount of neutral interstellar gas in this galaxy.

Hydroxyl (OH) was the first interstellar molecule detected (1963, 1964), by several groups of radio astronomers, in the radio-frequency spectral region. It has four characteristic spectral lines with wavelengths near 18 cm. OH and CO, which has lines at 2.6 mm and 1.3 mm, are abundant interstellar molecules and are observed throughout the galaxy. They are found in dense clouds of interstellar matter, because only in such clouds do the atoms collide frequently enough to combine to form molecules.

In very dense interstellar clouds many more complicated interstellar molecules have been observed by their radio-frequency and far-infrared emission lines. These include water (H_2O), formaldehyde (H_2CO), methanol (CH_3OH), and ethanol (CH_3CH_2OH).

Dust Particles. Interstellar dust particles can be detected by the extinction of starlight. Extinction includes both absorp-

(Above) *The Horsehead Nebula, located in the belt of the constellation of Orion, is typical of dark nebulae. It comprises a large, dense, opaque region of dust silhouetted against a red emission nebula behind it. The blue nebulosity in the lower left is a reflection nebula.*

(Below) *The Pleiades open star cluster in the Taurus constellation is the best-known reflection nebula. Each bright star in the cluster is embedded in a blue nebulosity with a spectrum identical to that of the star, indicating reflection of starlight by surrounding dust particles.*

tion, in which light is actually destroyed by conversion into heat, and scattering, in which light's direction is changed, as by small water droplets. In both cases some light from a star shining through a cloud of interstellar particles does not reach the observer; for interstellar particles scattering is probably the more significant factor in the optical spectral region.

Very dense clouds of interstellar dust particles are seen as dark features silhouetted against the bright star field or nebula behind them. Examples are the dark nebulae discovered by Barnard, the "Gulf of Mexico" in the North American Nebula, and the dark Horsehead Nebula in Orion.

For small particles the extinction increases as the light's wavelength decreases, and light transmitted by a cloud of particles tends to have more long-wavelength radiation than incident light, that is, it tends to be redder (see INTERSTELLAR REDDENING). This reddening effect of small particles is very pronounced on Earth when the rising or setting Sun is seen through a long path in the Earth's atmosphere, containing many particles in the form of dust, smoke, or haze. A star's intrinsic color is known from its spectral type, which depends, like the color, primarily on its temperature. By finding a star's spectral type, measuring its actual color, and comparing this measurement with its intrinsic color, the amount of dust between the observer and the star can be measured. From the detailed way in which the amount of extinction produced by interstellar dust varies with wavelength, together with knowledge of the composition of interstellar matter, it can be gathered that the interstellar particles probably are a mixture of dielectric particles, composed largely of solid H_2O, CH_4, NH_3 with some metal impurities, silicate particles containing $MgSiO_4$ and $CaSiO_4$, and probably also graphite or silicon-carbide particles. An absorbed layer of H_2 may exist on the surfaces of interstellar particles, but most of their mass consists of elements heavier than H or He.

Because interstellar particles are not spherical but have elongated shapes, such as ellipsoids or rods, they may also polarize transmitted light. Such polarization is observed to be weakly present in many reddened stars and shows that the interstellar particles are elongated and also roughly aligned in regions of the galaxy, probably by large-scale magnetic fields.

Interstellar matter in our galaxy is distributed so that most of it is in or very close to the galactic plane. To a first approximation, interstellar matter can be thought of as forming a layer about 700 light-years thick and 60,000 light-years in diameter. Interstellar matter is not uniformly distributed within this layer, but tends to occur in various-sized clouds or condensations. In the inner part of the galaxy, closer to the galactic center, the clouds tend to be denser, and more of the interstellar matter is in the form of molecules. In the outer part of the galaxy, more of it is in atomic form. Only a small fraction of interstellar gas is ionized.

INTERSTELLAR MATTER IN OTHER GALAXIES

Interstellar matter can also be observed in other galaxies. The most direct method is the observation of individual galactic nebulae, or H II regions, which can be photographed in many nearby galaxies. The spectra of these nebulae show they are identical with ionized interstellar-matter clouds in our galaxy. Dust can also be recognized by its extinction effects in other galaxies, particularly in spiral galaxies seen nearly edge-on, because of the strong concentration of interstellar matter to the plane of the galaxy in which it is located. Radio measurements have detected the 21-cm emission line of interstellar hydrogen from many other galaxies.

In general, elliptical galaxies contain much less interstellar matter than our galaxy. They do not show any galactic nebulae, dust, or 21-cm line radiation. Most irregular galaxies contain far more interstellar matter than this galaxy; they are rich in galactic nebulae, dust, and 21-cm radiation. Spiral galaxies are intermediate; some are similar to this galaxy in interstellar-matter content, others contain significantly more or less interstellar matter, but almost always in the range between ellipticals and irregulars.

Photographs of spiral galaxies show that interstellar matter is strongly concentrated in spiral arms. The main defining features that make spiral arms visible on these photographs are the galactic nebulae and the high-luminosity stars, which recently formed from interstellar matter and are therefore mostly still immersed in it. This important discovery was made by Walter Baade, working at Mount Wilson Observatory in the early 1940s, when a World War II dimout in southern California made the skies particularly dark and astronomical photographs particularly effective.

Spiral arms in our galaxy are not easily recognized, because of the Earth's position close to the galactic plane. By identifying distant galactic nebulae and stellar associations, however, and by determining their distances accurately from the spectral types and magnitudes of their stars, the distribution of interstellar matter can be determined within a few thousand light-years of the Sun. It is found to be arranged in spiral arms, very similar to the spiral arms directly observed in other spiral galaxies.

Optical measurements cannot be pushed to larger distances in our galaxy's plane, because of the very strong extinction caused by dust in interstellar matter. Radio measurements, however, which are not subject to appreciable extinction, can be used to detect interstellar hydrogen throughout the galaxy by its 21-cm radiation. Radio measurements also show the presence of galactic nebulae, which emit highly excited radio-frequency lines of hydrogen throughout the galaxy. Although these radio measurements do not directly give the distances of the interstellar gas observed, the pattern of velocities measured by the shifts in wavelengths of the emission lines demonstrates that the gas lies in spiral arms everywhere except near the galaxy's center.

The physical mechanism responsible for the distribution of interstellar matter in a spiral pattern is not fully understood. It is certainly connected with the galaxy's rotation, which has a rate that varies with distance from the center of the galaxy. Large-scale magnetic fields may be involved in the spiral arms' production and maintenance. Another possibility is the density-wave theory, which attributes the spiral arms entirely to the interstellar gas's kinematical and gravitational effects.

INTERSTELLAR MATTER AND STELLAR EVOLUTION

Interstellar matter is the material from which new stars form. Our galaxy's more luminous stars have lifetimes that are short in comparison to the galaxy's age (see STELLAR EVOLUTION). They consume their supply of hydrogen so rapidly, converting it into helium by the nuclear reactions that provide the energy they radiate, that they cannot possibly have existed for 10 billion years.

Dense condensations in interstellar clouds are the nuclei that became gravitationally unstable and contract, forming a star or a group of stars by fragmentation. Young stars, such as high-luminosity O and B stars, are usually found in or close to interstellar matter. The only exceptions are high-velocity luminous stars, which have moved far from the interstellar gas clouds in which they formed.

At the end of their lifetimes, most stars return some of their mass to interstellar space. For example, a star of approximately solar mass discards an outer shell, which briefly becomes a planetary nebula; the stellar remnant, after a short, high-luminosity episode, becomes a white dwarf. A more massive star, at the end of its lifetime, becomes a supernova, consisting of a rapidly expanding shell of gas and a stellar remnant that probably becomes a neutron star. The planetary-nebula and supernova shells are slowed down by colliding with interstellar matter and merging with it. Probably other evolving stars, such as red giants, lose mass more gradually by "stellar winds," or flow of matter into space. Interstellar matter is a reservoir in which mass from evolving or evolved stars, often enriched in heavy elements by nuclear reactions, is captured and ultimately partly formed into new stars.

DONALD E. OSTERBROCK

Bibliography: Abell, George O., *Exploration of the Universe* (1969); Aller, Lawrence H., *Atoms, Stars, and Nebulae* (1971); Bok, Bart J. and Priscilla F., *The Milky Way* (1974); Heiles, Carl, "The Structure of the Interstellar Medium," *Scientific American*, January 1978; Osterbrock, Donald E., *Astrophysics of Gaseous Nebulae* (1974); Pasachoff, Jay M., *Contemporary Astronomy* (1977); Spitzer, Lyman, Jr., *Diffuse Matter in Space* (1978).

interstellar reddening

Interstellar reddening is the extinction effect that occurs when the light of distant stars passes through interstellar matter. Interstellar dust particles absorb and also scatter some of the light, reducing the amount transmitted to an observer. Absorption (destruction of light photons) and scattering (change in direction of light photons) together are called extinction. The amount of extinction by small particles generally increases as the wavelength of the light decreases, resulting in the transmitted light being richer in long-wavelength radiation than in short-wavelength radiation and therefore appearing redder than the original source. Familiar examples of this effect are the red color of the Sun seen near the horizon or the red color of distant streetlights on hazy or smoky nights, both results of extinction by particles in the Earth's atmosphere. Interstellar reddening is the same effect, caused by extinction by interstellar particles.

Some stars are very heavily reddened. Many distant hot blue stars in our galaxy, close to the central plane of the Milky Way, shine through so much interstellar dust that the light received from them is as red as the light, from much cooler stars, that has not suffered interstellar extinction.

DONALD E. OSTERBROCK

intertidal life [in-tur-ty'-dul]

Between the high and low tidemarks of marine coasts exists abundant and varied plant and animal life. Factors such as the type of rock, type of substrate, water temperature, protection from wave shock, and the interactions among various organisms determine the basic features of an intertidal community organization.

NORTH AMERICAN PACIFIC COAST
Splash Zone and Upper-Intertidal Zone. The rocky intertidal areas of temperate climates are easily visible. Regions such as the rocky shores of the North American Pacific coast can be

This illustration of a mixed rocky and sandy shore shows organisms from the Atlantic and Pacific coasts of North America. Fiddler crabs (1) burrow in sand along the Atlantic coast splash zone. Upper intertidal mollusks include the common periwinkle snail (2); Lister's keyhole limpet (4); Atlantic plate limpet (5); and, on the Pacific coast, the black tegula snail (3) and rough limpet (6). Barnacles (7) also inhabit this zone. Among the seaweeds, Fucus, or rockweed (9), often grows in rocky mid-intertidal areas; the red algae Gigartina (13) and Irish moss (12) typically form a zone between the rockweeds and the kelps, such as Laminaria (29; holdfast and stipe shown), which occupy the lowest intertidal zone. Seaweeds of the genera Ceramium (8), Codium (10), and Dasya (11) are usually found in lower intertidal and subtidal regions. The common sea star (16) preys on mollusks such as the blue mussel (15). Sea anemones (14, 19) occur in several zones. Lower intertidal animals include sea squirts (17) and sea grapes (20), both invertebrate chordates; sponges (18, 22); hermit crab (21), shown occupying a moon shell; rock crab (23); calico scallop (24), shown swimming; green sea urchin (25); sand dollar (26); blood star (27); and fanworm (28), a tube-dwelling polychaete worm.

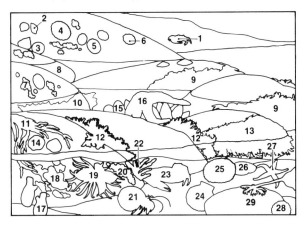

subdivided into four broad zones: the splash zone (supralittoral fringe), upper intertidal zone (upper mid-littoral), mid-intertidal zone (lower mid-littoral), and low intertidal zone (infralittoral fringe). Highest above the waves, the splash zone is rarely covered by water for any length of time. Animals living in this zone, such as shore crabs and large isopods, are primarily adapted to terrestrial life. Splash pools dry up in summer and flood from freshwater runoff in winter; as a result, these pools contain only a few hardy animals such as the splash pool copepod, *Tigriopus.*

Below this zone lies the upper intertidal, often covered by rough acorn barnacles and carnivorous snails of the genus *Nucella*, which prey on the barnacles, and a relatively sparse covering of leafy green and stubby brown seaweeds (algae). Periwinkle snails, turban snails, and limpets inhabit this zone and graze on the film of microscopic algae covering the hard rock substrate. The barnacles would easily overpopulate and completely cover everything if their predators and accidental disturbances did not occasionally clear some empty space for the other organisms.

Mid-Intertidal Zone. Below these two zones, in the mid-intertidal zone, a broad band of mussels often forms a bed several inches thick. Many varieties of algae are common in this zone. The common starfish continually feeds on mussels, which would otherwise abound throughout all the available mid-intertidal space. Mussels cannot withstand the dry conditions of the upper intertidal zone; they are thus unable to press upon the barnacles and other organisms of the upper zone. Within the mussel bed live many polychaete worms, snails, and crabs. Along headlands exposed to the roughest surf, gooseneck barnacles and sea palm algae sometimes replace mussels as the dominant life forms.

Low Intertidal Zone. In the low intertidal zone both plant and animal life reach their greatest diversity. Algal species of this region include red coralline algae and several types of large kelp that are characterized by straplike fronds. These plants form massive holdfasts, under which dwell many worms as well as snapping shrimp and porcelain crabs. Thick beds of sea urchins often abound here. Their predator, the giant sunflower starfish, moves actively about, causing the sea urchins to loosen their grip. In moist and shady areas beneath overhanging rocks masses of sponge colonies, sea squirts, bryozoans, and hydroids cover the rocks. In protected areas deep tide pools often contain large sea anemones that capture food from the passing currents; hermit crabs compete for snail shells to occupy; and large crabs and small octopuses act as predators on many animals. Numerous fishes and small shrimps swim in the large tide pools.

ATLANTIC COAST

Along the rocky shores of New England the same intertidal zones occur as along the Pacific coast, but the diversity of life is much less. The Atlantic shores of North America largely consist of spacious sandy beaches that protect muddy bays and estuaries behind barrier islands. Sandy beaches of these coasts actually are deserts in terms of visible life. The few forms that survive are often quite abundant, however. Bean clams, mole crabs, and razor clams rapidly burrow in the shifting sands of the outgoing waves. Ghost crabs and beach-hopper amphipods help clear these beaches of the wrack that accumulates with the ebbing tide.

MARSHES

Along both American coasts the quiet waters of bays and ES-TUARIES are lined with marshes of pickleweed (genus *Salicornia*) or spartina grass. In these marshes dense populations of fiddler crabs undermine the banks with a honeycomb of burrows. Oyster banks often line the lower edge of the intertidal marsh and form hiding places for many crabs and snails as well as the only hard substrate available for sponges and the other encrusting forms. The mud flats appear sterile, but exploration with a shovel and sieve quickly uncovers the extensive burrow systems of large clams, mud shrimp, many polychaete worms, as well as peanut worms and echiurans. Most of these animals eat either by filtering the water at high tide or by deposit feedings—siphoning up the microscopic food particles that accumulate on the surface of the mud.

Within the burrows small crabs, shrimp, and even a few species of small fishes often live as harmless guests.

Because intertidal life is so diverse and so accessible, research on these organisms continues to provide major contributions to modern ecological studies.   ARMAND KURIS

Bibliography: Carefoot, Thomas, *Pacific Seashores* (1977); Kozloff, E. N., *Seashore Life of Puget Sound, the Strait of Georgia, and the San Juan Archipelago* (1973); Ricketts, E. F., Calvin, J., and Hedgpeth, J., *Between Pacific Tides*, 4th ed. (1968); Southward, A. J., *Life on the Sea-Shore* (1965); Stephenson, T. A. and Anne, *Life between Tidemarks on Rocky Shores* (1972).

intervention

Intervention, in INTERNATIONAL LAW, is diplomatic or military interference by one nation in the affairs of another without that nation's consent. It is considered illegal under customary international law, as well as in many treaties. Intervening countries usually state that they are intervening to protect their own nationals or to defend themselves against aggression by the other country. Intervention is legal only when done for humanitarian reasons (prevention of genocide) or under the "collective intervention" terms of the United Nations charter to preserve international peace and security.

In CIVIL LAW, intervention is a procedure through which a person whose rights are affected by a lawsuit may become a party to that lawsuit. Such a person can join with the plaintiff or with the defendant or can intervene with a claim adverse to both parties.

intestine

The intestine is the part of the DIGESTIVE SYSTEM in vertebrates that extends from the stomach to the anus and is divided into distinctive sections for handling the processes of digestion and absorption of food and the elimination of waste.

In the adult human the intestine is divided into the small and large intestines. The small intestine is a tightly coiled, hollow tube about 6 m (20 ft) in length and made up of the DUODENUM, the jejunum, and the ileum, in that order. The large intestine, which is also a coiled tube, is joined to the ileum at a region called the cecum, about 1.5 m (5 ft) in length, and consists of the colon and rectum. The great length of the intestine is an adaptation that provides an extensive surface for efficiently breaking down digestible foods and absorbing the products. Some organisms, notably teleost (bony) fish, have numerous supplementary sacs known as caeca, and sharks and a few other fish possess a so-called spiral valve, which is a membranous sheet traversing the intestine. In land vertebrates generally, however, the surface of the small intestine is supplemented by elevations of its lining, or mucous membrane, to form fingerlike folds called villi.

Small Intestine. The duodenum in mammals is notable for its role in the ENDOCRINE SYSTEM because it produces HORMONES such as cholecystokinin, which causes the GALLBLADDER to release bile, a substance that aids in the digestion of fat; secretin, which stimulates the PANCREAS to release digestive enzymes; and enterogastrone, which inhibits the secretion of hydrochloric acid by the STOMACH after the stomach contents have passed into the duodenum.

At the end of the cecum is a small dead-end structure called the APPENDIX. In such animals as the horse and cow, which subsist solely on grasses and other plants, the cecum is large and an important site for the digestion of tough plant fibers (cellulose) by its specialized bacterial population. In humans the cecum and appendix have no important function.

The intestine is surrounded by layers of smooth muscle, a circular layer on the inside and a longitudinal layer on the outside. The contractions of the various muscles propel the contents of the intestine from one segment to the next, sometimes delaying movement to enhance the digestive or absorptive processes. The small intestine is the site of digestion and absorption of nutrients and retention of waste materials. Very few digestible substances reach the large intestine.

Large Intestine. The colon performs the vital function of absorbing water and salts from the undigested residues and passing them into the bloodstream so that they are not lost

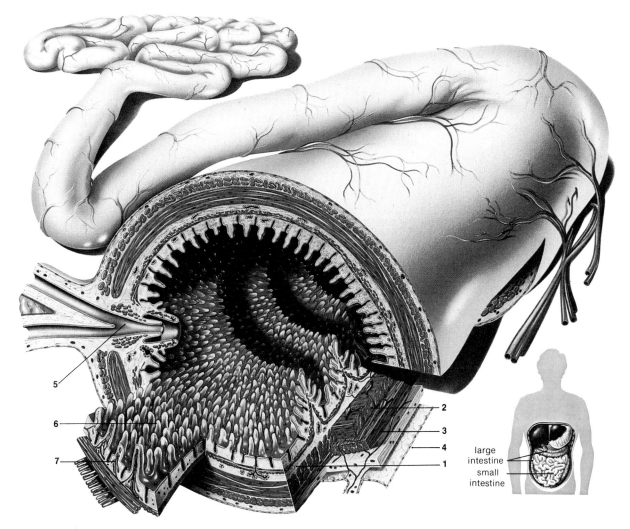

The small intestine completes the digestion of food delivered from the stomach and selectively absorbs the food into the blood and lymph vessels. About 7 m (23 ft) in length, the small intestine is folded and coiled into a compact mass within the abdominal cavity. The intestinal wall is lined with an inner mucosal layer (1), circular (2) and longitudinal (3) layers of smooth muscle, and an outer layer of connective tissue (4). The muscular layers contract in a wavelike motion (peristalsis), which pushes food forward in the intestines. Pancreatic juice and bile enter the small intestine from the hepatopancreatic duct (5) and break down food into simple components; the digested food then is absorbed by villi (6), fingerlike projections that carpet the inner surface of the intestines. Each villus contains a lacteal (7), which has blood and lymph vessels that carry digested food to the rest of the body. Waste matter with some digested food passes from the small intestine into the large intestine, where food is absorbed and waste matter is excreted by way of the colon and rectum.

through the anus. A too rapid passage of material through the colon does not permit adequate absorption of water and results in DIARRHEA. If unchecked, diarrhea leads to dehydration and loss of salts that can be fatal, especially in infants. An unusually slow passage through the large intestine, on the other hand, may lead to excessive removal of water and cause CONSTIPATION, which is characterized by a hard mass of undigested residues.

The normal bowel movement, or defecation, begins with the stimulation by feces of sensory nerve receptors in the rectum. The nerve receptors trigger a complex reflex action, which results in relaxation of the sphincter muscles at the junction of the rectum and anus, allowing defecation unless a conscious effort is made to override the reflex.

ROY HARTENSTEIN

Bibliography: Creamer, Brian, ed., *The Small Intestine* (1974); Davenport, H. W., *Physiology of the Digestive Tract: An Introductory Text*, 4th ed. (1977); Friedman, M. H., ed., *Functions of the Stomach and Intestine* (1974); Morton, J. E., *Guts: The Form and Function of the Digestive System* (1967).

See also: DIGESTION, HUMAN.

Intolerable Acts

The Intolerable Acts was an American label for the laws sponsored by Lord NORTH's ministry and enacted by the British Parliament in 1774 in response to the BOSTON TEA PARTY. Also called the Coercive Acts, they were a major factor contributing to the outbreak of the AMERICAN REVOLUTION.

The Boston Port Act (March 31) closed the harbor to commerce pending compensation by the city for the destroyed tea. The Massachusetts Government Act (May 20) made the upper house of the legislature appointive by the crown, increased the governor's patronage powers, provided that juries be summoned by sheriffs rather than elected, and banned all town meetings not authorized by law or gubernatorial approval. The Impartial Administration of Justice Act (May 20) made possible a change of venue to another colony or to England for crown officers charged with capital crimes while performing official duties. Two acts that were not specifically related to Massachusetts were also deemed "intolerable" by Americans. The Quartering Act (June 2) authorized civil officers to requisition houses and empty buildings to house royal troops where barracks were unavailable or unsuitable. The QUEBEC ACT (June 22) granted civil government and religious liberty to the Roman Catholic inhabitants of the former French colony and extended the Canadian boundary to the Ohio River.

Although intended primarily to prevent disorder in Massachusetts, the Intolerable Acts united Americans in a common cause and led to the First CONTINENTAL CONGRESS.

LARRY R. GERLACH

Bibliography: Ammerman, David, *In the Common Cause: American Response to the Coercive Acts of 1774* (1974).

Intracoastal Waterway   [in-truh-koh'-stul]

The Intracoastal Waterway is a 4,800-km-long (3,000-mi) watercourse for shipping and pleasure vessels along the Atlantic and Gulf coasts of the United States; it utilizes the protected bays, inlets, and sounds of the ocean, rivers, and artificial channels. The Atlantic Intracoastal Waterway stretches about 3,000 km (1,900 mi) from Boston to Key West, Fla. The CHESAPEAKE AND DELAWARE CANAL, Cape Cod Canal, and Albemarle and Delaware Canal are major components of the waterway, which passes Trenton, N.J., Norfolk, Va., and Miami, Fla.

The Gulf Intracoastal Waterway begins at Apalachee Bay on Florida's west coast and flows for 1,800 km (1,100 mi) to Brownsville, Texas (at the border with Mexico), passing Mobile, Ala., New Orleans, La., and the Texas port cities of Port Arthur, Galveston (part of the Houston port complex), and Corpus Christi.

The original plan for the Intracoastal Waterway called for a canal in northern Florida connecting the two branches; a 1971 presidential order, however, prevented its construction for environmental reasons. The toll-free system connects with the Hudson River and NEW YORK STATE BARGE CANAL and the Mississippi River. The waterways are used to haul petroleum and petroleum products, manufactured goods, and foodstuffs. The U.S. Army Corps of Engineers maintains the system.

SARAH FUSFELD

introspection

Introspection is the consideration of one's own inner experiences, or "seeing in." Systematic introspection, an organized system for reporting personal experiences under special conditions, was a research method of structural psychology, the dominant school of psychology from about 1880 to 1920. In modern investigations of human behavior, introspection is usually replaced or supplemented by techniques of observation.

introversion: see EXTRAVERSION-INTROVERSION.

intrusive rock: see IGNEOUS ROCK.

intuition   [in-too-ish'-uhn]

Intuition is the knowledge of a concept, truth, or solution to a problem, which is arrived at apparently spontaneously, without conscious steps of reasoning or inquiry. One explanation of intuition is that it is the result of a special faculty, or ability, or a special sympathy with the object known. Some philosophers and psychologists claim that human phenomena can be understood only by special intuition; many psychologists, however, attribute intuition to a thought process that occurs too fast for a person to be conscious of it. For instance, numerous minimal cues may be rapidly integrated, making possible identification of the present experience in relation to past experiences.

Inuit: see ESKIMO.

invention

Invention is an act of creativity that results in a device, process, or technique novel enough to produce a significant change in the application of technology. The application is fundamental to invention. Credit for invention has frequently been claimed for someone who conceived an idea, but the inventor is the person who not only had the idea but worked out the method of putting it into practice. Thus LEONARDO DA VINCI conceived of flying machines and self-propelled vehicles and showed great ingenuity in working out possible designs, but he did not invent either the airplane or the automobile.

The element of novelty has various forms; it may be a new device or process, or even material, but it may also consist of a combination of existing knowledge in a manner not previously thought of. James WATT added a separate condensing chamber—a new device—to Thomas NEWCOMEN's atmospheric engine and created the steam engine; the basic patent of the Wright brothers (see WRIGHT, ORVILLE AND WILBUR) was their method of warping the wings in coordination with rudder movements in order to attain lateral stability, essentially a combination of existing techniques. Novelty is so difficult to define that in modern times it usually has to be determined in each specific case by patent offices and ultimately by courts of law.

The characteristics of inventiveness are as difficult to define as novelty. In modern times, when inventors have been identified, they usually appear to share the following qualities: an insatiable curiosity; determination in pursuit of their ideas, sometimes to the point of obsession; technical training or native technical skill; some familiarity with science; and the indefinable trait called *creativity*.

Theories of Invention. The two general theories of invention are the deterministic and the individualistic. The deterministic theory holds that when economic, technical, and cultural conditions are ripe, an invention will be made by one inventor or another; who does it is just historical accident. This theory has some support in the numerous instances of simultaneous and independent invention, such as the Bessemer-Kelly process of making steel (1857) and the Hall-Héroult process for reducing aluminum (1886). It also helps to explain the competing claims that emerged over the invention of the steamboat, the electric telegraph, the incandescent lamp, and the airplane. The theory is also plausible because timing is unquestionably important in invention. Leonardo had brilliant insights, but the Italy of his day lacked the level of technology or the economic structure required to make his ideas operative. Also, since inventors normally want reward or at least recognition, they are likely to focus on projects that are reasonably attainable and for which there is a recognizable need or demand.

Nevertheless, determinism does not sufficiently account for invention. It does not explain the emergence of a creative genius who has the insight that others miss, or of an inventor such as Oliver EVANS, whose automated grist mill (1785) run by water power and whose steam road vehicle (1805) were demonstrated in operation but were ahead of their time. These failures of the deterministic theory give rise to the individualistic theory of invention, which identifies the individual as the most important element in the inventive process.

Patents. Inventiveness can be found throughout history. The wheel and axle, definitely a conscious invention and not a technological accident, dates from about 3000 BC. Only within the last 500 years, however, has invention come to be recognized as an activity deserving encouragement by society. The first known PATENT was issued in Florence, Italy, in 1421, and Venice enacted the first general patent law in 1474. The general model for patent systems in the Western world was the English Statute of Patents and Monopolies (1623), which specifically gave the right of patent protection to the first inventor of a new device or technique. The Constitution of the United States followed the accepted pattern of the Western world; in Article I, Section 8, clause 8, it empowers Congress "to promote the progress of science and useful arts by securing for limited times to authors and inventors the exclusive right to their respective writings and discoveries."

Inventiveness in History. These patent systems came before the rise of modern industrialism, which they undoubtedly helped to bring about by stimulating inventiveness. For the first time in history, inventors were recognized as individuals deserving social approval and entitled to reward.

Invention has also flourished in other periods. Medieval Europe showed great ingenuity in applying wind and water power and developing gearing, and China in the same period had even greater technical achievements. But most technical progress during this period was in minor increments, which were kept closely guarded secrets by the craft guilds; even with the great breakthrough inventions like gunpowder, the magnetic compass, and papermaking, neither the name of the individual inventor nor the date of the invention is known.

Although no simple explanation can be made for the subsequent focusing of inventive leadership in western Europe, it seems clear that by the time of the Renaissance inventiveness had come to be more highly regarded in the West than in China. Continuing step-by-step advances in technology were important because successful invention requires an adequate background of technical competence. By the 18th century not only was invention encouraged, but also the level of European technology was capable of making the ideas work.

Both European and American patent systems have been based on the premise that invention is an individual act, and at the time the systems were created, this assumption was accurate enough. The increasing complexity of modern technology, however, has inevitably affected the inventive process. Technological change had to become systematized, with organized effort directed to identified objectives. In the 20th century this process has become known as research and development (R & D).

This change is succinctly expressed in Alfred North Whitehead's statement that the greatest invention of the 19th century was the invention of the method of invention. Whitehead referred to the growth of organized research, which was becoming prominent by the end of the 19th century. Even Thomas A. EDISON, the personification of the self-taught inventive genius, did his most important work with the aid of a well equipped laboratory at Menlo Park, N.J., and a trained technical staff. The enormous growth of R & D in the 20th century has led some observers to conclude that the individual inventor is obsolete, but this position is not substantiated by the facts. The research laboratories have developed such outstanding achievements as radar (U.S. Naval Research Laboratory, 1922), nylon (Dupont, 1938), and transistors (Bell Laboratories, 1948). On the other hand, television, the Polaroid camera, the jet engine, the ball-point pen, and the Xerox copying machine all originated with individual inventors working on their own.

In reality the laboratory and the individual are more complementary than competitive. A good research laboratory possesses resources that an individual working independently cannot match. However, through history most technological progress has come as incremental minor improvements and refinements rather than through major inventions, and organized research is well suited for this kind of development. Organization, however, may inhibit originality and creativity, so the seminal discoveries are still likely to be made by inventors in the classic individualistic tradition.

Although the lack of information about invention and inventors in previous stages of history makes accurate comparison between periods and societies difficult, some similarities emerge. The qualities that characterize inventors can be found among all peoples and at all times, and these qualities are responsive to the values placed by a society on technological skill and achievement. The most prolific era of invention began with the INDUSTRIAL REVOLUTION of the 18th century; each new technical advance has provided the foundation for others. The pace of invention has steadily accelerated, both by individual inventors and through organized research, because as the technology becomes more complex, both the opportunity and the need for invention become greater.   JOHN B. RAE

Bibliography: Aitken, Hugh G. J., *Syntony and Spark: The Origins of Radio* (1976); Baker, R., *New and Improved: Inventors and Inventions that Have Changed the Modern World* (1978); De Bono, Edward, *Eureka: An Illustrated History of Inventions from the Wheel to the Computer* (1974); Gilfillan, S. C., *The Sociology of Invention* (1970); Jewkes, John, et al., *The Sources of Invention*, 2d ed. (1971); Morison, Elting E., *Men, Machines and Modern Times* (1966); National Geographic Society, *Those Inventive Americans* (1971); Stein, Ralph, *The Great Inventions* (1976).

See also: SCIENTIFIC RESEARCH; TECHNOLOGY; TECHNOLOGY, HISTORY OF.

Invercargill [in'-vur-kar'-gil]

Invercargill (1977 est. pop., 49,900), the southernmost New Zealand city, is located in Southland County on the southern coast of South Island. It is situated along the Waihopai River, about 175 km (110 mi) southwest of Dunedin. Invercargill is the commercial center for locally produced farm products. Textile weaving and lumbering are also important. The city was founded in 1856 and served as the capital of the former Otago province from 1861 to 1930.

Inverness (city) [in-vur-nes']

Inverness is a town in the HIGHLAND administrative region of northern Scotland. It has a population of 36,600 (1974 est.). Located near Moray Firth on the River Ness, Inverness is the eastern terminus of the Caledonian Canal. A seaport and commercial center surrounded by rich farmland, Inverness is also a tourist site. The capital of the ancient kingdom of the Picts, Inverness became a chartered burgh in the 12th century and a royal burgh in the 13th century. Abertarff House, one of its many 16th- and 17th-century buildings, now contains a Gaelic museum. Nearby is the battlefield of Culloden, where Prince Charles Edward Stuart was routed by the English in 1746, during the Jacobite uprising.

Inverness (county)

Inverness is a former county of northwestern Scotland that included many of the islands of the HEBRIDES. The burgh of Inverness was its county town. The mainland section of the county, part of the mountainous area known as the HIGHLAND, is bisected southwest to northeast by the Caledonian Canal and a series of lakes, including Loch NESS. BEN NEVIS, Great Britain's highest peak (1,343 m/4,406 ft), is in Inverness. First inhabited by the Picts, Inverness came under Scottish rule in 1078. The clans of the area figured prominently in the Jacobite uprisings of the 18th century. Inverness was divided between the administrative regions of Highland and Western Isles during the 1975 reorganization of local government in Scotland.

inverse square law

Any natural law with the mathematical form $y = 1/x^2$ is an inverse square law because y varies inversely as the square of x. Many physical laws of this type exist, particularly where x represents a distance—for example, Newton's law of gravitation, Coulomb's law of electrostatics, and the intensity of light from a point source. In each case an effect diminishes uniformly from a point, analogous to an expanding sphere, and the area of a sphere's surface is proportional to the square of its radius.

See also: LAW, PHYSICAL.

inversion [in-vur'-zhuhn]

An inversion occurs whenever the normal decrease of atmospheric temperature or moisture or both with height changes anomalously over a relatively short vertical interval. Often inversions become sufficiently strong to produce a layer in the atmosphere where the temperature actually increases with height—that is, warm air covers cold air. Inversions, especially strong ones, limit the mixing upward of atmospheric pollutants, and thus they lower air quality if sources of contamination exist near the ground (see POLLUTION, ENVIRONMENTAL). Such strong inversions often form under stagnant high-pressure systems in the middle and upper latitudes.

Nocturnal inversions are those that result from the night cooling of the lowest levels of the atmosphere. In the lower atmosphere a stable layer inversion caps the highly turbulent boundary layer that forms during sunny days over land, or when cold air blows over warmer ocean water. Over the trade wind region of the tropics, this inversion is called the trade-wind inversion. A frontal inversion occurs when warmer air overrides a synoptic-scale cold air mass.

At higher levels in the atmosphere the divisions between the troposphere and stratosphere (the TROPOPAUSE) and between the stratosphere and mesosphere (the stratopause) are also types of inversions.

Bibliography: Anthes, R. A., et al., *The Atmosphere*, 2d ed. (1978); Rosenberg, N. J., *Microclimate* (1974); Trewartha, Glenn T., *An Introduction to Climate*, 4th ed. (1968).

invertebrate [in-vurt'-i-brayt]

The invertebrate group is one of the two general categories of animals. The other group, vertebrates, includes those animals having backbones composed of a series of articulating vertebrae (fishes, amphibians, reptiles, birds, and mammals). Invertebrates lack vertebrae and include the remainder of the animal kingdom. The invertebrate group covers a wide range of organisms, from simple single-celled protozoans to those members of the phylum Chordata that lack a vertebral column. As such it is also an artificial category, splitting the phylum Chordata and including all the other phyla. Thus, invertebrates constitute almost the entire animal kingdom. Still, it is a useful category and unites a diverse assemblage of organisms that may be studied by a common approach distinct from the study of vertebrates.

HABITAT

In terms of habitat, distribution, and abundance, invertebrates are highly successful organisms. They occupy all habitats; the deepest samples from the deep-sea trenches include invertebrate animals. They are found in all types of marine substrates, from soft oozes to rocky bottoms. Swimming forms may be found at all depths of the sea and include forms specialized to live in the nutrient-poor, perpetually cold and sunless waters of the deep sea as well as a species specialized to live under the surface film of the open ocean. Invertebrates occur over a wide range of saline habitats, being common in fresh, brackish, and fully marine environments. Some specialized forms may also occur in hypersaline environments, where the salinity may greatly exceed full-strength seawater. These habitats occur in isolated lagoons along tropical coasts and pools high in the intertidal zone, where evaporation gradually increases their salinity.

Terrestrial habitats, including subterranean locations, are universally occupied by invertebrate forms. Even the air has an invertebrate fauna in insects and spiders. Some tiny spiders have been captured in high-altitude balloons.

In all of these habitats invertebrates may occupy a wide range of temperatures, from near 0° C (32° F) in the ocean depths to a few forms living in hot springs exceeding 55° C (131° F). Invertebrates also range over a wide series of oxygen conditions. Some are limited to richly oxygenated freshwater riffles while others may only be found in oxygen-free parasitic environments or oxygen-poor black sulfide muds.

Invertebrates also include many forms that live on or in other organisms. This category includes parasites that harm the host; commensals, which do not affect their host; and mutuals, which improve the condition of their host.

In all these habitats, invertebrate populations may reach astounding densities. Soil arthropods often attain densities of a half-million per square meter. The number of invertebrate species extant today is difficult to estimate. As many as 4.5 million species may exist, but only half have been named. Indeed, through habitat destruction, especially in the tropics, terrestrial species may be vanishing forever at a more rapid rate than scientists are discovering and describing them. The groups containing the largest number of species include the protozoans, roundworms, mollusks, and arthropods. All are estimated to have at least 100,000 species with only a fraction having been described. Among the arthropods, beetle species alone number at least 375,000.

FOSSIL RECORDS

Most invertebrate groups have ancient origins, and many have left a fossil record in old rocks. The study of the invertebrate fossil record is known as invertebrate paleontology.

The fossil record provides information of two kinds. Invertebrates with hard skeletal structures have left remains or imprints of them in the rocks by a process known as fossilization.

A more elusive record has been left by many soft-bodied, burrowing animals in the form of trace fossils, which are the remains of burrows, tubes, and track imprints in soft substrates that were gradually mineralized, leaving a permanent record.

The oldest invertebrate fossils date to the Precambrian Period of the Proterozoic geological epoch more than 530 million years ago. Fossils remaining from this period are few, and little is known of these life forms. Recent discoveries include a fossil clam believed to be more than 720 million years old. Fossil representatives of all major phyla with significant skeletal features have been found in the Cambrian Period (570–500 million years ago). The difference between the Precambrian and Cambrian periods may represent some unknown major event that led to the evolution of hardened skeletal structures for rapid movement (muscle attachments) or defense (armor).

As geological time passed, certain organisms that are extinct, or are a minor component today, flourished. The trilobites (related to modern horseshoe crabs) were dominant members of the Ordovician (500–425 million years ago) and Silurian Period (425–400 million years ago) faunas but then declined and were extinct by the end of the Permian Period (280–230 million years ago). Nautiloids, shelled squidlike mollusks, were an important component of these early periods. Today only the beautiful coiled *Nautilus* still exists. Some groups endured as faunal dominants for very long periods only to decline at a later date. The lamp shells (brachiopods) became abundant in the Ordovician Period and were a major marine group until the Paleocene Epoch of the Tertiary Period (65–55 million years ago). About 260 species of lamp shells remain today as compared with at least 12,000 described fossil forms.

Although most groups are as ancient as the Cambrian, the first traces of a few groups do not appear in the fossil record until a much later date. Primitive crustaceans are first seen in the Ordovician. Scorpions become the first air-breathing terrestrial animals by the Silurian, preceding the first vertebrate onto the uninhabited soil by about 50 million years. Primitive insects occur in the Devonian. Insects and arachnids (spiders, scorpions, and related groups) have greatly increased and continue to be important today.

Through examination of the fossil record we are able to obtain a glimpse into the life of the past. From fragmentary remains, paleontologists are able to describe the anatomy and even the ecology and behavior of these extinct forms, making use of the tantalizing fragments of evidence at their disposal. Description of the invertebrate fossil assemblages also has considerable economic importance as these associations and arrangements help geologists determine the age and type of different geological strata. These cues indicate, among other things, the oil-bearing potential of different regions.

Since the invertebrate group contains virtually the entire animal kingdom, it is not surprising that it includes bewilderingly diverse kinds of organisms. The following discussion proceeds generally from simple and primitive forms to more highly evolved types.

CLASSIFICATION

Protozoa. PROTOZOA are single-celled organisms. These individual cells are structurally much more complex, however, than any given cell in a multicellular organism. Protozoans are a common (30,000 described species), large group found in marine, freshwater, and terrestrial habitats and include many parasitic representatives, among them the causative agent of malaria, one of the most important human diseases.

Mesozoa. MESOZOANS are a small group (about 50 species) and entirely parasitic, one branch of which occurs only in the kidneys of octopuses and squids. These parasites consist of a small number of cells of merely a few cell types. Some zoologists regard them as genuinely primitive, whereas others classify them as degenerate flatworms.

Porifera. SPONGES (5,000 species) are simple, attached filter-feeding organisms. They are common in marine habitats; a few species are found in fresh water.

Coelenterata. COELENTERATES (10,000 species) include the jellyfishes, hydroids, sea anemones, and colonial corals. All are marine except for a few freshwater forms (including the hydra, the common pond dweller). The COMB JELLY (phylum Ctenophora, 80 species) is closely related to the coelenterates. All are marine, most being pelagic (deep-sea dwelling).

Platyhelminthes. FLATWORMS (nearly 13,000 species) are found in all habitats. This group includes the common planarian used extensively in the classroom and laboratory, as well as important parasitic groups, the flukes and tapeworms. Closely related are the RIBBON WORMS (phylum Nemertinea, 600 species), a mostly marine group with a very few freshwater, terrestrial, and parasitic members.

Pseudocoelomata. The pseudocoelomate phyla are mostly wormlike and are grouped together because they possess a few developmental similarities. SPINY-HEADED WORMS (phylum Acanthocephala, 300 species) are all parasitic. The adult worms are attached to vertebrate intestines. Life cycles are complex, involving two host species. The rotifers (1,500 species) are small freshwater organisms; a few are marine and parasitic. Gastrotrichs (phylum Gastrotricha, 150 species) are similar but are covered with bristles. They are inhabitants of fresh and marine water. The kinorhynchs (64 species) are all marine and are common in interstitial habitats, living in the fluid between the grains of mud or sand. The gnathostomulida (phylum GNATHOSTOMATA, 90 described species) are small wormlike animals living in the oxygen-poor environment of marine sands in shallow water. This poorly known habitat probably accounts for the fact that they escaped scientific detection until the mid-20th century. The roundworms, or NEMATODES (phylum Nematoda, 10,000 species described), are one of the most successful phyla. Parasitic members infect plants as well as every group of invertebrates and vertebrates (including human beings). Additionally, many are free-living marine, freshwater, and terrestrial types. With this great habitat diversity, nematodes are remarkable for their structural similarity. The gordian, or HORSEHAIR WORMS (phylum Nematomorpha, 250 species), are free-living aquatic forms as adults, but the juveniles are parasitic in the body cavities of arthropods.

Bryozoa. BRYOZOANS (4,000 species) are small, colonial, and mostly marine with a few freshwater representatives. They feed using a crescent-shaped crown of tentacles known as a lophophore. The small and structurally similar ENTOPROCTS (phylum Entoprocta) are sometimes included with the bryozoans although they show embryological similarities to the pseudocoelomates. Two other phyla also feed with a lophophore. The PHORONIDS are a small group (only 15 species), but they are often common animals in marine muds. Here, they live enclosed within a leathery or chitinous tube. The lamp shells, or BRACHIOPODS (phylum Brachiopoda, 260 species) are entirely marine and mostly deep-water inhabitants. They resemble clams but are attached to rocks by a flexible stalk and possess a lophophore.

Mollusca. The MOLLUSKS are a major phylum (130,000 species), including the snails, bivalves (clams and oysters), chitons, cephalopods (squids and octopuses), as well as a few minor groups. Mollusks have invaded every major environment, being found in marine, freshwater (snails and bivalves only), and terrestrial (snails only) habitats. A few snails are also parasitic. Mollusks include some of the largest invertebrates (giant clam and giant squid) and probably the most intelligent (squid and octopuses).

Annelida. The ANNELID worms (8,800 species) encompass many marine (polychaetes), freshwater, and terrestrial (earthworms and other oligochaetes) types and an important group of parasites (leeches). They all have many-segmented bodies and well-developed musculature. Three small phyla, all ma-

rine, are sometimes treated as annelid allies, the SPOONWORMS (phylum Echiura, 60 species), PEANUT WORMS (phylum Sipuncula, 275 species), and phylum Priapulida (8 species). All are burrowers, showing few remnants of their presumed former segmentation. The BEARDWORMS, phylum Pogonophora (80 species), are very elongate and dwell in deep-water sediments. Recognized in the early 20th century, recent evidence suggests that they are merely a type of polychaete annelid.

Onychophora. The ONYCHOPHORANS (65 species) are a curious "missing link" between the two great phyla Annelida and Arthropoda. They are small forms living under leaf litter of tropical forests.

Arthropoda. The ARTHROPODS (about 900,000 species) are enormously diverse. Recent work suggests that some of the major branches are not closely related and should be relegated to separate phyla. Arthropods include the chelicerates (trilobites, horseshoe crabs, spiders, scorpions, ticks, and mites). Present-day representatives are mostly terrestrial with ticks and mites representing important parasitic types. The crustaceans (fairy shrimp, ostracods, copepods, barnacles, shrimp, crabs, lobsters, pillbugs) are mostly marine, but also include important freshwater, terrestrial, and parasitic representatives. Millipeds and centipedes have only terrestrial representatives. The insects, however, include important freshwater and parasitic groups and a few marine forms. Insects dominate the terrestrial fauna. Among the parasitic insects are lice and fleas as well as a large group (more than 100,000 species) of wasps that are parasitoids of other insects. These parasitoid wasps look like parasites but they slowly devour the host and thus have a predatory character. Insects are also remarkable for their development of highly organized social colonies among the termites, ants, bees, and wasps.

Chaetagnatha. The ARROWWORMS (55 species) are a small group of transparent, unsegmented, pelagic predators. They feed on other marine planktonic animals.

Echinodermata. The ECHINODERMS (5,500 species) are the only major phylum limited solely to marine conditions. Included here are the sea lilies, sea cucumbers, sea urchins, sand dollars, starfish, and brittle stars. Acorn worms, or HEMICHORDATES (100 species), are also all marine. Most burrow in soft substrates.

Chordata. The final, partially invertebrate phylum encompasses three groups of seemingly dissimilar CHORDATES. Two are considered invertebrates, and the third and by far the largest is the vertebrates. All possess three distinctive features at some stage in their lives: a flexible stiffening notochord, a dorsal hollow nerve cord, and gill clefts. Of the two invertebrate groups, the urochordates (class Tunicata, 1,300 species) include the abundant, attached, filter-feeding sea squirts (tunicates) as well as some less well-known planktonic forms. Like the urochordates, the cephalochordates are entirely marine. Cephalochordates, however, are active swimmers, filter feeding while moving in and out of the sand along beaches in tropical and subtropical regions.

STRUCTURE AND FUNCTION

Because they are such a diverse group of organisms, many different schemes have been advanced to classify the invertebrates. Important features considered with regard to the greater complexity of the body plan are changes in the basic symmetry of the organism, its gut structure, the development of body cavities, and the increase in cell types and their arrangement in organ systems.

Body Plan. The cells of sponges and mesozoans are differentiated into a few cell types, and these tend to be organized into tissues, groups of similar cells having a coordinated function. There is no gut in these organisms, although in sponges water does move through a series of channels. The coelenterates show the next series of advances. Here, symmetry is radial (biradial in the comb jellies), a gut is present with a mouth but usually lacks an anal opening, and tissues are grouped into primitive organ systems such as the digestive system. All of the tissues tend to be arranged in outer and inner layers only.

In the flatworms the interior is filled with a solid mass of tissues and cells. Muscles tend to be extensively developed, and symmetry is now bilateral. With bilateral symmetry, the flatworms show the first signs of increasing cephalization, the tendency to group the sense organs and feeding structures at the anterior, or head, end. So situated, these features are now in a position to meet the environment. Ribbon worms are similar to flatworms but the gut is complete, with an anus.

The pseudocoelomates have developed the first primitive body cavity. It is not lined with a sheet of cells, like a peritoneum, and is thus not a true body cavity, or coelom. These phyla also exhibit well-developed and complete digestive tracts. Among the unique features of some pseudocoelomate groups is cell constancy, in which certain organs invariably consist of a constant number of cells.

The remaining phyla all have a coelom; although in some groups it is secondarily reduced. Because of the development of a coelomic body cavity, the higher invertebrates are able to attain life styles possible to only a limited extent in the primitive phyla. Here we see many strong swimmers and vigorous burrowers.

Based on details of embryological development the higher invertebrates are grouped into two main branches: the protostomes and the deuterostomes. In protostomes the mouth develops from the blastopore in the embryonic gut. In deuterostomes, the mouth develops an opening other than the blastopore, which becomes the anus. At the base of this separation lie the lophophorates, united in having a lophophore and sharing characteristics of both main branches. Protostomes include the annelids, annelid allies, mollusks, and arthropods, all closely related. The mollusks appear to have developed from a presumed annelid ancestor before segmentation (the serially repeated arrangement of many organs, typical of the annelids) was well developed. Segmentation allows for subsequent specialization of different segments for different functions: sensory perception, food capture, and respiratory, locomotive, and reproductive activities.

Among the arthropods, this specialization is carried to an extreme. Certain segments are fused together forming complex structures such as a head or an abdomen. The arthropod body cavity is greatly reduced. Only small cavities associated with the gonads, kidneys, and heart remain. It is replaced by a hemocoel, another type of functional body cavity filled with blood. A futher arthropodan elaboration is the sturdy exoskeleton, flexible and chitinized in most of the land-dwelling forms, sturdy and calcified in many marine arthropods. With this skeleton, arthropods also possess a series of jointed appendages. As do body segments, these appendages tend to serve specialized functions as mouth parts, walking legs, and swimming appendages.

Mollusks also show a reduction of their coelom in a manner similar to arthropods but have only traces of segmentation. In most groups a heavily calcified shell protects these animals from predators and environmental stress. In cephalopod mollusks (squids and octopuses) the shell is greatly reduced or absent. Cephalopods have highly developed muscular and nervous systems and rely on speed, agility, and intelligence instead.

The deuterostomes include the arrow worms, echinoderms, acorn worms, and the lower chordates. Relations here are obscure except that the last two groups appear to be more closely related. The vertebrates, being chordates, also appear on this branch. Echinoderms present an unusual body plan having reverted to radial symmetry. Certain echinoderm organ systems are without counterparts elsewhere in the animal kingdom. It has been suggested that if any of the phyla come from outer space, it is the echinoderms. Hemichordates are closely related to the chordates. Both have a specialized anterior chamber with gill slits serving the dual functions of filter feeding and respiration.

The body plan of certain parasitic forms differs greatly from that of their closest free-living relatives. Tapeworms and spiny-headed worms entirely lack a digestive tract. Food is absorbed through the general body surface. Parasites also tend to have prominent holdfasts, arrangements of hooks and suckers, to adhere to the host. As a result of the difficulty in locating hosts, parasitic forms often have outstanding reproductive capacities compared with related free-living forms.

Body Covering. The great structural diversity among invertebrates permits only a highlighting of common features here. Body surfaces may either consist of a delicate tissue layer or be covered with a tough and sometimes hard skeleton (for example, bryozoans, lamp shells, some annelids, mollusks, arthropods, and echinoderms). Only among the annelids and arthropods do we find terrestrial representatives; their external skeleton helps to prevent water loss, the chief stress produced by land environments. The integument of many invertebrates is often brilliantly colored, either providing camouflage or sometimes serving as a warning that the animal may be noxious. In the crustaceans, pigment granules occur in specialized cells, where they may be dispersed or contracted to permit gradual color change. In the cephalopod mollusks, pigment granules are found in little sacs operated by tiny sets of muscles. Here, color change can be instantaneous.

Bioluminescence. Representatives of several invertebrate phyla possess a capability for BIOLUMINESCENCE. Organs located in the integument emit cold light and are used for species-recognition signals or camouflage. The luminescent substances of animals may be either contained within cells or produced as secretions from groups of cells. Some animals produce their own light, whereas others contain bacteria or fungi that actually synthesize luminescent substances.

Circulatory System. Circulatory systems are absent in small species of all invertebrate phyla, because substances can be moved throughout the body via simple diffusion. These forms have an open circulation system. Body-cavity fluids also serve this distributory function. Most higher invertebrates have at least a partially closed circulatory system where the fluid moves through well-defined blood vessels at least part of the time. In these animals, hearts, acting as muscular pumps, are necessary organs. A well-developed closed circulatory system is perhaps best seen in annelid worms. Mollusks and arthropods have a partially closed system with hearts and a few large blood vessels, but each organ is ultimately bathed directly in blood.

Respiratory System. Like circulatory systems, respiratory systems are also associated with large size. Oxygen can diffuse directly through the general body surface of small organisms. Large aquatic animals (mollusks, arthropods, annelids, annelid allies, and echinoderms) all have evolved gill-like structures with enormously expanded surface areas to increase the rate of gas exchange. These structures are closely associated with the circulatory system to distribute oxygen directly to cells and remove waste gases. Terrestrial organisms have evolved more protected respiratory structures since exposed gills would quickly dry up on land. Land snails, scorpions, and spiders have evolved lunglike structures, called book lungs, and insects have a unique tracheal system of passageways leading from openings in the body surface to the vicinity of every body cell.

Excretory System. Excretory systems are a third organ system that tends to be most elaborately developed in large animals; simple diffusion suffices for small types. An excretory system basically involving a filtering structure leading to a duct that removes the wastes is found in most phyla above the coelenterates.

Nervous System. The nervous systems of invertebrates show a series of advances paralleling the evolution of the major vertebrate groups. Sponges have only a general sensitivity and no specialized sense organs. The coelenterates have a network of specialized nervous cells but are still capable of only general responses. Simple light receptors and balancing organs are also seen in this group. Flatworms have a well-defined nerve ladder and show coordinated responses to stimuli. Eyes are better developed but still only distinguish light from dark. Good images are formed only in mollusks, arthropods, and a few annelids, as compared to other invertebrates. The cephalopod eye is a remarkable parallel development to the vertebrate eye. A cornea, iris, lens, and associated musculature permit clear binocular images to be formed on the light-sensitive retina and carried thence to the well-developed brain for sensory processing. In association with their excellent vision, the nervous systems of these mollusks show other important advances. Giant nerve cells, having a width of about 1 mm (0.04 in), run the length of the body. Rapid conduction along these cells initiates the animal's rapid escape response.

Arthropods have a segmental nervous system with prominent nerve centers (fused ganglia) in each segment. Most crustaceans and insects possess compound eyes. Each eye is composed of many (sometimes hundreds) similar subunits. Each subunit is covered by a corneal layer and has a lens element and a few receptor cells. Light entering each of these subunits is prevented from passing to adjacent units by a series of pigmented cells between the subunits. Compound eyes seem to be particularly well suited to recognize rapid changes in movement, or detection of light and shade, rather than for the formation of images. In crustaceans the compound eyes are on movable stalks, and thus the visual field can be shifted or increased in size.

Many invertebrates show a wide variety of touch receptors, chemical sensors, and balance detectors in addition to light receptors. Sound production and reception appears to be largely limited to insects and crustaceans.

Echinoderms, while an advanced phylum in many respects, show only modest sensory capabilities related to their return to radial symmetry and a sedentary life-style.

In addition to nervous conduction, messages may also be transmitted through slower systems involving hormonal effects. These are perhaps best seen in the insects and crustaceans where the cyclical shedding of the exoskeleton is induced by the increase in concentration of the substance, ecdysone, in the blood. Maturation in insects is controlled by the level of juvenile hormone. A decrease in juvenile hormone production leads to maturation with cessation of growth in the adult insect.

Musculature. Sea anemones and higher invertebrates all have well-developed musculature. For worm-shaped organisms to be capable of subtle movements, locomotory muscles must be arranged in at least circular and longitudinal bands. The curious roundworms lack circular musculature. The whiplike movements imparted by antagonistic bands of only longitudinal muscles enables this group to be readily identified.

Reproductive System. All organisms must reproduce, and thus reproductive systems are well-defined even at the coelenterate level. In addition to gonads, most invertebrates have a wide variety of accessory reproductive structures. Ducts and channels permit movement of reproductive products. Sperm may be stored in the male reproductive system in seminal vesicles or in the female system in seminal receptacles. Forms producing shelled eggs, including flatworms, mollusks, and arthropods, have accessory glands to produce the shells and a storage chamber (uterus) to hold the finished product. Although many groups have separate male and female individuals, most flatworms, some mollusks, and a few arthropods have both sexes combined in a single individual. Reproductive development of both sexes may be simultaneous or sequential with first the male and then the female system maturing. Sex may be determined genetically or, in a few forms, such as slipper shell snails, sex may be environmentally determined. Among several of the lower invertebrates the primary form of reproduction is asexual, involving the division of the parent individual into two or more daughter individuals.

Regeneration. Most invertebrate phyla have excellent abilities to regenerate parts of the body if injured. The freshwater planarian flatworm can regenerate if cut into several pieces. More limited abilities typify other phyla. For example, crabs and shrimp are able to regenerate their appendages, but they must wait for the next time their exoskeleton is shed for this process to be completed.

Life Cycle. Many invertebrates have complicated life cycles. These developmental stages are often specialized for different functions. Many marine forms release numerous eggs that hatch as planktonic larvae, specialized for dispersal. Larval stages are followed by a habitat-selection stage, in which the organism attempts to settle in a habitat suitable for the development of the juvenile and adult forms. Between successive stages, these animals typically undergo complicated metamorphoses. Virtually every tissue and organ of a stage may be reorganized to form a new structure in the succeeding stage. Phyla with particularly complicated life cycles include the coelenterates, parasitic flatworms, chordates, and some arthropods (insects and crustaceans). ARMAND KURIS

Bibliography: Barrington, E. J., *Invertebrate Structure and Function* (1967); Barnes, R. D., *Invertebrate Zoology*, 3d ed. (1974); Gardiner, M. S., *The Biology of Invertebrates* (1972); Hyman, L. H., *The Invertebrates*, 6 vols. (1940-67); Meglitsch, P. A., *Invertebrate Zoology*, 2d ed. (1972); Russell-Hunter, W. D., *A Life of Invertebrates* (1979); Smith, E., et al., *The Invertebrate Panorama* (1971); Wells, M., *Lower Animals* (1968).

invertebrate zoology

Invertebrate ZOOLOGY is the study of the anatomy, physiology, behavior, and ecology of the INVERTEBRATES—animals lacking a backbone. The unicellular PROTOZOA are so distinctive that researchers of this group usually regard themselves as protozoologists rather than invertebrate zoologists. Insects are so numerous and economically important that this discipline has developed into a separate field of study, ENTOMOLOGY.

investiture controversy

In ecclesiastical tradition investiture is the conferring of symbols of higher office in the church to members of the church hierarchy, such as abbots of monasteries and bishops of dioceses. The question as to who should confer the symbols of office provoked a prolonged controversy during the high Middle Ages between the papacy and the secular rulers of Europe. When Christianity became the official state religion in the Roman Empire, the emperor approved and often nominated the higher clergy for office. In the medieval kingdoms, the secular rulers continued this practice; since bishops and abbots often held large estates (as feudatories of the crown) and performed secular as well as ecclesiastical functions, the monarchs had a crucial interest in maintaining control of

Henry IV, Holy Roman Emperor during the investiture controversy, kneels before two of Pope Gregory VII's most powerful allies, Abbot Hugo of Cluny and Countess Matilda of Tuscany, during his supplication to the pope. (Bibliotheca Apostolica Vaticana, Rome.)

their appointment. As papal power increased in the 11th and 12th centuries, the popes made a concerted effort to restore control of church offices and investiture to the hierarchy. This led to the investiture controversy.

Pope GREGORY VII (r. 1073–85) was the greatest of the reforming popes. Following upon the Benedictine Cluniac reform movement, the Gregorian reform movement enforced celibacy on the clergy and fought simony (the buying of church offices). Above all, Gregory battled for the freedom of the church from the secular powers. A synod of 1075 forbade all lay investiture of clergy, and from 1076 on Gregory fought all political control over the church. His chief opponent was Holy Roman Emperor HENRY IV, who could ill afford to have the German bishops become princes independent of the emperor. Henry attempted to depose Gregory, who responded (1076) by excommunicating Henry and declaring his office vacant. This action released all Henry's feudal vassals from their oaths of fealty. Faced with rebellion in Germany, Henry did penance before Gregory at Canossa (Jan. 25–28, 1077), forcing the pope to remove the ban of excommunication. The controversy continued, however, and effectively undermined the emperor's authority in Germany. Eventually Pope CALLISTUS II and Emperor HENRY V agreed to the compromise Concordat of Worms in 1122. The emperor guaranteed the free election of bishops and abbots and renounced the right to invest them with ring and staff, the symbols of their spiritual duties; however, in Germany (although not in Italy and Burgundy), the elections were to take place in the emperor's presence, and those elected were to pay homage to him as feudatories before consecration.

There was relatively little controversy over investiture in France, but in England, King HENRY I (r. 1100–35) struggled with Saint ANSELM, archbishop of Canterbury, over the same issue. The later Middle Ages saw the secular rulers reasserting their power once again against the papacy.   LEWIS W. SPITZ

Bibliography: Barraclough, Geoffrey, The Origins of Modern Germany, 2d ed. (1949; repr. 1966); Brooke, Z. N., Lay Investiture and its Relation to the Conflict of Empire and Papacy (1939); Morrison, Karl F., ed., The Investiture Controversy: Issues, Ideals, and Results (1971); Tellenbach, Gerd, Church, State, and Christian Society at the Time of the Investiture Controversy, trans. by R. F. Bennett (1959; repr. 1970).

See also: CHURCH AND STATE.

investment: see SAVING AND INVESTMENT.

investment banking

Investment banking is the distribution of new issues of STOCKS and BONDS to the investing public. An investment banking firm serves as an intermediary between the company or government agency issuing the security and the investors—insurance companies, mutual funds, pension funds, and the public—who buy them. In effect a financial wholesaler, an investment banking firm, buys a large block of securities from the issuer and sells it in smaller quantities to the public. Investment bankers may form a group or syndicate to market a large issue. In the process known as underwriting the bankers take responsibility for selling the securities at an agreed-upon price and establishing a permanent market for them. If they are unable to sell a security at the offering price listed, they may suffer a loss. Investment banking has no connection with the commercial or deposit BANKING SYSTEM. Investment banking enables the capital market system to function smoothly by making funds immediately available to businesses and providing investment opportunities.

Bibliography: Carosso, Vincent P., Investment Banking in America: A History, ed. by Martin V. Sears and Irving Katz (1970).

Invisible Man, The

The Invisible Man (1952), Ralph ELLISON's first novel, won a National Book Award and established Ellison as an important new talent. The novel focuses on an idealistic young Southern black man who recognizes the limitations on the social

role he is expected to play only after his forthrightness destroys his college career and ultimately jeopardizes his life. Gradually, after moving north to New York City, he realizes that he is altogether "invisible" to white society. Because even the Communists with whom he has become involved use him as a token, he concludes that there is no hope in political action. Finally, he chooses to live underground in a Harlem cellar.   CHARLOTTE D. SOLOMON

Bibliography: Reilly, John M., ed., Twentieth Century Interpretations of "Invisible Man" (1970); Trimmer, Joseph F., A Casebook on Ralph Ellison's "Invisible Man" (1972).

Io   [ee'-oh]

Io, the third-closest known satellite of the planet JUPITER, is the most volcanically active solid body known in the solar system. Photographs taken by the Voyager 1 spacecraft in 1979 revealed the existence of at least 8 active volcanos and more than 100 caldera on Io's surface. The most widely accepted theory posits that tidal forces generated within Io by the gravitational attraction of Jupiter and the other three Galilean satellites have melted most of the interior of Io and now cause a periodic rising and falling of the relatively thin remaining crust; the observed eruptions would thus represent the release of heat generated by this process. The primary constituent of the volcanic gases appears to be sulfur dioxide. Some of the volcanic products apparently escape into space to form, near Io's orbit, a plasma torus composed of sulfur and hydrogen ions.

Io is a 3,636-km-diameter (2,259-mi) body that appears in VOYAGER photographs as yellow, red, brown, black, and white. Orbiting Jupiter at a mean distance of 422,000 km (262,000 mi), it has a period of revolution of 1 day 18 hr 27 min 33.5 sec. Its surface temperature has been measured at $-148°$ C ($-235°$ F), although a 27° C (80° F) temperature was recorded by the Voyager spacecraft in the vicinity of a volcanic plume.   CRAIG B. WAFF

Bibliography: Beatty, J. Kelly, "The Far-Out Worlds of Voyager 1," Sky and Telescope, May and June 1979, and "Voyager's Encore Performance," Sky and Telescope, September 1979.

iodine   [y'-uh-dine]

Iodine, atomic number 53, symbol I, is a solid nonmetallic element of the HALOGEN family, a group that includes the elements fluorine, chlorine, and bromine. At room temperature iodine is a lustrous, blue-black, crystalline solid of atomic weight 126.9045.

Iodine is the least water-soluble halogen, but its solubility is appreciably increased in aqueous solutions of sodium iodide, due to the formation of polyiodide complex ions. It dissolves readily in alcohol, chloroform, carbon tetrachloride, and benzene.

HISTORY

Iodine was first observed in 1811 by Bernard Courtois, a saltpeter manufacturer. In his manufacturing process he used the ashes of various seaweeds washed ashore on the beaches of Normandy and Brittany. While washing these ashes in sulfuric acid he noticed a dark, solid precipitate. The precipitate sublimed upon heating, forming a violet vapor that condensed on cold surfaces as a dark, crystalline solid. Although he suspected the importance of this discovery, Courtois had neither equipment nor funds to carry out the investigation necessary to ascertain its true nature. He therefore asked Charles Bernard Desormes and Nicholas Clément to complete the work, and it was they who announced the discovery of a new element. In 1813, Sir Humphrey Davy's electrical experiments indicated the substance was, indeed, a new element. Further proof was supplied by Joseph Gay-Lussac's classic chemical experiments, and it was he who named the element for the color of its vapor.

In 1819, Jean Baptiste Dumas provided proof that iodine existed in the sponges that had long been used to treat GOITER. He also proposed that the element could be more advantageously ingested as a dilute alcoholic solution, as potassium iodide (KI), or dissolved in a potassium iodide solution. By 1820, data had been published linking kelp as a goiter treatment to the presence of iodine in this sea plant, and had begun a lifelong study of its physiological uses. In 1814, J. J. Colin advanced microanalytical chemistry by the discovery that the starch reaction with iodine produced a blue coloration so intense and so sensitive that iodine could be detected in amounts as low as one part in 400,000.

OCCURRENCE

Iodine is the 44th most abundant element in the cosmos, the 62d most abundant in the Earth's crust, and the 17th most abundant of those dissolved in seawater (gases excluded). Although scarce, iodine is widely distributed in nature, occurring in underground brines, rocks, soils, and essentially all living material even though apparently not necessary for life. Because of this general distribution and its low abundance, no large deposits of iodine exist; however, several living systems are able to concentrate it within themselves, thus becoming important sources. Examples are the sea plants and algae such as the Laminaria family. Because of the magnitude of the deposits, the Chilean nitrates, in which it is an impurity, are also important sources of iodine.

CHEMICAL PROPERTIES

Like all members of the halogen family iodine is very reactive, although it is somewhat less reactive than the other halogens. Both bromine and chlorine liberate free iodine from aqueous solutions of iodides by reactions similar to: $2NaI_{(aq)} + Br_{2(g)} \rightarrow 2NaBr_{(aq)} + I_{2(s)}$. Iodine vapor reacts directly with most metals to form metal iodides, similar to its reaction with nickel: $Ni + I_2 \rightarrow NiI_2$. Iodine also reacts with water (1) although the reverse reaction predominates at equilibrium; reaction (2) more accurately describes the chemical system:

$$I_2 + H_2O \rightleftharpoons 2H^+ + 2I^- + \tfrac{1}{2}O_2 \qquad (1)$$
$$I_2 + H_2O \rightleftharpoons H^+ + I^- + HOI \qquad (2)$$

Iodine reacts with hydrogen sulfide (H_2S) to liberate sulfur. Its reaction with phosphorus, arsenic, and antimony is similar to that with bismuth: $3I_2 + 2Bi \rightarrow 2BiI_3$. Oxygen compounds of iodine have been prepared having the formulas I_2O_4, I_4O_9, and I_2O_5, although it is probable that I_2O_4 is more correctly $(IO)IO_3$, and that I_4O_9 is $I(IO_3)_3$.

The several oxidation states available in iodine, -1, $+1$, $+3$, $+5$, and $+7$, help explain the interhalogen compounds (halogens combined with halogens) such as ICl, ICl_3, IF_5, IF_7, $K(IF_6)$, IOF_3 and IO_2F, all of which are stable at room temperature.

PRODUCTION

Iodine may be prepared in the laboratory by distilling potassium iodide (KI) or sodium iodide (NaI) with sulfuric acid and manganese dioxide:

$$2KI + 3H_2SO_4 + MnO_2 \rightarrow I_2 + 2KHSO_4 + MnSO_4 + 2H_2O$$

or by the reaction of potassium iodate (KIO_3) or sodium iodate ($NaIO_3$) with potassium iodide and sulfuric acid:

$$KIO_3 + 5KI + 3H_2SO_4 \rightarrow 3I_2 + 3K_2SO_4 + 3H_2O$$

Commercial iodine is produced principally (50%) from Chilean nitrate deposits containing about 0.2% calcium iodate ($Ca(IO_3)_2$) as an impurity. Iodine is recovered from solutions of the nitrate using sodium bisulfite ($NaHSO_3$) as a reducing agent. Other significant sources of iodine are underground brines such as those found in Michigan. The seaweeds that are able to concentrate the element are now less important in the United States but are still major sources of iodine in some countries.

USES

The principal use of iodine is in the health sciences. Almost from the year of its discovery it has been used to prevent goiter and now does so by the widespread use of sodium or potassium iodide additives to common table salt. Tincture of iodine has been used as a disinfectant, although iodine complexes now predominate in this application. Iodine complexed with surfactants are used in common sanitizers. Radio-

active iodine, ^{131}I, has found important use in tracer studies, including studies of the thyroid gland.

Other uses of iodine include its use in photographic papers, as tracers used to study stereochemistry, in dyes, as a catalyst, as an indicator in analytic chemistry, in engraving, in special soaps and lubricants, to seed clouds in rainmaking experiments, and as a measure of the degree of unsaturation of organic compounds. CHARLES HOWARD

Bibliography: Downs, A. J., and Adams, C. J., *The Chemistry of Chlorine, Bromine, Iodine and Astatine* (1975); Weeks, Mary E., *Discovery of the Elements*, 7th ed. (1968).

Iol [ee'-ohl]

Iol, at present-day Cherchel on the coast of Algeria, 96 km (60 mi) west of Algiers, was founded as a small Carthaginian port. Under Roman rule it prospered through its strategic location on Atlantic and Mediterranean trade routes. After annexation by Rome (33 BC), the city—renamed Caesarea after Augustus Caesar—was rapidly developed by King Juba II, who embellished it with a theater, baths, and high-quality copies of classical Greek and Hellenistic sculptures. The city became (AD 40) the capital of the province of Mauretania Caesariensis, supporting a population of about 100,000. Economic and political problems in the 3d and 4th centuries brought a decline that culminated in its destruction (429) by the VANDALS.

The rectilinear street plan, which focused on a central forum, was bounded by a city wall 7 km (4.5 mi) long. Continued occupation of the site has left visible only traces of the ancient structures. Two public baths, an aqueduct, several temples, a theater, amphitheater, and hippodrome have been identified, along with a lighthouse on the island protecting the harbor. Polychrome mosaics with scenes from Greco-Roman mythology and North African agricultural life have been recovered from villas in the city. JOHN P. OLESON

Bibliography: Raven, Simon, *Rome in Africa* (1969).

ion [y'-ahn]

An ion is an atom, a group of atoms, or a free subatomic particle that bears an electric charge. Atoms generally have the ability to capture additional electrons to form negative atomic ions ($Cl + e^- \rightarrow Cl^-$) or to lose electrons to form positive ions ($Ca \rightarrow Ca^{2+} + 2e^-$). In general, atoms tend to form a specific ion, positive or negative, singly or multiply charged.

Groups of atoms can form ions by the loss or gain of electrons, protons, or other ions:

$$O_2 \rightarrow O_2^+ + e^-$$
$$H_2O + H^+ (proton) \rightarrow H_3O^+$$
$$HgCl_2 + 2Cl^- \rightarrow HgCl_4^{2-}$$

Ions often have a very transient existence. In an electric discharge through gases, molecules are disrupted into ions but immediately reform into molecular combinations as soon as the electrical stress is over. Many ions can have a stable, permanent existence in the liquid or solid phase if they are in close proximity to oppositely charged ions. Salts, such as sodium chloride, are ionic solids. Seawater is a solution of many kinds of ions in a dynamic but stable system.

Ionization Energy. If sufficient energy is applied, electrons can be extracted from any substance. The energy may be supplied by particle-particle collisions, electrostatic fields or electromagnetic radiation. The amount of energy required to remove one electron from a neutral atom is its ionization energy, or ionization potential. The ionization energy of an element is measured by subjecting a gaseous sample of the element to a beam of electrons. The energy of the electron beam is increased until electrons are removed from the atoms. This energy level is called the *first ionization energy*. Sodium, for example, requires 5.1 electron volts (eV) for removal of the first electron from the atom: $Na + 5.1$ $eV \rightarrow Na^+ + e^-$. The elements of the alkali metal group, which contains sodium, have the lowest ionization energies. Next lowest are those of the alkali earth metals. Highest ionization energies are those of the inert gases, followed by the halogens.

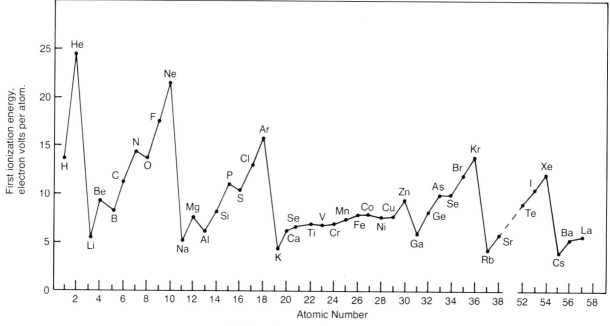

Relationship between the first ionization energy
and the number of the element.

Electron Affinity. Atoms also have an electron affinity, i.e., a tendency to gain electrons. When a neutral atom captures an electron, a negative ion results. Metals have relatively little electron affinity in contrast with nonmetals. Also, metal atoms lose electrons much more easily than do nonmetals. Consequently, many metals will react with nonmetals to form salts, compounds that are composed of ions. For example, sodium atoms will react with chlorine atoms in an ionization reaction to produce sodium ions and chloride ions: $Na + Cl \rightarrow Na^+ + Cl^-$. In contrast, atoms that have equal or relatively close electron affinities *share* electrons as they combine to form molecules. Two oxygen atoms will continue to form a neutral molecule, O_2.

Photolytic Ionization. Molecules and atoms can be ionized by radiation. This phenomenon is common in the upper atmosphere where highly energetic ultraviolet light and X rays are in abundant supply. An example is the ionization of oxygen by the absorption of ultraviolet light: O_2 + ultraviolet light $\rightarrow O_2^+ + e^-$. Many such photolytic ionization reactions have been characterized in the laboratory.

Solubility. Water is a universal solvent because of its ability to stabilize ions. The water molecule is *polar*, which means that its opposite ends are somewhat positively and negatively charged. This enables several water molecules to surround an ion and partially neutralize its charge. The positive ends of the water molecules in close proximity to a negative ion tend to decrease the intensity of the charge on that ion. Adjacent positive ions are similarly insulated, favoring the dissolution of ionic substances. This theory is in agreement with the fact that many salts will dissolve readily in water but will not dissolve in solvents composed of nonpolar molecules, such as carbon tetrachloride. Because of the high dielectric constant of water, which is a measure of the polarity of its molecules, many molecular materials will ionize when reacted with water. Hydrogen chloride, a molecular gas, will completely ionize when dissolved in water: $HCl + H_2O \rightarrow H_3O^+ + Cl^-$.

JOHN T. NETTERVILLE

Bibliography: Llewellyn-Jones, Frank, *Ionization and Breakdown In Gases* (1966); Pass, Geoffrey, *Ions in Solution 3: Inorganic Properties* (1973); Pauling, Linus, *The Nature of the Chemical Bond* (1960); Sienko, Mitchell, and Plane, Robert, *Chemistry*, 5th ed. (1976).

See also: CATION; ION EXCHANGE.

ion exchange

Ion exchange is a method of replacing one type of ion in a solution with another. Hard water containing calcium, iron, and magnesium ions can be made soft by passing the water through ZEOLITES, natural clay mixtures of sodium aluminosilicates. The resulting soft water will have sodium ions in an amount equivalent to the hard-water ions removed. Such reactions, called ion-exchange reactions, can be continued until the sodium ion is depleted in the zeolite: $2NaAlSi_2O_6 + Ca^{2+} \rightarrow Ca(AlSi_2O_6)_2 + 2Na^{2+}$. Many ion-exchange reactions are reversible. In the case of zeolite, the spent material can be recharged by flushing the zeolite—which contains the hard-water ion—with a concentrated solution of sodium chloride. The exchange is reversed and the zeolite is ready for reuse.

Deionized water is prepared by passing natural water first through a synthetic resin that exchanges hydrogen ions, H^+, for all cations and then through a resin that exchanges hydroxide ions, OH^-, for anions.   JOHN T. NETTERVILLE

Bibliography: Gymer, R. G., *Chemistry in the Natural World* (1977); Kunin, Robert, *Elements of Ion Exchange* (1960; repr. 1971).

See also: CHROMATOGRAPHY.

ion-exchange resin: see WATER SOFTENER.

ion propulsion: see ROCKETS AND MISSILES.

Ionesco, Eugène   [ee-oh-nes'-koh, u-zhen']

The Romanian-born Eugène Ionesco, b. Nov. 26, 1912, is one of the foremost playwrights of the THEATER OF THE ABSURD. The son of a Romanian father and a French mother, he spent most of his childhood in France, but in his early teenage years returned to Romania, where he qualified as a teacher of French and married in 1936. He returned to France in 1938 to complete his doctoral thesis. Caught by the outbreak of war in 1939, he settled there, earning his living as a proofreader for publishers.

Ionesco came to playwriting almost by chance. Having decided to learn English, he was struck by the emptiness of the clichés of daily conversation that appeared in his phrase

The French-Romanian dramatist Eugène Ionesco has created a body of avant-garde literature that has placed him in the forefront of the theater of the absurd. His plays, burlesques of bourgeois existence and parables of alienation, border on tragedy.

book. Out of such nonsensical sentences he constructed his first play, *The Bald Soprano* (1950; Eng. trans., 1958), which satirizes the deadliness and idiocy of the daily life of a bourgeois society frozen in meaningless formalities. Greatly surprised by the success of the play, Ionesco embarked on a career as a writer of what he called antiplays, which characteristically combine a dream or nightmare atmosphere with grotesque, bizarre, and whimsical humor. In his work the tragic and farcical are fused.

In *The Lesson* (1951; Eng. trans., 1958), a teacher gains domination over his pupil through his superior use of language, and finally kills her. In *The Chairs* (1952, Eng. trans., 1958), an old couple attempt to pass on their total life experience to humanity by inviting to a gathering a vast crowd of guests who never arrive but whose nonpresence is symbolized by a proliferation of empty chairs. Having convinced themselves that the crowd is assembled, the old people kill themselves, leaving the revelation of their message to an orator they have engaged who, as an added irony, turns out to be a feebleminded deaf-mute.

The image, typical of Ionesco, shows his frustrations as a dramatist who is trying to convey his life experience to a crowd of vacant chairs through the mediation of actors who do not understand his message. Similar images of despair concerning the isolation of the individual in the universe and the inevitability of death dominate Ionesco's work. His breakthrough into the English-speaking theater came with *Rhinoceros* (1959; Eng. trans., 1960), in which totalitarianism is depicted as a disease that turns human beings into savage rhinoceroses. The hero of this play, Bérenger, a simple sort of Everyman, who is also a self-image of Ionesco, reappears in *The Killer* (1958; Eng. trans., 1960), *Exit the King* (1962; Eng. trans., 1963), *A Stroll in the Air* (1963; Eng. trans., 1965), and *Hunger and Thirst* (1964; Eng. trans., 1966).

Elected a member of the Académie Française in 1970, Ionesco has also published theoretical writings, *Notes and Counternotes* (1962; Eng. trans., 1964); *Fragments of a Journal* (1966; Eng. trans., 1968); and a novel, *Le Solitaire* (1973), on which his 1971 film *La Vase* (with Ionesco playing the lead) was based. *Man With Bags*, Ionesco's most recent play, was produced in 1977.   MARTIN ESSLIN

Bibliography: Coe, Richard N., *Eugène Ionesco: A Study of His Work* (1968); Hayman, Ronald, *Eugène Ionesco* (1976); Lamont, Rosette C., comp., *Ionesco: A Collection of Critical Essays* (1973); Lewis, Allan, *Ionesco* (1972); Pronko, Leonard C., *Eugène Ionesco* (1965).

Ionia   [y-ohn'-ee-uh]

The term *Ionia* refers strictly to the central part of the west coast of ANATOLIA (western Turkey) where Ionic Greek was spoken, although the term is usually applied to the entire west coast. Many Mycenaean Greeks (see AEGEAN CIVILIZATION) emigrated to Ionia in order to escape the invading DORIANS (*c.*1100 BC). Their close contact with the more advanced civilizations of the East quickly raised the level of their culture. Trade and the arts and sciences flourished in Ionia, especially in MILETUS. In the 7th century that city, with a stupendous burst of energy, succeeded in Hellenizing the area around the Black Sea.

The Ionians were subjugated by CROESUS, ruler of the expanding kingdom of LYDIA, to the north of Ionia. In turn, the Persian king CYRUS THE GREAT conquered Croesus by 546 BC, which resulted in the subjugation of the Ionians. They attempted a revolt against DARIUS I in 499–494, but they were defeated and Miletus was destroyed. After the abortive invasion (480–479) of Greece by the Persian king XERXES I, the Ionians regained their freedom, becoming members of the DELIAN LEAGUE. But they soon came under the domination of Athens. In the 4th century, Ionia was at the center of a struggle between Greeks and Persians. When the collapse of the Athenian empire at the end of the 5th century BC created a power vacuum, the Persians extended their influence once again into the Aegean. ALEXANDER THE GREAT's conquest of the Persian Empire (334–325) freed Ionia, but its cities soon became the prey of contending Hellenistic monarchs. When one of them, Attalus III of Pergamum, died in 133 BC, he bequeathed his kingdom to Rome. Pergamum became the province of Asia and the Ionians Roman subjects. The Ionian cities continued to be important economic and cultural centers until they were conquered by the Ottoman Turks in the 15th century AD.   CHARLES W. FORNARA

Bibliography: Boardman, J., *The Greeks Overseas* (1964); Huxley, G. L., *The Early Ionians* (1966; repr. 1972).

Ionian Sea   [y-ohn'-ee-uhn]

The Ionian Sea is an arm of the MEDITERRANEAN SEA lying west of Greece and east of southern Italy. The Strait of Otranto, between Italy and Albania, is to its north. The Mediterranean's greatest depth, 4,846 m (15,900 ft), is found in the Ionian Sea.

ionic bonding: see CHEMISTRY.

ionium-thorium dating: see RADIOMETRIC AGE-DATING.

ionosphere   [y-ahn'-uhs-feer]

The ionosphere is the part of the Earth's upper atmosphere where ions and electrons are present in quantities sufficient to affect the propagation of radio waves. Such a region was first theorized in 1902 independently by the British physicist Oliver Heaviside (1850–1925) and by the American electrical engineer Arthur Edwin Kennelly (1861–1949), following Guglielmo MARCONI's success in sending a radio signal across the Atlantic Ocean on Dec. 12, 1901.

ORIGIN AND DESCRIPTION

The ionosphere originates from the solar X rays and ultraviolet radiation ionizing, or splitting, electrically neutral atmospheric molecules and atoms into negative electrons and positive ions. The ionosphere is concentrated in a region approximately 80 to 400 km (50 to 240 mi) above the Earth's surface. Above this region few ionizable particles exist; below it ionospheric absorption prevents penetration by the solar X rays and ultraviolet radiation.

Electron production occurs only during the daytime; electron losses, on the other hand, occur continuously. Electrons may lose their free existence by either of two different physical processes: recombination of a negative electron and a positive ion into an electrically neutral particle or attachment of an electron to a neutral particle. In the latter case the composite particle will have a mass 10,000 times greater than the electron; its motion and therefore its chance of collision will consequently be severely limited. At a given level, the large

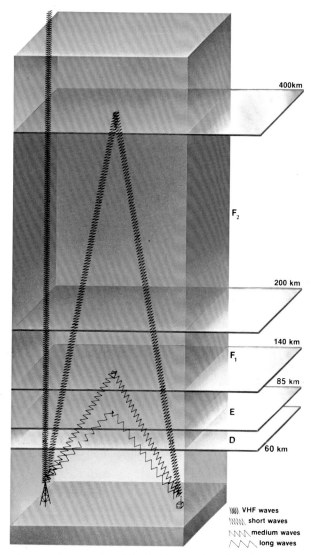

The ionosphere, a region of the Earth's atmosphere from about 80 km (50 mi) to 400 km (250 mi) altitude, is composed of several different layers of ions and electrons. Long-distance radio transmission on Earth depends on these layers. Very short, or VHF, radio waves pass through all the layers into outer space, but successively longer waves are reflected to Earth by different, lower layers. Because the ionization of each layer results from the Sun's radiation, the reflection characteristics of the layers will vary with the time of day or night.

daytime electron concentrations will be reduced 10 to 100 times at night.

The first observational evidence of the ionosphere came from the British scientists Edward Appleton and M. A. F. Barnett in 1925, and, more convincingly, from the Americans Gregory Breit and Merle Antony Tuve in 1926. The Breit-Tuve method is still used worldwide in ionospheric recorders. An exploring signal (frequency usually between 1 and 20 MHz) transmitted vertically upward is reflected downward by the ionosphere to a nearby receiver. The height of the reflecting level is obtained from the total travel time of the signal. The electron concentration N_e per cubic centimeter at the reflecting level is given by the formula $N_e = 1.24 \times 10^4 F^2$, with F the frequency of the signal wave in MHz. By varying the frequency an ionogram is obtained. A 10-MHz wave, for example, may reflect at 300 km (180 mi), indicating 1.24×10^6 electrons/cm^3 at that height. If, however, the concentration everywhere within the atmosphere is on some occasion less than 1.24×10^6 electrons/cm^3, then a signal of 10 MHz would

be transmitted vertically through all of the ionosphere, whether it came from the ground or from outer space.

The ionosphere has been classically subdivided into several regions. The D region, which disappears at night, is between 60 and 85 km (35 and 50 mi) of altitude. The E region, formerly the Kennelly-Heaviside layer, is between 85 and 140 km. The F_1 and F_2 regions occur above 140 km (85 mi) and merge at night; together they were formerly known as the Appleton layer. The D and E regions contain primarily molecular ionization; the F region is characterized primarily by atomic ionization, which produces equal numbers of electrons and atomic positive ions.

Ionospheric recorders stationed at the Earth's surface give excellent information on the electron profile (the concentration of electrons as a function of height) of the lower ionospheric half. A surface recorder can provide no information on the upper half, because a surface signal is reflected either by a level below the maximum electron concentration or not at all. The upper half is now better known than the lower, however, due to the placing of ionospheric recorders on satellites, beginning with the Canadian ALOUETTE satellite.

USE

Most commercial broadcasts are transmitted first along a horizontal path, but the signal will eventually enter the ionosphere due to the Earth's curvature. Because transmission is not vertical, fewer electrons are needed to reflect the signal back to the Earth's surface.

AM broadcasts (0.53-1.65 MHz) have a reflection level within the D region, but this layer is at a height near 80 km (50 mi). Here the air is still so dense—it burns up meteors and satellites—that the signal's energy is transmitted via the electrons to the many surrounding air molecules. The signal loses its strength and is said to have been absorbed. Ionospheric reflection cannot occur; only the ground wave can be received. The reception of AM stations during daytime is therefore limited by the curvature of the earth to a radius of less than 200 km (120 mi). At night the D region disappears, and the electron concentration required for reflection is now found about 50 km (30 mi) higher, where atmospheric particles are so far apart that virtually no absorption takes place. A San Francisco station can thus be heard at night from Alaska to Baja California. To avoid a nightly cacophony, most local stations have to shut down at sunset.

Long-distance ham-radio operators use a frequency of 3.75 MHz. Commercial short-wave transmissions have frequencies between 6 and 30 MHz. They are easily reflected by the E and F regions and then also by the Earth's surface, so that multiple hops are not uncommon, connecting points on opposite sides of the globe. During the long polar winter night, however, electrons may become so scarce that even short waves go through the skeleton ionosphere, and the result is a disruption—a polar-cap blackout—of long-distance communication. A radio fade-out may also occur under opposite circumstances. Charged particles from the Sun glide along the Earth's magnetic lines into the polar ionosphere, creating F-region-like electron concentrations in the D region; polar-cap absorption of signals results.

Still shorter waves (equivalent to higher frequencies) will penetrate the ionosphere whatever the original path. Only line-of-sight reception is possible without use of satellites. Examples of such high-frequency broadcasts include CB (27-28 MHz), TV channels 2-6 (54-88 MHz), FM (88-108 MHz), TV channels 7-13 (174-216 MHz), and UHF TV channels 14-83 (470-890 MHz).

The ionosphere was used for long-distance communication following World War I. In the coming century, however, such communication will occur mostly via satellites using such high frequencies that no ionospheric interference can occur. The role of the ionosphere in the 21st century may be mainly scientific—its high vacuum is an excellent laboratory to explore exactly how solar radiation affects atmospheric atoms.

WILLEM VAN DER BIJL

Bibliography: Banks, P. M., and Kocharts, G., *Aeronomy* (1973); Danilov, A. D., *Chemistry of the Ionosphere* (1970); Davies, K., *Ionospheric Radio Propagation* (1967); Giraud, A., and Petit, M., *Physics of the*

Earth's Ionosphere (1978); Ratcliffe, J. A., *An Introduction to the Ionosphere and Magnetosphere* (1972) and, as ed., *Fifty Years of the Ionosphere* (1976); Risbeth, Henry, and Garriott, O. K., *Introduction to Ionospheric Physics* (1969).

iora [y-ohr'-uh]

Ioras comprise four species of birds in the genus *Aegithina*, family Irenidae. They range from about 12.5 to 15 cm (5 to 6 in) in length. Ioras are dark green or black above, with yellow or green underparts, and prominent white wing bars in some species. Ioras are fruit- and insect-eating birds and inhabit the forests and forest edges and (one species) gardens of southeast Asia and the Philippines.   ROBERT J. RAIKOW

Iorga, Nicolae [yor'-gah, nee'-koh-ly]

Nicolae Iorga, b. June 17 (N.S.), 1871, d. Nov. 27 or 28, 1940, was a Romanian historian and statesman. First elected to parliament in 1907, he played an important role in Romanian politics, serving (1931–32) as prime minister under King CAROL II. An adversary of totalitarianism, Iorga was murdered by the fascist Iron Guard. He wrote hundreds of books, including a ten-volume history (1936–39) of the Romanians.
K. M. SMOGORZEWSKI

Bibliography: Oldson, William O., *The Historical and Nationalistic Thought of Nicolae Iorga* (1973).

Iowa

Iowa, an agricultural state located in the heart of the Midwest, is bordered by Wisconsin, Illinois, Missouri, Nebraska, South Dakota, and Minnesota. It represents a middle position economically, socially, and politically. Iowa even ranks in the middle (25th among the states) in both size and population. One of the last of the Midwestern states to be settled, it served as a bridge to the West. Its entrance into the Union (in 1846) as a free state was tied to the slavery question, and its people have reflected the changing mood of the nation—both in Civil War times and a century later—while not expressing extremes. Even its economic booms and busts have been middling in intensity, particularly in recent years.

LAND AND RESOURCES

Topography and Soils. Only about one-third of Iowa conforms to the popular stereotype of a flat landscape; most of the state is rolling to hilly land. Steep, rocky hills rise 100 to 125 m (330 to 380 ft) above the Mississippi River in the northeast, to an elevation of 335 m (1,100 ft), which is also the average elevation for the state. The lowest elevation, located along the Mississippi River in the southeast, is 146 m (480 ft); the maximum elevation is about 509 m (1,670 ft) in the northwest. Iowa's flatland is concentrated in the central portion north of Des Moines, where glacial deposits were left by the last retreating glacier. Pleistocene (Ice Age) materials cover the bedrock virtually everywhere in the state except along steep river bluffs and in the hilly northeast. The lake-dotted, irregular topography of the glacial drift lobe north of Des Moines reflects its recent origin. Here much of the land was poorly drained and marshy until reclaimed by farmers.

Rich prairie soils as much as 0.6 m (2 ft) thick cover most of the state and form the major resource base for agriculture. The rolling river valleys of the south and east have thinner and less fertile forest soils that contain less organic matter and are thus lighter in color than the prairie soils; these thinner soils are often severely eroded.

Rivers and Lakes. Numerous short rivers ranging in length from a few tens of kilometers to more than 160 km (100 mi) drain eastward into the MISSISSIPPI RIVER or westward into the MISSOURI RIVER. Those two large streams form the state's borders on the east and west, respectively. The Des Moines River (692 km/430 mi), the state's longest river, drains the centrally located Des Moines region, where the largest natural lakes and marshlands are found. The largest lake, Spirit Lake, is 6.4 km (4 mi) long and 5 km (3 mi) wide. Several large artificial reservoirs, including Rathbun, Red Rock, and Saylorville, have been constructed in recent years to aid in flood control.

IOWA

Capital and Largest City: Des Moines (1979 est. pop., 189,200)

Population: 2,890,100 (1979 est.). *Distribution*—57.2% urban, 42.8% rural; *density*, 20 persons per km² (51 per mi²); *increase* (1970-79) 2.3%; *population rank*, 25th

Area: 145,790 km² (56,290 mi²), including 904 km² (349 mi²) of inland water; *area rank*, 25th

Elevation: *Highest*—Ocheyedan Mound, 509 m (1,670 ft); *lowest*—Lee County, 146 m (480 ft)

Principal Products: *Manufacturing and industry*—chemicals, rubber, machinery, food products, metal products, farm equipment. *Agriculture*—beef and dairy cattle, hogs, sheep; corn, soybeans, oats; turkeys; eggs; greenhouse and nursery products. *Mining*—clay, coal, gypsum, sand and gravel

Government: *State legislature*—50 senators, 100 representatives. *Representation in Congress*—2 U.S. senators, 6 U.S. representatives

Number of Counties: 99

Statehood: Dec. 28, 1846; the 29th state

State Nickname: the Hawkeye State

State Bird: Eastern goldfinch

State Flower: Wild rose

State Tree: Oak

State Motto: Our Liberties We Prize and Our Rights We Will Maintain

Climate. Iowa's location deep in the continent's interior results in a climate characterized by temperature extremes and periodic droughts. Winter storms bring snowfalls that may total 61 cm (24 in) in the south to 100 cm (40 in) in the north, occasional hazardous blizzards, and extremely cold temperatures. Although average winter temperatures range from −10° C to −4° C (14° to 24° F), during storms temperatures may drop as low as about −34° C (−30° F). Summers are warm to hot and humid, with temperatures averaging in the lower 20°s C (mid-70°s F) throughout the state, which means daytime highs are often in the high 30°s (over 100° F).

Summer storms carry warm, moist air from the Gulf of Mexico, yielding in large part the 865-mm (34-in) average annual precipitation of the southeast, which declines to 635 mm (25 in) in the northwest. Droughts may occur throughout the state but are most common and severe in the northwest. The

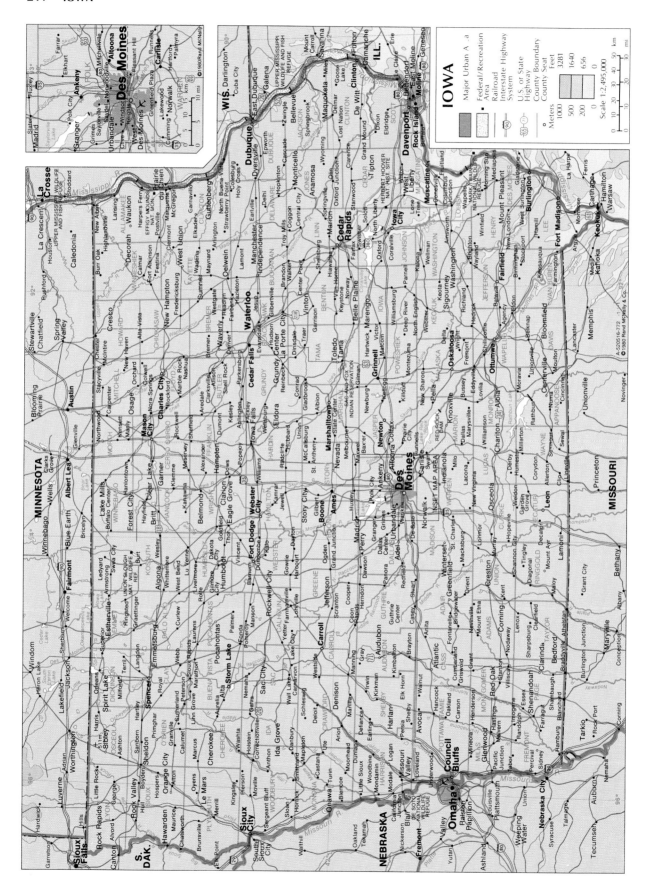

Des Moines, the capital and largest city of Iowa, is situated in the south central portion of the state at the junction of the Des Moines and Raccoon rivers. Originally established (1843) as a military garrison to control the Sauk and Fox Indians of the area, Des Moines has become a regional center for banking, printing, and manufacturing.

warm, humid air also results in about 40 to 50 thunderstorms and 15 tornadoes each summer.

Vegetation and Animal Life. Most of Iowa was originally covered by prairie grasslands, but they have now been replaced chiefly by cropland and pastureland. Deciduous forests of oak-hickory and maple-basswood, found mainly in the hilly south and east, have shrunk to less than 10,100 km² (3,900 mi²) as the land has been cleared for farming. White-tailed deer, game birds, and smaller forms of wildlife have adapted to dense agricultural settlement; but buffalo, cougars, and other large mammals succumbed decades ago to the pressure of people on the land.

Resources. The bulk of Iowa's water resources comes from streams, most of which are too small to provide an adequate water supply during drought years. About one-fourth of the water supply comes from under ground, chiefly from the glacial drift. Some wells penetrate as deeply as 900 m (3,000 ft) into the Paleozoic marine sediments that underlie the drift. These sedimentary rocks also provide mineral resources, especially along the river valleys where the drift is thinnest. Although more than 6.3 million metric tons (7 billion U.S. tons) of coal are thought to lie underground, deposits are thin and patchy and have a high sulfur content; consequently coal production is not important economically. Gypsum and stone

for construction have proved to be far more valuable resources in recent years, as have sand and gravel from the glacial drift.

PEOPLE

Iowa had an estimated population of 2,890,100 in 1979, giving an average population density of slightly less than 20 persons per km² (51 per mi²). The rural and small-town population is exceptionally evenly distributed across the state. Most of the larger cities are in the eastern half; the largest city, DES MOINES, the capital, is quite near the center of the state. Only SIOUX CITY and COUNCIL BLUFFS (across the Missouri from Omaha, Neb.) are located in the west. CEDAR RAPIDS and WATERLOO are the interior cities of the east; DAVENPORT, DUBUQUE, and several smaller cities line the banks of the Mississippi. Although 57% of the population is urban, small towns dominate; Iowa has almost 1,000 incorporated communities, most with fewer than 1,000 inhabitants.

Population growth has been very slow in recent decades, with only a 2.3% increase in 1970-79, far below the national average of 6.4% (1970-76). In the 1970s the net migration rate slowed to a 1.5% loss, down from a 6.6% net loss in the 1960s. Unlike the majority of the United States, most population growth in Iowa has taken place in the cities. The rural counties have lost population because of extensive out-migration, and some show a natural rate of decrease (an excess of deaths over births) due to an aging population; Iowa is third (following Florida and Arkansas) in the proportion of the population aged 65 and over.

The overwhelming majority of the population is native-born and of northwest European stock. Blacks (1.2% in 1970) are concentrated in the urban centers, particularly Des Moines and Waterloo. About 1,500 Fox Indians are located on or near the Mesquakie Settlement near Tama, and an approximately equal number live in Sioux City. Most of the population is Protestant, but Roman Catholics predominate in Dubuque and its surrounding area.

Education and Culture. The strength of Iowa's public educational system has resulted in the lowest illiteracy rate in the United States, since at least the turn of the century. Schools are consolidated in rural areas, but the declining number of pupils is currently creating pressures to close schools in both rural and urban districts. Seventeen public and 37 private institutions of higher learning are located in the state and serve as cultural centers.

The two major state universities date from the mid-19th century. The University of Iowa (1847) in IOWA CITY has earned a national reputation in the fine arts; it includes the renowned Writer's Workshop. Iowa State University (1858) in

Davenport, the seat of Scott County, is located in eastern Iowa along the Mississippi River. Davenport is the focus of an important industrial area commonly referred to as the Quad Cities, an urban agglomeration comprised of Davenport, Bettendorf, and the Illinois cities of Rock Island and Moline.

AMES specializes in basic sciences and agriculture (see IOWA, STATE UNIVERSITIES OF).

The major libraries are located at the state universities and in the larger cities.

Iowa counts Grant WOOD—the Midwestern regionalist painter who drew heavily on his Iowan heritage for his subjects—among its native sons. Des Moines and Iowa City have important art museums; presettlement and early white settlement are emphasized in museums in Cherokee and Decorah. The larger cities, notably Des Moines, Davenport, and Cedar Rapids, and the universities and colleges support theater, classical music, and dance. Because Iowa lacks large population concentrations, much of the population depends upon traveling artists and shows, a tradition that dates back to lecture circuits of the 19th-century and the CHAUTAUQUA movement (late 19th and early 20th centuries), providing education for adults.

Historical sites are associated largely with the settlement of the region and of the nation to the west. Noteworthy is the Herbert Hoover Presidential Library in West Branch, which includes not only official papers but also a preserved portion of the community, including the Hoover cabin, in which Iowa's only president was born (1874) and spent his early years. Preservation of many of Iowa's 19th-century buildings has become a popular concern in recent years.

Communications. Forty daily newspapers (with a total circulation of 900,100 in 1977) and nearly 400 weekly or biweekly newspapers are published in Iowa. Fourteen commercial television stations, 147 commercial radio stations, and publicly supported television, which reaches the great majority of the state's people, provide a complete communications network.

ECONOMIC ACTIVITY

Iowa was traditionally an agricultural state, and its economy is still inextricably tied to the fortunes of farming. Although manufacturing now exceeds farming in employment and financial return, most industrial development is based upon the agricultural sector. As in most parts of the United States, however, employment in the trade and services sector exceeds that of either manufacturing or agriculture. The economy's growth rate has been steady, with per-capita income slightly below the U.S. average. Years when profits from farm products are high and weather conditions are good are prosperous times for Iowa.

Agriculture. Iowa ranks second among the states in the value

Grain-fed beef cattle are among Iowa's chief agricultural commodities, with the state ranking second only to Texas in U.S. cattle production. About 75% of the state's agricultural income comes from raising cattle, hogs, and other livestock.

of agricultural production; it maintains this position because of its corn, soybeans, cattle, and hogs. Livestock feeding within the state consumes most of the grain, but much is shipped to other states or is exported abroad. Over $2 billion of the United States' $24 billion in farm exports in 1977 originated in Iowa; this figure highlights the importance of the state's productivity in the international balance of payments. Iowa's productivity derives from a combination of shrewd and innovative management, rich soils, and relatively flat land. Grain yields suffer during drought periods, however, and overproductivity often leads to cycles of poor farm prices and lowered incomes.

Manufacturing and Industry. Processing of food products accounts for nearly half (by value) of manufactured goods. In 1976 the value added by manufacturing was $7.8 billion dollars. In addition, manufacturing of farm equipment and chemicals for farm use is significant, as are the manufacture of other machinery, electrical products, and rubber products and printing and publishing. Most mining is of stone or gypsum, and most of the stone is used in local construction.

Corn, traditionally Iowa's most valuable cash crop, ripens in a field in Warren County, in the south central portion of the state. Iowa, also a major producer of soybeans, ranks third among all states in the value of its crops, trailing only California and Illinois.

Tourism. Most tourists visit Iowa while in transit, as the state contains little spectacular scenery to slow their pace. Residents, however, use the outdoors heavily, with fishing, hunting, boating, and camping focused in the 91 state parks and on federal reservoirs. Because of the lack of large urban centers, professional sports are unimportant. Instead, organized sports at the high school and the college levels are the center of attention for many residents.

Transportation. A dense network of roads was constructed to serve the evenly scattered farms. With more than 180,000 km (112,000 mi) of roads and nearly 13,000 km (8,000 mi) of railroad track (both mileages rank high among the states), Iowa has a denser transport network than can be supported and maintained adequately, and the trend is to reduce this mileage. Barge traffic on the Mississippi and Missouri rivers is becoming increasingly important for transporting farm products.

Energy. Although much coal is located under southern Iowa, most of this has a high sulfur content and is found in relatively small and scattered deposits. Coal from outside the state and natural gas are far more important in providing energy. Nearly half the electrical power comes from nuclear power plants.

GOVERNMENT AND POLITICS

The Iowa constitution dates from 1857; it provides the traditional separation of powers between executive, legislative, and judicial branches of government. The legislature is bicameral and consists of 50 senators who serve 4-year terms and 100 representatives who serve 2-year terms. The governor and other state executives are elected to 4-year terms. Counties and cities have separately elected officials and derive their authority from the state legislature.

Iowa has a long tradition of allegiance to the Republican party; that party has controlled the state legislature for 108 years. In recent years, however, Democrats have gained more support and have occupied the governorship for five terms, elected three senators, and controlled both the congressional delegation and the state legislature for varying periods of time.

Despite the traditional dominance of the Republican party, Iowans tend to be moderate rather than conservative; Republicans frequently occupy positions more liberal than the Democrats. Much of the credit for a liberal Republican position can be accorded to the influence of the *Des Moines Register*, a newspaper that is notable for its role in shaping public opinion on international as well as national issues.

HISTORY

Even as glacial ice was melting in central Iowa 13,000 years ago, it is believed that Paleo-Indians occupied the area. They hunted large, and now extinct, mammals such as mammoths and mastodons. Archaeological sites are rare for this early period, but it is clear that western Iowa valleys were occupied repeatedly by bison hunters as early as 10,000 BC. The Woodland Indian tradition began in eastern Iowa about 500 BC and continued to about AD 1000. These Indians are best remembered for their complex burial mounds—often in the form of an effigy of some animal—such as the mounds at Effigy Mounds National Monument (see MOUND BUILDERS). The small villages and incipient cultivation of the Woodland Indians gave way to post-Woodland cultures with larger settlements and a greater dependence upon cultivation.

European Exploration and Early Settlement. The first Europeans to see Iowa were the Frenchmen Louis JOLLIET and Jacques MARQUETTE, who traveled with their party down the Mississippi River in 1673. Had they penetrated to the interior of Iowa, they would have found a few thousand Indians living mostly along the larger streams. The first permanent white settler was Julien DUBUQUE, who mined lead along the Mississippi River, near the site of the city that bears his name, from 1788 to his death in 1810. After the LOUISIANA PURCHASE (1803) the land that was to become Iowa became part of the young United States, and the LEWIS AND CLARK EXPEDITION (1804–05) traveled the Missouri River en route to and from the Pacific. The SAUK and FOX (Mesquakie) tribes, forced into the Mississippi River valley from Wisconsin and Illinois by the oncoming pressure of white settlement, defeated the Iowa Indians

and occupied their lands in the late eighteenth and early nineteenth centuries. Following the BLACK HAWK WAR of 1832, the resistance of these tribes to white settlers was broken, and the land was now open to pioneer settlement. The first legal settlement west of the Mississippi took place in 1833, and population growth was rapid. Successive purchases from the Indians led to settlement throughout the area of the state in the 1830s and 1840s—but not without some confrontations, the last being the Spirit Lake Massacre of 1857. Just before this event (in 1856) the Mesquakies, who had been forced to move to Kansas, convinced the Iowa legislature to permit their repurchase of land along the Iowa River near Tama. The Mesquakie Settlement now covers about 13 km² (5 mi²).

Statehood and Settlement. The Territory of Iowa was created in 1838 despite some opposition in Congress, which attempted to tie territorial status to the annexation of Texas. Statehood was granted in 1846, with Southern congressional opposition again an issue; unwritten practice tied the admission of a free state to that of a slave state, in order to maintain a balance of power. Iowa's "partner" was Florida, which had been waiting since 1838 for a Northern free territory to become eligible. Iowa thus became the 29th state, with its capital at Iowa City, a site chosen by the first territorial governor as a compromise among the claims of the various Mississippi River towns that coveted the status. The capital was moved to Des Moines in 1857.

By 1850 nearly 200,000 people lived in Iowa, and by 1860 roughly 600,000 made their homes there. The majority of settlers came from the eastern Midwest states of Ohio and Indiana rather than from the East Coast. Thousands came from the border slave states; they primarily settled in southern Iowa. Many of Iowa's first white settlers had already made one or two previous moves and perhaps were not certain that Iowa would be their final home—not only new lands lay to the west but also the glitter of gold in the Rockies and beyond. Noteworthy among those who passed through Iowa in this period of early settlement were about 30,000 Mormons (in 1846), on their way to Utah by wagon and handcart.

The Civil War and Postwar Periods. In the pre-Civil War period Iowa was firmly Democratic. The war changed that, as antislavery forces finally coalesced into the new Republican party in 1856, turning Iowa into a virtual one-party state. With Republicans in the Senate, Iowa moved from isolationism on the slavery issue to a fervent antislavery position. John BROWN used Iowa and its Quaker communities as a base for his activities throughout the late 1850s, and six Iowans participated in his ill-fated attack at Harpers Ferry, W.Va., in 1859. During the Civil War, Iowa sent almost 80,000 soldiers to battle, a larger proportion of its population than any other Northern state; nearly half of all men of military age served during the war. Following the war suffrage was extended to blacks, and integrated schools were instituted.

Immigration to Iowa continued during the latter half of the 19th century, mostly by settlers from northwestern Europe. Iowans bought their land cheaply, often with the aid of credit from speculators, and paid dearly to improve it. The thick prairie sod required heavy plows pulled by many oxen; poor drainage was solved by cooperation—the formation of drainage districts—and by building ditches and underground tiles. Towns sprung up every few miles, evenly spaced on the physical landscape. From the outset farming was commercially rather than subsistence oriented, with corn rather than wheat the principal crop.

Because most agriculture was commercial, farmers needed railroads to get their produce to market. The railroads, which first arrived in 1867, proved to be as much an enemy to the individual farmers as a friend to their efforts to move their products because of their high freight rates. Regulation battles followed, and many farmers joined the GRANGER MOVEMENT to fight the railroads. These problems were not the only ones to be faced. Pests, diseases, and droughts plagued the settlers' crops, and depressions plagued their finances—in 1873, 1893, and most disastrously in the 1920s, leading to active rebellion when the Great Depression began in the early 1930s. The productive land also created opportunities for utopian ideals, and a number of communes established on this basis were founded. Only one survived into the 20th century—the AMANA SOCIETY—with its seven villages and more than 25,000 acres of land along the Iowa River. Even it was finally forced by economic pressure and cultural change to move from communistic ideals to capitalism in the early 1930s.

The Recent Period. Although Iowa has never been a leading industrial center, a number of enterprises became nationally successful as the need for a large farm population diminished. Laborers freed from the plow were mechanically adept and had a tradition of hard work behind them. Innovation, particularly hybridization of corn, and mechanization paved the way for more efficient and productive farming. Surplus population moved off the land, and the numbers of rural Iowans both on the farm and in the smaller towns declined. With the move to the cities came other social changes, and the long hold of the Republicans on the state political scene was broken. Today Iowa has a stable economy with a low growth rate, neither plunging to the depths with each new recession nor enjoying for long the dizzying heights of recovery. More than in most other parts of the nation, it holds a middle position, economically and socially, and this appears to be the role that Iowa is destined to play.   NEIL E. SALISBURY

Bibliography: Federal Writers' Project, *Iowa: A Guide to the Hawkeye State* (1938; repr. 1973); Hake, H. V., *Iowa Inside Out* (1968); Houlette, William, *Iowa, the Pioneer Heritage* (1970); Mills, G. S., *Rogues and Heroes from Iowa's Amazing Past* (1972); Nelson, H. L., *A Geography of Iowa* (1976); Posten, Margaret, *This Is the Place—Iowa*, 3d ed. (1971); Rosenberg, Morton M., *Iowa on the Eve of the Civil War* (1972); Ruhe, Robert V., *Quaternary Landscapes in Iowa* (1969); Sage, Leland L., *A History of Iowa* (1974); Wall, Joseph F., *Iowa: A Bicentennial History* (1978); Zielinski, John M., *Portrait of Iowa* (1974).

Iowa   (Indian tribe)

The Pahodja ("dusty roses"), a Siouan-speaking tribe of North American Indians, received their better-known name, Iowa, or Ayuhwa ("sleepy ones"), from their Sioux enemies. Closely related to the OTO and MISSOURI, all descended from the WINNEBAGO, they are traditionally believed to have originated in the Great Lakes region. After leaving there, the three tribes lived in present-day Illinois before moving to the Lower Missouri and separating into dialect groups. They farmed maize, beans, and squash supplemented by hunting and lived in villages consisting of rectangular bark dwellings. The tepee was used on summer excursions into the Great Plains. Clans were grouped into summer and winter moieties (complementary subdivisions). Sons inherited leadership and clan membership from fathers. Religion was organized by special societies; the GHOST DANCE was adopted in the 1880s, and the use of peyote later became widespread.

In 1804, Lewis and Clark found the Iowa living on the Platte River in a single village of about 800. Smallpox the year before had killed 100 of their tribespeople. The Iowa did not resist white expansion and ceded their land in 1824, 1836, and 1854, accepting a reservation in northeast Kansas; they then numbered about 500. Some Iowa were persuaded to relocate in Indian Territory (present-day Oklahoma) in the 1880s. The Iowa who remained in Kansas now number more than 600, although only 200 live on the reservation. Much intermarriage occurred in Oklahoma, and only about 100 Iowa remain there. Many descendants retain an Iowa identity and fought policies aimed at tribal termination in the 1950s.

ERNEST L. SCHUSKY

Bibliography: Indian Claims Commission, *The Sac, Fox and Iowa Indians*, 3 vols. (1974); Skinner, Alanson, *Ethnology of the Ioway Indians* (1926; repr. 1977).

Iowa, state universities of

The three state universities of Iowa are coeducational and offer both undergraduate and graduate degrees. The **University of Iowa** (1847; enrollment: 22,770; library: 2,100,000 volumes), at Iowa City, has programs in arts and sciences and colleges of dentistry, medicine, nursing, pharmacy, and journalism. **Iowa State University of Science and Technology** (1858; en-rollment: 22,800; library: 1,200,000 volumes), at Ames, is a land-grant institution. Among its schools are those of architecture, engineering, forestry, and veterinary medicine. It has an institute for atomic research. The **University of Northern Iowa** (1876; enrollment: 11,040; library: 461,000 volumes) is at Cedar Falls.

Iowa City

Iowa City lies along both banks of the Iowa River in eastern Iowa. With a population of 49,700 (1979 est.), it is the seat of Johnson County. It is the commercial center of an agricultural region dominated by cattle, grain, hogs, and poultry production. Area industries produce urethane foam and toiletries. Founded in 1839 as the capital of the Iowa Territory, it remained the seat of government until 1857. The establishment (1847) of the University of Iowa and the arrival of the railroad in 1855 assured its growth.

ipecac   [ip'-i-kak]

Ipecac, the dried roots and subterranean stems of one of several South American or Indian plants, contains a number of alkaloids. For medicinal uses the roots are ground into a powder from which a syrup or tincture (alcohol solution) can be made. Ipecac is used as an EMETIC (induces vomiting) when poisonous material has been ingested, but its use should be avoided if the poison is a petroleum product, an acid, or an alkali. It is used in expectorant mixtures to treat bronchitis, because it can liquefy mucous secretions.

RICHARD H. RUNSER

Iphigenia   [if-uh-juh-ny'-uh]

In Greek mythology, Iphigenia was the daughter of AGAMEMNON and CLYTEMNESTRA. When unfavorable winds detained the Greek army at Aulis from sailing for Troy, an oracle told Agamemnon that he must sacrifice Iphigenia to appease the anger of ARTEMIS, whose sacred stag he had killed. Agamemnon accordingly had Iphigenia brought to Aulis, where he performed the sacrifice. In another version of the story, Artemis substituted a deer at the last moment and carried Iphigenia in a cloud to Tauris, where she became a priestess of Artemis. Many years later Iphigenia escaped with her brother ORESTES to Attica, where she established a new temple to Artemis. Both versions of the story were used by EURIPIDES in his plays *Iphigenia in Aulis* and *Iphigenia in Tauris*.

Ipiutak   [ip-ee-oo'-tak]

Ipiutak, an archaeological site near Point Hope on the northwest coast of Alaska, is the name given a major prehistoric Eskimo culture of the first half of the first millennium AD. Excavations at the site have revealed the remains of more than 600 houses and a large burial ground. The Ipiutak economy was mainly based on caribou and seal hunting, with fowling and fishing of secondary importance. A great number of carefully worked arrows, harpoon heads, and other stone and antler implements were found in the open-hearthed, rectangular dwellings. Bows and arrows were important hunting tools. Neither blubber lamps nor pottery were known.

Ipiutak's remarkable cemetery consisted of wood coffins buried at depths of 0.5 to 1 m (1.5 to 3 ft), as well as burials in which the corpse was enclosed by logs placed directly on the surface of the tundra. The latter burials were especially rich in unusual grave goods, including ivory eyeballs, masks, animal figures, and bizarre openwork carvings. The style of these objects shows affinities with the OKVIK and Old Bering Sea cultures as well as with the so-called animal style art of the SCYTHIANS, suggesting links with Siberian cultural traditions. The Ipiutak site was discovered in 1939. Associated cultural remains have since been found at more southerly sites on CAPE KRUSENSTERN and on Seward Peninsula near Deering.

HANS-GEORG BANDI

Bibliography: Bandi, H. G., *Eskimo Prehistory*, trans. by A. E. Keep (1969); Larsen, H. E., and Rainey, F. G., *Ipiutak and the Arctic Whale Hunting Culture* (1948).

Iqbal, Muhammad [ik-bahl', muh-hahm'-uhd]

One of the greatest poets of the Indian subcontinent, Muhammad Iqbal, b. c.1877, was also a philosopher and Muslim political leader. He studied law and philosophy in Europe (1905–08) and, on his return to India, taught philosophy and literature, practiced law, and soon achieved fame as a poet. He wrote in both Persian and Urdu. The British knighted Iqbal in 1922 in recognition of his poetry. His works include *Asrār-e khūdī* (1915; translated as *The Secrets of the Self*, 1920, 1940), *Payām-e Mashriq* (The Message of the East, 1923), and *The Reconstruction of Religious Thought in Islam* (1934).

Iqbal also became active in Muslim politics, serving as a member of the Punjab Legislative Council (1926–30) and president of the MUSLIM LEAGUE (1930). One of the first to advocate a separate Muslim state in India, he has been called the spiritual father of Pakistan, where the anniversary of his death (Apr. 21, 1938) is a national holiday.

MARCUS FRANDA AND VONETTA J. FRANDA

Bibliography: Malik, Hafeez, ed., *Iqbal: Poet-Philosopher of Pakistan* (1971); Vahid, S. A., *Iqbal: His Art and Thought*, rev. ed. (1959).

IQ: see INTELLIGENCE.

IQSY: see INTERNATIONAL YEARS OF THE QUIET SUN.

Iráklion [ee-rah'-klee-awn]

Iráklion (Candia) is the largest city on Crete, with a population of 77,506 (1971). A seaport, it is the island's transportation, commercial, and tourism center. Wine, dried fruit, and grapes are major exports. Nearby are ruins of the Minoan city KNOSSOS. Iráklion's Archeological Museum is famous for its collection of MINOAN ART and relics.

The modern city was founded by Arabs in the 9th century. Iráklion, called Kandaq by the Arabs, became part of the Byzantine Empire in the 10th century; in 1300 it fell to Venetians, who renamed it Candia. It was conquered by Turks in 1669 and served as the capital of Crete until 1841. When Crete was incorporated into Greece in 1913 the city was renamed Iráklion.

Iran [ir-an']

Iran is the largest and most populous country in Southwest Asia. The nation possesses abundant petroleum resources and is also important because of its rapidly developing economy and strategic location. Iran shares a long land border with the USSR on the north; with a coastline 3,180 km (1,976 mi) long, it commands navigation on the PERSIAN GULF, the Strait of HORMUZ, and the Gulf of Oman in the south (see OMAN, GULF OF); and it shares borders with Turkey and Iraq on the west and with Afghanistan and Pakistan on the east. The country was known to the West as Persia, from the ancient Greek name Persis, but in 1935 the Iranian government requested use of the older and correct name, Iran, meaning "Land of the Aryans." Before 1979, when the shah of Iran, MUHAMMAD REZA SHAH PAHLAVI, was deposed and an Islamic republic was declared, Iran had been an independent monarchy (with a few interruptions) for over 2,500 years.

LAND AND RESOURCES

The topography of Iran consists mainly of a central plateau rimmed by high mountains; most of the country lies above 450 m (1,500 ft), and about 15% is over 2,000 m (6,500 ft). The only extensive lowlands, all restricted in width to between 15 and 115 km (10 and 70 mi), occur along the southern shores of the CASPIAN SEA and along the shores of the Gulf of Oman. About half of the country is dominated by the arid central plateau, with elevations ranging from 600 to 900 m (about 2,000 to 3,000 ft). The mountain ranges encircling the plateau are the ELBURZ MOUNTAINS and their structural continuation in the Talish Mountains and the Koppeh Dagh on the north, the ZAGROS MOUNTAINS on the southwest, and the Makran Range on the south. The highest mountains are in the Elburz, where Mount DEMAVEND, an extinct volcanic peak located northeast

of Tehran, rises to 5,671 m (18,605 ft), the highest point in Iran. One of the most extraordinary features of Iranian topography is an uninhabitable arid salt waste, the Dasht-e-Kavir, centered 485 km (300 mi) southeast of Tehran.

Soils. The soils used most extensively for farming in Iran are the rich brown forest soils found along the coastal regions of the Persian Gulf and the Caspian Sea. Elsewhere, soils suitable for farming are largely alluvial and limited to river valleys in mountainous areas and along the SHATT-AL-ARAB (the mouth of the Tigris-Euphrates). However, water availability rather than soil quality is the determining factor for agriculture, and large areas could be farmed if water were available.

Climate. Iran has a varied continental type of climate marked by extremes in both temperature and precipitation. Summers are extremely hot along the Persian Gulf, where temperatures of 49° C (120° F) are not uncommon. In inland areas, daytime highs also occasionally exceed 50° C (120° F) but fall rapidly at night. Winters are generally cold, except along the milder Caspian and Persian Gulf shores, with temperatures reaching below 0° C (32° F) on the plateau. In Tehran the average January temperature is 2° C (36° F), and the average for July is 30° C (86° F). Precipitation ranges from over 1,270 mm (50 in) in the northwestern Zagros and the Elburz mountains to less than 50 mm (2 in) in southeastern areas of the central plateau.

Drainage. The most important river in Iran is the Karun, which rises in the central Zagros and joins the Shatt-al-Arab at Khorramshahr. The Karun, which flows across a broad alluvial plain, is navigable to Ahvaz and is Iran's only navigable river. Three other rivers that maintain their flow all year are the Atrak in the northeast, which rises in the Koppeh Dagh

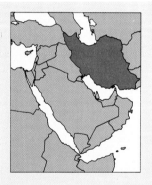

IRAN

Official Name: Islamic Republic of Iran
Capital and Largest City: Tehran (1976 est. pop., 4,200,000)
Area: 1,647,240 km² (636,000 mi²)
Elevation: *Highest*—Mount Demavend, 5,601 m (18,377 ft); *lowest*—sea level
Population: 35,808,000 (1979 est.). *Distribution*—47% urban, 53% rural; *density*, 22 persons per km² (56 per mi²); *annual rate of increase* (1970–79), 3.0%
Principal Languages: Persian, Turkish, Kurdish, Arabic
Principal Religions: Islam, Zoroastrianism, Judaism, Christianity, Baha'i
Principal Products: *Agriculture*—wheat, barley, rice, sugar beets, cotton, dates, raisins, tea, tobacco, sheep, goats. *Manufacturing and industry*—petroleum refining, textiles, petrochemicals, automobiles, cement, food processing, metal fabricating. *Mining*—petroleum, natural gas, iron, copper, coal, lead, zinc, chromite
Railroads: 4,601 km/2,859 mi (1978)
Roads: 12,060 km/7,494 mi (1977 paved)
Currency: 1 rial = 100 dinars

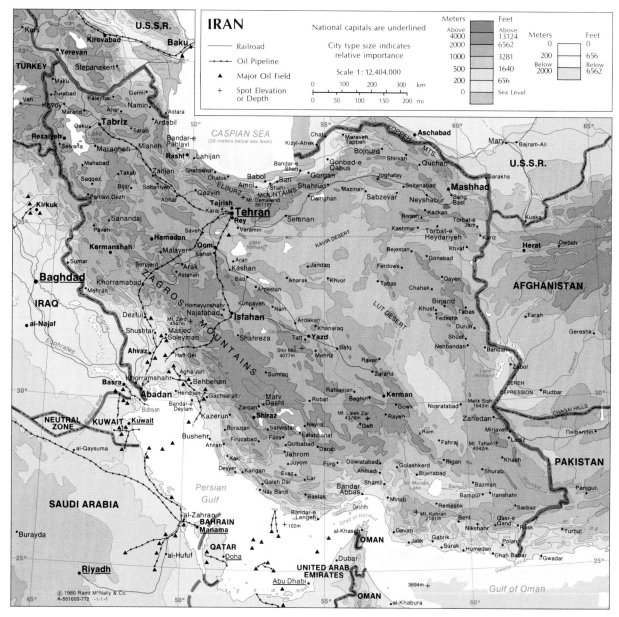

IRAN

National capitals are underlined

City type size indicates relative importance

Scale 1: 12,404,000

— Railroad
+-+-+ Oil Pipeline
▲ Major Oil Field
+ Spot Elevation or Depth

and flows into the eastern side of the Caspian Sea; the Safid, which flows through the Elburz to the south shore of the Caspian Sea; and the Araks in the northwest, which flows into the USSR before entering the western side of the Caspian Sea. Other rivers in Iran tend to dry up in summer and flow only intermittently. *Qanats*, or long underground water tunnels, are widely used to bring water from the mountains into the plateau.

Vegetation and Animal Life. About 10% of Iran is covered with forest, most of it deciduous and located in the mountains bordering the Caspian Sea. A variety of trees and shrubs also covers parts of the Zagros Mountains. Drier parts of the country are generally devoid of vegetation. Common trees in the oases are poplars, tamarisks, date palms, myrtles, and mulberries. On the plateau the fauna include wild boars, foxes, jackals, and a few lions and tigers in the wilder areas; numerous smaller animals; and, in the drier areas, a variety of lizards and other creatures adapted to arid conditions.

Resources. Iran is tremendously rich in minerals, especially petroleum and natural gas. In the 1970s it was the fourth-largest producer of oil in the world (after the USSR, the United

States, and Saudi Arabia), with an average output of 2 billion barrels per year. It is estimated that the petroleum reserves will last for 40 years. Most oil fields are located in the southwest, especially in Khuzestan province; some are under the waters of the Persian Gulf; and extensive discoveries have been made in other parts of the country. Natural gas supplies are also enormous, about 17 trillion m^3 (600 trillion ft^3), and constitute the world's second-largest reserves (after the USSR). Much of the natural gas is exported by pipeline to the USSR. In the 1970s iron and coal deposits were developed for use in the new steel industry, and large deposits of chromite, copper, lead, zinc, and salt are only beginning to be exploited on a large scale.

PEOPLE
The population of Iran is ethnically complex, and minority groups staunchly defend their provincial separatism and seek autonomy in local affairs. About two-thirds of the total population is descended from Aryan tribes who migrated to Iran from central Asia in the 17th century BC. The remaining one-third is composed mostly of Turks and Arabs, as well as small minorities of Armenians and Jews. The largest Aryan group

The Bakhtiari, a pastoral people of the Zagros Mountain region of southwestern Iran, have traditionally led a nomadic existence. In its efforts to promote cultural unity among its peoples, however, the Iranian government has discouraged their nomadic way of life.

are Persians, or Farsi, who constitute 63% of the total population and live mainly in the central plateau. Also of Aryan origin are the Gilani and Mazandarani, who live on the northern edge of the plateau and around the shores of the Caspian Sea. Many of Iran's important ethnic minorities (although also of Aryan descent) are nomadic and have strongly resisted culture change, with some even demanding separate nations; these groups include the KURDS, who live mainly in the northern Zagros Mountains; the BAKHTIARI and Lurs, who live in the southern half of the Zagros Mountains; and the BALU-CHI, who live in southeast Iran along the borders with Afghanistan and Pakistan. The largest Turkic-speaking group are the Azerbaijani, who live along the Soviet border in northwestern Iran. Arabs predominate in oil-rich Khuzestan province and along the Persian Gulf; and Armenians and Jews are concentrated in urban areas.

The official language is Persian, or Farsi, an INDO-EUROPEAN

language written in the Arabic script. The dialect of the Persians is considered standard and is quite unlike that spoken by the Gilani and Mazandarani. Related to Persian but different enough to be considered separate languages are Kurdish, Luri, and Baluchi. Azerbaijani is the most widely used of the Turkic languages, which belong to the URAL-ALTAIC LANGUAGE group. Arabic, a Semitic language, is widely spoken in Khuzestan province.

About 98% of all Iranians are Muslims; 93% are SHIITES, or members of the Shia sect of Islam. Iran is the world's center of Shiite Islam, and it is the official state religion. Most of the ethnic minorities, however, including Kurds, Baluchi, Turks, and Arabs, are SUNNITES, or members of the Sunni sect of Islam. Leadership of the Shiites rests with a priestly class of mullahs, whose leaders have great political influence and include about 400 ayatollahs, or "holy ones." The principal minority religions are BAHA'I, ZOROASTRIANISM (with about 25,000 adherents), Christianity (notably the NESTORIAN CHURCH), and Judaism.

Demography. Iran's population is predominantly rural, with 53% living in rural areas and 47% in urban areas. The largest urban center is TEHRAN, the capital, which has grown rapidly in recent decades. Other large urban centers are ISFAHAN, MASHHAD, SHIRAZ, and TABRIZ. The average population density is 22 persons per km² (56 per mi²); but large areas are uninhabited, and the population is concentrated along the southern shores of the Caspian Sea, the Atrek River valley in the northeast, the Karun River valley and Tigris-Euphrates delta in the southwest, and the mountain valleys of the northwest. The population, which was only 20,000,000 in 1960, has increased by 75% in the last two decades. This has resulted from a reduction in the death rate as a result of better health care, combined with a high birthrate (despite an official birth-control program under the shah).

Education and Health. Education is free and compulsory for all children between the ages of 6 and 11. Approximately one-fourth of all students continue their education in secondary and vocational schools, and one-tenth of these obtain higher education. The University of Tehran, established in 1934, is the largest of 17 universities. Under the shah, the government sent many students abroad, especially to the United States, for higher education. The illiteracy rate dropped from 80% in the mid-1960s to 37% in 1977 as a result of a governmental program launched in 1968 to raise literacy levels in rural areas and among women.

Iran's shortage of health facilities is reflected in a life expectancy at birth of 57 years (1976). In 1975 there were only 3.7 doctors and 14 hospital beds for every 10,000 inhabitants, with most health services concentrated in urban areas.

(Right) Tehran, the capital and largest city of Iran, is situated on a plateau in the north central portion of the nation. An ancient city, much of its expansion has occurred since the end of World War II.

(Below) Bars indicate the monthly ranges of temperature (red) and precipitation (blue) in Tehran, which has a steppe climate.

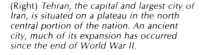
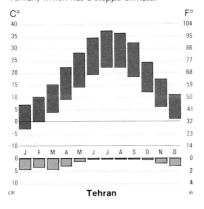

Tehran

The Arts. Iran's rapid pace of social and economic change in the 1960s and 1970s adversely affected many aspects of the nation's rich and indigenous culture. Poetry is traditionally the most important art form in Iran, and the 12th-century poet Omar KHAYYAM is perhaps the most famous (see PERSIAN LITERATURE). Music and architecture are also historically important; traditional forms of both have been influenced by Western styles in recent decades (see PERSIAN ART AND ARCHITECTURE). Iran is famous for its crafts, including ceramics and silver and gold metalwork, but the traditional industry of carpet-making seems to be in irreversible decline.

ECONOMIC ACTIVITY

During the 1960s and 1970s the shah attempted to transform Iran into a modern, industrial nation; the nation's petroleum revenues were reinvested in accordance with a series of ambitious development plans. Industrial expansion and diversification and land reform were actively pursued. As revenues increased following the world price rise in oil in the 1970s economic growth also accelerated, and Iran enjoyed an economic growth rate of about 10% a year, one of the highest in the world. This rapid growth created a prosperous middle class, but the consequent social and cultural dislocation was one of the causes of widespread social discontent that found expression in the upheavals of the 1979 revolution.

Manufacturing and Power. Manufacturing is now the leading source of revenue in Iran and employs more than 20% of the labor force. The principal industries are oil-related and include refining and the production of a wide range of petrochemicals. The principal oil-processing centers are ABADAN, Bandar-e-Shahpur, Ahvaz, Kharg Island, Shiraz, and Isfahan. Steel manufacturing began at Isfahan in 1973 and at Ahvaz in 1977; steel is now widely used in the production of automobiles, buses, trucks, tractors, washing machines, refrigerators, and electrical machinery. The textile industry, Iran's oldest major industry, is centered mainly in Isfahan and continues to produce cotton and woolen goods, but this industry has suffered from competition from synthetic fibers manufactured by the petrochemical industry.

In 1978, Iran produced 20 billion kW h of electricity, more than any other Middle-Eastern nation. About 25% is from hydroelectric plants, and the remainder is from thermal plants.

Agriculture and Fishing. Despite Iran's spectacular increase in industrial production, farming continues to employ about 36% of the labor force, although only about 12% of the land is suitable for agriculture. An additional 10% of the population are nomadic tribespeople dependent for their livelihood on their herds of sheep and goats; there was a total of over 35 million sheep and 14 million goats in 1976. In 1962 a major land-reform program redistributed much of the huge land holdings of absentee landlords to poor, landless peasants in an effort to raise the rural standard of living. Irrigation dams were also built; mechanization was encouraged, and the government attempted to establish huge, mechanized commercial farms. Most farming, however, continues to be unmechanized and inefficient, partly because 80% of all farms cover less than 11 ha (27 acres) each. Iran's farm output has not been able to keep pace with demands for food by the nation's rapidly growing population. Fishing is an important commercial activity along the Caspian Sea, where caviar is the principal product, and also along the Persian Gulf.

Transportation. Railroads serve the major cities of Tehran, Mashhad, and Tabriz in the north and connect with lines serving Qom (Qum), Ahvaz, Bandar-e-Shahpur, Khorramshahr, and Isfahan. The rail system connects with the European rail network, but there are no eastward connections with Afghanistan or Pakistan. The road system is extensive, the principal highway extending from the Turkish border at Bazargan through Tabriz, Tehran, and Mashhad and to Herat, in Afghanistan. The principal ports are Khorramshahr, Bandar-e-Shahpur, Bushehr (Bushire), and Bandar Abbas.

Trade. During most of the 1970s more than 90% of Iranian exports consisted of oil and oil products. Other exports were mainly textiles, carpets, cotton, and dried and fresh fruits. Imports accounted for half of Iran's exports, by value, giving Iran an extremely favorable balance of trade. The major trading partners are the United States, Japan, West Germany, and the United Kingdom.

GOVERNMENT

On Feb. 12, 1979, Muslim revolutionary forces led by the religious leader Ayatollah Ruhollah KHOMEINI proclaimed Iran an Islamic republic. Premier Mehdi Bazargan was appointed prime minister, but real power was retained by the Ayatollah Khomeini and an Islamic Revolutionary Council of his close advisors. On March 30–31, voters approved establishment of the republic in a national referendum. Drafts of a proposed constitution called for a parliamentary form of government,

The blue dome of the Masjid i Shah, or Royal Mosque, dominates this aerial photograph taken above the city of Isfahan, in central Iran. This outstanding example of Islamic architecture was constructed during the 17th century by command of Shah Abbas.

Iran's first steel mill, which has an annual capacity of 650,000 metric tons, was constructed near Isfahan with the assistance of the USSR and began operating in 1973. Many of Iran's industrial facilities have been built in cooperative efforts with foreign nations.

with a strong, elected president and an elected unicameral legislature, or *Majlis*; the SHARIA (Islamic law) as the basis of the nation's legal system; and a council of guardians, dominated by religious leaders. In a plebiscite held on December 2-3 the new constitution was overwhelmingly approved by Iranian voters. In January 1980 presidential elections were held, and the former finance minister, Abolhassan Bani-Sadr, was elected.

HISTORY

Many dynasties and empires have ruled over Persia, which at times has been at the center of vast empires extending through much of the Middle East (see PERSIA, ANCIENT). The modern Persian state traces its beginnings to CYRUS THE GREAT, who became the first of the ACHAEMENID emperors in 549 BC. In 330 BC, Persia became part of Alexander the Great's empire. It was subsequently part of the SELEUCID kingdom and then, beginning in 250 BC, of the Parthian empire (see PARTHIA). In AD c.224 the Parthian ARSACID dynasty was overthrown by the SASSANIANS, a Persian dynasty that ruled until the Arab conquest, which was completed in 641. The Arabs introduced Islam and incorporated Persia into the dominions of the caliphs (see CALIPHATE). In the 11th and 12th centuries the country came under the rule of the SELJUK Turks, who laid down the administrative and economic structure that persisted until the 20th century. Persia was overrun by the MONGOLS under GENGHIS KHAN in the 13th century and by TIMUR in the late 14th century.

In the 16th century, after a long period of disunity, Shah Ismail (r. 1502-24) founded the Safavid dynasty, which restored Persia as a political entity and established Shiism as the national religion. The greatest Safavid ruler was Shah ABBAS I, who reconquered (1603-23) substantial territories from the Ottoman Empire. The Afghans overthrew the Safavids in 1722, but Persian independence was restored (1736) by the despotic NADIR SHAH. His Afshar dynasty was followed (1750) by the Zand dynasty, which was overthrown in 1794 by the Qajars (Kajars), who held the throne until 1925.

The 19th century saw Iran come under increasing pressure from Russia in the north and from Britain, which was pushing westward from India and northward from the Persian Gulf. The Anglo-Russian Entente of 1907 (see TRIPLE ENTENTE) divided the country into a Russian zone of influence, a British zone, and a neutral zone. In 1908 petroleum was discovered. The decadent Qajar dynasty was unable to save the country from a state of virtual civil war and from foreign domination until the emergence of a strong leader in REZA SHAH PAHLAVI after World War I. The *Majlis* (parliament) elevated him to the throne in 1925. He reorganized the military forces, restored internal order, broke the power of the reactionary Shiite clergy, developed new industries, and revised the legal system. His reforms were facilitated by growing oil revenues.

In 1941 joint British-Soviet pressure forced the abdication of the allegedly pro-German Reza Shah. He was succeeded by his 22-year-old son, Muhammad Reza Pahlavi. In the early 1950s the power of the new shah was challenged by the nationalist leader Muhammad MOSADDEQ, who tried to take over the government and nationalized the oil industry, previ-

ously controlled by foreign interests. The shah was forced to flee the country briefly in 1953, but he returned shortly with strong backing from the Western powers; Mosaddeq was subsequently convicted of treason, and the shah emerged as a powerful and determined ruler. In 1954 a new arrangement with a consortium of Western oil companies was negotiated, giving Iran 50% of all profits (raised to 55% in 1970).

In 1963 the shah inaugurated an ambitious program of modernization and development known as the White Revolution. Its goals included land reform, emancipation of women, and rapid economic development. It also brought widespread social unrest and political opposition from the Shiite clergy, who saw their powers diminishing, and from other conservative elements. For many years order was maintained by a strongly centralized government, a well-equipped army, and the secret police known as SAVAK.

In 1978, however, conservative and radical forces both participated in street rioting, and revolution seemed imminent. Premier Jamshid Amouzegar and his successor Premier Jaafar Sharif-Emami both proved unable to end the riots, and in November 1978, in an attempt to restore order, the shah placed Iran under military rule. Political opposition continued, however, led by the Ayatollah Khomeini—who had lived in exile since 1964. Khomeini demanded the shah's abdication.

On Jan. 6, 1979, military rule was lifted, and Shahpur Bakhtiar was appointed premier. On January 16, the shah and his family left the country, and on February 1, Khomeini returned to a tumultuous welcome. Rioting intensified, and on February 11, when the army abandoned its support for the shah, the Bakhtiar government was deposed. On February 12, Iran was proclaimed an Islamic republic, with Mehdi Bazargan as premier of a transitional government. Hundreds of the shah's supporters and alleged members of the hated SAVAK were subsequently arrested, tried, and executed. Khomeini, who retained real power in the new republic, initiated policies to halt and reverse the Westernization of Iran.

Opposition to Khomeini's rule intensified among Iran's ethnic minorities—Arabs, Azerbaijanis, Baluchis, and Kurds. Kurds demanding autonomy revolted in March, and fighting continued until late August. In December fighting broke out in the city of Tabriz between Azerbaijani followers of the Ayatollah Shariat Madari and troops loyal to the Ayatollah Khomeini.

In October the shah, who had previously been in exile in Mexico, was admitted to a New York hospital for cancer treatment. On November 4 a group of militant Iranian students took about 60 American diplomatic personnel hostage at the American embassy in Tehran and demanded the return of the shah to Iran for trial. (Six Americans escaped during the takeover and took refuge in the Canadian embassy until January 1980, when they were smuggled out of Iran.) The Ayatollah Khomeini supported the students, and Bazargan resigned. American efforts to secure the release of the hostages included a plea to the International Court of Justice, the movement of U.S. warships to the Indian Ocean, and the freezing of Iranian assets in U.S. banks. The release on Nov. 19-20, 1979, of 13 hostages who were either black or female did little to alleviate the crisis. Although the shah left the United States for Panama in early December, the students refused to release the hostages and threatened to put them on trial for espionage. The crisis intensified when the USSR invaded neighboring Afghanistan in late December and subsequently vetoed a U.S.-sponsored trade embargo of Iran at the United Nations.   ARTHUR CAMPBELL TURNER

Bibliography: Amuzegar, Jahangir, *Iran: An Economic Profile* (1977); Armajani, Yahya, *Iran* (1972); Bill, James A., *The Politics of Iran* (1972); *Cambridge History of Iran*, 5 vols. (1968); Chubin, Shahram, *The Foreign Relations of Iran* (1974); Elwell-Sutton, L. P., *Modern Iran* (1976); Frye, Richard N., *The Heritage of Persia* (1963); Lenczowski, George, *Iran under the Pahlavis* (1977); Wilbur, Donald, *Iran: Past and Present*, 7th rev. ed. (1975); Zonis, Marvin, *The Political Elite of Iran* (1971).

See also: MIDDLE EAST; MIDDLE EAST, HISTORY OF THE.

Iraq   [ir-ak']

Iraq is a republic of Southwest Asia, extending northwest from the head of the PERSIAN GULF. It is bounded on the south by the gulf, Kuwait, and Saudi Arabia; on the west by Jordan and Syria; on the north by Turkey; and on the east by Iran. Iraq is a major petroleum producer. Formerly called MESOPOTAMIA ("the land between the rivers"), Iraq is the site of one of the most ancient centers of civilization. In the 7th century AD it became part of the Arab world. Under Ottoman Turkish rule from the 17th century until World War I, it was then under British mandate until 1932. Iraq achieved independence as a monarchy, but a violent revolution brought the establishment of a socialist republic in 1958.

LAND AND RESOURCES
The topography of Iraq has four main areas: lower Iraq, upper

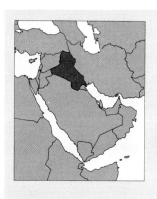

IRAQ

Official Name: Republic of Iraq
Capital and Largest City: Baghdad (1976 est. 2,969,000)
Area: 438,446 km² (171,267 mi²)
Elevation: *Highest*—Mt. Halgurd, 3,728 m (12,230 ft); *lowest*—sea level, along coast
Population: 12,470,000 (1978 est.). *Distribution*—65% urban, 35% rural; *density*, 28 persons per km² (73 per mi²); *annual rate of increase* (1970-76), 3.4%
Principal Languages: Arabic (official), Kurdish, Persian, Turkish
Principal Religions: Islam, Christianity, Judaism
Principal Products: *Agriculture*—wheat and barley, rice, dates, livestock. *Manufacturing and industry*—petroleum refining, textiles, brick and cement, sugar refining, food processing. *Mining*—petroleum, natural gas
Railroads: 2,203 km/1,368 mi (1972)
Roads: 6,490 km/4,030 mi (1978 paved)
Currency: 1 Iraqi dinar = 1,000 fils

Iraq, the northeast mountain region (part of KURDISTAN), and the western desert. Lower Iraq extends from the ridge between ar-Ramadi and BAGHDAD, the capital, southeastward for about 565 km (350 mi) to the Persian Gulf and encompasses the lower course of the TIGRIS and EUPHRATES river systems. These rivers are fundamental to the topography of Iraq. Near the gulf the rivers unite in the SHATT-AL-ARAB, but they are independent rivers throughout most of their courses, separated by a strip of land that at some points is more than 160 km (100 mi) in width. The plain of lower Iraq never exceeds 90 m (300 ft) in altitude. Baghdad is only 34 m (112 ft) above sea level, although over 500 km (310 mi) inland. The rivers run behind low levees, both natural and artificial. Their waters are distributed for irrigation through an extensive canal system.

Upper Iraq is 215 to 365 m (700 to 1,200 ft) high, composed primarily of rolling plains with fertile soil. The chief cities there are MOSUL and Kirkuk. Northeast of Kirkuk peaks in the mountain region rise to 3,730 m (12,240 ft). The western desert comprises about 35% of the total area of Iraq and extends from Kuwait along the Saudi Arabian border to Jordan and Syria. It is composed of heavily eroded rock of ancient origin. The soils of Iraq are heavy alluvial deposits in the Tigris-Euphrates Basin and very light soil elsewhere.

Climate. Aridity and summer heat characterize the climate of Iraq. In the lowlands, rainfall, occurring only between November and April, totals about 150 mm (6 in), whereas upper Iraq receives about 380-635 mm (15-25 in). The summer season in the plains is dry and excessively hot, with a persistent northwest wind (the *shamal*). The July mean temperature in Baghdad is about 34° C (93° F), with daily maxima from 43° to 49° C (110° to 120° F). The January average is 10° C (50° F), although temperatures of up to 27° C (81° F) have been recorded. In the uplands temperatures are more moderate, and mountain winters are cold.

Resources. Petroleum is the country's only substantial mineral resource. Natural gas and phosphate deposits are also present.

PEOPLE
Iraq has seen successive waves of conquest and immigration that have determined its ethnic diversity, but ARABS and Arabized elements of other ethnic strains make up about 71% of its present population. The largest, most visible minority is the more than 2,250,000 KURDS, who live in the northeast, speak their own language, and have a strong ethnic identity that has been a chronic problem for the Iraqi government. An important Persian minority lived within Iraq's borders, but half of these were repatriated to Iran in the early 1970s. Other minorities include Turks and Lurs.

Languages and Religions. Arabic is spoken almost universally, but Kurdish is commonly used in Kurdistan and Persian is used along the Iranian border. The dominant religion is Islam, evenly divided between the SUNNITES and SHIITES. Christians of various sects comprise about 4% of the population.

Demography. Vital statistics for Iraq lack reliability. Both emigration and immigration are low. The cities have grown rapidly since the 1950s as a result of rural-urban migration. The desert area is uninhabited except for BEDOUIN tribes.

Education and Health. A major expansion of educational facilities has taken place since 1958. About 20% of the population is literate. Approximately two-thirds of the boys and one-third of the girls attend school. Six universities have been established, all since 1957. Many Iraqis study abroad. Health services have been expanded, as part of the domestic policy of the recent socialist governments. Life expectancy is about 53 years at birth, and infant mortality is estimated at 28 per 1,000 live births.

Cultural Institutions. The traditional culture of Iraq developed from the broader Arab culture and is expressed in poetry and prose literature, dancing, and the design of rugs and artifacts. The Iraq Museum and Museum of Arab Antiquities in Baghdad house ancient relics. Ruins at BABYLON and NINEVEH attract tourists and archaeologists. Since the 1960s an attempt has been made to instill a distinct Iraqi culture.

ECONOMIC ACTIVITY
The economy of Iraq until recent decades was almost exclusively agricultural. However, increasing revenues from oil pro-

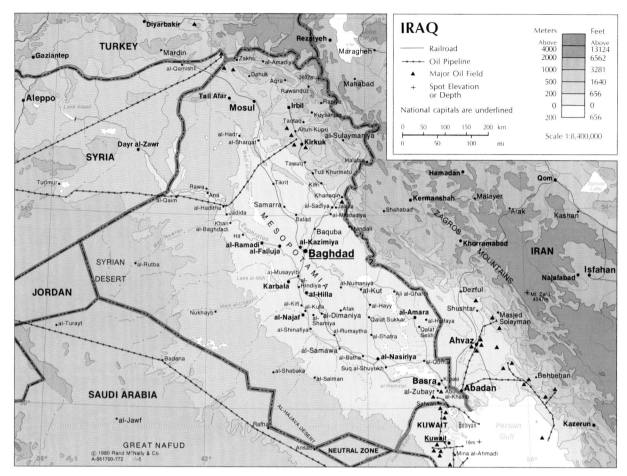

IRAQ

	Meters		Feet
Railroad	Above		Above
Oil Pipeline	4000		13124
▲ Major Oil Field	2000		6562
+ Spot Elevation or Depth	1000		3281
	500		1640
National capitals are underlined	200		656
	0		0
	200		656

Scale 1:8,400,000

duction have reduced the importance of agriculture. The development of industry and the upgrading of agriculture have been stressed in a succession of 5-year plans since 1965. The 1958 revolution led to the forced breakup of large estates for the creation of a class of smaller-landed proprietors.

Mining and Manufacturing. Petroleum is found in the north, northeast, and south; natural gas is also produced. Iraq's petroleum reserves are estimated at about 6% of the world total.

Current production averages 830 million barrels per year. The developer of the Iraqi oil industry was the British-dominated Iraq Petroleum Company. In 1972 all of Iraq's petroleum resources were nationalized. Iraq is a charter member of the ORGANIZATION OF PETROLEUM EXPORTING COUNTRIES.

Textile, steel, sugar, and cement plants are among Iraq's diversified industries. The Tigris River is the source for much of the hydroelectric power used by industry.

(Right) *Baghdad, the capital and largest city of Iraq, is located along the flood plain of the Tigris River in the central portion of the country. Baghdad's importance as a center of Islamic culture dates from the 8th century, when it became the seat of the Abbasid caliphate.*

(Below) *Bars indicate the monthly ranges of temperature (red) and precipitation (blue) in Baghdad, which has a steppe climate.*

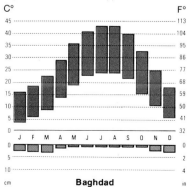

Baghdad

(Left) *The noria, a type of water wheel developed during Roman times, is still used in rural areas of Iraq to draw water for irrigation. In 1975 the Iraqi government, with the assistance of the Soviet Union, began work on a major river-control project that is expected to increase the amount of irrigated land and reduce damage from seasonal flooding. (Right) Although it receives no major tributaries along its course through Iraq, the Tigris River flows more swiftly and conveys a greater volume of water than the lengthier Euphrates, the nation's other major waterway.*

Agriculture. About 18% of Iraq's land is cultivated. Agriculture is dependent on irrigation in the south. Farther north rainfall is adequate for farming. Iraq is the world's largest producer of dates, grown mostly around the Shatt-al-Arab. Grains, beans, rice, and corn are grown; livestock raising is a traditional occupation.

Transportation and Trade. Road travel dominates transportation in Iraq. International airports are located near Baghdad and at BASRA. The Tigris and Euphrates are navigable.

Trade, primarily through the Gulf ports of Basra, Al Faw, and Umm Qasr, centers on petroleum exports, along with dates. Iraq imports machinery, transportation equipment, and sugar. Its principal trade partners are the USSR, France, and Italy. Because of its valuable petroleum exports, Iraq has a favorable trade balance.

GOVERNMENT

The overthrow of the monarchy in 1958 was followed by a succession of revolutionary socialist regimes that have ruled the country under a provisional constitution. Since the mid-1960s the Arab Socialist BAATH PARTY has controlled the nation. The Communist party is the only recognized political organization. The small governing junta is the 22-member Revolutionary Command Council (RCC).

In charge of the government since 1979 has been Saddam Hussein Takriti, who is president, chairman of the RCC, commander of the armed forces, premier, and secretary-general of the Baath party.

HISTORY

Iraq was one of the most ancient centers of urban civilization and settled cultivation. SUMER, AKKAD, ASSYRIA, and BABYLONIA all developed major civilizations in ancient Mesopotamia. In the early centuries AD, the area was part of various Persian empires. After the Arab conquest in the 7th century, Baghdad (founded in 762) became the seat of the CALIPHATE of the ABBASIDS. With the Mongol conquest by Hulagu in 1258, the country was virtually ruined.

In the 16th and 17th centuries control over Iraq was contested by the Ottoman and Persian empires. From 1638, however, Iraq was part of the OTTOMAN EMPIRE, although often

with some degree of autonomy. During World War I a British force occupied Iraq, and in 1920 it became a British mandate of the League of Nations, with FAISAL I of the Hashemite family as king. Following civil disturbances in the 1920s, the mandate was terminated in 1932, but the British maintained strong influence over Iraq until 1958.

Iraqi politics was dominated during the 1940s and '50s by the pro-Western leader Nuri es-Said, who initiated the modernization of Iraq. The country joined the CENTRAL TREATY ORGANIZATION in 1955, the only Arab state to do so. However, radical nationalist forces created a ferment that led to a military coup under Gen. Abdul Karim Kassem on July 14, 1958. A pro-Communist republic was proclaimed, and the royal family, along with Nuri es-Said, were murdered.

Since 1958 the history of Iraq has largely been one of extremism and violence, along with substantial economic development. The Kassem regime collapsed in 1963, and Col. Abdul Salam Aref assumed control. By the end of that same year Aref had ousted Baath party extremists from the governing council. Upon his death in 1966 his brother assumed control. He in turn was succeeded, after a 1968 coup by the Baathist Ahmad Hassan al-Bakr. In the past two decades Iraq has been subject to insurrection by the Kurdish independence movement. In 1972 the nation signed a treaty of alliance with the USSR, but recent moves have suggested a drift from the Communist bloc. Iraq participated in the ARAB-ISRAELI WAR of 1973 and has maintained a consistently hostile stance toward Israel. After al-Bakr suffered a heart attack in 1976, effective control of the government passed to Gen. Saddam Hussein Takriti, who formally succeeded al-Bakr in 1979.

ARTHUR CAMPBELL TURNER

Bibliography: Atiyyah, Ghassan R., *Iraq, 1908–1921* (1975); Fernea, Elizabeth W., *Guests of the Sheik: An Ethnography of an Iraqi Village* (1969); Ireland, P. W., *Iraq* (1970); Khadduri, Majid, *Independent Iraq* (1960), *Republican Iraq* (1970), and *Socialist Iraq* (1978); Langley, K. M., *The Industrialization of Iraq* (1961); Penrose, Edith, *Iraq* (1978); Roux, Georges, *Ancient Iraq* (1965).

See also: MIDDLE EAST; MIDDLE EAST, HISTORY OF THE.

Iredell, James   [ire'-dul]

James Iredell, b. Oct. 5, 1751, d. Oct. 20, 1799, was an American jurist and an associate justice of the U.S. Supreme Court. He played a leading role in North Carolina's ratification (1788) of the federal Constitution. In 1790, President Washington appointed Iredell to the newly established U.S. Supreme Court, on which he served until his death.

Bibliography: McRee, Griffith J., *The Life and Correspondence of James Iredell* (1857; repr. 1949).

Ireland

The Republic of Ireland (Eire) covers almost 85% of the island bearing its name. DUBLIN is its capital. Twenty-six of the island's 32 counties are within the Republic. The six northeastern counties form NORTHERN IRELAND, which is part of the United Kingdom. This partition dates from 1920–22, before which the whole island was under British rule. Ireland is separated from Great Britain by the IRISH SEA. The Atlantic Ocean surrounds it on the north, west, and south.

The Republic of Ireland is primarily suited to agricultural activities, although industry is increasing in importance. Recently discovered deposits of lead, silver, zinc, and copper are mined. The pleasant scenery, unspoiled countryside, and unhurried way of life attract many vacationers.

LAND AND RESOURCES

Physically, Ireland is a detached fragment of the European mainland, separated from it by the shallow seas of the continental shelf. Most of the country is a lowland less than 150 m (500 ft) above sea level and underlain by limestone rocks of Carboniferous age. The surface is covered by glacial drift, a legacy of the Pleistocene ice age. In places the drift has been shaped into distinctive landforms, as in long gravel ridges (eskers) of the midlands and hundreds of small hills (drumlins) that form a continuous belt across the island from Clew Bay in the west.

The central lowland is surrounded by a discontinuous rim of mountains. The oldest of these, mainly of Cambrian and Precambrian age, can be found in the north and west of the country, the remnants of a mountain range that once was a chain extending from Ireland through Scotland to Scandinavia. Quartzite rocks give rise to rugged mountain scenery as in Errigal (752 m/2,466 ft) and Muckish (670 m/2,197 ft) in DONEGAL; Croagh Patrick (765 m/2,510 ft) in MAYO; and the Twelve Bens or Pins in County GALWAY. A former ice cover has steepened many of the slopes and scoured river valleys, some of which, like Killary harbor in Mayo, have been flooded by the sea to form fjords.

IRELAND

Official Name: Republic of Ireland
Capital and Largest City: Dublin, 567,866 (1971)
Area: 70,282 km² (27,136 mi²)
Elevation: *Highest*—Carrantuohill, 1,041 m (3,414 ft); *lowest*—sea level, along the coast
Population: 3,364,881 (1979). *Distribution*—52.2% urban, 47.8% rural; *density*, 48 persons per km² (124 per mi²); *annual rate of increase* (1971–79), 1.5%
Principal Languages: English, Irish (Gaelic)
Principal Religions: Roman Catholic, Anglican
Principal Products: *Agriculture*—livestock and dairy products, barley, potatoes, oats, sugar beets, hay and wheat, turnips. *Manufacturing and industry*—food processing, brewing, textiles, chemicals and pharmaceuticals, machinery and transportation equipment. *Mining*—lead, zinc, natural gas, peat, silver, copper
Railroads: 2,009 km/1,248 mi (1976)
Roads: 80,139 km/49,775 mi (1975 paved)
Currency: 1 Irish pound = 100 pence

In the south of Ireland a series of parallel ridges of Devonian sandstone, separated by valleys floored with Carboniferous limestones and shales, are a continuation of the Hercynian structures of central Europe and Brittany. The ridges rise in elevation westward, culminating at Carrantuohill, the highest mountain in the country. The Lakes of Killarney, famous for their scenic beauty, are situated in that area. A geologically recent depression of the land allowed the sea to enter the

(Left) *The neoclassical dome of the Four Courts (center, partially obscured), headquarters of Ireland's judiciary, is one of the major architectural landmarks crowding the River Liffey in Dublin. Dublin is Ireland's capital, largest city, and cultural center.*

(Below) *Bars indicate the monthly ranges of temperature (red) and precipitation (blue) of Dublin, Ireland. Moderate temperatures, year-round rainfall, and high humidity account for Ireland's verdure.*

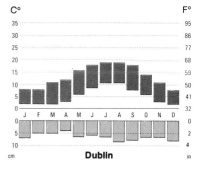

Dublin

North America and Great Britain continued over the next hundred years; by 1930 the population numbered little more than half the 1845 figure. Since 1961, the population has been increasing at an average of about 1% per annum. Ireland's density is fifth-lowest of all European nations.

A distinctive feature of Ireland's rural population today is the low proportion to the total population of people in the 15-to-45-year age group. This low level results from the departure of working-age persons to seek employment in the cities or overseas.

The population is fairly evenly distributed throughout the country. Higher densities can be found along the western seaboard, an area of small farms on poor land. Lower densities are associated with larger farms on the more fertile land in the east.

Only 52% of the population live in towns of 1,500 inhabitants or more. Dublin, together with its seaport of DÚN LAOGHAIRE, has more than one-fifth of the country's total population. Second in importance is the city of CORK, followed by Limerick, WATERFORD, and GALWAY, all port cities. The largest inland town is KILKENNY, with 9,838 inhabitants. The most urbanized areas of the country are the south and east; the population is increasing in these areas while densities elsewhere are declining. Migration has led to serious rural depopulation in the extreme west and in the LEITRIM and ROSCOMMON areas near Lough Allen.

Education. Elementary education is compulsory and free between the ages of 6 and 15 in schools financed by the state but managed by the various religious denominations. Postprimary education is provided by privately owned, state-subsidized schools and by state-owned comprehensive and vocational schools. Third-level education is provided by five teacher training colleges, nine regional technical colleges, a National Institute for Higher Education in Limerick, and two universities. The National University, founded in 1909, has constituent colleges in Dublin, Cork, Galway, and Maynooth. The latter is also a pontifical college. The University of Dublin was founded in 1592 and has one college, TRINITY COLLEGE.

Health. Ireland has a comprehensive health service. Persons in the lower income groups and their dependents are entitled to general medical care, hospitalization, and specialized treatment at government expense. Financial assistance for medical care is provided by the government on the basis of economic need. Adequate hospital accommodations are available, and the doctor-patient ratio approximates one to 1,000. Ireland's birthrate is 21.6 per 1,000, the death rate is 10.5 per 1,000, and the infant mortality rate is 14.6 per 1,000 live births. The chief cause of death is heart disease, accounting for 32% of all fatalities.

The Arts. A considerable body of literature written in the Irish language exists, dating from the 6th century; much of it is based on a rich oral tradition preserving the sagas of ancient Ireland. Gaelic literature continued to be common until the 17th century, when the use of English became more widespread. An Anglo-Irish writing style began with Jonathan SWIFT; in succeeding centuries many Irish writers and dramatists have become noteworthy, including Oliver GOLDSMITH, Richard Brinsley SHERIDAN, Oscar WILDE, James JOYCE, George Bernard SHAW, and Samuel BECKETT. The development of the ABBEY THEATRE as the National Theatre of Ireland is associated with the work of Lady GREGORY, William Butler YEATS, Sean O'CASEY, John Millington SYNGE, James STEPHENS, and many others who, even though they wrote in English, drew their inspiration from Gaelic traditions and Irish rural life. For additional information, see IRISH LITERATURE; IRISH LITERARY RENAISSANCE.

Ireland is noted for its early Christian art in both metalwork and illuminated manuscripts. An example of the former is the Ardagh Chalice and, of the latter, the BOOK OF KELLS; both date from the 8th century (see CELTIC ART). The most noteworthy architectural structures of the country are the round towers and early Celtic churches built between 700 and 1150. A few of the great castles constructed by the Anglo-Norman invaders dating from 1170 are still intact, but most now lie in ruins. In contrast to these fortified buildings, elegant Georgian architecture dating from 1729 provides Dublin with many fine squares and public buildings. Merrion Square, Trinity College, the Custom House, the Four Courts, and the Bank of Ireland (formerly the parliament buildings) are examples.

The main learned societies in the country are the Royal Irish Academy, founded in 1785, and the Royal Dublin Society, dating from 1731. The latter is concerned with the fostering of agriculture, science, and the arts; two major agricultural shows are held annually on its grounds at Ballsbridge.

ECONOMIC ACTIVITIES

Throughout its history Ireland has been an agricultural country. Farming remains the largest single economic activity, employing 20% of the work force. Almost 90% of the farms cover less than 250 ha (100 acres); 90% of the agricultural land is under pasture or hay. Dairying, usually by cooperatives, predominates in the south and in the north midlands; beef cattle are raised on the small farms in the west and fattened on the larger farms of the east. Sheep graze on the uplands. The main crops are barley for feeding and for malting, oats, wheat, potatoes, and sugar beets.

Fishing employs 4,500 part-time and 2,000 full-time workers. The chief fish caught are cod, whiting, plaice, sole, haddock, herring, and mackerel. Lobsters, prawns, periwinkles, and other shellfish abound along the rocky coasts and have a ready market on the European continent. In an effort to improve fishing facilities, the government has designated five ports for special development. Howth on the east coast, Dunmore East on the south coast, and Castletown Bere, Galway, and Killybegs in the west.

(Left) *Although Ireland's saucer-shaped central plain prevents effective drainage, farming is the principal economic activity.*

(Below) *A family of shepherds drives a small flock along a rural road in County Tipperary, which contributes much of the more than 4 million sheep raised in Ireland for export.*

Ireland has long traditions in dairying, brewing, and textile weaving, but these activities employ only a small fraction of the population. In the 1930s the new state encouraged local industry, placing tariffs on imported goods so small-scale industries could develop to serve local needs. By 1950 this market had been saturated, and a decline in development necessitated a major change in government policy. Foreign-owned firms, especially those with export potential, were induced to locate in the country.

In 1959 a special industrial estate was established at Shannon, close to the international airport, where goods are imported and exported without customs restrictions. Forty factories, employing 4,500 workers, are now located there. Manufacturing currently employs 19% of the country's total work force; 47,000, or 24%, are employed in the production of food and drink. Electric power is available everywhere from the national grid. Imported coal and petroleum generates 67%, local peat and coal 25%, and hydropower 8%.

Ireland maintains an economy of both public and private enterprises. The electric power network, along with the chemical, steel, and sugar industries, are state controlled. Unemployment remains high in the country; the inflation rate had been reduced to 6% by mid-1978.

Ireland has an extensive system of public roads, forming a dense network throughout the country. Railroads radiate from Dublin and provide passenger and freight facilities to all the major towns; the roads, however, now carry a much greater volume of traffic. Dublin is the chief seaport, handling about two-thirds of the seaborne trade. Numerous car ferries ply frequently between various British and Irish ports, and a direct car and passenger ferry travels from Rosslare to Le Havre, France. The number of passengers using the cross-channel ferries is 1.9 million annually, while an additional 2 million travel by air, 371,000 of these on the transatlantic services. International airports are located at Dublin, Cork, and Shannon, with direct services to the United States and Canada as well as to nine European countries. Public transportation is state owned, including Aer Lingus, the national airline.

A government corporation controls and operates the country's radio and television service. Irish-language radio stations broadcast from Kerry, Galway, and Donegal counties.

The United Kingdom is Ireland's chief trading partner, accounting for about 50% of external trade. In addition, the United States and West Germany are important to the Irish foreign trade market.

More than one-third of all exports are agricultural products; machinery and woolen textiles are also significant exports. Imports are dominated by manufactured goods, petroleum, and coal. Heavy dependence on costly imported fuel has created a balance-of-payments deficit. Tourism, valued at more than $100 million in 1977, has become an important source of foreign currency.

GOVERNMENT

In the late 18th century, Ireland achieved self-government under an Anglo-Irish Protestant Ascendancy, but the Act of Union, effective in 1801, abolished the Dublin Parliament and linked Ireland politically with Britain. The modern independent state of Ireland dates from 1921 when, after a long and bitter struggle, the Irish Free State (Saorstat Éireann) was created. A new constitution was adopted on Dec. 29, 1937, making Ireland a member of the Commonwealth. It was not until 1949 that the Free State was declared a republic and separated from the Commonwealth. The Republic of Ireland is a parliamentary democracy. Its constitution provides for a nonexecutive president elected by direct vote for a 7-year term. The national parliament is the Oireachtas, consisting of the president and two houses, Dáil Éireann and Seanad Éireann. Dáil Éireann's 148 members are elected through a system of proportional representation by means of the single transferable vote. The electorate is composed of all Irish citizens over the age of 18.

The Seanad, or upper house, has 60 members, 11 of whom are nominated by the taoiseach, or prime minister. The remaining 49 are elected, 6 by the universities and 43 from panels of candidates selected on a vocational basis. The govern-

ment is headed by the taoiseach, who is appointed by the president on the nomination of the Dáil Éireann. The taoiseach, in turn, nominates from 7 to 15 Dáil members to form his cabinet. The life of the Dáil is 5 years, unless dissolved by the president on the advice of the taoiseach. Constitutional changes can be made only by a referendum to the people, as was done in 1971 when Ireland planned to become a member of the EUROPEAN ECONOMIC COMMUNITY.

Ireland had 4 ancient provinces: LEINSTER, MUNSTER, CONNACHT, and Ulster. Today, the Republic of Ireland is divided politically into 27 county councils (TIPPERARY is divided for administrative purposes), 4 county borough corporations, 7 borough corporations, 49 urban district councils, and 28 town commissions. Local officials are elected for 5-year terms.

The two major political parties, both conservative in outlook, are FIANNA FÁIL, founded by Eamon DE VALERA in 1926, and the FINE GAEL party, formally established in 1933. The former won the general election of 1977. In December 1979, Charles J. Haughey succeeded Jack LYNCH as prime minister.

The political leaders of Ireland today must face the economic problem of high unemployment. Ireland's admission to the EEC in 1973 was encouraged by its government to provide easier access to the markets of member nations. Domestically, however, the country has found no easy solution to the problems related to Northern Ireland and the terrorist activities of the IRISH REPUBLICAN ARMY.   JOSEPH P. HAUGHTON

Bibliography: Chubb, Basil, *The Government and Politics of Ireland* (1970); De Breffny, Brian, ed., *The Irish World: The Art and Culture of the Irish People* (1977); Figgis, Allen, *The Encyclopedia of Ireland*, ed. by Victor Meally (1968); Freeman, Thomas W., *Ireland: A General and Regional Geography*, 3d ed. (1965); Gillmor, Desmond, *A Systematic Geography of Ireland* (1971); Haughton, Joseph P., ed., *Atlas of Ireland* (1979); Kennedy, Kieran, and Dowling, Brendan, *Economic Growth in Ireland* (1975); Kennedy, Robert E., *The Irish: Emigration, Marriage and Fertility* (1973); Mitchell, G. F., *Irish Landscape* (1976); O'Donnell, J. D., *How Ireland Is Governed*, 5th ed. (1965); Orme, O. R., *Ireland* (1970); Whittow, J. B., *The Geology and Scenery in Ireland* (1974).

Ireland, history of

The first human settlements in Ireland, an island lying on the western fringe of Europe, were made relatively late in EUROPEAN PREHISTORY, around 6000 BC.

Early Gaelic Ireland. Sometime between about 600 and 150 BC, Celtic peoples from western Europe, who came to be known as GAELS, invaded Ireland and subdued the previous inhabitants. The basic units of Gaelic society were the *tuatha*, or petty kingdoms, of which perhaps 150 existed in Ireland. The *tuatha* remained independent of one another, but they shared a common language, Gaelic (see CELTIC LANGUAGES), and a class of men called *brehons*, who were learned in customary law and helped to preserve throughout Ireland a remarkably uniform but archaic social system. One reason for the unique nature of Irish society was that the Romans, who transformed the Celtic societies of Britain and other societies on the Continent with their armies, roads, administrative system, and towns, never tried to conquer Ireland.

MEDIEVAL IRELAND

Another consequence of Ireland's isolation from Romanized Europe was the development of a distinctive Celtic type of Christianity. Saint PATRICK introduced mainstream Latin Christianity into the country in the 5th century AD, but the system of bishops with territorial dioceses, modeled on the Roman Empire's administrative system, did not take secure root in Ireland at this time. While the autonomous *tuath* remained the basic unit of Gaelic secular society, the autonomous monastery became the basic unit of Celtic Christianity. During the 6th and 7th centuries the Irish monasteries were great centers of learning, sending out missionaries such as saints COLUMBA and COLUMBAN to the rest of Europe. What was for most of Europe the Dark Ages was for Ireland the golden age. Religious art, such as the Ardagh Chalice and the BOOK OF KELLS and other illuminated manuscripts, flourished alongside secular, even pagan, artistic achievements like the Tara Brooch and the great Irish epic *Tain Bo Cuailgne* (The Cattle Raid of Cooley).

The Viking Invasions. In the late 8th century, VIKINGS from Scandinavia began to raid Ireland. Other parts of Europe at about this time were responding to such pressures by developing the system of FEUDALISM, but the Gaelic society did not lend itself to such development. It lacked the heritage of Roman law that provided the framework for feudal institutions elsewhere. Moreover, the elaborate kinship arrangements by which both property-holding and succession to leadership roles were regulated by brehon law may have impeded the exchange of land for military service, which is the fundamental bargain underlying the feudal system. Eventually, Gaelic society did manage to organize resistance: in 1014, Irish forces led by King BRIAN BORU decisively defeated the Vikings at the Battle of Clontarf.

Brian's tenure (1002–14) of the honorific title "high king of Ireland" is sometimes misunderstood as the seed time of a national monarchy. Actually, the high king's power throughout much of Ireland was insubstantial. Without the infrastructure of feudalism even such a leader as Brian could not make the transition from symbolic kingship to effective monarchy that was beginning in other parts of Europe. Meanwhile, although Viking power was broken, the Vikings had left their mark upon the country by founding Ireland's first cities, including DUBLIN, LIMERICK, and WATERFORD.

The Anglo-Norman Conquest. Even such unity as there had been under Brian had disappeared by the time Ireland faced its next challenge. This challenge came from the highly effective feudal monarchy that had been founded in England by WILLIAM I (William the Conqueror) after his invasion of that country in 1066 from Normandy in France. In 1171, William's descendant HENRY II took advantage of an earlier letter from Pope ADRIAN IV authorizing Henry to make himself overlord

Ireland in the late 12th century was ruled by two aristocracies: Gaelic chieftains in the north and west and Anglo-Norman barons in the east. Although Henry II was recognized as feudal lord in 1175, the English monarchy failed to realize control of either ruling group.

Ireland after 1170
Showing the Principal Irish Clans and Norman Families

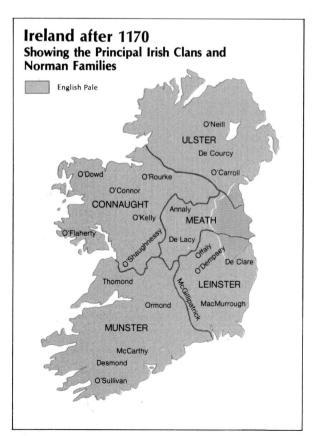

English Pale

ENGLISH PLANTATION (SETTLEMENT) OF IRELAND

Planted before the reign of Elizabeth

Planted during the reign of Elizabeth I, 1558-1603

Planted during the reign of James I, 1603-25

The plantations of Ireland, begun under Queen Mary I in the central plain and vigorously conducted under Elizabeth I in Munster (1584) and James I in Ulster (1608) saw the eviction and execution of thousands of native Irish.

of Ireland in order to bring the Irish church more into line with Roman standards. Several Anglo-Norman barons, with their retainers, had already seized large parts of Ireland when Henry went to Ireland with an army to receive the formal submission of those barons and of most of the Irish kings.

In those areas where the Anglo-Norman barons settled and drove out the native Gaelic aristocracy, they established a feudal system like that which their ancestors had brought from Normandy to England. The result, however, was not an effective centralized monarchy such as Norman feudalism had fostered in England. The English monarchy was usually distracted from Irish affairs by more pressing concerns such as the HUNDRED YEARS' WAR (1338–1453) and therefore did not effectively subordinate to royal authority even the Anglo-Norman colony. Thus, one may think of Ireland in the late Middle Ages as consisting of three concentric regions: (1) Dublin and its immediate hinterland (eventually called the PALE), the only area in which the English government really exercised authority; (2) a broad arc of territories beyond the Pale, which were the quasi-independent fiefs of the great Anglo-Norman lords; and (3) a further arc of territories along the western coast of Ireland that retained Gaelic customs and remained completely outside English rule.

The English colony in Ireland reached its greatest extent in the early 14th century, after which Gaelic society enjoyed considerable resurgence, partly by winning territories back from the colonists but mainly through the transformation of the Anglo-Normans into an "Anglo-Irish" aristocracy. As the Anglo-Normans intermarried with the Gaelic population and adopted the Gaelic language and customs, they gradually became "more Irish than the Irish." The Statutes of Kilkenny (1366) were an unsuccessful attempt to arrest this process and to define the area of English control.

The Anglo-Norman conquest hastened reforms that brought the Irish church more into line with Roman standards. English legal practices and civil administration were introduced, and, although it served only the Anglo-Irish colony, an Irish parliament modeled on the English one was created in the late 13th century. Because of the colony's propensity to support the Yorkist side in the Wars of the ROSES (1455-85), England's HENRY VII forced an Irish parliament of 1494-95 to adopt Poynings's Law, which gave the English Privy Council a veto over legislation proposed in future Irish parliaments.

By the end of the Middle Ages it was clear that the Anglo-Norman conquest was a failure, and in the 16th century the English monarchs HENRY VIII, MARY I, and ELIZABETH I made concerted efforts to reconquer Ireland by military expeditions and by the establishment (or plantation) of colonies of English settlers in Ireland. Henry's severance of the ties between the Church of England and the papacy, however (see REFORMATION), complicated the reconquest. In Ireland, unlike England, there was virtually no indigenous sympathy with the Protestant reformers among either the Gaelic Irish or the Anglo-Irish. Thus the Church of Ireland was legally transformed into a Protestant church rejected by the overwhelming majority of the population.

MODERN IRELAND

The most determined resistance to reconquest came from the Gaelic chieftains of Ulster (the northeastern quarter of the island), led by Hugh O'Neill, 2d earl of TYRONE, at the end of Elizabeth's reign. In suppressing their rebellion between 1595 and 1603, English forces devastated the Ulster countryside. Once these chieftains had submitted, however, King JAMES I of England was willing to let them live on their ancestral lands as English-style nobles, but not as petty kings within the old Gaelic social system. Dissatisfied with their new roles, the chieftains took ship to the Continent in 1607. This "flight of the earls" gave the English crown a pretext to confiscate their vast lands and sponsor scattered settlements of British Protestants throughout west and central Ulster (the Ulster Plantation). The crown's actions indirectly encouraged the much heavier unsponsored migration of Scots to the coastal counties of Down and Antrim. These settlements account for the existence in present-day Ulster of numerous Protestants (many of them Scottish Presbyterians) of all social classes.

Elsewhere in modern Ireland, Protestantism has been confined to a small propertied elite, many of whose members were the beneficiaries of further confiscations a generation after the Ulster Plantation. The pretext for these new confiscations was the rebellion of the Gaelic Irish in Ulster against the British settlers in 1641. Indeed, this rebellion triggered the ENGLISH CIVIL WAR, which put an end to King CHARLES I's attempt to create an absolutist state (represented in Ireland by the policies of his lord deputy, Thomas Wentworth, 1st earl of STRAFFORD). When the Puritan party defeated Charles, their leader, Oliver CROMWELL, quickly imposed (1649-50) English authority on Ireland. Cromwell repaid his soldiers and investors in the war effort with land confiscated largely from the Anglo-Irish Catholics of the Irish midlands who had joined the rebellion hesitantly and only to defend themselves against Puritan policies.

The Protestant Ascendancy. Hoping to recover their lands and political dominance in Ireland, Catholics took the side of the Catholic king JAMES II in England's GLORIOUS REVOLUTION of 1688 and thus shared in his defeat by WILLIAM III at the Battle of the BOYNE in 1690. The Irish Protestant elite consolidated its victory over what was left of a Catholic elite by enacting a number of Penal Laws designed to exclude the latter from property and power. Protestants had not, however, won for their parliament the powers that the landed elite of England

The Battle of the Boyne (1690), portrayed by Jan Wyck, resulted in decisive victory for William III over Irish and French forces backing the deposed king James II. Final defeat of the remaining Irish forces a year later brought about the systematic persecution of Irish Catholics. (National Museum of Ireland, Dublin.)

had won for theirs in the Glorious Revolution. Furthermore, British trade policies discriminated against Ireland, and many of the Scottish Presbyterians in Ulster began to emigrate to America, where their descendants became known as the "Scotch-Irish." In 1782 a "Patriot" party led by Henry GRATTAN and backed by an army of Protestant volunteers persuaded the British government to amend Poynings's Law to give the Irish Parliament legislative independence, including the right to establish Ireland's own tariff policy.

The Revolutionary Era. The reforms of 1782 did not extend far

(Left) Daniel O'Connell, whose efforts to mobilize Irish Catholics did much to bring about Catholic emancipation (1829), dramatized the Irish position when he was elected (1828) to Parliament in defiance of the restrictive British Test Act.

(Below) Irish tenants evicted from their lands during the great famine of 1845 to 1849 crowd about the work house in this contemporary engraving.

enough in a democratic direction to satisfy such intellectuals as Wolfe TONE and many of the Presbyterian merchants and farmers of the north, who were prompted by the French Revolution to form the Society of UNITED IRISHMEN. The United Irishmen allied themselves with the Catholic "Defender" cells that had recently originated out of sectarian conflict in County Armagh and spread throughout the south. A rebellion in 1798 was quickly put down, but it convinced the British government to end Ireland's separate political institutions. Members of the Irish Parliament were cajoled and bribed into passing the Act of Union (1800), which provided for a single Parliament for the British Isles. Catholics, who had been granted the right to vote in 1793, were encouraged to believe that the united Parliament would grant them the right to hold parliamentary seats. Not until 1829, however, when faced with a menacing agitation for CATHOLIC EMANCIPATION led by Daniel O'CONNELL, did Parliament grant this right.

The Growth of Irish Nationalism. Ironically, as the state moved toward neutrality between the two religions during the 19th century, the sectarian division of Irish society was taking on new significance as a "nationality" difference. In the 1830s, when O'Connell started a new movement to repeal the Act of Union, he received practically no support from those northern Presbyterians whose fathers had been United Irishmen. Its growing prosperity as an outpost of industrializing Britain made the city of BELFAST increasingly committed to the legislative union with Britain. Meanwhile, those parts of Ireland where most Catholics lived lagged badly behind Britain and northeast Ulster in economic development, as was dramatically demonstrated in the 1840s, when the failure of the potato crop for several successive years produced a devastating famine. Between 1841 and 1851, Ireland's population fell from 8.2 million to 6.6 million through starvation, disease, and emigration—especially to the United States.

The famine arrested temporarily the growth of nationalism in the Catholic community—in 1848 a rebellion promoted by dissidents from O'Connell's movement ended in farce—but its long-term effect was to strengthen Irish nationalism. In rural Ireland the generation that came of age following the famine experienced modestly rising prosperity and a rapidly increasing awareness of the greater affluence enjoyed by British (and Ulster Protestant) beneficiaries of industrialization—conditions that were favorable to the emergence of a vigorous popular demand for national self-government. Such a demand was enthusiastically supported by the Irish emigrant community in the United States, some members of which had formed an arm of the secret revolutionary society of FENIANS.

The Home-Rule Movement. The agricultural depression of the late 1870s interrupted the rise in prosperity, and the resulting agrarian discontent was harnessed to emerging nationalist aspirations by Charles Stewart PARNELL. Under Parnell's leadership an Irish nationalist party, demanding home rule—a separate Irish parliament within the Union—and land reform, was able to win every parliamentary seat having a Catholic majority. This solid bloc of votes gave Parnell and his successor, John REDMOND, powerful leverage in British politics whenever neither British party had a clear majority in the House of Commons. By exploiting such a situation in 1910-14, the Irish party finally forced the enactment of a HOME RULE BILL—but it also evoked the Ulster Covenant, by which northern Protestants vowed to resist home rule by force. Paramilitary forces were being organized by both sides, and civil war seemed imminent when World War I intervened. Home rule was enacted in 1914 but suspended until the end of the war, when it was understood that Ulster would receive some special treatment.

From the 1890s, nationalism found expression in an IRISH LITERARY RENAISSANCE. The poet William Butler YEATS, the playwrights Sean O'CASEY and John Millington SYNGE, and others turned their attention to uniquely Irish subjects and traditions. Writers, students, and Gaelic-language enthusiasts associated with this cultural revival tended to gravitate toward SINN FEIN, a political movement founded by Arthur GRIFFITH.

The Division of Ireland. Frustration arising from the postponement of home rule led to the 1916 EASTER RISING in Dub-

lin. Although a military failure, this rebellion brought a new generation of potential leadership to public attention. At the end of World War I, Sinn Fein candidates, who had pledged not to attend Parliament, won all but six of the Catholic seats away from the more moderate Irish party and set themselves up as a revolutionary parliament, Dáil Éireann, in Dublin. While guerrilla warfare by the IRISH REPUBLICAN ARMY (IRA) and reprisals by crown forces were under way in Ireland, the British government attempted to produce an alternative to the Home Rule Act. This 1920 Government of Ireland Act set up separate parliaments for Northern Ireland and Southern Ireland, although only the former ever functioned.

Dáil Éireann refused to accept the new legislation, and following a ceasefire in 1921 its representatives negotiated a treaty making the Irish Free State a self-governing dominion within the British COMMONWEALTH OF NATIONS and allowing the Northern Ireland Parliament to take the six northern counties out of the dominion. Because some members of the Dáil and of the IRA felt honor-bound to accept nothing less than a republic "externally associated" with the Commonwealth, a civil war broke out between protreaty and antitreaty factions, led respectively by Michael COLLINS and Eamon DE VALERA. The antitreaty faction was defeated.

THE IRISH FREE STATE; EIRE; THE REPUBLIC OF IRELAND
The state composed of the southern 26 of Ireland's 32 counties has had three different names, which reflect the stages by which the goals of the defeated antitreaty side were actually attained during the generation after the civil war.

The Irish Free State. Under the 1922 constitution framed by the protreaty side, the first prime minister was William T. Cosgrave (1880–1965; see COSGRAVE family). De Valera's republican party refused to sit in the Dáil because of the required oath of allegiance to the British crown. Despite the difficulties

(Left) *Eamon de Valera spearheaded efforts to establish an independent Irish republic during the turbulent post–World War I period.*

(Below) *Street fighting of the Easter Rising of Apr. 24, 1916, continued for six days, as approximately 1,500 Irish held out against British forces in Dublin. When 15 leaders of the revolt were subsequently executed, Irish public opinion changed dramatically to support the radical republican movement.*

of governing a state whose very legitimacy was rejected by the major opposition party, the Cosgrave government managed to set up a well-functioning administration and to accomplish some modest reforms. In 1927, however, de Valera reconciled his conscience to taking the oath while denying that he was doing any such thing. After the 1932 election his FIANNA FÁIL party (with Labour party support) was able to form a government, and as prime minister until 1948, and again in 1951–54 and 1957–59, he consolidated his party's dominance over Cosgrave's party, FINE GAEL. One by one de Valera set about breaking the remaining constitutional links with Britain.

Eire. In 1937 a new constitution drafted by de Valera was adopted. The new state, Eire, was a republic in all but name, but it remained formally within the British Commonwealth. During World War II de Valera followed a policy of neutrality, which was supported by the overwhelming majority of the southern population.

The Republic of Ireland. In 1948, John A. Costello (1891–1976), a Fine Gael leader who succeeded de Valera as prime minister in a coalition government, introduced legislation by which the South became a republic outside the Commonwealth. In the 1950s the republic began to turn away from constitutional struggles and toward a greater concern with economic development. The attempt to achieve economic self-sufficiency, which had been such a prominent feature of de Valera's policy in the 1930s, gradually gave way to policies of interdependence. Under Fianna Fáil prime minister Sean Lemass (1899–1971; served 1959–66), the republic entered into a free-trade agreement with Britain. The decision to enter the EUROPEAN ECONOMIC COMMUNITY (Common Market) in 1973 was backed by both the Fianna Fáil, led by John LYNCH (prime minister, 1966–73, 1977–79), and the Fine Gael, led by Liam Cosgrave (William Cosgrave's son; prime minister, 1973–77).

Feudalism had been the essential ingredient of state building that Ireland lacked in the Middle Ages; nationalism may be the essential prerequisite for successful state building in a democratic age. The nationalism that had been growing among Catholics for a century was a prime factor that enabled the South to overcome the bitterness of civil war and achieve stable democratic institutions.

NORTHERN IRELAND

Whereas the southern Irish state was born out of a positive nationalist demand, Northern Ireland arose out of a negative defensive reaction on the part of a people who never quite became nationalists of any sort. This difference helps in understanding why Northern Ireland failed, where the South of Ireland succeeded, at the enterprise of state building. Not being nationalists, Ulster Protestants had no vision of a national fulfillment in which all conflicts would be resolved; on the contrary, they assumed that conflict was inevitable and that constant vigilance was required on the part of the ORANGEMEN and the "Special Constabulary" into which their paramilitary force of 1912–14 had been transformed. This assumption that their state would always be rejected by their "enemies" dissuaded the Unionist governments elected by the Protestant majority from 1921 to the 1970s from even trying to win the allegiance of the Catholic minority. Members of that minority, however, were convinced by nationalist ideology that sooner or later Irish unity would be attained; they refused to face the fact that partition was a reality that would not go away. Thus in the north the assumptions of both Catholics and Protestants tended to inhibit reconciliation.

Nevertheless, several economic factors more conducive to rapprochement were at work in the decades after World War II. The decline of Northern Ireland's traditional industries (shipbuilding, linen, agriculture) turned the government's attention to industrial development. Educated Protestants—notably Terence O'Neill (b. 1914), who served as prime minister (1963–69)—realized that better relations with the republic and with its own Catholic minority were important to potential investors. O'Neill's overtures struck a responsive chord in the republic, which was coming to prefer prosperity and interdependence with its neighbors to austere self-sufficiency.

The postwar growth of the British welfare state gave many

British soldiers and civilians under fire from the Irish Republican Army take cover in Belfast, Northern Ireland. The antagonism between Ulster's large Catholic minority and Protestant majority erupted into intensive violence in 1969, continuing throughout the 1970s.

northern Catholics a practical reason for accepting the British connection. Unfortunately for O'Neill, such acceptance was expressed not so much in votes for him as in demonstrations for "British rights" led by Bernadette Devlin (b. 1947) and others beginning in 1968. In turning their attention from "Irish unity" to "British rights," northern Catholics were making an important, if hesitant, step toward rapprochement.

Not all northern Protestants were ready for rapprochement: a section of them, represented by the Rev. Ian PAISLEY, were unwilling to accept the premise that Catholics might ever cease to be enemies. O'Neill resigned in the face of attacks from these "loyalists" and was succeeded by James Chichester Clark (b. 1923), who requested British troops to keep the peace between civil rights demonstrators and extremist Protestant mobs. Even with the backing of troops, the state was collapsing, and its inability to provide minimal protection for its Catholic citizens led to the recrudescence of the IRA first as a community defense force and then as an assailant of the crumbling state. The decision of Brian FAULKNER, who became prime minister in 1971, to intern IRA suspects without trial led to increasing violence. The final dissolution of the Northern Irish state was recognized by the imposition of "direct rule" from London in March 1972.

The crisis dragged on because no effective state replaced the rickety one that had collapsed in 1969–72. The governments of Great Britain and the Republic of Ireland attempted in 1973 to create a new "power-sharing" government of Protestants and Catholics, but it had no chance of success because it was not allowed to exercise the security powers by which its Catholic members might have proved to the majority that they were not "enemies." In May 1974 the power-sharing government was brought down by a Protestant general strike. Nevertheless, lacking a true nationalism, the Protestant community has not taken the initiative to reerect a state on its own terms by a unilateral declaration of independence.

DAVID W. MILLER

Bibliography: Beckett, James C., *The Making of Modern Ireland, 1603–1921* (1966); Curtis, Edmund, *History of Ireland*, 7th ed. (1964); de Paor, Maire and Liam, *Early Christian Ireland* (1958); Herity, Michael, *Ireland in Prehistory* (1977); Lydon, James, and MacCurtain, Margaret, eds., *The Gill History of Ireland*, 13 vols. (1972–75); Lyons, F. S. L., *Ireland since the Famine* (1971); Moody, T. W., and Martin, F. X., *The Course of Irish History* (1967); Moody, T. W., Martin, F. X., and Byrne, F. J., eds., *A New History of Ireland*, 9 vols. (1976–   ); O'Brien, Conor Cruise, *The Shaping of Modern Ireland* (1970) and *States of Ireland* (1972); Rumpf, E., and Hepburn, A. C., *Nationalism and Socialism in Twentieth-Century Ireland* (1977).

See also: IRELAND; IRISH LITERATURE; NORTHERN IRELAND.

Ireland, John   (clergyman)

John Ireland, b. Ireland, 1838, d. Sept. 25, 1918, was an American Roman Catholic churchman who became widely known in his day for defending changes that benefited the common people. He emigrated to the United States as a child. After theological studies in France, he was assigned to the cathedral in Saint Paul, Minn. (1861), and rose steadily from curate to bishop in less than 15 years. He proved to be a vigorous and bold controversialist, defending experiments in education that allowed Catholic children to attend public schools full-time and receive religious instruction in a parochial setting in addition. As archbishop (from 1888), Ireland brought about many changes in his own diocese to encourage popular support of Catholicism, and he supported many social reforms for the country as a whole.   HENRY WARNER BOWDEN

Bibliography: Moynihan, James H., *The Life of Archbishop John Ireland* (1953).

Ireland, John   (composer)

The English composer John Nicholson Ireland, b. Aug. 13, 1879, d. June 12, 1962, studied (1893–1901) under Sir Charles Stanford at the Royal College of Music in London and pursued further studies in Durham until 1905. Thereafter he lived mostly in London, composing, teaching at the Royal College of Music, and serving (1904–26) as church organist in Chelsea. Inspired by German romanticism and Celtic legend as well as by the world of nature, Ireland was also influenced by French impressionism and Russian and English folk music. Most of his music consists of short pieces such as his songs set to poems by Thomas Hardy and A. E. Housman. His larger works include a piano concerto (1930), the symphonic rhapsody *Mai-Dun* (1921), and *A London Overture* (1936).

F. E. KIRBY

Bibliography: Longmire, John, *John Ireland, Portrait of a Friend* (1969).

Ireland, Northern: see NORTHERN IRELAND.

Irenaeus, Saint   [y-ruh-nee'-uhs]

Saint Irenaeus, b. Anatolia, *c.*140–60, d. *c.*200, known as the father of Catholic theology, is the most important theologian of the 2d century AD. In his youth, he became a disciple of Saint Polycarp of Smyrna. Later he served as bishop of Lugdunum (Lyon) in Gaul.

Irenaeus is known through several extant works, as well as by his influence on later Christian writers of the patristic era. He was a man of peace and of tradition. His major efforts were spent in combating GNOSTICISM, and his great work, *Adversus haereses* (Against Heresies), was written for this purpose. He developed the doctrine of recapitulation (*anakephalaiosis*) of all things in Jesus Christ in opposition to the teachings of gnostics such as VALENTINUS and Basilides. A staunch defender of the apostolic tradition, Irenaeus was the first Father of the Church to systematize the religious and theological traditions of the church, so far as they existed. In the Quartodeciman controversy over the date for the observance of Easter, he argued for diversity of practice in the unity of faith. Feast day: June 28.   AGNES CUNNINGHAM

Bibliography: Nielsen, Jan Tjierd, *Adam and Christ in the Theology of Irenaeus of Lyons* (1968); Wingren, Gustaf, *Man and the Incarnation: A Study in the Biblical Theology of Irenaeus*, trans. by Ross MacKenzie (1959).

Irene, Byzantine Empress

Irene, b. *c.*752, d. Aug. 9, 803, was the first woman to rule (797–802) the Byzantine Empire. She married Leo IV in 768 and, on his death in 780, became regent and co-emperor with her son Constantine VI. A strong opponent of ICONOCLASM, she convened the Seventh Ecumenical Council (787; see NICAEA, COUNCILS OF) which restored icon veneration. In 797, ambitious and restless, she had her son blinded and began to rule in his stead. Military failures and rumors that she planned to marry Charlemagne aroused opposition, however, and Irene was deposed (802) and sent to a convent; Nicephorus I succeeded her as emperor (802–11). Irene is considered a saint by the Greek Orthodox church.   C. M. BRAND

Bibliography: Diehl, Charles, *Byzantine Empresses*, trans. by Harold Bell and Theresa de Kerpely (1963).

Irian Barat: see IRIAN JAYA.

Irian Jaya   [ir'-ee-uhn jah'-yuh]

Irian Jaya, formerly West New Guinea, West Irian, or Irian Barat, is an Indonesian province encompassing the western half of NEW GUINEA and bordering islands in the Arafura Sea, Ceram Sea, and Pacific Ocean. Its capital is Jayapura; the province has a population of 1,025,331 (1975 est.). The east-west trending Maoke Mountains, reaching 5,029 m (16,500 ft), divide the province. Most inhabitants are primitive Papuans, some of whom still practice cannibalism and headhunting. They subsist on fishing and hunting, and on taro, bananas, and sweet potatoes. The climate is tropical, with heavy rains during the monsoon. Formerly part of the Dutch East Indies, Irian Jaya was administered by Indonesia after 1963 under authority of the United Nations. After a 1969 plebiscite, Indonesia formally annexed the area.

iridium   [ir-id'-ee-uhm]

Iridium is a dense, brittle, hard, silver-white precious metal. A chemical element, its symbol is Ir, atomic number 77, and atomic weight 192.22. The discovery of iridium was announced in 1804 by Smithson Tennant, who named the metal from the Latin *iris*, meaning "rainbow." Iridium is not found in nature in pure form but as osmiridium, an alloy with osmium and platinum. Many radioactive isotopes of iridium have been created in the laboratory. The pure metal cannot be dissolved by most acids, including aqua regia. Iridium is used in platinum alloys for jewelry and surgical pins; because of its resistance to corrosion, it is used in aircraft spark plugs.

Iris   [y'-ris]

In Greek mythology, Iris, the daughter of Thaumas and Electra, was the goddess of the rainbow and a messenger from the gods to humankind. The rainbow was her bridge between heaven and earth. Iris was represented in art as a beautiful young woman in a long tunic with golden wings attached to her shoulders.

iris

A large group of popular outdoor ornamentals are commonly known as iris, flag, or Fleur-de-Lis. Because of their multicolored flowers, the genus was named after Iris, the personification of the rainbow in Greek mythology. This genus comprises about 200 species that are mostly distributed in the northern temperate zone, the majority being native to Asia. About 30 species grow wild in North America, predominantly in the eastern United States and the Mississippi delta region. Irises belong to the family Iridaceae, which also includes crocuses, freesia, and gladiolus.

Structure. The irises are perennial herbs that are divided into two divisions, those arising from bulbs and those from horizontal underground rhizomes. They have linear, grasslike or swordlike leaves, and large, showy flowers that are regular and, despite their elaborate appearance, relatively simple. The ovary is connected to a short tube that is attached to three sepals, known as falls because they usually droop. The upper surface of each fall is usually bearded or crested. Three petals, called standards, alternate with the sepals and are upright. Three styles, which are petallike extensions of the ovary, arch over the base and midsection of each fall. Between each style and fall is a single stamen, which is the male organ of the flower. The arrangement of the style and fall ensures cross-pollination of the flowers by insects. As an insect moves through the passageway between the style and fall, it deposits pollen from the previous flower on the stigma near the tip of the style. It then reaches the stamen, brushing against the flower's pollen and carrying it off to other flowers.

Varieties and Uses. Many horticulturally important species, hybrids, and cultivars are grown. The common garden irises of the United States are usually divided into bearded, beard-

Irises are colorful, orchidlike flowers that have been cultivated into numerous hybrids, including (clockwise from left) *the tall, bearded iris,* I. germanica, *which has prominent gold tufts at the base of its petals; the Siberian iris,* I. sibirica, *which has upright petals and no beard; the Japanese iris,* I. kaempferi, *a beardless, fringed hybrid; and blue flag,* I. cristata, *a small, beardless, and crested iris.*

less, and crested irises, all of which are rhizomatous, and bulbous varieties. Bearded irises, which are by far the most popular group, are native to the Old World and have been widely cultivated since ancient times. The Fleur-de-Lis, or German iris, *Iris germanica*, is the species of bearded iris that is most commonly grown. It is a source of orris root, used in perfumes and tooth powders. Although not as popular, many of the beardless irises, native to Asia, are also cultivated. This group includes the Japanese iris, *I. kaempferi*, the Siberian iris, *I. sibirica*, and the oriental iris, *I. orientalis*. Bulbous irises, mostly native to the Mediterranean region, are the florists' irises that are grown in greenhouses for cut flowers in winter. Two common species are the Tangiers iris, *I. tingitana*, and the Spanish iris, *I. xiphium*. Very few crested irises are cultivated in the United States. The slender iris, *I. gracilipes*, is a crested iris that is occasionally grown in rock gardens.

JOHN E. EBINGER

Bibliography: Price, Molly, *The Iris Book* (1966; repr. 1973); Randall, Harry, *Irises* (1969); Warburton, Bee, ed., *The World of Irises* (1977).

Irish art: see CELTIC ART.

Irish elk

The Irish elk, genus *Megaloceros*, a giant European deer, is now extinct. Its antlers were about 3.9 m (13 ft) across, greater in size than those of any other deer; the body size was that of a large moose. Fossil remains, primarily from Irish peat bogs, date from the Pleistocene Epoch—2,500,000 to 10,000 years ago.

EVERETT SENTMAN

Irish Free State: see IRELAND, HISTORY OF.

Irish Gaelic language: see CELTIC LANGUAGES.

Irish Literary Renaissance

The Irish Literary Renaissance, also known as the Irish Revival and the Celtic Renaissance, was a literary movement sparked by a growing consciousness of a Celtic identity separate from English influence; it was bound up with Ireland's struggle for political independence. Beginning toward the end of the 19th century and continuing into the early decades of the 20th century, it was inspired by the past glories of the Gaelic bards, Irish mythology and legends, and the simplicity of peasant folkways. Among its most gifted writers were the poets William Butler YEATS, George William RUSSELL (pseudonym, Æ), and Padraic COLUM; the prose writers George MOORE and James STEPHENS; and the dramatists John Millington SYNGE, Lady GREGORY, Lennox ROBINSON, and Sean O'CASEY. The revival restored and preserved a literary past and led to the creation of an indigenous contemporary literature.

The renaissance began when the Gaelic League was formed in 1893 to rekindle interest in Ireland's cultural past and particularly in Gaelic language and literature. Such works as *The Ballad Poetry of Ireland* (1845) by Charles Gavan Duffy (1816–1903), the seminal two-volume *History of Ireland* (1878 and 1880) by Standish James O'Grady (1846–1928), and *A Literary History of Ireland* (1892) by Douglas Hyde (1860–1949) supplied an historical perspective for the movement. In 1888, Yeats collected and edited *Poems and Ballads of Young Ireland*, and in 1891–92 he was instrumental in founding the Irish Literary Society, which gave the movement a creative center. Yeats was the most prominent figure of the Irish Literary Renaissance. In mystical poems such as those in *The Wanderings of Oisin* (1889), in symbolic plays like *The Land of Heart's Desire* (1894), and in stirring essays he invoked the spirit of Irish myth and legend. In 1899, Yeats, Moore, Lady Gregory, and Edward Martyn (1859–1924) established the Irish Literary Theatre, a forerunner of the ABBEY THEATRE, where the plays of the movement were presented.

Bibliography: Boyd, Ernest, *Ireland's Literary Renaissance* (1916; repr. 1968); Fallis, Richard, *The Irish Renaissance* (1967); Loftus, Richard J., *Nationalism in Modern Anglo-Irish Poetry* (1964).

(Below left) *William Butler Yeats, generally considered Ireland's greatest lyric poet, led the Irish Literary Renaissance with his efforts to reawaken Celtic literary traditions.* (Center) *Augusta, Lady Gregory, a dramatist whose translations of Celtic legends also influenced the movement, codirected the Abbey Theatre with Yeats and George Russell.* (Right) *The poet George Russell (pseudonym A.E.) was active as a playwright, editor, and director. The three portraits were painted by Jack Yeats, brother of the poet. (National Gallery, Dublin.)*

Irish literature

Irish literature encompasses literature in two languages; Irish, more exactly, Irish Gaelic, and English. The literature written in Irish may be classified as Early or Modern. Early Irish literature has survived in a large number of manuscripts and is traditionally classified by subject matter. The Ulster cycle, which includes texts composed as early as the 7th century, comprises several heroic tales in verse and prose recounting the exploits of CUCHULAIN and the company of the Red Branch knights. The Red Branch has been identified with an ancient northern kingdom roughly corresponding to the modern province of Ulster. The FENIAN CYCLE, which includes later texts, consists of heroic tales, most of them about Finn McCool and the *Fianna*. The *Fianna* were bands of warriors who, unlike the Red Branch knights, lived outside the tribe and indeed outside society, although they were recognized by the law. The language of the Ulster cycle is Old Irish; the tales relate to northern Ireland, are heroic in temper, and are obviously the products of an aristocratic class. The language of the Fenian cycle is Middle and Modern Irish; the tales relate to southern Ireland, are romantic in temper, and ostensibly are the products of a subject class. Early Irish literature also comprises the Mythological cycle, about gods and goddesses of the Celtic pantheon; the Historical cycles, which deal with recognizably historical figures; and tales described as voyages, such as "The Voyage of Mael Duin," adventures, such as "The Adventure of Bran, Son of Febal," or visions, such as "The Vision of Adamnan."

Modern Irish literature begins with Geoffrey Keating (c.1570–c.1650), whose *History of Ireland* may have been the last important work in Europe to circulate extensively in manuscript form as copies of it continued to be made until the 19th century. After Keating, Modern Irish literature has consisted primarily of poems. Two of the most important of these poems, written in the 18th century, are Michael Comyn's "Oisin in the Land of Youth," based on a Fenian theme, and Brian Merriman's "The Midnight Court," a masterpiece of contemporary satire dealing with a perennial problem in Ireland, the unwillingness of the men to take wives. By the mid-19th century, however, the Gaelic-speaking audience for such poetry had been greatly reduced by centuries of English conquest and by the potato famine of the 1840s, which decimated the rural population through death and emigration. A movement to revive the Irish language began at the end of the century, and Irish writers began to write in Irish again. Today a small but distinctive body of literature is written in Irish.

Although Irish authors such as the dramatists William CON-GREVE and George FARQUHAR wrote within the mainstream of English literature during the 17th century, Irish literature in English—what is usually but somewhat unsatisfactorily described as Anglo-Irish literature—begins in the 18th century with Jonathan SWIFT, author of GULLIVER'S TRAVELS and *A Tale of a Tub*; and with Oliver GOLDSMITH, author of the poem "The Deserted Village" and the novel THE VICAR OF WAKEFIELD. In the 19th century, writing in English was limited largely to members of the ruling class, called in Ireland the Ascendancy. These writers included such novelists as Maria EDGEWORTH and Charles Lever, such poets as Samuel Ferguson and William Allingham, and the dramatist Oscar WILDE. Yet Thomas MOORE, the Irish writer most widely read during the century and known as the national poet of Ireland, was the son of a Catholic grocer. The novelists William Carleton, and John and Michael Banim were of peasant stock; and Gerald Griffin was Catholic but, like Moore, from a prosperous family.

With the Celtic revivalism of the second half of the 19th century, the literature in English began to take its inspiration from Irish tradition, a development culminating at the end of the century in the founding, by William Butler YEATS and others, of the Irish Literary Renaissance. In what might be called the manifesto of that movement Yeats asked, "Can we not build up a national literature which shall be none the less Irish in spirit from being English in language?" His answer was *yes*, by writing in an "English which shall have an indefinable Irish quality of rhythm and style," that is, in English as it is spoken in Ireland. Because the Irish peasant of western Ireland still spoke Irish and was considered a direct link with the past and thus with Gaelic literary tradition, the dialect Yeats called for turned out to be largely a peasant dialect, especially as used in the plays of Lady GREGORY and John Millington SYNGE, produced at the ABBEY THEATRE in Dublin.

The Irish Literary Renaissance was enormously successful, not only because talented people, some indeed with genius, responded to Yeats's appeal, but also because the historical timing was propitious. Ireland, responding to the nationalist impetus that had swept European countries, was moving toward revolution and the establishment of its political independence. A small nation of only 4 million produced within a generation some of the foremost poets, dramatists, and novelists of this century in Yeats, Synge, Sean O'CASEY, James JOYCE, and Samuel BECKETT. Conor Cruise O'BRIEN could justly claim that for a time Dublin was the literary center of the English-speaking world.   DAVID H. GREENE

Bibliography: Alspach, Russel K., *Irish Poetry: From the English Invasion to 1798*, 2d ed. (1960); Carroll, Donald, ed., *New Poets of Ireland* (1963; repr. 1977); Dillon, Myles, *Early Irish Literature* (1948); Ellis-Fermor, Una, *The Irish Dramatic Movement*, 2d ed. (1954); Fallis, Richard,

(Below left) *James Joyce, one of the most influential writers of the 20th century, used such radical literary techniques as stream-of-consciousness prose in his explorations of the sordid Dublin milieu of his childhood.* (Center) *Sean O'Casey, a leading playwright of the Irish Literary Renaissance, achieved great success at the Abbey Theatre with his tragicomic portraits of the Irish poor.* (Right) *Samuel Beckett, a member of Joyce's Paris circle, wrote of his Dublin experience before embracing the French language and existentialist thought.*

The Irish Renaissance (1977); Finneran, Richard J., *Anglo-Irish Literature: A Review of Research* (1976); Flanagan, Thomas J. B., *The Irish Novelists, 1800–1850* (1959); Hogan, Robert, *After the Irish Renaissance* (1967); Howarth, Herbert, *The Irish Writers, 1880–1940* (1958); Taylor, Geoffrey, *Irish Poets of the Nineteenth Century* (1951); Thomson, Derick, *An Introduction to Gaelic Poetry* (1974).

Irish moss

Irish moss, *Chondrus crispus*, is a purplish to pink red plant in the red ALGAE division, Rhodophycophyta. These algae are highly branched, crinkled, and somewhat flattened. Their life cycle is characterized by a complicated ALTERNATION OF GENERATIONS peculiar to red algae. Irish moss is commonly found in intertidal zones and deeper, offshore waters on both sides of the North Atlantic.

Irish Republican Army

The Irish Republican Army (IRA) is the latest of the organizations founded during the past 2 centuries to fight for the independence and unity of Ireland. In 1798, Wolfe TONE directed his UNITED IRISHMEN in an unsuccessful rebellion against British rule. Following another abortive uprising in 1848, the Irish Republican Brotherhood (IRB or FENIANS) launched a long and fruitless campaign to wrench Ireland loose from the union with Britain. Toward the end of the 19th century the Irish nationalists concentrated on parliamentary action to secure home rule for Ireland. Militant Protestant opposition to the Third HOME RULE BILL, however, provoked the formation (1913) of the nationalist Irish Volunteers. This group joined with the IRB in the EASTER RISING (1916).

Veterans of the Easter Rising formed the core of the Irish Republican Army, which was organized (1919) by Michael COLLINS. As the military wing of the SINN FEIN party, it battled for 2 years with the undisciplined auxiliary British forces known as the Black and Tans. After the founding (1922) of the Irish Free State, many IRA members continued to fight the new Irish government, of which Collins was a member until he was assassinated in August by republican extremists. The IRA objected to Ireland's continued association with Britain as a dominion and even more to the separation of Protestant NORTHERN IRELAND from the new state. Although the civil war ended in 1927 and the Irish State asserted full sovereignty in 1937, the IRA remained in existence as an underground organization.

For the next 30 years IRA activities were sporadic. During World War II its members conspired with German agents but without practical effect. After the war they launched periodic bombing attacks in England and Northern Ireland, but the organization was weak and divided. Finally in 1969 the IRA split into two groups: the moderates, or officials, who decided to shift to political methods aimed at achieving a united socialist Ireland; and the radicals, or provisionals, who continued to espouse terrorism.

In 1969, British troops were sent to Northern Ireland to protect the minority Roman Catholic community from the increasingly violent Protestant reaction to Catholic civil rights demands. The army, however, soon antagonized the Catholics, appearing to side with the Protestants. Taking advantage of this disaffection, the IRA provisionals launched a terrorist guerrilla campaign against the British troops and the Protestant community. A murderous civil war ensued, and despite occasional truces, the gun battles, assassinations, and bombings continued. Under the leadership of Seán MacStiofáin, the IRA provisionals vowed to keep trying to bomb Ulster into a United Ireland. In 1979 they were apparently responsible for the murder of Earl Mountbatten of Burma.

Bibliography: Bell, J. B., *The Secret Army*, rev. ed. (1980).

See also: IRELAND, HISTORY OF.

Irish Sea

The Irish Sea is a roughly circular arm of the North Atlantic Ocean bounded by Wales, England, and Scotland on the east and by Ireland to the west. About 210 km (130 mi) in diameter, the sea covers about 103,600 km² (40,000 mi²) and has a mean depth of 60 m (200 ft). It joins the Atlantic through the North Channel, between Ireland and Scotland, in the north, and through the SAINT GEORGE'S CHANNEL in the south. The ISLE OF MAN and Anglesey are its principal islands. The sea's largest ports are Dublin and Liverpool.

Irish setter

The Irish, or red, setter originally had a red and white coat. Bred for bird hunting in the early 19th century, the setter is today prized as a pet and a show dog.

The Irish setter, originating as a gun dog in Ireland before 1800, was at that time primarily red and white in color. Its solid red coat was developed in Ireland and England during the 1800s. The ancestry of the Irish setter is unknown, but speculation credits a variety of breeds as its progenitors: the Irish water spaniel, English setter, Gordon setter, springer spaniel, and pointer. The Irish setter stands approximately 63.5 to 68.5 cm (25 to 27 in) high at the shoulders and weighs about 27 kg (60 lb). It has a mahogany to rich chestnut-red coat, which is thick, straight, and as free from curl as possible. Feathering is present on the ears, chest, legs, and tail. Although this feathering is desirable in a show dog, it is a handicap in the field.   JOHN MANDEVILLE

Bibliography: Brearly, Joan, *This Is the Irish Setter* (1975); Thompson, William C., *The New Irish Setter*, 3d ed. (1968).

Irish terrier

The Irish terrier is a rough-coated, generally reddish breed standing about 46 cm (18 in) high at the shoulders and weighing approximately 12 kg (27 lb). It has a long head, flattened skull, and small V-shaped ears that drop forward toward the eyes. Its tail is docked. Its wiry coat should be solid red, golden red, red wheaten, or wheaten (yellowish).

The Irish terrier is a most versatile dog. In addition to being a pet and watchdog, it is adept at hunting large and small game and is an accomplished retriever; it was also used as a messenger and sentinel during both world wars.

The Irish terrier has a curious history in that there is no definite mention of the breed prior to 1875, even though an Irish terrier club was founded in 1879 to promote the breed. It is obvious, therefore, that the breed or earlier variants of it were known in Ireland for many years previously. The Irish terrier has been used as a guard dog and as a hunter of small game and vermin.   JOHN MANDEVILLE

Bibliography: Kidd, George, *Your Irish Terrier* (1978).

Irish water spaniel

The Irish water spaniel, a large-sized sporting dog, is considered the oldest breed native to Ireland. A thick coat of tight ringlets provides this accomplished swimmer and retriever—the largest of all spaniels—with excellent insulation in cold water.

The Irish water spaniel, a curly-coated, medium-sized dog, reaches about 60 cm (24 in) in height at the shoulders and 30 kg (65 lb) in weight. Its coat, always solid liver in color, is a dense mass of crisp ringlets. Its head is covered by a topknot, which consists of long, loose curls. The tail is thick near the root and bears dense curls along the first 5 to 8 cm (2 to 3 in), but from there to the tip it tapers to a fine point and is covered only with short, smooth hair. The Irish water spaniel originated in Ireland. The breed's fondness for water and its dense oily coat that protects it from the cold make it ideally suited for duck retrieving.   JOHN MANDEVILLE

Bibliography: American Kennel Club, *The Complete Dog Book*, 15th ed. (1975).

Irish wolfhound

The Irish wolfhound, originally bred to hunt wolves and deer, can move with great speed and grace despite its massive size. The Irish wolfhound makes a formidable hunter.

The Irish wolfhound is the tallest of the breeds recognized by the American Kennel Club. Males must be at least 81 cm (32 in) in height at the shoulders and 54.5 kg (120 lb) in weight; females, 76 cm (30 in) and 47.5 kg (105 lb). Dogs of 91.5 cm (36 in) and even more and 68 kg (150 lb) are relatively common. The coat is wiry and of one color, with various shadings; it may be gray, brindle, red, black, white, or fawn. In recent times the Irish wolfhound has been used to hunt wolves, deer, and other large game. The origins of the modern breed of Irish wolfhound undoubtedly trace back to ancient times; large, greyhound-type hunting dogs were known in Ireland and Britain at least 2,000 years ago. By the early 1860s, the breed had dwindled to near extinction. It was only through the determined efforts of Capt. G. A. Graham, an officer in the British army, that the breed was saved.   JOHN MANDEVILLE

Bibliography: Donovan, John A., *You and Your Irish Wolfhound* (1977); Starbuck, Alma, *The Complete Irish Wolfhound*, 3d ed. (1969).

Irkutsk   [ir-kootsk']

Irkutsk is the capital of Irkutsk oblast in the Russian SFSR of the USSR. It is situated in southern SIBERIA, on the Angara River, near its outlet from Lake BAIKAL. The city has a population of 550,000 (1979). It is named for the small Irkut River, which enters the Angara here. Irkutsk is one of Siberia's largest cities, situated on the TRANS-SIBERIAN RAILROAD, and serves as a supply base for the development of Siberian resource areas to the north.

The city's industries produce transportation equipment and machinery for gold mining and other extractive industries and process mica mined in Siberia. Power needs are met, in part, from a hydroelectric station built here on the Angara River in 1956. One of the largest consumers of power is an aluminum plant at Shelekhov, just southwest of Irkutsk. The A. A. Zhdanov University (1918) and many research institutes train specialists for the development of Siberian resources. During the Russian advance through Siberia, a fort was founded in Irkutsk in 1661. It became a major administrative and economic center in the 18th and 19th centuries. Its importance was enhanced after the railroad arrived in 1898.

     THEODORE SHABAD

iron   [y'-urn]

Iron, a silvery white solid metal, appears in the periodic table as a TRANSITION ELEMENT. Its atomic number is 26, and its atomic weight is 55.847. Its chemical symbol, Fe, is derived from *ferrum*, the Latin word for iron. Iron is unique among the elements in the abundance of its ores and the vast number of useful alloys that can be formulated with iron as the major constituent. Iron is also biologically important; it is the central atom in heme, the oxygen-carrying portion of HEMOGLOBIN found in blood.

Elemental iron has been known since prehistoric times. Although how early humans first learned to extract the element from its ores is still debated, scientists are fairly certain that early, highly prized samples of iron were obtained from meteors. Several references to "the metal of heaven"—probably iron—have been found in ancient writings. By approximately 1200 BC, iron was being obtained from its ores; this achievement marks the beginning of the IRON AGE. Even with the dependence today on plastics, concrete, aluminum, and fiberglass, iron and its alloys remain crucial in the economies of modern countries.

OCCURRENCE
In its various compounds, iron is the fourth most abundant element (5.1%) in the Earth's crust. Evidence exists that the molten core of the Earth is primarily elemental iron. Iron has four natural isotopes; the most abundant is ^{56}Fe (91.66%), which occurs with ^{54}Fe (5.82%), ^{57}Fe (2.19%), and ^{58}Fe (0.33%).

Iron occasionally occurs naturally in its pure or uncombined form (see NATIVE ELEMENTS), but is abundant in combination with other elements, as oxides, sulfides, carbonates, and silicates. Iron ores are naturally occurring compounds of iron from which the metal can easily be recovered in significant quantity (see IRON AND STEEL INDUSTRY). Iron pyrite (FeS_2) is a yellow, crystalline mineral called fool's gold because of its goldlike appearance.

PHYSICAL PROPERTIES
In its pure form, iron is rather soft and is malleable and ductile at room temperature. It melts at 1,535° C and boils at 3,000° C. Pure iron can exist in two structural types, or allotropic forms.

At room temperature, the iron atoms are arranged in a body-centered cubic lattice called the α-form, which is transformed at 910° C into a cubic close-packed structure called the γ-form. At 1,390° C iron returns to a body-centered cubic structure, called the δ-form.

Iron at room temperature exhibits ferromagnetism, a strong magnetic behavior that the metal may retain even in the absence of an external, applied magnetic field. When iron is heated to 768° C, it loses this property and exhibits paramagnetism, a weaker attraction to an applied magnetic field (see MAGNETISM). Between 768° and 910° C, iron is said to be in its β-form, which is not a different allotropic form of iron.

Although pure iron does conduct electricity, compared to other metals used for that purpose, such as copper or aluminum, it is a poor conductor.

CHEMICAL PROPERTIES
Easily oxidized, iron reacts directly with most common nonmetallic elements, forming compounds in which iron is in the +2 or +3 oxidation state: FeO, Fe_2O_3, FeF_3, $FeCl_3$, $FeBr_3$, FeI_2, and FeS. At high temperatures, iron also absorbs hydrogen and nitrogen and forms phosphides, carbides, and silicides.

In the absence of water, and under various conditions, iron reacts with oxygen. Finely divided iron burns in air once it is ignited. Larger pieces of iron react with oxygen in dry air at temperatures above 150° C to form the mixed oxides Fe_2O_3 and Fe_3O_4. At temperatures above 575° C and at low concentrations of oxygen, FeO is formed.

Corrosion. Perhaps the most important chemical reaction of iron, at least from an economic standpoint, is the least desirable one: the reaction of iron, water, and oxygen to form hydrated iron oxide, or rust. The CORROSION of iron has been studied carefully, and the formation of rust is known to be an electrochemical reaction.

For rust to form at room temperature, three components in addition to iron must be present: oxygen, water, and an electrolyte (an ionic substance dissolved in the water). Iron that is partially immersed in salt or fresh water usually rusts more rapidly than does iron that is totally immersed. In the atmosphere, the formation of rust begins when the relative humidity exceeds 50%. The presence of air pollutants, particularly the oxides of sulfur, greatly increases the rate at which rust forms. In the presence of air and water, sulfur dioxide forms sulfuric acid that attacks and oxidizes the iron. Because rust on the surface of iron is porous, the metal surface beneath the rust also reacts.

The formation of rust may be inhibited by coating the surface of the metal with paint or certain other chemicals, or by covering the metal with another metal such as zinc (galvanized iron) or tin (the derivation of "tin" cans).

Aqueous Solutions. The chemistry of iron in the +2 or +3 oxidation state is complex; many oxidizing and reducing agents are capable of interconverting the various compounds of Fe^{2+} and Fe^{3+}. For example, the reactions of a solution of potassium ferrocyanide, $K_4Fe(CN)_6$, with Fe^{3+} and a solution of potassium ferricyanide, $K_3Fe(CN)_6$, with Fe^{2+} both yield a dark blue solid. The product of the first reaction is called Prussian blue, and the other, Turnbull's blue; both have identical compositions—$KFeFe(CN)_6$.

Solutions of iron ions exhibit various chemical and physical properties characteristic of many transition metals. When ferrous sulfate (iron in the +2 oxidation state is called ferrous iron) is dissolved in water, the pale green $Fe(H_2O)_6^{2+}$ ion is formed. When ferric nitrate (iron in the +3 oxidation state is called ferric iron) is dissolved, the product is the pale violet $Fe(H_2O)_6^{3+}$ ion, which differs from the former ion only by having one less electron. Like most iron ions in solution, both

ions are paramagnetic; that is, solutions containing them are attracted by external fields. A seemingly endless number of chemical compounds, both ions and neutral molecules, can replace the water molecules associated with iron in solution. If cyanide ions (CN^-) are added to solutions of the ions mentioned above, the products are ferrocyanide ion, $Fe(CN)_6^{4-}$, and ferricyanide ion, $Fe(CN)_6^{3-}$, respectively. A change in the magnetic properties of iron occurs when ferrocyanide is formed. Solutions containing this ion are diamagnetic; that is, they are weakly repelled by a magnetic field. By contrast, solutions of the ferric compound are weakly paramagnetic.

Iron in the +6 oxidation state can be made by reacting solutions of ferric ion with strong oxidizing agents to produce FeO_4^{2-}, a reddish purple ion, which is also weakly paramagnetic.

Organometallic Compounds. Iron in its various oxidation states readily combines with many carbon compounds to form organometallic compounds. Finely divided iron reacts with carbon monoxide under pressure to form the yellow liquid iron pentacarbonyl, $Fe(CO)_5$. This transition metal carbonyl, like many others, contains the metal in a zero oxidation state. The compound is the starting material for thousands of iron compounds in unusually low oxidation states (including some that are formally negative). On decomposition, iron pentacarbonyl yields samples of very pure iron.

A new type of organometallic compound was discovered in 1951. If ferrous chloride, $FeCl_2$, is reacted with cyclopentadiene (C_5H_6) in the presence of a strong organic base, the orange crystalline compound ferrocene, $(C_5H_5)_2Fe$, is the product. This compound, which has a highly stable structure, is called a "sandwich" compound because the iron atom is strongly held between the two flat C_5H_5 rings. In this case, it is not useful to attempt to assign an oxidation state to iron. The characterization of this compound has led to extensive transition metal organometallic chemistry.

ALLOYS
Iron is abundant and easily obtainable from its ores. Its desirable mechanical and magnetic properties, as well as its resistance to corrosion, may be improved by mixing iron with other elements, frequently metals, to form ALLOYS, substances that may be simple mixtures of elements; solid solutions, in which the atoms of one substance occupy definite positions relative to the other substances; or as intermetallic compounds.

Perhaps the most important alloy of iron is steel, which contains up to approximately 2% carbon. Steels that contain about 0.25% carbon are called mild steels; those with about 0.45% carbon are medium steels; and those with 0.60% to 2% carbon are high-carbon steels. Within this range, the greater the carbon content, the greater the tensile strength of the steel. The hardness of steel may be substantially increased by heating the metal until it is red hot and then quickly cooling it, a process known as quench hardening. An important component of many steels is cementite, Fe_3C, a carbon-iron compound. Mild steels are ductile and are fabricated into sheets, wire, or pipe; the harder medium steels are used to make structural steel. High-carbon steels, which are extremely hard and brittle, are used in tools and cutting instruments.

At carbon contents below that of steel is wrought iron, which is nearly pure iron. Because of its low carbon content (usually below 0.035%) it is forgeable and nonbrittle. Iron of high carbon content (3 to 4%), obtained when pig iron is remelted and cooled, is called cast iron. If cast iron is cooled quickly, hard but brittle white cast iron is formed; if it is cooled slowly, soft but tough gray cast iron is formed. Because it expands while cooling, cast iron is used in molds.

The addition of other materials in alloys—for example, manganese or silicon—also increases the hardness of steel. The inclusion of tungsten permits high-speed drills and cutting tools to remain hard even when used at high temperatures. The inclusion of chromium and nickel improves the corrosion resistance of the steel and, within certain limits of composition, is called stainless steel. A common stainless steel contains 0.15% carbon, 18% chromium, and 8% nickel and is used in cooking utensils and food-processing equipment. The inclusion of silicon, ranging from 1 to 5%, results in an alloy that is hard and highly magnetic. An alloy with co-balt is used for permanent magnets.   NORMAN V. DUFFY

Bibliography: Cotton, Frank A., and Wilkinson, Geoffrey, *Basic Inorganic Chemistry* (1976); Dennis, William H., *Foundations of Iron and Steel Metallurgy* (1967); Nicolls, D., *The Chemistry of Iron, Cobalt and Nickel* (1973); Pounds, N. J., *The Geography of Iron* (1959); Swank, James M., *History of the Manufacture of Iron in All Ages* (1964).

Iron Age

The Iron Age marks the period of the development of TECH-NOLOGY, when the working of iron came into general use, re-placing bronze as the basic material for implements and weapons. It is the last stage of the archaeological sequence known as the three-age system (Stone Age, Bronze Age, and Iron Age).

Although iron is a commoner metal than copper or tin, the technique of iron SMELTING is more complicated than that with the other ores, requiring repeated hammering at red heat to expel slag impurities (primarily stone fragments) before wrought iron can be produced. Precisely when and where iron was first smelted remains unknown. It is possible that the process was discovered accidentally, when local sources of copper and tin with which to make bronze were becoming scarce. Occasional objects of smelted iron are known from as early as 3000 BC in the ancient Near East and predynastic Egypt, but these objects were inferior in hardness to compara-ble objects produced in bronze.

True iron metallurgy began among the HITTITES in eastern Anatolia at some time between 1900 and 1400 BC. The art of iron smelting was perfected by the time of the fall of the Hit-tite empire (*c.*1200 BC), and by 1000 BC iron objects and the knowledge of iron metallurgy had spread throughout the Near East and the Mediterranean and westward into Europe. This development marked the end of the Near Eastern Bronze Age, although bronze working was still in use for various rit-ual or prestige objects.

After about 900 BC the widespread mass production of iron implements gave rise to large-scale folk migrations that ex-tended widely over the continents of Asia and Europe. The beginning of the European Iron Age varied from place to place, depending upon available sources of raw materials. Outside of Greece, the earliest use of iron in Europe occurred about 800–750 BC in the late URNFIELD CULTURE of central Eu-rope and northern Italy (see VILLANOVANS). Following the Urn-field culture came the HALLSTATT period (700–450 BC) of the European Iron Age. In about 500 BC the technique of forging iron tools and jewelry was introduced in Europe, a technique that remained virtually unchanged until the Middle Ages. The Celtic migration of about 450 BC, commonly referred to as the LA TÈNE phase of Celtic culture, marked the division between the Early and Late Iron Age in Europe. The end of the prehis-toric Iron Age was heralded by the Roman expansion in the Alpine area as far as the Danube River (*c.*15 BC).

Elsewhere in the world, the Iron Age appeared in China by about 600 BC, spreading widely during the course of the War-ring States period (403–222 BC). The Chinese developed supe-rior blast furnaces and technical apparatus with which to pro-duce cast iron, techniques not employed in Europe until the Middle Ages. Early iron artifacts in China included swords and other weapons as well as implements of common use, such as axes, adzes, sickles, hoes, and other equipment that revolutionized Chinese agriculture.

In Africa, iron objects found in tombs of the ancient king-dom of MEROË date from the 6th century BC, although large-scale iron smelting did not occur there until the 4th cen-tury BC. Ironworking spread to the area of Lake Chad by the 2d century AD and thence to the rest of Africa. Ironworking was unknown in the New World until the arrival of the Euro-peans.   RALPH S. SOLECKI

Bibliography: Cunliffe, Barry, *Iron Age Communities in Britain*, 2d ed. (1978); Hodges, Henry, *Technology in the Ancient World* (1970); Knauth, Percy, *The Metalsmiths* (1974); Oliver, R. A., and Fagan, B. M., *Africa in the Iron Age* (1975); Reynolds, P., *Life in the Iron Age* (1975).

Iron Cross: see MEDALS AND DECORATIONS.

Iron Curtain

The *Iron Curtain* is a phrase that came to mean, after World War II, the economic, social, and military barriers created against the West by the Union of Soviet Socialist Republics and the Communist-dominated countries of Eastern Europe. The phrase first received wide currency when Winston CHURCHILL said (Mar. 5, 1946), in a speech at Westminster Col-lege in Fulton, Mo., "From Stettin in the Baltic to Trieste in the Adriatic, an iron curtain has descended across the continent."

Iron Gate

The Iron Gate, the deepest gorge in Europe, is on the DANUBE RIVER on the Romania-Yugoslavia border. It is about 3 km (2 mi) long and 168 m (550 ft) wide. Cutting through the Car-pathian and Balkan mountains, the Iron Gate has cliffs that rise more than 790 m (2,600 ft) above the river. In 1972 sluices to aid navigation and a hydroelectric plant were completed.

Iron Guard

The Iron Guard was a Fascist organization founded in Roma-nia in 1927. A paramilitary group that used assassination freely, it was proscribed in 1933 but reemerged as a powerful force in the late 1930s despite the execution of its leaders by CAROL II in 1938. In 1940 the Iron Guard helped bring Ion AN-TONESCU to power, but he suppressed the organization in 1941 and thousands of Guardists were killed. It never recovered.
                    K. M. SMOGORZEWSKI

iron lung

The iron lung was the first widely used mechanical device ca-pable of artificial respiration. Invented by Philip Drinker of Harvard University during the 1930s, the iron lung was used initially to ventilate patients who could not breathe spontane-ously. Many of these patients were victims of respiratory pa-ralysis caused by poliomyelitis.

The iron lung consists of a large metal tank in which the patient's entire body is placed, with the exception of the head. A rubber collar fits tightly around the patient's neck, thus minimizing air leakage. As the pressure in the tank is in-creased, the chest is compressed; this forces air out of the lungs. When the pressure in the tank is decreased, the chest expands, and air is drawn into the lungs. Through the use of alternating high and low pressures in the tank, a patient can be artificially ventilated for prolonged periods of time.
                    THEODORE H. STANLEY, M.D.

See also: RESPIRATOR; RESUSCITATOR.

iron and steel industry

The iron and steel industry is made up of hundreds of large and small businesses, some of which are basic steel producers and others which form steel into finished products. The num-ber of basic steel producers is limited and ranges from the large, fully integrated companies that operate IRON ore mines, coal mines, coke ovens, blast furnaces, steelmaking furnaces, and a variety of rolling mills to medium-sized producers who make steel in electric furnaces and thus depend on scrap rather than iron ore and coal, and electric furnace steel pro-ducers who operate smaller units called minimills. The wide range of activities that characterize the iron and steel industry as a whole constitutes an important part of modern techno-logical civilization.

IRON

Iron is one of the most widely distributed and abundant ele-ments in the Earth's crust, constituting about 5% of the total. It is estimated that world supplies of iron ore are adequate for at least 100 years in spite of a projected increase in pro-duction that could double during the next quarter of a cen-tury. In addition to ores that are economically and physically obtainable at present, there are almost unlimited quantities of iron-bearing materials from which iron can be recovered as

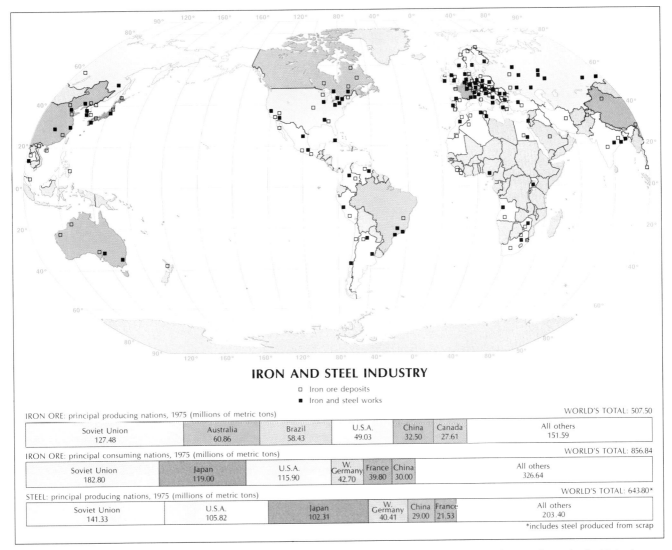

IRON AND STEEL INDUSTRY

□ Iron ore deposits
■ Iron and steel works

IRON ORE: principal producing nations, 1975 (millions of metric tons)						WORLD'S TOTAL: 507.50
Soviet Union 127.48	Australia 60.86	Brazil 58.43	U.S.A. 49.03	China 32.50	Canada 27.61	All others 151.59

IRON ORE: principal consuming nations, 1975 (millions of metric tons)						WORLD'S TOTAL: 856.84
Soviet Union 182.80	Japan 119.00	U.S.A. 115.90	W. Germany 42.70	France 39.80	China 30.00	All others 326.64

STEEL: principal producing nations, 1975 (millions of metric tons)						WORLD'S TOTAL: 643.80*
Soviet Union 141.33	U.S.A. 105.82	Japan 102.31	W. Germany 40.41	China 29.00	France 21.53	All others 203.40

*includes steel produced from scrap

new mining techniques are developed and improvements in transportation and ore handling are employed.

Iron Ore. The development of present iron ore deposits began millions of years ago when most of the world was under water. Immense quantities of sediment, some rich in iron, settled out through the ages. These age-old, iron-bearing marine sediments form the basis of the major usable iron deposits in the world today. After these deposits were incorporated into the crust of the Earth, they were gradually moved closer to the surface by the drift of the continents and the upheaval of sediment layers on the sea bottoms.

The ore formed in this way is not pure iron but a mixture of iron oxide and other deposits in varying proportions. A working definition of iron ore might be "rust plus dirt." In practical economic terms, iron ore is that part of the total iron in the Earth's crust that is economically available for industry. It is usually found in chemically combined forms, such as iron oxides, carbonates, sulfides, and silicates, in that order of importance.

Iron ore reserves are found worldwide. Areas with more than 1 billion metric tons of reserves include, in order of decreasing amounts, Australia, Brazil, Canada, the United States, Venezuela, South Africa, India, the USSR, Gabon, France, Spain, Sweden, and Algeria. The ore is found in varying grades, ranging from 20% to 70% iron content.

North America has been fortunate in its ore deposits, which are found in commercially usable quantities in 22 states in the United States and in 6 Canadian provinces. In the United States the most abundant supplies, discovered in the early 1890s, are located in the Lake Superior region around the Mesabi Range. Other large deposits are found in Alabama, Utah, Texas, California, Pennsylvania, and New York. These deposits, particularly the Mesabi Range reserves, seemed inexhaustible in the 1930s, when an average of 30 million tons of ore were produced annually from that one range. The tremendous demand for iron ore during World War II virtually tripled the output of the Mesabi Range and severely depleted its deposits of high-grade ore.

After the war a serious question arose about the future supply of easily mined, high-grade ores because it was projected that the Mesabi Range, which had been the mainstay of the iron-ore industry for over half a century, would be depleted in 25 years at the current rate of production.

Faced with this critical problem, the steel and ore companies of the United States undertook a twofold program to provide ore for the future. This program consisted of a worldwide search for new deposits and a drive to develop techniques that would upgrade the large, known reserves of low-grade ores such as taconites and jaspers. The effort met with success. Large deposits of rich ore, acceptable for blast furnace use, were found in Brazil, Australia, Canada, Venezuela, West Africa, and South Africa.

Two new upgrading techniques that have been developed are sintering and pelletizing. Sintering is used when ore is too

fine to be charged directly into the furnace; the ore is agglomerated with a mixture of coal and coke breeze (a powder) so that it forms a clinkerlike substance. Sintering permits
the passage of air through the blast furnace burden, whereas
very fine particles of ore would make the air passage difficult.
Pelletizing is used to increase the iron content of low-grade
ores such as taconites and jaspers, which average from 20% to
30% iron in their natural form; after being crushed, screened,
ground, and concentrated, the ore is formed into small round
balls called pellets, which have an iron content of 60% or
more. As a result, these ores, which were once considered
uneconomical and almost useless, supply in their upgraded
state a very substantial percentage of steel industry needs.

Two methods are employed in mining iron ore (see MINING
AND QUARRYING). Underground mining is the least economical
and may take place at depths well in excess of 300 m
(1,000 ft). The recent discoveries of iron ore made in the postwar period, however, involve reserves that are located close
to the surface; the most widely used method of mining today
is open-pit mining. In this process a layer of overburden is
removed, exposing the ore body. Huge shovels dig the ore,
which is loaded into trucks or railroad cars and carried out at
very low cost. The equipment is immense and requires extensive capital investment. The shovels are capable of taking
150 m³ (200 yd³) in one bite, while the trucks can handle
100 tons in one load. The recently developed mines in Australia, Brazil, South Africa, Canada, and West Africa are open-pit
mines.

Ironmaking. Iron is made by refining iron ore to a point
where it reaches 90% to 95% purity. Refining has been
achieved in a number of ways through the centuries, dating
back as far as the 2d millennium BC.

Iron production was at first extremely limited because of
the slow and difficult methods used to refine ore. At first
lumps of iron were heated in contact with charcoal, producing a pasty mass mixed with a great deal of SLAG. This was
hammered into a semifinished bar and then further worked
into finished products. In the Middle Ages a change was
made in the production method; sufficient heat was applied
to smelt the ore and produce liquid iron, which was then cast
into useful shapes.

The current method of smelting iron is in the BLAST FURNACE,
which was developed in a crude form during the Middle
Ages. The furnace was a stone structure built in the form of a
truncated pyramid into which iron ore, charcoal, and a flux-
ing material, usually limestone, were charged. Combustion
was aided by a blast of cold air blown in at the base of the
furnace. This operation changed little anywhere in the world
until about 1840, when anthracite coal was used for fuel in
place of charcoal, and the air blast was heated.

The construction of the furnace also changed at about that
time. The short, square-based stone stack was replaced by a
tall, cylindrical structure made of wrought-iron plates and
lined with firebrick. These furnaces were larger and increased
the production of iron considerably. In 1839 the new-style
furnaces were reportedly able to produce 28 tons of foundry
iron in a week. Stone-structure furnaces were limited to less
than half that tonnage. In the 1870s and '80s anthracite was
gradually replaced by COKE made from BITUMINOUS COAL. Furnaces grew larger and by 1900 were capable of producing
more than 200 tons of molten pig iron per day.

During the 20th century significant improvements in blast
furnace structure and practice (but not in the basic process)
have resulted in tremendous production increases. The blast
furnace remains essentially a giant stove with a shell lined
with firebrick. It features a furnace stack, which is over 30 m
(100 ft) in height and 12 m (40 ft) in diameter at the hearth,
and 3 or 4 stoves—used to preheat the air—which are almost
as high as the furnace stack. Facilities are also provided for
handling and charging iron ore, coke, and limestone into the
top of the vertical stack; as they descend they are met by a
rising volume of hot gas formed by combustion of the coke
with air preheated to 1,000° C (1,800° F) and blown in under
pressure through openings called tuyères, which are located
at the base of the stack. The carbon monoxide from the burn-

ing coke reduces the iron oxide to iron, while the limestone
removes impurities from the ore. At the base of the furnace
the molten iron is tapped into ladles capable of holding
300 tons.

The blast-furnace process operates 24 hours a day, 7 days a
week. This continuity is essential to efficient operation; if the
furnace is shut down, several days are often required before
smooth operation is restored. The raw materials are constantly
being charged into the top to replace the gasified carbon and
the molten products that are removed from the furnace. The
furnace is tapped about 4 times every day, at intervals of 5 or
6 hours; the iron drawn off leaves the furnace in a fiery
stream at 1,500° C (2,700° F). The size of the furnace determines the amount drawn off at each tap. For the large, average furnace in the United States producing 3,000 tons per
day, each tap yields about 800 tons. The new 10,000-ton-per-
day furnaces have 4 tapholes, and the tapping process is almost continuous.

The blast-furnace process is one of the most efficient in the
industrial world, since 90% of the iron contained in the ore is
recovered in molten pig iron. Of the other 10%, some goes
into slag, and some becomes flue dust combined with the gas
at the top of the furnace. Most of this flue dust is recovered,
agglomerated into chunks resembling clinkers by sintering,
and recharged into the furnace. Thus, the total recovery of
iron often exceeds 95% of that contained in the ore.

Uses of Iron. Until 1870 very little steel was produced either
in the United States or in the rest of the world. Iron was the
end product, and it had a multiplicity of uses. Perhaps the
greatest use was in railroad rails and railroad car wheels. Iron
was used in construction, but only to a limited extent because most of the buildings were relatively small and made
from stone, brick, or wood. Ships were also made of wood.
Iron had significant uses in the form of nails and wire, and in
sheets plated with tin, called tin plate, which were used for
food containers.

With the advent of steel, most of the iron came to be used
as raw material for the production of steel, and that remains
its principal use today. Of the total production of 101 million
tons of pig iron from U.S. blast-furnace plants in 1973, 96
million tons were used for steelmaking, while the remaining
5 million tons were used for other purposes.

Today the principal use of blast-furnace iron that is not
turned into steel is for cast products. The iron is purchased by
foundries (see FOUNDRY) in solid form and then melted together with scrap to make castings for a number of industries.
Some of the principal items are motor blocks for the automobile industry, heavy machinery castings, water and drainage
pipe, construction castings, and a variety of smaller castings
used in the railroad and automobile industries.

STEEL PRODUCTION

As it comes from the blast furnace, iron contains about 5%
carbon and is too brittle for many applications. Most of this
carbon must be removed along with small portions of other
elements, such as phosphorus, silicon, and aluminum, to give
the resultant material its strength and flexibility. In a number
of instances, small amounts of other elements, such as manganese, molybdenum, chromium, and nickel, are added during the process.

Steel, which is the result of this refining process, can be defined as relatively pure iron containing less than 1.7% carbon.
Although steel has been known for centuries, its production
was extremely limited until the invention of the Bessemer
process in the late 1850s. Before that time steel was principally produced in small containers called crucibles or by a ce-
mentation process that consisted of placing iron bars in a
charcoal furnace. In the crucible process, molten iron was
mixed with charcoal and refined in a refractory-lined pot.
Production was so limited that the amounts of steel produced
were measured in pounds. Statistics from 1860 record some
11 thousand tons of steel produced in the United States, compared to almost a million tons of iron produced in the same
year.

The Bessemer Process. The Bessemer process, which gave
birth to the modern steel industry, is a pneumatic process

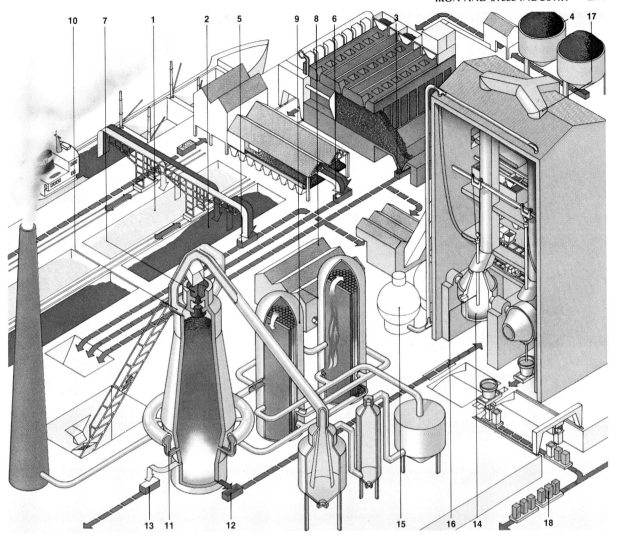

The production of steel, the most widely used of all the metals, is essentially a two-stage process. It involves the initial production of an impure form of iron from an ore composed primarily of iron oxide and varying amounts of silica and compounds of sulfur, phosphorus, and manganese. The extracted iron, called pig iron, is hard and brittle and contains several percent of carbon, as well as small amounts of silicon, manganese, sulfur, and phosphorus remaining from the original ore. A small amount of pig iron is made into different types of cast iron by remelting and cooling it under carefully controlled conditions. Most pig iron, however, is converted into steel by removing the impurities and later adding small but definite amounts of carbon and selected substances—particularly manganese, chromium, molybdenum, and vanadium—to produce alloys with specific properties that make them suitable for various uses. For reasons of economy, present iron and steel production facilities are generally combined in one large plant. Modern integrated iron and steel plants use such large amounts of coke that they are usually located near coal mines. Other raw materials, such as limestone (1) and iron ore (2) are brought in by train or ship. Before extraction of iron from the ore is begun, coke (3) is produced by controlled burning of coal (4). Specific amounts of correctly sized coke, ore, and limestone (5), and a sintered mixture of finely powdered ore, limestone, and coke (6) are then blended and charged into the top of a blast furnace (7). Air from a pumphouse (8) is preheated in heat exchangers (9) by hot gases (10) from the blast furnace and blown into the bottom of the furnace through tuyeres, or nozzles (11). A series of complicated reactions converts the ore into molten pig iron, which is tapped off (12) periodically at the bottom of the furnace into containers for further purification and conversion into steel. The limestone, which reacts with impurities to form a slag that floats on the liquid iron, is also removed (13). The pig iron, which still contains excessive impurities, is mixed with limestone and refined in a basic oxygen furnace (14) into which oxygen from a tank (15) is blown through a water-cooled metal tube, or lance (16). Some of the remaining impurities form a slag, which is withdrawn after a definite period of time. Carbon and other impurities are converted to gases, which are drawn off (17) and freed of pollutants before being discharged into the air. Predetermined amounts of carbon and alloying metals are added to the purified iron to form steel with specific properties. The final steel is poured into ladles and cast into ingots (18), which are shipped to manufacturers for rolling and forging into numerous products.

that forces air through a bath of molten iron in a pear-shaped vessel. The oxygen in the air is brought into contact with the carbon in the iron and reduces the carbon content to the desired level. The process was developed in the late 1850s by the Englishman Henry BESSEMER. At about the same time an American, William Kelly, developed a similar process. After a sharp contest between the two, Kelly was granted priority by the United States Patent Office, but the dispute was finally resolved by an agreement to merge the two interests. The first Bessemer converter in the United States, a very small vessel

capable of producing approximately 2 tons of steel at one time, was installed at Wyandotte, Mich., in 1864.

Acceptance of the process was slow at first, so that by 1870 the annual output of Bessemer steel in the United States was a mere 42 thousand tons. Production grew rapidly thereafter, rising to 1.2 million tons in 1880.

The principal application of Bessemer steel in the last century was for railroad rails, since it had been discovered that rails made of steel were far more durable than those made of iron. The transition from iron to steel rails was made rapidly.

In 1872, 906,000 tons of iron rails were produced, compared with 94,000 tons of steel rails. In 1877 steel-rail production stood at 432,000 tons, whereas iron rails had dropped to 322,000 tons. By 1890 there were virtually no iron rails produced.

The Open-Hearth Process. The open-hearth process of steel-making, referred to in Europe as the Siemens-Martin process, was first introduced in the United States in 1868 (see SIEMENS family). It makes use of a rectangular, boxlike structure lined with brick, forming a shallow basin, or hearth, into which materials are charged. The charge consists of large quantities of scrap and molten pig iron, and the fuel, either gas or oil, is introduced through openings at the ends of the furnace.

The new process was accepted slowly until 1895. In that year almost 1.3 million tons of steel were produced by this process; its expansion in the next 5 years, however, was so rapid that by 1900 output of open-hearth steel had tripled to 3.8 million tons.

Although the new process took much longer to refine steel than did the Bessemer converter, it had a number of advantages. The open hearth could: (1) use large amounts of scrap, up to 80 and 90% of the charge, whereas the scrap in the Bessemer converter was limited to 10% of the charge; (2) refine iron made from ore containing significant amounts of phosphorus, which was not possible in the Bessemer converter; (3) be controlled and tested during the process by sampling the steel, which was impossible with the Bessemer converter because it belched forth hot flames; and (4) produce less brittle steel than the Bessemer converter, which contained nitrogen from the air that was passed through the molten iron.

The second advantage was particularly important because most of the ore in the United States had a higher percentage of phosphorus than the Bessemer converter could remove when that ore had been smelted into iron. A disadvantage of the open hearth was that it took a longer period of time (8 to 10 hours) to complete the process; the Bessemer converter accomplished its objective in approximately half an hour.

In the 20th century the open hearth became the dominant steelmaking process, while the Bessemer process declined almost to the point of extinction. In the postwar period from 1946 to 1958, open-hearth steel constituted 90% of total production, whereas Bessemer steel accounted for less than 5%. In 1968 the last significant amount of Bessemer steel was produced in the United States. Open-hearth furnaces were capable of producing 400 tons at a time, while the Bessemer converter rarely reached 35 tons.

In a new process developed during the last two decades, oxygen is injected into the open-hearth furnace through a tube built into the roof, accelerating the process considerably by shortening the production time to 5 or 6 hours.

Basic Oxygen Process. The basic oxygen process, one of the greatest technological breakthroughs in the steel industry during the 20th century, revolutionized the production of steel by reducing the time required in the normal open-hearth from an average of 8 or 9 hours to 45 minutes. This new method also required less investment and appreciably reduced operating costs. The process was developed in Austria after World War II and was installed in 1953 at the Voest plant in Linz. The vessel in which the steel is made is pear shaped, resembling the Bessemer converter. It is tilted to receive the charge, which consists of scrap and hot metal, and then brought to an upright position. An oxygen tube is lowered into the converter to a point about 2 m (6 ft) above the metal bath; from this position it blows 54 to 58 cubic m (1,700 to 1,800 cubic ft) of oxygen for each ton of steel produced. The actual blowing time is about 22 minutes, with an equal amount of time required to fill and empty the vessel. The full cycle is completed in about 45 minutes.

In the United States the process uses from 25% to 28% scrap with the remainder of the charge in molten iron. The Japanese practice uses much less scrap—an average of about 12%, although at times as low as 5%—and, consequently, much more iron.

The first vessels installed at Linz had a 30- to 35-ton capacity, as did the first vessels installed in the United States in 1954 at the Detroit plant of the McLouth Steel Corporation. Since that time the capacity of the vessels has increased tremendously; many operations throughout the world today are capable of producing between 300 and 350 tons at one time.

The basic oxygen process has spread rapidly worldwide and now constitutes approximately 60% of world steel production. In the United States this figure is about 65% and in Japan between 80% and 85%. Because this process requires a substantial amount of molten pig iron, it must be operated in conjunction with a blast furnace, which, in turn, is supported by coke ovens. The investment for the entire process is very large primarily because of the high cost of installing coke ovens and blast furnaces.

Electric Furnace. The first commercial production of steel in an ELECTRIC FURNACE was recorded in France in 1900, and the initial installation of the process in the United States was in 1906 at the Halcomb Steel Company in Syracuse, N.Y. This furnace, tiny by comparison with today's units, had an output limited to 4 tons of steel per charge.

The electric-furnace process uses scrap iron almost exclusively as a raw material. The scrap is placed in the furnace—a round deep receptacle lined with refractory brick—while the roof is off. The roof is replaced, and electrodes are lowered through holes in the roof until they are in contact with the scrap charge. Once the power is turned on, tremendous heat is generated as arc temperatures reach 3,300° C (6,000° F). This heat melts the scrap into new steel in a matter of a few hours with an electric power consumption of approximately 500 kW h per ton of steel produced.

Acceptance of the process at first was confined to the production of alloy steels. Attempts to produce carbon steel during the second decade of the century met with limited success because of the inability to compete with the open-hearth furnace.

Shortly before World War II a number of units were used to produce carbon steel with significant success, both physically and economically. This practice continued in the postwar period; electric furnaces were used to produce larger and

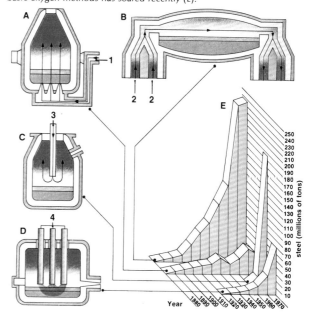

Of the major methods for producing steel from iron, the Bessemer process (A), in which air (1) is blown through molten iron, is now rarely used. Burning gases containing an excess of air (2) are used in the open-hearth furnace (B) to heat the iron charge from above. In the basic oxygen process (C) oxygen (3) is blown onto the molten charge. Arcing carbon electrodes (4) in electric furnaces (D) develop the temperatures needed to melt iron in the absence of oxygen and produce steels containing easily oxidized additives. Although most of the world's steel has been produced in open hearths since 1880, use of basic oxygen methods has soared recently (E).

larger tonnages of carbon steel. In 1955 about 4.3 million tons of carbon steel were produced by electric furnaces as opposed to 3.7 million tons of alloy steel. In 1977 electric-furnace steel accounted for a total of 27.9 million tons, of which 8.4 million tons were alloy and stainless and 19.5 million tons were carbon steel.

In order to produce these large tonnages, electric furnaces increased both in number and size. In the late 1940s they averaged 30 to 40 tons per charge; by 1978 there were a number of furnaces capable of producing 200 tons per charge, and two in the United States capable of producing 400 tons or more.

In addition to the furnace, a considerable amount of electrical equipment, including a large transformer, is necessary to provide the electric power. Although the entire plant represents a sizable capital investment, the investment is small in comparison with the capital required for the basic oxygen process, which must be supported by blast furnaces and coke ovens. As the electric furnace uses scrap, which is gathered rather than produced, only a small investment is required for scrap processing and handling facilities.

Despite limitations on the amount of such scrap available and on the availability of electric power in some areas of the world, there is a growing trend to install electric furnaces for more and more steel production. Until recently, the largest electric-furnace plant had the capacity to produce 2 million tons annually; in 1979 a 4-million-ton electric-furnace plant opened in Venezuela. Electric furnaces have been installed in a number of developing countries throughout the world, where they provide a means for establishing a steel-making operation on a relatively small scale with a limited investment. Most of these operations consist of furnaces capable of producing between 25 and 50 tons at one time.

A substitute for scrap, a material called sponge iron, was recently developed. It is made from iron ore combined with gas to reduce the ore's oxygen content and raise its iron content to better than 90%. This direct reduction process uses NATURAL GAS and, consequently, is employed only in those areas of the world where natural gas is abundant. Another process, not widespread as yet, uses coal. In the Middle East several programs are under way that call for the installation of equipment to produce sponge iron as well as the electric furnaces in which it will be used to make steel.

In 1974, a year of record steel output, worldwide production of electric-furnace steel was 137 million tons. This will probably increase to 215 million tons by the mid-1980s.

STEEL PROCESSING

Immediately after molten steel is poured from the furnace into a ladle at a temperature of about 1,600° C (3,000° F), it passes through one of two processes: ingot production or continuous casting.

Ingot Production. The molten steel can be discharged into ingot molds and allowed to solidify into ingots, which are tall, rectangular shapes weighing from less than a ton to 100 or more tons. After solidification, the molds are stripped off and the ingots are placed in a covered pit, called a soaking pit, where they are heated to an even temperature. Upon removal from the pit they pass through a primary rolling mill, which is a massive piece of equipment that can be powered by as much as 15,000 hp. This mill, called either a slabbing or blooming mill, reduces the ingots to a bloom or slab. A bloom is a square section usually more than 15 by 15 cm (6 by 6 in), varying in length up to 9 m (30 ft). A slab is a rectangular-shaped section that can vary in width from 50 to 200 cm (20 to 80 in) and in thickness from 5 to 30 cm (2 to 12 in). Blooms are further processed into smaller square sections, 13 by 13 cm (5 by 5 in) or less, called billets. These three classifications, blooms, billets, and slabs, constitute what is known as semifinished steel.

Continuous Casting. A recent technological breakthrough is continuous casting, a process in which the liquid steel is poured into a machine called a continuous caster, which produces a semifinished form without the intermediate ingot, soaking pit, and blooming or slabbing mill operations. Developmental work on the process began in the 1940s, but was

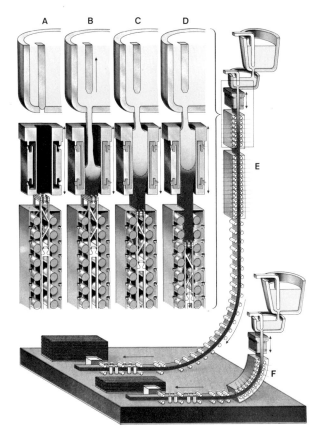

In the continuous casting of steel rods and bars, molten steel from a reservoir (A) is poured into a water-cooled copper mold (B). A plug at the bottom of the mold is withdrawn (C), bringing with it the partially solidified bar, which is cooled by water sprays as it is drawn between metal rolls (D). Earlier casting machines (E) required considerable headroom to accommodate their long, straight cooling sections. Newer machines (F) use short, curved cooling sections. After cooling, the bars are cut into whatever lengths are required.

not successful until the early 1950s. Since that time a large number of units have been put in place throughout the world, and close to one-third of the steel made is processed through them rather than by the ingot operation.

Semifinished steel made either by ingot or continuous casting is reheated to a temperature of about 1,200° C (2,300° F) and is then processed into many finished steel products on a variety of rolling mills. These include hot-strip and cold-strip sheet mills and plate, rail, pipe, rod, bar, and structural mills. The most significant of these is the hot-strip mill, which, in the United States, processes somewhat more than half of the semifinished steel.

Hot-Strip Mill. The hot-strip mill consists of a series of consecutive stands each containing huge rolls that squeeze the slab successively until it is reduced in thickness from its original size (from 5 to 30 cm/2 to 12 in) to less than 3.175 mm (⅛ in). The strip is elongated from the original slab length of 4.5 to 10 m (15 to 33 ft) to over 900 m (3,000 ft). The width usually remains the same as that of the original slab. This ribbon of steel comes off the hot-strip mill and is coiled and allowed to cool. It can be cut to usable lengths, usually up to 3.5 m (12 ft), and sold as hot rolled sheets or in coil form.

There are 38 wide hot-strip mills in the United States, 11 of which have been built since 1962. Total power in the newer mills is over 100,000 hp, and the strips emerge from the last stand at the rate of 1,200 m (4,000 ft) per min.

Cold-Strip Mill. The product of the hot-strip mill, excluding that sold as hot-rolled sheets, is cleansed of its surface oxides by means of an acid bath in a process called pickling. The coil is then introduced at room temperatures into a cold-strip mill, which usually consists of five stands of rolls that reduce it to a thin sheet 1.588 mm (one-sixteenth of an inch) or less thick. As the product comes off the cold mill in the form of a coil, it is usually too stiff for many uses and must be softened by a heat-treating process called ANNEALING. To restore some stiffness in the steel after this process is complete, the product is passed through another mill called the temper mill. Most coils are sold as cold-rolled sheets. Some are coated with zinc and sold as galvanized sheets; others are plated with tin and sold as tinplate, which is used principally for cans and other containers.

Plate Mills. Semifinished slabs are further processed into plates on a rolling mill, usually with one set of rolls having a reversible rotation. The slab is passed back and forth through the rolls until it reaches the desired thickness and length. Plates are produced in a variety of sizes, varying in thickness from 6.350 mm ($\frac{1}{4}$ in) to 30 cm (12 in), and in width from 76 cm (30 in) to 535 cm (210 in).

In a year of strong steel demand, plate consumption in the U.S. economy is approximately 10 million tons. The product has a wide variety of uses in construction, in the manufacture of machinery, railroad cars, and ships, and in the production of large-diameter line pipe for the transmission of oil and gas.

Structural Mills. A number of blooms and, in some cases, ingots are rolled directly into structural shapes on rolling mills, which, unlike the flat rolls on a strip-and-plate mill, have rolls that are grooved and shaped to yield the structural shapes desired. A large variety of structural shapes are made; they range from beams that weigh 135 kg (300 lb) per ft to very light structural sections used in the construction of single-story buildings. Structural mills usually have a series of consecutive rolls, so that the shape of the final product is arrived at gradually as it passes from one set of rolls to the next.

Rail Mills. Rails were the predominant steel product during the 19th century. The nature of transportation has changed to such an extent that there are only four major rail mills operating in this country today. These mills take an ingot or a bloom and, through a series of rolls that are grooved and formed to shape the rail, produce railroad rails in lengths of 12 m (39 ft) and 24 m (78 ft). The rails are then processed further as they are hardened and straightened. The average rail produced weighs 64 kg (132 lb) per yd.

Bar Mills. The term *bar* encompasses a wide variety of steel products and shapes. In years of strong demand, U.S. bar production has amounted to a total of 16 million tons. Bars are produced by both large and small steel-makers and are put to many uses, including concrete reinforcing bars for construction and special cold-finished bars for the manufacture of machines and machine tools. Bar mills usually consist of a number of consecutive stands, as many as 18 to 20. The semifinished form used to produce a bar is, for the most part, a billet, 13 by 13 cm (5 by 5 in) or smaller. There are about 80 bar mills in operation throughout the nation's steel industry.

Wire and Wire Rod Mills. The semifinished billet can be rolled down through a series of as many as 20 consecutive stands into a round section about 13 mm ($\frac{1}{2}$ in) in diameter and more than 5,000 m (16,500 ft) in length. This section is called a rod and comes from the mill in coil form. The wire rod mills operate at extremely high speeds; the newest installations spew out rods at 4,500 m (15,000 ft) per minute. This material is then drawn through a die and formed into wire.

Seamless Pipe Mills. In this process the semifinished bloom is rolled into a round, solid section. It is then heated and its center pierced, so that a hollow is formed without a seam. The section is processed further to produce seamless pipe, which has a number of applications, particularly in oil-well drilling and as oil-well casing. The absence of a welded seam gives the pipe sufficient strength to be used in drilling wells 3,000 m (10,000 ft) deep. It is also used in other applications where high pressure is involved, such as boiler tubes.

USES OF STEEL

Steel today has a multiplicity of uses, ranging from fine piano wire to heavy girders for bridges. Consequently, it plays a key role in modern life.

In the last decade an average of about 90 million tons of domestically produced steel products have been consumed in the U.S. economy each year. About 21% was used by the automotive industry, 19% by construction, 17% by machinery, 7% by containers, 3.5% by the railroads, and 20% by the steel service centers, which act as a distributing arm of the steel industry. A number of other industries consume small percentages.

Up to 1890 most of the steel produced was processed into rails, but as overall output grew and other uses were found, rails constituted an ever-diminishing proportion of the steel market. In the first 2 decades of the 20th century, shipbuilding, heavy construction, and machinery were significant markets for steel. In the 1920s, as the automobile and appliance industries grew to substantial proportions, more and more sheet steel was used. This increased use brought a shift to the lighter sheet steels, which were necessary for automobile bodies, refrigerator cabinets, small appliances, and furniture. The significance of light, flat, rolled-steel products can be judged by the fact that they constituted 51% of all the steel shipped in 1973, a record year. Bars accounted for 16.2%, plates 8.7%, structural shapes 6.4%, pipe and tubing 8.2%, wire 2.9%, railroad rails and other materials 1.4%, and semifinished products 5.1%.

Alloy steels contain percentages of elements other than iron, which give them special properties to function in a variety of applications for which normal carbon steel would be inadequate. The alloying elements that are introduced into the furnace as the steel is being refined include aluminum, chromium, cobalt, columbium, molybdenum, nickel, titanium, tungsten, and vanadium. The percentages of these elements vary and often total as much as 50% of the final product.

Alloy steels are called specialty steels by the industry and are usually divided into three categories—STAINLESS STEEL, tool steel, and alloy steel. In 1976 alloy-steel shipments amounted to 8.1 million tons, stainless-steel shipments were 1 million tons, and tool-steel shipments were 76,000 tons. Outstanding properties of alloy steels include their resistance to heat, abrasion, and corrosion; they find many applications in sections of chemical plants, petroleum refineries, power plants, and jet engines. Because stainless steels are also relatively rustproof, they are used both for their strength and for their decorative qualities, in such applications as the bright trim on automobiles and buildings, and for household and commercial equipment. Silicon steel has been used since the turn of the century in the production of electric motors, generators, and transformers. Tool steels have a limited production that rarely surpasses 100,000 tons a year in the United States. They are used for such applications as high-speed drills, cutting edges, and parts of machinery subject to severe wear.

WILLIAM T. HOGAN

Bibliography: Cockerill, A., and Silberton, A., *The Steel Industry* (1974); Dennis, W. H., *Foundations of Iron and Steel Metallurgy* (1967); Hogan, William T., *Economic History of the Iron and Steel Industry in the United States* (1971); Lewis, W. David, *Iron and Steel in America* (1976); Pounds, Norman, *Geography of Iron and Steel* (1968); Russell, Clifford S., and Vaughan, William J., *Steel Production: Processes, Products and Residuals* (1976); Swank, James H., *History of the Manufacture of Iron in All Ages* (1892; repr. 1965); Szekely, Julian, *The Future of the World's Steel Industry* (1976) and "Toward Radical Changes in Steelmaking," *Technology Review*, February 1979; Wertime, Theodore, *Coming of the Age of Steel* (1962).

ironweed

Vernonia, commonly referred to as ironweed, is a widely distributed plant genus of more than 500 species in the family Compositae. It includes herbs, vines, and shrubs. Ironweed heads have purple, white, or pink disk florets, and the leaves are usually alternate and toothed. *V. noveboracensis* is native to eastern North America.

DIANNE FAHSELT

ironwood

Ironwood is the common name for about 35 small- to medium-sized trees and shrubs and refers to the hard, heavy wood that has been used traditionally for making items such as tool handles, mallets, and even arrowheads. Native to North America, ironwoods include the Eastern HOP HORNBEAM, *Ostrya virginiana,* and the American HORNBEAM, *Carpinus caroliniana.*   DIANNE FAHSELT

ironwork, ornamental

Although iron was used decoratively during the IRON AGE and in classical times, very little early work has survived. During the Roman occupation of Britain (AD c.43–425), wrought iron was used for tools, weapons, and furnishings. During the following centuries such objects were frequently damascened—elaborately decorated with inlaid patterns of gold and silver—and used as ceremonial objects and gifts. By the 11th century the Anglo-Saxons and Scandinavians had begun to exploit the decorative possibilities of wrought iron in a new way—in complex hinges that secured and ornamented the doors of churches and cathedrals. A century later hingework based on English models was produced in France and then emulated in Germany and elsewhere in Europe.

By the 13th century iron ornament in scrolls and arabesques covered church doors. These decorations included three-dimensional forms such as dragons' heads and leaves whose surfaces were decorated with stamped work—scored, chiseled, or punched into the hot metal with tools—as in the Gate of Saint Anne in Notre Dame de Paris. Thirteenth-century Venetian ironwork, the earliest in Italy, consisted of screens pierced with Islamic-style geometric patterns, which were cut into unheated metal. This technique spread throughout Europe and appeared in the screen (1425–31) of Henry V's tomb in Westminster Abbey, London, by Roger Johnson.

The next 3 centuries were a period of great activity in European decorative ironwork. French smiths combined hot and cold working techniques in an elaborate baroque style of rich scrollwork in *C, S,* and *G* forms. This flamboyant French style was introduced into England in the late 17th century by Jean TIJOU, who worked at Chatsworth (1688–89) and Hampton Court (1689–99), producing staircase balustrades and park gates. During the 18th century staircases in French houses were especially imposing, and among the most celebrated was the grand wrought-iron staircase (1766–68) of the Palais Royal, Paris, designed by Pierre Contant d'Ivry (1698–1777). In the late 18th century elaborate ironwork was inexpensively cast rather than handwrought. By 1810 the Industrial Revolu-

Jean Tijou's intricately ornamented sanctuary screen (c.1695-1707) in Saint Paul's Cathedral, London, is representative of the rich baroque decoration he introduced to English wrought ironwork.

tion had transformed the character of the metal industries. Cast iron was mass-produced on a commercial scale, and because even small household and architectural fittings were cast, the art of the decorative smith declined.

REVIEWED BY KATHRYN B. HIESINGER

Bibliography: Frank, Edgar B., *Old French Ironwork* (1950); Lister, Raymond, *Decorative Wrought Ironwork in Great Britain* (1957; repr. 1970); Magnani, Franco, *Ornamental Metalwork* (1967); Meilach, Dona Z., *Decorative and Sculptural Ironwork* (1977); Robertson, E. Graeme and Joan, *Cast Iron Decoration: A World Survey* (1977); Southwork, Susan and Michael, *Ornamental Ironwork: An Illustrated Guide to Its Design, History and Use in American Architecture* (1978).

irony

Derived from the Greek *eironeia* ("simulated ignorance"), the term *irony* refers to a rhetorical device in which the intention is in sharp contrast to the literal meaning. The realization of this intended interpretation depends on a knowing audience participating or collaborating with the author or speaker.

Irony most likely originated with a character type in the Old Comedy, a seeming simpleton who asked questions and said less than he knew. In Socratic irony, the speaker pretends to be naive and makes opponents expose their confused or false conceptions by asking them deceptively simple questions.

For a while irony was associated with a "dissembler," but it soon came to be recognized as a habit of discourse, or conceit, that realizes a rhetorical strategy. For example, Jonathan Swift's *A Modest Proposal,* an ironic attack on the attitudes of the English rulers, argues that to alleviate the famine in Ireland, English landlords should purchase and eat the children of the poor. In this respect it is closely associated with SATIRE; irony is the method by which satire achieves its particular purpose. The use of the innocent narrator in *Huckleberry Finn* is also an example of the use of irony as a rhetorical strategy.

Situational irony reveals a striking incongruity between what is expected and what results, as when a pickpocket discovers that his or her pocket has been picked. The concept of the twist of fate was long recognized but was not called irony until about the 19th century. Dramatic irony, a special instance of situational irony, occurs when a character is ignorant of a situation that is known to the spectators. When Oedipus, for example, prays that the unknown killer of Laius be eternally cursed, he is ironically cursing himself; the audience knows that Oedipus is blind to the fact that he is the killer.

Verbal irony admits of varying degrees. The New Critics have used the term to designate incongruities resulting from the special use of words. For example, in the phrase "the short and simple annals of the poor," *annals* has an ironic ring because annals are usually long records of the rich and powerful.

The term *irony* has been increasingly used in the 20th century to describe a sense of detachment—an attitude of mind held by an observer or author when that person abstracts himself or herself from the scene and views everything impartially. Thomas Mann's work is often described as ironic in this sense.

Bibliography: Booth, Wayne C., *A Rhetoric of Irony* (1974); Knox, Norman, *The Word Irony and Its Context, 1500-1755* (1965); Muecke, D. C., *The Compass of Irony* (1969) and *Irony* (1970); States, Bert, *Irony and Drama: A Poetics* (1971).

Iroquois League [ir'-uh-kwoy]

The Iroquois League was a union of Iroquoian-speaking North American Indian peoples, originally composed of the SENECA, CAYUGA, ONONDAGA, ONEIDA, and MOHAWK Indians. The TUSCARORA became the sixth member of the league in the early 18th century. The tribes occupied a territory comprising what is now New York's Mohawk Valley and Finger Lakes region, bordered on the north by Lake Ontario and the Adirondacks and on the south by the Catskills and what today approximates the New York–Pennsylvania state line.

Although the precise date of the league's founding is un-

The Iroquois League, a confederacy of American Indian nations comprised of the Mohawk, Onondaga, Oneida, Seneca, Cayuga, and, after 1722, the Tuscarora tribes, is shown at an intertribal council in an idealized engraving by Joseph Lafitau. (New York Public Library.)

known, some historians suggest that the confederacy was probably formed by the early 16th century. According to Iroquois legend, the league was founded by Deganawidah, a leader of divine status, who persuaded the original Five Nations to give up intertribal warfare marked by blood feud and cannibalism. Historians of Indian culture view its formation as a defensive response to warfare with neighboring Huron and other Algonquian-speaking tribes. The prophet HIAWATHA (fl. c.1550), Deganawidah's earthly spokesman, doggedly traveled among the five tribes in an attempt to unify them. His persistence succeeded, and the tribes united in what proved to be a nearly invulnerable political alliance until its eventual collapse during the American Revolution. Sporadic warfare and raiding against tribes outside the league afforded opportunities for young Iroquois warriors to earn prestige and honor. Initially, conquest and the gaining of economic and political advantages were of secondary importance. Eventually, however, in dealings with the British and French and, later, the British and the colonists, the league skillfully played off opposing parties against one another and subjugated neighboring tribes for both economic and territorial gains. Before its collapse in the late 18th century, the Iroquois League dominated lands as far west as the Mississippi River.

The league was modeled after already existing family, clan, and community organizations; its aim was not only to unite its members through symbolic kinship relationships but to maintain the autonomy of individual tribal members. The league's Grand Council consisted of 50 life-appointed male sachems, or peace chiefs, who were nominated by the headwoman of certain sachem-producing lineages in each clan. The Onondaga had 14 sachems, the Cayuga 10, the Oneida and Mohawk 9 each, and the Seneca 8. After lengthy ratification procedures, the council members became responsible for keeping the internal peace, representing the body of tribes to outsiders, and coordinating tribal activities in unified warfare against nonmembers.

Major decisions were reached through unanimity, compensating for otherwise unequal tribal representation. An individual sachem could be deposed through impeachment proceedings initiated by his lineage's headwoman. Some historians claim that the highly democratic political organization of the Iroquois League may have served as a model for the compilers of the United States Constitution.

JAMES W. HERRICK

Bibliography: Fenton, William N., ed., *Parker on the Iroquois* (1968); Graymont, Barbara, *The Iroquois in the American Revolution* (1972); Hunt, George T., *The Wars of the Iroquois* (1940; repr. 1960); Morgan, Lewis H., *League of the Ho-De-No-Sau-Nee, or Iroquois* (1851; repr. 1962).

irradiation: SEE RADIOLOGY; RADIATION THERAPY.

irrational number

An irrational number is a NUMBER that is not a RATIONAL NUMBER—that is, not the quotient of two integers. Deciding whether or not a particular number is irrational is a problem that has perplexed mathematicians throughout the ages, starting with the Greeks in the 6th century BC. The Greeks proved that such numbers as $\sqrt{2}$ and $\sqrt{3}$ are irrational; it was not until 1761, however, that Johann Lambert proved that π (the number PI) is irrational. The irrational numbers themselves are divided into two classes: the algebraic numbers and those that are not algebraic, which are called TRANSCENDENTAL NUMBERS. The algebraic irrational numbers are defined as irrational numbers that are roots of POLYNOMIAL equations with integer coefficients, for example, $\sqrt{2}$ and $\sqrt[3]{5}$. WILLIAM W. ADAMS

Bibliography: Courant, Richard, and Robbins, Herbert, *What is Mathematics* (1941), Niven, Ivan, *Numbers: Rational and Irrational* (1961).

Irrawaddy River [ir-uh-wahd'-ee]

The Irrawaddy River (Iyawadi-Nmai), 2,095 km (1,300 mi) long, flows through central Burma. Its drainage basin covers more than 410,000 km² (158,000 mi²), and its delta is the rice bowl and population center of Burma. The river rises in the mountains of northern Burma as the headstreams Mali and Nmai, which join to the north of Myitkyina. Between Myitkyina and MANDALAY, a distance of 585 km (365 mi), the Irrawaddy passes through three deep gorges, or defiles—one to the north and two to the south of Bhamo, an important river port. Just below Mandalay is the Ava Bridge, the only span over the river. About 130 km (80 mi) below Mandalay the Chindwin River flows into the Irrawaddy. The river's enormous delta begins about 290 km (180 mi) from the ANDAMAN SEA. There monsoonal precipitation reaches about 2,540 mm (100 in) per year. The outer edge of the delta contains many mangrove-covered islands protected from the sea by dikes. The major delta city is RANGOON, Burma's capital.

irredentism [ir-i-den'-tizm]

Irredentism, a term of Italian origin, refers to movements in any country that demand the incorporation into their states of foreign-ruled territories that they regard as belonging to them by reason of ethnic, cultural, or historical ties. The term was first used in the 1870s by Italian nationalists who called for the annexation of Italian-speaking communities in Austrian-held Trieste, Trentino, Istria, and south Tyrol. More extreme irredentists claimed, in addition, Corsica and Nice, which were part of France, and Malta, which was under British rule.

The continuing agitation for *Italia irredenta* ("unredeemed Italy") was a strong influence on Italian foreign policy in the late 19th and early 20th centuries—especially from 1900 to 1914. Although Italy was part of the Triple Alliance with Germany and Austria-Hungary, it eventually entered World War I on the side of the Entente powers. Consequently, Italy realized most of its irredentist goals at the Paris Peace Conference in 1919.

See also: ITALY, HISTORY OF.

irreversible processes: SEE REVERSIBLE AND
IRREVERSIBLE PROCESSES.

irrigation [ir-i-gay'-shuhn]

Irrigation is the practice of artificially supplying water to land to sustain the growth of crops. An ancient agricultural technique, irrigation may have been practiced as early as 5000 BC along the banks of such regularly flooding rivers as the Nile, by digging channels to extend the area covered by the flood, and by erecting dikes to trap water on the land after the river had subsided. The development of diversion dams and of water-lifting machines permitted the irrigation of lands lying above those normally reached by floodwaters. Ancient remnants of these structures have been found in Egypt, Babylonia, China, Phoenicia, Peru, Mexico, India, and the United

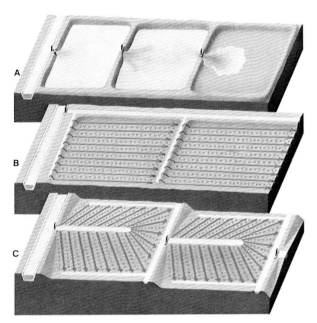

In the oldest, most basic irrigation method (A), fields are subdivided into basinlike sections, which are flooded as needed. In furrow irrigation, or infiltration (B), fields are divided into ridges and furrows, and controlled amounts of water are discharged into each furrow through a network of sluice gates or siphons. Irrigation by natural flow (C) requires that each field be built up into a gently sloping ridge. Water is then released from a channel that runs along the top of each ridge and percolates down the slope.

States. Modern irrigation systems are still based on these two key engineering innovations.

DIVERSION DAMS AND WATER-LIFTING MACHINES

The diversion dam supplies water from a stream to a canal system at an elevation above the lands to be irrigated. Often a reservoir for storage is included in the system. The canals follow the natural land contours, so that water flows by gravity to the fields.

Water-lifting machines were developed to lift water directly from streams or from canals to irrigate higher-lying fields. The *shaduf* in Egypt, and its counterpart in many other early agricultures, is simply a bucket and a counterweight attached to the ends of a pivoted pole. The bucket is pulled down, filled by hand, and then lifted by the counterweight. ARCHIMEDES' SCREW, a large hand-turned screw within a wooden cylinder, lifts water on its wide threads from the end dipped in the stream. The Persian wheel consists of a chain of buckets that pass over a vertical wheel and dip into the water. This vertical wheel is turned by a horizontal wheel rotated by a draft animal. The filled buckets are tipped into a trough or canal leading to the fields.

MODERN IRRIGATION SYSTEMS

Water distribution systems are of two broad types: surface and closed-conduit distribution systems.

Surface Irrigation. In surface irrigation systems, the entire land surface may be covered with water (flood irrigation), or the water may be restricted to small ditches called furrows or rills (furrow irrigation). Both flood and furrow irrigation are used on naturally sloping, ungraded fields, although the effectiveness of water absorption by the soil is improved if the fields are graded to a uniform slope. Recently the practice of dead-level surface irrigation—grading fields to a zero slope—has been introduced to improve irrigation uniformity. This practice requires a water stream large enough to cover the field or to fill the furrows in a time period that is short compared to the time required for the water to infiltrate the soil. Dead-level surface irrigation is presently limited to arid climates, where waterlogging of the soil is not a potential problem.

Closed-Conduit Irrigation. Closed-conduit irrigation systems use pipes to distribute water over wide areas or to the ground area around each plant. These systems can apply water uniformly, and they permit frequent light irrigations that maintain the desired level of moisture in the soil. Sprinkler systems distribute water by pumping it through a network of pipes that are either laid on the ground or lifted above the field; often the pipes are on wheels or other devices that permit the network to be moved from field to field. Bubbler irrigation supplies water through a small pipe that periodically delivers equal quantities to small basins at each plant or group of plants. Drip, or trickle, irrigation uses narrow plastic tubes that deliver small quantities of water frequently, but at an extremely slow rate, to the soil around the roots of each plant.

(Above) Most of the world's rice is planted in fields similar to this flood-irrigated Asian rice paddy. After being properly prepared, the field is flooded, often by diverting river water. The rice seedlings are then removed from seedling beds and planted in the field by hand.

(Right) The furrow method of irrigation is commonly used in the cultivation of corn and other close-growing crops. Small, gradually sloping furrows are plowed between the rows of corn and supplied with water from a ditch through a system of siphon tubes. The water is absorbed into the soil as it flows down the slope.

(Above) *Sprinkler systems are often used to water alfalfa and other crops requiring frequent light irrigation. The water is sprayed as a fine mist or as small droplets through sprinkler nozzles spaced at intervals along parallel rows of pipes connected to a central water pump.*

(Below) *Center-pivot irrigation systems use rotating sprinklers to spray water uniformly over circular fields. Such systems are effective where water supplies are limited. Shown here is an arid region of Texas, where alfalfa and wheat are grown using center-pivot irrigation.*

This type of irrigation, widely used in the United States, Australia, and Israel, has had spectacular results. Drip systems use less water than other closed-circuit systems, supplying the precise amount needed to replace transpired plant moisture and the water that is evaporated from the soil. They also reduce the problem of soil salinity and create impressive crop yields.

PROBLEMS ASSOCIATED WITH IRRIGATION

Salt accumulation and waterlogging are the most severe problems caused by irrigation. Dissolved salts are present in small quantities in all irrigation water. As the water evaporates or is used by plants, the salt content of the water remaining in the soil increases. This remaining water may percolate down to

COUNTRIES WITH THE MOST IRRIGATED LAND

Country	Irrigated Land		Percent of Farmed Land
	Thousand Hectares	Acres	
China	76,500	184,400,000	69
India	38,969	93,900,000	24
United States	21,489	51,800,000	11
Pakistan	12,400	30,000,000	57
USSR	11,500	27,700,000	5
Indonesia	6,800	16,400,000	38
Iran	5,251	12,700,000	31
Mexico	4,200	10,100,000	18
Iraq	4,000	9,600,000	39
Italy	3,500	8,400,000	29
Thailand	3,170	7,600,000	11
Afghanistan	2,900	7,000,000	30
Egypt	2,852	6,900,000	100
Japan	2,626	6,300,000	48
Sudan	2,520	6,100,000	25

the ground-water aquifer, which then becomes saltier. A few irrigated regions have sufficient natural drainage to prevent the water table from rising into the plant-root zone. But in many areas, the extra input to the aquifer as a result of percolation from irrigated fields and the seepage from unlined canals and reservoirs eventually exceeds the natural drainage capacity. Once the water table rises to within several feet of the surface the salty water moves to the ground surface by capillary action, and, as it evaporates, leaves behind a thin deposit of salt. Even if the aquifer itself does not become saline, the excess water in the root zone of the soil retards crop growth.

Historically, salt accumulation and the waterlogging caused by inadequate drainage have taken a huge toll where agriculture has been based on irrigation. Mesopotamia's once-productive farmlands now bear some of the world's lowest crop yields because the crops grow on waterlogged, salty fields. The world's largest irrigation enterprise, the Indus Basin in Pakistan, is in serious danger as water tables rise to the surface and salt accumulates. More than one-third of the world's irrigated land (including some of the lush cropland in California's Imperial Valley) is being undermined by salinity.

If irrigated lands in semiarid regions are to remain permanently productive, two steps are necessary. Water tables must be kept at distances well below the surface, by reducing the seepage of irrigation water and by installing artificial drainage. Irrigation must also be managed so that a small additional increment of water passes through the soil around plant roots to leach salts below the root zone.

STEPHEN L. RAWLINS

MAJOR IRRIGATION SYSTEMS OF THE WORLD

Irrigation is now practiced on every continent. The world total is approximately 231 million irrigated ha (569 million acres), which represents about 15% of all farmed lands. Some irrigation is necessary for most agricultures, and it is crucial for nations like Egypt, where all farmlands are irrigated. In addition, the production from irrigated agriculture supplies a far greater proportion of the world's food than its acreage represents. High-value crops such as vegetables, fruits, and nuts are often produced by irrigation, and the yield may be double the harvest from equally fertile but nonirrigated land. At present, five nations account for 71 percent of the world's total irrigated farmland: China, with the largest irrigated area; India; the United States; Pakistan; and the USSR.

China. Irrigation has been practiced in China since at least the 3d century BC. The Tukiang Dam on the Min River, for example, which still supplies water to some 202,000 ha (500,000 acres), was constructed about 300 BC. In China, as in most Asian countries, the basic irrigation crop is rice, a semiaquatic plant that must be kept under flooded conditions during the growing season. In addition to rice, cotton and wheat are among the major irrigated crops. About two-thirds of China's arable land is now under irrigation.

Although many Chinese rivers are tapped for irrigation, the major rivers, the YANGTZE and the HWANG HO, supply much of the country's irrigation water through a system of dams and reservoirs that also function as flood control units. The government of the People's Republic of China has been particularly active in bringing more land under irrigation, and the annual production in the Yangtze and Hwang Ho basins has doubled, and in some cases tripled, since 1949 as the result of an ambitious program of dam construction.

India. India has the second largest irrigation system in the world. The GANGES RIVER basin in northern India accounts for a number of large irrigation projects. Most of the rivers in northern India flow year-round; when they are swollen with melted snow from the Himalayas, they spill over their low banks into an extensive system of irrigation canals. Southern Indian rivers are high only during the monsoon season, and until recently, surface irrigation was limited mostly to the delta areas. Diversion dams that store the monsoon flow and canals to channel the water are being built, however.

In addition to river waters, much of India depends on well water for irrigation. At one time, most well irrigation used Persian wheels turned by bullocks to move the water from the wells to irrigation canals. Motor-driven pumps are rapidly replacing the Persian wheel, and since the 1960s, hundreds of thousands of driven, or tube, wells have been added to the irrigation system.

Since independence in 1947, about 700 large irrigation projects have been undertaken in India, although not all were completed by the late 1970s. The total amount of land under irrigation has increased by more than 50 percent during the last 30 years.

The United States. Early irrigation, practiced by the Indians of the Southwest, consisted of digging wide furrows to carry water from streams to fields. Spanish settlers improved upon the method, extended irrigation to larger areas, and introduced the first dams and reservoirs into the New World.

Prior to the mid-19th century, however, most irrigation projects involved relatively small amounts of land. In 1847, Mormon settlers in Utah constructed a widespread system of irrigation canals and, by 1860, had placed more than 6,500 ha (16,000 acres) under irrigation. Other important 19th-century irrigation ventures included the more than 12,000 ha (30,000 acres) brought under irrigation by members of the Union Colony, a Colorado settlement established in 1870. The first U.S. government irrigation project was the construction (1868) of an irrigation system on the Mojave Indian reservation in Arizona. The building of irrigation projects in the western states flourished in the late 1800s. By 1900 nearly 3.6 million ha (9 million acres) were under irrigation.

Variations in rainfall divide the United States into a humid East and a relatively dry West. Except along the northern Pacific coasts and in the Rocky Mountains, the western half of the country has an average annual precipitation of less than 50.8 cm (20 in). Thus, irrigation is overwhelmingly concentrated in the western 17 states, which possess more than 90 percent of the total irrigated land. The U.S. Bureau of Reclamation, which has been responsible for several of the most important irrigation projects, operates only in the western states. The U.S. Army Corps of Engineers (see ENGINEERS, CORPS OF) is also actively engaged in dam building and other irrigation construction.

The United States has more irrigated land than any other country in the Western Hemisphere—21.5 million ha (51.8 million acres), or about 11 percent of all U.S. farmland. Ten percent of all U.S. farms, about 237,000 farms, are irrigated.

Pakistan. Nearly three-quarters of Pakistan's farmland is irrigated, and the prosperity of the country is dependent on the Indus River and its system of irrigation canals. These canals were built largely by the British during their control of the Indian subcontinent. Unfortunately, many of them were constructed without sufficient drainage, and soil waterlogging and salinization are increasing problems. Because of poor drainage, by the mid-1970s more than 10 percent of Pakistan's farmland had gone out of production.

The USSR. Although only 5 percent of USSR farmland was irrigated by the late 1970s, the country ranks fifth in the world in the total area under irrigation. Most of the irrigation projects are located in Caucasia and central Asia. Under the Virgin Lands program in the 1950s and early '60s, large areas of semiarid land were brought under irrigation.

The Middle East. Wide-scale irrigation is practiced in many of the more arid Middle Eastern countries, especially along the Nile and the Tigris-Euphrates rivers, and in Israel. The Middle Eastern countries with the largest irrigated land areas are Iran, Egypt, Turkey, and Iraq. Egypt's irrigation system is the oldest in the world. Modern irrigation projects in Egypt on the NILE RIVER include the ASWAN HIGH DAM and the Asyūt Barrage. The Nile and its two main tributaries, the White Nile and the Blue Nile, are also used to irrigate large tracts of cropland in Sudan.

In Israel almost 25 percent of the land under cultivation is irrigated. The major irrigation development, the National Water Carrier, channels surplus water from the Sea of Galilee south to the Negev Desert through a system of pipelines and canals. The Israelis have pioneered in the search for new water sources—from the sea, through desalination projects, and from the air, through new dew-trapping techniques—and they have made better use of existing water supplies, especially through drip irrigation.

Bibliography: Cantor, L. M., *A World Geography of Irrigation* (1970); Clark, Colin, *The Economics of Irrigation*, 2d ed. (1970); Downing, Theodore E., and Gibson, McGuire, eds., *Irrigation's Impact on Society* (1974); Hagan, R. M., et al., *Irrigation of Agricultural Lands* (1967) and *Successful Irrigation* (1969); Israelson, Orson, and Hansen, Vaughn E., *Irrigation Principles and Practices*, 3d ed. (1962); Pair, C. H., *Sprinkler Irrigation*, 4th ed. (1975); Shoji, Kobe, "Drip Irrigation," *Scientific American*, November 1977; Smythe, William E., *Conquest of Arid America* (1969); Yaron, B., et al., *Arid Zone Irrigation* (1973); Zimmerman, Josef D., *Irrigation* (1966).

Irtysh River   [ir-tish']

The Irtysh River, a major waterway of Central Asia, runs for 4,248 km (2,639 mi). It originates on the southwestern slopes of the ALTAI MOUNTAINS in Sinkiang province, China. From there it flows west as the Black Irtysh into the Kazakh SSR of the Soviet Union, where it broadens into Lake Zaisan. It then winds northwest across the steppes of Kulanda and Ishim into Soviet Siberia, where it joins the OB RIVER near Khanty-Mansiysk as the Ob's main tributary. The chief tributaries of the Irtysh are (on the right bank) the Narym, Bukhtarma, Om, and Tara rivers and (on the left bank) the Osha, Ishim, Tobol, Vagai, and Konda rivers.

The Irtysh is navigable and is used by steamships. Industrial cities along the river include OMSK, Khanty-Mansiysk, Tobolsk, Tara, Pavlodar, Semipalatinsk, and Ust-Kamenogorsk. Hydroelectric power stations along the Irtysh supply energy for the mining and smelting of the many minerals found along the upper river. Commercially important fish abound in its waters.

Irving, Edward

Edward Irving, b. Aug. 4, 1792, d. Dec. 7, 1834, a Scottish minister, was one of the founders of the Catholic Apostolic church. Educated at Edinburgh, he became a minister of the Church of Scotland and preached with great success in London. After he came into contact with a group headed by Henry Drummond which was devoted to eschatological speculations, Irving began to preach the imminence of the SECOND COMING OF CHRIST. His writings on Christ, in which he deemed the human nature of Christ as sinful, led to his excommunication (1830) and his expulsion from the ministry (1833).

In 1832 he joined with others in forming the Catholic Apostolic church. The members, known for a while as Irvingites, believed that the Second Coming was near and tried to restore the biblical organization of the church in preparation for Christ's return. The movement was somewhat influential in Britain until 1900; it then spread to Europe and the United States. Membership in the church is about 50,000 at the present time, with over half of the members in Germany.

FREDERICK A. NORWOOD

Bibliography: Shaw, P. E., *The Catholic Apostolic Church* (1946).

Irving, Sir Henry

Through his talents as actor and innovative stage manager, Sir Henry Irving was instrumental in establishing the Lyceum as London's most notable theater in the late 19th century. In 1895, Irving became the first actor to be knighted, a remarkable honor at a time when theatrical performers were not highly regarded by English royalty.

Actor, manager, and director Henry Irving (stage name of John Henry Brodribb, b. Feb. 6, 1838, d. Oct. 13, 1905) was the foremost theatrical figure on the London stage during the latter half of the 19th century. Born in Somerset and educated for a career in commerce, he spent four years as a clerk in a London countinghouse before making his stage debut (1856) at the age of 18 in a provincial theater. For nine years he toured the provinces, returning to London in 1866. The role of Mathias in Leopold Lewis's melodrama The Bells at the Lyceum Theatre in 1871 made Irving famous, and in 1878 he took over the management of the theater, which during his tenure became the most notable in London.

Irving's repertoire consisted of Shakespearean works and conventional melodrama; he avoided new works. Nevertheless, he gained great prestige as an actor and manager, although he was never free from adverse criticism for his mannerisms and occasional excesses. He was not handsome, and his voice lacked flexibility, but his interpretations were always interesting and provocative. An important element of acting for Irving was movement, and he was a master of timing and byplay. His most noteworthy performances were in the roles of Hamlet (1874); Shylock (1878)—to the Portia of his leading lady Ellen TERRY; Malvolio (1884) in Twelfth Night; the leads in Tennyson's The Cup (1881) and Becket (1893); and Iachimo (1896) in Cymbeline. He was knighted in 1895, the first actor to be accorded this honor.

Irving made many theatrical innovations; he was one of the first directors to abandon the grooves that for 200 years had been the usual method of shifting scenery on the stage, and he made an art of stage lighting; he was the first English producer to darken the auditorium during performances. He also paid careful attention to costumes, even those of minor characters and extras. His greatest period was the decade between 1878 and 1888. His Macbeth in 1889, with Ellen Terry as Lady Macbeth, was not a great success, and from this time on his star was on the wane. In 1901 he played Coriolanus, but he retired from the Lyceum the next year. Tours of Canada and the United States in 1903 preceded his final tour (1905) of the English provinces, where he died after a performance of Becket.					ANDREW KELLY

Bibliography: Archer, William, Henry Irving, Actor and Manager: A Critical Study (1883; repr. 1970); Bingham, Madeleine, Henry Irving: The Greatest Victorian Actor (1978); Craig, Edward Gordon, Henry Irving (1930; repr. 1969); Irving, Laurence, Henry Irving: The Actor and His World (1951); Stoker, Bram, Personal Reminiscences of Henry Irving, 2 vols. (1906; repr. 1970).

Irving, John

John Irving, b. Exeter, N.H., Mar. 2, 1942, is an author and college professor whose sprawling fourth novel, The World According to Garp (1978), earned him a huge following and a National Book Award nomination. The story of an eccentric feminist and her writer son, it displays the same delight in language and narrative exuberance that characterized his previous novels, Setting Free the Bears (1968), The Water-Method Man (1972), and The 158-Pound Marriage (1974). Irving, who also writes short stories, was writer-in-residence at the University of Iowa from 1972 to 1975 and today teaches English at Mount Holyoke College.

Irving, Robert

Robert Augustine Irving, b. Winchester, England, Aug. 28, 1913, has been the principal conductor and music director of the New York City Ballet since 1958. After graduating from Oxford and the Royal College of Music, he taught piano (1936–40) at Winchester College and was associate conductor (1945–48) of the BBC Scottish Orchestra before becoming principal conductor at Sadler's Wells (now Royal) Ballet at Covent Garden. During that period he also composed the music for the New York Theatre Guild's production of As You Like It (1949) and for several documentary films.
					BARBARA NEWMAN

Irving, Washington

The career of Washington Irving, b. New York City, Apr. 3, 1783, d. Nov. 28, 1859, America's first successful professional man of letters, coincided with the early development of a distinctive national literature. Although he was influenced by such English models as Joseph Addison, Oliver Goldsmith, and Sir Walter Scott, Irving won an international reputation as a distinctively American prose stylist and helped promote the literary efforts of his compatriots both at home and in Europe. In light of his cosmopolitan achievements, William Makepeace Thackeray described him as "the first ambassador sent by the new world of letters to the old."

In an attempt to restore his failing health and also to further his education, Irving traveled in Europe from 1804 to 1806. Upon his return to New York he resumed his study of law, but his interest in it waned as he devoted himself increasingly to literature. His youthful comic talents were best expressed in the sprightly Salmagundi papers (1807–08) and in A History of New York (1809), the latter purporting to be the work of Diedrich Knickerbocker.

In 1815, Irving sailed again for Europe and began a 17-year sojourn, during which he gained international prominence. The Sketch-Book (1819–20), which he signed with the pseudonym Geoffrey Crayon, was an immediate popular and critical success. Its calculatedly miscellaneous contents included essays and sketches about the countryside and folk customs of England, two essays about the American Indian, and two American tales—The LEGEND OF SLEEPY HOLLOW and RIP VAN WINKLE. The Sketch-Book revealed glimpses of Irving's inclination to satire, but its humor was predominantly playful and gentle, and its tone reflective and sentimental. Like its successors, Bracebridge Hall (1822) and Tales of a Traveller (1824), it

Washington Irving, whose earliest works lampooned pretentious society in both the Old World and his native Hudson River valley, was one of the first Americans to win international recognition as an author. Among the best known of his short stories are "Rip Van Winkle" and "The Legend of Sleepy Hollow," which appeared in The Sketch-Book (1819–20).

was light literature, written mainly for amusement.

Seeking to broaden his reputation, Irving took up residence (1826) in Spain, where he wrote his *History of the Life and Voyages of Christopher Columbus* (1828) and *A Chronicle of Granada* (1829). This three-year interlude in Spain also bore fruit in *The Alhambra* (1832), an evocative collection of legends and sketches.

Upon his return (1832) to the United States, Irving was tumultuously welcomed by his compatriots, and for the rest of his career he enjoyed their virtually unanimous esteem. He contributed a series of distinctly indigenous works to the national literature: *A Tour on the Prairies* (1835), an autobiographical account; *Astoria* (1836), a narrative about John Jacob Astor's ill-fated commercial enterprise on the northwest Pacific Coast; and *The Adventures of Captain Bonneville, U.S.A.* (1837).

Irving never married, but in 1834 he purchased the nucleus of Sunnyside, a small estate on the Hudson River, and made it a place of resort for members of his extensive family. Here he began work on *The Life of George Washington*, which he regarded as the crowning achievement of his literary career. This work was interrupted when he was appointed (1842) U.S. minister to Spain, an office in which he served with distinction for four years. Upon his return to Sunnyside, Irving devoted himself primarily to work on *Washington*, which was published in five volumes between 1855 and 1859. Sustained effort on this task seriously undermined Irving's health, and he died only a few months after its completion.

WAYNE R. KIME

Bibliography: Hedges, William, *Washington Irving: An American Study, 1802-1832* (1965); Irving, Pierre M., *The Life and Letters of Washington Irving*, 4 vols. (1863-64; repr. 1967); Johnston, Johanna, *Heart That Would Not Hold: A Biography of Washington Irving* (1971); Kime, Wayne, *Pierre M. Irving and Washington Irving: A Collaboration in Life and Letters* (1977); Reichart, Walter, *Washington Irving and Germany* (1957); Wagenknecht, Edward, *Washington Irving: Moderation Displayed* (1962); Williams, Stanley, *The Life of Washington Irving*, 2 vols. (1935; repr. 1971).

Irwin, James

The American astronaut James Benson Irwin, b. Pittsburgh, Pa., Mar. 17, 1930, was the eighth man to walk on the Moon. Irwin was an Air Force pilot when selected as an astronaut in 1966. During the APOLLO 15 flight in 1971, his only mission in space, he and commander David SCOTT spent nearly 67 hours on the lunar surface, including more than 18 hours accumulated over three moon walks. Irwin and Scott also operated the first LUNAR ROVER vehicle. Irwin resigned from NASA and from the Air Force in 1972 and established the High Flight Foundation, an evangelical organization. In 1973, Irwin published his autobiography, *To Rule the Night*.

DAVID DOOLING

Isaac

The biblical patriarch Isaac was the promised son of the aged ABRAHAM and SARAH and the father by Rebecca of the twins ESAU and JACOB. When Isaac was a boy, he was almost sacrificed by his obedient father, but God spared the boy. This story (Genesis 22) may illustrate ancient Israel's rejection of child sacrifice. Serving as a bridge in the patriarchal tradition, Isaac is also an important character in the Jacob story. According to Genesis 27, Jacob and his mother, Rebecca, deceive the old and feeble Isaac into giving his final blessing to Jacob instead of the firstborn Esau. In the Bible, God is called the God of Abraham, Isaac, and Jacob.

Isaac, Heinrich   [ee'-zahk]

Heinrich Isaac, b. *c.*1450, d. Mar. 26, 1517, was one of the most celebrated and prolific composers of the Renaissance Flemish school. He had already achieved some prominence when he settled (1484) in Florence, where, except for sojourns in Rome and Austria, he remained until his death. His secular music, which includes songs in French, German, Italian, and Latin as well as instrumental pieces, reflects his abil-

ity to absorb the musical traditions of the different countries in which he lived. But it is his sacred music—comprising masses and motets written in the polyphonic style of his native Flanders—that best reveals his genius and the total mastery of his art. Isaac's most famous work is the *Choralis Constantinus*, a collection of more than 300 settings of mass propers for all Sundays and many feast days of the liturgical year. It contains 5 settings of the ordinary of the mass as well.

FRANK A. D'ACCONE

Bibliography: Reese, Gustave, *Music in the Renaissance*, 2d ed. (1959).

Isaac I Comnenus, Byzantine Emperor
[kahm-nee'-nuhs]

Isaac I, *c.*1005-*c.*1061, ruled the BYZANTINE EMPIRE from 1057 to 1059 as the representative of the military aristocracy. With the help of the army, the populace of Constantinople, and the patriarch MICHAEL CERULARIUS, he deposed Michael VI Stratioticus, who had the support of the bureaucrats. Isaac ably defended the empire against the PECHENEGS. He quarreled with Cerularius, however, and deposed him in 1058, thus losing popularity. In 1059, stricken with a sudden illness, Isaac abdicated in favor of Constantine X Ducas and retired to a monastery.

C. M. BRAND.

Isaac II Angelus, Byzantine Emperor

Isaac II, b. *c.*1155, d. February 1204, was raised to the throne of the BYZANTINE EMPIRE in 1185 by a mob rising up against the tyrant Andronicus I Comnenus. Isaac ruled until he was deposed and blinded in 1195 by his elder brother Alexius III. In 1203 the Fourth CRUSADE restored him to the throne as coemperor with his son Alexius IV, but they were both overthrown in January 1204.

During his first reign Isaac fought successfully against invading Normans from Italy (1185), but he could not overcome the rebellious Walachians and Bulgarians nor prevent Holy Roman Emperor FREDERICK I from passing through his lands on the Third Crusade. In his second reign Isaac was senile, a helpless pawn of others.

C. M. BRAND

Bibliography: Brand, Charles M., *Byzantium Confronts the West, 1180-1204* (1968).

Isabella I, Queen of Castile   (Isabella the Catholic)

Isabella, b. Apr. 22, 1451, the daughter of King John II of Castile, laid the foundations for the unification of Spain into one kingdom by her marriage to FERDINAND II of Aragon. During the troubled reign (1454-74) of her brother, Henry IV, Isabella had been the object of many dangerous intrigues, but she was ultimately recognized as heir in 1468. On Oct. 19, 1469, she married Ferdinand, heir to the throne of Aragon, and on Dec. 13, 1474, she was crowned queen of Castile and León. Isabella and her husband were known as the Catholic kings.

Isabella I, queen of Castile (1474-1504), appears in this portrait by Bartolomé Bermejo. Her marriage to Ferdinand II of Aragon laid the foundation of the unified Spanish state. Isabella sponsored the voyages of Christopher Columbus and thus gained for Spain its first foothold in the New World. (Royal Palace, Madrid.)

Isabella's policies within Castile set the pattern of Spanish domestic policy for generations to come. Aided but not dominated by her husband, who had few political rights in Castile, she enlisted the nobility in restoring order to the countryside and reformed both the court and the royal administration. Her deep religious convictions made her a guiding spirit behind the founding (1487) of the Spanish INQUISITION and the expulsion (1492) of the Jews, but they also led her to support Cardinal Francisco JIMÉNEZ DE CISNEROS in his efforts to reform the church. The queen took an active part in the wars leading to the conquest (1492) of GRANADA, the last Moorish stronghold in Spain. She also supported Christopher COLUMBUS, whose discoveries in the New World led to the establishment of a Spanish empire in America. As a patron of scholarship, Isabella did much to introduce humanism to Spain. Few monarchs have been as popular in their own time or as venerated since.

Isabella's last years were clouded by the deaths of her son, her eldest daughter, and her infant grandson, and by increasing concern over the stability of her second daughter, JOAN THE MAD. At her death on Nov. 24, 1504, she left Castile to Joan, under the regency of Ferdinand. The Spanish kingdoms were finally united (1516) under Joan's son Charles I, who was to become Holy Roman Emperor CHARLES V.

WILLIAM S. MALTBY

Bibliography: Fernández-Armesto, Felipe, Ferdinand and Isabella (1975); Mariéjol, J. H., The Spain of Ferdinand and Isabella, trans. by Benjamin Keen (1961); Prescott, W. H., History of the Reign of Ferdinand and Isabella (1838).

Isabella II, Queen of Spain

Civil war and revolt marked the reign (1833-68) of Isabella II of Spain. Her conservative leanings and her personal life contributed to her eventual deposition.

Isabella was born on Oct. 10, 1830, the daughter of FERDINAND VII and his fourth wife, María Cristina. Isabella was proclaimed queen on Ferdinand's death (1833), but her succession was contested by her uncle Don Carlos. Civil war between her followers and his (the CARLISTS) lasted until 1839. In 1846, Isabella married her cousin Francisco de Asís de Borbón, but she did not live with him, preferring her lovers.

During Isabella's tumultuous personal reign revolts and coups continued; they were caused by demands for reform among army officers, the middle classes, and the urban poor. Their demands were resisted, however, by the queen, most generals, and the wealthy. Isabella's most effective prime ministers were two generals, Ramón María Narváez (1800-1868) and Leopoldo O'Dónnell (1809-67). Increasingly proclerical and conservative, the queen was forced into exile in 1868 after an uprising of liberal officers led by Gen. Juan PRIM overthrew the government. In 1870 she abdicated her rights in favor of her son Alfonso (later ALFONSO XII). Isabella died in Paris on Apr. 9, 1904.

DANIEL R. HEADRICK

Bibliography: Aronson, Theo, Royal Vendetta: The Crown of Spain 1829-1965 (1966).

Isabey, Jean Baptiste   [ee-zah-bay']

The French miniaturist Jean Baptiste Isabey, b. Apr. 11, 1767, d. Apr. 18, 1855, exemplified the brilliant and flattering style of court portraiture in the late 18th and early 19th centuries. Soon after arriving (1786) in Paris, Isabey met with great success in gaining commissions from the court of Louis XVI, including one from Marie Antoinette. His elegant and highly personalized portraits, which owe much to the works of J. H. Fragonard, continued to find official favor throughout the Napoleonic and Bourbon Restoration periods, with the empresses Josephine and Marie Louise and the kings Charles X and Louis Philippe all employing his talents.

Bibliography: Osmond, Marion W., Jean Baptiste Isabey, the Fortunate Painter (1947).

Isaiah, Book of   [y-zay'-uh]

The Book of Isaiah is the first and longest of the books of the Major Prophets in the Old Testament of the BIBLE. It derives its name from the prophet Isaiah, who lived in Jerusalem, perhaps of aristocratic origin. His prophetic career spanned half a century, from around 742 BC to at least 701. The book, however, contains the work of more than one man. Scholars now generally agree that chapters 1 to 35, known as First Isaiah, can be ascribed either to Isaiah himself or to his disciples; chapters 36 to 39 have been taken directly from II Kings 18:13-20:18. Chapters 40 to 55, known as Second Isaiah, or Deutero-Isaiah, were the work of an anonymous prophet-poet during the latter part (c.545-540 BC) of the Babylonian exile. Chapters 56 to 66, known as Third Isaiah, or Trito-Isaiah, were written by authors unknown in detail but working around the end of the 6th century (525-500 BC) or the beginning of the 5th (500-475 BC). Some of the material may be derived from a period even later than these times (c.375-250 BC).

First Isaiah falls roughly into four periods: (1) From 747 to 736 BC the prophet speaks about internal political and economic policy; (2) in 736-735 he addresses the crisis caused by the Syro-Ephraimite War, an attempt to force Jerusalem into an anti-Assyrian alliance; (3) after a period of silence, he speaks again, addressing himself to the attempt of King HEZEKIAH to free himself from status as a vassal to Assyria (716-711); (4) again after a time of silence, Isaiah speaks of Hezekiah's second attempt to establish political independence (705-701). The writings from these periods fall into seven collections of sayings on themes of sin, judgment, and deliverance from the judgment. The Immanuel prophecies (chapter 6-12) are well known to Christians, who interpret them as references to Christ.

Second Isaiah comprises poems of various genres: oracles of deliverance, hymns, prophetic legal speech designed to show that the God of Israel alone is God, and discussion forms designed to repel opposition. In addition, the material of Second Isaiah contains the passages about the Servant of the Lord, also interpreted by Christians as references to Christ (42:1-4; 49:1-6; 50:4-9; 52:13-53:12).

Third Isaiah includes 14 independent sayings concerning the operation of the restored Temple, with corresponding emphasis on the sabbath and cult. The material comprises a short prophetic liturgy (56:9-47:13), an oracle of promise (57:14-21), an exhortation and promise (58:1-12), prophetic invective and threat (65:1-2), and a promise (65:8-25). The final chapter contains a prophetic denunciation of the Temple and a rejection of the sacrificial cult, as well as three prophetic sayings that announce an imminent end and its results. Isaiah contains some of the most beautiful and best-known passages in the Bible. Two manuscripts of the book were found among the DEAD SEA SCROLLS.

GEORGE W. COATS

Bibliography: Knight, G. A. F., Prophets of Israel: Isaiah (1962); Rosenbloom, J. R., The Dead Sea Isaiah Scrolls (1970); Whedbee, J. W., Isaiah and Wisdom (1971).

Iselin, Columbus O'Donnell

The American physical oceanographer Columbus O'Donnell Iselin, b. New Rochelle, N.Y., Sept. 25, 1904, d. Jan. 6, 1971, is best known for his research on oceanic circulation, particularly of the Gulf Stream, as well as for his work on subsurface temperature and salinity distribution. He proved (1926) that the Labrador Current was considerably narrower than had been thought. A professor of physical oceanography at Harvard as well as at the Massachusetts Institute of Technology, Iselin served on the staff of the Woods Hole Oceanographic Institution from 1932 and became its director in 1940.

Isenheim Altar: see GRÜNEWALD, MATTHIAS.

Isère River   [ee-zair']

The Isère River rises in the Alps of southeastern France at an elevation of 2,400 m (7,900 ft) above sea level. It flows west and then southwest for 290 km (180 mi), until it joins the RHÔNE RIVER above Valence. Its major tributaries are the Arly and the Arc. GRENOBLE is the largest city along the Isère, and the river is important for hydroelectric power.

Isfahan   [is-fah-hahn']

Isfahan (also Esfahan) is the second largest city of Iran and the capital of Isfahan province. The city is located at an altitude of 1,590 m (5,216 ft) on the north bank of the Zayandeh River about 320 km (200 mi) south of Tehran. The population is 671,825 (1976). Annual temperatures average 2° C (36° F) in January and 28° C (83° F) in July; rainfall averages 355 mm (14 in).

Isfahan is a transportation center, as Iran's main north-south and east-west roads intersect there. The city has long been famous for its traditional handicrafts; filigree and metal-work, carpets, and hand-printed textiles are produced. The old art of tile making has been revived for use in restoring Isfahan's many historical monuments. A modern industrial complex manufactures steel and textiles. The University of Isfahan (1966) is located there.

First known as a city during the Sassanian period, Isfahan was conquered in 642 by the Arabs, who made it a provincial capital. During the mid-11th century the SELJUKS captured Isfahan and made it the capital of their vast empire in 1051. In 1387, TIMUR conquered the city and killed many of the inhabitants. Isfahan reached its zenith after 1598, when Shah ABBAS I chose the city as the capital of the Safavid dynasty. Abbas built many of the monuments that remain today. Isfahan fell into a long decline beginning in 1722 when it was captured by Afghans. In the reign of REZA SHAH PAHLAVI (1925–41) it was revived as an industrial center. Isfahan's many landmarks include the Masjid-i-Shah (Royal Mosque) and Shayk Lutfullah mosque, the Royal Palace, and many gardens and squares.   ARTHUR CAMPBELL TURNER

Isherwood, Christopher   [ish'-ur-wud]

Christopher Isherwood, a British novelist, achieved literary recognition with his Berlin Stories (1946), a series of works based on the author's experiences in Germany during the 1930s. These works, which form the basis of the musical Cabaret, contain vivid character portrayals and chronicle the social climate in Berlin during the rise of nazism.

Christopher William Bradshaw-Isherwood, b. Cheshire, England, Aug. 26, 1904, is a novelist and a writer of nonfiction. His work is largely autobiographical or quasi-autobiographical. While a school boy in Surrey, he began a lifelong friendship with the poet W. H. AUDEN. In 1928 he began to study medicine but soon left the University of London to visit Auden in Germany. Living there off and on until 1933, Isherwood came to understand the social and political climate of pre-Hitler Germany, which he described in *Mr. Norris Changes Trains* (1935), *Sally Bowles* (1937), and *Goodbye to Berlin* (1939). The drama *I Am a Camera* (1951) and the musical *Cabaret* (1966) came from his writings on Germany.

In 1939, Isherwood immigrated to the United States, settled in California, and became a U.S. citizen in 1946. Over the years he has worked on film scripts in Hollywood and has adapted plays for television.

Down There on a Visit (1962), which some critics consider his best novel, centers on Isherwood's life in Germany, Greece, England, and California. *Kathleen and Frank* (1971), culled from his parents' letters and diaries, is his effort to un-derstand his family and his early childhood. Homosexual love, once hinted at in his writings, later became a central concern. *A Single Man* (1964), *A Meeting by the River* (1967), and *Christopher and His Kind* (1976) are explicitly concerned with homosexuality.   RICHARD A. JOHNSON

Bibliography: Finney, Brian, *Christopher Isherwood:* (1979); Fryer, Jonathan, *Isherwood* (1978); Heilbrun, Carolyn, *Christoper Isherwood* (1970); Piazza, Paul, *Christopher Isherwood* (1978).

Ishikawa Takuboku   [ee-shee-kah'-wah tah-koo-boh'-koo]

Ishikawa Takuboku, b. Ishikawa Hajime, Oct. 28, 1885, d. Apr. 13, 1912, was a Japanese writer best known for the traditional tanka poems he published in *A Handful of Sand* (1910; Eng. trans., 1934) and *A Sad Toy* (1912; Eng. trans., 1962). Poems showing a modern European influence appeared in *Akogare* (Aspiration, 1905) and *Yobiko to kuchibue* (Piping and Whistling, 1913). Takuboku's novels and essays were less popular than his verse. His diary, documenting a life of poverty and disease, was published in 1948–49.

Ishmael   [ish'-may-el]

According to Genesis 16, Ishmael was the son of the patriarch ABRAHAM by the Egyptian handmaiden HAGAR. When Abraham's supposedly barren wife SARAH finally bore ISAAC, a rivalry developed between Sarah and Hagar and thus between the two half brothers, Isaac and Ishmael.

Cast out into the wilderness, Ishmael was the ancestor of the nomadic Arabian Ishmaelites, arranged, like the Israelites, into twelve tribes. Because Islam traces its lineage from Abraham through Ishmael and Judaism and Christianity trace their lineages through Isaac, Muslims, Jews, and Christians are all spiritual "children of Abraham."

Ishtar

In Babylonian and Assyrian mythology, Ishtar was the principal goddess and the queen of heaven. She was worshiped by the Phoenicians as ASTARTE, by the Sumerians as Inanna, and by other peoples of the region under various names. A composite of many earlier goddesses, Ishtar was both the compassionate mother of all life, who brought fertility and relief from sickness, and the lustful goddess of sexual love and of war. These contrasting attributes are reflected in the story that she caused the great flood and then was sorry about it. The best-known legend about her is that of her imprisonment by Allatu, queen of the underworld, where Ishtar had gone to visit her lover, Tammuz, the god of vegetation. Ishtar was later identified with the Greek APHRODITE and the Roman VENUS.

Isidore of Seville, Saint

Isidore of Seville, b. c.560, d. Apr. 4, 636, was a Spanish churchman and encyclopedist who is generally regarded as the last of the western Fathers of the Church. He succeeded (600) his older brother, Leander, as archbishop of Seville and presided (633) over the fourth national Council of Toledo. Isidore exercised a wide influence throughout Spain, bringing about unity between orthodox Christian Romans and Arian Goths. He fostered learning and culture, promoted the education of clergy, and preserved for the Middle Ages the intellectual riches of earlier centuries.

Isidore was a compiler rather than an original thinker. His encyclopedic writings covered all of the areas of knowledge of the time and were used as textbooks by students and as sources by authors during the Middle Ages. His best-known works are *Etymologiae* (Origins), a compendium of classical knowledge, and *Historia de Regibus Gothorum, Vandalorum et Suevorum* (History of the Reigns of the Goths, Vandals, and Suevi), an important chronicle of the time. His scriptural and theological writings earned him a place among the Doctors of the Church. Known for his outstanding charity to the poor, he was canonized in 1598. Feast day: Apr. 4.

AGNES CUNNINGHAM

Bibliography: Bréhaut, E., *An Encyclopaedist of the Dark Ages* (1912).

Isidorus of Miletus   [iz-i-dohr'-uhs]

Isidorus of Miletus is the name of a Byzantine architect who, with ANTHEMIUS OF TRALLES, built (AD 532–37) in Constantinople the church of HAGIA SOPHIA for the emperor Justinian I. Like his better-known partner, Isidorus of Miletus was an academic rather than a professional architect. He taught stereometry and physics at the universities of Alexandria and Constantinople and wrote an annotated work on vaulting. When the original dome of Hagia Sophia collapsed in 558, his son or nephew Isidorus the Younger built the new dome, this time with a steeper curvature.

Bibliography: Krautheimer, Richard, *Early Christian and Byzantine Architecture* (1965).

Isis   [y'-sis]

In Egyptian mythology, Isis was the mother goddess of fertility and nature. Her worship was combined with that of her brother and husband, OSIRIS, and her son HORUS. She is often depicted wearing on her head the horns of a cow, encircled by either a lunar or solar disk. Her worship originated in Egypt, and by Hellenistic times she had assimilated the attributes of the major Greek divinities DEMETER and APHRODITE. By the period of the Roman Empire, she had become the most prominent deity of the Mediterranean basin, as her temple at Pompeii attests.

Isis's cult focused on the celebration of the mysteries associated with the death and resurrection of Osiris. In The GOLDEN ASS (AD c.155), Lucius APULEIUS, an African priest of Isis, left an excellent account of her appearance and mystery cult; in a dream or during initiation, Apuleius saw Queen Isis rise with the moon from the sea. In this text she has many titles, including queen of heaven, earth, and the underworld, and mother of wheat.

During the early centuries AD the cult of Isis was a formidable contender with the newly founded Christian religion. Despite purges of the followers of Isis, her worship continued well into the 6th century AD   NORMA L. GOODRICH

Bibliography: Budge, E. A., *Gods of the Egyptians*, 2 vols. (1904; repr. 1969); Witt, R. E., *Isis in the Graeco-Roman World* (1971).

Islam   [iz'-luhm]

Islam, a major world religion, is customarily defined in non-Islamic sources as the religion of those who follow the Prophet Muhammad. The prophet, who lived in Arabia in the early 7th century, initiated a religious movement that was carried by the ARABS throughout the Middle East. Today, Islam has adherents not only in the Middle East, where it is the dominant religion in all countries (Arab and non-Arab) except Israel, but also in other parts of Asia, Africa, and, to a certain extent, in Europe and in the United States. Adherents of Islam are called Muslims (sometimes spelled Moslems).

The Name and Its Meaning. The Arabic word *al-islam* means the act of committing oneself unreservedly to God, and a Muslim is a person who makes this commitment. Widely used translations such as "resignation," "surrender" and "submission" fail to do justice to the positive aspects of the total commitment for which *al-islam* stands—a commitment in faith, obedience, and trust to the one and only God (ALLAH). All of these elements are implied in the name of this religion, which is characteristically described in the KORAN (Arabic, Qur'an; the sacred book of Islam) as "the religion of Abraham." In the Koran, ABRAHAM is the patriarch who turned away from idolatry, who "came to his Lord with an undivided heart" (37:84), who responded to God in total obedience when challenged to sacrifice his son (37:102–105), and who served God uncompromisingly. For Muslims, therefore, the proper name of their religion expresses the Koranic insistence that no one but God is to be worshiped. Hence, many Muslims, while recognizing the significance of the Prophet Muhammad, have objected to the terms *Muhammadanism* (or Mohammedanism) and *Muhammadans* (or Mohammedans)—designations used widely in the West until recently—since they detect in them the suggestion of a worship of Muham-

mad parallel to the worship of Jesus Christ by Christians.

Numbers. Estimates of the world population of Muslims range from a low of 580 million to a high of 908 million; 750 million is a widely used medium. Notwithstanding the significant variations in these estimates, there seems to be a consensus that the world population of Muslims rose by at least 100 million between 1967 and 1977, and some observers believe a similar increase took place in the preceding decade. This significant expansion, due largely but not entirely to the general population growth in Asia and Africa, is gradually reducing the numerical difference between Christians (the largest religious community in the world) and Muslims, whose combined totals make up more than 40 percent of the world population.

Origin. While many Muslims vehemently oppose the language that the Prophet Muhammad is the "founder" of Islam—an expression which they interpret as an implicit denial of God's initiative and involvement in the history of Islam's origins—none would challenge that Islam dates back to the lifetime (570–632) of the Prophet and the years in which he received the divine revelations recorded in the Koran. At the same time, however, most of them would stress that it is only in a sense that Islam dates back to the 7th century, since they regard their religion not as a 7th-century innovation, but as the restoration of the original religion of Abraham. They would also stress that Islam is a timeless religion, not just because of the "eternal truth" that it proclaims but also because it is "every person's religion," the natural religion in which every person is born.

Islam's Comprehensive Character. When applied to Islam, the word religion has a far more comprehensive meaning than it commonly has in the West. Islam encompasses personal faith and piety, the creed and worship of the community of believers, a way of life, a code of ethics, a culture, a system of laws, an understanding of the function of the state—in short, guidelines and rules for life in all its aspects and dimensions. While many Muslims see the SHARIA (the "way," denoting the sacred law governing the life of individuals as well as the structures of society) as fixed and immutable, others make a clear distinction between the unchangeable message of the Koran and the mutable laws and regulations for Muslim life and conduct. Throughout history, practices and opinions have differed with regard to the exact way in which Islam determines life in all its aspects, but the basic notion of Islam's comprehensive character is so intrinsic to Muslim thought and feeling that neither the past history of the Muslim world nor its present situation can be understood without taking this characteristic into consideration.

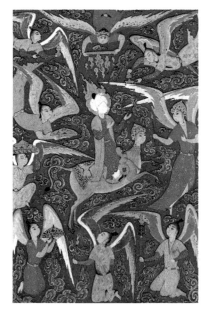

In this 16th-century Persian miniature the prophet Muhammad is escorted by angels as he ascends into heaven on the winged creature Buraq. In Islamic legend this heavenly ascension (miraj) *is preceded by* Muhammad's *nocturnal purification and journey* (isra) *from Mecca to Jerusalem. Various interpretations of Muhammad's night journey and ascension include the Sufi Muslim belief that they constitute an allegory of the soul's acquisition of spiritual wisdom.*

This miniature from a manuscript by Mirza Muhammad Refi portrays the prophet Muhammad with the angel Gabriel and the first four caliphs. At the bottom of the painting is a ladder that leads to heaven from the Kaaba sanctuary in Mecca, where the sacred black stone is enclosed. In Islamic faith, Mecca is revered as the place where heavenly power directly touches the Earth.

According to Muslim jurists, the *sharia* is derived from four sources—the Koran; the *sunna* ("customs") of the Prophet, which are embodied in the *hadith* ("tradition"); *qiyas* ("analogy"; the application of a decision of the past, or the principles on which it was based, to new questions); and *ijma* ("consensus"; the consensus of the community of believers, who, according to a saying of the Prophet, would not agree on any error).

HISTORY AND SPREAD OF ISLAM
The Prophet. Muhammad was born in 570 in MECCA, a trading center in western Arabia. About 610 he received the first of a series of revelations that convinced him that he had been chosen as God's messenger. He began to preach the message entrusted to him—that there is but one God, to whom all humankind must commit themselves. The polytheistic Meccans resented Muhammad's attacks on their gods and finally he emigrated with a few followers to MEDINA. This migration, which is called the Hegira (Hijrah), took place in 622; Muslims adopted the beginning of that year as the first year of their lunar calendar (Anno Hegirae, or AH).

At Medina Muhammad won acceptance as a religious and military leader. Within a few years he had established control of the surrounding region, and in 630 he finally conquered Mecca. There, the KAABA, a shrine that had for some time housed the idols of the pagan Meccans, was rededicated to the worship of Allah, and it became the object of pilgrimage for all Muslims. By the time of his death in 632, Muhammad had won the allegiance of most of the Arab tribespeople to Islam. He had laid the foundation for a community (*umma*) ruled by the laws of God.

The Koran records that Muhammad was the Seal of the Prophets, the last of a line of God's messengers that began with Adam and included Abraham, Noah, Moses, and Jesus. He left for the future guidance of the community the words of God revealed to him and recorded in the Koran, and the *sunna*, the collective name for his opinions and decisions as recorded in the tradition literature *(hadith)*.

A Rapidly Growing Empire, 632–750. After the death of Muhammad, a successor (*khalifa*, or caliph; see IMAM) was chosen to rule in his place. The first caliph, the Prophet's father-in-law, ABU BAKR (r. 632–34), initiated an expansionist movement that was carried out most successfully by the next two caliphs, UMAR I (r. 634–44) and Uthman (r. 644–56). By 656 the CALIPHATE included the whole Arabian peninsula, Palestine and Syria, Egypt and Libya, Mesopotamia, and substantial parts of Armenia and Persia. Following the assassination of Uthman, the disagreements between those upholding the rights of the fourth caliph, ALI (r. 656–61), the Prophet's son-

in-law, and their opponents led to a division in the Muslim community between the SHIITES and the SUNNITES that still exists today. When the governor of Syria, MUAWIYA I, came to power after the murder of Ali, the Shiites refused to recognize him and his successors.

Muawiya inaugurated an almost 90-year rule by the UMAYYADS (661–750), who made Damascus their capital. A second wave of expansion followed. After they conquered (670) Tunisia, Muslim troops reached the northwestern point of North Africa in 710. In 711 they crossed the Strait of Gibraltar, rapidly overran Spain, and penetrated well into France until they were turned back near Poitiers in 732. On the northern frontier Constantinople was besieged more than once (though without success), and in the east the Indus River was reached; the Islamic empire now bordered China and India, with some settlements in the Punjab.

Rival Dynasties and Competing Capitals (Baghdad, Córdoba, Cairo), 750–1258. In 750, Umayyad rule in Damascus was ended by the ABBASIDS, who moved the caliphate's capital to Baghdad. The succeeding period was marked more by an expansion of horizons of thought than by geographical expansion. In the fields of literature, the sciences, and philosophy, contributions by such Muslim scholars as al-KINDI, al-FARABI, and Ibn Sina (AVICENNA) far surpassed European accomplishments of that time.

Politically, the power of the Abbasids was challenged by a number of rival dynasties. These included an Umayyad dynasty in Córdoba, Spain (756–1031); the FATIMIDS, a dynasty connected with the ISMAILIS (a Shiite sect), who established

This 13th-century miniature from the Baghdad school portrays a caravan of pilgrims making the hajj (pilgrimage) to Mecca, the birthplace of the prophet Muhammad and the holiest city of Islam. Islam requires each Muslim to take the hajj at least once.

(909) themselves in Tunisia and later (969-1171) ruled Egypt; the ALMORAVIDS and the ALMOHADS, Muslim Berber dynasties that successively ruled North Africa and Spain from the mid-11th to the mid-13th century; the SELJUKS, a Muslim Turkish group that seized Baghdad in 1055 and whose defeat of the Byzantines in 1071 led indirectly to the Christian CRUSADES (1096-1254) against the Islamic world; and the AYYUBIDS, who displaced the Fatimids in Egypt and played an important role in the later years of the Crusades.

The Abbasids were finally overthrown (1258) in Baghdad by the MONGOLS, although a family member escaped to Egypt, where he was recognized as caliph. While the brotherhood of faith remained a reality, the political unity of the Muslim world was definitely broken.

Two Great Islamic Powers: The Ottomans and the Moguls, 15th-18th Century.
The Ottoman Turkish dynasty, founded by OSMAN I (c.1300), became a major world power in the 15th century, and continued to play a very significant role throughout the 16th and 17th centuries. The BYZANTINE EMPIRE, with which Muslim armies had been at war since the early days of Islam, came to an end in 1453 when Ottoman sultan MEHMED II conquered Constantinople. That city then became the capital of the OTTOMAN EMPIRE.

In the first half of the 16th century, Ottoman power, already firmly established over all Anatolia and in most of the Balkans, gained control over Syria, Egypt (the sultans assumed the title caliph after deposing the last Abbasid in Cairo), and the rest of North Africa. It also expanded significantly northwestward into Europe, besieging Vienna in 1529. The defeat of the Ottoman navy in the Battle of LEPANTO in 1571 was not, as many in Europe hoped, the beginning of a rapid disintegration of the Ottoman Empire; more than one hundred years later, in 1683, Ottoman troops once again besieged Vienna. The decline of the empire becomes more visible from the late 17th century onward, but it survived through World War I. Turkey became a republic under Kemal ATATÜRK in 1923, and the caliphate was abolished in 1924.

The MOGULS were a Muslim dynasty of Turko-Mongol origin who conquered northern India in 1526. The Mogul Empire reached the climax of its power in the period from the late 16th century until the beginning of the 18th century. Under the emperors AKBAR, JAHANGIR, SHAH JAHAN, and AURANGZEB, Mogul rule was extended over most of the subcontinent, and Islamic culture (with a strong Persian flavor) was firmly implanted in certain areas. The splendor of the Moguls is reflected in a special way in their architecture. In the 18th century Mogul power began to decline. It survived, at least in name, however, till 1858, when the last sultan was dethroned by the British.

Two Examples of the Coming of Islam in Frontier Areas: Indonesia and West Africa.
While there may have been sporadic contacts from the 10th century onward with Muslim merchants, it was only in the 13th century that Islam clearly established itself in Sumatra, where small Muslim states formed on the northeast coast. Islam spread to Java in the 16th century, and then expanded, generally in a peaceful manner, from the coastal areas inward to all parts of the Indonesian archipelago. By the 19th century it had reached to the northeast and extended into the Philippines. Today there are 140 million Muslims in Indonesia, constituting 90 percent of the population.

Islam penetrated West Africa in three main phases. The first was that of contacts with Arab and Berber caravan traders, from the 10th century onward. Then followed a period of gradual Islamization of some rulers' courts, among them that of the famous MANSA MUSA (r. 1312-27) in Mali. Finally, in the 16th century the Sufi orders (brotherhoods of mystics; see SUFISM), especially the Qadiriyya, Tijaniyya, and Muridiyya, as well as individual saints and scholars, began to play an important role. The 19th century witnessed more than one JIHAD (holy war) for the purification of Islam from pagan influences, while later in the 19th century and in the first half of the 20th century, Muslims formed a significant element in the growing resistance to colonial powers. In the post-colonial period Islam plays an important role in Nigeria, Senegal, Guinea, Mali

and Niger, while there are smaller Muslim communities in the other states in West Africa.

Islam in Modern History.
Napoleon's invasion of Egypt in 1798, followed three years later by the expulsion of the French troops by the combined British-Ottoman forces, is often seen as the beginning of the modern period in the history of Islam. The coming to power of MUHAMMAD ALI (r. 1805-49) and the modernization of Egypt under his leadership was the beginning of a long struggle throughout the Muslim world to reestablish independence from the colonial powers and to assume their place as autonomous countries in the modern world. Resistance to foreign domination and an awareness of the need to restore the Muslim community to its proper place in world history are integral parts of the pan-Islamic efforts of JAMAL AL-DIN AL-AFGHANI as well as the nationalist movements of the 20th century.

The political, social, and economic developments in the various countries with Muslim majorities show significant differences. For example, Turkey and many of the Arab countries have become secular republics, whereas Saudi Arabia is virtually an absolute monarchy, ruled under Muslim law. Iran was ruled from 1925 to 1979 by the Pahlavi dynasty, which stressed secularization and westernization. Growing resistance from the Muslim community, which is overwhelmingly Shiite, culminated in the forced departure of the shah and the establishment of an Islamic republic under the leadership of the Ayatollah KHOMEINI. However, while opinions differ in regard as to how Islam can continue to function in modern societies as a force relevant to all aspects of life, the great majority of Muslims hold fast to the notion of the comprehensive character of Islam as well as to its basic theological doctrines.

ISLAMIC DOCTRINES
Islamic doctrines are commonly discussed and taught widely—often by means of a catechism, with questions and answers—under six headings: God, angels, Scriptures, messengers, the Last Day, and predestination. The Muslims' notion of God (Allah) is, in a sense, interrelated with all of the following points and will be referred to below. Some of the angels (all of whom are servants of God and subject to him) play a particularly important role in the daily life of many Muslims: the guardian angels; the recording angels (those who write down a person's deeds, for which he or she will have to account on Judgment Day); the angel of death; and the angels who question a person in the tomb. One of those mentioned by name in the Koran is Jibril (see GABRIEL, angel), who functioned in a special way as a transmitter of God's revelation to the Prophet. The importance of the Muslim recognition of Scriptures other than the Koran and of messengers other than Muhammad will be referred to below.

The promise and threat of the Last Day, which occupy an important place in the Koran, continue to play a major role in Muslim thought and piety. On the Last Day, of which only God knows the hour, every soul will stand alone and will have to account for its deeds. In the theological discussions of the Last Day and, in general, of the concept of God, a significant issue has been whether the descriptions in the Koran (of HEAVEN and HELL, the vision of God, God being seated on the throne, the hands of God, and so on) should be interpreted literally or allegorically. The majority view accepts the principle of literal interpretation (God *is* seated on the throne, he *has* hands), but adds the warning and qualification that humans cannot state and should not ask how this is the case, since God is incomparable (*bila kayf,* "without how"; *bila tashbih,* "beyond comparison").

The last of the six articles, PREDESTINATION, is also a theocentric issue. Because the divine initiative is all-decisive in bringing humans to faith ("had God not guided us, we had surely never been guided," 7:43), many concluded that God is not only responsible for guiding some but also for not guiding others, allowing them to go astray or even leading them astray. In the debate of later theologians on these questions, the antipredestinarians were concerned less with upholding the notion of human freedom and, therefore, of human dignity, than with defending the honor of God. According to

(Left) *The Great Mosque of Samarra, which was constructed during the 8th-century reign of the Abbasid caliph al-Mutawakkil, is the largest mosque in the world. Its 52-m (170-ft) spiral-shaped minaret stands apart from the mosque itself. The minaret's atypical form is reminiscent of the ziggurats of pre-Islamic Mesopotamia. The call for Muslim prayer is sounded each morning from the minaret.*

these thinkers—the Qadarites and the Mutazilites, of the 8th to 10th centuries—the Koranic message of the justice of God "who does not wrong people" (". . .they wrong themselves," 43:76) excluded the notion of a God who would punish human beings for evil deeds and unbelief for which they themselves were not really responsible. The major concern of their opponents was to maintain, against any such reasoning, the doctrine of the sovereign freedom of God, upon whom no limits can be placed, not even the limit of "being bound to do what is best for his creatures." Two important theologians of the 10th century, al-Ashari (d. 935) and al-Maturidi (d. 944), formulated answers that would mark for the centuries to come the traditional (Sunni) position on these points. Although one's acts are willed and created by God, one has to appropriate them to make them one's own. A recognition of a degree of human responsibility is combined with the notion of God as the sole creator, the One and Only.

Around this concept of the unity of God another debate arose on the essence and attributes of God; it focused on the question whether the Koran—God's speech—was created or uncreated. Those who held that the Koran was created believed that the notion of an uncreated Koran implied another eternal reality alongside God, who alone is eternal and does not share his eternity with anyone or anything else. Their opponents felt that the notion of a created Koran detracted from its character as God's own speech. The Sunni position that emerged from these discussions was that the Koran as written down or recited is created, but that it is a manifestation of the eternal "inner speech" of God, which precedes any articulation in sounds and letters.

None of the theological issues referred to above can be understood fully unless the sociopolitical context of these doctrinal debates is taken into consideration. The interrelation between theological positions and political events is particularly clear in the first issues that arose in the history of Islam. Reference has already been made to the division between the Shiites and the Sunnites. The Shiites were those who maintained that only "members of the family" (Hashimites, or, in the more restricted sense, descendants of the Prophet via his daughter, FATIMA and her husband Ali) had a right to the caliphate. Another group, the Kharijites (literally "those who seceded"), broke away from Ali (who was murdered by one of their members) and from the Umayyads. They developed the doctrine that confession, or faith, alone did not make a person a believer and that anyone committing grave sins was an unbeliever destined to hell. They applied this argument to the leaders of the community, holding that caliphs who were grave sinners could not claim the allegiance of the faithful.

(Left) *The elaborate interior of this 16th-century mosque at Edirne, Turkey, reflects the influence of Persian art and architecture. The person in prayer is facing the mosque's mihrab (prayer niche), which designates the direction of Mecca, the place toward which all Muslims face in prayer.* (Right) *Shoes are removed before entering mosques, as in this scene before the mosque of the dancing dervishes in Konya, Turkey. Dervishes are Islamic monks who are involved in mystical practices.*

Pilgrims at a mosque in Kano, Nigeria, attend a communal prayer gathering during Ramadan, the ninth month of the Muslim year, during which fasting is observed in the daylight hours. Through the activities of Arab and Berber caravan traders, Islam spread into West Africa and was established as a major religion.

While the mainstream of Muslims accepted the principle that faith and works must go together, they rejected the Kharijite ideal of establishing here on earth a pure community of believers, insisting that the ultimate decision on whether a person is a believer or an unbeliever must be left to God. Suspension of the answer till Judgment Day enabled them to recognize anyone accepting the "five pillars" (see below) as a member of the community of believers, and to recognize those Muslims who had political authority over them, even if they objected to some of their practices.

ISLAMIC WORSHIP, PRACTICES, AND DUTIES

To what extent faith and works go together is evident from the traditional listing of the basic duties of any Muslim, the "five pillars" of Islam: *shahada*, the profession of faith in God and the apostleship of Muhammad; *salat*, the ritual prayer, performed five times a day facing Mecca; *zakat*, almsgiving; *sawm* (fasting), abstaining from food and drink during the daylight hours of the month of RAMADAN; and *hajj*, the pilgrimage to Mecca, incumbent on every believer who is financially and physically able to undertake it. The witness to God stands here side by side with the concern for the poor, reflected in almsgiving. The personal involvement of the individual believer, expressed most clearly in the formulation of the *shahada*, "I witness there is no God but God, and Muhammad is the messenger of God," is combined with a deep awareness of the strength that lies in the fellowship of faith and the community of all believers, significant dimensions of both the ritual prayer and the pilgrimage.

Muslim worship and devotion is not limited to the precisely prescribed words and gestures of the *salat*, but finds expression also in a wealth of personal prayers, in the gathering of the congregation in the central mosque on Fridays, and in the celebration of the two main festivals: Id al-Fitr, the festival of the breaking of the fast at the end of Ramadan; and Id al-Adha, the festival of the sacrifice (in memory of Abraham's willingness to sacrifice his son). The latter, observed on the 10th day of the month of pilgrimage, is celebrated not only by the participants in the pilgrimage, but also simultaneously by those who stay in their own locations. The interpretations of *jihad* (literally, "striving" in the way of God), sometimes added as an additional duty, vary from sacred war to striving to fulfill the ethical norms and principles expounded in the Koran.

ISLAMIC VIEWS OF OTHER RELIGIONS

Islam is definitely an inclusivistic religion in the sense that it recognizes God's sending of messengers to all peoples and his granting of "Scripture and Prophethood" to Abraham and his descendants, the latter resulting in the awareness of a very special link between Muslims, Jews, and Christians as all Abraham's children. Throughout history there have been believers who discerned the Truth of God and responded to him in the right manner, committing themselves to him alone. Of these "Muslims before Muhammad," the Koran mentions, among others, Abraham and his sons, Solomon and the queen of Sheba, and the disciples of Jesus. This inclusiveness is also expressed in the Muslim recognition of earlier Scriptures, namely, the Taurat (Torah) given to Moses, the Zabur (Psalms) of David, and the Injil (Gospel) of Jesus.

This recognition of other prophets besides Muhammad and other Scriptures besides the Koran is coupled with the firm conviction that the perfection of religion and the completion of God's favor to humanity have been realized in the sending down of the Koran, the sending of Muhammad as "the Seal of the Prophets," and the establishing of Islam. People's reactions and response to this final criterion of truth became, therefore, the evidence of their faith or unbelief. Those who, on the basis of what they had previously received from God, recognize the message of the Koran as the ultimate Truth show themselves thereby as true believers, while those who reject it prove themselves to be unbelievers, no matter by what name they call themselves.   WILLEM A. BIJLEFELD

Bibliography:

GENERAL: Abdul-Rauf, Muhammad, *Islam: Creed and Worship* (1975); Cragg, Kenneth, *The House of Islam* (1975); Gibb, H. A. R., *Mohammedanism* (1949; repr. 1975); Hitti, Philip K., *Islam, A Way of Life* (1970); Lewis, Bernard, ed., *Islam and the Arab World* (1976); Morgan, Kenneth W., ed., *Islam: The Straight Path* (1958); Nasr, Seyyed Hossein, *Ideals and Realities of Islam* (1966; repr. 1972); Rahman, Fazlur, *Islam*, 2d ed. (1979); Schacht, Joseph, and Bosworth, C. E., eds., *The Legacy of Islam*, 2d ed. (1974); Watt, W. Montgomery, *What Is Islam?* (1968).

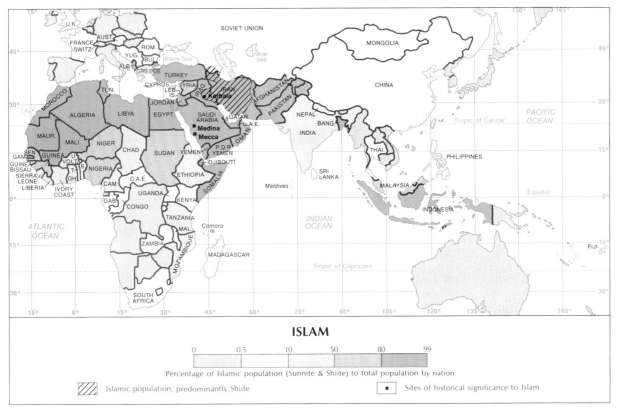

ISLAM

| 0 | 0.5 | 10 | 50 | 80 | 99 |

Percentage of Islamic population (Sunnite & Shiite) to total population by nation

///// Islamic population, predominantly Shiite   ■ Sites of historical significance to Islam

ISLAM IN MODERN HISTORY: Cragg, Kenneth, *Counsels in Contemporary Islam* (1965); Rosenthal, Erwin I. J., *Islam in the Modern National State* (1965); Smith, Wilfred C., *Islam in Modern History* (1959).
SOCIOLOGY OF ISLAM AND ETHNOGRAPHICAL DATA: Levy, Reuben, *The Social Structure of Islam* (1957; repr. 1965); Weeks, Richard V., ed., *Muslim Peoples: A World Ethnographic Survey* (1978).

See also: AFRICA, HISTORY OF; ASIA, HISTORY OF; MIDDLE EAST, HISTORY OF THE.

Islam, Nation of: see BLACK MUSLIMS.

Islam in the West, World Community of:
see BLACK MUSLIMS.

Islamabad   [is-lum-uh-bahd']

Islamabad, the capital city of Pakistan, is located in the northeastern part of the country, near the Himalayas. The city covers 65 km² (25 mi²) and has a population of 277,318 (1972). Islamabad's climate is hot and desertlike: the annual average temperature is 22° C (71° F), and average annual rainfall is 915 mm (36 in). Islamabad, whose name means City of Peace, is a new city, built between 1960 and 1975 to replace KARACHI as the capital. Nearby RAWALPINDI served as the interim capital (1959–67) until the new capital was completed. Islamabad is divided into eight districts; the government's administrative buildings make up the central district, which is surrounded by commercial, residential, and educational zones. Industrial and green zones encircle the city.

Islamic art and architecture

Islamic art and architecture refers to artistic achievements in those lands where, from the 7th century on, ISLAM became the dominant faith. The Islamic tradition encompasses the arts of the Middle East, North Africa, Spain, Anatolia and the Balkans, Central Asia, and northern and central India, from the time each of these areas became Muslim—as early as AD 622 in parts of Arabia and as late as the 15th century for Istanbul,

parts of the Balkans, and central India. Generally excluded from consideration in this context are the arts of sub-Saharan and eastern Africa, Indonesia, Malaysia, the Philippines, and Muslim parts of China. These areas did not adopt Islam until relatively late, generally after the 16th century, and by that time the artistic creativity of the central Muslim lands had weakened; their arts tend to be closer to local traditions.

GENERAL CHARACTERISTICS
During the most creative millennium in Islamic art (about 650–1650) certain key features emerged that came to characterize the Islamic style of art and architecture. These shared characteristics appeared despite the differences in environment between such diverse lands as Mediterranean Spain, steppic Central Asia, mountainous Algeria, arid Arabia, and the subtropical Indus Valley, and despite cultural diversity of such distant ethnic groups as Arabs, Berbers, Persians, Turks, and Indians. The developing Islamic tradition drew on complex artistic inheritances that included Late Roman art, Early Christian art of the Byzantines and the Copts, and Sassanian art of Persia, and on lesser influences from Mongol, Central Asian, and Indian sources.

Function of Art. From its inception Islamic art was an art created for the setting of daily life. Most religious architecture, notably the MOSQUE and the MINARET, was built less as a testimonial to Allah than as a place where people could best express their piety and learn the precepts of the faith. In addition to that used to decorate buildings, Islamic painting developed primarily in the form of book illustration and illumination. Such painted works were generally created not as ends in themselves but to help explain a scientific text or to enhance the pleasure of reading history or literature.

In the field of the decorative arts the Islamic style is distinguished by the novelty and extraordinary quality of techniques used in the making of utilitarian objects. These techniques include the application of lustrous glazes and rich colors in ceramics and glassware; intricate silver inlays that transform the surfaces of bronze metalwork; lavish molded stucco and carved wood wall panels; and endlessly varied motifs woven into textiles and rugs. In nearly all instances the

with imagination is it possible to reconstruct the secluded life of the 9th-century imperial palaces at Samarra, or the pleasure pavilions of the Safavids in Iran, such as the 17th-century Ali Qapu and Chehel Sutun in Isfahan. An exquisitely ornamented and rare rock-crystal ewer, preserved in the San Marco Museum, Venice, provides a hint of the richness of 10th- and 11th-century Fatimid art in Cairo; the countless treasures in the Topkapi Palace Museum, Istanbul, attest to the enormous wealth of the Turkish Ottomans.

Decorative Character of Art. A fundamental characteristic of much Islamic art is its powerfully decorative or ornamental quality. A variety of arbitrary geometric, floral, or other types of designs—such as the swirling, interlaced ARABESQUE—tend to predominate over specific motifs taken from nature or from an idealized version of the natural world. Although there are exceptions, the vast majority of motifs, decorating everything from architectural monuments to manuscript borders, do not seem to bear direct relation to a visually perceived reality. Even CALLIGRAPHY, the art of beautiful handwriting, often seems removed from the meaning of the words depicted; it functions instead more as an element in the overall decorative design. In this decorative tendency Islamic art contrasts sharply with the representational art of the West, in which precise iconographic meanings are attached to most artistic forms.

Whether in fact the Muslim world may also have sought to transmit a concrete message through its abstract forms is a subject of debate among scholars. Several possiblities have been suggested. One is that the Muslims tended to reject the representation of the visible in their art to emphasize that visible reality is but an illusion and that Allah alone is true. Abstraction thus became a way to make a very specific theological point. Another theory holds that an art which sought above all to enhance the setting of human activities, rather than to order human behavior or beliefs, was by necessity compelled to develop abstract forms rather than forms with a single obvious meaning.

The Court of Lions, one of two main courtyards located in the 14th-century Alhambra Palace, Granada, Spain, is one of the most articulate examples of Islamic architecture. The elaborate interior decoration includes a profusion of delicate muqarna work.

objects decorated—whether ewers, cooking cauldrons, candlesticks, or pen cases—served fundamentally practical purposes; their aesthetic effect was aimed above all at making the daily activities or architectural setting more pleasurable.

Sources of Patronage. The vast majority of surviving examples of Islamic art reflect the patronage of a wide social spectrum, most of the patronage coming from the urban world of the great Islamic cities. From Córdoba in Spain to Samarkand in Central Asia, the cities were the centers of Islamic learning and of mercantile wealth. Of the thousands of ceramic objects excavated in the Persian city of Nishapur, the celebrated lusterwares from Fatimid Cairo, or the many inlaid bronzes from Herat (Afghanistan) or Mosul (Iraq), most were made for the bourgeoisie of the cities. The styles of these objects reflect the preferences of these urban dwellers; the variations in quality presumably reflect local variations in price and standards of appreciation.

In addition to the arts created for the urban strata of the Islamic world there was a splendid art of kings and emperors. Little has been preserved of this regal art, however, and only

(Left) *This 12th-century bronze incense burner from Gurgan, Iran, is representative of the highly decorative metalwork of the Seljuk period. Kufic inscriptions, such as that encircling the animal's chest, are common embellishments to all forms of Islamic artistic expression. (Archaeological Museum, Tehran.)* (Below) *This relief tilework from a late-14th century mausoleum at Fathabad, Uzbekistan, typifies the articulation of architectural inscription of the Timurid period. (Victoria and Albert Museum, London.)*

An excellent example of the difficulty involved in even defining this problem lies in the *muqarnas* (sometimes called the honeycomb or stalactite motif), a form of ceiling decoration composed of small, three-dimensional units invented in Iran in the 10th century and eventually found everywhere from Spain to India. The *muqarnas* appears at first glance to be an arbitrary and strictly ornamental architectural motif. In Iranian domes of the late 11th and 12th centuries, however, the *muqarnas* ceiling carries a structural significance, in which the parts of the design are carefully aligned with support thrusts from the dome. In the intricately faceted ceilings of the Moorish ALHAMBRA outside Granada or the Cappella Porlatina (Palantine Chapel) in Palermo, inscriptions and the particular sequence of designs indicate that the *muqarnas* ceiling was meant to symbolically represent the dome of heaven. Other existing examples show that many seemingly abstract motifs in Islamic art carried subtle layers of meaning discernible either through their context or through an inscription.

Iconoclastic Tendency. Another characteristic of Islamic art is what is generally called its iconoclasm, or rejection of the representation of religious images and other living beings. In many ways the term *iconoclasm* is not an appropriate one because no formal doctrinal statement against such representations appeared in the Koran but only in the Hadith (traditions), a later writing. Even there the statements are incidental and partial (the decoration of baths or floors, for example, are exempted from the prohibition). Nevertheless, it is true that early Islamic art modified the art of previous centuries by tending to avoid the representation of humans and animals. Whether this reluctance was derived from a still undetected religious prohibition or from a search for a cultural identity distinct from the identities of other traditions remains a matter of scholarly debate.

Primacy of Calligraphy. The art of calligraphy played a preeminent role throughout the world of Islam. Because of its association with the divine revelation, the Arabic alphabet be-

A leaf from a Koran manuscript (c.900) displays the angular Kufic script used for sacred texts until the 11th century. The Islamic emphasis on literature led to the development and perfection of vigorous and remarkably decorative calligraphic styles. (Nelson Gallery of Art and Atkins Museum of Fine Arts, Kansas City, Mo.)

came the vehicle for such diverse languages as Persian and Turkish. In addition, Islamic culture in general was highly verbal, therefore, unusual attention was given to the transformation of writing into a visually appealing expression of aesthetic forms. From the sharp angles of early Kufic to the flowing rhythms of later Persian *shekasteh* script or to the formal compositions of an Ottoman *tughra* (imperial emblem), many different systems of proportions between letters, relationships between parts of letters, and arrangements of words were developed. The impact of a fascination with writing appeared throughout the Islamic world: ceramics, metal objects, textiles, and architecture all acquired calligraphic forms as a universally appreciated means of decoration.

HISTORICAL DEVELOPMENT

Although no universally accepted chronology of Islamic art and architecture exists, the following three major periods are generally recognized: the Formative period (650–1000), Middle period (1000–1250), and Late period (1250 on).

The Formative Period. From about 650 to 1000—under the Umayyad and early Abbasid CALIPHATES as well as of the first local dynasties in Spain, Egypt, and eastern Iran—the Muslim

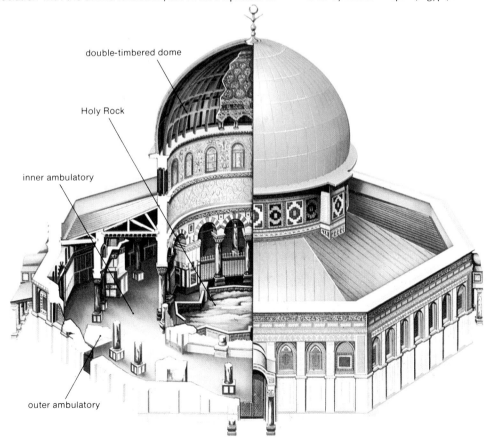

double-timbered dome

Holy Rock

inner ambulatory

outer ambulatory

The Qubbat al-Sakhra, or Dome of the Rock, Jerusalem, is one of the earliest and most important Islamic shrines. Constructed (691) by the Umayyad caliph Abd-al-Malik, the octagonal structure more closely resembles Christian architecture than it does Islamic. A double colonnade of Corinthian columns divides the interior into two concentric ambulatories focusing on the al-Sakhra, or Holy Rock, significant to Islamic, Judaic, and Christian tradition. The interior is lavishly decorated with quartered marble and naturalistic glass mosaics; the mosaics originally covering the exterior surfaces were replaced by ceramic decoration during the 16th century. The double-timbered dome is covered at present with sheets of gilded aluminum.

world created its own identifying forms, from mosques to the abstract design known as the arabesque. Major monuments from this period are found throughout the Islamic world—the mosques of Córdoba, Ibn Tulun in Cairo, Damascus, Samarra, and Dome of the Rock in Jerusalem; private palaces like Khirbat-al-Mafjar in Palestine; royal palaces like Samarra's in Iraq; the urban architecture of Baghdad; tin-glazed ceramics in Iraq, Egypt, and northeastern Iran; woodwork and rock-crystal carving in Egypt; carved ivories in Spain. However, the most influential and perhaps most creative area was Iraq, which remained the center of the Muslim world until the early part of the 11th century. Although some of the more imaginative ceramics have been found in Nishapur in eastern Iran, it was probably in Iraq that the technique of lusterware originated (9th century), along with other uniquely Islamic forms of decorative art.

The Middle Period. The year 1000 marks the beginning of the Middle period of Islamic art. During this brilliant period, cut short by the Mongol invasion during the early 13th century, a large number of local styles were formed. Eastern Iran, western Iran, Iraq, Egypt, Anatolia (newly conquered by the Seljuks), North Africa, and Spain all acquired their own stylistic and iconographic peculiarities, which corresponded to political and social differences between provinces and the weakening of central authority. Cairo, Nishapur, Herat, Isfahan, and the Anatolian center of Konya rivaled the early Islamic capital city of Baghdad in cultural and artistic importance. Yet common threads were maintained in the art of these diverse centers. In almost all Islamic cities an architecture of citadels and city walls rather than of palaces reflected the new power of a military elite. Next to the single mosques were built small private mosques, mausoleums for holy men, and *madrasahs* (schools of law and theology) or *khanqahs* (semimonastic establishments for holy men and women). This proliferation of architectural complexes in Islamic cities illustrates the growing complexity of the Muslim religious system during this period. Throughout the Muslim world a new emphasis was given to external forms of architecture (minarets, gates, and domes) as well as to the *muqarnas*.

New or reinvented techniques in the decorative arts—*minai*, or enameling in ceramics, luster painting in glass, and silver inlays in metalwork—made it possible to increase the number and character of illustrated topics. Quite suddenly in the latter part of the 12th century, during this period of intense artistic creativity, books began to be illustrated. The reasons for this proliferation of new forms of representation are difficult to assess. In part it reflected new contacts with other cultures (India and the Christian West), but it probably also reflected an internal need for more complex expressions of a

This manuscript page (c.1250) from the Abbasid period, depicting a fanciful representation of the archer associated with Sagittarius positioned between the Moon and Jupiter, reflects the interest in astrological science that thrived in Islamic civilization from the 8th to the 13th century. Scientific treatises constituted a large part of the manuscript tradition of the Abbasid period. (Bibliothèque Nationale, Paris.)

richer culture. The Middle period was also an era when mysticism began to affect all aspects of Muslim piety and when local cultural traditions, especially those in Iran, began to reassert themselves.

Late Period. After the devastating Mongol invasions of 1220-60 the Muslim world became more strictly divided both politically and culturally. The separate geopolitical entities that emerged tended to remain independent of each other although still frequently subject to common influence. West to east, the principal independent cultural areas were the Muslim West, the area comprising Egypt, Palestine, and Syria; the Ottoman Empire; Iran; and Muslim India.

In the Muslim West, Islam slowly disappeared from Spain, culminating in the fall of Granada in 1492, but was maintained in North Africa. Moorish art is distinguished primarily by brilliant geometrical ornamentation adorning mostly private, interiorized, architectural monuments. This striking decorative tradition was maintained by the Mudéjars, Moors remaining in Spain after its reconquest by the Christians, and exerted a strong influence on later Spanish styles of craftwork and architectural decoration. Except for the unique masterpiece of the 14th-century Alhambra palace, however, most of western Islamic art tended to be conservative and repetitive, with limited novelties in the art of objects. (See MOORISH ART AND ARCHITECTURE.)

From 1258 to 1517 the area comprising Egypt, Palestine, and Syria was ruled by the unique system of military slaves known as the MAMELUKES. Its major artistic achievement was in archi-

(Below) A Syrian enamelled flask (c.1300; British Museum, London) features the lavish arabesques and geometric patterns characteristic of the highly sophisticated art produced under the Mamelukes, as the elegant lines (left) of the Masjid-i shah mosque (1612-38), Isafan, Iran, epitomize the symmetrical architecture of the Safavids.

This miniature (1485), by the Herat calligrapher and artist Mirak Naqqash, illustrates a scene from the "Khusrau and Shirin" segment of Nezami's Khamseh, a 12th-century dramatic poem. Naqqash's work, in its precise execution and unified design, exemplifies the Herat style of manuscript illumination. (Chester Beatty Library, Dublin.)

tecture, as attested by the multitude of Mameluke monuments still extant in the cities of Cairo, Jerusalem, and to a lesser degree, Damascus and Aleppo. For complex economic and social reasons the affluent classes invested in vast architectural projects that transformed these cities. The buildings are traditional in function, but their forms and techniques—superb stonework, brilliantly decorated gates and minarets, complex domes—display a level of sophistication and quality hitherto unknown in the Islamic world. A characteristic example, ranked among the masterpieces of world architecture, is the immense madrasah of Sultan Hasan in Cairo. Built around a square court surmounted by four lofty cross vaults, it houses the mausoleum of the sultan, crowned by a huge cupola.

The Ottoman dynasty, having begun in western Anatolia, conquered the Balkans and took Constantinople in 1453 and nearly all Islamic lands around the Mediterranean by 1520. A strong, centralized state, the Ottoman Empire concentrated its creative energies on the development of a uniquely logical mosque architecture. As early as the 14th and 15th centuries, in Bursa and Iznik, the Ottomans chose to use the single dome as the focal compositional element of their monuments. This fascination with the cupola was in large part inspired by the Byzantine church of HAGIA SOPHIA (which was converted into a mosque) and culminated in the 16th-century masterpiece of the Suleiman (Süleymaniye) mosque in Istanbul. Its architect, SINAN, created numerous monuments in Edirne and Istanbul, which in turn became types adapted for use from Yugoslavia to Egypt. Ottoman decorative art, especially ceramic objects and tiles, and miniature painting are largely derivative of other traditions, although many examples are noteworthy for the exceptional precision of their execution.

Of all the Islamic lands Iran was most strongly affected by

the Mongol invasions, but this traumatic experience led to a rejuvenation of the arts, despite continuous political upheavals. Under the Ilkhanids (1280–1336), the Timurids (1370–1502), and Safavids (1502–1712), and several other minor dynasties, Persian architecture exhibited a whole gamut of styles ranging from the grandiloquent monumentality of the Sultaniyah mosque to the intense piety of Samarkand's mausoleums, to the colorful brilliance of the monuments around Isfahan's Masjid-i-Shah mosque. It was an imaginative, inventive, accretive tradition remarkably attuned to the composition of Persian religious thought. Especially impressive is the development of Persian painting. From the Shah-Nama (Book of Kings) to lyrical poems of Nizami, Persian literature was illuminated through a striking array of painting styles—rough and brutal in the early part of the 14th century, poetically complex in the 15th century, and marked by precisely observed details of everyday life in later times. (See PERSIAN ART AND ARCHITECTURE.)

Farther east, after several centuries of rule by various military dynasties, Islamic India reached its apogee under the MOGULS (1526–1707). Their architecture was often inspired by Persia but rapidly acquired its own identity through the use of local materials and techniques. The Mogul achievements in architecture are most impressive in such celebrated buildings as the TAJ MAHAL or the urban complex of FATEHPUR SIKRI. The Persian influence was also strongly felt in painting in the early years, but soon Mogul art became uniquely inspired by the remarkable precision and human insights apparent in native Indian traditions of painting. (See MOGUL ART AND ARCHITECTURE.)

OLEG GRABAR

Bibliography: Arnold, Thomas W., Painting in Islam (1928; repr. 1965); Aslanapa, Oktay, Turkish Art and Architecture (1971); Ettinghausen, Richard, Arab Painting (1962) and, as ed., Islamic Art in the Metropolitan Museum (1972); Goodwin, Godfrey, A History of Ottoman Architecture (1971); Grabar, Oleg, The Formation of Islamic Art (1973); Gray, Basil, Persian Painting (1930; repr. 1971); Grube, Ernest J., The World of Islam (1967); Hoag, John D., Islamic Architecture (1977); Kühnel, Ernest, Islamic Art and Architecture (1966); Lane, Arthur, Early Islamic Pottery (1957) and Later Islamic Pottery, 2d ed. (1971); Rice, David T., Islamic Art (1965); Welch, S. C., Persian Painting (1976); Wilkinson, Charles K., Nishapur: Pottery of the Early Islamic Period (1973).

island arc

An island arc is a long, narrow, and usually curved chain of volcanic islands, found in the western Pacific and North Atlantic oceans. In a geographic sense the term refers only to the dry, visible parts of the islands. Geologically, however, a far more extensive feature is referred to, because the geologist is concerned with the underwater roots of these islands. A single island arc consists of a single chain of volcanic islands. Less common, double island arcs have two chains, an outer, often submerged, sedimentary formation and an inner volcanic one.

Island arcs occur where two plates of the lithosphere converge (see PLATE TECTONICS). They are most common at boundaries between oceanic and continental plates, but some, such as the TONGA, the KERMADEC, and the MARIANA ISLANDS, occur between two oceanic plates. At convergent boundaries one of the plates (always the oceanic one) is subducted, or thrust beneath, the other, and it then descends into the mobile upper mantle, or asthenosphere, usually at an angle of 30° to 60°. The subduction zone is marked by a deep sea trench parallel to, but several hundred kilometers oceanward of, the island arc. Subduction, which may occur at rates as high as 10 cm (4 in) per year, creates great earthquakes beneath the inner wall of the trench, where the two plates are in contact.

At a depth of 100 to 150 km (60 to 90 mi), part of the descending lithosphere melts and reacts with the surrounding asthenosphere to form the magma that rises and erupts through the VOLCANOES of the arc. In the region between the arc and trench, marine sediments rapidly accumulate as a result of erosion from the arc and the scraping off of sediments from the oceanic plate as it is subducted.

Although some arcs, such as the Tonga and the Kermadec Islands in the southwest Pacific, are relatively straight, most are curved and always convex towards the subducted oceanic plate side. Within the concave area behind an island arc, a marginal basin may form on the seafloor. The growth of such basins by SEAFLOOR SPREADING creates marginal seas that occupy the area between the arc and the adjacent continental shelf. The BERING SEA, the Sea of OKHOTSK, and the Sea of Japan (see JAPAN, SEA OF), lying behind the Aleutian, Kuril, and Japanese island arcs, respectively (see ALEUTIAN ISLANDS; JAPAN; KURIL ISLANDS; RING OF FIRE), are examples of such seas. These seas may eventually be filled in by volcanic buildup and erosion, and thus extend the continent oceanward. By this or other processes the volcanic arc may eventually occur within the continent, as do the South American ANDES, the Middle Americas arc in Central America, and the CASCADE RANGE of northern California, Oregon, and Washington. Many mountain ranges, such as the SIERRA NEVADA of California, are the remnants of ancient island arcs that are no longer active.

CHRISTOPHER H. SCHOLZ

Bibliography: Sugimura, A., and Uyeda, S., *Island Arcs* (1973); Talwani, Manik, and Pitman, Walter C., eds., *Island Arcs, Deep Sea Trenches and Back-Arc Basins*, vol. 1 (1977).

Isle of Man

The Isle of Man, a crown possession of the United Kingdom, lies in the Irish Sea 48 km (30 mi) west of England. A rocky, indented coast gives way to gentle hills that rise to a maximum height of 620 m (2,034 ft) at Snaefell. The island covers 572 km² (221 mi²). The climate is mild with an average temperature of 8° C (46° F); precipitation averages 1,143 mm (45 in) annually. The population is 60,496 (1976). Douglas, the capital, is the largest town, with a population of 19,897 (1976).

Agriculture (grains and root vegetables), dairying, and sheep raising are important industries, but tourism forms the base of the island's economy. Although under the administration of the British Home Office, the island has its own bicameral legislature, the Court of Tynwald, the world's oldest continuous parliament, which in 1979 celebrated its 1,000th anniversary. The Isle of Man has no income tax, and this has attracted many immigrants from Great Britain.

Inhabited from Neolithic times, the island became a refuge of Irish missionaries after the 5th century. Norsemen took the island during the 9th century and sold it to Scotland in 1266, but since the 14th century it has been held by England. Manx, the indigenous Celtic language, is still spoken by a small minority.

Bibliography: Corran, H. S., *Isle of Man* (1977); Kinvig, R. H., *The Isle of Man: A Social, Cultural, and Political History* (1975).

Isle of Pines

The Isle of Pines (Spanish: Isla de Pinos) lies in the Caribbean Sea, 56 km (35 mi) from Cuba, to which it belongs. It covers an area of 2,227 km² (860 mi²) and has a population of 37,000 (1973 est.). Fishing and citrus farming are the main economic activities. A large prison is located there. Claimed formerly by the United States (1898–1907), it has belonged to Cuba since 1925.

Isle of Wight

The Isle of Wight is an island county off the southern coast of Hampshire, England. Newport is the administrative center. The area is 381 km² (147 mi²), and the population is 111,000 (1978 est.). The Medina, Western Yar, and Eastern Yar rivers cut deeply into its chalk uplands, which reach their greatest height (240 m/787 ft) at Saint Boniface Down. A mild, sunny climate and arable lowlands aid agriculture. Agriculture, shipbuilding, aircraft manufacturing, and tourism are the economic mainstays. The island's points of interest include Bronze Age mounds, monoliths believed to be from the Neolithic period, Roman villas, Quarr Abbey, Carisbrooke Castle, where Charles I was imprisoned (1647–48), and Osborne House, Queen Victoria's seaside home. The resort town of Cowes is famous for its annual yachting regattas.

Bibliography: Wilson, Lawrence P., *Portrait of the Isle of Wight* (1965).

Ismail Pasha   [is-mah-eel' pah'-shuh]

Ismail Pasha, b. Dec. 31, 1830, d. Mar. 2, 1895, ruled Egypt (1863–79) under the suzerainty of the Ottoman Empire, receiving the hereditary title of khedive (viceroy) in 1867. Because of the increased value of the Egyptian cotton crop during the U.S. Civil War, Ismail was able to secure foreign credits for such projects as the completion of the SUEZ CANAL, the extension of Egyptian control over the Sudan, the construction of irrigation facilities, and the modernization of education. His policies led to an enormous foreign debt, however, and in 1875, Ismail was forced to sell his interest in the Suez Canal to Great Britain. Because he refused to cooperate fully with reforms suggested by a French-British Debt Commission, the Ottoman sultanate replaced him in 1879 with his son TAWFIQ PASHA. Ismail's policies had so weakened Egypt financially and politically that Britain was soon able to occupy the country (in 1882) following the outbreak of an Egyptian nationalist revolt.

Bibliography: Crabitès, Pierre, *Ismail: The Maligned Khedive* (1933); Rowlatt, Mary, *Founders of Modern Egypt* (1962).

Ismailis   [is-mah-eel'-eez]

The Ismailis are members of a sect of Muslim SHIITES who recognize Ismail as the seventh and last IMAM until the return of his son at the end of time. They are also called Sabiyah, or Seveners. The sect originated after the death (765) of the sixth Shiite imam, Jafar ibn Muhammad. Most Shiites accepted his younger son, Musa al-Kazim, as his successor; the Ismailis were those who supported his older, disinherited son, Ismail. The sect attained its greatest influence under the FATIMIDS, who claimed descent through Ismail's son from FATIMA, daughter of the Prophet Muhammad. This dynasty, established in Tunis in 908, ruled in Egypt from 969 to 1171. Late in the 11th century a split occurred between the Mustalis, who recognized al-Mustali as the caliph-imam (concentrated in Egypt, Yemen, and India), and the Nizaris, named for Mustali's brother Nizar, with strongholds in Iran and Syria. The latter, who became known as the ASSASSINS in Crusader stories, remained in power until the late 13th century. A subsection, under the AGA KHAN, moved to India in 1840.

In their interpretation of the Koran, the Ismailis distinguish between exoteric and esoteric knowledge, that is, between knowledge for the public and knowledge for the initiated. The same distinction finds organizational expression in the Ismaili hierarchy from the imam, who alone has perfect knowledge, by way of the *dais* (missionaries) to the believers at various levels of knowledge and insight.   WILLEM A. BIJLEFELD

Bibliography: Lewis, Bernard, *The Assassins* (1967) and *The Origins of Ismā'īlism* (1940).

See also: DRUZES; ISLAM.

Isocrates   [y-sahk'-ruh-teez]

Isocrates, 436–338 BC, was a Greek teacher of rhetoric and political philosophy. In Athens he opened (*c*.393 BC) the first permanent institution of higher education in the liberal arts. Isocrates' younger contemporaries, the philosophers Plato and Aristotle, regarded him as a superficial and misguided SOPHIST, but he trained many leaders of 4th-century Greece, including the general Timotheus and the historians Ephorus and Theopompus. He published a series of pamphlets in oratorical form, setting forth his moral and political ideas; these contributed to the definition of HELLENISM, or Greek culture, and helped make the training of an orator the goal of ancient education.

Isocrates' works were elaborated with great care, but achieved smoothness of style at the expense of vigor of expression. The *Panegyricus* (380 BC), in which Isocrates urged the Greeks to accept Athenian leadership in a campaign against Persia, is the most famous of his works. Later, in the *Philippus* (346 BC), Isocrates urged Philip of Macedon to assume leadership in the continuing struggle against Persia. Of Isocrates' orations, 21 are extant.   GEORGE KENNEDY

Bibliography: Isocrates, *Orations*, 3 vols., trans. by George Norlin and La Rue Van Hook (1945); Jaeger, Werner, *Paideia*, vol. 3, trans. by Gilbert Highet (1944); Kennedy, George, *The Art of Persuasion in Greece* (1963).

isoelectric point   [y-soh-ee-lek'-trik]

When dissolved in water, macromolecules such as protein or DNA may have a net positive or negative electrical charge. The charge, which depends on the pH (degree of acidity) of the solution, can be neutralized, or even reversed, by adjusting the pH. The isoelectric point of a substance is the pH of a solution at which the macromolecule has no net charge. The significance of the isoelectric point is that an uncharged molecule will not migrate when an electrical field is applied (a separation technique known as ELECTROPHORESIS). The isoelectric point thus helps chemists identify and purify the substance.   JOHN T. NETTERVILLE

Bibliography: Stryer, Lubert, *Biochemistry* (1975).

isohyet   [y'-soh-hy-uht]

An isohyet is a line on a weather map connecting points with equal rainfall or snowfall during a given time period. Isohyets are prepared for individual storms (to aid in flood prevention), for days (including daytime versus nighttime comparisons), and for rainy seasons. Isohyets are also used on world maps to indicate annual wet, dry, and intermediate rain regimes. Orientation of mountain ridges and valleys and the height of mountains result in very complex precipitation patterns. The construction of safe reservoirs and dams requires the careful use of isohyets for accurate watershed evaluation.   HERBERT RIEHL

isolationism

Isolationism is a foreign policy by which a nation deliberately makes no permanent alliances or commitments and tries to avoid all involvement beyond its borders. The term is most closely identified with the foreign policy of the United States from the American Revolution to World War II.

In an effort to secure independence from foreign intervention and to achieve a sense of national unity, the founders of the United States warned against the disruptive influences of attachments to European countries by U.S. citizens. George Washington asked in his Farewell Address in 1796: "Why, by interweaving our destiny with that of any part of Europe, entangle our peace and prosperity in the toils of European ambition, rivalship, interest, humor, or caprice? It is our true policy to steer clear of permanent alliances with any portion of the foreign world . . . we may safely trust to temporary alliances for extraordinary emergencies." The MONROE DOCTRINE (1823) reaffirmed America's intention not to interfere in European affairs and cautioned the nations of Europe not to intervene in the Western Hemisphere.

The United States could pursue an isolationist policy because of special circumstances that existed during the 19th century. An ocean was an effective barrier to the powerful nations of Europe, the British navy was interested in maintaining freedom of the seas, and the European powers were embroiled in their own affairs. The U.S. government, therefore, saw no contradiction between an isolationist policy toward Europe and a policy of expansion in the Western Hemisphere and even outward to Asia.

American isolationism was breached in 1898 by the Spanish-American War and again by World War I. After that war, the United States reverted to a policy of isolationism, only to have it shattered by World War II and its aftermath, when U.S. power and the changes that occurred in the world situation made it difficult for the country to remain aloof from foreign commitments.   RITA J. IMMERMAN

Bibliography: Bemis, Samuel Flagg, *A Diplomatic History of the United States*, 5th ed. (1965); Bemis, Samuel Flagg, and Griffin, G. G., *A Guide to the Diplomatic History of the U.S., 1775–1921* (1935); Strauss, Wallace P., *Isolation and Involvement: An Interpretive History of American Diplomacy* (1972).

isomer   [y'-suh-mur]

If a particular chemical formula or composition represents two or more distinct compounds, each is called an isomer. Although the term was first used by the German chemist Jöns Jakob Berzelius for organic molecules, isomerism also exists in inorganic compounds, such as complexes (see COMPLEX, chemistry).

Chain isomerism exists among the alkanes, or molecules possessing a chain of carbon atoms, because the chain may be straight or branched. Although the properties of isomers of a given formula are similar, the compounds are nonetheless distinct.

Position isomerism occurs because not all hydrogen atoms in a molecule are equivalent. The substitution of another element for one of these hydrogens or the loss of adjacent pairs to form multiple bonds at more than one possible location can give rise to isomeric structures. Thus, propyl alcohol (C_3H_7OH) can be either of two types, one with the hydroxyl group (OH) attached to a terminal carbon atom and the other in which it is attached to the middle carbon. A substituted benzene ring, such as toluene ($C_6H_5CH_3$), can add another substituent to any of the other five carbon atoms; because two pairs are equivalent, there are only three possible isomers, ortho, meta, and para. The location of the double bond in ALKENES and the triple bond in ALKYNES determines another form of positional isomerism.

Functional group isomerism refers to compounds whose class cannot be determined from the formula alone. The formula C_3H_8O may be either an ETHER or either of the two propyl alcohols. The same is true for formulas indicating an unsaturated hydrocarbon, which may represent an alkyne, a diene, an allene, or a cyclic compound.

Geometric isomerism refers to molecules in which the atoms are attached in the same order but have different spatial relationships. CIS-TRANS ISOMERISM, common in alkenes, refers to asymmetry across the double bond. The important study of optical isomerism is discussed under STEREOCHEMISTRY.   STEPHEN FLEISHMAN

See also: CONFIGURATION.

isometric system   [y-suh-met'-rik]

CRYSTALS belong to the isometric system if they have three mutually perpendicular axes of equal length. Five symmetry classes exist in this system. Crystals in this system must have at least 4 threefold symmetry axes. The most symmetric class—the hexoctahedral—under this system contains a center of symmetry, 3 fourfold symmetry axes (coincident with the crystallographic axes), 4 threefold symmetry axes (body diagonals), and 6 twofold symmetry axes (between the centers of the cube edges). The isometric class containing the fewest symmetry elements—the tetartoidal—possesses only the 4 threefold symmetry axes and 3 twofold symmetry axes that are coincident with the crystallographic axes.

Only crystals in the isometric system are isotropic; that is, their physical properties do not vary according to crystallographic direction. Isotropic minerals thus have a single index of refraction and appear dark when viewed with crossed Nicols in the polarizing MICROSCOPE (see OPTICAL MINERALOGY). Consequently, identification of isotropic minerals usually rests on their optical properties in reflected rather than transmitted light.

Common minerals occuring in the isometric system include COPPER, DIAMONDS, GARNETS, GOLD, HALITE (common salt), and PYRITE.   JOAN FITZPATRICK

isometrics

Isometrics is a method of exercise in which stress is created in stationary muscles. Isometrics may be performed by pushing or pulling an immovable object or by contracting or tightening opposing flexor and extensor muscles. Most exercises, such as calisthenics, running, or swimming, involve muscle tension through a range of movements and are called isotonics. The advantages of isometric exercise are that no specialized equipment is required and that only a few minutes each day are needed to produce noticeable results.

The benefits of isometric exercise are limited because each exercise only affects one specific point in the range of a muscle's movement; a regimen of isometrics fails to develop stamina, quickness, or flexibility. Some critics of isometrics contend that these exercises contribute to weight gain, muscle hypertrophy, and stiffness. In order to attain all-around physical fitness, isometrics should be combined with running, isotonic exercise, and other vigorous exercises.

isomorph   [y′-soh-mohrf]

Isomorphs are two or more compounds that have similar chemical composition and crystal structures. Atoms of similar size can replace one another in the crystal structure, often forming a complete isomorphous, or SOLID-SOLUTION, series with a continuous chemical variation from one pure compound to the other. Notable examples of isomorphs include the ARSENATE, FELDSPAR, and vanadate minerals, the ARAGONITE and CALCITE groups of carbonate minerals, the BARITE group of sulfate minerals, the SPINEL group of oxide minerals, and the APATITE group of phosphate minerals.

See also: PARAMORPH; POLYMORPH; PSEUDOMORPH.

isomorphism   [y-soh-mohr′-fizm]

An isomorphism is a one-to-one correspondence between two mathematical objects, systems, or sets. Such a correspondence shows that their mathematical structures are essentially the same. The concept of isomorphism is basic to much of modern mathematics. Although it arose in connection with algebraic systems such as FIELDS, RINGS, and groups, its usefulness has been extended to other branches of mathematics. Isomorphic systems have identical structure, even if they have completely different types of elements or a different order of elements; therefore, such systems cannot be distinguished from any abstract point of view. Although the elements of two isomorphic systems are in a one-to-one correspondence, they are not necessarily identical: the set consisting of the fingers on the right hand is isomorphic to, but not identical with, the set of fingers on the left hand.   AVNER ASH

Bibliography: Adler, Irving, *Groups in the New Mathematics* (1967).

See also: GROUP THEORY; SET THEORY.

isoniazid: see ANTIBIOTICS.

isopod   [y′-suh-pahd]

Isopods are members of the order Isopoda in the class Crustacea. The order includes about 4,000 species, most of which are marine, some of which live in fresh water, and some of which (pill bugs and wood lice) are the most successful of the few terrestrial crustaceans. Most isopods are 5 to 15 mm (0.2 to 0.6 in) long, but *Bathynomus giganteus* may exceed 36 cm (14 in). The body of an isopod is usually flat from top to bottom, with a shieldlike head region, unstalked eyes, and various paired appendages on the thorax and abdomen. These appendages are used for locomotion, respiration, and repro-

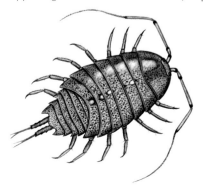

The rock slater, Ligia oceanica, *is a European wood louse. It is representative of Isopods, an order of terrestrial crustaceans. Isopods generally lack an outer shell and have a segmented, flattened body and seven pairs of legs.*

duction; the foremost pair (the maxillipeds) is used for feeding.

The majority of isopods are free-swimming, omnivorous scavengers. Quite a few are parasitic and may be found in the gill chambers of shrimp, on the skin or in the mouths of fish, or in similar sites. Their mouthparts have been modified into piercing appendages for sucking blood and body fluids. Many terrestrial forms contain the enzyme cellulase or cellulose-digesting bacteria in their gut to aid in the digestion of wood and bark.

The terrestrial wood lice have successfully invaded a number of land habitats but still must prevent drying out in order to survive. They usually live in damp or protected habitats, such as beneath stones or in bark or leaf mold. Most are nocturnal and avoid light and are able to detect small changes in humidity.

Bibliography: Schultz, George A., *How to Know the Marine Isopod Crustaceans* (1969).

isoprene   [y′-suh-preen]

Isoprene is a five-carbon conjugated diene; it is of industrial importance because it is the basic chemical unit of natural rubber. Thus it is the major ingredient used to make certain types of synthetic RUBBER and other elastomers. Isoprene does not occur in nature in monomeric form but is widespread in multiples of the C_5H_8 unit, which are known as TERPENES. Common terpenes include phytol, menthol, the carotenoids (vitamin A), and the sterols (cholesterol).

$$CH_2{=}\overset{\overset{\textstyle CH_3}{\textstyle |}}{C}{-}CH{=}CH_2 \quad \text{isoprene}$$

Isoptera   [y-sahp′-tur-uh]

Isoptera is the insect order comprising the TERMITES. Cockroaches, of the order Orthoptera, are believed to be the most closely related insect species. Termites are superficially similar to ants and usually live in and eat wood. They digest the wood cellulose with the aid of protozoans, and sometimes bacteria, in their digestive tracts.

isostasy   [y-sahs′-tuh-see]

Isostasy is a condition of balance that exists between different portions of the Earth's crust. The lighter rocks of the crust float on the heavier, plastic rocks of the mantle and either rise relatively higher or sink relatively lower, depending on their density and volume. Mountain chains, for example, are composed of large volumes of rocks of relatively low density that therefore rise to great heights. As this large volume is eroded away, the mountain chain continues to rise, at a progressively lower rate and to successively lesser heights, until both the root—the large volume of low-density rock below the land surface—and the mountain have been entirely consumed. The Himalayas have a large volume of material beneath them; the root of the Appalachians, on the other hand, has almost disappeared.

Continents have formed because their crust is generally lighter and thicker than oceanic crust and therefore rises to a higher level. The weight of a large temporary mass of material, such as glacial ice, may cause a portion of the crust to sink. When the mass is removed—by melting, for instance, if it is glacial ice—the continent rises back up, or rebounds. Most portions of the northern hemisphere that were covered by glacial ice during the last ice age (the Pleistocene glaciation) are still rebounding today, 10,000 years after the ice melted.   R. D. HATCHER, JR.

See also: EARTH, STRUCTURE AND COMPOSITION OF.

isotherm   [y′-soh-thurm]

An isotherm is a line that connects points that have the same temperature at a given instant or have the same average temperature over a certain period of time. Such a line may be drawn on a horizontal map of land or sea; on a vertical section through the atmosphere, the ocean, or a portion of the Earth; or on a thermodynamic diagram.

Isothermal maps are now used primarily to estimate temperatures at various locations. Consequently, a former practice of converting the cooler temperatures of plateaus and mountain regions to sea-level equivalents, by use of an average lapse rate, is now waning. ARNOLD COURT

Bibliography: Barry, R. G., and Perry, A. H., *Synoptic Climatology: Methods and Applications* (1973).

isothermal process [y-soh-thurm'-ul]

In thermodynamics, an isothermal process involves heat or energy transfer in which a system's temperature remains constant. A common isothermal process is the boiling of water, which occurs at 100° C (212° F). An ideal gas undergoing an isothermal process reacts according to Boyle's law, in which the product of the gas pressure and volume remains constant. In addition to isothermal processes, many other constant-property processes are important in thermodynamics. For example, isobaric processes occur at constant pressure, isochoric processes at constant volume, and isentropic processes at constant entropy. GARY S. SETTLES

isotope [y'-suh-tohp]

The term *isotope* (from the Greek word meaning "same place") defines atoms that have the same number of protons but a different number of neutrons; that is, they are atoms of the same element that have different masses. Their atomic number (proton number) is the same, but their mass numbers (the total number of protons and neutrons in the nucleus) vary. Lighter elements tend to possess fewer isotopes (hydrogen has 3), while heavier elements tend to have more isotopes (polonium has 27). Several ways of denoting isotopes are used; ^3_1H, ^3H, H^3, and hydrogen-3 all symbolize TRITIUM, a radioactive isotope of hydrogen that has one proton and two neutrons. The superscript indicates the mass number; the subscript denotes the atomic number.

Types of Isotopes. There are two major types of isotopes, stable and unstable. Stable isotopes do not undergo radioactive decay, but rather persist in nature. Unstable isotopes—radioisotopes or radionuclides—undergo radioactive decay toward a more energetically stable form.

Stable isotopes, of which there are approximately 280, make up most of the natural elements of the Earth. The major component of an element is usually one stable isotope accompanied by minor amounts of other stable and unstable isotopes. Sometimes an element, such as chlorine, is composed of more than one stable isotope in quantity; therefore, certain elements may have several atomic masses that differ greatly. Twenty-one elements have only one isotope, and therefore consist of only one kind of atom.

Radioisotopes are of two major types, natural and artificial. Natural radioisotopes, of which there are only 25, were formed during the creation of the Earth; the only radioisotopes left from that time are those which decay very slowly. New radioisotopes are constantly being created; some are members of a decay series in which unstable isotopes decay to other unstable isotopes until a stable isotope is reached, and some are produced continuously in the Earth's atmosphere by cosmic-ray bombardment. The rate of decay of these types of isotopes has reached an equilibrium with their rate of formation. Tritium (^3H) is an example of a rapidly decaying isotope, while carbon-14 is an example of a more slowly decaying radioisotope produced in this fashion. Both are formed by the cosmic-ray bombardment of nitrogen-14.

Synthesis of Isotopes. Artificial production of radioisotopes was first achieved in 1934 when Frédéric and Irène Curie-Joliot converted aluminum-27 into phosphorus-30. More than 1,800 artificial radioisotopes have been produced since 1934 using several techniques based on the bombardment of stable nuclei with various particles. A new isotope is formed with an accompanying ejection of nuclear particles and/or the emission of electromagnetic radiation.

Particle ACCELERATORS generate high-energy particles that cause nuclear transformations of stable elements. Examples are the linear accelerator and the cyclotron. NUCLEAR REACTORS cause nuclear transformations by direct neutron bombardment. Fission of uranium-235 yields as final products molybdenum-95, lanthanum-139, two neutrons, and about 200 MeV of thermal energy. The neutrons then interact with other uranium nuclei, creating new radioisotopes. Other neutron sources such as radium-beryllium sources and neutron generators have also been used in the production of new radioisotopes. Neutron generators, which are portable, economical, and versatile, are of two types: positive-ion bombardment, which releases neutrons, and electron bombardment.

The most popular method of isotopic separation is gaseous diffusion. Since isotopes differ slightly in mass, they diffuse at slightly different rates. The lighter isotopes concentrate and can eventually be purified. Separation can also be achieved by other methods, including chemical exchange, evaporation, and electromagnetic interaction.

Applications. Many uses have been found for isotopes, both industrially and scientifically. Industrial applications include the synthesis of ethyl bromide from hydrogen bromide and ethylene using cobalt-60 gamma radiation, polymerization cross-linking with beta or gamma radiation, vulcanization of rubber, and curing or hardening of paint films. DEUTERIUM (^2H), a stable isotope of hydrogen, is used in the preparation of heavy water (deuterium oxide), which is used to moderate nuclear reactors. Other applications include liquid-flow monitoring, mechanical-wear analysis, X-ray analysis, age-dating in water sources, thickness gauging, and food sterilization.

Research applications of isotopes are numerous, with ^{14}C, ^{13}C, ^2H, ^3H, ^{15}N, and others used in biological tracer experiments. Cobalt-60 is used in radiation therapy of tumors, and iodine-131 in hyperthyroid treatment as well as other medical uses. In analytical chemistry, activation analysis is performed by neutron irradiation of a sample, which converts a particular element in the sample to a known radioisotope. Measurement of the radioactivity provides an accurate and precise quantitation of the original element under analysis.
RONALD D. JOHNSON

Bibliography: Duncan, James F., and Cook, G. B., *Isotopes in Chemistry* (1968); Hendree, W. R., *Radioactive Isotopes in Biological Research* (1973); Lederer, Michael C., et al., *A Table of Isotopes*, 6th ed. (1967); Romer, Alfred, *Radiochemistry and the Discovery of Isotopes* (1970); Weast, R. C., ed., *Handbook of Chemistry and Physics*, 58th ed. (1977).

See also: RADIOACTIVITY; TRANSMUTATION OF ELEMENTS.

isotopic tracer: see NUCLEAR MEDICINE.

Isozaki Arata [ee-soh-zah'-kee ah-rah'-tah]

The avant-garde architect Isozaki Arata, b. 1931, has demonstrated in a series of important Japanese public buildings his imaginative mastery and synthesis of various Western and Japanese influences. After working (1954–63) in Kenzo TANGE's office, Isozaki opened his own atelier in 1963. His early works (the Oita Prefectural Library, 1966, and the initial portion of the Oita Medical Center, 1960), executed in roughly cast coarse concrete, were composed of large-scale horizontal and vertical forms reminiscent of traditional Japanese timber-beam architecture. More recently, simple geometric volumes have dominated his designs. The sleek aluminum Gunma Prefectorial Museum of Fine Arts (1974) in central Honshu is composed of a system of cubes; semicircular vaults reminiscent of 18th-century Parisian toll houses surmount the Kitakyushu Central Library (1975), Fukuoko, and the Fushimi Country Clubhouse, Kyoto.

Bibliography: Boyd, Robin, *New Directions in Japanese Architecture* (1968); Ross, Michael Franklin, *Beyond Metabolism: The New Japanese Architecture* (1978).

Israel

The State of Israel, an independent nation in southwest Asia, is located between the eastern shores of the Mediterranean Sea and the head of the Gulf of AQABA, an arm of the Red

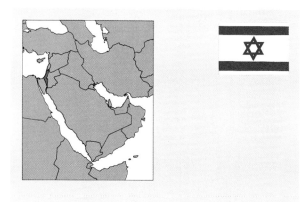

ISRAEL

Official Name: State of Israel
Capital and Largest City: Jerusalem (1976 est. pop.,
355,500)
Area: 20,701 km² (7,993 mi²)
Elevation: *Highest*—Mount Meron, 1,208 m (3,963 ft);
lowest—Dead Sea, 396 m (1,300 ft) below sea level
Population: 3,712,000 (1979 est.). *Distribution*—85% urban, 15% rural; *density*, 179 persons per km² (464 per
mi²); *annual rate of increase* (1970-77), 2.8%
Principal Languages: Hebrew, Arabic, English
Principal Religions: Judaism, Islam, Christianity
Principal Products: *Agriculture*—citrus fruits, vegeta-
bles, beef and dairy products, poultry products.
Manufacturing and industry—food products; textiles;
chemicals; metal products; rubber; electrical equip-
ment; machinery; plastics; diamond cutting. *Min-
ing*—potash, phosphate rock
Railroads: 783 km/486 mi (1976)
Roads: 4459 km/2769 mi (1978 paved)
Currency: 1 shekel = 100 agorot

Sea. Israel was established on May 14, 1948, as a Jewish state
on land that had been part of the British mandate for PALES-
TINE. Historically, it is considered the Holy Land for Christians,
Jews, and Muslims.

Since 1948, Israel has fought four wars with its Arab neighbors, who refused to recognize the State of Israel. At the end
of the first war (1949) Israel occupied substantially more territory than had been allocated in the 1947 United Nations plan
that partitioned Palestine into two states: one Jewish and one
Arab. The eastern and northern quarters of JERUSALEM, the
WEST BANK of the Jordan River, the GAZA STRIP, SINAI, and the
Golan Heights were brought under Israeli control as a result
of the war of 1967. By the terms of a peace treaty signed with
Egypt in 1979, Israel is to return all of Sinai to Egypt. Despite a
history dominated by hostilities, in little more than three decades of existence Israel has transformed its land and developed a modern, technologically advanced, and highly urbanized society.

LAND
Israel and the Israeli-occupied West Bank of the Jordan extend southward along the Mediterranean shore of Asia,
412 km (256 mi) to ELAT at the head of the Gulf of Aqaba.
Together they extend inland for about 100 km (63 mi) to the
Rift Valley. The Rift Valley is a continuation of Africa's Great
Rift Valley and is occupied in part, from north to south, by
the Hula Valley (Lake Hula was drained in the 1950s); the Sea
of GALILEE, which lies 209 m (676 ft) below sea level; the JOR-
DAN RIVER; and the DEAD SEA, with the world's lowest land elevation (−396 m/ − 1,300 ft). The Araba Valley occupies the
rift between the Dead Sea and the Red Sea to the south. The
Rift Valley is associated with ancient volcanic rocks and hot
springs.

The southern half of Israel west of the Rift Valley, mostly

The Golan Heights, on the border between Syria and Israel, rise above the eastern edge of the Great Rift Valley, a huge fault extending from the Middle East into East Africa. During the Six-Day War of 1967, Syrian artillery situated on the heights battered Israeli territory in the surrounding lowlands. The strategic mountains were seized in an armored assault and remained in Israel's possession until 1974.

desert, is known as the NEGEV. North of the Negev, occupying most of Israel and the West Bank, is a mountainous region. The mountains rise to 1,208 m (3,963 ft) on Mount Meron, located in the far north near Safad, and have an average elevation of 600 m (2,000 ft). The mountains are divided by the northwest-southeast trending Plain of ESDRAELON that extends from HAIFA to Beth Shean on the edge of the Rift Valley. North of Esdraelon are the hills of Galilee; to the south, partly in the West Bank area, are Samaria and Judea.

The Dead Sea (so named because of its extreme salinity) is considered the location of the biblical settlements of Sodom and Gomorrah. In 1947 the oldest surviving biblical manuscripts, the Dead Sea Scrolls, were discovered in the nearby caves of Qumran.

The principal lowland is a narrow coastal plain, 5 to 15 km (3 to 9 mi) wide, along the shores of the Mediterranean Sea. North of Haifa it is known as the Plain of Zebulun; between Haifa and TEL AVIV it forms the Plain of SHARON; and south of Tel Aviv, the Plain of Judea.

Soils. The steeper mountain slopes that cover much of Israel have been severely eroded and are mostly barren. The best soils are alluvial, found in the Hula, Jordan, and Kishon valleys and the Plain of Esdraelon. The soils of the coastal plain are fertile but sandy, requiring large quantities of water and fertilizer to be productive. Terra rossa soils, found in many upland limestone areas, tend to be shallow, stony, and suitable only for pasture and nonmechanized farming. Only 20% of the total land area is arable, and 40% of this is irrigated.

Climate. Israel's climate is Mediterranean in the north and arid in the south. In summer the entire area is dominated by a subtropical high that brings cloudless skies and no precipitation. In winter, the southern half of the country remains under the subtropical high, but weather in the northern half is influenced by cyclonic depressions that pass over the Mediterranean, bringing moderate rainfall. Precipitation in the north averages 700 mm (28 in), falling primarily from October to March. Rainfall amounts diminish rapidly to the south. Be-

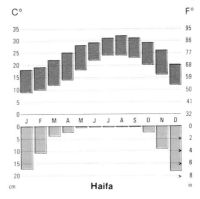

Bars indicate monthly ranges of temperatures (red) and precipitation (blue) in Haifa, one of Israel's principal seaports. Haifa has a Mediterranean climate.

The adjoining Mediterranean cities of Tel Aviv, which was founded by Jews from Jaffa in 1909, and the ancient port of Jaffa merged in 1950 to form Israel's largest urban center. The promontory on which the old section of Jaffa is situated appears in the background.

yond BEERSHEBA and GAZA desert conditions predominate.

Average summer temperatures range between 18° and 32° C (65° and 90° F) over most of the country. Winters are mild, with temperatures averaging 14° C (57° F) along the coast and 9° C (48° F) in the mountains. The Rift Valley is about 9° C (15° F) warmer than the rest of the nation during the winter. The Dead Sea area is one of the hottest regions in the world.

Drainage. Israel's most important river is the Jordan, 200 km (120 mi) long. Its principal tributary is the Yarmuk. The only other permanent rivers are the 32-km-long (20-mi) Yarkon and part of the 43-km-long (27-mi) Kishon, both of which flow to the Mediterranean. Other water courses are usually dry and hold water only after heavy rainfall. The waters of the Sea of Galilee are fresh; those of the Dead Sea are saltier than the ocean and rich in minerals.

In addition, Israel has large groundwater resources. The National Water Carrier distributes groundwater and water from the Sea of Galilee by way of the Kinneret-Negev Conduit, as far south as Beersheba.

Natural Vegetation and Wildlife. Little remains of Israel's natural vegetation and indigenous animal life. The natural forest cover had already disappeared in ancient times, but recent reforestation of the uplands has covered 550 km² (211 mi²) with new forests consisting mainly of pine trees. Wildlife, too, is being restored through protective laws and the establishment of animal preserves for migrating birds, deer, and gazelles.

Resources. Israel has no deposits of coal, only small deposits of petroleum and natural gas, and no rivers suitable for the generation of hydroelectric power. Copper ore mining at Timna has been abandoned. Israel's principal minerals are potash, produced by evaporation of Dead Sea water; phosphates; and limestone.

PEOPLE

Israel was established in 1948 as a homeland for Jews, and the Jewish population now forms 85% of the total within the 1949 borders. Of these, Jews born in Israel, known as *Sabras*, account for 48%, and immigrants, *Olim*, 52%. The immigrants come from many different national backgrounds. Those from

the urbanized societies of Europe and North America constitute 27% of the total population. Immigrants from the predominantly Islamic culture areas of Asia and North Africa, who constitute 25% of the total population, often face problems of adjustment to Israel's democratic and technologically advanced society. The non-Jewish population consists mainly of Arabs, who make up 14% of the total population, and DRUZES, who account for 1.2%. Both groups are concentrated in Galilee, and Arabs constitute a majority in the territories occupied since 1967.

Language. The official languages of Israel are Hebrew and Arabic. The great majority of Jews speak Hebrew in public, but in their homes use their native tongue. English is widely used as a second language.

Religion. Freedom of religion and the inviolability of the holy places and centers of worship for all religions is guaranteed by law. For the Jewish population, supreme religious authority is vested in the Chief Rabbinate, made up of a chief rabbi from the ASHKENAZIM and one from the SEPHARDIM, along with the Supreme Rabbinical Council. Small Jewish minorities who reject the rabbinic tradition and law include about 12,000 KARAITES, who live in the vicinity of Ramla near Tel Aviv, and about 500 SAMARITANS living in Holon and Nablus.

Israel's Arab minority is 75% Muslim and 25% Christian. Also followers of Islam are the CIRCASSIANS, a small group brought to the region in the 19th century from the Caucasus and now concentrated in the Galilee villages of Kafr Kama and Rehaniya. The Druzes broke away from Islam in the 11th century and practice their own secret religion. Israel is also the center of the BAHA'I faith.

Demography. The population density in Israel is one of the highest in the world, if the Negev is excluded. It is also one of the world's most highly urbanized nations, with 85% of the total population living in urban centers. The three largest cities are Jerusalem, Tel Aviv, and Haifa. About 9% of the Jewish population live in rural areas, but these rural settlements play a major role in Israeli life. Approximately 4% of the country's population live in 349 cooperative villages, called *moshavim*; about 3% live in 235 collective villages called *kibbutzim* (singular, KIBBUTZ), operated on a communal basis. In addition, there are 56 *moshavot* based on private enterprise. A very small minority live in 28 *moshavim shittuphiyim* where production is based on a communal effort as in the kibbutz, but households remain private units. In 1979, 629,000 Arabs

Two farmers work in a field covered with sheets of plastic in Upper Galilee. Although this area in northern Israel receives more rain than most of the country, some valuable crops require the plastic covering to reduce the amount of water lost from the soil through evaporation.

High-rise apartment complexes ring the old city of Jerusalem, the capital of Israel. The city, which was partitioned between Jordan and Israel from 1948 until 1967, is regarded as holy by three monotheistic faiths—Judaism, Christianity, and Islam.

and 5,000 Jews lived in the occupied West Bank area.

The population is increasing twice as rapidly among the non-Jews as among Jews. Immigration was a factor in the rapid increase of the Jewish population before 1970, but the increase was virtually balanced by emigration toward the end of the 1970s. In 1977 the birthrate was 23.3 per 1,000 for Jews and 39.8 per 1,000 for non-Jews; the death rate was 7.7 per 1,000.

Education and Health. Israel ranks among the world's most highly developed nations in providing educational and health services. Education is free and compulsory between the ages of 5 and 15; parental income determines fees for children attending postprimary schools. Higher education is provided in the Technion-Israel Institute of Technology (1912) in Haifa and at five universities, including the Hebrew University of Jerusalem (1918). The Weizmann Institute of Science in Rehovoth is a major scientific research center.

In 1975, Israel had 129 hospitals, containing more than 23,000 beds. Health-care costs for the overwhelming majority of the population were covered by health-insurance programs. Major communicable diseases are under control, and the death rate is one of the lowest in Asia. The infant mortality rate is 23 per 1,000 live births.

The Arts. One of Israel's greatest cultural achievements is its revival of the HEBREW LANGUAGE, which has been adapted for modern use with the aid of Jerusalem's Academy for the Hebrew Language, founded in 1953. Modern Israeli literature is now written in Hebrew, and all plays performed are either translated into or originally written in Hebrew (see HEBREW AND YIDDISH LITERATURE). Israeli architects are working to develop a national style and design. For about 25 years the German Bauhaus style was emulated, but the strongest influence is the style of Israeli architect Moshe Savdi, creator of Habitat (in Montreal). The Israel Philharmonic Orchestra enjoys world renown. Five other orchestras and many choral and chamber music groups are active in the country. Archaeology is pursued not only by professionals but also by amateurs as a hobby. Many relics are housed in the nation's museums, especially the Israel Museum in Jerusalem.

ECONOMIC ACTIVITY
In the early years immediately following independence, resources were scarce and rationing was imposed. Real economic growth did not occur until the second half of the 1950s as overseas capital became available for investment. From that time until 1973 the gross national product grew at an annual rate of 10%. After 1973 its growth rate declined to only 1% per year, and the economy was adversely affected by inflation, currency devaluations, the world petroleum crisis, and military expenditures.

The Histadrut, the General Federation of Labor in Israel, is the nation's largest organization with voluntary membership. It supervises the health service and maintains large interests in all sectors of the economy.

Manufacturing and Mining. By 1977, 23% of the labor force was employed in mining and manufacturing. Tel Aviv and Haifa are the principal manufacturing centers, but industrial facilities are dispersed throughout the nation. The major industries are food processing and the manufacture of textiles, chemicals, fertilizers, machinery, electrical goods, and electronic and precision equipment. Diamond cutting and polishing is the principal export-oriented industry.

Mining is not economically significant. The principal mineral product is potash, extracted from the Dead Sea. Small natural gas deposits are worked at the southern end of the Dead Sea, and small quantities of crude petroleum, supplying less than 1% of national consumption, are produced in the Heletz region southeast of Ashqelon.

Energy. Israel is totally dependent on petroleum for its energy needs. Most was imported through the port of Elat and piped from there to Ashqelon, and then on to refineries at Haifa and Ashdod. This source dried up with the revolution in Iran. In 1978 installed electrical capacity was 2.8 million kW, and production reached 13.5 billion kW h. The major centers for generation of electricity are Haifa, Tel Aviv, and Ashdod.

Agriculture, Forestry, and Fishing. Only 6% of the labor force is engaged in agriculture, forestry, and fishing. The amount of land cultivated and irrigated has steadily increased since 1948, primarily through creation of new communal and collective settlements.

Poultry and dairy farming have also expanded, along with increased output of citrus, olives, grapes, cotton, vegetables, and flowers. Citrus, especially Jaffa oranges, and early vegetables and flowers are important export items. Forestry is commercially insignificant, but reforestation is actively promoted in the interest of soil and groundwater conservation. Fishing in the immediate area is of minor importance.

Transportation. All transportation facilities are state controlled. Rail transportation is poorly developed, and none of the country's waterways are navigable. Accordingly, most passenger and freight traffic moves by road. Israel's two ports on the Mediterranean are Haifa and Ashdod; Elat serves as the port for the Red Sea and Indian Ocean. El-Al, the Israeli airline, flies from Ben-Gurion Airport near Tel Aviv, the principal international airport. Domestic flights are operated by Arkia Israel Inland Airlines.

Communications. The Israeli government controls the broadcasting industry of the country, consisting of 24 radio and 15 television stations, plus an instructional television system.

Newspaper publishing is limited to Tel Aviv and Jerusalem. The four dailies headquartered in Jerusalem are printed in languages other than Hebrew. Tel Aviv has 18 dailies, 11 of which are in Hebrew. The remaining seven are each printed in a different foreign language.

Trade. Israel's imports usually exceed exports in value. The deficit is made up in part by revenues from tourism, financial aid, and foreign investment. Diamonds are the leading export, followed by manufactured goods, chemicals, and citrus. The principal imports are machinery, crude petroleum and petroleum products, uncut diamonds from South Africa, food, iron and steel, and chemicals. Israel enjoys special trading privileges in the EUROPEAN ECONOMIC COMMUNITY (EEC), and most trade takes place with its members and the United States.

GOVERNMENT

Israel is a parliamentary democracy, with legislative powers vested in the Knesset, a unicameral parliament of 120 members elected for 4-year terms, pending dissolution. The cabinet, which holds executive power, is chosen by the prime minister. No constitution has yet been adopted, but a number of basic laws serve together as the fundamental law. All citizens over the age of 18 are eligible to vote. Votes are cast for national lists of candidates submitted by each of the political parties. Usually more than 10 political parties are successful in an election, and the governments are based on coalitions. Until 1968 the Mapai party dominated Israeli politics, led by David BEN-GURION, Moshe SHARETT, and Levi ESHKOL. In 1968, Mapai merged with Rafi and Achdur Avoda to form the Labor party. The new party remained dominant under Golda MEIR and Yitzhak RABIN until 1977, when Likud, a coalition of rightwing parties led by the Heruth (Freedom) party came to power under Menachim BEGIN. The president is head of state, a position of high prestige but limited constitutional power. The president is elected for 5 years and may be reelected. Israel's presidents have included Chaim WEIZMANN, Itzhak BEN-ZVI, Zalman Shazar, Ephraim Katzir, and, since 1978, Yitzhak Navon.

Israel is divided administratively into six districts: Central, Haifa, Jerusalem, Northern, Southern, and Tel Aviv. Local government consists of 31 municipal corporations, 115 local councils, and 49 regional councils. Local officials are elected for 4-year terms.

HISTORY

The modern state of Israel was established in territory that had been granted as a League of Nations mandate to Britain following World War I. The creation of a Jewish homeland was an objective of ZIONISM, a movement that developed politically in the 19th century. In the BALFOUR DECLARATION of 1917 the British government pledged its support for this goal, and the declaration was incorporated into the terms of the mandate over Palestine, which took effect in 1923. Serious violence soon arose between the Arabs and the Jews, and the British, who had made promises to both groups, were unable to satisfy either. Upheavals brought about by World War II and the decimation of European Jewry stimulated action toward the creation of a Jewish homeland. In November 1947 the United Nations voted to divide Palestine into Jewish and Arab states. The British withdrew from the area on May 13, 1948, conceding failure in achieving peace between the Jews and Arabs. On May 14, Israel proclaimed its independence. On May 15, the Arabs attacked, refusing to recognize both the partition of Palestine and the new nation. Since the partition, Israel's boundaries have been redrawn along truce lines established by cease-fire agreements following the several ARAB-ISRAELI WARS.

The first 5 years of existence were a time of improvisation. Israel's resources were strained to meet the needs of the Jewish immigrants who swelled the population from 650,000 to 1.3 million in the first 3 years, and to fight the Arabs. A period of organization marked the years between 1953 and 1956. Immigration slowed to 30,000 persons a year, and overseas funds, along with restitution money paid by West Germany after 1952 for Nazi war crimes, made possible planned development of agriculture, irrigation, settlements, and industry.

Following the Suez-Sinai War of 1956, Israel enjoyed a period of consolidation and economic growth. In the Six Day War of 1967, it occupied the Sinai Peninsula and the Gaza Strip as well as the Golan Heights and the West Bank of Jordan. Israel refused to leave the occupied territories until permanent peace treaties were signed. Another period of economic expansion followed, with new growth in immigration, industry, and trade. Israel held off a surprise Arab attack in the Yom Kippur War of 1973, but it subsequently began a period of economic retrenchment as inflation accompanied the need to reequip military forces and pay for petroleum imports. In 1977 a right-wing government under Menachim Begin assumed control. Fighting continued sporadically, especially along the Lebanese border, but hopes for peace with the Arabs rose after President Anwar al-SADAT of Egypt visited Jerusalem in November 1977. On Mar. 26, 1979, a peace treaty was signed with Egypt, and Israeli troops began a scheduled gradual withdrawal from the Sinai to new defense positions in the Negev.   YEHUDA KARMON

Bibliography: Brecher, Michael, *The Foreign Policy System of Israel* (1972); Dupuy, Trevor N., *Elusive Victory: The Arab-Israeli Wars, 1947-1974* (1978); Eban, Abba, *My Country: The Story of Modern Israel* (1972); Elizur, Yuval, and Salpeter, Eliahu, *Who Rules Israel?* (1973); Elon, Amos, *The Israelis* (1971); Gervasi, F. H., *The Case for Israel* (1967); Halevi, Nadav, and Klinov-Malul, Ruth, *The Economic Development of Israel* (1968); Karmon, Yehuda, *Israel, a Regional Geography* (1971); Likhovski, Eliahu, *Israel's Parliament: The Law of the Knesset* (1971); Orni, Efraim, and Ofrat, Elisha, *The Geography of Israel*, 3d ed. (1971); Samuel, Edwin, *The Structure of Society in Israel* (1969); Schoenbrun, David, *The New Israelis* (1973); Sykes, Christopher, *Cross Roads to Israel: Palestine from Balfour to Begin* (1965); Urofsky, Melvin I., *We are One: American Jewry and Israel* (1978).

Israel, Kingdom of

The Kingdom of Israel was the name both of the united kingdom of the Israelites under Kings SAUL, DAVID, and SOLOMON (c.1020-c.922 BC) and of the political unit formed by the ten northernmost Israelite tribes when they revolted against the Davidic dynasty after the death of Solomon. The territory of the latter included what was left of the Davidic dynasty's holdings east of the Jordan River, and extended south to a few kilometers north of Jerusalem, the capital of JUDAH, where the Davidic dynasty still held power. The northern kingdom's own capital moved several times until King Omri finally established it permanently at Samaria c.875 BC.

The first king of Israel, the northern kingdom, was JEROBOAM, a former official of Solomon, but neither he nor any of his successors was able to establish a stable dynastic succession such as existed in Judah. Throughout its short history Israel was continually rocked by bloody dynastic changes. The small nation was constantly harassed by strong enemies and experienced only two brief periods of expansion in the 9th and 8th centuries before it was destroyed by Assyria in 722-721 BC.   J. J. M. ROBERTS

Bibliography: Bright, John, *A History of Israel* (1972); Buccellati, Giorgio, *Cities and Nations of Ancient Syria* (1967).

Israeli-Arab Wars: see ARAB-ISRAELI WARS.

Israëls, Jozef   [ees'-rah-els, yoh'-zef]

Jozef Israëls, b. Jan. 27, 1824, d. Aug. 10, 1911, a leader of the Hague school, was a Dutch genre painter and landscapist. He studied with Jan Adam Kruseman in Amsterdam and François Edouard Picot in Paris. Although Israëls's style evolved through the major idioms of the period, he is best known for his sympathetic portrayals of peasants and fisherfolk; he has been called "the Dutch Millet." His works, reminiscent of Rembrandt in lighting and brushwork, influenced a generation of Dutch painters.

Bibliography: Colmjon, Gerben, *The Hague School*, trans. by C. Buddingh (1951).

Istanbul   [is-tan-bool']

Istanbul is Turkey's largest city, its largest port, and its industrial, commercial, cultural, and tourism center. The city, long known as Constantinople, occupies a strategic location at the entrance to the Black Sea on the traditional crossroads between Europe and Asia; it covers an area of 254 km² (98 mi²). The population of the city proper is 2,547,364; the metropolitan area's population is 4,500,000 (1979).

Istanbul has spread from the old city, on a triangular peninsula jutting into the Sea of MARMARA, into both the European and Asian areas surrounding it. The Golden Horn inlet is to its north, the BOSPORUS to the east, and the Sea of Marmara to the south. Within the city lie seven hills with flat tops and

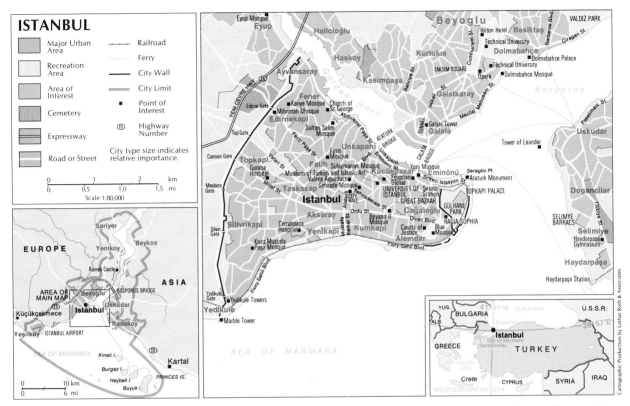

ISTANBUL

Major Urban Area	Railroad
Recreation Area	Ferry
Area of Interest	City Wall
Cemetery	City Limit
Expressway	(E5) Highway Number
Road or Street	City type size indicates relative importance.

Point of Interest ■

Scale 1:80,000

0   1   2   km
0   0,5   1,0   1,5   mi

steep sides. The annual average temperature is 14° C (57° F), and the annual rainfall averages 800 mm (32 in).

Contemporary City. The vast majority of Istanbul's population is Turkish and Muslim. Among the other residents are Greeks, Armenians, small numbers of other Christians, and Jews. The population is increasing rapidly because of a high birthrate and an influx of large numbers of immigrants from within Turkey.

Istanbul is Turkey's foremost industrial center. Textiles, flour, tobacco, cement, glass, and soap are produced. Over 1 million tons of imports and more than 250,000 tons of exports passed through its port in 1970.

The city's mayor is appointed by the president of Turkey and serves as the administrator for both the municipality and

Istanbul's Galata Bridge, which spans the Golden Horn, links the historic quarter of Stamboul with the commercial district of Beyoglu. The Yeni Camii (right), or New Mosque, a multidomed structure with twin minarets, was constructed between 1597 and 1663.

province. Istanbul University has an enrollment of 33,000. The Palais de la Culture d'Istanbul (1969) is the home of the city's symphony orchestra and opera and also houses an art gallery. Among the many museums are the Archaeological Museum of Istanbul, the Topkapi Palace Museum, and the Museum of Turkish and Islamic Art. There are many public parks, including the Hippodrome, now a public garden. The city's most famous monument is HAGIA SOPHIA (537), originally a Byzantine church, later a mosque, and now a museum. Istanbul's many mosques include the Süleymaniye, the Mihrimah, and others designed by the architect Mimar SINAN in the 16th century. The Bosporus Bridge, a 1,074-m (3,524-ft) suspension bridge connecting the European and Asian parts of the city, was opened in 1973.

History. Istanbul has been the capital of three states: the BYZANTINE EMPIRE, the OTTOMAN EMPIRE, and the Turkish Republic. It was founded (c.660 BC) as BYZANTIUM by Greeks from Megara. The Persian king DARIUS I took the city in 512 BC. Sparta captured it in 479 BC, lost it to Athens, but regained it in 405 BC. For about 675 years Sparta, Macedonia, Rhodes, and Rome contended for the city. The Roman emperor Septimius SEVERUS virtually destroyed the city in AD 196, but rebuilt it. In 324, CONSTANTINE I, the Great, chose the city for the new capital of the entire Roman Empire. Named Constantinople for the emperor, the city was enlarged and walls were added for protection. As the capital of the Byzantine Empire (as the eastern half of the Roman Empire came to be known), Constantinople became Europe's preeminent city, a position it held until the mid-11th century. It was subjected to attacks by the Persians (626), Arabs (673–77, 717–18), Bulgars (813, 924), Russians (860, 941, 1043), and Pechenegs (1090–91). None were successful, however, until the armies of the Fourth CRUSADE attacked and plundered the city in 1204.

The Crusaders established the Latin Empire of Constantinople (see CONSTANTINOPLE, LATIN EMPIRE OF). It lasted until 1261, when the Byzantines regained control. Thereafter, as the Byzantine Empire declined, so did its capital. The fall of Constantinople to the Ottoman sultan MEHMED II in 1453 marked the end of the Byzantine state.

Constantinople then became the seat of government for the

Ottoman sultans, whose court was called the Sublime Porte. Mehmed began (1462) construction of the palace of Topkapi Sarayi. In the reign of SULEIMAN I (1520–66) the architect Sinan embellished the city with numerous mosques and other buildings. The sultans continued to build lavishly through the 19th century.

The Ottoman Empire was dissolved in October 1918; by 1920 Turkey was forced to cede all its European territory except for Constantinople and its environs. The Allies held control of the city from the end of World War I until Turkish nationalists overthrew the sultan in 1922. Constantinople was officially renamed Istanbul in 1930. In the late 1970s the city suffered increasingly from pollution.   IRA M. SHESKIN

Bibliography: Asimov, Isaac, *Constantinople: The Forgotten Empire* (1970); Lewis, Bernard, *Istanbul and the Civilization of the Ottoman Empire* (1963); Maclagan, Michael, *The City of Constantinople* (1968); Mayne, Peter, *Istanbul* (1967).

Isthmian Games   [is'-mee-uhn]

The Isthmian Games, which began about 582 BC, were one of the four great athletic festivals of ancient Greece. The games were held biennially in the spring of even years on the Isthmus of Corinth at the Sanctuary of Poseidon, the sea god. Competitions in athletics, horse racing, oratory, and music were held, and the winners received a crown of dry, wild celery. Legend traces the origin of the games to either Sisyphus, king of Corinth, or to Theseus, king of Athens. Archaeological digs have disclosed ruins of the temple, stadium, and theater used in the games. The games ceased in the Christian era.

Bibliography: Harris, H. A., *Sport in Greece and Rome* (1972).

Istria   [is'-tree-uh]

Istria is a mountainous peninsula in northern Yugoslavia that penetrates the northern Adriatic Sea. It is about 96 km (60 mi) long and is bounded on the west by the Gulf of Venice and on the east by the Kvarner gulf. A coastal strip in the northwest that includes the city of TRIESTE belongs to Italy. Istria is 3,890–5,180 km² (1,500–2,000 mi²) in area; its highest elevation is 1,396 m (4,580 ft) at Mount Ucka. The coastline is irregular and rocky, with deep harbors and many offshore islands. The most significant of these is Brijoni (Italian: Brioni), where a health resort is located. Grape cultivation, forestry, fishing, and cattle raising are the major economic activities. Coal, quartz, and bauxite are mined. PULA, the major city and seaport, is a shipbuilding center.

Istria was ruled by the Illyrians until the 2d century BC, when it was taken over by the Romans. The Byzantines continued to claim the area until the 8th century AD. The peninsula was later divided between Austrian and Venetian control, but in 1797, Austria secured all of Istria. Italy was given sovereignty over Istria at the end of World War I. In 1947, however, control over most of the peninsula passed to Yugoslavia. The status of Trieste, as part of Italy, was settled in 1954.

Itagaki Taisuke   [ee-tah'-gah-kee ty'-soo-kay]

Itagaki Taisuke, b. Apr. 17, 1837, d. July 1919, was a Japanese social reformer, educator, and statesman. Of noble birth, he advanced to military commander of the large Tosa feudal domain and was involved in the overthrow of the TOKUGAWA shogunate and the MEIJI RESTORATION in 1868. As an official in the new government, Itagaki called for broader representation; although he participated in several cabinets, he often resigned in protest. He founded the first political club, the first national organization with a wide following (Aikokusha, "Society of Patriots," 1875), a school, and then, in 1881, the Jiyuto, or Liberal party, of which he became the figurehead.

ITA: see INITIAL TEACHING ALPHABET.

Italian art and architecture

The Italian artistic tradition is perhaps the richest of any single Western nation. For centuries Italy was an influential center of artistic production, setting the standards that European and American art tended to follow and exporting artists to work for enlightened and powerful patrons abroad. Many styles that characterize epochs in the history of Western art first arose in Italy, and through its inexhaustible inventiveness, Italian art has helped stimulate other countries to develop national art forms responsive to their own particular institutions, customs, and tastes. The character of Italian art was profoundly affected by the church and ruling families and by classical antiquity, which often provided inspiration for new styles through surviving architecture, sculpture, and painting. Italian art comprises many distinct regional schools; its diversity reflects temperamental and cultural differences within a country historically divided in many separate states. Florence, Pisa, Siena, Rome, Venice, Bologna, Naples, Urbino, and Milan were artistic centers that frequently engaged in spirited rivalry and had individual influence that waxed and waned with the passage of time.

A decline in the unrivaled position and prestige that Italian art had enjoyed since the Renaissance began to take place in the later part of the 18th century, brought about by the flowering of artistic centers in France, England, and Germany. Nonetheless, Italy has sustained a rich continuity in the visual arts to the present day. The importance of futurism to 20th-century art is widely recognized, and the changing historical perspective of recent years has encouraged exploration of the neglected accomplishments of 18th- and 19-century Italian artists.

ARCHITECTURE

Romanesque Churches. Monumental building in Italy all but ceased for several centuries following the Lombard invasion and the fall (751) of the Byzantine capital at Ravenna (see BYZANTINE ART AND ARCHITECTURE). Large-scale projects, especially ecclesiastical building, were resumed in the 11th century in a style that came to be known as Romanesque (see ROMANESQUE ART AND ARCHITECTURE) because of its dependence on the architecture of ancient Rome. The church of Sant' Ambrogio in Milan (begun c.1130), which incorporates an Early Christian basilical plan, contains the earliest example of ribbed-groin roof vaulting (see ARCH AND VAULT). Tuscan Romanesque is exemplifed by Pisa's Cathedral (begun 1063) with its octagonal baptistry (begun 1153) and cylindrical CAMPANILE, bell tower (1174–1372), or Leaning Tower—a group of buildings remarkable for their height and rich exterior decoration of white and polychromed marble and multitiered colonnades. In Florence the church of San Miniato al Monte (c.1018–1207) and the domed octagonal Baptistery (consecrated 1059) are simple geometric structures elaborately patterned with framed panels of multicolored marble (see BAPTISTERY). The major seaport of Venice, like parts of south-

Tuscan Romanesque architecture is represented by the Cathedral (begun 1063), baptistery (begun 1153), and famous Leaning Tower (1174–1372) of Pisa. All three buildings display a stylistic continuity and are finely decorated with white and polychrome inlaid marble.

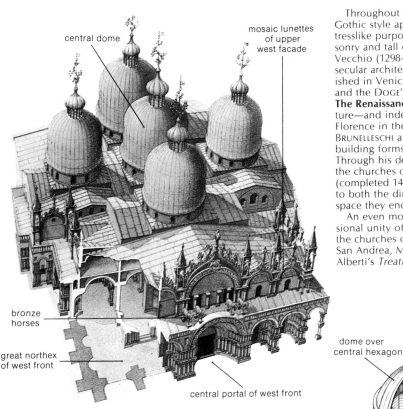

central dome

mosaic lunettes
of upper
west facade

bronze
horses

great northex
of west front

central portal of west front

campanile

dome over
central hexagon

nave

exterior of striped marble

west facade

(Above) *Saint Mark's Basilica (begun 1063),
in Venice reflects the Byzantine influence
on Venetian architecture. Constructed on
the site of a 9th-century basilica, Saint
Mark's features a five-domed Greek cross
plan derived from the Church of the
Apostles, Istanbul. Its interior decoration of
glass mosaics and colored marble is typically
Byzantine. (Right) The Siena Cathedral
(begun 1226) is one of the most
accomplished expressions of Italian Gothic
style, which, influenced by both antique and
Byzantine traditions, never attained the
elaboration of the Gothic architecture of
northern Europe. The feature most
representative of these influences is the
domed central hexagon. Both the interior
and exterior are noted for the brilliant use
of colored marble.*

Throughout central and northern Italy a unique secular Gothic style appeared in town halls and palaces; their fortresslike purpose was emphasized by massive rusticated masonry and tall crenellated defensive towers as in the Palazzo Vecchio (1298-1313), Florence. An extremely light and elegant secular architecture—tinged with Oriental influences—flourished in Venice in such palaces as the Ca'd'Oro (begun 1421) and the DOGE'S PALACE (begun c.1345).

The Renaissance. A major turning point in Italian architecture—and indeed in all Western architecture—occurred in Florence in the early 15th century, when the architect Filippo BRUNELLESCHI applied classical principles to contemporary building forms (see RENAISSANCE ART AND ARCHITECTURE). Through his designs for the Pazzi Chapel (begun c.1429) and the churches of San Lorenzo (begun 1421) and San Spirito (completed 1428), he brought a sense of measured proportion to both the dimensions of architectural members and the space they enclosed.

An even more thorough realization of the three-dimensional unity of ancient Roman construction was achieved in the churches of San Francesco, Rimini (begun c.1450), and San Andrea, Mantua (begun 1470), by Leon Battista ALBERTI. Alberti's *Treatise on Architecture* (1485; Eng. trans., 1726, repr.

ern Italy and Sicily, which also maintained strong connections with the eastern Mediterranean, continued to build churches in a Byzantine style, with a central plan and domed interior richly decorated with gold mosaic, as in SAINT MARK'S CHURCH (begun 1063).

The Gothic Period. The persistence of strong classical traditions prevented complete acceptance of Gothic architecture in Italy (see GOTHIC ART AND ARCHITECTURE). Monastic buildings such as the Cistercian Abbey of Fossanova (consecrated 1208) introduced the style, which later assumed distinct local forms, exemplified by the facade of the Cathedral of Orvieto (begun 1290) and by the nearly contemporary but utterly different Duomo or cathedral and church of Santa Croce, Florence (begun 1295). The largest of the Italian Gothic cathedrals, Milan (begun c.1386), most closely resembles later northern examples, but in general Italian Gothic architecture retained a clarity and simplicity of horizontal space, avoiding the soaring vertical scale and ornamental complexity of French and English cathedrals.

1955) was to remain a cornerstone for the continued development of rational architecture based on classical theory.

The culmination of Early Renaissance innovation took place in Rome, where Donato BRAMANTE succeeded in balancing the massive shapes and voids of his Tempietto for the courtyard of San Pietro in Montorio (1502) and of the new centrally planed SAINT PETER'S BASILICA, Rome (begun 1506), thus creating the phase known as High Renaissance. MICHELANGELO crowned Saint Peter's with a graceful cupola, completed in 1590 after his death, one of his many architectural designs of colossal grandeur that announced both the fulfillment and the eventual decline of the monumental harmony of the High Renaissance.

Some fine buildings of the second half of the 16th century were based in part on Michelangelo's inventions. In Rome, Giacomo Barozzida VIGNOLA's Church of the Gesù (begun 1568) anticipated baroque architecture, while in Florence architects such as Giorgio VASARI and Bartolommeo AMMANATI experimented with unorthodox and theatrical arrangements

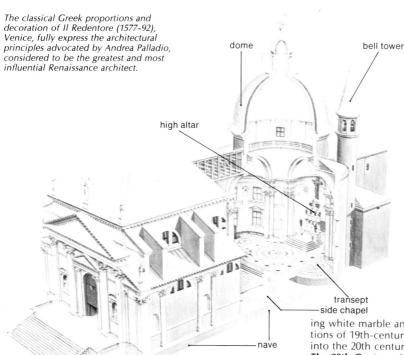

The classical Greek proportions and decoration of Il Redentore (1577-92), Venice, fully express the architectural principles advocated by Andrea Palladio, considered to be the greatest and most influential Renaissance architect.

dome

high altar

bell tower

transept
side chapel

nave

(Above) *Francesco Borromini's facade of San Carlo alle Quattro Fontane (1665-1667), in Rome, exemplifies high baroque architecture. Borromini departs from the traditional flat facade and creates an illusion of movement.*

related to the Mannerist style of painting and sculpture (see MANNERISM). In numerous churches, palaces, and villas built in and near Venice, Andrea PALLADIO strictly interpreted ancient Greek and Roman modes of building, and through his immensely influential writings on architecture, codified classical principles for later generations in Italy and throughout Europe and North America.

The Baroque Period. In baroque architecture the earlier search for harmonious arrangement within a given repertoire of forms was replaced by a desire for energetic movement, richness of effect, and bold contrasts. Baroque architects animated exterior walls and interior space, preferring rounded, oval, or curving forms to the rectilinear stability of their predecessors. Colored marbles and gilded ornament, often used in combination with elaborate, illusionistic ceiling paintings and sculpture, gave startling new life to the treatment of interiors (see BAROQUE ART AND ARCHITECTURE).

In the Roman churches of San Carlo alle Quattro Fontane (1638-1667), Sant' Ivo (1642-50), and Sant' Agnese (begun 1653), Francesco BORROMINI developed an extravagant style notable for the surprising juxtaposition of unorthodox forms. In Piedmont this imaginative style was carried on by Guarino GUARINI and Filippo JUVARRA. Two of the most famous landmarks of late baroque architecture, reflecting a concern for the design of public monuments, fountains, and squares, are Nicola SALVI's Trevi Fountain (1732-62) and the Spanish Steps (1723-25) in Rome by Francesco De SANCTIS.

Neoclassicism and the 19th Century. The neoclassical style (see NEOCLASSICISM, art) was represented in Naples by Pietro Bianchi (1787-1849) and in Rome by Giuseppe Valadier (1762-1839), who redesigned the Piazza del Popolo (1813-31). Although the authority of the classical order persisted throughout the 19th century, it competed with architectural styles derived from other cultures and periods. The result was a historical or eclectic style of architecture, usually characterized by elaboration of sculpted detail and strong contrasts of light and shadow, which may be seen in Guiseppe Calderini's (1837-1916) Palace of Justice, Rome (1888-1910), and the Victor Emmanuel Gallery (1865-77) in Milan by Guiseppe Mengoni (1829-77). With the creation of Guiseppe Sacconi's (1854-1905) superbly bombastic Monument of Victor Emmanuel II in Rome (1884-1911), an elaborate confection of gleam-

ing white marble and gilt bronze statuary, the grandiose traditions of 19th-century historical architecture were extended into the 20th century.

The 20th Century. Italian architecture of the 20th century has tended to parallel the development of the international BAUHAUS style, particularly in industrial northern Italy, where architectural principles were reappraised in the light of modern needs and new materials and techniques of construction. The "Group of Seven," formed in 1926 under the leadership of Giuseppe Terragni (1904-43) in Milan, produced buildings that are notable for their austere and functional style. The Florence railway station (1934-36) by Giovanni Michelucci (1891-   ) and the stadium (1930-32) in Florence by Pier Luigi NERVI were examples of successes achieved before the advent of the swollen, pseudo-Roman style of Fascist architecture. Postwar Italian architecture has continued to flourish in response to the country's changing social and economic requirements. Despite the proliferation of undistinguished urban buildings, excellent works have been produced by Gio PONTI and as a result of the engineering innovations of Nervi, for example, the Pirelli Building in Milan (1955-58).

SCULPTURE

Romanesque and Gothic Periods. Church construction provided Romanesque sculptors with opportunities to ornament doorways, capitals, and church furniture with scenes from sacred legends and the Bible. In Lombardy the primitive and rustic vigor of the sculpture executed by Guglielmo for Modena Cathedral (early 12th century) echoes the massiveness of Romanesque architecture. Benedetto ANTELAMI, whose mature work adorns the Baptistery of Parma (1196-1260), evolved a highly refined personal style. A particularly vigorous school of sculpture was founded at Pisa by Nicola PISANO. His marble pulpit (1260) in the Baptistery at Pisa reflects a profound knowledge of classical sculpture, which he emulates in his free-standing solid human forms. Italian sculpture was only marginally affected by Gothic style, but some influence of the graceful poses and fine descriptive detail of the northern Gothic can be discerned in the work of Nicolo Pisano's son Giovanni and Lorenzo Maitani (d. 1330).

The Renaissance. Lorenzo GHIBERTI, a pivotal figure in the transition from the elegant Late Gothic International Style, demonstrated in his second pair of bronze doors (1424-52) for the Baptistery of Florence Cathedral a new interest in the classical rendering of human forms and their relationship to existing space.

DONATELLO's marble statues of *Saint Mark* (1411-13; Or San Michele, Florence) and *Saint George* (c.1415; Bargello, Florence) and *A Prophet* (1423-25; Museum of the Duomo, Flor-

The Adoration of the Magi *(1410–17), a panel from the bronze north door of the Florence baptistery, was one of the first works executed by the sculptor Lorenzo Ghiberti. The north door, sculpted in a style imitating Andrea Pisano's south door, reflects the Late Gothic tradition, as opposed to the classical style embodied in Ghiberti's mature work on the baptistery's east door.*

ence) for the campanile of Florence Cathedral demonstrate the remarkable evolution of early Renaissance sculpture, which emancipated figures from their architectural surroundings and gained an unprecedented ability to depict human movements and emotions. The sculptural reliefs of Donatello and Ghiberti rationalized pictorial space, using it as a supporting framework for narrative.

Luca della Robbia (see DELLA ROBBIA family) developed popular, brightly glazed terra-cotta sculpture, and other new forms of the period included the portrait bust and small bronzes of the type associated with Antonio del Pollaiuolo (see POLLAIUOLO family), which reestablished a taste for individual cabinet-pieces for private collectors. Important contributions were made by Andrea del VERROCCHIO and Andrea SANSOVINO, but it was Michelangelo, working in Florence (DAVID), Rome (Tomb of Julius II), and again in Florence (Medici Tombs), who dominated High Renaissance sculpture. The awesome spiritual and physical power of Michelangelo's mature works seems to have exhausted his personal energies as well as the tradition of HUMANISM that reached its full fruition in the art, literature, and philosophy of his time. Later sculptors such as Benvenuto CELLINI and Giovanni da BOLOGNA cultivated the virtuosity and fanciful invention of the Mannerist

style, wherein elaborate complexes of architectural, painting, and sculptural elements prefigure an important aspect of baroque style.

The Baroque Period. The supreme artist of the baroque, Giovanni Lorenzo BERNINI, exercised his talent in both architecture and sculpture. His individual figures are charged with movement and emotion, and in larger projects such as the Cornaro Chapel, Santa Maria della Vittoria, Rome (1645–52), and the Baldachino (1624–33) and the Altar of the Throne (1656–66) of Saint Peter's, Rome, he created elaborate spectacles that compel attention (see ALTAR). Italian sculpture of the later 17th and much of the 18th century remained conservative, however—devoted to minor variations of established baroque subjects and styles.

From Neoclassicism to the Present Day. Neoclassicism, which emerged in the mid-18th century, was slower to reveal itself in sculpture than in painting, but with the appearance of Antonio CANOVA, sculpture once again became preeminent among the arts. Canova was the last Italian artist to achieve fame and worldwide recognition in his own day comparable to that of Michelangelo and Bernini. The enormous success of such sculptures as the *Monument to Clement XIV* (1783–87; Santi Apostoli, Rome), *Cupid and Psyche* (1793; Louvre, Paris), and the *Three Graces* (1816; Hermitage, Leningrad) was based on an original reformulation of ancient models, to which was added an unrivaled delicacy of execution and finish.

Other significant achievements of 19th-century sculpture include the modified classicism of Lorenzo Bartolini (1777–1850), the naturalistic observation of Vincenzo Gemito's (1852–1922) genre works, and the impressionist technique of Medardo ROSSO in his wax sculptures.

At the beginning of the 20th century a reaction to traditional forms brought about the powerful but short-lived avant-garde movement known as FUTURISM; whose theoretical inspiration lay in the aesthetic of the machine and the increasingly frenetic pace of 20th-century life. The most famous manifestation of futurism in sculpture was Umberto BOCCIONI's bronze figure, *Unique Forms of Continuity in Space* (1913; Museum of Modern Art, New York City), which evokes a sense of solid masses moving through space. After World War I new personalities appeared, including Giacomo MANZÙ, noted for portraiture, and Marino MARINI and Alberto GIA-

(Far left) *Michelangelo's* David *(1501–04; Accademia, Florence), a magnificent marble sculpture, exemplifies the powerful conception of human beauty and spirituality realized in all his work.* (Left) *The classical grace of 16th-century sculpture was succeeded by the vigorous movement seen in baroque sculpture. Bernini's* Apollo and Daphne *(1622–24; Galleria Borghese, Rome) illustrates his superb ability to evoke motion and feeling.*

A further development in the representation of movement is seen in Umberto Boccioni's Unique Forms of Continuity in Space *(1913; Museum of Modern Art, New York City), a bronze by one of the progenitors of the futurist movement.*

COMETTI, whose works recalled Etruscan sculpture and reaffirmed the importance of Italy's ancient past.

PAINTING

The Late Middle Ages. Responding to strong Byzantine influence during the 13th century, Italian artists turned their attention to painting as a monumental art form. From CIMABUE on the history of Italian painting can be regarded as a series of rapid advances caused by the initiative of individual genius.

A confrontation of local styles and of old and new traditions can be observed in the works of DUCCIO DI BUONINSEGNA and GIOTTO DI BONDONE. Duccio's masterpiece, the *Maestà* Altarpiece (1308–11; Museo dell'Opera del Duomo, Siena), is a lavish example of Italian Gothic altar painting, incorporating in its separate wood panels paintings of the Virgin and saints with narrative scenes from the life of Christ. Its abundant gold-covered backgrounds, detailed narratives, and delicate, graceful style are the mark both of Duccio's personal manner and the northern-derived Gothic style, which continued to flourish among the conservative painters of Siena and elsewhere.

It was Giotto who brought about the first major revolution

in Italian painting. This great artist's ability to adapt traditional formulas of representation, to dispense with many of the purely ornamental elements of medieval art, and to establish his images on observed reality is best exemplified by his frescoes in the Arena Chapel, Padua (1304–13). He was able to instill his figures with a convincing sense of mass, weight, and movement within an implied space and to motivate their actions by the depiction of human emotions. Although without an immediate successor, Giotto's example inspired later Renaissance innovators, who were to transform the nature of Western pictorial art in their turn.

The Renaissance. Florence was the cradle of early Italian Renaissance painting, and MASACCIO dominated this field just as Bruneslleschi and Donatello did theirs. His frescoes of the Holy Trinity in Santa Maria Novella (1428) and of New Testament scenes in the Brancacci Chapel (c.1425), Santa Maria del Carmine, Florence, acquired a startling unity from their logical rendering of mass, light, and space. Spatial perspective, which was considered an important principle of the new rational style of painting, was developed by Paolo UCCELLO in Florence, Andrea MANTEGNA in Padua and Mantua, and at San

The Mona Lisa, or La Gioconda (begun 1503), is Leonardo da Vinci's most famous painting. The subtle delicacy of this work is an example of the sfumato technique Leonardo perfected, and its subject and symbolic meaning have long been topics of speculation. Leonardo, whose intellect engaged with all aspects of Renaissance learning, is considered one of the greatest figures of all time. (Louvre, Paris.)

(Above) Giotto di Bondone's The Kiss of Judas (1304–50), from his monumental fresco cycle in the Scrovegni (Arena) Chapel in Padua, reflects Giotto's compositional genius and ability to create dramatic tension. By abandoning static Byzantine styles, Giotto became a pivotal figure in Italian art. (Left) The Baptism of Christ (c.1450–55) reveals the symmetry and perfection of light and form introduced into early Renaissance painting by Piero della Francesca. (National Gallery, London.)

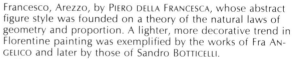

Francesco, Arezzo, by PIERO DELLA FRANCESCA, whose abstract figure style was founded on a theory of the natural laws of geometry and proportion. A lighter, more decorative trend in Florentine painting was exemplified by the works of Fra ANGELICO and later by those of Sandro BOTTICELLI.

The inquiring spirit of the Renaissance was nowhere better demonstrated than in the universal genius of LEONARDO DA VINCI. In paintings such as the *Madonna of the Rocks* (begun 1483; Louvre, Paris), *The Last Supper* (1495–98; Santa Maria delle Grazie, Milan), and the *Mona Lisa* (begun 1503; Louvre) Leonardo was able to unite form and space by the technique of sfumato, or soft blending. RAPHAEL's paintings of Madonnas and frescoes in the Vatican, Rome (1509–14), defined the ideal and harmonious beauty of the High Renaissance for all time. In the same period Michelangelo's SISTINE CHAPEL ceiling (1508–12) introduced a new dimension of physical and spiritual power to painting.

Venice was also an important center of High Renaissance art, producing a school that included Giovanni Bellini (see BELLINI family) and GIORGIONE, painters who, although less scientifically inclined than the Florentines, were unrivaled in their sense of color and lyrical feeling. TITIAN, a master of psychological insight and the greatest painter of 16th-century Venice, explored the potential of oil painting to the full in portraits, altarpieces, and mythological subjects drenched with light and color. Virtuosity was also the hallmark of Tin-

The spiritual power and impressive dignity of Renaissance art found its greatest expression in the Sistine Chapel frescos (1508-12) of Michelangelo. This detail from The Creation of Adam *is one of nine panels depicting scenes from Genesis. The frescos, painted to create the impression of painted sculpture, are framed by the cornices of the chapel ceiling. (Left) Raphael's* The Virgin and Child with Saint John the Baptist and Saint Nicholas of Bari *(c.1505) achieves religious intensity through simple, unified composition. (National Gallery, London.)*

the time-honored system of artistic training through workshop apprenticeship.

During this period the volatile genius Michelangelo Merisi da CARAVAGGIO became celebrated for an unorthodox style of religious painting that included naturalistic depictions of figures and scenes of common life. His paintings *The Calling of Saint Mathew* (c.1599) and *The Conversion of Saint Paul* (1600-01) in the Roman churches of San Luigi dei Francesi and Santa Maria del Popolo, Rome, incorporated startling effects of foreshortened perspective. Another characteristic feature of Caravaggio's style—the dramatic contrast of deep shade and bright light—was adopted widely throughout Italy and Europe and became the hallmark of a school of 17th-century Neapolitan painters. This tenebrist style was better adapted to easel painting, however, than to the large-scale illusionistic ceiling frescoes produced by such baroque masters as Pietro da CORTONA and Giovanni Battista GAULLI (see ILLUSIONISM).

The baroque style persisted in the 18th century. In Venice an attractive mode of view painting was practiced by CANALETTO and Francesco GUARDI, and the grand manner of Italian

(Left) The rich texture and suffused light of Titian's The Crowning with Thorns *(c.1570), in which a violent scene is endowed with a sense of noble suffering, typify the artist's mature style. Titian was one of the most influential artists of the Venetian Renaissance. (Alte Pinakothek, Munich.)*

(Below) The Calling of Saint Matthew (c.1599), a work that relates a sacred story in a mundane, immediately recognizable tavern setting, exemplifies the vitality, naturalism, and drama characteristic of Caravaggio's work. (San Luigi dei Francesi, Rome.)

toretto, who filled dozens of Venetian churches and palaces with acres of vivid canvases.

So great were the accomplishments of these painters of the first half of the 16th century that their classic authority was almost immediately acknowledged. Giorgio VASARI, the first art historian, wrote a famous account of his predecessors and contemporaries, *Lives of the Artists* (1550; Eng. trans., 1912-14), tracing the development of Italian art from the late Middle Ages. Vasari was also a distinguished artist in the elegant and artificial Mannerist style, which, despite its attractiveness, passed with the advent of baroque painting at the close of the 16th century.

The Baroque Period. In their grand ceiling fresco (1597-1604)—centered on the Triumph of Bacchus and Ariadne—for the Gallery of the Farnese Palace, Rome, the brothers Annibale and Agostino Carracci (see CARRACCI family) reasserted the figural and compositional values of ancient and High Renaissance art. Their search for ideal beauty was empowered with a new energy and exuberance, manifested by massively proportioned figures, deeply receding spaces, and diagonal, closely framed composition. The private academy founded by the Carracci family in Bologna—where classical theory was established as the basis for study of live models and the art of the ancients and Renaissance masters—was the prototype of many similar academic institutions, which were later established throughout Europe and replaced

baroque fresco painting attained its final glory in the work of Giovanni Battista TIEPOLO (see TIEPOLO family), accented by the airiness and elegance of the French ROCOCO STYLE.

Neoclassicism and the 19th Century. The Roman neoclassical movement of the mid-18th century was a reaction to the artificiality of the art of the immediate past. Maturing more rapidly in theory than in practice, this movement was inspired by the writings of the German archaeologist Johann WINCKELMANN, by discoveries at the ancient cities of POMPEII and HERCULANEUM, and by the participation of several non-Italian painters, principally Anton Raphael MENGS and Gavin HAMILTON. The skilled draftsman Pompeo Girolamo BATONI, an important painter of this period, was only partially allied to the neoclassical movement, and he eventually became a successful portrait painter with numerous foreign patrons.

The neoclassicism of Vincenzo Camuccini (1771–1844), Andrea Appiani (1754–1817), and Pietro Benvenuti (1769–1844) was succeeded by a succession of styles, including purism, led by Tommaso Minardi (1787–1871), and the historical romanticism of Francesco Hayez (1791–1892). A realist school was developed at Posilippo under the leadership of Domenico Morelli (1826–1901), and in mid-century a group known as the MACCHIAIOLI began to paint landscapes and genre scenes (see GENRE PAINTING) in the manner of the French impressionists.

The 20th Century. At the beginning of this century experi-

Piazza d'Italia *(1912) epitomizes the mysterious atmosphere evoked by the metaphysical paintings of Giorgio de Chirico. A major influence on early surrealist painters, Chirico's style evokes mysterious empty spaces and archetypal symbols.*

ments in futurist (see FUTURISM) painting were carried out by Boccioni, Gino SEVERINI, Giacomo BALLA, and Carlo CARRÀ. A personal compromise between modern abstract principles and traditional linear representation was evolved by Amedeo MODIGLIANI, and a new phenomenon called metaphysical painting became known through the dreamlike surrealist compositions of Giorgio de CHIRICO. Modernism continues to challenge tradition, as in the austerely simple and formalistic works of Giorgio Morandi (1890–1964).

Bibliography: Blunt, Anthony, *Artistic Theory in Italy, 1450–1600* (1940; rcpr. 1956); Chastel, André, *The Flowering of the Italian Renaissance* (1965) and *Italian Art* (1963); Freedberg, Sidney, *Painting in Italy: 1500–1600* (1970); Hartt, Frederick, *History of Italian Renaissance Art* (1969); Keller, Harold, *The Renaissance in Italy,* trans. by Robert E. Wolf (1969); Klein, Robert, and Zerner, Henri, *Sources and Documents in Italian Art: 1500–1600* (1964); Martin, Marianne W., *Futurist Art and Theory: 1909–1915* (1968); Meeks, Carroll L. V., *Italian Architecture, 1750–1914* (1966); Meiss, Millard, *Painting in Florence and Siena After the Black Death* (1951); Pope-Hennessey, John, *An Introduction to Italian Sculpture,* 5 vols. in 3 parts, 2d ed. (1971); Seymour, Charles, *Sculpture in Italy: 1400–1500* (1966); Smart, Alistair, *The Renaissance and Mannerism in Italy* (1971); Venturi, Lionello, *Italian Painting,* 3 vols., trans. by Stuart Gilbert (1950–52); Waterhouse, Ellis K., *Italian Baroque Painting* (1962); White, John, *Art and Architecture in Italy, 1250–1400* (1966); Wittkower, Rudolf, *Art and Architecture in Italy, 1600–1750,* 3d ed. (1973), and *Studies in the Italian Baroque* (1975).

See also: ARCHITECTURE; ART; CATHEDRALS AND CHURCHES; FOUNTAINS; FURNITURE; GARDEN; GOLD AND SILVER WORK; HOUSE (in Western architecture); JEWELRY; MONASTIC ART AND ARCHITECTURE; PAINTING; PALACE; SCULPTURE.

Italian greyhound

The Italian greyhound is a breed of dog similar to the true greyhound in form but smaller in all proportions. These dogs

(Above) La Salute, Venice *(c.1740–50) is representative of Canaletto's precisely executed vedute ("views") of Venice. These scenes, meticulously detailed and remarkably sensitive to the atmosphere of the city, contributed to a growing interest in landscape painting. (Emil G. Buhrle Foundation, Munich.)*

(Left) *Modigliani's* Seated Nude *(c.1917) exemplifies the fluid line, elongated form, and tonally unified composition characteristic of his work. (Courtauld Institute, London.)*

The Italian greyhound, a miniature version of the true greyhound, was known as the royal palace dog in aristocratic circles during the 16th century. Its petite, small-waisted body and dainty, high-stepping movement make it one of the most graceful of the toy breeds.

stand 15-25 cm (6-10 in) at the shoulder and weigh 3-4.5 kg (7-10 lb). Italian greyhounds are long-legged and have a smooth coat, laid-back ears, and long tail. Any color and markings are acceptable for show except tan markings normally found on black and tan dogs of other breeds.

There is evidence that the Italian greyhound was popular in the days of ancient Pompeii, and it is evident that the breed is a miniature greyhound, intentionally dwarfed in ancient times to be a pet. The breed was brought to England during the reign of Charles I in the 17th century. Because of its antiquity, the precise ancestry of the breed is unclear.

JOHN MANDEVILLE

Bibliography: American Kennel Club, *The Complete Dog Book*, 15th ed. (1975).

Italian language: see ROMANCE LANGUAGES.

Italian literature

If Italian literature, over its 900-year history, can be characterized, it is by its fidelity to tradition, respect for style, and concern for political and social questions. Most prominent Italian writers have been well educated—disciplined by the study of the classics. At the same time, Italians have recurrently displayed an aptitude for formal innovation and thematic pioneering that has been fruitful for European letters as a whole. As proof of this contention, it is sufficient to cite the achievement of Petrarch in lyric poetry, the groundbreaking sociopolitical studies of Machiavelli, or the chivalrous romance perfected by Ariosto. These names also suggest the period in which Italian literature was preeminent; from the mid-14th century through the High Renaissance the influence of Italian writers was widespread and seminal. Although this primacy was lost at the end of the 16th century, each generation since has brought forth figures of international resonance.

A specifically Italian literature was late in developing primarily because Latin, both as a spoken and as a written language, survived in the peninsula longer than elsewhere in Europe. The first Italian writers were members of the so-called Sicilian School. Flourishing at the court of Emperor Frederick II (r. 1208-50), these poets adapted the amatory substance of the Provençal troubadours to their lyrics, adding their own stylistic refinements. The idealized Lady of their verses was given philosophical and religious significance by their successors Guido GUINICELLI and Guido CAVALCANTI and achieved immortality in the BEATRICE of DANTE ALIGHIERI and the Laura of PETRARCH.

After Frederick's death the Italian muse moved northward, and a wider range of themes—social, political, and religious—becomes apparent in the works of the Tuscan Guittone d'Arezzo (c.1230-c.1294) and JACOPONE DA TODI, whose devotional verse was popular in style. All these motifs were fused in Dante's richly complex DIVINE COMEDY, a perfect reflection of the 13th-century world view and unquestionably the greatest poem of the Middle Ages. It was Dante's use of his native Tuscan dialect that ultimately established it as the literary language of Italy. Petrarch brought to his sonnets and songs, especially those of the *Canzoniere* (Song Book), a deep emotional commitment and a technical mastery that remains unsurpassed. The bulk of his work, however, was written in Latin. As a prime mover in the new HUMANISM, he was dedicated to a deeper appreciation of the classics, one of the principal facets of the RENAISSANCE, especially as it unfolded in Italy. Giovanni BOCCACCIO, a friend and admirer or Petrarch, while chiefly celebrated for the sprightly prose, well-plotted tales, and cynical wit of his DECAMERON (1351-53), also pioneered in the invention of a number of poetic genres that were widely imitated abroad. The lively *Novelle* (c.1378-c.1395), or short stories, of Franco Sacchetti (c.1332-1400) further developed the genre mastered by Boccaccio.

Although the cult of Latin tended to overshadow the vernacular in the 15th century, Italian writers of talent were not lacking. The versatile Leon Battista ALBERTI, better known as an architect, published a lengthy treatise, *On the Family* (1433-39); its wisdom and rationality reflected the abiding concern of Italian letters with social and ethical topics. Toward the end of the century the Florentine tyrant Lorenzo de'Medici (1449-92) and his protégé Angelo Poliziano (see POLITIAN) excelled in lyric, narrative, and satirical verse. The semipopular Carolingian epic was polished and exploited by Luigi PULCI in his comic *Morgante Maggiore* (1483) and by Matteo Maria BOIARDO in his well-known *Orlando Innamorato* (left unfinished in 1487).

The major cities of Italy achieved full autonomy in the 15th century and under their *signori* became centers of great wealth and culture, enjoying a precarious liberty that endured until the foreign invasions of the early 16th century. These were the years of the High Renaissance, which produced innumerable writers of rare originality. In 1532, Ludovico ARIOSTO finished his romantic epic, ORLANDO FURIOSO. Nicolò MACHIAVELLI's The PRINCE (1532), unique among political works of the period in examining the real, rather than the ideal, bases of a sovereign's power; Baldassare CASTIGLIONE's *The Courtier* (1528), with its vivid description of Renaissance court life and manners; and Jacopo SANNAZARO's pastoral idyll *Arcadia* (1502), roughly contemporaneous works, all exercised an important influence on literature internationally. High Renaissance Italian writers also included Cardinal Pietro BEMBO, who

Dante (right) *and Petrarch* (below) *were two of the greatest poets of the 14th century. Dante, reflecting the culmination of medieval thought, and Petrarch, anticipating that of the Renaissance, helped form the vernacular into a mode of literary expression.*

exemplified the PLATONISM of the times; the historian of the contemporary Italian wars, as well as of his native Florence, Francesco GUICCIARDINI; the satirist Pietro ARETINO; the short-story writers Matteo BANDELLO and Giovanni Francesco STRAPAROLA; and the genius MICHELANGELO, whose sonnets rival his paintings in their depth of feeling and vigor of expression.

Italy's golden age came to an end with the loss of political liberty that was experienced when most of Italy fell under the domination of Spain. Intellectual freedom also suffocated under a doctrinaire Church as it attempted to contain the spread of the Protestant Reformation. The tensions of the times are evident in the writings of the philosopher Giordano BRUNO as well as in the last great poetic work of the century, Torquato TASSO's epic *Jerusalem Delivered* (1581). In *Aminta* (1573), Tasso contributed to the popularity of the pastoral play, a genre also represented by the *Pastor Fido* (1590) of Giovanni Battista GUARINI.

In the baroque twilight of the early 17th century, the flamboyant Neapolitan poet Giambattista MARINI, alone among Italian writers, received international recognition. The mock-epic *The Rape of the Bucket* (1622) by Alessandro Tassoni (1565-1635), nevertheless, has a certain vivacity and may well have influenced Alexander Pope's The RAPE OF THE LOCK; the poets Gabriello Chiabrera (1552-1638), Fulvio Testi (1593-1646), and Francesco Redi (1626-98) also show originality and vigor.

The early years of the 18th century produced three able dramatists: Pietro METASTASIO, a deft composer of melodramas and librettos; Carlo GOLDONI, whose well-made comedies still hold their own on the stage; and Carlo GOZZI, who adapted the COMMEDIA DELL'ARTE to his own romantic uses.

Social concerns inspired the work of the economic reformer Pietro Verri (1728-97), of Giambattista VICO—the most powerful intellect of his century—whose cyclical interpretation of history helped establish the discipline on a modern, scientific basis, and of the satirical poet Giuseppe PARINI.

Toward the end of the century a new note was sounded by the dramatist Vittorio ALFIERI, whose plays, though classic in form, were already romantic in mood and informed by the nationalist spirit of the coming RISORGIMENTO. The era was perhaps best epitomized by the Venetian soldier-poet Ugo FOSCOLO in works that blend romantic emotion, classical discipline, and patriotic passion.

A strong element of Christian piety colors the work of Alessandro MANZONI, the leader of Italian romanticism (see ROMANTICISM, literature), chiefly famous for his semirealistic, semiromantic historical novel *I promessi sposi* (1825-27; trans. as *The Betrothed*, 1828). The most gifted and lyrical voice of the century belonged to the poet Giacomo LEOPARDI, who employed traditional verse forms for his uniquely seductive blend of passionate spontaneity and linguistic precision. Other writers of note in the early 19th century include the historical novelists Tommaso Grossi (1790-1853) and Francesco Guerrazzi (1804-73). Because of Italy's growing struggle for independence and national unification, the writings of such political theorists as Vincenzo GIOBERTI, Massimo D'Azeglio (1798-1866), and especially the great patriot Giuseppe MAZZINI also assumed significance at the time. Following unification, which was crowned by the seizure (1870) of Rome by the royal troops of the house of Savoy, literary activity intensified.

Giosuè CARDUCCI, a poet of social commitment and also a distinguished critic, was the greatest lyrical talent to emerge in the second half of the century. Toward the end of the century the more personal verse of Giovanni PASCOLO became popular. In the 1880s and 1890s the Italian novel was ably represented by two great writers: the master of VERISMO, Giovanni VERGA, celebrated for his evocations of Sicilian life, and the subtle psychologist Italo SVEVO.

Antonio FOGAZZARO, author of *Piccolo Mondo Antico* (1896; trans. as *The Patriot*, 1906), and Matilde Serao (1856-1927), with her colorful observations of Neapolitan life, also wrote novels of note. By far the most versatile and certainly the most prominent of all Italian writers during the period, however, was Gabriele D'ANNUNZIO, novelist, poet, and dramatist, as well as duelist, patriot, and dilettante. His soaring lyrics together with his flamboyant personal life and controversial political activism kept his influence alive into the 1930s.

The early years of the 20th century witnessed the emergence of Luigi PIRANDELLO, already known for his novels, as one of modern DRAMA's most innovative figures. His cerebral plays questioning the nature of reality and anticipating the thrust of later EXISTENTIALISM retain their flavor and popularity today. Pirandello's work shows some affinity with the "grotesque" theater of his time, of which Luigi CHIARELLI, Pier Maria ROSSO DI SAN SECONDO, and Massimo BONTEMPELLI (1878-1959) were leading exponents. The symbolic dramas of Ugo BETTI have also had an influence far beyond the confines of Italy.

In lyric poetry, three successive schools appeared: the crepuscolari, or "twilight" poets, of the early 20th century, chief among them Guido Gozzano (1883-1916), Sergio Corazzini (1887-1907), and Marino Moretti (b. 1885); the short-lived, clamorous futurists (see FUTURISM), captained by Filippo Tommaso MARINETTI; and the hermetics, whose origins may be found in the early verses of Giuseppe UNGARETTI and who flourished unobtrusively during the Fascist era. Less easy to categorize are the original and irrational poetry of Dino Campana (1885-1932) and the sensitive, autobiographical verse of Umberto SABA.

The novel in the early part of the century was represented by the Sardinian regionalist Grazia DELEDDA, winner of the 1926 Nobel Prize for literature, and the Tuscan realist Federigo TOZZI. At the same time the writings of the great philosopher, critic, and historian Benedetto CROCE attracted an international audience, while the polemical essays and *Life of*

Gabriele D'Annunzio, one of the most vivid and prolific of the fin de siècle *writers, was flamboyantly active in Italian politics and dominated Italian literature during the first quarter of the 20th century. D'Annunzio's facile lyricism, sensuality, and technical skill, seen most brilliantly in* Alcione *(1904), are evident throughout his many works.*

Alberto Moravia, one of Italy's leading contemporary novelists, explores the alienation and decadence of modern society in his works. The Conformist *(1951), following Italy's long tradition of social and political literature, treats the effects of his country's fascist regime under Mussolini and is one of his most acclaimed novels.*

Christ (1921; Eng. trans., 1923) of Giovanni Papini (1881–1956) also enjoyed a great if ephemeral vogue.

In spite of censorship during Mussolini's years in power (1922–43), many writers continued to express themselves with some degree of freedom under fascism. Overt criticism of the regime, however, was ventured mainly by such exiles as the socialist novelist Ignazio SILONE, author of *Bread and Wine* (1937; Eng. trans., 1962), and the critic and novelist Giuseppe Antonio BORGESE; within Italy, the social commentator Carlo LEVI wrote his perceptive *Christ Stopped at Eboli* (1945; Eng. trans., 1947) from government-enforced exile in the south, while the novelist Elio VITTORINI, the father of NEOREALISM, was temporarily imprisoned (1943) for his Marxist-oriented writings. Many prominent figures espoused the regime—Pirandello, Bontempelli, and Ungaretti among them. The discontent of such able novelists as Alberto MORAVIA, who in the postwar years became Italy's most prolific and popular novelist and who in *The Conformist* (1951; Eng. trans., 1952) exposed the suffocating destructiveness of the regime, or of Corrado ALVARO, author of *Revolt in Aspromonte* (1930; Eng. trans., 1962), though evident to a perceptive reader, was expressed only obliquely in the 1930s and early 1940s. Riccardo Bacchelli (b. 1891) during this period turned to the historical novel, while the mischievous realism of Aldo Palezzeschi (1885–1974), who began his career as a twilight poet, had no political undertones.

The fall of fascism brought a new flowering to Italian letters. Reflecting Italian literature's traditional bias toward social and political concerns, the *Letters from Prison* (1947; selections trans., 1973) and *Prison Notebooks* (1948–51; selections trans., 1971) of Antonio GRAMSCI, prewar Italy's leading Marxist theoretician, became bestsellers a decade after his death and exerted a powerful influence on European intellectuals. Among neorealist novelists, Cesare PAVESE and Vasco PRATOLINI came to the fore; they were joined by new recruits to neorealism, many, such as Giorgio BASSANI, the sensitive author of *The Garden of the Finzi-Continis* (1962; Eng. trans., 1965), and Natalia GINZBURG, in *A Light for Fools* (1952; Eng. trans., 1957), drawing on their memories of the war and of the partisan resistance in their fiction.

The novel of fantasy was represented by Dino BUZZATI and Italo CALVINO, while a sophisticated regionalism, characterized by varying styles and intents, was cultivated by Carlo Cassola (b. 1917), the satirical Vitaliano BRANCATI, Michele Prisco (b. 1920), Lionello Sciscia (b. 1921)—perhaps the most talented writer of his generation—and Fulvio Tomizza (b. 1935). The conventional novel of middle-class crises and problems was given a new twist by Guido Piovene (1907–76), Mario Soldati (b. 1906), and Alba De Cespedes (b. 1911). Paradoxically, the two Italian novels that enjoyed the greatest international success in the postwar period were written by members of the older generation; *That Awful Mess in Via Merulana* (1958; Eng. trans., 1965), a riotous and polysemous detective story, by Carlo Emilio GADDA, and *The Leopard* (1956; Eng. trans., 1960), a sad and disillusioned historical novel, by Giuseppe Tomasi di LAMPEDUSA, were both sui generis.

In poetry the older hermetics won worldwide recognition when Salvatore QUASIMODO in 1959 and Eugenio MONTALE in 1975 won the Nobel Prize in literature. In recent years a more "open" school of poets has come forth, among them Vittorio Sereni (b. 1913) and Pier Paolo PASOLINI, the latter also a noted film director and Communist. A versatile writer of the era, the poet, novelist, and critic Edoardo Sanguineti (b. 1930), has assumed the role of spokesman for the avant-garde in contemporary letters.

In the drama, the theater of Eduardo DE FILIPPO is notable for its color, while Diego Fabbri (b. 1911) has created a number of well-made plays. If the harvest among playwrights is otherwise slight, the reason is probably that so much creative dramatic talent has been channeled into the cinema, in which Italy has won international renown over the last three decades.   THOMAS G. BERGIN

Bibliography: Bondanella, Peter and Julia, *Dictionary of Italian Literature* (1979); Burckhardt, Jacob, *The Civilization of the Renaissance in Italy*, 2d ed., trans. by S. G. C. Middlemore (1965); Cippico, Antonio, *The Romantic Age in Italian Literature* (1918); Donadoni, Eugenio, *A History of Italian Literature*, 2 vols., trans. by Richard Monges (1969); De Sanctis, Francesco, *History of Italian Literature*, 2 vols., trans. by Joan Redfern (1931; repr. 1968); Fletcher, J. B., *Literature of the Italian Renaissance* (1934); Garin, Eugenio, *Italian Humanism*, trans. by Peter Munz (1965; repr. 1975); Martin, M. W., *Futurist Art and Theory, 1909–1915* (1968); Molinaro, J. A., ed., *Petrarch to Pirandello* (1973); Pacifici, Sergio, *A Guide to Contemporary Italian Literature* (1962; repr. 1972) and *The Modern Italian Novel*, 3 vols. (1967, 1973, 1979); Riccio, J. M., *Italian Authors of Today* (1970); Salvatorelli, Luigi, *The Risorgimento: Thought and Action* (1970); Venturi, Franco, *Italy and the Enlightenment* (1972); Whitfield, John H., *A Short History of Italian Literature* (1960); Wilkins, Ernest H., *A History of Italian Literature*, rev. ed. by Thomas G. Bergin (1974).

Italian music

Italy has played a major role in the development of Western music. Scholars can only speculate about what the music of Roman antiquity sounded like; no notated music from Roman times has been preserved. The earliest known Italian music is bound up with the history of the Catholic church. The two great centers of liturgical and musical reform in Italy in the first millennium were Milan and Rome. Saint Ambrose (*c*.333–97), bishop of Milan, imported several musical practices from Syria, including the custom of antiphonal singing (see ANTIPHON). He was also the author of a number of HYMNS; Saint Augustine credits him with the introduction of hymn singing in the West.

MIDDLE AGES

The most important figure in the reformation and codification of musical ritual of the Church was Gregory the Great, pope from 590 to 604. Though he is now admired more as an organizer than a creator, the common custom of referring to all sacred CHANT as "Gregorian" chant is a continuing tribute to his efforts in this field. Another figure of great importance for the orderly and uniform transmission of chant was the Benedictine monk GUIDO D'AREZZO.

With the development of poetry in the vernacular, which made use of rhythmic accent and rhyme, a new body of music arose that was based on this poetry. Among the first pieces using Italian texts are the *laude spirituali*, the earliest of which date from the 13th century. The following century witnessed a remarkable flourishing of secular music, with important advances in rhythmic notation and POLYPHONY. Theorists of the time spoke of a new art—an *ars nova*. The earliest known notated polyphonic music in Italy comes from the 14th century. The principal forms were the MADRIGAL, the caccia (a piece dealing with the chase, or hunting), and the ballata. The outstanding composer of this period was Francesco LANDINI. Blind from childhood, Landini was widely admired as a poet, philosopher, and astrologer as well as a composer and performer on several instruments.

RENAISSANCE

During the 15th and much of the 16th century Italy functioned largely as an importer of musical talent. Nevertheless, toward the end of the 15th century, distinctively Italian secular music began to reappear at some of the Italian courts. In Florence, during the time of Lorenzo de'Medici (1448–92), carnival celebrations were enriched by *canti carnascialeschi* (carnival songs). In Mantua composers developed the *frottola*, a homophonic (chordal), clearly phrased, strophic piece. The carnival songs and *frottole* were significant in preparing the ground for the 16th-century madrigal, one of the great flowerings of Italian musical art.

In the earlier part of the 16th century madrigals were written by French and Netherlandish composers as well as Italians such as Costanzo Festa (1490–1545). The late madrigal, written in the last third of the century, was dominated by the Italians Luca MARENZIO, Carlo GESUALDO, and Claudio MONTEVERDI. Sacred music developed in two main centers—Rome and Venice. The Roman school is epitomized in the works of Giovanni Pierluigi da PALESTRINA. Working under the influence of the Counter Reformation, Palestrina wrote several hundred motets and 105 masses. The Venetian school had its founding father in the Flemish composer Adrian WILLAERT, who was di-

This engraving (1554), from the title page of Palestrina's first mass, shows the composer offering the work to Pope Julius III, to whom it was dedicated. Palestrina's many settings of the mass represent the culmination of 16th-century polyphonic liturgical music.

A 19th-century cartoon portrays Gaetano Donizetti, one of the century's most prolific composers, writing music with both hands. Of Donizetti's 75 operas, the tragic Lucia di Lammermoor (1835) and the brilliantly comic The Daughter of the Regiment (1840) and Don Pasquale (1843) are among the most highly acclaimed. Donizetti's music, greatly influenced by Rossini, was in turn an important precursor of Verdi's operas.

rector of music at Saint Mark's Cathedral from 1527 to 1562. Willaert, his student Andrea Gabrieli, and Andrea's nephew Giovanni Gabrieli (see GABRIELI family) developed a polychoral (multiple choruses) style of composition that gave special force to the contrast and opposition (both spatial and aural) of mixed groups of performers.

Venice was also an important center of music printing from as early as the beginning of the 16th century. The *Odhecaton*, printed by Ottaviano dei Petrucci in 1501, is the first printed collection of part songs. Petrucci printed more than 50 volumes of secular and sacred vocal music as well as a few volumes of music for the lute.

BAROQUE

The period of Italy's greatest musical influence throughout Europe lasted from the end of the 16th to the middle of the 18th century. During this time new attitudes toward the relationship of text and music and toward the states of mind most suitable for expression in music generated changes in the treatment of dissonance, rhythm, and texture. The resulting style of the BAROQUE MUSIC affected old genres and brought forth several new ones, such as the opera, oratorio, cantata, concerto, and sinfonia.

The earliest operas that have survived complete are *Euridice* by Jacopo PERI and Giulio CACCINI, performed in Florence in 1600, and *Rappresentazione di Anima e di Corpo* by Emilio de Cavalieri (c.1550–1602), performed in Rome in 1600. Peri, Caccini, and Cavalieri were all associated with a group of

Claudio Monteverdi, one of Italy's most acclaimed composers, was a major figure in the transition from the Renaissance tradition of polyphony to baroque drama and compositional innovation. In Orfeo (1607), one of the first operas, and in L'Incoronazione di Poppea (1642), Monteverdi developed the techniques of recitative, complex orchestration, and characterization that form the basis of operatic drama. He appears here in a portrait by Domenico Fetti.

Florentine humanists called the Camerata, who hoped to achieve in their own time the great effects attributed to music by the ancient Greeks. To accomplish this goal they instituted a style of reciting in music, the *stile recitativo* (RECITATIVE), that allowed the text to be projected with clarity. The voice was accompanied by chords notated in a shorthand called FIGURED BASS. The full expressive possibilities of the new style were first demonstrated by Monteverdi in his opera *Orfeo* (1607).

Rome was a center of operatic composition from about 1620 until the late 1630s. In 1637 the first public opera house opened in Venice, and until the end of the 17th century, Venice was the operatic capital of Italy. Some of the finest Venetian operas were written by Monteverdi and his pupil Pier Francesco CAVALLI. Other offspring of the new style were the cantata, similar to an operatic scene, and the oratorio, a musical presentation of a sacred subject.

One of the characteristics of baroque music was the development of an idiomatic style of writing for various instruments. The greatest keyboard composer at the turn of the 17th century was Girolamo FRESCOBALDI, organist at Saint Peter's in Rome.

Throughout the baroque era Italy was preeminent both in the manufacture of violins and in the composition and performance of music for them. Some of the greatest violin makers of all times flourished in that age; they were members of the AMATI, STRADIVARI, and GUARNERI families, all of whom worked in Cremona. The texture that was favored in the second half of the 17th century called for two treble instruments, most often violins, and a melodic bass instrument such as the cello with a keyboard instrument filling in the harmonies. The term trio sonata designated music written for such an ensemble, and some of the finest examples were written by Arcangelo CORELLI.

Orchestral music also had its origins in the baroque era. The interest in exploiting contrasting masses of sound was brought to fruition in the concerto. The term *concerto grosso* describes a piece built on the contrast between a larger and a smaller group of instruments; Corelli composed some of the best examples of the genre. The most important composers in the development of the solo concerto, which contrasts a single player with a group, were Giuseppe TORELLI, Tommaso ALBINONI, and Antonio VIVALDI.

The most important composer of operas at the turn of the century was Alessandro Scarlatti (see SCARLATTI family), who wrote more than 100. *Opera seria* (see OPERA) was cultivated by German composers as well as Italians such as Niccolò JOMMELLI and Tommaso Traetta (1727–79). Comic opera made great advances in the hands of Giovanni PERGOLESI, Niccolò PICCINNI, Giovanni PAISIELLO, and Domenico CIMAROSA.

Instrumental music was not abandoned in the second half of the 18th century. The Milanese composer Giovanni Battista SAMMARTINI won international fame for his symphonies. The

Verdi, one of the most brilliant composers of the 19th century, presented La Traviata, *a poignant tragedy based on* La Dame aux camélias, *(1848) a novel by Alexandre Dumas fils. Although initially a failure,* La Traviata *later became one of Verdi's most popular works. Verdi's operas, including such masterpieces as* Il Trovatore *(1853) and* Aïda *(1871), are noted for their lyricism and dramatic power.*

concerto was cultivated by Giovanni Battista VIOTTI, an Italian working in France and England. Luigi BOCCHERINI, an Italian who spent much of his career in Spain, wrote a large quantity of chamber music.

19TH CENTURY

The most commanding figure in Italian opera at the beginning of the 19th century was Gioacchino ROSSINI. In two decades Rossini created nearly 40 operas, fairly evenly divided between the serious and the comic genres. He is best known for his comic masterpiece *The Barber of Seville* (1816). Rossini's last opera, *William Tell* (1829), was written for Paris, where he resided from 1824 until 1837 and from 1855 until his death in 1868.

After Rossini's premature withdrawal from operatic composition, two younger men, Vincenzo BELLINI and Gaetano DONIZETTI, came to prominence. Bellini's art is one of refined and expressive lyricism, although in his best works, such as *Norma* (1831), dramatic values are not neglected. Donizetti's more robust temperament was at home both in comic works such as *Don Pasquale* (1843) and tragic works such as *Lucia di Lammermoor* (1835).

For a half century, beginning in the 1840s, Italian opera was dominated by Giuseppe VERDI, the representative of the musical and the nationalistic aspirations of the Italian people. Verdi's career unfolded during the period in which Italy finally achieved independence and unification; many of his operas dramatize, implicitly or explicitly, the struggle against tyranny

and oppression. Verdi frequently drew the plots of his operas from the works of the finest European playwrights—among them Hugo, Schiller, and Shakespeare. The best known Verdi operas include *Rigoletto* (1851), *Il Trovatore* (1853), *La Traviata* (1853), *Aida* (1871), and *Otello* (1887). Most of his works are tragic, but his final opera, *Falstaff* (1893), is a comedy.

The librettist for *Otello* and *Falstaff* was Arrigo BOITO, a significant composer in his own right, whose major work is the opera *Mefistofele* (1868). The heroic operas of Verdi gave way in the 1890s to a style known as VERISMO (realism), which emphasized sordid settings and violent contrasts. The landmark works of verismo are Pietro MASCAGNI's *Cavalleria rusticana* (1890) and Ruggero LEONCAVALLO's *I Pagliacci* (1892), but it was Giacomo PUCCINI who achieved the most continuous success. Puccini was an accomplished eclectic composer with an astute sense of the theater. He blends veristic elements with sentimentality in *La Bohème* (1896), with fancy costumes in *Tosca* (1900), and with exoticism in *Madama Butterfly* (1904).

20TH CENTURY

Of the generation of composers who came to maturity at the turn of the 20th century, the most significant were Gian Francesco MALIPIERO, Ildebrando PIZZETTI, Ottorino RESPIGHI and Alfredo Casella (1883–1947). These men had in common an interest in the renewal and active cultivation of instrumental music, which had been comparatively neglected in the 19th century. In a clear rejection of the works of the verismo composers, they turned for their inspiration to compositions of the Italian Renaissance and baroque period or to Gregorian chant. The most important representatives of the next generation, Luigi DALLAPICCOLA and Goffredo PETRASSI, manifested in their works closer contacts with contemporary composers outside of Italy. Petrassi was most influenced by Paul Hindemith and Igor Stravinsky. Dallapiccola, once he became acquainted with the works of Arnold Schoenberg and Anton Webern, incorporated TWELVE-TONE techniques into a distinct personal style.

Italian composers today are working in virtually all the current trends—SERIAL MUSIC, ELECTRONIC MUSIC, ALEATORY MUSIC, and collage techniques. Most prominent among the avant-garde composers are the late Bruno MADERNA, Luigi NONO, Luciano BERIO, and Sylvano Bussotti (b. 1931).

CHARLOTTE GREENSPAN

Bibliography: Brown, Howard M., *Music in the Renaissance* (1976); Bukofzer, Manfred, *Music in the Baroque Era* (1947); Dent, Edward, *Music of the Renaissance in Italy* (1933); De Robeck, Nesta, *Music of the Italian Renaissance* (1928; repr. 1969); Einstein, Alfred, *The Italian Madrigal*, 3 vols. (1949; repr. 1971); Grout, Donald J., *History of Western Music*, rev. ed. (1973), and *A Short History of Opera*, 2d ed. (1965); Lang, Paul H., ed., *Contemporary Music in Europe* (1965); Levarie, Siegmund, *Musical Italy Revisited* (1963; repr. 1973); Palisca, Claude, *Baroque Music* (1965); Reese, Gustave, *Music in the Middle Ages* (1940) and *Music in the Renaissance*, rev. ed. (1959).

See also: RENAISSANCE MUSIC.

Italian Somaliland: see SOMALIA.

Italian Wars

Between 1494 and 1559, the HABSBURG rulers of Spain and the Holy Roman Empire fought the VALOIS kings of France for control of Italy in a series of conflicts known as the Italian Wars. These conflicts weakened Italy but helped to spread its RENAISSANCE culture to other areas of western Europe.

After the Peace of Lodi (1454), a precarious balance of power had been maintained among the chief Italian states: Florence, Milan, Naples, the papacy, and Venice. This equilibrium was upset when Ludovico Sforza (see SFORZA family) of Milan appealed to France for aid against a secret league of Florence and Naples. The French king CHARLES VIII descended (1494) into Italy with his army, expelled the Florentine ruler Piero de'Medici (see MEDICI family), and entered Naples in February 1495. Threatened by a coalition of Italian states allied with Emperor MAXIMILIAN I and King FERDINAND II of Aragon, Charles soon withdrew.

One of the most dramatic scenes in Giacomo Puccini's Tosca *(1900), Tosca's murder of Scarpia at the close of the second act, was used to illustrate this poster. Puccini's musically expressive and vividly theatrical operas continue to be frequently performed, and Puccini is considered one of Italy's most successful operatic composers.*

A period of intermittent warfare followed, during which the Spanish general Gonzalo FERNANDEZ DE CÓRDOBA conquered (1503-04) Naples, bringing southern Italy under Spanish control whereas France dominated the northern half of the peninsula. Soon Venice seemed to pose a new threat, and in response France, the empire, the papacy, and Spain formed (1508) the League of Cambrai. Following its victory at Agnadello (1509), the League conquered all of Venice's mainland possessions. The League soon fell apart, however, and Venice gradually recovered its empire. In 1512 the Habsburgs restored the Medici to Florence and in 1515 were defeated by the French at the battle of Marignano. By the Treaty of Noyon (1516) France received Milan, but renounced its claim to Naples.

During the 1520s, France and the empire continued to fight over Lombardy, but the defeat of the French and the capture of their king, FRANCIS I, at Pavia (1525; see PAVIA, BATTLE OF) doomed French influence in Italy. The League of Cognac, formed in May 1526, allied France, Florence, Milan, Venice, and the papacy against the Habsburgs in an attempt to reverse the effects of Pavia, but Spanish pikemen quickly conquered Milan and, in May 1527, sacked Rome. France continued to meddle in Italian affairs until the Treaty of CATEAU-CAMBRÉSIS (Apr. 3, 1559), by which all French claims in Italy, except in Savoy, were renounced. The Spanish Habsburgs were left free to dominate the severely weakened Italian peninsula until the early 18th century.

BENJAMIN G. KOHL

Bibliography: Green, Vivian H., *Renaissance and Reformation*, 2d ed. (1964); Taylor, F. L., *Art of War in Italy, 1494 to 1529* (1921; repr. 1973).

Italo-Turkish War

Italy's attempt to annex the Turkish North African provinces of Cyrenaica and Tripolitania (which comprise modern Libya) resulted in the Italo-Turkish War of 1911-12. In an era of imperial expansion, Italian leaders, including Premier Giovanni GIOLITTI—humiliated by defeat (1896) in Ethiopia and jealous over French success in taking Tunisia (1881) and Morocco (1911)—determined to build a colonial empire as an outlet for Italy's surplus population.

On Sept. 29, 1911, Italy, alleging mistreatment of Italians in Libya, declared war on the failing Ottoman (Turkish) Empire. Italy landed troops in Libya, seizing Tripoli and other coastal towns, and in November declared it to be Italian territory. Fighting continued in Libya, where Turkish forces were backed by the Arab population, and Italy widened the war to Rhodes and the other Dodecanese Islands off the coast of Turkey to force Turkey to submit. Faced with rebellion in the Balkans (see BALKAN WARS), Turkey conceded and signed the Treaty of Ouchy (or Treaty of Lausanne) on Oct. 18, 1912. This treaty allowed the Turks some religious authority in Libya but made the country an Italian protectorate. Contrary to the provisions of the treaty, Italian forces remained on the Aegean islands. The Italo-Turkish War weakened the Ottoman Empire and upset the fragile balance of power in Europe, thus contributing to the outbreak of World War I, in 1914.

DONALD S. BIRN

Bibliography: Askew, William C., *Europe and Italy's Acquisition of Libya, 1911-1912* (1942); Whittam, J. R., *The Politics of the Italian Army, 1861-1918* (1977).

Italy

Italy, officially the Italian Republic, is an independent nation in southern Europe. It extends southward from the Alps to the MEDITERRANEAN SEA, forming a narrow, 1,100-km-long (700-mi), boot-shaped peninsula reaching almost to the northern coast of Africa. The peninsula is bordered by the LIGURIAN SEA and the TYRRHENIAN SEA on the west, the IONIAN SEA on the south, and the ADRIATIC SEA on the east. It is advantageously located to control traffic between the eastern and western basins of the Mediterranean. The national territory includes the two large islands of SARDINIA and SICILY; the smaller offshore islands of CAPRI, ELBA, and Ischia; the Lipari (Aeolian) Islands;

ITALY

Official Name: Italian Republic
Capital and Largest City: Rome (1977 est. pop., 2,897,800)
Area: 301,205 km² (116,300 mi²)
Elevation: *Highest*—Monte Rosa, 4,634 m (15,203 ft). *lowest*—sea level, along the Mediterranean Sea coast
Population: 56,867,000 (1979 est.). *Distribution*—78% urban, 22% rural; *density,* 189 persons per km² (489 per mi²); *annual rate of increase* (1970-77), 0.7%
Principal Languages: Italian (official), German, French, Slovene
Principal Religion: Roman Catholicism
Principal Products: *Agriculture*—wheat, rice, potatoes, olives, grapes, citrus fruit, peaches, tomatoes; pigs, cattle, sheep. *Manufacturing and industry*—machinery, automobiles, iron and steel, chemicals, food processing, textiles, shoes. *Mining*—natural gas, petroleum, lignite; iron pyrites; sulfur
Railroads: 20,689 km/12,856 mi (late 1970s)
Roads: 254,393 km/158,077 mi (late 1970s paved)
Currency: 1 Italian lira = 100 centesini

the islands of Pantelleria, Linosa, Lampione, and Lampedusa in the Strait of Sicily between Sicily and Africa; and—by agreements with Yugoslavia in 1954 and 1975—TRIESTE and the northern sections of ISTRIA. Located on the Italian peninsula are two small independent enclaves—VATICAN CITY, in Rome, and the Republic of SAN MARINO, near RIMINI. Italy is bordered on the northwest by France, on the north by Switzerland, on the northeast by Austria, and on the east by Yugoslavia. The capital is ROME.

The name *Italy* was already in use during Roman times and came into the Latin language from the ancient Oscan tongue, which in turn may have taken it from a southern Greek dialect. Its etymology is linked to a Greek word meaning "calf," and according to a modern interpretation it is a reference to Calabria in southern Italy, where early inhabitants adopted the calf as their symbol.

The modern Italian state dates from 1861, when the title king of Italy was conferred on VICTOR EMMANUEL II, king of Sardinia. Before that time, Italy consisted of separate states which have retained a strong sense of regional identity and are identifiable today in the nation's 20 administrative regions. Eight of these states are located in northern (or Upper) Italy: EMILIA-ROMAGNA, FRIULI-VENEZIA GIULIA, LIGURIA, LOMBARDY, PIEDMONT, TRENTINO-ALTO ADIGE, VALLE D'AGOSTA, and VENETO. Six are in central Italy: ABRUZZI, LATIUM, MARCHE, MOLISE, TUSCANY, and UMBRIA. Southern Italy contains four: APULIA, BASILICATA, CALABRIA, and CAMPANIA. The other two states

ITALY

- Major Urban Area
- Railroad
  Glacier
- ＋ Spot Elevation
  or Depth

National capitals are underlined

City type size indicates
relative importance

Meters	Feet
Above 4000	Above 13124
2000	6562
1000	3281
500	1640
200	656
0	0
200	656
Below 2000	Below 6562

Scale 1:6,145,000

0   50   100   150 km
0   50   100 mi

WEST GERMANY
Salzburg
Basel
Zurich
LIECH.
Innsbruck
AUSTRIA
SWITZERLAND
Graz
Bern
Merano
Brenner Pass
1374m
Bressanone
Brunico
Ljubljana
Domodossola
Bormio
Livigno
Bolzano
Pieve di
Cadore
Zagreb
Verbania
Trento
Belluno
Udine
Monfalcone
Como
Bergamo
Vicenza
Padua
Venice
Trieste
YUGOSLAVIA
Milan
Brescia
Verona
Rijeka
FRANCE
Turin
Piacenza
Parma
Bologna
Ravenna
Genoa
APENNINES
Modena
Rimini
SAN MARINO
Nice
MONACO
Florence
Ancona
LIGURIAN
SEA
Livorno
Perugia
Macerata
ADRIATIC
SEA
Dubrovnik
CORSICA
(France)
Ajaccio
Rome
Pescara
L'Aquila
APENNINES
Naples
Foggia
Bari
Brindisi
Taranto
Lecce
SARDINIA
Cagliari
TYRRHENIAN
SEA
Cosenza
Catanzaro
IONIAN
SEA
Reggio
di Calabria
Palermo
Messina
SICILY
Catania
Syracuse
ALGERIA
Tunis
MEDITERRANEAN   SEA
TUNISIA
MALTA   Valletta

© 1980 Rand McNally & Co.
A-551800-772

The village of Valle d'Ayas is situated in the Valle d'Aosta autonomous region in northwestern Italy. Its location in the Italian Alps has made it an important tourist area. The unique cultural character of the region is a result of its predominantly French-speaking population.

The Dolomites, a principal range of the eastern Alps, are located in northeast Italy, between the Adige and Piave river valleys. The mountains are characterized by their distinctly sharp outlines, which were produced by erosion of the dolomite limestone.

are the island regions of Sardinia and Sicily.

Italy has been historically important since Roman times, and millions of tourists are attracted each year to its ancient cities and art treasures. Modern Italy is an important industrial nation and a leading member of the EUROPEAN ECONOMIC COMMUNITY (EEC), commonly known as the Common Market. Italy's rapid growth since 1950 has been referred to as the "Italian miracle"; the term is apt, because Italy has developed with few economic assets other than an abundant, skilled labor force.

LAND

Italy can be divided topographically into three parts—continental, peninsular, and insular Italy. Continental Italy, in the north, includes the broad, triangular-shaped North Italian Plain—Italy's only large lowland—and the high mountains of the Alps, which curve along the northern border in a broad arc about 1,300 km (2,080 mi) long and 150 to 250 km (240–400 mi) wide. These mountains extend from Savona, on the Ligurian coast, to near Trieste in the east. The highest

peaks in the Alps are west of the SIMPLON PASS (linking Domodossola and Brig, Switzerland) and include Gran Paradiso, which rises to 4,061 m (13,323 ft) south of Aosta; Mont Blanc (see BLANC, MONT), the highest mountain in Europe, on the border with France; the MATTERHORN, on the border with Switzerland; and Monte Rosa (see ROSA, MONTE), Italy's highest point. The central Alps, located between the Simplon Pass on the west and the Resia Pass on the east, rise over 3,300 m (10,800 ft) in the Lepontine Alps and to 4,049 m (13,346 ft) farther east in the Bernina Alps. Italy's eastern Alps include the Ötztal and Carnic Alps, forming parts of the border with Austria; the Dolomites, rising wholly within Italy to 3,342 m (10,965 ft) in Marmolada; and the Julian Alps, located primarily in Yugoslavia.

Peninsular Italy encompasses all of the Italian peninsula south of the North Italian Plain and the junction of the Ligurian Alps with the APENNINES at Savona. The Apennines form the backbone of the peninsula and reach their highest elevation in the central or Abruzzi Apennines. In the northern and central sections of the peninsula, the highest mountains are close to the Adriatic coast. Broad lowlands, backed by the rolling hills of the pre-Apennines, border the Tyrrhenian coast in Tuscany and Latium. In the south, the highest mountains are close to the Tyrrhenian coast, which is rocky, steep, and indented south of Naples. VESUVIUS, Europe's only active mainland volcano, is near Naples.

Insular Italy includes Sardinia, Sicily, and many smaller islands off their shores. Sardinia covers an area of 23,812 km² (8,930 mi²) and rises to a high point of 1,834 m (6,016 ft) in the ancient granite massif of Gennargentu. Sicily covers an area of 28,812 km² (10,804 mi²) and rises to 3,262 m (10,703 ft) in Mount ETNA. Northern Sicily is traversed by high mountains geologically related to the Apennines. This chain reappears across the Sicilian Channel as the ATLAS MOUNTAINS of northern Africa. Two active volcanoes—STROMBOLI and Vulcano—located on islands off the north coast of Sicily, together with frequent earthquakes felt throughout Italy, attest to the geologic youth of the Alpine chain and the Apennines. Only Sardinia is composed primarily of ancient rocks.

Soils. The richest and most productive soils for agriculture are the alluvial soils of the North Italian Plain and the smaller river valleys of the peninsula. Well suited for forestry and pas-

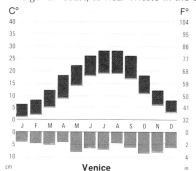

Venice

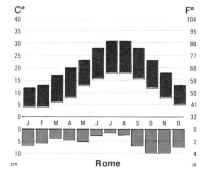

Rome

The climate graphs of Venice (left) and Rome (right) reflect the differences between these two Italian cities. Bars indicate the monthly ranges of temperatures (red) and precipitation (blue) of the marine west-coast climate of Venice and the Roman Mediterranean climate.

ture are the brown podzolic soils, which developed under an original forest cover and are found throughout the Apennines. Regosols have developed on the weathered volcanic deposits of Tuscany and Latium and on the lower slopes of active volcanoes. Red soils are common in Apulia and in other limestone areas in the south.

Climate. Except for the Alps, which have a mountain climate that varies with altitude, Italy has a continental climate in the north and a Mediterranean climate in the south. Summer temperatures average 24° C (75° F) for July throughout the nation, but winter temperatures range from a January average of 1° C (33° F) at BOLZANO in the north to 7° C (45° F) at Rome, and 12° C (53° F) at Palermo on Sicily. The annual temperature range between summer and winter is greatest in the north (typical of a continental climate) and least in the south. Precipitation ranges from 889 mm (35 in) at Trieste to 610 mm (24 in) in Palermo. It is concentrated during the winter in the south (typical of a Mediterranean climate) and during the warmer part of the year in the north.

Six climatic subregions may be distinguished. The Alpine zone is characterized by harsh winters, abundant precipitation, frequent snow, and cool summers. The lowlands of the North Italian Plain experience harsh winters with long periods of frost, warm summers, precipitation concentrated in spring and fall, and intense fog in fall and winter. The coastal Tyrrhenian region has mild winters and hot, dry summers. The Adriatic coast has a climate similar to that of the Tyrrhenian coast but tends to be drier and colder in winter. The Apennines are climatically similar to the North Italian Plain. The islands have a typically Mediterranean climate, with hot, dry summers and mild winters during which some rainy days can be expected.

Drainage. The main Italian waterway is the 652-km-long (405-mi) PO RIVER, which drains most of the North Italian Plain and enters the Adriatic Sea about 56 km (35 mi) south of Venice. The ADIGE RIVER, Italy's second longest, has a length of 410 km (255 mi) and flows into the Adriatic Sea north of the Po. In the peninsula, the main river is the 405-km-long (253-mi) TIBER RIVER, which flows from the Tuscan-Emilian Apennines through Rome and Ostia to the Tyrrhenian Sea. Also important in the peninsula is the 241-km-long (151-mi) ARNO RIVER, flowing through Tuscany and the cities of Florence and PISA before entering the Ligurian Sea.

The largest lakes in Italy are in the Alps and pre-Alps and are of glacial origin. The largest is Lake GARDA, with an area of 370 km² (142 mi²); others are Lake MAGGIORE, and Lake COMO. The largest lakes of the peninsula are Lake Trasimeno (Lake of Perugia) and Lake Bolsena, which was formed in an extinct volcanic crater.

Vegetation and Animal Life. About one-fifth of Italy is forested, with deciduous trees predominating in the North Italian Plain and needle-leaf trees at higher altitudes. The typical lowland Mediterranean woodland is a mixture of holm oaks, cork trees, maritime pines, cypresses, oleasters (wild olive), carobs, laurels, and myrtles. Forests of chestnut and oak are characteristic of cooler areas; they occur at elevations of about 1,000 m (3,000 ft) in the Alps, 1,100 m (3,600 ft) in the northern Apennines, and 1,800 m (5,900 ft) in Sicily. Above these limits are mainly beech trees, pines, and white fir. In the Alps at altitudes above 1,000 m (3,000 ft) forests of larch, spruce, and pine are found. Between the tree line (limit of tree growth) and the snow line stretch extensive alpine pastures. Heath is common on the North Italian Plain.

The principal large animals found wild in Italy today are the brown bear, which inhabits the Alps and the Abruzzi mountains; wolves, found in the Apennines; wild boars, found in Sardinia; red deer, chamois, roe deer, and Alpine ibex, in Gran Paradiso National Park; and fallow deer and mouflons, on Sardinia. The most numerous birds are larks, crows, and wrens. Hawks, buzzards, eagles, and other birds of prey can be seen in some upland areas. Gran Paradiso and Circeo national parks are important centers for the conservation of endangered animal species.

Resources. Except for sulfur and mercury, Italy has only small deposits of minerals needed for industry. Minor coal deposits are located in Sardinia, and some lignite is mined in Tuscany, Umbria, and Basilicata. Petroleum and natural gas are found in Sicily, and a large natural gas field underlies much of the North Italian Plain. Abundant hydroelectric power is produced on rivers flowing from the Alps. This form of energy is increasingly important in the south as dams are built to regulate the flow of local rivers. Forests occupy about 21% of the total land area, arable land 53%, and pastures 17%.

PEOPLE

The Italian people are among the most ethnically homogeneous in Europe. Nearly all are of Italian origin and speak Italian or dialects and languages related to Italian. These dialects vary considerably from region to region and are considered separate languages in the case of Sardinian, spoken by about 1.2 million people in Sardinia; Friulian, a Rhaeto-Romanic language spoken by about 520,000 people in the northeastern district of Friuli; and Ladin, a Rhaeto-Romanic language spoken in the mountains of the Alto Adige. The principal non-Italian minorities are 260,350 (1971) German-Italians, who live in the Alto Adige (formerly Austria's South TYROL) and speak the German dialects of Austria and Bavaria; and 53,000 Slavic Italians, scattered in several areas in Friuli and Venezia-Giulia. In addition, some isolated minority groups live in southern Italy, including Greek-speaking communities in parts of Apulia and Calabria; Albanian colonies in Sicily and Calabria; and Serbo-Croatian communities in parts of Molise. French is spoken in the Aosta valley.

Religion. Most Italians are Roman Catholics. Roman Catholicism was established as Italy's official religion by the LATERAN TREATY between Vatican City and Italy on Feb. 11, 1929; however, this legal status was abolished in 1976. Protestants constitute a small minority of about 180,000, and Jews number about 35,000.

Demography. Italy has the fifth highest population density in Europe. Densities over 100 persons per km² (260 per mi²) occur in most of the North Italian Plain; the Ligurian coast; the Arno Valley and northern Tuscany; the hilly Adriatic regions of Marche, Abruzzi, and Molise; most of Umbria, Latium, Calabria, and Apulia; and many coastal areas in Sicily. The sparsely populated areas are the Alpine uplands, parts of the Apennines in Liguria and Calabria; and the marshes of Tuscany and Latium.

This aerial view shows the Tyrrhenian Sea, an arm of the Mediterranean Sea, along the coast of Calabria, the southernmost region of the Italian peninsula. Many factors have hindered the economic development of this predominantly mountainous area.

The city of Venice, built on 118 islands in the Lagoon of Venice, is famous for its distinctive canals and bridges and its history as an Italian artistic center and European maritime power. This view of the city shows the pollution problems caused by nearby industry.

Italy's current birthrate of 13.2 per 1,000 and death rate of 9.6 per 1,000 approximate the average in Europe. Both rates have dropped dramatically since the 19th century. In the decade 1961–71, Italy's population increased by 6.9%, a rate similar to that maintained since the first census in 1861. During this period, the population of central and northern Italy grew by 9.5% while that of the south grew by only 1.4%, an indication that internal migration from south to north is continuing despite government efforts to develop the south and slow this migration. Between 1957 and 1971, an estimated 4.2 million of a total Mezzogiorno (south) population of 19 million migrated northward, most in search of greater economic opportunity.

About 48% of the population live in urban areas. More than 30% live in the 47 cities that have more than 100,000 inhabitants. The largest city is Rome. MILAN, NAPLES, and TURIN each have more than one million inhabitants. Other large cities are GENOA, PALERMO, BOLOGNA, FLORENCE, CATANIA, and VENICE.

Emigration has long been a feature of Italy's population. Between 1861 and 1965, an estimated 26.5 million Italians emigrated, primarily to the United States, Argentina, and Brazil. Only 6 million returned. Since World War II, emigration has continued but mainly by workers leaving temporarily for employment in other European nations—particularly West Germany and Switzerland. Only about 25% of all migrants during this period emigrated permanently overseas.

Education and Health. Education is free and compulsory between the ages of 6 and 14. Children between the ages of 11 and 14 attend middle school, and those who graduate may continue their education in a classical or scientific high school, in a teacher training school, or in one of a variety of technical schools that prepare students for specific careers. Only a small number of students go on to study at a university. The principal universities are at Rome, Naples, Milan, Bologna, Turin, and Palermo. According to the 1971 census, about 5.2% of the total population over the age of 6 were illiterate and had completed no school course, 27% could read but had completed no school course, 44.3% had graduated from elementary school, 14.7% had a diploma from middle school, 6.9% had a high school diploma, and 1.9% possessed university degrees.

Health costs for most Italians are covered by compulsory insurance programs. In 1975 there was one physician for every 482 inhabitants, about average for Europe. The principal causes of death were cancer, heart disease, and cerebrovascular disease. The infant mortality rate in 1977 was 17.6 per 1,000 live births. In 1976, 1,945 hospitals, with 584,000 beds, served the country. Many are run by Catholic religious orders.

Cultural Institutions. Academies are an important feature of intellectual life in Italy. Among the more prominent are the ACCADEMIA DEI LINCEI, founded in Rome in 1603; the National Academy of Saint Luke for fine arts, founded in the 14th century; Florence's Accademia Nazionale della Crusca (1582) for philological, lexicographical, and grammatical studies; and the National Academy of Saint Cecilia for music, founded in Rome in 1566. The leading research institute for mathematics, physics, and natural sciences is the National Research Council of Italy (1923). The leading libraries are the National Central Library (1747) in Florence, containing 4 million books; Rome's Victor Emmanuel II National Central Library, with 2.5 million volumes; and the Central State Archives (1871) in Rome, con-

The city of Palermo, which was originally settled as an ancient Phoenician commercial port between the 8th and 6th century BC, is the capital of Sicily, the largest island of the Mediterranean Sea. Such sights as this street vendor are commonly found throughout the city.

taining 120,000 volumes. Museums and art galleries can be found in all the larger towns. Among the most famous are the PITTI PALACE, UFFIZI, and National Museum in Florence; the Gallerio Borghese, Villa Giulia, Capitoline Museum, and National Gallery of Modern Art, in Rome; and the Accademia in Venice. The Università Italiana per Stranieri, founded in 1925 in Perugia, offers courses in the history of Italian civilization and the Italian language for foreign students.

ECONOMIC ACTIVITY
Modern industry developed in Italy at the beginning of the 20th century, about 100 years later than in other parts of Western Europe. This delay resulted in part from a lack of industrial raw materials, especially coal and other fuels. Other factors retarding industrialization were the survival into the 19th century of ancient feudal social structures and the political fragmentation that hindered the development of a single national market. Early industrialization was concentrated mainly in the northwest, where industrial agglomeration in the iron and steel, shipbuilding, engineering, and textile industries continues. The rest of Italy remained industrially underdeveloped and primarily agricultural until economic growth rapidly accelerated in the 1950s.

Governmental participation in industrial development continues. Through autonomous public organizations, an estimated one-third to one-half of all production by privately managed and competing companies is directed by the state. In addition, programs such as the Southern Development Fund offer special financial incentives to companies locating in the south. These programs are part of the government's efforts to lessen the socioeconomic disparity between north and south.

Manufacturing and Mining. In 1975 manufacturing contributed more than 40% to the gross national product and employed about 43% of the economically active population. About 30% of all industrial workers live in Lombardy, and another 14% live in Piedmont. Veneto, Emilia-Romagna, and Tuscany each have 8% of the industrial labor force. Italy's principal industries are the steel, automotive engineering, chemical, and textile industries. In 1975 steel output was 22 million metric tons (20 million net tons), 11 times the produc-

Milan, Italy's second largest city and a major industrial center of the northern portion of the country, has since the Middle Ages been a major financial and commercial center. The Galleria, a glass-roofed shopping arcade, also serves as a social meeting place.

tion at the end of World War II. The principal steel-making centers are TARANTO, Genoa, Naples-Bagnoli, and Piombino. The automobile industry is located in BRESCIA, MODENA, Milan, and Turin. Italy also exports sewing machines, typewriters, motor scooters, bicycles, mopeds, power tools, calculators, refrigerators, radios, and televisions. Airplanes are manufactured in Turin, and ships are built at ANCONA LA SPEZIA, Genoa, Naples, Trieste, and Venice. The production of petrochemicals such as plastics, fertilizers, and synthetic rubber is concentrated in the natural gas fields of the North Italian Plain and Sicily. The textile industry, important as early as the Middle Ages, was traditionally dependent on imported wool and cotton. Since the discovery of natural gas and petroleum, a synthetic fiber and fabric industry has developed. Florence and Milan are leading textile and garment centers. Artisans play an important role in the Italian economy and receive assistance from the government. Glass, pottery, lace, carved marble, and gold and silver filigree work are among the most famous hand-crafted products.

Petroleum and natural gas are the leading minerals produced, but local output supplies only a fraction of the nation's needs. Most petroleum is extracted in the Sicilian district of Ragusa. Natural gas underlies much of the North Italian Plain and parts of Sicily. Other minerals, far less important in terms of total value, include marble, quarried as in Michelangelo's time at Carrara; lead and zinc, mined in Sardinia; sulfur, in Sicily; and bauxite, mined mainly in the south.

Energy. Petroleum is the principal fuel consumed, and about 80% is imported. In 1977, Italy produced 166.5 billion KW h of electricity. About 73% of all electricity was generated in thermal electric power plants, fueled by petroleum and natural gas; 25% by hydroelectric installations primarily along Alpine rivers; and 2% from nuclear plants. Hydroelectric power output stayed about the same during the decade 1965–75 while total electrical production nearly doubled.

Agriculture. About 15% of the labor force is employed in agriculture, which contributed more than 7% to the gross national product in 1976. Slightly more than half of all land is used for farming, but productivity is low because only 29% of the land devoted to farming is in the fertile North Italian Plain; the rest is in the agriculturally marginal hill and mountain areas. Agricultural production is further limited by lack of investment capital for modern equipment, by a preponderance of tenant-farmed estates in the south, and by the small size of most farm units.

The principal crops are wheat, which is grown throughout the nation, and corn and rice, grown mainly in the North Italian Plain where water is available in summer for irrigation of the rice crop. Olives, grapes, citrus fruits, peaches, and other tree crops are characteristic of Italian agriculture, especially in the typically Mediterranean central and southern regions. Early spring vegetables, grown near Naples and other southern areas, command high prices when shipped to northern Europe. Flowers are a specialty crop along the Ligurian coast. Livestock accounts for about 40% of all agricultural production by value, but Italy must import large quantities of meat, primarily from France and Germany. Dairy cattle dominate in the Alps and in the provinces of Emilia-Romagna, Lombardy, and Tuscany, and sheep and goats are raised in the hilly, drier areas of the south and in Sardinia and Sicily.

Fishing and Forestry. Many small fishing ports line Italy's long coast, but the Mediterranean is not abundant in fish. The 1977 catch of 337,994 metric tons (306,561 net tons) was insufficient to meet the nation's needs. Some fishing fleets work in the Atlantic Ocean, but most fishers use small boats and outdated equipment. Forestry is of only minor importance, and Italy must import most of its wood.

Transportation. Road and freeway traffic is increasing as more Italians purchase automobiles, and the highway (*autostrade*) system now covers 4,800 km (2,983 mi). The most important freeway is the 1,250-km-long (781-mi) highway linking Milan, Rome, Naples, and REGGIO DI CALABRIA, breaking the historic isolation of many southern communities. About half of the 20,088 km (12,483 mi) of railroad is electrified, and the fast, efficient service on many of the state-run lines provides an al-

(Above) *The landlocked region of Umbria in central Italy is divided into the provinces of Perugia and Terni. This fertile mountainous region is used extensively for growing crops and the raising of livestock.*

(Left) *Montferrat is a historic area located in the wine-producing Piedmont region of northwestern Italy, where the fertile Po River valley yields grapes and cereals.*

ternative to highway travel. International air traffic is centered on Rome, located on international air traffic routes serving Europe and Asia. The Po River, navigable as far as CREMONA, is Italy's only natural inland water route. Small canals are used for transportation in Venice and in the North Italian Plain.

Communications. The broadcasting industry of Italy is state-owned. Within the country, 135 AM and 660 FM radio stations operate, along with 900 television stations. Of the 76 daily newspapers published in Italy, 32 have headquarters in either Rome or Milan.

Trade. Italy's imports are dominated by industrial raw materials, petroleum, meat, and cereal grains. The principal exports are manufactured goods and craft items, along with fruits and vegetables. Italy usually suffers a trade deficit, but the difference is offset by its large and profitable tourist industry and by money sent by Italian citizens working abroad. The principal ports are Genoa, Trieste, Taranto, Venice, Savona, and Naples. Petroleum is imported primarily through Augusta. A pipeline from Algeria, by way of Tunisia, to Sicily is under construction. Italy's principal trading partners are other members of the EEC, especially West Germany, France, the Netherlands, Belgium, Luxembourg, and the United Kingdom. Other trade partners include the United States, and—for petroleum imports—Saudi Arabia, Iran, and Iraq.

GOVERNMENT

In a referendum vote held on June 2, 1946, Italy's monarchy was abolished and the Italian Republic established. The constitution was adopted on Dec. 22, 1947, and took effect on Jan. 1, 1948. According to the constitution, executive power lies with the cabinet, and legislative powers are vested in a parliament consisting of a 630-member chamber of deputies and a 322-member senate. Except for a few life members of the senate (including former presidents and five prominent citizens nominated by the president), both houses are elected directly by universal adult suffrage for 5-year terms unless dismissed earlier. The president of the republic is head of state and is elected to a renewable 7-year term by a joint session of Parliament and three delegates from each of the regional legislatures. Executive power rests with the council of ministers (cabinet) headed by the prime minister appointed by the president.

Each of the 20 regions has an elected council, a president, and a *qiunta regionale* that exercises executive power and is responsible to the regional council. Five of the regions—Friuli-Venezia Giulia, Sardinia, Sicily, Trentino–Alto Adige, and Valle d'Aosta—are granted special autonomous status by the constitution.

The principal political party is the Christian Democratic party, which has led or participated in every government since 1945. The second largest party is the Communist party, which was excluded from the government from 1947 to 1977. Other parties include the Republican, Italian Socialist, and Social Democratic parties.
PAOLO MIGLIORINI

Bibliography: Acquaviva, Sabino, and Santuccio, Mario, *Social Structure in Italy: Crisis of a System* (1976); Adams, J. C., *The Government of Republican Italy*, 3d ed. (1972); Allen, Kevin J., and Stevenson, Andrew A., *An Introduction to the Italian Economy* (1974); Allum, P. A., *Italy: Republic Without Government?* (1973); Barnes, Samuel H., *Representation in Italy: Institutionalized Tradition and Electoral Choice* (1977); Carlyle, Margaret, *The Awakening of Southern Italy* (1962); Dickenson, Robert E., *The Population Problem in Southern Italy* (1977); Nichols, Peter, *Italia, Italia* (1974); Tannenbaum, Edward R., and Noerther, E. R., eds., *Modern Italy* (1974); Tilly, Charles, et al., *The Rebellious Century, 1830–1930* (1975); Walker, Donald S., *A Geography of Italy*, 2d ed. (1967); Woolf, S. J., ed., *The Rebirth of Italy, 1943–50* (1972).

See also: ITALIAN ART AND ARCHITECTURE; ITALIAN LITERATURE; ITALIAN MUSIC.

Italy, history of

Since earliest times the history of Italy has been influenced by cultural and political divisions resulting from the peninsula's disparate geography and by circumstances that made Italy the scene of many of Europe's most important struggles for power.

EARLY ITALY

Recent excavations throughout Italy and Sicily have revealed evidence of human activity during the Paleolithic and Mesolithic periods. By the beginning of the Neolithic period (c.5000 BC), the small communities of hunters of earlier times had been replaced by agricultural settlements, with some stock breeding and widespread use of stone implements and pottery. Painted vessels that seem to have been influenced by contemporary styles in Greece have been found at Castellaro Vecchio on the island of Lipari.

The Bronze Age. By 2000 BC new immigrants from the east had introduced metalworking into southern Italy and Sicily; the northern Italian Polada culture of the same period left evidence of strong links with cultures north of the Alps. During the Bronze Age (c.1800–1000 BC), much of central and southern Italy had a unified culture known as the Apennine, characterized by large agricultural and pastoral settlements; on the southeastern coast and in Sicily evidence indicates trading contacts with the Mycenaeans. After c.1500 BC, in the Po Valley to the north, the terramara culture—with its villages constructed on wooden piles, its advanced techniques of bronze working, and its cremation rites—rose to prominence.

(Below) *This 3rd-century AD relief portrays Roman legionaries in battle with Germans, with whom they came into direct conflict in securing the provinces of the Roman Empire bordering the Rhine and the Danube rivers. Subsequent barbarian invasions contributed to the final collapse of the empire in the 5th century AD. In AD 476 the German chief Odoacer deposed the last Roman emperor in the West, Romulus Augustulus.*

(Above) *The Etruscan civilization flourished from the 8th to the end of the 6th century BC in central Italy and the Po Valley. This painted clay plaque exemplifies the Orientalizing phase of Etruscan archaic painting. It was found in a tomb near Cerveteri and dates from the late 6th century BC. (Louvre, Paris.)*

By the time of the introduction of iron into Italy (c.1000 BC), regional variations were well established.

The Etruscans. The diverse cultural patterns of the early Iron Age were further complicated in the late 8th century BC by the arrival of Greek colonizers in the south and in Sicily and by the appearance of the ETRUSCANS in central Italy and the Po Valley. Historians generally agree that Etruscan culture was the result of outside (probably eastern) influence on indigenous peoples; the source, degree, and chronology of that outside influence remain uncertain. By the end of the 7th century BC, LATIUM and part of CAMPANIA had joined central Italy under Etruscan rule. As the Etruscans expanded their rule, many city-states were founded by the Italians.

ROMAN ITALY
According to later Roman historians, the city of ROME, founded in c.753—probably by local LATINS and SABINES—was ruled by Etruscan kings from 616 BC. But after the expulsion of the last of these kings, Lucius TARQUINIUS SUPERBUS in 510 BC, and the foundation of the Roman republic in 509, the power of the Etruscans declined as the Romans began the unification of Italy (see ROME, ANCIENT). This process reached its final stage in 89 BC, when the right of Roman citizenship was extended throughout Italy, with the consequent diffusion of Roman institutions and the Latin language and culture from the Alps to Sicily.

The Roman Empire. The Roman Empire began effectively with the defeat of Mark ANTONY and CLEOPATRA in 31 BC by the man who would later become Emperor AUGUSTUS. During the following centuries the increasing extent of the Roman possessions outside Italy and the complexity of the imperial bureaucracy resulted in a decline in the importance of Italy itself, a process accelerated by the growing number of emperors born outside Italy, whose allegiances lay elsewhere. The Edict of Caracalla (AD 212 or 213), which extended Roman citizenship to nearly all free provincials throughout the empire, further undermined Italy's special status. In 330, Emperor CONSTANTINE I transferred his capital from Rome to Constantinople, built on the site of Byzantium. Italy's administrative autonomy was lost shortly afterwards when two dioceses were joined with that of Africa to form a single prefecture. The loss of temporal power, however, was to some degree compensated for by the growing importance of Italy as a center of Christianity: starting in the 2d century AD several bishoprics were founded—in Milan, Ravenna, Naples, Benevento, and elsewhere—in addition to that of Rome.

After 476, when the Germanic chieftain ODOACER deposed the last western emperor, Romulus Augustulus (r. 475-76),

military control of Italy passed into barbarian hands. Under the Ostrogothic king, THEODORIC (r. 493-526; see GOTHS), in practical terms Italian political and social ties were with the West, in spite of continuing theoretical ties with the BYZANTINE EMPIRE. By 553, however, internal feuds permitted the Byzantine emperor JUSTINIAN I to regain control. Peninsular Italy was administered from its capital at RAVENNA as merely one division of the empire, although the Byzantines gradually and grudgingly admitted the ecclesiastical primacy of Rome in the West.

THE MIDDLE AGES
During the early Middle Ages, Italian ties with the "New Rome" of the East (Constantinople) were first threatened and later severed after a series of invasions from the west and north into Italy. The severing of ties with the East was confirmed by the eventual emergence of the PAPACY and the Italian cities as powers in their own right.

The Lombards. After the Ostrogoths, another Germanic people, the LOMBARDS, arrived in Italy—in 568; their control soon spread from the north to Tuscany and Umbria, although much of southern and eastern Italy remained in Byzantine hands. The Lombards were resisted chiefly by the popes—most notably GREGORY I (r. 590-604)—who acted as de facto political and military as well as ecclesiastical leaders and held a band of land stretching across the peninsula that later became the PAPAL STATES. By the end of the 7th century, papal resistance had induced the Lombards to consolidate their power in northern and central Italy, where they achieved a high degree of political unification. Meanwhile, the unrest in the Byzantine centers in the south reflected the disturbances taking place in Byzantium itself (see ICONOCLASM), and popular revolts broke out in Rome, Naples, Venice, and elsewhere. Thus by 728 the Lombards, under Liutprand (r. 712-44), were able to extend their influence in spite of further papal attempts at intervention. During Liutprand's reign, many of the Lombards converted from ARIANISM to Roman Catholicism. By this time they were accepting many other elements of Roman culture, including the Latin language; their law and administration reflected both Roman and Germanic influences (see GERMANIC LAW).

The Franks. The success of the Lombards, however, was temporary. Under the pretense of restoring to the papacy its lost territories, Pope Stephen II (r. 752-57) invited the FRANKS, still another Germanic tribe, to invade Italy. In 774 the Franks expelled the Lombard rulers; Lombard territory passed into the hands of the Frankish ruler CHARLEMAGNE, who was crowned emperor in Rome on Dec. 25, 800.

This 15th-century miniature by Jean Fouquet depicts the coronation in Rome of the Frankish ruler Charlemagne by Pope Leo III on Christmas day 800. Italy was a part of Charlemagne's empire and of its successor, the Holy Roman Empire, a key factor in the country's medieval history.

The following century was characterized by continual feuding between Franks and Byzantines, the chief beneficiaries being the SARACENS, newly arrived from North Africa. These Arabs originally came to assist rebels against the Byzantine Empire. The Saracens remained to conquer (827-78) Sicily, however, and to establish outposts in southern Italy; in 846 they launched an attack on Rome itself. The collapse of the Carolingian empire in the 9th century, at the same time as the resurgence of Byzantium under the Macedonian dynasty, caused a brief return to eastern influence.

The Ottonians. This constant alternation of power was temporarily ended by the arrival in Italy—once again by papal invitation—of the German king OTTO I, who was crowned Holy Roman emperor in 962 (see HOLY ROMAN EMPIRE). The Ottonian dynasty fell, however, shortly after 1000, leaving in the north a vacuum to be exploited by the local small landowners and town merchants. Meanwhile, local insurrections weakened the Saracens' hold on the southern coastal cities, although the Arabs remained strong in Sicily.

The Rise of the Italian City-States. In this climate of political and social fragmentation, individual Italian cities began to assert their autonomy. During the 11th century an elaborate pattern of communal government began to evolve under the leadership of a burgher class grown wealthy in trade, banking, and such industries as woolen textiles. Many cities—especially FLORENCE, GENOA, PISA, MILAN, and VENICE—became powerful and independent CITY-STATES. Resisting the efforts of both the old landed nobles and the emperors to control them, these COMMUNES hastened the end of feudalism in northern Italy and spawned deeply rooted identification with

The city of Naples, a commercial and cultural center of sourthern Italy, is depicted in this 15th-century painting. The city, then the capital of the kingdom of Naples, was seized from the Angevins by Alfonso V of Aragon in 1442 and briefly captured by the French in 1494.

the city as opposed to the larger region or country. The cities were often troubled by violent and divisive rivalries among their citizens, the most famous being the papal-imperial struggle—between the GUELPHS AND GHIBELLINES, the supporters respectively of the popes and the emperors. Despite such divisions, however, the cities contributed significantly to the economic, social, and cultural vitality of Italy.

The Kingdom of Sicily. Unlike the north, with its network of vigorously independent urban centers, southern Italy experienced a significant consolidation after its conquest by the NORMANS. Bands of these invaders arrived in Italy early in the 11th century. Starting *c.*1046, ROBERT GUISCARD and his successors expelled the Saracens and Byzantines and carved a powerful domain out of APULIA CALABRIA, Campania, and Sicily. Although the Norman territories remained a fief of the papacy, papal overlordship became a mere formality in the 12th century—especially after 1127, when ROGER II united the southern part of the peninsula with Sicily; he assumed the title of king of Sicily in 1130 (see NAPLES, KINGDOM OF; SICILY).

While the Normans were consolidating their rule in southern Italy, the papacy and the Holy Roman Empire continued their struggle for dominance in northern and central Italy. In

(Above) *Rivalries among the Italian city-states, which began to emerge in the 11th century, led to internal wars and domestic fragmentation. In 1494, Charles VIII of France invaded Italy, beginning the Italian Wars (1494-1559), which brought long periods of foreign occupation.*

1077, Pope GREGORY VII humbled Holy Roman Emperor HENRY IV at Canossa during the INVESTITURE CONTROVERSY. Later, Pope ALEXANDER III successfully supported an alliance of northern cities known as the Lombard League against the efforts of Emperor FREDERICK I (Barbarossa; r. 1152–90) of the HOHENSTAUFEN dynasty to impose imperial authority over them. Early in the 13th century the Hohenstaufen FREDERICK II succeeded in uniting the thrones of German and Norman Sicily. Although Pope INNOCENT III (r. 1198–1216) opposed the emperor and advanced far-reaching claims of political and religious supremacy, Frederick established one of the wealthiest and most powerful states in Europe, centering on his brilliant court at PALERMO, with its great cultural innovations.

The papal-imperial conflict culminated in 1262 with a papal invitation to Charles of Anjou, brother of King Louis IX of France, to conquer Sicily. Charles, the founder of the ANGEVIN dynasty of Naples, ruled from 1266 as CHARLES I, king of Naples and Sicily. French rule, which introduced feudalism to the south at a time when it was weakening elsewhere, was highly unpopular, and in 1282 a successful revolt (the SICILIAN VESPERS) resulted in the separation of Sicily from the mainland. PETER III of Aragon was made king of Sicily while the former Norman domains on the mainland remained under Angevin rule as the Kingdom of Naples. In the 15th century both kingdoms became Spanish possessions; they were then reunited under the title Kingdom of the TWO SICILIES.

THE ITALIAN RENAISSANCE AND FOREIGN DOMINATION

After 1300 both the papacy and the Holy Roman Empire turned their attention away from Italy. The emperors concentrated on German affairs while the popes met increasing resistance—especially from the French—as they tried to assert their authority in Europe. For much of the 14th century the papacy was situated outside Italy—at Avignon, in southern France.

The weakening of papal and imperial authority accompanied great intellectual changes in Italy. An intellectual revival, stimulated in part by the freer atmosphere of the cities and in part by the rediscovery of ancient Greek and Latin writings, gave rise to the humanist attitudes and ideas that formed the basis of the RENAISSANCE. About the same time, many of the communal governments of the city-states fell under the rule of dictators called *signori*, who curbed their factionalism and became hereditary rulers. In Milan the VISCONTI family rose to power in the 13th century, to be succeeded by the SFORZA family in the mid-15th century—a few decades after the MEDICI family had seized control of Florence. Meanwhile the ESTE family ruled Ferrara from the 13th through the 16th century. Although they subverted the political institutions of the communes, the *signori* (who became known as *principi*, with royal titles) were instrumental in advancing the cultural and civic life of Renaissance Italy. Under the patronage of the Medici, for example, Florence became the most magnificent and prestigious center of the arts in Italy. During the 14th and 15th centuries, Italian thought and style influenced all Europe.

As the larger cities expanded into the surrounding countryside, absorbing many of the smaller cities, they involved themselves in the complex international politics of the age. The frequent wars between city-states brought to Italy the mercenary leaders known as the CONDOTTIERI and ultimately resulted in foreign intervention. In 1494, CHARLES VIII of France invaded Italy (see ITALIAN WARS), signaling the beginning of a period of foreign occupation that lasted until the 19th century. By 1550 almost all Italy had been subjugated by the Habsburg ruler CHARLES V, who was both Holy Roman emperor and king of Spain; when Charles abdicated in 1555–56, dividing the Habsburg territories between his brother Emperor FERDINAND I and his son PHILIP II of Spain, Italy was part of the latter's inheritance. Spain remained the dominant power in Italy until Austria replaced it after the War of the SPANISH SUCCESSION (1701–14).

In the 18th century some areas of Italy achieved independence. SAVOY (the Kingdom of Sardinia after 1720) annexed SARDINIA and portions of LOMBARDY (see SARDINIA, KINGDOM OF); in 1735 the Kingdom of the Two Sicilies became an independent monarchy under the junior branch of the Spanish

In 1734, Naples and Sicily were conquered by the Spanish Bourbon prince Charles, who ruled the two kingdoms until his succession to the Spanish throne (as Charles III) in 1759. He is shown meeting with Pope Benedict XIV, who agreed to lessen church power in Naples.

Bourbon dynasty. Italy itself, however, no longer played a central role in European politics.

ITALIAN UNIFICATION

In the 18th century, as in the Renaissance, intellectual changes began to break down traditional values and institutions. Enlightenment ideas from France and Britain spread rapidly, and from 1789 the French Revolution excited liberal Italians.

The Napoleonic Era in Italy. Europe was soon involved, however, in a series of wars (see FRENCH REVOLUTIONARY WARS; NAPOLEONIC WARS) that eventually involved Italy. Between 1796, when troops under General Napoléon Bonaparte (see NAPOLEON I) invaded Italy, and 1814, when they withdrew, the entire peninsula was under French domination. Several short-lived republics were proclaimed early in the period. After two decades of Napoleon's modern but often harsh rule, profound changes took place in Italy; many Italians began to see the possibilities of forging a united country free of foreign control. Following the restoration of European peace in 1815, Italy consisted of the Kingdom of Sardinia (Piedmont, Sardinia, Savoy, and Genoa); the Kingdom of the Two Sicilies (including Naples and Sicily); the Papal States; and TUSCANY and a series of smaller duchies in north central Italy. Lombardy and Venetia were now controlled by the Austrians.

The Risorgimento. The repressive and reactionary policies imposed on Italy by the Austrian leader Klemens, Fürst von METTERNICH, and the Congress of Vienna (see VIENNA, CONGRESS OF) aggravated popular discontent, and the expansion of Austrian control in Italy stimulated intense antiforeign sentiment. These conditions gave rise to the Italian unification movement known as the RISORGIMENTO. Revolutionaries and patriots, especially Giuseppe MAZZINI, began to work actively for unity and independence. A series of unsuccessful revolts led in the 1820s by the CARBONARI, a conspiratorial nationalist organization, and in the 1830s by Mazzini's Young Italy group, provided the background for the REVOLUTIONS OF 1848, felt in every major Italian city and throughout Europe. Charles Albert, king of Sardinia (1831–49), declared war on Austria and, along with some other Italian rulers, gave his people a constitution; but both the war of liberation and the revolutionary republics set up in Rome, Venice, and Tuscany were crushed by Austria in 1849. Charles Albert abdicated in favor of his son, VICTOR EMMANUEL II, who retained the Sardinian constitution.

Unity. Under the progressive, liberal leadership of Camillo Benso, conte di CAVOUR, Sardinia led Italy to final unification.

The Italian patriot and hero of the Risorgimento, Giuseppe Garibaldi, is portrayed leading his volunteer army of Red Shirts in his Sicilian campaign (1860). Garibaldi's conquest of Sicily and southern Italy led to a unified Kingdom of Italy (1861) under King Victor Emmanuel II.

In 1859, after gaining the support of France and England, Cavour, in alliance with the French emperor NAPOLEON III, seized Lombardy; in 1860 all of Italy north of the Papal States—except Venetia—was added to Sardinia. Giuseppe GARIBALDI, a popular hero and guerrilla leader, led an expedition of 1,000 "Red Shirts" to Sicily in the same year and subsequently seized the southern part of peninsular Italy, which with Sicily constituted the Kingdom of the Two Sicilies. Garibaldi turned his conquests over to Victor Emmanuel, and in 1861 the Kingdom of Italy was proclaimed. Only Venetia and Rome were not included in the new state (the former was added in 1866 and the latter in 1870). Italians at last had their own country.

THE KINGDOM OF ITALY

The new nation faced many serious problems. A large debt, few natural resources, and almost no industry or transportation facilities combined with extreme poverty, a high illiteracy rate, and an uneven tax structure to weigh heavily on the Italian people. Regionalism was still strong, and only a fraction of the citizens had the right to vote. To make matters worse, the pope, angered over the loss of Rome and the papal lands, refused to recognize the Italian state. In the countryside, banditry and peasant anarchism resulted in government repression, which was often brutal. Meanwhile during the 1880s a socialist movement began to develop among workers in the cities. The profound differences between the impoverished south and the wealthier north widened. Parliament did little to resolve these problems: throughout this so-called Liberal Period (1870–1915), the nation was governed by a series of coalitions of liberals to the left and right of center who were unable to form a clear-cut majority. (The most notable leaders of the period were Francesco CRISPI and Giovanni GIOLITTI.) Despite the fact that some economic and social progress took place before World War I, Italy during that time was a dissatisfied and crisis-ridden nation.

In an attempt to increase its international influence and prestige, Italy joined Germany and Austria in the TRIPLE ALLIANCE in 1882; in the 1890s Italy unsuccessfully tried to conquer Ethiopia; and in 1911 it declared war on Turkey to obtain the North African territory of Libya (see ITALO-TURKISH WAR). After the outbreak of WORLD WAR I in 1914, Italy remained neutral for almost a year while the government negotiated with both sides. In 1915, Italy finally joined the Allies, after having been promised territories that it regarded as *Italia irredenta* (unliberated Italy; see IRREDENTISM). The country was unprepared for a major war, however; aside from a few victories in 1918, Italy suffered serious losses of men, matèriel, and morale (see CAPORETTO, BATTLE OF). Moreover, despite the efforts of Vittorio Emmanuele ORLANDO at the PARIS PEACE CONFERENCE, the treaties that followed the war gave Italy only Trentino and Trieste—a small part of the territories it had ex-

pected. These disappointments produced a powerful wave of nationalist sentiment against the Allies and the Italian government.

THE FASCIST PERIOD

Italy was plunged into deep social and political crisis by the war. Veterans, unemployed workers, desparate peasants, and a frightened middle class demanded changes, and the 1919 elections suddenly made the Socialist and the new Popular (Catholic) parties the largest in parliament. While extreme nationalists agitated for territorial expansion, strikes and threats of revolution unsettled the nation.

The Rise of Fascism. In 1919, in the midst of these unsettled conditions, Benito MUSSOLINI, a former revolutionary socialist, founded a new movement called FASCISM. Through a combination of shrewd political maneuvering and widespread violence perpetrated by Mussolini's BLACKSHIRT squads, the Fascists gained increasing support. In October 1922, after the Fascists had marched on Rome, King VICTOR EMMANUEL III named Mussolini prime minister. Within four years, Mussolini had become a dictator, destroying civil liberties, outlawing all other political parties, and imposing a totalitarian regime on the country by means of terror and constitutional subversion. Public works projects, propaganda, militarism, and the appearance of order gained Mussolini considerable prestige, and the LATERAN TREATY with the papacy in 1929 gave the *duce* (as he was called) a wide measure of popularity.

Fascist Expansionism. Mussolini's foreign policy, based on aggression and expansion, moved Italy closer to war during the 1930s. In 1935–36 the Italian army invaded and conquered

The unification of Italy, which had experienced political disunity since the 5th century, began with the Sardinian seizure of Lombardy from Austria in 1859. The Kingdom of Italy was proclaimed in 1861, and Venetia and Rome were included in 1866 and 1870, respectively.

UNIFICATION OF ITALY 1859-70

Kingdom of Sardinia until 1859	Added October and November 1860
Added November 1859	Joined 1866 (Venetia) and 1870 (Rome)
Added March 1860 following plebiscite	Ceded to France March 1860

Cartographic Production by Lothar Roth & Associates

Benito Mussolini, known as Il Duce, was the Fascist dictator of Italy from 1922 to 1943. He is shown leading his Blackshirt brigade in their march on Rome in 1922. At first Mussolini worked with King Victor Emmanuel III; soon, however, he assumed dictatorial powers.

ETHIOPIA, and in 1936, Italy sent troops to support Francisco Franco in the SPANISH CIVIL WAR. Later that year Mussolini and Adolf HITLER, the National Socialist dictator of Germany, established the Rome-Berlin AXIS; in 1939, Italy took Albania, and the two dictators then concluded a military alliance known as the Pact of Steel. In June 1940, 9 months after the outbreak of WORLD WAR II in Europe, Italy entered the conflict on Germany's side.

World War II. Mussolini's war effort met with setbacks and defeats on all fronts; in July 1943 the Allies invaded Sicily. The Fascist leadership turned against Mussolini, and the king forced him to resign. Rescued by German paratroopers, Mussolini escaped to Salò in northern Italy, where he established a puppet government (the Italian Social Republic) under German protection. In the south, the king and his new prime minister, Pietro BADOGLIO, surrendered to the Allies in September and then joined in the war against Germany. A fierce and heroic anti-Fascist resistance movement fought in the German-occupied north for two years while underground political leaders organized the anti-Fascists into the Committee of National Liberation (CLN). The Allies pushed the German armies out of Italy with great difficulty, and in April 1945 the partisans captured and executed Mussolini.

POSTWAR ITALY

Between 1945 and 1948 a new Italian nation emerged from the disaster of fascism and war. In June 1946 a popular election abolished the monarchy in favor of a republic; a new constitution was adopted the next year. The Christian Democrats, the Communists, and the Socialists became the strongest political parties in the country. The largest of these parties, the Christian Democrats, first under the leadership of Alcide DE GASPERI, dominated the Italian government after 1948. De Gasperi stressed industrial growth, agricultural reform, and close cooperation with the United States and other Western nations. With massive U.S. aid, Italy underwent a remarkable economic recovery that saw rapid industrial expansion and a sharp increase in the standard of living. Italy joined the NORTH ATLANTIC TREATY ORGANIZATION in 1949, the European Coal and Steel Community (see EUROPEAN COMMUNITY) in 1951, and the Common Market (see EUROPEAN ECONOMIC COMMUNITY) in 1958.

In the late 1970s many serious problems still faced the Italians, including chronic inflation and widespread demands for social and political justice. Labor unrest, student demonstrations, and violence frequently unsettled the country, and the political situation reflected this unstable condition. After 1962, when the Christian Democrats formed a coalition with the Socialists (the "opening to the left"), the strength of the Christian Democrats diminished in favor of the Communists, who received about one-third of all votes in the 1970s and controlled many local governments.

Acts of organized terrorism from the extreme left (especially from the Red Brigades) made the political situation increasingly volatile in the 1970s. The Christian Democrats were unable to maintain their working majority in parliament without the support of the Communists. Whether the Communists would form a coalition government with the Christian Democrats (the so-called "historical compromise") remained a crucial political issue in Italy; the kidnapping and murder of Christian Democratic leader Aldo MORO by Red Brigade terrorists in 1978 made the question vital to the future of the country.   PHILIP V. CANNISTRARO AND JOHN J. REICH

Bibliography: Boak, Arthur, and Sinnigen, William, *A History of Rome to A.D. 565*, 6th ed. (1977); Croce, Benedetto, *A History of Italy, 1871-1915*, trans. by Cecilia M. Ady (1929; repr. 1963); Hay, Denys, *The Italian Renaissance and Its Historical Background* (1961); Hearder, Harry, and Waley, D. P., eds., *A Short History of Italy* (1963); King, Bolton, *A History of Italian Unity*, 2 vols. (1924; repr. 1967); Mack Smith, Denis, *Italy: A Modern History*, rev. ed. (1969); Procacci, Giuliano, *A History of the Italian People*, trans. by Anthony Paul (1971); Randall-MacIver, David, *Italy Before the Romans* (1928; repr. 1972); Waley, D. P., *The Italian City-Republics* (1969); Whyte, A. J., *The Evolution of Modern Italy* (1965); Wiskemann, Elizabeth, *Italy Since 1945* (1971).

See also: ITALIAN ART AND ARCHITECTURE; ITALIAN LITERATURE.

Ithaca   (Greece)   [ith'-uh-kuh]

Ithaca (Greek: Itháki), a mountainous island in the Ionian Sea, forms, with nearby Cephalonia, a *nome* (department) of Greece. Ithaca has an area of 96 km² (37 mi²) and a population of 4,156 (1971). Olives, grapes, and currants grow in the poor volcanic soil; fishing is a major industry. Ithaca has been traditionally associated with Odysseus of Homer's *Odyssey*.

Ithaca   (New York)   [ith'-uh-kuh]

Ithaca (1979 est. pop., 31,500) is the seat of Tompkins County, New York. Located at the southern tip of Cayuga Lake in the Finger Lakes region, it is the southern terminus of the NEW YORK STATE BARGE CANAL system. It is an agricultural center for the area's dairy and poultry farms; industries in the city manufacture business machines and research instruments. It was settled about 1790 and was incorporated as a city in 1888. Ithaca is the site of CORNELL UNIVERSITY (1865) and Ithaca College (1892).

Ito Hirobumi   [ee'-toh hee-roh'-boo-mee]

Ito Hirobumi, b. October 1841, was a leading Japanese statesman after the MEIJI RESTORATION. His father, a peasant, had been adopted by a lower-class samurai in Choshu. Ito was an aide to Kido Takayoshi, one of the organizers of the Satsuma-Choshu alliance that overthrew the shogunate in 1868.

Ito served in several important posts in the new Meiji government. He went on the Iwakura mission (1871-73) to study Western government and technology and to work on the revision of treaties with Western countries. On his return, he opposed the invasion of Korea and took a lead in the movement to modernize Japan.

In 1878, after the powerful Okubo Toshimichi was assassinated, Ito succeeded him as home minister. In 1881 he persuaded his rival OKUMA SHIGENOBU, a key minister, to resign and exacted from the oligarchic government a promise to adopt a constitution and a more representative form of government. In preparation for drafting the Meiji Constitution of 1889, Ito headed another mission (1882-83) to Europe to study European governments, especially the Prussian system. After his return, he helped reorganize the peerage and created a cabinet system.

Ito served as Japan's first prime minister under the new cabinet system (1885-88) and headed the privy council that ratified (1889) the constitution. He was prime minister again in 1892-96, 1898, and 1900-01. In 1900 he founded the Seiyukai party in the Diet. After the RUSSO-JAPANESE WAR of 1904-05, Ito became resident general in Korea, which had become a protectorate of Japan.

Despite Ito's moderate policies, a Korean nationalist assassinated him at Harbin, Manchuria, on Oct. 26, 1909, an act that precipitated the Japanese annexation of Korea.

WILLIAM B. HAUSER

Bibliography: Akita, George, *Foundations of Constitutional Government in Modern Japan, 1868-1900* (1967); Kengi Hamada, *Prince Ito* (1936); Scherer, A. B., *Three Meiji Leaders: Ito, Togo, Nogi* (1936).

Iturbi, José   [ee-toor'-bee]

The pianist and conductor José Iturbi, b. Valencia, Spain, Nov. 28, 1895, is best known for his interpretations of Spanish music and for his appearances in several American musical films during the 1940s. He studied at the Paris Conservatory, and after a successful concert career in Europe he made his United States debut in 1928, touring the country. He again toured the United States in 1930, giving recitals and performing with leading symphony orchestras, and from 1936 to 1944 he was conductor of the Rochester (N.Y.) Philharmonic. He frequently performed with his pianist sister, Amparo Iturbi (1898-1969), in duo-piano concerts.

Discography: Albeniz, I., *Suite Espanola* (nos. 3 and 5); Granada, E., *Allegro di Concierto in C* and *Spanish Dances* (3).

Iturbide, Agustín de   [ee-toor-bee'-day, ah-goos-teen' day]

Agustín de Iturbide, b. Sept. 27, 1783, d. July 19, 1824, was an army officer who declared Mexican independence from Spain and who for a short time served (1822-23) as emperor of Mexico. From an upper-class background, Iturbide as a youth attended the seminary in his home town, Valladolid (now Morelia, Mexico); however, he soon dedicated himself to a military career, becoming an officer in the viceregal army. When rebellion against Spain, led by Miguel HIDALGO Y COSTILLA and José María MORELOS Y PAVÓN, broke out in 1810, Iturbide, like most other aristocratic Mexicans, supported the Spanish government. For more than ten years he fought to quell the independence movement, gaining a reputation for being not only brave and dashing, but also unscrupulous, avaricious, and cruel. In 1820 he was appointed to lead an army against Vicente Guerrero's insurgent band in southern Mexico. Because he and the Mexican elite feared that Spain would introduce liberal reforms, however, Iturbide instead came to terms with the insurgents in 1821, overthrew the viceroy, and, on Sept. 27, 1821, proclaimed Mexico an independent constitutional monarchy according to the conservative Plan de Iguala (Feb. 24, 1821). In the following year he proclaimed himself emperor of Mexico, but he was overthrown in March 1823 by the revolutionary forces led by Antonio López de SANTA ANNA and went into exile in Italy. In

Agustín de Iturbide, a leader of Mexican conservative revolutionary forces, established Mexico's independence from Spain by the 1821 Treaty of Córdoba. The following year he was proclaimed emperor of Mexico. He was overthrown by a liberal counterrevolution and was forced to abdicate in 1823.

1824, Iturbide tried to reestablish himself in power, but he was arrested, tried, and executed as a traitor.   ROBERT PATCH

Bibliography: Caruso, J. A., *The Liberators of Mexico* (1954); Robertson, William S., *Iturbide of Mexico* (1952; repr. 1968).

Ivan III, Grand Duke of Moscow   (Ivan the Great)

Ivan III, b. Jan. 22, 1440, was grand duke of Moscow from 1462 until 1505. Known as Ivan the Great, he began the unification and centralization of the Russian lands under Moscow. After a tumultuous childhood and youth, Ivan succeeded his father, Vasily II. During Ivan's reign the declining Khanate of the GOLDEN HORDE made several attempts to reimpose its rule on Russia; in 1480, Ivan, repelling a Tatar invasion, finally freed Moscow from domination by the TATARS. In that same year he suppressed a rebellion at home. During the 1470s and 1480s, Ivan absorbed Moscow's old rivals in the north, Novgorod and Tver, as well as other territories, and established a unified rule over what had been a divided Russia. He also fought Lithuania (1492-94 and 1500-03) in an attempt to reconquer the Ukraine but was only partly successful. During Ivan's reign, Moscow was the site of an impressive building campaign directed by Italian artists and artisans.

After the death (1467) of his first wife, Ivan married (1472) Sophia, a Byzantine princess and niece of the last Byzantine emperor. Following the marriage, Ivan developed a complicated court ceremonial based on the Byzantine model and began to use the title of *tsar* (a variation of the word *caesar*). After a long period of vacillation, and, amid plots and rebellions by rival contenders for the throne, Ivan finally chose (1502) his eldest son by Sophia as his successor. Ivan died on Oct. 27, 1505, and was succeeded by this son, VASILY III.

DONALD L. LAYTON

Bibliography: Fennell, John L. I., *Ivan the Great of Moscow* (1961); Grey, Ian, *Ivan the Third and the Unification of Russia* (1964).

Ivan IV, Grand Duke of Moscow and Tsar of Russia   (Ivan the Terrible)

The first Russian ruler to be crowned tsar and to hold that official title was Ivan IV, known as the Terrible. He centralized the administration of Russia and expanded the boundaries of the Russian empire.

Ivan was born on Aug. 25, 1530, in Moscow, the son of VASILY III, grand duke of Moscow, who died in 1533 when Ivan was only three years old. Ivan's mother, Yelena Glinskaya, who was from a leading BOYAR, or noble, family, established a regency, but it soon degenerated into intrigue, denunciation, and wild violence as rival boyars disputed the dominance of the Glinsky family.

Following Yelena's death in 1538 strife and misrule continued. Ivan, who suffered from poor health, was largely ignored, his education neglected. In 1547, Ivan was crowned, not as grand duke but as tsar. In the same year, he married Anastasia Romanov, and although he was to marry several more times following her death in 1560, Ivan was never able to recapture the happiness he had enjoyed with Anastasia. (The ROMANOV dynasty, which ruled Russia from 1613 to 1917, traces its claim to the throne from their union—through Anastasia's brother, Nikitu.)

The years 1547 through 1560 are usually considered the constructive period of Ivan's reign, although the exact date that he assumed de facto control from the aristocracy is in dispute. He appointed an advisory council, founded (1549) a national assembly, enacted reforms in local government (approved by the advisory council), drew up (1550) a new law code, and standardized the responsibilities and duties of the aristocracy. Ivan annexed two of the three Tatar states in Russia—Kazan (1552) and Astrakhan (1556)—the first non-Slavic states in the empire. Thus Russian control of the Volga River and access to the Caspian Sea was assumed. Expansion to the east, beyond the Ural Mountains, also began during this period. (Before Ivan's death Russia had established itself in Siberia.) In addition, trade contacts with the English, French, and Dutch were begun.

Anastasia's death in 1560 marked the end of Ivan's constructive policies. Increasingly powerful, Ivan turned against his advisors—convinced that they, backed by the boyars, had caused her death. Threatening to abdicate unless the boyars were punished for their greed and treachery, Ivan abandoned Moscow in 1564, settling in the village of Aleksandrovsk. Confused and frightened, the people of Moscow begged Ivan to return and rule over them. He eventually agreed to do so on two conditions: he was to have the right to punish traitors and wrongdoers, executing them when necessary and confiscating their possessions; and a political and territorial subdivision—the *oprichnina*—was to be established, managed entirely at the discretion of the tsar.

The *oprichnina* included most of the wealthy towns, trade routes, and cultivated areas of Russia and was, therefore, a stronghold of wealthy old boyar families. To Ivan's select bodyguard, the *oprichniki*, fell the task of destroying many of these great lords. Contemporary estimates of the number killed are from 400 to as high as 10,000. Only a few of the old boyar families survived. Those who were not killed were ruined by Ivan's political and economic reforms. Ivan controlled this personal territory until 1572.

In foreign affairs, too, turmoil and disaster marked the latter part of Ivan's reign. Russia attempted, unsuccessfully, to gain access to the Baltic Sea in the Livonian War (1557–82) with Poland-Lithuania.

Ivan died on Mar. 18, 1584. Although the transition from Ivan to his son and successor, Fyodor I, was relatively easy and quiet, Moscow was, according to most observers, on the verge of anarchy as a result of Ivan's policies.

DONALD L. LAYTON

Bibliography: Graham, Stephen, *Ivan the Terrible* (1933; repr. 1968); Grey, Ian, *Ivan The Terrible* (1964); Platonov, Sergei Federovich, *Ivan the Terrible*, ed. and trans. by Joseph L. Wieczynski (1974); Waliszewski, Kazimierz, *Ivan the Terrible*, trans. by Mary Loyd (1904; repr. 1966); Wipper, Robert, *Ivan Grozny*, trans. by J. Fineberg, 3d ed. (1947).

Ivanchenkov, Aleksandr   [ee-vahn-chenk'-awf]

The Soviet civilian cosmonaut Aleksandr Ivanchenkov, b. Sept. 28, 1940, was the flight engineer in the second crew to visit the Salyut 6 space station. He graduated (1964) from the Moscow Aviation Institute and was working in a design office when he was selected (1970) to be a cosmonaut. He was probably part of the backup crews of Soyuz 16 and 19. Ivanchenkov and Col. Vladimir Kovalenok, the flight commander, were launched into space on June 15, 1978, aboard SOYUZ 29, which docked with SALYUT 6 the following day. During their stay within the space station they were joined for brief periods by the crews of Soyuz 30 and 31 and were resupplied with food, water, and air by the Progress 2, 3, and 4 automatic supply crafts. The cosmonauts used two furnaces for technical experiments, made extensive observations of the Earth's surface, conducted various biological experiments, and tested new astro-orientation and space-navigation optical experiments. On July 29, Ivanchenkov and Kovalenok went outside the space station to retrieve biopolymer-sample canisters, install radio-sensitive plates, and inspect a micrometeorite detection system. The length of the mission—140 days—set a new space endurance record. The Soyuz 29 spacecraft was brought back to Earth on September 3 by the Soyuz 31 crew, while Ivanchenkov and Kovalenok returned aboard the Soyuz 31 craft, which landed 180 km (112 mi) southeast of Dzhezkazgan, Kazakhstan, on November 2.   CRAIG B. WAFF

Bibliography: Hooper, Gordon R., "Missions to Salyut 6," pts. 5–8, *Spaceflight*, March, May, July, August–September 1979.

Ivanhoe   [y'-vuhn-hoh]

Set in 12th-century England, *Ivanhoe* is the first of Sir Walter SCOTT's novels in which the action takes place outside Scotland. Scott's principal concern in *Ivanhoe* is to show the noble idealism of chivalry along with its often cruel and impractical consequences. The work also introduces some of Scott's most memorable characters, among them Richard the Lion-hearted, the Jewess Rebecca, and the Knight Templar Sir

Brian de Bois-Guilbert. Long one of Scott's most popular novels, *Ivanhoe* colorfully depicts medieval panoply in the age of the Third Crusade and offers narrative excitement by means of such episodes as the tournament at Ashby-de-la-Zouche and the siege of Torquilstone.   R. L. ABRAHAMSON

Ivanov, Georgy   [ee-vahn'-awf]

Georgy Ivanov was the first Bulgarian cosmonaut and the fourth non-Soviet to fly aboard a Soviet spacecraft. A major in the Bulgarian air force, he began astronaut training in 1978 as part of the Soviet Intercosmos program. At the time of his flight aboard SOYUZ 33 (April 11–13, 1979), Ivanov was 38 years old. He and fellow crewmember N. N. Rukavishnikov, a Russian, had planned to dock their Soyuz spacecraft with the SALYUT 6 space station, but malfunctions in the Soyuz main propulsion system forced them to abort their mission and return to Earth along a high-stress reentry profile that subjected them to an 8 g deceleration, twice that normally experienced. They landed safely in the Kazakhstan steppes, about 2,900 km (1,800 mi) southeast of Moscow.   CRAIG B. WAFF

Ivanov, Lev Ivanovich

Lev Ivanovich Ivanov, b. Feb. 18 (N.S.), 1834, d. Dec. 11 (N.S.), 1901, was a dancer and choreographer in the Imperial Theaters of Saint Petersburg (now Leningrad). In 1852 he became a member of the Imperial Ballet but did not gain promotion to premier danseur until 1869; he retired as a dancer in 1893. During his artistic career he also served as stage manager, ballet master, and teacher. His most significant contribution to ballet history, however, was his choreography, which in the classical purity of its symphonic form influenced later choreographers like George Balanchine. Always working under the shadow of the dictatorial Marius Petipa, Ivanov created the Polovetsian Dances for Aleksandr Borodin's opera *Prince Igor* (1890). Ivanov was also responsible for portions of several of Petipa's major ballets—the entire *Nutcracker*, following Petipa's precise scenario (1892), and acts 2 and 4 of *Swan Lake* (1895).   ANN FARKAS

Bibliography: Roslavleva, Natalia, *The Era of the Russian Ballet* (1966).

Ivanov, Vsevolod Vyacheslavovich   [ee-vahn'-awf, vuh-sev'-uh-luht vee-e-chis-lahv'-uh-vich]

A Russian novelist, b. Lebyazhye, Siberia, Feb. 24 (N.S.), 1895, Vsevolod Vyacheslavovich Ivanov in 1920 was one of the members of the Petersburg group, the Serapion Brothers, and subsequently an ornamentalist in his search for a special artistic language whose words would have value independent of their practicality. His early novels, *Partizany* (Partisans, 1921) and the well-known *Armoured Train No. 14-69* (1922; Eng. trans. of 1927 play, 1933), deal with the Russian Civil War (1918–23), which Ivanov describes as a clash of brutal and elementary forces inherent in Russian history. For this treatment he came under the fire of official critics in the late 1920s. His later works, the autobiographical novel *Adventures of a Fakir* (1935; Eng. trans., 1935) and *Vzyatiye Berlina* (The Taking of Berlin, 1945), are written in the style of socialist realism. The former presents a colorful picture of Ivanov's life in a number of professions, including the circus.

Bibliography: Maguire, Robert A., *Red Virgin Soil* (1968); Struve, Gleb, *Russian Literature Under Lenin and Stalin, 1917–1953* (1971).

Ives, Burl   [yvz]

Folksinger and actor Burl Icle Ivanhoe Ives, b. Jasper County, Ill., June 14, 1909, began to learn his art as a child from his folksinging family. As a youth, he hoboed around the country, reaching New York in 1937. A series of bit acting parts, and nightclub stints as an increasingly popular singer, led in 1940 to his own radio show, "The Wayfaring Stranger," to a number of successful recordings, and, from 1945, to a career in Hollywood. Ives starred in the New York production of Tennessee Williams's *Cat on a Hot Tin Roof* (1955) and in the film of the play (1958). He won an academy award for his role in *The Big Country* (1958).

Ives, Charles Edward

Charles Ives, a 20th-century American composer, was among the first to use the innovative devices polytonality and polyrhythm that dominate later musical composition. He often used traditional American melodies in his compositions, including hymn tunes, patriotic songs, and marches. A highly successful executive, Ives did not publish many of his works until late in life.

Considered by many to have been America's greatest composer, Charles Edward Ives, b. Danbury, Conn., Oct. 20, 1874, d. May 19, 1954, typified in his life and music much of the New England tradition. Ives's father, George, a noted Civil War band director with a boldly inquiring mind, was a key influence on the composer's approach to life and music. After comprehensive musical studies with his father, Ives received traditional academic training from Horatio Parker at Yale University (1894–98). Ives was also deeply influenced by the writings of Ralph Waldo Emerson, Nathaniel Hawthorne, the Alcotts, and Henry David Thoreau, which inspired his remarkable Second Piano Sonata: Concord, Mass., 1840–60 (1909–15). Each of the four movements of this sonata bears the name of one of the above authors as its title. Ives frequently quoted hymns and popular, patriotic, and ragtime music in his compositions, but he adapted these borrowings to new formal and sound contexts that were either misunderstood by tradition-minded listeners or regarded as curiosities. At a surprisingly early date he used or created many of the important 20th-century composing techniques that are still used, notably polytonality and polyrhythmic textures. Ives's self-conscious view of himself as a composer in a society that generally held a disdainful view of music as a profession was probably one of the reasons for his decision to earn his living in the insurance business. The firm of Ives and Myrick (founded 1907) became a famous insurance agency in New York City. A heart attack in 1921 and a diabetic condition forced Ives to virtually cease composing; he retired from business in 1930.

In the 30 or so years of his creative activity (about 1890–1921), Ives composed more than 500 works, about a third of which were left incomplete. He produced nearly 70 instrumental pieces for large ensembles; the most significant of these are his four numbered symphonies, three orchestral sets (sometimes called symphonies), including Three Places in New England (1903–14), and two overtures (Emerson and Browning). He also wrote music for chamber or theater orchestra, including marches, ragtime pieces, and The Unanswered Question (1908), several sets of songs for voices or instruments or both, and music for band (primarily marches). Other works include two sonatas for piano, five for violin (of which four are numbered), two string quartets, a piano trio, many miscellaneous pieces for a variety of instrumental combinations, numerous piano pieces (including experimental "studies"), several piano duets, organ music (voluntaries, preludes, and variations, including Variations on "America"), music for the theater, much choral music (sacred and secular), and more than 200 solo songs with piano accompaniment. The wide variety of his songs alone gives a broad overview of Ives's shorter forms and the techniques of composition that spanned his entire creative career. Under

the leadership of a pianist and Ives specialist, John Kirkpatrick, an effort is being made to publish Ives's complete works.

DELMER D. ROGERS

Bibliography: Cowell, Henry and Sidney, Charles Ives and His Music, rev. ed. (1969); Hitchcock, H. Wiley, Ives (1977) and An Ives Celebration, ed. by H. Wiley Hitchcock and Vivian Perlis (1974); Ives, Charles, Essays Before a Sonata, The Majority, and Other Writings, ed. by H. Boatwright (1970), and Memos, ed. by John Kirkpatrick (1972); Perlis, Vivian, Charles Ives Remembered (1974); Rossiter, Frank R., Charles Ives and His America (1975); Wooldridge, David, From the Steeples and Mountains: A Study of Charles Ives (1974).

See also: AMERICAN MUSIC.

Ivory Coast

Ivory Coast is a West African nation, located on the Gulf of Guinea. It is bordered by Ghana on the east, Upper Volta and Mali on the north, and Guinea and Liberia on the west. Formerly a territory within FRENCH WEST AFRICA, it achieved independence on Aug. 7, 1960. Its natural resource base and stable government give Ivory Coast good potential for economic growth.

LAND AND PEOPLE

The terrain of Ivory Coast rises gradually from the Gulf of GUINEA northward in four east-west zones: the littoral strip, rainforest, savanna, and tableland. The littoral strip, reaching as far as 50 km (30 mi) inland, is characterized by lagoons separated from the ocean by long sandbars. North of these lagoons, a cross-country rainforest belt some 300 km (185 mi) wide gives way to wooded savanna. Tablelands in the northernmost areas approach elevations of about 400 m (1,300 ft),

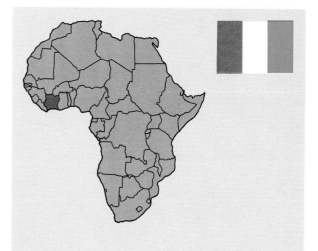

IVORY COAST

Official Name: Republic of Ivory Coast
Capital and Largest City: Abidjan (1976 est. pop., 850,000)
Area: 322,463 km² (124,504 mi²)
Elevation: Highest—Mount Nimba, 1,752 m (5,747 ft); lowest—sea level along Gulf of Guinea
Population: 7,365,000 (1979 est.). Distribution—21% urban, 79% rural; density, 21 persons per km² (54 per mi²); annual rate of increase (1970–76), 2.6%
Principal Languages: French (official), tribal languages
Principal Religions: Traditional religions, Islam, Roman Catholicism
Principal Products: Agriculture—coffee, cocoa beans, bananas, timber, pineapples, yams, palm oil, corn, rubber. Manufacturing and industry—food and wood products; tobacco; textiles; chemicals; plastics; metal products; rubber. Mining—diamonds, manganese
Railroads: 652 km/405 mi (1976)
Roads: 2,200 km/1,370 mi (1976 paved)
Currency: 1 franc CFA = 100 centimes

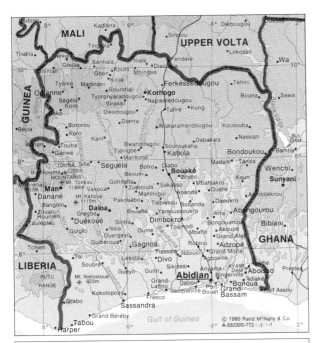

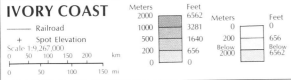

IVORY COAST

——— Railroad

+ Spot Elevation

Scale 1:9,267,000

Meters	Feet
2000	6562
1000	3281
500	1640
200	656
0	0

Meters	Feet
0	0
200	656
Below 2000	Below 6562

ing and forestry occupy more than 50% of the land area and employ about 80% of the labor force. Mineral production is restricted to diamonds, but a foreign consortium has been established to extract and process the nation's iron ore reserves, and petroleum drilling has begun in the Gulf of Guinea. Light manufacturing industries process the raw materials of the country.

Ivory Coast has a favorable trade balance. Exports include cocoa from processed cacao beans, coffee, and timber. Petroleum, iron and steel, machinery, and transport equipment are imported. Its principal trading partners include France, the United States, and the Netherlands. Ivory Coast is an associate member of the European Economic Community. Heavy

with occasional peaks rising more than 900 m (2,950 ft). The highest altitudes are found near the Guinean-Liberian border. The country's four main rivers are the Komoé, Bandama, Sassandra, and Cavally.

The climatic zones of the country vary with topography. The subequatorial south is characterized by high humidity and a temperature range of 26°–28° C (79°–82° F). Precipitation averages 2,000 to 3,000 mm (80 to 120 in) annually, occurring primarily from April to November. The forest zone has lower humidity, temperature variations from 15° to 40° C (59° to 104° F), and rainfall of 1,000 to 2,500 mm (40 to 100 in), which decreases to the north. Temperatures drop with increasing elevations in the north, but a hot, dry wind from the Sahara desert prevails in the winter.

Wildlife includes antelope, giraffes, hyenas, lions, elephants, monkeys, pigmy hippopotamuses, crocodiles, and snakes, as well as numerous species of birds. Forests, particularly of hardwood such as mahogany, constitute the country's greatest resource other than agricultural lands. Diamonds and iron ore are found in quantities sufficient for mining.

The country's more than 60 ethnic groups form seven main divisions: the AKAN, mainly in the southeast; the KRU, in the southwest; the Lagoon or Kwa, along the littoral; the MANDE, nuclear and peripheral, and the SENUFO throughout the north; and the Lobi in the central regions. About 1,500,000 non-Ivorian Africans live in the country, particularly immigrants from Upper Volta, Mali, and Guinea, as well as 50,000–60,000 French and 25,000–30,000 Lebanese. Bouaké (1974 est. pop., 156,000) is the only large city other than ABIDJAN, the capital.

Infant mortality is high (164 per 1,000 live births); life expectancy at birth is 44 years. Although stress has been placed on education, literacy is about 20%, or 65% at primary school level. The university at Abidjan was established in 1964.

ECONOMIC ACTIVITY

Ivory Coast has one of Africa's most diversified and wealthy economies. It is the world's third-largest producer of coffee and cacao; together with hardwoods and bananas, these crops account for 75% of all export earnings. Plantation farm-

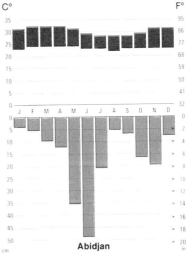

Abidjan

(Above) *Abidjan, the capital and largest city of Ivory Coast, was the administrative center of the French Ivory Coast colony between 1934 and 1960, when the nation achieved independence. The city has become a major port since 1950, when the Vridi Canal was completed.*

(Left) *Bars indicate monthly ranges of temperatures (red) and precipitation (blue) of Abidjan, the capital of Ivory Coast. The tropical wet climate is typical of countries in the equatorial zone.*

borrowing (principally from France) for development projects, however, has created a large foreign debt. In 1979, with inflation and unemployment rates of 20% per year, Ivory Coast had a per capita gross domestic product of $940.

HISTORY AND GOVERNMENT

Little is known of Ivory Coast's history before European involvement in the ivory and slave trades. French missionary contact in Ivory Coast began as early as 1637, but an official French protectorate was not established until 1843-45, when treaties were concluded with local chiefs. Ivory Coast became a French colony in 1893 and was a constituent of French West Africa from 1904 until 1958. It was made an overseas territory in 1946, and its inhabitants were given French citizenship. Ivory Coast was proclaimed a republic within the FRENCH COMMUNITY in December 1958; in 1960 it became independent.

Ivory Coast is a republic, with a president elected for a 5-year term, an appointed cabinet, and a unicameral national assembly of 120 members, popularly elected for 5-year terms. Members of the judiciary are chosen by the president. The country is divided into 24 departments, each headed by a centrally appointed prefect and subdivided into a total of 127 subprefectures.

Ivory Coast has been led since 1959 by Félix HOUPHOUËT-BOIGNY, who was elected president in 1960 and last reelected in 1975. His Parti Democratique de la Côte d'Ivoire is the country's only legal political party. Ivory Coast has been generally favorable to the West in its policies and strongly anti-Communist.

FRANKLIN PARKER

Bibliography: Cohen, Michael A., *Urban Policy and Political Conflict in Africa: A Study of the Ivory Coast* (1974); Thompson, Virginia, *West Africa's Council of the Entente* (1972); Zolberg, Aristide R., *One-Party Government in the Ivory Coast* (1974).

ivory and ivory carving

Ivory is the smooth, solid, usually white material that makes up the tusks of elephants and the tusks and teeth of walruses, sperm whales, narwhals, hippopotamuses, and wild boars. Exceptionally durable if it is not exposed to extremes of temperature or humidity, ivory may be carved and shaped with wood-cutting tools. It is one of the oldest carving materials, and carved ivory objects have been found that date back more than 20,000 years.

More fibrous than bone, ivory is actually modified dentine. The elephant tusk is built up of layers of ivory, and when cut in section it shows the distinctive pattern of hair-thin curving lines—a structure resembling the precise lines left on metal by engine turning—that gives ivory its fine grain and elasticity. A large proportion of the tusk is buried in the bone socket of the skull and is hollow for part of its length, narrowing to thread diameter toward the point of the tusk. A very dense material, ivory has close, compact pores filled with a gelatinous substance that produces a glowing finish when the ivory surface is polished.

Types of Ivory. The hardest ivory is obtained from elephants inhabiting the western part of Africa. Ivory from elephants in eastern Africa is generally softer, more densely white, and more easily carved. On the average, African male elephant tusks measure 2 m (6 ft) in length and weigh about 23 kg (50 lb). The tusk of the much smaller Asian elephant averages 1.5 m (5 ft) in length and weighs around 16 kg (35 lb). Asian tusks from India are no longer permitted to be imported into the United States, and most commercial ivory comes from the African elephant, *Loxodonta africana*.

Ancient mammoth and elephant ivory found embedded in frozen river beds and along the Arctic Ocean was once used in great quantity. Parcels of Siberian mammoth ivory weighing from 10 to 20 tons were common in the ivory markets of the 1890s. Today what little fossil ivory remains comes from Alaska.

Walrus ivory was used for centuries by European ivory carvers, and the North European walrus herds were hunted to the point of extinction by ivory traders in the late Middle Ages.

Walrus tusks may grow to 0.6 m (2 ft) in length, and weigh as much as 3.7 kg (8 lb). Texture is considerably less dense than that of elephant ivory, and the tusk is hollow for much of its length.

Ancient Egyptian ivory carvers often used the extremely hard hippopotamus ivory, which must first be steeped in acid to remove its outer casing of enamel. Because of its hardness, dentists in ancient Rome used hippopotamus ivory to make dentures; and modern Japanese carvers prize its close grain and pure whiteness.

Ivory obtained from the teeth of the sperm whale has limited attraction for carvers because the teeth are relatively small. The single large tusk of the Arctic narwhal, sometimes 2.5 m (8 ft) long, is of good color and texture, but its spiral groove and a deep cavity running almost its entire length makes working difficult. Nevertheless, narwhal ivory is widely used in Japan.

Various substitutes for ivory are in common use. The most important is vegetable ivory, made from the fruit of the South American ivory nut palm, *Phytelephas macrocarpa*. In present-day Japan, vegetable ivory is often carved and stained to simulate mellow old ivory. Celluloid and plastics also serve as substitutes for ivory and have largely replaced genuine ivory for such uses as buttons, billiard balls, and piano keys.

Ivory Carving. Prehistoric peoples fashioned sculptured or incised designs from bone or ivory. By 4000 BC the Egyptians had achieved a highly developed art of ivory carving, which included freestanding objects, incised designs on flat surfaces, mosaics, inlay, and ivory panels with designs carved in relief. The colossal statues of gods made by the ancient Greeks were fashioned of hammered gold, with painted ivory faces, hands, and feet of a composite material called chrys-elephantine. In Roman and Byzantine times ivory came to be

The Byzantine diptych of the consul Anastasius (c.517), a hinged writing tablet, embodies the boldly carved, balanced design typical of ivories produced at Constantinople between the 4th and 6th centuries. (Cabinet des Médailles, Paris.)

A stylized ivory mask from Benin, the capital of a Nigerian kingdom that flourished between the 14th and 17th centuries, represents the divine king or oba who was both a political ruler and an object of cult worship. Dating from the 16th century, the "classical" period of Benin art, the mask shows the detailed carving and naturalistic conception that distinguish Benin ivory sculpture. (Museum of Primitive Art, New York City.)

ivy

The Canary Island ivy (left), H. canariensis variegata, has large leaves that are edged in white. Two varieties of the common ivy are H. helix "Caenwoodiana" (center) and H. helix "Manda's Crested" (right).

appreciated for its own inherent qualities, and the painting or staining of ivory carvings began to lose importance.

Ivory carving rose to a very high level in Europe, particularly in the Early Christian, Byzantine, and Carolingian eras. The small, portable carvings provided a means whereby stylistic trends spread from one area to another. The ivory carvings of the Byzantine period, for example, inspired the stone Romanesque sculptures of France. The Gothic style, which flourished from the late 13th through the 15th century, produced a wealth of carvings, especially in the form of relief plaques on caskets, altarpieces, and reliquaries.

In the Orient ivory carving is a very ancient art. Early Chinese ivories from the Shang dynasty (c.1558–1027 BC) include ornamental plaques and pieces of inlay. Ivory was valued as much as gold or jade; workshops established in the 17th century in Peking to supply carved ivory to the court produced a wealth of fine ivory objects, and their tradition continues to the present day. Japanese ivory carvers of the 8th century created superlative ivories, but surviving examples are extremely rare, and the ivory art of Japan is usually assessed from work dating from the 18th century to the present (see NETSUKE). India, the Near East, and most countries of southern Asia retain a deeply rooted ivory-carving tradition.

In North America, Eskimo ivory carving dates back at least 2,000 years. Ivory, bone, antler, and tooth were all used to create utilitarian and shamanistic objects, many of them highly decorated.

African ivory art is rooted in the remote past, particularly in the Ivory Coast and Congo regions where carvings ranged from elaborate knife handles to entire elephant tusks completely carved in relief.

Contemporary ivory carvers are still active in many parts of the world, and their productions bear comparison with fine antique ivories, except that they lack the charm of age and the mellow, soft sheen of old ivory.

Bibliography: Beckwith, John, *Ivory Carving in Early Medieval England* (1972); Beigbeder, Oliver, *Ivory* (1965); Carrà, Massimo, *Ivories of the West* (1970); Eastham, Barry C., *Chinese Art Ivory*, rev. ed. (1976); Natanson, Joseph, *Early Christian Ivories* (1953); Wilson, Derek, and Ayerst, Peter, *White Gold: The Story of African Ivory* (1976); Woodhouse, Charles P., *Ivories: The Collector's History and Guide* (1976).

See also: SCRIMSHAW.

Trailing plants that belong to the genus *Hedera*, family Araliaceae, are usually known as ivies. The English ivy, *H. helix*, native to Eurasia, is an evergreen vine with handsome, glossy leaves. It is a hardy, dependable climber that clings to walls or the ground by means of aerial roots. Varieties of *H. helix* include: "baltica," a very hardy plant; "conglomerata," a slow-growing dwarf variety; "hahn's self-branching," used as ground cover because of its very dense growth; and "minima," which has small leaves and is used primarily for decorative purposes indoors. Algerian ivy, or Canary Island ivy, *H. canariensis*, is an attractive ivy from the Canary Islands that thrives in gardens of the southeastern United States.

Other species with ivylike leaves and growth habits are: American ivy or five-leaved ivy, *Parthenocissus quinquefolia*; Boston or Japanese ivy, *P. tricuspidata*; Cape ivy, *Senecio macroglossus*; German ivy, *S. mikanioides*; ground ivy, *Glechoma hederacea*; poison ivy, *Rhus toxicodendron*; and ivy geranium, *Pelargonium peltatum*.

Bibliography: Pierot, Suzanne W., *The Ivy Book: The Growing and Care of Ivy and Ivy Topiary* (1974).

Ivy League

The Ivy League is a group of seven universities and one college in the northeastern United States: Brown, Columbia, Cornell, Dartmouth, Harvard, Pennsylvania, Princeton, and Yale. All but Cornell were established before the American Revolution, and all have very selective admissions standards. Social and athletic competition among the colleges dates from the late 19th century. The concept of the league began when policies for athletic competition were set down in 1956. Ivy League college presidents, directors of athletics, and other officers meet periodically to discuss common problems of admissions, financial aid, and administration.

Bibliography: Tobias, Andrew, et al., *Ivy League Guide Book* (1968).

Iwo Jima   [ee'-woh jee'-muh]

Iwo Jima is the largest of three islands that make up Japan's Volcano group. Located about 1,210 km (750 mi) south of Tokyo, it has an area of 21 km² (8 mi²) and a maximum elevation, on Mount Suribachi, of 166 m (546 ft). About 1,000 Japanese live on the island.

Volcanic in origin, Iwo Jima has soil suitable for growing

sugarcane, making a sugar refining industry possible. Sulfur mining is a major activity.

Japan annexed the Volcano Islands in 1887 and used them as a major military base during World War II. In February 1945, U.S. Marines launched a costly battle to capture Iwo Jima; a photograph of the American flag being raised on Suribachi was the basis for the famous sculpture in Arlington National Cemetery. The U.S. Navy controlled Iwo Jima until its return to Japan in 1968.

Bibliography: Newcomb, Richard F., *Iwo Jima* (1965).

IWW: see INDUSTRIAL WORKERS OF THE WORLD.

Ixion   [iks'-ee-ahn]

In Greek mythology, Ixion, king of the Lapiths, was traditionally considered the first murderer of a kinsman. He refused to pay his father-in-law, Eioneus, the promised price for his bride, Dia, and finally murdered him by throwing him into a fiery pit. To purify Ixion of this sin, ZEUS invited him to Olympus; there Ixion tired to violate HERA, but she was transformed into a cloud. From Ixion's union with the cloud was born either the CENTAURS or their father, Centaurus, depending on the version of the legend. In punishment, Ixion was bound to a fiery, eternally revolving wheel.

Ixtacihuatl   [ees-tah-see'-wah-tul]

Ixtacihuatl, Mexico's third-highest mountain, is located about 55 km (35 mi) southeast of Mexico City in the SIERRA MADRES. One of its three volcanic cones rises 5,386 m (17,671 ft) above sea level. The pinnacles suggest a reclining figure, thus its popular name, "sleeping woman." It last erupted in 1868.

Izapa   [ee-sahp'-ah]

Izapa, an archaeological site located east of Tapachula in the southeastern Chiapas state, Mexico, contains important remains of pre-Columbian civilization. A ceremonial center in Early Formative times (1500–800 BC), it is composed of more than 80 scattered earthen temple mounds faced with cobblestones. Located in its labyrinth of courts and plazas are elaborately carved stone monuments (steles) dating mainly from the Late Formative (300 BC–AD 150) and Proto-Classic (AD 150–300) eras.

The Izapa art style is thought to represent a cultural link between the OLMEC (1000–300 BC) and the Classical MAYA (AD 300–900) civilizations. Prominent features include complex depictions of various secular activities and distinctive representations of deities, notably the large-lipped god of rain and lightning, an adaptation of the Olmec were-jaguar and a forerunner of the long-nosed Mayan rain god.

JAMES W. HERRICK

Bibliography: Thompson, J. Eric S., *The Rise and Fall of Maya Civilization* (1954); Tax, Sol, ed., *The Civilizations of Ancient America* (1951; repr. 1967).

İzmir   [iz-mir']

İzmir (formerly Smyrna) is a city in west central Turkey on the Aegean Sea at the eastern end of the Gulf of İzmir. The population of the city proper is 636,834; that of the metropolitan area is 955,000 (1975). İzmir has a mean July temperature of 27° C (81° F), a mean January temperature of 8° C (47° F), and a mean annual precipitation of 719 mm (28 in).

The excellent port facilities and the introduction of the railroad contributed to early industrialization. Textile, cigarette, soap, and food processing plants are found there. Agricultural products and carpets are major exports. The city is the home of Aegean University (1955) and an archaeological museum. The agora (marketplace), the ancient aqueducts, and splendid beaches attract tourists to the city.

İzmir, first settled about 3000 BC, was an Aeolian, then an IONIAN, colony in the 11th century BC. Destroyed by about 600 BC, it was refounded in the 4th century BC by Alexander the Great's successors ANTIGONUS I and LYSIMACHUS. It came under Roman rule late in the 1st century BC. Attacked by the Arabs in the 7th century, the city fell to the Seljuks in the late 11th century. From 1204 to 1261 it was part of the Byzantine state of NICAEA. In 1424 it was incorporated into the OTTOMAN EMPIRE. At the end of World War I İzmir was occupied by Greek forces, and the Treaty of Sèvres (1920) awarded the city and its surrounds to Greece. Turkish nationalist forces captured the city in September 1922, and its large Greek population fled. The Treaty of Lausanne (1923; see LAUSANNE, TREATY OF) gave İzmir to the new Turkish republic.   IRA M. SHESKIN

Izvestia   [iz-ves'-tee-uh]

The official newspaper of the USSR since the Russian Revolution, *Izvestia* (English, "news") is published by the Supreme Soviet Presidium, the legislative branch of the Soviet government. Its news coverage generally reflects the government's viewpoint. The other major newspaper in the USSR is PRAVDA.

JOHN D. MITCHELL

J

J/j, the tenth letter of the English alphabet, is one of the few relatively modern additions to the Semitic-Greek-Etruscan-Latin line of development that gave rise to the alphabet. The letter *J/j* was derived from the letter *I/i* by the addition of a curved stroke at the bottom.

J/j occurs as early as the 14th century AD, but its early use was only ornamental, created by the lengthening of *I/i*, especially in initial position. Eventually, *J/j* came to contrast with *I/i* to distinguish the consonant *y* from the vowel *i*, both of which were represented by the letter *I/i* in Latin. This differentiation was not fully established in English until the 17th century, however.

Because of early French influence, the letter *J/j* has the pronunciation *dzh* in modern English speech, as in *jet* and *jury*. This sound is partially shared by the letter *G/g* and is the voiced counterpart of *ch* (*tsh*). In German, *J/j* has only the sound of consonantal *y*, a sound found in a few English words such as *hallelujah*.   I. J. GELB AND R. M. WHITING

2 PHOENICIAN	**ETRUSCAN**
EARLY HEBREW	**EARLY LATIN**
EARLY ARAMAIC	**CLASSICAL LATIN**
EARLY GREEK	**GERMAN-GOTHIC**
CLASSICAL GREEK	

MODERN LATIN

Jabbar, Kareem Abdul: see ABDUL-JABBAR, KAREEM.

Jabotinsky, Vladimir   [yab-uh-tin-skee']

Vladimir Jabotinsky, b. Russia, Oct. 18 (N.S.), 1880, d. Aug. 3, 1940, was a militant Zionist leader in Palestine during the British mandate period. In 1920 he helped organize the Haganah, the Jewish self-defense movement against the Arabs in Palestine. Believing existing Zionist organizations to be too passive, he formed (1925) the World Union of Zionist Revisionists, which advocated the creation of a Jewish state on both sides of the Jordan by force, if necessary. In the 1930s some of Jabotinsky's followers founded the Irgun Zvai Leumi, an underground group that made terrorist attacks on both the British and the Arabs.

Bibliography: Schechtman, Joseph B., *The Vladimir Jabotinsky Story*, 2 vols. (1956–61).

jacamar   [jak'-uh-mahr]

Jacamars are about 15 species of neotropical birds, family Galbulidae, frequently found in wooded areas. They measure 13 to 28 cm (5 to 11 in) in length and have metallic plumage and long, thin bills. Jacamars feed primarily on butterflies in midair, and they nest in burrows that they scrape in the ground.

jacana   [jak'-uh-nuh]

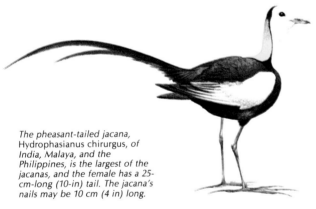

The pheasant-tailed jacana, Hydrophasianus chirurgus, *of India, Malaya, and the Philippines, is the largest of the jacanas, and the female has a 25-cm-long (10-in) tail. The jacana's nails may be 10 cm (4 in) long.*

The jacanas are 7 species of pantropical, ploverlike birds (family Jacanidae) with greatly elongated toes that enable them to walk, and sometimes even nest, on floating vegetation. They are polyandrous—large, dominant females lay several clutches of eggs, and a different male incubates each clutch and raises the young. The American jacana, *Jacana spinosa*, which ranges from Mexico to Argentina, measures 20 to 25 cm (8 to 10 in) in length and has cinnamon-red coloration with bright green wing patches.   GEORGE J. WALLACE

jacaranda   [jak-uh-ran'-duh]

The genus *Jacaranda*, family Bignoniaceae, comprises about 50 species of trees and shrubs having blue or blue violet flowers and fine, fernlike leaves. Native to the American tropics, some species are grown in greenhouses or homes as potted plants. In Brazil an extract of the bark is used for the treatment of syphilis.   DIANNE FAHSELT

jack

A jack is a type of mechanism that is used to press against an object, moving it if it is free, or exerting pressure on the object if it is fixed. Common types of jacks are the lever jack, the screw jack, and the hydraulic jack; all three produce a sizable mechanical advantage, so that the applied force of a person is multiplied, resulting in a larger force being exerted on

a heavy body. The lever jack is essentially a LEVER combined with a ratchet device that prevents the object from slipping back down during the reverse motion of the lever. The object is thus raised a small amount each stroke. In the screw jack, or jackscrew, the turning of a screw (by the use of a lever) causes the screw, which is fitted into a threaded base, to move upward as it rotates. A hydraulic jack makes use of the properties of an enclosed liquid to exert a large force on a piston in a large cylinder by applying a smaller force to the piston of a smaller cylinder (see HYDRAULIC SYSTEMS).

jack-o'-lantern

One species of poisonous mushroom, *Clitocybe illudens*, is known as the jack-o'-lantern fungus. The name is derived from its gills, which become luminescent during active growth periods. It is characterized by crowded, narrow gills and the lack of a veil. It fruits during late summer and early fall. The jack-o'-lantern fungus is distributed throughout eastern North America to the southern United States and to the Pacific coast; it also occurs in southern Europe.

jack-in-the-pulpit

Jack-in-the-pulpit, A. atrorubens, *derives its name from the way the flower looks, like a clergyman giving a sermon in his pulpit. In fall, a cluster of bright-red berries appear, which are unpleasantly bitter and hot to the taste.*

Arisaema triphyllum, family Araceae, is a plant species most commonly referred to as jack-in-the-pulpit. This herbaceous perennial grows in damp or shady places. The inflorescence is a densely flowered spadix surrounded by a large bract known as the spathe. In the fall, red berries are borne in a dense, egg-shaped cluster. The plants are monoecious; each season, however, flowers of just one sex are produced. For about two years staminate flowers are formed; in subsequent seasons pistillate flowers are produced. The transition from male to female is said to be slowed in dry sandy soil and facilitated in rich soils.

Calcium oxalate crystals accumulate in the rhizome and, if taken into the mouth by a human, will cause irritation and a burning sensation. Pawnee Indians pulverized and dried the roots and dusted the powder on their temples to relieve headaches. The roots have also been used as a source of flour, but they must be processed first in order to dispel the "acrid principle." They can be boiled and crushed into cakes and then baked or steamed, or they may be cut into thin slices and allowed to dry for a few weeks and then eaten raw.   DIANNE FAHSELT

Jack the Ripper

Jack the Ripper was the name popularly given to a London murderer who killed seven prostitutes in the East End between Aug. 7 and Nov. 10, 1888. The murderer's identity has never been discovered, although some have suggested that he was the duke of Clarence, Queen Victoria's grandson. The name *Jack the Ripper* came from letters received by the police and presumed to have been written by the killer. He struck at night while his victim was walking the street, cutting her throat and then mutilating her body with the skill of a surgeon.

Jack the Ripper became a staple theme of mysteries and

horror stories, and one such novel, *The Lodger* (1913), by Marie Belloc Lowndes, has been made into three motion pictures.

Bibliography: Farson, Daniel, *Jack the Ripper* (1972); Harrison, Michael, *Clarence: Was He Jack the Ripper?* (1972); Rumbelow, Donald, *The Complete Jack the Ripper* (1975).

jackal [jak'-ul]

The golden jackal, C. aureus, resembles a small wolf. It feeds on plants, insects, and other small animals and carrion left by the larger predators.

Jackal is the name applied to several carnivorous mammals in the genus *Canis*, dog family, Canidae, which includes the dog and the wolf. They inhabit brush country, deserts, and grasslands. Jackals are about 90 cm (3 ft) long, including the bushy 35-cm (14-in) tail, and weigh about 10.8 kg (24 lb). They have erect ears, fairly long legs, and a slinking gait. The Asiatic, or golden, jackal, *C. aureus*, is found from Turkestan through the Near East and North Africa. The black-backed jackal, *C. mesomelas*, and the side-striped jackal, *C. adustus*, inhabit eastern and southern Africa. Night hunters, jackals kill small mammals and poultry and often eat carrion. They hide in brush or in a hole during the day and howl in the evening, like a coyote. Litters consist of 2 to 7 pups.   EVERETT SENTMAN

Bibliography: Bueler, Lois E., *Wild Dogs of the World* (1973); Fox, Michael, ed., *The Wild Canids* (1975).

jackdaw [jak'-daw]

The jackdaw, *Corvus monedula*, family Corvidae, order Passeriformes, is a crowlike bird of Europe, Asia, and North Africa. It is black with a gray nape and measures about 33 cm (13 in). Jackdaws are most common in open, rocky country, along seashores, and around human dwellings or ruins. They nest colonially in holes in trees, rocks, and buildings.

ROBERT J. RAIKOW

jacks

Jacks, or jackstones, is a children's game using 6 to 12 six-pointed jacks and a rubber ball. A player throws the ball in the air and tries to pick up increasing numbers of jacks with each toss. Jacks is of prehistoric origin and is played worldwide. Games similar to jacks are depicted in ancient Greek art, and in pre-Christian Rome jacks was a gambling game. In other parts of the world, seeds, stones, bones, or filled bags are used by adults and children of both sexes to play games similar to jacks. Only in the United States and Canada is jacks considered a girl's game.

Bibliography: Weigle, Marta, *Jacks and Jacks Games* (1970).

Jackson (Michigan)

Jackson is a city on the Grand River in southern Michigan. The seat of Jackson County, it has a population of 42,700 (1979 est.). Manufactures include auto and aircraft components. The city, settled in 1829 and named for President Andrew Jackson, was the site of the founding of the Republican party in 1854.

Jackson (Mississippi)

Jackson, the capital and largest city of Mississippi, is situated on the Pearl River. It is one of two seats of Hinds County (the other is Raymond) and has a population of 190,700 (1979 est.). Jackson is a railroad and distribution center; manufactures include textiles, glass, and electronic equipment. Several colleges are located in the city. Nearby Ross Barnett Reservoir provides recreational facilities.

Established as a trading post in 1792, the site was selected for the state capital in 1821 and named for Andrew Jackson. In the mid-1800s the city served as an important rail junction, but it was nearly destroyed by Gen. William Sherman's forces during the Civil War. The capitol building survived and is now a museum. A new capitol, modeled after the U.S. Capitol, was completed in 1903. Growth was spurred in the 20th century by the convergence of new rail lines on Jackson and the opening of natural-gas fields in the 1930s. In 1979 heavy rains caused severe flooding of the Pearl River in Jackson.

Jackson, Alexander Young

A member of the GROUP OF SEVEN, the Canadian landscape painter Alexander Young Jackson, b. Montreal, Oct. 3, 1882, d. 1973, specialized in scenes of the rugged Canadian wilderness. After studying at the Art Institute of Chicago and in Europe, Jackson settled (1913) in Toronto, where he joined (1920) the Group of Seven. Jackson seldom used human figures in his work, and when they do appear—Indians, Eskimos, and fishermen—they are insignificant when compared to the power and majesty of nature. *Valley of the Gouffre River* (1933; McMichael Canadian Collection, Kleinburg, Ontario) is a typical example of his work.   ABRAHAM A. DAVIDSON

Bibliography: Jackson, A. Y., *A Painter's Country: The Autobiography of A. Y. Jackson* (1958); Mellen, Peter, *The Group of Seven* (1970).

Jackson, Andrew

Andrew Jackson, a frontier general and Indian fighter, was elected seventh president of the United States on a platform that proclaimed him the champion of democracy and of the common man. Jackson served two terms of office (1829-37) that were marked by bitter controversies over state rights, nullification, the tariff, the spoils system, Indian removal, and banking policies. A man of strong convictions, iron will, and fiery temperament, Jackson used the presidential power vigorously and left his mark on the era, often termed the "Age of Jackson."

EARLY POLITICAL AND MILITARY CAREER

Born Mar. 15, 1767, in the Waxhaw settlement on the border of North Carolina and South Carolina, Jackson was orphaned at the age of 14. After reading law and gaining admission to the bar in North Carolina, he migrated to Nashville, Tenn., where he allied himself with the powerful political faction led by William BLOUNT. In 1791, Jackson married Rachel Donelson Robards; both he and Rachel mistakenly believed that she and her first husband had received a legal divorce. When they discovered their error, they remarried (1794).

Jackson served as a delegate to the Tennessee constitutional convention in 1796 and as congressman from Tennessee (1796-97). His congressional career was undistinguished, marked primarily by his fierce opposition to the Washington administration's conciliatory stance toward Great Britain and the Western Indian tribes. Jackson was elected U.S. senator in 1797, but financial problems forced his resignation and return to Tennessee in less than a year. After serving (1798-1804) as a Tennessee superior court judge, he retired from the bench to devote all his energies to business ventures and to his plantation, the Hermitage, near Nashville. His political career seemed to be over. For a time he appeared willing to aid Aaron BURR in his secret project in the West—but his involvement in Burr's conspiracy led only to embarrassment. Jackson's efforts to gain appointment as governor of Louisiana were rebuffed by the Jefferson administration.

The WAR OF 1812 dramatically changed Jackson's political fortunes. In 1814, Jackson, a major general in the Tennessee decimated an invading British army. Coming at the end of a war marked by military ineptness and humiliating defeats, Jackson's victory was seized upon by a public hungry for vindication of national honor. (News that the British and the Americans had signed a peace treaty on Dec. 24, 1814, in Ghent, Belgium, reached the United States a few days later.) The Battle of New Orleans made Andrew Jackson a legend and a symbol of American virtue.

Jackson was called into action in 1817 against the Seminole Indians. In the spring of 1818 (in the First SEMINOLE WAR) he pursued the Indians into Spanish Florida, where he apparently exceeded his instructions by deposing the Spanish authorities and executing two British subjects: one a young officer, the other an elderly Scottish trader whom he charged with aiding the Indians. Jackson subsequently insisted that his actions had the tacit prior approval of the Monroe administration, and efforts of his enemies to secure his censure by Congress failed. His actions helped lead to the U.S. acquisition of Spanish Florida in 1819. Jackson resigned his army commission in 1821 and served briefly as territorial governor of Florida in the same year.

RETURN TO POLITICS

In 1822 the Tennessee legislature nominated Jackson for the presidency; the following year it elected him to the U.S. Senate. He soon became involved in the presidential campaign of 1824. He almost won the presidency, but the election of 1824 was bitterly contested. The demise of the FEDERALIST PARTY, discredited by its opposition to the War of 1812, had left the nation with a one-party system. The Democratic-Republicans were unable, however, to agree on a common presidential candidate. The congressional caucus nominated Georgia's William H. CRAWFORD. Local party organizations and state legislatures, however, in addition to Jackson, placed in candidacy John Quincy ADAMS of Massachusetts, Henry CLAY of Kentucky, and John C. CALHOUN of South Carolina, who soon withdrew to seek the vice-presidency. The popular and electoral votes were indecisive because no candidate received a majority. Although Jackson led in both tallies, the House of Representatives chose John Quincy Adams as president. Jackson's supporters charged that Adams's election was the result of a "corrupt bargain" with Henry Clay, whom Adams named secretary of state.

During the Adams administration, Jackson's supporters, aided by Vice-President Calhoun and Sen. Martin VAN BUREN, built a powerful political machine dedicated to Jackson's election in 1828. That machine became the nucleus of the DEMOCRATIC PARTY. Critical of Adams's nationalist policies and lack of concern for STATE RIGHTS, the Jackson organization represented Old Hickory as champion of the common man. They attacked Adams and Clay for the "corrupt bargain" that, they alleged, revealed the aristocratic principles of Adams and Clay and their contempt for democracy. Adams's supporters in turn attacked Jackson for the irregularity of the first years of his marriage and portrayed him as an ignorant and uncouth barbarian. Yet the Jacksonian Democracy was triumphant in 1828. In an election marked by mudslinging and character assassination on both sides, Jackson defeated Adams's bid for a second term.

THE PRESIDENCY

Saddened by the death of his wife late in 1828, Jackson, although close to his first secretary of war, John H. EATON, relied more heavily on his KITCHEN CABINET, a group of unofficial advisors, than on his official cabinet.

Rotation in Office. President Jackson sought to make government more sensitive to the will of the people through his principle of "rotation in office." Proclaiming that no person should regard officeholding as a right, Jackson declared all intelligent citizens equally qualified to serve and announced his intention to protect the nation from a permanent aristocratic officeholding clique by removing long-term officeholders. Although only a minority of federal officials (estimated at no more than ten percent) were actually removed by Jackson, his political foes charged him with seeking to corrupt the civil service for political reasons and dubbed his principle of "rotation in office" the "spoils system" (see PATRONAGE).

ANDREW JACKSON
7th President of the United States (1829–37)

Nickname: "Old Hickory"
Born: Mar. 15, 1767, Waxhaw area, on N.C.-S.C. border
Profession: Lawyer, Soldier
Religious Affiliation: Presbyterian
Marriage: August 1791 (2d ceremony, Jan. 17, 1794), to Rachel Donelson Robards (1767–1828)
Children: None
Political Affiliation: Democrat
Writings: *Correspondence of Andrew Jackson* (7 vols., 1926–35), ed. by J. S. Bassett and J. F. Jameson
Died: June 8, 1845, Nashville, Tenn.
Buried: The Hermitage, Nashville, Tenn.

Vice-President and Cabinet Members

Vice-President: John C. Calhoun (1829–32); Martin Van Buren (1833–37)
Secretary of State: Martin Van Buren (1829–31); Edward Livingston (1831–33); Louis McLane (1833–34); John Forsyth (1834–37)
Secretary of the Treasury: Samuel D. Ingham (1829–31); Louis McLane (1831–33); William J. Duane (1833); Roger B. Taney (1833–34); Levi Woodbury (1834–37)
Secretary of War: John H. Eaton (1829–31); Lewis Cass (1831–36)
Attorney General: John M. Berrien (1829–31); Roger B. Taney (1831–33); Benjamin F. Butler (1833–37)
Postmaster General: William T. Barry (1829–35); Amos Kendall (1835–37)
Secretary of the Navy: John Branch (1829–31); Levi Woodbury (1831–34); Mahlon Dickerson (1834–37)

militia, was ordered to march against the pro-British faction of the CREEK Indians. Assisted by pro-American Indian allies, he crushed Creek resistance at Horseshoe Bend (March 1814). He then forced all the Indians of the region, friends and foes alike, to surrender enormous tracts of land in both Alabama and Georgia. Impressed by his stunning victory, the federal government placed Jackson in command of the defense of New Orleans. Old Hickory, as Jackson was known to his admirers, organized the defense of the city and on Jan. 8, 1815,

State Rights. Although Jackson declared his belief in state rights and in limitations on the activities of the federal government, he was inconsistent in applying these principles. In 1830 he vetoed a bill appropriating funds to construct a road between Maysville and Lexington entirely within Kentucky, the state of his rival Henry Clay. Since many of Jackson's supporters in Western states favored internal improvements at federal expense, however, his administration increased rather than limited federal spending for road, canal, and harbor construction.

In another case, that of the CHEROKEE Indians of Georgia, Jackson effectively supported a state rights position (and asserted his independence of the Supreme Court). Despite two U.S. Supreme Court decisions (1831 and 1832) upholding the rights of the Cherokee nation against the state of Georgia, which was attempting to destroy Cherokee sovereignty and take the Indians' land, Jackson refused to intervene on behalf of the Indians. Many tribes were resettled west of the Mississippi while he was in office. The removal of the Cherokee was finally accomplished (1838–39) by a forced trek westward during the administration of Jackson's successor, Martin Van Buren.

The Tariff Question and Nullification. Jackson's followers were divided on the tariff question. Southerners were generally opposed to a protective tariff and had supported Jackson in the belief that he would lower duties drastically from the levels established in 1828; but Jacksonians in other areas tended to be protectionists. In 1832 his administration approved only modest reductions in duties (see TARIFF ACTS). On Nov. 24, 1832, however, South Carolina, acting on the doctrine of NULLIFICATION espoused by Vice-President Calhoun, declared the federal tariff laws of 1828 and 1832 null and void and prohibited the collection of tariffs in South Carolina after Feb. 1, 1833. Jackson, in his Nullification Proclamation of Dec. 10, 1832, declared his intent to enforce the law but also promised to seek further downward adjustment of the tariff. In 1833, Congress passed both a force bill, empowering Jackson to coerce South Carolina, and a compromise tariff. Other southern states failed to rally to the support of South Carolina, which accepted the new tariff (but not the force bill), and the threat of disunion was averted.

Economic Policy. Although Jackson had not made the Second BANK OF THE UNITED STATES an issue in the 1828 election, he soon announced his belief that the bank, a private corporation established in 1816 and operating under a federal charter, had failed to provide a stable currency, had favored the privileged few at the expense of the common people in its financial operations, and had received a charter in violation of the Constitution. The bank's charter was not due to expire until 1836, but in July 1832 the president of the bank, Nicholas BIDDLE, encouraged by Jackson's political enemies—particularly Henry Clay and Daniel WEBSTER—pushed a bill through Congress granting recharter. Jackson quickly vetoed the bill. The bank recharter was a major issue in the 1832 presidential election, in which Jackson (with Martin Van Buren as his running mate) overwhelmingly defeated Clay.

Jackson's war against the Bank of the United States extended throughout his second term of office. Angered by Biddle's use of bank funds to support anti-Jacksonian candidates, Jackson ordered federal deposits withdrawn from the bank in 1833. When two secretaries of the treasury refused to comply, Jackson, in another bold assertion of presidential power, removed both. That action earned him the censure of the Senate and, along with his use of the presidential veto, prompted his foes to charge him with abuse of power.

Although Jackson destroyed the Second Bank of the United States by withdrawing government money, his administration failed to develop a coherent national banking policy. In many states, especially in the South and West, state-chartered banks engaged in irresponsible and speculative issuance of paper currency—a policy that Jackson and other hard-money advocates opposed. (The federal government issued no paper legal tender prior to the Civil War.) Thus during the mid-1830s the United States was swept by a land boom. Sales of federal lands soared, helping to wipe out the national debt and creating a large federal surplus. By 1836, however, the boom was becoming increasingly speculative. Alarmed and determined to curb extensive use of paper currency issued by private state-chartered banks, Jackson, in the Specie Circular of 1836, forbade further purchases of federal land or payment of federal debts in any currency except federally issued coins. His actions, which created a demand for specie that led to many bank failures, were opposed by conservatives in the business community; they charged him with responsibility for disrupting the economy and blamed him for the ensuing Panic of 1837.

Foreign Policy. Jackson's foreign policy was marked by firm defense of American interests in forcing the French government to pay long-overdue spoliation claims and reopening the British West Indian trade. Although personally sympathetic to the American-organized rebellion of Texas against Mexico, Jackson took a cautious stance on Texan independence. He was reluctant to split the Democratic party in a domestic controversy over the expansion of slavery or to go to war with Mexico. Jackson did not recognize the Lone Star Republic until the day before he left office in 1837; he left the troublesome problem of Texas annexation to his successors.

LAST YEARS AND INFLUENCE
Even after his retirement, Jackson was a powerful force in the Democratic party. He switched his support from his successor, Van Buren, to James K. Polk, who won the Democratic nomination and subsequently the presidency in 1844. Jackson died at the Hermitage on June 8, 1845.

A symbol of the self-made man and the virtues of the American frontier, he helped shape both an important concept—that of mass democracy—and a powerful political organization, the Democratic party. Of his many accomplishments, Jackson's strengthening of the powers of the presidency has probably been the most enduring. The first president to proclaim himself the elected representative of all the American people, Jackson did not hesitate to use the power of veto. (He vetoed 12 bills, more than all of his predecessors combined.) His use of the powers of removal and of executive orders paved the way for the modern American presidency.   ALFRED A. CAVE

Bibliography: Bassett, John S., *The Life of Andrew Jackson* (1931; repr. 1967); Davis, Burke, *Old Hickory: A Life of Andrew Jackson* (1977); James, Marquis, *Andrew Jackson: Portrait of a President*, 2 vols. (1937); Meyers, Marvin, *The Jacksonian Persuasion* (1957); Remini, Robert V., *Andrew Jackson* (1966) and *Andrew Jackson and the Course of American Empire, 1767–1821* (1977); Rogin, Michael, *Fathers and Children: Andrew Jackson and the Subjugation of the American Indian* (1975); Schlesinger, Arthur M., *The Age of Jackson* (1945); Sellers, Charles, *Andrew Jackson: A Profile* (1971); Van Deusen, Glyndon G., *The Jacksonian Era* (1959).

Jackson, Charles

An American novelist best known for his frank exploration of alcoholism in *The Lost Weekend* (1944; film, 1945), Charles Reginald Jackson, b. Summit, N.J., Apr. 6, 1903, d. Sept. 21, 1968, has shown an interest in psychopathology or aberrant behavior in much of his work. *The Fall of Valor* (1946) deals with homosexuality, and *The Outer Edges* (1948) deals with the crime of a child molester.   F. M. PAULSEN

Jackson, Glenda

The English actress Glenda Jackson, b. May 9, 1936, made her stage reputation as the demented Charlotte Corday in Peter Weiss's *Marat/Sade* (1964; film, 1966), directed by Peter Brook. In 1971 she scored notable successes as the brittle divorcee in the film *Sunday, Bloody Sunday* and as Queen Elizabeth I in the BBC-TV production of *Elizabeth R*. Her performances have earned her two Academy Awards as best actress, for *Women in Love* (1969) and *A Touch of Class* (1972).

Jackson, Helen Hunt

An American poet, essayist, and novelist, Maria Helen Hunt Fiske Jackson, b. Amherst, Mass., Oct. 15, 1830, d. Aug. 12, 1885, is best known for the novel *Ramona* (1884), a fictionalized romance about Indian life in California. A lifelong friend of Emily Dickinson, Jackson sometimes published under a pseudonym, but most of her work was unsigned. In addition to *Ramona*, Jackson's works include *Verses* (1877) and *A Century of Dishonor* (1881), a study of the U.S. government's injustice to the Indians.

Bibliography: Banning, Evelyn, *Helen Hunt Jackson* (1973).

Jackson, Henry M.

Henry Martin "Scoop" Jackson, b. Everett, Wash., May 31, 1912, became a U.S. senator from the state of Washington in 1953. He was reelected in 1958, 1964, 1970, and 1976. A liberal in domestic policy, he supported larger defense expenditures and advocated more unyielding policy toward the USSR than many other liberals. He coauthored the Jackson-Vanik amendment, which tied improved trade terms with the USSR to the liberalization of Jewish emigration policies by that country. In 1972 and 1976 he campaigned unsuccessfully for the Democratic presidential nomination. Jackson practiced law before being elected to the U.S. House of Representatives in 1940, where he served six terms.

Bibliography: Ognibene, Peter J., *Scoop: The Life and Politics of Henry M. Jackson* (1975).

Jackson, Jesse L.

Rev. Jesse Jackson, an American Baptist minister and civil rights activist, attained a national reputation as the organizer of two minority-assistance programs, Operation Breadbasket and PUSH (People United to Save Humanity). In 1979, Jackson embarked on a controversial tour of the Middle East, where he met with Arab leader Yasir Arafat to discuss a solution to the conflict between Israel and the Palestine Liberation Organization.

Jesse Louis Jackson, b. Oct. 8, 1941, became one of the most influential black leaders of the 1970s. A Baptist minister, he was active in the Southern black protest movement with Martin Luther King, Jr., during the early 1960s. Jackson organized and directed the Chicago branch of Operation Breadbasket (1966–77), a group dedicated to eliminating racial discrimination in employment and business dealings, and founded PUSH (People United to Save Humanity) to advance the interests of blacks and other disadvantaged groups. In 1979 he visited both South Africa, where he urged unity among South African blacks in combating the regime, and the Middle East, where he called for Israeli recognition of the Palestine Liberation Organization.

Bibliography: Drotning, Philip T., and South, Wesley W., *Up from the Ghetto* (1970); Reynolds, Barbara A., *Jesse Jackson: The Man, the Movement, the Myth* (1975).

Jackson, Mahalia

Mahalia Jackson, b. New Orleans, Oct. 26, 1911, d. Jan. 27, 1972, was the most famous gospel singer of her time. Like many other black singers, Jackson began by singing in a church choir; but unlike those who moved into the pop-music field, she continued to sing GOSPEL MUSIC throughout her career. She first attracted national attention with recordings

made in 1945; at the time of her death she had sung in countries as far removed from the gospel idiom as Japan and India. Her voice was as magnificent as Bessie Smith's, and, although her music is sacred and Smith's is most secular, their techniques are similar.

Bibliography: Jackson, Jesse, *Make a Joyful Noise unto the Lord* (1974); Jackson, Mahalia, and Wylie, Evan, *Movin' On Up* (1966).

Discography: *The Great Mahalia Jackson; In That Great Gettin' Up Mornin'; In Concert; What The World Needs Now.*

Jackson, Reggie

Reginald Martinez Jackson, b. Wyncote, Pa., May 18, 1946, is an American baseball player who became one of the sport's most talented and publicized figures of the 1970s. Jackson joined the Kansas City Athletics in 1967 and became a star after the team moved to Oakland in 1968, hitting 29 home runs in his first full season and 47 the following year. Although he helped Oakland win 3 straight world championships (1972–74) his catankerous personality often overshadowed his hitting performances. He was traded to Baltimore in 1976, then acquired by the New York Yankees as a free agent in 1977; he helped the Yankees win 2 World Series (1977–78). Jackson tied a World Series record by hitting 3 home runs in 1 game.

Bibliography: Jackson, Reggie, *Reggie Jackson's Scrapbook*, ed. by Robert Kraus (1978).

Jackson, Robert Houghwout

Robert Houghwout Jackson, b. Spring Creek, Pa., Feb. 13, 1892, d. Oct. 9, 1954, was an associate justice of the U.S. Supreme Court (1941–54) who believed in judicial restraint and the defense of civil liberties. After studying at Albany Law School, he was admitted to the bar without a law degree. He was appointed to a series of posts by President Franklin D. Roosevelt, including solicitor general (1938) and attorney general (1940). Jackson also served as U.S. chief counsel at the Nuremberg war crimes trials (1945–46).

Bibliography: Gerhart, Eugene C., *America's Advocate: Robert H. Jackson* (1958); Jackson, Robert H., *The Case Against the Nazi War Criminals* (1945) and *The Supreme Court in the American System of Government* (1955); Schubert, Glendon, ed., *Dispassionate Justice: A Synthesis of the Judicial Opinions of Robert H. Jackson* (1969).

Jackson, Sheldon

Sheldon Jackson, b. Minaville, N.Y., May 18, 1834, d. May 2, 1909, was the leading Protestant missionary in Alaska at the close of the 19th century. He served first as a Presbyterian minister and missionary in Minnesota and the Rocky Mountain territories, where he imported prefabricated churches from the East into lumber-poor areas. From 1884 to the end of his life he worked in Alaska as a missionary and public servant, for which he was called the "Bishop of All Beyond." He was Alaska's first federal superintendent of public instruction, bringing educational opportunities to whites, Indians, and Eskimo. At his urging the U.S. government imported reindeer from Siberia for domestication by the Eskimo.

MARK A. NOLL

Bibliography: Lazell, J. Arthur, *Alaskan Apostle* (1960).

Jackson, Shirley

Shirley Jackson, b. San Francisco, Dec. 14, 1919, d. Aug. 8, 1965, was an American short-story writer and novelist. Innovatively mixing the conventions of the gothic tale with sophisticated psychology, she produced stories of chilling evil, which she perceived under the surfaces of everyday life. Her short story, "The Lottery," caused a sensation when it appeared in *The New Yorker* in 1948 and remains a classic of civilized horror. Her best-known novels are *The Haunting of Hill House* (1959) and *We Have Always Lived in the Castle* (1962). More of her stories, part of a novel, and three lectures appeared in *Come Along With Me* (1968), edited by her husband, Stanley Edgar Hyman, after her death.

Jackson, Stonewall

Thomas "Stonewall" Jackson, a military officer who first distinguished himself during the Mexican War, became one of the finest Confederate field commanders of the Civil War. Jackson is best remembered for his tactically brilliant Shenandoah Valley campaign of 1862, during which he threatened the federal capital while tying down a Union army that otherwise might have advanced on Richmond.

Thomas Jonathan "Stonewall" Jackson, b. Clarksburg, Va., now W.Va., Jan. 21, 1824, d. 1863, a Confederate general in the American Civil War, is held second only to Robert E. LEE in the affection and esteem of Southerners. He was left an orphan at an early age but later graduated (1846) from West Point. He fought with distinction in the Mexican War and resigned from the army to teach at the Virginia Military Institute.

During his 10 years of teaching (1851-61), Jackson's first wife died and he remarried. He became a zealous Presbyterian and was sometimes called "Deacon Jackson." Austere in personal habits, he also became something of an eccentric. Imagining one side of his body to weigh more than the other, he often walked or rode with one arm raised to restore his balance. He stood while eating to straighten his intestinal tract and thus aid digestion.

In 1861, Jackson joined the Confederate army. In July, at the first battle of BULL RUN, he won his famous nickname. As the Confederates fell back before a Northern attack, Jackson and his brigade stood firm—"like a stone wall," according to Gen. Barnard Bee.

In the spring of 1862, Jackson commanded a Confederate army in the Shenandoah Valley. By a brilliant campaign of hard marching and hard fighting, he defeated Federal generals whose combined strength was several times his own. He then joined Robert E. Lee, who was trying to drive another Northern army away from Richmond. In the Seven Days battles (June 1862; see PENINSULAR CAMPAIGN), however, Jackson was physically exhausted, and his performance was slow and ineffective. Later, at the Second Bull Run (August) and at the battles of ANTIETAM (September) and FREDERICKSBURG (December), he contributed greatly to a remarkable string of Southern victories.

At CHANCELLORSVILLE the following spring, Jackson fought his last and greatest battle: On May 2, 1863, with over half the available Confederate troops under his command, he made a crushing attack on the exposed flank of the Federal army. As he returned from a night reconnaisance, however, he was shot by some of his own men who mistook him for an enemy. Pneumonia developed as a result of his wounds, and he died on May 10, 1863. A brilliant tactician, Jackson was the ablest of Lee's generals; his loss was a great blow to the Confederacy. Lee wrote, "I know not how to replace him."

RICHARD M. MCMURRY

Bibliography: Chambers, Lenoir, *Stonewall Jackson*, 2 vols. (1959); Henderson, G. F., *Stonewall Jackson and the American Civil War* (1896; new ed., 1961); Tanner, Robert G., *Stonewall in the Valley* (1976); Tate, Allen, *Stonewall Jackson: The Good Soldier* (1957); Vandiver, Frank E., *Mighty Stonewall* (1957; repr. 1974).

Jackson, William Henry

A native of Keesville, N.Y., William Henry Jackson, b. Apr. 4, 1843, d. June 30, 1942, won renown for his pioneering photographs of the Indians and the terrain of the American frontier. Settling in Omaha, Nebr., in 1866, Jackson photographed along the route of the Union Pacific Railroad, and later worked (1870-78) for the Haden Geological Survey before establishing (1879) the Jackson Photographic Co. in Denver, Colo. His autobiography, *Time Exposure*, was published in 1940.

KEITH F. DAVIS

Bibliography: Forsee, Aylesa, *William Henry Jackson: Pioneer Photographer of the West* (1964); Jackson, Clarence S., *Picture Maker of the Old West: William Henry Jackson* (1947); Newhall, Beaumont, and Edkins, Diana, *William H. Jackson* (1974).

Jackson Hole

Jackson Hole is a valley in Grand Teton National Park, northwestern Wyoming. A long, narrow valley, about 80 km (50 mi) long and 10 to 13 km (6 to 8 mi) wide, it lies east of the Teton Mountains and west of the Wind River Range, at an elevation of 2,134 m (7,000 ft). Jackson Hole is watered by the Snake River, which meets Jackson Lake to the north. The area was settled in the late 1880s and named for David Jackson, an American trapper. It is noted for abundant wildlife—one of the largest elk herds in North America winters there. The resort town of Jackson, southeast of the valley, is the gateway to Jackson Hole.

Jackson Laboratory

The Jackson Laboratory, formerly the Roscoe B. Jackson Memorial Laboratory, is an independent, nonprofit research laboratory in Bar Harbor, Maine. Founded in 1929, it conducts research on cancer, heredity, organ transplantation, immunity, behavior, reproduction, and metabolism. The laboratory produces more than 2 million genetically standard mice annually for use by researchers throughout the world.

Jacksonville

Jacksonville is a major transportation and commercial center in northeast Florida. Located on the St. Johns River, 35 km (22 mi) from the Atlantic coast, the city has a population of 539,000 (1979 est.). Jacksonville and Duval County merged in 1968, creating the nation's fourth-largest city in area, 1,984 km² (766 mi²). Jacksonville has an average January temperature of 13° C (55° F) and an average July temperature of 28° C (82° F). Precipitation averages 1,295 mm (51 in) annually.

Jacksonville is the leading deepwater port on the southern U.S. Atlantic coast. In 1976 its harbor handled over 5 million tons of goods. It is a major coffee and automobile importing center. Large shipyards and the Cecil Field Naval Air Station occupy the waterfront. Industrial products include lumber, paper, chemicals, and processed food. Jacksonville is also a rail hub and a prominent finance and insurance center. The city's institutions of higher education include Jacksonville University (1934). The Gator Bowl (a major football stadium seating over 70,000 people), the Cummer Gallery of Art, and Jacksonville Art Museum are frequented by residents and tourists. In 1564, French Huguenots led by René Goulaine de LAUDONNIÈRE established Fort Caroline on the St. Johns River; the site is now marked by Fort Caroline National Monument. The city of Jacksonville was laid out in 1822, after the United States had acquired the area from Spain. It was named for Florida's first territorial governor, Andrew Jackson. Growth was impeded by the second Seminole War (1835-42), the Civil War, a yellow fever epidemic in 1888, and a fire in 1901. In the years 1870-90, Jacksonville developed into a major resort and experienced its first building boom.

TRUMAN A. HARTSHORN

Jacob

In the Bible, Jacob was the grandson of ABRAHAM and SARAH, the son of ISAAC and REBECCA, and the traditional ancestor of all Israel. Jacob obtained his prominence in the line of Abraham by tricking his elder twin brother ESAU out of both his birthright and his paternal blessing (Gen. 25:29–34; 27:1–41). As he fled from the enraged Esau, Jacob had a dream at Bethel of angels ascending and descending a ladder to heaven (Gen. 28:10–22). He married his cousins RACHEL and Leah and worked 20 years for their father, Laban, in Haran. He later wrestled with an angel, who gave him the name Israel (Gen. 32:22–32), and was reconciled with Esau. Jacob's 12 sons were the ancestors of the 12 tribes of Israel; Jacob's favorite was JOSEPH.

Bibliography: Weisel, Elie, *Messengers of God* (1976).

Jacob, François   [zhah-kohb']

François Jacob, a French biologist, b. June 17, 1920, contributed to the knowledge of how genes function and was awarded, along with French biologists Jacques MONOD and André LWOFF, the 1965 Nobel Prize for physiology or medicine. At the Pasteur Institute in 1958, Jacob and Monod proposed that molecules of ribonucleic acid (RNA) carried the genetic message from the deoxyribonucleic acid (DNA) in the nucleus to the ribosomes, or sites of protein synthesis in cells. They also found that not all genes function directly in protein synthesis but that some, which they called operator genes, function to regulate the activity of other protein-synthesizing genes.

Jacob, Georges

Georges Jacob, 1739–1814, was the founder of one of France's most celebrated families of furniture makers, who dominated the Parisian luxury furniture industry for three generations. Made a master in 1765, Jacob became the leading chairmaker of the Louis XVI period and counted among his clients members of the French and foreign courts. In 1787, Jacob provided furniture for Queen Marie Antoinette's bedroom at the Trianon, Versailles. His innovations in chairmaking included the use of mahogany, the curved "sabre" leg, and lighter seat frames. In 1788, Jacob made chairs in a neoclassical style for the painter Jacques Louis David.

See also: STYLES OF LOUIS XIII–XVI.

Jacobean literature   [jak-uh-bee'-uhn]

Jacobean literature is the term used for the corpus of English writings produced during the reign (1603–25) of James I ("Jacobus" in Latin). A strikingly restless, pained, and analytical literary age, it witnessed a high point in dramatic development in the forms of tragedy, satire, and romance. Shakespeare during this time wrote three of his great tragedies—*Othello, King Lear* and *Macbeth*—and vied with Francis BEAUMONT and John FLETCHER in romantic comedy. Ben JONSON was the master of satire and, with John DONNE, dominated the age's nondramatic poetry. Jonson's polished classical verse linked the previous Elizabethans to the later CAVALIER POETS, and Donne's witty and theatrical metaphysical style generated a new poetic mode. English prose was evolving into the "plain style" heralded by Francis BACON's *Essays* and the King James translation of the Bible.   EILEEN JORGE ALLMAN

Bibliography: Bush, Douglas, *English Literature in the Earlier Seventeenth Century* (1945).

Jacobean style   [jak-uh-bee'-uhn]

Jacobean style is the term sometimes used to describe the phase of English architecture of the 17th century that follows the ELIZABETHAN STYLE. It is generally characterized by the use of Renaissance motifs in English building and a final turning away from Gothic forms. At its best the Jacobean style is a fanciful imaginative style that assimilates motifs from a wide variety of sources, including the English medieval tradition and the Renaissance motifs of Flanders and Italy. In date it corresponds roughly with the reign of James I (1603–25).

Strapwork—a type of flat, pierced ornament—is a very common feature, as are pilasters and columns, which are often used one on top of another in a manner derived from Flem-

ish models. Many buildings in this style can be found in Oxford and Cambridge colleges. The Jacobean style was revived in the 19th century. One of its attractions for Victorian architects was that it could be justified as a purely English style, and this appealed to those concerned about a national spirit in architecture.

Bibliography: Summerson, John, *Architecture in Britain: 1530–1830* (1953); Whiffen, Marcus, *Elizabethan and Jacobean Architecture* (1952).

Jacobi, Carl Gustav Jacob   [jah-kohb'-ee]

Carl Gustav Jacob Jacobi, b. Dec. 10, 1804, d. Feb. 18, 1851, was a German mathematician. He obtained his Ph.D. in 1825 and taught mathematics at the University of Königsberg from 1826 until his death, becoming a full professor in 1832. Jacobi's reputation as an excellent teacher attracted many students. He introduced the seminar method to teach students the latest advances in mathematics. Jacobi was a prolific writer. His *Fundamenta nova theoria functionum ellipticarum* (New Foundations of the Theory of Elliptic Functions, 1829) and its later supplements made basic contributions to the theory of elliptic functions.   ARTHUR SCHLISSEL

Bibliography: Bell, Eric T., *Men of Mathematics* (1937).

Jacobi, Friedrich Heinrich   [yah'-kohb-ee]

The German philosopher Friedrich Heinrich Jacobi, b. Jan. 25, 1743, d. Mar. 19, 1819, known during his life primarily as an opponent of German idealism, is now considered a precursor of EXISTENTIALISM. Beginning his career as a merchant, he later turned to philosophy and religion and endeavored to defend his own version of Christian theism. Jacobi advocated the romantic view that God dwells within humans and reveals himself through our feelings, not our reason. Stressing feeling and faith over reason, he became a strong critic of Enlightenment views, deism, and especially of the then-current idealism. In turn, he suffered the harsh and devastating attack of idealists Immanuel Kant, Johann Gottlieb Fichte, Friedrich Schelling, and Georg Wilhelm Hegel. Not a consistent or systematic thinker, Jacobi presented his views in the form of novels, *Allwill* (1775) and *Woldemar* (1777).

Jacobi was much influenced by David Hume. In addition to opposing the idealists, Jacobi criticized the view of Baruch Spinoza, which he thereby popularized.   NICHOLAS CAPALDI

Bibliography: Crawford, Alexander W., *The Philosophy of F. H. Jacobi* (1905); Wilde, Norman, *Friedrich Heinrich Jacobi* (1894).

Jacobi, Lotte

Lotte Jacobi, b. 1896, is a Berlin-born photographer who became known in the 1920s and '30s for her bold and original portraits of prominent personalities from the world of art, the stage, film, and dance. Many of her subjects, including Bertolt Brecht and Kurt Weill, were associated with German expressionism, and Jacobi herself employed surrealist and cubist effects in her portraits. Less successful after she immigrated to New York in 1935, Jacobi nevertheless won a small group of discerning admirers and in the 1950s began experimenting with photograms (photographs made without a camera) and "photogenics" of abstract forms. Her photographs were exhibited at New York City's International Center of Photography in 1979.

Jacobins   [jak'-uh-binz]

During the FRENCH REVOLUTION, the Jacobins were members of the Society of the Friends of the Constitution, a political group that met from 1790 to 1794 in the former Dominican, or Jacobin, monastery in Paris. Members of the many local societies throughout France that became affiliated to the mother society in Paris were also called Jacobins. Through repeated secessions and purges, the Jacobins became identified with ardent patriotism, with secular and democratic republicanism, and with the adoption of ruthless minority government in times of emergency. Identified also with Maximilien de ROBESPIERRE, they were suppressed soon after his execution.

Bibliography: Brinton, Crane, *The Jacobins* (1930; repr. 1961).

Jacobite church [jak'-uh-byt]

A body of Monophysite Christians, living primarily in Syria, Iraq, and India, the Jacobite church takes its name from Jacob (James) Baradai (d. 578), bishop of Edessa, who organized a separate church, opposed to the Orthodox episcopate of Eastern Christendom. Together with the Copts of Egypt, the Armenians, and the Ethiopians, the Jacobites reject the doctrine of the Council of Chalcedon (451; see CHALCEDON, COUNCIL OF) on the "two natures in one person" of Christ and prefer to define Christ's person as "one nature" (see MONOPHYSITISM). Modern historians generally consider that their doctrine, as elaborated in the 6th century by Severus of Antioch and Philoxenus of Mabbug, is not essentially different from that of Saint CYRIL OF ALEXANDRIA, whom Orthodox, Roman Catholics, and Monophysites equally venerate as a Father of the Church. Their rejection of the Council of Chalcedon, however, still keeps the Jacobites separated from the main bodies of Christendom.

The head of the Jacobite church bears the title of patriarch of Antioch and resides in Homs, Syria. His flock has been gradually reduced by the various stormy events in the Middle East. The MALABAR CHRISTIANS of India, also often designated as "Jacobites," have established their own patriarchate.

JOHN MEYENDORFF

Bibliography: Attwater, Donald, *The Christian Churches of the East* (1948).

Jacobites [jak'-uh-byts]

After Britain's GLORIOUS REVOLUTION of 1688 the adherents of the exiled STUART king JAMES II and his Roman Catholic descendants were known as Jacobites. The major support for their cause was in Scotland and Ireland, where the Jacobites continued to resist after the accession to the throne of WILLIAM III and MARY II in 1689. William, however, defeated the Scottish Jacobites under Viscount DUNDEE at Killiecrankie (1689) and the Irish Jacobites in the Battle of BOYNE (1690).

When James II died in 1701, his son, James Edward (known as the Old Pretender; see STUART, JAMES FRANCIS EDWARD), was recognized as king of England and Scotland by Spain and France. He first attempted an invasion of Scotland in 1708, but it was a total fiasco. More serious was the Jacobite rising of 1715, which took place after the accession of the Hanoverian GEORGE I and had support in England as well as Scotland. Nonetheless, the Scottish Jacobites were defeated at Preston in Lancashire on November 13, and by the time James Edward landed in Scotland on Dec. 22, 1715, the cause was lost. He departed on Feb. 4, 1716.

In 1745 his son, Charles Edward (Bonnie Prince Charlie or the Young Pretender; see STUART, CHARLES EDWARD), sailed to Scotland and raised certain Highland clans. He defeated Sir John Cope at Prestonpans on Sept. 21, 1745, but was later routed at Culloden Moor on Apr. 16, 1746. Charles Edward fled from Scotland, and with him went the last of the Jacobite hopes.

CHARLES H. HAWS

Bibliography: Petrie, Sir Charles, *The Jacobite Movement*, rev. ed. (1959); Prebble, John, *Culloden* (1961).

Jacobs, W. W.

The English short-story writer William Wymark Jacobs, b. Sept. 8, 1863, d. Sept. 1, 1943, is particularly remembered for his chilling horror story, "The Monkey's Paw" (1902). Jacobs is also known for his often humorous tales of the London dockland, published in *Many Cargoes* (1896), *Captains All* (1905), and *Night Watches* (1914).

ROBIN BUSS

Jacob's ladder

Jacob's ladder is the common name for approximately 25 species of annual or perennial plants constituting the genus *Polemonium* in the phlox family, Polemoniaceae. These plants have reclining stems or underground rhizomes and bear blue, purple, yellow, or white funnel-shaped flowers. A Eurasian perennial grown as an ornamental and now also found wild

in eastern North America is *P. caeruleum*, which grows to 1 m (3 ft) high and bears clusters of typically bright blue flowers with yellow stamens.

Jacob's Pillow Dance Festival

The Jacob's Pillow Dance Festival is a summer performance series at Jacob's Pillow, the former Ted SHAWN retreat in Lee, Mass., which developed out of informal performances by Shawn and his Men Dancers beginning in 1933. The festival itself was organized in 1940; at first it was directed by others, but Shawn eventually gained complete control. Programs at the Pillow were noted for their diverse content, including ballet, modern, and ethnic dance, and for the many companies given important exposure there. The festival declined in quality near the end of Shawn's life but has been revived and continued since his death.

EDWARD RICCO

Bibliography: Terry, Walter, *Ted Shawn: Father of American Dance* (1976)

See also: DANCE; DENISHAWN; MODERN DANCE; ST. DENIS, RUTH.

Jacob's staff

The Jacob's staff, also known as the fore staff and later as the cross staff, was an instrument that was used by early astronomers and navigators to measure angles and the altitude of the Sun and stars. It was described by astronomer LEVI BEN GERSHON in 1342 and was the most popular tool of the navigator until the end of the 16th century. The staff, of square cross section, was held against the navigator's cheek bone; a cross piece was moved along the staff until the ends of the cross bar appeared to touch the horizon and the Sun or a star simultaneously. Each side of the staff was marked with a different scale of degrees; four cross pieces of different lengths were provided with the instrument.

RODERICK S. WEBSTER AND MARJORIE WEBSTER

Bibliography: Stimson and Daniel, *The Cross Staff: Historical Development and Modern Use* (1977).

Jacobsen, Arne [yah'-kohp-sen, ar'-neh]

The Danish architect Arne Jacobsen, b. Feb. 11, 1902, d. Mar. 21, 1971, produced some of the most elegant and meticulous buildings of modern Scandinavia. Initially influenced by Erik Gunnar ASPLUND, Jacobsen began as an architect of private houses and later turned to public commissions. He produced three distinguished town halls: Aarhus (1939–42), Søllerød (1940–42), and Rødovre (1955). The first two are more classical in their use of expanses of concrete and large, evenly spaced windows, while the third features an extremely long, unbroken, elegantly detailed facade of glass and steel, and terminal walls of black stone. The SAS Royal Hotel and Air Terminal (1958–60), a particularly smooth and sophisticated application of INTERNATIONAL STYLE technique, was Copenhagen's first skyscraper. The tradition of Scandinavian craftsmanship evident in the details of Jacobsen's buildings is also apparent in his designs for furniture and household articles of the 1950s.

ANN VAN ZANTEN

Bibliography: Dyssegaard, Soren, ed., *Arne Jacobsen: A Danish Architect* (1972); Faber, Tobias, *Arne Jacobsen*, trans. by E. Rockwell (1964).

Jacobsen, Jens Peter [yah'-kohp-sen, yens pay'-tur]

The Danish poet, novelist, and translator Jens Peter Jacobsen, b. Apr. 7, 1847, d. Apr. 30, 1885, published what is often considered the first literary example of Danish naturalism. The story, "Mogen" (1872; Eng. trans., 1921), shows the influence of Georg Brandes, whom Jacobsen had heard lecture at the University of Copenhagen. Jacobsen's two novels, *Fru Marie Grubbe* (1876; Eng. trans., 1914) and *Niels Lyhne* (1880; Eng. trans., 1896), explore the tensions between abstract social or religious positions and actual psychological reality. The German poet Rainer Maria Rilke was among those influenced by his poetry. Trained in the life sciences, Jacobsen was also the first Danish translator of the writings of Darwin. In the early 1870s he contracted the tuberculosis that eventually led to his death. .

Bibliography: Gustafson, Alrik, *Six Scandinavian Novelists*, 2d ed. (1966); Mitchell, Philip M., *A History of Danish Literature* (1957).

Jacobson's organ

A nasal structure, Jacobson's organ consists of a thin plate of bone (vomer) and the nasal bone, which forms the bridge of the nose. Most developed in snakes, it has chemically sensitive nerve endings in vertebrates and responds to a narrow range of odors. Present in human embryos, Jacobson's organ degenerates as the nervous system matures.

Jacopone da Todi   [yah-koh-poh'-nay dah toh'-dee]

An important Italian religious poet of the Middle Ages, Jacopone da Todi, originally surnamed dei Benedetti, b. *c.*1230, d. Dec. 25, 1306, became a Franciscan monk about 1278. As a member of the so-called spiritual faction of his order, he opposed Pope BONIFACE VIII, and this led to his excommunication and five-year imprisonment. During this time he composed many of the canticles, or *laudi*, for which he is remembered. The liturgical poem *Stabat Mater Dolorosa* is also often attributed to Jacopone.

Jacquard, Joseph Marie   [zhah-kar']

The French inventor Joseph Marie Jacquard, b. July 7, 1752, d. Aug. 7, 1834, built the first successful LOOM for weaving patterned fabrics. This loom, which used a system of punched cards to produce a pattern, was a forerunner of the computer. Several inventors had improved the draw, or pattern, loom when Jacquard undertook his work about 1800. His creation gave impetus to the development of the textile industry and paved the way for the fully automatic loom. Jacquard's loom was demonstrated to Napoleon I and patented in 1804. It won for its inventor both royalties and a pension. Although Jacquard and his invention were opposed by silk workers, the loom was gradually accepted and became used worldwide. The punched cards used in it were adopted (1835) by the British inventor Charles BABBAGE for his calculator and by Herman HOLLERITH for use in tabulating the 1890 U.S. census.

See also: SPINNING; WEAVING.

Jacqueline of Hainaut   [jak'-wuh-leen, en-oh']

Jacqueline of Hainaut, b. July 25, 1401, d. Oct. 9, 1436, countess of Holland, Zeeland, and Hainaut, surrendered control of her three counties to her cousin PHILIP THE GOOD, duke of Burgundy, in 1428 and thus contributed to the Burgundian domination of the Low Countries. Before inheriting (1417) the counties from her father, Jacqueline married (1415) Jean de Touraine, second son of Charles VI of France. Later she married John IV, duke of Brabant (1418), and Humphrey, duke of Gloucester (1422; see GLOUCESTER, HUMPHREY, DUKE OF) in order to protect her territories from Philip. Abandoned by Humphrey, she was forced to sign over her lands to Philip by the Treaty of Delft (1428). Jacqueline remained titular countess until 1433, when Philip forced her abdication for marrying without his consent.

Jacquerie   [zhahk-uh-ree']

The Jacquerie was a French peasant insurrection in 1358. During the HUNDRED YEARS' WAR the French peasants suffered in the extensive pillaging of the countryside by English soldiers and were further victimized by the financial exactions of their own nobles. On May 21, 1358, an uprising began near Compiègne, northeast of Paris. Led by Guillaume Cale, or Carle, the peasants destroyed castles and slew their occupants. They joined forces with another rebel group from Paris, led by Étienne Marcel, but both groups were routed on June 9 and 10. Savage reprisals followed.

Bibliography: Tuchman, Barbara, *A Distant Mirror* (1978).

jade

(Left) Jade *is a term given to two distinct minerals—the common amphibole, nephrite, and the rare pyroxene, jadeite. Both are found as compact groups of matted, fibrous crystals in various colors.*

(Below) *Jade has been carved into ornaments and tools by various cultures. This carved jade ornament from China is typical of the intricate shapes and designs for which Chinese artisans have long been noted.*

Jade, a translucent ornamental material, has been carved since ancient times. Jade carving has flourished in China since 2000 BC, notably during the Chou dynasty and the Ch'ien-lung era of the Ch'ing dynasties. The Chinese have ascribed to this GEM many human virtues. The Han scholar Hsü Shen, for example, asserted that its bright yet warm luster typified charity; its translucency, revealing inner color and markings, represented rectitude; its pure and penetrating note when struck displayed wisdom; its ability to break but not bend exemplified courage; and its sharp edges, not intended for violence, symbolized equity. Jade ornaments and tools also have been carved by the Mesoamerican Maya and Aztec, the Maori of New Zealand, the Alaskan Eskimo, and by inhabitants of India since the 17th century.

Jade consists of two separate silicate mineral species: nephrite, and the less common but more valued jadeite. Both are monoclinic. Nephrite has a splintery fracture, vitreous or silky luster, and dark-colored inclusions. A calcium and ferromagnesian silicate ($Ca_2(Mg, Fe)_5Si_8O_{22}$ $(OH,F)_2$), nephrite is the massive form of actinolite and tremolite (see AMPHIBOLE). It forms translucent-to-opaque, mottled-green, compact aggregates composed of interwoven long, thin fibers. Hardness is 5–6, and specific gravity is 3.0–3.1. Nephrite occurs in rocks subjected to low-grade metamorphism.

Jadeite has a granular fracture, a glassy or pearly luster, and a pitted or polished surface. A PYROXENE mineral, jadeite is a sodium aluminosilicate ($NaAlSi_2O_6$). It occurs as transparent-to-opaque compact lenses, veins, or nodules that vary in color due to impurities: the white through emerald- or apple-green, red, blue, and brown varieties contain calcium; the dark-green to blackish varieties (chloromelanite) contain iron. Hardness is 6½–7, and specific gravity is 3.3–3.5. Jadeite occurs in rocks once subjected to deep-seated metamorphism and subsequently uplifted and eroded.

Bibliography: Chu, Arthur and Grace, *The Collectors' Book of Jade* (1978); Goette, John A., *Jade Lore*, 2d ed. (1976); Gump, Richard, *Jade: Stone of Heaven* (1962); Hansford, S. Howard, *Chinese Jade Carving* (1950); Schedel, J. J., *The Splendor of Jade* (1974).

jadeite: see JADE.

Jadwiga, Queen of Poland   [yahd-vee'-gah]

Jadwiga, b. c.1373, d. July 17, 1399, reigned as queen of Poland from 1384 to 1399. The younger daughter of the Hungarian King LOUIS I, who ruled Poland from 1370 to 1382, she was elected queen by the Polish nobles in order to separate Poland from Hungary, which was inherited by her older sister, Maria. In 1386 the young Jadwiga married Jogaillo, grand duke of Lithuania, who was baptized a Christian and crowned king of Poland as Władysław II (or V). Although it produced no children, this marriage eventually brought the unification of Poland and Lithuania (see JAGELLO dynasty). Jadwiga, a gentle woman of poor health, restored the University of Kraków and is venerated as a saint in Poland.

K. M. SMOGORZEWSKI

Bibliography: Kellogg, Charlotte, *Jadwiga, Queen of Poland* (1936).

jaeger   [yay'-gur]

Jaeger is the common name for predatory sea birds of the genus *Stercorarius*, family Stercorariidae. Jaegers breed on Arctic Ocean shores and winter on the warmer seas of the world. They are swift, agile fliers that hunt small birds and mammals and harass other sea birds during flight in order to steal their food.

WILLIAM SANFORD

Jaffa   [jaf'-uh]

Jaffa (Hebrew: Yafo) is the old city of the TEL AVIV-JAFFA metropolis. Located in west central Israel on the Mediterranean Sea, it has been an important commercial seaport since 2000 BC. Before the establishment of the state of Israel, Jaffa was predominantly Arab, but in 1947-48 most Arabs left and the city was partially destroyed. In 1950, Jaffa and its modern Jewish suburb Tel Aviv were incorporated into one city. At present, Jaffa is a center of tourism and entertainment. During the 1970s its Manshiye quarter became a banking and commercial district.

Originally a Phoenician city, Jaffa was taken over by Egypt in 1472 BC and was made a provincial capital. In the 4th century BC it was conquered by Alexander the Great, and in AD 68 it was destroyed by the Roman emperor Vespasian. During the 12th century Jaffa was the site of several battles between the Crusaders and the Muslims. After the Ottomans took the city in the 16th century the port regained importance. In 1799, Jaffa was occupied by Napoleon.

Jagan, Cheddi   [jah'-gahn, ched'-ee]

The Guyanese political leader Cheddi Jagan, b. Berbice, British Guiana, Mar. 22, 1918, was the first premier (1961-64) of British Guiana (now Guyana). After studying at U.S. universities he entered politics in 1947. He founded (1950) Guyana's first political party, the People's Progressive party, with Forbes BURNHAM (later prime minister); Jagan was head of the government for 6 months in 1953 until Great Britain suspended the constitution. He served as minister of trade and industry (1957-61; his wife at the same time served as minister of labor, health, and housing) and as opposition leader (1964-73, 1976-78).

Bibliography: Jagan, Cheddi, *The West on Trial: My Fight for Guyana's Freedom* (1966); Simms, Peter, *Trouble in Guyana* (1966).

Jagello   (dynasty)   [yah-gel'-loh]

The dynasty of Jagello (Polish: *Jagiello*; Lithuanian: *Jogaillo*) ruled Poland and Lithuania (1386-1572), Hungary (1440-44, 1490-1526), and Bohemia (1471-1526). It took its name from Jogaillo (c.1350-1434), grand duke of Lithuania, who in 1386 married JADWIGA, queen of Poland, and thus brought about the Christian conversion of Lithuania and the eventual union of Poland and Lithuania.

Jogaillo, who became King Władysław II (or V) of Poland, was succeeded by his oldest son, Władysław III (or VI), who also reigned as king of Hungary (1440-44), and then, after a brief interregnum, by his younger son, CASIMIR IV (r. 1447-92). Casimir was followed by his three sons in succession: John I (r. 1492-1501), Alexander I (r. 1501-06), and SIGISMUND I (r. 1506-48). The last Jagello ruler of Poland was SIGISMUND II (r. 1548-72).

Another son of Casimir's became king of Bohemia (1471) and then Hungary (1490) as Ladislas II. He was succeeded in both countries by his son, LOUIS II (r. 1516-26).

Under the Jagello rulers the Poles and Lithuanians won joint victories over the TEUTONIC KNIGHTS (1410, 1466) and fought against the expanding power of Muscovite Russia. Finally, by the Union of Lublin in 1569, the two nations formally merged in the Polish-Lithuanian Commonwealth, with one king and a common parliament. The great age of the commonwealth was the 16th century, when it enjoyed peace, prosperity, and cultural flowering. Its decline began not so much with the end (1572) of the male Jagello line and the implementation of elective monarchy, as with the ruinous 17th-century wars.

ANNA M. CIENCIALA

Bibliography: Reddaway, W. W., ed., *Cambridge History of Poland*, vol. 1 (1950; repr. 1971).

jaguar   [jag'-war]

The jaguar is the largest member of the cat family, Felidae, found in either North or South America. Formerly designated either *Panthera onca* or *Felis onca*, the jaguar is now classified as *Leo onca*. In Latin America it is commonly called a *tigre*; the term *jaguar* is derived from its native Indian name.

A male jaguar may reach 1.8 m (6 ft) in length (head and body) with a 75-cm-long (2.5-ft) tail, and may weigh nearly 180 kg (400 lb). Its coat ranges from grayish to reddish tan

The jaguar, L. onca, the largest cat found in the Americas, looks like a leopard but is more heavily built. The solitary jaguar establishes its own territory, and males and females disregard each other except during mating season.

and is spotted like that of a leopard, with body spots grouped into small circles, or rosettes; unlike the leopard, however, the jaguar's rosettes surround one or more solid spots. The jaguar is also more stoutly built than the leopard, with a larger, broader head.

Jaguars are found from the southwestern United States to Patagonia in southern Argentina. They inhabit marshes, scrub brush areas, and both temperate and tropical forests. They feed on a wide variety of large and small animals and also occasionally prey on domestic animals; very rarely, they have become man-eaters. Jaguars breed once a year, in no particular season in the tropics. After a gestation period of about 14 weeks usually 1 to 4 young are born. EVERETT SENTMAN

Bibliography: Perry, Richard, *The World of the Jaguar* (1970).

jaguarundi [jag-wuh-ruhn'-dee]

The jaguarundi, or eyra, is a tropical American cat, *Felis yagouaroundi*, found from northern Mexico to northern Argentina. It somewhat resembles a large weasel, having a long, slender body, a wedge-shaped head, short legs, and a long tail. Jaguarundis may reach 1.3 m (51 in) in total length, including a 60-cm-long (24-in) tail. They may stand 30 cm (12 in) high at the shoulders and weigh up to 9 kg (20 lb). Two color phases occur, a red and a dark gray or brownish. Newborn jaguarundis are spotted. EVERETT SENTMAN

Jahangir, Mogul Emperor of India [juh-huhn-geer']

Jahangir, or Jehangir, b. Aug. 31, 1569, d. Oct. 28, 1627, the fourth Mogul emperor of India, ruled from 1605 to 1627. He was the son of AKBAR and the father of SHAH JAHAN, the builder of the Taj Mahal. Although he rebelled against his father in 1599, Jahangir continued Akbar's expansionist policies after his succession; he fought long wars in the Deccan but won little new territory.

Like his father, Jahangir was a patron of the arts, especially painting and poetry. Otherwise, however, he was a cruel tyrant and, despite his Muslim faith, a drunkard and opium user. Pursuing his private pleasures, he left the running of his empire mostly to his Persian wife, Nur Jahan, who became the strong-willed dispenser of imperial justice. Jahangir's last years were troubled by frequent rebellions by his son, Prince Khurram (later Shah Jahan). It was to Jahangir's court that England first dispatched an ambassador, Sir Thomas Roe, in 1615. MARCUS FRANDA AND VONETTA J. FRANDA

Bibliography: Hansen, Waldemar, *The Peacock Throne: The Drama of Mogul India* (1972); Pandey, Awadh Bihari, *Later Medieval India: A History of the Mughals* (1962); Prasad, Beni, *History of Jahangir* (1923).

Jahiz, Abu Uthman Amr al- [jah'-his, ah'-boo oot'-mahn ahm'-ur ahl]

The Arabic writer Abu Uthman Amr al-Jahiz, b. *c.*776, d. 868, was deeply involved in the theological, literary, and scientific discussions of his age. His 7-volume masterpiece *Kitab al-hayawan* (Book of Animals) goes beyond zoology to a study of animals in Arab culture and lore. His prolific writings also include *Kitab al-bayan wa't-tabyin* (Book of Eloquence and Exposition) and *Kitab al-bukhala* (Book of Misers). These works have been translated into French, and selections from his works appear in Charles Pellat's *The Life and Works of Jahiz* (1969).

Jahn, Friedrich Ludwig [yahn]

Friedrich Ludwig Jahn, b. Aug. 11, 1778, d. Oct. 15, 1852, was a German nationalist educator and the father of GYMNASTICS. In 1811, as an anti-Napoleonic move, he organized group outdoor exercises to strengthen German youth and to raise national morale. The movement emphasized the German folk tradition, and it spread rapidly. Jahn introduced new gymnastic apparatuses such as the horizontal bar, the side horse, the balance beam, and the parallel bars. After the fall of Napoleon, Jahn's movement was suppressed, and he was arrested

by the reactionary government. Later released, he was given an Iron Cross in 1840 and elected to the revolutionary German parliament of 1848.

Jähn, Sigmund [yahn]

Sigmund Jähn, the first East German cosmonaut, was 41 years old and an air force lieutenant colonel at the time of his flight aboard Soyuz 31. A native of the German town of Rautenkranz, he graduated from his country's flying school and was selected (1976) for the Soviet Intercosmos program. Jähn, the third non-Soviet cosmonaut, and Valery Bykovsky, the Soviet flight commander, were launched on Aug. 26, 1978, and docked a day later with the Salyut 6 space station. They returned to Earth on September 3 aboard the Soyuz 29 craft brought up earlier by cosmonauts Alexander Ivanchenko and Vladimir Kovalenok, who remained aboard Salyut 6. CRAIG B. WAFF

Jahnn, Hans Henny [yahn, hahns hen'-ee]

The German writer and organ builder Hans Henny Jahnn, b. Dec. 17, 1894, d. Nov. 29, 1959, was a major experimenter in fictional and dramatic form between World Wars I and II; he was particularly inclined toward sexual imagery. His best-known plays are *Pastor Ephraim Magnus* (1919) and *Medea* (1926). He gained a much greater international reputation, however, as a designer and builder of organs. His post-World War II works, principally fiction, include the trilogy *Fluss ohne Ufer* (River without Shore, 1949–61), of which only the first book, *The Ship* (1949; Eng. trans., 1961), has been translated. Although Jahnn influenced the German expressionists, he was not identified with any literary movement.

jai alai [hy'-ly]

Jai alai is a form of handball for singles or doubles competition played on a court with one or three walls. Players use a curved wicker basket (cesta) for returning the ball. The game is played most seriously in Mexico City, Havana, and Miami, Fla., and on a less competitive level in southern Europe and Connecticut. The players are professionals, and wagering is common.

The game is derived from either the Aztecs or a Basque variation of handball. It developed in Spain, was imported to Cuba in 1900, and arrived in Miami in 1924.

The ball (pelota) is made of hard, wound rubber covered by linen thread and two layers of goatskin; it is 2 in. (5 cm) in diameter and travels about 240 km/h (150 mph).

The standard rules are similar to handball rules, except the court (fronton) is much larger—176 ft (53.7 m) long. There is one more player (or team) than the number of game points. If a player loses a point he is eliminated, and the next player comes on the court. The first player to reach game point wins. In Miami an alternative form of scoring is used in which 8 competitors play for 5 points. A player sits down when he has won 3 points; the first 3 players to do so compete in a playoff to determine the match winner.

Bibliography: Hollander, Zander, and Schulz, David, *The Jai Alai Handbook* (1978).

jail: see PRISON.

Jainism [jy'-nizm]

Jainism is a religious faith of India that is usually said to have originated with Mahavira, a contemporary of the Buddha (6th century BC). Jains, however, count Mahavira as the last of 24 founders, or Tirthamkaras, the first being Rishabha. The 1971 census of India counts 2,600,000 Jains, mostly concentrated in the western part of India. Jainism has been present in India since Mahavira's time without interruption, and its influence has been significant.

The major distinction within Jainism is between the Digambara and Svetambara sects, a schism that appears to date from about the 1st century AD. The major difference between them is that whereas the Svetambaras wear white clothes, the Digambaras traditionally go naked. Fundamentally, however, the views of both sects on ethics and philosophy are identical.

The most notable feature of Jain ethics is its insistence on noninjury to all forms of life. Jain philosophy finds that every kind of thing has a soul; therefore strict observance of this precept of nonviolence (*ahimsa*) requires extreme caution in all activity. Jain monks frequently wear cloths over their mouths to avoid unwittingly killing anything by breathing it in, and Jain floors are kept meticulously clean to avert the danger of stepping on a living being. Jains regard the intentional taking of life, or even violent thoughts, however, as much more serious. Jain philosophy posits a gradation of beings, from those with five senses down to those with only one sense. Ordinary householders cannot help harming the latter, although they should strive to limit themselves in this regard by refraining from eating meat, certain fruits, or honey or from drinking wine. In addition Jain householders are expected to practice other virtues, similar to those in HINDUISM. The vows taken by the Jain monks are more severe. They eventually involve elements of ASCETICISM: fasting, peripatetic begging, learning to endure bodily discomfort, and various internal austerities constituting a Jain variety of YOGA. Jainism is unique in allowing the very spiritually advanced to hasten their own death by certain practices (principally fasting) and under specified circumstances.

Jain philosophy is based on a fundamental distinction between living and nonliving matter. Living souls are divided into bound and liberated; the living souls are found in both mobile and immobile loci. Nonliving matter is composed of *karman* or very fine particles that enter a soul and produce changes in it, thus causing its bondage. This influx of *karman* is induced by activity and has to be burned off by experience. *Karmans* are of infinitely numerous varieties and account for all distinctions noted in the world. By nonattachment, however, an individual can prevent influx of further *karmans* and thus escape from the bonds of action. A soul, which is thought of as having the same size as its body, at liberation has lost the matter that weights it down and thus ascends to the top of the universe, where it remains forever.

Jainism recognizes no supreme deity; its ideal is the perfection attained by the 24 Tirthamkaras. Numerous temples have been built celebrating the perfected souls; a notable example is the temple at Mount Abu in Rajasthan.   KARL H. POTTER

Bibliography: Chatterjee, A. K., *A Comprehensive History of Jainism* (1978); Gopalan, Subramania, *Outlines of Jainism* (1973); Jain, J. P., *Religion and Culture of the Jains* (1976); Mehta, Mohan Lal, *Outlines of Jaina Philosophy* (1954); Stevenson, S. T., *The Heart of Jainism* (1915; repr. 1970); Williams, R. H. B., *Jaina Yoga* (1963).

Jaipur   [jy'-pur]

Jaipur, the capital and largest city of Rajasthan state in western India, is located about 300 km (190 mi) southwest of Delhi. The city has an area of approximately 206 km² (80 mi²), and its population, 613,144 (1971), makes it the 13th-largest city in the country. Jaipur, which lies at an altitude of about 427 m (1,400 ft), occupies a strategic position on the eastern flanks of the Aravalli Range on the trade routes from Gujarat to Agra and Delhi. Jaipur's summer temperature reaches a mean maximum of 42° C (108° F), but in winter the mean is only 18° C (64° F). The annual rainfall is about 610 mm (24 in), but millet, barley, and chickpeas are nevertheless grown in the surrounding area. Jaipur is noted for its jewelry, printed cloth, and enamelware. Rajasthan University was established there in 1947.

Jaipur was planned and founded in 1727 by Maharaja Sawaii Jai Singh II. Although his plan was not followed completely, Jaipur's regular layout, nine rectangular blocks with a gridiron street pattern, is unusual for an Indian city of its size. A masonry wall, 6 m (20 ft) high with eight gates, surrounds the city. Jaipur is called the pink city because most of its buildings are of light red sandstone. Landmarks include the city palace, which contains Chandra Mahal and the Jantar Mantar, an 18th-century astronomical observatory with masonry instruments; and the Hawa Mahal, or Hall of Winds, a beautifully sculptured five-story building.

Jakarta   [juh-kart'-uh]

Jakarta (Djakarta), the capital of Indonesia, has a population of 6 million (1978 est.), the largest of any urban center in Southeast Asia and one of the largest in the world. It is located on the alluvial plain of the Liwung River in northwestern Java. The city is coextensive with its metropolitan area, Djakarta Raya, covering 578 km² (223 mi²) and forming a special capital region. The city has expanded from the Kota, or Old City, and now includes the modern port of Tanjung Priok, 10 km (6 mi) to the east.

Jakarta lies within a humid, tropical region. Monthly temperature averages vary little from the annual mean of 26° C (79° F). Maximum rainfall occurs in summer, with an average of 1,788 mm (70 in) falling annually.

The majority of the city's residents are Muslims from west, central, and east Java. In the last 30 years, heavy in-migration, primarily from the densely populated rural areas of Java, has accounted for much of the rapid growth. Jakarta is the major industrial and commercial center in Indonesia, with textiles and food processing among its more important industries. Jakarta's port is the nation's center for waterborne international trade, and its airport handles both domestic and overseas flights.

Jakarta is also the cultural center of Indonesia. The Museum of Indonesian Culture (1778) houses both ancient and modern works of art. The University of Indonesia (1950) and nine private universities are located there.

Jakarta, the capital and largest city of the Republic of Indonesia, lies on the northwestern coast of Java along the Liwung River. The city, formerly known as Batavia, was the colonial capital of the Netherlands East Indies until Indonesia won its independence in 1949.

Jakarta was settled as a trading center by Hindus and Buddhists from India about the 5th century. The Portuguese dominated the area in the 14th century, but they were ousted by the sultan of Bantam in 1527. He named the city Djajakerta, meaning "glorious fortress."

In 1619 the Dutch under Jan Pieterszoon Coen captured the city, fortified it, and named it Batavia. The city became the capital of the Dutch East Indies. Dutch architectural styles were introduced, as was a system of canals (kalis). For a time during the Napoleonic Wars British rule prevailed. The Netherlands controlled the area from 1815 until 1949, when Indonesia became independent and Jakarta was chosen as its capital. The city was occupied by the Japanese during World War II.   RICHARD ULACK

Jakobson, Roman [yah'-kub-suhn, roh'-mahn]

The linguist Roman Jakobson, b. Moscow, Oct. 11 (N.S.), 1896, has contributed to virtually every aspect of language study. His early books and articles dealt with aphasia and language acquisition. As a member of the PRAGUE SCHOOL, Jakobson wrote on the relation of language to literature and culture. His recent publications include *Main Trends in the Science of Language* (1973) and six volumes of selected writings (1962–78).   DAVID YERKES

Jalapa [hah-lah'-pah]

Jalapa (Jalapa Enríquez), the capital of Veracruz state in east central Mexico, is situated in the Sierra Madre Oriental. Its population is 183,200 (1976 est.). The city thrives as a market for the region's coffee and tobacco crops. Tourism is also important. During the Spanish colonial era Jalapa was a trading center. Veracruzana University was founded there in 1944.

Jalisco [hah-lees'-koh]

Jalisco, a mostly mountainous state in west central Mexico, is traversed by the Sierra Madre Occidental. It has an area of 80,137 km² (30,941 mi²) and a population of 4,157,000 (1976 est.); its capital is GUADALAJARA. The narrow coastal plain on the Pacific Ocean, where the climate is hot and humid, rises to a high plateau with numerous volcanic peaks. The state has large silver and gold deposits. Its principal agricultural products include corn, wheat, beans, tobacco, and citrus fruits; stock raising is also important. Jalisco was conquered by the Spanish in 1529 after great Indian resistance. In the 1820s it was an important stronghold during the independence movement.

jam and jelly

Jam is a confection made by cooking fruit and sugar until a mixture with a fairly thick consistency is achieved. Jellies are fruit juices cooked with sugar to form a firm gel, using the PECTIN of the fruit itself or added pectin to aid the gelling process. Fruit preserves are whole or sectioned fruits cooked in a thick, clear, sugar syrup. Citrus preserves are called marmalades. The smooth, semisolid fruit butters and the thick-to-solid fruit pastes are made from varying concentrations of fruit pulp and sugar. In addition to the fruit and sugar, federal standards permit the use of citric, tartaric, or other food-derived acids to improve gelling and to stabilize color and flavor. Other permitted sweeteners include corn syrup and dextrose. No artificial flavors or colors are permitted except in mint and cinnamon jellies.

The commercial manufacture of preserves and jellies is similar. The fruits or juices, pectin, and sugar are blended, heated, and pumped to a vacuum pan, where rapid boiling at 60° C (140° F) protects the fruit's color and flavor as the water content evaporates. When the mixture reaches the required degree of thickness, the food-acid mix is added. The finished product is immediately packed into jars, sterilized, cooled in a water spray, dried, labeled, and cartoned.

In 1975 the United States consumed 233 million kg (514 million lb) of fruit jams and jellies. Of this total, 8 percent was marmalade, and the balance was equally divided between jams and jellies. Grape jelly is the most popular commercial product, with 30 percent of total sales; strawberry preserves and apple jelly rank second and third.

Jam and jelly making is a simple way to preserve fruit, and the techniques described here are used, on a smaller scale, in many home kitchens.   JAY C. MUSSER

Bibliography: Byron, May, *Jams and Jellies* (1975); Johnson, Arnold, and Peterson, Martin, eds., *Encyclopedia of Food Technology* (1974).

Jamaica [juh-may'-kuh]

Jamaica, a nation in the West Indies, occupies the third largest island in the Caribbean Sea. Located south of Cuba and west of Hispaniola, Jamaica is slightly larger than the island of Hawaii. KINGSTON is its capital.

JAMAICA

Official Name: Jamaica
Capital and Largest City: Kingston (1977 est. pop., 600,000)
Area: 11,422 km² (4,409 mi²)
Elevation: *Highest*—Blue Mountain, 2,256 m (7,402 ft); *lowest*—sea level, along the Caribbean Sea coast
Population: 2,217,000 (1979 est.). *Distribution*—31% urban, 63% rural; *density*, 190 persons per km² (503 per mi²); *annual rate of increase* (1970–77), 1.6%
Principal Language: English
Principal Religions: Anglican, Baptist, Church of God, Roman Catholic, Methodist
Principal Products: *Agriculture*—bananas, coffee, ginger, pimento, sugar. *Manufacturing and industry*—asbestos products, cement, chemicals, metal products, rum, cotton textiles, tobacco, sugar. *Mining*—alumina, bauxite, ceramic clay, silica sand, gypsum
Railroads: 330 km/205 mi (1979)
Roads: 7,600 km/4,723 mi (1979 paved)
Currency: 1 Jamaican dollar = 100 cents

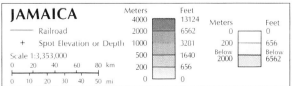

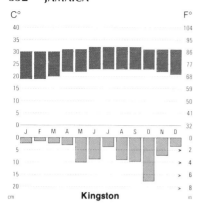

Kingston

(Above) *Bars indicate monthly ranges of temperature (red) and precipitation (blue) of Kingston, Jamaica. The tropical wet climate is modified by coastal influences.*

(Right) *The Blue Mountains of eastern Jamaica provide lush scenery and respite from the heat and humidity of the coast. Blue Mountain attains the island's highest elevation at 2,256 m (7,402 ft).*

LAND

Jamaica, about 235 km (146 mi) long by 82 km (51 mi) at its widest point, is bisected by highlands, trending east and west, that cover 80% of the island. The highest elevations are in the Blue Mountains to the east. The coastal plains are wider and more arid to the south. Most of the soil of the island, particularly in the central section, contains abundant amounts of limestone, making cultivation difficult. Rainwater does not remain near the surface but percolates through the limestone soil to unusable depths. The island has few large rivers; only the Black River is navigable. Mean annual temperatures are about 27° C (80° F) on the coast. Annual rainfall averages 1,955 mm (77 in), but it reaches 5,080 mm (200 in) in some mountainous regions. Jamaica has a great diversity of vegetation, although much of the land has been cleared for agriculture.

PEOPLE

The population of Jamaica consists mostly of descendants of African blacks, plus several small East Indian, Chinese, and European minorities. The official language is English, but most of the rural population speaks a Creole dialect. Population is concentrated on the coastal plains; the highlands are nearly uninhabited. A high birthrate and low death rate have resulted in high population densities in recent years. Anglicans and Baptists are the largest religious groups. Approximately 5% of the population are Roman Catholics. The RASTAFARIAN religion originated in Jamaica. The administrative center for the University of the West Indies (1948) is near Kingston. The Institute of Jamaica (1879) in Kingston has a library and museum of native history.

ECONOMIC ACTIVITY

Most Jamaicans are employed in agriculture or mining. Sugar, tropical fruits, coffee, cacao, and spices are grown in quantity for export through the ports of Kingston and Montego Bay. Jamaica has recently developed a profitable mining industry. It ranks second in the world in the production of bauxite and alumina, which are exported to Canada, Norway, and the United States for refining into aluminum. A petroleum refinery is under construction. Other industries include sugar processing, textiles, printing, and chemicals.

The lack of indigenous energy sources has slowed industrial development in Jamaica; also, recent outbreaks of violence have damaged the important tourist industry. Economic growth in 1978 was −2%. Inflation and unemployment have been running at high levels, and the balance-of-payments deficit is large.

GOVERNMENT

Jamaica became an independent member of the Commonwealth of Nations in 1962. Executive power within Jamaica's government lies with a 19-member cabinet headed by a prime minister responsible to the parliament. The People's National party, closely associated with the MANLEY family, is presently in power. Local government consists of 14 parishes.

HISTORY

Jamaica was discovered by Christopher Columbus on May 4, 1494, and was subsequently settled by the Spanish. Spain ruled the island until 1655, when a British expedition captured the island. Formal British control was confirmed in 1670 by the Treaty of Madrid.

Arawak Indians, who inhabited the island at the time of Columbus's arrival, had died off, so African slaves were imported to work the sugarcane fields. With the abolition of slavery in Jamaica in 1833, the plantations declined and the freed men took to peasant farming. In 1958, Jamaica formed the West Indies Federation with nine other British possessions, but it withdrew in 1961, a move that led to the eventual collapse of the Federation. Jamaica's withdrawal was urged by Sir Alexander BUSTAMANTE, a labor leader who became prime minister when Jamaica achieved full independence in 1962. British legislation in 1967 stopped an exodus of Jamaicans to the United Kingdom, thus eliminating one route of emigration from the country.   THOMAS MATHEWS

Bibliography: Boot, Adrian, and Thomas, Michael, *Jamaica: Babylon on a Thin Wire* (1977); Braithewaite, Edward, *The Development of Creole Society in Jamaica, 1770-1820* (1971); Campbell, Mavis C., *The Dynamics of Change in a Slave Society. A Sociopolitical History of the Free Coloreds of Jamaica* (1976); Hurwitz, Samuel J. and Edith F., *Jamaica: A Historical Portrait* (1971); Kuper, Adam, *Changing Jamaica* (1976); Lacey, Terry, *Violence and Politics in Jamaica, 1960-70* (1977); Manley, Michael, *The Politics of Change: A Jamaican Testament* (1974); Nettleford, Rex, *Manley and the New Jamaica* (1972) and *Identity, Race and Protest in Jamaica* (1972).

Jamal al-Din al-Afghani

The Muslim teacher and political activist Jamal al-Din al-Afghani, b. 1839, d. Mar. 9, 1897, sought to promote pan-Islamism as a force to combat European domination of the Muslim world. Of obscure origin, he was politically active in Afghanistan (1866–68) and later taught in Istanbul (1870–71) and Cairo (1871–79). Advocating a liberal theology and democratic socialism, he gathered a group of followers in Cairo but was deported in 1879. In Paris (1883–86) he coedited a pan-Islamic journal with his disciple Muhammad 'Abduh. After a period of travel he returned to Persia in 1889, but his attempts to achieve legal and social reform brought him into conflict with the shah, Nasir al-Din, and he was forced to leave. He ended his career in Istanbul, from where he was accused of instigating the assassination (1896) of Nasir al-Din. Since his death al-Afghani has served as an inspiration for many Islamic reform and nationalist movements.

Bibliography: Keddie, Nikki R., *An Islamic Response to Imperialism* (1968); Kedourie, Elie, *Afghani and 'Abduh* (1966).

Jamalzade, Mohammed Ali   [jam'-ahl-zah-day, moh-ham'-ed ah'-lee]

The Iranian writer Mohammed Ali Jamalzade, b. *c.*1895, is credited with introducing the modern short story into Iranian (Persian) literature. The son of a leading figure in the Iranian national revival, he studied abroad and then joined a progressive group of Iranian liberals. His first short-story collection, *Yeki bud va yeki nabud* (There Was Once—Or Was There?, 1921), was significant in Iranian literature as the first attempt to present a realistically critical view of Iranian society. Jamalzade's later works, published mainly after 1941, include the novel *Dar ol-majanin* (House of Fools, 1942) and many collections of stories and essays, such as *Kohne va nou* (The Old and the New, 1959). Jamalzade is also a translator; his translations of his own stories have appeared in English and European periodicals.   MARCIA E. MAGUIRE

James, Saint   (the "brother" of Jesus Christ)

In the Bible, James is listed first among the "brothers of Jesus," a relationship often posited as that of stepbrothers or cousins, but was not a follower of Jesus during his early ministry (Matthew 3:31–35; Matt. 12:36–50; John 7:5). He became a believer after the resurrected Christ appeared to him (I Corinthians 15:7), and was regarded as an apostle (Galatians 1:19). Later he became a leader in the Jerusalem church (Gal. 1:19; 2:9; Acts 15:13–29), and tradition describes him as Jerusalem's first bishop. Roman Catholic tradition identifies him with Saint James the Lesser, and he is possibly the author of the Epistle of James. As a minister to the Jews, James opposed the imposition of Jewish law on gentile converts, but encouraged Jews to observe it (Acts 12:17; 15:13–21; 21:18; Gal. 2:9, 12). According to the historian Josephus, James was stoned to death in AD 62.   DOUGLAS EZELL

James, Saint   (James the Great)

Together with his brother Saint JOHN, Saint James was among the first disciples called by Jesus (Matt. 4:21). These sons of Zebedee, called the Boanerges ("Sons of Thunder"), joined the brothers PETER and ANDREW, also fishermen by trade, in a close inner circle around Jesus. James, Peter, and John were the only disciples present, for example, at the TRANSFIGURATION (Luke 9) and near Jesus in the Garden of Gethsemane. James was martyred under Herod Agrippa I (Acts 12). According to legend, his bones were taken to Spain, and his shrine at SANTIAGO de Compostela was one of the most important pilgrimage centers in the Middle Ages. Feast day: Apr. 30 (Eastern); July 25 (Western).

James, Saint   (James the Lesser)

Saint James the Lesser was the Apostle James, son of Alphaeus and disciple of Jesus (Mark 3:18). His mother, Mary, was one of the women at the crucifixion and at the tomb (Matt. 10:3; 27:56, Mark 15:40; 16:1; Acts 1:13). This James is sometimes identified with James the "brother of Jesus," although this and other identifications are unproven. Feast day: Oct. 9 (Eastern); May 3 (Western, since 1969).

James, Epistle of

The Epistle of James, the first of the general letters (Catholic epistles) of the New Testament of the BIBLE, is an exhortation to Christian patience and obedience. The book, more a sermon than a letter, uses 54 imperatives in 108 verses to call its readers to responsible living that accords with what they profess. Traditionally, JAMES, "the Lord's brother," has been accepted as the author, which would date the book between AD 45 and 50 and would account for its primitive Christology. Some scholars, however, claim that it comes much later from the hand of another and date the book from late 1st century to early 2d century.

Although accepted by the church from the 2d century, James was reluctantly admitted into the Protestant New Testament canon. Martin Luther rejected the book as "a right strawy epistle," because he thought that James contradicted Saint Paul's view of justification by faith alone. Paul, however, was emphasizing the inappropriateness of works for salvation whereas James spoke of works that issue from faith. For both, the essentials are the same, and both were probably dealing independently with a traditional topic of Jewish belief.
                      DOUGLAS EZELL

James, Henry

The American writer Henry James, one of the most influential figures in the development of the modern novel, appears here in a portrait by John Singer Sargent. James's meticulously crafted works, which often treat the theme of innocence and corruption, are characterized by subtle observation and psychological perceptiveness.

An influential force in the development of literary realism, the American novelist, short-story writer, travel essayist, and critic Henry James, b. New York City, Apr. 15, 1843, d. London, Feb. 28, 1916, enjoyed a long, productive career, during which he achieved international stature as a writer. He wrote 22 novels, 113 tales, 15 plays, the equivalent of about 10 books of criticism, 7 travel books, 3 autobiographical volumes, and 2 biographies. Approximately 15,000 of his letters are extant.

James's parents—Henry James, Sr., a rich, eccentric philosopher, and Mary Walsh James, who was loving and practical—had four other children, including psychologist-philosopher William James. By 1861 young Henry had crossed the Atlantic Ocean six times with his purposely rootless parents; lived in France, England, Switzerland, Germany, and New England; and studied literature and languages, including French, which he spoke flawlessly. James stayed out of the Civil War because of a back injury and soon became a celibate, detached observer of the international social scene.

James's long apprenticeship may be dated from 1864 to 1875. At the age of 21 he published his first works, an anonymous short story and an unsigned book review. He wrote more reviews and easily found magazine outlets for his early short fiction. In 1869 he took his first European trip as an adult, going from England to Switzerland and then Italy, which ultimately became his favorite country. In 1872, James escorted an aunt and sister to Europe but stayed on alone, writing and roaming, for two years. A winter in New York was productive but mainly helped him decide to live permanently abroad. After publishing his first two books (short stories and travel essays, both 1875) and completing his first mature novel (*Roderick Hudson*, 1876), he set sail for Paris.

From this time through 1881, James was highly popular. In Paris he met Ivan Turgenev (a unique professional influence upon him), Gustave Flaubert, Guy de Maupassant, and Émile Zola, among other writers. During this phase of his career, James wrote *The American* (1877), about a man whose Yankee dollars fail to buy him admission to French society. Feeling unwelcome in Paris, James moved (1876) to "the great grey Babylon," London, where he soon met Alfred Lord Tennyson, Robert Browning, George Eliot, William Morris, Leslie Stephen, and many others. He gained notoriety with his immensely admired short novel DAISY MILLER (1878), about an innocent, socially naive American girl destroyed by European mores. He also published (1879) the first book-length treatment of Nathaniel Hawthorne and began his first masterpiece, The PORTRAIT OF A LADY (1881).

Between 1882 and 1895, James published several experimental short stories and three long novels but was unsuccessful in his attempts to write popular drama. The tales include "The Liar," "The Lesson of the Master," "The Pupil," "The Real Thing," and "The Middle Years." The novels, all political in subject, are *The Bostonians* (1886), about the feminist movement in post–Civil War New England; *The Princess Casamassima* (1886), featuring international anarchists in and out of London; and *The Tragic Muse* (1890), which contrasts art (painting and acting) with politics (including diplomacy). When these books failed commercially James tried to conquer the London stage, but his most ambitious play, *Guy Domville* (1895), was also a failure.

From 1896 until World War I, when the Anglo-French cultural community he revered was shattered, James was extremely active. He bought an 18th-century house south of London and wrote and entertained there. He produced streams of fiction, a two-volume biography (1903) of the American expatriate sculptor William Wetmore Story, autobiographical material, and *The American Scene* (1907). His short fiction of the period includes *The Turn of the Screw* (1898), "The Beast in the Jungle" (possibly James's finest tale), "The Birthplace," and "The Jolly Corner."

Three long novels of this major phase of his career would alone assure the author's fame. *The Wings of the Dove* (1902) contrasts a rich young American with European fortune hunters who are ultimately shamed by the dying heroine's charity. The AMBASSADORS (1903), which James called "the best, 'all round,' of my productions," describes the initiation of an aging American into the relativistic ethics of the Old World in "huge iridescent" Paris. The GOLDEN BOWL (1904) verbosely analyzes father-daughter and adulterous relations, all symbolized by the glittering, flawed bowl.

James next revised about half of his fiction for a sumptuous edition (1907–09), complete with 18 profound critical prefaces. *The American Scene* (1907), reflecting his first visit to the United States since the death of his parents in 1882, is one of the subtlest travel books ever written.

Henry James was a writers' writer, psychologically penetrating and technically innovative. He is at his best when he throws inexperienced Americans into European sociocultural complexities and when he fictionalizes artists and writers. He was, in the words of Joseph Conrad, "the historian of fine consciences," especially those of women—wealthy young Americans expanding in leisure's sunlight even while threatened by the fictive constructs of James's "imagination of disaster." He develops the restricted point of view absorbingly; characterizes through picturesque, dramatic scenes; and is a wizard at the use of ambiguity. An unstoppable James boom started in the 1930s and gained momentum during and just after World War II. James ignored too many elements of workaday American life ever to be popular with the masses. He has, however, influenced literary geniuses as diverse as Joseph Conrad, Edith Wharton, James Joyce, Virginia Woolf, William Faulkner, and Graham Greene. James is idolized as "the Master" by readers who admire his superb craftsmanship.   ROBERT L. GALE

Bibliography: Anderson, Charles R., *Person, Place, and Thing in Henry James's Novels* (1977); Cargill, Oscar, *The Novels of Henry James* (1961); Edel, Leon, *Henry James,* 5 vols. (1953–72); Gale, Robert L.,

"Henry James," in *Eight American Authors,* ed. by James Woodress (1971); Hocks, Richard A., *Henry James and Pragmatistic Thought* (1974); Matthiessen, F. O., *Henry James: The Major Phase* (1944); Winner, Viola Hopkins, *Henry James and the Visual Arts* (1970).

James, Jesse

Jesse James, b. Clay County, Mo., Sept. 5, 1847, one of the most famous outlaws of the American West, acquired a Robin Hood reputation among the people of his region. At the age of 15, during the Civil War, he joined a band of pro-Confederate guerrillas led by William C. Quantrill. After the war he formed a gang with his brother, Frank, and several other men. They held up banks, stagecoaches, and trains until 1876, when the gang was decimated trying to rob a bank in Northfield, Minn. The two brothers escaped and formed a new gang. On Apr. 3, 1882, Jesse was shot and killed by a fellow gang member for a reward. Frank later surrendered; he was tried and acquitted twice.

Bibliography: Briehan, Carl W., *The Complete Authentic Life of Jesse James* (1953); Ernst, John, *Jesse James* (1976); Settle, William A., Jr., *Jesse James Was His Name* (1966); Walker, Henry J., *Jesse James, the Outlaw* (1961).

James, P. D.

P. D. James is the pen name of Phyllis Dorothy James White, b. Aug. 3, 1920, an English civil servant and detective novelist. Her series of books, featuring Adam Dalgliesh of the C.I.D. (Criminal Investigation Department of Scotland Yard), has won consistently high critical praise and has been compared with the work of Margery Allingham and Dorothy Sayers. In such novels as *Cover Her Face* (1962), *Unnatural Causes* (1967), *Shroud for a Nightingale* (1971), and *Death of an Expert Witness* (1977), James often uses medical backgrounds, with which her work has familiarized her, and she is as concerned with the spiritual condition of her characters as with their legal guilt or innocence.

James, Thomas

Thomas James, *c.*1593–*c.*1635, was an English navigator whose account of his journey in search of the NORTHWEST PASSAGE probably inspired Samuel Taylor Coleridge's poem The RIME OF THE ANCIENT MARINER. Sailing on the *Henrietta Maria,* James set out from Bristol in May 1631 and returned in October 1632 after visiting Greenland and the southern extension of Hudson Bay (named James Bay in his honor). His *Strange and Dangerous Voyage* was published in 1633.   ROBIN BUSS

Bibliography: MacInnes, Charles M., *Captain Thomas James and the Northwest Passage* (1967).

James, William

The American philosopher and psychologist William James, b. New York City, Jan. 11, 1842, d. Aug. 26, 1910, was one of the

William James, a leading American philosopher and psychologist and the brother of novelist Henry James, extended the philosophy of pragmatism developed by Charles Peirce to include religious commitments and nonrational choices. His highly literary works did much to establish pragmatism as an influential American philosophy.

founders and leading proponents of PRAGMATISM. He was the son of philosopher Henry James, Sr., and brother of novelist Henry James. He attended schools in Europe and in 1861 entered Harvard College. He received his degree 3 years later and began studies at Harvard Medical School. At Harvard, he was a member of "The Metaphysical Club," an informal group that met to discuss philosophy and included Charles PEIRCE, Oliver Wendell HOLMES, JR., and Chaunsey Wright, all of whom were to become well known in the pragmatist movement.

After receiving his medical degree, James suffered a period of illness, but in 1873 he was able to accept an appointment as instructor in anatomy and physiology at Harvard. Two years later he began teaching psychology, and in 1879, philosophy. James remained at Harvard, with only a few interruptions in his academic career, until his resignation in 1907. The works of Herbert Spencer and John Stuart Mill were important influences in James's early thinking; Henri Bergson was important both personally and philosophically in his later years, as was John Dewey, who carried on the leadership of the pragmatist movement after James's death.

In his famous work *The Principles of Psychology* (1890), James developed the view, in opposition to the more traditional ASSOCIATIONISM, that consciousness functions in an active, purposeful way to relate and organize thoughts, giving them a streamlike continuity.

In the history of psychology, James's theory of mind is called functionalism. James had established an international reputation in psychology before his main focus turned to philosophy, and many of his philosophical views have their roots in his psychological studies.

James elaborated his theory of pragmatism in works such as *Pragmatism: A New Name for Some Old Ways of Thinking* (1907) and *The Meaning of Truth: A Sequel to Pragmatism* (1909). He considered pragmatism to be both a method for analyzing philosophic problems and a theory of truth. He also saw it as an extension of the empiricist attitude (see EMPIRICISM) in that it turned away from abstract theory and fixed or absolute principles and toward concrete facts, actions, and relative principles.

James considered philosophies to be expressions of personal temperament and developed a correlation between "tough-minded" and "tender-minded" temperaments and empiricist and rationalist positions in philosophy. Theories, he felt, are "instruments" that humans use to solve problems and should be judged in terms of their "cash value" or practical consequences for human conduct.

He developed the notion of truth as a "leading" that is useful: it can change as human experience changes. The morality, as well as the truth, of an idea or action should be judged, according to James, in a similar way—in terms of its outcome in human experience.

In *The Will to Believe* (1897) and *The Varieties of Religious Experience* (1902), James examined the problem of belief in cases in which no immediate evidence exists on which to base one's belief. He concluded that in the area of religious commitment, belief can create its own truth through the effects created in the experience of the believer by his "willing nature." Belief in God is thus pragmatically justified if it makes a positive difference in the experience of the believer.

In *A Pluralistic Universe* (1909) and *Essays in Radical Empiricism* (1912), James developed his metaphysical position: there is no fixed external world to be discovered by our minds but instead a "humming-buzzing confusion" that we organize through experience. The universe, as well as our knowledge of it, is continuously evolving. Never complete, it cannot be reduced to a single underlying substance.

James's writing is characterized by a lucid, easily readable style, and he has had a wide popular readership.

SANDRA B. ROSENTHAL

Bibliography: Allen, Gay W., *William James: A Biography* (1967); Ayer, A. J., *The Origins of Pragmatism* (1969); Brennan, Bernard P., *William James* (1968); Grattan, C. Hartley, *Three Jameses* (1962); Perry, Ralph B., *The Thought and Character of William James*, 2 vols. (1935; repr. 1974); Reck, Andrew J., *Introduction to William James* (1967).

James Bay

James Bay is the southern extension of HUDSON BAY situated between the provinces of Quebec and Ontario, Canada. The shallow bay is 445 km (275 mi) long and 217 km (135 mi) wide. Numerous rivers (including the La Grande, Eastmain, Moose, Nottaway, Albany, and Attawapiskat rivers) enter the bay, giving it a low saline water content. The largest of the many islands in the bay is Akimiski. Much of the bay's shoreline is reserved for wildlife protection; small settlements include Fort George, Nouveau-Comptoir, Eastmain, and Fort-Rupert. The bay was discovered in 1610 by Henry Hudson and was named for Capt. Thomas James, who explored the bay in 1631.

James River

The James River is formed in west central Virginia by the confluence of the Jackson and Cowpasture rivers. It zigzags eastward 547 km (340 mi) through the Blue Ridge Mountains and enters Chesapeake Bay through the 8-km-wide (5-mi) estuary of HAMPTON ROADS. The river is navigable by ocean vessels to Richmond, about 160 km (100 mi) upstream. In 1607, Jamestown Island in the lower river was the site of the first permanent English settlement in America.

James I, King of Aragon   (James the Conqueror)

James I, b. Feb. 2, 1208, d. July 27, 1276, ruled the Spanish kingdom of Aragon from 1213 and greatly expanded his dominions. After a turbulent minority, James, the son of Peter II (r. 1196–1213), undertook the conquest of the Muslim kingdom of Majorca in 1229. This campaign was the first stage in the extension of Aragonese power into the western Mediterranean. When he completed the conquest of the Muslim kingdom of Valencia in 1238, he had brought the kingdom of Aragon (Aragon, Catalonia, Valencia) to the limits it would retain in the peninsula for the rest of the Middle Ages. James's attempts in later years to partition his realms among his sons were the cause of great discord. His son PETER III succeeded him to the Aragonese throne.   JOSEPH F. O'CALLAGHAN

Bibliography: Forster, John, trans., *The Chronicle of James I, King of Aragon, Surnamed the Conqueror*, 2 vols. (1883); Shneidman, J. Lee, *Rise of the Aragonese-Catalan Empire, 1200–1350* (1970).

James II, King of Aragon

James II (called James the Just), b. 1264, d. Nov. 2, 1327, was king of Aragon (1291–1327) and king of Sicily (1285–95). His father, PETER III, seized Sicily from CHARLES I of Naples in 1282 during the revolt known as the SICILIAN VESPERS. After Peter's death (1285), James's older brother, Alfonso III, became king of Aragon, and James became king of Sicily. On Alfonso's death (1291), James became king of Aragon. He continued to rule Sicily until 1295, when he signed an agreement with Pope BONIFACE VIII and Charles II of Naples exchanging Sicily for Corsica and Sardinia, ending French claims in Aragon, and arranging a marriage with Charles's daughter Bianca.

Bibliography: Shneidman, J. Lee, *The Rise of the Aragonese-Catalan Empire: 1200–1350*, 2 vols. (1970).

James I, King of England

James I, the only child of MARY, QUEEN OF SCOTS, was the first king to rule both England and Scotland, the latter as James VI. Born on June 19, 1566, James was only 15 months old when he succeeded his mother to the Scottish throne. He received an excellent education from tutors such as George BUCHANAN and, after a tumultuous minority, began his personal rule of Scotland in 1583. During the next 20 years James successfully asserted his position as head of church and state in Scotland, outwitting the nobles who conspired against him. Being eager to succeed the childless ELIZABETH I to the English throne, he merely protested when his mother was executed for treason against Elizabeth in 1587. James went to Scandinavia in 1589 to bring home his bride, Anne of Denmark, who bore him several children but annoyed him by becoming a Roman Catholic.

James I, the first Stuart king of England, offended his subjects by his arrogant disregard of Parliament, his policy of conciliation with Catholic Spain, and his excessive reliance on court favorites. An arrogant man who staunchly defended the divine right of kings, James ruled without Parliament for more than half his reign and thus helped create the crisis confronted by his son, Charles I.

James II, the last Stuart king of England, succeeded his brother, Charles II, in 1685 despite efforts to exclude him from the throne for his openly Catholic faith. His suspension of laws forbidding Catholics to hold office and his rule without Parliament so alienated his subjects that he was forced to flee the country in the bloodless Glorious Revolution of 1688.

In 1603, James became the first STUART king of England, and he devoted himself almost entirely to English affairs thereafter. Although raised as a Presbyterian, he immediately antagonized the rising Puritan movement (see PURITANISM) by rejecting a petition for reform of the Church of England at the Hampton Court Conference (1604). Roman Catholic hostility, manifested in the attempt (1605) by Guy FAWKES to blow up both king and Parliament, did not dissolve the English suspicion that James was pro-Catholic because he had concluded peace with Spain in 1604. The suspicion was intensified when James took only ineffective diplomatic steps to secure the restoration of his Protestant son-in-law, Elector Palatine FREDERICK V, after he had been deposed in the Thirty Years' War.

Initially guided by Robert Cecil, 1st earl of SALISBURY, an able chief minister, James subsequently allowed his court favorites—first Robert Carr, earl of Somerset, and later George Villiers, 1st duke of BUCKINGHAM—effective control. The role of these ministers complicated James's stormy relations with Parliament. That body's conception of its rights, especially in financial matters, clashed with the king's view of the royal prerogative.

Confident in his own wisdom and experience, James avoided hard work, preferring to hunt. He was fortunate in having the services of Lionel Cranfield, earl of Middlesex, a former merchant, who looked after the royal finances until he was impeached (1624) for corruption at the behest of Buckingham. Parliament also impeached (1621) another able minister, Francis BACON, and blocked James in his attempts to arrange a formal Anglo-Scottish union and to exchange his rights to feudal dues for a permanent grant of revenue from Parliament.

James wrote books about kingship, theology, witchcraft, and tobacco and commissioned the Authorized (King James) Version of the Bible. He died on Mar. 27, 1625, having warned his son and heir, CHARLES I, of future dangers to the monarchy from Parliament.

MAURICE ASHLEY

Bibliography: Akriff, George P., Jacobean Pageant: The Court of King James I (1962; repr. 1967); Bingham, Caroline, The Making of a King: The Early Years of James VI and I (1968); Davies, Godfrey, The Early Stuarts (1937; corrected repr. 1952); Fraser, Antonia, King James Sixth and First (1975); McIlwain, C. H., ed., Political Works of James VI (1918); Smith, Alan G. R., ed., Reign of James VI and I (1973); Willson, David H., James VI and I (1956; repr. 1967).

James II, King of England, Scotland, and Ireland

James II, b. Oct. 4, 1633, d. Sept. 5, 1701, the second son of CHARLES I, reigned as king of England, Scotland, and Ireland from 1685 to 1688, when he was overthrown by the GLORIOUS REVOLUTION. James, a Stuart (see STUART family), was in exile from 1648 in the aftermath of the English Civil War. He

served with distinction in the armies of France and Spain during the 1650s. After his brother, CHARLES II, was restored to the throne in 1660, James fought bravely as lord high admiral in the ANGLO-DUTCH WARS. James's conversion (about 1671) to Roman Catholicism caused the House of Commons to attempt, unsuccessfully, to exclude him from the throne. He succeeded Charles unopposed, however, on Feb. 6, 1685.

James's reign lasted only 4 years. In 1687 and 1688, in a tactless attempt to procure liberty of conscience for all his Christian subjects, he issued two declarations of indulgence, which alienated the Church of England. He also evaded the TEST ACT of 1673 by promoting Catholics to high office and military commissions. In 1688 he put seven bishops on trial for refusing to order his declarations to be read in all the churches, but the bishops were acquitted. All of these actions contributed to his overthrow, which was finally precipitated by the birth of his son in June 1688. The prospect of a Catholic succession led the Protestant opposition to invite James's Dutch Protestant nephew and son-in-law, William of Orange, to come to England. He assumed the crown as WILLIAM III, and his wife, James's older daughter, became MARY II.

Although James's opponents saw him as a tyrant, acting as a tool of the expansionist Catholic LOUIS XIV of France, it was not tyranny but stupidity and cowardice that brought his downfall. After fleeing to France early in 1689, he assembled an Irish-French army in an attempt to restore himself, but in 1690 his army was defeated by William at the Battle of the BOYNE in Ireland. James spent his last years in France, seeking forgiveness for his sins and hoping that his renunciation of the throne would merit him eternal salvation.

MAURICE ASHLEY

Bibliography: Ashley, Maurice, James II (1978); Ogg, David, England in the Reigns of James II and William III (1955); Turner, Francis C., James II (1948).

James I, King of Scotland

James I, b. July 1394, d. Feb. 20, 1437, became titular king of Scotland in 1406. His father, ROBERT III, shortly before his death (1406), had sent James to France for safety, but the young prince was captured en route by the English, who detained him until 1424. During James's absence Scotland was governed by James's uncle, Robert Stuart, 1st duke of Albany (d. 1420), and later by Albany's son, Murdoch, neither of whom ruled effectively. In his last year of captivity, James married Joan Beaufort, a cousin of Henry V of England.

After James's return (1424) to Scotland, he quickly subdued the powerful nobility, executing many, including Murdoch (1425). He also reorganized Scotland's financial administration and improved the judicial system by appointing an advocate to represent the poor in court. James was assassinated in the Dominican friary at Perth, apparently at the instigation of rival claimants to the throne; but he was succeeded by his son

James II. James I is generally considered to be the author of *The Kingis Quair* ("The King's Book"; rev. ed. by John Norton-Smith, 1971), a long poem about his captivity and about his romance with Joan.   CHARLES H. HAWS

Bibliography: Balfour-Melville, E. W. M., *James I: King of Scots, 1406-1437* (1936); Dickinson, William Croft, *Scotland from the Earliest Times to 1603*, 3d ed. (1977); Donaldson, Gordon, *Scottish Kings* (1967).

James IV, King of Scotland

James IV, b. Mar. 17, 1473, d. Sept. 9, 1513, one of the most energetic of Scotland's STUART monarchs, personified the ideal of the Renaissance king. A patron of the arts and education, he encouraged such diverse endeavors as alchemy, architecture, and printing. James, who succeeded his father, James III, in 1488, extended royal administration and justice and raised Scotland's status in European politics.

Continuing Scotland's pro-French diplomacy, James, beginning in 1495, supported Perkin Warbeck's claims to the English throne. Border clashes with England followed, but in 1497 the two countries signed a 7-year truce. The truce was strengthened in 1503 when James married Margaret Tudor, the daughter of HENRY VII of England. This union prepared the way for the ultimate succession of a Stuart to the English throne (see JAMES I, KING OF ENGLAND). In 1512, however, Scotland renewed its French alliance, and when HENRY VIII invaded France in 1513, James marched into northern England. He was defeated and killed in the Battle of Flodden. James was succeeded by his son, James V.   CHARLES H. HAWS

Bibliography: Dickinson, W. C., *Scotland from the Earliest Times to 1603*, 3d ed. (1977); Mackie, Robert L., *King James IV of Scotland* (1958; repr. 1976).

James V, King of Scotland

James V, b. Apr. 10, 1512, d. Dec. 14, 1542, was the seventh Stuart king of Scotland (1513-42), the son of JAMES IV. In 1514, James V's mother, Margaret Tudor, daughter of England's Henry VII, married Archibald Douglas, 6th earl of Angus (see DOUGLAS family). John Stuart, duke of Albany, became regent, and a power struggle ensued among factions controlled by Albany, Angus, and Margaret. For a time, Angus, a pro-English Protestant supporter, held James prisoner (1526-28).

When James reached his majority, he sided with Scotland's pro-French Catholic faction against the English. On Jan. 1, 1537, he married Madeleine, the daughter of FRANCIS I of France, and received a large dowry. She died the following July, and James married (1538) Mary of Guise (see GUISE family). His aggressive, vindictive policies lost him the support of the nobility, weakening his army and contributing to his defeat by the English at Solway Moss in 1542. Soon after this battle, he died at Falkland Palace, leaving a week-old daughter, MARY, QUEEN OF SCOTS, to succeed him.

                                                 CHARLES H. HAWS

Bibliography: Donaldson, Gordon, *Scotland: James V-James VII* (1965).

James VI, King of Scotland: see JAMES I, KING OF ENGLAND.

Jameson, Sir Leander Starr

Sir Leander Starr Jameson, b. Feb. 9, 1853, d. Nov. 26, 1917, a British colonial administrator in Africa, led a disastrous raid into the Boer Republic of the TRANSVAAL in 1895. The Jameson Raid intensified the hostility between the Boers and British that led to the SOUTH AFRICAN WAR (1899-1902).

A physician, Jameson immigrated to South Africa in 1878, became a close friend of Cecil RHODES, and in 1891 assumed office as administrator of Mashonaland, now part of Zimbabwe (Rhodesia). On Dec. 29, 1895, Jameson led a raiding party into the Transvaal, hoping to join forces with the discontented non-Boer Europeans (called *uitlanders*) in that state to overthrow the government of President Paul KRUGER. The force of volunteers was soon captured. Although the raid was not approved by the British government, Rhodes was clearly implicated and forced to resign as prime minister of Cape

Colony; British Colonial Secretary Joseph CHAMBERLAIN was cleared of charges of involvement, but he probably knew of the conspiracy. After a prison term in Britain, Jameson served as prime minister of the Cape Colony from 1904 to 1908.

                                                     L. H. GANN

Bibliography: Colvin, I. D., *The Life of Jameson*, 2 vols. (1922); Van der Pole, Jean, *The Jameson Raid* (1951).

Jamestown

Jamestown, Va., founded in 1607, was the first English settlement in North America. After initial hardships, the settlers found an export crop in tobacco and established the first representative government of the colonies. The drawing depicts the city as it was in 1622.

Jamestown, the first permanent English settlement in North America, was situated on a marshy peninsula (now Jamestown Island) in the James River of Virginia. An expedition sent by the LONDON COMPANY selected the site principally on the basis of its strategic military location.

About 100 men, under the leadership of Capt. Christopher Newport, settled at Jamestown on May 14, 1607; they faced continual disappointment. In the first 7 months they were nearly wiped out by disease and famine, but Capt. John SMITH revived the settlement in 1608. After the severe winter of 1609-10 (the "starving time"), the settlers were prevented from abandoning Jamestown only by the arrival in June of the governor, Lord DE LA WARR, with supplies and additional men.

Instead of spending their time growing the crops necessary for survival, the settlers quarreled with one another and searched fruitlessly for gold, silver, and a westward passage to the Pacific. They discovered, however, that the land was suited to the cultivation of an important cash crop, tobacco. The settlers managed to turn the Indians of the POWHATAN Confederacy against them—despite the marriage (1614) of John ROLFE to POCAHONTAS, the daughter of Chief Powhatan. Of many Indian attacks, the most serious came on Mar. 22, 1622, when Indians led by Opechancanough massacred 347 people. Charging mismanagement, the crown recalled the London Company's charter in 1624, and Jamestown, with the entire colony of Virginia, came under royal control.

A representative assembly, the House of Burgesses, had been established at Jamestown in 1619. Although the settlement was burned to the ground on Sept. 19, 1679, during BACON'S REBELLION, Jamestown remained Virginia's capital until 1699, when WILLIAMSBURG became the seat of government. Jamestown soon fell into decay. The present fort at Jamestown, now part of Colonial National Historical Park, is a reconstruction.   RICHARD R. BEEMAN

Bibliography: Craven, Wesley F., *The Southern Colonies in the 17th Century, 1607-1689*, 2d ed. (1970); Morgan, Edmund S., *American Slavery, American Freedom: The Ordeal of Colonial Virginia* (1975).

Jamnitzer   (family)   [yahm'-nit-sur]

The Jamnitzer family of goldsmiths and jewelers were in large part responsible for making Nuremberg the major European center for ornamental GOLD AND SILVER WORK for most of the 16th century.

Wenzel Jamnitzer I, 1508-85, who moved from Vienna to Nuremberg about 1530, was the most accomplished artist of the family, and his style evolved from High Renaissance to Mannerism in his long lifetime. His most significant contribution was the incorporation of direct castings of such natural objects as shells, fishes, and plants into his pieces.

Albrecht Jamnitzer, d. 1555, Wenzel's brother and partner, in addition to goldsmithing, also made jewelry and cast bronze, and, with his brother, probably made watches and scientific instruments.

Hans Jamnitzer II, c.1538-1603, Wenzel's son, continued to work in the same styles as his father and uncle, and achieved a considerable reputation as a master goldsmith throughout northern Europe.

Christoph Jamnitzer, 1563-1618, Hans's son, continued the tradition of his father and grandfather and produced the most opulent and original gold and silver work in the Mannerist style. He also published (1610) an influential pattern book of designs that epitomizes Mannerism at its most extreme.

Bibliography: Hayward, J. F., *Virtuoso Goldsmiths and the Triumph of Mannerism, 1540-1620* (1976).

Janáček, Leoš   [yahn'-ah-chek, lay'-ohsh]

Leoš Janáček, b. July 3, 1854, d. Aug. 12, 1928, is generally considered the greatest Czech-Moravian composer since Dvořák and among the most original of the postromantics. He was born in Moravia, the son of a schoolmaster and organist. Trained as a choirboy, he was directing choirs by age 16. He studied composition in Prague (1875) and in Leipzig and Vienna (1879-80). From 1881 to 1919 he worked in Brno as teacher and conductor, his compositions attracting little attention. He also studied Czech folk music and developed theories on projecting the rhythms and inflections of the Czech language in music, which he applied to his operas and other vocal works.

Throughout his career Janáček composed numerous orchestral, chamber, piano, vocal, and choral works, culminating in his two surviving string quartets (1923, 1928); a wind sextet, *Mládí* (1924); a symphonic poem, *Taras Bulba* (1915-18); the spectacular *Sinfonietta* (1926); and the nationalistic *Glagolitic Mass* (1926). His vocal works, especially the operas, are perhaps Janáček's most original productions. The opera *Jenufa* (1894-1903) is a compelling treatment of human character. A pair of one-act comedies, *Mr. Brouček's Excursions* (1908-17), was followed, after the dramatic song-cycle *The Diary of One Who Vanished* (1917-19), by another masterpiece, *Kátya Kabanová* (1919-21). His last three operas were the whimsical *The Cunning Little Vixen* (1921-23), the gloomy *Makropulos Affair* (1923-25), and the grimly powerful *From the House of the Dead* (1927-28). Only in 1916, with the Prague production of *Jenufa*, did Janáček at last win recognition from his fellow Czechs, including a professorship in Prague (1919-25). His international reputation has grown steadily since his death, particularly in recent decades through recordings of his works.

JOHN. W. BARKER

Bibliography: Ewans, Michael, *Janáček's Tragic Operas* (1978); Hollander, Hans, *Leoš Janáček: His Life and Work*, trans. by Paul Hamburger (1963); Janáček, Leoš, *Letters and Reminiscences*, ed. by Bohumír Štědroň, trans. by Geraldine Thomsen-Muchová (1955); Vogel, Jaroslov, *Leoš Janáček, His Life and Works*, trans. by Geraldine Thomsen-Muchová (1962).

Jane Eyre   [air]

One of the classics of 19th-century English literature, *Jane Eyre* (1847), by Charlotte Brontë (see BRONTË family), introduced a new kind of heroine in the plain but passionate governess for whom the novel is named. Forced to earn a living in the only way open to respectable middle-class women in Victorian England, Jane nevertheless yearns for love and autonomy amidst seemingly hopeless surroundings, and struggles to assert herself as a human being against society's repressive codes. Reflecting something of Brontë's own un-

happy youth, the novel recounts Jane Eyre's love for her enigmatic, rather Byronic master, Edward Rochester. The realism with which Jane's position is portrayed is combined with both melodrama and romance to permit a satisfactory resolution to the story: the eventual marriage of Jane and Mr. Rochester following the death of his mad, sequestered wife.

JANET M. TODD

Bibliography: Blom, Margaret, *Charlotte Brontë* (1977); Oldfield, Jenny, *"Jane Eyre" and "Wuthering Heights": A Study Guide* (1976).

Janequin, Clément   [zhahn-eh-kan']

Clément Janequin, b. 1485, d. c.1560, was one of the principal composers of the Parisian school of the Renaissance. He was active in Bordeaux before becoming a singer in the royal chapel in Paris. Although Janequin composed much church music, it was his chansons (published from 1528 on) that established his reputation. These are charming miniature pieces, harmonically simple and formally concise, with strongly rhythmic melodies. His fame, however, rests chiefly on his longer descriptive chansons, in which sounds such as the noises of battle ("La guerre," also known as "La Bataille") and bird calls ("Le chant des oiseaux") are effectively depicted.

FRANK D'ACCONE

Bibliography: Reese, Gustave, *Music in the Renaissance*, 2d ed. (1959).

Janet, Pierre   [zhah-nay']

Pierre Marie Félix Janet, b. May 30, 1859, d. Feb. 24, 1947, was a French psychologist who studied hysterical neuroses. He was appointed director of the Salpêtrière, a mental hospital in Paris, by his former teacher Jean Martin Charcot. While professor (1902-36) at the Collège de France, he united clinical and academic psychology. He emphasized the psychological rather than the physical causes of hysteria. Janet postulated a continuum between lower and higher mental acts, including unconscious acts.

Bibliography: Mayo, Elton, *Some Notes on the Psychology of Pierre Janet* (1948).

Janeway, Elizabeth   [jayn'-way]

An American novelist and editor, Elizabeth Hall Janeway, b. Oct. 7, 1913, began chronicling the lives of career women in the 1940s and in the 1970s became a respected commentator on feminism. She is known especially for her anthology *Man's World, Woman's Place: A Study in Social Mythology* (1971) and as the editor of *Women: Their Changing Roles* (1973). The best known of her fictional works is the novel *Daisy Kenyon* (1945), which was made into a film in 1947.

Janissaries   [jan'-ih-sair-eez]

The Janissaries, an elite infantry corps in the army of the OTTOMAN EMPIRE, was established by Sultan MURAD I in the late 14th century. The corps was manned by Christian slaves who were forced to convert to Islam. In the 15th century, MURAD II and MEHMED II intensified recruitment and training of the Janissaries under the *devshirma* system. The corps became the most powerful part of the army. Until the 17th century the Janissaries were subject to severe discipline and were required to remain unmarried and to reside in barracks. They were paid salaries to keep them closer to central control than was possible with the feudal cavalry. Starting in the 17th century, however, discipline and effectiveness declined. Members married, abandoned their training, and occupied most of their time as merchants and artisans. The corps continued to play an active role in politics, however, making and breaking sultans, extorting payments from town and country alike, and blocking reform efforts. Its members were massacred and the corps abolished by MAHMUD II in 1826.   STANFORD J. SHAW

Bibliography: Shaw, Stanford J., *History of the Ottoman Empire and Modern Turkey*: vol. 1, *Empire of the Gazis: The Rise and Decline of the Ottoman Empire, 1280-1808* (1976) and vol. 2 (coauthored with Ezel Kural Shaw), *Reform, Revolution, and Republic: The Rise of Modern Turkey 1808-1975* (1977).

Jannings, Emil [yahn'-ings]

A distinguished German actor best known for the pathos he brought to his portrayals of defeated, broken men, Emil Jannings, originally named Theodor Friedrich Emil Janenz, was born in Brooklyn, N.Y., July 26, 1886, but grew up in Europe, where he died Jan. 2, 1950, his reputation tarnished because of his wartime cooperation with the Nazis. Trained by Max Reinhardt for the stage, Jannings entered films in 1914, and briefly enjoyed success at the end of the silent era in Hollywood, where he won an Academy Award (the first given) for his role in *The Way of All Flesh* (1927). His greatest parts, however, were in such German-language films as F. W. Murnau's *The Last Laugh* (1924) and *Faust* (1926), E. A. Dupont's *Variety* (1925), and Josef von Sternberg's *Blue Angel* (1930), opposite Marlene Dietrich.

Jansenism [jan'-sen-izm]

The theological position known as Jansenism was probably the single most divisive issue within the Roman Catholic church between the Protestant Reformation and the French Revolution. The doctrine took its name from the Flemish theologian and bishop of Ypres, Cornelius Jansen (1585–1638), who summarized his ideas on GRACE and free will in his posthumously published treatise, the *Augustinus* (1640). Relying on the strictest possible interpretation of one aspect of Saint AUGUSTINE's philosophy, Jansen argued in favor of absolute PREDESTINATION, in which humans are perceived as incapable of doing good without God's unsolicited grace and only a chosen few are believed to receive SALVATION. In this respect, the doctrine closely resembled CALVINISM, although the Jansenists always vigorously proclaimed their attachment to Roman Catholicism. As Jansenism was elaborated in France, especially by Jansen's friend Jean DUVERGIER DE HAURANNE, the abbot of Saint-Cyran, and by the latter's protégé Antoine ARNAULD, it also entailed an austere form of piety and a rigorously puritanical morality. From the 1640s, the spiritual center of Jansenism became the convent of Port-Royal-des-Champs (near Paris) where numerous nobles, parlementarians, and intellectuals favorable to the movement made religious retreats.

Almost from the beginning, the Jansenists aroused the hostility both of the JESUITS, who opposed the theology and moral teachings of the group, and of the French royal government, who associated the Jansenists with the opposition "Devout party" and with the rebellions of the FRONDE (1648–53). As early as 1653, five propositions supposedly found in the Jansenist position were condemned by Pope Innocent X. In 1713, under intense pressure from King LOUIS XIV, Pope CLEMENT XI issued the bull *Unigenitus* condemning 101 propositions in a treatise by another French Jansenist, Pasquier Quesnel (1634-1719). The French king closed Port-Royal-des-Champs in 1709 and had it razed to the ground in 1710.

During the 18th century, Jansenism acquired a much broader following among the lower French clergy and spread to other areas of Europe, notably Spain and Italy. The Jansenists increasingly allied themselves with the Gallicans in the French PARLEMENTS in an effort to force the calling of an ecclesiastical council to reconsider the pope's condemnation (see GALLICANISM). The greatest triumph of the Jansenists came in the 1760s when the parlements forced the suppression of the Jesuits in France. But thereafter the movement declined in importance. Only a small group of Jansenists survived into the 19th century.   T. TACKETT

Bibliography: Abercrombie, Nigel J., *The Origins of Jansenism* (1936); Clark, Ruth, *Strangers and Sojourners at Port Royal* (1972); Sedgwick, A., *Jansenism in Seventeenth-Century France* (1977); Van Kley, Dale, *The Jansenists and the Expulsion of the Jesuits from France* (1975).

Jansky, Karl [jan'-skee]

The American radio engineer Karl Guthe Jansky, b. Norman, Okla., Oct. 22, 1905, d. Feb. 14, 1950, was the first to detect radio waves from an extraterrestrial source—a discovery that initiated the science of RADIO ASTRONOMY. After graduating with a degree in physics from the University of Wisconsin, he joined the staff of the Bell Telephone Laboratories in Holmdel, N.J., in 1928. Assigned to identify the sources of atmospheric static that interfered with ship-to-shore and transatlantic communication, Jansky built a linear directional antenna and with it distinguished three types of interference. One was due to local squalls and thunderstorms; another, to distant storms; the third, detected in 1931, moved around the sky each day. Jansky perceived that this third source was extraterrestrial and later determined that its direction was nearly identical with that of the center of the Galaxy in the constellation of Sagittarius. He ended his radio astronomy work in 1937, after the telephone company rejected, as financially unjustifiable, his proposal for a 100-ft (30-m) dish-shaped aerial.   CRAIG B. WAFF

Bibliography: Hey, J. S., *The Evolution of Radio Astronomy* (1973; repr. 1975); Pfeiffer, John, *The Changing Universe: The Story of the New Astronomy* (1956); Verschuur, Gerrit L., *The Invisible Universe* (1974).

Janson, H. W.

Horst Woldemar Janson, b. Leningrad, Oct. 4, 1913, is a distinguished American art historian and critic. He studied at Hamburg, Munich, and Harvard (A.M. 1938, Ph.D. 1942) universities and has been professor of fine arts at New York University since 1949. Janson is best known for his study *History of Art*, a standard text for art survey courses. He has also written *The Sculpture of Donatello* (1957) and numerous other scholarly works on art history.   PHIL PATTON

Bibliography: Esterow, M., "Conversations with H. W. Janson," *Art News*, September 1975.

Janssen, Jules [zhahn-sen', say-zar']

The French astronomer Pierre Jules César Janssen, b. Feb. 22, 1824, d. Dec. 23, 1907, was an early investigator in the fields of astronomical spectroscopy and photography, especially as applied to the Sun. He first demonstrated the absorption effect of the Earth's atmosphere on the solar spectrum and, independently of Sir Joseph Norman LOCKYER in England, discovered a spectroscopic method to study solar prominences in daylight. As first director of Meudon Observatory, near Paris, Janssen compiled an atlas of solar photographs taken from 1876 to 1903.

The Abbey of Port-Royal-des-Champs, a convent of Cistercian nuns, was one of the primary centers of Jansenism, a reform movement within the Roman Catholic church. The abbey was destroyed in 1710 as part of the attempt to suppress the movement.

Janus [jayn'-uhs]

In Roman mythology, Janus was the doorkeeper of heaven and the god of beginnings and endings. He was originally a supreme deity and in later mythology was second only to JU-PITER. Janus was the mediator of prayers and petitions to the other gods. His blessing was asked at the beginning of every day, month, and year, and the first month of the year, January (Latin, Januarius), was named for him. He also presided over the sowing of crops. Roman commanders departed to war through the doors of his temple in the forum, which were closed only in time of peace. Janus was represented in art with two faces, one looking east and the other west, symbolizing his knowledge of the past and the future.

Japan

Japan is one of the world's leading industrial and trading nations and the first Asian nation to develop a technologically advanced industrial economy. It is a small country compared with nations such as the United States but is significantly larger than the United Kingdom, East and West Germany combined, and all other major European nations except Sweden, France, and Spain.

Before World War II, Japan was the center of an empire that at times included Taiwan, Korea, Manchuria, much of eastern China, southern Sakhalin island, and the Marshall and Mariana islands of the southwest Pacific. Today, following concessions of territory at the end of the war, Japan, greatly reduced in size, consists of four main islands—Hokkaido, Honshu, Shikoku, and Kyushu—and hundreds of lesser islands that stretch in a series of arcs for nearly 3,000 km (1,875 mi) along the eastern edge of the Asian mainland.

JAPAN

Official Name: Japan
Capital and Largest City: Tokyo (1976 est. pop., 11,600,000)
Area: 381,945 km² (147,470 mi²)
Elevation: *Highest*—Mt. Fuji, 3,776 m (12,388 ft); *lowest*—sea level, along the coast
Population: 115,493,000 (1979 est.). *Distribution*—76% urban, 24% rural; *density*, 302 persons per km² (783 per mi²); *annual rate of increase* (1970-77), 1.2%
Principal Language: Japanese
Principal Religions: Shinto, Buddhism
Principal Products: *Agriculture*—rice, wheat, barley, potatoes, soybeans, tobacco, sugar, mulberry bushes (for silkworms), fruits and vegetables, cows and pigs. *Manufacturing and industry*—iron and steel, refined copper, lead, and zinc, machine tools, transportation equipment, appliances, electronic equipment, precision and optical instruments, cement, chemicals, textiles, processed foods, fishing. *Mining*—natural gas, limestone, copper, coal, lead, chromite, zinc, clay
Railroads: 21,892 km/13,603 mi (1976)
Roads: 338,343 km/210,246 mi (1976 paved)
Currency: 1 yen = 100 sen

The snowcapped cone of Mount Fuji, which rises to an elevation of 3,776 m (12,388 ft), is the highest point in Japan. Mount Fuji is considered sacred and is a traditional goal for Buddhist pilgrims. Lake Yamanaka lies at the base of Fuji.

Japan's closest neighbor is the USSR; Sakhalin island, a Soviet possession, reaches to within 50 km (31 mi) of Hokkaido across the narrow Soya (La Perouse) Strait. The nearest mainland neighbor is South Korea, which lies about 200 km (124 mi) west of Japan across the Korea Strait. To the southwest is Taiwan; and to the north, the mainland of the USSR.

The name Japan is the romanized version of the Japanese name *Nihon* or *Nippon*, which means "Land of the Rising Sun." The islands were known to European traders during the 15th century, but during the TOKUGAWA period (1603-1868), an era of isolation, Japan developed a highly original and distinctive culture. The country reopened contact with the outside world under the MEIJI RESTORATION (1868-1912). Contact and trade with the West was resumed, and on the basis of this trade, Japan, which possesses few industrial raw materials, developed into one of the world's leading industrialized nations. Japan waged war against the Allies during World War II, but surrendered after the atomic bombing of HIROSHIMA and NAGASAKI in 1945. The country achieved a rapid recovery and is once again one of the world's leading economic powers.

LAND AND RESOURCES

Japan's four main islands, which together constitute 98% of the total area, are HOKKAIDO, in the north; HONSHU, the largest and most populous, located in the center; and the southern islands of KYUSHU and Shikoku. The two southern islands are separated from the main island of Honshu by the protected waters of the INLAND SEA, which has been Japan's core for over 2,000 years. Also integral parts of Japan are more than 3,000 islands and islets, including Iki and Tsushima, located in the narrow Korea Strait; Awaji, located in the Inland Sea between Shikoku and Honshu; and Sado, located off the northwest coast of Honshu. OKINAWA, the RYUKYU ISLANDS, a long island chain located southwest of Kyushu, was administered by the United States after World War II but was restored to Japan in 1972. Located almost 500 km (375 mi) away in the Pacific Ocean are the Marcus, Bonin, and Volcano (including

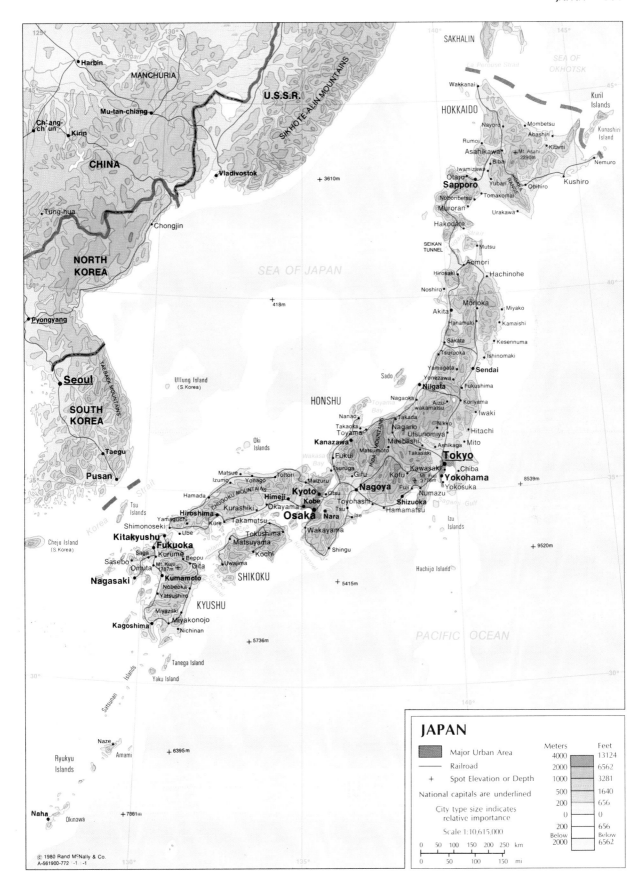

SAKHALIN

SEA OF
OKHOTSK

Kuril
Islands

La Perouse Strait

Wakkanai

HOKKAIDO

Kunashiri
Island

Nayoro
Mombetsu
Abashiri
Kitami

Rumoi
Asahikawa
+Mt. Asahi
2290m

Nemuro

Otaru
Iwamizawa
Bibai
Yubari
Obihiro
Kushiro

Sapporo
Noboribetsu
Tomakomai
Urakawa

Muroran

Hakodate

Tsugaru Strait

SEIKAN
TUNNEL

Mutsu

Aomori

Hirosaki
Hachinohe

Noshiro

HONSHU

Morioka
Miyako

Akita
Kamaishi

Hanamaki

Sakata
Kesennuma

Tsuruoka
Ishinomaki

Yamagata
Sendai

Sado
Yonezawa
Fukushima

Nagaoka
Niigata
Aizu-
wakamatsu
Koriyama

Toyama Bay
Takada
Iwaki

Nanao
Nikko

Takaoka
Nagano
Hitachi

Toyama
Utsunomiya

Kanazawa
Maebashi
Mito

Matsumoto
Ashikaga

Fukui
Takasaki
Tokyo

Tsuruga
Kofu
Chiba

Gifu
Mt. Fuji
Yokohama

3776m
Yokosuka

Otsu
Numazu

Kyoto
Nagoya
Sagami Gulf

Kobe
Toyohashi
Shizuoka

Matsue
Tottori
Himeji
Tsu
Hamamatsu

Izumo
Yonago
Osaka
Nara
Ise

Hamada
Maizuru
Kurashiki
Okayama

Matsue
CHUGOKU MOUNTAINS
Wakayama
Izu
Islands

Yamaguchi
Takamatsu
Tokushima

Shimonoseki
Kure

Hiroshima
Matsuyama
Shingu

Kitakyushu
Ube

Fukuoka
Kochi
Hachijo Island

Saga
Kurume
Beppu

Sasebo
Mt. Kuju
Oita
SHIKOKU

Omuta
787m

Nagasaki
Kumamoto
Nobeoka

Yatsushiro

Miyazaki
KYUSHU

Miyakonojo

Kagoshima
Nichinan

PACIFIC OCEAN

+ 3610m

SEA OF JAPAN

+ 418m

+ 8539m

+ 9520m

+ 5415m

+ 5736m

Taneqa Island

Yaku Island

Satsunan Islands

Naze
Amami

+ 6395m

Ryukyu
Islands

Naha
Okinawa

+ 7861m

Harbin

MANCHURIA

U.S.S.R.

SIKHOTE-ALIN MOUNTAINS

Mu-tan-chiang

Ch'ang-
ch'un
Kirin

CHINA

Vladivostok

Tung-hua

Chongjin

NORTH
KOREA

Pyongyang

YABAEK MOUNTAINS

Seoul

Ullung Island
(S.Korea)

SOUTH
KOREA

Taegu

Oki
Islands

Pusan

Korea Strait

Tsu
Islands

Cheju Island
(S.Korea)

© 1980 Rand McNally & Co.
A-561900-772 -1 -1

IWO JIMA) island groups that were placed under U.S. administration after World War II and were returned to Japan in 1968. Japan disputes the claim by the USSR to some of the KURIL ISLANDS, which stretch northeastward from Hokkaido, and also the claim by Taiwan to the uninhabited Senkaku Islands located 344 km (213 mi) southwest of Okinawa in an area of rich seafloor petroleum deposits.

Japan's islands constitute part of the Circum-Pacific Ring—a tectonically unstable zone of volcanic activity and continuing mountain building that rims the Pacific Ocean. The islands that constitute Japan are actually the peaks of otherwise submerged mountain ranges. About 50 active volcanoes are known in Japan; every year about 1,500 minor earthquakes occur; and hot springs and other features of crustal instability are found. The most famous volcanic area is the Fuji-Hakone-Izu area, located near Tokyo. It is dominated by Mount FUJI, a dormant volcano and Japan's highest mountain, rising to 3,776 m (12,388 ft).

About 75% of Japan's land is mountainous and too steep for easy cultivation and settlement. The principal mountain ranges follow fault lines of great geologic complexity. Where two or more of these arcs intersect are knots of rugged mountains. One such node occurs in central Hokkaido (the Hokkaido Node), where the north-south arc from Sakhalin intersects a northeast-southwest trending arc that forms the Kuril Islands. A second mountain node (the Chubu Node) occurs in central Honshu and west of this is an east-west arc broken into two parallel faults between which the Inland Sea is located. The northern fault passes through western Honshu, and the southern fault is traceable through the Kii Peninsula of Honshu, the island of Shikoku and into Kyushu. A third (Kyushu) node is located in north-central Kyushu, from which run the Ryukyu Archipelago to the southwest and the aforementioned arcs to the northeast. Faults also line the sides of the Fossa Magna, a great rift valley that cuts across the core of the Chubu Node from northwest to southeast. To the north of the rift valley are the rugged Japan Alps, where several peaks rise to more than 3,050 m (10,000 ft).

Lowlands constitute only about 16% of the islands and are generally small, discontinuous, and found mostly in coastal

Hokkaido, the second largest and least populated of Japan's four major islands, is one of the most important fishing centers in the world. The northernmost island of Japan, Hokkaido is the country's chief winter resort and was the site of the 1972 Winter Olympic Games.

The undulating terrain of Honshu island is typical of Japan's mountainous topography. Only 16% of Japan's land is arable. In areas such as this in northern Honshu terraces are constructed to increase the amount of land available for cultivation.

areas. The largest is the Kanto Plain, where Tokyo and surrounding cities are located. Other major cities also grew up on lowlands: Nagoya on the Nobi Plain and Osaka and Kyoto on the lowlands of Kansai. Many small coastal plains surround the Inland Sea.

Soils. The most productive soils are developed on alluvium that has accumulated to considerable depths in all of the lowlands. For nearly 2,000 years these coastal soils have been carefully managed and enriched by the addition of plant, human, and animal wastes, and in recent years by large quantities of chemical fertilizers. The soils in the rest of Japan, as in many mountain areas, tend to be thin. Volcanic material is largely acidic (rather than basic) and supports only poor soils.

Climate. Japan has a range of climates typical of middle latitudes and similar to that of the east coast of most of North America. Hokkaido and the interior of northeastern Honshu have a humid continental climate, characterized by short, cool summers and long, cold, and often snowy winters. Summers become warmer and longer, and winters become shorter and milder toward the south, where subtropical conditions prevail. Demonstrating this latitudinal change in climate, Sapporo, on Hokkaido, has a January mean temperature of −6° C (21° F) and a July temperature of only 19° C (67° F); Niigata, in northern Honshu, has an average of 1° C (35° F) in January and 24° C (75° F) in July; Tokyo averages 3° C (38° F) in January and 26° C (76° F) in July; and Nagasaki, in the southwest, averages 6° C (42° F) in January and 26° C (79° F) in July.

Wind and rainfall patterns are primarily influenced by the monsoon system typical of East Asia. In winter, cold winds blow outward from the Asian continent, reaching Japan from the northwest and the Sea of Japan; in summer, warm, moist winds are drawn toward the Asian interior, blowing across Japan from the Pacific Ocean. As a result, coasts facing the Pa-

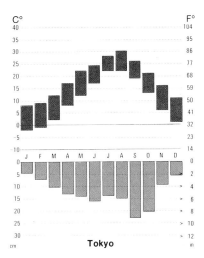

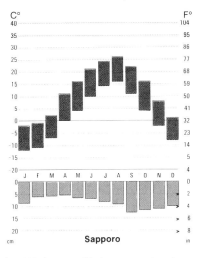

Annual climate charts for two cities in Japan illustrate distinct climate zones in that country. Bars indicate the monthly ranges of temperature (red) and precipitation (blue). Sapporo, located in the western portion of Hokkaido, Japan's northernmost major island, has a continental humid climate. The capital city, Tokyo, which is situated in east central Honshu on Tokyo Bay, has a subtropical humid climate.

cific receive the most precipitation from mid-June to mid-July, while the northeast coast receives heavy winter precipitation from the northwest monsoon, much of it in the form of snow. Average annual precipitation for most of Japan is 1,270 mm (50 in), with some mountain areas receiving up to 2,540 mm (100 in). The Inland Sea area is somewhat drier because it is protected by surrounding mountain chains; it receives only 1,016 mm (40 in) to 1,524 mm (60 in).

Japan's climate is also strongly influenced by two ocean currents and occasional storms and typhoons. The Japan Current (or Kuro Shio), a warm ocean current, flows northward through the islands; its warm waters moderate winter temperatures along the entire southern coast and, to a lesser extent, the southern coastal areas facing the Sea of Japan. By contrast, the cold Okhotsk Current originates in polar waters and flows southward along Hokkaido, contributing to the harsh climate of that island. Typhoons occur from late August to early October; they are accompanied by high winds and heavy rains often causing devastation, but the storms are also valued because they bring moisture during an otherwise dry season.

Drainage. Japan's rivers are short, swift, and shallow. Only 10 are more than 200 km (125 mi) long; thus navigation is limited to short stretches, usually near the sea. The longest river, the Shinano-gawa in west central Honshu, has a total length of only 367 km (228 mi). Drainage is mostly toward the Pacific and Inland Sea coastal regions, because of the general eastward tilt of the islands. Lakes fill less than 1% of the land area; only one, Lake Biwa (695 km²/268 mi²), is a prominent inland feature.

Vegetation and Animal Life. Forests cover about 70% of the total land area and more than 60% of each of the four main islands. Conifers, including fir, spruce, and larch, predominate on Hokkaido and the mountainous interior of northern Honshu. Mixed forest, with conifers such as cypress and hemlock and deciduous trees including oak, maple, birch, and ash, predominate in the warmer parts of Honshu. Subtropical evergreen vegetation predominates in the southwest and warmer parts of Kyushu and Shikoku. Natural vegetation is also widely interspersed with exotics (introduced species) including bamboo, giant cryptomeria, and camphor. Reforested areas are mostly planted with conifers, and these forests now account for one-third of the total wooded area.

The most common large animals are deer, bears, and boars. Native monkeys are widely found, as are many introduced smaller animals. Reptiles include snakes and lizards. The bird population includes the crown eagle, other birds of prey, and more than 400 additional species, both migratory and domestic.

Resources. Japan produces a wide range of metallic minerals, including chromite, zinc, manganese, copper, lead, molybdenum, and gold. Extensive deposits of low-grade coal are located on northwestern Kyushu and western Hokkaido; the coal is unsuitable for use in the iron and steel industry, how-

ever, and since the early 1960s has steadily lost ground to imported petroleum as a primary fuel. Small oil fields are located in Hokkaido and northern Honshu, but domestic production accounts for only 0.3% of total petroleum consumption. Hydroelectric power resources are abundant, because of the mountainous terrain and plentiful rainfall in upland areas. Nonmetallic minerals include clay and large amounts of gypsum.

PEOPLE
The dominant ethnic group is the Japanese, a Mongoloid people. The Japanese have developed a culture that was strongly influenced between the 3d and 10th century by contact with the Chinese and Koreans, contact with the West during the 16th century, isolation during the Tokugawa period (1603–1868), and renewed contact with the West and the rest of the world after 1854.

The largest minority group is the approximately 600,000 Koreans, who began settling in Japan mostly during the 1920s and have retained their language and culture. A smaller minority is the AINU, who live mostly in Hokkaido; they are the remnant of an indigenous people who were pushed northward through the islands over centuries of Japanese expansion from the Inland Sea region. The Buramkumin (or Eta) are ethnically Japanese but are often considered a separate group because they are descended from an ancient order of social outcasts; although they were given legal parity in 1868, they are often discriminated against, work in low-paying positions if their origins are known, and live in segregated communities. Okinawans, or inhabitants of the Ryukyu Islands, consider themselves Japanese, but they have some unique cultural elements, including language.

Spoken Japanese was long considered a unique language but is now known to bear a strong association with Korean. Written Japanese is complex, being derived from Chinese. Because the characters, or ideographs, used in written Chinese are inadequate to represent Japanese, parallel Kana (sets of phonetic syllabaries of 48 characters each) were developed during the 9th century. These can effectively transcribe Japanese but are usually used to supplement Chinese characters or to bridge the gap between the two languages. The Kanto dialect, spoken in the Tokyo area, is considered standard spoken Japanese. (See JAPANESE LANGUAGE.)

BUDDHISM, introduced from China during the 6th century, is followed by 75% of the population. SHINTO, the ancient Japanese and former state religion, is a parallel faith for most Japanese Buddhists. CONFUCIANISM, introduced during the 4th century, is also influential. About 1% of the population is officially listed as Christian, but Christianity may be more important than this figure suggests.

Demography. About 80% of the total population live on Honshu, 12% on Kyushu, 5% on Hokkaido, and 3% on Shikoku. The population is predominantly urban, with about 76% living in 645 cities mostly with populations of more than 30,000. The largest urban concentration is the Tokaido megalopolis. This

These Tokyo pedestrians wear both Japanese and Western clothing. Increased contact with the West has resulted in the adoption of many Western practices; despite these influences, however, traditional values are still an integral part of Japanese culture.

Graceful horizontal lines impart an air of serenity to these Buddhist temples in Kyoto. The capital of Japan from 794 until 1060, Kyoto is still one of the country's most important cultural and religious centers. Buddhism is among Japan's principal religions.

urban core on Honshu is an almost continuously inhabited and built up area along the Pacific corridor from Tokyo in the east to Kobe in the west, with extensions growing westward onto northern Kyushu and along the shores of the Inland Sea and to the east of Tokyo. Only 11 of Japan's 47 prefectures (the largest unit of government below the national level) are located in the urban core, but 45% of the total population lives in the region. Japan's 6 largest cities in order of population—TOKYO, OSAKA, YOKOHAMA, NAGOYA, KYOTO, and KOBE—dominate the area. The largest cities outside the core are SAPPORO, on Hokkaido; FUKUOKA and KITAKYUSHU on Kyushu; and KAWASAKI, on Kanto. All of these cities have more than 1 million inhabitants. Most urban growth has occurred since the 1920s, but urbanization has deep roots in Japan's past. Many cities have existed since the early years of the Tokugawa period. Edo (modern Tokyo), for example, had approximately 1 million inhabitants in 1721, Osaka and Kyoto each had about 500,000, and Kanazawa, Nagoya, and others 100,000 or more.

Japan's population is now nearly four times what it was in 1868 (30 million) and nearly twice as large as in 1920 (56 million). Since about 1952, however, the growth rate has slowed dramatically; the current rate, 1.3% (1977), is one of the lowest in Asia and similar to rates in other economically developed nations. The low death rate of 6.3 per 1,000 inhabitants (1976) reflects a high-quality medical system; the low birthrate of 16.3 per 1,000 inhabitants (1976) has been accomplished through a government-sponsored birth-control program and legalized abortion.

Japan has a population density of 302 persons per km² (783 per mi²), one of the highest in the world. The population is distributed unevenly over the land area, with almost the entire population crowded onto the 16% of land that is level enough for cultivation and settlement. As a result the number of people per cultivated unit is the highest in the world; congestion of living space, highways, railways, and industrial and agricultural space is a characteristic feature of Japanese life. The supply of adequate housing falls far short of demand, despite prodigious building programs by government and industry. Alleviating environmental pollution resulting from such concentrated development will be a source of concern for the Japanese for years to come.

Education and Health. Virtually the entire population is literate, and education is free and compulsory for all children between the ages of 6 and 15. Education after age 15 is a matter of individual choice, but more than 90% of all students, male and female, continue to high school and about one-third of all students attend an institution of higher education. The higher education system includes about 400 colleges and universities (half with graduate programs); about 500 junior colleges; and numerous technical schools that provide a wide range of practical training. Admission to most schools is highly competitive and based on performance in entrance examinations; the competition to enter a prestigious university is so severe that a large number of *juku* (extra-hour schools) operate to prepare students for the entrance examination. (See JAPANESE UNIVERSITIES.)

Medical facilities and training are highly developed in urban areas but are often limited elsewhere. In 1975 there were 8,379 hospitals, 73,915 general clinics, and 33,526 dental clinics. For each 100,000 citizens there were 1,185 hospital beds and 133 physicians. Life expectancy is among the highest in the world, 73 for males and 78 for females (1977). Tuberculosis, typhoid fever, and dysentery have been virtually eradicated. The principal causes of death today are stroke, cardiovascular diseases, and cancer. Infant mortality rates have declined from 124 per 1,000 live births in the 1930s to 9.7 per 1,000 in 1976.

Cars await shipment from the factory near Nagoya to other Japanese and foreign cities. Since World War II, Japan has become one of the most industrialized nations in the world and is a leading producer of ships, automobiles, trucks, steel, and electronics.

The Arts. Japanese pottery, clay statuary, and other Neolithic artifacts reveal an unusual sensitivity to aesthetic form and beauty, but most Japanese arts owe their greatest development to stimulus from China and the West. During the 6th century, when Buddhism was adopted from China, Japanese literature, architecture, painting, sculpture, theater, and other art forms were greatly influenced by contact with that culture. The Chinese impact remained strong, except perhaps in literature, until the end of the 16th century. During the isolated Tokugawa period, distinctly Japanese art forms developed, including the UKIYO-E (wood block print), KABUKI and other theater, and unique forms of architecture and exquisite landscape design. In later years, as art forms from many cultures including the West were adopted, an unmistakably Japanese touch was added to the imports.

Japanese artists now excel in many new fields, including Western music, photography, and architecture, but the rich artistic heritage of Japan's past continues to be reflected in modern machine-made ceramics, textiles, and the continuation of such ancient practices as the tea ceremony and Japanese flower-arranging arts. (See JAPANESE ART AND ARCHITECTURE; JAPANESE LITERATURE; JAPANESE MUSIC.)

ECONOMIC ACTIVITY

From the 13th to 16th century the Japanese became known as skillful navigators, traders, and pirates. In the 15th and 16th centuries, the Japanese conducted lively trade with Asia and the West, exporting manufactured goods and importing coinage and other necessities. Steel swords, made of a peerless-quality steel forged by techniques developed as a result of Japan's long martial tradition, were the chief export item. Foreign trade was halted during the Tokugawa period, but small Japanese industries continued to produce clothing, utensils, food products, guns, and other military hardware for the domestic market. At the same time, progress was made in the organization of a national system of marketing, management, trade, and finance. Thus, when seclusion ended, Japan already possessed the necessary infrastructures on which to build a modern system of industry, banking, and commerce.

Textiles were developed as the first leading industry, during the Tokugawa era, with some support from other light industries. Heavy industry was slow to develop because of the lack of adequate iron ore and coking coal but was stimulated by Japan's involvement in a series of wars beginning with the Sino-Japanese War of 1894–95 and culminating in World

War II. After the defeat of Japan in World War II, the economy was directed away from military needs, and the economic miracle that is the envy of developed and developing nations alike was accomplished. Japan overcame its deficiency of industrial raw materials and established one of the world's most productive modern economic systems. Despite industrial modernization traditional industries have continued as family enterprises, giving the nation a kind of dual industrial structure; the persistence of traditional forms as viable businesses, however, appears to be slowly weakening in the face of present economic conditions.

Manufacturing. Industry expanded rapidly after the 1950s, with a heavy emphasis on export items, and now employs about 25% of the labor force. The major industrial area is concentrated in Japan's urban core and stretches from Tokyo in the east through the coastal areas along the Inland Sea in the west to northern Kyushu. Japan ranks high as a world producer of manufactured goods and commands a large share of the world market for ships; iron and steel; automobiles, bicycles, mopeds, and other transportation equipment; machinery; chemicals; ceramics; cameras, precision goods, and optical equipment; and televisions, radios, and other electronic items. Much of manufacturing is concentrated in the hands of a relatively small number of large diversified concerns—including the giant Mitsubishi, Mitsui, Sumitomo, Toyota, and Nissan groups.

These sheaves of harvested rice are being hung on wooden racks to dry. Traditional methods of farming are still used in some parts of Japan. Rice constitutes the most important food crop; in 1976 rice accounted for more than one-third of the country's total agricultural output.

Whaling vessels are equipped to process fully an adult whale. Japan and the USSR continue to overhunt whales despite the regulation attempted by the International Whaling Commission, maintaining that whales provide a needed source of protein.

Power. In 1977, 537 kW h of electricity were produced. Imported petroleum accounts for 73% of all electricity generated in Japan and is the primary source of all energy. Coal provides 16.4% of all electricity, including only 3.4% produced from domestic coal. Water power accounts for 5.4% and atomic plants for 1.7%. In 1978, 16 atomic plants were in operation, 10 were under construction, and an additional 17 were planned.

Agriculture. Most Japanese farms consist of a number of small and scattered fields that add up to an average farm size of less than 1.2 ha (3 acres). Most farms are operated as family enterprises, and many are so small that they are run on a part-time basis, and by women and children, while male members of the family commute to other jobs in nearby urban areas. The growing season ranges from more than 250 days in the southwest to less than 120 days in Hokkaido. Thus, three crops a year are possible on lands in the warmer areas of Kyushu, Shikoku, and southwestern Honshu; two crops on most of southern Honshu; but only one on northern Honshu and Hokkaido. Winter cropping, however, now has become very limited or is extinct as it once was practiced. Irrigation, terracing, fertilizers, and other intensive cultivation methods are widely employed and provide Japan with some of the highest crop yields per cultivated area in the world. Rice, whose production is subsidized by the government, is the chief summer crop; wheat, barley, and potatoes were important dry-season and upland crops, but production recently has dwindled radically. Animal husbandry has been of minor importance, and little land is used as pasture. Chief commercial crops are mulberry bushes—the leaves are fed to silkworms—and tea, both of which are grown in upland areas. The silkworm-raising industry, concentrated in southern Honshu, has declined in the face of competition from synthetic textiles. Recently computer-monitored hydroponic farming for vegetables and fruit has become large scale.

Forestry and Fishing. Only about one-fourth of Japan's extensive forest cover is accessible for cutting, and production is inadequate to keep pace with the growing demand for wood, wood pulp, and wood products; Japan now imports more than half of its wood, much of it from Indonesia, India, and the Philippines.

Since the 1950s fishing has become a large-scale industry, and Japanese fishing fleets now operate in all the world's oceans. Japan leads the world in total quantity of fish caught and in 1976 landed 10.7 million metric tons (11.8 million U.S. tons) of fish—more than twice the amount landed by second-ranking Peru and one-seventh of the world's total fish catch. Coastal fishing is performed on a smaller scale, often as a family enterprise.

Transportation. Transportation has been a key to progress since the Tokugawa period, when highways were integrated and seaways improved in order to distribute the rice upon which the economy rested. After 1868 railroads became the principal means of transportation. Today railroads link all of Japan's major cities. Most are publicly owned and operated, but some important interurban and intraurban networks are privately owned. A 1,062-km-long (664-mi) high-speed rail line, with trains able to travel at 249 km/h (155 mph), links Tokyo with other cities in the urban core, including Yokohama, Nagoya, Kyoto, Osaka, Okayama, and Hakata (Fukuoka). It is to be supplemented by an 8,800-km-long (5,500-mi) super-express rail system now under construction and designed to supplement Japan's older, narrow-gauge rail system. Despite such construction, however, the railroads are continuing to lose traffic to automobiles and trucking; a highway culture threatens to dominate the future landscape of the nation.

Japan Air Lines, partially government operated, is the principal airline, and international airports are located at Tokyo, Osaka, Narita, and Fukuoka. Japan's merchant fleet is the second largest in the world (after Liberia) and includes the world's second-largest fleet of oil tankers and ore carriers. Yokohama, Kobe, and Nagoya are the leading ports.

Trade. Trade is central to the Japanese economy, owing to the scarcity of agricultural land and of industrial raw materials and fuel. Japan accounts for about 6.3% of all world imports by value, and for 6.8% of all world exports. The principal imports are metal ores, petroleum, coal, chemicals, machine equipment, and food. Exports include a wide range of machinery, textiles, iron and steel, optical instruments, automobiles, and electronic items. The export trade has become so successful in recent years that balance-of-payment problems have arisen with trading partners with competitive industries. This is especially true of the United States, Japan's single largest trading partner, which (during the 1970s) imported 25% more by value from Japan than it exported. Other leading trade areas are East Asia (especially South Korea, Taiwan, and China), which provides about 10% of all Japanese imports and absorbs more than 15% of the exports; Western Europe, which provides only 6% of the imports but takes 11% of Japan's exports; Saudi Arabia; Australia; Canada; and Indonesia. Japan's economy has been seriously affected by the increase in petroleum prices during the 1970s, but the country generally maintains a favorable trade balance and balance of payments.

GOVERNMENT

Japan is a constitutional monarchy, with a hereditary emperor and a parliamentary system of government. The present constitution was adopted on Oct. 7, 1946, and became effective on May 3, 1947. The emperor is ceremonial head of state with little governmental power; Emperor HIROHITO ascended the throne in 1926. Legislative power is vested in the Diet, a bicameral body composed of a House of Representatives with 511 members elected to 4-year terms, and a House of Councillors, whose 250 members serve 6-year terms. Executive power rests with the cabinet, which is headed by a prime minister, who heads the majority party in the Diet; in 1978, OHIRA MASAYOSHI succeeded FUKUDA TAKEO as prime minister. Since 1955 the majority political party has been the Liberal Democratic party, a generally conservative organization with strong agrarian roots that now holds about half the seats in both houses. The principal opposition party is the Socialist party, which controls about one-third of the seats in both houses. Small but significant parties reflecting extremes in the political spectrum include the Communist party and the Clean Government party, which has strong Buddhist ties.

Judicial powers rest with the supreme court, consisting of a chief justice and 14 other justices who are appointed by the government but who are subject to review in public referendums. Local government is by the 47 prefectures, each with its own elected governor and assembly and wielding a large measure of local autonomy. All citizens over the age of 20 are eligible to vote.   DAVID H. KORNHAUSER

Bibliography:

GENERAL: Livingston, Jon, et al., eds., *The Japan Reader*, 2 vols. (1973, 1974); Reischauer, Edwin O., *Japan* (1977) and *The Japanese* (1977); Richie, Donald, *Introducing Japan* (1978); Tiedemann, Arthur E., ed., *An Introduction to Japanese Civilization* (1974); Trewartha, Glenn T., *Japan* (1965).

PEOPLE, CULTURE AND SOCIETY: Benedict, Ruth, *The Chrysanthemum and the Sword* (1946; repr. 1967); Fukutake, Tadashi, *Japanese Rural Society*, trans. by R. P. Dore (1967); Ishida, Takeshi, *Japanese Society* (1971); Kornhauser, David H., *Urban Japan* (1976); Lebra, Takie S. and William P., eds., *Japanese Culture and Behavior* (1974); Whiting, Robert, *The Chrysanthemum and the Bat* (1977).

ECONOMICS: Clark, Rodney, *The Japanese Company* (1979); Kahn, Herman, and Pepper, Thomas, *The Japanese Challenge* (1979); Patrick, Hugh, and Rosovsky, Henry, eds., *Asia's New Giant* (1976); Vogel, Ezra F., *Japan as Number One: Lessons for America* (1979); Yoshino, M. Y., *Japan's Multi-National Enterprises* (1976).

POLITICS AND GOVERNMENT: Baerwald, H. H., *Japan's Parliament: An Introduction* (1974); Brzezinski, Zbigniew, *The Fragile Blossom* (1972); Gibney, Frank, *Japan* (1975); McNelly, Theodore, *Politics and Government in Japan* (1972); Richardson, Bradley M., *The Political Culture of Japan* (1974); Ward, Robert E., *Japan's Political System*, 2d ed. (1978), and *Political Development in Modern Japan* (1968).

Japan, history of

Modern knowledge about the first peoples to inhabit the Japanese archipelago has been pieced together from the findings of archaeologists and anthropologists and from the myths of ancient Japan. Although the date of the first human habitation is not known, anthropologists have identified one of the earliest cultures in Japan as the Jomon culture, which dates from about 8000 BC. A hunting and gathering culture, it used stone and bone tools and made pottery of distinctive design. In the 3d century BC, Jomon culture was disrupted by a new people, known as Yayoi, who probably emigrated from continental Asia. They introduced rice cultivation, primitive weaving, wheel-made pottery, domesticated horses and cows, and simple iron tools. Yayoi culture overlaid and fused with the earlier Jomon culture.

EARLY HISTORICAL PERIOD

The earliest written Japanese histories, the *Kojiki* (Record of Ancient Matters, 712) and the *Nihon shoki* (Chronicles of Japan, 720), include legends about the origins of the Japanese people and attribute the foundation of the state to a mythological emperor Jimmu in 660 BC. Another legend concerns the empress JINGO (AD c.169-269), who allegedly conquered Korea. These records provide more reliable chronicles of Japanese history from the 5th century.

Yamato Period. Beginning in the 3d or 4th century AD a new culture appeared—either from within Yayoi society or from the Asian mainland. Its leaders left massive tombs with pottery, figurines, armor, jewelry, weapons, and other evidence that they were mounted warriors with long iron swords and

Prince Shotoku Taishi, regent of Japan from 592 to 622, is depicted in this Chinese-style imperial portrait. When the centralized government established by the Yamato clan began to weaken, Taishi organized (604) a system of imperial government based on that of the Chinese T'ang dynasty.

bows. From this culture emerged rulers from the Yamato plain in the southern part of the main Japanese island of Honshu; they claimed descent from the sun goddess and achieved political unity—apparently in the mid-4th century. By placing the sun goddess at the head of the SHINTO deities the hereditary Yamato emperor reinforced his leadership position. Initially, the emperors ruled through alliances with other tribal chieftains, but the latter were gradually subordinated by a system of court ranking. This development was influenced by Chinese concepts of statecraft, learned through Japan's military endeavors in Korea. Japan also adopted Chinese script, and BUDDHISM was introduced from Korea about 538.

In the 6th century the centralized control of the Yamato court began to break down. At the end of the century, however, the regent Prince SHOTOKU TAISHI reasserted court authority. He promulgated (604) a 17-article constitution based on the Chinese political theory of centralized imperial government, redefining the sovereign's position in Chinese terms. Imperial authority was further asserted by the Taika reforms of 646, by which, following Chinese precedent, all land was claimed by the emperor and an elaborate taxation system was initiated. In 702 the Taiho Laws, comprising new civil and penal codes, were promulgated.

Nara Period. The first permanent capital was built at NARA in 710. In the following century tribal elites were replaced by a hereditary court aristocracy, and status became the basis for official influence. Japan was thus transformed from a tribal into an aristocratic culture. Court patronage made Buddhism a major force, which in turn reinforced state power. Nara was the center not only of government but of the major Buddhist temples; in 752 the statue of the Great Buddha (*Daibutsu*) was dedicated there. Buddhist priestly intrusion in state affairs provoked a reaction, however. Finally, Emperor KAMMU (r. 781-806) asserted imperial independence and established a new capital at Heian (modern KYOTO) in 794.

Heian and the Fujiwaras. In Heian, safe from Buddhist interference, imperial authority increased; however, the simplification of government that accompanied the move to Heian allowed the Fujiwara family to assert great influence. The Fujiwara had the privilege of intermarriage with the imperial house, and many emperors were married to Fujiwara women or were their sons. Fujiwara men proved capable administrators, and they used their family ties to dominate the government. In 858, Fujiwara Yoshifusa (804-72) had his grandson, the infant Emperor Seiwa, placed on the throne and made himself regent. Until the end of the 11th century the Fujiwara used the position of regent to dominate the emperors, adults as well as children.

Under imperial patronage two new Buddhist sects emerged in Heian. Tendai and Shingon, more Japanese in spirit than earlier Buddhist sects, ended the monopoly of the Nara Buddhist establishment. A reassertion of tribal, or clan, authority also accompanied the move to Heian. The imperial land system established by the Taika reforms decayed, and land increasingly fell into private hands. Aristocrats and religious institutions assembled huge tax-free estates (*shoen*). Private armies were created, and a class of rural warriors (SAMURAI) emerged.

Notable among the samurai class were the Taira and Minamoto families. Initially local military leaders, both clans were drawn into court politics. In 1156 they applied military force to settle a court dispute, and a war in 1159-60 left the Taira as the effective rulers. The Taira dominated court politics by force and by marital ties with the imperial line. In 1180, Taira Kiyomori placed his grandson Antoku on the throne, briefly reviving the Fujiwara practice of using the regency to dominate the government.

THE SHOGUNATES

In 1180 the Minamoto revolted against the Taira and in the Gempei War (1180-85) defeated them and established the Kamakura shogunate, the first of the military governments that would rule Japan until 1868. (See SHOGUN.)

Kamakura Period. The shogun Minamoto YORITOMO (r. 1192-99) assigned military governors and military land stewards to supplement the civil governors and estate offi-

(Above) Burning of the Sanjo Palace, *an illustration from the 13th-century saga* Heiji Monogatari (Tales of Heiji), *portrays a decisive event during the Heiji Wars (1159), when the Taira clan defeated the Minamoto. (Museum of Fine Arts, Boston.)* (Left) *Minamoto Yoritomo, depicted in this 12th-century portrait, conquered the Taira in 1185 and established the Kamakura shogunate, the first of the military governments that ruled until 1868. (Jingoji, Kyoto.)*

cials. While establishing military authority, however, Yoritomo failed to ensure the effective succession of his own family. His sons were first dominated, then eliminated, by the Hojo clan, which from 1203 held the position of *shikken* (shogunal regent).

After 1221, when the retired emperor Go-Toba failed in his attempt to overthrow the shogunate, military authority was increased. Warriors, while largely illiterate and unskilled in administration, proved effective governors. The Hojo upheld the military virtues on which the shogunate had been founded and proved apt successors to Yoritomo.

In 1274 and 1281 the shogunate was tested by two Mongol invasions (see MONGOLS). The Japanese warriors, assisted by storms that came to be described as divine winds (*kamikaze*), drove away the invaders. The Kamakura period was also one of spiritual awakening. Buddhism was simplified, and new sects—PURE LAND BUDDHISM, True Pure Land, and Lotus (see NICHIREN)—guaranteed salvation to all believers.

By the early 14th century, however, political and social stability were breaking down. In 1334 the Kamakura shogunate was destroyed when Emperor Go-Daigo reasserted imperial authority (the Kemmu Restoration). Many powerful military families such as the Ashikaga flocked to assist the emperor. He failed to reward them properly, however, and in 1336 he was driven from Kyoto and replaced by another puppet emperor. Go-Daigo established a rival court in Yoshino, and for 56 years there were two imperial courts.

Ashikaga Period. In 1338, Ashikaga Takauji was made shogun, creating the Ashikaga shogunate. The Ashikaga reached the height of their power under the third shogun, Yoshimitsu (r. 1368–94). He controlled the military aspirations of his subordinates and ended (1392) the schism within the imperial house.

The shogunate rested on an alliance with local military leaders (*shugo*), who gradually became powerful regional rul-

ers. The great *shugo*, however, became increasingly involved in the politics of the shogunate, and by the mid-15th century many had lost control of their provincial bases. Their weakness became apparent in the Onin War of 1467–77. Beginning as a dispute over the shogunal succession, it turned into a general civil war in which the great *shugo* exhausted themselves fighting in and around Kyoto, while the provinces fell into the hands of other *shugo* and eventually under the control of new lords called *daimyo*. The war effectively destroyed Ashikaga authority. The shogun Yoshimasa (r. 1440–73) simply turned his back on the troubles; he retired (1473) to his estate on the outskirts of Kyoto, where he built the Silver Pavilion (*Ginkaku*) and became the patron of a remarkable artistic flowering.

The Onin War marked the beginning of a century of warfare called the "Epoch of the Warring Country." In the provinces new feudal lords, the *daimyo*, arose. Independent of imperial or shogunal authority, their power was based on military strength. They defined their domains as the area that could be defended from military rivals. Ties were fixed by vassalage, and land holdings were guaranteed in return for military service. The *daimyo* concentrated their vassals in castle towns and left the villagers to administer themselves and pay taxes. The castle towns became market and handicraft industrial centers, and a new style of urban life began to develop.

This was the Japan found by the Europeans who began to visit the country after 1543. The Portuguese began trade in 1545, and in 1549 the Jesuit missionary Saint FRANCIS XAVIER introduced Roman Catholicism. Christianity conflicted with feudal loyalties, however, and was completely banned after 1639. At that point all Europeans, except the Dutch, were also excluded from Japan.

Period of Unification. Between 1560 and 1600, Japan was reunified by a succession of three great *daimyo*: Oda NOBUNAGA, Toyotomi HIDEYOSHI, and Tokugawa IEYASU. Nobunaga be-

Ashikaga Takauji established the Ashikaga shogunate in 1338, after driving the emperor Go-Daigo, whom he had earlier assisted, from the imperial court in Kyoto. The Ashikaga shogunate reached its height at the end of the century, under Ashikaga Yoshimitsu (r. 1368–94).

gan the military process in 1560 and by 1568 had extended his influence to Kyoto. He set up a puppet shogun and established control over central Japan. After Nobunaga's death (1582) during a rebellion, Hideyoshi continued the military unification of the country, completing the process in 1590. The use of firearms (supplied initially by the Europeans), the construction of fortified castles, the disarmament of the peasants, and a major land survey were the chief tools of pacification. When Hideyoshi died in 1598, centralized authority was secure, and the warrior class had been segregated from other members of society.

The third great unifier, Tokugawa Ieyasu, was a military leader who emerged as the guarantor of Hideyoshi's young heir, Hideyori. In 1600, Ieyasu defeated his military rivals at Sekigahara and asserted his predominance. He was appointed shogun in 1603, but in 1605 he turned that office over to his son and devoted the rest of his life to consolidating Tokugawa control. In 1615, Hideyori was attacked and finally eliminated, and when Ieyasu died the following year, the Tokugawa held unchallenged feudal supremacy over the whole country.

Tokugawa Period. From their castle town of Edo (modern TOKYO), the TOKUGAWA ruled Japan as shoguns until 1867. A careful distribution of land among their vassal *daimyo*, relatives, and outside *daimyo* ensured their control of the major cities—Kyoto, OSAKA, and NAGASAKI—and the chief mines. Thus they controlled the main economic centers and strategic military points, while unrelated *daimyo* administered some 250 autonomous domains. The *daimyo* spent half their time in Edo attending the shogun and left their families as hostages when they returned to their domains.

The Tokugawa period saw the flowering of urban culture and a monetized commodity economy. Edo had a population of over 1 million, and both Kyoto and Osaka had more than 400,000 people. The samurai stood at the top of a legally established four-class system. From illiterate warriors they were transformed into military bureaucrats who served both the shogunal and *daimyo* governments. Below them were the peasants, artisans, and merchants. Although despised, merchants became essential to urban life. A national market system developed for textiles, food products, handicrafts, books, and other goods. Osaka was the center of the national rice market, where *daimyo* exchanged their rice for cash to support their Edo residences and the traveling back and forth to their domains. After 1639 the Tokugawa pursued a policy of almost total seclusion from the outside world. Nagasaki, where the Chinese and the Dutch were allowed trading quarters (the Dutch on an offshore island), was the only point of contact with foreign countries.

By the 19th century considerable ferment existed in Japanese society. Peasant uprisings had become commonplace, and the samurai and even the *daimyo* were badly indebted to the merchant class. Thus the old socioeconomic system had virtually collapsed, while the shogunal government displayed increasing extravagance and inefficiency. In the early 1840s the national government attempted a series of reforms to improve economic conditions, but they were largely ineffectual.

(Above) *During the Tokugawa period (1600-1867) urban life flourished. This painting depicts a scene of daily life on the streets of Yoshiwara.*
(Left) *Under the Tokugawa shogunate Japan entered a period of isolation, which lasted until U.S. Commodore Matthew Perry arrived in 1853. The samurai then turned against the indecisive Tokugawa leadership and restored (1868) imperial government under the Meiji emperor.*

The shogunate, therefore, was already in a discredited position when U.S. Commodore Matthew PERRY forced Japan to abandon its seclusionist policy in 1854.

With the arrival of Perry's ships the Tokugawa shogun turned to the *daimyo* for advice and thereby undermined shogunal control over foreign policy. The imperial house, long excluded from politics, was drawn into the controversy, and the slogan "revere the emperor, expel the barbarians" was soon heard in the expanding political debate. In 1858 the shogun signed disadvantageous commercial treaties with the United States and several European countries. Tokugawa leadership was questioned, and numerous samurai attacks were made on the foreigners now allowed to enter Japan. By 1864 most activists realized that the foreigners' military power prevented their exclusion, and they turned against the Tokugawa instead. Samurai from the domains of Satsuma, Choshu, Tosa, and Hizen played major roles in pushing for reforms. In 1867 they finally forced the resignation of the shogun, and imperial government was restored under the young Meiji emperor in 1868 (see MEIJI RESTORATION).

MODERN JAPAN

The Meiji Period. In less than half a century Japan was transformed from a secluded feudal society into an industrialized world power. During the Meiji period, corresponding to the reign (1868–1912) of Emperor Meiji, centralized bureaucracy replaced the balance of power between the Tokugawa and the autonomous domains. A conscript army replaced the military authority of the samurai. Restrictions on residence and employment were abolished, and people flocked to Edo, now renamed Tokyo and adopted as the imperial capital. The government imported foreign advisors and technology for industrial, commercial, and educational purposes. Official missions were sent to examine modern Western societies. Adopting the slogan "rich country, strong army," Japan determined to gain a position of equality with the West.

(Left) *Under Emperor Meiji (Mutshito; r. 1868–1912), Japan was transformed from a secluded feudal society into a military and industrial world power. Rapid modernization occurred during the Meiji Restoration, and a constitution was promulgated in 1889.* (Right) *Japan's surprise attack on Port Arthur initiated the Russo-Japanese War (1904–05), a struggle over Korea and Manchuria. Japan's success won it recognition as a military power.*

Government stability was crucial to this objective. In 1873 a new tax system provided a secure revenue base and abolished the feudal land system. In 1877 the conscript army defeated a major samurai revolt led by SAIGO TAKAMORI, a leading figure in the imperial restoration. Inflation reduced the value of government revenues, and between 1881 and 1885 a rigorous deflation policy initiated by MATSUKATA MASAYOSHI stabilized the currency. Education was basic to Japan's emergence. Beginning with 40 percent male and 15 percent female literacy, the Meiji government required primary education for all children and established (1872) a centralized school system.

In 1881 domestic political pressure forced the oligarchical government to promise a constitution by 1889 and representative government by 1890. The statesman ITO HIROBUMI took charge of drafting the new constitution. A cabinet was established in 1885, a peerage was created, and in 1889 the constitution was promulgated as a gift from the emperor.

Japan thus became a constitutional monarchy, with a bicameral legislature (Diet) composed of a house of peers and an elected lower house. Suffrage was very limited, however; only 1 percent of the population was eligible to vote in the 1890 election. Moreover, the prime minister and cabinet were responsible only to the emperor, who was still regarded as a divine figure. Representative government evolved slowly, but the Diet had some control of the budget and gradually increased its authority.

Conflict between the Diet and the government leaders ceased during the SINO-JAPANESE WAR of 1894–95, in which Japan displayed its military superiority over the Chinese and secured control of Korea. The victory added to Japanese prestige, and in 1902, Japan concluded an alliance with Britain as an equal power.

In 1904–05, Japan and Russia fought over Manchuria and Korea. Victorious in this RUSSO-JAPANESE WAR, the Japanese added southern Sakhalin to their empire of Taiwan and the Ryukyu Islands; and in 1910 they formally annexed Korea. By 1905, therefore, Japan was a major military power in East Asia and an industrialized nation. When Japan entered World War I as an ally of Britain, the strains of industrialization were apparent in Japanese society.

World War I and the Interwar Years. During World War I, Japan seized several of the German holdings in East Asia, including the Chinese territory of Kiaochow. When the Chinese demanded the return of Kiaochow, the Japanese government responded with the Twenty-one Demands of January 1915, forcing Chinese acceptance of extended Japanese influence in China. In 1917, Japan extracted further concessions of rights in Manchuria and Inner Mongolia, setting the stage for its later open aggression against China.

In 1918, HARA TAKASHI became prime minister in the first cabinet based on a party majority in the Diet. Although the political parties were essentially controlled by business interests (see ZAIBATSU), they were a major step toward more democratic forms of government—a trend that was continued

by the expansion of the electorate in 1925 to include all males over 25.

Although repressive toward the growing labor movement, the party governments of the 1920s and after attempted modest reforms, cutting back the army and enacting some social legislation. They also pursued a less aggressive foreign policy than that of prewar Japan. At the WASHINGTON CONFERENCE of 1921–22, Japan signed a naval arms limitation treaty that replaced the Anglo-Japanese alliance and established a balance of power in the Pacific. In 1930 further naval limitations were agreed to at the London Naval Conference.

The Japanese military felt, however, that the politicians were compromising the nation's security and the emperor's right to supreme command. As the World Depression of the 1930s set in, the discontented began to rally to the cry of the militarists that the civilian governments were corrupt and that military expansion and the acquisition of new markets and sources of raw materials would cure Japan's economic ills. Right-wing terrorism increased (3 of Japan's 11 prime ministers between 1918 and 1932 were assassinated), and in 1931 Japanese officers in Manchuria acted without government authorization in precipitating the Mukden Incident and occupying Manchuria. Unable to stop the army, the civilian government accepted the establishment of the puppet state of MANCHUKUO in February 1932. Three months later military and civilian bureaucrats replaced party politicians in leading the government. From then until August 1945, the succession of cabinets and the young emperor HIROHITO, who had succeeded to the throne in 1926, were essentially the tools of the military extremists.

World War II. Japanese economic and political penetration of northern China proceeded against minimal Chinese resistance until 1937. In July 1937, however, the Second Sino-Japanese War began with a clash at the Marco Polo bridge near Peking. By 1940 the Japanese controlled eastern China and had established a puppet regime at Nanking. In the same year Japan allied with the Axis powers of Germany and Italy, which were already at war in Europe.

Having occupied the northern part of French Indochina in 1940, Japanese troops moved into southern Indochina in July 1941. The United States and Britain reacted to this move by imposing a total trade embargo on Japan. Faced with economic strangulation, Japan had the choice of withdrawing from Indochina, and possibly China, or continuing its expansion in order to secure oil supplies from the Dutch East Indies. The latter alternative would mean war with the United States, and Prime Minister KONOE FUMIMARO negotiated to avoid that contingency. In October 1941, however, Konoe was replaced by the more militant Gen. TOJO HIDEKI. On Dec. 7, 1941, Japanese forces launched simultaneous attacks on PEARL HARBOR in Hawaii, the Philippines, Hong Kong, and Malaya. The United States immediately declared war, and WORLD WAR II entered its worldwide phase.

At first the Japanese forces achieved great success, conquer-

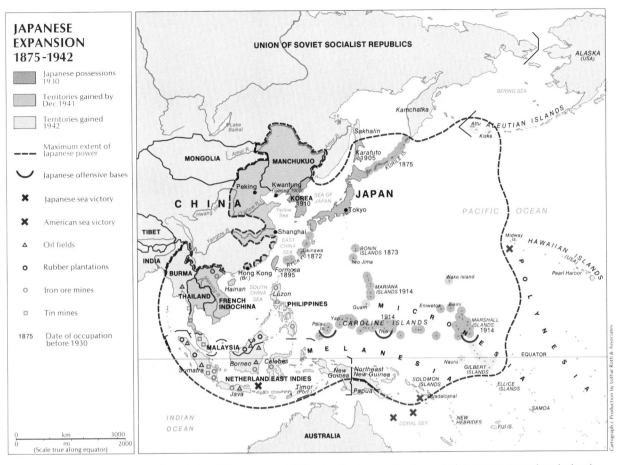

JAPANESE EXPANSION 1875-1942

Japanese possessions 1930

Territories gained by Dec. 1941

Territories gained 1942

Maximum extent of Japanese power

Japanese offensive bases

✖ Japanese sea victory

✖ American sea victory

△ Oil fields

○ Rubber plantations

◎ Iron ore mines

□ Tin mines

1875 Date of occupation before 1930

Cartograph c Production by Lothar Roth & Associates

This map shows Japanese expansion from the late 19th century until 1942, when the Japanese Empire reached its greatest extent. Japan's victories in the First Sino-Japanese (1894–95) and Russo-Japanese (1904–05) wars brought its first major territorial gains. In the 1930s, Japan began the systematic aggression that led to the Second Sino-Japanese War, and in the early years of World War II it overran most of Southeast Asia.

ing the Philippines, the Dutch East Indies, Malaya and Singapore, and Burma. The tide turned in June 1942, however, with the defeat of a Japanese fleet by the U.S. Navy at Midway Island in the Pacific. A war of attrition now began to force the Japanese back to their home islands. Japanese merchant shipping was disrupted, and industrial production declined as industries and cities were subjected to Allied bombing raids. Shortages of food and supplies increased along with military defeats. The atomic bombing of HIROSHIMA and Nagasaki on August 6 and 9 and the Soviet declaration of war on Aug. 8, 1945, were the final blows. Emperor Hirohito intervened and ordered the army to surrender unconditionally on Aug. 14, 1945.

Postwar Japan. The Allied occupation, under the command of U.S. Gen. Douglas MACARTHUR, lasted from 1945 to 1952 and resulted in political, social, and economic reforms. The emperor denied his divinity and was placed in a symbolic role. Government was democratized, and a new constitution with a bill of rights went into effect in 1947. Women received the vote and rights to property and divorce. The peerage was abolished, war criminals punished, and a massive purge of right-wing extremists (and later of Communists) conducted. The great *zaibatsu* concentrations of economic power were broken up, a major land reform was carried out, and education was liberalized. Article 9 of the constitution renounced the right to use force in foreign policy.

As millions of soldiers and civilians were repatriated from overseas, the devastated country experienced acute shortages of food, housing, clothing, and other goods and services. The government under YOSHIDA SHIGERU worked to implement re-

Kamikaze ("divine wind") forces were used during the last year of World War II as a new strategy for the failing Japanese military. Kamikaze pilots, who crashed their explosive-laden planes into enemy targets, first appeared (1944) at Leyte Gulf, the Philippines.

forms and achieve economic recovery. The outbreak of the Korean War (1950–53) aided that recovery by increasing Japanese exports. It also prompted the United States to press for rapid conclusion of a Japanese peace treaty. In 1951, Japan signed not only a peace treaty but a mutual defense treaty with the United States. It resumed full sovereignty in 1952 but continued to be very much under U.S. protection.

From 1954 until 1972 the Japanese economy expanded rapidly; the gross national product increased at a rate of over 10 percent annually. Building on its prewar industrial base, Japan imported modern technology and machinery. Factories were replaced, and economic development was the main focus of national policy. Central planning helped the government control the structure of the economy. Labor, resources, and capital were used where the growth potential was greatest, and by the early 1970s Japan was the world's largest producer of ships and a leader in the production of cars, steel, and electronic equipment.

Beginning in the 1960s the Liberal-Democrats, the conservative party that has dominated Japanese politics since 1954, began to feel increasing competition from the Socialist, Communist, Democratic-Socialist, and the Clean Government parties. Popular pressures for an improved quality of life and environmental protection challenged the emphasis on economic growth, and both right- and left-wing radicalism became more visible. Nonetheless, the Liberal-Democrats retained control, surviving a major corruption scandal that forced the resignation of Prime Minister TANAKA KAKUEI in 1974. The return of Okinawa, which had been under U.S. occupation since 1945, to Japan in 1972 signaled the end of Japanese subordination to the United States. Japan handled the U.S. rapprochement with Communist China in 1972 by establishing its own diplomatic ties with that long-time enemy. Highly dependent on imported petroleum, Japan also weathered the crises brought on by the Arab cutbacks in oil exports in 1973–74 and in the late 1970s, maintaining its position as the world's third-largest economy. The strong ties between Japan and the U.S. and European markets are likely to continue, while Japan's economic role in relation to the developing nations will probably increase. WILLIAM B. HAUSER

Bibliography: Beasley, W. G., *The Meiji Restoration* (1972) and *The Modern History of Japan,* 2d ed. (1974); Borton, Hugh, *Japan's Modern Century: From Perry to 1970,* 2d ed. (1970); Brown, Delmer M., *Nationalism in Japan* (1955); Duus, Peter, *The Rise of Modern Japan* (1976); Hall, John W., *Japan: From Pre-History to Modern Times* (1970); Latourette, Kenneth, *History of Japan,* rev. ed. (1957); Morton, W. Scott, *Japan: Its History and Culture* (1970); Murdoch, James, *A History of Japan,* 3 vols. (1926; repr. 1964); Neumann, William L., *America Encounters Japan* (1963); Reischauer, Edwin O., *Japan: The Story of a Nation,* rev. ed. (1974), and *The Japanese* (1977); Sansom, George A., *A History of Japan,* 3 vols. (1958–63), *Japan: A Short Cultural History,* rev. ed. (1962), and *The Western World and Japan* (1950; repr. 1974); Toland, John, *The Rising Sun: The Decline and Fall of the Japanese Empire, 1936–1945* (1970); Yoshida, Shigeru, *Japan's Decisive Century: 1867–1967* (1967).

Japan, Sea of

The Sea of Japan (Japanese: Nihon-Kai) separates the Japanese islands from the Asian mainland. It is about 1,600 km (1,000 mi) long, has an area of 1,000,000 km² (389,000 mi²), and reaches a maximum depth of 3,750 m (12,300 ft). The Tsushima archipelago and the shallow Korea Strait form its southwestern boundary. To the west are South and North Korea, and to the northwest, the USSR. The main Japanese island, Honshu, whose coastline is heavily industrialized, is located to the east. The sea's most important port is the Soviet city of Vladivostok. The sea is extensively fished.

Japan Trench: see OCEANIC TRENCHES.

Japanese art and architecture

The art and architecture of Japan bears the imprint of that country's unusual geographic location, separated from Korea by about 160 km (100 mi) and from China by about 800 km (500 mi). This location has both protected Japan from foreign

This terra-cotta figurine, dating from the late Jomon period of the first millennium BC, may represent a fertility symbol. The intricate and imaginative decoration and impressed cord-patterns are also characteristic of Jomon ware. Both the pottery and figurines of the late Jomon period are thought to reveal the influence of mainland cultures. (Takeo Nakazawa Collection, Tokyo.)

invasion and enabled its rulers to close or open the doors to contacts with other nations almost at will. Thus, during periods of cultural extroversion such as the 7th and 8th centuries, the 14th and 15th centuries, and, more recently, from 1868 to the present day, Japan has seen the massive influx of foreign culture. During such periods the arts produced in Japan have exemplified the adulation of foreign culture, whereas during the intervening periods of cultural introversion imported modes have become transformed into what can be considered to be typically Japanese art forms. In general, the latter display a lack of interest in rational philosophies and, instead, show a predominant concern for highly aesthetic and emotive forms. "Harmony is to be valued," said the influential royal art patron SHOTOKU TAISHI (c.593–622); perhaps this more than any other single concept may be said to lie at the heart of Japanese culture.

Early Cultures: Jomon, Yayoi, and Tumulus Periods. Evidence of Stone Age culture in Japan dates back at least to 70,000 BC. However, the earliest ceramic culture, known by its cord-pattern wares as Jomon, is now dated from about 7500 to 300 BC. The predominantly hunting-fishing-gathering culture of the Jomon people, which appears to have originated in northeast Asia, produced distinctive ceramic wares in a great number of small communities throughout Japan. These wares vary from the early conical and cylindrical types found in northeastern Japan and Hokkaido to the elaborately decorated, sculpturesque wares from the 4th and 3d millennia BC that are found principally in central Japan. From this period onward a number of small clay figurines are also found, which may be associated with fertility and mortuary rites. It appears also that by this time forms of primitive agriculture were practiced, particularly in central Japan, and that the more elaborate sculpturesque wares may have been associated with agricultural rituals. The wares of the late Jomon period (2d millennium to 500 BC) suggest a new influx of continental influence, notably in northeastern Japan.

The culture of the Yayoi people (c.300 BC–AD 300) shows a marked change in orientation and is more recognizably Japanese in character. Wet-rice cultivation and bronze technology appear to have been introduced from Korea by way of Kyushu. As opposed to the robust vigor of Jomon wares, Yayoi ceramics are made with finer clay, are turned on a wheel, and are generally more utilitarian in character, having more casual and at times elegant decoration. The large settlements of the Yayoi people, centered in southwestern and central Japan, appear to have become increasingly stratified under religious leaders. Bronze weapons, mirrors, and bells, originally close to their Asian prototypes, were evidently used in rituals that led to the exaggeration of their forms; the bells, especially, suggest the growth in authority of powerful clans that may have governed large areas.

During the Tumulus period, lasting from the 4th through the 6th century, the increasing concentration of power in the hands of the great clans of central Japan, symbolized by massive mounded tombs, culminated in the unification of the nation under the imperial clan. Whereas the artifacts such as mirrors found in the earlier tombs indicate continuation of the ritual orientation of the Yayoi culture, the later tombs contain equestrian trappings and weaponry suggestive of invasion or infiltration by a warlike Mongoloid people from northeast Asia. The culture of the later Tumulus period is most vividly represented in the *haniwa* clay figures that were set around the center and later the borders of the great tombs. These lively, mass-produced grave guardians include figures of shamans, crowned figures, soldiers, court ladies, dancers, houses, ships, and animals; they provide very literal images of the daily life of this period and, in addition, seem to indicate a much changed attitude toward the afterlife.

Mid-6th to Early 8th Century. In the mid-6th century, Buddhism and Chinese learning reached Japan in the form of official emissaries and gifts from the Korean kingdom of Paekche. After some resistance from native factions the acceptance of foreign learning and Buddhism was actively promoted by Prince Shotoku during his regency (593–622), heralding 200 years of regular contact with the Asian mainland. Monasteries such as the now-lost Hokoji and Wakakusa-dera were built and furnished with bronze images of Buddhas made by immigrant Korean artisans such as the Tori group. The *Shaka Triad* (Horyuji, Nara), made in 623 by Tori Busshi as a votive offering in memory of Prince Shotoku, is a fine example of the Korean version of styles found in early-6th-century sculptures at LUNG-MEN in China. Other statues from the first half of the 7th century preserved in the Horyuji include the painted wooden statues of the *Kudara Kwannon* and the *Yumedono Kwannon*, a popular deity of compassion and mercy, and the *Four Celestial Kings*, guardians of the four directions and protectors of the state.

In the latter half of the 7th and the early 8th century contact with China became more frequent, and the more refined and elegant sculptural styles of early-7th-century China are reflected in works such as the *Tachibana Shrine* (c.710; Horyuji, Nara). In this sculpture the complex iconography of Amida, the Buddha of the Western Paradise, is expressed in the triad of Amida and two bodhisattvas seated on lotus pedestals rising from a pond; behind them is a low-relief bronze screen depicting a tranquil scene of the souls reborn in the Western Paradise.

Nara Period (710–784). With the establishment in 710 of the new capital of NARA, modeled after Ch'ang-an, the Chinese capital during the T'ang dynasty (618–907), the building of temple-monasteries reached a peak. Older temples such as

(Left) *Juxtaposed with the kondo is the 7th-century Gojunoto, or five-storied pagoda, of the Horyuji temple and monastery compound. The pagoda, with its masonry foundation and exterior bracketing, is typical of the Buddhist-inspired Chinese architecture of the T'ang dynasty.*

(Below) *The detailed modeling of this mid-8th-century painted clay figure of the Shukongojin, a ferocious guardian deity brandishing a thunderbolt in the Hokkedo of the Todaiji, Nara, expresses the realistic treatment afforded the sculpture of the late Nara period.*

Avalokitesvara is the central figure of the mid-7th century wall painting of the Amida Triad in the kondo, or Golden Hall, of Nara's Horyuji Monastery. The introduction of Buddhism in the 7th century resulted in the increased cultural influence of China. This painting reflects the rich modeling and attention to ornamental detail characteristic of T'ang Chinese art.

the Yakushiji were rebuilt in the new site; the Horyuji, burned in 670 and rebuilt shortly afterward, was equipped with huge mural paintings in its Golden Hall, and many new temples were constructed. Dominant among them was the great Todaiji, whose colossal *Great Buddha*, or *Daibutsu*, a cast bronze image more than 16 m (53 ft) high, was completed in a grand opening ceremony in 752.

By contrast with the more introspective design of 7th-century temples in which a five-storied PAGODA had often occupied the central place, the centerpiece in the Todaiji is the great Golden Buddha Hall, now flanked by twin pagodas placed like watchtowers at the outer edges of the expansive courtyard. Resembling Chinese palaces, the compound was evidently designed to impress contemporaries as a symbol of the divine power of the emperor in his role as leading delegate of the Roshana (all-powerful) Buddha. Buddhist sculptures in such buildings, executed in bronze, painted clay, and dry lacquer, closely reflect Chinese prototypes in their vigorous blend of ideal and real forms; this is especially notable in the statues of guardian deities that often surrounded the central images on the altar. Other important relics of this period are the household effects of Emperor Shomu, dedicated by his wife to the Todaiji and stored in the temple storehouse known as the Shosoin in 756. These decorated objects, mostly Chinese imports, provide rich testimony of the cosmopolitan arts of T'ang China, reflecting T'ang contact with the Eastern Mediterranean, Persia, India, and Central Asia.

Early Heian Period (784–897). The early Heian period, named after the new capital at Heian-kyo (KYOTO), was strongly influenced by the introduction of esoteric Buddhism, or *Mikkyo*. Monasteries of the Tendai and Shingon sects were built outside the capital, often in remote locations such as Mt. Koya. The pantheon of esoteric deities that were represented in sculpture and painting led to a new burst of energy in the arts. MANDALA paintings, representations in diagram form of esoteric doctrines concerning the inseparable nature of the physical and spiritual universe, were executed on huge silk hangings, either drawn in gold and silver line or painted in a rich variety of colors. Groups of deities derived from the mandalas were represented in sculptural form within certain halls. Sculpture tended to be made from a single block of wood and became heavier and more sensuous in appearance, emphasizing solemnity and spiritual force. Among the deities favored for individual paintings, the images of the ferocious Fudo and the Five Mighty Bodhisattvas were worshiped individually or in groups of five.

Late Heian Period (897–1185). During the late Heian period, also called the Fujiwara period, PURE LAND BUDDHISM arose. This sect, with its beatific visions of the Western Paradise governed by the Buddha Amida, proved more attractive than the esoteric Buddhist sects to the aesthetic and pleasure-oriented Heian courtiers. Paintings centered attention on the welcoming figure of Amida and his heavenly troupe of music-making bodhisattvas coming to carry the believer to paradise at the moment of death. The same group was represented in sculptural form, now using a multiblock technique in wood that allowed for greater refinement of execution. The Hoodo or Phoenix Hall of the Byodoin temple at Uji, completed (1053) with sculpture by JOCHO and his studio, is a fine example of a Heian villagarden transformed into an enchanting image of paradise on earth.

The greatest achievement of the late Heian period may be said to lie in the development of native traditions in secular painting and CALLIGRAPHY. Satiated with deep drafts from the fount of T'ang culture during the Nara period, Japan was ready to sever its dependence on the continent; official contacts ceased after 894, and thereafter native traditions rapidly bloomed. During this period the term *yamato-e* ("paintings of Japanese themes") is recorded in connection with paintings of famous places and themes from Japanese poetry, as opposed to *kara-e* ("paintings of Chinese themes"). Although works from the 9th and 10th centuries are all lost, an 11th-century landscape painting on a folding screen from the Jingo-ji, Kyoto (now in the Kyoto National Museum), reveals an early blend of the two modes; the poet's hut in the foreground of the Chinese type of landscape scene is rendered in *kara-e* style, while the rolling hills behind reveal the emotive abstraction native to *yamato-e*.

Abbreviation of the cumbersome usage of Chinese characters as phonetic symbols led to the emergence of the phonetic kana script. This distinctive form of Japanese calligraphy developed at the hands of Heian noblewomen into a respectable mode for poems, diaries, and romances. The ability to compose short Japanese poems, written in a cultivated hand, became a requirement in social exchanges, resulting in the emergence in the 11th century of major masters of the kana script, such as Fujiwara no Yukinari. Thereafter, classical Japanese poems came to be rendered on increasingly finely decorated paper, as seen in the famous *Thirty-Six Poets* anthology (c.1120; Tokyo National Museum).

Heian noblewomen also appear to have originated a subtle style for illustrating their courtly romances. The horizontal hand-scroll illustrations (now widely dispersed) of Lady Murasaki's epic TALE OF GENJI (c.1010), produced by a team of painters and calligraphers working in the early 12th century, is the finest surviving example of the *onna-e* (ladies'-style painting). In largely interior scenes with the roofs removed, action is centered on the affairs of the heart. A symphonic array of human emotions, with a pervasive pathos, is conveyed by the carefully chosen postures and masklike facial expressions of the main characters. The inclining of diagonals and the slight disturbance of hangings provides occasional indications of tragedy, and rich opaque colors suggest mood.

In contrast to the delicate, emotive style of the Genji scrolls is the racy narrative style of *otoko-e* (gentlemen's-style painting), in which action is as lively as the humor of the caricature. This tradition, seen in works such as the *Legends of Mt. Shigi* scroll (late 12th century; Chogosonshiji, Nara), developed from the style of painting that appeared in 8th-century Buddhist propaganda scrolls. Another highly developed tradition of Buddhist scroll painting during the Heian period is that of the animal cartoons, in which frolicking animals parody the popular human entertainments of the day in witty, deftly drawn scenes.

The delicate beauty of the Hoodo, or Phoenix Hall, of the Byodoin temple at Uji, near Kyoto, built during the 11th century, reflects the "Pure Land" aesthetic of the Heian period. The Hoodo, which houses the sculptor Jocho's magnificent gilded wood image of the Amida Buddha, evokes the serenity and refinement of the Western Paradise.

This 12th-century illustration, traditionally attributed to Takayoshi, is from Lady Murasaki's Tale of Genji *(c.1010), the earliest complete novel in the world. The scrolls illustrating this work are among the finest examples of* yamato-e, *a style of painting that arose during the late Heian period. (Masuda Collection, Tokyo.)*

Kamakura Period (1185–1333). When the eastern-based Minamoto clan established supremacy in 1185, a new political capital was established at Kamakura. The reign of Minamoto YORITOMO, who gained the title of shogun (generalissimo) in 1192, marked the start of seven centuries of rule by military dictators. The rebuilding of the Nara temples of Todaiji and Kofukuji (destroyed by fire in 1180) provided opportunities for revitalization in religious art. The Todaiji restoration, aided partly by contributions from the new rulers and mainly by the popular fund-raising campaign of priest Chogen, included the recasting of the colossal bronze *Great Buddha* (1182–85), under the direction of technicians from Sung China, and the rebuilding of the Great Buddha Hall and the Great South Gate in a new Sung Chinese-inspired style known as *Tenjikuyo.*

The Nara-based school of sculptors descended from Jocho gained ascendancy in the competition for contracts during this period of rebuilding in Nara. Typified by Kokei, his son UNKEI, and Unkei's son Tankei, this school produced numerous works of sculpture in Nara and Kyoto. The new style represented a blending of the naturalistic vigor derived from Nara-period antecedents with a humanistic realism that evidently suited the pragmatic tenor of warrior-dominated society. A fine example is seen in Unkei's *Nio* (1203), one of the colossal wooden guardian figures standing at the Great South Gate of the Todaiji. As a result of renewed contact with China, Sung influence is also evident in Kamakura sculpture, notably in the works of Kaikei, whose style combines dignified realism with aesthetic grace.

In paintings as in sculpture, the trends toward greater realism and humanism favored the emergence of a lively tradition of realistic portraiture. The personalities of great generals such as Yoritomo, members of the aristocracy, and even the emperor were fully expressed in the new form of painting called *nise-e* ("likeness paintings") that emerged during the Kamakura period. New developments in narrative hand scrolls included a focus on the vigorous portrayal of military history such as the Heiji wars of 1159–60 and the abortive Mongol invasions of 1274 and 1281, and on the vivid and sometimes bizarre depiction of Buddhist hell scenes. Another popular subject of Kamakura scroll paintings were the biographies of famous evangelist priests, as seen in En-i's *Biography of Ippen Shonin* (1299; Tokyo National Museum), in which Sung Chinese influence is evident.

The transmission of ZEN BUDDHISM from China to Japan in the early 13th century created a significant new impetus in religious painting. The pragmatic, fundamentalist doctrines of Zen, stressing meditation as the most reliable path to realiza-

tion of Buddhahood, appealed to the warrior class, with the result that Chinese monks such as Lan-ch'i Tao-lung and Wu-hsüeh Tsu-yüan were invited to head the newly built Kenchoji (1253) and Enkakuji (1282) monasteries in Kamakura. With such figures came Sung monastic architectural style and a variety of painting styles associated with the Zen sect, notably the highly personalized portraits of Zen masters (*chinso*). By the early 14th century, Japanese monk-painters such as Mokuan (d. 1343) went to China for extended periods, becoming the direct inheritors of Ch'an (Zen) painting traditions in China. Prominent among such works were paintings of the free and uncommitted saints, eccentrics such as Pu-tai, Han-shan, and Shih-te. With the advent of Chinese literati monks such as I-shan I-ning (d. Japan, 1317), schooled in Chinese literature and philosophy, scholasticism began to flourish in Zen circles, resulting in literati-oriented paintings of orchids and bamboo by monks such as Tesshu (d. 1366) and Bonpo (1348–c.1420).

Muromachi (or Ashikaga) Period (1338–1573). The Ashikaga shoguns ruled from the Muromachi district of Kyoto beginning in 1338. They relied on Zen monks as intermediaries in

(Left) *the Daibutsu, or Great Buddha (1252) of the Kotoku temple at Kamakura is a heroic representation of the Amida Buddha.*

(Below) *The stylistic influence of the Sung dynasty is seen in such works of the late Heian period as* Portrait of Jion Daishi *(mid-11th century; Yakushiji, Nara). This silk painting is a cult image of a T'ang-dynasty priest frequently depicted in Sung art who was revered by members of the Japanese Hoos sect.*

(Left) *The decorative style which developed during the Momoyama period is exemplified by* Pine Trees and Eagle, *a screen attributed to Kano Eitoku. Characterized by bold, horizontal patterns and brilliant colors against a gold-leaf background, such works were designed to illuminate the interiors of the castles of the military leaders of the period. (Academy of Art, Tokyo.)*

foreign relations and were equally influenced by their tastes in literature and art. Collecting Chinese paintings and art objects became a passion with the shogun Yoshimitsu (1358-1408), who indulged in elaborate ceremonial displays of his collection, setting a pattern for later shoguns. The painters of the Ashikaga mortuary temple, the Shokokuji, came to form a virtual academy with a variety of functions, including the procuring of paintings for the shogun's collection. The priest-painters JOSETSU, SHUBUN, and their associates in the first half of the 15th century formulated a national style based on Chinese styles of the Southern Sung painting academy. A notable example is Shubun's *Studio of the Three Worthies*—pine, bamboo, and plum (1418; Seikado Foundation, Tokyo). This 15th-century tradition of "poem paintings," usually symbols of seclusion in the form of rustic huts, surmounted by numerous eulogies in Chinese verse, gradually gave way to an increasing interest in landscape painting for its own sake. Paintings on screens and sliding doors (*fusuma*) in monastic and secular buildings began to reflect the tastes of the shoguns. Nature themes such as the popular *Eight Views of the Hsiao and Hsiang Rivers*, as well as other paintings of landscape and of bird-and-flower motifs, tended to be arranged within a four-seasons frame reflecting native Japanese tastes; formal and more cursive styles were allocated according to the formal or less formal function of the rooms.

With the decline of centralized Ashikaga power beginning in the mid-1400s came diversified patronage in provincial courts. One of the greatest masters of landscape painting was SESSHU, who had studied at the Shokokuji, left Kyoto before the Onin civil war (1467-77), visited China with an official mission, and later settled in Yamaguchi, founding there an influential school of monochrome painting. Kenko Shokei, after studying in Kyoto with Geiami (1478-80), headed a school in Kamakura. Soga-school painters descended from Shubun's line worked for the Asakura clan in Echizen, and the Kano school, headed by MOTONOBU, developed a widely patronized decorative orthodoxy. The works of the 16th-century master SESSON, as exemplified in his boldly painted *Hawk on a Pine Tree* (Tokyo National Museum), presage trends toward more martial styles favored by the warring daimyos (great lords) of the succeeding Momoyama period.

Momoyama Period (1573-1614). The Kano school found its most eager patrons in the parvenu military dictators of the Momoyama period (so named after a grandiose castle of the ruler HIDEYOSHI). In 1576 the warlord NOBUNAGA commissioned Kano EITOKU to decorate his Azuchi castle with gigantic murals of flowering trees, Confucian sages, and other subjects. Although pillaged in 1582, Nobunaga's castle set a pattern of ostentatious decoration that was followed by his successor Hideyoshi in the decoration of Osaka castle (1582), the Jurakudai castle-palace (1587), and the Momoyama castle near Fushimi (1594). Eitoku and his pupils developed the *konpeki* style, using rich mineral colors over thick gold leaf to produce dazzling images of flowering trees, birds and flowers, and animals. Murals and screens in this bold, polychrome

(Right) *This early 17th-century teapot of Oribe ware, a thinly glazed ceramic, reflects the rough form and deliberately asymmetrical decoration favored during the Momoyama period. It was during this period that the ritual of the tea ceremony crystallized into a disciplined art. (Seattle Art Museum.)*

style were generally reserved for grand reception halls, whereas monochrome ink paintings in a vigorous decorative mode were often preferred for the more private rooms of the castle. These styles were further developed by SANRAKU and Sansetsu (1589-1651) in the early 17th century.

The drinking of green tea, introduced from China in the 12th century, was initially practiced by Zen monks to prevent drowsiness; by the Muromachi period the practice had become an elite form of secular gathering, known as the tea ceremony, at which imported art objects were often displayed. During the 15th century standards of taste associated with such gatherings became established by curator-painters attached to the shogun's household. In the Momoyama period, lavish ostentation gave way to more intimate gatherings at which the new patrons of art, the rich merchants of Sakai (Osaka) and Kyoto, could mingle with SAMURAI warriors on an equal basis.

A simple, mat-covered room in a rustic yet elegant hut within the confines of a small garden became a favored environment for appreciation of the tea-drinking ceremony and the few chosen art objects being displayed. The secluded, highly restrained Tai-an in Kyoto, designed by the great tea master Rikyu (1520-91), is a classic example of teahouse architecture. Humble Korean bowls came to be favored over the more refined Sung Chinese tea wares, and emotionally evocative paintings such as those by the famous Chinese artist MU CH'I became prime favorites. Increasing demand for tea wares led to the development of the native Japanese *Seto* and *Mino* wares, in which rustic simplicity belies a subtle charm. The organic, deliberately rough-textured *raku* wares of Kyoto, favored by Hideyoshi, are considered the epitome of the quality of *wabi* (quiet simplicity) that was inextricably linked with the cult of tea.

Early Edo Period (1615-88). Early in the 17th century, IEYASU established the capital of the Tokugawa shogunate at Edo (present-day Tokyo). During the early years of the Edo (or Tokugawa) period (1615-1868), a renaissance and transformation of Heian aristocratic traditions was achieved by the

(Right) *Ogata Korin illuminated the decorative style of the early Edo period with richly dramatic lacquer work and screens such as* Irises, *one of a pair of screens considered his masterpiece. The bold design and brilliant colors, unified by a golden background and reflecting elements of yamato-e style, are characteristic of Korin's work. (Nezu Museum, Tokyo.)*

school of decorative art and painting called Rimpa. A curious artistic alliance between courtly and upper bourgeois tastes appeared in the work of KOETSU, SOTATSU, and others, possibly as a reaction against the repressive feudal regime and the ostentatious, militaristic art forms demanded by its rulers. Honnami Koetsu emerged from a family of sword appraisers as a practitioner of the tea ceremony, *sarugaku* dance, and *renga* linked verse and a master of calligraphy. Granted (1615) an estate at Takagamine in Kyoto by the Tokugawa shogun, he presided over an artistic colony that produced decorated paper, lacquer ware, brushes, and ceramics. Koetsu's raku teabowls are considered among the most powerful and evocative ever produced, and his lacquers reveal an unfettered genius for design.

Koetsu's contemporary Sotatsu, master of the Tawaraya painting shop in Kyoto, produced paper for calligraphy and fans richly decorated with paintings evoking themes from Heian poetic romances. His screen paintings such as the work depicting the pine-topped islands of Matsushima (Freer Gallery, Washington, D.C.), one of Japan's most famous scenic views, demonstrate the lyricism of his masterly designs. His innovative ink wash techniques (*tarashikomi*) opened new directions for emotive expression. In the *Deer Scroll* (early 17th century; Seattle Art Museum), classical poems are inscribed by Koetsu on paper richly decorated with gold and silver renderings of deer herds by Sotatsu; in its bold approach to traditional subject matter, this collaborative work well exemplifies the early Edo-period rejuvenation of classical Japanese tastes in a free and ebullient contemporary style. Ogata KORIN, a major heir of this traditon, executed sumptuously decorated gold screens and lacquered objects characteristic of the extravagant tastes of the rich merchant class of his time. His brother Ogata KENZAN produced ceramics that combined dramatic designs with the conventions of calligraphy and lyrical painting.

The Tosho-gu mausoleum of Tokugawa Ieyasu at Nikko, built in 1617–19 and expanded (1634–36) by the third Tokugawa shogun, was designed with the express purpose of deifying in perpetuity the founder of the Tokugawa regime. Its extraordinarily ornate decoration with elaborate relief work and lavish use of gold, lacquer, and rich colors provides an overwhelming statement of shogunal power. A marked contrast is found in the classical elegance and restraint of the imperial villas of this period. The Katsura villa of Prince Hachijo Toshihito, built in the 1620s, is the earliest of these, combining an exquisite classical garden with rustic teahouses and dignified simplicity in the main residence. Closely related are the Sento Palace garden and Shugaku-in detached palace, in whose design Emperor Gomizuno-o, increasingly circumscribed by shogunal edicts, took an active part. Such villas symbolize the role of the court, now confined to the practice and patronage of a variety of fine arts.

Later Edo Period: Genroku Era (1688–1703) to 1868. The tradition of genre paintings featuring popular life and festivals, typified by screen compositions of life in and around Kyoto,

(Right) *One of the greatest ceramicists of the Edo period, Ogata Kenzan, Korin's brother, developed a highly personal art style in his wares, many of which were created for use in the tea ceremony. Kenzan's work is exemplified by this single peony motif accompanied by boldly executed calligraphy. (Nelson Gallery of Art and Atkins Museum of Fine Art, Kansas City, Mo.)*

(Below) *Miyagawa Choshun's painting,* A Beauty, *treats a subject characteristic of Ukiyo-e, the courtesan, as one of the representatives of the "floating," or transient, world. This style of genre painting culminated in the Ukiyo-e woodblock prints of the Genroku era.*

(Above) *Sharaku's satiric prints, exemplified by* The Actor Segawa Kikunojo *(1794), marked a culmination of the figural Ukiyo-e style of the late 1700s. (Private collection.)*

(Below) *The bold coloring and imaginative compositions that distinguish the work of Hokusai are seen in* "Mount Fuji on a Clear Day" *(c.1825), one of a series of prints contained in Thirty-Six Views of Mount Fuji (c.1823–29). Hokusai, considered one of the most brilliant representatives of the Ukiyo-e school of the early 19th century, contributed greatly to Ukiyo-e's increasing focus on national landscape. (Musée Guimet, Paris.)*

was patronized by both the feudal establishment and the urban bourgeoisie in the 16th and 17th centuries. Out of this tradition emerged the yet more popular art of UKIYO-E ("pictures of the floating world"). During the heyday of popular entertainment, the Genroku era (1688–1703), hand-colored woodblock prints began to appear celebrating the pleasures of the Yoshiwara or gay quarter of Edo. Thereafter, prints of individual courtesans and of popular theater, or KABUKI scenes, were produced in great numbers. Rudimentary color printing prevailed until Suzuki HARUNOBU's polychrome prints of 1765 elevated the medium to new levels of artistic expression. His lyrical, idealized female figures were later surpassed by the statuesque geisha type of Torii KIYONAGA. During this period Kitagawa UTAMARO perfected the languid sensuousness of his prints of beautiful women, and the greatest actor prints were produced, notably in the incisive, satirical work of Toshusai SHARAKU.

Sumptuary edicts prohibiting "licentious material" and restrictions on travel in the 18th century contributed to the rise of landscape prints; the prodigious genius of Katsushika HOKUSAI was expressed in such brilliantly innovative landscape series as the *Thirty-six Views of Mount Fuji* (c.1823–29), while Ando HIROSHIGE gave rein to a lyrical mode in works such as his *Fifty-three Stations of the Tokaido* (1833). Following the printmakers' experiments with "perspective prints" based on Dutch prints, the 18th-century painter Maruyama OKYO adapted Western naturalist methods to the medium of decorative paintings, founding the Kyoto Shijo school. Ito Jakuchu (1713–1800) combined zoological curiosity with dynamic design in sharply delineated, brocadelike paintings such as *Fowl and Hydrangea* (Imperial Household Collection, Tokyo).

The 18th century also saw the rise of the "southern school" (*nanga*) painters, inspired by literati painting traditions in China. Early masters such as Gion Nankai (1687–1761) emerged from among scholars serving in the Confucian schools. With the spread in Japan of Chinese painting manuals such as the *Mustard Seed Garden*, the presence of Chinese painters in Nagasaki, and the influence of erudite Chinese monks at monasteries near Kyoto, the literati movement gained momentum among the urban bourgeoisie as a sanctioned alternative to the academic traditions of the KANO school. Ike no TAIGA's eclectic blend of Chinese and native Rimpa traditions during a career of extraordinary creativity served to define the nature of the *nanga* school in Japan. Yosa no BUSON, who became a noted master of haiku, contributed

to *nanga* a poetic and intimate spirit more attuned to native aesthetics. The personal spirit of the modern age began to assert itself in the evocative works of Uragami GYOKUDO and the uninhibited style of Mokubei (1767–1833). In Edo the passion for Western learning sparked the Western influence on *nanga* seen in the works of Tani BUNCHO and Kazan (1793–1841).

Modern Period (1868 to the Present). The determined modernization of Japan during the Meiji period (1868–1912) was accompanied by the rapid introduction of an enormous variety of European forms of art and architecture. Palatial buildings, such as Tokyo's Akasaka palace, modeled (1909) after Versailles, appeared in many large cities. With later political developments, increasingly national adaptations of Western forms of architecture emerged as Japan approached World War II. Sculpture revealed a similar hybrid variety of Western-oriented forms, closely reflecting rapid social and political changes. In painting the most lasting of the hybrid forms emerged, in part through the encouragement of the American scholar Ernest FENOLLOSA. In this tradition, called *nihonga* ("Japanese painting"), traditional pigments and an instinct for emotive design are combined with techniques of Western realism. The works of painting masters such as Yokoyama Taikan (1868–1958), Kobayashi Kokei (1883–1957), and Maeda Seison (1885–1977) preserve most clearly the cultural identity of Japan through a period of extraordinary change and diversity.

RICHARD STANLEY-BAKER

Bibliography:

GENERAL WORKS: *The Heibonsha Survey of Japanese Art,* 31 vols. (1972–76); Murase, Miyeko, *The Arts of Japan* (1977); Paine, Robert T., and Soper, Alexander C., *Art and Architecture of Japan,* rev. ed. (1975); Swann, Peter C., *An Introduction to the Art of Japan* (1958); Warner, Langdon, *The Enduring Art of Japan* (1952); Yashiro, Yukio, *2000 Years of Japanese Art* (1958).

SPECIAL STUDIES: Akiyama, Terukazu, *Japanese Painting* (1961); Alex, William, *Japanese Architecture* (1963); Ienaga, Saburo, *Japanese Art: A Cultural Appreciation,* trans. by Richard L. Gage (1978) and *Painting in the Yamato Style* (1973); Kawakita, Michiaki, *Modern Currents in Japanese Art,* trans. by Charles S. Terry (1974); Kidder, Jonathan Edward, *Early Japanese Art* (1964) and *Japanese Temples* (1964); Michener, James A., *Japanese Prints: From the Early Masters to the Modern* (1963); Munsterberg, Hugo, *The Art of Modern Japan* (1978) and *Folk Arts of Japan* (1958); Noma, Seiroku, *The Arts of Japan: Ancient and Medieval,* trans. by John Rosenfield (1966); Swann, Peter, C., *The Art of Japan:*

From Joman to the Tokugawa Period (1966); Teiji, Ito, *Traditional Domestic Architecture of Japan* (1972); Tempel, Egon, *New Japanese Architecture* (1970); Toda, Kenji, *Japanese Painting* (1970).

Japanese beetle

Japanese beetles, *Popillia japonica*, are small, shiny beetles that were accidentally brought into the United States from Japan in the early 1900s and are now serious pests to many agricultural and ornamental plants. The beetles range in color from metallic green to bronze or copper.

Japanese bobtail cat

The Japanese bobtail, Japan's traditional good-luck cat, is a brightly colored calico with a truncated "pom-pom" tail.

The Japanese bobtail cat is an old breed unrelated to the somewhat similar Manx cat. Like the Manx, its hind legs are longer than the front ones, but when the Japanese bobtail stands relaxed, its hind legs are kept slightly bent so that the back is almost level. Its tail, never absent as in the Manx, is short, about 5 to 7.5 cm (2 to 3 in) long. The bobtail's coat comes in a variety of colors, but in Japan the traditional *Mi-Ke* is a tricolor of black, red, and white. The Japanese bobtail cat was brought to the United States about 1968.

EVERETT SENTMAN

Japanese chin

The Japanese chin, or spaniel, with its short muzzle, long-haired coat, and curved, plumy tail, resembles the more popular Pekingese. Originating in China but developing in Japan, this breed was introduced to the West when four of the toy dogs were given to Commodore Perry by the emperor of Japan in 1853.

The Japanese chin was registered with the American Kennel Club as the Japanese spaniel until 1977, when its name was officially changed to Japanese chin. There is little doubt that the Japanese chin, the Pekingese, and several other related breeds are of ancient Chinese origin and that the Japanese chin reached Japan long ago. The Japanese chin is a small, long-legged, long-coated breed. It has a short muzzle, prominent eyes, a large forehead, and a plumed tail carried over its back. The Japanese chin may reach 25 cm (10 in) in height at the shoulders and 4 kg (9 lb) in weight. Its coat color is white with reddish or black markings.

JOHN MANDEVILLE

Japanese giant salamander

The Japanese giant salamander, *Andrias japonicus*, of the family Cryptobranchidae, is the world's largest salamander, reaching a length of 1.6 m (5.25 ft). It is long-lived; the first living specimen ever sent to Europe was maintained for 52 years. This salamander is found only on the southern end of the Japanese island of Honshu, in cold mountain streams. The skin of this species contains many blood vessels and is apparently used in respiration, absorbing oxygen from the water. The Japanese giant salamander retains certain larval features. Fertilization is external.

JONATHAN CAMPBELL

See also: HELLBENDER.

Japanese language

Japanese is the language of nearly 115 million people living on the four home islands of Honshu, Kyushu, Shikoku, and Hokkaido, as well as on Okinawa and many other smaller islands to the south. It is also the native language of many residents of Hawaii, Brazil, and several other parts of the world that have had significant numbers of Japanese immigrants.

The earliest written records of Japanese consist of a few names appearing in late 5th-century inscriptions; the first substantial literary texts date from the 8th century. The language of the earliest texts is called Old Japanese. Middle Japanese extends to the end of the 16th century, bridging the wide differences in grammar and lexicon between Old Japanese and the modern language, the earliest forms of which appear in texts from about 1600. Old Japanese differed from both Middle and modern Japanese in many ways. Its sound system, for example, had eight different vowels, while the present-day language of Tokyo has only five. Old Japanese, however, lacked the contrast between long and short vowels that is so important to modern Japanese.

In all its historical forms Japanese is now understood to be one of the branches of the URAI-AITAIC family, the major language stock of Asia. Thousands of languages resulted from the prehistoric breakup and diffusion of Ural-Altaic; some of the important present-day representatives are Turkish, Mongolian, Manchu, and Korean as well as Japanese.

Old Japanese made a sharp distinction between the standard, prestige language of the court at Nara and what were already designated the Eastern dialects. Similar distinctions have been important in Japanese ever since. The many surviving dialects of modern Japan are classified as those of Eastern Japan, with Tokyo as the focal point; those of Western Japan, in the area of Osaka and Kyoto; and those of the island of Kyushu.

Since the middle of the last century, however, the language of an educated elite in Tokyo has been used as the official standard in schools, for most writing, and more recently, on radio and television. As a result of this official policy, the Tokyo language is rapidly replacing local dialects and now serves as a common medium for all regions. The past century has also seen an increasingly strong tendency to employ, for literary purposes, forms close to those of the spoken language. In earlier periods, literary forms were clearly differentiated from those used in speech.

Since earliest times Japanese has been written with characters borrowed from China. Phonetic signs were later added to this script by altering and simplifying a few of the borrowed Chinese characters; today both the original Chinese characters and the Japanese phonetic signs are used together in the most complex writing system of any developed nation. Minimal basic literacy for the modern language requires mastery of at least 1,850 different characters. Despite the obvious economic and educational burden of such a system, no significant movement is afoot to abolish or even significantly reform the traditional writing.

ROY ANDREW MILLER

Bibliography: Chaplin, Hamako Ito, *A Manual of Japanese Writing*, 3 vols. (1967); Jorden, Eleanor H., *Beginning Japanese*, 2 vols. (1962–63); Martin, Samuel E., *A Reference Grammar of Japanese* (1975); Miller, Roy Andrew, *The Japanese Language* (1967), and *Japanese and the Other Altaic Languages* (1971).

Japanese literature

Japanese literature is noteworthy for the rapidity with which it began to flourish after the development of a writing system, for its rich variety of literary forms, and for its continuing vitality and complex development under the influence of Western literature. The major work of classical Japanese literature is the early-11th-century novel TALE OF GENJI (Eng. trans., 1925-33), considered by many critics to be the first true novel of psychological depth and complexity written anywhere in the world.

The style of NŌ DRAMA, or Noh drama—restrained dance drama with lyrical, poetic texts and masked actors—has excited considerable interest in the modern West, exerting influence on Ezra Pound and W. B. Yeats. The 17-syllable poetic form, the HAIKU, has become well known outside Japan through its influence on symbolist poets, and the works of many modern Japanese novelists have found a wide Western audience through translation.

The Heian period (794-1185), which takes its name from the establishment of the capital at Heian-kyō, was the high point of purely indigenous prose fiction. Poetry in the classical 31-syllable *waka* form flourished between the 10th and 14th centuries, in part because of imperially commissioned anthologies. The most famous of these were the *Kokinshū* of 905 (Eng. trans., 1922) and the *Shinkokinshu* of 1205. The great dramatic works of Nō date from the 14th and 15th centuries, while the 17th and 18th centuries were the peak period for the BUNRAKU and KABUKI theaters.

Beginnings. The origins of Japanese literature lie in oral poetry and mythology, and the earliest surviving work in Japanese, the *Kojiki* (Record of Ancient Matters), transforms such myths into written form, explaining the cosmology of the Japanese and justifying the legitimacy of the ruling house as descendants of the sun goddess. The mid-8th-century *Man'yōshu* (Collection of Ten Thousand Leaves) is a compendium of some 4,500 poems in several forms, including both *waka* and longer poems.

The idea of compiling such early works was unquestionably inspired by Chinese models, but these two works mark the beginning of native Japanese literature and are written in a cumbersome writing system based on Chinese in which the characters are used sometimes for their meanings and sometimes for sound alone.

By the 9th century the development of *kana*, a syllabic writing system better suited to Japanese, helped foster advances in prose forms. The early-10th-century work *Tales of Ise* (Eng. trans., 1968) is a collection of poems with long prose contexts. *The Tosa Diary* (936; Eng. trans., 1912) is a prose travel diary by the courtier-poet Ki no Tsurayuki, who maintained the ruse of being a woman writer; in fact, the greatest prose works of the period were produced by women. Most famous are *The Tale of Genji* by MURASAKI SHIKIBU and *The Pillow Book* (c.1000; Eng. trans., 1967), a miscellany of various short comments by Sei Shōnagon (b. c.966).

A Period of Instability. The Gempei wars of 1180-85 brought an end to the comfortable, aesthetic life of courtier-poets and court ladies writing in the capital. These battles, in turn, were the subject of Japan's major epic, the *Tale of the Heike* (Eng. trans., 1975), a work of complex mixed oral and written origins that reached its current form in 1371. Collections of short tales, some religious, some secular in nature, enjoyed continuing popularity.

A few significant 14th-century works also continued the classical literary style. Most notable of these are *The Confessions of Lady Nijō* (1306; Eng. trans., 1973), by the imperial consort, Lady Nijō, and *Essays in Idleness* (c.1340; Eng. trans., 1967), by the Buddhist monk Yoshida Kenkō. Under government patronage, and largely through the writings of ZEAMI MOTOKIYO, Nō drama was transformed from rural folk entertainment into a highly literary, dramatic art that is still frequently performed today.

The Tokugawa Period. Some of the most notable works of the Tokugawa period (named after the shogun, or military governor, Tokugawa Iyeyasu and his successors of 1600-1867)

include the *haiku* and poetic travel accounts of BASHŌ; the plays of CHIKAMATSU MONZAEMON, author of Bunraku puppet texts of lasting literary value; and the witty fiction of IHARA SAIKAKU, with its dominant themes of lust and greed. Later Tokugawa fiction is best represented by the writings of UEDA AKINARI and Takizawa Bakin (1767-1848), whose work shows some influence from the flourishing Kabuki theater.

The Modern Period. Japanese literature of the modern period (1868 to the present) has absorbed the influence of Russian, Western European, and American literature while retaining a characteristically Japanese flavor. TSUBOUCHI SHŌYŌ published a critical monograph, *Shōsetsu Shinzui* (The Essence of the Novel, 1886), which introduced many ideas from Victorian literary criticism as standards for creating a modern style of literature for Japan.

Japanese critics of modern indigenous literature identify numerous schools, many related, in name at least, to various foreign trends. Regardless of school, however, much modern Japanese literature follows the first-person, *shi shosetsu* ("I-novel"), form.

Among well-known modern authors, MORI ŌGAI wrote novels that were often heavily romantic in mood, some based on his experiences in Germany, others dealing with events in Japanese history. The naturalist SHIMAZAKI TŌSON is best known for *The Broken Commandment* (1906; Eng. trans., 1974), which deals with problems of discrimination in society. NATSUME SOSEKI's introspective, philosophical novels have assured his enduring public esteem. ABE KŌBŌ has produced surrealistic fiction and drama greatly influenced by Western avant-garde literature. Both TANIZAKI JUNICHIRO and the Nobel-Prize-winning KAWABATA YASUNARI, prolific writers whose careers spanned the years of the Second World War, have been extensively translated into English. The works of MISHIMA YUKIO—whose life of right-wing political activity, and eventual public suicide, electrified the nation—have also found an enthusiastic foreign audience. Comtemporary authors continue to produce a vast output of works in varied styles for an enthusiastic audience of avid readers.   SUSAN MATISOFF

Bibliography: Hibbett, Howard, *The Floating World in Japanese Fiction* (1959; repr. 1974) and, as ed., *Contemporary Japanese Literature* (1977); Hisamatsu, Sen Ichi, *Biographical Dictionary of Japanese Literature* (1976); Keene, Donald, *Japanese Literature: An Introduction for Western Readers* (1955), *Modern Japanese Novels and the West* (1961), *World Within Walls: Japanese Literature of the Pre-Modern Era, 1600-1867* (1976), and, as ed., *Anthology of Japanese Literature*, 2 vols. (1955, 1956); Janeira, A. M., *Japanese and Western Literature: A Comparative Study* (1970); Miner, Earl, *An Introduction to Japanese Court Poetry* (1961); Miyoshi, Masao, *Accomplices of Silence: The Modern Japanese Novel* (1974); Morris, Ivan, ed., *Modern Japanese Stories* (1961) and, as ed., *Dictionary of Selected Forms in Classical Japanese Literature* (1966); Putzar, Edward, *Japanese Literature: An Historical Outline* (1973); Rimer, J. Thomas, *Modern Japanese Fiction and Its Traditions* (1978); Yamanouchi, H., *The Search for Authenticity in Modern Japanese Literature* (1978).

Japanese music

The history of Japanese music begins in the 8th century. Music styles in Japan, like those of the West, have changed frequently in the last thousand years. Common characteristics found throughout this period, however, are as follows: (1) scales with five-tone (pentatonic) cores plus two auxiliary tones; (2) a chamber music sound ideal in which instruments can be heard separately rather than merged as in Western orchestras; (3) a maximum effect from a minimum amount of sound material; (4) music closely allied to verbal expression; (5) aural learning with limited use of detailed notations; (6) through-composed forms rather than forms that repeat or return to previous themes or sections; (7) an emphasis on melodic or rhythmic tension, with little harmony in the Western sense; (8) the use of melodic or rhythmic stereotyped patterns that tend to move in progressions, producing a sense of forward motion like that created in Western music by chords; and (9) a greater interest in the combination of standard materials than in "originality." Examples of these characteristics are described in the following survey.

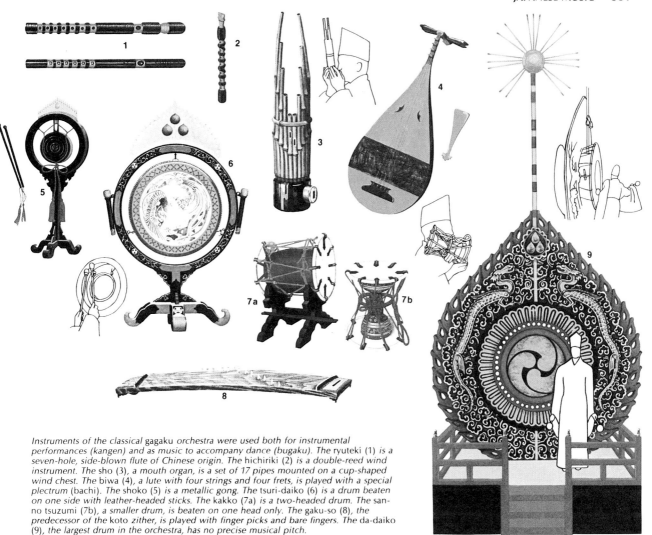

Instruments of the classical gagaku orchestra were used both for instrumental performances (kangen) and as music to accompany dance (bugaku). The ryuteki (1) is a seven-hole, side-blown flute of Chinese origin. The hichiriki (2) is a double-reed wind instrument. The sho (3), a mouth organ, is a set of 17 pipes mounted on a cup-shaped wind chest. The biwa (4), a lute with four strings and four frets, is played with a special plectrum (bachi). The shoko (5) is a metallic gong. The tsuri-daiko (6) is a drum beaten on one side with leather-headed sticks. The kakko (7a) is a two-headed drum. The san-no tsuzumi (7b), a smaller drum, is beaten on one head only. The gaku-so (8), the predecessor of the koto zither, is played with finger picks and bare fingers. The da-daiko (9), the largest drum in the orchestra, has no precise musical pitch.

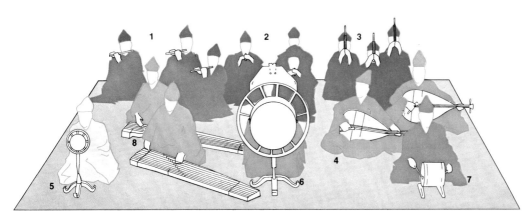

A classical Japanese gagaku orchestra is arranged in playing position, with percussion, wind, and string instruments. Gagaku was the official court music of Japan during the Nara (710–84) and Heian (794–1185) periods. Numbered parts include: three ryuteki (1), three hichiriki (2), three sho pipes (3), two biwa (4), one shoko (5), one tsuri-daiko (6), one kakko (7), two gaku-so (8).

The ryo and ritsu scales are derived from Buddhist chant (shomyo) and court music (gagaku), the first known sources of Japanese music. They originally came from Korea and China and gradually became "Japanized."

Ryo, like the yo scale of Japanese folk music, is close to Chinese models, whereas ritsu seems more Japanese in character. The in scale is commonly found in folk songs and in music after 1500.

Although gagaku orchestras include wind, string, and percussion instruments, their sound is similar to chamber music. The melody is played by flutes (ryuteki or komabue) and oboes (hichiriki); but the tone qualities and versions of the melody played by those two instruments are not the same, and thus they are heard separately. The mouth organ (sho) plays tone clusters to create another texture. The 13-stringed zither (koto) and the pear-shaped lute (biwa) play stereotyped patterns that mark off musical phrases, as do the sounds of the large hanging drum (*tsuri-daiko*), a small gong (*shoko*), and a horizontal drum struck on two heads (the *kakko* or the *san-no tsuzumi*). Flute and oboe notation consists of fingerings and dots to indicate basic percussion phrase markings, plus mnemonic syllables (*soga*). The parts are learned by singing the syllables before actually playing the instrument.

Maximum effect from minimum material is illustrated by the 14th- and 15th-century NŌ DRAMA. It uses few actors plus a unison chorus (*ji*) and an ensemble (*hayashi*) of flute (*nokan*), shoulder drum (*ko tsuzumi*), hip drum (*o tsuzumi*), and, in dance sections, a stick drum (*taiko*). The flute signals formal divisions or adds color while the drums play stereotyped patterns (*tetsuke*) in set orders.

When accompanying singing, these instruments also help to mark off the three-part divisions of a line that relate to the basic *jo* (introduction), *ha* (scattering), and *kyu* (rushing) formal design found in much Japanese music. Nō music, like most Japanese forms, is totally set and without improvisation, although there are different versions of the same piece in various guilds of musicians.

The *yo* and *in* scales appear frequently after 1500 as do solo instrumental pieces for the *shakuhachi* (end-blown flute) and the koto. *Sankyoku*, a genre of chamber music, is played by the koto combined with a plucked three-stringed samisen (or shamisen) and a *shakuhachi* or a bowed lute (*kokyu*). A vocal part is common, and even purely instrumental pieces tend to have evocative titles such as "Sound of the Deer" or "The Plover Bird."

In the puppet theater (*bunraku*) a narrative shamisen music is essential, whereas the KABUKI theater contains both narrative and lyrical genres, particularly *kiyomoto* and *nagauta*. Each genre uses a different shamisen, voice quality, and performer.

In dance pieces the singers and shamisen combine with the *hayashi* instruments of Nō drama. Off-stage music (*geza*) also adds color and meaning to the drama.

Since 1868, Western and traditional music (*hogaku*) have existed together in Japan. Public school music is primarily Western-oriented, although young people since the mid-20th century have shown increasing interest in indigenous styles. Today the best of both musical worlds can be heard in Japan.

WILLIAM P. MALM

Bibliography: Harich-Schneider, Eta, *A History of Japanese Music* (1973) and *Rōei: The Medieval Court Songs of Japan* (1965); Kishibe, Shigeo, *The Traditional Music of Japan* (1966); Malm, William, *Japanese Music and Musical Instruments* (1959) and *Nagauta: The Heart of Kabuki Music* (1963; repr. 1973); Piggot, Francis, *The Music and Musical Instruments of Japan* (1893; repr. 1971); Tanabe Hisao, *Japanese Music*, rev. ed. (1959).

Japanese mythology: see MYTHOLOGY.

Japanese newspapers

Japan has three national newspapers, all published in Tokyo: *Asahi Shimbun* ("the rising sun newspaper," 11.7 million circulation), *Yomiuri Shimbun* ("the read-and-sell newspaper," 9 million circulation), and *Mainichi Shimbun* ("the daily newspaper," 7 million circulation), which all publish morning and afternoon editions and account for half of the daily newspaper circulation in Japan. There are 110 other dailies, of which 13 are devoted to sports.

Japanese pagoda tree

Despite its name, the Japanese pagoda tree, *Sophora japonica*, is native to China and Korea. It is a member of the pea family, Leguminosae, and grows to 24 m (80 ft) high. Its leaves, which are shed in the fall, are divided into three to eight pairs of leaflets.

From July to September the tree bears yellowish white flowers in long clusters. The seed pods are about 8 cm (3 in) long and are narrowed between the seeds, giving them a necklace-like appearance.

The Japanese pagoda tree, Sophora japonica, *has yellowish white flowers and leaves divided into 7 to 17 oval leaflets. The fruit pods (right) are constricted between the seeds.*

Japanese universities

Universities in Japan were established as early as the 8th century AD, but it was only following the MEIJI RESTORATION (1868) that they began to assume their contemporary form. In 1877 the new government established the University of Tokyo by consolidating and restructuring several earlier institutions. In addition, the government established other institutions of research and higher education. At about the same time, a number of private individuals and groups also established educational institutions that eventually became universities. Initially all of these institutions, which sought to train civil servants and to introduce Western knowledge to Japan, enjoyed a similar status. In the early 1880s, however, the government began to solidify its program for national development, and, as a result, all state institutions of learning were favored.

In higher education the University of Tokyo was the only officially approved university. Founded in 1877, it was renamed the Imperial University in 1886 and was reorganized into faculties of law, letters, science, and medicine. By 1891, faculties of agriculture and engineering had been added, making it the first major institution in the world to grant university status to both these subjects. Japanese nationals replaced foreign personnel, and Japanese became the language of instruction. Subsequently, the government established six other imperial universities as well as a large number of lesser institutions. All were arranged in a generally recognized hierarchy, with the most important and prestigious institution, the University of Tokyo, receiving the largest budget and its graduates securing the most attractive jobs. This tradition continues today, with the result that nearly three-fourths of Japan's top civil servants are University of Tokyo graduates. Private institutions do not receive state subsidies. They make up a separate hierarchy, however, with Keio and Waseda universities at the top. Graduates largely join the private sector.

Japan's higher educational system underwent a major reform during the post–World War II American occupation so that in its more formal aspects it became similar to the American system. The university course of study was changed to four years to include a general education and a specialized education sequence. Junior colleges and graduate school courses were recognized; all prewar institutions had to be reorganized to conform to these regulations. In 1962 a new technical college, which provides a 5-year course for junior high school graduates, was recognized.

Enrollment of 250,000 students was recorded in all levels of higher education when the new university system started in 1950, and by 1976 there were over 2 million students, or 38 percent of all college-aged youth. The Japanese Ministry of Education provides the most recent (1975) data on the number of institutions and students:

NUMBER OF INSTITUTIONS

	National	Public	Private	Total
Technical colleges	54	4	7	65
Junior colleges	31	48	434	513
4-year universities	81	34	305	420
Total	166	86	746	998

NUMBER OF STUDENTS

	National	Public	Private	Total
Technical colleges	38,194	3,942	5,819	47,955
Junior colleges	13,143	17,973	322,666	353,782
4-year universities	357,772	50,880	1,325,430	1,734,082
Graduate schools	27,735	2,323	18,406	48,464
Total	436,844	75,118	1,672,321	2,184,283

This expansion has transformed Japanese higher education from an elitist system to one that enables young people from diverse social backgrounds to consider further education. Nevertheless, the traditional hierarchy remains, and many students apply to the most prestigious institutions.

TABLE 2: JAPANESE UNIVERSITIES

University and Location	Date Founded	Enrollment
National Universities		
Chiba University	1949	8,400
Hirosaki University	1949	4,300
Hiroshima University	1949	9,800
Hitotsubashi University, Tokyo	1875	4,000
Hokkaido University, Sapporo	1876	12,000
Kobe University	1949	11,100
Kyoto University	1897	15,100
Kyushu University, Fukuoka	1911	11,800
Nagasaki University	1949	5,500
Nagoya University	1939	8,700
Okayama University	1949	7,300
Osaka University	1931	13,000
University of the Ryukyus, Okinawa	1950	4,900
University of Tokyo	1877	19,000
Tokyo Metropolitan University	1949	4,500
Yamaguchi University	1949	7,000
Private Universities		
Chuo University, Tokyo	1885	35,100
Doshisha University, Kyoto	1875	20,900
Fukuoka University	1934	24,700
Hosei University, Tokyo	1880	30,700
Keio University, Tokyo	1858	26,000
Meiji University, Tokyo	1881	33,400
Nihon University, Tokyo	1889	102,200
Rikkyo University, Tokyo (St. Paul's University)	1874	13,000
Ryukoku University, Tokyo	1900	7,100
Tokai University, Tokyo	1942	27,600
Waseda University, Tokyo	1882	46,700

Various inadequacies in the educational programs of the universities, the high tuitions and special assessments charged by private universities, and general social problems have all contributed to the student protests that have periodically erupted on Japan's campuses. In the late 1960s these protests were so severe that at one point 144 universities temporarily suspended instruction. As a result, in 1970 the central government began to have public aid channeled to private institutions. Many universities took steps to democratize and rationalize their decision-making structures. Today Japan's universities are placing special emphasis on promoting more student and staff exchanges with overseas institutions in order to create more international educational and research environments.　　　　WILLIAM K. CUMMINGS

Bibliography: Aso, Makoto, and Amano, Ikuo, *Education and Japan's Modernization* (1972); Cummings, William K., Amano, Ikuo, and Kita-

mura, K., eds., *Changes in the Japanese University* (1979); Dowsey, Stuart J., *Zengakuren: Japan's Revolutionary Students* (1970); Nagai, Michio, *Higher Education in Japan: Its Takeoff and Crash* (1971); Passin, Herbert, *Society and Education in Japan* (1965).

Jarmo [jar'-moh]

Jarmo is an archaeological site named after the Kurdish village of Qallat Jarmo in the foothills of northern Iraq, about 55 km (35 mi) east of Kirkuk. It was excavated by the American archaeologist Robert BRAIDWOOD in 1948-55. Dated c.6750 BC, this early Neolithic settlement is important for its evidences of early plant and animal domestication. Excavators estimate that the total Neolithic population of Jarmo at any one time was as many as 150 people, living in 25 houses on about 1.5 ha (4 acres). Two kinds of domesticated wheat were found, and domesticated sheep and goats were identified. Braidwood's work at Jarmo formed the basis for his hypothesis that plant domestication and early farming in the Near East originated in the hilly flanks of northern Iraq's Zagros Mountains.　　　　RALPH S. SOLECKI

Bibliography: Braidwood, R. J., and Howe, Bruce, *Prehistoric Investigations in Iraqi Kurdistan* (1960).

Jarrell, Randall [jair'-ul]

One of the most accomplished of a gifted generation of American poets, Randall Jarrell, b. Nashville, Tenn., May 16, 1914, d. Oct. 15, 1965 (possibly a suicide), published his first book of poetry, *Blood from a Stranger*, in 1942. He then enlisted in the U.S. Air Force, serving for the remainder of World War II as a pilot or pilot trainer. The war loomed large in his second and third collections, *Little Friend, Little Friend* (1945) and *Losses* (1948); in many ways Jarrell remained a poet of suffering and loss. His works deal with people who are psychologically oppressed, trapped by guilt or bedeviled by fantasies, partly of their own making yet clearly beyond their control. His two final volumes, *The Woman at the Washington Zoo* (1960) and *The Lost World* (1965), turned to a world of children and of pained adults who are overwhelmed by their social destinies and mental struggles.

Jarrell taught English at several colleges, for 18 years (1947-65) at the University of North Carolina in Greensboro, and he was considered a brilliant critic. Two of his collections of essays, *Poetry and the Age* (1953) and *A Sad Heart at the Supermarket* (1962), were widely applauded, and a posthumous volume, *The Third Book of Criticism* (1969), contains many valuable insights. He was also a gifted translator of German poetry. *The Complete Poems* of Randall Jarrell was published in 1969.　　　　CHARLES MOLESWORTH

Bibliography: Ferguson, Suzanne, *The Poetry of Randall Jarrell* (1971); Lowell, Robert, et al., eds., *Randall Jarrell, 1914-1965* (1967); Rosenthal, M. L., *Randall Jarrell* (1972).

Jarry, Alfred [zhah-ree', ahl-fred']

Alfred Jarry, b. Sept. 8, 1873, d. Nov. 15, 1907, was a highly eccentric French dramatist, poet, and humorist who invented a pseudophilosophical system called "pataphysics," or the science of imaginary solutions. He is best known for his series of Ubu plays that included *King Ubu* (1896; Eng. trans., 1953), first produced by Firmin Gémier at the Théâtre de l'Oeuvre; *Ubu in Chains* (1900; Eng. trans., 1953); and *Ubu the Cuckold* (1944; Eng. trans., 1953). The farcical, antiheroic character of Ubu was based on young Jarry's physics teacher at his lycée in Rennes. A cruel, cowardly, and absurd figure, Ubu caricatured the ineptitude of the bourgeois and expressed Jarry's own hostility toward the established order. Other works by Jarry, such as the novels *L'Amour Absolu* (Absolute Love, 1899), *The Supermale* (1902; Eng. trans., 1977), and *The Gestures and Opinions of Doctor Faustroll* (1911; Eng. trans., 1965), contain a mixture of poetry and black comedy. Considered a precursor of Dada and surrealism for the exuberance of his personality and for his strange literary creations, Jarry influenced Antonin Artaud, Eugène Ionesco, Samuel Beckett, and Jean Genet.

Bibliography: Esslin, Martin, *The Theater of the Absurd* (1961); Shattuck, Roger, *The Banquet Years*, rev. ed. (1968).

jasmine [jaz'-min]

Common white jasmine, J. officinale, is a tropical and subtropical climbing shrub easily cultivated both outdoors (in warm climates) and in greenhouses. Its fragrant white flowers contain an essential oil used in making perfumes.

Jasmine is the common name given to a large number of plants, many of them unrelated. The poet's, or common, jasmine, *Jasminum officinale*, of the olive family, is a tropical and subtropical plant that probably originated in the Middle East and is now cultivated principally in France, Morocco, and Italy. The fragrant jasmine odor can be extracted (see ESSENTIAL OILS) and is one of the most widely used scents in the making of perfume. The flowers of Arabian jasmine, *J. sambac*, are used to scent and flavor tea. The nectar of the fragrant flowers of Carolina jasmine, *Gelsemium sempervirens*, is poisonous, although its dried roots are used in medicinal preparations as a sedative. ARTHUR O. TUCKER

Jason [jay'-suhn]

In Greek mythology, Jason was the son of Aeson and the leader of the Argonauts, who sought the GOLDEN FLEECE. After PELIAS, his uncle, usurped the throne of Iolcus, the young Jason was taken to the centaur CHIRON, who reared him on Mount Pelion. When, as a man, Jason claimed his kingdom, Pelias gave him the task of bringing to him the Golden Fleece. Jason ordered the construction of a 50-oared ship called the *Argo*, for which he assembled a crew including HERCULES, ORPHEUS, THESEUS, and other heroes. The voyages of Jason and the Argonauts were fraught with danger and adventure—storms at sea, seduction by beautiful women, the overcoming of mythical monsters—but at last they reached Colchis, the land of the Golden Fleece.

At Colchis, Jason yoked fire-breathing bulls, sowed the dragon's teeth of CADMUS, vanquished champions, and seized the fleece with the help of the princess MEDEA, with whom he returned to Iolcus. There they brought about the murder of Pelias but were expelled from the city by Pelias's son. After delivering the fleece to Orchemenus in Boeotia, Jason and Medea went to Corinth, where they lived as man and wife for many years. When Jason wished to marry Creusa (or Glauce), daughter of King Creon, Medea revenged herself by using her knowledge of magic and sorcery to burn to death both the father and daughter. For breaking his vow to Medea, Jason was condemned to wander the earth until, as an old man, he at last returned to Corinth. There he was accidentally killed when the prow of the *Argo* fell over and struck him. Versions of the story appear in Pindar's *Pythian Odes*, Ovid's *Metamorphoses*, and Apollonius of Rhodes's *Argonautica* (The Voyage of Argo). NORMA GOODRICH

jasper [jas'-pur]

Jasper is an opaque and fine-grained quartz. Colored red, yellow, brown, or off-white to gray by impurities, jasper has long been used as an ornamental stone because it takes a fine polish. The color of a streak made on a black jasper touchstone can determine with good accuracy the gold content of gold ores.

Jaspers, Karl [yahs'-purs]

Karl Jaspers, b. Feb. 23, 1883, d. Feb. 26, 1969, was a leading exponent of German EXISTENTIALISM. He studied law at Heidelberg and Munich and medicine and psychiatry at Berlin, Göttingen, and Heidelberg, where he received his M.D. in 1909. In his *General Psychopathology* (1913; Eng. trans., 1963) he offered a new classification of mental illnesses that has been influential in psychiatry. He became a professor of psychology at Heidelberg in 1916 and of philosophy there in 1921. During the Nazi regime he was relieved of his duties, but after the war in 1945 he was reinstated. He moved to the University of Basel in Switzerland in 1948. It was as a psychiatrist that Jaspers first studied philosophy, and all his later thought reflects this. His existential philosophy was influenced primarily by Friedrich NIETZSCHE and Søren KIERKEGAARD and only incidentally by Martin HEIDEGGER and Jean Paul SARTRE, who wrote most of their works after Jaspers had already published a good deal.

Jaspers presented his philosophy in a three-volume work, *Philosophy* (1932), and elaborated it in such later works as *Reason and Existenz* (1935; Eng. trans., 1955), *Existenzphilosophie* (1938), and *The Question of German Guilt* (1946; Eng. trans., 1947). His thought rests on the distinction between two states of being—*Dasein* and *Existenz*. *Dasein* (not to be confused with the meaning Heidegger gives it) refers to existence in an ordinary and minimal sense. It is concerned with the practical management of everyday life and known through objective scientific investigation. *Existenz* refers to the richness of authentic being. Jaspers defines it as the authentic self and as the experience of total freedom, of infinite possibility, and of loneliness. It is concerned with personal choice and known through individual insight or intuition. *Existenz* is inaccessible to traditional philosophic investigation, which quests for certainty. Only when such quests have been "shipwrecked" upon the limitations of *Existenz* can true philosophizing begin. Jaspers calls these limitations "boundary situations." They include death, suffering, guilt, chance, and conflict. Of these boundaries, the most important is death because the anticipation of death is the source not only of such negative emotions as dread but also of true relish for life. Experiences with such boundary situations force us to recognize the shallowness of *Dasein* and provide an introduction, says Jaspers, "to that shaking up of thought from which *Existenzphilosophie* must spring." Jaspers's examination of boundary situations constitutes an existentialist statement of the problem of evil.

In both outlook and method Jaspers was a strong subjectivist. Asserting that personal experience is the individual's only source of information about reality, he used his own experiences as the basis for philosophic generalization. Although

The German philosopher Karl Jaspers was one of the leading figures in modern philosophy. His prolific writings, which emphasize the uniqueness of the individual, reflect the influences of Søren Kierkegaard and are generally considered existentialist in content. Jaspers's inquiries led him to believe that "man is always more than what he knows, or can know, about himself."

Jaspers understood human *Existenz* as an individual state, he also believed that subjectivity was essentially social. One can discover one's authentic self only through reflection in someone else's authentic self. In fact philosophy is the disclosure of oneself through communication. Such communication requires what Jaspers called "philosophic faith," which involves a belief in personal freedom, the inadequacy of a person alone, and the transcendence of the ordinary world.

Jaspers was a religious existentialist. Although he believed that the open character of his own philosophy was opposed to the absolutism of traditional Christianity, the element of transcendence in his philosophy can be compared to that of traditional Christianity. Like Kierkegaard, he believed the "leap of faith" to be essentially absurd, in that nothing logically demonstrates that one should take this leap. Jaspers has a wide, nonacademic readership, and some theologians have shown an interest in his work.   THOMAS E. WREN

Bibliography: Ehrlich, Leonard H., *Karl Jaspers: Philosophy as Faith* (1975); Samay, Sebastian, *Reason Revisited: The Philosophy of Karl Jaspers* (1971); Schilpp, Paul A., ed., *The Philosophy of Karl Jaspers* (1957); Wallraff, Charles F., *Karl Jaspers: An Introduction to His Philosophy* (1970).

jaundice   [jawn'-dis]

Jaundice, a disorder symptomatic of several BLOOD and LIVER diseases, is characterized by yellowing of the skin and mucous membranes, particularly the white of the eyes. It is caused by the excess production or inadequate excretion of bilirubin, which is a yellow bile pigment that is formed from hemoglobin breakdown products after red blood cells decompose.

Because red blood cells continually wear out and break down, bilirubin is usually present, in small amounts, in blood plasma. It is excreted from the liver into the intestines through the bile ducts. Hemolytic jaundice occurs when red blood cells are destroyed excessively, as in some forms of anemia or sepsis (an infection of the bloodstream) or the transfusion of an incompatible blood type. Hepatogenous jaundice is caused by liver damage, particularly hepatitis, the ingestion or inhalation of toxic chemicals, or cirrhosis. Obstructive jaundice results from blockage of the bile ducts, usually by gallstones or tumors.

Newborn infants frequently develop mild hemolytic jaundice, which lasts several days until a normal excess of red blood cells is destroyed. Erythroblastosis fetalis, a serious form of jaundice in infants, generally is due to an RH FACTOR incompatibility. Adolescents and young adults who have a viral inflammation of the liver often develop jaundice; jaundice in middle-aged adults is commonly due to gallstones. In older adults jaundice may signal cancer of the liver or the bile ducts. It is often the first symptom of liver damage in alcoholics.

Bibliography: Schiff, Leon, ed., *Diseases of the Liver*, 4th ed. (1975).

Jaurès, Jean   [zhoh-res']

Jean Joseph Marie Auguste Jaurès, b. Sept. 3, 1859, d. July 31, 1914, an eminent French socialist, helped bring the various socialist factions of France into a single party. From a middle-class background, he taught philosophy at Toulouse before entering the Chamber of Deputies in 1885. As a leading supporter of Alfred Dreyfus in the prolonged DREYFUS AFFAIR, Jaurès won many converts to socialism, but he was attacked by Jules Guesde and other doctrinaire Marxists for attempting to attract bourgeois sympathizers and for supporting the bourgeois government of René WALDECK-ROUSSEAU. In 1905, Jaurès's efforts to bring together the five different schools of French socialists bore fruit with the creation of the Section française de l'internationale ouvrière (French section of the worker's international). In that year, however, the Second International (see INTERNATIONAL, SOCIALIST), which had facilitated the union, endorsed Guesde's position on participation in bourgeois politics.

In 1904, Jaurès founded *L'Humanité*, a leading left-wing newspaper. In his articles and in impassioned speeches, he urged reconciliation with Germany to prevent war. He was assassinated by a fanatical nationalist in Paris on the eve of World War I. Jaurès wrote a notable history of the French Revolution, *Histoire socialiste de la Révolution française* (1901-07).   P. M. EWY

Bibliography: Goldberg, Harvey, *The Life of Jean Jaurès* (1962).

Java   [jah'-vuh]

Java, the most important island of Indonesia, is located south of Borneo and Sumatra. The island is about 1,000 km (620 mi) long and has a maximum width of about 200 km (125 mi); its area is 125,740 km² (48,550 mi²). JAKARTA, the capital of Java and of Indonesia, on the northwestern coast, has a population of 4,576,000 (1971). The islands of Java and Madura, an associated island, have a population of 86,850,000 (1977 est.). Java is one of the most densely populated areas in the world, with 690 persons per km² (1,790 per mi²). Java is divided into three provinces and two districts, including the Jakarta federal district.

Java's topography is made up of longitudinal belts of limestone platforms, eroded volcanic mountains, volcanoes (35 of 112 are active), and alluvial valleys. Volcanic ash has created fertile soils. High temperatures, 19° C (66° F) to 37° C (98° F) at Jakarta, and heavy precipitation, averaging 1,755 mm (69 in) at Jakarta, characterize the island.

Most JAVANESE are farmers who tend the rice terraces that make up 40% of the cultivated land. Important commercial crops—rubber, coffee, tea, tobacco, cacao, and timber—are produced, and petroleum, coal, tin, gold, and silver are mined. Most of Indonesia's heavy industry is in Jakarta and SURABAYA, and BANDUNG is a textile center.

By AD 700, Java had been conquered by Indian princes. Indian influence reached its height with the MAJAPAHIT EMPIRE (founded 1293). Expanding Muslim influence led to the destruction of the empire in the early 16th century. The Dutch East India Company gradually gained control of the island in the early 17th century. It passed to the Dutch government in 1799, which retained it, except for occupations by the British (1811-16) and Japanese (1942-45), until Indonesian independence in 1950.   GARY A. KLEE

Java man

The remains of Java man, the first known fossils of the extinct species HOMO ERECTUS, were discovered (1891-93) by a young Dutch anatomist, Eugène DUBOIS, in a bank of the Solo River, at Trinil, Java. Dubois's finds consisted of a low, thick-boned, primitive-looking skullcap, with prominent brow ridges and a brain size only half that of modern humans, and a thighbone, which in contrast appeared entirely human in form. Following an earlier suggestion by the German biologist Ernst Haeckel, and to commemorate the humanlike thighbone, Dubois named his creature *Pithecanthropus erectus*, meaning "erect ape-man." This name was later changed to *Homo erectus*.

Java man's surprising combination of a primitive skullcap and a thoroughly modern-looking thighbone created much controversy among scholars of human evolution at the turn of the century. Subsequent finds in Africa of an earlier creature, AUSTRALOPITHECUS, more primitive still than *Pithecanthropus* but also clearly a hominid—and discoveries of additional fossils in Java—dated between about 700,000 and 1.5 million years ago—helped settle the debate. Java man is now recognized as belonging to the category *Homo erectus*, along with fossils from China, Europe, and Africa; on an evolutionary scale this species lies between the earlier *Australopithecus* and the later species *Homo sapiens*.   ALAN MANN AND NANCY MINUGH

Bibliography: Howells, William W., "Homo Erectus," *Scientific American*, November 1966; White, Edmund, and Brown, Dale, *The First Men* (1973).

Java Sea

The Java Sea is the part of the western Pacific Ocean between the islands of Borneo on the north and Java on the south. It covers 433,000 km² (167,000 mi²) and is shallow, with a mean depth of only 46 m (151 ft). The MAKASAR STRAIT connects it with CELEBES SEA.

Javanese [jah-vuh-neez']

Javanese, the largest group of Indonesians, occupy central and eastern Java, about two-thirds of the island. They numbered about 62,000, in the late 1970s, comprising about 60 percent of Indonesia's total population. Their language, affiliated with the Malayo-Polynesian linguistic family, has a rich literature dating back to the 10th century. By the 5th century Sumatra and Java had already been influenced by Indian civilization, including both Hinduism and Buddhism, and impressive Indianized kingdoms developed in these islands. Although the Javanese converted to Islam beginning in the 13th century, many indigenous and Hindu-Buddhist beliefs and practices are retained even today.

Most Javanese traditionally work as rice farmers, living in a village among their irrigated rice fields. A wide variety of other crops are also grown, including maize, manioc, sweet potatoes, peanuts, and soybeans. Some Javanese work in commercial plantations producing sugarcane, tea, tobacco, and other food products. The Javanese nobility whose ancestors once ruled their ancient kingdoms reside in large cities such as Jogjakarta. Genealogical descent is traced through both parents, and divorce and remarriage are frequent. Javanese dances, music (gamelan orchestra), dramas (shadow and puppet plays), woodcarvings, paintings, and textile decorations are world famous.   DONN V. HARTT

Bibliography: Geertz, Clifford, *The Religion of Java* (1960); Koentjaraningart, R. M., ed., *Villages in Indonesia* (1967); McVey, Ruth, *Indonesia*, rev. ed. (1967); Palmier, L. H., *Social Status and Power in Java* (1969); Smith, Datus, *The Land and People of Indonesia*, rev. ed. (1968).

Javanese language: see MALAYO-POLYNESIAN LANGUAGES.

javelin: see TRACK AND FIELD.

Javits, Jacob K. [jav'-its]

Jacob Koppel Javits, b. New York City, May 18, 1904, has served as U.S. senator from New York since 1957. A Republican, he became known for his leadership of the liberal wing of his party and for his advocacy of strong U.S. support for Israel. He served in the House of Representatives (1946-54) and as attorney general of New York (1954-57).

Bibliography: Douth, George, *Leaders in Profile* (1975).

jawfish

Jawfishes, family Opistognathidae, are about 24 to 30 species of small, colorful, large-mouthed marine fishes found in tropical and subtropical waters. Most are less than 15 cm (6 in) long, but *Opistognathus muscatensis*, of the Indo-Pacific, grows to 45 cm (18 in). In at least two species the large mouths are used to carry and incubate the eggs.

Jawlensky, Alexey von [yow-len'-skee, uhl-yik-syay' fuhn]

Alexey von Jawlensky, b. Russia, Mar. 25 (N.S.), 1864, d. Mar. 15, 1941, was a leading German expressionist painter. Educated at both military school and an art school, he became a captain of the Saint Petersburg Imperial Guards in 1889. His acquaintances in art circles led him to Munich in 1896, where he met a colony of Russian avant-gardists, including Wassily Kandinsky in 1897. Strongly influenced by German expressionism, Jawlensky, in his maturity, employed simplified shapes and bright, lush color to endow landscapes and portraits with intense, often anguished feelings. The impact of his imagery is heightened by the flickering, jagged quality of his brushstroke. He worked with Kandinsky and other members of *Der Blaue Reiter* (The Blue Rider) group but never

joined it. By the mid-1920s, his simplifications of form led to an extended series of masklike *Heads* that occupied him for the rest of his career.   CARTER RATCLIFF

Bibliography: Demetrion, James T., *Alexey von Jawlensky* (1964); Dube, Wolf-Dieter, *The Expressionists*, trans. by Mary Whittall (1972); Haftmann, Werner, *Painting in the Twentieth Century*, 2 vols. (2d ed., 1965).

Jaworski, Leon [juh-wor'-skee]

Leon Jaworski, b. Waco, Texas, Sept. 19, 1905, is a prominent Texas lawyer who led the last phase of the WATERGATE investigation that culminated in the resignation of President Richard M. Nixon in August 1974. Jaworski, named special prosecutor in November 1973, presented evidence to a federal grand jury that led to the indictment of seven important figures in the Nixon administration. He also successfully challenged Nixon's attempt to withhold White House tape recordings from use as evidence, in UNITED STATES V. RICHARD M. NIXON.

In 1977, Jaworski was appointed chief counsel of the House Ethics Committee to investigate alleged bribery of congressmen by officers of the government of South Korea but resigned after that government refused to cooperate.

Bibliography: Jaworski, Leon, *The Right and the Power* (1976) and, with Mickey Herskowitz, *Confession and Avoidance* (1979).

jay

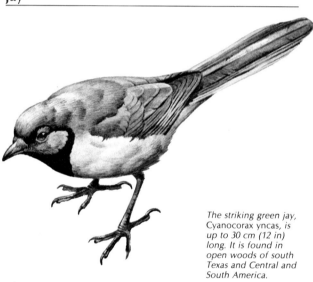

The striking green jay, Cyanocorax yncas, is up to 30 cm (12 in) long. It is found in open woods of south Texas and Central and South America.

The 35 species of jays, classified in the avian family Corvidae, are distributed throughout the Northern Hemisphere and South America. They measure 20 to 76 cm (8 to 30 in) in length and are usually crested and colorful; some species have very long tails. Jays eat a wide variety of foods, from seeds to eggs and young birds. Many jays give harsh, noisy calls; some can mimic other birds. A number of jays have elaborate social systems, sometimes involving a group of individuals taking care of young from a single nest.

Only two genera inhabit the Old World: the widespread common jay, *Garrulus glandarius*; and the Siberian jay, *Perisoreus infaustus*. The common jay, which has a distinctive brownish plumage and wing bands of black, blue, and white, is considered beneficial in dispersing tree seeds. Two well-known species that occur in North America are the gray jay, *P. canadensis*, which is found in northern and mountainous coniferous forests, and the blue jay, *Cyanocitta cristata*, which inhabits oak and pine regions of eastern and central North America. Most species, such as the green jay, *Cyanocorax yncas*, of Central and South America, occur in the tropics.
              GARY D. SCHNELL

Bibliography: Angell, Tony, *Ravens, Crows, Magpies and Jays* (1978); Bent, Arthur C., *Life Histories of North American Jays, Crows, and Titmice*, 2 vols. (1947).

Jay, John

John Jay, one of the leading figures of the early years of the American republic, was appointed as the first chief justice of the Supreme Court in 1789 and established procedures still observed by that judicial body. Jay was sent on a mission to London in 1794, where he negotiated the treaty that today bears his name, settling many outstanding differences between Great Britain and the United States.

The American statesman John Jay—the first chief justice of the U.S. Supreme Court—embodied the best of the moderate reform tradition. He initially favored limited resistance to Great Britain but supported the American Revolution after the signing of the Declaration of Independence. A seeker of social stability, he advocated a strong federal government and close ties to Britain during the early national period.

Born in New York City on Dec. 12, 1745, Jay grew up in a comfortable home, graduated from King's College (now Columbia University) in 1764, and four years later was admitted to the bar. He married (1774) into the influential Livingston family.

Jay began a brilliant career as a lawyer and soon became absorbed in public life. In prerevolutionary New York politics and as a delegate to the First and Second CONTINENTAL CONGRESS, he was a leading spokesman and strategist for the moderate faction, which sought measures of resistance to Great Britain short of independence. Once the Declaration of Independence had been adopted, however, Jay accepted it and worked earnestly in Congress and in New York City for the success of the American Revolution. New York's first state constitution (1777) was largely his work, and he took office under it as the state's chief justice in 1777.

Continuing to serve in Congress, Jay was elected its president in 1778. The next year he was appointed minister to Spain, embarking on fruitless negotiations to win Spanish recognition of American independence. In 1782, Jay went to Paris as one of the American peace commissioners. There, with Benjamin FRANKLIN and John ADAMS, he negotiated the peace treaty of 1783, which ended the Revolution.

He returned home in 1784 to serve as foreign secretary under the Articles of Confederation. He worked actively for adoption of the federal Constitution of 1787, most notably as one of the authors of The FEDERALIST. He became (1789) the first chief justice of the Supreme Court under the new Constitution, but his most important national service thereafter was to negotiate JAY'S TREATY (1794) with Great Britain. In the early 1790s he became a staunch Federalist (see FEDERALIST PARTY), favoring a strong national government sympathetic to the growth of commerce and industry. He resigned as chief justice to serve as governor of New York (1795–1801) and then refused further public office. He retired to his farm in Bedford, N.Y., where he supported the New York Antislavery Society, the American Bible Society, and other philanthropies. He died on May 17, 1829.   RALPH KETCHAM

Bibliography: Jay, John, *Correspondence and Public Papers*, 4 vols., ed. by Henry P. Johnston (1890–93; repr. 1970), and *John Jay: The Making of a Revolutionary: Unpublished Papers, 1745-1780*, ed. by Richard B. Morris (1975); Monaghan, Frank, *John Jay* (1935; repr. 1972); Morris, Richard B., *John Jay: The Nation and the Court* (1967); Smith, Donald L., *John Jay: Founder of a State and Nation* (1968).

Jaycees International   [jay'-seez]

An association of businessmen between the ages of 18 and 36, the Jaycees meet in local chapters and participate in programs of civic service and business education. Founded in Saint Louis, Mo., in 1915, as the Junior Chamber of Commerce, the organization was renamed the U.S. Jaycees in 1965 and by the 1970s had international chapters in about 80 countries. Membership in 1978 was more than 380,000. The U.S. Jaycees' charter excludes women from membership, although only six countries in the International have similar charters. A few dissident chapters in large U.S. cities have recruited women, but as late as 1978 the annual meeting voted to continue the exclusion.

Jay's Treaty

On Nov. 19, 1794, U.S. Chief Justice John JAY, acting in his capacity as special envoy, signed a treaty with Great Britain that proved advantageous to the new American nation—although it raised a storm of controversy in the months following its signing and subsequent passage by the U.S. Senate. By averting the threat of war, Jay's Treaty ensured Anglo-American trade and thus provided customs revenues to the new federal government.

Friction between Great Britain and its former colony had arisen from various sources. Despite the Treaty of Paris (1783), which had ended the American War for Independence, the British government had refused to evacuate the frontier forts in the Old Northwest (see NORTHWEST TERRITORY), and Americans believed that the British were encouraging the Indians to attack local settlers. The British, for their part, maintained that Americans had refused to pay prerevolutionary debts owed British creditors and to compensate loyalists for confiscated property. Anglo-American relations were further aggravated when Britain began seizing American ships and impressing American sailors into British service in its war against France.

Jay's Treaty secured the British evacuation of the frontier forts and a limited right of American ships to trade in the British West Indies. It referred the debt question and the settlement of boundary disputes to joint commissions, but it made no provision for settlement of the Indian issue, loyalist claims, or the impressment question. President George Washington pressed for ratification, and the treaty eventually passed through the Senate in June 1795, although the provision limiting American trade in the West Indies was removed. The treaty was denounced by the Democratic-Republicans for its concessions to Britain, however, and Jay was burned in effigy by indignant American mobs.   ROBERT H. FERRELL

Bibliography: Bemis, Samuel Flagg, *Jay's Treaty*, rev. ed. (1962).

jazz

Jazz is the only indigenous American musical form to have exerted an influence on musical development throughout the Western world. Created by obscure black musicians in the late 19th century, jazz was at first a synthesis of Western harmonic language and forms with the rhythms and melodic inflections of Africa. The African musical idiom present in black vocal music—SPIRITUALS, the work song, the field holler, and blues—was the structure through which popular tunes of the time were transmuted into jazz. The music was characterized by improvisation, the spontaneous creation of variations on a melodic line; by syncopation, where rhythmic stress is placed on the normally weak beats of the musical measure; and by a type of intonation that would be considered out of tune in Western classical music. (See BLUES for a discussion of this type of intonation.)

In its beginnings jazz was more an approach to performance than a body of musical compositions. The black marching bands of New Orleans, which often accompanied funeral processions, played traditional slow hymns on the way to the cemetery; for the procession back to town, they broke into jazzed-up versions of the same hymns, RAGTIME tunes, or syncopated renditions of popular marches. The instruments in the marching band—a cornet or a trumpet to carry the mel-

Louis Armstrong (center) joined King Oliver's Creole Jazz Band in 1922. Under the tutelage of Joe "King" Oliver, a prominent trumpeter who played in the New Orleans tradition, Armstrong became one of the foremost jazz trumpeters and vocalists of his time.

ody, with a clarinet and trombone to fill in, and a rhythm section of drums or a string bass—formed the nucleus of the first jazz bands, which usually added only a piano, guitar, or banjo.

DIXIELAND

The earliest recordings identified as jazz were made in 1917 in New York by the Original Dixieland Jazz Band under the leadership of Nick La Rocca. The members were white musicians from New Orleans, playing in a style that they learned from blacks in that city. Although the early jazz artists occasionally cut records, it was only when jazz bands traveled to Chicago and New York City that the music became available nationwide through recordings released by the major record companies. The first important recordings by black musicians were made in 1923, by King OLIVER's Creole Jazz Band, a group that included some of the foremost New Orleans musicians then performing in Chicago: Louis ARMSTRONG, Johnny and "Baby" Dodds, and Honore Dutrey.

Many white groups in Chicago and elsewhere adopted the style, among them the New Orleans Rhythm Kings and the Wolverines, led by Bix BEIDERBECKE. The characteristics of this early style, known as Dixieland, included a relatively complex interweaving of melodic lines among the cornet (or trumpet), clarinet, and trombone and a steady chomp-chomp beat from the rhythm instruments (piano, bass, drums). The texture was predominantly polyphonic. Most bands used no written notation, preferring "head" arrangements agreed upon verbally; improvisation was an indispensable factor.

During the 1920s jazz gained in popularity. The two most important recording centers were Chicago and New York, although all sections of the country were caught up in the dances that were closely associated with the music. The period itself became known as the Jazz Age.

In Chicago the most influential artists were members of small bands like the Wolverines. In New York, on the other hand, the trend was toward larger groups with two or more trumpets, one or two trombones, three or four reeds, plus a rhythm section. The larger groups played in revues and vaudeville shows and in large dance halls and theaters.

NEW YORK JAZZ

As the decade progressed, the performance styles in all groups featured more written arrangements and placed increasing emphasis on solo performance. Representative of the many players who led the outburst of jazz virtuosity that marked the 1920s were Sidney BECHET, Ferdinand "Jelly Roll" MORTON, Coleman HAWKINS, Armstrong, and James P. Johnson. Among the leaders in establishing the sound of the new big bands were Fletcher HENDERSON (with Don Redman, his arranger) and Edward Kennedy "Duke" ELLINGTON. It was

Henderson who developed the performance style that became known as SWING, featuring call-and-response patterns between brass and reeds, extensive use of the riff—the repetition of a motif—for ensemble work and as accompaniment for soloists, elaborate written arrangements, and the frequent insertion of improvised solos. Ellington extended the role of bandleader beyond mere arranging and into the area of composition, principally because of his need to provide music for the Cotton Club revues in Harlem. Many of his compositions were popular hits in their own time and have become standards for jazz players.

Another important facet of the jazz scene in New York was the production of vocal blues recordings marketed principally to blacks. Because of the unique form of the blues, many of the best jazz performers were used as back-up artists for the insertion of instrumental "comments" between the sung phrases. The most definitive singer of the period was Bessie SMITH, whose 1920s recordings are considered landmarks of vocal blues.

SWING

The dominant idiom of the 1930s and much of the 1940s was swing. Utilized almost exclusively for dancing, the music of the big bands borrowed heavily from the techniques introduced by Henderson. Among the most popular bands were those led by Benny GOODMAN, Glenn MILLER, Woody HERMAN, Tommy and Jimmy DORSEY, and Artie Shaw. As a counterpart of the highly arranged orchestrations of these New York-based bands, a Kansas City swing style developed under the influence of Count BASIE and Bennie Moten that emphasized a blues vocabulary and form as well as tempos of breakneck speed and an overwhelming use of riffs. Among the outstanding soloists associated with Kansas City was Lester YOUNG of the Basie band.

(Above) *Duke Ellington, a seminal figure in the history of jazz, introduced the "big band" sound to jazz with the brilliant compositions and arrangements performed by his 10-member band.*

(Left) *Bessie Smith, known as the Empress of the Blues, is considered by many the greatest blues singer in history. Bessie Smith combined the traditions of rural blues and spirituals with jazz and created a powerful style of blues singing still widely imitated.*

combine modern classical forms with jazz techniques. The style, known as "third stream," used improvisational segments interwoven with compositions scored for symphony orchestras and chamber groups, including string quartets. Musical forms identified with classical tradition were utilized—fugue, rondo, symphonic development. Polyphony became an important texture, best exemplified by the jazz fugues played by the MODERN JAZZ QUARTET.

JAZZ EXTREMES: THE 1960s

The jazz of the 1960s was in many ways a mirroring of the social ferment of that decade. Much of the performance was characterized by a search for freedom from melodic, harmonic, and rhythmic restraints. One of the leaders was Ornette Coleman, whose 1960 album, *Free Jazz*, set the tone of the decade. It featured eight musicians improvising individually and collectively without predetermined thematic material of any kind. The ultimate result was a breakdown in the traditional framework for improvisation, which had relied for decades on melodic variations based normally on a stated tune or harmonic progression. Cecil TAYLOR and others moved even farther away from traditional jazz practice and used atonality and other dissonances.

The leading figure of the decade was John COLTRANE. In many of his performances he abandoned tonality completely and improvised at length within a single scale structure or over a single chord or mode. His many followers cultivated an almost totally emotional style, extending the expressive range of their instruments to screaming, moaning, and piercing outbursts of passionate sound. As a result, the audience for jazz decreased dramatically and many critics expressed the fear that the art was doomed.

(Above) *Tommy Potter, Charlie Parker, Dizzy Gillespie, and John Coltrane are seen in performance (c.1950). The Parker-Gillespie combination produced some of the finest bop of the 1940s and early '50s. Under their influence such artists as Coltrane and Miles Davis evolved from the bop idiom into the progressive jazz of the 1960s. (Left) Miles Davis, a pioneer in cool jazz and modal jazz, also made major contributions to the development of electronic jazz.*

THE JAZZ REVOLUTION: BEBOP

In the early 1940s a rejection of the restrictive arrangements required by big-band style spread among jazz musicians. Under the leadership of Charlie PARKER, Dizzy GILLESPIE, Thelonious MONK, and others, a style known as bop, or BEBOP, emerged on the New York scene.

It represented a return to the small group concept of Dixieland, with one instrument of a kind rather than the sections used by swing groups. Emphasizing solos rather than ensembles, bop players developed an astounding degree of virtuosity. Bop was extremely complex rhythmically; it used extensions of the usual harmonic structures and featured speed and irregular phrasing. It demanded great listening skill, and its erratic rhythms made it unsuitable for dancing. Because of its sophistication, bop resulted in the first breakaway of jazz from the popular music mainstream. The style was adopted by many performers during the 1940s and 1950s but was rejected by others who preferred the more conservative techniques of swing.

Cool. One of the most important new jazz styles of the 1950s was known as "cool." Inaugurated by a group of highly trained academic performers under the leadership of Miles DAVIS, cool was a return to the carefully organized and scored principles of swing but without the latter's emphasis on call-and-response and riffing. The ensembles played frequently as an entire unit and included a number of new instruments in jazz: French horn, flute, baritone sax, flügelhorn, and others. The players rejected the emotional emphasis of bop as well as its exploitation of range and virtuosity. They preferred to play in the middle register, utilizing a smooth attack, little vibrato, and largely on-beat phrasing.

Third Stream. Closely allied to cool jazz was the attempt to

(Above) *Chick Corea, influenced during the 1960s by Miles Davis's avant-garde jazz, is one of the leading exponents of the jazz-rock fusion that ended the 1970s. Return to Forever, the group Corea organized in 1970, has featured such artists as Airto Moreira and Stanley Clarke.*

(Left) *George Benson has achieved widespread commercial success by blending jazz and rhythm and blues traditions with a funky popular style exemplified by Breezin' (1976).*

THE 1970s JAZZ REVIVAL

The decade of the 1970s, however, brought renewed interest in jazz, with a revival of many of the older, more traditional concepts and the addition of several new ones. The popularity of big bands, using many of the devices of swing, spread to high school and college campuses. Thad Jones, Mel Lewis, Woody Herman, and Count Basie provided the leadership for this renaissance of big-band style.

Many leading musicians, on the other hand, turned toward a fusion of ROCK MUSIC and jazz, trading on the overwhelming popularity of the 1960s rock innovations. Among the leaders in the fusion movement were Miles Davis, Herbie Hancock, Chick Corea, Wayne Shorter, and George Benson. Their music placed great emphasis on the use of electronic instruments, enlarged percussion sections, repeated melodic and rhythmic figures, and relatively long segments performed without any significant harmonic change.

Other leading players like McCoy Tyner experimented extensively with modal themes and drone effects, reflecting the black identification with Eastern religions and spiritualism. Large-scale dissonant compositions for jazz groups gained in popularity under the influence of men like Anthony Braxton and Sun Ra. At the same time, more traditional performers like the New Orleans Preservation Hall Jazz Band found enthusiastic audiences.

Although jazz is a peculiarly American black expression, it has been assimilated by white musicians not only as a performance style but also as a musical language that can be used in combination with more classical styles. Composers such as George GERSHWIN, Charles Ives, Darius Milhaud, Igor Stravinsky, and many others have made frequent use of jazz devices, including ragtime.

The mingling of jazz with more classical musical idioms has enriched the musical fabric of the entire 20th century.

DONALD IVEY

Bibliography: Blesh, Rudi, *Shining Trumpets*, rev. ed. (1975); Feather, Leonard, *The Encyclopedia of Jazz*, rev. ed. (1960); Feather, Leonard, and Gitler, Ira, *The Encyclopedia of Jazz in the Seventies* (1976); Hentoff, Nat, *Jazz Is* (1976); Hodeir, André, *Jazz: Its Evolution and Essence*, trans. by David Noakes (1956; repr. 1975); Jones, LeRoi, *Black Music* (1967); Ostransky, Leroy, *Understanding Jazz* (1977); Schuller, Gunther, *Early Jazz* (1968); Stearns, Marshall W., *The Story of Jazz* (1956; repr. 1977); Tanner, Paul, and Gerow, Maurice, *A Study of Jazz*, 3d ed. (1977); Tirro, Frank, *Jazz: A History* (1977); Williams, Martin T., *The Jazz Tradition* (1970).

JDL: see JEWISH DEFENSE LEAGUE.

Jeanneret, Charles Édouard: see LE CORBUSIER.

Jeans, Sir James

The English astronomer and physicist Sir James Hopwood Jeans, b. Sept. 11, 1877, d. Sept. 16, 1946, is best known for his work in statistical mechanics, his theory of the origin of the solar system, and his popularization of science. His early work on kinetic molecular theory led him to refine Rayleigh's law of the distribution of blackbody radiation. It has since been known as the Rayleigh-Jeans law. Although Jeans initially hoped to preserve classical physics, he was an early advocate of the quantum theory and helped to spread its acceptance.

The work of Jeans on the stability of rotating masses resulted in one of his most popular theories, now discounted, that planetary systems could not be formed from a rotating contracting mass. He proposed instead the collision hypothesis, in which a close encounter between two stars pulled the planetary matter from one star. The supposed rarity of such an encounter implied that our planetary system, and its accompanying life, must be unique. Jean's most popular works include *The Universe Around Us* (1929) and *The Mysterious Universe* (1930).

Bibliography: Milne, E. A., *Sir James Jeans* (1952).

jeep

The jeep is a small, 1¼-ton open-topped military car, first used by the U.S. Army in 1941. The name is derived from the Army's designation, General Purpose vehicle, or GP. The army jeep has a 71-hp engine, a speed of 105 km/h (65 mph), and, with its 4-wheel drive and high ground clearance, the capacity to travel over roads that might be impassable to ordinary vehicles.

The jeep was designed as a small, light, reconnaissance and command vehicle, but during World War II it was used in several roles. In addition to hauling supplies and acting as an emergency ambulance, it became an antiaircraft vehicle when heavy machine guns on steel mounts were added; a field-kitchen transporter; and a gun tractor for moving antitank guns. With the addition of waterproof hulls, some models were used as small, amphibious landing craft.

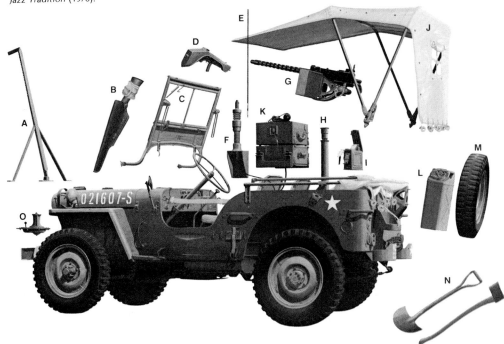

The jeep, a multipurpose, all-terrain vehicle introduced by the U.S. Army in 1941, carried an extraordinary amount of standard equipment: an antidecapitation wire interceptor (A), an M 1 rifle and ammunition holster (B), a hand-operated windshield wiper (C), a carbine rack (D), an antenna (E) and its mounting device (F), a Browning machine gun (G), its mounting device (H) and magazine (I), an all-weather hood (J), a radio transmitter-receiver (K), a spare fuel can (L), a spare wheel (M), survival tools—an axe and shovel—(N), and a capstan winch (O).

The jeep was made by several automobile companies during World War II and is produced today by one U.S. firm, American Motors Corporation, which uses the capitalized name as its trademark. In 1978, 175,000 jeeps were sold.

Bibliography: Olyslager Organization, Jeep: A Pictorial History (1970).

Jeffers, Robinson

The American poet John Robinson Jeffers, b. Pittsburgh, Pa., Jan. 10, 1887, d. Jan. 20, 1962, became closely associated with the rugged Pacific Coast, which provided the realistic setting for many of his poems, and noted for his modern adaptations of Greek and biblical myths.

After an extensive education, including an M.A. in literature and three years studying medicine, Jeffers published his first book, *Flagons and Apples* (1912), an undistinguished collection of love poems. The following year he moved to Carmel, Calif., where he deepened his knowledge of the classics and meditated on humanity's place in the universe. Under the influence of modern psychology, he began to adapt old stories to modern themes. "The Tower Beyond Tragedy" (1924) he derived from the *Oresteia*; "Solstice" (1935) and "Medea" (1937), from the Medea story; and "Tamar" (1924) and "Dear Judas" (1929), from biblical themes.

Jeffers repeatedly focused upon human self-importance and corruption, stressing the contrasting permanence of nature.

Bibliography: Bennett, Melba B., *The Stone Mason of Tor House* (1966); Brophy, Robert J., *Robinson Jeffers: Myth, Ritual and Symbol in His Narrative Poems* (1973; repr. 1976); Brother Antoninus, *Robinson Jeffers: Fragments of an Older Fury* (1968); Coffin, Arthur B., *Robinson Jeffers: Poet of Inhumanism* (1971); Jeffers, Robinson, *The Selected Letters of Robinson Jeffers, 1897–1962*, ed. by A. N. Ridgway (1968).

Jefferson, Joseph

The American actor Joseph Jefferson, b. Philadelphia, Feb. 20, 1829, d. Apr. 23, 1905, was most beloved for his portrayal of Rip Van Winkle, a role he played almost continuously from 1865 to 1880 in an adaptation by Dion Boucicault. He made his debut at the age of four, toured all over the world during his career, and retired in 1904 after 71 years on the stage. A master of stagecraft, he wrote at length on the art of acting in *The Autobiography of Joseph Jefferson* (1890; repr. 1964).

ANDREW J. KELLY

Jefferson, Territory of

The Territory of Jefferson, an unrecognized U.S. territory corresponding roughly to present COLORADO, was established following the discovery (1858) of gold there. On Aug. 1, 1859, the settlers met in convention to consider separation from the Kansas Territory, of which the area was then part.

The U.S. Congress, hamstrung by the slavery controversy, refused to consider a partition for territorial status, but the convention went ahead and adopted a constitution for the Jefferson Territory on October 24. The illegal government was unable to exert authority, however, and it was superseded in February 1861 when Congress formed the Territory of Colorado.

Jefferson, Thomas

Thomas Jefferson wished to be remembered for three achievements in his public life. He had served as governor of Virginia, as U.S. minister to France, as secretary of state under George WASHINGTON, as vice-president in the administration of John ADAMS, and as president of the United States from 1801 to 1809. On his tombstone, however, which he designed and for which he wrote the inscription, there is no mention of these offices. Rather, it reads that Thomas Jefferson was "author of the Declaration of American Independence, of the Statute of Virginia for religious freedom, and Father of the University of Virginia" and, as he requested, "not a word more." Historians might want to add other accomplishments—for example, his distinction as an architect, naturalist, and linguist—but in the main they would concur with his own assessment.

Early Life. Jefferson was born at Shadwell in what is now Albemarle County, Va., on Apr. 13, 1743. He treated his pedigree lightly, but his mother, Jane Randolph Jefferson, came from one of the first families of Virginia; his father, Peter Jefferson, was a well-to-do landowner, although not in the class of the wealthiest planters. Jefferson attended (1760–62) the College of William and Mary and then studied law with George WYTHE. In 1769 he began six years of service as a representative in the Virginia House of Burgesses. The following year he began building MONTICELLO on land inherited from his father. The mansion, which he designed in every detail, took years to complete, but part of it was ready for occupancy when he married Martha Wayles Skelton on Jan. 1, 1772. They had six children, two of whom survived into adulthood.

Jefferson's reputation began to reach beyond Virginia in 1774, when he wrote a political pamphlet, *A Summary View of the Rights of British America*. Arguing on the basis of natural rights theory, Jefferson claimed that colonial allegiance to the king was voluntary. "The God who gave us life," he wrote, "gave us liberty at the same time: the hand of force may destroy, but cannot disjoin them."

Declaration of Independence. Elected to the Second CONTINENTAL CONGRESS, meeting in Philadelphia, Jefferson was appointed on June 11, 1776, to head a committee of five in preparing the DECLARATION OF INDEPENDENCE. He was its primary author, although his initial draft was amended after consultation with Benjamin FRANKLIN and John Adams and altered both stylistically and substantively by Congress. Jefferson's reference to the voluntary allegiance of colonists to the crown was struck; also deleted was a clause that censured the monarchy for imposing slavery upon America.

Based upon the same natural rights theory contained in *A Summary View*, to which it bears a strong resemblance, the Declaration of Independence made Jefferson internationally famous. Years later that fame evoked the jealousy of John Adams, who complained that the declaration's ideas were "hackneyed." Jefferson agreed; he wrote of the declaration, "Neither aiming at originality of principle or sentiment, nor yet copied from any particular and previous writing, it was intended to be an expression of the American mind."

Revolutionary Legislator. Returning to Virginia late in 1776, Jefferson served until 1779 in the House of Delegates, one of the two houses of the General Assembly of Virginia—established in 1776 by the state's new constitution. While the AMERICAN REVOLUTION continued, Jefferson sought to liberalize Virginia's laws. Joined by his old law teacher, George Wythe, and by James MADISON and George MASON, Jefferson introduced a number of bills that were resisted fiercely by those representing the conservative planter class. In 1776 he succeeded in obtaining the abolition of entail; his proposal to abolish primogeniture became law in 1785. Jefferson proudly noted that "these laws, drawn by myself, laid the ax to the foot of pseudoaristocracy."

Jefferson was also instrumental in devising a major revision of the criminal code, although it was not enacted until 1796. His bill to create a free system of tax-supported elementary education for all except slaves was defeated as were his bills to create a public library and to modernize the curriculum of the College of William and Mary.

In June 1779 the introduction of Jefferson's bill on religious liberty touched off a quarrel that caused turmoil in Virginia for 8 years. The bill was significant as no other state—indeed, no other nation—provided for complete religious liberty at that time. Jefferson's bill stated "that all men shall be free to profess, and by argument to maintain, their opinions on matters of religion, and that the same shall in no wise diminish, enlarge, or affect their civil capacities." Many Virginians regarded the bill as an attack upon Christianity. It did not pass until 1786, and then mainly through the perseverance of James Madison. Jefferson, by then in France, congratulated Madison, adding that "it is honorable for us to have produced the first legislature who had the courage to declare that the reason of man may be trusted with the formation of his own opinions."

Wartime Governor of Virginia. In June 1779, Jefferson was

THOMAS JEFFERSON
3d President of the United States (1801-09)

Nickname: "Man of the People"; "Sage of Monticello"
Born: Apr. 13, 1743, Shadwell plantation, Goochland (now in Albemarle) County, Va.
Education: College of William and Mary (graduated 1762)
Profession: Lawyer, Planter
Religious Affiliation: None
Marriage: Jan. 1, 1772, to Martha Wayles Skelton (1748-82)
Children: Martha Washington Jefferson (1772-1836); Jane Randolph Jefferson (1774-75); infant son (1777); Mary Jefferson (1778-1804); Lucy Elizabeth Jefferson (1780-81); Lucy Elizabeth Jefferson (1782-84)
Political Affiliation: Democratic-Republican
Writings: *Writings* (10 vols., 1892-99), ed. by Paul L. Ford; *The Papers of Thomas Jefferson* (1950-), ed. by Julian P. Boyd, et al.; *Notes on the State of Virginia 1781* (1955), ed. by William Peden; *Autobiography* (1959), ed. by Dumas Malone
Died: July 4, 1826, Monticello, near Charlottesville, Va.
Buried: Monticello, near Charlottesville, Va.

Vice-President and Cabinet Members
Vice-President: Aaron Burr (1801-05); George Clinton (1805-09)
Secretary of State: James Madison
Secretary of the Treasury: Samuel Dexter (1801); Albert Gallatin (1801-09)
Secretary of War: Henry Dearborn
Attorney General: Levi Lincoln (1801-04); John Breckinridge (1805-06); Caesar A. Rodney (1807-09)
Secretary of the Navy: Benjamin Stoddert (1801); Robert Smith (1801-09)

elected governor of Virginia. His political enemies criticized his performance as war governor mercilessly. He was charged with failure to provide for the adequate defense of Richmond in 1780-81, although he knew a British invasion was imminent, and of cowardice and "pusillanimous conduct" when he fled the capital during the moment of crisis. In June 1781 he retired from the governorship. The Virginia assembly subsequently voted that "an inquiry be made into the conduct of

the executive of this state." Jefferson was exonerated: in fact, the assembly unanimously voted a resolution of appreciation of his conduct. The episode left Jefferson bitter, however, about the rewards of public service.

Money and the Ordinance of 1784. The death of his wife, on Sept. 6, 1782, added to Jefferson's problems, but by the following year he was again seated in Congress. There he made two contributions of enduring importance to the nation. In April 1784 he submitted *Notes on the Establishment of a Money Unit and of a Coinage for the United States* in which he advised the use of a decimal system. This report led to the adoption (1792) of the dollar, rather than the pound, as the basic monetary unit in the United States.

As chairman of the committee dealing with the government of western lands, Jefferson submitted proposals so liberal and farsighted as to constitute, when enacted, the most progressive colonial policy of any nation in modern history. The proposed ordinance of 1784 reflected Jefferson's belief that the western territories should be self-governing and, when they reached a certain stage of growth, should be admitted to the Union as full partners with the original 13 states. Jefferson also proposed that slavery should be excluded from all of the American western territories after 1800. Although he himself was a slaveowner, he believed that slavery was an evil that should not be permitted to spread. In 1784 the provision banning slavery was narrowly defeated. Had one representative (John Beatty of New Jersey), sick and confined to his lodging, been present, the vote would have been different. "Thus," Jefferson later reflected, "we see the fate of millions unborn hanging on the tongue of one man, and heaven was silent in that awful moment." Although Congress approved the proposed ordinance of 1784, it was never put into effect; its main features were incorporated, however, in the Ordinance of 1787, which established the NORTHWEST TERRITORY. Moreover, slavery was prohibited in the Northwest Territory.

Minister to France. From 1784 to 1789, Jefferson lived outside the United States. He was sent to Paris initially as a commissioner to help negotiate commercial treaties; then in 1785 he succeeded Benjamin Franklin as minister to France. Most European countries, however, were indifferent to American economic overtures. "They seemed, in fact," Jefferson wrote, "to know little about us. . . . They were ignorant of our commerce, and of the exchange of articles it might offer advantageously to both parties." Only one country, Prussia, signed a pact based on a model treaty drafted by Jefferson.

During these years Jefferson followed events in the United States with understandable interest. He advised against any harsh punishment of those responsible for SHAY'S REBELLION (1786-87) in Massachusetts. He worried particularly that the new CONSTITUTION OF THE UNITED STATES lacked a bill of rights and failed to limit the number of terms for the presidency. In France he witnessed the beginning of the French Revolution, but he doubted whether the French people could duplicate the American example of republican government. His advice, more conservative than might be anticipated, was that France emulate the British system of constitutional monarchy.

Secretary of State. When Jefferson left Paris on Sept. 26, 1789, he expected to return to his post. On that date and unknown to him, however, Congress confirmed his appointment as secretary of state in the first administration of George Washington. Jefferson accepted the position with some reluctance and largely because of Washington's insistence. He immediately expressed his alarm at the regal forms and ceremonies that marked the executive office, but his fears were tempered somewhat by his confidence in the character of Washington.

Jefferson, however, distrusted both the proposals and the motives of Secretary of the Treasury Alexander HAMILTON. He thought Hamilton's financial programs both unwise and unconstitutional, flowing "from principles adverse to liberty." On the issue of federal assumption of state debts, Jefferson struck a bargain with Hamilton permitting assumption to pass—a concession that he later regretted. He attempted, unsuccessfully, to persuade Washington to veto the bill incorporating a BANK OF THE UNITED STATES—recommended by Hamilton.

Jefferson suspected Hamilton and others in the emerging FEDERALIST PARTY of a secret design to implant monarchist ideals and institutions in the government. The disagreements spilled over into foreign affairs. Hamilton was pro-British, and Jefferson was by inclination pro-French, although he directed the office of secretary of state with notable objectivity. The more Washington sided with Hamilton, the more Jefferson became dissatisfied with his minority position within the cabinet. Finally, after being twice dissuaded from resigning, Jefferson did so on Dec. 31, 1793.

Brief Retirement. At home for the next three years, Jefferson devoted himself to farm and family. He experimented with a new plow and other ingenious inventions, built a nail factory, commenced the rebuilding of Monticello, set out a thousand peach trees, received distinguished guests from abroad, and welcomed the visits of his grandchildren. But he also followed national and international developments with a mounting sense of foreboding. "From the moment of my retiring from the administration," he later wrote, "the Federalists got unchecked hold on General Washington." Jefferson thought Washington's expedition to suppress the WHISKEY REBELLION (1794) an unnecessary use of military force. He deplored Washington's denunciation of the Democratic societies and considered JAY'S TREATY (1794) with Britain a "monument of folly and venality."

Vice-President. Thus Jefferson welcomed Washington's decision not to run for a third term in 1796. Jefferson became the reluctant presidential candidate of the Democratic-Republican party, and he seemed genuinely relieved when the Federalist candidate, John Adams, gained a narrow electoral college victory (71 to 68). As the runner-up, however, Jefferson became vice-president under the system then in effect.

Jefferson hoped that he could work with Adams, as of old, especially since both men shared an anti-Hamilton bias. But those hopes were soon dashed. Relations with France deteriorated. In 1798, in the wake of the XYZ AFFAIR, the so-called Quasi-War began. New taxes were imposed and the ALIEN AND SEDITION ACTS (1798) threatened the freedom of Americans. Jefferson, laboring to check the authoritarian drift of the national government, secretly authored the Kentucky Resolution (see KENTUCKY AND VIRGINIA RESOLUTIONS). More important, he provided his party with principles and strategy, aiming to win the election of 1800.

President. Jefferson's triumph was delayed temporarily as a result of a tie in electoral ballots with his running mate, Aaron BURR, which shifted the election to the House of Representatives. There Hamilton's influence helped Jefferson to prevail, although most Federalists supported Burr as the lesser evil. In his inaugural speech Jefferson held out an olive branch to his political enemies, inviting them to bury the partisanship of the past decade, to unite now as Americans.

Federalist leaders remained adamantly opposed to Jefferson, but the people approved his policies. Internal taxes were reduced; the military budget was cut; the Alien and Sedition Acts were permitted to lapse; and plans were made to extinguish the public debt. Simplicity and frugality became the hallmarks of Jefferson's administration. The LOUISIANA PURCHASE (1803) capped his achievements. Ironically, Jefferson had to overcome constitutional scruples in order to take over the vast new territory without authorization by constitutional amendment. In this instance it was his Federalist critics who became the constitutional purists. Nonetheless, the purchase was received with popular enthusiasm. In the election of 1804, Jefferson swept every state except two—Connecticut and Delaware.

Jefferson's second administration began with a minor success—the favorable settlement concluding the TRIPOLITAN WAR (1801-05), in which the newly created U.S. Navy fought its first engagements. The following year the LEWIS AND CLARK EXPEDITION, which the president had dispatched to explore the Louisiana Territory, returned triumphantly after crossing the continent. The West was also a source of trouble, however. The disaffected Aaron Burr engaged in a conspiracy, the details of which are still obscure, either to establish an independent republic in the Louisiana Territory or to launch an invasion of Spanish-held Mexico. Jefferson acted swiftly to arrest Burr early in 1807 and bring him to trial for treason. Burr was acquitted, however.

Jefferson's main concern in his second administration was foreign affairs, in which he experienced a notable failure. In the course of the Napoleonic Wars Britain and France repeatedly violated American sovereignty in incidents such as the CHESAPEAKE affair (1807). Jefferson attempted to avoid a policy of either appeasement or war by the use of economic pressure.

The EMBARGO ACT (Dec. 22, 1807), which prohibited virtually all exports and most imports and was supplemented by enforcing legislation, was designed to coerce British and French recognition of American rights. Although it failed, it did rouse many northerners, who suffered economically, to a state of defiance of national authority. The Federalist party experienced a rebirth of popularity. In 1809, shortly before he retired from the presidency, Jefferson signed the act repealing the embargo, which had been in effect for 15 months.

Later Life. In the final 17 years of his life, Jefferson's major accomplishment was the founding (1819) of the University of Virginia at Charlottesville. He conceived it, planned it, designed it, and supervised both its construction and the hiring of faculty.

The university was the last of three contributions by which Jefferson wished to be remembered; they constituted a trilogy of interrelated causes: freedom from Britain, freedom of conscience, and freedom maintained through education. On July 4, 1826, the 50th anniversary of the Declaration of Independence, Jefferson died at Monticello.   MORTON BORDEN

Bibliography: Boyd, Julian P., et al., eds., *The Papers of Thomas Jefferson*, 19 vols. (1950-   ); Brodie, Fawn, *Thomas Jefferson: An Intimate History* (1974); Chinard, Gilbert, *Thomas Jefferson: Apostle of Americanism* (1929); McDonald, Forrest, *The Presidency of Thomas Jefferson* (1976); Malone, Dumas, *Jefferson and His Time*, 5 vols. (1948-74); Nock, Albert J., *Jefferson* (1926); Peterson, Merrill D., *Thomas Jefferson and the New Nation* (1970); Schachner, Nathan, *Thomas Jefferson*, 2 vols. (1951); Smith, Page, *Jefferson: A Revealing Biography* (1976), Wills, Garry, *Inventing America: Jefferson's Declaration of Independence* (1978).

Jefferson Airplane

The ROCK MUSIC group Jefferson Airplane came out of San Francisco's HAIGHT-ASHBURY during that area's heyday as the center of the counter-culture movement. Founded in early 1965 by singer Marty Balin (b. Cincinnati, Jan. 30, 1943) and singer-guitarist Paul Kantner (b. San Francisco, Mar. 12, 1942), the band gained a large following after singer Grace Slick (b. Chicago, Oct. 30, 1939) joined the group in late 1966, bringing with her two popular American songs, "Somebody to Love" and "White Rabbit" (both released in 1967). From 1970 rifts between members caused a gradual disbanding, but in 1974 the group reformed under the name Jefferson Starship and released their extraordinarily successful album *Red Octopus* in 1975.

Jefferson City

Jefferson City, in central Missouri on the Missouri River, is the capital of the state and seat of Cole County. It has a population of 37,200 (1979 est.). Jefferson City is the center of trade for an agricultural region that grows grain and fruit and raises livestock. Manufactured goods include clothing, steel products, and processed food. The state and local governments are important employers.

The capitol, which was built (1911-18) in the Italian Renaissance style of Carthage marble, contains murals by painters N. C. WYETH and Thomas Hart BENTON and houses two museums. Lincoln University (1866), a state penitentiary, and a national cemetery are also located there.

A small river settlement when chosen as state capital in 1821, Jefferson City was laid out (1822) by Daniel M. Boone, son of the frontiersman, and developed slowly with railroad and river commerce. During the Civil War, because of its divided loyalties, the city was occupied by Union troops.

Jeffords, Thomas   [jef'-urdz]

Thomas Jeffords, b. Chautauqua County, N.Y., 1832, d. 1914, a U.S. army scout and stagecoach driver in Arizona, became a friend and agent of the Chiracahua APACHES. In 1872, Jeffords took part with Gen. Oliver O. HOWARD in negotiations with the Chiracahua chief, COCHISE, that helped secure for the Chiracahua a reservation in their southeastern Arizona homeland. At Cochise's request, Jeffords was named the reservation's agent, a post he held until the Chiracahua were transferred (1876) to another reservation.

Jeffrey, Francis

A Scottish critic and a successful lawyer, Lord Francis Jeffrey, b. Oct. 23, 1773, d. Jan. 26, 1850, helped found the *Edinburgh Review* in 1802 and served as its editor until 1829. A moderate Whig, he was hostile to many important new poets, and his criticism of Thomas Moore nearly led to a duel. Under his guidance, however, the *Review* helped to set the tone of literary journalism during the period.   ROBIN BUSS

Bibliography: Cockburn, Henry, *Life of Lord Jeffrey* (1852; repr. 1973).

Jeffreys, George Jeffreys, 1st Baron

The English judge George Jeffreys, b. between October 1644 and May 1645, was created Baron Jeffreys of Wem in May 1685. He gained notoriety for his part in the trials of the supporters of the duke of MONMOUTH's rebellion against King JAMES II in July 1685. In the trials, called the Bloody Assizes, nearly 200 persons were condemned to death and about 800 transported to the New World. Especially infamous was Jeffreys's insistence on a verdict of guilty for Alice Lisle, who was accused of harboring rebels; he also extorted money from many of the defendants. Nonetheless, in September 1685 he became lord chancellor. After the flight of King James in December 1688, Jeffreys was arrested; he died in the Tower of London on Apr. 18, 1689.

Bibliography: Helm, P. J., *Jeffreys* (1966); Keeton, G. W., *Lord Chancellor Jeffreys and the Stuart Cause* (1965).

Jeffreys, Sir Harold

The English astronomer and geophysicist Sir Harold Jeffreys, b. Apr. 22, 1891, is best known for his work on geophysics, the physics of the Earth. A graduate of Saint John's College, Cambridge, Jeffreys served there as Plumian professor of astronomy and experimental philosophy from 1946-58. He was one of the first to deduce times of travel for waves from earthquakes—a fundamental achievement in the study of the Earth's structure—and from this he hypothesized that the Earth had a liquid core. He investigated the thermal history of the Earth, stresses in its crust, and tidal friction.

Jeffreys's book *The Earth: Its Origin, History, and Physical Constitution* (1924) remained for many decades the best treatment of mathematical physics applied to the Earth, and it was still being reprinted in the late 1970s. His work on the Earth led Jeffreys to write *Scientific Inference* (1957) and *Methods of Mathematical Physics* (1946). His investigations also extended to planetary structure, the origin of the solar system, and the effect of the Earth's liquid core on nutation. He was knighted in 1953.   STEVEN J. DICK

Bibliography: Moore, Ruth, *The Earth We Live On* (1956).

Jeffries, James J.

James J. Jeffries, b. Carroll, Ohio, Apr. 15, 1875, d. Mar. 3, 1953, was an American heavyweight boxing champion who won the title in 1899 and defended it successfully six times, retaining it until he retired undefeated in 1905. A strong, intelligent boxer who made the defensive crouch popular, Jeffries knocked out Bob Fitzsimmons to earn the title. His defenses of the title included 2 victories over James J. Corbett and 1 over Fitzsimmons. His only loss against 20 wins and 2 draws was to Jack Johnson during a comeback attempt in 1910; Johnson knocked out Jeffries in the 15th round.

Jehangir: see JAHANGIR, MOGUL EMPEROR OF INDIA.

Jehoiakim, King of Judah   [jee-hoy'-uh-kin, joo'-duh]

According to the Bible, Jehoiakim was the king of Judah, the southern kingdom of ancient Israel, from 609 to 598 BC. When King JOSIAH died at Megiddo in 609, he was succeeded by his son Jehoahaz. The Egyptian pharaoh Necho, however, deposed Jehoahaz and placed Jehoiakim, also a son of Josiah, on the throne (II Kings 23). Judah subsequently came under Babylonian domination, but Jehoiakim rebelled about 601. He died shortly before NEBUCHADNEZZAR II took Jerusalem in 597. The prophet Jeremiah speaks of the reign of Jehoiakim (Jeremiah 36).

Jehoshaphat, King of Judah   [jee-hahsh'-uh fat]

Jehoshaphat, son and successor of Asa, was king of Judah, the southern kingdom of the ancient Israelites, from 873 to 849 BC. He became an ally of AHAB, king of Israel, and his successors, and during his reign, Judah and Israel agreed upon a treaty, ending the warfare dating from King Solomon. He was succeeded by his son Jehoram.

Jehovah: see GOD.

Jehovah's Witnesses   [juh-hoh'-vuhz]

Jehovah's Witnesses are a society of Christians who promote home study of the Bible, which they hold to be the complete Word of God. They believe that God's kingdom is an actual government now ruling in heaven that will soon restore the earth to its original paradisaic condition. They expect an early end to the present world system in a "great tribulation" from God that will rid the earth of wickedness and suffering. Following Armageddon will come a millennial reign over the earth by Jesus. The gaining of eternal life depends on complete obedience to Jehovah God and faith in the provision of Jesus Christ's ransom sacrifice. The Witnesses encourage adherence to the Bible's moral standards. Because of their neutrality as to affairs of secular government, their refusal to salute any flag, and their rejection of the practice of blood transfusion (which they believe is forbidden by the Bible), the Witnesses have been the subject of controversy.

The activities of Jehovah's Witnesses are coordinated by a governing body at international headquarters in Brooklyn, New York. In the more than 42,000 congregations worldwide, elders, male members meeting certain scriptural qualifications, preside as a body. Instruction and training are provided for all at five meetings a week, held primarily in "Kingdom Halls." The Watchtower Bible and Tract Society of Pennsylvania and the Watchtower Bible and Tract Society of New York, Inc., are the legal agencies of Jehovah's Witnesses. They print and distribute the Bible. Their principal periodical, *The Watchtower*, has a circulation of 8,300,000 copies in more than 100 languages.

The Witnesses acknowledge Jehovah God as their founder. The modern movement was organized in the 1870s by Charles Taze RUSSELL. By 1979, Jehovah's Witnesses numbered 2.2 million in more than 200 lands.   F. W. FRANZ

Bibliography: Cole, Marley, *Jehovah's Witnesses—The New World Society* (1955); Macmillan, A. H., *Faith on the March* (1957); Watchtower Bible and Tract Society, *Yearbook of Jehovah's Witnesses* (annual).

Jehu, King of Israel   [jee'-hyoo]

Jehu reigned as king of ancient Israel from 842 to 815 BC. He was anointed king by the prophet ELISHA, who instructed him to overthrow the wicked King AHAB (II Kings 9-10). With the army's support Jehu slaughtered the entire royal family and purged Israel of the idolatrous BAAL worship.

Jellicoe, Ann   [jel'-ih-koh]

Ann Patricia Jellicoe, b. July 15, 1927, is an English playwright who gained attention with her experimental work *The Sport of My Mad Mother* (1956). Trained as an actress and stage manager, she founded the Cockpit Theatre, London, in 1951, but she is best known for her play *The Knack* (1961; film, 1965), successful in both its stage and film versions.

Bibliography: McCrindle, Joseph F., ed., *Behind the Scenes* (1971).

jellyfish

A jellyfish is a free-swimming, sexually reproductive stage (medusa) found in the life cycle of certain species of COELENTERATES (phylum Cnidaria). It typically is shaped like a bell or inverted bowl from 3 mm to 2 m (0.12 in to 6.5 ft) in diameter. The bell's margin contains small sense organs that respond to light and gravity; the margin also bears tentacles the length and position of which vary considerably from species to species. The mouth is at the end of a projection called the manubrium, which hangs down within the center of the bell; the corners of the manubrium, in some species, extend into four or more oral arms. Much of the animal is composed of a firm, gelatinous middle layer (mesoglea), from which the common name *jellyfish* is derived.

Jellyfish feed on organisms ranging from plankton and fish to other jellyfish. They catch their prey by using nematocysts, small stinging organs present in the tentacles and oral arms. Rhythmic contractions of the bell's margins expel water from within the bell, and the animal moves forward by jet propulsion. Some species are strong swimmers, whereas others drift with the currents.

Jellyfish are of separate sexes and thus produce eggs or sperm. The fertilized egg develops into a planktonic planula larva, which is flattened and ciliated. Eventually the larva develops into a sedentary, asexually reproducing polyp. Most members of the class Hydrozoa possess a dominant polyp phase and a medusa, which, if present at all, is quite small. Large jellyfish belong to the class Scyphozoa, a group whose polyp stage is small and inconspicuous. In both classes new medusae are produced asexually by the polyp stage

Particularly in late summer, jellyfish often become abundant in coastal areas and are a nuisance to swimmers. The nematocysts of several species are not harmful to humans; other species such as sea nettles, however, can penetrate the skin, causing stings and subsequent rash. The most dangerous are certain boxlike jellyfish of the order Cubomedusae, found from the Philippines to tropical Australia; their stings have caused a number of fatalities.

A jellyfish, family Medusae, propels itself easily through the ocean by shooting water from its gelatinous, bell-like body. The jellyfish stings and paralyzes prey that wander into its curtain of tentacles.

A small, freshwater jellyfish, genus *Craspedacusta*, is sometimes seen in the late summer. It is only 15 to 20 mm (0.06 to 0.08 in) in diameter and is produced by a minute, asexually reproducing polyp that lives on the bottoms of lakes, ponds, and streams. The PORTUGUESE MAN-OF-WAR, sometimes mistakenly called a jellyfish, actually is a colony of polyplike and medusalike individuals that are attached to a gas-filled, floating membrane.   WENDELL K. PATTON

Bibliography: Bayer, Frederick M., and Owre, Harding B., *The Free-Living Lower Invertebrates* (1968); Hyman, Libbie H., *The Invertebrates*, vol. 1 (1940).

Jemison, Mary   [jem'-ih-suhn]

Mary Jemison, b. 1742, d. Sept. 19, 1833, was taken from her parents' frontier farm in Pennsylvania by an Indian raiding party in 1758. Known as the White Woman of the Genesee, she lived the rest of her life with the Seneca on the Genesee River in New York State, marrying two Seneca husbands. Her life story appears in J. E. Seaver's *Narrative of the Life of Mrs. Jemison* (1824; repr. 1967).

Jena   [yay'-nah]

Jena is a city of 100,979 people (1977) in southern East Germany, on the Saale River. With a temperate continental climate, Jena has an average January temperature of −1° C (30° F) and a July average of 19° C (66° F); precipitation is 600 mm (24 in). The site of the famous Schott and Zeiss glass plants, the town is noted for its production of optical instruments, lenses, astronomical equipment, and chemicals.

First mentioned in 9th-century documents, Jena was chartered in 1230 and flourished during the Middle Ages. Some of the city's medieval fortifications, Saint Michael's Church (begun 1390), and the 14th-century town hall remain. The Friedrich-Schiller University (1548) attracted Germany's most liberal philosophers and writers and was most prominent during the late 18th and early 19th centuries. Napoleon defeated the Prussian and Saxon armies on the northwest outskirts of the city on Oct. 14, 1806.

Jencks, Christopher

Christopher Sandys Jencks, b. Baltimore, Md., Oct. 22, 1936, is an American sociologist and educational consultant. He teaches at Harvard University's School of Education. With David RIESMAN, Jencks wrote *The Academic Revolution* (1968), a study of professionalization in higher education. In 1970 he devised the educational voucher plan, a controversial proposal that would allow parents to choose either a private or a public school for the publicly financed education of their children. His study, *Inequality: A Reassessment of the Effect of Family and Schooling in America* (1972), claimed that schooling has little effect on social mobility and that only direct social change can correct existing inequalities.

Jenkins, Charles Francis

The inventor Charles Francis Jenkins, b. near Dayton, Ohio, Aug. 22, 1867, d. June 6, 1934, pioneered in the early development of cinematography and television. He invented the phantascope, one of the earliest successful motion-picture projectors. He also designed (1925) an experimental television system based on a mechanical scene-scanning method, invented by Paul Nipkow. Jenkins was awarded more than 400 patents and was the founder and first president (1916) of the Society of Motion Picture Engineers.

Bibliography: Hylander, C., *American Inventors* (1934; repr. 1964).

Jenkins, Roy

Roy Harris Jenkins, b. Nov. 11, 1920, British politician and government minister, became president of the Commission of the European Community on Jan. 6, 1977. The son of a Welsh miner (later a Labour member of Parliament), Jenkins attended Oxford and was elected to Parliament in 1948 as a Labour member. He was minister of aviation (1964-65), home secretary (1965-67, 1974-76), and chancellor of the exchequer (1967-70). He has published works in biography and history, including *Asquith* (1964) and *Nine Men of Power* (1974).

K. M. SMOGORZEWSKI

Jenner, Bruce

Bruce Jenner, b. Mount Kisco, N.Y., Oct. 28, 1949, was an American track and field star who won the decathlon in the 1976 Olympic Games at Montreal with a record 8,618 points. It was the 3d time he had broken the world record in two years. As a youth he played football, ran track, and was a champion water-skier. Jenner first competed in a decathlon in 1970 and his rapid progress earned him a place on the 1972 U.S. Olympic team. In the years between Olympics he won 12 of the 13 decathlons that he participated in. After his Olympic victory, which was publicized by extensive television coverage, he parlayed his athletic success and good looks into an entertainment career, notably in breakfast-food commercials.

Bibliography: Jenner, Bruce, *Decathlon Challenge* (1977).

Jenner, Edward

Edward Jenner, b. May 17, 1749, d. Jan. 26, 1823, was an English physician responsible for a practical vaccination against smallpox. While practicing medicine in Berkeley, England, Jenner noticed that dairy maids who had contracted the relatively mild disease cowpox did not later contract smallpox. In 1796 he innoculated an 8-year-old boy with material taken from cowpox pustules and the boy developed cowpox. Several weeks later Jenner innoculated the boy with smallpox, but the disease failed to develop.

In 1798, Jenner published *An Inquiry into the Causes and Effects of the Variolae Vaccinae. . .* and later promoted smallpox vaccinations, the practice of which spread throughout the world, apparently eliminating this disease in the late 1970s.

Bibliography: Dolan, Edward F., *Jenner and the Miracle of Vaccine* (1960); Levine, Israel E., *Conqueror of Smallpox; Dr. Edward Jenner* (1960).

Jenney, William LeBaron

William LeBaron Jenney, b. Fairhaven, Mass., Sept. 25, 1832, d. May 14, 1907, was an influential American engineer and architect credited with developing a load-bearing frame of metal that made possible the development of the skyscraper. Jenney studied engineering at the Lawrence Scientific School in Cambridge, Mass., and at the École Centrale des Arts et Manufactures in Paris. During the Civil War he returned to the United States and rose to high rank as an engineer in the Union army. In 1866 he established an architectural practice in Chicago.

The disastrous Chicago fire of 1871 and the great growth of that city in the 1870s and '80s provided enormous opportunities for architects, and Jenney designed several important commercial and office buildings. His Home Insurance Building (1883-85; demolished 1931) is considered the first tall building in which a frame, or skeleton, of metal columns and beams replaced load-bearing walls. While this building was under construction, structural steel first became available in quantity and at reasonable prices so that Jenney was able to add a second innovation by making the upper portions of his structural skeleton of steel rather than of the weaker and more common cast iron.

Jenney also had an important role in training architects who later rose to great prominence in Chicago, including Daniel Hudson BURNHAM, William HOLABIRD, Louis SULLIVAN, and Martin Roche.

RON WIEDENHOEFT

Bibliography: Condit, Carl, *The Rise of the Skyscraper* (1952); Kingsford, P. W., *Builders and Building Workers* (1973).

Jensen, Arthur

Arthur Robert Jensen, b. San Diego, Calif., Aug. 24, 1923, is an American educational psychologist whose article "How Much Can We Boost IQ and Scholarly Achievement?" (1969) in the *Harvard Educational Review* aroused widespread controversy. "Compensatory education has been tried and it apparently has failed," Jensen claimed in the article. He attributed this failure largely to severe genetic limits to what educational intervention can achieve.

Jensen claimed that the observed gap in IQs between children of disadvantaged and more privileged backgrounds and between black and white children is largely due to genetic factors. His article met with a severely critical reception from many scholars.

Bibliography: Berube, M. R., "Jensen's Complaint," *Commonweal*, Oct. 10, 1969; Jensen, Arthur R., "What Is the Question? What Is the Evidence?" *Psychologists*, vol. 2, ed. by T. S. Krawiec (1974).

See also: INTELLIGENCE.

Jensen, Hans

The German physicist Johannes Hans Daniel Jensen, b. June 28, 1906, is known for his work on the shell structure theory of the nucleus, which states that protons and neutrons are arranged in shells like electrons. His conclusion, reached independently of Maria Goeppert MAYER, led to their collaboration on a joint publication on the shell theory. For this work Jensen, Goeppert Mayer, and Eugene WIGNER received the 1963 Nobel Prize for physics.

JAMES A. BOOTH

Jensen, Johannes Vilhelm [yen'-sen, yoh-hahn'-es vil'-helm]

The Danish novelist Johannes Vilhelm Jensen, b. Farsø, Jan. 20, 1873, d. Nov. 25, 1950, won the Nobel Prize for literature in 1944 for his six-part cycle *The Long Journey* (1908-22; Eng. trans., 1922-24), which explored the development of the human race from prehistoric times to Columbus's discovery of America. Jensen's interest in Darwinism, anthropology, and myth also found expression in poems, tales, and essays. He traveled widely, many of his tales growing out of visits to the United States and the Far East. Other novels include the historical trilogy *The Fall of the King* (1900-1901; Eng. trans., 1933), based on the life of Denmark's Christian II.

Bibliography: Nielsen, Marion L., *Denmark's Johannes V. Jensen* (1955).

Jerash: see GERASA.

jerboa [jur-boh'-uh]

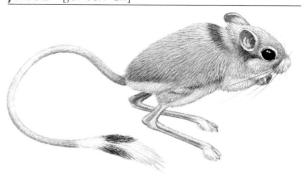

The desert jerboa, or Egyptian jerboa, Jaculus jaculus, *resembles a miniature kangaroo and can jump a few meters in one leap.*

Jerboas are jumping rodents of the family Dipodidae. There are 25 species, grouped into 10 genera, found in open, usually arid areas from northern Africa to northern China. Their hind legs are at least four times as long as their forelegs, and some species are capable of covering 2.5 m (8 ft) in a single leap. Jerboas range from 38 mm to 20 cm (1.5 to 8 in) in length; their tails may be 6 to 25 cm (2.5 to 10 in) long.

EVERETT SENTMAN

Jeremiah, Book of   [jair-uh-my'-uh]

The Book of Jeremiah, second of the Major Prophets or longer books of the prophetic collection of the Old Testament of the BIBLE, derives its name from the prophet Jeremiah who lived in Anathoth, on the outskirts of Jerusalem. His prophetic career ranged from about 626 BC, during the reign of Josiah, at least to the fall of Jerusalem (586 BC) and the deportation of the population; at this time Jeremiah was taken by the remaining Jewish community to Egypt, where he died. The career of Jeremiah embraced the period of Josiah's reformation (626-622 BC); the years of resurgent Judaic nationalism (608-597 BC); the period leading to the final demise of Judah (597-586 BC); and the time in Egypt.

The message of Jeremiah was a call to moral reform to establish a personal relationship between God and humankind. He advocated resignation in the face of political and religious crisis and denounced sin as a perversion of creation. He called urgently for repentance so that turning to God might lead to a new creation; he thus prefigured the New Testament notion of the "new covenant."

The Book of Jeremiah is composed of a collection of sayings, as well as autobiographical passages, the "confessions of Jeremiah." Considerable debate has developed over the designation of an original scroll containing Jeremiah's words in contrast to later rewriting of the scroll—both a rewriting engineered by Jeremiah and several successive editions of the book running through the Deuteronomistic period. To reconstruct the original scroll in detail does not seem possible. The "confessions," probably an original collection in its own right, includes the passages in 11:18-23; 12:1-6; 15:10; 17:14-18; 18:18-23; 20:7-13, 14-18, and perhaps also 15:15-20. The parallel for these "confessions" lies in the lamentation or complaint Psalms. They reveal Jeremiah's dramatic inner conflict in his struggle to surrender himself to God. In addition, the book contains some royal sayings (21:13-14; 22:1-7, 10, 13-19, 24-27, 28, 29-30); a minor collection "concerning the prophets"; one of optimistic sayings; and a group of oracles against foreign nations (46-51).   GEORGE W. COATS

Bibliography: Fohrer, Georg, *Introduction to the Old Testament*, trans. by David E. Green (1968); Holladay, W. L., "Jeremiah the Prophet," in *The Interpreter's Dictionary of the Bible Supplement* (1976); Soggin, J. Alberto, *Introduction to the Old Testament*, trans. by John Bowden, (1976).

Jerez de la Frontera   [hah'-rayth day lah frohn-tay'-rah]

Jerez de la Frontera is a city in southwestern Spain, 23 km (14 mi) northeast of Cádiz. Its population is 125,800 (1975). The city is famous for its sherry wines (the word *sherry* is derived from the English pronunciation of the city's name), its superior brandies, and Jerez horses. Originally a Roman colony, Jerez was held by the Moors from the early 8th century until its recapture by Alfonso X of Castile in 1264. A notable landmark is the Moorish Alcázar, an 11th-century palace rebuilt in the 14th century.

Jericho   [jair'-ih-koh]

Excavations at ancient Jericho, identified as Tell al-Sultan, 10 km (6 mi) north of the Dead Sea in Israeli-occupied Jordan, have revealed remains of the oldest city yet discovered by archaeologists. The earliest occupation of the site, dating from the 10th millennium BC, consists of remains of the NATUFIAN culture and includes what may have been a shrine. During the 8th millennium BC the site was greatly expanded under a culture known as the Aceramic, or Prepottery Neolithic A, and a wall standing 5.2 m (17 ft) high was erected around the settlement. On the west side were found remains of a round tower that stood 7 m (23 ft) high and included an internal flight of steps.

Four phases of reconstruction combined with the thickness of occupation debris testify to the long life of the early city. Following a break the next city was populated by a culture known as the Prepottery Neolithic B (7th-6th millennium BC). Houses of this phase were rectangular and had beaten earth

floors. That the two cultures represent different groups is shown by significant changes in both the architectural tradition and in the flint tools. Two possible shrines have been excavated belonging to this phase. Extraordinary finds of this period included plastered skulls with shells replacing the eyes. These skulls, found beneath the floors of houses, may have been connected with some form of ancestor cult.

In the ceramic stage of the Neolithic (6th-4th millennium BC) the dwellers lived in pits and produced a characteristic painted pottery. Early Bronze Age occupation (3100-2100 BC) was extensive and consisted of large, well-built homes. Tombs were constructed for mass burials, and in one such grave about 100 skulls were counted. Following the destruction of the Early Bronze Age settlement, occupation was resumed by people who have been identified with the AMORITES. They did not build a permanent settlement and buried their dead in shaft tombs, the variety of whose grave deposits may indicate tribal differences.

During the Middle Bronze Age (c.1900-1550 BC) houses consisting of small irregularly shaped rooms were built, and the city was fortified by an earthen rampart faced with plaster, surmounted by city walls. A huge retaining wall at the base of the slope existed in the final phase. Mass burials were excavated in a cemetery off the mound in shaft graves. The remains of wooden beds on which the deceased lay as well as pottery vessels containing food and drink have been found next to several of the bodies. The city was destroyed about 1560 BC by the Egyptians during their campaigns against the Hyksos. The remains of the Late Bronze Age and later periods were almost totally eroded away, and nothing remained of the walls that Joshua is alleged to have demolished (see JOSHUA, BOOK OF). Extensive excavations were conducted in 1930-36 by John GARSTANG for Liverpool University and in 1952-58 by Kathleen KENYON for the British School of Archaeology in Jerusalem.   JONATHAN N. TUBB

Bibliography: Garstang, John, and Garstang, J. B. E., *The Story of Jericho*, 2d ed (1948); Kenyon, Kathleen, *Amorites and Canaanites* (1966), *Archaeology in the Holy Land*, 3d. ed. (1970), *Digging Up Jericho* (1957), and *Excavations at Jericho*, 2 vols. (1960-65); Mellaart, James, *The Neolithic of the Near East* (1975).

Jeritza, Maria   [yuh-rits'-uh]

A Czech dramatic soprano, Maria Jeritza (or Jedlitzka), b. Oct. 6, 1887, had a brilliant voice and powerful stage magnetism. She made her debut (1910) as Elsa in Wagner's *Lohengrin* at Olomouc. From 1912 to 1935 she was prima donna of the Vienna State Opera, and from 1921 to 1932 she appeared at the Metropolitan Opera. She sang in the USSR and at all the great opera houses of Europe, often in roles created for her by composers. She was outstanding as Ariadne in Strauss's *Ariadne Auf Naxos* (1912), as Janáček's *Jenufa* (1918), as the empress in Strauss's *Die Frau Ohne Schatten* (1919), and as Marietta in Korngold's *Die tote stadt* (1921). Jeritza appeared in films during the 1930s in Hollywood, where she retired, and she made brief appearances in New York City and Vienna after World War II.   ELLA A. MALIN

Bibliography: Jeritza, Maria, *Sunlight and Song* (1924); Pleasants, Henry, *The Great Singers* (1966).

Jeroboam I, King of Israel   [jair-uh-boh'-uhm]

When ancient Israel split into two kingdoms after Solomon's death, Jeroboam was the first king of the ten northern tribes, from about 922 to 901 BC. Initially a trusted aide, Jeroboam led a revolt against SOLOMON and fled from his sudden wrath to Egypt. When the northern tribes refused allegiance to Solomon's son REHOBOAM, Jeroboam was named king; war resulted between the northern kingdom of Israel and the southern kingdom of Judah. Jeroboam fortified Shechem and waged continuous war on Judah. Choosing Dan and Bethel as alternative shrines to the south's Jerusalem, Jeroboam set up the golden calves at the shrines; the Bible (I Kings 12) interpreted this as idolatry. Upon his death he was succeeded as king by his son Nadab.

Bibliography: Bright, John, *A History of Israel*, 2d ed. (1972).

Jerome, Jerome K.

An English humorist, Jerome Klapka Jerome, b. May 21, 1859, d. June 14, 1927, is best remembered for his hilarious story of an accident-prone river excursion, *Three Men in a Boat* (1889). Jerome also enjoyed success as the author of a popular play, *The Passing of the Third Floor Back* (1908), and as the founder (1892) of the monthly *The Idler*.   ROBIN BUSS

Bibliography: Faurot, Ruth M., *Jerome K. Jerome* (1974).

Jerome, Saint

Saint Jerome in his Study (c.1450-55), a panel by the Italian Antonello da Messina, portrays the early church father and scholar at work. Jerome's translation of the Old Testament and much of the New formed the basis of the Vulgate, the Latin Bible used by the Roman Catholic church. (National Gallery, London.)

Jerome (Eusebius Hieronymus), c.347–420, was a Father of the Church and Doctor of the Church, whose great work was the translation of the Bible into Latin, the edition known as the Vulgate (see BIBLE). He was born at Stridon on the borders of Dalmatia and Pannonia of a well-to-do Christian family. His parents sent him to Rome to further his intellectual interests, and there he acquired a knowledge of classical literature and was baptized at the age of 19. Shortly thereafter he journeyed to Trier in Gaul and to Aquileia in Italy, where he began to cultivate his theological interests in company with others who, like himself, were ascetically inclined.

About 373, Jerome set out on a pilgrimage to the East. In Antioch, where he was warmly received, he continued to pursue his humanist and monastic studies. He also had a profound spiritual experience, dreaming that he was accused of being "a Ciceronian, not a Christian." Accordingly, he determined to devote himself exclusively to the Bible and theology, although the translator Rufinus (345–410), Jerome's close friend, suggested later that the vow was not strictly kept. Jerome moved to the desert of Chalcis, and while practicing more rigorous austerities, pursued his studies, including the learning of Hebrew. On his return to Antioch in 378 he heard Apollinaris the Younger (c.310–c.390) lecture and was admitted to the priesthood (379) by Paulinus, bishop of Antioch. In Constantinople, where he spent three years around 380, he was influenced by GREGORY OF NAZIANZUS.

When Jerome returned to Rome Pope DAMASUS I appointed him confidential secretary and librarian and commissioned him to begin his work of rendering the Bible into Latin. After the death (384) of Damasus, however, Jerome fell out of favor, and for a second time he decided to go to the East. He made brief visits to Antioch, Egypt, and Palestine. In 386, Jerome settled at Bethlehem in a monastery established for him by Paula, one of a group of wealthy Roman women whose spiritual advisor he had been and who remained his lifelong friend. There he began his most productive literary period, and there he remained for 34 years, until his death. From this period come his major biblical commentaries and the bulk of his work on the Latin Bible.

The writings of Jerome express a scholarship unsurpassed in the early church and helped to create the cultural tradition of the Middle Ages. He developed the use of philological and geographical material in his exegesis and recognized the scientific importance of archaeology. In his interpretation of the Bible he used both the allegorical method of the Alexandrian

and the realism of the Antiochene schools. A difficult and hot-tempered man, Jerome made many enemies, but his correspondence with friends and enemies alike is of great interest, particularly that with Saint AUGUSTINE. His greatest gifts were in scholarship, and he is a true founder of scientific biblical exegesis in the West. Feast day: Sept. 30 (Western).

ROSS MACKENZIE

Bibliography: Kelly, J. N. D., *Jerome, His Life, Writings, and Controversies* (1975); Steinmann, Jean, *Saint Jerome and His Times* (1959); Wiesen, David S., *St. Jerome as a Satirist* (1949; repr. 1964).

Jerome of Prague

Jerome, b. Prague, c.1370, d. May 30, 1416, a Bohemian church reformer and associate of John Huss, led the life of a wandering scholar. Educated at Prague, Oxford, Paris, Heidelberg, and Cologne, he became an advocate of John WYCLIFFE's views and acquainted (1401) Huss with these metaphysical and theological opinions. Brilliant in debate, Jerome became (1407) a spokesman for the Bohemian reform party in the university at Prague. When Huss was summoned before the Council of CONSTANCE, Jerome joined him. Although he was persuaded to renounce Wycliffe and Huss, he later withdrew his recantation and was burned at the stake for heresy.

JAMES D. NELSON

Jerrold, Douglas William

The English dramatist and journalist Douglas William Jerrold, b. Jan. 3, 1803, d. June 8, 1857, was the author of numerous melodramas and farces, as well as the founder and editor of several periodicals and a contributor to *Punch*. He served as a boy sailor in the British Navy during the Napoleonic Wars and then trained as a printer. His first play, *The Duellist*, written in 1818 and staged in 1821, was followed by such works as *Fifteen Years of a Drunkard's Life* (1828) and *Black-eyed Susan* (1829).   ROBIN BUSS

Bibliography: Kelley, Richard Michael, *Douglas Jerrold* (1972).

Jersey

Jersey, with an area of 117 km² (45 mi²) and a population of 74,470 (1976), is the largest and southernmost of the CHANNEL ISLANDS, a British dependency. It is located in the English Channel about 24 km (15 mi) west of the Normandy coast of France. Its capital is Saint Helier. Known for Jersey cattle, the island also supports the growing of potatoes, tomatoes, and greenhouse flowers for export and is a popular tourist resort. French is the official language.

jersey

Jersey is a general term for a variety of knitted fabrics made of wool, cotton, silk, or synthetic fibers. Weft-knitted jerseys, in which the yarn loopings run across the fabric, stretch both vertically and horizontally and are used for hosiery, gloves, nightgowns, and T-shirts. Warp-knitted jerseys stretch only along the width and are usually less elastic and more tightly woven than weft knits. Warp knits are used for dresses, shirts, and lingerie. The fabric name is derived from the English Channel Islands of Jersey, where the knitting of woolen cloth for fishers is an old cottage industry. In Britain sweaters are commonly called jerseys.   ISABEL B. WINGATE

See also: KNITTING; TEXTILE INDUSTRY.

Jersey cattle: see CATTLE AND CATTLE RAISING.

Jersey City

Located in northeastern New Jersey on the Hudson River opposite lower Manhattan, Jersey City is the seat of Hudson County and the state's second largest city, with a population of 231,000 (1979 est.). This busy port city (part of the Port of New York) has one of the most comprehensive transportation complexes on the Atlantic seaboard, making it a leading commercial and industrial center in the state (surpassed only by Newark). Chemicals, transportation equipment, and clothing manufacturing, and petroleum refining, are the major products of Jersey City's diversified industries. Jersey City has several colleges and a huge medical center.

First settled in 1618 by Dutch trappers, the area was acquired by Michiel Paux about 1629. About 1660, the stockaded village of Bergen was laid out. The site came under British rule in 1664. In the American Revolution the British-held fort at Paulus Hook was attacked and captured (1779) by Light-Horse Harry Lee. Jersey City, incorporated in 1820, was later expanded to include the former communities of Hudson City, Bergen, and Greenville. In 1916 a munitions warehouse on the Black Tom docks exploded, causing extensive damage; the incident was attributed to German saboteurs. Political boss Frank HAGUE was mayor of the city from 1917 to 1947.

Jerusalem   [juh-roo'-suh-lem]

Jerusalem (Hebrew: Yerushalayim; Arabic: Bayt al-Muqaddas), the capital of ISRAEL, is a holy city of Judaism, Christianity, and Islam. It is situated in the Judaean Hills, 55 km (35 mi) from the Mediterranean Sea. Jerusalem lies at an elevation of 745 m (2,440 ft) and covers an area of 109 km² (42 mi²). The population of the city is 355,500 (1976 est.), and that of the Jerusalem District, which includes the suburbs, is 392,100 persons (1976 est.). The growth of the city may be attributed to its location along a pass through the Judean Hills on an ancient trade route, and to its religious importance. For Jews, Jerusalem is the focus of their religious longing, the site of their ancient Temple, and their historical capital; for Christians, the city is the site of many of the events in the life of Jesus Christ; for Muslims, the city is their third holiest as the site from which Muhammad is said to have risen to heaven and the site of important mosques. Jerusalem's religious role makes tourism a major source of income. In 1949, at the end of the First ARAB-ISRAELI WAR, Jerusalem was partitioned between Israel and Jordan. In 1967, however, Israel won control of the entire city.

The rough topography of the city is due to the erosional power of the Kidron River, which has cut the narrow ridge of Mount Scopus (818 m/2,684 ft) and the Mount of Olives (808 m/2,652 ft). The ancient town's limestone base is dissected by the Valley of Bet Seita, the Tyropoeon Valley, and the Valley of Hinnom. Average annual rainfall is 510 mm (20 in); the mean July temperature is 24° C (75° F), and that of January is 9° C (48° F).

Contemporary City. Jews have constituted a majority of Jerusalem's population since about 1876; today they constitute about 75% of the population, and Arabs constitute about 20%. Both Hebrew and Arabic are spoken.

Jerusalem is divided into three sections: the Old City, New City (West Jerusalem), and East Jerusalem. The walled Old City, in the center, contains Muslim, Jewish, Christian, and Armenian quarters. The Old City was under Jordanian control from 1949 to 1967; during this period the Jewish quarter was destroyed, but it has recently been restored. Most of the narrow streets of the Old City are lined with shops where merchants sell foodstuffs and traditional handicrafts; homes are clustered around courtyards separated from the streets by high walls. Many of Jerusalem's religious landmarks are located in the Old City. The Western Wall (or Wailing Wall) is a small remaining portion of the original wall of Solomon's Temple. After the Jews were banished from the Temple Mount, the Western Wall became the most sacred place of Judaism. Atop the Temple Mount are the gold-domed Dome of the Rock (begun AD 661) and the silver-domed al-Aqsa (begun AD 710) mosques. The Via Dolorosa, a street in the Old City, is believed to be the site of the original Stations of the Cross. The Church of the Holy Sepulcher was begun in the 4th century AD and was rebuilt by the Crusaders beginning in 1099. The largest of Jerusalem's 160 parks is a 121-ha (300-acre) national park encircling the walls of the Old City.

The New City, built mostly by Jews, has expanded since the 19th century. This section was under Israeli control during the period of partition. Notable among the government buildings is the Knesset, seat of the Israeli parliament. The spacious campus of Hebrew University (1925), the nation's leading institution of higher learning, is located in the west. To the south is the Israel Museum, housing an art collection and an archaeological collection, as well as the Shrine of the Book, where the DEAD SEA SCROLLS are located. Further to the west, on the outskirts of the New City, are located modern high-rise apartment projects (primarily for immigrants) and the Hadassah Medical Center.

East Jerusalem, located just north of the Old City, is the modern Arab section. Although primarily a residential area, it is also the site of the Rockefeller Museum, with a fine archaeological collection.

Tourism is the major industry of the city, along with government-related functions. Industries include diamond cut-

Modern apartments dominate this view of Jerusalem, the capital of Israel. The city, which lies on the Judean Plateau west of the Dead Sea, was partitioned between Israel and Jordan until the Six-Day War of 1967, when Israeli forces occupied the Jordanian districts.

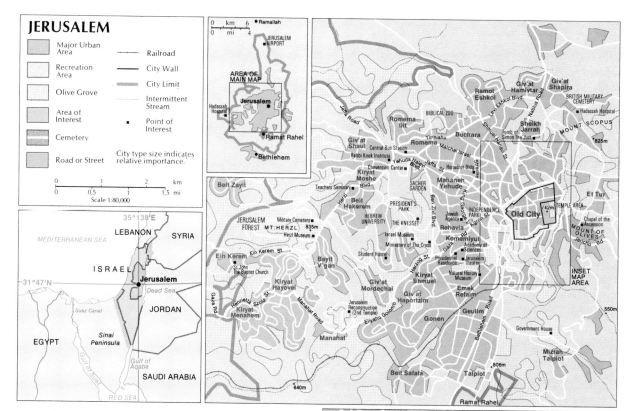

JERUSALEM

	Major Urban Area		Railroad
	Recreation Area		City Wall
	Olive Grove		City Limit
	Area of Interest		Intermittent Stream
	Cemetery	■	Point of Interest
	Road or Street		City type size indicates relative importance.

Scale 1:80,000

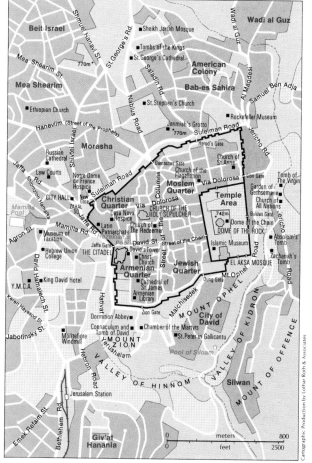

ting and polishing, home appliances, furniture, pharmaceuticals, chemicals, shoes, plastics, textiles and clothing, printing and publishing, and jewelry. The city is connected by rail and bus to Tel Aviv and is served by Mediterranean ports. Jerusalem is governed by a municipal council of 31 members elected to 4-year terms by proportional representation.

History. Jerusalem's history stretches back about 5,000 years. About 2500 BC, the Canaanites inhabited the city. Later, Jerusalem became a Jebusite citadel. When DAVID captured the city (c.1000 BC), the Jebusites were absorbed into the Jewish people. David made Jerusalem the capital of his kingdom, and SOLOMON built the first Temple to house the Ark of the Covenant. In 586 BC, the Babylonian NEBUCHADNEZZAR II destroyed Jerusalem and the Temple and exiled the Jews to Babylonia. Fifty years later (537 BC), CYRUS THE GREAT of Persia conquered Babylonia and permitted the Jews to return to Jerusalem and rebuild their Temple. Persia held the city until 333 BC, when ALEXANDER THE GREAT added Palestine to his empire. In 323 BC, PTOLEMY I of Egypt took Palestine into his kingdom.

About 198 BC, the Seleucid king ANTIOCHUS III conquered Judaea (of which Jerusalem was a part), making it tributary to Syria. The Jews later revolted under the leadership of Maccabees (see MACCABEES family) and defeated the Syrians. The Temple was reconsecrated in 165 BC, and the Maccabean, or Hasmonean, dynasty ruled until Rome took the city in 63 BC. The Romans set up a local dynasty, the house of Herod (see HEROD dynasty), to rule most of Palestine; Herod the Great (r. 40–4 BC) rebuilt much of Jerusalem, including the Temple. Roman governors, however, retained ultimate control; one of them, Pontius Pilate, authorized the execution of Jesus Christ. While suppressing a major Jewish revolt, the Romans destroyed the Second Temple in AD 70. In 135, after the failure of the BAR KOCHBA revolt, Jews were banished from Jerusalem. From the early 4th century, when Christianity became legal in the Roman Empire, Jerusalem developed as a center of Christian pilgrimage. The Church of the Holy Sepulcher and many other Christian shrines were erected. Except for a brief period of Persian rule (614–28) the city remained under Roman (later, Byzantine) control until 638, when the Muslim Arabs took Je-

Cartographic Production by Lothar Roth & Associates

Jerusalem is held sacred by three religions. Jews meet in prayer at the Wailing Wall, which contains stones from the original Temple built by King Solomon. Above the wall is the Dome of the Rock, believed by Muslims to mark the point from which Muhammad ascended to heaven. The Mount of Olives, in the background, is important in Christianity as the site of Gethsemane.

rusalem. The Arabs built (688–91) the Dome of the Rock mosque on the site of the Temple.

In the 11th century, Muslim toleration of both Jews and Christians gave way to persecution under the FATIMID caliph al-Hakim (r. 996–1021) and under the SELJUKS, who seized Jerusalem in 1071. European Christendom responded by launching the CRUSADES.

The Crusaders conquered Jerusalem in 1099 and established a Crusader state (see JERUSALEM, LATIN KINGDOM OF). SALADIN recaptured the city for the Muslims in 1187, and the Ayyubid and Mameluke dynasties ruled until 1517, when the Ottoman Empire took control.

In 1917 the British occupied Jerusalem, and it became the capital of mandated PALESTINE from 1923 until 1948. During this period the city saw Arab rioting against the Jews. The 1948 United Nations partition plan for Palestine called for the internationalization of the city. The Arabs rejected this resolution, and, from 1949, Jerusalem was divided into an Israeli and a Jordanian sector. The city remained divided until 1967, when Israel took the entire city following the Six Day War. The city is reunited today under Israeli government, which guarantees religious freedom and protection of all holy places.   IRA M. SHESKIN

Bibliography: Bellow, Saul, *To Jerusalem and Back: A Personal Account* (1976); Benvenisti, Meron, *Jerusalem: The Torn City*, trans. by Peretz Kidron (1977); Capa, Cornell, *Jerusalem: City of Mankind* (1974); Gilbert, Martin, *Jerusalem History Atlas* (1977); Hopkins, J. W., *Jerusalem: A Study in Urban Geography*, ed. by Charles F. Pfeiffer (1970); Thubron, Colin, *Jerusalem* (1976).

Jerusalem, Latin Kingdom of

The Latin Kingdom of Jerusalem was created in 1099 by the leaders of the First CRUSADE; it fell to the Muslims in 1291. At its greatest extent (c.1140) it included Palestine from the Gulf of Aqaba to Beirut and claimed sovereignty over the other Crusader states to the north, the principality of Antioch and the counties of Tripoli and Edessa. The history of the kingdom falls into two periods separated by the reconquest of Jerusalem by the Muslim leader SALADIN in 1187.

During its first phase (1099–1187) the kingdom had its capital at Jerusalem. The Crusaders initially chose GODFREY OF

BOUILLON as ruler (1099–1100). Although he took only the title of Defender of the Holy Sepulcher, his successors, beginning with his brother Baldwin I (r. 1100–18), used the royal title. They hoped to expand and consolidate their position in Palestine and, in particular, to capture the coastal towns, which the First Crusade had bypassed. With naval help from Venice, Genoa, and Pisa, they were successful in this effort.

Muslim Arab opposition was initially fragmented among various petty states. After 1128, however, the Arab states were gradually unified by outstanding leaders, the greatest being Saladin, who became the ruler of Egypt in 1169. Launching a holy war in 1187, he defeated the Crusaders at Hattin, regained Jerusalem for the Muslims, and besieged the remaining Crusaders in Tyre, Tripoli, and Antioch, and in a few castles elsewhere.

In 1189 the Christians undertook the Third Crusade in an attempt to recover Jerusalem. This Crusade, however, and later expeditions succeeded only in retaking the coastal towns and an adjacent strip of territory. Thus, from 1191 the capital of the Latin Kingdom was at Acre. The kingdom thereafter was torn by conflicts between the barons and their rulers; among the Venetian, Genoese, and Pisan colonists; and between the military orders of the HOSPITALERS and the TEMPLARS. The knights of these orders provided the only reliable armed force. The fall of Acre to the Egyptian MAMELUKES in 1291 marked the end of the kingdom.

The kingship of Jerusalem was held by various dynasties, including the ANGEVINS and HOHENSTAUFENS (notably Holy Roman Emperor FREDERICK II) and the house of Lusignan, which also ruled Cyprus and Lesser Armenia.   C. M. BRAND

Bibliography: Praver, Joshua, *The Crusaders' Kingdom* (1972); Riley-Smith, Jonathan, *Feudal Nobility and the Kingdom of Jerusalem, 1174–1277* (1973); Runciman, Steven, *A History of the Crusades*, 3 vols.

LATIN KINGDOM OF JERUSALEM c.1140

☐ Kingdom of Jerusalem   ☐ Other crusader states

(1951–1954); Setton, Kenneth M., ed., *A History of the Crusades*, 4 vols., 2d ed. (1969–1977); William of Tyre, *A History of Deeds Done Beyond the Sea*, trans. by Emily A. Babcock and A. C. Krey, 2 vols. (1943).

Jerusalem artichoke

The Jerusalem artichoke, H. tuberosus, is an autumn-blooming sunflower that is planted in garden beds and borders. Its tuberous roots (detail, right) are eaten as a vegetable and are a natural source of insulin.

Jerusalem artichoke is the common name for *Helianthus tuberosus*, a member of the sunflower family, Compositae. It is a perennial herb with edible potatolike roots. The plant is a native of North America and was cultivated by the Indians. The tubers store insulin, which forms fructose and can be used in the diet of diabetics. It is used more as a food in Europe than in North America.

Jespersen, Otto   [yes'-pur sen]

The noted Danish linguist Jens Otto Jespersen, b. July 16, 1860, d. Apr. 30, 1943, devoted the first part of his career to reforming his native language. In 1886 he founded a periodical to further the cause, and in 1901 he published a widely praised textbook on language teaching. During his tenure as professor of English at the University of Copenhagen from 1893 until his retirement in 1925, Jespersen produced a series of influential and highly original works on linguistics, notably *The Growth and Structure of the English Language* (1905), *A Modern English Grammar on Historical Principles* (7 vols., 1909–49), *Language: Its Nature and Development* (1922), and *The Philosophy of Grammar* (1924). He early advanced the view that a word's meaning can affect the development of its pronunciation.

Jessner, Leopold   [yes'-nur, lay'-oh-pohlt]

Director of the Berlin State Theater from 1919 to 1925, Leopold Jessner, b. Mar. 3, 1878, d. Oct. 30, 1945, was the leading advocate within Germany of theatrical expressionism in the period immediately following World War I. In opposition to the fluid harmony of classic productions and the detailed realism of the naturalists, Jessner encouraged an intense, highly stylized approach to acting and stage sets composed solely of simple geometric figures, such as the massive staircase (*Jessnertreppen*) in his production of *Richard III* (1921).

Bibliography: Bluth, Karl, *Leopold Jessner* (1928).

Jesuits' Estates Act   [jez'-oo-it]

The Jesuits' Estates Act, passed by the provincial legislature of Quebec in 1888, created a major political crisis in Canada. The legislation sought to settle the claims concerning the former properties of the Jesuits, which had passed to the crown after the dissolution (1773) of the order by the pope. A revived Jesuit order believed that it was entitled to this property or its value. The act of 1888 allocated $400,000 to the papacy

for distribution between the Jesuits and the Quebec bishops, while $60,000 was to go to the Protestant schools in Quebec. The Ontario Protestants immediately protested the act and demanded that the federal government of Sir John A. MACDONALD disallow it. The Macdonald government refused. This Roman Catholic–Protestant issue resurfaced in another form in 1890 in the MANITOBA SCHOOLS QUESTION.   P. B. WAITE

Bibliography: Dalton, R. C., *The Jesuit Estates Question, 1760–1888* (1968); Miller, J. R., *Equal Rights: The Jesuit Estates Act Controversy* (1979).

Jesuit Martyrs of North America

The Jesuit Martyrs of North America—Saints Jean de BRÉBEUF, Noël Chabanel (1613–49), Antoine Daniel (1601–48), Charles Garnier (1606?–1649), Isaac JOGUES, and Gabriel Lalemant (1610–49), all priests; and René Goupil (1608–42) and Jean de Lalande (d. 1646), laymen—were French missionaries who were killed by Indians in the 1640s. All of them worked among the HURON Indians, and all but one were put to death by the Hurons' enemies, the Iroquois (see IROQUOIS LEAGUE); Chabanel was killed by a Huron hostile to Christianity. The eight martyrs were canonized as a group (1930). Feast day: Oct. 19 (formerly Sept. 16).

Bibliography: Parkman, Francis, *The Jesuits in North America* (1895; repr. 1970); Kennedy, John H., *Jesuit and Savage in New France* (1950; repr. 1971).

Jesuits

The Society of Jesus, the largest Roman Catholic religious order, whose members are called Jesuits, was founded by Saint IGNATIUS LOYOLA. Noted for its discipline, based on the *Spiritual Exercises* of Ignatius, and for its lengthy training period of as much as 15 years, the society is governed by a general who lives in Rome. Jesuits do not wear a special habit and are not subject to local ecclesiastical authority. Professed members are bound by a vow of obedience to the pope.

The Jesuits began as a group of seven men who as students in Paris took (1534) vows of poverty and chastity. Ordained as priests, they placed themselves at the disposal of the pope, PAUL III, who gave formal approval to the society in 1540. Ignatius became (1541) its first general. The order grew so rapidly that at Ignatius's death (1556) the little band had expanded to nearly a thousand persons.

From the first, the Jesuits concentrated on foreign missions, education, and scholarship. Saint FRANCIS XAVIER, one of the original seven, was the first Jesuit to open the East to missionaries; Matteo RICCI and others followed at the court of China. Jesuits established missions throughout Latin America and founded a model commune for Paraguayan Indians. A remarkable account of the Jesuit mission to North America can be found in the *Jesuit Relations* (1632–73).

When the COUNTER-REFORMATION was launched, the Jesuit order was its driving force. During the Council of TRENT, several Jesuits, notably Diego Laínez, served as theologians. The English mission, a bold attempt to reclaim England for Catholicism during the reign (1558–1603) of Elizabeth I, was led by Edmund CAMPION and included the poet Robert SOUTHWELL. Jesuits established schools in almost every important European city and were leaders in education until the 18th century. Members of the society taught the sons of leading families and served as spiritual advisors to kings.

Because of the extent of the Jesuits' influence, powerful forces opposed them—forces composed of such unlikely allies as Blaise PASCAL and the Jansenists, VOLTAIRE, the Bourbon monarchs of France and Spain, and certain cardinals at the Vatican. These forces were instrumental in bringing about the suppression of the society (1773) by Pope CLEMENT XIV. Among the members of the order at that time was John CARROLL, who later became the first Roman Catholic bishop in the United States.

The Jesuit order was reestablished (1814) by Pope PIUS VII and resumed its work. Jesuit schools and universities, such as Georgetown, Fordham, and Saint Louis in the United States, were opened. In Europe, Jesuit traditions of learning were continued by the BOLLANDISTS, who were charged with compiling the lives of the saints; the Jesuits also published several periodicals and journals. Members of the order were in the forefront of many social and theological movements; several others undertook scientific pursuits, such as the study of earthquakes. Among noted modern Jesuits are the poet Gerard Manley HOPKINS, the paleontologist Pierre TEILHARD DE CHARDIN, John LaFarge (1880–1963), who worked for interracial justice, and the theologian John Courtney MURRAY.

CYPRIAN DAVIS, O.S.B.

Bibliography: Bangert, William, *A History of the Society of Jesus* (1972); Hollis, Christopher, *The Jesuits* (1968).

Jesus Christ

Jesus, or Jeshua ben Joseph, as he was known to his contemporaries, was a Jew who appeared as a prophet, a teacher, and a sage in Palestine about AD 30. His followers believed him to be the MESSIAH of Israel, the one in whom God had acted definitively for the salvation of his people (hence, the title CHRIST, a Greek rendition of the Hebrew *Meshiah*, meaning "anointed one"). This belief took distinctive form when, after the execution of Jesus by the Romans (acting on the recommendation of the Jewish authorities), he reportedly presented himself alive to some of his followers. The RESURRECTION of Jesus became a fundamental tenet of the religion that would soon be called CHRISTIANITY. According to Christian belief, Jesus was God made man (he was called both "Son of God" and "Son of Man" and identified as the second person of the TRINITY); his life and his death by crucifixion are understood to have restored the relationship between God and humankind—which had been broken by the latter's sinfulness (see ATONEMENT; ORIGINAL SIN); and his resurrection (the event celebrated by EASTER) affirms God's total sovereignty over his creation and offers humankind the hope of SALVATION.

These core beliefs about Jesus are summed up in the words of the Nicene Creed (see CREED): "I believe in one Lord Jesus Christ, the only-begotten Son of God, Begotten of his Father before all worlds, God of God, Light of Light, Very God of very God, Begotten, not made, Being of one substance with the Father, By whom all things were made: Who for us men, and for our salvation came down from heaven, And was incarnate by the Holy Ghost of the Virgin Mary, And was made man, And was crucified also for us under Pontius Pilate. He suffered and was buried, And the third day he rose again according to the Scriptures, And Ascended into heaven, And sitteth on the right hand of the Father. And he shall come again with glory to judge both the quick and the dead: Whose kingdom shall have no end."

THE HISTORICAL JESUS

The Christ-myth school of the early 20th century held that Jesus never lived but was invented as a peg on which to hang the myth of a dying and rising God. Yet the evidence for the historical existence of Jesus is good.

Non-Christian Sources. Among Roman historians, TACITUS (*Annals* 15.44) records that the Christian movement began with Jesus, who was sentenced to death by Pontius Pilate. SUETONIUS (*Claudius* 25.4) refers to the expulsion of the Jews from Rome because of a riot instigated by one "Chrestus" in AD c.48, and this is usually taken to be a confused reference to the Christians and their founder. PLINY THE YOUNGER (*Epistles* 10.96), writing to Emperor Trajan, says that the early Christians sang a hymn to Christ as God. Most of the Jewish evidence is late and anti-Christian propaganda, but an early reference in the Babylonian Talmud says that Jeshu ha-Noçri was a false prophet who was hanged on the eve of the Passover for sorcery and false teaching. The evidence from the historian JOSEPHUS is problematical. He recounts (*Antiquities* 20.9.1) the martyrdom of JAMES, "the brother of Jesus called the Christ," in AD 62. Another passage in the *Antiquities* (18.3.3) gives an extended account of Jesus and his career, but some features of it are clearly Christian interpolations. Whether this passage has an authentic nucleus is debated.

Thus the Roman sources show a vague awareness that Jesus was a historical figure as well as the object of a cult; the reliable Jewish sources tell us that he was a Jewish teacher who was put to death for sorcery and false prophecy and that he had a brother named James. The Jewish evidence is especially valuable because of the hostility between Jews and Christians at the time: it would have been easy for the Jewish side to question the existence of Jesus, but this they never did.

The Gospels. The Gospels According to MATTHEW, MARK, LUKE, and JOHN, the first four books of the New Testament of the BIBLE, are the principal sources for the life of Jesus. These works are primarily testimonies to the faith of the early Christian community, however, and have to be used critically as evidence for the historical Jesus. The methods include source, form, and redaction criticism. Source criticism studies the literary relationships between the Gospels, and the generally accepted view is that Mark was written prior to and was used by Matthew and Luke, and that Matthew and Luke also had another source in common, unknown to Mark, which consisted mostly of sayings of Jesus. Some would add two other primary sources, the material peculiar to Matthew and that peculiar to Luke. There is a growing consensus that the fourth Gospel, despite a heavy overlay of Johannine theology in the arrangement of the episodes and in the discourses, also enshrines useful historical information and authentic sayings of Jesus. Form criticism investigates the history of the oral traditions behind the written Gospels and their sources, whereas redaction criticism isolates and studies the theology of the editorial work of the evangelists.

These methods provide criteria to sift through the redaction and tradition and reconstruct the message and the mission of the historical Jesus. The criteria of authenticity are dissimilarity both to contemporary Judaism and to the teachings of the post-Easter church; coherence; multiple attestation; and linguistic and environmental factors. The criterion of dissimilarity establishes a primary nucleus of material unique to Jesus. The criterion of coherence adds other materials consistent with this nucleus. Multiple attestation—material attested by more than one primary source or in more than one of the forms of oral tradition established by form criticism—provides evidence for the primitivity of the Jesus tradition. Palestinian cultural background and Aramaic speech forms provide an additional test.

The Life of Jesus. Application of the critical methods described above reveals that the gospel tradition apparently started originally with Jesus' baptism by JOHN THE BAPTIST (Matt. 3:13–17; Mark 1:9–11; Luke 3:21–22; John 1:29–34). The stories concerning the birth of Jesus were probably later additions. These stories—the annunciations to MARY and JOSEPH, their journey to Bethlehem for the Roman census, and Jesus' birth there (Luke 2:1–7); the visits of the shepherds (Luke 2:8–20) and the three MAGI from the East (Matt. 2:1–12); and the flight of the family to Egypt to escape the massacre of young boys that had been ordered by King Herod (Matt. 2:13–23)—may be characterized conveniently, if

The baptism of Jesus Christ, depicted (1180) by the Romanesque artist Bonannus of Pisa, is one of several New Testament scenes portrayed on the bronze doors of Pisa Cathedral. Events from the life of Jesus were used extensively in the cathedral art of medieval Europe to provide both inspiration and instruction.

Jesus is shown preaching the Sermon on the Mount in this fresco by Fra Angelico. Jesus brought solace to a people accustomed to the tyrannies of foreign rule. (Monastery of San Marco, Florence.)

loosely, as "Christological midrash," expressions of Christological faith cast into narrative form. If there are any factual elements in them, these will be found among the items on which Matthew and Luke agree: the names of Mary, Joseph, and Jesus; the dating of Jesus' birth toward the end of the reign of Herod the Great (d. 4 BC); and, less certainly, the Bethlehem location of the birth. Some would add the conception of Jesus between the first and second stages of the marriage rites between Mary and Joseph; Christians interpreted this in terms of a conception through the Holy Spirit (see VIRGIN BIRTH).

Following his baptism by John the Baptist, Jesus embarked on a ministry of possibly three years duration, primarily in Galilee (he had grown up in the Galilean town of Nazareth). The Gospels record his choosing of 12 disciples (see APOSTLE), and he preached both to them and to the population at large, often attracting great crowds (as when he delivered the Sermon on the Mount, Matt. 4:25–7:29; cf. Luke 6:17–49). He proclaimed the kingdom of God—the inbreaking of God's final saving act through his own word and work (Mark 1:14; Matt. 12:28). He confronted his contemporaries with the challenge of this inbreaking reign of God in his parables of the kingdom (Mark 4). He laid down God's radical demand of obedience (Matt. 5:21–48).

In prayer Jesus addressed God uniquely as "Abba" (the intimate address of the child to his earthly father in the family), not "my" or "our" Father as in Judaism, and he invited his disciples in the LORD'S PRAYER to share the privilege of addressing God thus (Luke 11:2). He ate with the outcasts, such as tax collectors and prostitutes, and interpreted his conduct as the activity of God, seeking and saving the lost (as in the parables of the lost sheep, the lost coin, and the prodigal son, Luke 15). He performed exorcisms and healings as signs of the inbreaking of God's final reign, in triumph over the powers of evil (Matt. 11:4–6; 12:28).

Finally, Jesus went up to Jerusalem at the time of the Passover to deliver his challenge of imminent judgment and salvation at the heart and center of his people's life. One of the actions attributed to him there was the expulsion of the money-changers from the Temple (Matt. 21:12–17; Mark 11:15–19; Luke 19:45–46). Earlier, Jesus had incurred the hostility of the PHARISEES, who attacked him for breaking the Law and whom he denounced for their formalistic precepts and self-righteousness (Matt. 23:13–36; Luke 18:9–14). In Jerusalem his opponents were the other principal Jewish religious party, the SADDUCEES, who included the priestly authorities of the Temple. Aided by one of the disciples, JUDAS ISCARIOT, the authorities arrested Jesus in the Garden of Gethsemane. He was examined by the SANHEDRIN and handed over to the Roman governor, Pontius PILATE, who sentenced him to crucifixion. At

a time of considerable political unrest in Palestine and high messianic expectations among certain Jewish groups (for example, the revolutionary ZEALOTS), Jesus and his following undoubtedly appeared to represent some political threat.

The passion narratives of the Gospels contain major theological motifs. First Jesus' sufferings and death are presented as the fulfillment of God's will announced in the Old Testament writings. Second, the accounts of the LAST SUPPER, a farewell meal held before Jesus' arrest, proclaim the atoning significance of Jesus' death in the words over the bread and wine. Third, great emphasis is placed on the statement that Jesus died as Messiah or king. Fourth, some of the events described contain theological symbolism, for example, the rending of the Temple veil.

Jesus' Self-Understanding. Since titles of majesty were used only by the post-Easter church to proclaim Jesus, these titles cannot, by the criterion of dissimilarity, be used as firm evidence for the self-understanding of Jesus during his earthly ministry. That self-understanding has to be inferred indirectly from his words and works. In all of them Jesus confronts his

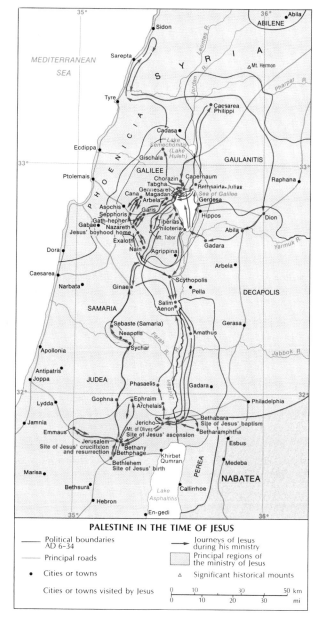

PALESTINE IN THE TIME OF JESUS

— Political boundaries AD 6–34
— Principal roads
• Cities or towns
Cities or towns visited by Jesus
→ Journeys of Jesus during his ministry
☐ Principal regions of the ministry of Jesus
△ Significant historical mounts

contemporaries with a great sense of authority (Mark 2:27; 11:27–33). This quality in Jesus evoked messianic hopes in his followers and messianic fears in his enemies. The hopes of his friends were shattered by the arrest and crucifixion of Jesus but restored and reinforced by the Easter event, faith in his resurrection on the third day following death and entombment.

During his earthly life Jesus was addressed as rabbi and was regarded as a prophet. Some of his words, too, place him in the category of sage. A title of respect for a rabbi would be "my Lord." Already before Easter his followers, impressed by his authority, would mean something more than usual when they addressed him as "my Lord." Jesus apparently refused to be called Messiah because of its political associations (Mark 8:27–30; Matt. 26:64, correcting Mark 14:62). Yet the inscription on the cross, "The King of the Jews," provides irrefutable evidence that he was crucified as a messianic pretender (Mark 15:26).

Although it is possible that Jesus' family claimed to be of Davidic descent, it is unlikely that the title "Son of David" was ascribed to him or accepted by him during his earthly ministry. "Son of God," in former times a title of the Hebrew kings (Psalms 2:7), was first adopted in the post-Easter church as an equivalent of Messiah and had no metaphysical connotations (Romans 1:4). Jesus was conscious of a unique filial relationship with God, but it is uncertain whether the Father/Son language (Mark 18:32; Matt. 11:25–27 par.; John passim) goes back to Jesus himself.

Most problematical of all is the title "Son of Man." This is the only title used repeatedly by Jesus as a self-designation, and there is no clear evidence that it was used as a title of majesty by the post-Easter church. Hence it is held by many to be authentic, since it passes the criterion of dissimilarity. Those who regard it as unauthentic see in it the post-Easter church's identification of Jesus with the "Son of Man" either of Daniel 7:13 or—if the title really existed there before Jesus—in Jewish apocalyptic tradition. One possible view, based on the distinction Jesus makes between himself and the coming "Son of Man" (Luke 12: 8–12; Mark 8:38), is that he invoked this figure to underline the finality of his own word and work—this finality would be vindicated by the "Son of Man" at the end. In that case the post-Easter church was able to identify Jesus with that "Son of Man" because the Easter event was the vindication of his word and work. The post-Easter church then formed further "Son of Man" sayings, some speaking in highly apocalyptic terms of his return in the Second Coming (for example, Mark 14:62; see SECOND COMING OF CHRIST); others expressing the authority exercised during the earthly ministry (for example, Mark 2:10, 28); and still others expressing his impending suffering and certainty of vindication (Mark 8:31; 9:31; 10:33).

CHRISTOLOGY

Although it is true that there was a basic difference between Jesus' message of the kingdom and the post-Easter church's message of him as the saving act of God, all of Jesus' words and work imply a Christology. Thus the critical quest for the historical Jesus yields a sufficient basis for the message of the post-Easter church and is therefore necessary to legitimate it.

Message of the Post-Easter Church. The Christology of the earliest Palestinian Christian community apparently had two focuses. It looked backward to the earthly life of Jesus as prophet and servant of God and forward to his final return as Messiah (Acts 3:21). Meanwhile Jesus was thought of as waiting inactively in heaven, to which he was believed to have ascended after the resurrection (Acts 1:9; see ASCENSION OF CHRIST). Soon their experience of the HOLY SPIRIT, whose descent is recorded in Acts 2, led the early Christians to think in terms of a two-stage Christology: the first stage was the earthly ministry and the second stage his active ruling in heaven. This two-stage Christology, in which Jesus is exalted as Messiah, Lord, and Son of God (Acts 2:36; Romans 1:4) is often called adoptionist. It is not the ADOPTIONISM of later heresy, however, for it thinks in terms of function rather than being. At his exaltation to heaven Jesus began to function as he had not previously. Another primitive Christological affirmation associates the birth of Jesus with his Davidic descent, thus qualifying him for the messianic office at his exaltation (for example, Romans 1:3). This introduced the birth of Jesus as a Christologically significant moment (see CHRISTMAS).

As Christianity spread to the Greek-speaking world between AD 35 and 50, further Christological perspectives were developed. The sending-of-the-Son pattern was one of them. This pattern is threefold: (1) God sent (2) his Son (3) in order to . . . (with a statement of the saving purpose—for example, Galatians 4:4–5). The birth narratives of Matthew and Luke combine the Davidic descent with the sending-of-the-Son Christology. Another major development of this period is the identification of Jesus as the incarnation of the heavenly wisdom of Jewish speculation (Proverbs 8:22–31; Sirach 24:1–12; Wisdom 7:24–30). Hence a three-stage Christology emerges: the preexistent wisdom or LOGOS (Word), who was the agent of creation and of general revelation and also of the special revelation of Israel, becomes incarnate in the life and death of Jesus of Nazareth, and then in the resurrection and exaltation returns to heaven (Philippians 2:6–11; Colossians 1:15–20; Hebrews 1:1–3; John 1:1–14). With this three-stage Christol-

(Left) Dirck Bouts's painting of Christ crowned with thorns, Ecce Homo (c.1460–70), portrays Jesus as the Suffering Servant of Old Testament prophecy while it evokes the pain of his trial and execution. Representations of the pathos of Christ's human suffering were seldom created before the early Renaissance. (Musée des Beaux-Arts, Dijon, France.)

(Right) The Crucifixion scene from the predella of Andrea Mantegna's San Zeno Altarpiece (1456–59) conveys the brutality of the crucifixion through its somber hues and rigid forms. (Louvre, Paris.)

ogy there is a shift from purely functional interpretation to the question of the being or person of Jesus. Thus the later phases of the New Testament lay the ground for the Christological controversies of the Patristic Age.

Christological Controversies of the Patristic Age. The rise of GNOSTICISM as a Christian deviation began in the 2d century and led to the development of DOCETISM, the view that the humanity of Jesus was apparent rather than real. Catholic Christianity insisted on his true humanity—hence the statement in the Apostles' Creed, "conceived by the Holy Ghost, born of the Virgin Mary."

In the 3d and 4th centuries there were some who continued to question the full humanity of Jesus and others who questioned his full deity. When Arius (see ARIANISM) denied that the preexistent Son, or Word, was fully God, the Council of Nicea (325; see NICAEA, COUNCILS OF) formulated a creed (the Nicene Creed) containing the phrases "of one substance with the Father" and "was made man." Next, Apollinarius, anxious to assert the Son's deity, taught that the Logos replaced the human spirit in the earthly Jesus (see APOLLINARIANISM). This teaching was condemned at the Council of Constantinople (381; see CONSTANTINOPLE, COUNCILS OF). Next, the theologians of the school of Antioch were so anxious to maintain the reality of Jesus' humanity that they seemed to compromise his deity. Thus THEODORE OF MOPSUESTIA and his pupil Nestorius (see NESTORIANISM) separated the deity from the humanity almost to the point of denying the unity of his person. To preserve this unity the Council of Ephesus (431; see EPHESUS, COUNCIL OF) affirmed that Mary was the "God-bearer" (*Theotokos*, later popularly rendered as "Mother of God"). EUTYCHES from the Alexandrian school then claimed that the two natures of Christ were, at the incarnation, fused into one. This view was ruled out at the Council of Chalcedon (451; see CHALCEDON, COUNCIL OF), which insisted that Christ was one person in two natures (divine and human) "without confusion, without change, without division and without separation."

Modern Christologies generally start "from below" rather than "from above," finding Jesus first to be truly human, and then discovering his divinity in and through his humanity: "God was in Christ, reconciling the world to himself" (2 Corinthians 5:19).

REGINALD H. FULLER

Bibliography: Augstein, Rudolf, *Jesus Son of Man*, trans. by Hugh Young (1977); Aulén, Gustaf, *Jesus in Contemporary Historical Research*, trans. by Ingalill H. Hjelm (1976); Bornkamm, Günther, *Jesus of Nazareth*, trans. by Irene and Fraser McLuskey (1960); Congar, Yves, *Jesus Christ*, trans. by Luke O'Neill (1966); Connick, Charles M., *Jesus: The Man, the Mission, and the Message*, 2d ed. (1974); Conzelmann, Hans, *Jesus*, trans. by J. R. Lord and ed. by John Reumann (1973); Fuller, Reginald H., *The Foundations of New Testament Christology* (1965); Goodspeed, Edgar J., *A Life of Jesus* (1950); Grant, Michael, *Jesus: An Historian's Review of the Gospels* (1977); Hahn, Ferdinand, *The Titles of Jesus in Christology*, trans. by Harold Knight and George Ogg (1969); Hanson, A. T., *Grace and Truth* (1975); Hengel, Martin, *The Son of God*, trans. by John Bowden (1976); Hick, John, ed., *The Myth of God Incarnate* (1976); Kasper, Walter, *Jesus the Christ* (1976); Keck, Leander E., *A Future for the Historical Jesus* (1971); Klausner, Joseph, *Jesus of Nazareth, His Life, Times and Teaching*, trans. by Herbert Danby (1925; repr. 1949); Pannenberg, Wolfhart, *Jesus: God and Man*, trans. by Lewis L. Wilkins and Duane A. Priebe (1977); Robinson, James M., *The New Quest of the Historical Jesus* (1959); Robinson, John A. T., *The Human Face of God* (1973); Schleiermacher, Friedrich, *Life of Jesus*, ed. by Jack C. Verheyden, trans. by S. MacLean Gilmour, rev. ed. (1974); Schoonenberg, Piet, *The Christ* (1971); Schweitzer, Albert, *The Quest of the Historical Jesus* (1906; repr. 1948).

jet

Jet, a black gemstone formed by the submersion of driftwood in seafloor mud, is a dense variety of lignite coal. Used since ancient times to make carved talismans, it has also been used as GEMS for mourning and for religious ceremonies, but has been replaced by the harder black tourmaline and black onyx.

jet propulsion

Jet propulsion is a type of propulsion in which the thrust is produced by generating a high-velocity jet of hot gases inside an engine and expelling it through a suitably shaped nozzle in the rear. The reaction produced is based on the third of Newton's laws of motion, which states that every action has an equal and opposite reaction. The mass of gases rushing out the rear propels the engine forward.

TYPES OF JET PROPULSION

Two types of engines based on jet propulsion are generally distinguished. The true rocket engine carries with it, in addition to its fuel, a supply of oxygen to burn that fuel (see ROCKETS AND MISSILES). The other type, called a jet engine, obtains its supply of oxygen from atmospheric air that it must take in. Its use is thus restricted to within the Earth's atmosphere. The jet engine itself can be divided into a number of types. The simplest is the RAMJET, in which the forward motion of the engine compresses the incoming air, fuel is injected and ignited in a combustion chamber, and the hot exhaust gases rush out the nozzle at the rear. In the turbojet, a turbine within the engine is driven by the high-speed gases; this

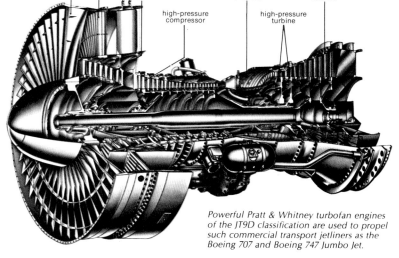

Powerful Pratt & Whitney turbofan engines of the JT9D classification are used to propel such commercial transport jetliners as the Boeing 707 and Boeing 747 Jumbo Jet.

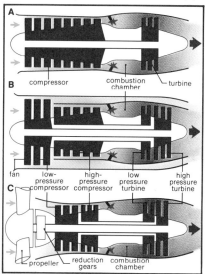

In a turbojet engine (A), thrust is provided by hot exhaust gases (red) produced by burning fuel with compressed air in a combustion chamber. Part of the gas flow powers a turbine that drives the compressor for the incoming air (blue). A turbofan engine (B) has an additional low-pressure turbine and compressor-fan combination to bypass part of the incoming air through ducts around the engine to provide extra thrust. In a turboprop engine (C), thrust is also obtained from a conventional propeller driven by the low-pressure turbine through reduction gears.

turbine runs a compressor to compress the incoming air. The gases, after they pass the turbine, continue out the nozzle to supply the propulsion. In the turboprop (turbo-propeller) engine, the turbine drives a propeller as well as the compressor. The propeller supplies most of the engine's thrust, although the exhaust gases provide a small contribution.

HISTORY

The first examples of jet propulsion were Hero of Alexandria's Aeolipile (AD c.70)—an elementary turbine driven by steam jets—and medieval Chinese rockets used as missiles against Kublai Khan. In the 19th century many jet engines were patented, but practical achievement awaited technological advances, notably heat-resisting metal alloys. No single person can be credited with the invention of jet propulsion. Among the pioneers are: for the rocket, Robert GODDARD of the United States, Hermann OBERTH and Wernher VON BRAUN of Germany, and Sergei KOROLEV and Konstantin TSIOLKOVSKY of the USSR; for the ramjet, René Leduc of France and Eugen Sänger and Otto Pabst of Germany; and for the turbojet, Sir Frank WHITTLE of Britain, Hans von Ohain and Max Adolf Müller of Germany, and Secondo Campini of Italy.

The first jet-propelled airplane to fly was a rocket-propelled tail-first glider flown in Germany on June 11, 1928; in the tail-first configuration, stabilizing fins are situated ahead of the wing. Two German research airplanes were built by Ernst Heinkel in 1939; the He 176 was flown on rocket power in June (precise date not recorded), and the He 178 was flown on turbojet power on August 24 (a short hop) and August 27 (the first full flight). The first jet fighter to fly was the He 280 on Apr. 5, 1941, and the first to enter service was Britain's Gloster Meteor in July 1944, though the German Messerschmitt Me 262 was the first to engage an enemy and was built in larger numbers than other jets of World War II. The first jet transport was the British de Havilland Comet, flown on July 27, 1949, and in regular passenger service beginning May 2, 1952.

Today nearly all combat airplanes are jet propelled, as are virtually all large civil transports. The favored type of engine is the turbofan, a turbojet with an oversized low-pressure compressor whose extra airflow is discharged as a relatively cool and slow propulsive jet, which shows better propulsive efficiency, reduced fuel consumption, and dramatically lower noise level than an ordinary turbojet engine. Modern aircraft jet engines are among the most compact sources of power known, other than one-shot devices (devices used only once) such as artillery or bombs. They have found applications driving air-cushion vehicles, warships, merchant ships, electric utility plants, pipeline pumps, and many other tasks calling for high sustained power with high reliability.   BILL GUNSTON

Bibliography: Hosny, A. N., *Propulsion Systems*, rev. ed. (1974); Kerrebrock, Jack L., *Aircraft Engines and Gas Turbines* (1977); Wilkinson, Paul H., *Aircraft Engines of the World* (1970).

Jet Propulsion Laboratory

The Jet Propulsion Laboratory (JPL), founded in 1936 and given its present name in 1944, is a government contract research facility that has been operated for the National Aeronautics and Space Administration by the California Institute of Technology since 1958. It is located in Pasadena, Calif., and has a staff of 4,200, of whom 1,700 are scientists. In the 1930s the laboratory helped carry out the early rocket work of Robert GODDARD. During World War II, JPL became a large research and development establishment. Since 1958, JPL has concentrated on work with unpiloted scientific missions to the Moon and the planets, as well as on research in physics, propulsion, electronics, and related subjects.

jet stream

A jet stream is a narrow, elongated core of air characterized by strong vertical and horizontal gradients of speed. It is often thousands of kilometers long, hundreds of kilometers wide, and a few kilometers deep. Jet streams vary in intensity—with the strongest having speeds surpassing 300 km/hr

(180 mph)—and in geographic location. Jet streams can be grouped roughly as tropospheric westerly, tropospheric easterly (particularly in the Eastern Hemisphere), and mesospheric.

Geographical and Temporal Variations. Jet streams may be highly variable in space and time. The mesospheric jet stream is strong and westerly (that is, blowing from the west) during winter, but it reverses to an easterly jet of comparable strength during summer. The altitude of its core is about 50 km (30 mi) in mid-latitudes. The tropical easterly jet stream, which occurs during summer, originates in the upper troposphere near Burma and extends to the west of Africa, some 10,000 km (6,000 mi) to the west. A weaker counterpart exists to the north of Australia during the Southern Hemisphere summer. Both are fairly constant in position and strength.

In both hemispheres a fairly continuous band of strong westerlies extends around the globe, with the most intense encountered usually on the eastern margins of continents. The tropospheric westerly jet streams achieve maximum strength at about 15 km (9 mi) altitude in winter, when the jets move to within 30° the equator. The weaker summer westerlies lie some 15° further poleward. A second class of jet stream is attached to the migratory weather systems that lie poleward of the winter westerly jet stream. Such systems are highly transient and are generally smaller in spatial extent than the basic westerly jet streams to which they are intimately related.

Climatologists in the past have referred to two distinct tropospheric westerly jet streams; the subtropical and the polar-front. The steadily improving data base, however, has failed to reveal a climatological double-jet structure except over Australia. The subtropical jet stream may be merely an interpretation of the winter position of the basic westerly maximum, whereas the polar-front jet streams are transients attached to the migratory weather systems.

Causes. WIND velocities are determined by the distribution of horizontal pressure differences, which in turn are governed by the temperature distribution. Consequently, regions of intense temperature gradients should be expected wherever winds occur in narrow bands. Such regions exist in a number of locations.

In middle and high latitudes, frontal zones demark the boundaries between air masses of differing character. At such interfaces of warm and cold air (regions of strong pressure gradient and, because of geostrophic considerations, of strong wind), jet streams develop with the same rapid variations in form as the fronts or weather systems to which they are attached.

A marked temperature gradient also exists between the equator and the pole. The resulting pressure gradient drives a meridional circulation called the HADLEY CELL. A flow of air from the equator to high latitudes moves along the upper branch of the cell. As the air slows down relative to the rotating Earth, weak easterly winds develop. The decreasing distance of the Hadley cell current to the rotational axis, together with the right-deviating effect of the Coriolis force (see CORIOLIS EFFECT), however, causes increasingly strong westerlies as the air parcels move poleward, resulting in a band of intense winds. The differentially heated continents and oceans, however, cause another form of temperature gradient that interferes and produces local concentrations of the temperature gradient. A wavelike structure of the westerly band results with centers of intense wind on the eastern side of the continents. Certain constraints, however, limit the strength of these subtropical jet streams. If they become too strong or narrow, large-scale turbulence, in the form of the familiar weather systems, is produced. Formation zones of the weather systems thus occur at the eastern edges of continents or the western sides of oceans.

Mesospheric jet streams are produced in a different manner. In the upper atmosphere an important constituent, ozone, absorbs incoming solar radiation. In the summer, maximum insolation occurs at high latitudes and correlates with the maximum concentration of ozone, so that polar regions are warmer than the equator. Geostrophic wind considerations imply that the wind is easterly. In the winter hemisphere, insolation is greatest at the equator and decreases rapidly towards the poles. In this case the equatorial regions are much warmer than those over the poles and a strong westerly mesospheric jet stream develops.

The tropical easterly jet stream also results from a unique situation. In the monsoon regions during summer, the precipitation that occurs in the ascending region liberates an enormous amount of latent heat, producing an upper-troposphere anomaly—air in these regions is warmer than air at the same height over the equator. Again, geostrophic-wind considerations dictate an intense easterly jet stream.

P. J. WEBSTER

Bibliography: Palmén, Erik Herbert, and Newton, Chester W., *Atmospheric Circulation Systems: Their Structure and Physical Interpretation* (1969); Reiter, Elmar R., *Jet-Stream Meteorology* (1963).

See also: ATMOSPHERE.

Jethro Tull   [jeth'-roh tuhl]

The British rock music group Jethro Tull is identified with the striking figure of Ian Anderson (b. Scotland, Aug. 10, 1947), its lead singer, guitarist, and flutist. Formed in 1968, the group produced a unique blend of blues and jazz, and their first album, *This Was Jethro Tull* (1968), brought them immediate recognition. The widely acclaimed album *Aqualung* was released in 1971, but *Thick as a Brick* (1972), which was conceived as a single piece of music, was praised for its complexity but criticized as cold and incomprehensible. Subsequent recordings received similar criticism, and the band retired until its successful return in the late 1970s.

jetty: see COASTAL PROTECTION.

jewelry   [joo'-ul-ree]

Jewelry, one of the oldest decorative arts, is a collective term for objects of personal adornment, prized both for their craftsmanship and for the intrinsic value of their precious materials. The earliest jewelry was probably amuletic, protecting its wearer from hostile forces, but as soon as social order developed, jewelry was used to denote rank—a function that survives today in regalia, badges of office, and military insignia. The social purpose of jewelry has been so important that during certain periods SUMPTUARY LAWS have regulated its use. The primary purpose of jewelry, however, is to adorn its wearer and enhance his or her glamour and sexual attraction. Generally, the more primitive the society, the more flamboyant the display of jewelry.

The character of the jewelry of a particular culture depends greatly on the raw materials that a region provides, on its climate—which dictates the nature of the clothing worn—and on its customs, both social and religious. Thus an abundance of gold and jade have determined the styles and symbolic uses of the jewelry of South and Central America. In India jewelry serves as both traditional decoration and as a family's financial investment. In the tropical regions of Africa, Central America, and the Pacific, jewelry is virtually all that is worn. In Japan, however, a country with a superb metalworking tradition, jewelry is hardly used, except for women's hair ornaments consisting of pins and combs of bamboo and lacquered wood.

THE ANCIENT WORLD

Virtually all modern kinds of jewelry—necklaces, earrings, rings, bracelets, and their ornaments—were in use as early as 2500 BC in the Sumerian civilization (see MESOPOTAMIAN ART AND ARCHITECTURE). Excavation of the royal tombs at Ur in Iraq has uncovered sophisticated jewelry such as a woman's headdress consisting of sheet-gold pendants on strings of lapis lazuli (c.2500 BC; British Museum, London). Sumerian goldsmiths used advanced metalworking techniques of coldhammering, casting, smelting, soldering, filigree, granulation, cloisonné, inlay, and lapidary work.

Ancient Egyptian jewelry served religious and royal purposes, as well as being used for decoration. Gold was the primary material in jewelry making, and it was usually ornamented with filigree designs. Semiprecious stones, such as carnelian, turquoise, and lapis lazuli, were widely used and magical significance was attributed to specific gems. This selection of Egyptian jewelry includes: rebus pectoral (1); faience collar (2); hinged bracelet (3); signet ring (4); bezel ring (5); shell pendant (6); and a pair of gold earrings (7).

Jewelry had begun to play an important role in Egyptian civilization (see EGYPTIAN ART AND ARCHITECTURE) by about 3000 BC. A wall painting from a Theban tomb of the late 15th century BC depicts a metalworker using tongs and a blowpipe to anneal gold. Alongside him other men are drilling stone beads with bow drills while another threads a bead collar. The tomb of TUTANKHAMEN (r. 14th century BC) contained numerous pieces of fine gold jewelry embedded with precious stones.

The art of fashioning gold jewelry reached the Mediterra-

Representative styles of Greek jewelry popular during the 4th century BC were: a bracelet of chased gold with filigree ornamentation (1); a gold ring carved in intaglio (2); a gold ring carved with a woman's profile (3); a gold spiral-shaped earring ending in a lion's head (4); and an elaborate gold earring with a filigree rosette and suspended pieces (5). The period of detailed goldwork began in Greece about 800 BC and reached its height during the classical period from 475 to 330 BC. In later developments, glass and colored stones were used as insets.

Greek and Etruscan styles exerted considerable influence on the jewelry of the Roman Empire. For the first time, however, hard stones such as emeralds and sapphires were used, and the popularity of gold filigree work waned. This selection exemplifies Roman jewelry worn during the 1st–3rd century AD: a gold snake bracelet (1); a necklace of gold and mounted stones (2); a gold fibula, used as a clasp (3); a gold earring with drop pendant set with garnets (4); and an oval ring incised with a standing figure (5).

During the Middle Ages polished precious stones and cameos were used in jewelry making throughout Europe. In the 13th century goldsmiths formed independent guilds. A selection of medieval and early Renaissance jewelry includes: a gold ring brooch (France, 13th century) (1); a 15th-century French hat badge portraying Charles V (2); an Ottoman jeweled cross (10th century) (3); an onyx cameo (Germany, mid-13th century) (4); and an Italian 15th-century belt buckle with decorations (5).

nean island of Crete from western Asia about 2400 BC. Diadems, hair ornaments, beads, bracelets, and complex chains have been found in Minoan tombs (see MINOAN ART). Asian techniques of filigree and granulation were introduced to Crete about 2000 BC, and evidence also indicates that Egyptian styles influenced Minoan jewelry. Minoan culture and its jewelry styles spread to the mainland of Greece, then dominated by the city-state of MYCENAE, about 1550 BC.

Metalworking techniques reached northern Europe by about 2000 BC, and the earliest jewelry found there dates from between 1800 and 1400 BC. These artifacts include lunulae—spectacular, crescent-shaped neck ornaments of beaten gold—most of which were found in graves in Ireland, where gold was once plentiful (see CELTIC ART). There is evidence that the Celtic and early British people were trading with the eastern Mediterranean races by this time, exchanging gold for faïence beads.

By 1200 BC jewelry making was flourishing in central and western Europe, where bronze as well as gold was frequently used to make jewelry, and the spiral was the most common motif of decoration. The fibula-brooch seems to have been invented at this time. Twisted gold torcs, modeled on Scandinavian bronze prototypes, were made in the British Isles and northern France from the 5th to the 1st century BC. These massive circlets for the neck were the characteristic ornament of the chiefs of the Celtic race. Celtic craftsmen also used enamel and inlay to decorate jewelry.

By the 7th century BC the ETRUSCANS of central Italy were also making fine gold jewelry. These people may have migrated from Anatolia, whence their metalworking skills seem to have been derived. The Etruscans brought to perfection the difficult technique of granulation, whereby the surface of the metal is covered with tiny gold grains.

Gold was plentiful in Greece during the Hellenistic Age (323–30 BC), and Greek jewelry of this period is characterized by its great variety of forms and fine workmanship in gold. Naturalistic wreaths and diadems were made for the head, and a variety of miniature human, animal, and plant forms were made up into necklaces and earrings. The so-called

Heracles-knot, of amuletic origin, was introduced, and remained a popular motif into Roman times. In the 3d century BC polychrome effects were achieved in gold jewelry by the use of colored stones and glass. At first garnets, chalcedonies, and carnelians were used and later emeralds, amethysts, and pearls. The engraving of CAMEOS also began at this time.

Jewelry continued to be made in Greek styles during the early Roman Empire, when the chief centers of production were Alexandria, Antioch, and Rome, to which Greek craftsmen had migrated. There was an increasing emphasis on the decorative use of stones and a relaxation of standards in gold work. For the first time the hardest stones were used—uncut but polished diamonds, sapphires, and, notably, emeralds from newly discovered Egyptian mines. Colorful jewelry was a striking characteristic of the Migration period (4th to 8th centuries AD), which followed the collapse of the Roman Empire. Mediterranean goldsmiths continued to produce jewelry of great refinement, but the jewelry of the European tribes dominates this period. Their primitive, primarily abstract styles of great splendor were worked in enamels and inlaid stones. The fibula-brooch reached extremes of size and elaboration. This is also the period of the penannular, or nearly circular, brooches of Ireland and Scotland, the finest-known example of which is the early-8th-century *Tara Brooch* (National Museum of Ireland, Dublin). From the 9th to the 13th century the technique of cloisonné enameling on gold was widespread, the finest pieces emanating from the workshops at Constantinople, the capital of the Byzantine Empire (see BYZANTINE ART AND ARCHITECTURE).

THE MIDDLE AGES AND THE RENAISSANCE
After the creation of Charlemagne's empire in AD 800 (followed by the Holy Roman Empire in 962) there was a fusion of northern and Mediterranean cultures, and the principal patrons of the arts were the emperor and the church. Jewelry design was based on the setting in gold of precious stones and pearls in colorful patterns. Precious stones, which were polished but still used in their natural form, were credited with talismanic powers; for instance the sapphire, symbolic of chastity and spiritual peace, was used for papal rings. Antique

The Renaissance pieces illustrated here exemplify the elaborate jewelry created by European artisans during the 16th century. This enameled gold pendant, set with rubies, emeralds, and pearls, represents Spanish goldwork (1). This English gem-studded enameled portrait bust of Elizabeth I was known as an Armada jewel (2). Pendants in unusual forms became popular during this time, typified by this fanciful Venetian ship pendant (3).

cameo gems were especially prized and often set in early medieval jewelry and given a Christian interpretation. Until this time European jewelry had been produced mainly in imperial and monastic workshops, but by the 13th century a system of independent guilds of goldsmiths had become established in European capitals, which suggests that the craft had become more widespread.

Gothic jewelry (see GOTHIC ART AND ARCHITECTURE) reflects the chivalrous ethic of aristocratic society in its symbolism and frequent use of amatory inscriptions. Jewelry, which has always had close affinities with modes of dress, frequently took the form of brooches and other fastenings such as belt clasps. The ring brooch, or fermail, which had originated in Anglo-Saxon times, became very popular and has survived in peasant jewelry. Pendants were occasionally used as RELIQUARIES. The use of earrings ceased entirely, because women wore elaborate jeweled headdresses that concealed the ears. About 1300, French jewelers began to use translucent enamels over engraved silver or gold.

In the 14th and 15th centuries jewelry was an important feature of both male and female attire. Notably fashionable during the first half of the 15th century were jewels composed of enameled gold figures, flowers, and foliage modeled in high relief and frequently interspersed with clusters of pearls. These exquisite works of art—which include *The Lennox*, or *Darnley Jewel*, of enameled gold set with sapphires (c.1570; Collection of Her Majesty the Queen, London)—are among the finest jewels ever made.

The affluence of the Spanish court during the 16th century, which was based on gold from colonies in the New World, set a standard for the other princely courts of Europe. At this time the art of engraving on metal was perfected, and thus designers were able to print and disseminate their ideas throughout Europe, with the result that it is extremely difficult to attribute 16th-century jewels to any particular country by their style. The earliest of these designers were Virgil Solis (1514–62) and Erasmus Hornick (c.1540–c.1583) of Nuremberg and the Frenchman Étienne Delaune (1520–c.1595). The most striking and influential of Hornick's designs were for figurative pendants of legendary subjects. A slightly later development of this style of pendant included a framework of abstract ornament or architectural elements, which dominated the form of the jewel and usually rendered it symmetrical. The engraved designs of Hans Collaert (1540–1622) are typical

of this style, which seems to have been used principally by south German jewelers. The most famous artist-goldsmith of this period was Benvenuto CELLINI, who worked first in his native Italy and later for Francis I of France, he is mainly known through his autobiography and sculptural work, because no jewelry has survived that can be ascribed to him with certainty.

FROM THE 17TH CENTURY TO THE PRESENT DAY

Figurative designs became less fashionable in the 17th century, when there was a shift of interest to formal designs using faceted gems and pearls. The uncut, or cabochon, gem is rarely found in jewelry after 1640. The Golconda diamond mines were opened in India during the 17th century, and Dutch merchants supplied diamonds for the European market. Consequently, Amsterdam became the center for the trading and cutting of gems and has remained so. By the middle of the 17th century the new, many-faceted "rose" style of cutting had superseded the old, square "table" cut. Stones were set in close proximity, and their settings played a smaller part in the overall effect. Silver was frequently used with diamonds to make the setting less visible. Delicate floral designs in enamel were used to decorate the backs of finer jewels. Since this time diamonds have tended to dominate jewelry.

Gilles Légaré (fl. c.1660), court jeweler to Louis XIV of France, was responsible for some of the finest designs of the late 17th century. Louis XIV was the last monarch to wear large numbers of jewels. Among Légaré's designs are the Sevigné, or bow ornament, a form of jewelry that has never lost its popularity, and girandole pendants, a form used for brooches and earrings that remained fashionable until the end of the 18th century. Black-enameled mourning jewelry and the memento mori jewel, a reminder of human mortality, reflected the somber Counter-Reformation mentality of the 17th century.

Eighteenth-century fashions were lighter and more frivolous. The sparkle of diamonds cut in the new "brilliant" style, invented in Venice between the end of the 17th and the beginning of the 18th century, echoed the glitter of the cut-crystal chandeliers at evening festivities. Other innovations of the

18th-century jewelry was characterized by lighter and more refined classical forms than earlier styles. The cutting and setting of precious stones to create sophisticated designs became the primary jeweler's art. Examples of 18th-century jewelry are: a chatelaine, or clasp, worn from the belt, to which watches, seals, and other personal articles could be attached (1); an English diamond "wheatear" brooch (2); a French shoe buckle, an essential part of male attire (3); and an earring of cut diamonds, an art first invented by the Venetians (4).

The eclectic taste of the Victorian era asserted itself in jewelry design as it did in all other arts. The setting of diamonds, which had become more abundant owing to the discovery of South African mines, reached a new height of technical perfection and highly stylized forms prevailed. This selection of 19th-century Victorian jewelry includes: a gold brooch set with turquoises, diamonds and other gems (1); a jet and gold pin (2); a gold, cameo and enamel earring (3); and an enameled gold brooch set with precious stones (4).

1869 and supplied an enormous market for jewelry among the newly rich of the United States and South America, who were principally interested in displaying their wealth. Large and valuable stones were often set *en solitaire* or as necklaces of single stones, called rivières. A somewhat mechanical technical excellence prevailed, and jewelry making became increasingly industrialized. The later prosperity of the 19th century also encouraged the growth of large commercial establishments that produced jewelry of superb craftsmanship. The most famous of these firms were those of Peter Carl FABERGÉ, which originated in Saint Petersburg, Russia, and of Charles Lewis TIFFANY in New York.

A movement devoted to reforming the applied arts came into being in the last half of the 19th century and began to affect jewelry about 1895. Although this development originated in the British ARTS AND CRAFTS MOVEMENT, the most progressive jeweler was the Frenchman René LALIQUE. His work was a return to the true goldsmith's tradition, and his designs in the ART NOUVEAU style can best be compared in brilliance to the imaginative jewelry of the Renaissance, although they are profoundly original and owe little to past styles.

The profession of the artist-jeweler has become firmly established in the 20th century, notably in Scandinavia, where Georg Jensen (1866–1935) set a high standard of artistry and craftsmanship in his simple mass-produced jewelry. Jewelry from the prestigious international houses, such as Cartier, Chaumet, Boucheron, Van Cleef and Arpels, and Tiffany, continue the conservative tradition of formal gem-set jewelry in which more regard is paid to ostentatious display than innovatory design. The future of jewelry is perhaps in the hands of the numerous independent artist-jewelers working in many parts of the world, who are now beginning to receive deserved attention from the public.   BETTY ELZEA

Bibliography: Aldred, Cyril, *Jewels of the Pharaohs* (1971); Coraelli, Filippo, *Greek and Roman Jewelry* (1970); Evans, Joan, *A History of Jewellery, 1100–1870*, 2d ed. (1970); Flower, Margaret C., *Victorian Jewelery*, rev. ed. (1973); Frégnac, Claude, *Jewelry from the Renaissance to Art Nouveau* (1965; repr. 1973); Gere, Charlotte, *Victorian Jewellery Design* (1973); Gregorietti, Giovanni, *Jewelry Through the Ages* (1969); Hughes, Graham, *Modern Jewelry: 1890–1963* (1963); Jessup, Ronald F., *Anglo-Saxon Jewellery* (1953); British Museum, London, *Jewelry Through 7,000 Years* (1976); Mason, Anita, and Packer, Diane, *An Illustrated Dictionary of Jewellery* (1974); Maxwell-Hyslop, K. R., *Western Asiatic Jewellery, c.3000–612 BC* (1971); Muller, Priscilla E., *Jewels in Spain, 1500–1800* (1972); Rogers, Frances, and Beard, Alice, *5,000 Years of Gems and Jewelry* (1940); Rosenthal, Renate, *Jewelry of the Ancient World* (1975); Rossi, Filippo, *Italian Jeweled Arts*, trans. by Elizabeth Mann Borgese (1958); Smith, Harold C., *Jewellery* (1908; repr. 1973); Steingraber, Erich, *Antique Jewelry* (1957).

See also: GEM CUTTING; RING (jewelry).

period included the informal spray of flowers entirely formed of stones, a type of jewel that required the utmost skill of the jeweler, and parures, matched sets of jewels consisting of necklace, earrings, and brooches or clasps of various sizes. Although, from 1725, there was an abundant new source of diamonds in Brazil, there was also a large demand for imitation, or paste, diamonds. Paris, the fashion center of the world, was severely disrupted by the French Revolution of 1789, and diamonds were unfashionable during the period of austere republicanism that followed, when only simple gold jewelry inspired by classical antiquity was worn.

Neoclassical designs were well suited to the imperial pomp of the First Empire (1804–14) of Napoleon I. His wife, Josephine, had a passion for antique cameos, which she had made into magnificent parures. Ornamental combs, worn at the back of the head, were added to parures. Diamonds soon returned to favor in the Napoleonic court, and there was a renewed interest in colored stones; but these were worn in rigidly formal settings, unlike those of the 18th century. The jewelry of the period immediately following the First Empire was bourgeois in character, as was every other decorative art. The fashion was for light filigree, or mechanically stamped-out gold jewelry, set with pale-colored semiprecious stones that produced a rich effect at a comparatively low cost. This style originated in Britain, where the domestically minded and sentimental Queen Victoria set the mood for British society. Much Victorian jewelry, such as lockets and brooches incorporating miniature portraits or locks of hair, was sentimental in feeling and low in intrinsic value. The Victorian enthusiasm for keepsakes led to a curious fashion for wearing jewelry made of woven human hair.

Nineteenth-century design was dominated by historical revivals. The GOTHIC REVIVAL inspired outstanding jewelry by François Désiré Froment-Meurice (1802–55) in France and the architect A. W. N. Pugin (1812–52) in England. France's fortunes increased with industrialization and, during the brief period of the Second Empire of Napoleon III (1852–70), the Parisian jewelers again rose to great heights of achievement. The Empress Eugénie had a preference for 18th-century styles and favored diamonds and pearls. Diamond setting reached a peak of technical virtuosity in the late 1860s with the monture illusion, an elaborate gem-encrusted framework associated with the jeweler Oscar Massin (b. 1829). During the same period, a vogue for archaeologically correct jewelry originated in Italy, following discoveries of Greek, Roman, and Etruscan gold jewelry.

South African diamonds were first brought to Europe in

jewelweed [joo'-ul-weed]

Jewelweed is either of two annual plants in the genus *Impatiens* in the balsam family, Balsaminaceae. The common jewelweed, *I. capensis*, grows 1.5 m (5 ft) tall, with long, coarsely toothed leaves and usually orange-yellow flowers spotted with reddish brown. It is found in moist sites from Newfoundland to Oklahoma and Florida. The pale jewelweed, *I. pallida*, is similar in appearance and habitat preference but grows to 2.5 m (8 ft) tall, with yellow flowers that are unspotted or lightly spotted with red. It is found from Newfoundland to Saskatchewan south to Kansas and Georgia. The upper two sepals of the jewelweed flower are small and green; the third and lower sepal is large and petallike and formed into a funnel with a pointed nectar-bearing tip, or spur. Three petals join the large sepal to form a "four-petaled" flower. Jewelweeds are also called touch-me-nots or snapweeds because the ripe seed pod opens at a touch, explosively expelling the seeds. Jewelweeds contain an antifungal agent, 2-methoxy-1, 4-napthoquinone, and juices from these plants were used by early settlers to treat athlete's foot and some types of skin infections and scalp disorders. The sap of these plants is also considered a remedy against poison ivy reactions.

Jewett, Sarah Orne   [joo'-et, orn]

An American writer who lived her entire life in South Berwick, Maine, Sarah Orne Jewett, b. Sept. 3, 1849, d. June 24, 1909, built her reputation on fiction that is usually set in the impoverished land and seascape of rural Maine. She educated herself, primarily by reading in her family's private library. Her stories and novels capture character, idiom, and natural conditions with a precision and clarity that resembles the work of Gustave Flaubert. Her best short stories are contained in her first major book, *Deephaven* (1877), and in the better-known collection *A White Heron and Other Stories* (1886). Her most ambitious work, *The Country of the Pointed Firs* (1896), is a novel that deals with the lonely lives of isolated people. She was awarded an honorary doctorate in literature by Bowdoin College in 1901, a year before a disabling accident put an end to her writing career.

Bibliography: Cary, Richard, *Sarah Orne Jewett* (1962).

jewfish

Jewfishes are large groupers of the sea bass family, Serranidae. Most commonly the name refers to *Epinephelus itajara*, also called the spotted jewfish, of the Atlantic Ocean. This fish reaches a maximum weight of 340 kg (750 lb). The name *jewfish* is also applied to several other similarly large, heavy-headed fishes of other families.

See also: GROUPER; SEA BASS.

Jewish Daily Forward

The *Jewish Daily Forward*, founded in 1897 in New York City, was once the wealthiest and most influential Yiddish-language newspaper in the United States. Edited by Abraham Cahan from 1903 to 1951, it supported democratic socialism and the Jewish labor movement. During World War I it reached an audience of nearly 200,000 readers; its current circulation is approximately 60,000.

Bibliography: Soltes, Mordecai, *The Yiddish Press: an Americanizing Agency* (1925; repr. 1950).

Jewish Defense League

Founded under the leadership of Rabbi Meir Kahane in 1968, the Jewish Defense League is a militant organization centered in New York City that uses radical tactics in the name of combating anti-Semitism and protecting Jews. The league has been especially active in protesting the USSR's treatment of Jews and its restrictions on Jewish emigration to Israel. More moderate Jewish leaders have been critical of the organization's violent methods.

Bibliography: Dolgin, Janet, *Jewish Identity and the J.D.L.* (1977); Kahane, Meir, *The Story of the Jewish Defense League* (1975).

Jewish Theological Seminary of America

Established in 1886, the Jewish Theological Seminary of America (enrollment: 525; library: 250,000 volumes) provides undergraduate and graduate training for men and women for the conservative rabbinate. The seminary, located in New York City and affiliated with the University of Judaism in Los Angeles, permits students to supplement their undergraduate work with courses at Columbia University.

Jews

The Jews are a people who trace their descent from the biblical Israelites and who are united by the religion called JUDAISM. They are not a race; Jewish identity is a mixture of ethnic, national, and religious elements. An individual may become part of the Jewish people by conversion to Judaism; but a born Jew who rejects Judaism or adopts another religion does not entirely lose his Jewish identity.

The word *Jew* is derived from the kingdom of Judah, which included 2 of the 12 Israelite tribes. The name *Israel* referred to the people as a whole and especially to the northern kingdom of 10 tribes. Today it is used as a collective name for all Jewry and since 1948 for the Jewish state. (Citizens of the state of ISRAEL are called Israelis; not all of them are Jews.) In the Bible, *Hebrew* is used by foreign peoples as a name for the Israelites; today it is applied only to the HEBREW LANGUAGE.

BIBLICAL PERIOD

The origin of the Jews is recounted in the Hebrew BIBLE (called the "Old Testament" by Christians). Despite legendary and miraculous elements in its early narratives, most scholars believe that the biblical account is based on historic realities. According to the Book of GENESIS God ordered the patriarch ABRAHAM to leave his home in Mesopotamia and travel to a new land, which he promised to Abraham's descendants as a perpetual inheritance. Although the historicity of Abraham, his son ISAAC, and his grandson JACOB is uncertain, the Israelite tribes certainly came to CANAAN (later Palestine) from Mesopotamia. Later they, or some of them, settled in Egypt, where they were reduced to slavery; they finally fled to freedom under the leadership of an extraordinary man named MOSES, probably about 1200 BC. After a period of desert wandering, the tribes invaded Canaan at different points, and over a lengthy period of time they gained control over parts of the country. (It is uncertain if there is any connection between the Hebrews and the Habiru mentioned in 14th-century BC Egyptian documents found at Tell el-AMARNA.)

Formation of a National Kingdom. For a century or more the tribes, loosely united and sometimes feuding among themselves, were hard pressed by Canaanite forces based in fortified strongholds and by marauders from outside. At critical moments tribal chieftains (traditionally called judges) rose to lead the people in battle. But when the PHILISTINES threatened the very existence of the Israelites, the tribes formed a kingdom under the rule (1020–1000 BC) of SAUL, of the tribe of Benjamin. Saul died fighting the Philistines, and was succeeded by DAVID of the tribe of Judah.

David crushed the Philistine power and established a modest empire. He conquered the fortress city of JERUSALEM, which up to that time had been controlled by a Canaanite tribe, and made it his capital. His son SOLOMON assumed the

Moses leads the Jews across the Red Sea in this illustration from a German-Jewish prayerbook (1427). According to biblical tradition, God parted the waters of the Red Sea to allow the Jews safe passage. Pursuing Egyptians drowned when the waters returned to normal.

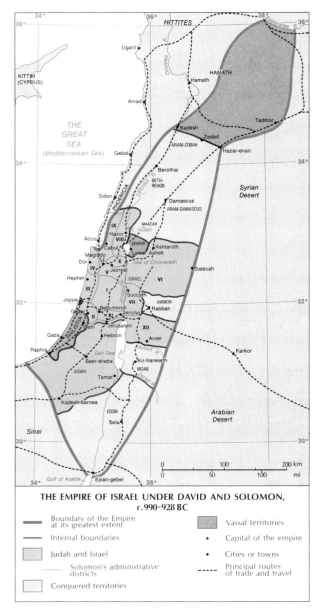

THE EMPIRE OF ISRAEL UNDER DAVID AND SOLOMON, c.990–928 BC

Boundary of the Empire at its greatest extent		Vassal territories
Internal boundaries	★	Capital of the empire
Judah and Israel	•	Cities or towns
Solomon's administrative districts	-----	Principal routes of trade and travel
Conquered territories		

The empire of Israel during the reigns of Kings David and Solomon (10th century BC) is shown in this map. During David's reign, Israel became a Near Eastern power. His son and successor, Solomon, built cities, expanded trade, and made political alliances.

trappings of a potentate and erected the Temple in Jerusalem, which became the central sanctuary of the distinctive monotheistic Israelite religion and ultimately the spiritual center of world Jewry.
Division, Conquest, and Exile. The national union effected by David was shaky. The economically and culturally advanced tribes of the north resented the rule of kings from pastoral Judah, and after Solomon's death the kingdom was divided (see ISRAEL, KINGDOM OF; JUDAH, KINGDOM OF). The larger and richer northern kingdom was known as Israel; Judah, with Benjamin, remained loyal to the family of David. Israel experienced many dynastic changes and palace revolutions. Both Israel and Judah, located between the empires of Egypt and Assyria, were caught in the struggle between the two great powers. Assyria was the dominant empire during the period of the divided kingdom. When Israel, with Egyptian encour-

agement, tried to throw off Assyrian rule, it was destroyed and a large number of its inhabitants were deported (722 BC). Judah managed to outlive the Assyrian Empire (destroyed c.610), but the Chaldean (Neo-Babylonian) Empire that replaced it also insisted on control of Judah. When a new revolt broke out under Egyptian influence, the Chaldeans under NEBUCHADNEZZAR II destroyed Jerusalem and burned the Temple (587 or 586 BC); the royalty, nobility, and skilled craftsmen were deported to Babylonia (see BABYLONIAN CAPTIVITY).

Loss of state and Temple, however, did not lead to the disappearance of the Judeans, as it did in the northern kingdom. The peasantry that remained on the land, the refugees in Egypt, and the exiles in Babylonia retained a strong faith in their God and the hope of ultimate restoration. This was largely due to the influence of the great PROPHETS. Their warnings of doom had been fulfilled; therefore, the hopeful message they began to preach was believed. The universal prophetic teaching assured Jews that they could still worship their God on alien soil and without a temple. Henceforth the Jewish people and religion could take root in the dispersion (see DIASPORA) as well as in the homeland.
Return to Palestine. CYRUS THE GREAT of Persia conquered Babylonia in 536 BC. Subsequently he permitted the exiles to return to Judah and rebuild the Temple. (Many chose, however, to remain in Mesopotamia, where the Jewish community existed without interruption for more than 2,500 years until the virtual elimination of Jewish presence in Iraq after World War II.) Leadership of the reviving Judean center was provided largely by returning exiles—notably Nehemiah, an important official of the Persian court, and Ezra, a learned priest (see EZRA AND NEHEMIAH, BOOKS OF). They rebuilt the walls of Jerusalem and consolidated spiritual life by a public ceremony of allegiance to the TORAH (Law of Moses) and by stringent rules against mixed marriage. In the following centuries leadership was provided mainly by priests, who claimed descent from Moses' brother AARON; the high priest usually represented the people in dealings with the foreign powers that successively ruled the land.

HELLENISTIC AND ROMAN PERIODS
The available information about the Persian period is meager. ALEXANDER THE GREAT conquered Palestine in 322; his successors, the Macedonian rulers of Egypt (the Ptolemies) and Syria (the SELEUCIDS); vied for control of this strategically important area; eventually the Syrians won. Hellenistic influences penetrated Jewish life deeply, but when the Seleucid king ANTIOCHUS IV tried to impose the worship of Greek gods upon the Jews, a rebellion ensued (168 BC).
The Maccabees. The popular revolt was led by the MACCABEES a provincial priestly family (also called Hasmoneans). By 165 they recaptured the Temple, which had been converted into a pagan shrine, and rededicated it to the God of Israel. Hostilities with Syria continued; but Simon, the last of the Maccabean brothers, consolidated his power and was formally recognized in 131 BC as ruler and high priest. His successors took the title of king and for about a century ruled an independent commonwealth. Dynastic quarrels, however, gave the Roman general POMPEY THE GREAT an excuse to intervene and make himself master of the country in 63 BC.
The Herodians. In subsequent decades a family of Idumaean adventurers (see HEROD dynasty) ingratiated themselves with the successive Roman dictators; with Roman help, Herod the Great made himself ruler of Judea, eventually (37 BC) with the title of king. Able but ruthless, he was hated by the people, although he rebuilt the Temple with great magnificence. The Romans allowed Herod's sons less authority and in 6 BC put the country formally under the control of their own officials, known as procurators.

New spiritual forces emerged during the Maccabean and Herodian periods. The leadership of hereditary priests was contested by laymen distinguished for their learning and piety, who won the respect and support of the people. The priestly conservatives came to be known as SADDUCEES, the more progressive lay party as the PHARISEES. The latter came to dominate the SANHEDRIN, which was the highest religious and legal authority of the nation.

Burdened by excessive taxation and outraged by acts of brutality, the Judeans became more and more restive under Roman rule, all the more because they were confident that God would ultimately vindicate them. Revolutionary groups such as the ZEALOTS emerged calling for armed revolt. The Sadducees were inclined to collaborate with the Romans; the Pharisees advocated passive resistance but sought to avoid open war.

THE ERA OF REVOLTS AND THE MISHNAH AND TALMUD

The Great Revolts. In AD 66 the moderates could no longer control the desperate populace, and rebellion against Roman tyranny broke out. After bitter fighting the Romans captured Jerusalem and burned the Temple in 70; at MASADA the Zealots held out until 73, when most of the 1,000 surviving defenders killed themselves to defy capture by the Romans. As a result of the revolt thousands of Jews were sold into slavery and thus were scattered widely in the Roman world. The last vestiges of national autonomy were obliterated.

The Pharisaic leaders, shortly thereafter given the title of RABBI (Hebrew, "my teacher"), rallied the people for a new undertaking—the reconstruction of religious and social life. Using the institution of the SYNAGOGUE as a center of worship and education, they adapted religious practice to new conditions. Their assembly, the Sanhedrin, was reconvened at Jabneh, and its head was recognized by the Romans and given the title of patriarch; the Diaspora Jews accepted his authority and that of the Sanhedrin in matters of Jewish law. The leaders of the Jabneh period included JOHANAN BEN ZAKKAI, GAMALIEL OF JABNEH, and AKIBA BEN JOSEPH.

Many Diaspora Jewish communities rebelled against Rome early in the 2d century; however, their rebellions were crushed, with much bloodshed. Still more bitter was the revolt of Palestinian Jewry led by BAR KOCHBA in 132; it was put down after three years of savage fighting. For a time thereafter observance of basic Jewish practices was made a capital crime, and Jews were banned from Jerusalem. Under the Antonine emperors (138–92), however, milder policies were restored, and the work of the scholars was resumed, particularly in Galilee, which became the seat of the patriarchate until its abolition (c.429) by the Romans. There the sages called tannaim completed the redaction of the MISHNAH (oral law) under the direction of JUDAH HA-NASI.

Babylonian Community. In the 3d and 4th centuries scholarly activity in Palestine declined as a result of bad economic conditions and oppression by Christian Rome. Meanwhile, two Babylonian pupils of Judah ha-Nasi had returned home, bringing the Mishnah with them, and established new centers of learning at Sura and Nehardea. A period of great scholarly accomplishment followed, and leadership of world Jewry

This detail from the arch built by the Emperor Titus to commemorate his conquest of Palestine in AD 70, which still stands in Rome, shows the looting of Jerusalem's Temple by Roman soldiers. The Temple, rebuilt for a third time during the reign of Herod, was destroyed.

passed to the Babylonian schools. The Babylonian TALMUD became the standard legal work for Jews everywhere. Babylonian Jewry enjoyed peace and prosperity under the Parthian and Sassanian rulers, with only occasional episodes of persecution. In addition to the heads of the academies, the Jews had a secular ruler, the exilarch.

This situation was not significantly changed by the Muslim conquest of the Persian empire. At the end of the 6th century, the heads of the academies had adopted the title of gaon (Hebrew, "excellency"), and the next four centuries are known as the gaonic period; communities throughout the world turned to the Babylonian leaders for help in understanding the Talmud and applying it to new problems. About 770 the sect of KARAITES, biblical literalists who rejected the Talmud, appeared in Babylonia. Despite the vigorous opposition of the great SAADIA BEN JOSEPH GAON and other leaders, the Karaites continued to flourish for centuries in various lands; today the sect has only a few small remnants.

THE MIDDLE AGES

The Sephardim. The last influential gaon died in 1038, but as the eastern center was declining, creative forces emerged in North Africa and especially in Muslim Spain. The Christian Visigoths had all but exterminated the Spanish Jewish communities dating from Roman times, but the tolerant Arab rulers who conquered southern Spain were generally reasonable in their treatment of the Jews. (The Jews of Spain, Portugal, and the Middle Eastern countries and their descendants are known as SEPHARDIM. They differ somewhat in their rituals, customs, and life-style and in their pronunciation of Hebrew from the ASHKENAZIM, Jews of other European countries and their descendants.) Jews participated in the Arab cultural renaissance. They wrote in Arabic on science, philosophy, grammar, and rhetoric; they also produced notable biblical commentaries, legal works, and outstanding Hebrew poetry. (Among the scholars of this period were Solomon IBN GABIROL, JUDAH HA-LEVI, LEVI BEN GERSHON, and the great MAIMONIDES.) But this golden age was not entirely without problems. Muslim religious leaders and many of the common people resented the authority entrusted to Jewish statesmen and bankers. In the 12th century the ALMOHADS, a fanatical sect from North Africa, took control of Muslim Spain, and the Jews had to choose between Islam, martyrdom, and flight. Many found a precarious refuge in northern Spain, where Christian rulers found Jews useful to them in their effort to reconquer the peninsula.

Fanaticism continually stirred the Spanish mobs. In 1391 thousands of Jews were massacred and thousands more were converted by force or accepted baptism to save their lives. These "new Christians" (also known as Marranos, Spanish for "swine") were suspected of practicing Judaism in secret; it was largely to ferret out these Marranos that the INQUISITION was introduced. Many Marranos rose to high posts in the court and in the church, but they were constantly spied on, and many perished in the autos-da-fé, festive celebrations in which heretics were burned at the stake. Such tragic events stimulated the spread among Spanish Jews of the mystical doctrines of KABBALAH.

Once the last Muslim rulers were driven out and Spain was united under FERDINAND II and ISABELLA I, all professing Jews had to choose between baptism and expulsion. In August 1492 most of them left Spain in search of new homes. Under Spanish pressure, Portugal expelled its Jews in 1498. The exiles found refuge in North Africa, Italy, and especially in the Ottoman Empire, including the Balkans.

The Ashkenazim. Jews had lived in Italy, Germany, France, and the Low Countries since Roman times and in England since the Norman Conquest (1066). They were generally secure during the early Middle Ages, and because they had ties with other Jews in distant lands, they played a considerable role in international trade. Conditions changed drastically, however, during the CRUSADES (beginning 1096), when whole communities in France and Germany were massacred. During the Black Death (1347–51; see BUBONIC PLAGUE), Jews were accused of poisoning wells; further violence was roused by accusations of ritual murder and of desecrating the Eucharist.

Sacred symbols from the Kabbalah are shown in this drawing of hands from the Shefa Tal *by 17th-century German Kabbalist Sabbatai Horowitz. Kabbalists knew God through feeling rather than intellect and believed the scriptures held secrets.*

Nevertheless, Jews were needed in the very countries that persecuted them. Medieval Christian doctrine forbade Christians to take interest on loans; as a result, Jews were required to engage in money lending. The royal treasuries took a large part of the profits, and the Jews bore the popular resentment against usurers. In general, they were excluded from ownership of land and from the guilds that controlled the skilled trades.

When Christian money lenders learned to collect interest under other names, Jews were no longer needed. They were expelled from England in 1290 and from France in 1306 and, finally, in 1394. In the German states, life for Jews was difficult and uncertain. Many moved eastward into Poland, which lacked a middle class with the financial and commercial skills Jews could provide.

The Ashkenazim were not exposed to a broad secular culture such as the Jews of Spain (and Provence) had enjoyed. Theirs was a simple intense piety that repeatedly found expression in martyrdom. Their scholars produced important commentaries on the Bible and Talmud, and works on Kabbalah.

EARLY MODERN PERIOD
The Ghetto. Jews had long been accustomed to living in neighborhoods of their own, for security and for ready access to a synagogue. From the 16th century, however, they were systematically compelled to live in walled enclosures, to be locked in at night and on Christian holidays, and to wear a distinguishing badge when outside the walls. The Jewish quarter of Venice (established 1516) was called the GHETTO, and this local name became a general term for such segregated areas. Cut off from normal relations with non-Jews, few Jews had any idea of the cultural revival of the Renaissance (except in Italy; see ABRAVANEL, ISAAC BEN JUDAH; ABRAVANEL, JUDAH) or of the scientific advances in the 16th and 17th centuries. Even in the field of Jewish law they tended to a rigid conservatism.

In Poland and Lithuania, social conditions also had a segregatory effect. The Jews continued to speak a German dialect, mixed with many Hebrew words and with borrowings from Slavic languages—now known as Yiddish (see GERMANIC LANGUAGES; HEBREW AND YIDDISH LITERATURE). Intellectual life was focused on study of the Talmud, in which they achieved extraordinary mastery. They enjoyed a large measure of self-government, centralized in the Council of the Four Lands.

Persecutions became more frequent, however, inspired by competition from the growing Christian merchant class and by overly zealous churchmen. In 1648 a rebellion of Cossacks and Tatars in the Ukraine—then under Polish rule—led to an invasion of Poland, in which hundreds of thousands of Jews were massacred. Polish Jewry never recovered from this blow.

A little over a century later, Poland was partitioned (1772, 1793, 1795) among Prussia, Austria, and Russia, and most of Polish Jewry found itself under the heartless rule of the Russian tsars.

Sectarian Responses to Persecution. In 1665 a Turkish Jew named SABBATAI ZEVI proclaimed himself MESSIAH. Throughout the years there had been a number of such messianic claimants, but none had received more than local support. Sabbatai's announcement, however, evoked an unheard-of response; thousands of Jews from all over Europe and the Middle East sold their belongings and went to join Sabbatai in Palestine. Under threat of death Sabbatai adopted Islam, and the movement collapsed.

An outgrowth of the Sabbatean movement was the sect founded in 18th-century Poland by Jacob FRANK. The latter ultimately converted to Roman Catholicism, and his sect died out early in the 19th century.

Poland was also the birthplace of HASIDISM, the mystical sect founded by BAAL SHEM TOV. Although condemned by the rabbinic leadership, most notably by ELIJAH BEN SOLOMON, it established deep roots and became a significant social factor in the life of East European Jewry.

TOWARD EMANCIPATION
The successful revolt of the Netherlands against Spain during the 16th century encouraged a number of Marranos to flee Spain and Portugal and to settle in Amsterdam, where they formally returned to Judaism. Members of this Sephardic group later founded the Jewish communities in England, even before they were formally readmitted in 1656, and the New World; they were soon followed by larger numbers of Ashkenazim.

Western Developments. Some 18th-century liberals began to advocate an improvement of Jewish status; at the same time Moses MENDELSSOHN and a few other Jews were urging their coreligionists to acquire secular education and prepare themselves to participate in the national life of their countries. Such trends were intensified by the French Revolution. The French National Assembly granted (1791) Jews citizenship, and Napoleon I, although not free from prejudice, extended these rights to Jews in the countries he conquered, and the ghettos were abolished. After Napoleon's fall (1814–15), the German states revoked the rights he had granted the Jews, but the struggle for emancipation continued.

Equal rights were achieved in the Netherlands, and more slowly in Great Britain. Germany and Austria, even after 1870, discriminated against Jews in military and academic appointments; in these countries much popular hostility continued, now called ANTI-SEMITISM and supposedly justified on racial

In 1665, Nathan of Gaza hailed as Messiah the Jewish ascetic Sabbatai Zevi, who had arrived in Palestine with a small following proclaiming 1666 as the millennium. The Sabbatian movement grew rapidly, attracting adherents all over Europe. This German engraving (1666) depicts a multitude of Jews being led from exile to the Holy Land.

rather than religious grounds. In the American colonies the Jews had suffered relatively minor disabilities; with the founding of the United States, Jews became full citizens—although in a few states discriminatory laws had to be fought.

Jews entered the life of the Western world with keen enthusiasm; they contributed significantly to commercial, scientific, cultural, and social progress. But the old structure of Jewish life was severely damaged: community controls became less effective, and neglect of religious observance, mixed marriage, and conversion to Christianity occurred. In response to such challenges, new modernist versions of Judaism were formulated; these movements originated in Germany and had their greatest development in North America.

Persecution in Russia. In Russia hopes of improvement were soon abandoned; the government engaged in open war against Jews. Under Nicholas I (r. 1825–55), 12-year-old Jewish boys were drafted into the army for terms of more than 30 years (whereas other Russians were drafted at 18 for 25 years); and Jewish conscripts were treated with the utmost brutality to make them convert to Christianity.

After 1804, Jews were allowed to reside only in Poland, Lithuania, and the Ukraine; Russia proper was closed to them. This PALE of settlement was later made smaller. From 1881 on, anti-Jewish riots (POGROMS), tolerated and sometimes instigated by the government, sent thousands fleeing to Western Europe and the Americas. Because Russia refused to honor the passports of American Jews, the United States abrogated a trade treaty in 1913.

In response to these policies, new trends appeared in Russian Jewry. A movement of Jewish nationalism expressed itself in a revival of Hebrew as a secular language and in a few attempts at colonization in Palestine. A Jewish socialist movement, the Bund, appeared in urban centers, stressing the Yiddish language and folk culture.

THE 20TH CENTURY

The Jewish population of Western Europe and the United States grew rapidly through immigration from Eastern Europe. Jews shared in the prosperity of these expanding nations, the older settlers helping newcomers make a fresh start. Various forms of economic and social discrimination persisted, however, and racial anti-Semitism became well organized and highly vocal.

Zionism and Palestine. The violent outburst of hatred that accompanied the DREYFUS AFFAIR in France inspired Theodor HERZL to launch the movement of ZIONISM, which sought to establish a Jewish state. Its chief support came from East Eu-

Jewish refugees from Europe wave a flag bearing the Star of David from the deck of a ship attempting to dock in Palestine in 1947. The severe immigration quotas imposed by the British mandate authorities led to confrontations between the Zionists and the administration.

ropean Jews; elsewhere Herzl's proposals were considered impractical and a threat to newly won civil status.

During World War I, East European Jews suffered heavily from troops on both sides. American Jewry now found itself for the first time the leading element in the world Jewish community, bearing the major responsibility for relief and reconstruction of the ravaged centers. The peace treaties guaranteed equal rights to minorities in the newly constituted or reconstituted countries, but these agreements were not consistently upheld with regard to Jewish minorities, and colonization in Palestine expanded considerably.

In the BALFOUR DECLARATION of 1917, Great Britain announced its support for a Jewish national home; this purpose, approved by the Allied governments, was embodied in the mandate for PALESTINE that Britain assumed after the war. British agents had secretly made contradictory promises to Arab leaders, however, and growing Arab nationalism expressed itself in anti-Jewish riots in Palestine in 1920–21 and 1929. In the latter year leading non-Zionist Jews, convinced that Palestine alone offered hope for impoverished and oppressed millions (since Western nations had rigidly restricted immigration), joined with the Zionists to form the Jewish Agency to assist and direct Jewish settlement and development in Palestine.

Soviet and Nazi Anti-Semitism. The Communist Revolution of 1917 did not end the sufferings of the Jewish population in Russia. Much of the fighting in the Civil War of 1918–20 took place in the Ukraine, where the White Russian armies conducted savage pogroms in which thousands of Jews were massacred. Although discriminatory decrees were abolished and anti-Semitism was banned as counterrevolutionary under the Soviet system, Judaism suffered the same disabilities as other religious groups. After the fall of Leon TROTSKY, the old anti-Semitism was revived as a government policy.

In Germany the Weimar Republic for the first time abolished all official discrimination against Jews. The republic was unpopular, however, and anti-Semitism was popular. Calculated use of anti-Semitism as an instrument was a major factor in Adolf HITLER's rise to power in 1933, whereupon the German Jews were immediately disfranchised, robbed of possessions, deprived of employment, barred from the schools, and subjected to physical violence and constant humiliation. Once World War II occupied the attention of the democracies, Hitler and his supporters attempted "the final solution," the complete extermination of the Jews (see HOLOCAUST). About 6 million Jews—almost a third of their total number—were massacred, starved, or systematically gassed in CONCENTRATION CAMPS. In addition to destroying so many individual lives, the Holocaust eradicated the communities of Central

This portrait of Theodor Herzl was painted in 1903, one year before the great Zionist leader died. Herzl outlined his plan for establishing a homeland for the Jews in a pamphlet, The Jewish State, published in 1897. In 1949, Herzl was reburied on Mount Herzl near Jerusalem.

On May 14, 1948, in Tel Aviv, the Jewish National Council established the new state of Israel, with Chaim Weizmann as president and David Ben Gurion (reading Israel's new Declaration of Independence) as prime minister. In the background is a portrait of Theodor Herzl.

and Eastern Europe, which had been the chief centers of learning and piety for nearly a thousand years.

Establishment of Israel. The Western democracies all but closed their doors to refugees. Britain meanwhile had gradually abandoned the Balfour Declaration, reducing the number of Jews admitted to Palestine while making concessions to Arab leaders who had supported the Nazis in World War II. After repeated outbreaks of violence, investigations, and abortive British plans, Britain announced that it was giving up the mandate, and the United Nations adopted a resolution calling for the partition of Palestine into Jewish and Arab areas.

On May 14, 1948, the State of ISRAEL was proclaimed. Since then Israel has fought four wars against Arab coalitions to establish and preserve its independence (see ARAB-ISRAELI WARS). A peace treaty (Mar. 26, 1979) between Israel and Egypt was not accepted by the other Arab states.

The Diaspora since World War II. Although the USSR voted for the UN partition resolution in 1947, it has since become markedly anti-Israel in its policies. A great resurgence of Jewish self-consciousness, however, has occurred within Soviet Jewry. Deprived of religious education, isolated from Jews of other lands, and subject to many serious forms of discrimination, thousands of Jews in the USSR have found ways to affirm their Jewish commitment; a considerable number have succeeded in emigrating to Israel and to the United States.

Since World War II the Jews of the United States have achieved a degree of acceptance without parallel in Jewish history. Education and economic discrimination have largely disappeared, and Jews play a significant role in intellectual and cultural life. The elimination of social barriers has led to a high rate of mixed marriage. During the same period there has been a substantial growth in synagogue affiliation, a vast expansion of Jewish studies in the universities, and fervid support for the state of Israel.

Recent estimates put the total number of Jews at about 14 million, of whom over 5 million reside in the United States, more than 2 million in the USSR, and over 3 million in Israel. France has about 650,000 Jews, Great Britain more than 400,000, and Argentina about 300,000. The once-substantial communities in North Africa and the Middle East have been reduced to small fragments; the few left in Syria and Iraq have suffered severe persecution. Most of these Oriental Jews have settled in Israel, but those of Algeria, being French citizens, have mostly gone to metropolitan France.

BERNARD J. BAMBERGER

Bibliography: Baron, S. W., A Social and Religious History of the Jews, 15 vols. (1952-73); Ben-Sasson, H. H., ed., A History of the Jewish People (Eng. trans., 1976); Borchsenius, Poul, The History of the Jews (1965); Cohen, Bernard L., Jews Among the Nations (1978); Eban, Abba, My People (1968); Finkelstein, Louis, The Jews: Their History, Culture and Religion, 3 vols., 4th ed. (1970-71); Gay, Ruth, Jews in America (1965); Patai, Raphael, The Jewish Mind (1977); Raddock, Charles, Portrait of a People, 2d ed. (1967); Roth, Cecil, The Jewish Contribution to Civilization, 3d ed. (1956), and A Short History of the Jewish People, rev. ed. (1969); Sachar, A. L., A History of the Jews, rev. ed. (1967); Sklare, Marshall, ed., The Jew in American Society (1974).

Jew's harp

The Jew's harp (its name possibly corrupted from jaw's harp) is a simple metal percussion instrument (bamboo in Oceania). The clothespin- or horseshoe-shaped frame is held between the teeth, a strip of metal (or bamboo) is vibrated by strumming with a finger, and various overtones are produced by changes in the oral cavity. Found in many parts of the world, the instrument has ancient roots and was introduced into Europe from Asia about 1350.   ELWYN A. WIENANDT

Jezebel   [jez'-uh-bel]

Jezebel, d. c.843 BC, was a Phoenician princess and wife of AHAB, the king of ancient Israel. According to 1 Kings 18 and 19, Jezebel fostered the worship of the Phoenician god BAAL and supported 450 prophets of Baal. When ELIJAH opposed her and stirred up popular sentiment against the pagan prophets, she decreed his death, forcing him to flee. Jezebel was killed when her eunuchs threw her from a palace window at the order of King JEHU; her body was eaten by dogs, as Elijah had prophesied.

Jhabvala, R. Prawer   [jahb-vah'-lah, prah'-wur]

One of India's foremost English-language novelists, Ruth Prawer Jhabvala, b. Cologne, Germany, May 7, 1927, writes mildly satirical novels that deal compassionately and intelligently with middle-class Indian life. She went to England as a refugee with her Polish-German parents in 1939 and, after receiving an M.A. degree in English from London University, married an Indian architect and moved to Delhi. Her novels include To Whom She Will (1955; publ. in the United States as Amrita, 1956), A Backward Place (1965), A New Dominion (1973; publ. in the United States as Travelers), and Heat and Dust (1975). Jhabvala is also the author of short stories and of such screenplays as that for James Ivory's Shakespeare-wallah (1965).   GAUTUM DASGUPTA

Jidda   [jid'-uh]

Jidda (1974 pop., 561,104) is a port city on the Red Sea in the HEJAZ region of western Saudi Arabia. It is Saudi Arabia's leading business and diplomatic center. Steel, petroleum, cement, clothing, and pottery are the city's major industries. Because of its location, 72 km (45 mi) west of MECCA, it is the port of entry for millions of Muslims on pilgrimage to Mecca; tourism is therefore an important industry. King 'Ahd al-Aziz Private University (1967) is here.

Old Jidda was founded by Caliph Uthman about 646. Present-day Jidda, which is north of the original site, is about 300 years old. Ruled by Turkey until 1916, it was briefly part of the Kingdom of Hejaz. King IBN SAUD conquered the area in 1925.

jig

The jig, a folk dance that was often a part of European peasant celebrations of the 16th century, is today most closely associated with Ireland. Performing to lively fiddle or bagpipe music, the dancer keeps an erect torso while executing rapid, springy steps. Jig tempos and forms were used as the basis of the gigue, a movement in the instrumental SUITE of the 17th century.

jigsaw puzzle

A jigsaw puzzle is a collection of interlocking pieces that can be joined together to form a picture. Simple puzzles, made for children, consist of a few large pieces; more complex puzzles, made for more sophisticated solvers, may consist of 1,000 or more pieces. Most puzzles contain from 300 to 750 pieces. The ease or difficulty of solving a puzzle depends on the number of pieces, their shapes and shadings, and the design of the picture. Modern jigsaw puzzles are manufactured in two layers; the top is a reproduction of a painting or color photograph, and the bottom is a backing of wood or cardboard. The puzzle is cut into pieces.

Jigsaws are not used to make modern puzzles; instead, a die press stamps out the pattern, after which the pieces are separated and packaged. With the exception of custom-made puzzles, most jigsaw puzzles are mass-produced. These are usually rectangular or circular, whereas custom-made puzzles may be unique.

The creation of the modern jigsaw puzzle took place in England in the early 1760s when John Spilsbury, a British printer, glued an engraving of a map to a backing of wood and cut the result with a marquetry saw. He quickly sold this and other puzzles and advertised them as educational devices. Other printers followed his example, and soon dissected maps were joined by dissected depictions of alphabets, biblical events, past and present celebrities, historical scenes, and other designs. The black-and-white puzzle enjoyed popularity until the early 19th century, when color lithography came into use. Jigsaw puzzles remained relatively costly until the late 1800s, when the implementation of the die press made mass-produced puzzles, and low prices, possible. The popularity of jigsaw puzzles fluctuated until the Depression of the 1930s, when the demand for inexpensive home entertainment made jigsaw puzzles a flourishing, and eventually permanent, source of amusement in the United States.   FRANCENE AND LOUIS SABIN

Bibliography: Sabin, Francene and Louis, The One, the Only, the Original Jigsaw Puzzle Book (1977).

jihad   [jih-hahd']

In Islam, the duty of each Muslim to spread his religious beliefs is termed *jihad*. Although the word is widely understood to mean a "holy war" against nonbelievers, jihad may also be fulfilled by a personal battle against evil inclinations, the righting of wrongs, and the supporting of what is good.

Jim Crow laws

Jim Crow laws, named for an antebellum minstrel show character, were late-19th-century statutes passed by the legislatures of the Southern states that created a racial caste system in the American South. Although slavery had been abolished, many whites at this time believed that nonwhites were inherently inferior and to support this belief sought rationalizations through religion and science. The U.S. Supreme Court was inclined to agree with the white-supremacist judgment and in 1883 began to strike down the foundations of the post–Civil War RECONSTRUCTION, declaring the CIVIL RIGHTS ACT of 1875 unconstitutional. In 1896 it legitimized the principle of "separate but equal" in its ruling PLESSY V. FERGUSON.

The high court rulings led to a profusion of Jim Crow laws. By 1914 every Southern state had passed laws that created

This 19th-century cartoon illustrates conflict between black and white passengers in a railroad car. Jim Crow laws became prevalent in the American South in the late 1800s following the Reconstruction period. These laws legalized racial segregation in virtually every public facility and were not repealed until the 1950s, when they were declared unconstitutional.

two separate societies—one black, the other white. This artificial structure was maintained by denying the franchise to blacks through the use of devices such as GRANDFATHER CLAUSES, poll taxes, and literacy tests. It was further strengthened by the creation of separate facilities in every part of society, including schools, restaurants, streetcars, health care institutions, and cemeteries.

The first major blow against the Jim Crow system of racial segregation was struck in 1954 by the Supreme Court's decision in BROWN V. BOARD OF EDUCATION OF TOPEKA, KANSAS, which declared segregation in the public schools unconstitutional. In the following decade the system slowly crumbled under the onslaught of the civil rights movement. The legal structure of segregation was finally ended by the civil rights legislation of 1964–68.   RONALD L. LEWIS

Bibliography: Williamson, Joel, ed., The Origins of Segregation (1968); Woodward, C. Vann, The Strange Career of Jim Crow, 3d rev. ed. (1974).

See also: INTEGRATION, RACIAL.

Jiménez, Juan Ramón   [hee-may'-nayth, hwahn rah-mohn]

Juan Ramón Jiménez, b. Dec. 24, 1881, d. May 29, 1958, was one of the most influential Spanish poets of the 20th century. After studying in Cádiz and Seville, he went to Madrid in 1900, where, under the influence of Rubén Darío, Gustavo Bécquer, and the French symbolists, he produced several volumes of verse which identified him with the Spanish modernist movement. In *Almas de Violeta* (Violet Souls, 1900), *Ninfeas* (Water Lilies, 1900), and *Arias tristes* (Sad Airs, 1903), he displayed the preoccupation with love, natural beauty, and death that haunted all his later work.

A sojourn (1905–11) in his native Andalusia inspired the ornate *Elejías* (Elegies, 1908) as well as his most famous work, the prose poem collection *Platero and I* (1914–17; Eng. trans., 1957). The influential *Diario de un poeta recién casado* (Diary of a Recently Married Poet, 1917) signaled his departure from the rich textures of the elegies and the beginning of his experiments with free verse and the spare style of his later poetry.

Jiménez's subsequent volumes, illustrating both this denuded style and a growing mysticism, include *Eternidades* (Eternities, 1918), *Piedra y cielo* (Stone and Sky, 1919), *La estación total* (All Seasons in One, 1946), and *Animal de fondo* (Animal of the Depths, 1949). He also wrote the personal sketches collected in *Españoles de tres mundos* (Spaniards of Three Worlds, 1942) and translated Blake, Eliot, and (with his American-born wife) Rabindranath Tagore.

After leaving Spain during the Spanish Civil War, Jiménez traveled widely in the Americas, lecturing at various universities until settling in Puerto Rico in 1951. In 1956 he received the Nobel Prize for literature.

Bibliography: Fogelquist, Donald F., Juan Ramón Jiménez (1976); Jiménez, Juan Ramón, Selected Writings, trans. by H. R. Hays, ed. by Eugenio Florit (1957), and Three Hundred Poems, 1903–1953, trans. by Eloise Roach (1962); Young, Howard T., Juan Ramón Jiménez (1967).

Jiménez de Cisneros, Francisco   [hee-may'-nayth day thees-nay'-rohs, frahn-thees'-koh]

The Spanish cardinal, statesman, and grand inquisitor Francisco Jiménez (or Ximenes) de Cisneros, b. 1436, d. Nov. 8, 1517, initiated important reforms of the Spanish clergy that helped to eradicate much of the kind of corruption later criticized in Germany by Martin Luther during the REFORMATION. After studying at the University of Salamanca, Jiménez was ordained a priest. In 1484 he abandoned the secular clergy to join the Franciscan order. He became confessor to Queen ISABELLA I of Castile in 1492 and archbishop of Toledo in 1495.

In 1499, Jiménez began a ruthless campaign of converting the Moors, burning a million priceless Arabic manuscripts, and provoking the Muslim revolt of 1499–1500. Appointed cardinal and head of the INQUISITION in Castile by Isabella's widower, FERDINAND II of Aragon, in 1507, Jiménez financed and led the conquest (1509) of Moorish Oran. In 1508 he founded the university at Alcalá de Henares. He also supervised the compilation of the Complutensian Polyglot Bible (1514–17), which displayed parallel columns of text in various languages. After Ferdinand's death in 1516, Jiménez, as regent of Castile, managed the accession of Charles I (later Holy Roman Emperor CHARLES V) to the Spanish throne.

Jiménez de Quesada, Gonzalo   [hee-may'-nayth day kay-sah'-dah, gohn-zahl'-oh]

Gonzalo Jiménez de Quesada, b. c.1496, d. Feb. 16, 1579, a Spanish conquistador, founded the city of BOGOTÁ. He arrived on the northern coast of South America in 1535 as chief magistrate of the colony of Santa Marta. The following year he headed an expedition that went inland in search of the legendary city of gold, EL DORADO. With 900 men, he advanced about 725 km (450 mi) up the Magdalena River valley through different and varied terrain; many in the expedition died during the 8-month trek. Finally penetrating the central plain of Colombia in 1537, Jiménez conquered the kingdom of the CHIBCHA Indians and discovered great mineral wealth. He founded (1538) the city of Santa Fé de Bogotá to facilitate the further accumulation of gold and emeralds.

Jiménez returned to the coast in 1539 and went to Spain to claim the territory he had discovered, which he called NEW GRANADA. Rebuffed by the Spanish crown because of rival claims, he finally received (1549) only the honorary title of marshal of New Granada. Returning to South America, Jiménez struck out from Bogotá in search of El Dorado again in 1569. He spent 3 futile years in the plains crossed by the Orinoco River (in present-day Venezuela) before returning to Bogotá bankrupt and ill. He died, a leper, a few years later. Jiménez is thought by some to have been the model for Cervantes' Don Quixote.

Bibliography: Graham, R. B., *The Conquest of New Granada: Being the Life of Gonzalo Jiménez de Quesada* (1922; repr. 1973).

jimsonweed   [jim'-suhn-weed]

Jimsonweed, or common thorn apple, *Datura stramonium*, family Solanaceae, is a widespread annual weed common to roadsides and pastures. It grows up to 1.6 m (5.3 ft) tall, and the white to violet flowers are funnel shaped. The jimsonweed contains poisonous alkaloids and is a source of the drug stramonium, which is used for relaxing bronchial muscles in the treatment of asthma and bronchial complaints. Seed and plant extracts have been used in Europe to treat a number of disorders, including rheumatism and epilepsy.

DIANNE FAHSELT

Jingo

Jingo, c.169–c.269, also known as Jingu Kogo, was the semilegendary empress of Japan during the period of Japanese expansion into southern Korea. She is supposed to have been the wife of Chuai (r. 192–200) and regent for her son Ojin. Although most of her attributes—such as her ability to control tides—are legendary, historians believe that Japanese women exerted a powerful influence on politics in that period and that some parts of Jingo's history are probably based on fact.

Jinnah, Muhammad Ali   [jin-uh, muh-hahm'-ud ah'-lee]

Muhammad Ali Jinnah, b. Dec. 25, 1876, d. Sept. 11, 1948, led the Indian Muslims in the years before independence and founded the state of Pakistan. A brilliant, prosperous, westernized lawyer, Jinnah began his political activities in the 1906 session of the INDIAN NATIONAL CONGRESS party. In 1913 he joined the All-India MUSLIM LEAGUE. He left the Congress party in 1920 because of differences with its leader Mahatma GANDHI, who opposed the Muslim demand for a separate communal electorate and advocated policies of noncooperation. Thereafter Jinnah used the Muslim League to propagate his views and to demand political equality for India's large

Muslim minority. During the 1920s and early '30s, Jinnah continued to seek a rapprochement between Hindus and Muslims.

By the late 1930s, however, converting the poetic concept of the word Pakistan—meaning "land of the pure"—into a political slogan, Jinnah was advocating the idea of a separate independent state for the Indian Muslims. His struggle bore fruit in 1947 when the Indian subcontinent was partitioned into two states: Muslim Pakistan and Hindu India.

Jinnah—having won himself the popular title of *Qaid-i-Azam* ("the great leader")—became the first governor general of Pakistan. Although he served only a year in that post before his death, his detractors argue that he paved the way for a series of bungling successor governments and military coups by his inability to work with others and to follow democratic norms.

MARCUS FRANDA AND VONETTA J. FRANDA

Bibliography: Bolitho, Hector, *Jinnah* (1954); Sayeed, Khalid B., *Pakistan: The Formative Phase, 1857-1948*, 2d ed. (1968).

See also: INDIA, HISTORY OF.

jinni   [jin'-ee]

In Arab and Muslim folklore, a jinni (often anglicized as *genie*) is a desert or wilderness spirit that can assume human or animal form and exercise supernatural powers. Often, as in the tale of ALADDIN's lamp in the *Arabian Nights*, it serves a summoner who knows the correct magical words or gesture. Most jinni are ugly, evil demons, but some are beautiful and good. Their ruler is Suleiman, or Solomon, and the foremost of them is Iblis, the prince of darkness.

jinrikisha: see RICKSHA.

jitterbug

The jitterbug, an uninhibited, acrobatic dance, reached the height of its popularity during the SWING era of the 1930s and '40s. A dance for couples, it could range from a sedate series of steps—including variations of the Lindy hop, the shag, and the BLACK BOTTOM—to a wild improvisation using swings, lifts, and turns. Jitterbugging was also called jiving, and jitterbug music, jive.

Jívaro   [hee'-vah-roh]

The Jívaro are a South American Indian people who inhabit the *montaña* region of Ecuador. Of uncertain linguistic affiliation, the Jívaro have never been conquered. Throughout their history they have fought among themselves in intercommunity blood feuds; they are popularly known for their practice of taking the heads of their enemies (see HEADHUNTING). Their population numbers approximately 8,000.

Jívaro are shifting horticulturalists who grow manioc, maize, beans, and sweet potatoes. They also engage in hunting and fishing. A typical community consists of a single, large, elliptically shaped house containing a man, his wives, and their children; occasionally, two or more large households occupied by close relatives are established within a few hundred meters of each other. The community is usually abandoned after about five years, as the residents move to cultivate new, fertile areas.

Jívaro religion is animistic and involves SHAMANISM, witchcraft, and the use of hallucinogens. The Jívaro are thought to believe in a supreme deity and a creation myth involving Sun, Moon, and flood, a belief that is similar to those of many indigenous South American peoples.

LOUIS C. FARON

Bibliography: Harner, Michael J., *The Jívaro, People of the Sacred Waterfalls* (1972); Steward, Julian H., and Faron, Louis C., *Native Peoples of South America* (1959).

Joachim, Joseph   [yoh'-ah-kim, yoh'-sef]

The Hungarian violinist and composer Joseph Joachim, b. June 28, 1831, d. Aug. 15, 1907, was an influential musician and a close friend of Johannes Brahms. After early years in Hungary and Vienna he lived in Germany and studied for a time with Ferdinand David in Leipzig. His wide-ranging concertizing included numerous visits to England, where he was especially popular. In 1869 he organized the celebrated Joachim Quartet. Brahms, who greatly valued Joachim's musical advice, dedicated his violin concerto to him, as did Dvořák. Joachim's compositions include three violin concertos, of which the *Hungarian Concerto* (1857) is the best known.

Bibliography: Bickley, Nora, ed. and trans., *Letters to and from Joseph Joachim* (1914; repr. 1972); Chapin, Victor, *The Violin and Its Masters* (1969).

Joachim, Saint

Saint Joachim was the husband of Saint ANNE and the father of the Virgin MARY. He is not mentioned in the Bible. The nonbiblical *Gospel of James*, an apocryphal book, is the only source of information about him. Feast day (shared with Saint Anne): July 26 (Western); Sept. 9 (Eastern).

Joan, Pope

Pope Joan was a legendary female pope who supposedly ruled the church as John VIII from 855 to 858, between the pontificates of Leo IV (847-55) and Benedict III (855-58). Another version of the story places her election at about the year 1100. According to the legend, a learned woman in male disguise became the papal notary and was eventually elected pope. Her sex was discovered when she gave birth during a papal procession. Some variations of the story record her name as Agnes or Gilberta. Although the legend was widely believed during the Middle Ages, it has since been totally discredited. A literary treatment of the subject is Lawrence Durrell's *Pope Joan* (1960; adapted from a Greek work by Emmanuel Royidis).

Joan of Arc, Saint

Joan of Arc (French, Jeanne d'Arc), b. *c.*1412, was a French peasant girl who led the French army against the English during the HUNDRED YEARS' WAR. Called the Maid of Orléans, she is a French national heroine and patron saint.

When Joan was about 13 years old she began to hear "voices" (which she later identified as those of Saint Catherine, Saint Margaret, and Saint Michael) that gave her the mission of liberating France from English domination. She kept the messages secret for about 5 years, and only in 1429 did she leave her home in Domrémy, Champagne, and travel with an escort to the court of the dauphin, later King CHARLES VII, who had been deprived of his rights as heir to the French throne by the Treaty of Troyes of 1420. At that time the English were besieging Orléans. After a group of theologians tested her, Charles was persuaded to reassemble his troops

The French visionary Joan of Arc, here portrayed (1854) by J. A. D. Ingres, revived the hopes of French troops when she led them to victory over the English during the Hundred Years' War. Captured in 1430, she refused to deny her claim to divine inspiration and was burned as a heretic. Her conviction was later overturned, and she was canonized in 1920. (Louvre, Paris.)

and place them under Joan's command in an expedition to relieve the city. In 8 days during May 1429, she lifted the siege that had lain on Orléans for 8 months. In June 1429, Joan and her troops were able to break through to Reims, where she persuaded Charles to hold his coronation. The relief of Orléans and the crowning of the dauphin revived French hopes.

Against Joan's advice, a period of military inactivity followed, but in the spring of 1430, Joan resumed her campaigns. In May, while attempting to relieve Compiègne, she was captured by the Burgundians, who sold her to the English. The latter, who wanted her executed but were reluctant to accept the responsibility for such an action, turned her over to a church court in Rouen. There she was tried on charges of heresy and witchcraft, and the judges declared her visions diabolical. After months of interrogation, Joan was tricked into admission of guilt. She soon retracted her confession, however, and was condemned as a relapsed heretic. On May 30, 1431, she was burned at the stake in Rouen. When French fortunes were finally restored, Joan was rehabilitated in a formal trial (1456) called for by Charles VII, who had done nothing to save her while she was alive.

Joan of Arc has been the subject of much art and literature. There are monuments to her memory in many French cities and towns. In Rouen, a statue stands on the spot in the marketplace where she was executed. She was canonized in 1920. Feast day: May 30.   THOMAS E. MORRISSEY

Bibliography: Guillemin, Henri, *Joan, Maid of Orleans* (1973); Lightbody, Charles W., *The Judgements of Joan* (1960); Lucie-Smith, Edward, *Joan of Arc* (1977); Michelet, Jules, *Joan of Arc*, trans. by Albert Guérard (1957); Pernoud, Régine, *Joan of Arc By Herself and Her Witnesses* (1969); Sackville-West, Victoria, *Saint Joan of Arc* (1936).

Joan the Mad, Queen of Castile

Joan the Mad, or Juana la Loca, b. Nov. 6, 1479, d. Apr. 11, 1555, was the daughter of the Spanish monarchs FERDINAND II of Aragon and ISABELLA I of Castile. She was already insane when she succeeded (1504) to her mother's throne, and a regency was set up by her father. Her husband, the Habsburg PHILIP I of Castile, whom she had married in 1496, reigned briefly in 1506. On Philip's death, Ferdinand resumed control until his own death in 1516, when Joan's son, later Holy Roman Emperor CHARLES V, became joint ruler of Castile with Joan. She lived most of her life in seclusion at Tordesillas castle.

Joan I, Queen of Naples

Joan I, b. 1326, d. May 22, 1382, succeeded her grandfather King Robert I on the Neapolitan throne in 1343. As a result of her involvement in the murder (1345) of her cousin and husband, Andrew, she earned the enmity of his brother, King LOUIS I of Hungary, and she was driven out of Naples in 1348. She returned in 1352, but the remainder of her reign was troubled, in part by intrigues surrounding her subsequent marriages and in part by struggles between Louis of Anjou and Charles of Durazzo to secure her throne. Deposed by Pope URBAN VI in 1380, she was murdered on the orders of Charles, who succeeded her as CHARLES III.

                                            JAMES M. POWELL

See also: NAPLES, KINGDOM OF.

Job, Book of   [johb]

The Book of Job, in the Old Testament of the BIBLE, is a complex wisdom writing that uses a blend of prose and poetry in dramatic form to explore the perennial problem of innocent suffering and God's justice. The principal figure of the book is Job, a pious Jew afflicted with disease and stripped of all his goods. The free and imaginative transformations of the Job figure are literarily and imaginatively comparable to Shakespeare's treatment of Hamlet and Goethe's use of Faust. The identity of the author, usually dated 600-400 BC, is completely unknown.

Throughout the drama, Job asserts his innocence of wrong, thereby rejecting the traditional view that suffering is the result of sin. The humble and patient Job who bears his sufferings as proofs of piety, however, becomes the raging and insistent Job pressing relentlessly for divine vindication in the dialogue that forms the main part of the book (chaps. 3-31). The argument is pursued through three cycles of speeches in which Job's three friends—Eliphaz, Bilbad, and Zophar—chide the hero and he, in answering them, challenges God. Job's final self-defense and call upon the deity is answered by God's speech from a whirlwind in which Job is invited to trust in the divine omniscience and power. This direct experience of the mysteries of God leaves Job at peace with himself. Although no final solution to the problem is offered, the author clearly rejects traditional explanations of suffering. It is a moot point whether he offers a positive answer to questions about suffering and divine justice.

The unity of the book is debated. Many interpreters assign the prologue and epilogue to an earlier or later hand, and it is widely assumed that the poem on wisdom (chap. 28) and the speeches (chaps. 32-37) of a fourth friend (Elihu) inserted after the dialogues were added later, because they interrupt the flow of the argument.   NORMAN K. GOTTWALD

Bibliography: Gordis, Robert, *The Book of God and Man* (1965); Johnson, L. D., *Out of the Whirlwind: The Major Message of Job* (1971).

Job Corps

The Job Corps is a United States government agency that provides vocational training, remedial education, health care, and personal counseling to disadvantaged youth in order to enable them to find work. It is managed by the Employment and Training Administration of the Department of Labor and was established by the Economic Opportunity Act of 1964 as part of the Johnson administration's WAR ON POVERTY program. The Job Corps is now included as Title IV of the Comprehensive Employment and Training Act (CETA) of 1973. In 1978 it had a budget of $175 million.

Drawing on the experience of the Civilian Conservation Corps, which provided public works employment for 2.6 million young men between 1933 and 1942, the Job Corps trains 45,000 youths per year at 58 centers throughout the United States. Each center trains 100 to 2,000 young men and women between 16 and 21 years of age, generally high-school dropouts from low-income families. Training usually lasts for 6 months but may be extended to 2 years. About 60% of all Job Corps members are black, while 11% are Hispanic; 73% are men; and about 70% score below a sixth-grade reading level on entry.

On graduating, Job Corps members are helped to find employment by federal and state employment agencies and the Job Corps-sponsored Graduate Aid to Employment (GATE), which has centers located in 13 cities. About 90% of the graduates find work or go back to school.

Bibliography: Levitan, Sar A., and Johnston, Benjamin H., *The Job Corps: A Social Experiment That Works* (1976).

Jocho   [joh'-choh]

Jocho, d. 1057, was a famous Buddhist sculptor of the Fujiwara (late Heian) period (987-1185) in Japan. The first in a family line of gifted professional sculptors, he is credited with perfecting a technique that allowed great refinement in wood sculpting. To his hand is attributed one of the period's finest surviving works, the magnificent gilt-wood statue of Amida Buddha, in the Byodoin temple's Phoenix Hall at Uji, near Kyoto.

Jochum, Eugen   [yoh'-kuhm, oy'-guhn]

The distinguished German conductor Eugen Jochum, b. Nov. 1, 1902, is known as one of the foremost interpreters of Mozart and Bruckner. He studied (1924-25) with Sigmund von Hausegger. After conducting in various German cities, Jochum became conductor (1934-49) of the Philharmonic Orchestra and State Opera in Hamburg. He was coconductor (1961-63) of the Concertgebouw Orchestra in Amsterdam, and he has been guest conductor of most of the leading European and American orchestras, touring with several. From 1969 to 1977 he was chief conductor of the Bamberg Symphony. He is currently conductor laureate of the London Symphony Orchestra and permanent guest conductor of the Concertgebouw Orchestra, the West Berlin Opera and Philharmonic Orchestra, and the Chicago Lyric Opera.

Discography: Beethoven, L. v., *Symphonies Nos. 1-9*; Brahms, J., *Symphonies Nos. 1-4*; Bruckner, A., *Mass No. 3, Motets, Symphonies Nos. 1-9*, and *Te Deum*; Haydn, F. J., *Symphonies Nos. 93-104*; Mozart, W. A., *Symphony No. 41*; Schubert, F., *Symphony No. 8*.

Jodrell Bank Experimental Station: see
NUFFIELD RADIO ASTRONOMY LABORATORIES.

joe-pye weed   [joh-py']

Joe-pye weed comprises a few species of perennial herbs of genus *Eupatorium*, family Compositae. Leaves are opposite, and large, rounded inflorescences occur with many small flowers. Flowers are pink to purple. The plants are often found growing in moist places or meadows in eastern North America. They contain cyclic organic compounds known as lactones and sesquiterpenes and were once widely used as domestic medicine during the 19th century. The rhizomes were used to treat kidney ailments and urinary dysfunctions, and a decoction was used as an aphrodisiac.

DIANNE FAHSELT

Joel, Book of   [joh'-ul]

The Book of Joel, a prophetic book of the Old Testament of the BIBLE, derives its name from the prophet Joel. Nothing other than his name is known about the prophet. The date of composition was probably between 400 and 350 BC, although some scholars place it much earlier (9th-7th century BC). The book falls into two sections. The first (1:1-2:17) gives an account of a plague of locusts and a drought that ravaged Judah as a symbol of divine judgment. The second (2:18-3:21) promises the gift of the spirit of the Lord for the entire population and declares final judgment on all nations, with protection and fertility for Judah and Jerusalem. The passage on the outpouring of God's Spirit (2:28-32) is cited in Saint Peter's Pentecost sermon in Acts 2:17-21.   GEORGE W. COATS

Joffre, Joseph Jacques Césaire   [zhawf, zhoh-zef' zhahk say-zair']

Joseph Jacques Césaire Joffre, b. Jan. 12, 1852, d. Jan. 3, 1931, was commander in chief of the French Army at the outbreak of World War I. He had received that post in 1911, as one of a new group of republican officers elevated in response to the DREYFUS AFFAIR.

When war broke out in August 1914, Joffre's plan for a French offensive into Alsace-Lorraine was frustrated by the speed of the German advance through Belgium into northeastern France. An orderly retreat enabled the Allies to regroup and counterattack, however, in the First Battle of the MARNE (Sept. 5-10, 1914). For this victory, Joffre was hailed as the savior of France.

Joffre's failure to provide further victories led to increasing criticism, however. After the costly battles of Verdun and the Somme in 1916 (see SOMME, BATTLE OF; VERDUN, BATTLE OF), Joffre was transferred to an advisory position, which he left on Dec. 26, 1916. He was made a marshal of France on the same day. Joffre's *Memoirs* was published in translation in 1932.

P. M. EWY

Bibliography: Dawbarn, Charles, *Joffre and His Army* (1916); Joffre, Joseph, *My March to Timbuktu* (1915); King, Jere C., *Generals and Politicians: Conflict Between France's High Command, Parliament and Government, 1914-1918* (1951).

Joffrey Ballet   [jahf'-ree]

The Joffrey Ballet, an energetic ensemble without stars, performs an eclectic repertory under the direction of Robert Joffrey. From 1954 to 1962, Joffrey presented mainly his own choreography, using several company names for a constantly growing group of dancers. In 1962 the group came under the sponsorship of Rebekah Harkness and greatly expanded their activities with her help. Harkness withdrew her support early in 1964, and a new company was formed later in the same year.

After a well-received season at the City Center Theater in 1966 they were invited to become the official resident ballet company. In this new period of security, Joffrey expanded the repertory with revivals of important works. These have included Kurt Jooss's *Green Table* (1967), Leonid Massine's *Parade* (1973), Frederick Ashton's *A Wedding Bouquet* (1978), and Vaslav Nijinsky's *L'Après-midi d'un Faune* (1979). Gerald Arpino, associate director, has choreographed numerous works for the company, including *Olympics* (1966) and *Trinity* (1968), to rock music.

Contemporary choreographers who have worked with the Joffrey Ballet include Anna Sokolow, Eliot Feld, and Twyla Tharp, who choreographed *Deuce Coupe* and *As Time Goes By* in 1973.

In 1970, Joffrey II was formed, an apprentice group for young dancers serving as an intermediate stage between the American Dance Center, the company's school, and the parent company.   MICHAEL ROBERTSON

jogging: see RUNNING AND JOGGING.

Jogues, Saint Isaac   [johg]

Isaac Jogues, b. Jan. 10, 1607, d. Oct. 18, 1646, was a French Jesuit missionary to the North American Indians. He became a novice in the Society of Jesus in 1624, was ordained a priest in 1636, and in the same year left France for Canada. Sent to preach among the HURONS in the Georgian Bay area, he was entrusted with the construction of Fort Sainte Marie I. In 1642, when returning from a visit to Quebec, Jogues was captured and mutilated by Mohawk warriors; he was released the following year only with the help of a Dutch trader. Returning to Quebec in 1644, Jogues spent two years at Montreal before he was named a French ambassador of peace to the Mohawks. His mission to the Mohawk country in the late spring of 1646 appeared to be succeeding; but after he had returned there in the autumn, he was slain by a hostile war-

rior. He was canonized in 1930 as one of the JESUIT MARTYRS OF NORTH AMERICA. Feast day: Sept. 26.   F. J. THORPE

Bibliography: Birch, J. J., *The Saint of the Wilderness: St. Isaac Jogues* (1936).

Johanan ben Zakkai   [joh-han'-uhn ben zak'-ay-y]

Johanan ben Zakkai, fl. 1st century AD, was a Jewish leader who contributed to the reconstitution of Jewish communal life in Palestine after the destruction (AD 70) of the Second Temple. Johanan reconvened the SANHEDRIN at Jabneh, where it became both an executive organ and an academy for the study of the TORAH. He was succeeded as head of the Sanhedrin by GAMALIEL OF JABNEH.

Bibliography: Neusner, Jacob, *A Life of Rabbai Yoachanan Ben Zakkai* (1962).

Johannes von Tepl   [yoh-hahn'-es fuhn tep'-ul]

Johannes von Tepl, c.1350–1415, was a schoolmaster and lawyer successively in Tepl, Saaz, and Prague. His *Der Ackermann aus Böhmen*, written soon after 1400 and translated in 1947 as *Death and the Ploughman*, is a dialogue in alternating chapters between a newly bereaved ploughman and Death. The form suggests humanism, but the devotional content remains medieval. The work was copied and reprinted many times in the next 150 years, but its literary and cultural significance as a major example of pre-Reformation German prose was not realized until the early 20th century.   PAUL SALMON

Johannesburg   [joh-han'-es-burg]

Johannesburg is the largest city in South Africa. It is situated 1,753 m (5,750 ft) above sea level on the Witwatersrand, a ridge of gold-bearing hills in the southern Transvaal. Johannesburg lies about 160 km (100 mi) southwest of Pretoria. The city population is 654,682, and the metropolitan area population is 1,432,643 (1970). Like all South African cities, Johannesburg is racially segregated, with the white suburbs spreading northward. The largest African, Coloured, and Asian townships (to the South) are, respectively, Soweto (1977 est. pop., 1,000,000), Nancefield, and Lenasia. The townships are administered by the municipality. The mean temperature is 10° C

Johannesburg, founded in 1886 as a gold-mining camp, is South Africa's financial center as well as its largest city. During the 1970s Soweto, one of the black townships of Johannesburg, was the scene of violent racial disturbances resulting from South Africa's apartheid policies.

(50° F) in July and 20° C (68° F) in December; the city receives about 760 mm (30 in) of rainfall annually.

Johannesburg is the administrative headquarters of many mining, banking, industrial, and commercial concerns and is the home of the South African Stock Exchange (1887). Its industries (metallurgical, engineering, printing, food processing) contribute about one-fifth of the nation's total output. Gold production is declining, but gold-related industries and general manufacturing are expanding. The city has numerous branch offices of governmental institutions and consular offices. Johannesburg forms the hub of South Africa's major urban-industrial region called the Rand. Landlocked, it has road, rail, and air service with all major cities, and the nearby Jan Smuts Airport is South Africa's main port of entry.

Johannesburg is home of the English-language University of the Witwatersrand (1903), the Rand Afrikaans University (1966), and the Witwatersrand College for Advanced Technical Education (1925). Union Observatory (1903) is a major astronomical station. The major tourist attractions are the Zoological Gardens, the Carlton Centre, the Africana Museum, and the Melrose Bird Sanctuary.

Johannesburg was settled when gold mining began there in 1886. As a mining and gold-processing center, it grew rapidly. The city was originally part of the Boer-controlled Transvaal, but after the SOUTH AFRICAN WAR (1899–1902), it passed to the British.

Johannsen, Albert   [joh-han'-sen]

The American petrographer Albert Johannsen, b. Belle Plaine, Iowa, Dec. 3, 1871, d. Jan. 11, 1962, is best known for the meticulous detail of his quantitative mineralogical classification (now abandoned) of igneous rocks. His four-volume *Descriptive Petrography of the Igneous Rocks* (1931–38) is still a standard reference.

John, Saint

Saint John, a Galilean fisherman and the son of Zebedee, was one of the Twelve APOSTLES. John and his brother, Saint JAMES (the Great), were called Boanerges, or Sons of Thunder, by Christ. Several passages in the BIBLE imply that this describes their intense loyalty and aggressive zeal (Mark 9:38; Luke 9:49, 54). John was one of the inner circle among the Twelve. Saint PETER, James, and John witnessed the TRANSFIGURATION (Matt. 17:1; Mark 9:2; Luke 9:28) and went to GETHSEMANE with Jesus (Matt. 26:37; Mark 14:33).

Many people believe that John was the beloved disciple referred to in the fourth gospel. If so, he was beside Jesus at the LAST SUPPER (John 13:23), was asked to care for Jesus' mother MARY (John 19:26), and was the first to comprehend Jesus' RESURRECTION (John 20:2–9). John had a prominent role in the early church (Acts 1:13, 8:14). Traditionally, five New Testament books are ascribed to him: the fourth gospel, three Epistles, and the Book of REVELATION. Feast day: Dec. 27 (Western); Sept. 26 (Eastern).   DOUGLAS EZELL

John, Augustus

The British portraitist Augustus John, b. Jan. 4, 1878, d. Oct. 31, 1961, was one of a number of brilliant students from the Slade School of Art, London, which he attended from 1894 to 1898, who changed the direction of British art in the 20th century. His early work was in the Slade tradition of figure compositions and fine drawing. After a stay in Paris he came to admire Pierre Puvis de Chavannes and Pablo Picasso; later, in association with J. D. Innes, his style became freer and more colorful. He lived a bohemian life, touring in a horse-drawn caravan, and became the epitome of the modern artist, exhibiting at the New English Art Club and in the ARMORY SHOW (1913) in New York City.

After service as a war artist in World War I, John found fashionable success with his portraits of famous people such as *George Bernard Shaw* (1915; Fitzwilliam Museum, Cambridge), *T. E. Lawrence* (1919; Tate Gallery, London), *Thomas Hardy* (1923; Fitzwilliam Museum), and *Tallulah Bankhead*

(1930; National Portrait Gallery, Washington, D.C.). John became a member of the Royal Academy in 1928, resigned in 1938, and was reelected in 1946.   MALCOLM CORMACK

Bibliography: Easton, Malcolm, and Holroyd, Michael, *The Art of Augustus John* (1974); Holroyd, Michael, *Augustus John*, 2 vols. (1974–75); John, Augustus, *Chiaroscuro* (1952) and *Finishing Touches* (1964).

John, Elton

Elton John, b. Reginald Kenneth Dwight in England, Mar. 25, 1947, is among the most successful pop singer-pianist-composers of the 1970s. He has worked with lyricist Bernie Taupin for most of his career; their collaborations, lavishly staged and performed exhuberantly by John, have won him stardom. Since his first recording (1969), he has sold over 80 million albums worldwide. He made a successful tour of the USSR in May 1979.   JONATHAN KAMIN

Bibliography: Nutter, David, *Elton: It's a Little Bit Funny* (1977); Tatham, Dick, and Jasper, Tony, *Elton John* (1976).

John, Epistles of

The Epistles of John are three letters in the New Testament of the BIBLE traditionally ascribed to Saint JOHN the apostle. They are classed with the General, or Catholic, Epistles because they are addressed to a general readership rather than to specified churches or individuals. The first epistle bears no clue to its authorship, but in the other two epistles the author calls himself "the elder." The three letters were probably written in the Roman province of Asia (western Anatolia) toward the end of the 1st century.

The first epistle should probably be understood as a general pamphlet written to churches in Anatolia. Its message is about life, meaning eternal life, life in fellowship with God through faith in JESUS CHRIST. The book was written to give a series of standards by which people can know that they possess eternal life. Two features stand out in the series of tests. First, the validity of the INCARNATION is affirmed against those who claimed special knowledge (see DOCETISM; GNOSTICISM) and denied that Christ came in the flesh (1 John 4:2–3). The second feature of the test is love. The true follower of Christ is to love as Christ loved (1 John 2:6; 4:7–12, 19).

The second epistle, the shortest book of the Bible, is a note to a church addressed as the "elect lady." In this letter the message of 1 John is applied to a local church situation. The people are warned about teachers with special knowledge. They are encouraged to be hospitable toward one another. The third epistle is a personal word to Gaius, a follower of the truth. He is encouraged to show kindness to traveling believers who pass his way.   DOUGLAS EZELL

Bibliography: Vine, W. E., *Epistles of John* (1970).

John, Gospel According to

The Gospel According to John is the fourth book of the New Testament of the BIBLE. In style, language, and content, it differs dramatically from the Gospels of MATTHEW, MARK, and LUKE—called the synoptic Gospels. Unlike these Gospels, the fourth Gospel opens with a philosophical prologue (John 1:1–18). It identifies the LOGOS, or Word, with Christ and introduces the themes to be developed in the Gospel. Further comparisons show that the synoptic Gospels describe the ministry of Christ mainly in Galilee, with reference to only one Passover; but John situates most of the events in Judea and refers to three Passovers. Thus it is from John's Gospel that one concludes that Jesus' ministry lasted 3 years. In the synoptic Gospels, parables are Jesus' vehicle for teaching; in John, long discourses are used. Although John omits significant events such as the Temptation of Christ and the TRANSFIGURATION, he relates a number of events in Jesus' life not found in the synoptic Gospels.

By the time the fourth Gospel was written, in the latter half of the 1st century, Christianity had shifted from Jerusalem to the Aegean world. The thought of the day was directed more to universal truths than to historical facts. With the development of GNOSTICISM, the idea of the spirit was stressed, and the idea of the material was deemphasized. Weaving into his message concepts like truth, light, life, spirit, and word, John aimed to teach that God's eternal truth had become incarnated for the SALVATION of humankind in events that happened once for all. He could not overlook historical events because he believed that in Christ the eternal had become flesh and dwelt among humankind. For John, the true meaning of the eternal could only be understood through the REVELATION of God in the historical person JESUS CHRIST.

According to a tradition dating from the second half of the 2d century, the author of the Gospel was Saint JOHN, the Apostle. Many are still convinced of the tradition's accuracy. Others, while acknowledging that John the Apostle is the source behind the Gospel, refer to John the Elder, a disciple of John, as the author.   DOUGLAS EZELL

Bibliography: Dodd, C. H., *The Interpretation of the Fourth Gospel*, rev. ed. (1960); Howard, Wilbert F., *Christianity According to St. John* (1943); Scott, E. F., *The Fourth Gospel*, 2d ed. (1930).

John of Austria, Don

Don John of Austria, b. Feb. 24, 1547, d. Oct. 1, 1578, was the illegitimate son of Holy Roman Emperor CHARLES V and the half brother of King PHILIP II of Spain. After fighting against the MORISCOS in Granada (1569), he commanded the naval force of Spain, Venice, and the papacy that crushed the Turkish fleet in the Battle of LEPANTO on Oct. 7, 1571. Appointed Spanish governor of the Low Countries in 1576, Don John could not subdue the DUTCH REVOLT either by concessions or by war. He was succeeded on his death by Alessandro FARNESE.

Bibliography: Stirling-Maxwell, Sir William, *Don John of Austria* (1883).

John the Baptist, Saint

Saint John the Baptist, a Jewish prophet, was the forerunner of JESUS CHRIST. He was the son of Zachariah, a priest of the Temple, and of Elizabeth, a kinswoman of Mary, the mother of Jesus. Little is known of John prior to his public ministry, except that his birth was miraculously foretold (Luke 1:13-20). John achieved recognition as a prophet in the region of the lower Jordan Valley, where he attracted disciples. His public ministry began with the proclamation of a baptism of repentance in preparation for the MESSIAH. Throngs came to be baptized, among them his cousin Jesus of Nazareth, whom John recognized as the Messiah.

When John spoke against the marriage of Herod Antipas (see HEROD dynasty) to Herodias, his brother's wife, Herod imprisoned John. John was executed after Herodias had instructed her daughter, SALOME, to request his head as a reward for her dancing (Mark 6:17-29). Herod later believed that Jesus was John the Baptist risen from the dead (Mark 6:14-16; 8:27, 28). Feast day: June 24.   DOUGLAS EZELL

Bibliography: Black, Matthew, *The Scrolls and Christian Origins* (1961); Kraeling, Carl Hermann, *John the Baptist* (1951); Matthews, Robert, *The Life and Ministry of John the Baptist* (1972).

John Baptist de La Salle, Saint   [duh-lah-sahl']

Saint John Baptist de La Salle, b. Apr. 30, 1651, d. Apr. 7, 1719, was a French educator and the founder of the Institute of the Brothers of Christian Schools, popularly known as Christian Brothers. Ordained a priest in 1678, he was a canon of the cathedral at Reims until 1683, when he resigned as canon to devote himself to organizing schools for poor children. The following year, he founded a religious order devoted to teaching. Distinguished as a pioneer of training colleges for teachers and in the use of the vernacular in teaching, he ranks among the outstanding educators of modern times. Canonized in 1900, he is the patron saint of schoolteachers. Feast day: Apr. 7.

John Birch Society

The John Birch Society is an ultraconservative, anticommunist organization in the United States. Founded in 1958 by Robert Welch, Jr., a retired candy manufacturer, it is organized into

3,500 local chapters with perhaps 50,000 members. The society actively campaigns for U.S. withdrawal from the United Nations, for repeal of the income tax and social security laws, and for withdrawal of U.S. recognition of the USSR, among other right-wing causes. The organization is named for John Birch, a Baptist missionary and an intelligence officer in the U.S. Army, who was killed by the Chinese Communists on Aug. 25, 1945. Society members honor Birch as the first American casualty of the cold war.

Bibliography: Broyles, J. Allen, *The John Birch Society* (1964).

John Bull   (locomotive)

The *John Bull* was a LOCOMOTIVE built in England by Robert Stephenson & Company and exported to the Camden & Amboy Railroad (in New Jersey) in 1831. When Isaac Dripps, master mechanic for the Camden & Amboy, found that the engine had a tendency to derail, he installed a two-wheel pony truck that also included the first locomotive pilot, or "cow-catcher." The front guiding wheels were able to direct the locomotive in the direction of the track and thus reduced the likelihood of derailment.   JOHN F. STOVER

Bibliography: Jensen, Oliver, *The American Heritage History of Railroads in America* (1975); McPherson, James A., and Williams, Miller, eds., *Railroads: Trains and Train People in American Culture* (1976).

John Bull   (personification):   see BULL, JOHN.

John of the Cross, Saint

Saint John of the Cross, b. June 24, 1542, d. Dec. 14, 1591, a Spanish mystic and poet, is considered by many the greatest Western authority on MYSTICISM and one of Spain's finest lyric poets. He entered a CARMELITE monastery in 1563 and was ordained a priest in 1567. Dissatisfied with the laxity of the order, he began to work for the reform of the Carmelites. With Saint TERESA OF ÁVILA, he founded the Discalced Carmelites. Friction with the hierarchy led to his imprisonment (1577) in the monastery of Toledo. He escaped in 1578 and later served as prior of Granada (1582-88) and of Segovia (1588-91).

Saint John combined the imagination and sensitivity of a poet with the precision and depth of a theologian and philosopher trained in the tradition of Saint Thomas AQUINAS. These two factors contributed toward making his writings powerfully descriptive and analytical of the mystical experience. His most important writings are *The Spiritual Canticle*, written during his imprisonment in 1578; *The Ascent of Mt. Carmel* and *Dark Night of the Soul*, written shortly afterward; and *The Living Flame of Love*, completed by 1583. These poems deal with the purification of the soul—through detachment and suffering—in its mystical journey toward God and give a detailed description of the three stages of mystical union: purgation, illumination, and union. Saint John was canonized in 1726 and declared a Doctor of the Church in 1926. Feast day: Dec. 14.   JOAN A. RANGE

Bibliography: Brenan, Gerald, *St. John of the Cross* (1973); Sencourt, Robert, *Carmelite and Poet* (1944).

John Damascene, Saint   [dam'-uh-seen]

Saint John Damascene, b. c.675, d. Dec. 4, 749, was a Syrian Christian theologian who synthesized the doctrines of the Eastern FATHERS OF THE CHURCH. His father served in Damascus under the Muslim caliph as a treasury official, a high office to which John succeeded. Around 715 he entered the monastery of Saint Sabas (Mar Saba) near Jerusalem, where he studied theology and was ordained a priest. Between 726 and 730, Byzantine Emperor LEO III issued edicts against the cult of images. John became a leading figure in the defense of icons in the iconoclastic controversy (see ICONOCLASM).

Among his many writings the *Fountain of Knowledge* is the main work. It is divided into three parts—a study of Greek philosophy, a history of heresies, and an exposition of the teaching of the Eastern Fathers on the central Christian doctrines. John is a Doctor of the Church. Feast Day: Dec. 4.   ROSS MACKENZIE

Bibliography: Cassidy, F. P., *Molders of the Medieval Mind* (1944).

John Dory

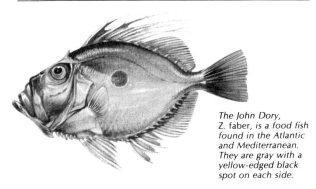

The John Dory, Z. faber, is a food fish found in the Atlantic and Mediterranean. They are gray with a yellow-edged black spot on each side.

The John Dory, *Zeus faber*, or the European John Dory, is a solitary, midwater marine fish of the family Zeidae found in the temperate waters from the British Isles southward to the African coasts and into the Mediterranean Sea. It is distinguished by a large, eyelike spot—black circled by a yellow ring—located in the center of its body. Another identifying feature is the presence of short spines along the bases of the anal and dorsal fins, as well as commonly found along the belly midline. Older fish develop long filaments on the first eight to ten spiny rays of the dorsal fin. The John Dory is occasionally found near the surface among floating debris, and it ambushes small fish with its large, engulfing mouth. It matures in its fourth year and may attain a weight of up to 20 kg (44 lb).

Zeus japonicus (Indo-Pacific water), *Z. nebulosa* (Japanese water), and the American John Dory, *Zenopsis ocellata* (Atlantic coast of North America), are other species in the dory family. These fish rarely exceed a length of 0.9 m (3 ft). Dories are commercially caught and marketed where they occur. They are considered a delicacy by some, whereas others consider them suitable only for fish meal.   CAMM SWIFT

John The Fearless, Duke of Burgundy

John the Fearless, b. May 28, 1371, d. Sept. 10, 1419, was the oldest son of PHILIP THE BOLD and the first cousin of King CHARLES VI of France. In 1396 he was a leader of a crusade against the Turks that ended disastrously at Nicopolis (now in Bulgaria). John succeeded his father as duke of Burgundy in 1404 and became count of Flanders on his mother's death (1405); he was thus the leading prince of the Low Countries. He also struggled with his cousin Louis of Orléans (see OR-LÉANS family) for control of the resources of the French government. Virtually excluded from power in Paris, he had Louis murdered in 1407, provoking a disastrous civil war. After a period of dominance in France (1408-13), he was again excluded from power until 1418. In that year he took advantage of French defeats by the English in the HUNDRED YEARS' WAR to seize Paris. The following year, however, he was assassinated while negotiating with the dauphin (the future CHARLES VII).   JOHN B. HENNEMAN

Bibliography: Vaughan, Richard, *John the Fearless: The Growth of Burgundian Power* (1966).

See also: ARMAGNACS AND BURGUNDIANS.

John of Gaunt, Duke of Lancaster   [gawnt, lang'-kuhs-tur]

John of Gaunt, b. March 1340, d. Feb. 3, 1399, was the fourth son of King EDWARD III of England. Through marriage (1359) to Blanche, heiress of Lancaster, he secured her large holdings and became duke of Lancaster. After Blanche's death he married (1371) Constance, heiress of PETER I of Castile, and claimed the Castilian crown. He was a leading English magnate under his nephew RICHARD II, but his military campaigns in Europe kept him out of the major domestic conflicts of that reign. Gaunt supported John WYCLIFFE for a time and pa-

tronized Geoffrey CHAUCER. In 1386 he invaded Castile, but he surrendered his claim in 1388. In 1396, Gaunt married his mistress Catherine Swynford and legitimized his children by her (see BEAUFORT family). Gaunt's son by Blanche became King HENRY IV and thus founded the royal house of Lancaster (see LANCASTER family).   GEORGE HOLMES

Bibliography: Armitage-Smith, Sidney, *John of Gaunt* (1904; repr. 1964).

John Henry

The legend about the black American railroad worker John Henry, who died from exertion after successfully competing with a hammer and steel bit against an automated steam hammer, originated about 1870, soon after steam hammers were introduced on railroad construction sites in the Allegheny Mountains. John Henry's legend, which may have some factual basis, is celebrated in stories and songs.

John Jay College of Criminal Justice: see NEW YORK, CITY UNIVERSITY OF.

John Maurice of Nassau   [mor'-is, nas'-aw]

John Maurice, count of Nassau–Siegen, b. June 17, 1604, d. Dec. 20, 1679, was called "the Brazilian" because he governed the Dutch colony in Brazil at the height of its power and prosperity. He was a cousin of the Dutch stadtholders MAURICE OF NASSAU and FREDERICK HENRY of Orange, under whose command he served in the Dutch army from 1621 until 1636. In the latter year he was named governor of Brazil, newly conquered from the Portuguese. His ambitious plans for the development of the colony proved too costly for the Dutch West India Company, which recalled him in 1644. Thereafter he commanded Dutch armies in the final stages of the Thirty Years' War and served the elector of Brandenburg as governor of Cleves. His residence at The Hague, known as Mauritshuis ("Maurice's House"), later became a world-famous museum.   HERBERT H. ROWEN

Bibliography: Boxer, C. R., *The Dutch in Brazil, 1624-1654* (1957).

John Nepomucene, Saint   [ne-poh-muh-seen']

Saint John Nepomucene, b. *c.*1345, d. Mar. 20, 1393, was a Bohemian martyr who is the patron saint of the Czechs. As vicar general to the archbishop of Prague, he opposed the attempts of King Wenceslas IV of Bohemia to create a new bishopric for one of the king's favorites. The king had him tortured and drowned in the Vltava (Moldau) River when John failed to comply with his wishes. According to a tradition declared unfounded in 1961, Saint John was put to death for refusing to betray Wenceslas's wife, Queen Sophia, by revealing her confessional secrets. He was canonized in 1729. Feast day: May 16.

John Paul I, Pope

John Paul I, b. Oct. 17, 1912, d. Sept. 28, 1978, was pope (Aug. 26 to Sept. 28, 1978) for only 34 days. His name was Albino Luciani. Patriarch of Venice from 1970, he had not played a prominent role in international church affairs before his election to succeed PAUL VI as pope. His friendly and spontaneous manner, however, won immense affection for him almost immediately. He abandoned the traditional coronation ceremony with the triple tiara and substituted for it a simple investiture with the pallium (a white woolen stolelike band), to symbolize the pastoral nature of the papal office. John Paul I seemed conservative on doctrinal and disciplinary matters but made no major pronouncements on them.   JOHN W. O'MALLEY

Bibliography: Greeley, Andrew M., *The Making of the Popes 1978* (1979); Hebblethwaite, Peter, *The Year of Three Popes* (1979).

John Paul II, Pope

John Paul II, b. May 18, 1920, was elected pope on Oct. 16, 1978, succeeding John Paul I, who had reigned only 34 days. His name was Karol Wojtyla. Archbishop of Kraków in Poland

Pope John Paul II, the first non-Italian pontiff in 456 years, has delighted many with his personal charm and bold leadership. His papacy has combined a rigid defense of traditional doctrine with a condemnation of theological radicalism.

when elected, he became the first non-Italian pope since the Dutchman ADRIAN VI (r. 1521–23).

Born to working-class parents in the small town of Wadowice, he did his studies at the University of Kraków and in an underground seminary during the difficult years of World War II. His enthusiasm while a student for the theater and for sports (especially skiing and soccer) were to remain with him for the rest of his life. After his ordination to the priesthood in 1946, he studied philosophy in Rome and in 1953 began teaching ethics at the Catholic University of Lublin. As a philosopher he became an expert on phenomenology, on which he published several works.

Wojtyla was named auxiliary bishop of Kraków in 1958 and archbishop in 1964; in 1967 he was created a cardinal by Pope Paul VI. As a prelate he was noted in Poland and elsewhere for his ability to deal with the Communist government in a way that was both firm and effective. His most dramatic success against governmental resistance was in building a church at Nowa Huta, a new industrial town intended by Communist planners to be a model Socialist city.

Wojtyla's election as pope came as a complete surprise, at the end of the second day of voting in the conclave. He made an immediately favorable impression on the international radio and television audiences by his control of Italian, English, and other foreign languages and by his friendly manner. During the early months of his pontificate, he made clear his support of the stance of his predecessors against the marriage of the clergy and similar issues, yet he issued no major pronouncements on doctrinal or disciplinary matters. His most important undertaking during this period was his visit to Mexico, Jan. 26–31, 1979, where he opened the third general assembly of Latin American bishops at Puebla. In Mexico the pope emphasized the church's support of the poor and disenfranchised in their struggle against their oppressors, but he rejected a Marxist analysis of the problem.

In June 1979, John Paul made a triumphant 9-day visit to Poland, the first by a pope to a Communist country. Although he refrained from direct political statements, his entire tour—and the fervent popular welcome he received—constituted a challenge to the Communist regime. In late September–early October of the same year he traveled to Ireland and the United States. Of all recent popes, John Paul II has brought to the papal office the richest combination of academic training, pastoral experience, physical vigor, and political accomplishment.

JOHN W. O'MALLEY

Bibliography: Greeley, Andrew M., *The Making of the Popes 1978* (1979); Hebblethwaite, Peter, *The Year of Three Popes* (1979) and, with Ludwig Kaufman, *John Paul II* (1979); Oran, James, *The People's Pope* (1979).

John of Salisbury   [sawlz'-bur-ee]

John of Salisbury, b. *c.*1115, d. Oct. 25, 1180, was an English scholastic philosopher and humanist. After studying in Paris under Peter ABELARD, he was appointed secretary to Theobald and later to Thomas BECKET, successive archbishops of Canterbury. John became bishop of Chartres in 1176. His chief writings are the *Policraticus*, a treatise on questions of CHURCH AND STATE, in which he defended the supremacy of the church; and the *Metalogicon*, a defense of the study of philosophy and the liberal arts. Although his writings demonstrate little philosophic originality, they shed important light on the history of the time.

Bibliography: Webb, Clement C., *John of Salisbury* (1932; repr. 1971).

John II Comnenus, Byzantine Emperor
[kuhm-nee'-nuhs, biz'-uhn-teen]

John II Comnenus, b. 1088, d. Apr. 8, 1143, succeeded his father, ALEXIUS I, as ruler of the BYZANTINE EMPIRE in 1118. A gifted soldier and statesman, he temporarily restored the fortunes of the empire. He reestablished imperial authority in the Balkans by defeating the PECHENEGS in 1122, controlling the Serbs, and checking Hungarian expansion. His alliance with Holy Roman Emperor LOTHAIR II countered the threat from the NORMANS in southern Italy.

In the east John conquered the Armenian state of CILICIA in 1137 and forced the Latin principality of Antioch to acknowledge his suzerainty. He was succeeded by his son MANUEL I COMNENUS.

John V Palaeologus, Byzantine Emperor
[pay-lee-ahl'-uh-guhs]

John V Palaeologus, b. November 1331, d. Feb. 16, 1391, succeeded his father, Andronicus III, as ruler of the BYZANTINE EMPIRE in 1341. He was deposed in 1347 by John VI Cantacuzenus, who reigned until 1354. When John V recovered his throne, he found the empire exhausted by civil wars. The Ottoman Turks, who had occupied western Anatolia, were expanding into Thrace and Bulgaria. The Serbs under STEPHEN DUŠAN seized the western Balkans. To secure Western aid against the Turks, John agreed (1369) to a reunion of the Eastern and Western churches. Nonetheless, the Turks were further strengthened by their victory (1371) over the Serbs at the Maritza, and John soon had to pay tribute to the Ottomans. Deposed by his son Andronicus IV from 1376 to 1379 and by John VII in 1390, he was back on the throne at his death, when he was succeeded by MANUEL II.

Bibliography: Head, Constance, *Imperial Twilight: The Palaiologos Dynasty and the Decline of Byzantium* (1977).

John VI Cantacuzenus, Byzantine Emperor
[kan-tuh-kyoo'-zen-uhs]

John VI Cantacuzenus, b. *c.*1295, d. June 15, 1383, ruled the BYZANTINE EMPIRE from 1347 to 1354. Until the death (1341) of Andronicus III, Cantacuzenus served as chief minister; he then revolted against the regency for John V Palaeologus, proclaiming himself emperor. To support his rebellion, he introduced Ottoman Turkish troops into Europe.

After John V's restoration in 1354, Cantacuzenus became a monk, although he continued to advise the government; he also composed a history of his own times, defending his role.

C. M. BRAND

Bibliography: Nicol, Donald M., *The Byzantine Family of Kantakouzenos (Cantacuzenus), ca. 1100–1460* (1968).

John, King of England

The youngest son of HENRY II and ELEANOR OF AQUITAINE, John, b. Dec. 24, 1167, succeeded his brother RICHARD I as king on May 27, 1199. John's reign is notable for his difficulties with the church and the barons; the king's conflict with the latter resulted in MAGNA CARTA.

King John's arbitrary policies so antagonized the English barons that they mustered an army to force him to yield to their demands, embodied in the Magna Carta (1215), which he is shown signing. This document served as a foundation of modern civil and political rights.

John's character was not attractive—he was hedonistic, mercurial, personally unstable, suspicious, and unforgiving. Yet he had many commendable qualities—he was highly intelligent, well versed in law and government, efficient, and sophisticated. His greatest shortcoming, in view of his contemporaries, was that he was no warrior, in an age when kings were expected to be great fighters. Moreover, John's difficulties stemmed largely from the policies of his father and brother. Richard had bequeathed financial bankruptcy and a ruinously expensive war in France. John also bore the brunt of baronial reaction to the centralization of government, a policy initiated by his predecessors, though continued with enthusiasm by him.

Early in his reign John lost most of the English possessions in France; by 1206, PHILIP II of France had conquered Anjou, Normandy, and Brittany. In that year John also became embroiled in a quarrel with the church by refusing to accept the election of Stephen LANGTON as archbishop of Canterbury. The pope placed England under interdict (in effect, closing the churches) until John abandoned the fight in 1213 and accepted papal vassalage.

The king took this step to strengthen his hand against the barons, with whom trouble had been building since 1208. The failure of John's expedition to Poitou in 1214, however, coupled with the defeat of his ally, Holy Roman Emperor OTTO IV, in the Battle of BOUVINES, gave the English barons their excuse for rebellion. In June 1215 the barons forced the king to accede to their demands for the restoration of feudal rights in the famous document called Magna Carta. The civil war was resumed soon after, however, and continued at the time of John's death on Oct. 18-19, 1216. John was succeeded by his young son, HENRY III. JAMES W. ALEXANDER

Bibliography: Holt, James C., *King John* (1963); Jolliffe, J. E. A., *Angevin Kingship*, 2d ed. (1963); Poole, A. L., *From Domesday Book to Magna Carta*, 2d ed. (1955); Warren, W. L., *King John* (1961; repr. 1978).

John II, King of France   (John the Good)

John II, b. Apr. 16, 1319, d. Apr. 8, 1364, the elder son of PHILIP VI, assumed a major role in French government by 1348 and became king in 1350. John waged war against both England (see HUNDRED YEARS' WAR) and domestic rebels led by his son-in-law, Charles the Bad, king of Navarre. He was criticized for his lowborn and corrupt advisors. In September 1356, John was captured by EDWARD, THE BLACK PRINCE in the Battle of Poitiers. To ransom him from the English under the terms of the Treaty of BRETIGNY (1360), the French paid the first regular peacetime taxes in their history. When his hostage son broke parole, John returned to England late in 1363 and died there. JOHN B. HENNEMAN

Bibliography: Fowler, Kenneth, *The Age of Plantagenet and Valois* (1967); Perroy, Édouard, *The Hundred Years War* (1945; trans. 1951).

John I, King of Hungary   (John Zápolya)

John Zápolya, b. 1487, d. July 22, 1540, was one of the two rival kings of HUNGARY in the period following the Battle of MOHÁCS (1526). In the chaos after the death (1490) of MATTHIAS CORVINUS, John became the leader of the so-called national party of the Hungarian nobility. As the governor of TRANSYLVANIA (1511-26), he helped put down the Dózsa peasant uprising in 1514, but he failed to appear at the Battle of Mohács, where Turkish victory ended Hungary's unity and independence for centuries.

Although elected king by his supporters in 1526, John was never able to consolidate his rule against his rival, the future Holy Roman emperor FERDINAND I. In the Treaty of Várad (1538) he agreed to leave his section of Hungary to Ferdinand, but Turkish pressure and the birth (1540) of his son, John Sigismund (John II), made him change just before his death. John I was a weak and vacillating ruler whose policies contributed to Hungary's prolonged division. S. B. VARDY

Bibliography: Kosáry, D. G., and Vardy, S. B., *History of the Hungarian Nation* (1969); Sinor, Denis, *History of Hungary*, 5th ed. (1977).

John II, King of Hungary   (John Sigismund Zápolya)

John Sigismund Zápolya, b. July 7, 1540, d. Mar. 14, 1571, was titular king of Hungary, as John II, from 1540 to 1570 and the first prince of Transylvania from 1556 until his death. Although elected king immediately after the death (1540) of his father, John I, he never ruled more than the eastern section of Hungary, and that only under Turkish protection. During John's minority, power was exercised by Friar György Martinuzzi (until 1551) and later, when John was recognized by the Turks as ruler of Transylvania, by his mother, Isabella (1556-59). In 1570, John gave up the royal Hungarian title. Under his rule Transylvania became largely Calvinist and was separated from Hungary—a separation that lasted for a century and a half. S. B. VARDY

Bibliography: Kosáry, D. G., and Vardy, S. B., *History of the Hungarian Nation* (1696); Sinor, Denis, *History of Hungary*, 5th ed. (1977).

John II, King of Poland   (John Casimir)

John II, b. Mar. 21, 1609, d. Dec. 16, 1672, ruled Poland from 1648 to 1668. The younger son of SIGISMUND III, John Casimir pursued a military career before becoming a Jesuit novice (1646) and a cardinal (1647). He gave up his cardinal's hat, however, to succeed his brother, Władysław IV, as king.

John's reign was marked by constant wars with Sweden, Russia, Prussia, and the Ottoman Empire. He was a pretender to the Swedish throne, and this fact gave Sweden's King CHARLES X a formal pretext for invading Poland. John rallied popular support against the Swedes in 1655-60, but his country was devastated and the crown bankrupted. In return for support from Brandenburg, John recognized the state's sovereignty over East Prussia in 1657. Poland also lost the eastern Ukraine to Russia in 1667. John worked on projects for government reform, but in 1668 he was forced to abdicate. He lived his last years in Nevers, France, supported by Louis XIV. Michael Wisniowiecki succeeded John to the Polish throne. ANNA M. CIENCIALA

Bibliography: Marcinkowski, K., *The Crisis of the Polish-Swedish War, 1655-1660* (1951); Reddaway, W. W., et al., eds., *Cambridge History of Poland*, vol. 1 (1950).

John III, King of Poland   (John Sobieski)

John Sobieski, b. Aug. 17, 1629, d. June 17, 1696, ruled Poland as King John III from 1674 to 1696. He is best known for saving Vienna from the Turks on Sept. 12, 1683, thereby achieving the last great Polish military victory before the Partitions of Poland in the 18th century.

A Polish noble, John studied at Kraków and toured Europe in 1646-48. He married (1655) Marie Casimiere d'Arguien and was devoted to her to the end of his life; his collected letters to her are a classic of Polish literature. As commander of the

Polish army, he defeated the Turks at Chocim (Khotin) in 1673, and this feat led to his election the following year as successor to King Michael (Wisniowiecki). John tried to strengthen the crown with French help. When he failed to do so, he opted for cooperation with Austria and, after defeating the Turks before Vienna, tried to build an anti-Turkish league. This attempt also failed. John was a patron of the arts, and his palace at Wilanów is a monument of baroque art and architecture.   ANNA M. CIENCIALA

Bibliography: Morton, John B., *Sobieski, King of Poland* (1932); Reddaway, W. W., et al., eds., *Cambridge History of Poland*, vol. 1 (1950).

John I, King of Portugal   (John the Great)

John I, b. Apr. 11, 1357, d. Aug. 14, 1433, ruled Portugal from 1385 to 1433, a period that saw the beginning of Portuguese overseas expansion. The illegitimate son of PETER I, John came to the throne in a revolt against the regency established by the widow of his half brother, Ferdinand I (see FERDINAND I, KING OF PORTUGAL), on behalf of Ferdinand's daughter Beatrice, the wife of John I of Castile. John's defeat of the Castilians in the Battle of Aljubarrota in 1385 assured Portuguese independence although a formal peace was not concluded until 1411. In 1387, John married Philippa of Lancaster, daughter of JOHN OF GAUNT. Ably advised by his chancellor, João das Regras, and his military commander, Nuno Álvares PEREIRA, John strengthened the powers of the monarchy and of the merchants and lesser nobles at the expense of the higher aristocracy. Not content with ruling a stable and prosperous, albeit small, kingdom, John took advantage of Portugal's maritime position to encourage shipbuilding and overseas trade. In 1415 a major expedition seized the strategic harbor and trading city of Ceuta on the coast of Morocco, and in the 1420s the Portuguese began to settle the Madeira Islands, stepping-stones toward the South Atlantic. John was succeeded as king by his eldest son, Edward I; John's sons, especially HENRY THE NAVIGATOR, continued Portuguese patronage of overseas exploration.   DANIEL R. HEADRICK

Bibliography: Prestage, Edgar, *The Chronicles of Fernão Lopes and Gomes Eannes de Zurara* (1928).

John II, King of Portugal   (John the Perfect)

John II, b. May 3, 1455, d. Oct. 25, 1495, who ruled Portugal from 1481 to 1495, earned the nickname "the Perfect" for his assertion of power over the aristocracy and for his patronage of the arts and of overseas expeditions. His father, Alfonso V, placed him in charge of explorations in 1474. John sent Diogo CAM down the coast of Africa (1482–84), Bartolomeu DIAS around the Cape of Good Hope to the Indian Ocean (1487–88), and Pedro de Covilhão to the Middle East (1487–93), but he rebuffed the Genoese Christopher COLUMBUS in 1484. As king, John strengthened royal authority, confiscating property belonging to his rivals from the house of BRAGANÇA. He admitted into Portugal thousands of Jews after their expulsion from Spain in 1492. His reign brought prosperity to the towns of Portugal. In 1494, John agreed to the Treaty of TORDESILLAS, which divided the New World between the Spanish and the Portuguese. He was succeeded by his brother-in-law and cousin, MANUEL I.   DANIEL R. HEADRICK

Bibliography: Sanceau, Elaine, *The Perfect Prince* (1959).

John III, King of Portugal   (John the Pious)

John III, b. June 6, 1502, d. June 11, 1557, succeeded his father, MANUEL I, to the Portuguese throne in 1521. In 1525 he married Catherine, sister of Holy Roman Emperor Charles V. A strong Roman Catholic, sometimes called "the Pious," John allowed the establishment of the INQUISITION (1536) and the Jesuits (1540) in Portugal and encouraged the arts and literature. During his reign Lisbon became one of the largest, richest, and most cosmopolitan cities of Europe. While the king spent lavishly on extravagant luxuries and futile wars in Morocco, however, Portugal's economy, population, and naval power began to decline. John was succeeded by his young grandson, SEBASTIAN.   DANIEL R. HEADRICK

John IV, King of Portugal

John IV, b. Mar. 18, 1604, d. Nov. 6, 1656, became king of Portugal in 1640 as a result of the revolution against Spanish rule that reestablished Portuguese independence. Since 1580, Portugal had been ruled by Spanish kings, and since the 1620s the Portuguese had found Spanish taxes and conscription oppressive. John, as duke of BRAGANÇA, was the wealthiest landowner and most powerful aristocrat in Portugal. In December 1640, after the successful national revolt against PHILIP IV of Spain, he was crowned king; he was recognized by the Cortes (representative assembly) in January 1641. John proved to be hard-working and cautious, respectful of the Cortes, and shrewd in diplomacy. Victory over the Spanish at Montijo (1644) confirmed Portuguese independence, although the threat of reconquest remained strong; Spain did not recognize Portugal's independence until 1668. During John's reign, Portugal regained Angola and Brazil but lost its Asian colonies to the Dutch. John was succeeded by his son Alfonso VI.
DANIEL R. HEADRICK

John V, King of Portugal   (John the Magnanimous)

John V, b. Oct. 22, 1689, d. July 31, 1750, succeeded his father, PETER II, to the Portuguese throne in 1706. After the conclusion (1713) of the War of the SPANISH SUCCESSION, Portugal remained at peace except for a naval campaign against Turkey in 1717. Gold and diamonds from Brazil gave John the wealth to finance much building. He also patronized the arts, made endowments, and maintained a magnificent court. At the same time, however, the Portuguese government and economy stagnated. John's son, Joseph I, succeeded him.

John VI, King of Portugal

John VI, b. May 13, 1767, d. Mar. 10, 1826, king of Portugal from 1816, survived—rather than shaped—the tempestuous events of his times. When his mother, Queen Maria I, became insane in 1792, John took over her duties, becoming regent in 1799. Portugal long remained untouched by the influences of the French Revolution and the Napoleonic Wars. In 1807, however, as a French Army advanced across Spain, the royal family and court fled to Brazil. They remained there even after the British had driven the French out of Portugal (1811) and John had succeeded to the throne on Maria's death (1816). In 1820 a liberal revolt, patterned after the Spanish revolution of the same year, broke out in Portugal. The following year John was persuaded to return to Portugal, leaving his son Pedro (later Emperor PEDRO I) as regent of Brazil. In 1825 he recognized Brazil's independence. Having accepted a liberal constitution, John subsequently faced continuing intrigues and political discontent. His indulgent, irresolute personality encouraged ambitious conspirators to use the monarchy for their own ends. After John's death, his daughter Maria Isabel became regent for Pedro, who ruled Portugal briefly as Peter IV.   DANIEL R. HEADRICK

John XXII, Pope

John XXII, b. c.1245, d. Dec. 4, 1334, was pope from 1316 to 1334. He was a Frenchman named Jacques Duèse. After his election he established the papal residence at Avignon, where he remained until his death. John's pontificate was filled with conflicts, both theological and political. The FRANCISCANS were divided over the interpretation of poverty; a radical group, called Spiritual Franciscans, held that the practice of evangelical poverty was absolute and could not be modified. When John condemned the rigid view of the Spirituals, they sought the help of the pope's enemy, Holy Roman Emperor LOUIS IV, who in 1328 set up as antipope a Spiritual Franciscan, Pietro Rainalducci, under the name of Nicholas V. The rivalry was short-lived, however; in 1329, John excommunicated and imprisoned Nicholas. John was a capable administrator who asserted papal authority over imperial affairs throughout his pontificate.   DAVID HARRY MILLER

Bibliography: Mollat, Guillaume, *The Popes of Avignon*, trans. by J. Love (1963).

John XXIII, Pope

John XXIII's reign (1958–63) as the 261st pope of the Roman Catholic church was liberal and innovative, and his sincerity and simplicity endeared him to a wide range of people. He sought to depoliticize and reinvigorate the church and in 1962 convened Vatican II, the first ecumenical council in almost 100 years.

John XXIII, b. Nov. 25, 1881, d. June 3, 1963, was pope from 1958 to 1963. His name was Angelo Giuseppe Roncalli. One of 13 children of a tenant farmer of Sotto il Monte (near Bergamo), he studied in Bergamo and in Rome, where he was ordained a priest in 1904. After serving as secretary to the bishop of Bergamo and teaching theology in the local seminary, he became a military chaplain during World War I. He began his long career in the Vatican diplomatic corps when he was appointed (1925), with the title of archbishop, to be the apostolic visitor to Bulgaria. Pope PIUS XI named him apostolic delegate to Turkey and Greece in 1935. As nuncio to France (1944-53), Roncalli dealt with the delicate controversies concerning the hated VICHY GOVERNMENT and problems between conservatives and liberals, especially the worker-priest movement. He was also Vatican observer at UNESCO (1946–53). In 1953 he was made a cardinal and named patriarch of Venice. His energetic half decade there ended in his 77th year.

When he was elected pope, Roncalli seemed to be a compromise candidate because of his advanced years. His reign was full of surprises. John XXIII left the Vatican often to visit Italian churches, hospitals, and prisons. His common touch and jovial warmth inspired great popular affection. The Second VATICAN COUNCIL, announced in 1959, initiated an *aggiornamento*, or modernization, of the church. Even before Vatican II began, John steered the Roman Catholic church toward the eventual goal of reunion with other Christians, creating (1960) the Secretariat for Christian Unity. During the council, which began in October 1962 with 2,600 prelates present, three dozen Protestant and Orthodox representatives were observers. Curialists and other conservatives were unable to thwart revision of formulas and discipline that had been established 400 years earlier at the Council of Trent.

John XXIII supported use of the vernacular in the LITURGY and other progressive reforms discussed during the council. During his pontificate, he sought rapprochement with Communist governments. He also enlarged the College of CARDINALS and promoted the development of regular native hierarchies in former European colonies. Among his encyclicals, *Mater et Magistra* (1961) dealt with economic problems and social reforms, and *Pacem in Terris* (1963) discussed peace among nations based on justice, freedom, and the right organization of society. The process of change begun by John presented an enormous task to his successor, Paul VI, who presided over the council's conclusion. The personal writings of John include his memoirs, *Journal of a Soul* (1964; Eng. trans., 1965), and *Pope John XXIII: Letters to his Family* (1968; Eng. trans., 1970). The process of his beatification, the first step toward canonization, was begun in 1965.

Bibliography: Elliott, Lawrence, *I Will Be Called John: The Biography of Pope John XXIII* (1973); Hatch, Alden, *A Man Named John* (1963); Hayles, E. E., *Pope John and His Revolution* (1965); Johnson, Paul, *Pope John 23rd* (1974).

John XXIII, "Antipope"

During the Great SCHISM of the West, John XXIII, b. *c.*1370, d. Nov. 22, 1419, the second pope of the Pisan line, reigned (1410-15) in competition with the rival claimants of the Roman (Gregory XII) and the Avignon (BENEDICT XIII) lines. Named Baldassare Cossa, he studied law and served as an administrator in the Curia. While he was endeavoring to end the schism, he was elected pope himself in May 1410.

John's most important achievement was the summoning of the Council of Constance (see CONSTANCE, COUNCIL OF). It deposed (May 1415) him and secured the removal of the other papal claimants, thus bringing to an end the Great Schism that had divided the Western church for almost 40 years. The legitmacy of John's original claim to the papal office has remained a disputed question to the present day; this was acknowledged by Angelo Roncalli when he adopted the name John XXIII on election to the papacy in 1958.

Bibliography: Oakley, Francis, *Council Over Pope* (1969).

Johns, Jasper

Jasper Johns, b. Allendale, S.C., May 15, 1930, is a major modern artist who changed the course of ABSTRACT EXPRESSIONISM and reexamined the relation between works of art and physical objects. He settled in New York in 1952. Three paintings from his first one-man show in 1958, including *Target with Four Faces* (1955), were purchased by the Museum of Modern

The American artist Jasper Johns's encaustic Flag on an Orange Field *(1957) represented a pivotal transition from abstract expressionism to the revived representationalism of Pop art and subsequent related trends in modern art. (Wallraf-Richartz Museum, Cologne.)*

Art, New York City. He worked for a time creating window displays for New York City stores and was part of a circle of young artists that included Robert Rauschenberg. Johns's early paintings contained much of the imagery for which he later became famous: the American flag, in its familiar or in unfamiliar colors; the map of the United States; and the target. Johns was strongly influenced by Marcel Duchamp, who displayed prosaic objects such as a urinal, a bottle rack, and a bicycle wheel as art.

Johns also incorporated "found" objects in his work, selecting flat materials to place on flat canvas, thus removing the conventional distinction between the surface of a painting and the object represented. In his first paintings Johns put the short active strokes of abstract expressionism to quite a different purpose: to contrast the craft of painting with universal, mechanically reproduced images such as maps, targets, and stenciled numbers or letters. In the 1960s, Johns began making prints such as his series of numerals, rendered singly and in patterns.

Johns's sculpture *Painted Bronze* (1964; Leo Castelli Gallery, New York City), which consists of two beer cans—one manufactured, the other a plaster and bronze facsimile—also points out the ambiguous relation between reality and the illusions of art.   PHIL PATTON

Bibliography: Crichton, Michael, *Jasper Johns* (1977); Field, Richard S., *Jasper Johns: Prints 1970-1977* (1978); Kozloff, Max, *Jasper Johns* (1968); Steinberg, Leo, *Other Criteria* (1972).

Johns Hopkins University, The

Established in 1876, The Johns Hopkins University (enrollment: 3,200; library: 2,100,000 volumes) is a private coeducational institution in Baltimore, Md., and the first in the United States to be formed as a university, with graduate study and research. Qualified students may pursue graduate degrees before completing their undergraduate work. Associated with the university are a hospital (1889) and a medical school (1893), The Peabody Institute of Music (1857), and the School of Advanced International Studies, which is located in Washington, D.C., with a campus in Bologna, Italy. The Johns Hopkins University Press (1878) is America's oldest university press in continuous operation.

Bibliography: Hawkins, Hugh, *Pioneer: A History of the Johns Hopkins University 1874-1889* (1960); Sharkey, Robert P., *Johns Hopkins: Centennial Portrait of a University* (1975).

Johnson, Andrew

Andrew Johnson became the 17th president of the United States after the assassination of Abraham LINCOLN, on Apr. 15, 1865. As president he was the focal point of a struggle over how to restore the Union after the Civil War. The contest over RECONSTRUCTION became so bitter that he was impeached by the House of Representatives and tried before the U.S. Senate, which ultimately found him not guilty of the charges.
Early Life. Johnson was born in Raleigh, N.C., on Dec. 29, 1808. His family, already poor, was left destitute by the death of his father 4 years later. When he was 14 his mother apprenticed him to a tailor. Johnson never received a formal education; he learned the rudiments of reading and writing from the foreman in his place of work. In 1826, Johnson and his family moved to eastern Tennessee, and a year later he opened his own tailor shop in Greeneville. On May 17, 1827, Johnson married Eliza McCardle, the daughter of a shoemaker. She furthered his education, teaching him arithmetic and improving his reading and writing.

Ambitious to rise from his humble origins and resentful all his life of those at the pinnacle of society, Johnson and his friends founded a political organization that soon replaced Greeneville's traditional leaders. Attracted by Andrew JACKSON's antiaristocratic rhetoric, Johnson was an important figure in Tennessee Democratic politics by the 1830s. Representing the mostly nonslaveowning small farmers of the eastern Tennessee hill country, he successfully challenged the western Tennessee cotton planters who usually controlled the party.

ANDREW JOHNSON
17th President of the United States (1865-69)

Born: Dec. 29, 1808, Raleigh, N.C.
Profession: Tailor; Public Official
Religious Affiliation: None
Marriage: May 17, 1827, to Eliza McCardle (1810-1876)
Children: Martha Johnson (1828-1901); Charles Johnson (1830-63); Mary Johnson (1832-83); Robert Johnson (1834-69); Andrew Johnson (1852-79)
Political Affiliation: Democrat; Unionist
Writings: *Papers of Andrew Johnson* (1967), ed. by L. P. Graf and R. W. Haskins
Died: July 31, 1875, Carter's Station, Tenn.
Buried: Greeneville, Tenn.

Vice-President and Cabinet Members
Vice-President: None
Secretary of State: William H. Seward
Secretary of the Treasury: Hugh McCulloch
Secretary of War: Edwin M. Stanton (1865-68); John M. Schofield (1868-69)
Attorney General: James Speed (1865-66); Henry Stanbery (1866-68); William M. Evarts (1868-69)
Postmaster General: William Dennison (1865-66); Alexander W. Randall (1866-69)
Secretary of the Navy: Gideon Welles
Secretary of the Interior: John P. Usher (1865); James Harlan (1865-66); Orville Browning (1866-69)

Having served as alderman (1829-30) and then mayor (1831-33) of Greeneville, he became a state representative (1835-37, 1839-41) and senator (1841-42). Johnson then served his state as U.S. congressman (1843-53), governor (1853-57), and finally U.S. senator (1857-62).

Johnson was a radical Jacksonian, as distinguished from more conservative western Tennessee Democratic leaders. As such he believed passionately that government at every level should interfere as little as possible in people's lives, no matter how desirable the benefits of government action might seem. Moreover, he was convinced that the U.S. Constitution imposed such limitations on the national government.

As a Southerner Johnson defended SLAVERY in the conflicts of the 1840s and '50s, taking the strong STATE RIGHTS position that Congress could not prevent its spread to territories of the United States. Accordingly, in 1860 he supported the proslavery Democratic presidential candidate, John C. BRECKINRIDGE. When the Southern states began to secede after the victory of the antislavery Republican candidate, Abraham Lincoln, however, Johnson denied that secession could be undertaken legally. He therefore fought unsuccessfully to keep Tennessee in the Union and refused to resign his place in Congress—the only Southern senator to remain loyal to the United States. When Union forces occupied part of Tennessee in 1862, Lincoln appointed Johnson military governor there.

In 1864 the Republicans, seeking to balance the UNION PARTY ticket with a prowar Southern Democrat, chose Johnson to be Lincoln's running mate in the presidential election. Thus in 1865, Johnson became vice-president of the United States.

Presidency. Succeeding to the presidency after Lincoln's assassination, Johnson tried to restore the Union with as little change as possible beyond the abolition of slavery. Following Lincoln's Reconstruction plan, he pardoned nearly all Southerners for their parts in the rebellion and let them reorganize their state governments, urging Congress to permit representatives who passed tests of loyalty to take their old seats. When Congress refused to agree, Johnson broke with the Republican party.

Like most white Southerners of his time, Johnson was a racist who believed whites should have firm control over society and government. As a believer in state rights, he also thought that Congress had no power to interfere in the Southern states' internal affairs. He therefore opposed Republican legislation to protect the rights of ex-slaves in the South and tried unsuccessfully to prevent Congress from replacing the Southern state governments he had authorized with new ones. In 1868 the struggle between Johnson and Congress came to a head. In defiance of the TENURE OF OFFICE ACT, which Congress had passed over presidential veto in 1867, Johnson attempted to fire his secretary of war, Edwin M. STANTON. Congress responded by impeaching the President for "high crimes and misdemeanors." After a trial lasting several months (March–May 1868), the Senate found Johnson not guilty. (The tally was only one vote shy of the two-thirds majority needed for conviction; seven Republicans had voted with the Democrats for acquittal.) Johnson's power had been broken, however, and he spent the remainder of his term in impotent frustration. Foreign affairs achievements, such as Secretary of State William H. SEWARD's purchase (1867) of Alaska, had been overshadowed by Johnson's domestic troubles.

Later Life. When his term ended in 1869, Johnson returned to Tennessee, where he soon was again in conflict with the old leaders of the Democratic party. He rebuilt his eastern Tennessee Democratic organization, and after several unsuccessful candidacies for Congress, he was again elected to the U.S. Senate in 1875. He died shortly afterwards, however, on July 31, 1875.

For many years historians viewed Johnson as a president who was too tactless to carry out the appropriately mild Reconstruction policy he had inherited from Lincoln. His integrity and courage were later recognized, but most historians now fault him for being insensitive to the legitimate concern Northerners felt that the rights of Southern blacks be protected and that loyal officials govern the South.

MICHAEL LES BENEDICT

Bibliography: Benedict, Michael Les, *The Impeachment and Trial of Andrew Johnson* (1973); Gerson, Noel B., *The Trial of Andrew Johnson* (1977); Johnson, Andrew, *Papers*, 4 vols., ed. by Leroy P. Graf and Ralph W. Haskins (1967–76); Jones, James S., *Life of Andrew Johnson* (1975); Lomask, Milton, *Andrew Johnson* (1960); McKitrick, Eric L., *Andrew Johnson and Reconstruction* (1960) and, as ed., *Andrew Johnson: A Profile* (1969); Mantell, Martin E., *Johnson, Grant, and the Politics of Reconstruction* (1973); Smith, Gene, *High Crimes and Misdemeanors: The Impeachment and Trial of Andrew Johnson* (1977); Thomas, Lately, *The First President Johnson: The Three Lives of the Seventeenth President of the United States of America* (1968); Winston, Robert W., *Andrew Johnson, Plebeian and Patriot* (1928; repr. 1969).

Johnson, Charles Spurgeon

Charles Spurgeon Johnson, b. Bristol, Va., July 24, 1893, d. Oct. 27, 1956, was a sociologist and the first black president of Fisk University (1946–56). Much of Johnson's life was devoted to the study and improvement of relations between blacks and whites. His books include *The Negro in Chicago* (1922), *Growing Up in the Black Belt* (1941), and *Patterns of Negro Segregation* (1943).

Bibliography: Robinson, W. S., *Historical Negro Biographies* (1968).

Johnson, Eastman

Eastman Johnson's handling of light and color shown by In the Fields *(c.1875–80) illustrates the rich luminosity characteristic of his work. Johnson was one of the most successful and sensitive of the late-19th-century genre painters. (Detroit Institute of Fine Arts.)*

Jonathan Eastman Johnson, b. Lovell, Maine, July 29, 1824, d. Apr. 5, 1906, was an important American painter of portraits and scenes of country life. He was apprenticed to a lithographic draftsman about 1840 and then spent 9 years as a successful crayon portraitist before studying (1849–51) painting at the Dusseldorf Akademie in Germany. From 1851 to 1855 he resided at The Hague studying 17th-century Dutch masters, imitating their naturalism so effectively in portraits that he would be called the American Rembrandt.

On his return to the United States his first major successes were *The Old Kentucky Home* (1859; New-York Historical Society, New York City) and *Corn Husking* (1860; Everson Museum, Syracuse, N.Y.). In the 1860s he painted in a freer style a series of subjects dealing with maple sugaring in Maine, followed in the 1870s by a series dealing with cranberry picking in Nantucket, Mass. In their integration of figures with landscape, atmospheric light and color, and sincerity of feeling, these paintings constitute Johnson's best work and represent a major achievement in American art. An excellent example is *The Cranberry Harvest* (1880; Timkin Art Gallery, San Diego, Calif.). A decline in the sales of his genre subjects made Johnson turn almost exclusively to portraiture in the mid-1880s. Although Johnson's work lacks the consistency of his great contemporaries Winslow Homer and Thomas Eakins, at his best he closely approaches their high level of accomplishment.

DAVID TATHAM

Bibliography: Baur, John, *American Genre Painter, Eastman Johnson, 1824–1906* (1940); Hills, Patricia, *Eastman Johnson* (1972).

Johnson, Edward

The Canadian operatic tenor Edward Johnson, b. Aug. 22, 1881, d. Apr. 20, 1959, was general manager of the Metropolitan Opera from 1935 to 1950. He made his operatic debut in 1912 in Padua, Italy, and 2 years later joined the La Scala Opera, where, under Arturo Toscanini, he sang the first performance in Italian (1914) of Wagner's *Parsifal*. From 1919 to 1922 he sang with the Chicago Opera, after which he became a member of the Metropolitan Opera, where he remained until his retirement as manager in 1950. Johnson sang the traditional tenor repertoire as well as roles created for him such as Deems Taylor's *Peter Ibbetson*. He became a U.S. citizen in 1922. During his management of the company, Johnson introduced a large number of new American singers, including Jerome Hines, Robert Merrill, Eleanor Steber, and Risë Stevens.

Bibliography: Mercer, Ruby, *The Tenor of His Time: Edward Johnson of the Met* (1976).

Johnson, Emily Pauline

Emily Pauline Johnson, b. Mar. 10, 1862, d. Mar. 7, 1913, also called *Tekahionwake*, or "the Mohawk Princess," was a Mohawk Indian poet. Born and educated at the Six Nations Reserve in Ontario, she was a great-granddaughter of the British colonial leader Sir William JOHNSON and Molly Brant. She began writing early and in 1895 published her first volume of verse, *White Wampum*. Her collected poems were published under the title *Flint and Feather* (1912).

Bibliography: Foster, Anne, *The Mohawk Princess, Being Some Account of the Life of Tekahion-Wake (E. Pauline Johnson)* (1931).

Johnson, Eyvind

A prolific Swedish novelist, Eyvind Johnson, b. July 29, 1900, d. Aug. 15, 1976, was, like some other writers of his generation such as Harry Edmund Martinson and Vilhelm Moberg, largely self-educated. His early life in northern Sweden provided the material for a renowned series of novels, including *Nu var det 1914* (1934; trans. as *1914*, 1970). When this work was published, he had already produced eight novels and three collections of short stories.

Johnson's postwar fiction explores a wide range of historical periods—ancient Greece in *Strändernas svall* (1946; trans. as *Return to Ithaca*, 1952), 17th-century France in *Drömmar om rosor och eld* (Dreams about Roses and Fire, 1949), and the age of Charlemagne in *Hans nådes tid* (1960; trans. as *The Days of His Grace*, 1965). Johnson was made a member of the Swedish Academy in 1957 and in 1974 shared the Nobel Prize for literature with Harry Martinson.

ROBIN FULTON

Bibliography: Orton, Gavin, *Eyvind Johnson* (1972).

Johnson, Fenton

The reputation of the American poet Fenton Johnson, b. Chicago, May 7, 1888, d. Sept. 17, 1958, rests on a small number of widely anthologized poems. In the years just before the Harlem Renaissance, Johnson, in such poems as "The Scarlet Woman," "The Minister," and "Tired," voiced scathing bitterness at the plight of black Americans. His *Visions of the Dusk* (1915; repr. 1971) and *Songs of the Soil* (1916; repr. 1969) have recently been reissued.

Johnson, Hiram Warren

Hiram Warren Johnson, b. Sacramento, Calif., Sept. 2, 1866, d. Aug. 6, 1945, was a U.S. progressive Republican political leader and one of the founders of the BULL MOOSE PARTY. An attorney, he achieved prominence by prosecution of the San Francisco political boss Abraham Ruef. Johnson was elected governor of California in 1910. He held that office until 1917, when he entered the U.S. Senate, serving there until his death. As governor, Johnson effected broad social and economic reforms, including women's suffrage, and broke the political power of the Southern Pacific Railroad.

After helping to found the Progressive, or Bull Moose, party, Johnson was Theodore ROOSEVELT's running mate in the latter's unsuccessful bid for the presidency in 1912. In 1916, Johnson refused to support the Republican presidential candidate, Charles Evans HUGHES. As a result, Hughes lost California, and hence the election, to the Democratic candidate, Woodrow Wilson.

Senator Johnson was a leading contender for the 1920 Republican presidential nomination, but after the party chose Warren G. HARDING, he refused to be considered for the vice-presidential nomination. Johnson supported Franklin D. Roo-

sevelt and the Democrats in the 1932 election and generally favored the NEW DEAL domestic programs. He was a lifelong isolationist who opposed U.S. participation in the League of Nations and entry into World War II. On his deathbed he voted against the charter of the United Nations.

Bibliography: Olin, Spencer C., Jr., *California's Prodigal Sons: Hiram Johnson and the Progressives, 1911-1917* (1968).

Johnson, Jack

John Arthur Johnson, b. Galveston, Tex., Mar. 31, 1878, d. June 10, 1946, was an American heavyweight boxer who became the first black to hold the world title. Because he was black, flamboyant, and outspoken, Johnson incurred much hostility when he won the title by defeating Tommy Burns in Australia in 1908. He was convicted in 1913 for violating the Mann Act and took sanctuary in Europe. Meanwhile, the white-controlled boxing world began its search for a "great white hope" to regain the title from the champion. In desperate need of money, Johnson fought 2 m-1 cm (6 ft-7 in) Jess Willard in Havana in 1915, losing the title when he was knocked out in the 26th round. The ex-champion later claimed that the fight was fixed. Johnson fought in exhibitions almost up to the time of his death. He had a career record of 80 victories, 7 losses, 14 draws, and 13 no-decisions in 114 bouts.

Bibliography: Farr, Finis, *The Life and Times of Jack Johnson* (1964); Johnson, Jack, *Jack Johnson: In the Ring and Out—An Autobiography*, ed. by Damon Runyon, et al. (1978).

Johnson, James Weldon

James Weldon Johnson, an American writer and diplomat of the early 20th century, compiled anthologies of black American poetry and songs before publishing his free-verse work God's Trombones *in 1927. The first black to be admitted to the Florida bar, he was a founder and secretary of the NAACP. His essays and writings form a substantial contribution to black American culture.*

James Weldon Johnson, b. Jacksonville, Fla., June 17, 1871, d. June 26, 1938, was an author, editor, social reformer, and a leader of the HARLEM RENAISSANCE of the 1920s. He graduated from Atlanta University in 1894 and became principal of a school for blacks in his hometown of Jacksonville, Fla. He was the first black admitted (1897) to the Florida bar. From 1906 to 1912 he was a consul in Venezuela and Nicaragua. He later became executive secretary of the National Association for the Advancement of Colored People. From 1930 until his death, he was professor of creative literature at Fisk University in Nashville, Tenn. He published a novel called *Autobiography of an Ex-Coloured Man* (1912); an autobiography; and several books of verse.

Bibliography: Levy, Eugene D., *James Weldon Johnson, Black Leader* (1973).

Johnson, John Harold

John Harold Johnson, b. Arkansas City, Ark., Jan. 19, 1918, founded EBONY and other magazines for black American readers. His family moved from Arkansas to Chicago's South Side in 1933. After high school he went to work as an office boy for a black-owned life insurance company, eventually becoming chairman of the board. In the meantime he founded Ne-

gro Digest in 1942 (later called *Black World*), *Ebony* in 1945, *Tan* in 1950 (later *Black Stars*), *Jet* in 1951, and *Ebony, Jr.* in 1973. The five magazines had a circulation of 2.6 million in 1975. He also entered the fields of book publishing, radio broadcasting, and cosmetics. His personal business enterprises grossed $34 million in 1974.

Bibliography: Drotning, Phillip T., and South, Wesley W., *Up From the Ghetto* (1970).

Johnson, John Rosamond

The American composer and bass singer John Rosamond Johnson, b. Jacksonville, Fla., Aug. 11, 1873, d. Nov. 11, 1954, wrote in collaboration with his brother, the poet James Weldon Johnson, "Lift Every Voice and Sing" (1900), known as the Negro national anthem. He sang in music halls and in operas in London, and toured (1930–32) Europe and the United States in programs of Negro spirituals. He also sang the role of Lawyer Frazier in early productions of George Gershwin's *Porgy and Bess.* Johnson's compositions include a ballet, *African Drum Dance*, and much vocal music, and he provided the musical arrangements for *The Book of Negro Spirituals* (1925) and *The Second Book of Negro Spirituals* (1927), both compiled by his brother. In 1937 he published *Rolling Along in Song*, a history of black music.

Johnson, Lyndon B.

Lyndon Baines Johnson became the 36th president of the United States on the assassination of John F. KENNEDY in November 1963. A skilled promoter of liberal domestic legislation, he was also a staunch believer in the use of military force to help achieve the country's foreign policy objectives. His escalation of American involvement in the VIETNAM WAR eroded his popular standing and led to his decision not to run for reelection to the presidency in 1968.

Early Life. Johnson was born on Aug. 27, 1908, near Johnson City, Tex., the eldest son of Sam Ealy Johnson, Jr., and Rebekah Baines Johnson. His father, a struggling farmer and cattle speculator in the hill country of Texas, provided only an uncertain income for his family. Politically active, Sam Johnson served five terms in the Texas legislature. His mother had varied cultural interests and placed high value on education; she was fiercely ambitious for her children.

Johnson attended public schools in Johnson City and received a B.S. degree from Southwest Texas State Teachers College in San Marcos. He then taught for a year in Houston before going to Washington in 1931 as secretary to a Democratic Texas congressman, Richard M. Kleberg.

During the next 4 years Johnson developed a wide network of political contacts in Washington, D.C. On Nov. 17, 1934, he married Claudia Alta Taylor, known as "Lady Bird." A warm, intelligent, ambitious woman, she was a great asset to Johnson's career. They had two daughters, Lynda Byrd, born in 1944, and Luci Baines, born in 1947.

In 1933, Franklin D. ROOSEVELT entered the White House. Johnson greatly admired the president, who named him, at age 27, to head the National Youth Administration in Texas. This job, which Johnson held from 1935 to 1937, entailed helping young people obtain employment and schooling. It confirmed Johnson's faith in the positive potential of government and won for him a coterie of supporters in Texas.

In 1937, Johnson sought and won a Texas seat in Congress, where he championed public works, reclamation, and public power programs. When war came to Europe he backed Roosevelt's efforts to aid the Allies. During World War II he served a brief tour of active duty with the U.S. Navy in the Pacific (1941–42) but returned to Capitol Hill when Roosevelt recalled members of Congress from active duty. Johnson continued to support Roosevelt's military and foreign-policy programs.

During the 1940s, Johnson and his wife developed profitable business ventures, including a radio station, in Texas. In 1948 he ran for the U.S. Senate, winning the Democratic party primary by only 87 votes. (This was his second try; in 1941 he had run for the Senate and lost to a conservative opponent.)

LYNDON BAINES JOHNSON
36th President of the United States (1963–69)

Nickname: "LBJ"
Born: Aug. 27, 1908, near Johnson City, Tex.
Education: Southwest Texas Teachers College (graduated 1930)
Profession: Teacher, Public Official
Religious Affiliation: Disciples of Christ
Marriage: Nov. 17, 1934, to Claudia Alta ("Lady Bird") Taylor (1912-   )
Children: Lynda Bird Johnson (1944-   ); Luci Baines Johnson (1947-   )
Political Affiliation: Democrat
Writings: *The Vantage Point: Perspectives of the Presidency, 1963-1969* (1971)
Died: Jan. 22, 1973, near Johnson City, Tex.
Buried: Near Johnson City, Tex.

Vice-President and Cabinet Members
Vice-President: Hubert H. Humphrey (1965–69)
Secretary of State: Dean Rusk
Secretary of the Treasury: C. Douglas Dillon (1963–65); Henry H. Fowler (1965–69)
Secretary of Defense: Robert S. McNamara (1963–68); Clark Clifford (1968–69)
Attorney General: Robert F. Kennedy (1963–65); Nicholas Katzenbach (1965–67); Ramsey Clark (1967–69)
Postmaster General: John A. Gronouski (1963–65); Lawrence F. O'Brien (1965–68); W. Marvin Watson (1968–69)
Secretary of the Interior: Stewart L. Udall
Secretary of Agriculture: Orville L. Freeman
Secretary of Commerce: Luther H. Hodges (1963–65); John T. Connor (1965–67); Alexander B. Trowbridge (1967–68); Cyrus R. Smith (1968–69)
Secretary of Labor: W. Willard Wirtz
Secretary of Health, Education, and Welfare: Anthony J. Celebrezze (1963–65); John W. Gardner (1965–68); Wilbur J. Cohen (1968–69)
Secretary of Housing and Urban Development: Robert C. Weaver (1966–69)
Secretary of Transportation: Alan S. Boyd (1967–69)

The opposition accused him of fraud and derisively tagged him "Landslide Lyndon." Although challenged, unsuccessfully, in the courts, he took office in 1949.

Senator and Vice-President. Johnson moved quickly into the Senate hierarchy. In 1953 he won the job of Senate Democratic leader. The next year he was easily reelected as senator and returned to Washington as majority leader, a post he held for the next 6 years despite a serious heart attack in 1955.

The Texan proved to be a shrewd, skillful Senate leader. A consistent opponent of civil rights legislation until 1957, he developed excellent personal relationships with powerful conservative Southerners. A hard worker, he impressed colleagues with his attention to the details of legislation and his willingness to compromise.

In the late 1950s, Johnson began to think seriously of running for the presidency in 1960. His record had been fairly conservative, however. Many Democratic liberals resented his friendly association with the Republican president, Dwight D. Eisenhower; others considered him a tool of wealthy Southwestern gas and oil interests. Either to soften this image as a conservative or in response to inner conviction, Johnson moved slightly to the left on some domestic issues, especially on civil rights laws, which he supported in 1957 and 1960. Although these laws proved ineffective, Johnson had demonstrated that he was a very resourceful Senate leader.

To many northern Democrats, however, Johnson remained a sectional candidate. The presidential nomination of 1960 went to Senator John F. Kennedy of Massachusetts. Kennedy, a northern Roman Catholic, then selected Johnson as his running mate to balance the Democratic ticket. In November 1960 the Democrats defeated the Republican candidates, Richard M. NIXON and Henry Cabot Lodge, by a narrow margin.

Johnson was appointed by Kennedy to head the President's Committee on Equal Employment Opportunities, a post that enabled him to work on behalf of blacks and other minorities. As vice-president, he also undertook some missions abroad, which offered him some limited insights into international problems.

Presidency. The assassination of President Kennedy on November 22, 1963, elevated Johnson to the White House, where he quickly proved a masterful, reassuring leader in the realm of domestic affairs. In 1964, Congress passed a tax-reduction law that promised to promote economic growth and the Economic Opportunity Act, which launched the program called the WAR ON POVERTY. Johnson was especially skillful in securing a strong CIVIL RIGHTS ACT in 1964. In the years to come it proved to be a vital source of legal authority against racial and sexual discrimination.

In 1964 the Republicans nominated Senator Barry M. GOLDWATER of Arizona as their presidential nominee. Goldwater was an extreme conservative in domestic policy and an advocate of strong military action to protect American interests in Vietnam. Johnson had increased the number of U.S. military personnel there from 16,000 at the time of Kennedy's assassination to nearly 25,000 a year later. Contrasted to Goldwater, however, he seemed a model of restraint. Johnson, with Hubert H. HUMPHREY as his running mate, ran a low-key campaign and overwhelmed Goldwater in the election. The Arizonan won only his home state and five others in the Deep South.

Johnson's triumph in 1964 gave him a mandate for the Great Society, as he called his domestic program. Congress responded by passing the MEDICARE program, which provided health services to the elderly, approving federal aid to elementary and secondary education, supplementing the War on Poverty, and creating the Department of Housing and Urban Development. It also passed another important civil rights law—the Voting Rights Act of 1965.

At this point Johnson began the rapid deepening of U.S. involvement in Vietnam; as early as February 1965, U.S. planes began to bomb North Vietnam. American troop strength in Vietnam increased to more than 180,000 by the end of the year and to 500,000 by 1968. Many influences led Johnson to such a policy. Among them were personal factors such as his

temperamental activism, faith in U.S. military power, and staunch anticommunism. These qualities also led him to intervene militarily in the Dominican Republic—allegedly to stop a Communist takeover—in April 1965. Like many Americans who recalled the "appeasement" of Nazi Germany in the 1930s, Johnson thought the United States must be firm or incur a loss of credibility.

While the nation became deeply involved in Vietnam, racial tension sharpened at home, culminating in widespread urban RACE RIOTS between 1965 and 1968. The breakdown of the interracial civil rights movement, together with the imperfections of some of Johnson's Great Society programs, resulted in Republican gains in the 1966 elections and effectively thwarted Johnson's hopes for further congressional cooperation.

It was the policy of military escalation in Vietnam, however, that proved to be Johnson's undoing as president. It deflected attention from domestic concerns, resulted in sharp inflation, and prompted rising criticism, especially among young, draft-aged people. Escalation also failed to win the war. The drawn-out struggle made Johnson even more secretive, dogmatic, and hypersensitive to criticism. His usually sure political instincts were failing.

The New Hampshire presidential primary of 1968, in which the antiwar candidate Eugene MCCARTHY made a strong showing, revealed the dwindling of Johnson's support. Some of Johnson's closest advisors now began to counsel a de-escalation policy in Vietnam. Confronted by mounting opposition, Johnson made two surprise announcements on Mar. 31, 1968: he would stop the bombing in most of North Vietnam and seek a negotiated end to the war, and he would not run for reelection.

Johnson's influence thereafter remained strong enough to dictate the nomination of Vice-President Humphrey, who had supported the war, as the Democratic presidential candidate for the 1968 election. Although Johnson stopped all bombing of the North on November 1, he failed to make real concessions at the peace table, and the war dragged on. Humphrey lost in a close race with the Republican candidate, Richard M. Nixon.

Retirement. After stepping down from the presidency in January 1969, Johnson returned to his ranch in Texas. There he and his aides prepared his memoirs, which were published in 1971 as *The Vantage Point: Perspectives of the Presidency, 1963-1969.* He also supervised construction of the Johnson presidential library in Austin. Johnson died on Jan. 22, 1973, 5 days before the conclusion of the treaty by which the United States withdrew from Vietnam.   JAMES T. PATTERSON

Bibliography: Evans, Rowland, and Novak, Robert, *Lyndon B. Johnson, The Exercise of Power: A Political Biography* (1966); Geyelin, Philip, *Lyndon B. Johnson and the World* (1966); Goldman, Eric F., *The Tragedy of Lyndon Johnson* (1969); Johnson, Lady Bird, *White House Diary* (1970); Kearns, Doris, *Lyndon Johnson and the American Dream* (1976); Schandler, Herbert, *The Unmaking of a President: Lyndon Johnson and Vietnam* (1977); White, Theodore, *The Making of the President—1964* (1965); Wicker, Tom, *JFK and LBJ: The Influence of Personality Upon Politics* (1968; repr. 1970).

Johnson, Philip

Philip Cortelyou Johnson, b. Cleveland, Ohio, July 8, 1906, has been one of the most influential forces in America as critic, historian, and designer. After graduating (1927) from Harvard College, where he studied philosophy and Greek, Johnson became director of the architecture department of the newly founded Museum of Modern Art in New York City. There he and architectural historian Henry-Russell HITCHCOCK introduced (1932) the American public to the achievements of recent European design through the seminal exhibition, and its accompanying book, *The International Style: Architecture since 1922* (see INTERNATIONAL STYLE, architecture).

In the 1940s Johnson began architectural practice. After returning to Harvard University to study architecture, he designed a number of notable houses that showed the pervasive influence of Ludwig Mies van der Rohe. The outstanding example is his own residence, the Glass House (1949) in New

Philip Johnson's "glass house" (1949–50) in New Canaan, Conn., a transparent structure interrupted only by a central utility unit, unites interior and exterior through glass walls. The design exemplifies the International Style of architecture.

Caanan, Conn., a single room entirely walled in glass and set in parklike surroundings. Yet Johnson's architecture cannot be easily categorized. Such designs as the Hodgson House (1951) in New Caanan openly derive from Miesian principles, yet other structures such as the Wiley (1953) and Boissonas (1956) houses in the same town reflect a concern for the use of local materials and picturesque siting.

Throughout his career Johnson has used his keen knowledge of history to create a mode of expression in apparent contradiction to the International Style. In such designs as the Amon Carter Museum (1961) in Fort Worth, Tex., and the Sheldon Art Gallery (1963) in Lincoln, Neb., Johnson experimented with the use of such classical elements as symmetrical plans and templelike facades. His recent buildings are no longer neutral, glazed containers; Yale's Kline Science Center (1965) in New Haven, Conn., has a massive masonry tower set in an arcaded court; Pennzoil Place (1976) in Houston, Tex., has a sharp, picturesque roof silhouette recalling earlier American skyscrapers. His design (1978), with his partner John Burgee, for the new New York City headquarters of American Telephone & Telegraph Company—a 60-story, pink granite office tower set on a gigantic colonnade and topped with a colossal broken pediment—aroused a storm of controversy and has been seen by critics as a total rejection of the International Style. In 1979, Johnson was awarded the Pritzker Prize for architecture.   LEON SATKOWSKI

Bibliography: Cook, John W., and Klotz, Heinrich, *Conversations with Architects* (1973); Hitchcock, Henry-Russell, *Philip Johnson: Architecture 1949-1965* (1966); Jacobus, John M., *Philip Johnson* (1962); Johnson, Philip, *Writings*, ed. by Robert Stern and Peter Eisenman (1978); Johnson, Philip, and Hitchcock, Henry-Russell, *The International Style* (1932; rev. ed., 1966).

See also: POSTMODERN ARCHITECTURE.

Johnson, Rafer

Rafer Lewis Johnson, b. Hillsboro, Tex., Aug. 18, 1934, was an American track and field star who was considered one of the greatest decathlon competitors of all time. At age 19 he won the decathlon in the Pan American Games, and the following year he placed second in the event in the 1956 Olympic Games. He proceeded to dominate decathlons during the next 4 years, culminating his success by setting a world record at the 1960 Olympics in Rome. A student leader as well as an athlete at the University of California, Los Angeles, Johnson retired from sports in 1960 and devoted himself to public service.

Johnson, Reverdy

The U.S. statesman Reverdy Johnson, b. Annapolis, Md., May 21, 1796, d. Feb. 10, 1876, was reputed to be one of the ablest constitutional lawyers of his time. He served most notably as counsel for the slave-owning defendant in the DRED SCOTT V. SANDFORD case. Johnson was U.S. attorney general (1849–50) and served twice as U.S. senator from Maryland (1845–49, 1863–68). He backed Andrew Johnson's RECONSTRUCTION program and was instrumental in persuading the Senate to vote against the president's impeachment. In 1868–69, Reverdy Johnson served as minister to Great Britain; in that capacity

he negotiated the Johnson-Clarendon Treaty in settlement of the ALABAMA CLAIMS. The Senate rejected the treaty, however, largely for partisan reasons.

Bibliography: Steiner, Bernard C., *The Life of Reverdy Johnson* (1914; repr. 1970).

Johnson, Richard M.

Richard Mentor Johnson, b. near what is now Louisville, Ky., Oct. 17, 1780, d. Nov. 19, 1850, was vice-president of the United States (1837–41) under Martin VAN BUREN. He was admitted to the bar in his native Kentucky in 1802. Johnson served in the U.S. House of Representatives (as a Democratic-Republican, 1807–19, and as a Democrat, 1829–37) and in the Senate (1819–29). His career was aided by his claim that he had killed the Indian chieftain TECUMSEH at the Battle of the Thames (1813).

A man of rough frontier manners and unconventional habits, Johnson won Andrew JACKSON's support as the vice-presidential nominee in 1836. His candidacy was unacceptable to Southerners, however, who were offended by his efforts to introduce his mulatto daughters into polite society. Despite Van Buren's decisive majority, Johnson received only a plurality of the electoral vote and was chosen vice-president by the U.S. Senate. His vice-presidential career was undistinguished. In 1840 he was denied renomination by the Democratic Convention, which chose no vice-presidential candidate.
ALFRED A. CAVE

Bibliography: Meyer, Leland W., *Life and Times of Col. Richard M. Johnson of Kentucky* (1932).

Johnson, Samuel   (philosopher)

Samuel Johnson, b. Oct. 14, 1696, d. Jan. 6, 1772, was an American philosopher and clergyman. A Congregationalist minister, he was converted (1722) to Anglicanism and received ordination in the Church of England in 1723. He was one of the founders of King's College (later Columbia University), New York City, and its first president (1754–63). A friend of George BERKELEY, he became the leading exponent of Berkeley's IDEALISM in America. With Berkeley, Johnson held that the sensible world is made up of the ideas people receive from God and that what is commonly thought to be matter is actually in the mind as passive ideas. His principal works are *Introduction to Philosophy* (1731) and *Elementa Philosphica* (1752).   E. DARNELL RUCKER

Bibliography: Ellis, Joseph, *The New England Mind in Transition* (1973); Schneider, Herbert and Carol, eds., *Samuel Johnson, President of King's College*, 4 vols. (1929; repr. 1972).

Johnson, Samuel   (writer)

Samuel Johnson, lexicographer, essayist, poet, and critic, was the leading English writer of the second half of the 18th century. The period is now called the Age of Johnson in recognition of his eminence. His achievements are so diverse that they are not easily summarized. He wrote the first English dictionary based on historical principles; he produced the first editorially intelligent edition of Shakespeare's plays; his literary criticism, after suffering a long period of disesteem, is now correctly ranked with the finest in English; as a moralist

Samuel Johnson, poet, critic, and essayist, is considered one of the greatest figures of 18th-century England. Johnson is as well known for his gargantuan personality, revealed in Boswell's famous biography, as for his brilliant and incisive literary style, exemplified in his Dictionary of the English Language *(1755), the 1765 edition of* Shakespeare, *and his* Lives of the Poets *(1779-81).*

he has always been admired. Thanks to James BOSWELL's massive, brilliant LIFE OF SAMUEL JOHNSON (1791), his personality and conversational powers have entertained thousands who have never read his writings. Yet it is as a writer that Johnson remains important: he has been called the greatest man of letters in English literature.

Johnson was born in Lichfield on Sept. 18, 1709, and died in London, which became his home after 1737, on Dec. 13, 1784. Though constitutionally robust, he suffered throughout life from bodily afflictions. To these were added poverty (which compelled him to leave Oxford without a degree) and mental disturbance. At 21 he suffered the first of two mental breakdowns, which left him with a lifelong dread of insanity, death, and religious damnation.

He tried teaching school but hated it, was attracted to law but lacked the necessary diploma, and settled for writing because writing was what he could do. His first book was a translation (1735) of *A Voyage to Abyssinia* by a Portuguese Jesuit; it was typical of the literary hackwork Johnson produced to support himself for 20 years. In 1738 he joined the staff of *The Gentleman's Magazine*, for which he wrote poetry—both in Latin and English—and essays. As occasion required, he also produced prefaces, reviews, encyclopedia articles, and biographies; one of the latter, his life of the notorious minor poet Richard Savage (1744), achieved considerable popularity. His talents so impressed the London publishers that in 1747 they commissioned him to write *A Dictionary of the English Language* (1755). While working on this mammoth project, he also wrote his chief poem, *The Vanity of Human Wishes* (1749), a satire in imitation of the Roman poet Juvenal; saw his tragedy *Irene* produced (1749); and composed a powerful series of periodical essays, *The Rambler* (1750-52), on which his reputation as a probing anatomist of human nature is largely based.

In 1756, Johnson turned to editing Shakespeare. By the time *The Plays of William Shakespeare* appeared (1765), he had also produced a second series of essays, *The Idler* (1758-60), and a comic romance, *Rasselas* (1759), his finest satire on the human propensity to hopeful self-delusion. He had also experienced a second breakdown (1766); been awarded a government pension (1762); and made two friends who were to become his principal biographers: James Boswell and Hester Thrale. With Mrs. Thrale he found domestic comforts that his life had not hitherto afforded. (His wife of 17 years had died in 1752.) With Boswell he made a tour (1773) of the Hebrides that produced a travel book, *A Journey to the Western Islands of Scotland* (1775).

Johnson's last and greatest work was again the result of a publisher's commission. Paid to supply prefaces to an edition of 52 English poets from Abraham Cowley to Thomas Gray, he wrote a massive set of biographies and criticisms, *The Lives of the Poets* (1779-81). The 10-volume work sums up Johnson's two main interests as a writer: man and literature. His biographies treat the poets as tragicomic representatives

of human aspiration and its ultimate defeat. His criticism of their works is an extraordinarily honest, and sometimes withering, estimate of their value; its impact on readers is indicated by the fact that for two centuries Johnson's judgments have provoked controversy.

Johnson cultivated a literary style of sonorous distinction. He became a master of the personified generality: his sentences give life to terms like *envy, hope,* and *malice.* This style confers upon his moral writings—especially the essays of *The Rambler* and *The Vanity of Human Wishes*—an air of exceptional authority. His conversation, if Boswell's famous renderings are accurate, was distinguished by a similar power and also by such epigrammatic brilliance that many of his recorded sayings have achieved the status of proverbs.

WILLIAM MCCARTHY

Bibliography: Bate, W. Jackson, *Samuel Johnson* (1977); Fussell, Paul, *Samuel Johnson and the Life of Writing* (1971); Greene, D. J., *Samuel Johnson* (1970); Halliday, F. E., *Dr. Johnson and His World* (1968); Hodgart, Matthew, *Samuel Johnson and His Times* (1963); Irwin, George, *Samuel Johnson: A Personality in Conflict* (1971); Johnson, Samuel, *Letters,* 3 vols., ed. by R. W. Chapman (1952), *Selections of Johnson's Writings,* ed. by Bertrand Bronson, 3d ed. (1974), and *Yale Edition of the Works of Samuel Johnson,* 10 vols., ed. by E. L. McAdam, et al. (1958-   ); Krutch, Joseph W., *Samuel Johnson* (1944; repr. 1963).

See also: CRITICISM, LITERARY; DICTIONARY; PIOZZI, HESTER LYNCH.

Johnson, Tom Loftin

The American municipal reformer Tom Loftin Johnson, b. Kentucky, July 18, 1854, d. Apr. 10, 1911, served four terms (1901-09) as mayor of Cleveland, Ohio. An inventor, Johnson made a fortune in streetcar lines and steel, then turned to politics, serving (1891-95) in the U.S. House of Representatives as a Democrat from Ohio. As mayor of Cleveland he was noted for his fiscal rectitude, his battles against political bosses, and his farsighted reform measures—including aid to the poor and improved sanitary facilities. A follower of Henry GEORGE, he pressed for municipal ownership of public utilities. Although Johnson did not see this plan carried out, it was later widely adopted by many cities. His autobiography, *My Story*, was published in 1913.

Johnson, Uwe [yohn'-zohn, oo'-vay]

One of West Germany's leading novelists, Uwe Johnson, b. July 20, 1934, was raised in East Germany after World War II but left in 1959 when he encountered difficulties publishing his first novel, *Speculations about Jacob* (1959; Eng. trans., 1963), which dealt simultaneously with the alienation of the individual and with the division of Germany. Both *The Third Book about Achim* (1961; Eng. trans., 1967) and *Two Views* (1965; Eng. trans., 1966) continued to focus on the lack of communication between East and West, in a style strongly influenced by Joyce and Faulkner. Johnson's greatest achievement to date is a series of novels entitled *Anniversaries* (1970-74; Eng. trans., 1975), which trace the wanderings of a young German woman who eventually immigrates to America.

JACK ZIPES

Bibliography: Boulby, Mark, *Uwe Johnson* (1974).

Johnson, Walter Perry

Walter Perry Johnson, b. Humboldt, Kans., Nov. 6, 1887, d. Dec. 10, 1946, was an American professional baseball player whose pitching record is one of the most impressive in the sport's history. Johnson won 20 or more games in 12 of his 21 major league seasons—his best years were 1912, when he won 32 games, and 1913, when he won 36 games—and set unequaled career records for strikeouts (3,508) and shutouts (113). He also led the American League in strikeouts 12 times, and he pitched the second highest number of career victories—416. All of his major league pitching (1907-27) was for the Washington Senators, a perennially mediocre team, which makes Johnson's records even more remarkable.

Bibliography: Allen, Lee, *The American League Story* (1962; repr. 1965); Associated Press Eds., *Sports Immortals* (1974).

Johnson, Sir William

Sir William Johnson, b. 1715, d. July 11, 1774, an American co-lonial fur trader, land speculator, soldier, and Indian agent, exerted crucial influence on the IROQUOIS LEAGUE during the last two FRENCH AND INDIAN WARS (1744–63). Born in Ireland, Johnson went to New York about 1738 under the sponsorship of his uncle, Sir Peter Warren. Settling in the lower Mohawk Valley, he soon became involved in trading and negotiating with the Indians, who came to call him Warraghiyagey ("doer of great things"). Appointed to the New York provincial council in 1750, Johnson participated in the ALBANY CONGRESS in 1754.

During King George's War (1744–48), Johnson had orga-nized Indian war parties against the French. Commanding a provincial army at Lake George after the resumption of war, Johnson defeated an invading French force under Ludwig Au-gust, Baron Dieskau, in August 1755. For that achievement he was made a baronet and was soon appointed (1756) superin-tendent for northern Indian affairs.

Johnson was also involved in the taking of Fort Niagara (1759) and in Gen. Jeffrey AMHERST's successful campaign against Montreal (1760). Subsequently he played a construc-tive role in several important negotiations with Indians, most notably during PONTIAC'S REBELLION (1763–66) and in conclud-ing the Treaty of Fort Stanwix (1768), by which the Iroquois ceded extensive territory to the British. Johnson died during an Indian conference at his home, Johnson Hall, near the pre-sent Johnstown, N.Y.   DOUGLAS EDWARD LEACH

Bibliography: Hamilton, Milton Wheaton, *Sir William Johnson* (1976); Pound, Arthur, and Day, R. E., *Johnson of the Mohawks* (1930); Sulli-van, J., et al., eds., *The Papers of Sir William Johnson*, 13 vols. (1921–62).

Johnson, William Samuel

William Samuel Johnson, b. Stratford, Conn., Oct. 7, 1727, d. Nov. 14, 1819, was one of the framers of the U.S. Constitution and president (1787–1800) of Columbia College (later Colum-bia University). He was the son of Samuel Johnson, the first president of Columbia, originally called King's College. A Connecticut lawyer, he served on the governor's council, as the colony's agent in London (1767–71), and as judge of the superior court (1772). During the American Revolution, John-son was suspected of pro-British sympathies, but he eventu-ally accepted the break with England. He played an influential role at the Constitutional Convention in 1787 and was one of the two Connecticut signers of the Constitution. While pres-ident of Columbia, Johnson also served as U.S. senator from Connecticut (1789–91).

Bibliography: Beardsley, E. Edwards, *Life and Times of William Samuel Johnson* (1876; repr. 1972); Groce, George C., Jr., *William Samuel John-son: Maker of the Constitution* (1937).

Johnson Foundation: see ROBERT WOOD JOHNSON FOUNDATION.

Johnson Space Center

The Lyndon B. Johnson Space Center, Houston, Tex., is the development, training, and operations center for U.S. manned space missions. It was named in 1973 by act of Congress, in remembrance of President Johnson's support for space re-search. The installation began as the Space Task Group, an autonomous unit of Goddard Space Flight Center at Langley Research Center, Hampton, Va. The group was then assigned with development of the one-man Mercury spacecraft. Fol-lowing President John F. Kennedy's commitment in 1961 to land a man on the moon, plans were announced to build a manned-spacecraft center.

The new center was given responsibility for manned space missions, including design, development, and testing of manned spacecraft, the training of astronauts, the coordina-tion of tracking stations around the world, and mission con-trol. The APOLLO, GEMINI, and SKYLAB missions were directed

from mission control. During 1974–79, it was modified to sup-port the development and operation of the reusable SPACE SHUTTLE.   DAVID DOOLING

Johnston, Albert Sidney

Albert Sidney Johnston, b. Feb. 2, 1803, d. Apr. 6, 1862, was a Confederate general in the U.S. Civil War. He graduated from West Point in 1826 but in 1834 left the U.S. Army to go to Texas. He served as commander of the Texan army (1837–38) and then as secretary of war (1838–40) of the Texas republic. Johnston was recommissioned into the U.S. Army in 1849 and commanded forces in the UTAH WAR (1857–58). In 1861 he joined the Confederacy and was given the impossible task of defending the area between the Appalachian Mountains and the Mississippi River. He was killed at the Battle of SHILOH. Al-though highly regarded by Jefferson DAVIS and others, John-ston died too early to permit a realistic evaluation of his abili-ties as a general.   RICHARD M. MCMURRY

Bibliography: Roland, Charles P., *Albert Sidney Johnston: Soldier of Three Republics* (1964).

Johnston, Denis

A leading figure in the modern Irish theater, William Denis Johnston, b. June 18, 1901, was director of the Dublin Gate Theatre from 1931 to 1936. He is best known for his plays dealing with the Irish temperament in the period following Irish independence, especially *The Old Lady Says No* (1929), *The Moon in the Yellow River* (1931), and *A Bride for the Unicorn* (1933). In the United States he has taught at Smith College (1961–66), the University of Iowa (1967–68), University of California (1970–71), New York University (1971–72), and elsewhere. His autobiography, *Nine Rivers from Jordan*, ap-peared in 1953, and his *Collected Plays* (2 vols.) in 1960.   ROBIN BUSS

Johnston, Franz

The Canadian landscape painter Franz (Frank) Johnston, b. 1888, d. July 9, 1949, was a founding member of the GROUP OF SEVEN. Trained in Toronto and later at the Pennsylvania Acad-emy of the Fine Arts in Philadelphia, Johnston's restrained renderings of northern Ontario, in particular the Algoma re-gion, display his exceptional drawing abilities. Frequently, however, his landscapes are simply decorative and anecdotal. During World War I, he documented the role of the Cana-dian armed forces in Europe. In 1921 he moved from Toronto to Winnipeg to become principal of its School of Art. He re-signed from the Group of Seven in 1924 but continued as a successful painter for the rest of his life.   DAVID WISTOW

Bibliography: Mellen, Peter, *The Group of Seven* (1970); National Gal-lery of Canada, Ottawa, *The Group of Seven* (1971).

Johnston, Joseph E.

Gen. Joseph E. Johnston is regarded, after Robert E. Lee, as the most able military strategist of the Confederacy. Johnston conducted a masterful series of retreating engagements against the numerically superior Union army of William T. Sherman. He was eventually forced to formally surrender the Army of Tennessee, the final Confederate army in the field, on Apr. 26, 1865.

Joseph Eggleston Johnston, b. Prince Edward County, Va., Feb. 3, 1807, d. Mar. 21, 1891, was a Confederate general in the U.S. Civil War. After graduating from West Point in 1829, he served with distinction in the Second Seminole War and in the Mexican War. In April 1861 he resigned from the U.S. Army and joined the Confederacy. After coming to the aid of P. G. T. BEAUREGARD at the First Battle of BULL RUN (July 1861), Johnston became commander of the Army of Northern Virginia. He was wounded (May 1862) during the PENINSULAR CAMPAIGN and replaced by Robert E. LEE. By then Johnston and President Jefferson DAVIS had quarreled bitterly over Johnston's rank in the army and over matters of strategy.

In 1863, Johnston assumed command of the Department of the West, but he was unable to prevent the fall of Vicksburg in July. In December he succeeded Braxton BRAGG as commander of the Army of Tennessee. Outnumbered and constantly outmaneuvered by the Federals under William T. SHERMAN in the ATLANTA CAMPAIGN, he fell back to Atlanta, exposing important areas of the Confederacy to invasion. In July 1864, Davis replaced him with John Bell HOOD. After Lee became general in chief in February 1865, he restored Johnston to his command; Johnston surrendered to Sherman in April.

Johnston held several political offices after the war. Despite considerable intelligence and ability, he was a petulant, secretive man, more disposed to see and complain about difficulties than to seize opportunities.　　　　RICHARD M. MCMURRY

Bibliography: Govan, Gilbert E., and Livingood, James W., *A Different Valor* (1956; repr. 1973).

Johnston, Samuel

Samuel Johnston, b. Dundee, Scotland, Dec. 15, 1733, d. Aug. 17, 1816, was a political leader of North Carolina during the American Revolution and the early national period. A lawyer, he served in the colonial assembly and in 1770 drafted the so-called Bloody Act under which Gov. William Tryon suppressed the REGULATORS' revolt. Johnston supported the rebellion against British rule, but he was a conservative force in North Carolina's four provincial Congresses (1774–76). He represented North Carolina in the Continental Congress (1781–82) and served as governor of the state (1787–89), U.S. senator (1789–93), and superior court judge (1800–03).

Johnstown

Johnstown, a city in southwestern Pennsylvania, is located in a deep valley at the confluence of the Conemaugh River and Stony Creek. Its population is 38,000 with 174,200 in the metropolitan area (1979 est.). Johnstown is a major center for the mining of bituminous coal and the manufacture of iron, steel, and metal products. It is the site of the University of Pittsburgh at Johnstown.

Johnstown was laid out in 1800. In 1831–34, Johnstown grew as the terminus of the Allegheny Portage Railroad, which hauled canal barges piggyback for 58 km (36 mi) on railroad cars. During the second half of the 19th century, it was the nation's leading steel manufacturing center. Johnstown has often suffered from disastrous floods, most notably in 1889 (when 2,200 people died), 1936, and 1977.

Bibliography: McCullough, David, *Johnstown Flood* (1970).

JOIDES

The Joint Oceanographic Institutions for Deep Earth Sampling, or JOIDES, is an organization that was established in early 1964 by the Lamont (now Lamont-Doherty) Geological Observatory of Columbia University, the Institute of Marine Science (now the Rosenstiel School of Marine and Atmospheric Science) of the University of Miami, the Scripps Institution of Oceanography of the University of California, and the Woods Hole Oceanographic Institution. These institutions were later joined by the departments of oceanography at the University of Rhode Island, the University of Washington, Oregon State University, and Texas A & M, and the Institute of Geophysics at the University of Hawaii.

JOIDES drilled (1965) a line of 6 geological exploratory wells as deep as 1 km (0.6 mi) in the Blake Plateau, a broad flat bottom feature extending several hundred kilometers east off the continental shelf bordering Florida. The National Science Foundation, impressed with the success of this venture, began funding (1966) the DEEP SEA DRILLING PROJECT (DSDP) proposed by JOIDES. The objectives of DSDP are to drill, recover, and study cores of sediment and basaltic crust beneath the deeper parts of the oceans.

Through 1979, this project, extended several times, has cost about $150 million. After funding became international, with contributions of $1 million a year from the Soviet Union, West Germany, France, the United Kingdom, and Japan, DSDP was renamed (1975) the International Program of Ocean Drilling (IPOD).

Bibliography: Heirtzler, J. R., and Maxwell, A. F., "The Future of Deep Ocean Drilling," *Oceanus*, Summer 1978; West, Susan, "DSDP: 10 Years After," *Science News*, June 24, 1978.

joint

A joint is a fracture in rock along which little or no fault displacement has occurred. The term dates from mining jargon in Britain, where miners once regarded rocks as being "joined" along fractures. Indeed, no mining or quarrying would be possible without the joints that are present in all exposed rocks.

Many joints occur in regularly spaced systems of parallel sets. Some are closely spaced, every few centimeters or less, whereas others are meters apart. Some are short in extent, barely a few centimeters in any direction; others extend for great distances. The pattern and distribution of joints determine directions of weakness in rocks, and they may control the movement of groundwater, petroleum, and mineralizing solutions. Joints are commonly classified according to their relation to other structures: bedding joints are parallel to bedding; normal joints are perpendicular, or nearly so, to bedding or other layering; cross joints are at a large angle to structures such as FOLDS or ore bodies. Also, the strikes of strike, dig, and oblique joints are, respectively, parallel, perpendicular, and at an oblique angle to the bedding. Closely spaced joints may resemble rock cleavage, although with a clear distinction: cleavage planes are potential planes of parting in rocks, whereas in joints the rock has actually lost cohesion and its breaking strength has been exceeded. Where cleavage is present, however, joints tend to form parallel to cleavage planes.

The breaking strength of a rock can be exceeded in two modes. At extension joints, which may carry vein fillings, the two "walls" move apart slightly; at shear joints, which tend to grade into faults, the walls move past each other. Some joints formed in extension carry plumose structures (delicately sculptured, feather-shaped patterns) on their faces. Cooling of some volcanic rocks produces extension joints arranged in hexagonal prisms; such columnar jointing is especially evident at Devil's Tower, Wyoming.

Bibliography: Billings, Marland P., *Structural Geology*, 3d ed. (1972); Hobbs, Bruce E., et al., *An Outline of Structural Geology* (1976).

joints

Any union between adjacent BONES is a joint, whether or not movement of the bones is possible. The many joints in the human body differ from each other in shape and in structure and are classified into three main types: fibrous, cartilaginous, and synovial. The study of joints constitutes the science of "arthrology."

Joint classifications are based on the manner in which the adjacent bones are attached to each other. In fibrous joints the bones are held together only by LIGAMENTS, a type of fibrous connective tissue. Cartilaginous joints are those in which the bones are attached to each other by CARTILAGE, a different and special type of connective tissue. The synovial joints are freely movable and are sometimes referred to as diarthroses. The ends of bones are covered by cartilage, but there is a space, the joint cavity, between them, and the en-

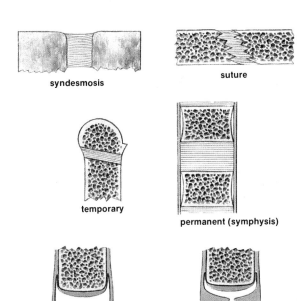

The three structural types of joints are fibrous (top), cartilaginous (center), and synovial (bottom). Fibrous joints include syndesmoses (left), such as that between the borders of the radius and ulna in the forearm, and the immovable sutures (right) found in the skull. Cartilaginous joints include the temporary (left) joint between the end and shaft of a growing bone and permanent (right) joints, or symphyses, such as the intervertebral discs. Most of the joints in the body are synovial, characterized by one or more cavities, with (right) or without (left) menisci that divide the cavity in two. These cavities contain a fluid that protects and lubricates the joint.

also upon the kind of movements permitted. Some of these joints, including the knee, have a fibrocartilaginous disk, or meniscus, that partially or completely divides the joint cavity into two cavities. Movements in these joints may occur around a single axis, two axes, many axes, or without regard to any axis.

When movement occurs around a single axis, or limited to a single plane, either transverse or longitudinal, it is a uniaxial joint. One type of uniaxial joint is the hinge (ginglymus) joint. The humeroulnar articulation in the elbow illustrates movement around a single transverse axis, but because some side-to-side motion is possible the elbow is not a true hinge joint. The pivot (trochoid) joint may be illustrated by the articulation between the proximal (upper) end of the radius and the ulna in the elbow. Here the head of the radius rotates within a ring formed by a ringlike ligament and a groove in the ulna bone.

When movement is permitted around two transverse axes set at right angles to each other, the joint is said to be biaxial. In these joints there is no rotation around a longitudinal axis. The joint between the mandible (lower jaw bone) and the temporal bone of the skull is a biaxial joint. The joint be-

Classification of joint articulations is based on the kind of movement they permit. The elbow (1) is essentially a hinge joint, or ginglymus, allowing movement in a single transverse axis. The pivot, or trochoid, joint found at the upper end of the ulna and radius (2) permits motion around a longitudinal axis. It is shown here in two different positions. A condyloid joint, such as the articulation between the jaw and the skull (3), and a saddle joint, such as the thumb (4), are biaxial joints. The hip (5), a ball and socket joint, can move in an indefinite number of axes. The articulating surfaces of the vertebrae (6), or spinal column, provide examples of gliding, or nonaxial, joints.

tire area is enclosed by an articular capsule. The capsule is made up of a tough, fibrous outer layer and a thinner, more delicate inner layer known as the synovial membrane. The cavity is filled with a slightly viscous fluid, the synovial fluid, that resembles the white of an egg to a certain degree.

Fibrous Joints. There are two subtypes of fibrous joints: syndesmoses and sutures. In syndesmoses the bones are attached by an interosseous (between bones) membrane or ligament, and some movement of the bones is possible. The union between spinous processes of the vertebrae in the spinal column is one example of this kind of joint. Sutures occur between bones of the skull. The articulating ends of bones have bony processes that interlock with each other to a varying degree in the different types of sutures. A sutural ligament or membrane is found between the bony processes. In sutures there can be very little or no movement. The roots of teeth fitting into alveoli (sockets) of the jawbone are sutures. The periodontal membrane between the root and its bony wall allows the orthodontist to reposition teeth by applying gentle pressure over a period of time.

Cartilaginous Joints. Cartilaginous joints are also subdivided into two subtypes. A primary (temporary) joint is present between the end (epiphysis) and the shaft (diaphysis) of a growing long bone such as the humerus. Normally this epiphyseal cartilage ossifies into bone by the time the bone has reached its adult size. In some bones this change does not take place until the person has reached the late teens. A good example of a permanent (secondary) cartilaginous joint is that located between the bodies of the vertebrae in the spinal column. In these symphyses the ends of the articulating bones are covered by hyaline cartilage and held together by softer, more pliable, fibrocartilage and reinforced by ligaments.

Synovial Joints. The synovial joints are more freely movable and are more variable in structure than other joints. Classification depends on the shapes of the articulating surfaces and

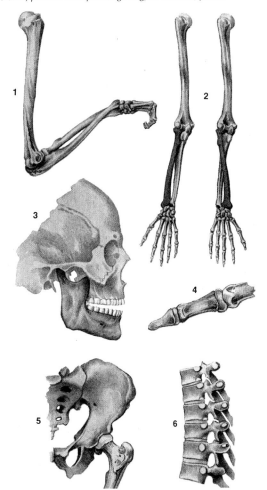

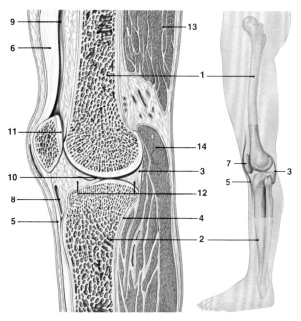

The knee is the largest and most complicated joint in the human body. The femur (1) and tibia (2) are joined at the back and sides by the capsular ligament (3), which is continuous with the periosteum (4), or outer membrane, of the bones. In front, the patellar ligament (5) and tendon of the quadriceps muscle (6) attach to the patella (7), or knee cap. The bursae (8, 9) and articular cavity (10), filled with synovial, or lubricating, fluid, increase mobility of the joint, as does the cartilage (11), which covers the articulating surfaces of the bones. The menisci (12) and ligaments lend stability to the knee. The biceps muscle (13) controls flexion and lateral rotation of the knee; the gastrocnemius muscle (14) controls ankle flexion.

tween the metacarpal bone of the thumb and a carpal bone of the wrist is of the saddle-joint type. Here the articulating surfaces are shaped somewhat like the surfaces of a saddle and fit together reciprocally.

The ball-and-socket, or enarthrodial, articulations are polyaxial. In this type of joint, motion may occur around an indefinite number of axes. The hip joint and the joint of the shoulder are illustrative of this type. A hemispherical, or globular-shaped, process on one bone fits into a cuplike cavity in the other. Almost any kind of motion can occur, limited only by soft tissues such as ligaments and muscles.

In the nonaxial, or plane-surfaced, joints a plane or slightly convex surface on one bone lies in contact with another plane or slightly concave surface on another bone. Movement is a sliding or gliding action. The degree of movement may be restricted by ligaments only or by both ligaments and bony processes around the articulating surfaces. Examples of this group include the articular facets on vertebrae, articulations between carpal bones in the wrist, and those between tarsal bones in the foot.

All joints of the body are vulnerable to injury and also to damage by diseases such as arthritis (SEE BONE AND JOINT DISEASES). Some of the joints when severely damaged may be replaced by artificial joints (prostheses). Orthopedic surgeons have had considerable success in replacing certain joints, notably the hip. Knee-joint replacements have also been undertaken but with somewhat less success. Prostheses have been devised for a few other joints as well.   PRESSLEY L. CRUMMY

Bibliography: Grollman, Sigmund, *The Human Body: Its Structure and Physiology*, 4th ed. (1978); Memmler, Ruth L., and Wood, Dena L., *The Structure and Function of the Human Body*, 2d ed. (1977); Simon, William, ed., *The Human Joint in Health and Disease* (1978).

Joint Chiefs of Staff: see DEFENSE, U.S. DEPARTMENT OF.

joint-stock company   [joynt-stahk']

A joint-stock company is a type of partnership having many of the attributes of a corporation. Like a corporation, a joint-stock company has shares that may be transferred from one owner to another. Also, as in a corporation, management is centralized in a board of directors who are elected by the partners (shareholders). A joint-stock company differs from a corporation in that the former's shareholders are personally liable for the company's debts. Historically, many of the famous chartered companies—the British EAST INDIA COMPANY, for example—were joint-stock companies. In recent times, because statutes in most of the United States have made it relatively easy to form corporations, the joint-stock company has not been widely used as a form of business organization.

joint tenancy   [joynt ten'-uhn-see]

A joint tenancy is a type of coownership of PROPERTY, usually land; it is distinguished from other types of coownership in that each joint tenant owns the undivided whole and the coownership contains a right of survivorship. Survivorship means that upon the death of one joint tenant, his or her interest automatically passes to the remaining joint tenant or tenants rather than passing to heirs as in a tenancy in common. Another characteristic of a joint tenancy is that rents and profits, if any, belong to all of the joint tenants.

Joint tenancies tend to be disfavored under the law. In most states of the United States, a joint tenancy can be defeated by one of the tenants conveying the interest to a third person. This severs the joint tenancy and creates in its place a tenancy in common. In some states the right of survivorship in a joint tenancy has been abolished by statute. Others have merged joint tenancies and tenancies in common into a single interest containing more of the characteristics of a tenancy in common. Still others allow for both types of coownership, but a presumption is created in favor of the tenancy in common. To defeat the presumption, the relevant document must specify that the interest is a joint tenancy with a right of survivorship.

Joinville, Jean, Sire de   [zhwahn-veel', zhawn, seer duh]

Jean, Sire de Joinville, b. c.1224, d. Dec. 24, 1317, was a French chronicler who wrote the *Histoire de Saint Louis* (final form, 1309), the principal source on the life of LOUIS IX of France. The work's main section is a lively account of the Seventh CRUSADE (1248-54), on which Joinville accompanied Louis.

Bibliography: Joinville, Jean de, *The Life of St. Louis by John of Joinville*, trans. by René Hague (1955).

Jókai, Maurus   [yoh'-koy, mou'-ruhs]

A most accomplished and prolific author of romantic fiction, Maurus (Mór) Jókai, b. Feb. 18, 1825, d. May 5, 1904, established the novel as a genre in Hungary. *Black Diamonds* (1870; Eng. trans., 1894), which develops the concept of an ideal man, and *Az aranyember* (1873; trans. as *A Modern Midas*, 1884), which uses the Midas motif, are considered his best works.   ALBERT TEZLA

Jolas, Betsy

The French composer Betsy Jolas, b. Aug. 5, 1926, received her musical studies in the United States (Bennington College, 1945-46) and in Paris as a pupil of Darius Milhaud in composition, and of Oliver Messiaen in musical analysis. She has worked with serial, aleatory, and spatial music (in which performers are stationed at various distances from one another). Her compositions include: *Quatuor II*, for coloratura soprano, violin, viola, and cello (1964); *Diurnes*, for a chorus of from 12 to 72 voices (1970); and *Lassus Ricercare*, for 10 instruments (1970). Since 1971 she has taught at the Paris Conservatory as a substitute for Messiaen during his tours.   DIKA NEWLIN

Bibliography: Vinton, John, ed., "Betsy Jolas," *Dictionary of Contemporary Music* (1974).

Joliot-Curie, Frédéric [zhol-yoh′-koo-ree′, fray-day-reek′]

The French physicist Jean Frédéric Joliot, b. Mar. 19, 1900, d. Aug. 14, 1958, was known for his work in nuclear science. He and his wife, the former Irène Curie, adopted the name Joliot-Curie when they married. In 1931, the year after he obtained his doctorate from the University of Paris, Joliot-Curie began four years of close collaboration with his wife that culminated in their discovery of artificial RADIOACTIVITY in 1934. For this achievement they shared the 1935 Nobel Prize for chemistry. During this period Frédéric and Irène Joliot-Curie obtained important results that were instrumental in the discovery (1932) of the neutron by the English physicist James CHADWICK.

In early 1939 the German radiochemists Otto HAHN and Fritz Strassmann published data proving that the impact of a neutron can cause the nucleus of a uranium atom to split into two nuclei of comparable mass. Within a few days of this, Joliot-Curie obtained decisive proof of the phenomenon of fission. He then determined the number of neutrons released per fission event and showed that a chain reaction among uranium atoms was possible, a chain reaction that can release enormous amounts of energy. During WORLD WAR II Joliot-Curie was involved in the French Resistance. A leader in reorganizing French science after 1945, he directed the effort to develop France's atomic energy program.

ROBERT PAUL

Bibliography: Goldsmith, Maurice, *Frédéric Joliot-Curie, A Biography* (1976); Weart, Spencer R., *Scientists in Power* (1979).

Joliot-Curie, Irène

The French physicist Irène Joliot-Curie, b. Sept. 12, 1897, d. Mar. 17, 1956, is known for her pioneering work in RADIOACTIVITY and nuclear science. The daughter of Marie and Pierre CURIE, discoverers of radium, Irène began (1921) her career as an assistant at the Radium Institute of the Sorbonne where she studied the ejection of alpha rays from polonium. Using the world's largest supply of polonium, Irène, working with her husband Frédéric, was the first to detect radiation far stronger than that from any other lightweight element. In 1932, James Chadwick identified this radiation as being that of the neutron.

Irène and her husband continued their work with alpha particles and in 1934 discovered that the irradiation of aluminum by alpha particles produces a new, unstable isotope of phosphorus. This was the first instance of artificial radioactivity, for which Irène and Frédéric Joliot-Curie were awarded the 1935 Nobel Prize for chemistry. In 1937, Irène Joliot-Curie was appointed professor at the Sorbonne. The next year she and P. P. Savic showed that the irradiation of uranium with slow protons produces a new radioisotope. This work led Otto HAHN and Fritz Strassmann in 1939 to perform experiments confirming the reality of nuclear fission. From 1946, Irène Joliot-Curie was professor and director of the Radium Institute.

ROBERT PAUL

Bibliography: Opfell, Olga S., *Lady Laureates* (1978).

Jolivet, André [zhoh-lee-vay′, ahn-dray′]

The French composer André Jolivet, b. Aug. 8, 1905, d. Dec. 20, 1974, was as a young man strongly drawn to painting, writing, and music. He was Edgard Varèse's only composition pupil (1928-30). In 1936, Jolivet, Olivier Messiaen, Daniel-Lesur, and Yves Baudrier founded *Jeune France* ("Young France"), a group dedicated to the creation of a humane, national (but not nationalistic), truly contemporary music free of all "artificial quests." A successful lecturer, conductor, and teacher, Jolivet produced many orchestral and chamber works, including several symphonies and concertos. His style was eclectic, making use of many 20th-century techniques. Like his teacher Varèse, Jolivet was much concerned with the exploration of orchestral timbres. His long, sensitively constructed melodic lines have been highly praised.

DIKA NEWLIN

Jolliet, Louis [joh-lee-et′]

Louis Jolliet, 1645-1700, was a French-Canadian explorer who, with Father Jacques MARQUETTE, opened the Great Lakes and Mississippi Valley to European influence. Originally intending to become a Jesuit, he attended the Jesuit seminary in Quebec but then studied hydrography in France. He became (1669) a fur trader in the Lake Superior region.

In 1672 the Comte de FRONTENAC commissioned Jolliet to find the "great western river" described by Indians. With Marquette, he left Michilimackinac in May 1673 and followed the Fox and Wisconsin rivers to the Mississippi, which they canoed down as far as the Arkansas River. Jolliet's subsequent explorations of the lower Saint Lawrence, Labrador, and Hudson Bay persuaded his superiors to appoint him royal hydrographer for Canada in 1697. He executed many notable charts of the area.

Bibliography: Delanglez, Jean, *Life and Voyages of Louis Jolliet, 1645-1700* (1948); Eifert, Virginia L., *Louis Jolliet, Explorer of Rivers* (1961); Hamilton, Raphael N., *Marquette's Explorations: The Narratives Reexamined* (1970); Severin, Timothy, *Explorers of the Mississippi* (1967); Steck, Francis B., *The Jolliet-Marquette Expedition, 1673* (1927).

Jolson, Al [johl′-suhn]

The singer Al Jolson, b. Asa Yoelson in Lithuania, c.1886, d. Oct. 23, 1950, immigrated with his family to Washington, D.C., around 1895. After a long apprenticeship as a singer in burlesque, minstrel shows, and vaudeville, he won (1911) his first important role in the Broadway show *La Belle Paree*. Jolson's style was notable for its vigor and volume, its blatant sentimentality, and for his use of blackface, a leftover theatrical convention from the already moribund minstrel show. His work—especially his film roles, beginning with *The Jazz Singer* (1927), the first major sound picture—won him a large audience during his lifetime. Jolson was awarded the Congressional Medal of Merit posthumously for his many overseas tours of wartime army camps, the last at the beginning of the Korean War in 1950.

Bibliography: Friedland, Michael, *Jolson* (1972).

Discography: *Best of Al Jolson: Steppin' Out* and *California, Here I Come* (1911-29).

Joly, John [jahl′-ee]

The Irish geologist and physicist John Joly, b. Nov. 1, 1857, d. Dec. 8, 1933, often invented new apparatus to carry out his research. Joly graduated in 1882 from Trinity College, Dublin, where he became a demonstrator in engineering and physics and, from 1897 until his death, a professor of geology. Joly invented a steam calorimeter to measure the specific heat of minerals, a diffusion photometer, a meldometer to determine the melting point of minerals, a method for color photography, and a cancer-treatment method using radiation. He calculated the age of the Earth based upon the rate of increase in the sodium content of the oceans, and he later used radioactive methods to date geological formations.

Bibliography: Burchfield, Joe D., *Lord Kelvin and the Age of the Earth* (1975).

Jommelli, Niccolò [yoh-mel′-lee, nik-koh-loh′]

Niccolò Jommelli, b. Sept. 10, 1714, d. Aug. 25, 1774, was an eminent Italian opera composer of the Neapolitan school. He was a follower of Allessandro Scarlatti, but developed a more serious style than most of his contemporaries, making more effective use of the orchestra, using richer harmony, and depending less on the invariable "da capo" aria, which he considered undramatic. He was among the first to make consistent use of orchestral accompaniment in recitative. His style had some influence on the formation of the classical style of the later 18th century. From 1753 to 1769 he was court music director in Stuttgart. In addition to about 60 operas, Jommelli composed much church music.

FARLEY K. HUTCHINS

Bibliography: Long, Alan Bligh Yorke, *Music At Court: Four 18th Century Studies* (1954).

Jonah, Book of

The Book of Jonah, in the Old Testament of the BIBLE, is one of the works of the Minor Prophets. Unlike the other prophetic books, it is not a book written by a prophet but is a narrative about a prophet. Jonah seems to be the prophet mentioned in 2 Kings 14:25 who lived during the reign of Jeroboam II (*c*.785 BC). The book is anonymous and was probably composed during the 4th century BC.

A short novella, the book describes how Jonah sought to evade God's command to go to Nineveh, the capital of Assyria, to preach repentance. He booked passage on a ship to Tarshish, only to have his flight brought to an end by a divinely ordained storm. Thrown overboard and swallowed by a great fish, Jonah was vomited up on shore after three days and nights. He then obeyed God's command and preached in Nineveh. When the population responded to his preaching and repented, God changed his plan to destroy the city. Divine mercy was thus shown to possess a distinctly universal dimension. The purpose of the book, then, was primarily didactic, dramatizing God's care for Jews and Gentiles alike. It was a polemic against the exclusivism that was beginning to dominate Judaic theology, depicted so clearly by Jonah himself.   GEORGE W. COATS

Bibliography: Ellul, Jacques, *The Judgment of Jonah*, trans. by Geoffrey Bromiley (1971); Martin, Hugh, *The Prophet Jonah* (1952; repr. 1979).

Jonathan

Jonathan was the eldest son of King SAUL and a respected warrior who captured a Philistine outpost single-handedly. He was killed during Saul's last campaign against the Philistines (1 Samuel 13-31). Jonathan and the future king DAVID became close friends when David entered the service of Saul.

Jones, Anson

Anson Jones, b. Jan. 20, 1798, d. Jan. 9, 1858, was the last president of the Texas Republic. He fought in the Texas Revolution and served (1837-41) in the House and Senate of the Texas Congress before becoming the republic's secretary of state under President Sam HOUSTON. He was elected to succeed Houston in 1844. Jones resigned (February 1846) after the formal annexation of Texas by the United States.

Jones, Bobby

Robert Tyre Jones, Jr., b. Atlanta, Ga., Mar. 17, 1902, d. Dec. 18, 1971, was the greatest amateur golfer and perhaps the greatest golfer ever. He entered the U.S. Amateur tournament in 1916 at the age of 14 but did not win a major tournament until 1923, when he won the U.S. Open. In the ensuing years Jones won a succession of championships. He won the U.S. Open again in 1926 and 1929; the U.S. Amateur in 1924, 1925, 1927, and 1928; and the British Open in 1926 and 1927. He

Bobby Jones hits a fairway shot on his way to winning the 1926 British Open. Jones, who never lost his amateur status, retired after his most successful season, 1930, when he won the Amateur and Open championships of both the United States and Great Britain.

was the first golfer to win both the U.S. Open and the British Open in the same year (1926). In 1930 he achieved the first and never-repeated Grand Slam of golf by winning the British Amateur, British Open, U.S. Open, and U.S. Amateur tournaments all in the same year. In eight years Jones won 13 of the 27 major tournaments that he entered. He never became a professional golfer and retired from tournament play in 1930 to practice law. He entered business with his father for a time, and he later, in cooperation with investment banker Cliff Roberts, designed a new golf course in Augusta, Ga. The course, now known as the Augusta National Golf Club, has been since 1934 the site of the Masters tournament, one of the most prestigious events on the professional golf tour. Jones's health began to fail, and in 1948 he underwent a painful back operation. Slow paralysis set in, and he spent his last few years confined to a wheelchair.   HOWARD LISS

Bibliography: Jones, Robert Tyre, *Golf Is My Game* (1960); Klein, Dave, *Great Moments in Golf* (1971); Lardner, Rex, *The Great Golfers* (1970); Scott, Tom, and Cousins, Geoffrey, *The Golf Immortals* (1969).

Jones, Casey

"Casey," or John Luther, Jones, b. Fulton County, Ky., Mar. 14, 1864, d. Apr. 30, 1900, an engineer for the Illinois Central Railroad, became a hero of American railroad men and was immortalized in song after his death, in a collision near Vaughan, Miss. According to tradition, he saved the lives of his passengers by remaining at the throttle to brake his train.

Jones, George

A crusading publisher of the *New York Times*, George Jones, b. Poultney, Vt., Aug. 16, 1811, d. Aug. 12, 1891, began planning with Henry Jarvis RAYMOND the "ideal daily" newspaper in the early 1840s when the two men were employed at Horace Greeley's newly founded *New York Tribune*. In 1843, Jones became a banker in Albany, N.Y., while Raymond went to work for the *Morning Courier and New-York Enquirer*. By 1851 they had managed to accumulate the astounding sum of $100,000 to purchase the *Times*, called until 1857 the *New York Daily Times*. After Raymond's death, with Louis J. Jennings as editor, Jones's *Times* exposed the infamous "Boss" Tweed and the scandalous Tammany Hall political maneuverings.   RICHARD HIXSON

Bibliography: Tebbell, John, *Media in America: A Social and Political History* (1975).

Jones, Henry Arthur

Considered a daring writer in his time, the English dramatist Henry Arthur Jones, b. Sept. 20, 1851, d. Jan. 7, 1929, has since declined in popularity and impact. His early work includes a number of social-problem plays, among them *Saints and Sinners* (1884), *The Masqueraders* (1894), and *Michael and His Lost Angel* (1896). Jones later turned increasingly to well-constructed comedies. He also wrote dramatic criticism and theory, including *The Renascence of the English Drama* (1895) and *The Theatre of Ideas* (1915).   ROBIN BUSS

Bibliography: Jones, Doris, *The Life and Letters of Henry Arthur Jones* (1930; repr. 1971).

Jones, Inigo   [in'-ig-oh]

The buildings and designs of Inigo Jones, baptized July 19, 1573, d. June 21, 1652, established in England the principles of ancient classical architecture as interpreted during the Italian Renaissance by Andrea Palladio.

Little is known of Jones's early life, but it is probable that he was first trained as a painter. Between 1598 and 1604, and again in 1613, Jones traveled extensively in Italy, acquiring a knowledge of mannerist painting and an enthusiasm for ancient classical architecture, which he knew both firsthand and through study of the buildings and writings of Palladio. From 1604 to 1611 he designed costumes and sets for court masques, many in collaboration with the dramatist Ben Jonson. From 1615 to 1642 he was surveyor of the king's works, first under James I and then Charles I. His earliest surviving structure, the Queen's House at Greenwich, is the first strictly classical English building. Jones's greatest monument is the Banqueting Hall (1619–22), all that remains of his additions to the Palace of Whitehall, London. It consists of a single interior space in the form of a double cube. He planned the first town square in London in Covent Garden (1631–35) and worked on numerous other projects, which included country houses and the restoration of Saint Paul's Cathedral (1634–42, destroyed in the great London fire of 1666). As advisor in the remodeling of Wilton House, Wiltshire, he left the imprint of his style on the work of his nephew and assistant, John Webb, who executed the building and its interior design (c.1650).

The outbreak of civil war in 1642 removed the opportunities for royal patronage on which his career had been founded. He was captured by Cromwell's forces in 1645 and released after paying a heavy fine. Immediately after Jones's death his example was emulated only by Webb, but his later influence on English architecture was profound. The Palladian principles of design that Jones imported to England reached fruition in the work of Sir Christopher Wren, and the designs of William Kent.   VALENTIN TATRANSKY

Bibliography: Bloomfield, Reginald, *Six Architects* (1935; repr. 1969); Collier, John Payne, *Inigo Jones* (1928); Loftie, William J., *Inigo Jones and Wren* (1893); Orgel, Stephen, and Strong, Roy, *Inigo Jones: The Theatre of the Stuart Court*, 2 vols. (1973); Summerson, John, *Inigo Jones* (1966); Triggs, Harry Inigo, *Some Architectural Works of Inigo Jones* (1901); Wittkower, Rudolf, *Palladio and Palladianism* (1974).

Jones, James

James Jones, b. Robinson, Ill., Nov. 6, 1921, d. May 9, 1977, one of the most notable novelists of the World War II generation, became famous overnight with *From Here to Eternity* (1951; film, 1953), a powerful, often shocking picture of the lives of Hawaii-based U.S. Army personnel in the days preceding the attack on Pearl Harbor. Winner of a National Book Award, it was written in a style that, although seldom graceful, nevertheless had the force of absolute fidelity to its subject. Two later Jones novels form part of a war trilogy: *The Thin Red Line* (1962; film, 1964) and *Whistle* (1978). Of his other works—which include *The Pistol* (1958), *Go to the Widow-Maker* (1967), *The Merry Month of May* (1971), and *A Touch of Danger* (1973)—*Some Came Running* (1957; film, 1958), a novel of post–World War II American small-town life, was the most successful.   MARCUS KLEIN

Bibliography: Hopkins, John R., ed., *James Jones: A Checklist* (1974); Morris, Willie, *James Jones: A Friendship* (1978); Paris Review (periodical), *Writers at Work: The "Paris Review" Interviews*, 3d series (1967).

Jones, James Earl

The actor James Earl Jones, b. Arkabutla, Miss., Jan. 17, 1931, played numerous Shakespearean roles before earning acclaim—and a Tony Award—as the black boxing champion Jack Jefferson in *The Great White Hope* (1968; film, 1970). As a member of the New York Shakespeare Festival, he has appeared as Caliban in *The Tempest* (1962), as Othello (1964), and as Lear (1973). He has also done television work and several movies.

Jones, John Paul

John Paul Jones was a sailor-of-fortune who became an American naval hero during the AMERICAN REVOLUTION. Born on July 6, 1747, he was the son of a Scottish gardener and was originally named John Paul. At the age of 12 he entered the British merchant marine. Sailing aboard merchantmen and slavers, he received his first command in 1769. In 1773, however, he murdered a mutinous crewman at Tobago in the West Indies and fled to North America, adopting the name Jones.

In 1775 two friendly members of the Continental Congress obtained for Jones a lieutenant's commission in the Continental Navy. The following year he became captain of the sloop *Providence*.

John Paul Jones, an American naval hero of the Revolutionary War, stands ready for battle in this contemporary engraving. Jones's raids on British warships earned him the French Mérite Militaire, making him the only officer in the American armed services to be so decorated.

Sailing to France aboard the 18-gun *Ranger* in 1778, Jones received from the French the first salute given to the new American flag by a foreign warship. During the spring he terrorized the coastal population of Scotland and England by making daring raids ashore.

His reputation in Paris greatly enhanced, Jones received from the French government a converted French merchantman, which he renamed *Bonhomme Richard* (*Poor Richard*) in honor of Benjamin Franklin.

Setting sail at the head of a small squadron on Aug. 14, 1779, Jones captured 17 merchantmen off the British coast and on September 23 fell in with a convoy of British merchant vessels escorted by H.M.S. *Serapis* and *Countess of Scarborough*. Challenging the *Serapis*, Jones deftly maneuvered the *Bonhomme Richard* alongside the larger British vessel and lashed the two ships together. With the muzzles of their guns touching, the two warships fired into each other's insides. Although his smaller vessel was on fire and sinking, Jones rejected the British demand for surrender; "I have not yet begun to fight," he replied. More than three hours after the bloody battle began, the *Serapis* surrendered, and Jones took command of it.

Although lionized in Paris and Philadelphia, Jones encountered such stiff political rivalry that he never again held a major American command at sea. In 1788, Russian empress CATHERINE II appointed him rear admiral in the Russian navy, and he served in the Black Sea until political intrigue resulted in his discharge (1790). Jones lived quietly in Paris until his death on July 18, 1792.   KENNETH J. HAGAN

Bibliography: Abbazia, Patrick, *John Paul Jones, America's First Naval Hero* (1976); De Koven, Anna, ed., *Life and Letters of John Paul Jones*, 2 vols. (1913); Lorenz, Lincoln, *John Paul Jones, Fighter for Freedom and Glory* (1943); Morison, Samuel E., *John Paul Jones* (1959).

Jones, LeRoi: see BARAKA, IMAMU AMIRI.

Jones, Margo

Margo Jones, b. Livingston, Tex., 1913, d. July 24, 1955, was an American theatrical producer and director who in 1947 established in Dallas the country's first professional theater-in-the-round. Its work was described by Jones in her book *Theatre-in-the-Round* (1951).

A champion of regional, repertory, and experimental theater, Jones also worked in New York, most notably as a co-director of Tennessee Williams's first Broadway production, *The Glass Menagerie* (1944).

Jones, Robert Edmond

Robert Edmond Jones, b. Milton, N.H., Dec. 12, 1887, d. Nov. 26, 1954, was one of the major forces in American theatrical design in the first half of the 20th century. His sets for Anatole France's *The Man Who Married a Dumb Wife* (1915) had a revolutionary effect on stagecraft in the United States and began a movement away from realism toward suggestion and mood. He designed sets for many of the plays of Eugene O'Neill and together with O'Neill and Kenneth Macgowan managed the Provincetown Playhouse and the Greenwich Village Theatre after 1923. He was the first American to design for the BALLET RUSSES DE SERGE DIAGHILEV (1916), and he began to work in color films in 1933. With Macgowan he wrote *Continental Stagecraft* (1922; repr. 1964), which introduced European theatrical innovations to the United States. Jones also wrote *The Dramatic Imagination* (1941).

ARNOLD ARONSON

Bibliography: Pendleton, Ralph, ed., *The Theatre of Robert Edmond Jones* (1977).

Jones, Rufus Matthew

Rufus Matthew Jones, b. South China, Maine, Jan. 25, 1863, d. June 16, 1948, was an American Quaker philosopher and social reformer. He taught philosophy at Haverford College from 1893 until 1934. Attempting to emancipate Quakers from what he defined as a parochial evangelism, Jones argued that the Society of FRIENDS (Quakers) combined mysticism and social reform. He served (1893–1912) as editor of the *Friends' Review* (renamed *American Friend*), wrote four of the 7-volume Rowntree series on the history of the Society of Friends, and helped found (1917) and later served as chairman of the American Friends Service Committee. The committee, which grew out of an attempt to provide alternative service to conscientious objectors in World War I, continues to engage in a wide range of relief activities in the United States and abroad. Jones wrote more than 50 books, many of them about the Quakers and mysticism.

J. WILLIAM FROST

Bibliography: Fosdick, H. E., ed., *Rufus Jones Speaks to Our Time: An Anthology* (1951); Vining, E. G., *Friend of Life, the Biography of Rufus M. Jones* (1958).

Jones, Samuel Milton

Samuel Milton Jones, b. Wales, Aug. 3, 1846, d. July 12, 1904, was an industrialist and political reformer. Jones was brought to the United States as a small child and claimed he received only 30 months of schooling in his life. After working in the oil business, he became wealthy manufacturing oil-drilling equipment; he gave his employees an 8-hour day and cooperative health insurance and became known as "Golden Rule" Jones. Elected Republican mayor of Toledo, Ohio, in 1897, he undertook municipal reforms that lost him the 1899 Republican nomination; he was reelected in 1901 and 1903 as an independent.

Bibliography: Frederick, Peter J., *Knights of the Golden Rule* (1976); Jones, Samuel Milton, *The New Right* (1899) and *Letters of Love and Labor*, 2 vols. (1900–01); Tager, Jack, *The Intellectual as Urban Reformer* (1968); Warner, Hoyt, *Progressivism in Ohio, 1897–1917* (1964).

Jones, Spike

The bandleader and composer Lindley "Spike" Jones, b. Long Beach, Calif., Dec. 14, 1911, d. May 1, 1964, was a drummer with several Hollywood-based bands before organizing his own group, The City Slickers, in 1942. Specializing in bizarre antics and corny humor, the band used sound effects as well as their instruments to create musical mayhem. Their wartime recording of "Der Fuehrer's Face," which featured a derisive Bronx cheer, and their lunatic renditions of romantic ballads ("Chloe," for example) were instant hits during the 1940s and '50s.

DONALD IVEY

Jones, Sir William

The English linguist and jurist Sir William Jones, b. Sept. 28, 1746, d. Apr. 27, 1794, revolutionized the study of language when he argued that Sanskrit, Greek, Latin, and several other languages were all descended from an earlier, extinct tongue—Indo-European. Jones had already mastered ten languages when he turned his attention to law, publishing the widely used *An Essay on the Law of Bailments* in 1781. He went out to Calcutta as a Supreme Court judge in 1783 and had learned 20 more languages by the time of his death 11 years later.

DAVID YERKES

Bibliography: Cannon, Garland, *Oriental Jones: A Biography* (1964) and, as ed., *Letters of Sir William Jones*, 2 vols. (1970); Pedersen, Holger, *Linguistic Science in the Nineteenth Century* (1931); Sebeok, Thomas, ed., *Portraits of Linguists* (1967).

See also: HISTORICAL LINGUISTICS; INDO-EUROPEAN LANGUAGES.

Jonestown

Jonestown, a 364-ha (900-acre) agricultural commune in northwestern Guyana, was the site of the largest mass suicide in modern history. Its origin and demise are associated with James Warren "Jim" Jones, leader of the People's Temple, an American religious cult. Jones, b. Lynn, Ind., 1931, was intensely attracted to religion at an early age. After briefly attending Indiana University he founded his own church, the Christian Assembly of God, in Indianapolis in the late 1950s; he soon changed its name to the People's Temple. In 1965, Jones and 100 followers moved the People's Temple to Redwood Valley, north of San Francisco. The cult grew rapidly, soon numbering several thousand members.

In 1971 the People's Temple moved its headquarters to San Francisco. At this time the organization was engaged in legal aid, drug rehabilitation, and sponsoring medical care and soup kitchens for the poor. It held colorful revival-style meetings which drew large crowds. The People's Temple's monetary assets grew to several million dollars. Increasingly, however, the cult came to center on its charismatic, idealistic, power hungry, and extremely unstable leader, whose power over his followers grew to dangerous proportions. A harsher and harsher discipline emerged within the cult, beatings became common, money was extorted from members, and sexual promiscuity grew.

In 1975, Jones and his followers helped in the election of San Francisco mayor George Moscone, and Jones was made chairman of the San Francisco Housing Authority in 1976. His increasingly prominent political activities drew attention to the People's Temple. In July 1977, with a California magazine about to expose the group's darker side, Jones and 800 followers fled to "Jonestown," the site in Guyana purchased by the cult in 1974.

In Jonestown, Jim Jones and the cult deteriorated rapidly. Members were given inadequate food and forced to work as long as 11 hours a day. They were guarded by Jones's armed security guards, cut off from the outside world, and forced to listen to Jones's increasingly bizarre, rambling sermons. In November 1978, California congressman Leo Ryan and a group of reporters flew to Jonestown to investigate reports that members were being held there against their will. On November 18, Ryan and several reporters were murdered, after which Jones ordered the commune members to commit mass suicide by poisoning. Some persons apparently drank the poison voluntarily, while others were forced. In all, more than 900 cult members died.

Bibliography: Kilduff, Marshall, and Javers, Ron, *The Suicide Cult* (1978); Krause, Charles A., and the Staff of the Washington Post, *Guyana Massacre* (1978); Lane, Mark, *The Strongest Poison* (1980); Maguire, John, and Dunn, Mary Lee, *Hold Hands and Die* (1978).

See also: RELIGIOUS CULTS.

Jong, Erica   [jawng]

The novelist, poet, and feminist, Erica Mann Jong, b. New York City, Mar. 26, 1942, won overnight success with her candidly erotic, best-selling novel *Fear of Flying* (1973); for this work, Jong was both acclaimed for writing openly about a woman's sexual drives and needs, and censured as a pornographer. The further sexual misadventures of Jong's heroine, Isadora Wing, and her eventual satisfying relationship with a younger man, form the basis of a second novel, *How to Save Your Own Life* (1977). Jong's poetry includes the volumes *Fruit and Vegetables* (1971), *Half-Lives* (1973), and *Loveroot*

Erica Jong is an American novelist and poet who writes in a bold but humorous mode. Her works explore the fears of women who attempt to redefine their social and sexual roles.

Photo Jill Krementz © 1974

(1975), works that give voice, sometimes erotically, sometimes ironically and brashly, to the values, questions, and tensions of contemporary society.

Jongkind, Johan Barthold [yawng'-kint, yoh'-hahn bar'-tohlt]

The Dutch landscape painter, watercolorist, and graphic artist Johann Barthold Jongkind, b. June 3, 1819, d. Feb. 27, 1891, was with Eugène Boudin a precursor of French impressionism. After studying at The Hague Art School with Andreas Schelfhout, he went (1846) to Paris on the recommendation of Eugène Isabey, who influenced his early work. Jongkind admired the artists of the Barbizon school and became friendly with Camille Corot, Charles Daubigny, and Constantin Troyon, but his own style of landscape painting was derived more from the precedents of 17th-century Dutch landscapists. He painted the flat, low-lying countryside, as well as numerous scenes of the rivers and seacoasts of the Netherlands and France in an increasingly free manner, for example, *Moulins à Rotterdam* (1870; Musée des Beaux-Arts, Reims, France). His creation of the effects of light and atmospheres and his technique of loose, colorful brush strokes greatly influenced the impressionists, especially Claude Monet. Jongkind died in a mental institution and was buried in France, his adopted country.   PHILIP GOULD

Bibliography: Bakker-Hefting, Victorine, *J-B. Jongkind* (1962); Gesson, George, *Johan-Barthold Jongkind, 1819-1891* (1955).

Jonker, Ingrid [yawng'-kur]

Ingrid Jonker, b. Sept. 19, 1933, d. by drowning, July 19, 1965, was a South African poet whose unhappy adolescence was reflected in many of her poems. Her first volume of poetry, *Ontvlugting* (Flight, 1956), attracted attention, but her second work, *Rook en oker* (Smoke and Ochre, 1963), won her the Afrikaanse Pers Award and brought her general recognition. *Kantelson* (trans. as *Selected Poems*, 1968), published posthumously in 1966, included early poems and others written just before her death.

jonquil [jawng'-kwil]

The jonquil, *Narcissus jonquilla*, is a single species of narcissus, native to southern Europe and Algeria. It bears small golden yellow flowers with short cups of cream, yellow, or orange; produces rushlike leaves; and is distinguished by its sweet fragrance. The term *jonquil* is sometimes used inaccurately to describe others members of the genus *Narcissus*.
                                                    CHARLES L. WILSON

Jonson, Ben

Ben Jonson, one of the great English poets of the 17th century and one of the greatest comic dramatists of any century, ex-

erted a lasting impact on both English poetry and stage comedy. Both in his poems and in his plays Jonson fused a passionate classicism—a respect for form, a veneration for the ancients—with a teeming, vivacious realism. His comic masterpieces, VOLPONE and *The Alchemist*, show humanity as a parade of rogues and fools verging on monomania, each character exhibiting one or two traits—greed, jealousy, religious fanaticism—developed to an abnormal degree.

Born c.June 11, 1572, Jonson was educated at the famous Westminster School but did not go on to Oxford or Cambridge; rather, after a brief, unwilling apprenticeship to his bricklayer stepfather, and military service in Flanders, he gravitated toward the theater. He first tried his hand as an actor, a capacity he evidently showed little talent for. He then became a playwright; his career was embattled at every point, and he was imprisoned (1597) for his part in a lost satiric comedy declared seditious by the authorities.

Jonson pioneered in a form of corrective comedy known later as the "comedy of humors." The term was derived from his own first significant venture in the form, *Every Man In His Humour* (1598). His intent was to expose the humors, or follies, of men in the hope that his audiences, seeing their own defects ridiculed on the stage, would mend their ways.

His classical tragedy *Sejanus* (1603), based on Roman history, offered a powerful picture of dictatorship in action but embroiled Jonson anew with the authorities and angered the sensation-loving London spectators with its slow-moving, declamatory style. The experience, however, taught Jonson the usefulness of making conspiracy the mainspring of a plot, and in three of the four great comedies that followed—*Volpone, or the Fox* (1606), *Epicene, or The Silent Woman* (1609), and *The Alchemist* (1610), the fourth being *Bartholomew Fair* (1614)—he utilized the conspiracy to expose human baseness and the lengths to which self-destructive folly could go. His last plays (1616-33), dismissed by Dryden as "dotages," suggest that he was losing touch with his playhouse audiences. During the same years, however, he continued to compose brilliant court masques, an art form he had already revolutionized and made aesthetically and philosophically serious for the first time.

Jonson also wrote much nondramatic poetry, chiefly satiric epigrams in the manner of Martial, and verse epistles addressed to friends and patrons, which expounded the ideals of honesty, loyalty, courtesy, and conviviality. His notebook of critical comments, collected after his death under the title *Timber, Or Discoveries* (1640), did much to cement Jonson's reputation as the first "literary dictator" in English.

Passionately gregarious, Jonson maintained close friendships throughout his life with fellow writers and patrons of literature. Formidably contentious as well, he also made many enemies, engaged in literary quarrels, and defended his art against rivals and detractors. His conversion to Roman Catholicism—a dangerous move in a country that prided itself on having recently thrown off the yoke of Rome—brought

Ben Jonson, an English satirist, is considered, after Shakespeare, the most influential dramatist of the Elizabethan stage. Jonson's early works, such as Every Man In His Humour (1598), playfully exaggerate and examine human shortcomings. Under attack by critics, Jonson abandoned his gentle touch in Volpone (1606), a thinly veiled castigation of his enemies.

him briefly into the orbit of government espionage at the time of the Gunpowder Plot (1605), an experience he seems to have commemorated in his second classical tragedy, *Catiline* (1611). Although the play failed in the theater, later in the century it held readers spellbound with its veiled analogy between the ancient Roman conspiracies and the intrigues of the Jesuits in 17th-century England.

The accession of Charles I to the throne in 1625 brought Jonson on evil days. The new king preferred to entrust the production of court masques to Jonson's rival, the architect and stage designer Inigo Jones. The theatergoing public hissed his comedy *The New Inn* in 1629, by which time Jonson had suffered a paralytic stroke from which he never fully recovered. Although he continued to read and write, he spent his last years bedridden, visited by the coterie of younger admirers known as the "Sons of Ben." He died on Aug. 6, 1637, and was buried in Westminster Abbey under the inscription, "O Rare Ben Jonson." JONAS A. BARISH

Bibliography: Barish, Jonas A., *Ben Jonson and the Language of Prose Comedy* (1970) and, as ed., *Ben Jonson: A Collection of Critical Essays* (1963); Baskervill, Charles R., *English Elements in Jonson's Early Comedy* (1911; repr. 1967); Herford, C. H., Simpson, Percy and Evelyn, eds., *Ben Jonson: The Man and His Work*, 11 vols. (1925–52); Knights, L. C., *Drama and Society in the Age of Jonson* (1937; repr. 1968); Orgel, Stephen, *The Jonsonian Masque* (1965); Swinburne, Algernon C., *Study of Ben Jonson* (1889; repr. 1969); Trimpi, Wesley, *Ben Jonson's Poems: A Study of the Plain Style* (1962); Partridge, Edward B., *The Broken Compass: A Study of the Major Comedies of Ben Jonson* (1958; repr. 1976).

Joos van Cleve   [yohs vahn klay'-veh]

The Flemish painter Joos van Cleve, *c.*1485–1540, trained in his native town of Kleve, West Germany, before moving to Antwerp, where he became a master painter in 1511. Little is known of his life, but he is thought to have left Antwerp and traveled abroad, probably to the court of the French king Francis I at Fontainebleau, between 1528 and 1535. Several portraits of Francis have been attributed to Joos, who is chiefly known as a portraitist and painter of religious subjects. Two paintings of the *Death of the Virgin* (Munich Cathedral and Wallraf-Richartz Museum, Cologne), both dated 1515, are almost certainly by him. Although these works are characteristically Flemish, his later work reveals the influence of Italian Mannerism, with which he may have come into contact at Fontainebleau.

Bibliography: Friedlaender, Max J., *From Van Eyck to Bruegel*, ed. by F. Grossmann, trans. by Marguerite Kay, 3d ed. (1969).

Joos van Ghent   [yohs' vahn gent]

Joos van Ghent, *c.*1430–*c.*1476, also known as Justus van Ghent or Joos van Wassenhove, was one of the few 15th-century Flemish painters known to have worked in Italy. Little is known of his early life, but documents indicate that he was admitted to the Antwerp Painters' Guild in 1460 and that four years later he was painting in Ghent. While in Ghent, he became friends with Hugo van der Goes, whom he may have taught. Sometime after 1465 he went to Italy, where he was employed by the great Renaissance art patron Frederigo da Montefeltro, the duke of Urbino. Joos's work at Urbino reflects the influence of Netherlandish masters Rogier van der Weyden and Dirk Bouts but without the typical Flemish concern for realistic detail. His *Communion of the Apostles* (*c.*1472–74; National Gallery, Urbino) typifies his eclectic style, in which an Italianate feeling for monumentality and spatial harmony coexisted with Flemish precision and clarity.

Bibliography: Friedländer, Max J., *Early Netherlandish Painting*, vol. 3, trans. by Heinz Norden (1968); Panofsky, Erwin, *Early Netherlandish Painting*, 2 vols. (1953).

Jooss, Kurt   [yohs, koort]

Kurt Jooss, b. Jan. 12, 1901, d. May 22, 1979, was an important figure in the world of German dance, not only because of his long career as a leading choreographer, teacher, and artistic director but also because of his early and enduring resistance to totalitarianism from the moment the Nazis seized power in

1933. Outside of Germany, his fame is largely based on a single work, *The Green Table* (1932), which remains after nearly 50 years a chilling indictment of war.

Jooss, who studied with Rudolf von LABAN and subsequently became his assistant, acquired international renown in 1932, when *The Green Table* won first prize at a choreographic competition in Paris. In 1933 the Jooss Dance Company, originally called the Essen Dance Theater, was established in England and toured Europe and the Americas. During most of World War II the company was confined to Britain, and it disbanded in 1947. Returning to Essen in 1949, Jooss formed another company—which lasted until 1953—and established a school, from whose direction he retired in 1968. He also briefly took charge (1954–55) of the ballet in Düsseldorf. At the Salzburg Festival in 1968 he enjoyed a success with his skillful choreography for Emilio de'Cavalieri's *La Rappresentazione di anima e di corpo* (The Representation of the Soul and the Body, 1600), presented in the 18th-century Collegiate Church. Jooss's works remain in the repertoire of several companies, including the JOFFREY BALLET.   DALE HARRIS

Bibliography: Coton, A. V., *The New Ballet* (1946).

Joplin, Janis   [jahp'-lin, jan'-is]

The rock singer Janis Joplin, b. Jan. 19, 1943, overwhelmed audiences with the anger, passion, and sexual intensity of her singing, a unique rock interpretation of blues styles. As lead singer with the rock group Big Brother and the Holding Company, she gained instant fame at the 1967 Monterey Pop Festival, and her recordings, especially the song "Me and Bobby McGee," were widely popular. She died on Oct. 4, 1970, of a heroin overdose.   JONATHAN KAMIN

Bibliography: Friedman, Myra, *Buried Alive: The Biography of Janis Joplin* (1973); Landau, Deborah, *Janis Joplin: Her Life & Times* (1971).

Joplin, Scott

Scott Joplin, b. Texas—possibly in Texarkana, where he was raised—Nov. 24, 1868, d. Apr. 1, 1917, was the most celebrated composer of instrumental RAGTIME. Although his family was poor—his parents had been slaves—the young Joplin studied classical piano as a child; he later worked as a dance musician, and at about the age of 20 he became an itinerant pianist, traveling throughout the Midwest. He published his first composition, the song "Please Say You Will," in 1895; other sentimental songs and marches followed. His "Maple Leaf Rag" (1899) became the most popular piano rag of the period, securing for Joplin a modest lifetime income from royalties and the title "King of Ragtime." Altogether, he published some 60 compositions, of which 41 are piano rags; the balance consists of songs, marches, and the opera *Treemonisha* (1911), produced unsuccessfully in concert form in 1915 but revived successfully 57 years later. During his lifetime, Joplin was never acknowledged as a serious composer. Rec-

The American composer Scott Joplin helped develop the syncopation and rhythmic diversity characteristic of the musical genre known as ragtime. The film The Sting *(1973), which featured Joplin's music, excited renewed interest in his life and work. He was posthumously awarded the 1976 Pulitzer Prize in music.*

ognition came posthumously, however, with the republication (1972) of his music, a Pulitzer Prize (1976), and acclaim from both the popular and the scholarly communities.

EDWARD A. BERLIN

Bibliography: Berlin, E. A., *Ragtime: A Musical and Cultural History* (1979); Blesh, R., and Janis, H., *They All Played Ragtime*, 4th ed. (1971); Haskins, J., and Benson, K., *Scott Joplin* (1978); Joplin, Scott, *The Collected Works of Scott Joplin*, 2 vols., ed. by Vera Brodsky Lawrence (1972).

Jordaens, Jacob   [yor'-dahns, yoh'-kohp]

The baroque artist Jacob Jordaens, b. May 19, 1593, d. Oct. 18, 1678, has been called the quintessential painter of 17th-century Flemish life. He was a student of Adam van Noort's. Although Jordaens never had the opportunity for a trip to Italy, his lusty figure style took shape under the impact of Michelangelo Caravaggio as well as his two great Flemish contemporaries, Peter Paul Rubens and Sir Anthony van Dyck. Unlike Rubens and van Dyck, whose art reflected their lives as courtiers, Jordaens was the painter of burgher and peasant life. A homelier, down-to-earth spirit predominates even in his mythological paintings such as *Triumph of Bacchus* (late 1640s; Kassel Gallery, Germany) and in religious works such as *Christ Driving the Money Changers from the Temple* (*c.*1657; Louvre, Paris). Among his most famous works is the warm and hearty *The King Drinks* (*c.*1638–40; Fine Arts Museum, Brussels). Jordaens was a leading member of the Calvinist community De Olytak (The Olive Branch), but he continued to receive many commissions from Roman Catholic churches. He also designed numerous tapestries and decorative cycles.

Bibliography: d'Hulst, R. A., *Jordaens Drawings*, 4 vols. (1974); Jaffe, Michael, *Jacob Jordaens 1593–1678* (1969).

Jordan

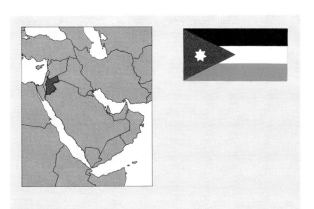

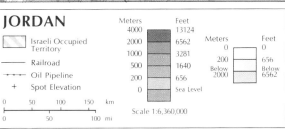

JORDAN

☐ Israeli Occupied Territory
— Railroad
+‑+‑+ Oil Pipeline
+ Spot Elevation

Meters	Feet
4000	13124
2000	6562
1000	3281
500	1640
200	656
0	Sea Level

Meters	Feet
0	0
200	656
Below 2000	Below 6562

Scale 1:6,360,000

JORDAN

Official Name: The Hashemite Kingdom of Jordan
Capital and Largest City: Amman (1977 pop., 732,587)
Area: 97,740 km² (37,738 mi²)
Elevation: *Highest*—Jabal Ramm 1,754 m (5,755 ft); *lowest*—Dead Sea 396 m (1,300 ft) below sea level
Population: 3,008,000 (1979 est.). *Distribution*—51% urban, 49% rural; *density*, 31 persons per km² (77 per mi²); *annual rate of increase* (1970–76), 3.2%
Principal Languages: Arabic (official); English
Principal Religions: Islam (official); Christianity
Principal Products: *Agriculture*—wheat, barley, tomatoes, citrus fruit, watermelons, eggplants; sheep and goats, cattle. *Manufacturing and industry*—cement, petroleum refining, ceramics, cigarettes, beverages, pharmaceuticals, leather, paper, soap. *Mining*—phosphate, potash, salt
Railroads: 1,073 km/666 mi (1977)
Roads: 4,825 km/2,996 mi (1977 paved)
Currency: 1 Jordanian dinar = 1,000 fils

The Hashemite Kingdom of Jordan is an Arab nation in southwest Asia at the northwest corner of the Arabian Peninsula. A small country, Jordan is slightly larger in size than the state of Kentucky. Although its official area is 97,738 km² (37,738 mi²), the portion of the country west of the Jordan River covering 5,439 km² (2,099 mi²) has been occupied by Israel since the Arab-Israeli War of 1967. Jordan is bounded on the west by Israel, on the north by Syria, and on the east by Iraq and Saudi Arabia. Only a 19-km (12-mi) southern coastline on the Gulf of AQABA, a northern arm of the Red Sea, prevents the country from being completely landlocked. The maximum east-west and north-south dimensions are approximately equal—370 km (230 mi)—when the West Bank area is included. AMMAN, the capital and dominant city, is located about 40 km (25 mi) east of the JORDAN RIVER.

Since the creation (1948) of the state of Israel, Jordan has experienced a large influx of Palestinian refugees, straining the nation's meager resource base. The 1979 Egyptian-Israeli accord provided for a 5-year period of negotiation to decide the final status of the Israeli-occupied West Bank territory.

LAND

Of Jordan's pre-1967 area, about 10% is arable, more than 75% is desert, and 1% is forested. Jordan is composed of three major landform regions: the Palestinian uplands, the Jordan Valley, and the Transjordan Plateau. To the west of the Jordan River are the Palestinian uplands—the dissected, low, limestone hills of Judea and Samaria. This southern extension of the mountains of Lebanon has an average elevation of 915 m (3,000 ft). Where soft marls exist, the hills are low and rounded. Sinkholes, caves, and dissected gorges are common.

Separating the Palestinian uplands from the plateaus to the east is the flat-floored valley of the Jordan River. This area is part of the GREAT RIFT VALLEY. The DEAD SEA, the saltiest lake on earth, occupies the lowest portion of this depression. Only 108 km (67 mi) separate the Sea of Galilee (see GALILEE, SEA OF) in the north from the Dead Sea in the south; but the Jordan River, connecting the two lakes, meanders to such a degree that its course is twice that distance.

The largest region in Jordan is the Transjordan Plateau, a great upthrust block that is part of the Arabian Plateau. Its western edge forms a 610 to 915 m (2,000 to 3,000 ft) escarpment above the Jordan River. It rises to a maximum height of 1,753 m (5,750 ft) near Aqaba. Geologically recent lava flows cover portions of northern and eastern Jordan. Wheat grows well where this rock has weathered to form rich, brown soils, and where moisture is sufficient. The fertile, alluvial soils of the Jordan River valley and the alkaline soils that accumulate in the valleys to the west are also agriculturally important. The SYRIAN DESERT covers most of the northeast. Scarcity of water in the uplands and inefficient agricultural methods result in low crop yields.

Climate. A Mediterranean climate characterizes much of Jordan. The summers are long, hot, and dry, and the winters mild with periods of precipitation. The northern and western parts of Jordan receive more moisture than the south and east. Light snow occasionally falls in the Jerusalem area and the northern uplands.

The deserts of southern and eastern Jordan receive as little as 50 mm (2 in) of rainfall annually. Temperatures here are more extreme than in the western and northern regions where yearly precipitation averages 400 mm (16 in). In the Jordan Valley, summer daytime temperatures reach 32° C (90° F), and winter nighttime temperatures drop below freezing, while the Palestinian Hills average a low of 7° C (44° F) and a high of 31° C (87° F) in summer.

Drainage. The Jordan River is the heart of the country's drainage system. Many of its tributaries originate in the mountains of southern Lebanon and Syria. The Transjordan Plateau to the east is dissected by the deep valleys of intermittent streams draining into the Jordan River. The largest tributary entering from the east is the Yarmuk, a permanent river that follows part of the border between Syria and Jordan. Wells provide additional water throughout much of the country,

The winding Jordan River flows from the Golan Heights to the Dead Sea. Following the Arab-Israeli War of 1967, the river was established as the border between Israel and Jordan. The former Jordanian territory west of the river was known in biblical times as Judea and Samaria.

but drilling is expensive and frequently beyond locally available technology.

Vegetation. Much of Jordan is dry, and the ground is generally rocky with sparse vegetation. Patches of coniferous forests are found in the northwest; willow, oleander, and tamarisk grow along the lower Jordan River valley. Low shrubs, thorny bushes, and seasonal grasses dot the semiarid regions and the desert margins. Forest cover is possible in the wetter regions.

Wildlife. Wild boars, ibex, foxes, jackals, wildcats, hyenas, wolves, hare, and some panthers can be found in isolated gorges, particularly south of the Sea of Galilee. Birds are plentiful. The steppe and desert areas of eastern Jordan have little game.

PEOPLE

The majority of the people living east of the Jordan River are descendants of BEDOUIN Arabs, while those to the west of the Jordan are of mixed ancestry. Most are of Semitic origin. Arabic is the official language, although English is widely used. Islam is the state religion. Sunni Muslims vastly outnumber both Shiite Muslims and Christians; most of the latter are members of the Eastern Orthodox church. Almost twice as many Jordanians live east of the Jordan River as on the West Bank. In 1976, Jordan's East Bank population included approximately 850,000 registered refugees from Palestine and about 70,000 nomadic or seminomadic Bedouins. In the more humid northern and western areas the people live in towns and villages, while Bedouins inhabit the deserts and the steppes. After Amman, important urban centers in the East include Aqaba, Irbid, Madaba, Ramtha, Salt, and Zarqa. Major cities in the Israeli-occupied West Bank territory are BETHLEHEM, HEBRON, Janin, Jericho, Nabulus, and Ram Allah.

Education and Health. In 1976 the vast majority of all 6- to 11-year-olds were enrolled in the more than 1,800 free elementary schools. Compulsory schooling lasts for 9 years. Palestinian refugee children are educated by the United Nations Relief and Works Agency. The University of Jordan (1962) is located in Amman, but many students study abroad. About 55% of the population is literate. The government provides medical and welfare assistance.

ECONOMIC ACTIVITY

When Jordan lost the West Bank to Israel in 1967, the country lost more than half of its population, its best agricultural land, and its greatest tourist attractions. It also gained 300,000 more refugees, many of whom were unable to find employment. As a result, economic development has been slowed.

Manufacturing. In 1979, Jordan had a GNP per capita of $870. Although Jordan produces cement, refined petroleum, cigarettes, olive oil, soap, leather, and clay, most industry has not developed far beyond the handicraft stage. Obstacles to industrial development include the paucity of natural resources, the limited local market, prohibitive transport costs, and lack of energy resources such as hydroelectric power and petroleum reserves. Imported petroleum supplies most of Jordan's energy. The 1976–80 Five Year Plan stresses mining and transport. Phosphate, salt, potash, limestone, gypsum, and marble are extracted.

Agriculture. Approximately 80% of the settled population is engaged in farming. Wheat, barley, lentils, vegetables, melons, and citrus fruits are the chief crops, but corn (maize), sesame, tobacco, olives, dates, and nuts are also grown. Because they can survive on sparse grass cover, goats and sheep are the most important livestock. Cattle raising takes place in the river valleys, and camels survive in the deserts. Small catches of fish are taken at Aqaba and from the Jordan and Yarmuk rivers. Many farmers are small landowners, although tenancy is still common. In 1967, Jordan completed the East Ghor Canal Project that uses water from the Yarmuk River for irrigation. Subsequent land reform, along with improved water management and cultivation practices, vastly strengthened Jordan's agricultural base.

Transportation. Almost 4,825 km (3,000 mi) of paved roads and more than 1,600 km (1,000 mi) of gravel roads link Jordan's villages and towns. The government operates a railroad that runs northward from just south of Ma'an through Am-

(Right) *Amman, known in the Bible as Rabbath Ammon, capital of the Ammonites, had declined to little more than a village when Emir Abdullah made it the capital of Transjordan in 1921. Today Amman is the capital and largest city in Jordan and is an industrial and commercial center.*

(Below) *Bars indicate the monthly ranges of temperatures (red) and precipitation (blue) in Amman, the capital of Jordan. The region surrounding Amman, in western Jordan, has a steppe climate, which is influenced by the Mediterranean Sea to the east and the Arabian Desert to the west.*

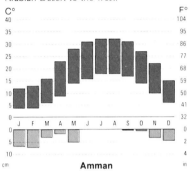

Amman

The Nabataeans, an ancient Arab tribe, established their capital at Petra during the 4th century BC, where it remained until the Roman occupation in AD 106. Their tombs, carved in the cliffs above Petra, were discovered in the 19th century.

man to the Syrian border. An international air terminal is located at Amman. The Trans-Arabian oil pipeline runs for 177 km (110 mi) through Jordan en route from Saudi Arabia to the Mediterranean coast of Lebanon. Radio and television stations are government operated. Two privately owned newspapers are published daily in Amman.

Trade. In international trade, Jordan's imports habitually exceed exports. Annual grants-in-aid from Arab states and the United States help to offset this trade deficit. The Arab states and India are Jordan's most important foreign customers. Agricultural crops, particularly vegetables, and phosphates are the primary exports. The United Kingdom, the United States, and West Germany supply Jordan with foods, machinery, textiles, and military equipment.

GOVERNMENT
Jordan is a constitutional monarchy. Its constitution, adopted in 1952, provides for a prime minister appointed by the king. A cabinet is named by the prime minister. The king also selects the 30 members of the Senate for 4-year terms. The 60 members of the House of Representatives are elected by the people for 4-year terms. Citizens over 20 may vote. The judges of the separate Muslim and Christian religious courts are appointed by the king. Jordan is divided into 8 districts called *muhafaza*, each headed by a centrally appointed governor. Three of the districts are in the Israel-occupied West Bank. In 1976, because Israeli occupation of the West Bank had called into question the validity of the government's structure, the lower house was dissolved and elections postponed indefinitely.

HISTORY
Village life in Jordan dates from at least 8000 BC at JERICHO. Hebrew states developed on the hills west of the Jordan River, while the small states of EDOM, GILEAD, MOAB, and Ammon were settled east of the Jordan River. The area was frequently invaded by the Assyrians, Egyptians, Babylonians, and Persians.

In the 4th century BC the northern area was incorporated into the kingdom of the SELEUCIDS, but the south was ruled by the Arab tribe of Nabataeans, who established their capital at PETRA. The Romans displaced the Seleucids in the 1st century BC, but Petra did not fall to Rome until AD 106.

The Muslim Arabs dominated from the 7th century until the 16th century, except for an interlude of Crusader control (see JERUSALEM, LATIN KINGDOM OF). The Ottoman Turks conquered the area in 1517 and retained control until the end of World War I.

After the Turkish defeat in World War I, the territory of Jordan became part of the short-lived Syrian kingdom of FAISAL I (later king of Iraq). After Faisal's defeat by French forces in 1920, Transjordan was incorporated into Britain's League of Nations' mandate of PALESTINE. Transjordan was treated separately from Palestine, however, and its residents were assured that it would not be affected by the establishment of a Jewish homeland in the future. ABDULLAH, Faisal's brother, was chosen to rule Transjordan in 1921. He cooperated closely with the British, who helped create the Arab Legion, a small army later commanded by Sir John GLUBB. In 1928 a treaty with

Britain made Transjordan a constitutional monarchy. A second treaty with the British on Mar. 22, 1946, created the Hashemite Kingdom of Transjordan.

Transjordan opposed the partition of Palestine and joined the other ARAB LEAGUE nations in fighting the new Israeli state in 1948 (see ARAB-ISRAELI WARS). By the end of the war it occupied a section of West Bank territory designated for the Arabs in the United Nations partition plan. The country's name was changed to Jordan in 1949, and in 1950 it formally annexed the West Bank territory, including Old Jerusalem.

Abdullah was assassinated in 1951, and a year later his son Talal was forced to abdicate in favor of Talal's son HUSSEIN I. Hussein established greater independence from Britain, especially after 1956, but his relations with the other Arab countries were somewhat strained.

In the Six-Day War of June 1967, Jordan's forces were routed by the Israelis, who then occupied the West Bank territories. As a result Jordan, which already had many Palestinian refugees, received a new influx. Guerrilla groups were formed among the refugees, and they not only challenged the authority of Hussein but made Jordan a target for Israeli attacks. In 1970 civil war erupted between government and guerrilla forces, and the following year Hussein succeeded in destroying the guerrilla bases in Jordan. At the Arab Summit conference in Rabat in 1974, however, Hussein was forced to agree that the West Bank should become an independent Palestinian state following Israeli withdrawal from the disputed territory. Provisions were made in the 1979 treaty between Israel and Egypt for the negotiation of a permanent settlement regarding control over the West Bank. Jordan, however, like the other Arab states, condemned the treaty.

J. ROWLAND ILLICK

Bibliography: Copeland, Paul W., *The Land and People of Jordan* (1972); Faddah, Mohammad I., *The Middle East in Transition: A Study of Jordan's Foreign Policy* (1974); Glubb, John B., *Syria, Lebanon and Jordan* (1967); Johnston, Charles, *The Brink of Jordan* (1972); Mishal, Shaul, *West Bank/East Bank: The Palestinians in Jordan, 1949–1967* (1978); Kanovsky, Eliyahu, *The Economic Development of Jordan* (1976); Nyrop, Richard F., et al., *Area Handbook for the Hashemite Kingdom of Jordan* (1974); Patai, Raphael, *The Kingdom of Jordan* (1958); Vatikiotis, P. J., *Politics and the Military in Jordan: A Study of the Arab Legion, 1921–1957* (1967).

Jordan, Barbara

Noted for her eloquent speaking style, Barbara Jordan, b. Houston, Tex., Feb. 21, 1936, was a Democratic representative from Houston to the U.S. House of Representatives from 1973 to 1979. As a member of the House Judiciary Committee she impressed nationwide TV audiences during the impeachment hearings concerning President Richard Nixon in 1974. Jordan graduated from Texas Southern University (1956) and was the first black student at Boston University Law School (1956–59). She served as the only woman and the only black in the Texas State Senate (1966–72) and was consulted by President Lyndon B. Johnson on civil rights legislation. She chose not to

Barbara Jordan, the first black U.S. congresswoman from the deep South, defended the cause of the poor and promoted civil-rights legislation during her six years as a representative of Texas. A dynamic speaker and a former lawyer, she served on the House Judiciary Committee during the Nixon impeachment proceedings.

run for reelection to Congress in 1978; since leaving the House, Jordan has written an autobiography and taught at the University of Texas.

Bibliography: Jordan, Barbara, with Shelby Hearon, *Barbara Jordan: A Self-Portrait* (1979).

Jordan, Camille   [zhor-dahn', kah-meel']

The French mathematician Marie Ennemond Camille Jordan, b. Jan. 5, 1838, d. Jan. 22, 1922, was highly regarded by his contemporaries for his work in algebra and group theory. He is best remembered today for his proof that a simply closed CURVE divides a plane into exactly two regions. He originated the concept of functions of bounded variation and is known especially for his definition of the length of a curve. He also generalized the criteria for convergence of Fourier series (see FOURIER ANALYSIS).

Jordan studied mathematics at the École Polytechnique and from 1873 taught there and at the Collège de France. He was particularly interested in the theory of finite groups. Two of his best-known students, Sophus LIE and Felix KLEIN, drew upon Jordan's studies of the groups of all movements in three-dimensional space to produce their own theories of continuous and discontinuous groups.   J. W. DAUBEN

Jordan, June

June Jordan, b. Harlem, N.Y., July 9, 1936, is a noted American poet and educator who, with Terri Bush, has edited a collection of the writings of black and Puerto Rican children, *Voice of the Children* (1970). *His Own Where* (1971), a collection of paintings of black people, features poetic commentary by Jordan. She has also written works for young adults, including *Dry Victories* (1972). The latest collection of her disciplined, intense poetry is *Things That I Do in the Dark* (1977). Jordan's honors include the 1970–71 Prix de Rome in Environmental Design.

Jordan River

The Jordan River (Hebrew: Iha-Yarden; Arabic: Nahr al-Urdunn), the longest river of Israel and Jordan, meanders for 359 km (223 mi) from Mount HERMON to the DEAD SEA. It drains an area of 16,000 km² (6,000 mi²). The headwaters of the Jordan descend from the Anti-Lebanon Mountains and join in the Hula Basin. The river flows along the west side of the Golan Heights to the Sea of GALILEE (Lake Tiberias) at 209 m (686 ft) below sea level. Following the 1967 Arab-Israeli War, the river formed the border between Israel and Jordan south of the Sea of Galilee. After receiving its main tributary, the Yarmuk, it winds sluggishly through the Ghor depression to the north end of the Dead Sea (295 m/1,296 ft below sea level), where it empties.

The Jordan is not used for navigation because it is shallow and has a twisted course. It is very important, however, for irrigation in a hot and arid region. Cereal, corn, peanut, and fruit crops are grown there. The Hula Basin, previously a huge swamp, was drained in the 1950s and is now productive agricultural land. Diversion of the Jordan's waters for irrigation and hydroelectric power remains a matter of dispute between Israel and Jordan. The main crossing point is the Allenby Bridge on the road from Jerusalem to Amman.

The Jordan River valley was one of the earliest sites of wheat cultivation in the world. Its oldest settlement is JERICHO, dating from about 8000 BC. Of great importance in biblical times, the river was the site of Jesus' baptism.

Jørgensen, Jen Johannes   [yur'-gen-sen, yen yoh-hahn'-es]

The Danish poet and biographer Jen Johannes Jørgensen, b. Nov. 6, 1866, d. May 29, 1956, began his career as a follower of the proponent of naturalism George BRANDES, but later abandoned naturalism for mysticism and symbolism. After becoming a Roman Catholic in 1896, he devoted himself to writing lives of the saints, notably Francis of Assisi (1907; Eng.

trans., 1912) and Catherine of Siena (1915; Eng. trans., 1938). His seven-volume autobiography (1916-28) was translated into English in 1928-29.

Bibliography: Jones, W. Glyn, *Johannes Jørgensen* (1969).

Joseph

Joseph, the 11th son of JACOB and the first son of Jacob's favorite wife, RACHEL, is the biblical hero in the drama of Genesis 37-50. Joseph's favored status and his coat of many colors, a gift from his father, caused his brothers to be jealous, and they staged his accidental "death." Joseph was actually taken to Egypt, where his ability to interpret dreams brought him into favor with the pharaoh. Joseph became a high Egyptian official. When, during a famine, his unsuspecting brothers sought grain in Egypt, the forgiving Joseph—whom his brothers did not at first recognize—arranged a family reunion. Thus the whole family of Jacob moved to Egypt and lived there until the Exodus.

Joseph, Chief

Chief Joseph was one of the Nez Percé Indian chiefs responsible for the tribe's skillful retreat from pursuing U.S. Army troops during the Nez Percé War (1877). Under his leadership the small band successfully eluded and then withstood attacks from the army during a retreat of more than 1,600 km (1,000 mi) from Oregon to Montana, where they were forced to surrender only 48 km (30 mi) from the Canadian border.

Chief Joseph, c.1840-1904, was a chief of the NEZ PERCÉ Indian tribe. He is remembered principally for his leadership during the hostilities that broke out between the U.S. Army and the Nez Percé in 1877. Friendly with the whites until then, the Nez Percé had once occupied much territory in the region where Washington, Oregon, and Idaho adjoin. Under the terms of the Stevens Treaty of 1855, the Nez Percé agreed to cede much of their land to the U.S. government in return for the guarantee of a large reservation in Oregon and Idaho. When gold was discovered (1863) in Oregon, however, the government demanded that the Nez Percé relinquish this part of the reservation also. Chief Joseph resisted but later agreed to move peacefully with his people to the Lapwai Reservation in Idaho.

Fighting broke out in 1877 when young Nez Percé warriors retaliated for what they considered outrageous acts by the white settlers. In the war that followed, Joseph showed remarkable skill in military tactics by defeating larger U.S. forces in several battles. He then led his people on a retreat of more than a thousand miles over mountainous terrain in an effort to reach Canada. On Sept. 30, 1877, however, federal troops overtook the Nez Percé only 48 km (30 mi) from the border. Because most of his warriors were dead or wounded and his people were starving, Chief Joseph surrendered, saying, "I will fight no more forever." Sent to the Indian Territory in Oklahoma, the Nez Percé were allowed to return to Idaho in 1883-84. Joseph died on the Colville Indian Reservation in the state of Washington.   KENNETH M. STEWART

Bibliography: Beal, Merrill D., *"I Will Fight No More Forever"* and *Chief Joseph and the Nez Perce War* (1963; repr. 1973, 1975).

Joseph, Father

François Leclerc du Tremblay, b. Nov. 4, 1577, d. Dec. 18, 1638, known as Father Joseph, was a French Capuchin friar who was the advisor of the statesman Cardinal RICHELIEU. Known as the *éminence grise,* "gray eminence," he carried out sensitive diplomatic missions and is thought to have influenced French entry into the Thirty Years' War.

Joseph, Saint

Saint Joseph was the husband of MARY, the mother of Jesus Christ. Given prominent attention in the first two chapters of Matthew and Luke, Joseph is portrayed as a carpenter in Nazareth, a righteous descendant of Bethlehem's David, and a kind husband and father. Although little else is known of his life, Joseph's faithful cooperation in the birth of Christ earned him sainthood. He is venerated by Orthodox and by Roman Catholics, who consider him the patron saint of workers. Feast days: May 1 (Western); first Sunday after Christmas (Eastern).

Joseph Andrews

The History of the Adventures of Joseph Andrews and of his Friend, Mr. Abraham Adams (1742) was the first of Henry FIELDING's novels. Begun as a burlesque of Samuel Richardson's PAMELA, the book developed into what Fielding saw as a new kind of English comic novel, or "comic epic poem in prose," modeled on Cervantes' *Don Quixote* and substituting social satire and literary playfulness for the emotional and didactic intensity of Richardson. Dismissed after resisting the lustful advances of his London employer Lady Booby, Joseph sets out to return to the country and to marry his sweetheart Fanny. En route he meets Parson Adams, with whom he shares a series of comic adventures. Like Don Quixote, they are innocent and courageous figures, and the novel satirizes the knaves and fools who persecute them. Many of these are both traditional comic characters and representative 18th-century English social types as Fielding saw them. In the end, Joseph is revealed to be the son of a gentleman, kidnapped as a baby by gypsies; the book concludes happily as he and Fanny marry. A film version of *Joseph Andrews* was released in 1977.   JOHN RICHETTI

Bibliography: Battestin, Martin C., *The Moral Basis of Fielding's Art: A Study of Joseph Andrews* (1959); Goldberg, Homer, *The Art of Joseph Andrews* (1969).

Joseph of Arimathea   [ar-ih-muh-thee'-uh]

In the New Testament, Joseph of Arimathea was a rich, devout member of the Sanhedrin who would not consent to that body's decision to put Jesus Christ to death (Matt. 27:57; Mark 15:43; Luke 23:50, 51). After the crucifixion of Jesus, Joseph asked the Roman procurator Pontius Pilate for Jesus' body and, with the assistance of Nicodemus, buried the body in a garden tomb near Golgotha (John 19:38-42; Matt. 25:57-60). Joseph became a popular figure in apocalyptic literature. Medieval legends connect Joseph with the Holy Grail (see GRAIL, HOLY) and with Glastonbury, England, where his staff was believed to have taken root and grown into a thorn tree that flowered every Christmas Eve.   DOUGLAS EZELL

Bibliography: Griffith, Leonard, *Gospel Characters* (1976).

Joseph I, Holy Roman Emperor

Joseph I, b. July 26, 1678, d. Apr. 17, 1711, king of Hungary from 1687, succeeded his father, LEOPOLD I, as emperor in 1705. The War of the SPANISH SUCCESSION continued throughout his reign, and the imperial armies under EUGENE OF SAVOY won victories in Italy, Germany, and Flanders. Joseph's death, without male issue and the succession of his brother CHARLES VI, however, altered the course of the war. The allies who had earlier supported Charles's claim to the Spanish throne abandoned him, fearing a united Spain and Austria. During Joseph's reign the Hungarian revolt led by Ferenc II Rákóczy was finally suppressed in 1711.

Joseph II, Holy Roman Emperor

Joseph II, b. Mar. 13, 1741, d. Feb. 20, 1790, became emperor and coregent of the Habsburg monarchy with his mother, MARIA THERESA, after the death of his father, FRANCIS I, in 1765. When his mother died in 1780, he inherited the crowns of Bohemia and Hungary. Ruling by himself from then on, Joseph pursued a policy of centralization and reform designed to enhance the power of his state and the welfare of his subjects.

Driven by a passion for reason and order, he was intolerant of opposition. He created a secret police and employed military force to implement the thousands of laws and edicts that flooded out of the Vienna court. With his curious blend of humanitarian ideals and autocratic methods, Joseph II exemplified all of the characteristics usually associated with 18th-century enlightened despotism.

Joseph's reform program included the abolition of serfdom, freedom of the press, the elimination of torture and the death penalty, and an attempt to establish equality before the law. He tried to ease the fiscal burdens of the lower classes by introducing a single tax based on land. He granted official toleration to Protestants and Jews and dissolved the monasteries of contemplative Catholic orders, earmarking their revenues for the support of hospitals. In his relentless efforts to unify the administrative structure of his monarchy, Joseph sought to diminish the influence of provincial diets (legislatures) as well as the special privileges of the aristocracy. He decreed the use of German for governmental business throughout his domains, including his distant possessions in Italy and the Austrian Netherlands.

Fourteen years before the French Revolution, Joseph warned his sister MARIE ANTOINETTE, queen of France: "The revolution, if you fail to avert it, will be an atrocious one." His own actions, however, provoked widespread discontent among the peoples he ruled. At the time of his death he faced mounting unrest in his Austrian and Bohemian lands and open revolt in Hungary and the Low Countries. While some of his reforms survived, many were revoked by his successor, LEOPOLD II.   JOHN A. MEARS

Bibliography: Bernard, P. P., *Joseph II* (1968); Blanning, T. C. W., *Joseph II and Enlightened Despotism* (1970); Padover, Saul K., *Revolutionary Emperor: Joseph Second of Austria*, rev. ed. (1967).

Josephine

Josephine became empress of France as the consort of NAPOLEON I. Born in Martinique on June 23, 1763, she was originally named Marie Josèphe Rose Tascher de La Pagerie. She married Alexandre, vicomte de Beauharnais in 1779 and had two children by him, Eugène and Hortense (see BEAUHARNAIS family). Their marriage became one of estrangement and mutual infidelity.

After Beauharnais was guillotined (1794), Josephine became a leading figure in the salon society of Paris. She met Napoléon Bonaparte and married him on Mar. 9, 1796, to assure security and social position for herself and her children. However, she soon became involved in numerous affairs, scandalizing the Bonaparte clan.

Josephine was crowned empress by Napoleon in 1804, but her failure to bear him a male heir led to the annulment of their marriage in 1810. She withdrew to Malmaison and lived in imperial style until her death on May 29, 1814. Josephine contributed to Napoleon's success by serving as a link with the French bourgeoisie and by organizing her court without the stifling regulations of formal European courts.

DONALD D. HORWARD

Bibliography: Castelot, André, *Josephine*, trans. by Denise Folliot (1967); Epton, Nina, *Josephine: The Empress and Her Children* (1976); Knapton, Ernest, *Empress Josephine* (1963).

Josephson, Brian David

The English physicist Brian David Josephson, b. Jan. 4, 1940, shared the Nobel Prize for physics in 1973 for his theoretical predictions regarding the quantum tunneling of a super-current through a thin insulating barrier separating two superconductors. Josephson earned his Ph.D. degree in physics at Cambridge University in 1964 and has taught and conducted research there since 1967.

Bibliography: Anderson, Philip W., "How Josephson Discovered his Effect," *Physics Today*, Nov. 1970.

Josephus, Flavius   [joh-see'-fuhs, flay'-vee-uhs]

Flavius Josephus, b. AD 37, d. after 93, was a Jewish historian whose works are invaluable sources for the history of the Jews under Roman domination. A Pharisee, originally named Joseph ben Matthias, he reluctantly joined the revolt against Rome in AD 66 and served as commander in Galilee until captured by the Romans in 67. Through the patronage of Vespasian, he later became a Roman citizen. Josephus's *The Jewish War* (75-79), a description of the tragic events of the revolt, is based to a large extent on his firsthand knowledge. His *Jewish Antiquities* (93), although covering the history of the Jews from the Creation on, gives a particularly full account of the Maccabees and the dynasty of Herod. Josephus has been criticized for his subservience to the Romans, but he was a passionate defender of Jewish religion and culture, as shown in his apologia entitled *Against Apion* as well as in his historical works.

Bibliography: Josephus, Flavius, *Works*, Loeb Classical Library ed., trans. by H. St. John Thackeray, R. Marcus, and L. H. Feldman (1926-65); Thackeray, H. St. John, *Josephus, the Man and the Historian* (1929); Williamson, Geoffrey A., *The World of Josephus* (1965).

Josetsu   [joh-sayt'-soo]

Japanese landscape artist Josetsu, fl. 1405-18, was a master of *suibokuga*, or Chinese-style ink painting. Little is known of his life, except that he was a Zen priest at Shokoku-ji in Kyoto and the teacher of SHUBUN.

A colophon to Josetsu's *Catching a Catfish with a Gourd* (Taizoin, Myoshinji, Kyoto) refers to its being in a "new style," which presumably means the incorporation of a Southern Sung–type landscape setting into an illustration of a Zen allegory. Other works attest to his mastery of the Southern Sung styles of MA YÜAN and LIANG K'AI.

BARBARA BRENNAN FORD

Bibliography: Fontein, Jan, and Hickman, Money, *Zen Painting and Calligraphy* (1970).

Joshua, Book of   [jahsh'-oo-uh]

Joshua is the sixth book of the Old Testament of the BIBLE. It is named for the leader who succeeded MOSES and led Israel in the successful conquest of CANAAN, the Promised Land. The book is divided into three parts: the conquest of Canaan during Joshua's three major campaigns (chaps. 1-12), including the fall of Jericho (chap. 6), the siege of Gibeon, and Joshua's victory while the sun and moon stood still (chap. 10); the division of Canaan by tribes (chaps. 13-22); and Joshua's farewell speeches and death (chaps. 23-24).

The Book of Joshua forms part of the Deuteronomistic History, the collective name given by scholars to the books of DEUTERONOMY, Joshua, JUDGES, 1 and 2 SAMUEL, and 1 and 2 KINGS, all of which appear to have been compiled by the same editor or editors.

This history was recorded during the time of Josiah (c.640-609 BC) and revised around 550 BC. Joshua is based on earlier sources, however; some parts of the text date from the premonarchial period. Because the book was edited almost 600 years after the conquest of Canaan (c.1225 BC), the story of that conquest must be used with caution as a historical source.   J. J. M. ROBERTS

Bibliography: Soggin, J. A., *Joshua, A Commentary* (1972).

Joshua tree

The Joshua tree, *Yucca brevifolia*, a yucca plant belonging to the family Agavaceae, is found in North American desert and

The Joshua tree, Y. brevifolia, *with its unusually shaped branches and spiked leaves, adds beauty to the deserts of southern California.*

semidesert areas. It has bayonetlike leaves (stiff with long points) and showy white flowers, which are fragrant at night. The flowers are borne on a tall stalk.   DIANNE FAHSELT

Josiah, King of Judah   [joh-sy'-uh]

Josiah was the king of Judah, ancient Israel's southern kingdom, from c.640 to 609 BC. According to 2 Kings 22 and 23, his reign was noted for religious reforms. A book of the law, the core of the biblical book of DEUTERONOMY, was discovered in the Temple during repair work. This law prohibited all altars outside Jerusalem and thus made the worship of Baal and other foreign gods practically impossible. Josiah died at Megiddo in a battle with Egypt. His attempts to restore the kingdom of David were unsuccessful.

Josquin des Prez   [zhohs-kan' day pray']

Josquin des Prez, b. c.1440, d. Aug. 27, 1521, was a celebrated composer of the Renaissance and one of the most influential figures in the history of Western music. Born in the region of Hainaut (in present-day Belgium), he probably received his musical training at Cambrai, France. In 1459 he became a singer at the cathedral in Milan and was employed there until the end of 1472. He then passed into the service of Galeazzo Sforza, duke of Milan. After Galeazzo's death in 1476, Josquin joined the entourage of the duke's brother, Cardinal Ascanio Sforza, with whom he remained probably until September 1486, when he became a papal singer in Rome. He then began a period of traveling in Italy, France, and the Low Countries. In the papal chapel again from June 1489 through November 1494, he was nominated for several important benefices by the pope. After a period in France (1501) and then in Italy (1503-04) at the court of Ferrara, Josquin returned to Hainaut in May 1504, where he served as provost of the local church at Condé until his death.

Josquin's mastery of every important musical genre of his time is evidenced by his surviving works, which include 19 masses, about 100 motets, some 70 French chansons, and a handful of instrumental pieces and Italian frottole (part songs). These were published widely both during his lifetime and long after his death. His musical style was the product of two cultures: the north, where he was born and educated and to which he later returned and the south, where he reached artistic maturity and spent many of the most productive years of his life. The techniques and styles of the two regions coexist in his music, and he had recourse to them throughout his long career.

In many of his works the contrapuntal artifices of the Franco-Netherlanders and the chordal, harmonically controlled style of the Italians are fused into a rich and expressive musical language that has as its primary goal the perfect

union of words and music. These works set a standard for composers of the later Renaissance that was often emulated but never surpassed.   FRANK A. D'ACCONE

Bibliography: Brown, Howard Mayer, *Music in the Renaissance* (1976); Lowinsky, Edward E., ed., *Josquin des Prez* (1976); Reese, Gustave, *Music in the Renaissance*, rev. ed. (1959).

Jotunheimen   [yoh'-tun-hay-men]

The Jotunheimen (Norwegian for "home of the giants"), the highest mountain group in Scandinavia, is located in south central Norway. It extends for about 110 km (70 mi) from the Jostedalsbreen ice cap and is surrounded by lakes. Glittertind, topped by a glacier, is the tallest peak, with an elevation of 2,481 m (8,104 ft). The setting for many Scandinavian legends, the sparsely populated Jotunheimen is now a tourist center attracting skiers and mountain climbers.

joule   [jool]

The joule is the unit of energy or work in the mks (meter-kilogram-second) system of units. It is the WORK done when a force of 1 newton acts through a distance of 1 meter, and is thus synonymous with a newton-meter of work. One joule is equivalent to 1 watt-second, 10^7 ergs, 0.7376 foot-pounds, and 9.48×10^{-4} Btu.

Joule, James Prescott

The British physicist James Prescott Joule, b. Dec. 24, 1818, d. Oct. 11, 1889, is known for his contributions to the science of thermodynamics. In his first major publication (1840), Joule stated that the amount of heat produced by an electric current is proportional to the product of the resistance of the wire and the square of the current. In his study of electrical, chemical, and mechanical energy, Joule observed that the amount of heat produced by each form of energy is proportional to the energy expended. In 1843 he determined a value for the coefficient of equivalence, the amount of energy needed to produce a unit of heat. In 1852, Joule and William Thomson (Lord KELVIN) observed that when a gas expands without performing work, its temperature falls. This Joule-Thomson effect was later applied to refrigeration technology.   SHELDON J. KOPPERL

Bibliography: Crowther, James C., *British Scientists of the Nineteenth Century* (1935); Thomson, Thomas, ed., *The Scientific Papers of James Prescott Joule*, 2 vols. (1884-87); Wood, Alexander, *Joule and the Study of Energy* (1925).

Joule-Thomson effect   [jool'-tahm'-suhn]

The Joule-Thomson effect describes the temperature change of a gas undergoing an ADIABATIC throttling process. Throttling is a thermodynamic process by which the pressure of a flowing gas is reduced, usually by forcing it through a small orifice or a partially closed valve. In throttling, most gases at ordinary initial temperatures experience a Joule-Thomson temperature drop. This is accompanied by an irreversible ENTROPY increase and loss of energy availability.

The Joule-Thomson effect is the principle of most refrigeration, air conditioning, and air liquefaction equipment. It was first identified during 1852-62 by James P. Joule and William Thomson.   GARY S. SETTLES

Bibliography: Van Wylen, Gordon, and Sonntag, Richard, *Fundamentals of Classical Thermodynamics* (1976).

Journal of the American Medical Association

With 250,000 subscribers, most of them physicians, the *Journal of the American Medical Association* is the official publication of that organization. Established in 1848, the *Journal* is published weekly; it contains reports on clinical medicine and professional news and directories.

journalism

Traditionally journalism is regarded as the collecting, writing, editing, and publishing of news, or comment upon news in

NEWSPAPERS and periodicals. The scope of journalism has, however, expanded to include the presentation of material of current interest or wide popular appeal in a variety of media, notably radio and television—which are commonly referred to as electronic journalism.

OVERVIEW

Despite the expanded definition of journalism, timeliness remains the principal concern of the journalist, whose main functions are reporting the news and offering interpretive comments. The purpose of the journalist is to report events as they appear at the moment of writing or speaking, not to give a definitive analysis of a situation. Although a journalist may write an account that is entertaining as well as newsworthy, one who writes principally to entertain is not a journalist.

Journalism has sometimes been called "literature in a hurry," a description that recognizes the journalist's skill and also suggests that the necessarily hurried nature of the product might lead one to expect poor and careless writing. Dictionary definitions of journalism that emphasize such terms as *hasty, incomplete, inaccurate,* and *transitory* describe journalistic failure rather than the sense of social responsibility and professional discipline that characterizes good journalism. Historians have often found that on-the-spot reports of great events not only have literary impact but also are remarkably accurate and complete, containing valid assessments of the importance of the event.

Forms of Journalism. The oldest and most widely identified form of journalism is print journalism. Periodicals printed at regular and stated intervals, including daily and weekly newspapers, journals, and magazines, are in this category, as are pamphlets, newsletters, and books that focus on public affairs. Equally a part of journalism are the news reports and commentaries delivered on television and radio, as well as these media's public-affairs documentaries and direct broadcasts of news events. Newsreels, motion-picture documentaries, and videotape also qualify.

Adjuncts to the mass media that perform journalistic roles include the wire services, which collect and distribute news and pictures to the newspapers, broadcast stations, and news magazines; and the syndicates, which offer background news and pictures, commentary, and entertainment features.

The Journalistic Community. Most commonly identified as journalists are reporters, writers, editors, photographers, and columnists who work for newspapers, news agencies, syndicates, news magazines, and magazines devoted largely to public affairs. Reporters, writers, editors, news announcers, commentators, cinematographers, and photographers in radio, television, and film are also journalists, but they tend to associate themselves with the media that they represent. All are, however, part of the journalistic community, commonly referred to as the press and once known widely as the FOURTH ESTATE, whose principal function was to observe and comment upon the conduct of government. This definition of the journalistic community can be expanded to include writers in magazines and the authors of public-affairs books, who offer a deeper and more detailed examination of subjects than is possible in daily journalism. The broadcast journalist is limited by demands of immediacy in reporting news and by the confines of space and time. If newspapers elect to do so, they can present far more coverage, with more opportunity for interpretation, than the broadcast media can. On the other hand, television can have greater impact and reach larger audiences.

HISTORY

Journalism in the broad sense of the communication of news in a permanent form is probably as ancient as the development of writing itself. The origins of journalism in the Western world are, however, generally traced to Rome.

Early Development. In imperial Rome the Roman Senate posted the ACTA DIURNA, which reported official actions, news of personages, deaths, and gladiators' contests. Scribes made up to 2,000 copies to dispatch throughout the empire. Fifteen centuries passed before similar journalism appeared in other parts of Europe.

Beginning in the 8th century AD, however, China developed a systematic program for collecting information, a program that was to last for 1,200 years. The brilliant T'ang dynasty produced a monthly report called the *Tching-pao;* it became a weekly in 1361 and a daily in 1830. Printed from wooden blocks until Pi Sheng made (c.1045) movable ideographs from baked clay, it was reproduced on paper invented by the Chinese. The *Tching-pau* (called the *Peking Gazette* as a daily) disappeared with the empire in 1911, but China's inventions prospered in western Europe.

There Johannes GUTENBERG made movable type from lead in the 1450s and adapted a winepress for printing. Before 1500 every large city in Europe had a printing press. The development of printing provided a way to distribute the news traditionally disseminated by news hawkers, ballad singers, one-item broadsheets, and letter writers such as those employed by the great banking and trading houses.

European Roots. Three news sheets printed in Germany in 1609 are the oldest known newspaper copies to survive. The publication of corantos carrying foreign news was generally permitted, and Amsterdam led in their printing. Thomas ARCHER, Nicholas Bourne, and Nathaniel Butter introduced the coranto to London in 1622; shortly afterward it became the *Weekly Newes.* The first Paris weekly, the *Gazette,* began in 1631. The Swedish court paper, which was started in 1645 and holds the current record for continuous publication, still appears.

Early journalism operated under grave handicaps: government licensing, bans on reporting domestic governmental news, and the stern laws of criminal seditious libel. William CAXTON had established the first English press in 1476; in 1530, Henry VIII instituted a licensing system that lasted until 1695. During Oliver Cromwell's Commonwealth (1649–60), journalism was relatively free to report the contending sides, and John Milton wrote his great plea for freedom of expression, AREOPAGITICA (1644). London's first daily, Samuel Buckley's *Daily Courant,* began in 1702. As English intellectual activity flowered, the famed essay papers sold widely; Joseph ADDISON and Sir Richard STEELE led with the *Tatler* and *Spectator.* Daniel Defoe's *Review* and Jonathan Swift's *Examiner* probed sociopolitical issues as did Dr. Samuel Johnson and John Wilkes. The TIMES first appeared in London in 1785; another surviving great paper, the *Neue Zürcher Zeitung* of Zurich, dates from 1780.

Beginnings of American Journalism. The English colonists in America imported their first printing press to Cambridge in 1638 for Harvard College. An exiled Londoner, Benjamin HARRIS, printed one issue of *Publick Occurrences* in Boston in 1690, but it was promptly banned for saying too much. John CAMPBELL's *News-Letter* of 1704 was properly cautious. The best colonial papers were James Franklin's *New England Courant* (1721–26) and Benjamin FRANKLIN's *Pennsylvania-Gazette* (1729), both well printed and emulating London literary models.

Before and during the Revolutionary War, Samuel Adams used the *Boston Gazette* to promote the patriot cause, assisted by Isaiah THOMAS and his *Massachusetts Spy.* The sedition trial (1735) of John Peter ZENGER in New York and his acquittal had paved the way for printers to advocate revolution in the colonial weeklies of 1776, although not all of them were anti-British. Postwar reaction, however, brought the ALIEN AND SEDITION ACTS of 1798 and caused harassment of journalists until the concept of seditious libel finally expired in the United States around 1800.

19th-Century Expansion. Methodical efforts to collect the news had been made by the beginning of the 19th century. As journalism expanded on both sides of the Atlantic, the need for cooperative newsgathering became apparent. Shipping and business news began to be collected in coffeehouses located in coastal cities. A semaphore system for speeding news across the continent augmented horse expresses and boats. The first major news agency, Agence Havas, was founded (1835) in Paris by Charles Havas.

In the United States, Samuel Topliff began to meet incoming sailing ships to gather European news for his coffeehouse. The New York dailies soon competed with harbor boats and used pony expresses and homing pigeons to speed the flow of news from other ports and the capital in Washington. In the 1830s railroads became available for enterprising news collectors, and, in 1844, Samuel F. B. Morse perfected the magnetic telegraph, which overcame the problems of long-distance communication. England and France were joined underwater by cable in 1851, New York and London in 1866.

To share the costs of gathering foreign and Washington news, the New York dailies founded (1848) the New York Associated Press. Three more agencies, named for their founders, followed: Dr. Bernhard Wolff's Berlin agency (1849), Paul Julius REUTER's in London (1851), and Guglielmo Stefani's in Turin (1853). Soon all four of these agencies and Agence Havas were interchanging news.

Faster and improved printing presses were needed if more popularly supported dailies than the limited-interest mercantile and politically oriented papers were to develop. A steam-operated printing press developed (1811) for the *Times* of London by Friedrich Koenig of Saxony was soon improved upon by David Napier and America's Hoe and Company, headed by Richard HOE. When Benjamin Henry DAY proved that a paper specializing in human-interest news and selling for a penny could make money, the first mass-circulation journalism was at hand. His *New York Sun*, founded in 1833, used new presses, and its sales reached 30,000 by 1837—as many copies as all the rest of its 11 New York daily competitors had sold in 1833. James Gordon BENNETT combined the new enterprise spirit of the mercantile papers and the human-interest style of the *Sun*, making his *New York Herald* (founded 1835) the leading penny paper in the next decade.

A major function of journalism beyond news enterprise was commenting on the news and exercising opinion leadership. This function was characteristic of the colonial weeklies and the political papers that appeared with the new government, such as the Whig *National Intelligencer* (founded 1800) and Andrew Jackson's *Washington Globe* (founded 1830). Horace GREELEY's *New York Tribune* (founded 1841) set the pace in the mid-19th century with its emphasis upon serious discussion, editorial argument, and interpretation of events. Henry J. RAYMOND gave The NEW YORK TIMES (founded 1851) a more conventional tone, using the *Times* of London as a model and emphasizing deeper coverage of European social and political change.

The American Civil War provided daily news stories; the war-generated economy spurred journalism in the North, even as blockade and scarcity impeded it in the South. Faster and larger presses and the use of stereotype plates (first used by Hoe and Company in 1861) to run the same edition on duplicate presses enabled the leading New York papers to expand their readership. New papers prospered in Cincinnati and Chicago; dailies in Boston, Philadelphia, and Baltimore vied with the New York dailies in coverage of war news.

Between 1865 and 1900 a dynamic capitalism utilizing vast resources and new machines transformed the American economy. The change manifested itself in urbanization; the development of national networks of railroad, telegraph, and telephone lines; harnessing of electricity for light and power; and an improved and more extensive educational system. As part of this transformation, the number of daily and weekly newspapers as well as magazines and their combined circulation increased during the last three decades of the 19th century.

The new, emerging society needed a new journalism—one that concentrated increasingly on impartial news reporting, avoiding partisan political entanglements, crusading in the public interest, and catering in style and subject matter to the concerns of a new audience of working people, immigrants, and city dwellers. The architect of that New Journalism was Joseph PULITZER, an immigrant who devoted his immense intellectual capacity to journalism. He founded (1878) the ST. LOUIS POST-DISPATCH and gave the *New York World* preeminence after 1883 by developing liberal, aggressive editorial pages and combining popular appeal and a crusading spirit in news reporting. Edward Wyllis SCRIPPS developed a similar approach in the Middle West. William Randolph HEARST, who gained prominence in San Francisco and after 1895 chal-

lenged Pulitzer in New York, was the most sensational and bombastic in his support of labor unions and attacks on big business. A circulation battle between Pulitzer and Hearst ensued and brought the name of YELLOW JOURNALISM to the era.

Magazines became an important force in the reform era at the turn of the century. Some of the most influential were Edwin Lawrence GODKIN's NATION, Cyrus H. K. CURTIS's LADIES HOME JOURNAL, and the hard-hitting *Collier's* and *Cosmopolitan*. Among the most outstanding was S. S McCLURE's monthly, which carried Ida M. TARBELL's exposé of the Standard Oil Company and Lincoln STEFFEN's "Shame of the Cities." These were the journalists that Theodore Roosevelt labeled MUCKRAKERS, and they wore the label proudly.

By the turn of the century, journalism instruction had begun in several leading universities. Journalism schools were organized at the University of Missouri (1908) and Columbia University (1912).

MODERN JOURNALISM
The publisher Viscount Alfred Harmsworth NORTHCLIFFE rocked British journalism in 1896 with his sensationalized *Daily Mail*, forerunner of the popular tabloids in Britain during the 20th century. The *Daily Telegraph*, begun in 1855 as Britain's first penny daily, became a quality competitor to the *Times*, the MANCHESTER GUARDIAN (founded 1821), and the *Morning Post* (1772–1937). In Paris Le FIGARO (founded 1826) held its place in circulation, and *France-Soire* (founded 1844) achieved the largest evening circulation in France, while Le MONDE took over *Le Temps*'s opinion leadership after World War II. The great *Frankfurter Zeitung* (1856) reappeared as the *Frankfurter Allgemeine Zeitung* in 1949. With the *Times*, the *Guardian*, and *Le Monde* it ranked among world leaders in newspaper journalism.

News Agencies. The major world news agencies grew in size and importance. Reuters of Britain followed the lines of empire to Africa and Asia; Havas and its post-World War II successor, Agence France-Presse, became a second worldwide competitor. The United States developed the other news agencies: the Associated Press (AP), reorganized in 1900; the United Press (UP), founded by Scripps in 1907; and the International News Service, founded by Hearst in 1909 and merged with UP to form United Press International (UPI) in 1958. In the 1970s, AP and UPI collected and distributed news in more than 100 countries, using satellites, radio teleprinters, cables, and teletype circuits to transmit words or pictures around the world within one minute. Other nations had national news services, the most important of which was Tass in the USSR.

Expansion and Consolidation. A great expansion of the media took place when broadcasting and motion pictures appeared by the 1920s. The same decade ushered in the tabloid era. The popular NEW YORK DAILY NEWS was founded in 1919; under Joseph Medill Patterson it became for a time the second-largest daily in the world, before television made inroads on the sales of big-city papers. Robert R. McCORMICK's CHICAGO TRIBUNE, affiliated with the *Daily News*, had the largest circulation of any standard daily.

Among magazines, De Witt WALLACE's READER'S DIGEST (founded 1922) exceeded 18 million in circulation. Highly successful examples of journalism were Henry LUCE's newsmagazine TIME and his LIFE magazine, the leader in photojournalism until the 1970s. Challenging the *New York Times* among the most prestigious newspapers were Katharine GRAHAM's WASHINGTON POST and Otis CHANDLER's LOS ANGELES TIMES, which also united to form a major news agency.

Group ownership of newspapers and conglomerate media ownerships became problems for journalism. In 1935 one newspaper owner, William Randolph Hearst, controlled about 13% of daily circulation and about 24% of Sunday sales. Although the largest daily circulation controlled by one group owner 40 years later was only 6%, the approximate percentage of total daily circulation controlled by group owners had jumped from 41% to 71%. The conglomerates reflected similar consolidation. Samuel NEWHOUSE owned 30 dailies, 11 magazines, and 12 broadcast stations. The *Los Angeles Times* owned giant dailies on Long Island and in Dallas, the *Sporting News*, two cable systems, and three book firms. Rupert

MURDOCH, the Australian owner of 88 worldwide newspapers, in 1977 acquired the *New York Post* and The VILLAGE VOICE, as well as NEW YORK MAGAZINE and *New West*.

Organizations of journalists began to create the means for organized negotiations with owners. Britain's INSTITUTE OF JOURNALISTS, formed in 1884, was joined later by the National Union of Journalists (founded 1907). In France the chief association was the Federation Nationale de la Presse Française. Among the other organizations are the American Newspaper Guild, organized in 1933 and mainly including the staffs of larger dailies and news agencies; the AMERICAN SOCIETY OF NEWSPAPER EDITORS, founded in 1922; and the INTERNATIONAL PRESS INSTITUTE.

Recent Developments. Three characteristics of journalism in the 1960s and 1970s were the intensification of investigative reporting, the rise of alternative forms of journalism, and the development of a writing style to which the term *New Journalism* was reapplied.

The 1960s saw widespread social and political unrest, attacks on the "establishment," criticism of the Vietnam War, racial crisis, and youth protests. Young journalists created underground papers; others practiced advocacy journalism on standard papers and forcefully urged the investigation of social inequalities, business inefficiency or corruption, political machines, and public institutions. The climax came with the determined reporting by the *Washington Post*, which led to the uncovering of the Watergate scandal. Growing out of the movement were journalism reviews, new critical magazines, and improved investigative reporting throughout the press.

Responding to the public interest in much the same spirit as the New Journalism of the late 19th century, the New Journalism of the 1960s involved a new style of nonfiction reportage. Generally it attempted to obtain a view of events from inside the source, instead of relying on the standard information-gathering approach. Its practitioners focused on writing style and quality of description. Among its leaders were Tom Wolfe, Jimmy Breslin, Gay Talese, Truman Capote, and Norman Mailer. Among their vehicles were ESQUIRE, HARPER's, the *Village Voice*, the *New York Herald Tribune* (until its demise in 1966), and *New York Magazine* under editor Clay S. FELKER.

Both print and electronic journalism continue to flourish. In 1978 the United States had approximately 1,760 dailies with a circulation of over 60 million; more than 8,000 weeklies with about 37 million circulation; and 9,782 other periodicals of all types. In 1977, AM radio stations totalled 4,574; FM stations, 3,007; and television stations, 725.   EDWIN EMERY

Bibliography: Agee, Warren K., et al., *Introduction to Mass Communications*, 6th ed. (1979); Desmond, Robert W., *The Information Process: World News Reporting to the Twentieth Century* (1978); Emery, Edwin and Michael, *The Press and America*, 4th ed. (1978); Epstein, Edward J., *Between Fact and Fiction: The Problem of Journalism* (1975); Halberstam, David, *The Powers That Be* (1979); Head, Sydney, *Broadcasting in America*, 3d ed. (1976); Hohenberg, John, *The Professional Journalist*, 3d ed. (1973); Knightly, Phillip, *The First Casualty: From the Crimea to Vietnam: The War Correspondent as Hero, Propagandist and Myth Maker* (1975); Kobre, Sidney, *The Development of American Journalism* (1969); Mills, Nicolaus, *The New Journalism* (1974); Mott, Frank Luther, *American Journalism*, 3d ed. (1962); Pember, Don, *The Mass Media in America*, 2d ed. (1977); Pickett, Calder, *Voices of the Past* (1977); Tebbel, John, *The Media in America* (1974); Wood, James P., *Magazines in the United States*, 3d ed. (1971).

See also: PRESS AGENCIES AND SYNDICATES; RADIO AND TELEVISION BROADCASTING.

Jouvet, Louis   [zhoo-vay', lwee]

One of the greatest French stage actors between the world wars, Louis Jouvet, b. Dec. 24, 1887, d. Aug. 16, 1951, also excelled as a director, scenic and lighting designer, and theorist of acting. Jouvet is best remembered for his roles in plays by Molière and by Jean Giraudoux, whose work he introduced to French audiences, and for his 1923 creation of the comically sly Dr. Knock in Jules Romain's play of the same name. In films Jouvet was especially notable as the priest in *La Kermesse Héroïque* (1935) and as Mosca in *Volpone* (1941).

Joy of Cooking

A cookbook that ranks with Fannie Farmer's *Boston Cooking School Cookbook* (1896) in its impact on the American diet, *Joy of Cooking* has clarified American cooking techniques and considerably enlarged the American cuisine. Written in 1931 by Irma Starkloff Rombauer and her daughter Marion Rombauer Becker (who also provided the original illustrations), the work—now in its 13th edition—is an encyclopedic compendium of classic American and European recipes, lucid explanations of culinary techniques, and detailed discussions of every important aspect of food preparation. A perpetual best-seller, the book to date has sold about 8,000,000 copies.

See also: COOKING.

Joyce, James

Few writers have so profoundly influenced the course of literature as the Irish poet and novelist James Joyce. Since 1922, the year of the publication of ULYSSES, Joyce has been acknowledged as the supreme innovator of modern fiction, the writer who gave the novel a new subject and a new style. The author of *Ulysses* is not a narrator describing a subject outside himself. He is a recorder of what is sometimes called "the stream of consciousness"—the haphazard progress of reflection, with all its paradoxes, irrelevancies, and abrupt shifts of interest. By this means Joyce made his characters the authors of his work while, as creator of both them and their thoughts, he viewed their actions down the long perspective of history and myth, imposing structure on what, at first, seems merely random. To some of the first readers of *Ulysses* it seemed that Joyce had portrayed the human condition in its entirety. To T. S. Eliot the book had "the importance of a scientific discovery." Edmund Wilson called him "the great poet of a new phase of human consciousness." The dissenting voices were mostly those of moralists shocked by Joyce's sexual and scatological frankness. In the 1980s this no longer seems worth noticing, but it is important to remember that *Ulysses* has been legally available in the United States only since 1933.

James Augustine Aloysius Joyce, the eldest of ten children of John Joyce, a tax collector, was born in a suburb of Dublin on Feb. 2, 1882. His father, whose coarse but occasionally charming character is given fictional form in A PORTRAIT OF THE ARTIST AS A YOUNG MAN, was a heavy drinker and a fugitive from debt. The family moved many times while Joyce attended Clongowes Wood College, a respectable boarding school, and Belvedere College, a Dublin day school. Both were Jesuit institutions, and Joyce's Catholic upbringing, intended to prepare him for the priesthood, left an indelible mark on his writing. Stephen Dedalus, the autobiographical hero of *A Portrait*, bids farewell to family, country, and religion, but as he does so, he names the subjects that were to occupy all Joyce's fiction.

In 1898, Joyce entered University College, Dublin, where he graduated four years later with a degree in modern languages. He then left for Paris to study medicine but was soon recalled by his mother's final illness. In Dublin he worked as a

The Irish author James Joyce was the seminal influence on the development of the 20th-century novel. Joyce's innovations included stream of consciousness writing, erudite wordplay, and the use of literary epiphany. Joyce's novel Ulysses (1922), regarded as his masterpiece, fused the Homeric tradition with the modern literary sensibility.

teacher, published a few poems and sketches, and won a prize in a music contest. Like his father, Joyce had a fine tenor voice. In June 1904 he met Nora Barnacle, a girl from the west of Ireland who was working as a waitress in a Dublin hotel. She was to remain his lifelong companion, although they did not marry until 1931, long after the birth of their two children. In October 1904 they left for Pola (also Pula) on the Adriatic coast of Italy, where Joyce had been offered a job as a language teacher. For the next ten years they lived in Pola, Trieste, and briefly, in Rome—where Joyce spent an unhappy period as a bank clerk.

Joyce first thought of himself as a poet, and while still a student he had written numerous poems and prose sketches in his notebooks. These sketches, which he called "epiphanies," were the embryo of his later work. In an epiphany—literally a "showing forth" of inner truth—Joyce hoped to portray the nature of reality so faithfully as to reveal its significance without further comment. This was, in fact, an extreme form of the naturalism that Joyce admired in other writers: Gustave Flaubert and Henrik Ibsen. Before leaving Dublin he had begun work on Stephen Hero (1944), a sprawling and formless autobiographical work that later became the basis of A Portrait. His first publication, however, was Chamber Music (1907), a volume of poems that owes much to the French symbolists and to the tradition of the "art song." The imagery of Joyce's poems is delicate but not sufficiently anchored in reality: he found his true métier when describing the sights and smells of Dublin, or, in an unforgettable passage from A Portrait, the color of the dirty bath water at his boarding school. In Trieste, and later in Zurich, Switzerland, Joyce found a publisher for Dubliners (1914)—a volume of short stories—and A Portrait—which first appeared in serial form (1914-15) in The Egoist, a British avant-garde magazine. He also began to plan Ulysses. In 1914 he wrote Exiles (1918), his only play.

Ulysses was the culmination of Joyce's earlier career; the fulfillment of the pledge made by Stephen Dedalus at the end of A Portrait: "to forge in the smithy of my soul the uncreated conscience of my race." Through his work with epiphanies Joyce had regarded this task as a long encounter with reality, the literal texture of Dublin life. Ulysses, a single day in the lives of two Dubliners—June 16, 1904—makes Dublin as familiar a place as the London of Charles Dickens. Joyce visited his native city for the last time in 1912, but his imagination never left it.

In 1919, Joyce returned to Trieste but soon after moved to Paris on the instigation of the poet Ezra POUND, who was by now an enthusiastic champion of Joyce's work, as were many other European and American writers. Ulysses found a charitable publisher in Sylvia Beach—an American who ran a Paris bookstore, Shakespeare and Company—and Joyce became the most respected writer of his time. Hampered by increasing blindness and the mental illness of his daughter, Joyce began work on "Work in Progress," sections of which appeared in the Paris journal transition. Anna Livia Plurabelle (1928), Tales Told of Shem and Shaun (1929), and Haveth Childers Everywhere (1930) were also parts of Joyce's last work, Finnegans Wake (1939), whose final appearance, unlike that of Ulysses, caused disappointment and puzzlement.

In Finnegans Wake technique overshadows content and imposes difficulties of comprehension that few readers have been able to surmount. In this work a Dublin night follows the Dublin day of Ulysses. The book is the record of a dream in which the sleeper recalls not only an actual Irish landscape but also an extensive intellectual tradition stretching from Homer to modern psychology. It neither begins nor ends, for the last sentence leads back into the first, and its intention, expressed in the curious language of the book, is to encompass "allspace in a notshall."

The outbreak of war forced Joyce to leave Paris in 1939. He lived for a brief period near Vichy, then moved once again to Zurich, where he died on Jan. 13, 1941, following a surgical operation.   HOWARD BATCHELOR

Bibliography: Adams, Robert M., Surface and Symbol: The Consistency of James Joyce's Ulysses (1962); Anderson, Chester G., James Joyce and His World (1968); Benstock, Bernard, James Joyce: The Undiscover'd Country (1977); Burgess, Anthony, Joysprick: An Introduction to the Language of James Joyce (1975) and Re Joyce (1968); Ellmann, Richard, The Consciousness of Joyce (1977), James Joyce (1959), and Ulysses on the Liffey (1973); Gilbert, Stuart, James Joyce's Ulysses, 2d ed. (1955); Goldberg, S. L., The Classical Temper: A Study of James Joyce's Ulysses (1961); Hart, Clive, Structure and Motif in Finnegans Wake (1962); Joyce, James, Letters, 3 vols., vol. 1 ed. by Stuart Gilbert (1957), vols. 2 and 3 ed. by Richard Ellmann (1966); Kain, Richard, Fabulous Voyager (1947); Levin, Harry, James Joyce, rev. ed. (1960); Litz, A. Walton, James Joyce (1966); Peake, Charles, James Joyce: The Citizen and the Artist (1977); Potts, Willard, ed., Portraits of the Artist in Exile: Recollections of James Joyce by Europeans (1979); Staley, Thomas F., ed., James Joyce Today: Essays on the Major Works (1966).

See also: STREAM OF CONSCIOUSNESS NOVEL.

Joyce, William: see LORD HAW-HAW.

József, Attila   [yoh'-zhef, ah'-til-ah]

Attila József, b. Budapest, Apr. 11, 1905, d. Dec. 3, 1937, was Hungary's first truly proletarian poet and one of the greatest Hungarian poets of the 20th century. The son of a simple soapmaker who deserted his family, József was brought up in harsh poverty by his mother, a washerwoman. He had an almost schizophrenic drive to alter the existing order of things, and his seven volumes of poetry reflect a profound sympathy for the exploited Hungarian working classes. József committed suicide, having been troubled by mental illness throughout his life.   AGNES HUSZAR VARDY

Bibliography: Nyerges, Anton N., Poems of Attila József (1973).

Juan Carlos I, King of Spain   [hwahn kar'-lohs]

Juan Carlos I de Borbón y Borbón, b. Rome, Jan. 5, 1938, became king of Spain on Nov. 22, 1975. A grandson of King Alfonso XIII, he was formally designated heir apparent to the throne and successor to Generalissimo Francisco Franco in 1969; he took the throne on Franco's death. Under Juan Carlos, Spain has become a democratic constitutional monarchy. In 1962, Juan married Princess Sophia of Greece.

Juan Chi   (Ruan Ji)   [hwahn jee]

One of the Seven Sages of the Bamboo Grove, Juan Chi, AD 210-263, was one of the few who escaped involvement and persecution in one of China's most politically turbulent ages. Like his friend, Chi K'ang, he also sought refuge in drinking and reputedly led a life of decadence. In his writings he employed allegory and double entendre. He is best known for 82 poems entitled Yung-huai shih, translated into English as Poems of Solitude (1960).   ANGELA JUNG PALANDRI

Bibliography: Holzman, Donald, Poetry and Politics: the Life and Works of Juan Chi (1976).

Juan de Fuca, Strait of   [hwahn duh fyoo'-kuh]

The Strait of Juan de Fuca, an inlet of the Pacific Ocean, separates Vancouver Island in British Columbia from the state of Washington. The strait is about 161 km (100 mi) long and 18-27 km (11-17 mi) wide; the U.S.-Canada border runs through the center. The strait links PUGET SOUND and the Strait of Georgia with the Pacific Ocean.

Juana Inés de la Cruz, Sor   [hwahn'-ah een-ays' day lah kroos']

Sor (or Sister) Juana Inés de la Cruz, b. Juana Inés de Asbaje y Ramírez de Santillana, Nov. 12, 1648, d. Apr. 17, 1695, was a Mexican intellectual, dramatist, and lyrical poet whose talents made her one of the central figures of the Mexican baroque period. A precocious child who had learned to read at age three and Latin by age nine, she first served as a lady-in-waiting at the court of the viceroy. She took religious vows at the age of 17 and thereafter devoted her life to writing and meditation. When ordered by the bishop of Puebla to refrain from intellectual pursuits, she wrote her Respuesta a Sor Filotea (Reply to Sister Philotea, 1691), a defense of women's right to knowledge and a signal document in the history of the emancipation of her sex.

She wrote five plays—two comedies and three religious allegories, or autos sacramentales—of which *El Divino Narciso* (The Divine Narcissus, 1690) is the most important. Also well known as a poet, Sor Juana wrote many lyrics and sonnets on both religious and worldly themes, in addition to a highly sophisticated long poem, *Primero sueño* (First Dream, 1680). Both her poetry and plays reveal the influence of the peninsular Spanish poets Luis de Góngora y Argote and Pedro Calderón de la Barca.   EDWARD MULLEN

Bibliography: Flynn, Gerard C., *Sor Juana Inés de la Cruz* (1971).

Juana La Loca: see JOAN THE MAD.

Juárez: see CIUDAD JUÁREZ.

Juárez, Benito   [hwar'-ays, bay-nee'-toh]

Benito Juárez, the first Mexican president of Indian descent, took part in the overthrow of the dictator Santa Anna and became president of the liberal government in 1858. His efforts to transfer power to mestizos and his victory over the French-sponsored regime of Emperor Maximilian made him a national hero.

The 19th-century Mexican statesman Benito (Pablo) Juárez is remembered as a leader of the resistance against foreign invasion and a champion of Mexican liberalism. Born in San Pablo Guelatao, Oaxaca, on Mar. 21, 1806, Juárez was the son of Zapotec Indian peasants, who died when he was three. In his early years he spoke only his native Zapotec language and received no education. At the age of 12, however, he abandoned his village to join his sister in Oaxaca City, where he learned Spanish and was educated by a Franciscan. He eventually studied law and in 1831 entered politics.

Juárez became a judge in 1841 and from 1847 to 1852 was governor of Oaxaca. Exiled in 1853 by the government of SANTA ANNA, he lived in New Orleans until 1855. When Santa Anna was overthrown in 1855, Juárez became minister of justice. In this capacity he was responsible for a law (Ley Juárez) curtailing the privileges of the Mexican clergy. When President Ignacio Comonfort resigned in the face of conservative opposition to the constitution of 1857, Juárez succeeded him.

As president from 1858, Juárez led the liberals to victory over the conservatives in the War of the Reform (1858–60) and began the nationalization of property owned by the Roman Catholic church. When the French invaded in 1862 Juárez headed the resistance and carried on the struggle until the French-imposed empire of MAXIMILIAN fell in 1867. He was reelected president in 1867 and 1871, but his death on July 18, 1872, cut short his second term.

Despite the autocratic tendencies he displayed in his last years, Juárez is a national hero in Mexico because of his decades-long struggle to establish democracy and because of his resistance to the French invaders.   ROBERT PATCH

Bibliography: Atwater, James D., and Ruiz, Ramón E., *Out from Under: Benito Juárez and Mexico's Struggle for Independence* (1969); Roeder,

Ralph, *Juárez and His Mexico: A Biographical History*, 2 vols. (1947; repr. 1968); Smart, Charles Allen, *Viva Juárez! A Biography* (1963).

Judah   [joo'-duh]

In the Bible, Judah, the fourth son of JACOB and Leah, was the father of the tribe of Judah, one of the 12 tribes of Israel. The account of his life is recorded in Genesis 29–49. He persuaded his brothers to sell JOSEPH to the Ishmaelites rather than kill him (Gen. 37). Along with his brothers, Judah received the blessing of Jacob before his death (Gen. 49). His tribe led the Exodus and gave its name to the kingdom of Judah, which includes the city of Jerusalem. From his line came the family of David, to which Jesus belonged.

DOUGLAS EZELL

Judah, Kingdom of

When King SOLOMON died in 922 BC, ancient Israel was divided into the southern kingdom of Judah and the northern kingdom of Israel. Comprising the tribes of Benjamin and Judah, the southern kingdom outlasted its northern rival, perhaps because of the strength of its capital, Jerusalem. Judah collapsed in 587 BC when it was overrun by the Babylonians.

Judah, Theodore D.

Theodore Dehone Judah, b. Bridgeport, Conn., Mar. 4, 1826, d. Nov. 2, 1863, was a railroad engineer who promoted the construction of the first railroad across the Sierra Nevada. After attending the Rensselaer Polytechnic Institute, Judah worked for several railroads in the East before moving to California in 1854. He became active in public discussions about a transcontinental link and was a leader in bringing together Collis P. Huntington, Leland Stanford, and the other organizers of the Central Pacific Railroad Company, the company that built the western section of the transcontinental railroad in the 1860s. Judah broke with his associates in 1863, however. He contracted typhoid or yellow fever while crossing the Isthmus of Panama.

Judah ha-Levi   [joo-duh hah-lee'-vy]

The Hebrew poet and philosopher Judah ha-Levi, b. before 1075, d. 1141, grew up in Islamic Spain, traveled widely, and, led by an intense Jewish nationalism, set out for the land of Israel. Evidence points to his death in Egypt, although according to legend he was trampled at the gates of Jerusalem. His approximately 800 surviving poems include love songs, eulogies, and religious works. His philosophical tract, the *Kuzari* (trans. as *The Book of Argument and Proof In Defense of the Despised Faith*, 1905), is a polemic that defends the principles of Judaism and contrasts them with those of Aristotelian philosophy, Christianity, and Islam. In modern times ha-Levi has exerted a strong influence on Heinrich Heine, as well as on various Jewish authors.   LAWRENCE H. SCHIFFMAN

Bibliography: Efros, I. I., *Judah Halevi as Poet and Thinker* (1941); Kayser, Rudolf, *The Life and Time of Judah Halevi*, trans. by Frank Gaynor (1949); Noveck, Simon, ed., *Great Jewish Personalities in Ancient and Medieval Times* (1959).

Judah ha-Nasi   [joo'-dah ha-nah'-see]

Judah ha-Nasi, c.135–c.220, was the patriarch of the Jewish community in Palestine who was responsible for the final redaction of the MISHNAH (Oral Law). He was the last of the tannaim, the Jewish sages who had engaged in the compilation of the Oral Law since the time of HILLEL (fl. 30 BC–AD 10). The Mishnah, as edited by Rabbi Judah, served as the foundation of both the Palestinian and the Babylonian TALMUD.

Judaism   [joo'-day-izm]

Judaism, the religion of the JEWS, claims over 14 million adherents throughout the world. It is the oldest living religion in the Western world. Historically, Judaism served as the matrix for Christianity and Islam, the other two great monotheistic religions, which together with Judaism claim half the world's population as adherents.

BELIEFS

Judaism was the first religion to teach MONOTHEISM, or belief in one God. This belief is the basis of Judaism and is summed up in the opening words of the Shema, recited daily: "Hear O Israel, the Lord our God, the Lord is One" (Deut. 6.4). Jews believe that God's providence extends to all people but that God entered into a special COVENANT with the ancient Israelites. They do not believe that they were chosen for any special privileges but rather to bring God's message to humanity by their example. Belief in a coming MESSIAH has been a source of optimism for Jews.

The beliefs of Judaism have never been formulated in an official creed; Judaism stresses conduct rather than doctrinal correctness. Its adherents have a considerable measure of latitude in matters of belief, especially concerning the messianic future and immortality. Judaism is a this-world religion; its objective is a just and peaceful world order on earth. This hope is assured by the belief that God is the Lord of history as well as of nature.

The basic source of Jewish belief is the Hebrew BIBLE (called the "Old Testament" by Christians), especially its first five books, called the TORAH or the Pentateuch. The Torah was traditionally regarded as the primary revelation of God and his law to humanity; it is considered as valid for all time. Its laws were clarified and elaborated in the oral Torah, or the tradition of the elders, and were eventually written down in the MISHNAH and TALMUD. Thus, Judaism did not stop developing after the Bible was completed. The traditional Jewish prayer book is an important result of this process of development, reflecting the basic beliefs of Judaism as well as changes in emphasis in response to changing conditions. During the Middle Ages, systematic codes of talmudic law were compiled. Jewish literature—legal, ethical, philosophic, mystical, and devotional—is virtually endless.

PRACTICES

Judaism has a system of law, known as HALACHAH, regulating civil and criminal justice, family relationships, personal ethics and manners, social responsibilities—such as help to the needy, education, and community institutions—as well as worship and other religious observances. Some laws once deemed very important, for example, laws governing the offering of sacrifice and most rules of ceremonial defilement and purification, have not been practiced since the destruction of the Second Temple in Jerusalem in AD 70.

Individual practices still widely observed include the dietary laws (see KOSHER); rules concerning the marital relationship, daily prayer, and study; and the recital of many blessings, especially before and after meals. The SABBATH and festivals are observed both in the home and in the SYNAGOGUE, a unique institution for prayer and instruction that became the model for the church in Christianity and for the mosque in Islam. Traditionally observant Jews wear *tefillin*, or PHYLACTERIES, on their forehead and left arm during morning prayers, and affix to their doorposts a mezuzah, a little box containing a parchment scroll inscribed with passages of the Torah that emphasize the unity of God, his providence, and the resulting duty of serving him. In accordance with biblical law, men wear a fringed shawl (*tallith*) during prayer. Covering the head is a widespread custom.

The Jewish religious calendar, of Babylonian origin, consists of 12 lunar months, amounting to about 354 days. Six times in a 19-year cycle a 13th month is added to adjust the calendar to the solar year. The day is reckoned from sunset to sunset.

The Sabbath, from sunset Friday to sunset Saturday, is observed by refraining from work and by attending a synagogue service. Friday evening is marked in the home by the lighting of a lamp or candles by the woman of the household, the recital of the kiddush (a ceremonial blessing affirming the sanctity of the day) over a cup of wine, and the blessing of children by parents. The end of the Sabbath is marked by parallel ceremonies called havdalah. Similar home ceremonies occur on the festivals.

The holidays prescribed in the Torah are the two "days of awe," ROSH HASHANAH (New Year) and YOM KIPPUR (Day of Atonement), and three joyous festivals, PASSOVER, SHAVUOTH (Feast of Weeks), and the Feast of TABERNACLES. Later additions are the festive occasions of CHANUKAH and PURIM, and the fast of the Ninth of Av (*Tishah be-Av*), commemorating the destruction of the Temple.

On the 8th day after birth, male children are circumcised as a sign of the covenant with Abraham; the boy is named during the ceremony (see CIRCUMCISION). Girls are named at a synagogue service. At the age of 13, a boy is deemed responsible for performing the commandments (BAR MITZVAH). To mark his new status, the bar mitzvah takes part in the Bible readings during a synagogue service. (The synagogue service is sometimes popularly referred to as the bar mitzvah.) A similar ceremony for girls (*bat mitzvah*) is a recent innovation. Somewhat older is the confirmation ceremony for both sexes introduced by Reform Judaism; it is usually a class observance on or near Shavuoth.

Judaism has characteristic, but not unparalleled, customs concerning marriage and death and mourning. The importance attached to recital of the KADDISH prayer by mourners dates from the Middle Ages. The prayer itself is much older and was originally recited as the conclusion of a sermon; it is related in thought and language to the "Lord's Prayer" of Christians. After the disasters during the First Crusade, the Jews of central and later eastern Europe introduced a memorial service on Yom Kippur and on other holidays; they also began to observe the anniversary of the death of parents.

HISTORY

In the biblical account, the patriarchs ABRAHAM, ISAAC, and JACOB received the revelation of the one, true God, who promised special protection to the Israelite tribes (of whom there were 12, descended from the 12 sons of Jacob, who was also called Israel).

Origins. Many 19th-century scholars held that monotheism gradually emerged out of POLYTHEISM, the evolution being complete only with the great prophets in the 8th century BC and later. Today many are convinced that monotheism was already a reality in the days of MOSES (13th century BC) and that later prophets developed more fully only the ethical and spiritual implications of the belief. All the Israelite tribes agreed on the worship of one God named Yahweh (see GOD); they shared the memory of slavery in Egypt, the deliverance under Moses, and the Mosaic covenant and revelation at Sinai. Although some practices were borrowed from surrounding peoples (agricultural festivals, civil jurisprudence), the Israelite religion was kept pure of paganism through the strenuous efforts of the prophets. Unparalleled in any other

Moses descends Mount Sinai, bringing the Israelites the Torah, or Written Law, which is contained in the first five books of the Bible. Authorship of these books is traditionally ascribed to Moses, who received the divine revelation on Mount Sinai. (Illumination from the Sarajevo Haggadah, 13th century.)

A prophecy made by the prophet Isaiah to King Hezekiah of Judah is recorded on the imperial crown of the Holy Roman Empire (c.962). Isaiah prophesied during the period when Israel was overrun by Assyria. Many of his prophetic warnings dealt with the threat of military invasion.

Near Eastern religion are Judaism's prohibition of images, observance of the Sabbath, dietary laws, legislation guaranteeing support of the poor as a matter of right, and protection of slaves and animals against cruelty. When a loose tribal confederation was replaced by a national state under Kings SAUL and DAVID a national Temple in Jerusalem helped unify the people spiritually. After the division of the kingdom following the death (c.933) of SOLOMON, the northern kingdom of Israel also had national shrines (see ISRAEL, KINGDOM OF; JUDAH, KINGDOM OF).

Prophets. The PROPHETS exercised decisive influence on all development in Israel. From the time of the 11th-century-BC prophet Samuel, they ceased to be mere soothsayers and became more and more national leaders, speaking in the name of God (the Hebrew word for prophet is *navi*, meaning "spokesman"). They upheld strict principles of justice and humanity, criticizing bluntly the most powerful forces in the nation. They warned of national disaster unless a radical improvement of religious and moral standards was realized. The reform movement led by King JOSIAH (c.640–609 BC), based on the Book of DEUTERONOMY, was probably undertaken under prophetic influence; the reforms included abolishing all local shrines and sanctuaries and limiting sacrifice to the Temple in Jerusalem. This dramatized belief in one God and reduced the importance of sacrifice in the daily life of the worshiper. The gap left by the abolition of the local shrines was eventually filled by the establishment of the SYNAGOGUE, but there is no clear reference to this new institution until some four centuries later. The most mature and eloquent expression of prophetic ideals is found in the recorded speeches of the later prophets, beginning in the 8th century BC with the prophet Amos.

The Exile and Foreign Influences. The fall of both kingdoms and the BABYLONIAN CAPTIVITY (586–538 BC) were perceived as a confirmation of the prophetic predictions and therefore of the truth of their message. Thus the Israelites were prepared to listen to the prophets of hope who now appeared, promising not only national restoration but also the ultimate redemption of all peoples from idolatry, injustice, and war.

Returning exiles were leaders in the revival of the Palestinian center (now confined to the area of the former southern kingdom of Judah) and the building of the Second Temple. The high priests usually served as official representatives to the Persian government and to the succeeding empires. In the middle of the 5th century BC, the final form was given to the Torah—in the opinion of many scholars, a composite of laws, narratives, and poems dating from different periods, but with beginnings going back to Moses; and the people formally accepted the Torah as the rule for their life. Shortly thereafter the SAMARITANS broke away from the main body of Judaism; small numbers of this sect still survive.

During this period, prophecy waned and finally disap-

peared, but the writings of the great prophets were compiled and accepted as sacred literature. Other books were composed—notably, wisdom literature, such as JOB—and many of them were eventually included in the Bible.

Some elements of Persian religion were incorporated into Judaism: a more elaborate doctrine of ANGELS; the figure of SATAN; and a system of beliefs concerning the end of time, including a predetermined scheme of world history, a final judgment (see JUDGMENT, LAST), and the RESURRECTION of the dead. These ideas were expounded in many visionary documents called apocalypses; none of them was included in the Hebrew Bible except the Book of DANIEL (see APOCALYPSE THEME; APOCALYPTIC LITERATURE; ESCHATOLOGY).

Hellenism and Judaism. Following the conquests of Alexander the Great (d. 323 BC), Judea (as Judah came to be called) passed under the rule of Alexander's Egyptian successors (the Ptolemies) and later his Syrian successors (the Seleucids). Under these Hellenistic rulers, Jewish life was changed both inwardly and outwardly, in Palestine and in the growing DIASPORA. In Alexandria, which acquired a large Jewish population, novel forms of Judaism emerged. The Bible was translated into Greek (the SEPTUAGINT), the first of innumerable translations. New explanations of the Torah were devised in the 1st century AD by PHILO OF ALEXANDRIA.

The Greek language and customs also affected Palestinian Jewry; the Jewish emphasis on study may be in part the result of Greek influence. But while many Jews were attracted to pagan customs and attitudes, the majority resisted these trends. The attempt of the Seleucid king ANTIOCHUS IV to impose the Greek religion by force aroused open rebellion led by the MACCABEES, a Jewish priestly family. During the short period of Judean independence under the Maccabees (also called Hasmoneans) a movement of proselytizing began that was apparently not organized but was nevertheless energetic. Large numbers of persons, disillusioned with the old pagan cults, adopted Judaism formally or attached themselves unofficially to the synagogue.

The Sects. The worldliness of the later Maccabees alienated most of their subjects, and effective leadership passed more and more to pious and learned laymen, especially after the Romans established control in 63 BC. These laymen formed the party of the PHARISEES (separatists); democratic in spirit, the Pharisees sought to adapt the laws of the Torah to changing needs, utilizing old popular traditions (oral Torah), which they expanded by the free method of MIDRASH, or verse-by-verse interpretation of scripture. Their opponents, the SADDUCEES, were drawn largely from the wealthy classes and from the priesthood; conservative in religious matters, the Sadducees interpreted scripture strictly, disregarding the oral tradition and popular customs, and rejecting the doctrine of resurrection. The Pharisees were followed by the majority; all subsequent Judaism was pharisaic, and the roots of Christianity and Islam are found in pharisaic Judaism. (The ESSENES were a sort of right-wing, monastic splinter group of the Pharisees; they probably wrote the DEAD SEA SCROLLS.)

Talmudic or Rabbinic Judaism. After the disastrous revolt against Rome in AD 66–70, the pharisaic leaders, whose successors bore the title RABBI, rallied the people around the synagogue and the academies of learning. Through centuries of effort (recorded in the Mishnah, Talmud, and many works of midrash) they produced a disciplined and loyal Jewish community.

The earliest Christians differed from other Jews chiefly in their belief that Jesus was the messiah. But under the leadership of Saint Paul and others, gentile Christianity soon became dominant, and the break between the two religions became complete. When the Roman Empire became officially Christian in the 4th century AD, the Jews became subject to many discriminatory laws, including a prohibition against seeking or even accepting converts.

In the 4th century, religious and legal leadership was assumed more and more by the Babylonian center of learning; and from the 5th century, the Babylonian Talmud was generally accepted as the authoritative source of law. Thereafter world leadership remained with the Babylonian scholars; the

Rabbi Akiva (AD c.40-135), who began his study of the Torah at age 40, eventually became the greatest Jewish scholar of his day. His recording of the oral law provided a basis for the Mishnah. This page from a 13th-century Spanish prayerbook shows Akiva instructing his pupils.

heads of the academies, called *Gaonim* ("excellencies"), provided information and advice on legal and other questions to the Diaspora communities. In the 8th century, the sect of KARAITES broke away, rejecting tradition and rabbinic authority, and seeking to live by the letter of the biblical law. After four centuries of vigorous activity, the sect declined; today only remnants survive.

Philosophy and Mysticism. By AD 1000, the Babylonian center was in decline, but new centers of Jewish culture emerged in North Africa and in Muslim Spain. (The Spanish Jews, together with the oriental communities, came to be known as SEPHARDIM, and those of Christian Europe as ASHKENAZIM. The two groups differ somewhat in liturgical forms, in the pronunciation of Hebrew, in their music, and in many customs.) Under tolerant rulers, Jews participated actively in the Arabic cultural renaissance. In addition to commentaries on the Bible and Talmud, they also wrote extensively on grammar, science, and philosophy, usually in Arabic, and produced outstanding poetry in Hebrew, both religious and secular.

Although the first important Jewish philosopher was the Gaon SAADIA in Baghdad (10th century), nearly all of his important successors were of Spanish origin, including the preeminent MAIMONIDES. These philosophers were scholastics, like their Muslim and Christian contemporaries, drawing largely on the works of Aristotle and the Neoplatonists. Like Philo, they tended to explain difficult Bible passages as allegories. Their writings were welcomed by intellectuals trying to

harmonize revealed religion with the new scientific learning. But the masses were not interested in them, and many of the orthodox leaders regarded the new doctrines as subversive. After the death of Maimonides, his admirers and detractors waged a bitter struggle in Christian Spain and the Provence. His last important successor, Chisdai Crescas (d. 1410), undertook a critique of Aristotle in the interest of simple faith.

More lasting and widespread was the influence of KABBALAH ("tradition"), a term that includes various mystical doctrines and practices. Mystical elements appear in the old apocalypses and in talmudic and gaonic literature. There were mystical movements in Europe as well, culminating in the 13th and 14th centuries in southern France and northern Spain. A wealth of kabbalistic writings was produced, including the *Zohar* ("splendor") of Moses de Leon (13th century).

There are many kabbalistic systems. In addition to true mystical experience, they contain mythological and magical elements, reinterpretations of biblical and talmudic passages and of prayers and commandments, Neoplatonic ideas, and messianic speculations. The tragedies that befell the Jews of Spain, culminating in the expulsion of 1492, called for stronger comfort than rational philosophies could offer. This was in some measure provided by Kabbalah, with its enthralling mysteries and increasing emphasis on messianism. The Jews of central and eastern Europe also cultivated Kabbalah. These communities were unsurpassed in talmudic learning; French scholars contributed much to biblical studies also. They introduced a number of legal changes to improve the status of women including a formal ban on polygamy.

The Darmstadt Haggadah, a Passover prayerbook dating from the 15th century, is richly illustrated. A Passover feast, or seder (bottom), is prepared each year to commemorate the deliverance of the Jews from Egypt. During the feast, pages from the Haggadah are read.

Kabbalist scholars, seeking higher understanding through mysticism, put great emphasis on the magical significance of numbers and letters. The ushpizin prayer belongs to the Kabbalah. Ushpizin, from an Aramaic word meaning "guest," refers to the seven prophets who visited the tabernacle during the Sukkot festival. (Israel Museum, Jerusalem.)

(Left) *During a synagogue service, the Torah, richly sheathed in silk and precious metals, is removed from the Ark and presented to worshipers. Traditionally, services are held twice a day. In addition, the synagogue serves as a gathering place for communal functions.*

(Below) *The first synagogues were built in Babylonia and Egypt in the 3d century BC. Prague's Altneu Synagogue, erected in the 12th century AD, is one of the oldest remaining in Europe. In front of its Ark of the Covenant burns the Eternal Light, symbolizing the permanence of faith.*

The 17th century saw a revival of Jewish life in Palestine. An attempt to revitalize the legal system by creating a new SANHEDRIN, or central court, was unsuccessful. But a 17th-century mystical revival had a profound effect on Jewish thought and liturgy. The messianic speculations of this new Kabbalah, taught by Isaac LURIA, and the massacres of Polish Jewry in 1648 formed an explosive combination; in 1665 a Turkish Jew, SABBATAI ZEVI, proclaimed himself the messiah. There had been many such messianic claimants over the centuries, but they never achieved more than a local following; Sabbatai's announcement, however, shook world Jewry. Thousands of believers left their homes to join him in Palestine. When Sabbatai broke under threats and accepted Islam, there was widespread disillusionment and despair. Yet a substantial number of believers kept up an underground Sabbatean movement for over a century, finding kabbalistic justifications for their leader's apostasy and awaiting his triumphant return.

A more positive mystical movement arose in eastern Europe in the 18th century. It was founded by BAAL SHEM TOV and was known as HASIDISM. Its leaders were versed in the mysteries of Kabbalah, but they addressed themselves to the unlearned masses, teaching them a simple and joyous faith and encouraging them to express their religious feelings in ecstatic song and dance. Initially opposed by the rabbinic leaders as heretical, Hasidism survived such attacks and is today regarded as representative of extreme Orthodoxy. The movement declined for a time because it fostered "the cult of personality" and encouraged superstition, but it seems to have regained vitality in some American cities and in Israel.

Modern Developments. Except for these mystic stirrings, Jewish life from the 16th to the 19th centuries—the GHETTO period—was rather torpid. But gradually modern scientific and philosophic ideas penetrated the ghetto. These influences began to be felt in the West during the 17th century. The Enlightenment of the 18th century witnessed discussion of improving the situation of Jews and led to their emancipation under the impact of the American and French revolutions. Though progress in Germanic lands was slow and disappointing, and in eastern Europe and in the Muslim lands virtually nonexistent, the impact of new ideas was felt everywhere among Jews. The Jewish community no longer provided its members with political status. Wherever Jews received citizenship, the old Jewish community lost its authority; in the New World it had never existed, and in Russia it was dissolved by government order in 1844. No longer subject to community discipline, confused by new social and intellec-

tual conditions, Jews were uncertain of their place in the modern world.

One response was *Haskalah*, the Hebrew word for "Enlightenment," which sought to bring modern knowledge and ideas to large numbers of Jews, using chiefly writings in modern Hebrew. Moses MENDELSSOHN made the pioneer effort in 18th-century Berlin. His program—to combine modern education with strict Orthodox practice—was ineffective; his efforts led rather to assimilation, even to Christian baptism for worldly advancement. In Austrian Poland (Galicia), Haskalah was more fruitful, resulting in new efforts to study Jewish history and literature by modern critical methods ("the science of Judaism"), a trend continued with great success in Germany. In Russia, the attempt at popular education, with the slogan "Be a Jew at home and a man elsewhere," was soon recognized as futile because of the government's viciously anti-Jewish policies. In its place, a movement for Jewish nationalism arose—first expressed in secular literature in Hebrew—decades before the rise of political ZIONISM. Later a strong socialist movement developed in urban centers, and these Jewish socialists spoke in Yiddish, the folk language, rather than in Hebrew.

In the West, Enlightenment led to attempts at religious reconstruction, partly as a response to spreading indifference and apostasy that ghettoized Orthodoxy could not check. The first reforms were external, to provide a more decorous and attractive synagogue service, with portions of the service read in the language of the country, organ and choral music, and the revival of preaching. These changes aroused Orthodox opposition and sometimes government intervention. The Reformers had recourse to the newly developing "science of Judaism," showing that Judaism had always grown and changed. Eventually they developed a modernist theology, rejecting the literalist understanding of Scripture and the changeless authority of the halachah. They upheld a doctrine of progressive revelation, equating the revelation of God with the education of the Jewish people and of all humanity. They rejected the traditional prayers that asked for a return to the land of Israel and the restoration of sacrifices. Instead of a personal messiah, they envisioned a messianic age of brotherhood and peace; and instead of bodily resurrection, they taught a purely spiritual immortality. They discarded many traditional observances as no longer meaningful, modified others, and introduced new ones, such as confirmation. They also affirmed the equality of women in religious matters. A second group of modernists held similar theoretical views, but retained traditional practice with only limited modifications; they became the spiritual fathers of Conservative Judaism in the United States.

All parties, including the Orthodox Jews in western countries, were perfervid in patriotism toward their several lands. All were deeply affected by 19th-century liberalism—optimistic, universalistic, and convinced of the reality of progress. The modernist movements, starting in Germany, had only modest success in Europe, but expanded greatly in North America. They have since acquired followers in Latin America, South Africa, Australia, and Israel. The terms Reform, Liberal, Progressive, Conservative, and Reconstructionist are used in various countries with varying shades of meaning; all designate nonorthodox versions of Jewish religion.

New forms of Jewish community and synagogue organization, mostly on a voluntary basis, emerged in the 19th century. The old rabbinic academies (Yeshivoth) confined instruction to the Talmud and its commentaries. At this time modern rabbinical seminaries were established whose students were exposed to the whole range of Jewish history and lore and were required to obtain a university degree as well. Important works were written on Jewish theology, displaying Kantian and post-Kantian influences. Completely new were trends toward a secularist understanding of Jewish life, more or less completely rejecting religion and finding a substitute in nationalistic and cultural activities.

The prevailing liberal, optimistic mood gradually cooled as official oppression and widespread hatred continued in eastern Europe while ANTI-SEMITISM also flourished in the West. Jewish thinkers exhibited an increasing sense of the tragic element in human life, in the style of existentialism. The trend toward Jewish nationalism took concrete form in the movement of Zionism. Initially opposed by many religious leaders of all parties and by the Jewish socialists, Zionism was vindicated by the march of events, culminating in the HOLOCAUST. World Jewry, despite many divisions and disagreements, is today united in concern and support for the State of Israel, which was established in 1948.

At present, because of political circumstances, rigid Orthodoxy is the only form of Judaism officially recognized in Israel, for example, in solemnizing marriages and in military chaplaincy. But a large part of the population is remote from formal religion, and the modernist versions have difficulty making their message heard.

In the USSR, there has been an extraordinary revival of Jewish self-affirmation despite harsh repression. In the Western

world, despite loss of members, mixed marriages, and a serious drop in the Jewish birthrate, religious institutions are flourishing. The number of synagogues and synagogue members increased dramatically after World War II. There has been a remarkable resurgence of Orthodoxy after a long period of decline, and modernist groups are placing greater emphasis on tradition and ceremony.   BERNARD J. BAMBERGER

Bibliography: Agus, Jacob, *The Evolution of Jewish Thought* (1959); Baeck, Leo, *The Essence of Judaism*, rev. ed. (1948); Bamberger, B. J., *The Story of Judaism*, 3d ed. (1971); Blau, Joseph L., *Modern Varieties of Judaism* (1966); Cohen, Arthur A., *The Natural and Supernatural Jew* (1962); Finkelstein, Louis, *The Jews: Their History, Culture, and Religions*, 4th ed. (1971); Glazer, Nathan, *American Judaism*, 2d ed. (1973); Goldin, Judah, *The Jewish Expression* (1970); Heschel, Abraham J., *God in Search of Man* (1955; repr. 1972); Meyer, Michael, *The Origins of the Modern Jew* (1967); Neusner, Jacob, *The Life of the Torah: Readings in the Jewish Religious Experience* (1974) and *The Way of the Torah: An Introduction to Judaism*, 2d ed. (1974); Silver, D., and Martin, B., *A History of Judaism*, 2 vols. (1974).

Judas, Saint: see THADDAEUS, SAINT.

Judas Iscariot   [joo'-duhs is-kair'-ee-uht]

Judas Iscariot was the Apostle who betrayed JESUS CHRIST to the authorities. According to Matthew 27:4, Judas, distraught over Jesus' condemnation, returned his reward of 30 pieces of silver and hanged himself. According to Acts 1:18, Judas bought a field with the money, but fell headlong in it, injured himself, and died. His surname may indicate that he belonged to the Sicarii, a radical political group.

Bibliography: Gartner, Bertil, *Iscariot* (1971).

Judas tree

Judas trees, *Cercis*, comprise several small, fast-growing deciduous trees or shrubs with clustered pink to purplish pea-like flowers that bloom in spring (thus the common name, redbud). They belong to the pulse family, Fabaceae. The leaves are heart-shaped or rounded and the fruits are flat pods. Judas trees grow well in semishade and are often used in ornamental plantings. The flowers have a sharp, acid flavor and are used in salads. The buds, flowers, and young pods can be fried in butter or pickled.   DIANNE FAHSELT

Judd, Donald

Donald Judd, b. Excelsior Springs, Mo., June 3, 1928, is an American sculptor and writer and one of the earliest exponents and theoreticians of what is termed MINIMAL ART, a movement that began in New York City during the early 1960s. Judd, who began his career as a painter, wrote a number of influential articles during the early 1960s; in these, he emphasized the "objectness," or the simple concreteness of sculptural form, and the immediacy, or wholeness, of the sculptor's "specific objects," which are "seen at once and not part to part." From about 1964 to the present, Judd has been making neutral, modular, or monolithic geometric objects, chiefly cubes and boxes of stainless steel, aluminum, plexiglass, and wood, in fulfillment of his minimalist goals.
          BARBARA CAVALIERE

Bibliography: Agee, William C., *Don Judd* (1968); Smith, Brydon, ed., *Donald Judd* (1975).

Jude, Epistle of   [jood]

Jude is a short book of the New Testament of the BIBLE, consisting of 25 verses. The author is commonly believed to have been the Apostle Jude (or THADDAEUS). However, as verse 17 implies that the Apostles are already dead, the authorship and date of composition are uncertain. The book may have been written as late as AD 100.

The text is a warning to its recipients against teachers promoting doctrines leading to immorality. Some scholars suggest that the teachers were proponents of GNOSTICISM. A distinctive characteristic of this letter is its use of citations from the Assumption of Moses and the Book of Enoch, works classified as PSEUDEPIGRAPHA.   DOUGLAS EZELL

Jude the Obscure

Jude the Obscure (1895), first published serially in 1894–95, is the most unrelentingly pessimistic of Thomas HARDY's major novels. The central character, the stonemason Jude Fawley, is destroyed by the tension between his spiritual and corporal aspirations, and his failure to find either material or romantic satisfaction illustrates what Hardy, in the book's preface, called "the tragedy of unfulfilled aims." The novel outraged Hardy's contemporaries because of its attacks on the Anglican church, the English educational system, and marital traditions.

Bibliography: Cox, Reginald Gordon, ed., *Thomas Hardy: The Critical Heritage* (1970).

judge advocate general: see MILITARY JUSTICE.

Judges, Book of

Judges, the seventh book of the Old Testament of the BIBLE, traces Israel's history from the death of Joshua, the lieutenant and successor of MOSES, to the beginning of the monarchy under SAUL. Its title is derived from the figures who serve as the protagonists in most of the book. Their Hebrew designation is normally translated "judge," but the word has a broader meaning and should perhaps be translated "ruler." Where sufficient information is related about individual "judges," they consistently appear in the role of war leader or ruler, not judge. DEBORAH, the prophetess, however, may be an exception, and some scholars hold that the minor judges, mentioned only in lists, were officials of the tribal league with judicial functions quite distinct from the role of the major figures like GIDEON and SAMSON. These major figures appear to have been of only regional importance and may have overlapped chronologically; the neat chronological structure of the book based on their succession is certainly late and artificial. Judges is part of the Deuteronomistic History, the name given by scholars to the books of DEUTERONOMY, JOSHUA, Judges, 1 and 2 SAMUEL, and 1 and 2 KINGS, all of which appear to share the same complex history of composition. Many early oral and written sources, including the premonarchical song of Deborah, were incorporated into the general editorial framework provided by the final editor of the history in the time of Josiah (c.640–609 BC).   J. J. M. ROBERTS

Bibliography: Gray, John, *Joshua, Judges, and Ruth* (1967).

judgment

A judgment is a decision of a COURT of law, usually based on a conclusion derived from the evidence presented at a trial. The judgment settles finally and authoritatively the issues in dispute before the court. Judgments can be appealed to higher courts and may be set aside by them. A judgment is valid only if it is decided in a competent court that has legal jurisdiction.

Special kinds of judgments include a default judgment (the defendant does not appear and defend the case) and a confessed judgment (the defendant admits to the claim against him or her).

Judgment, Last

The concept of a final judgment on humankind at the end of history is found in Judaism and Christianity, Islam, and Zoroastrianism. It holds an important place in Judaic tradition, in which God's judgment is regarded as operative both within history and at its end. The consummation of history is called the Day of the Lord, which is a day of judgment upon all who are unfaithful to God.

Christian ESCHATOLOGY owes much to this Hebrew tradition. The New Testament freely employs the language and imagery of Jewish APOCALYPTIC LITERATURE. It affirms the expectation that (in the language of the historic creeds) Christ "will come again with glory to judge both the quick and the dead." Many different interpretations of the meaning of this affirmation have been offered and, in particular, of the symbolic language employed in the New Testament to describe the in-

describable. But there is little doubt that the apostolic writers believed in the SECOND COMING OF CHRIST and the Great Judgment Day as a manifestation of Christ's eternal victory.

CHARLES W. RANSON

judicial review

Judicial review is the power of courts to decide the validity of acts of the legislative and executive branches of government. If the courts decide that a legislative act is unconstitutional, it is nullified. The decisions of the executive and administrative agencies can also be overruled by the courts as not conforming to the law or the Constitution.

The U.S. Constitution does not explicitly mention judicial review. The power was first asserted by Chief Justice John Marshall in 1803, in the case of MARBURY V. MADISON. Relying in part on Alexander Hamilton's writings in *The Federalist*, no. 78, Marshall asserted that the judiciary logically and of necessity had the power to review congressional and executive actions. This follows from the premise (stated in Article VI of the U.S. Constitution) that the Constitution is the supreme law of the land and that courts, in deciding cases, must be able to make final and binding interpretations of the law. Subsequently the states adopted the same view, and their superior courts commonly nullify acts of legislatures or governors that conflict with the state constitutions.

Constitutions adopted by other countries, such as Germany, Italy, India, and Pakistan, often provide for some form of judicial review. Great Britain does not recognize judicial review; the final authority in British law is Parliament.

In exercising their power, justices of the U.S. SUPREME COURT have sometimes been accused of writing their own political views into the Constitution. Their overturning of some of the New Deal legislation of the 1930s brought proposals to reorganize the Court. For this reason, some justices have urged the Court to be restrained in exercising its power. The Court generally observes the principle that any attack upon the validity of a statute must overcome a presumption of its constitutionality. The Court has also stated that it will not judge the wisdom of particular legislative and executive actions and will avoid political questions, but these principles have been interpreted differently by different justices.

Bibliography: Mason, Alpheus, and Beaney, William, *The Supreme Court in a Free Society* (1968).

Judith, Book of [joo'-dith]

A book of the Old Testament in versions of the BIBLE based on the Greek SEPTUAGINT, Judith is included with the APOCRYPHA in the Authorized and Revised Standard versions; it does not appear at all in the Hebrew Bible. The work of an unknown author, the book is a fictitious account of the deliverance of Israel from a foreign army by Judith, the devout and beautiful heroine who first beguiled and then beheaded the Assyrian commander Holofernes. The book is dated to the Maccabean period in the 2d century BC. Although the besieged city of Bethulia is described as being in Samaria, Samaritans are curiously unmentioned. Deliberate anachronisms, such as calling the Babylonian king Nebuchadnezzar "king of the Assyrians," were probably intended to signal readers that Judith is not exact history but a call to celebrate recent victories of the Maccabees and to inspire further resistance to Hellenizing enemies. The ritual scrupulosity of the heroine suggests an early pharisaic origin for the book.

NORMAN K. GOTTWALD

judo: see MARTIAL ARTS.

Judson, Adoniram [juhd-suhn, ad-uh-ny'-ruhm]

Adoniram Judson, b. Malden, Mass., Aug. 9, 1788, d. Apr. 12, 1850, was an American Baptist missionary and linguist who published a now-standard Burmese-English dictionary and translated the Bible into that language. He graduated from Brown University and Andover Seminary and was ordained as a Congregationalist minister before traveling in the first contingent of American evangelists to the Far East in 1812. En route he became convinced that the standard practice of baptizing infants was wrong, and he joined the Baptists on arrival in India.

Settling in Burma, Judson slowly overcame governmental opposition and widespread indifference among the local populace. After 20 years of severe trials, including disease and imprisonment, he published (1834) his translation of the Bible; 15 years later he issued a complete Burmese-English dictionary, which made the work of later missionaries much easier. Judson's long-suffering example inspired many others to volunteer for similar service around the world. The Judson Memorial Church in New York City bears his name.

HENRY WARNER BOWDEN

Bibliography: Anderson, Courtney, *To the Golden Shore: The Life of Adoniram Judson* (1956).

Jugurtha, King of Numidia [joo-gur'-thuh, noo-mid'-ee-uh]

Jugurtha, c.160–104 BC, a grandson of MASINISSA, was adopted as joint heir by King Micipsa, who was Jugurtha's uncle and Masinissa's successor. On Micipsa's death (118), Jugurtha murdered one of the other two heirs and seized the second's capital at Cirta, thus uniting NUMIDIA under his rule. In the fray some Italians were killed, and Rome launched (112) the Jugurthine War to avenge their deaths. Jugurtha made peace in 111, but war was renewed after he murdered another rival. First under Quintus Caecilius METELLUS NUMIDICUS and then under Gaius MARIUS, the Romans were unable to subdue Jugurtha until he was betrayed by his father-in-law, Bocchus of Mauretania, in 105. Jugurtha was executed in a Roman prison.

Juilliard, Augustus D. [jool'-yard]

Augustus D. Juilliard, b. at sea between France and the United States, Apr. 19, 1836, d. Apr. 25, 1919, was a merchant and banker who left most of his fortune to music schools and to the support of opera. Beginning his career in the textile industry, Juilliard acquired interests in woolen mills, silk mills, and cotton mills and became a powerful figure in the New York financial world. He was a devotee of the opera. At the end of his life he was president of the Metropolitan Opera and Real Estate Company. The Juilliard Foundation supports the eminent school of music named for him and contributes to other musical activities. Juilliard also gave extensively to the American Museum of Natural History.

Juilliard School, The

As the educational arm of Lincoln Center for the Performing Arts in New York City, The Juilliard School, with both undergraduate and graduate divisions, offers broad professional training in music, dance, and drama. Housing the Juilliard American Opera Center (established 1969-70), several orchestral, chamber, and choral ensembles (made up of students and faculty), and four auditoriums, the school is a popular center for concerts and opera. Drama and dance departments were added in 1968. The Juilliard String Quartet was founded in 1946. Peter MENNIN has been president since 1962.

The Juilliard Music Foundation was incorporated in 1920 with the aid of a bequest from Augustus D. Juilliard, a New York textile manufacturer. Four years later The Juilliard School of Music was established, and in 1926 it merged with the Institute of Musical Art, which had been founded by Frank Damrosch in 1905. William Schuman was president of the school from 1945 until 1962, when he became president of Lincoln Center.

jujitsu: see MARTIAL ARTS.

jujube [joo'-joob]

Jujube, *Ziziphus*, is any of several deciduous or evergreen trees or shrubs widely distributed in tropical, subtropical, or temperate regions. They belong to the family *Rhamnaceae*. The Chinese jujube, *Z. jujuba*, is a small, deciduous tree that has been cultivated for at least 4,000 years in China. It bears a small, dark fruit with white flesh that, eaten fresh, dried, or

The common jujube, often called the Chinese jujube or the Chinese date, Z. jujuba, bears a datelike fruit that ripens in late fall.

candied, is one of China's chief fruits. The tree is also grown in the Mediterranean area and in parts of the United States, for example, in California and Texas, as well as in Mexico, sometimes as an ornamental. The pit or stone is sometimes eaten as a nut. The Indian jujube, *Z. mauritiana*, a small, thorny evergreen, differs from the Chinese jujube in that the underside of the leaf is covered with dense hairs. The plant is widespread in tropical Africa and Asia, particularly the drier regions. The fruits, rich in vitamin C and eaten fresh or dried, are also made into a drink.

DIANNE FAHSELT

jukebox [jook'-bahks]

The jukebox is a coin-operated phonograph that plays records of the customer's choice. The first jukebox was installed in San Francisco's Palais Royal Saloon in 1899. A converted Edison electric phonograph, it was equipped with four listening tubes and four coin slots. The modern jukebox offers a selection of up to 200 long-playing records, has a permanent stylus, and plays in stereophonic sound.

The term *jukebox* was first used in the late 1930s. Jook, a word of African origin used by blacks in the American South, referred to brothels where nickel-in-the-slot machines were often found.

The growing American enthusiasm for SWING music during the 1930s led to a proliferation of jukeboxes in bars, diners, and drugstores, and brought new prosperity to the recording industry, which had languished during the previous two decades.

Julian, George Washington

George Washington Julian, b. Wayne County, Ind., May 5, 1817, d. July 7, 1899, was a U.S. congressman who opposed slavery and its extension. An Indiana lawyer, he entered (1845) the state legislature as a Whig. In 1848, after joining the antislavery FREE-SOIL PARTY, he was elected to the House of Representatives and there vigorously opposed the COMPROMISE OF 1850. Julian lost his seat in Congress but accepted nomination for the vice-presidency on the 1852 Free-Soil ticket. In 1856 he joined the new Republican party, became one of its early leaders, and in 1860 was again elected to Congress for the first of five consecutive terms. During the Civil War, Julian pressed hard for the emancipation of slaves and supported the Homestead Act. In the Reconstruction period, he advocated black suffrage and played a leading role in the impeachment trial of Andrew Johnson. Later an advocate of women's rights, he joined the Liberal-Republicans in 1872 and the Democrats in 1876.

JAMES BREWER STEWART

Bibliography: Riddleburger, Patrick, *George Washington Julian* (1964).

Julian day

The Julian day is the unit of a chronological system in which any date is measured by counting the number of days from an arbitrary zero day, Jan. 1, 4713 BC, at noon, Greenwich time. Joseph Scaliger created the system in 1582, believing that the Earth was created in 4713 BC. It is now used mostly in astronomy to calculate the number of days between two widely separated periodic events, such as eclipses. The Julian date (JD) of Jan. 1, 1980 (at noon), is JD 2,444,240.

Julian the Apostate, Roman Emperor

Flavius Claudius Julianus, called Julian the Apostate, b. AD 331 or 332, d. June 26, 363, was the last pagan Roman emperor. A nephew of CONSTANTINE I, he survived the purge in which his father was killed upon Constantine's death (337) but was exiled to remote Cappadocia. There he rejected the Christian faith in which he had been baptized and embraced the traditional pagan cults.

Following the execution of his half brother Gallus in 354, Julian was unexpectedly appointed caesar in his place the following year. He remained on good terms with the emperor CONSTANTIUS II until 360, when he refused to supply troops for the war against the Persians and subsequently demanded an equal share in the government. Only the death (361) of Constantius prevented another civil war.

Succeeding Constantius as emperor, Julian attempted to rescind privileges the Christian church had enjoyed under his predecessors and to restore paganism through proclamations and philosophical discourses. Whether the failure of these efforts, which only the educated few could have appreciated, would have inspired a persecution is uncertain. Julian died while campaigning against the Persians, and his policies were abandoned by his Christian successor, Jovian.   JOHN W. EADIE

Bibliography: Bowersock, G., *Julian the Apostate* (1978); Browning, R., *The Emperor Julian* (1976); Head, C., *The Emperor Julian* (1976).

Juliana, Queen of the Netherlands
[joo-lee-an'-uh]

Juliana, b. Apr. 30, 1909, succeeded to the throne of the Netherlands on Sept. 6, 1948, following the abdication of her mother, Queen WILHELMINA. She married (1937) Prince BERNHARD OF LIPPE-BIESTERFELD; they had four daughters. The eldest, Princess Beatrix, b. Jan. 31, 1938, is heir presumptive to the throne.

Julius Caesar   [jool'-yuhs see'-zur]

William SHAKESPEARE's *Tragedy of Julius Caesar*, written and first performed in 1599 and published in 1623, is closely based on Plutarch's *Lives*, translated by Sir Thomas North as *The Lives of the Noble Grecians and Romans* (1579). *Julius Caesar* is a convincing re-creation of Roman history, and the speeches of Brutus, in particular, evoke the clarity and rationality of Roman philosophy and republican virtue. Brutus is an early example of the Shakespearean tragic protagonist: a good, thoughtful man who blunders in practical life. His assassination of Caesar, undertaken for the public good, is construed as an envious murder and precipitates a civil war. Antony, however, is a thoroughly political figure who sways the mob in his funeral oration for Caesar and so turns the "tide in the affairs of men" against the conspirators.
MAURICE CHARNEY

Bibliography: Palmer, John, *Political Characters of Shakespeare* (1945); Ure, Peter, ed., *Julius Caesar: A Collection of Critical Essays* (1969).

Julius II, Pope

Julius II, b. Dec. 5, 1443, d. Feb. 21, 1513, was pope from 1503 to 1513. His name was Giuliano della Rovere. A nephew of Pope SIXTUS IV, he was elected pope after a long career in ecclesiastical politics.

In 1506 he consolidated control over the PAPAL STATES and enlarged his temporal power by the conquest of Perugia and Bologna. Shortly thereafter Julius assumed successful leader-ship in Italy of a campaign to drive out the French invaders (see ITALIAN WARS). In 1511, he formed the Holy League against France; it included Spain, England, Switzerland, Venice, and the papacy. King LOUIS XII responded by convoking a council at Pisa to depose the pope. With the avowed intention of reforming the church, Julius replied to the schismatic council of Pisa by calling the Fifth LATERAN COUNCIL in 1512. The cardinals who had sided with Louis were removed from their positions, and Gallicanism was condemned.

Although criticized and satirized for his military undertakings, Julius II was a sincere and vigorous churchman. He was also a patron of great Renaissance artists such as Donato BRAMANTE, whom he commissioned as the first architect for the new SAINT PETER'S BASILICA; RAPHAEL, to whom he entrusted the painting of the papal apartments; and MICHELANGELO, who frescoed for him the ceiling of the SISTINE CHAPEL.
JOHN W. O'MALLEY

Bibliography: Gobineau, Joseph, *Golden Flower*, trans. by B. R. Redman (1924).

July Revolution

In July 1830 an insurrection in France forced the abdication of CHARLES X and brought LOUIS-PHILIPPE to the throne. The culmination of liberal middle-class opposition to the reactionary Charles, the revolution was precipitated by Charles's issue of the repressive July Ordinances. One of the leading liberal activists was Adolphe THIERS.

Jumbo

Jumbo, whose name has entered the English language as an adjective, was the great African male elephant acquired by P. T. BARNUM from the London Zoological Society in 1882. The purchase outraged Britishers but proved a gold mine for the Barnum & Bailey Circus. Jumbo's skeleton is at the American Museum of Natural History in New York City.   A. H. SAXON

Jummu and Kashmir: see KASHMIR.

Jumna River: see YAMUNA RIVER.

jumping plant louse

Jumping plant lice comprise over 1,000 species of tiny insects, 2–5 mm (0.08–0.2 in) in length, that resemble miniature cicadas and are active jumpers. They belong to the family Psyllidae, order HOMOPTERA. Some are serious pests of orchard trees and garden plants. On infested plants, the nymphs of many species produce large amounts of a waxy secretion resembling cotton or wool. Some of these insects form small, beadlike galls on hackberry leaves.   DONALD J. BORROR

junco   [juhn'-koh]

The slate-colored junco, J. hyemalis, is a sparrow common to eastern regions of North America.

Juncos are any of several North American birds that belong to the finch family, Fringillidae. They are approximately 15 cm (6 in) in size, with pink bills and white outer tail feathers. The yellow-eyed junco, *Junco phaeonotus*, has a dark upper bill and pale lower bill. The dark-eyed junco, *hyemalis*, found from Mexico to the arctic, includes the slate-colored, Oregon, and white-winged races, until recently considered separate species. The most common form, the slate-colored junco, is dark gray above and on the breast and flanks and has a white belly. The white-winged junco is similar but has white wing bars, and the Oregon junco is brown on the back and flanks.

WILLIAM F. SANDFORD

June bug

June "bugs," also called June beetles, vary in size but are heavy-bodied oval or elongated beetles. Members of the sub-family Melolonthinae, family Scarabaeidae, they are usually brown and are commonly found around lights. Most June bugs belong to the genus *Phyllophaga*. The adults defoliate deciduous trees, and the larvae, commonly called white grubs, eat roots of a variety of plants, including small grains, grasses, corn, potatoes, and strawberries. The life cycle can require two to three years to complete.

ROBERT NOVAK AND GEORGE B. CRAIG

Juneau   [joo'-noh]

Juneau, the capital of Alaska, lies between Gastineau Channel and the slopes of Mounts Juneau and Roberts in the Alaska Panhandle. Juneau's population is 19,200 (1979 est.). In 1970 the island town of Douglas merged with Juneau, making Juneau the largest city in area in the United States, covering 8,049 km² (3,108 mi²). The climate is rainy and mild, with an average temperature of 4° C (40° F) and average annual precipitation of 1,397 mm (55 in). Juneau has an ice-free harbor, an airport, and a seaplane base. The state and federal governments are major employers; lumbering, fishing, and tourism are also important to the economy. The Alaska Historical Library and Museum house a notable collection of Indian and Eskimo artifacts.

Juneau experienced rapid growth after 1880, when two miners, Joseph Juneau and Richard Harris, discovered gold nearby. In 1900 the city became the capital of the territory of Alaska; on Alaska's admission to the Union in 1959, Juneau became the state capital.

juneberry

Juneberry, or serviceberry, *Amelanchier*, in the rose family, Rosaceae, is any of 25 species of shrubs or small trees, native to northern temperate regions. Some are planted for their white or pinkish blooms, which appear in early spring. The small, dark-blue fruit is of particular value to birds as food, although it is also collected by humans. Indians used the fruit in making bread and dried cakes. The fruits can also be used in pies and jelly. The wood is used, to some extent, to make tool handles and other items.

DIANNE FAHSELT

Jung, Carl   [yung]

Carl Gustav Jung, b. July 26, 1875, d. June 6, 1961, was a Swiss psychiatrist who founded analytical psychology. The issues he dealt with arose in part from his personal background, which is vividly described in his autobiography, *Memories, Dreams, Reflections* (1961). Throughout his life Jung experienced periodic dreams and visions with striking mythological and religious features, and these experiences shaped his interest in myths, dreams, and the psychology of religion. For many years Jung felt he possessed two separate personalities: an outer public self that was involved with the world of his family and peers and a secret inner self that felt a special closeness to God. The interplay between these selves formed a central theme of Jung's personal life and contributed to his later emphasis on the individual's striving for integration and wholeness.

The Swiss psychiatrist Carl Jung dedicated his life as scholar and therapist to the founding of analytical psychology during the early 20th century. His pioneering work in the exploration of myth and dreams in relation to the human psyche recognized the important link betweeen symbols and psychology.

Following his medical training in Basel and early years of practice at the Burghölzi Mental Hospital in Zurich, where he conducted studies of word association, Jung was deeply influenced by Sigmund Freud's writings on mental illness and dreams. From 1907 to 1913, Jung maintained close ties to Freud, and in 1911, Jung became the first president of the Internationale Psychoanalytische Gesellschaft (International Psychoanalytic Association). Theoretical disputes, chiefly concerned with the significance of sexuality in human life, finally led to Jung's breaking off the relationship with Freud.

Theory of Motivation and Personality. Jung felt that the emphasis of psychoanalysis on erotic factors led to a one-sided, reductionistic view of human motivation and behavior. He proposed that motivation be understood in terms of a general creative life energy—the libido—capable of being invested in different directions and assuming a variety of different forms. The two principal directions of the libido are known as extraversion (outward into the world of other people and objects) and introversion (inward into the realm of images, ideas, and the unconscious). Persons in whom the former directional tendency predominates are extraverts, while those in whom the latter is strongest are introverts. Jung also proposed that people could be grouped according to which of four psychological functions is most highly developed: thinking, feeling, sensation, or intuition. Transformations of libido from one sphere of expression to another—for example, from sexuality to religion—are accomplished by symbols that are generated during personality change.

Theory of Symbols. Jung viewed symbol creation as central to understanding human nature, and he explored the correspondences between symbols arising from the life struggles of individuals and the symbolic images underlying religious, mythological, and magical systems of many cultures and eras. To account for the many striking similarities between independently originating symbols in individuals and across cultures, he suggested the existence of two layers of the unconscious psyche: the personal and the collective. The personal unconscious comprises mental contents acquired during the individual's life that have been forgotten or repressed, whereas the collective unconscious is an inherited structure common to all humankind and composed of the archetypes—innate predispositions to experience and symbolize universal human situations in distinctively human ways. There are archetypes corresponding to situations such as having parents, finding a mate, having children, and confronting death, and highly elaborated derivatives of these archetypes populate all the great mythological and religious systems of the world. Toward the end of his life Jung also suggested that the deepest layers of the unconscious function independently of the laws of space, time, and causality, giving rise to paranormal phenomena such as clairvoyance and precognition.

Theory of Therapy. In Jungian therapy, which deals extensively with dreams and fantasies, a dialogue is set up between the conscious mind and the contents of the unconscious. Patients are made aware of both the personal and collective (archetypal) meanings inherent in their symptoms and difficulties. Under favorable conditions they may enter into the individuation process: a lengthy series of psychological transformations culminating in the integration of opposite tendencies and functions and the achievement of personal wholeness.   GEORGE ATWOOD

Bibliography: Bennet, E. A., *What Jung Really Said* (1971); Brome, Vincent, *Jung* (1978); Hall, Calvin S., and Nordby, Vernon A., *A Primer on Jungian Psychology* (1973); Jacobi, Jolande, *The Psychology of C. G. Jung*, 7th ed. (1968); Jung, Carl G., *The Collected Works of Carl G. Jung*, 20 vols. (1953-75), and *Man and His Symbols* (1968); McGuire, William, ed., *The Freud/Jung Letters* (1974); Moreno, Antonio, *Jung, Gods and Modern Man* (1970); Stern, Paul, *C. G. Jung: The Haunted Prophet* (1976).

Jungfrau   [yung'-frow]

The Jungfrau is a famous peak in the Bernese ALPS, on the border of the Bern and Valais cantons of Switzerland. Noted for its graceful contours and the dazzling whiteness of its snow cover (Jungfrau in German means "virgin"), it rises to a height of 4,158 m (13,642 ft). Aletsch Glacier lies on its south side, which was first ascended in 1927. The eastern side was climbed in 1811. Tourists and winter sports enthusiasts can ascend by rail to the Jungfraujoch, a mountain saddle at 3,454 m (11,332 ft), which is also the site of a scientific research observatory.

Jungle, The

The Jungle (1906), a novel by Upton SINCLAIR, is a particularly graphic example of "muckraking" fiction (see MUCKRAKERS). The book centers on the life of a Lithuanian immigrant, Jurgis Rudkus, who finds work in the Chicago stockyards. As the story proceeds, the unsanitary, exploitative conditions of the stockyards are fully documented. Working in such a barbaric environment, Rudkus becomes completely demoralized and debased, until he becomes a socialist. The novel caused a public outcry when published and is believed to have been instrumental in the passage of the Pure Food and Drug Act of 1906. Corrective labor regulation, however, did not come for another 30 years.   CHARLOTTE D. SOLOMON

Jungle Book, The

The Jungle Book (1894) is a group of stories by the English writer Rudyard KIPLING. They relate the history of an Indian boy, Mowgli, who strays from his village and is reared by a family of wolves. Mowgli's intelligence and manual dexterity make him valuable to the animals, who defend him from the perils of the wilderness. Mowgli learns the complex "Law of the Jungle" and in turn imparts human qualities to the animals. Although ostensibly a work for children, *The Jungle Book* has found many appreciative adult readers, some of whom have regarded it as an allegory of colonial government. Kipling repeated his success with *The Second Jungle Book* (1895).

jungle and rain forest

Jungle and *rain forest* are terms that are often used synonymously but with little precision. The more meaningful and restrictive of these terms is *rain forest*, which refers to the climax or primary forest in regions with high rainfall (greater than 1.8 m/70 in per year), chiefly but not exclusively found in the tropics. Rain forests are significant for their valuable timber resources, and in the tropics they afford sites for commercial crops such as rubber, tea, coffee, bananas, and sugarcane. They also include some of the last remaining areas of the Earth that are both unexploited economically and inadequately known scientifically.

The term *jungle* originally referred to the tangled, brushy vegetation of lowlands in India, but it has come to be used for any type of tropical forest or woodland. The word is more

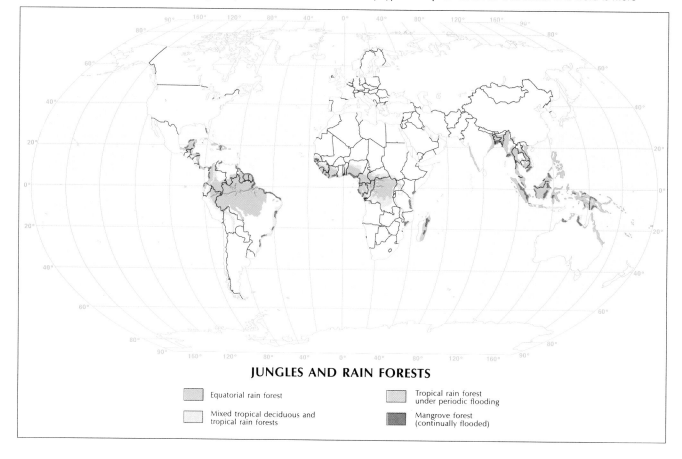

JUNGLES AND RAIN FORESTS

Equatorial rain forest

Mixed tropical deciduous and tropical rain forests

Tropical rain forest under periodic flooding

Mangrove forest (continually flooded)

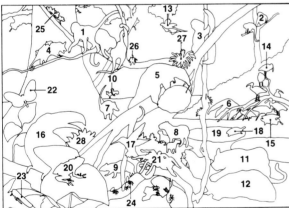

Animals of a South American rain forest include: black-capped capuchins (1), Cebus appella, and howler monkeys (2), Alovatta seniculus; the three-toed sloth (3), Bradypus tricactylus; and the opossum (4), Didelphis marsupialis. The tamandua (5), Tamandua tetradactyla, is related to the great anteater (6), Myrmelophaga tridactyla. Other inhabitants are the brown coatimundi (7), Nasua narica; the capybara (8), Hydrochoerus hydrochaeris, and the paca (9), Cuniculus paca; and the red brocket deer (10), Mazama americana. A jaguar (11), Panthera onca, strikes its prey, a tapir (12), Tapirus terrestris. Birds include: the scarlet macaw (13), Ara macao; the scarlet ibis (14), Eudocimus ruber, and the roseate spoonbill (15), A. ajaia; the keel-billed toucan (16), Ramphastos sulfuratus; and the ruby-topaz hummingbird (17), Chrysolampis mosquitus. Other animals are: a South American river turtle, the Arrau (18), Podocnemis expansa, shown on a giant lily pad (19), Victoria amazonica; the arrow poison frog (20), genus Dendrobates; the bird-eating spider (21), family Aviculariidae; a rare butterfly (22), Heliconius ethillus; a leaf hopper (23), family Cicadellica; and leaf-cutter ants (24), genus Atta. Three epiphytic plants are two orchid genera, Oncidium (25) and Cattleya (26), and a bromeliad (27). Cephaelis (28) carpets the floor.

meaningful if limited to the dense, scrubby vegetation that develops when primary rain forest has been degraded by destructive forms of logging or by cultivation followed by abandonment.

Tropical rain forest is characterized by broadleaf evergreen trees forming a closed canopy, an abundance of vines and epiphytes (plants growing on the trees), a relatively open forest floor, and a very large number of species of both plant and animal life. The largest trees have buttressed trunks and emerge above the continuous canopy, while smaller trees commonly form a layer of more shade-tolerant species beneath the upper canopy. The maximum height of the upper canopy of tropical rain forests is generally about 30 to 50 m (100 to 165 ft), with some individual trees rising as high as 60 m (200 ft) above the forest floor.

The largest areas of tropical rain forest are in the Amazon basin of South America, in the Congo basin and other lowland equatorial regions of Africa, and on both the mainland and the islands off Southeast Asia, where they are especially abundant on Sumatra and New Guinea. Small areas are found in Central America and along the Queensland coast of Australia.

The degree of human interference that has occurred in tropical rain forests varies markedly from place to place. In some areas, such as on the island of Java, the lowland primary forest has been almost totally removed and replaced with rice fields or with plantation crops such as rubber and sugarcane. Other forests, especially in Brazil and New Guinea, still remain largely undisturbed over considerable areas.

In vast portions of upland tropical forests throughout the world the practice of "shifting cultivation" has caused deterioration of the primary forest; in this primitive system of agriculture the trees are killed in a plot of a few acres that is cropped for two or three seasons and then abandoned. If the original plot is cultivated again before the primary vegetation has reestablished itself, the result is a progressive deterioration of the forest leading to coarse grass or jungle.

Temperate rain forests, growing in higher-latitude regions having wet, maritime climates, are less extensive than those of the tropics but include some of the most valuable timber in the world. Notable forests in this category are those on the northwest coast of North America, in southern Chile, in Tasmania, and in parts of southeastern Australia and New Zealand. These forests contain trees that may exceed in height those of tropical rain forests, but there is less diversity of species. Conifers such as REDWOOD and Sitka spruce tend to predominate in North America, while their counterparts in the southern hemisphere include various species of EUCALYPTUS, *Araucaria*, and *Nothofagus* (Antarctic beech).

WILLIAM C. ROBISON

Bibliography: Bates, Marston, *Where Winter Never Comes* (1952); Batten, Mary, *The Tropical Forest* (1973); Meggers, Betty J., et al., eds., *Tropical Forest Ecosystems in Africa and South America* (1973); Odum, H. I., and Pigeon, R. F., eds., *A Tropical Rain Forest* (1970); Perry, Richard, *Life in Forest and Jungle* (1976); Richards, P., *The Life of the Jungle* (1970) and *The Tropical Rain Forest* (1952; repr. 1979).

Juni, Juan de   [hoo'-nee, hwahn day]

Juan de Juni, c.1507–1577, was a master of intensely expressive sculpture in Renaissance Spain. Born in France, he arrived in León, Spain, in 1533, and later also worked in Salamanca, Zamora, and Valladolid. His early portrait medallions (1536) on the facade of San Marcos, León, display a northern sobriety, although his characteristic emotionalism is seen in the splendid polychromed wood *Pietà* group *The Entombment of Christ* (completed 1544; Valladolid Museum, Spain). Juni was also an important designer of altars, such as the Antigua Altar (completed 1560) in the Valladolid Cathedral.

EDWARD J. SULLIVAN

Bibliography: Alcolea, Santiago, *Spanish Sculpture* (1969); Kubler, George, and Soria, Martín, *Art and Architecture in Spain and Portugal and Their American Dominions, 1500 to 1800* (1959).

junior colleges: see COMMUNITY AND JUNIOR COLLEGES.

junior high school: see MIDDLE SCHOOLS AND JUNIOR HIGH SCHOOLS.

juniper   [joon'-ih-pur]

Junipers, *Juniperus*, are evergreen trees or shrubs belonging to the cypress family, Cupressceae. They include approximately 35 species found throughout the Northern Hemisphere from the Arctic Circle to Mexico and the West Indies, Azores, Canary Islands, North Africa, Abyssinia, the mountains of tropical East Africa, the Himalayas, China, and Formosa.

Juniper bark is usually thin and scales off in longitudinal strips. Leaves are awl-shaped, closely pressed, and scalelike. The wood is fragrant, usually highly colored, reddish brown, and very durable. An essential oil is distilled from the wood and used for perfume and, sometimes, in medicine. Juniper leaves have powerful diuretic properties, and the characteristic taste of gin is derived from juniper berries. The common juniper, *J. communis*, is a small tree that is found in the colder northern areas of the Northern Hemisphere, and many are grown as landscape plants. Red "cedar," *J. virginiana*, is the most important juniper native to the United States. Its wood is the main source of "cedar" lining used to mothproof closets.

Junius   [joon'-ee-uhs]

Junius was the pseudonym of the author of a series of political lampoons published in the *London Public Advertiser* between Jan. 21, 1769, and Jan. 21, 1772. With eloquent wit and sarcasm, the essays—commonly called the "Letters of the Junius"—denounced the government of King George III and many of its major officials, including the prime minister, Lord NORTH. Since that time dozens of writers have been tentatively identified as Junius, among them such eminent figures as Edward Gibbon, John Wilkes, Edmund Burke, and Thomas Paine. But Sir Philip Francis, then a clerk in the war office, is currently considered the likeliest candidate.

Bibliography: Cannon, John, ed., *The Letters of Junius* (1978); Cordasco, Francesco, *A Junius Bibliography* (1973).

junk

By the late Middle Ages the ancient Chinese sailing ship had evolved into the junk, one of the world's strongest and most seaworthy ships. (The term probably is derived from the Chinese *Ch'uan*, "boat," via Malay *djong*.) The junk is notable for two innovations in shipbuilding, the construction of the hull and the rigging of the sails. Lacking three components—the keel as well as the stemposts and sternposts (upright beams at the bow and the stern)—that are basic to other types of ships, the junk has a hull that is partitioned off by solid plank walls, or bulkheads, running both lengthwise and crosswise, dividing the junk into watertight compartments and giving it structural rigidity. (Crosswise bulkheads were not adopted in the West until the 19th century.) The lack of a keel is compensated for by using a deep, heavy rudder mounted so that it can be raised and lowered. The sails, made of narrow, horizontal sheets of linen or of matting panels, are carried on masts numbering from one to five. Each panel has its own

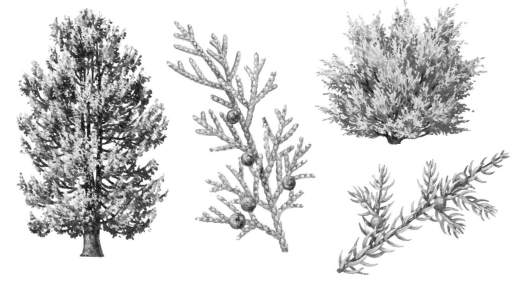

The juniper is a small, coniferous tree that has scaly leaves and berrylike cones, each of which contains one to six seeds. The western juniper (left), J. occidentalis, is found in the Sierra Nevada mountains of California. The common juniper (right), J. communis, is found throughout temperate and cold northern climates.

The junk, a sailing vessel used primarily for coastal trade, features a projecting bow and high stern. Junks have been used in eastern Asia for thousands of years.

sheet, or line; the numerous lines help distribute the wind's force, and each sail can be quickly spread or closed.

By the 9th century, Chinese junks were carrying merchants to Indonesia and India. Marco Polo, in his *Travels* (1298), describes such a junk and praises its system of bulkheads. By the 15th century, junks had sailed as far as eastern Africa, and in 1848 a junk sailed from China by way of Cape Horn to Boston, New York City, and London.   FRANCES GIES

Bibliography: Worcester, G. R., *Junks and Sampans of the Yangtze* (1971).

Junkers   [yunk'-urz]

The name *Junker*, derived from a German term meaning "young lord," was applied to the aristocracy of PRUSSIA, which became the ruling elite of the German Empire created in 1871. The Junkers, descendants of the medieval German knights who conquered the territory east of the Elbe River, owned huge feudal estates in eastern Germany. When the rulers of Brandenburg-Prussia began to centralize government in the 17th century, the Junkers lost some of their feudal privileges, but they were compensated with a monopoly on the military and administrative services. This situation persisted after the unification of Germany under the Prussian monarchy, and the Junker values of extreme conservatism and militarism permeated the German government until 1918. Junker hostility helped undermine the Weimar Republic (1918–33) and thus contributed to the rise of Adolf Hitler. Many Junker estates remained in existence until the Soviet occupation of eastern Germany at the end of World War II.

Juno   (mythology)

In Roman mythology, Juno, the wife and sister of JUPITER, was the queen of heaven. Like HERA, her Greek counterpart, she was the goddess of marriage and the protectress of women. She also presided over the finances of the Roman state, and the mint was located in her temple on the Capitoline Hill. A festival, the Matronalia, was celebrated in her honor on March 1.

Juno   (rocket)

Juno I was the rocket that placed the first U.S. artificial satellite, EXPLORER I, into orbit on Jan. 31, 1958. The 29,030-kg (64,000-lb) four-stage rocket stood 24.7 m (81.3 ft) tall and had a lift-off thrust of about 369,000 newtons, or 37,648 kg

(83,000 lb). The rocket was a development of the JUPITER-C rocket, which in turn had been based on the REDSTONE medium-range ballistic missile built under the direction of Werner von Braun at the Army Ballistic Missile Agency. So that Juno I could be used as a satellite launcher, a fourth-stage Baby Sergeant motor was added to Jupiter C; this allowed the rocket to achieve an orbital velocity of 28,157 km/h (17,500 mph).

Juno II was a four-stage satellite and space-probe launcher based on a Jupiter intermediate-range ballistic missile (IRBM) that had its body lengthened by 0.91 m (3 ft) to allow enough propellant for 20 seconds extra burning time. It carried an arrangement of Baby Sergeant upper stages similar to the Jupiter IRBM. The weight was about 64,856 kg (121,000 lb).

KENNETH GATLAND

Junot, Andoche   [zhoo-noh', ahn-dohsh']

Andoche Junot, b. Oct. 23, 1771, d. July 29, 1813, was a French general during the NAPOLEONIC WARS. He rose through the ranks and served as aide-de-camp to Napoléon Bonaparte (later NAPOLEON I) in Italy and Egypt. In 1807, Junot opened the Peninsular War with his invasion of Portugal. He was rewarded for his entry into Lisbon with the title duc d'Abrantès. Following a defeat in 1808 by the future duke of WELLINGTON, however, he was forced to evacuate Portugal. Despite later military service against Spain, Austria, and Russia, Junot never regained his reputation. He became mentally unstable and committed suicide.

junta   [hun'-tuh]

Junta, a Spanish word meaning council or committee, is the name given to a small group of people who rule a country, usually after a revolution or coup d'état. A junta may assume control for the purpose of restoring order in times of national turbulence, or it may have the aim of instituting reforms or reversing policies of a previous government. Juntas usually count among their members high-ranking military officers and tend to advocate a conservative or moderate approach. Juntas either govern by decree or form governments that will carry out their wishes. Although juntas have most commonly been associated with Spanish-speaking countries of the New World, the term *junta* has international application. In 1952, for instance, a military junta took over the Egyptian government. One of the members was Gamal Abdel Nasser, who became (1954) Egypt's prime minister and who subsequently took control of the country. In earlier centuries the word *junta* generally referred to a governing group, a meaning somewhat different from the one it has today. In 16th-century Spain *junta* was the name given to numerous government consultative committees. Spanish resistance to Napoleon's invasion in 1808 during the Peninsula War was organized by provincial and national juntas. In English history the word *junto* (a variant of *junta*) was used to describe the Whig faction in late-17th-century England.

Bibliography: Janowitz, Morris, *Military Institutions and Coercion in the Developing Nations*, 2d ed. (1977); Woddis, Jack, *Armies and Politics* (1977).

Jupiter   (mythology)

In Roman mythology, Jupiter was the king of the gods and the lord of life and death. He was also called Jove. Jupiter was the son of SATURN and Rhea, the husband of JUNO, and the father of MINERVA. The Romans identified him with the Greek god ZEUS, but he retained to some degree his own distinctive character. Unlike Zeus, for example, he never came to visit humankind on earth. Jupiter was usually represented in art sitting on an ivory throne and holding a sheaf of thunderbolts. The eagle and the ox were sacred to him. His most celebrated temple was on the CAPITOLINE HILL in Rome.

Jupiter   (planet)

Jupiter is the fifth planet from the Sun. Named for the Roman ruler of the gods, Jupiter is brighter than any star in the sky, attaining a magnitude of −2.5 at opposition. Because Jupiter's orbit is greater than the Earth's, it can remain above the horizon all night.

Surface Appearance. Even in a small telescope, Jupiter presents a complex image, revealing dark regions near the poles, a bright zone at the equator (which at times becomes extremely narrow), and a series of approximately four dark belts and four bright zones in parallel bands in each hemisphere. In the south tropical zone near −22° latitude lies the GREAT RED SPOT. An oval that varies in size and is now 38,500 km (24,000 mi) long and 13,800 km (8,500 mi) wide, the spot's smaller dimension is greater than the Earth's diameter. Usually brick red, at times the color of the spot fades and nearly disappears. The Great Red Spot has been observed for more than 300 years and is possibly a permanent feature of the planet.

The bright zones on Jupiter are generally yellowish or whitish, and the darker belts brownish or reddish. In a large telescope, when the atmosphere is very steady, a more intricate structure of spots, plumes, waves, and festoons begins to appear, and local spots appear that are white, blue, gray, or black. The true complexity of Jupiter's surface becomes apparent in space-probe pictures of the planet.

Astronomical Data. Jupiter revolves around the Sun at an average distance of 778,330,000 km (483,340,000 mi) in an almost circular orbit (eccentricity 0.0484) inclined to the plane of the ecliptic by only 1°18'. Jupiter is 143,200 km (88,900 mi) in diameter at its equator, which is 11.23 times the diameter of the Earth and almost one-tenth the diameter of the Sun. The planet is highly flattened, and its polar diameter is only 134,600 km (83,600 mi). The polar axis is inclined only 3°7' from perpendicular to the orbit. The flattening is the natural result of rapid rotation, the Jovian day being less than 10 hours. The velocity of a point at the equator due to rotation is 12.6 km/s (28,200 mi/h) which is greater than the ESCAPE VELOCITY at the Earth's equator. With Jupiter's mass being 317.9 times that of Earth (1.9 × 10²⁷ kg or 2.1 × 10²⁴ tons), the effective gravitational pull (gravity minus centrifugal force) is 2.34 times as great as Earth's. Yet the planet is so large that its mean density is only 1.32 g/cm³, one-quarter that of Earth.

Jupiter's rotational period is difficult to define. The visible clouds near the equator rotate with an average period of 9 hr 50 min 30 sec, called the System I period. More than 10° from the equator, the average is nearer the System II period of 9 hr 55 min 41 sec, but in fact individual cloud systems have their own small, peculiar motions, and the precise periods are given for reference in catalogs and ephemerides. Recently, a System III period of about 9 hr 55 min 30 sec has been determined from the rotation period of the Jovian magnetic field as measured by radio astronomers, and this is generally used as the planet's true rotation period. Because Jupiter may be fluid throughout, except possibly for a small rocky core, no better period may ever be derived than that of the magnetic field of the planet.

Atmosphere. Detailed knowledge of Jupiter's atmosphere has come from ultraviolet, visible, infrared, and microwave spectroscopy and radiometry from Earth, the *Pioneer 10* and *11* flights in 1973 and 1974, and the *Voyager 1* and *2* flights in 1979. Radar returns have come from Jupiter's larger satellites, but microwave radiation falling on the planet appears to be absorbed by atmospheric gases such as ammonia.

The major atmospheric constituents are molecular hydrogen (H_2) and helium (He) in a ratio near 89 to 11 by number of molecules, which is virtually the solar ratio. The uncertainty in the helium abundance is rather large, however, and errors of 100 percent in the helium abundance are possible. The most important minor components in the visible atmosphere are methane (CH_4), approximately 1×10^{-3} of the abundance of molecular hydrogen, and ammonia (NH_3), approximately 2×10^{-4} of the abundance of molecular hydrogen.

Other minor constituents that have been identified include ethane (C_2H_6), acetylene (C_2H_2), phosphine (PH_3), carbon monoxide (CO), and water (H_2O). The first two of these are probably created by photolysis (dissociation of a gas by electromagnetic radiation, in this case methane by the Sun, followed by reaction of the products) in the Jovian upper atmosphere. Water has been seen only near a wavelength (5 microns) that is especially free of absorptions and that allows penetration to a depth where water remains unfrozen. Tentative identification has also been made of germanium tetrahydride (GeH_4). Three molecules involving isotopes of hydrogen or carbon have been confirmed: CH_3D, HD, and $^{13}CH_4$, where D is a deuterium hydrogen atom.

Models of Jupiter's atmosphere must be two-dimensional if they are to account for the banded appearance of the planet. The light-colored zones appear to be regions of high clouds in which warmer "air" is rising, and the darker belts are relatively clear regions of sinking cooler "air" that allow views to greater atmospheric depth. These clouds are ammonia cirrus,

(Left) *This montage of Jupiter and its four largest, or Galilean, moons was assembled from photographs taken by Voyager 1 in early March 1979. In order of increasing distance from Jupiter, Io (upper left) is closest, followed by Europa (center), Ganymede, and Callisto (lower right).*

(Below) *The presence of a thin ring of debris around Jupiter was first recorded by* Voyager I *on Mar. 4, 1979. This image of the ring was photographed (July 10) by* Voyager 2. *The ring is too tenuous to be visible from Earth. A fainter ring is visible within the brighter ring and may extend to the cloud tops.*

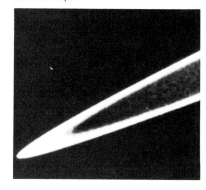

The highly turbulent and complex nature of Jupiter's cloud-top features is illustrated in this photograph of the region near the Great Red Spot taken by the Voyager 2 spacecraft on July 3, 1979. The Great Red Spot is a gigantic hurricane system that rotates counterclockwise with one revolution every 6 days. Although it has varied in width from 2 to 3 times the size of the Earth and in color intensity during the 300 years that it has been observed, it has always remained at the same latitude.

clouds of ammonia crystals with their bases near 145 K (−198° F). The visible surface in the belts is a second cloud layer near 225 K (−54° F), probably ammonium hydrosulfide (NH₄SH), only partially obscured by ammonia crystals. Occasional dark spots that appear in the belts are holes to greater depths where temperatures are 310 K (99° F) or more. Water has been detected spectroscopically through such holes. The forces driving these motions are not well understood, nor are any of the large-scale motions on the planet.

Jupiter's Rings. Jupiter is the third planet in the solar system (after Saturn and Uranus) known to be encircled by a ring. The ring was discovered in a single photograph taken by *Voyager 1* in March 1979 and confirmed by *Voyager 2* four months later. Too faint to be seen from Earth, the ring consists of many small particles about 10 microns in size. Most of the material is concentrated in a region about 6,500 km (4,000 mi) wide, compared to the 80,000-km (49,000-mi) width of Saturn's rings. The outer edge of the ring is about 57,000 km (35,000 mi) from Jupiter's upper regions and well inside the orbit of Amalthea, the innermost moon. At least one scientist has speculated that material may be circling Jupiter from the ring down to the surface.

The Interior. All contemporary models of Jupiter's interior include a rocky core at a uniform temperature. Only with such a core could the helium abundance be kept down to approximately solar values, and only such a core could be responsible for the form of the planet's gravitational field. Above the core is a region of metallic hydrogen mixed with helium and a solar abundance of "ices" (solid water, methane, and ammonia). Metallic hydrogen is the stable phase of hydrogen at pressures above a few million atmospheres, at which point all of its electrons become stripped from the protons. It is an excellent conductor. Above the metallic hydrogen layer is one of mixed molecular hydrogen and helium. Separate hydrogen-rich and helium-rich layers are possible at temperatures less than about 8,000° C (14,400° F) in the molecular layer, where the fluids may become immiscible. The excess power radiated by Jupiter is convected from the interior, where it is produced by one or more of several effects.

Magnetic Field. Two regions of Jupiter's interior should show good electrical conductivity: the metallic hydrogen phase and the bottom of the molecular hydrogen layer, where high pressures destroy its insulating gap and valence electrons can flow freely. Moderately good electrical conductivity in a fluid in complex motion is needed for generation of a planetary magnetic field. *Pioneers 10* and *11* carried magnetometers that added detail to a model of Jupiter's magnetic field already suggested by radio astronomers from their studies of Jupiter's radiation. Near Jupiter the field can be described as a dipole field with its axis tilted about 10° from Jupiter's rotational axis

and displaced about one-tenth of the planetary radius from the center of the planet.

The maximum field strength at Jupiter's surface is 14.4 gauss in the northern hemisphere and 10.8 gauss in the southern hemisphere, compared to 0.58 and 0.68 gauss at Earth's magnetic poles. Earth's field is also tipped and displaced by 11°24′ and 0.07 radii, in a simple dipole description. The Jovian field actually arises in the upper metallic and lower molecular hydrogen regions and not in the center of the planet. Farther from the planet the field lines are stretched out nearly radially because of a ring of charged particles circling Jupiter from about 20 to 60 radii outward.

Satellites. Jupiter has its own miniature solar system of 13 or more satellites. The four largest were discovered in January 1610 by Galileo and are easily seen with 7×50 binoculars. In 1892, a tiny fifth satellite was found, visually through the 36-in (91-cm) Lick refracting telescope, close to the planet. Since then, eight more small satellites have been found photographically, four revolving in prograde (direct) orbits around Jupiter at distances near 11.5 million km (7 million mi) and four revolving in retrograde (backward) orbits near 23 million km (14 million mi). Charles T. Kowal, who in September 1974 found satellite XIII, also discovered in October 1975 a probable 14th, but its angular separation from Jupiter soon grew so small that insufficient observations were obtained for a reliable orbit, and the body was lost; it was rediscovered by the *Voyager 2* spacecraft in July 1979. Jupiter's small satellites have always been given Roman-numeral designations upon discovery. Formal names were officially accepted for nine of them only in 1976.

Other than the Galilean satellites, only JV, JVI, and JVII have received any study other than for positions and visual magnitudes because the others are so small and faint. Infrared measurements of JV, JVI, and JVII indicate all are dark objects, having visual geometric albedos of only 0.02, 0.03, and 0.03. These values indicate diameters of roughly 240, 170, and 80 km (150, 105, and 50 mi).   RAY L. NEWBURN, JR.

Bibliography: Asimov, Isaac, *Jupiter: The Largest Planet* (1973); Burns, J. A., *Planetary Satellites* (1977); Gehrels, T., ed., *Jupiter* (1976);

CHARACTERISTICS OF JUPITER

Mean distance from Sun	778,330,000 km (483,340,000 mi)
Length of year	11.86 years
Length of day	9 h, 50 min, 30 sec
Inclination of axis	3° 05′
Equatorial diameter	143,200 km (88,900 mi)
Mass compared to Earth	317.9
Specific density (water-1)	1.32
Atmosphere	hydrogen, helium
Mean temperature	−127° C (−198° F)

JUPITER'S SATELLITES

Satellite		Year of Discovery	Apparent Magnitude	Average Distance from Jupiter km	mi	Period of Revolution	Radius km	mi
JV	Amalthea	1892	14.1	181,000	112,000	0.498	160	100
JI	Io	1610	5.0	422,000	262,000	1.769	3,636	2,260
JII	Europa	1610	5.3	671,000	417,000	3.551	3,060	1,900
JIII	Ganymede	1610	4.6	1,070,000	665,000	7.155	5,220	3,240
JIV	Callisto	1610	5.6	1,880,000	1,168,000	16.689	4,890	3,040
JXIII	Leda	1974	20.	11,100,000	6,898,000	238.7	~6	~4
JVI	Himalia	1904	14.8	11,500,000	7,146,000	250.6	~100	~60
JVII	Elara	1905	16.4	11,700,000	7,270,000	259.7	~24	~15
JX	Lysithea	1938	18.4	11,900,000	7,395,000	263.6	~16	~10
JXII	Ananke	1951	18.9	21,200,000	13,174,000	631.1	~16	~10
JXI	Carme	1938	18.0	22,600,000	14,043,000	692.5	~18	~11
JVIII	Pasiphae	1908	17.7	23,500,000	14,600,000	738.9	~20	~12
JIX	Sinope	1914	18.3	23,700,000	14,700,000	758.	~18	~11

Pasachoff, Jay, *Astronomy Now* (1978); "Voyager 2," *Science News*, July 14, 1979; Wetterer, Margaret K., *The Moons of Jupiter* (1971); Wolfe, J. H., "Jupiter," *Scientific American*, September 1975.

See also: PLANETS; SATELLITE.

Jupiter (rocket)

Jupiter is the name given to two different ROCKETS, one (Jupiter C) a modified REDSTONE rocket that was the basis for the Juno I satellite launches, and the other an intermediate-range ballistic missile (IRBM) later developed into Juno II. Both were under the control of the Army Ballistic Missile Agency.

The Jupiter C, first launched on Sept. 20, 1956, to test nose-cone materials for the Jupiter IRBM under development, was a Redstone rocket lengthened by 2.44 m (8 ft) to a total length of 23.5 m (77.3 ft). Its original LO_2/ethyl alcohol PROPELLANTS were changed to liquid oxygen and Hydyne, a mixture of 60% unsymmetrical dimethylhydrazine and 40% diethylene triamine. Two solid-propellant stages were clustered in a spinning "tub" on the separable nose of the vehicle, which contained the guidance platform. Stage 2 had an outer ring of 11 solid-propellant rocket motors; stage 3 had a second cluster of three of these motors (Baby Sergeants) inside.

The Jupiter IRBM, first test-launched at Cape Canaveral on Mar. 1, 1957, was a liquid-propellant (LO_2/kerosene) rocket. It stood 18.4 m (60.3 ft) tall, had a diameter of 266.7 cm (105 in), and a launch weight of approximately 49,900 kg (110,000 lb). Maximum design range was 2,575 km (1,600 mi). The later development of lightweight thermonuclear warheads and the desire to have missiles concealed in nuclear submarines resulted in the more compact solid-propellant POLARIS missile, and Jupiter production was terminated.   KENNETH GATLAND

Jura [jur'-uh]

The Jura, a mountain range of the Alpine system (see ALPS), form a natural boundary between France and Switzerland. The range extends 200 km (125 mi) from the Rhône River gorge near Geneva, north to the Rhine River near Basel. The narrow, parallel ridges reach a maximum width of 65 km (40 mi). Average elevation is about 860 m (2,800 ft), and the maximum elevation is 1,723 m (5,650 ft) at Crêt de la Neige, in France.

The Jura was formed in two stages: during the early Tertiary Period when the Alps originated and during the Jurassic Period (the latter period is named for the mountains). The ridges and furrows of fossiliferous limestone conceal many underground rivers and caverns. Principal above-ground rivers include the Ain, the Doubs, and the Loire. The heavily forested slopes support stands of oak, beech, fir, and sycamore maple. Pulp, paper, and lumber industries are important, as are watchmaking and other skilled manufacturing, dairying, and tourism. Transportation routes, which from Roman times have followed the transverse gorges called *cluses*, are augmented by modern tunnels and roads cut through the ranges.

Jurassic Period [jur-as'-ik]

The Jurassic Period, from about 190 to 140 million years ago, is the middle division of the MESOZOIC ERA of geologic time. The name, introduced (1829) by the French geologist Alexandre BRONGNIART, refers to the chalk sequence in the rock strata of the Swiss-French Jura Mountains. Stratigraphers have subdivided the Jurassic system into the following stages:

Upper	Portlandian Kimmeridgian Oxfordian Callovian
Middle	Bathonian Bajocian
Lower	Aalenian Toarcian Pliensbachian Sinemurian Hettangian

PALEOTECTONICS AND GEOGRAPHY

At the beginning of the Jurassic Period, the various parts of the supercontinent of Gondwanaland—South America, Africa, India, Antarctica, and Australia—were still connected to one another. They remained so until the late Jurassic (160 to 135 million years ago), when CONTINENTAL DRIFT began to rift them apart. A vast, shallow sea, the Tethys, separated Gondwanaland from the protocontinents of Europe and Asia at this time.

Great thicknesses of marine sediments were accumulating in belts of sinking crust (geosynclines), one of which, occupied by the Tethys Sea, extended from the Mediterranean to Iran, the Himalayas, and Indonesia. In the Alpine, or Northern Tethyan geosyncline, thicknesses of Jurassic sediment, containing a large variety of facies, were deposited. (Jurassic facies patterns are complex, and changes in thickness are commonly abrupt.) The geology of the Alpine region became further complicated by normal faulting, which produced a complex pattern of uplifted and downwarped blocks. Within the central and western areas of the Tethyan geosyncline, thick sequences composed primarily of marine facies were deposited. In central Iran, however, significant nonmarine strata have been found, indicating tectonic activity there.

In the circum-Pacific geosynclinal belt, graywacke, shale, siliceous sediments, and volcanics, rocks characteristic of eugeosynclines, were deposited. In some places the deposits accumulated to thicknesses of several thousand meters. A geosynclinal belt extended across northeast Siberia, where detrital sediments were deposited.

Shallow seas spreading from the Tethys, the Arctic, and the

Atlantic invaded much of northwest Europe early in Jurassic time but retreated by the close of the period. In the Indian Ocean, shelf seas occupied the coastal region of eastern Africa and the western half of Madagascar. Shelf seas also occupied various embayments in western Australia.

In North America, shallow marine transgressions originating from the Arctic Ocean covered the present area of the Rocky Mountains, eventually reaching as far south as Utah. These seas had completely retreated by the end of the Jurassic. The Gulf of Mexico formed during this period, a fact indicated by the presence of Jurassic marine rocks in the southern United States, eastern Mexico, and northern Central America.

In western North America, PLATE TECTONICS triggered an orogeny as the eastern Pacific plate, driven under the American plate along a subduction zone, exerted compressional forces that deformed the geosynclinal belt of western Nevada,

producing the Sierra Nevada. This orogeny, accompanied by intrusion of batholiths, affected a great belt extending northward through British Columbia and central Alaska.

Worldwide orogenic (mountain-building) activity increased significantly over that of the preceding Triassic and heralded the intense activity of the Cretaceous. The Crimea and the Caucasus underwent orogenesis. Much of China was affected by some form of diastrophism during the Jurassic. New Zealand underwent final orogenesis in the Late Jurassic, as did the geosynclinal belt extending across northeast Siberia.

With few exceptions, Jurassic climates seem to have been remarkably equitable. In the western United States, arid conditions are indicated by thick deposits of dune sand, which accumulated, especially in Utah, before transgression of the inland sea from the north. No evidence of Jurassic glaciation has been found.

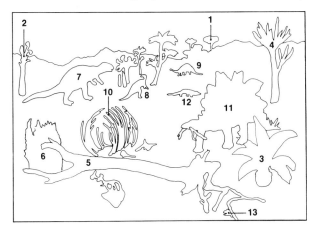

Jurassic life forms have been well documented by fossils found in the Morrison Formation, layers of sedimentary rock that were deposited from Montana to Arizona as newly formed mountains to the west were eroded. The prevalent flora of the Jurassic Period were gymnosperms, or plants with naked seeds: conifers (1) and tree ferns, or cyads (2), both abundant during the period; the similar cycadeoids, or Bennittatales (3); Williamsonia (4), a type of cycadeoid; and gingko trees (5), deciduous gymnosperms that developed to their present form more than 175 million years ago. Horsetails (6) and ferns were also abundant. During this period of approximately 54 million years the great dinosaurs flourished. At least 69 species have been identified from the Morrison Formation, including the ferocious Allosaurus (7), an active carnivore, and the herbivores Camptosaurus (8), Brontosaurus (9), Camarasaurus (10), and Stegosaurus (11). Crocodiles (12) much like the modern reptile existed at this time. The Jurassic Period saw the development of primitive mammals (13), which had first appeared during the late Triassic. Approximately 25 species of these small mammals have been identified from Jurassic rock formations. These were not to develop and gain ascendency until the late Cretaceous Period, when dinosaurs disappeared for reasons that are still uncertain.

Jurassic plant fossils of worldwide distribution and widespread coal deposits are evidence of a moist climate that was probably warmer and more uniform than at present, although from studying the growth rings on fossil trees, experts have determined that seasons did exist.

Jurassic rocks have yielded moderate amounts of mineral resources, including iron ore and petroleum in western Europe and coal in Scotland and Greenland. Petroleum is also obtained from Jurassic rocks in North America, Morocco, and Saudi Arabia.

LIFE

The FOSSIL RECORD clearly shows that the Jurassic was a time of great abundance and diversity of life. In contrast to the Triassic, nearly all major invertebrate fossil groups exist in a great diversity of forms. The dominant invertebrate group, the ammonites, had a great resurgence after nearly becoming extinct at the close of the Triassic. The Jurassic was also a time of especially marked development and modernization of the bivalved mollusks.

The vertebrate life of the Jurassic consisted primarily of reptiles. The best known, the DINOSAURS, lived both on land (saurischians and ornithischians) and in the seas (ichthyosaurians and plesiosaurians). Some of the most famous finds of terrestrial dinosaurs have come from the Morrison Formation, a sequence of freshwater sediments deposited in Utah, Colorado, Wyoming, and Montana. Turtles and crocodiles also made their appearance in the Jurassic.

The last environmental domain uninhabited by the vertebrates was the air. This changed in the Jurassic with the appearance of the PTERODACTYLS and other pterosaurs (flying reptiles). The first bird, ARCHAEOPTERYX, also appeared during this time. Mammals, which first appeared in the Late Triassic, diversified into at least five orders during the Jurassic.

Jurassic plants were surprisingly uniform throughout the

Reptiles of the Jurassic Period not only conquered the land but also evolved to fill the air and sea. Some dinosaurs that had adapted to terrestrial life returned to the sea, including Plesiosaurus (1), a turtlelike creature with a long neck and flippers. Ichthyosaurus (2), a marine reptile existing in the Triassic Period, reached a length of up to 7.5 m (25 ft) during the Jurassic Period. Crocodiles, such as Steneosaurus (3), first appeared at this time and have changed little in the ensuing 140 million years. These sea creatures fed upon the newly developed banjo fish (4) and other fishes. Shrimp and small lobsters inhabited Jurassic seas, along with belemnites (5), cousins of the modern squid. One of the most significant developments of the period is the appearance of the first bird, Archaeopteryx (6). Although covered with feathers, the crow-sized creature retained reptilian teeth, claws, and tail. Winged reptiles, such as Pterodactylus (7) and Rhamphorhynchus (8), had neither feathers nor scales, their wings consisting of a leathery skin supported on a single extended digit. Two dinosaurs inhabiting shoreline environments were Homeosaurus (9) and the tiny Compsognathus (10), which attained a length of only 60 cm (2 ft). The fossil remains of the dinosaurs have been found in parts of every continent except Antarctica.

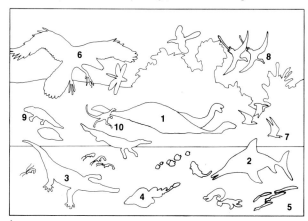

JURASSIC ROCK FORMATIONS

Primary formations

Land deposits

Ice sheet

The smaller map shows the estimated positions
of the continents during Jurassic times.

world. The principal types of flora were the CYCADS (the most characteristic type), ginkgoes, conifers, and ferns.

BERNHARD KUMMEL

Bibliography: Arkell, W. J., *Jurassic Geology of the World* (1956); Hallam, A., *Jurassic Environments* (1975); Kummel, Bernhard, *History of the Earth*, 2d ed. (1970); McKee, E. D., et al., *Paleotectonic Maps of the Jurassic System* (1956).

See also: EARTH, GEOLOGICAL HISTORY OF; EVOLUTION; PALEOGEOGRAPHY.

jurisdiction: see COURT.

jurisprudence: see LAW.

jury

A jury is a body of lay men and women randomly selected to determine facts and to provide a decision in a legal proceeding. The jury is of Frankish origin, beginning with Charlemagne's *inquisitio*, which had an accusatory and interrogatory function. Trial by jury was brought to England by the Normans in 1066. Jurors were witnesses summoned from the vicinity of the crime, and they were used as part of the proof of innocence or guilt. In the 14th century the role of the jury finally became that of judgment of evidence. By the 15th century trial by jury became the dominant mode of resolving a legal issue. It replaced such primitive forms of resolution as trial by ordeal, in which a person could prove innocence by enduring a test by fire or boiling water.

English influence and settlers brought the custom of jury trial to America. Deprivation of the "benefits of trial by jury" was a specific complaint mentioned in the American Declaration of Independence, and the right to a jury in federal courts was established in the U.S. Constitution. Article III provides for trial by jury in Federal criminal cases; the 5TH AMENDMENT, the 6TH AMENDMENT, and the 7TH AMENDMENT provide respectively for the rights to presentment or indictment of a GRAND JURY, to trial in criminal prosecutions by an impartial jury of the state in which the crime has been committed, and to trial by jury in COMMON LAW suits where the value in controversy exceeds twenty dollars. The Supreme Court in *Duncan* v. *Louisiana* (1968) declared through the 14TH AMENDMENT that the jury trial is a constitutional right applicable to all criminal trials—state or federal—in which the punishment may exceed six months. There is, however, no constitutional right to a jury trial for petty offenses (*Dyke* v. *Taylor Implement Mfg. Co.*,

1968), defined as those leading to less than six months of punishment (*Codispoti* v. *Pennsylvania*, 1974). The jury must be representative of the community, and exclusion of one class or group, such as blacks (*Norris* v. *Alabama*, 1935), women (*Taylor* v. *Louisiana*, 1975), or Mexican-Americans (*Castaneda* v. *Partida*, 1977) has been held by the Supreme Court to be unconstitutional.

The Supreme Court has held that there is no constitutional right that a jury be composed of the traditional 12 members (*Williams* v. *Florida*, 1970), or that its verdict be unanimous (*Apodaca* v. *Oregon*, 1972). In 1978 the Court ruled that juries of less than 6 persons were unlawful. The right to a jury can be waived by the defendant. In America there are two types of juries. The grand jury decides whether an indictment should be brought against one suspected of committing a crime. The PETIT JURY, so called because it has a maximum of twelve members (the grand jury often exceeds that number), decides a civil or criminal case.

The mechanics of the American jury system vary with each state, but its function does not. Once selected and sworn, the juror is questioned by the attorneys, the judge, or both as to background or possible bias. This is known as a voir dire examination. If an attorney believes there is a reason a juror should not sit on this jury, that juror can be challenged "for cause" and replaced by another juror. The attorneys have additional challenges, for which no reason must be given before dismissing a juror from a case. These are called "peremptory challenges." Use of these limited "peremptory challenges" and the selection of the jury are important parts of each trial.

The jury always deliberates in private and is not compelled to reveal its reasons for a decision. After the verdict is announced, usually by the foreman, a jury can be "polled." Each juror is asked in open court whether the verdict delivered by the foreman is his or her own. Occasionally a jury will be "sequestered," or separated from society so that its members are protected from being influenced by publicity concerning a case to which they have been assigned. If the jury cannot agree on a decision, a "hung" jury results. The case must then be retried before a different jury.

In a civil case, such as a personal injury action, the jury determines liability and the amount of the award. In most criminal cases the jury renders a verdict of innocence or guilt, but the judge sentences the defendant. In some states, juries may determine punishment in capital cases.

More than 90 percent of all jury trials are held in America. Many urge the curtailment or elimination of the jury trial as an amateurish, inefficient means of determining a legal issue. Others defend it as an essential part of American freedom.

Throughout the world the jury trial is limited. In England and the United States the jury trial has declined in favor of trial by judge. The French Revolution of 1789 initiated jury trials on continental Europe, and this spread to other civil-law countries, but only for criminal trials. In the 20th century, jury trials have been abandoned or eliminated in most civil-law countries.

KENNETH P. NOLAN

Bibliography: Bloomstein, Morris J., *Verdict: The American Jury System* (1972); Kalren, Henry, Jr., and Zeisel, Hans, *The American Jury* (1966); Moore, Lloyd E., *The Jury: Tool of Kings, Palladium of Liberty* (1973); Simon, Rita James, ed., *The Jury System in America* (1975)

See also: COURT; LEGAL PROCEDURE.

Justice, U.S. Department of

The U.S. Department of Justice is the federal government's legal office. It is headed by the cabinet-rank ATTORNEY GENERAL, who is responsible for the enforcement of federal laws, represents the government in all legal matters, and gives advice and opinions to the president and the heads of the executive departments. The Justice Department also includes the FEDERAL BUREAU OF INVESTIGATION and a number of other bureaus and agencies.

Assisting the attorney general are the deputy attorney general, the associate attorney general, and the solicitor general. The last handles government cases in the Supreme Court.

The department has six divisions, each headed by an assist-

ant attorney general, that are devoted primarily to legal affairs. The Antitrust Division is responsible for enforcing the federal antitrust laws. The Civil Division represents the government in civil lawsuits arising from the commercial and governmental activities of federal agencies. The Criminal Division is responsible for enforcing about 900 federal criminal statutes. Other legal divisions are the Civil Rights Division, the Land and Natural Resources Division, and the Tax Division.

The department also contains the Federal Bureau of Prisons, the Board of Parole, the Immigration and Naturalization Service, the Board of Immigration Appeals, the Drug Enforcement Administration, and the Law Enforcement Assistance Administration, which assists state and local governments in improving law-enforcement procedures.

The Department of Justice was established in 1870. The office of attorney general was created by the Judiciary Act of 1789, which also set up the federal court system. In 1978 the department had about 55,000 employees and a budget of $2.5 billion.

Bibliography: Huston, Luther A., *Department of Justice* (1967); Jahnige, T. P., and Goldman, S., eds., *The Federal Judicial System* (1968).

justice of the peace

A justice of the peace is a public official with limited judicial power. Justices of the peace are usually elected officials in the United States, although in some states they are appointed. They usually have the power to try minor criminal cases and civil cases involving small amounts of money. Their other duties include issuing arrest and search warrants, holding preliminary hearings in criminal cases, holding inquests, and performing marriage ceremonies. The office was created in 14th-century England, where the first justices of the peace were powerful agents of the king, responsible for keeping the peace in each county.

Justin Martyr, Saint

Saint Justin Martyr, *c.*100–*c.*165, is recognized as one of the most important early Christian writers. A Samarian, he studied in different schools of philosophy—Stoic, Peripatetic, Pythagorean, and Platonic—before becoming a Christian. Justin took up the task of making a reasoned defense of Christianity to outsiders. He went to Rome and opened a school of philosophy. Justin is the reputed author of a vast number of treatises, but the only authentic remaining works are two *Apologies*, his *Dialogue with Trypho the Jew*, and fragments of *On the Resurrection*. Justin was beheaded, probably in 165. Feast day: June 1.

Bibliography: Barnard, L. W., *Justin Martyr: His Life and Thought* (1967).

Justine

Justine; or, The Misfortunes of Virtue (1791) is a novel by Comte Donatien Alphonse François de SADE, known as the Marquis de Sade. Justine, the heroine, holds tenaciously to her innocence and virtue, vexing and exciting the men around her and causing her deep suffering. Her worldly and corrupt sister, on the other hand, lives happily as a prostitute. *Justine* tends at times to become a catalog of sexual activity, but the novel illustrates de Sade's belief that self-restraint is not in accord with human nature, which has a fundamental need to inflict pain. De Sade's ideas have influenced many writers, notably Baudelaire and Lautréamont.

JOSEPH A. REITER

Bibliography: Gorer, Geoffrey, *The Life and Ideas of the Marquis de Sade* (1963; repr. 1978); Hackel, Roberta J., *De Sade's Quantitative Moral Universe* (1976); Praz, Mario, *The Romantic Agony*, trans. by Angus Davidson (1951; repr. 1970).

Justinian Code   [juhs-tin'-ee-uhn]

The Justinian Code was part of a collection of ROMAN LAW, known as the *Corpus Juris Civilis* ("Body of Civil Law"), prepared during the reign of the Byzantine emperor Justinian I (r. 527–65). In the 6th century AD the mass of Roman legal material that had accumulated in 1,000 years of development was generally unavailable to those who needed it, and it frequently contained contradictions. Early in his reign Justinian established three committees, under the general chairmanship of his chief legal advisor, Tribonian, to gather and edit the legal material.

One committee collected all the laws that had emanated from the emperors themselves. These form the *Code*, which appeared in 12 books in 529 and contains mainly public, administrative, and criminal law. Another committee collated and removed contradictions from the writings of the foremost Roman legal experts to form the *Digest*. This work contains more than 9,000 extracts arranged in 50 books. This distillation of legal expertise heavily influenced the development of European law. A third committee prepared a textbook, the *Institutes*, for beginning students. It is still used and has been a model for later texts. The *Corpus* also includes *Novellae*, which were later enactments of Justinian and two of his successors.
                                    FRANK BOURNE

Bibliography: Jolowicz, H. F., *Historical Introduction to the Study of Roman Law*, 3d ed. (1972); Kunkel, Wolfgang, *An Introduction to Roman Legal and Constitutional History*, 2d ed., trans. by J. M. Kelly (1973).

Justinian I, Byzantine Emperor (Justinian the Great)

Justinian I, or Justinian the Great, ruled the BYZANTINE EMPIRE from 527 to 565 as one of its greatest emperors. Born c.482 near Scupi (the modern Skopje, Yugoslavia), he was originally named Petrus Sabbatius. Educated in Constantinople by his uncle Justin, an army officer, he became a power behind the throne when his uncle became emperor as Justin I in 518. Justinian married (525) THEODORA, whose support was to be vital to him, and in 527 succeeded Justin to the throne.

Justinian's aim was the restoration of the earlier Roman Empire by reconquest of areas lost to the Germanic tribes. With the help of his general BELISARIUS, he regained North Africa from the VANDALS (533–34) and, after a lengthy war (535–54), Italy from the Ostrogoths (see GOTHS). Justinian also acquired southeastern Spain. Repeated wars with the SASSANIAN Persians, however, usually ended with the Byzantines buying peace; and the Slavs occupied much of the Balkan Peninsula.

To finance his wars, Justinian extorted heavy taxes from his subjects. He also improved the system of justice by the codification of Roman law in the celebrated Justinianic Code. After the great Nika riot and fire in Constantinople (532), he rebuilt HAGIA SOPHIA with extraordinary magnificence. He intervened repeatedly in theological quarrels to reconcile eastern MONOPHYSITES and western Catholics, but without success (see CONSTANTINOPLE, COUNCILS OF). At his death on Nov. 15, 565, Justinian left an exhausted empire but also enduring monuments in the form of Hagia Sophia and his code of law. His contemporary PROCOPIUS OF CAESAREA wrote the history of the reign.
                                    C. M. BRAND

Bibliography: Barker, John W., *Justinian and the Later Roman Empire* (1966; repr. 1976); Browning, Robert, *Justinian and Theodora* (1971).

Justus of Ghent: see JOOS VAN GHENT.

jute   [joot]

Jute is the fiber from the inner bark of *Corchorus capsularis*, a tall, annual, Asiatic plant cultivated almost exclusively in India and Pakistan. Although it can be grown in hot, humid areas, its cultivation has not yet been mechanized; therefore, substantial hand labor is required to prepare the fiber. Because of the high labor costs involved, attempts to raise jute in the Florida Everglades have been unsuccessful.

Jute is one of the cheapest natural textile FIBERS and is second only to cotton in world consumption. (Other important woody fibers are flax and hemp.) The plant grows to a height of 0.6–3.6 m (2–12 ft); the stalks will produce up to five times

more fiber than the flax plant. After harvesting, the stalks are steeped in running water for several days to loosen the fibers by retting, or rotting, the outer bark. The retted, dried stems are then kneaded and crushed to separate the fibers.

The yellowish jute fibers, which may reach a length of 3 m (10 ft), are thick, brittle, and harsh to the touch. Coarser grades of jute are made into gunny sacking, a rough, heavy fabric used as a wrapping material; into scrim, an open-weave bagging used for packing vegetables; or into ROPE and twine. Finer grades are woven into carpets, shirting, and coat linings. Jute threads are used as backing and binding for carpets. Burlap, a coarse, plain-weave fabric often used for inexpensive slipcovers and draperies, is also made of jute.

Because jute does not bleach or dye well and is one of the weakest of the plant fibers, its use is limited. It will disintegrate with prolonged exposure to moisture or when alkaline laundry detergents are used. In the United States it has been partially replaced by SYNTHETIC FIBERS.   ISABEL B. WINGATE

Bibliography: Atkinson, R. R., *Jute: Fibre to Yarn* (1965); Kirby, R. H., *Vegetable Fibers* (1963).

Jutland   [juht'-luhnd]

Jutland (Danish: Jylland) is the peninsula on which mainland Denmark is located; it is bounded on the west by the North Sea, on the north by the SKAGERRAK, and on the east by the KATTEGAT and the Lille Baelt. The southern part of the peninsula is part of the West German state Schleswig-Holstein, but the term *Jutland* usually refers only to the Danish part. Danish Jutland, including several offshore islands, covers an area of 29,766 km² (11,493 mi²). It is a low area, usually not more than 30 m (100 ft) above sea level and has a mild climate with cool winters and warm summers.

The World War I Battle of Jutland (1916) between British and German fleets was fought off the peninsula's North Sea coast.

Jutland, Battle of

The Battle of Jutland, from May 31 to June 1, 1916, was the only major naval engagement in WORLD WAR I. A preliminary encounter in the North Sea between the battle-cruiser squadrons of the British admiral David Beatty and the German Franz von Hipper was followed by a full-scale battle between the two main fleets, the British under Adm. Sir John Jellicoe and the German under Adm. Reinhard Scheer. Although the battle was strategically indecisive, the Germans displayed greater tactical skill and suffered lighter losses. On the other hand, the German high fleet did not leave port again for the duration of the war.

Bibliography: Bennett, Geoffrey, *The Battle of Jutland* (1964); Costello, John, and Hughes, Terry, *Jutland 1916* (1977); Marder, Arthur J., *From Dreadnought to Scapa Flow*, vol. 3, *Jutland and After* (1966).

Jutra, Claude   [zhoo-trah', klohd]

The Canadian filmmaker Claude Jutra, b. Mar. 11, 1930, is recognized for his style of combining documentary and cinéma-vérité techniques. After studying medicine, Jutra attended the Théâtre du Nouveau Monde in Montreal, made short films, then joined the National Film Board of Canada and collaborated with Norman McLaren on *A Chairy Tale* (1957). Later he worked with Jean Rouch and has also been associated with the Radio Canada television series *Images en boîte*. His fiction films, *Mon oncle Antoine* (1970) and *Kamouraska* (1972), show a close reading of character. Jutra was the founding president of L'Association professionnelle des cinéastes.

Juvarra, Filippo   [yoo-var'-ah, fee-leep'-poh]

Filippo Juvarra, b. 1678, d. Jan. 31, 1736, was one of the greatest Italian architects of the early 18th century. Although many of his most important buildings are in northern Italy, he also worked in Lucca, Naples, Lisbon, London, Paris, and Madrid. He received his early training in the studio of Carlo Fontana in Rome, where he lived from about 1703 to 1714. There he also executed many designs for stage scenery. In 1714 he was made first architect to the king of Piedmont. In the many churches, palaces, and private residences that he built in and near the capital city, Turin, Juvarra evolved a distinctive personal style that drew on a variety of architectural precedents without being merely eclectic.

The Palazzo Madama in Turin (1718-21) has a richly decorated facade that has been compared with the garden facade of the Palace of Versailles. In contrast the simple, classical lines of the Stupinigi Castle (1729-33), which is built on a star-shaped plan, create an imposing, monumental effect. In 1717, Juvarra began work on his masterpiece of ecclesiastical architecture, the church and monastery complex at Superga (completed 1731), in which the classical Michelangelesque style of the church contrasts with the massive yet elegant design of the abbey. In 1735, Juvarra submitted his designs for the new royal palace at Madrid, which he envisaged as an enormous three story structure comprising 19 courtyards. He traveled to Spain to oversee the work, but he died there suddenly before the project had begun.   EDWARD J. SULLIVAN

Bibliography: Collier, W., "French Influence on the Architecture of Filippo Juvarra," *Architectural History*, 6 (1963); Pommer, Richard, *Eighteenth Century Architecture in Piedmont: The Open Structures of Juvarra, Alfieri and Vittone* (1967); Wittkower, Rudolf, *Art and Architecture in Italy: 1600-1750*, rev. ed. (1973).

Juvenal   [joo'-vuh-nul]

Juvenal, the anglicized name of Decimus Iunius Iuvenalis, AD c.60-130, was the last of the great Roman satirists. Although few of the details of his life that have been transmitted are reliable, it appears that he grew up in Aquinum (later the home of Thomas Aquinas) and came to Rome to make a living as a teacher during the reign of Domitian (81-96). The poet's constant rhetorical declamation on sensational fictitious topics, combined with the actual outrages of Domitian's last years before his assassination, led Juvenal to moral protest through SATIRE. As soon as Domitian was dead, Juvenal published a series of poems that lashed out at the corruption, vices, follies, and excesses of imperial Rome, masking his concern with the contemporary city by explicit allusions to the dead emperor. Whether Juvenal was successful or not cannot be known for only MARTIAL alludes to him, in epigrams that antedate Juvenal's earliest publication. Similarly, scholars have no reason to trust the later story that Juvenal suffered exile for his outspokenness and died wretchedly in Egypt, the victim of Emperor Hadrian's malevolence. Writing over a period of 30 years, growing older in a Rome that fared variously under Domitian, Nerva (96-98), Trajan (98-117), and Hadrian (117-138), Juvenal himself moderated his themes in his later satires. This can be seen through comparing his two most famous poems; in Satire 3 he attacks contemporary Rome as a decadent un-Roman horror, but in Satire 10 he discourses on the vanity of all men's wishes regardless of time or nationality. Brilliant in invective and parody, passionate and bitter in tone, Juvenal is the Roman satirist most admired and imitated by later writers.   WILLIAM S. ANDERSON

Bibliography: Green, Peter, *The Shadow of the Parthenon: Studies in Ancient History and Literature* (1972); Highet, Gilbert, *Juvenal the Satirist* (1954); Scott, Inez G., *The Grand Style in the Satires of Juvenal* (1927).

See also: LATIN LITERATURE.

juvenile delinquency

Juvenile delinquency is lawbreaking by nonadult persons. It includes crimes such as murder or robbery, as well as some offenses, such as truancy or certain sexual acts, that are illegal only when committed by juveniles. The definition of *juvenile* varies from state to state, but the term most commonly refers to someone under 18 years of age.

Delinquency is a major social problem. Between 1960 and 1974 the number of juvenile court cases rose 146 percent in the United States, whereas the number of juveniles rose only 32 percent in that period. According to U.S. national crime statistics, juveniles accounted for nearly half of those arrested for major property crimes in 1975. Delinquents are likely to come from a background of poverty, to belong to a racial or ethnic group that experiences discrimination, and to live in an urban area. They are more often male than female.

Causes of Delinquency. Criminologists who study juvenile delinquency attempt to explain it in several ways. One theory is that children from the poorest part of society lack opportunities to develop in socially acceptable ways and turn to delinquency as a substitute. Another theory is that delinquency is learned behavior, acquired by associating with people who have little respect for the law. A third explanation is that juveniles who are caught and labeled delinquent by the authorities are likely to continue to break the law because that label makes it harder for them to be law-abiding. Other explanations stress biological or psychological causes. No theory, however, satisfactorily explains all delinquency.

Juvenile Justice. Police departments often employ special officers who handle many juvenile cases informally, without making arrests. Once arrested, a juvenile normally appears before a juvenile court. Because juvenile courts have been traditionally less concerned with legal guilt or innocence than with helping the offender, they have been more informal than adult criminal courts. At the end of the court hearing, the offender may be assigned a probation officer, who tries to provide guidance for the young offender and to encourage more acceptable social behavior.

If the judge feels the case is serious enough, the offender may be sentenced to a correctional institution. Juvenile correctional institutions vary in size, setting, and facilities. They usually offer work training and try to instill a sense of social responsibility. The State of New Jersey takes young offenders to visit prisons, where they learn from the inmates some of the realities of prison life. Although most juveniles who come into contact with the juvenile justice system do not become adult criminals, a large proportion are not rehabilitated and do commit further violations.

Juvenile rights in the United States have become increasingly defined in recent years. The U.S. Supreme Court has held, for example, that the DUE PROCESS clause of the 14th Amendment requires that juveniles accused of criminal offenses have the right to counsel, to confront and cross-examine witnesses, and to protection against self-incrimination (*In re Gault*, 1967). The Court has also held that conviction must be by "proof beyond a reasonable doubt" (*In re* Winship, 1970) and that juveniles may not be placed in double jeopardy (*Breed* v. *Jones*, 1975). At the same time the standards of the juvenile justice system have also become more severe. The Supreme Court has held that due process does not assure the right of trial by jury in a state juvenile court proceeding (*McKeiver* v. *Pennsylvania*, 1971). Juvenile court proceedings have become more adversarial in nature, and newspapers may publish the name of a child subject to juvenile court proceedings. In some states juveniles of a certain age may be tried as adults for certain crimes.   JOEL BEST

Bibliography: Davis, Samuel M., *Rights of Juveniles: The Juvenile Justice System* (1974); Gibbons, Don C., *Delinquent Behavior*, 2d ed. (1976); Griffin, Brenda S., and Griffin, Charles T., *Juvenile Delinquency in Perspective* (1978); Sanders, William B., *Juvenile Delinquency* (1976).

juvenile hormone

Juvenile hormone, a chemical produced by the endocrine system of insects, controls transformation of an immature form (larval stage) into an adult form. In the immature form, juvenile hormone, also called neotenin, is produced by the corpora allata in the brain. A high level of the hormone preserves larval characteristics and prevents development of adult characteristics at each molt, or growth stage. A low level allows larval-to-pupal development (see PUPA). Thereafter juvenile hormone is absent, and METAMORPHOSIS to the adult stage is allowed.   STEPHEN C. REINGOLD

Bibliography: Wigglesworth, V. B., *Insect Hormones* (1970).

juvenile justice: see JUVENILE DELINQUENCY.

Jylland: see JUTLAND.